SECOND EDITION

DRAMA AND DISCUSSION

Edited by

STANLEY A. CLAYES

Loyola University of Chicago

PRENTICE-HALL, INC., *Englewood Cliffs, New Jersey*   07632

Library of Congress Cataloging in Publication Data

CLAYES, STANLEY A. date– comp.
  Drama and discussion.

  1. Drama—Collections. I. Title.
PN6112.C578 1978   808.82   77–750
ISBN   0-13-219030-3

Printed in the United States of America

Cover courtesy of the Chicago Art Institute.

10   9   8

PRENTICE-HALL INTERNATIONAL, INC., *London*
PRENTICE-HALL OF AUSTRALIA PTY. LIMITED, *Sydney*
PRENTICE-HALL OF CANADA, LTD., *Toronto*
PRENTICE-HALL OF INDIA PRIVATE LIMITED, *New Delhi*
PRENTICE-HALL OF JAPAN, INC., *Tokyo*
PRENTICE-HALL OF SOUTHEAST ASIA PTE. LTD., *Singapore*
WHITEHALL BOOKS LIMITED, *Wellington, New Zealand*

CONTENTS

PART TWO
Comedy 287

PART THREE
Modern Tragicomedy and Irony 469

Outsiders

PART FOUR
Essays 625

PREFACE

The revision of this selection of plays and essays is the result of attempts to reduce its level of difficulty and to arrange the plays in ways that will make the forms of drama more meaningful to students. The changes to reduce difficulty are to more modern plays, more American plays, more comedies and tragicomedies, and to fewer essays, more of them dealing with specific difficulties in the plays. Plays that have long been popular with students have been added—*Oedipus the King*, *Tartuffe*, *Major Barbara*, *The Playboy of the Western World*, and *A View from the Bridge*. From the theatre of the absurd there is now Pinter's *The Dumb Waiter* as well as Beckett's *All that Fall*. And for the discussion of experimental theatrical techniques three short plays of one-act length illustrate the possibilities of balletic stylization in Lorca's *The Love of Don Perlimplín*, the flashback in Bullins' *A Son, Come Home*, and cinematic background in O'Neill's *Hughie*. While these three plays are not difficult, they do require the reader to visualize. The stage is used in these plays in entirely different ways, and visualizing them imaginatively is essential to perceiving their different ways of meaning.

While the categories of Tragedy, Comedy, and Modern Tragicomedy and Irony in this book indicate something the plays in each group have in common, the differences, the unique features of each of the plays, are a more important subject for discussion. There is no need to study the plays in the order they are presented, but the nature of tragedy, for example, is going to be clearer if the tragedies are read together than if they are read, mixed with comedies and tragicomedies, in their historical place. Reading the tragedies together will then make clearer the differences in their historical and personal styles. It is the same with the sub-headings. Such sub-headings as Avengers direct attention to a common element in each play's conception as the basis for bringing into focus differences, sometimes sharp contrasts, in style, technique, theme, and attitude. No one disputes that *The Libation Bearers* and *Hamlet* are tragedies, but we are much more likely to observe how different they are. We use the similarities as a basis for perceiving contrasts.

The essays and prose pieces, both those that follow plays and those at the end of the book, are not parts of a total view of drama but should provide a basis for discussions approaching the plays from various perspectives. The prose pieces following the plays were selected with more attention in this edition to providing students with aids to understanding. As in the previous edition there are sometimes brief prose pieces (introductions, prefaces, letters, and notes) by editors, authors, and translators, but half of the plays in this edition are followed by extensive discussions of the plays. Two of these approach the plays from the director's point of view. While we can assume that Brecht's director's notes for *Mother Courage* are definitive, Kazan's for *A Streetcar Named Desire*, though they were the basis for the very successful original production, are now debatable as the best approach to that play. The comparatively long essays that follow the short plays by Lorca, Pinter, and Bullins provide a background for understanding their innovative styles. Elsewhere what follows the plays was chosen to provide students with information or an attitude that will lead to something important in the play.

The essays and extensive prose excerpts in Part Four are commonly cited in discussions of the forms of drama. Definitions of tragedy, comedy, and tragicomedy, which have never been defined to the satisfaction of all, vary in perspective and emphasis because there is great variety among the plays in each category, some elements more important in some plays than in others. With the shifting perspectives from which different plays must be approached, students need generalizations of a higher order than those that are particularly relevant for particular plays. The presence here of excerpts from Aristotle, Langer, and Frye, as well as Sewall's complete essay, should enable students not only to follow more easily allusions to them but to encounter first hand descriptive analyses of critical importance in the evolving definitions of tragedy and comedy. For particular styles of tragicomedy, Frye on the ironic form, Brecht on epic theatre, and Oates on the absurd should help to keep these distinctions clear.

Because no anthology can include everything that might for various reasons seem desirable, let me suggest some plays that would make interesting complements and contrasts to those here. For tragedy a study of the other two plays of the *Oresteia, Agamemnon* and *The Eumenides,* or the *Electra* of both Sophocles and Euripides would make a useful basis for independent reading and writing projects. Shakespeare's *Othello* illustrates the action of the con man in a tragic context, and Shaw's *Saint Joan* and O'Neill's *A Long Day's Journey into Night* are important modern tragedies available separately. For comedy Aristophanes' *Lysistrata* shows a very early use of gamesmanship by women who seem surprizingly modern. For tragicomedy many popular absurdist plays, available separately but not available to anthologists, might supplement those here. I think particularly of the gamesmanship in Edward Albee's *The Zoo Story* and *Who's Afraid of Virginia Woolf* and in Pinter's *The Homecoming* and of the analysis of the human condition in Beckett's *Waiting for Godot.*

My debt to others begins with Martin S. Stanford, who as an editor at Appleton-Century-Crofts, was a partner in the conception of the first edition, providing both encouragement and important contributions. For this edition I am particularly indebted to the following friends, students, and colleagues, who looked at various parts of the manuscript at various stages and were kind enough to put kindness aside and tell me what they really thought: Robert Mann, William Heilig, Paul Lombardo, Barbara High, Meredith Christensen, James Graham-Luján, Suzanne Gossett, John Nabholtz, Anthony LaBranche, Rita Clarkson, and John Gerrietts. Sound advice based on years of experience is invaluable, but my gratitude feels greatest to Dipti Shah for cheerfully working some typing into her busy schedule and for being interested, intelligent, and efficient.

S.A.C.

PART ONE

TRAGEDY

Tragedy is one form of drama. Definitions of tragedy vary from the traditional, which lean heavily on Aristotle and the practice of Sophocles and Shakespeare, to more recent and comprehensive definitions that include the practice of some modern playwrights. The definitions and discussions by Aristotle, Langer, Frye, and Sewall at the end of this book approach the problem of definition in different ways. Each of the twentieth century approaches assumes the importance of Aristotle and starts anew to construct a description of tragedy that will include the great variety of tragic styles that have evolved in many nations in the twenty-four centuries since Aristotle wrote of the tragedy of ancient Greece. In many definitions tragedy must affirm a spiritual order beyond the human. The tragedies of Aeschylus and Sophocles, performed originally at religious festivals, present the reality of a cosmic order transcending the human with the revelations of oracles which speak a mysterious truth; in the final play of the *Oresteia* Athena literally comes on the stage to establish justice. In Shakespearean and modern tragedy the mysterious presence of cosmic power may be only intimated. Northrop Frye refers to the heroes' communion "with something beyond which we can see only through them." But even when the hero seems oblivious to the existence of a transcendent order, the tragedy may, as Sewall suggests, be "witness to the cosmic mystery," may develop in its audience a sense "that justice exists somewhere in the universe."

Tragedy as a form of drama abstracts its essential form from the resistance of the tragic spirit to the human condition. It is the human condition not only to be involved in the process of growth, decline, and death but to be aware of that involvement and to question its meaning. As we mature we become aware of the limits of our opportunities. We learn to shape our lives, shrink our hopes, to an evolving sense of our identity and our place in an imperfect world. As we accept limitations and fulfill the expectations of others, we participate, even as we acquiesce, in the formation of our identity—and our fate. But the fate of the tragic hero is different from ours. "Be reasonable," says the voice of moderation. "No," says the tragic spirit. We accept our fate; the tragic hero sacrifices himself in an attempt to have another fate. The tragic condition, then, from which tragedy as a form of drama abstracts its essential form, is to resist the necessities of the human condition without any real possibility of success—though in a tragedy the audience must hope with the hero. The audience is thus a witness to a triumphant action of the tragic spirit.

Aristotle's assertion of the central importance of the action in tragedy puzzles those whose interest is drawn to the hero or heroine. Because modern tragedy differs from the Greek in its focus on the interplay of social and personal forces that explain the hero's choices and create his destiny, we are more likely to see character as of central importance in modern drama. But we would miss

1

Aristotle's point if we did not see that, whether the hero's motives are examined or not, the action is the element that most clearly defines the tragedy because the common denominator is a process. All tragic heroes are involved in a process larger than they can see objectively, and the action of all tragedy shows the hero involved to move from ignorance (or incomplete awareness) to knowledge (or greater awareness) of that process. It begins in aspiration and over-confidence inherent in the aspiration, and it moves to error, reversal of expectation, improved awareness, and defeat. The process has been elaborated in as many plots as we have tragedies, the best and the worst, even though our interest is more often in the particular, the details of particular situations and the individual hero who hesitates and is divided as he acts.

Many of the greatest tragic heroes have virtue, power, and nobility, but they all act in error. Aristotle's opinion was that the hero's fall must be the result of *hamartia*, a miscalculation, an error, the result of imperfect knowledge. *Hubris* is Aristotle's term for the hero's pride, the overconfidence, that enables him to ignore warnings to be moderate. These terms help us to discuss why the hero falls, but when mechanically applied they may make a great tragedy look like a moral treatise. Too much concentration on error seems to argue that the hero ought to have done nothing; but the hero who does not act is no hero. Instead of oracles as the agents of prophesy, Shakespearean and modern drama use other characters to warn and caution the hero. Like the Greek chorus, they caution moderation and register wonder, but the hero cannot be both exceptional and moderate. The only alternatives are, as W. H. Auden has pointed out, to be the hero or "one of the chorus," to be wondered at or to stand in wonder.

"Tragedy as a mechanism," according to Kenneth Burke, "is based upon a calamitous persistence in one's ways." The persistence of the hero or heroine, whether they are admirable, villainous, or pathetically mistaken, gives form to the tragedy, because their persistence in error forces events to turn against them. Persistence is essential both to the hero's flaw and to his virtue. The heroic nature of his energy is defined by the way it exceeds ordinary human limits, but the force of his will, his pride, turns circumstances against him. The possibility of avoiding the catastrophe, as the hero persists, becomes first the probability and then the inevitability that the catastrophe will occur. This change from hope to inevitability is implicit in Susanne Langer's analogy between tragic structure and the change from growth to decline exhibited as the structure of the history of all living things: "the act that constitutes the protagonist's tragic error or guilt is the high-water mark of his life, and now the tide recedes." Parallel to the structural change in the protagonists' fortunes is the recognition, and sometimes reconciliation, that occurs in many of the greatest tragedies as heroes and heroines move from ignorance to knowledge. The knowledge may be knowledge of themselves and their error as well as of the mysterious ways of their gods. Santayana, who greatly preferred heroes reconciled to their cosmos, describes our experience: "Tragedy, the knowledge of death, raises . . . our mortal wills into harmony with our destiny, with the wages of existence, and with the silence beyond." But sometimes, often in modern tragedy, we wait for the hero to come to his senses and he never does. He simply defies human limitations, comes to no greater awareness and acceptance, as Hamlet does, and leaves the recognitions to us. Even divided in his own mind, as we often are, and perceiving defeat, the hero persists, and as we watch him struggle and suffer we recognize the greatness of his spirit; his heroic quality, shown in his endurance and his resistance to necessity, leads us less to pity a human being like ourselves than to wonder at one who, in turbulence and suffering, in daring and protest, caught between certainty and self-doubt, is of another order of humans.

THE HERO AND FATE

Aristotle, in the fourth century B.C., using the plays of his time as examples—*Oedipus the King* as his prime example—developed a set of principles, entitled *The Poetics*, for a well constructed tragedy. Probably written as a set of lecture notes, *The Poetics* still has a great influence on how we look at tragedy today. It does not seem particularly useful to speculate about whether Aristotle would have said different things if he had known the tragedies of Shakespeare, written twenty centuries later, nor to blame Shakespeare for not always following the model of *Oedipus the King*, but it is useful to observe what interested Aristotle, and critics ever since, about it. The action of the play is complex, probable, and inevitable; it is presented in a plot structured to reversal of expectation (*peripateia*), resulting in suffering, and completed in recognition; and it imitates the action of a hero whose fate is not something imposed on him but something he incurs by his own choices, something forseen by power beyond human comprehension and recognized too late. Aristotle proposed pity and fear as the proper effect of tragedy: pity for the suffering humans and fear for "someone like ourselves."

Although Oedipus falsely assumes that he has escaped his fate in going to Thebes from the home of his "parents" in Corinth, this error does not account for his downfall. The prophecy did not set conditions under which the downfall could be avoided but declared that it would happen. A hidden necessity would work itself out. We may argue that something hidden in Oedipus cooperated with the process, but we should be a long way from modern tragedy where psychological and social forces can be clearly identified as the cause of doom. *Oedipus*, as it shows the hero continue to act and make decisions on the assumption of his innocence, demonstrates not why Oedipus acted but the terrifying power of the gods and the ignorance of man. It moves, as Aristotle said it should, according to necessity, but it demonstrates as well a test of the hero's exceptional character. Oedipus wants his own fate; he resists necessity. Certain of his nobility, he persists, ignores warnings, and only finally recognizes that his actions have fulfilled the fate foretold.

THE HEROINE AND SOCIETY

Heroes and heroines of modern tragedy are not conceived in the proportions of classical heroes but closer to those of the common man, whose power to choose is limited and whose gods are never clear. Hamlet's "divinity that shapes our ends" is not only less clear but less mysterious in modern tragedy because less present in the awareness of the hero. The tragic situations of modern heroes and heroines have a social and psychological explanation, but because, in the best modern tragedies, that explanation is never complete, necessity and inevitability still have a mysterious source in the psyche of the hero who chooses and acts. This modern analogy to the great cosmic mystery that the classical hero confronted is present in the ghosts of Ibsen's title.

Of the modern plays classified in this book as tragedies, *Ghosts* is closest to the classical idea. Its plot has been observed by Francis Fergusson to be the same as that of *Oedipus*: both central tragic figures pursue the truth about past errors only to discover themselves as the guilty ones. In *Ghosts* the original error has a social explanation but one that is incomplete. It explains that Mrs. Alving's decisions were determined by the ideas of a middle-class morality she thought she had outgrown, but it does not explain why she is still controlled by the ghosts of those ideas. Her recognitions like those of Oedipus confront her with something inscrutable.

Another kind of modern tragedy places its emphasis on the hero's struggle—the resistance to necessity—and leaves recognitions to come from the audience's side of the stage. Having lost much of their classic nobility, modern heroes and heroines are shown to have been so shaped by the past and by a particularized social condition (a convergence of ethnic, economic, and moral imperatives) that they cannot choose other than they choose and still be themselves. From their choices their tragedy takes its form from the conflict between the necessity in the will of the hero or heroine and the necessity in the laws of nature and the imperatives of society. The hero must not only resist accepting these necessities but give the audience the impression that he might succeed. Mere acceptance is pathetic, not tragic; and endurance seems heroic only when it involves a refusal and a plan that has some chance. The plan may seem doomed to the audience, but as they hold their fears in abeyance and hope with the hero, as they refuse to give up hope and refuse to accept what must be, their own tragic spirit is engaged. But the definitive element in the structure of a tragedy is stated in Aristotle's principle of peripety: what the hero does to avoid his fate produces the opposite of the result expected. At the heart of the reversal of fortune is the hero's own action. As the audience perceives that inevitability, it begins to sense, even in modern tragedy, that he has "thrown a switch in a larger machine." (Northrop Frye). Tragic irony is thus the result of the hero's action and the inevitability of his acting against his purposes.

The fates of both Mrs. Alving and Blanche DuBois are instances of the modern heroine (or hero) as part victim and part guilty of complicity in her fate. The plots differ: the plot of *Ghosts* moves to Mrs. Alving's discovery of her complicity; the plot of *A Streetcar Named Desire* shows Blanche to resist and even in defeat refuse to yield. Though they are entirely different women, each accepts some responsibility—and suffers guilt—for her past action; and in roles that are adversary and sacrificial, each asserts an importance of the individual spirit that her society would deny.

Blanche DuBois seems to be merely a pathetic victim, but *A Streetcar Named Desire* is structured on extreme contrasts that require a complex and ironic response. Unbalanced productions that stress her weaknesses and present Stanley as an irresistible natural force fail to recognize that Stanley is a force to be resisted. So long as we see Blanche's chance of a new life with Mitch as a real possibility, Blanche engages in a tragic contest in resisting Stanley. She does all the wrong things—with the result that she generates his hostility and his exposure of her. But the tragic irony in her self-defeating action is qualified by the pathetic impression she makes. She is so self-deceived (and fails so pathetically to embody the civilization that she fights for) that audiences are more likely to see her as pathetic than as tragic. Her awareness is severely limited, and her escape into madness makes impossible any final recognition of her real situation. We can, however, watch her cooperate in the working out of her fate with some modern equivalent of pity and terror, pity for one who is clearly deceived and terror at the awful price to be paid for self-deception.

AVENGERS

In *The Libation Bearers* the crime to be avenged is so terrible, and Orestes with Apollo on his side is so certain, that we feel that something in the nature of things will put right the dislocation caused by the crimes of Clytemnestra and Aegisthus. This process in the nature of things of putting things right is called Dike, usually understood to be retribution; but retribution suggests a single action, whereas Dike, in adjusting one dislocation, often creates another. Kitto translates Dike as "the way in which things regularly happen." Dike restores balance, and Orestes, as the agent of Dike, restores the balance in one way and, by killing his mother, upsets it in another. Killing his mother is a crime against a different principle of justice protected by the Furies, who judge the fact of matricide and not Orestes' reason for it, and he thus invokes the demand for revenge by the Furies, who are also agents of Dike. Their demand, the last in a long series of cries for vengeance in the story of the House of Atreus, is resolved by Athena, goddess of Justice, in the last play of the trilogy.

Revenge tragedy is as old as the *Oresteia*,

and from the audience's perspective there has always been some ambivalence about the relationship of revenge and justice in tragedy, about the idea that blood cancels a blood debt, that one crime creates justice for another. Revenge and its appeal to our most primitive sense of justice is common in all kinds of drama. One slap repays another in a Punch and Judy slapstick farce, and comic plots are often built on the exposure of tricksters and con men beaten at their own game. In comedy there can be justice on earth, and humans may be given their deserving. In tragedy another source of justice, beyond human comprehension, is evoked. Dike is at work. Whether he is wrong or right, the tragic avenger's attempt to establish justice, to kill and to die for it, involves him in a process with an ironic structure, a process hidden from him and fatal to him which he activates in his attempt to put things right. Hamlet seems to be aware of the process. The way his tragedy compares and contrasts to Greek revenge tragedy is discussed by H.D.F. Kitto in "*Hamlet* and Greek Drama," the essay that follows *Hamlet*.

It is a long way from the majesty of Oedipus to Eddie Carbone, but there are similarities. Both act with a sense of the justice of their actions, but in error, and both fall into error and come to their tragic end fulfilling their own sense of their own identity as just and generous people. Both mistakenly assume that they know who they are, but Eddie Carbone is a smaller man in the shrunken cosmos of modern naturalism. He echoes the great tragic heroes when, entering the final fight, he declares "I want my name." He claims, like Oedipus, an identity he has already destroyed, but it was never the majestical identity of Oedipus, and though he resists, with tragic irony, inevitabilities that he helped to create, he never attains the self-knowledge that Oedipus does. The revenge he took against Rodolfo and Marco generates, as with the operations of Dike, the revenge Marco takes against him, and Eddie dies concerned only that he has been misunderstood, betrayed by a law of his own nature that he never understands. But the play's resolution leads its audience to a recognition, not of the great cosmic mystery of ancient tragedies, nor to the small, clear moralities of melodrama, but to the unknown, to the dark potentialities of human nature to betray itself.

THE HERO AND FATE

ŒDIPUS THE KING

Sophocles

translated by H. D. F. Kitto

CHARACTERS

ŒDIPUS, King of Thebes
PRIEST OF ZEUS

From *Sophocles: Three Tragedies*. Antigone, Oedipus the King, Electra, translated by H.D.F. Kitto. Copyright © 1962 by Oxford University Press. Reprinted by permission.

CREON, brother of Iocasta
TEIRESIAS, a Seer
IOCASTA, Queen of Thebes
A CORINTHIAN SHEPHERD
A THEBAN SHEPHERD
A MESSENGER
Chorus of Theban citizens
Priests, Attendants, etc.

Scene: Thebes, before the royal palace

The date of the first production is unknown; probably about 425 B.C., some fifteen or twenty years after the Antigone. *The sequel,*

*Oedipus at Colonus, was written much
later and was first produced after Sophocles'
death in 406 B.C. The three plays therefore
in no real sense make a trilogy; for example,
Creon appears in each, and in each is quite a
different sort of man.*

*The tetralogy of which the present play
formed part gained the second prize; the
first was awarded to an otherwise unknown
Philocles, a nephew of Aeschylus. There is
no need to blame the Athenian judges for not
recognizing a superb play when they saw
one: its fellows in the tetralogy (two more
tragedies and a satyr-play) may well have
been inferior.*

OEDIPUS. My children, latest brood of
    ancient Cadmus,
What purpose brings you here, a
    multitude
Bearing the boughs that mark the
    suppliant?
Why is our air so full of frankincense,
So full of hymns and prayers and
    lamentations?
This, children, was no matter to entrust
To others: therefore I myself am come
Whose fame is known to all—I, Oedipus.
—You, Sir, are pointed out by length of
    years
10 To be the spokesman: tell me, what is in
    Your hearts? What fear? What sorrow?
        Count on all
    That I can do, for I am not so hard
    As not to pity such a supplication.
PRIEST. Great King of Thebes, and sovereign
        Oedipus,
    Look on us, who now stand before the
        altars—
    Some young, still weak of wing; some
        bowed with age—
    The priests, as I, of Zeus; and these,
        the best
    Of our young men; and in the
        market-place,
    And by Athena's temples and the shrine
20 Of fiery divination, there is kneeling,
    Each with his suppliant branch, the rest
        of Thebes.

The city, as you see yourself, is now
Storm-tossed, and can no longer raise its
    head
Above the waves and angry surge of
    death.
The fruitful blossoms of the land are
    barren,
The herds upon our pastures, and our
    wives
In childbirth, barren. Last, and worst of
    all,
The withering god of fever swoops on us
To empty Cadmus' city and enrich
Dark Hades with our groans and
    lamentations.   30
No god we count you, that we bring our
    prayers,
I and these children, to your palace-door,
But wise above all other men to read
Life's riddles, and the hidden ways of
    Heaven;
For it was you who came and set us free
From the blood-tribute that the cruel
    Sphinx
Had laid upon our city; without our aid
Or our instruction, but, as we believe,
With god as ally, you gave us back our
    life.
So now, most dear, most mighty Oedipus,   40
We all entreat you on our bended knees,
Come to our rescue, whether from the
    gods
Or from some man you can find means
    to save.
For I have noted, *that* man's counsel is
Of best effect, who has been tried in
    action.
Come, noble Oedipus! Come, save our
    city.
Be well advised; for that past service
    given
This city calls you Saviour; of your
    kingship
Let not the record be that first we rose
From ruin, then to ruin fell again.   50
No, save our city, let it stand secure.
You brought us gladness and deliverance
Before; now do no less. You rule this
    land;

Better to rule it full of living men
Than rule a desert; citadel or ship
Without its company of men is nothing.

OEDIPUS. My children, what you long for,
    that I know
Indeed, and pity you. I know how cruelly
You suffer; yet, though sick, not one of
    you
60 Suffers a sickness half as great as mine.
Yours is a single pain; each man of you
Feels but his own. My heart is heavy with
The city's pain, my own, and yours
    together.
You come to me not as to one asleep
And needing to be wakened; many a tear
I have been shedding, every path of
    thought
Have I been pacing; and what remedy,
What single hope my anxious thought
    has found
That I have tried. Creon, Menoeceus' son,
My own wife's brother, I have sent to
70   Delphi
To ask in Phoebus' house what act of
    mine,
What word of mine, may bring
    deliverance.
Now, as I count the days, it troubles me
What he is doing; his absence is
    prolonged
Beyond the proper time. But when he
    comes
Then write me down a villain, if I do
Not each particular that the god discloses.

PRIEST. You give us hope.—And here is
    more, for they
Are signalling that Creon has returned.

OEDIPUS. O Lord Apollo, even as Creon
80   smiles,
Smile now on us, and let it be
    deliverance!

PRIEST. The news is good; or he would not
    be wearing
That ample wreath of richly-berried
    laurel.

OEDIPUS. We soon shall know; my voice
    will reach so far:
Creon my lord, my kinsman, what
    response
Do you bring with you from the god of
    Delphi?

Enter CREON

CREON. Good news! Our sufferings, if they
    are guided right,
Can even yet turn to a happy issue.

OEDIPUS. This only leaves my fear and
    confidence
In equal balance: what did Phoebus say? 90

CREON. Is it your wish to hear it now, in
    public,
Or in the palace? I am at your service.

OEDIPUS. Let them all hear! Their sufferings
    distress
Me more than if my own life were at
    stake.

CREON. Then I will tell you what Apollo
    said—
And it was very clear. There is pollution
Here in our midst, long-standing. This
    must we
Expel, nor let it grow past remedy.

OEDIPUS. What has defiled us? and how are
    we to purge it?

CREON. By banishing or killing one who
    murdered, 100
And so called down this pestilence upon
    us.

OEDIPUS. Who is the man whose death the
    god denounces?

CREON. Before the city passed into your
    care,
My lord, we had a king called Laius.

OEDIPUS. So have I often heard.—I never
    saw him.

CREON. His death, Apollo clearly charges us,
We must avenge upon his murderers.

OEDIPUS. Where are they now? And where
    shall we disclose
The unseen traces of that ancient crime?

CREON. The god said, Here.—A man who
    hunts with care 110
May often find what other men will
    miss.

OEDIPUS. Where was he murdered? In the
    palace here?
Or in the country? Or was he abroad?

CREON. He made a journey to consult the
    god,
    He said—and never came back home
    again.
OEDIPUS. But was there no report? no fellow
    traveller
    Whose knowledge might have helped you
    in your search?
CREON. All died, except one terror-stricken
    man,
    And he could tell us nothing—next to
    nothing.
OEDIPUS. And what was that? One thing
120   might lead to much,
    If only we could find one ray of light.
CREON. He said they met with brigands—
    not with one,
    But a whole company; they killed Laius.
OEDIPUS. A brigand would not *dare*—unless
    perhaps
    Conspirators in Thebes had bribed the
    man.
CREON. There *was* conjecture; but disaster
    came
    And we were leaderless, without our king.
OEDIPUS. Disaster? With a king cut down
    like that
    You did not seek the cause? Where was
    the hindrance?
CREON. The Sphinx. *Her* riddle pressed us
130   harder still;
    For Laius—out of sight was out of mind.
OEDIPUS. I will begin again; *I*'ll find the
    truth.
    The dead man's cause has found a true
    defender
    In Phoebus, and in you. And I will join
    you
    In seeking vengeance on behalf of Thebes
    And Phoebus too; indeed, I must: if I
    Remove this taint, it is not for a stranger,
    But for myself: the man who murdered
    him
    Might make the same attempt on me;
    and so,
140   Avenging him, I shall protect myself.—
    Now you, my sons, without delay, arise,
    Take up your suppliant branches.—
    Someone, go

And call the people here, for I will do
What can be done; and either, by the
    grace
Of God we shall be saved—or we shall
    fall.
PRIEST. My children, we will go; the King
    has promised
All that we came to ask.—O Phoebus,
    thou
Hast given us an answer: give us too
Protection! grant remission of the plague!
[*Exeunt* CREON, PRIESTS, *etc.* OEDIPUS *remains*
    Enter the CHORUS *representing the citizens*
    of Thebes

Strophe 1

CHORUS.
Sweet is the voice of the god, that
(*mainly dactyls:* $\frac{4}{4}$)[1]   sounds in the 150
    Golden shrine of Delphi.
    What message has it sent to Thebes? My
    trembling
Heart is torn with anguish.
Thou god of Healing, Phoebus Apollo,
How do I fear! What hast thou in mind
To bring upon us now? what is to be
    fulfilled
From days of old?
Tell me this, O Voice divine,
Thou child of golden Hope.

Antistrophe 1

First on the Daughter of Zeus I call for 160
Help, divine Athene;
And Artemis, whose throne is all the
    earth, whose
Shrine is in our city;
Apollo too, who shoots from afar:
Trinity of Powers, come to our defence!

[1]The translator has added musical indications of
tempo to the lyrical choral passages to indicate the
tempo at which they might have been sung.

If ever in the past, when ruin threatened
  us,
You stayed its course
And turned aside the flood of Death,
O then, protect us now!

Strophe 2

170 (*agitated:* $\frac{3}{8}$) Past counting are the woes we
  suffer;
  Affliction bears on all the city, and
  Nowhere is any defence against
    destruction.
  The holy soil can bring no increase,
  Our women suffer and cry in childbirth
  But do not bring forth living children.
  The souls of those who perish, one by one,
  Unceasingly, swift as raging fire,
  Rise and take their flight to the dark
    realms of the dead.

Antistrophe 2

  Past counting, those of us who perish:
180 They lie upon the ground, unpitied,
  Unburied, infecting the air with deadly
    pollution.
  Young wives, and grey-haired mothers
    with them,
  From every quarter approach the altars
  And cry aloud in supplication.
  The prayer for healing, the loud wail of
    lament,
  Together are heard in dissonance:
  O thou golden Daughter of Zeus, grant
    thy aid!

Strophe 3

(*mainly iambic:* $\frac{3}{8}$) The fierce god of War has
  laid aside
  His spear; but yet his terrible cry
  Rings in our ears; he spreads death and
190   destruction.

Ye gods, drive him back to his distant
  home!
  For what the light of day has spared,
  That the darkness of night destroys.
  Zeus our father! All power is thine:
  The lightning-flash is thine: hurl upon
    him
  Thy thunderbolt, and quell this god of
    War!

Antistrophe 3

  We pray, Lord Apollo: draw thy bow
  In our defence. Thy quiver is full of
  Arrows unerring: shoot! slay the
    destroyer!
  And thou, radiant Artemis, lend thy aid! 200
    Thou whose hair is bound in gold,
  Bacchus, lord of the sacred dance,
    Theban Bacchus! Come, show thyself!
  Display thy blazing torch; drive from
    our midst
  The savage god, abhorred by other gods!
OEDIPUS. Would you have answer to these
  prayers? Then hear
My words; give heed; your help may
  bring
Deliverance, and the end of all our
  troubles.
Here do I stand before you all, a stranger
Both to the deed and to the story.—What 210
Could I have done alone, without a clue?
But I was yet a foreigner; it was later
That I became a Theban among
  Thebans.
So now do I proclaim to all the city:
If any Theban knows by what man's hand
He perished, Laius, son of Labdacus,
Him I command to tell me all he can;
And if he is afraid, let him annul
Himself the charge he fears; no
  punishment
Shall fall on him, save only to depart 220
Unharmed from Thebes. Further, if any
  knows
The slayer to be a stranger from abroad,
Let him speak out; I will reward him,
  and

Besides, he will have all my gratitude.
But if you still keep silent, if any man
Fearing for self or friend shall disobey me,
This will I do—and listen to my words:
Whoever he may be, I do forbid
All in this realm, of which I am the King
And high authority, to shelter in their
230   houses
Or speak to him, or let him be their
    partner
In prayers or sacrifices to the gods, or
    give
Him lustral water; I command you all
To drive him from your doors; for he it is
That brings this plague upon us, as the
    god
Of Delphi has but now declared to me.—
So stern an ally do I make myself
Both of the god and of our murdered
    king.—
And for the man that slew him, whether
    he
Slew him alone, or with a band of
240   helpers,
I lay this curse upon him, that the wretch
In wretchedness and misery may live.
And more: if with my knowledge he be
    found
To share my hearth and home, then
    upon me
Descend that doom that I invoke on him.
This charge I lay upon you, to observe
All my commands: to aid myself, the god,
And this our land, so spurned of Heaven,
    so ravaged.
For such a taint we should not leave
    unpurged—
The death of such a man, and he your
250   king—
Even if Heaven had not commanded us,
But we should search it out. Now, since
    'tis I
That wear the crown that he had worn
    before me, ·
And have his Queen to wife, and
    common children
Were born to us, but that his own did
    perish,

And sudden death has carried him
    away—
Because of this, I will defend his cause
As if it were my father's; nothing I
Will leave undone to find the man who
    killed
The son of Labdacus, and offspring of   260
Polydorus, Cadmus, and of old Agênor.
On those that disobey, this is my curse:
May never field of theirs give increase, nor
Their wives have children; may our
    present plagues,
And worse, be ever theirs, for their
    destruction.
But for the others, all with whom my
    words
Find favour, this I pray: Justice and all
The gods be ever at your side to help
    you.
CHORUS-LEADER. Your curse constrains me;
    therefore will I speak.
I did not kill him, neither can I tell   270
Who did. It is for Phoebus, since he laid
The task upon us, to declare the man.
OEDIPUS. True; but to force the gods against
    their will—
That is a thing beyond all human power.
CHORUS-LEADER. All I could say is but a
    second best.
OEDIPUS. Though it were third best, do not
    hold it back.
CHORUS-LEADER. I know of none that reads
    Apollo's mind
So surely as the lord Teiresias;
Consulting him you best might learn the
    truth.
OEDIPUS. Not even this have I neglected:
    Creon   280
Advised me, and already I have sent
Two messengers.—Strange he has not
    come.
CHORUS-LEADER. There's nothing else but
    old and idle gossip.
OEDIPUS. And what was that? I clutch at
    any straw.
CHORUS-LEADER. They said that he was
    killed by travellers.
OEDIPUS. So I have heard; but no one
    knows a witness.

CHORUS-LEADER. But if he is not proof
  against *all* fear
  He'll not keep silent when he hears your
  curse.
OEDIPUS. And will they fear a curse, who
  dared to kill?
CHORUS-LEADER. Here is the one to find
290 him, for at last
  They bring the prophet here. He is
  inspired,
  The only man whose heart is filled with
  truth.

        Enter TEIRESIAS, *led by a boy*

OEDIPUS. Teiresias, by your art you read
  the signs
  And secrets of the earth and of the sky;
  Therefore you know, although you
  cannot see,
  The plague that is besetting us; from this
  No other man but you, my lord, can
  save us.
  Phoebus has said—you may have heard
  already—
  In answer to our question, that this plague
300 Will never cease unless we can discover
  What men they were who murdered
  Laius,
  And punish them with death or
  banishment.
  Therefore give freely all that you have
  learned
  From birds or other form of divination;
  Save us; save me, the city, and yourself,
  From the pollution that his bloodshed
  causes.
  No finer task, than to give all one has
  In helping others; we are in your hands.
TEIRESIAS. Ah! what a burden knowledge
  is, when knowledge
310 Can be of no avail! I knew this well,
  And yet forgot, or I should not have
  come.
OEDIPUS. Why, what is this? Why are you
  so despondent?
TEIRESIAS. Let me go home! It will be best
  for you,

And best for me, if you will let me go.
OEDIPUS. But to withhold your knowledge!
  This is wrong,
  Disloyal to the city of your birth.
TEIRESIAS. I know that what you say will
  lead you on
  To ruin; therefore, lest the same befall
  me too . . .
OEDIPUS. No, by the gods! Say all you
  know, for we
  Go down upon our knees, your suppliants. 320
TEIRESIAS. Because *you* do *not* know! I never
  shall
  Reveal my burden—I will not say *yours.*
OEDIPUS. You know, and will not tell us?
  Do you wish
  To ruin Thebes and to destroy us all?
TEIRESIAS. *My* pain, and yours, will not be
  caused by me.
  Why these vain questions?—for I will
  not speak.
OEDIPUS. You villain!—for you would
  provoke a stone
  To anger: you'll not speak, but show
  yourself
  So hard of heart and so inflexible?
TEIRESIAS. You heap the blame on me; but
  what is yours   330
  You do not know—therefore *I* am the
  villain!
OEDIPUS. And who would not be angry,
  finding that
  You treat our people with such cold
  disdain?
TEIRESIAS. The truth will come to light,
  without *my* help.
OEDIPUS. If it is bound to come, you ought
  to speak it.
TEIRESIAS. I'll say no more, and you, if so
  you choose,
  May rage and bluster on without
  restraint.
OEDIPUS. Restraint? Then I'll show none!
  I'll tell you all
  That I can see in you: I do believe
  This crime was planned and carried out
  by you,   340
  All but the killing; and were you not
  blind

I'd say your hand alone had done the murder.

TEIRESIAS. So? Then I tell you this: submit yourself
To that decree that you have made; from now
Address no word to these men nor to me
You are the man whose crimes pollute our city.

OEDIPUS. What, does your impudence extend thus far?
And do you hope that it will go scot-free?

TEIRESIAS. It will. I have a champion—the truth.

OEDIPUS. Who taught you that? For it was
350   not your art.

TEIRESIAS. No; you! You made me speak, against my will.

OEDIPUS. Speak what? Say it again, and say it clearly.

TEIRESIAS. Was I not clear? Or are you tempting me?

OEDIPUS. Not clear enough for me. Say it again.

TEIRESIAS. You are yourself the murderer you seek.

OEDIPUS. You'll not affront me twice and go unpunished!

TEIRESIAS. Then shall I give you still more cause for rage?

OEDIPUS. Say what you will; you'll say it to no purpose.

TEIRESIAS. *I* know, *you* do not know, the hideous life
Of shame you lead with those most near
360   to you.

OEDIPUS. You'll pay most dearly for this insolence!

TEIRESIAS. No, not if Truth is strong, and can prevail.

OEDIPUS. It is—except in you; for you are blind
In eyes and ears and brains and everything.

TEIRESIAS. You'll not forget these insults that you throw
At me, when all men throw the same at you.

OEDIPUS. You live in darkness; you can do no harm
To me or any man who has his eyes.

TEIRESIAS. No; *I* am not to bring you down, because
Apollo is enough; he'll see to it.   370

OEDIPUS. Creon, or you? Which of you made this plot?

TEIRESIAS. Creon's no enemy of yours; you are your own.

OEDIPUS. O Wealth! O Royalty! whose commanding art
Outstrips all other arts in life's contentions!
How great a store of envy lies upon you,
If for this sceptre, that the city gave
Freely to me, unasked—if now my friend,
The trusty Creon, burns to drive me hence
And steal it from me! So he has suborned
This crafty schemer here, this mountebank,   380
Whose purse alone has eyes, whose art is blind.—
Come, prophet, show your title! When the Sphinx
Chanted her music here, why did not *you*
Speak out and save the city? Yet such a question
Was one for augury, not for mother wit.
You were no prophet then; your birds, your voice
From Heaven, were dumb. But I, who came by chance,
I, knowing nothing, put the Sphinx to flight,
Thanks to my wit—no thanks to divination!
And now you try to drive me out; you hope   390
When Creon's king to bask in Creon's favour.
You'll expiate the curse? Ay, and repent it,
Both you and your accomplice. But that you
Seem old, I'd teach you what you gain by treason!

CHORUS-LEADER. My lord, he spoke in anger; so, I think,
Did you. What help in angry speeches? Come,

This is the task, how we can best discharge
The duty that the god has laid on us.
TEIRESIAS. King though you are, I claim
the privilege
400 Of equal answer. No, I have the right;
I am no slave of yours—I serve Apollo,
And therefore am not listed *Creon's* man.
Listen—since you have taunted me with
blindness!
You have your sight, and yet you cannot
see
Where, nor with whom, you live, nor in
what horror.
Your parents—do you know them? or
that you
Are enemy to your kin, alive or dead?
And that a father's and a mother's curse
Shall join to drive you headlong out of
Thebes
And change the light that now you see
410 to darkness?
Your cries of agony, where will they not
reach?
Where on Cithaeron will they not
re-echo?
When you have learned what meant the
marriage-song
Which bore you to an evil haven here
After so fair a voyage? And you are
blind
To other horrors, which shall make you
one
With your own children. Therefore, heap
your scorn
On Creon and on me, for no man living
Will meet a doom more terrible than
yours.
OEDIPUS. What? Am I to suffer words like
420 this from him?
Ruin, damnation seize you! Off at once
Out of our sight! Go! Get you whence
you came!
TEIRESIAS. Had you not called me, I should
not be here.
OEDIPUS. And had I known that you would
talk such folly,
I'd not have called you to a house of
mine.

TEIRESIAS. To you I seem a fool, but to
your parents,
To those who did beget you, I was wise.
OEDIPUS. Stop! Who were they? Who *were*
my parents? Tell me!
TEIRESIAS. This day will show your birth
and your destruction.
OEDIPUS. You are too fond of dark
obscurities. 430
TEIRESIAS. But do you not excel in reading
riddles?
OEDIPUS. I scorn your taunts; my skill has
brought me glory.
TEIRESIAS. And this success brought you to
ruin too.
OEDIPUS. I am content, if so I saved this
city.
TEIRESIAS. Then I will leave you. Come,
boy, take my hand.
OEDIPUS. Yes, let him take it. You are
nothing but
Vexation here. Begone, and give me
peace!
TEIRESIAS. When I have had my say. No
frown of yours
Shall frighten *me*; you cannot injure me.
Here is my message: that man whom
you seek 440
With threats and proclamations for the
death
Of Laius, he is living here; he's thought
To be a foreigner, but shall be found
Theban by birth—and little joy will this
Bring *him*; when, with his eyesight
turned to blindness,
His wealth to beggary, on foreign soil
With staff in hand he'll tap his way along,
His children with him; and he will be
known
Himself to be their father and their
brother,
The husband of the mother who gave
him birth, 450
Supplanter of his father, and his slayer.
—There! Go, and think on this; and if
you find
That I'm deceived, say then—and not
before—

That I am ignorant in divination.
[*Exeunt severally* TEIRESIAS *and* OEDIPUS

Strophe 1

CHORUS. The voice of god rang out in the
    holy cavern,
Denouncing one who has killed a King—
    the crime of crimes.
    Who is the man? Let him begone in
    Headlong flight, swift as a horse!

(*anapaests*) For the terrible god, like a
    warrior armed,
Stands ready to strike with
460   a lightning-flash:
    The Furies who punish crime, and
    never fail,
    Are hot in their pursuit.

Antistrophe 1

The snow is white on the cliffs of high
    Parnassus.
It has flashed a message: Let every
    Theban join the hunt!
    Lurking in caves among the mountains,
    Deep in the woods—where is the man?

(*anapaests*) In wearisome flight, unresting,
    alone,
An outlaw, he shuns Apollo's shrine;
    But ever the living menace of the god
470   Hovers around his head.

Strophe 2

(*choriambics*) Strange, disturbing, what the
    wise
Prophet has said. What can he mean?
Neither can I believe, nor can I
    disbelieve;
I do not know what to say.
I look here, and there; nothing can I
    find—

No strife, either now or in the past,
Between the kings of Thebes and Corinth.
A hand unknown struck down the King;
Though I would learn who it was dealt
    the blow,
That *he* is guilty whom all revere—   480
How can I believe this with no proof?

Antistrophe 2

Zeus, Apollo—they have knowledge;
They understand the ways of life.
Prophets are men, like me; that they can
    understand
More than is revealed to me—
Of that, I can find nowhere certain proof,
Though one man is wise, another foolish.
Until the charge is manifest
I will not credit his accusers.
I saw myself how the Sphinx challenged
    him: 490
He proved his wisdom; he saved our city;
Therefore how can I now condemn him?

Enter CREON

CREON. They tell me, Sirs, that Oedipus the
    King
Has made against me such an accusation
That I will not endure. For if he thinks
That in this present trouble I have done
Or said a single thing to do him harm,
Then let me die, and not drag out my
    days
With such a name as that. For it is not
One injury this accusation does me;   500
It touches my whole life, if you, my
    friends,
And all the city are to call me traitor.
CHORUS-LEADER. The accusation may
    perhaps have come
From heat of temper, not from sober
    judgement.
CREON. What was it made him think
    contrivances
Of mine suborned the seer to tell his lies?

CHORUS-LEADER. Those were his words; I do not know his reasons.

CREON. Was he in earnest, master of himself,
When he attacked me with this accusation?

CHORUS-LEADER. I do not closely scan what kings are doing.—
But here he comes in person from the palace.

Enter OEDIPUS

OEDIPUS. What, *you*? You dare come here? How can you find
The impudence to show yourself before
My house, when you are clearly proven
To have sought my life and tried to steal my crown?
Why, do you think me then a coward, or
A fool, that you should try to lay this plot?
Or that I should not see what you were scheming,
And so fall unresisting, blindly, to you?
But you were mad, so to attempt the throne,
Poor and unaided; this is not encompassed
Without the strong support of friends and money!

CREON. This you must do: now you have had your say
Hear my reply; then yourself shall judge.

OEDIPUS. A ready tongue! But I am bad at listening—
To you. For I have found how much you hate me.

CREON. One thing: first listen to what I have to say.

OEDIPUS. One thing: do not pretend you're not a villain.

CREON. If you believe it is a thing worth having,
Insensate stubbornness, then you are wrong.

OEDIPUS. If you believe that one can harm a kinsman
Without retaliation, you are wrong.

CREON. With this I have no quarrel; but explain
What injury you say that I have done you.

OEDIPUS. Did you advise, or did you not, that I
Should send a man for that most reverend prophet?

CREON. I did, and I am still of that advice.

OEDIPUS. How long a time is it since Laius . . .

CREON. Since Laius did *what*? How can I say?

OEDIPUS. Was seen no more, but met a violent death?

CREON. It would be many years now past and gone.

OEDIPUS. And had this prophet learned his art already?

CREON. Yes; his repute was great—as it is now.

OEDIPUS. Did he make any mention then of me?

CREON. He never spoke of you within my hearing.

OEDIPUS. Touching the murder: did you make no search?

CREON. No search? Of course we did; but we found nothing.

OEDIPUS. And why did this wise prophet not speak *then*?

CREON. Who knows? Where I know nothing I say nothing.

OEDIPUS. This much you know—and you'll do well to answer:

CREON. What is it? If I know, I'll tell you freely.

OEDIPUS. That if he had not joined with you, he'd not
Have said that I was Laius' murderer.

CREON. If he said this, I did not know.—But I
May rightly question you, as you have me.

OEDIPUS. Ask what you will. You'll never prove *I* killed him.

CREON. Why then: are you not married to my sister?

OEDIPUS. I am indeed; it cannot be denied.

CREON. You share with her the sovereignty of Thebes?

OEDIPUS. She need but ask, and anything is hers.

CREON. And am I not myself conjoined
    with you?

OEDIPUS. You are; not rebel therefore, but
    a traitor!

CREON. Not so, if you will reason with
    yourself,

    As I with you. This first: would any man,

    To gain no increase of authority,

    Choose kingship, with its fears and
    sleepless nights?

    Not I. What I desire, what every man

    Desires, if he has wisdom, is to take

    The substance, not the show, of royalty.

    For now, through you, I have both
570   power and ease,

    But were I king, I'd be oppressed with
    cares.

    Not so: while I have ample sovereignty

    And rule in peace, why should I want
    the crown?

    I am not yet so mad as to give up

    All that which brings me honour and
    advantage.

    Now, every man greets me, and I greet
    him;

    Those who have need of you make much
    of me,

    Since I can make or mar them. Why
    should I

    Surrender this to load myself with that?
580   A man of sense was never yet a traitor;

    I have no taste for that, nor could I force

    Myself to aid another's treachery.

        But you can test me: go to Delphi; ask

    If I reported rightly what was said.

    And further: if you find that I had
    dealings

    With that diviner, you may take and
    kill me

    Not with your single vote, but yours and
    mine,

    But not on bare suspicion, unsupported.

    How wrong it is, to use a random
    judgement

    And think the false man true, the true
590   man false!

    To spurn a loyal friend, that is no better

Than to destroy the life to which we
    cling.

This you will learn in time, for Time
    alone

Reveals the upright man; a single day

Suffices to unmask the treacherous.

CHORUS-LEADER. My lord, he speaks with
    caution, to avoid

    Grave error. Hasty judgement is not sure.

OEDIPUS. But when an enemy is quick to plot

    And strike, I must be quick in answer too.

    If I am slow, and wait, then I shall find   600

    That he has gained his end, and I am
    lost.

CREON. What do you wish? To drive me
    into exile?

OEDIPUS. No, more than exile: I will have
    your life.[2]

CREON. ⟨When will it cease, this monstrous
    rage of yours?⟩

OEDIPUS. When your example shows what
    comes of envy.

CREON. Must you be stubborn? Cannot
    you believe me?

OEDIPUS. ⟨You speak to me as if I were a
    fool!⟩

CREON. Because I know you're wrong.

OEDIPUS.   Right, for myself!

CREON. It is not right for me!

OEDIPUS.   But you're a traitor.

CREON. What if your charge is false?

    [2]The next two verses, as they stand in the MSS., are impossible. Editors are agreed on this, though no single remedy has found general acceptance. The MSS. attribute v. 624 (v. 605 here) to Creon, and v. 625 (v. 606 here) to Oedipus. I can make no real sense of this: the only φθόνος, 'envy', that is in question is the envy of his royal power that Oedipus is attributing to Creon; and the words ὑπείξων 'yield', 'not to be stubborn', and πιστύσων, 'believe', must surely be used by Creon of Oedipus, not by Oedipus of Creon. Since a translator who hopes to be acted must give the actors something to say, preferably good sense, and cannot fob them off with a row of dots, I have reconstructed the passage by guesswork, putting my guesses within brackets. I have assumed that two verses were lost, one after v. 623 and one after v. 625, and that the wrong attribution of vv. 624 and 625 followed almost inevitably.

610 OEDIPUS.   I have to govern.
CREON. Not govern badly!
OEDIPUS.   Listen to him, Thebes!
CREON. You're not the city! I am Theban
  too.
CHORUS-LEADER. My lords, no more! Here
  comes the Queen, and not
    Too soon, to join you. With her help,
    you must
  Compose the bitter strife that now
  divides you.

Enter IOCASTA

IOCASTA. You frantic men! What has
  aroused this wild
    Dispute? Have you no shame, when
    such a plague
  Afflicts us, to indulge in private quarrels?
  Creon, go home, I pray. You, Oedipus,
  Come in; do not make much of what is
  nothing.
CREON. My sister: Oedipus, your husband
620 here,
    Has thought it right to punish me with
    one
  Of two most awful dooms: exile, or death.
OEDIPUS. I have: I have convicted him,
    Iocasta,
  Of plotting secretly against my life.
CREON. If I am guilty in a single point
  Of such a crime, then may I die accursed.
IOCASTA. O, by the gods, believe him,
    Oedipus!
    Respect the oath that he has sworn, and
    have
  Regard for me, and for these citizens.

  (*In what follows, the parts given to the
  chorus are sung, the rest, presumably,
  spoken. The rhythm of the music and dance
  is either dochmiac, 5-time, or a combination
  of 3- and 5-time.*)

Strophe

630 CHORUS. My lord, I pray, give consent.
    Yield to us; ponder well.
  OEDIPUS. What is it you would have me
    yield?

CHORUS. Respect a man ripe in years,
    Bound by this mighty oath he has sworn.
OEDIPUS. Your wish is clear?
CHORUS.   It is.
OEDIPUS.   Then tell it me.
CHORUS. Not to repel, and drive out of our
    midst a friend,
    Scorning a solemn curse, for uncertain
    cause.
OEDIPUS. I tell you this: your prayer will
    mean for me
    My banishment from Thebes, or else my
    death.
CHORUS. No, no! by the Sun, the chief of
    gods,   640
    Ruin and desolation and all evil come
    upon me
  If I harbour thoughts such as these!
  No; our land racked with plague breaks
    my heart.
    Do not now deal a new wound on
    Thebes to crown the old!
OEDIPUS. Then let him be, though I must
    die twice over,
    Or be dishonoured, spurned and driven
    out.
  It's your entreaty, and not his, that moves
  My pity; he shall have my lasting hatred.
CREON. You yield ungenerously; but when
    your wrath
    Has cooled, how it will prick you!
    Natures such   650
  As yours give most vexation to themselves.
OEDIPUS. O, let me be! Get from my sight.
CREON.   I go,
  Misjudged by you—but these will judge
    me better [*indicating* CHORUS].
                              [*Exit* CREON

Antistrophe

CHORUS. My lady, why now delay?
    Let the King go in with you.
IOCASTA. When you have told me what has
    passed.
CHORUS. Suspicion came.—Random words,
    undeserved,
    Will provoke men to wrath.

IOCASTA. It was from both?

CHORUS.   It was.

IOCASTA.   And what was said?

CHORUS. It is enough for me, more than
660   enough, when I
    Think of our ills, that this should rest
        where it lies.

OEDIPUS. You and your wise advice,
        blunting my wrath,
    Frustrated me—and it has come to this!

CHORUS. This, O my King, I said, and say
        again:
    I should be mad, distraught,
    I should be a fool, and worse,
    If I sought to drive you away.
    Thebes was near sinking; you brought
        her safe
    Through the storm. Now again we pray
        that you may save us.

IOCASTA. In Heaven's name, my lord, I too
670   must know
    What was the reason for this blazing
        anger.

OEDIPUS. There's none to whom I more
        defer; and so,
    I'll tell you: Creon and his vile plot
        against me.

IOCASTA. What has he done, that you are
        so incensed?

OEDIPUS. He says that I am Laius' murderer.

IOCASTA. From his own knowledge? Or has
        someone told him?

OEDIPUS. No; that suspicion should not fall
        upon
    Himself, he used a tool—a crafty prophet.

IOCASTA. Why, have no fear of *that*. Listen
        to me,
680   And you will learn that the prophetic art
    Touches our human fortunes not at all.
    I soon can give you proof.—An oracle
    Once came to Laius—from the god
        himself
    I do not say, but from his ministers:
    His fate it was, that should he have a son
    By me, that son would take his father's
        life.
    But he was killed—or so they said—by
        strangers,
    By brigands, at a place where three ways
        meet.

As for the child, it was not three days old
When Laius fastened both its feet together 690
And had it cast over a precipice.
Therefore Apollo failed; for neither did
His son kill Laius, nor did Laius meet
The awful end he feared, killed by his son.
    So much for what prophetic voices
        uttered.
Have no regard for them. The god will
        bring
To light himself whatever thing he
        chooses.

OEDIPUS. Iocasta, terror seizes me, and
        shakes
My very soul, at one thing you have said.

IOCASTA. Why so? What have I said to
        frighten you?   700

OEDIPUS. I think I heard you say that
        Laius
Was murdered at a place where three
        ways meet?

IOCASTA. So it was said—indeed, they say
        it still.

OEDIPUS. Where is the place where this
        encounter happened?

IOCASTA. They call the country Phokis, and
        a road
From Delphi joins a road from Daulia.

OEDIPUS. Since that was done, how many
        years have passed?

IOCASTA. It was proclaimed in Thebes a
        little time
Before the city offered you the crown.

OEDIPUS. O Zeus, what fate hast thou
        ordained for me?   710

IOCASTA. What is the fear that so oppresses
        you?

OEDIPUS. One moment yet: tell me of Laius.
    What age was he? and what was his
        appearance?

IOCASTA. A tall man, and his hair was
        touched with white;
    In figure he was not unlike yourself.

OEDIPUS. O God! Did I, then, in my
        ignorance,
    Proclaim that awful curse against myself?

IOCASTA. What are you saying? How you
        frighten me!

OEDIPUS. I greatly fear that prophet was
        not blind.

But yet one question; that will show me
720   more.
IOCASTA. For all my fear, I'll tell you what
    I can.
OEDIPUS. Was he alone, or did he have
    with him
    A royal bodyguard of men-at-arms?
IOCASTA. The company in all were five;
    the King
    Rode in a carriage, and there was a
    Herald.
OEDIPUS. Ah God! How clear the picture
    is! . . . But who,
    Iocasta, brought report of this to Thebes?
IOCASTA. A slave, the only man that was
    not killed.
OEDIPUS. And is he round about the palace
    now?
IOCASTA. No, he is not. When he returned,
730   and saw
    You ruling in the place of the dead King,
    He begged me, on his bended knees, to
    send him
    Into the hills as shepherd, out of sight,
    As far as could be from the city here.
    I sent him, for he was a loyal slave;
    He well deserved this favour—and much
    more.
OEDIPUS. Could he be brought back here—
    at once—to see me?
IOCASTA. He could; but why do you desire
    his coming?
OEDIPUS. I fear I have already said,
    Iocasta,
740   More than enough; and therefore I will
    see him.
IOCASTA. Then he shall come. But, as your
    wife, I ask you,
    What is the terror that possesses you?
OEDIPUS. And you shall know it, since my
    fears have grown
    So great; for who is more to me than you,
    That I should speak to *him* at such a
    moment?
     My father, then, was Polybus of
     Corinth;
    My mother, Merope. My station there
    Was high as any man's—until a thing
    Befell me that was strange indeed, though
    not

Deserving of the thought I gave to it.   750
A man said at a banquet—he was full
Of wine—that I was not my father's son.
It angered me; but I restrained myself
That day. The next I went and
    questioned both
My parents. They were much incensed
    with him
Who had let fall the insult. So, from them,
I had assurance. Yet the slander spread
And always chafed me. Therefore secretly,
My mother and my father unaware,
I went to Delphi. Phoebus would return   760
No answer to my question, but declared
A thing most horrible: he foretold that I
Should mate with my own mother, and
    beget
A brood that men would shudder to
    behold,
And that I was to be the murderer
Of my own father.
            Therefore, back to Corinth
I never went—the stars alone have told me
Where Corinth lies—that I might never
    see
Cruel fulfilment of that oracle.
So journeying, I came to that same spot   770
Where, as you say, this King was killed.
    And now,
This is the truth, Iocasta: when I
    reached
The place where three ways meet, I met
    a herald,
And in a carriage drawn by colts was
    such
A man as you describe. By violence
The herald and the older man attempted
To push me off the road, I, in my rage,
Struck at the driver, who was hustling me.
The old man, when he saw me level with
    him,
Taking a double-goad, aimed at my head   780
A murderous blow. He paid for that, full
    measure.
    Swiftly I hit him with my staff; he rolled
    Out of his carriage, flat upon his back.
    I killed them all.—But if, between this
    stranger
    And Laius there was any bond of
    kinship,

Who could be in more desperate plight
  than I?
Who more accursèd in the eyes of
  Heaven?
For neither citizen nor stranger may
Receive me in his house, nor speak to me,
790 But he must bar the door. And it was
  none
But I invoked this curse on my own head!
And I pollute the bed of him I slew
With my own hands! Say, am I vile?
  Am I
Not all impure? Seeing I must be exiled,
And even in my exile must not go
And see my parents, nor set foot upon
My native land; or, if I do, I must
Marry my mother, and kill Polybus
My father, who engendered me and
  reared me.
800 If one should say it was a cruel god
Brought this upon me, would he not
  speak right?
  No, no, you holy powers above! Let me
Not see that day! but rather let me pass
Beyond the sight of men, before I see
The stain of such pollution come upon
  me!
CHORUS-LEADER. My lord, this frightens me.
  But you must hope,
  Until we hear the tale from him that saw
  it.
OEDIPUS. That is the only hope that's left
  to me;
  We must await the coming of the
  shepherd.
810 IOCASTA. What do you hope from him,
  when he is here?
OEDIPUS. I'll tell you: if his story shall be
  found
  The same as yours, then I am free of
  guilt.
IOCASTA. But what have *I* said of especial
  note?
OEDIPUS. You said that he reported it was
  brigands
Who killed the King. If he still speaks of
  'men',
It was not I; a single man, and 'men',
Are not the same. But if he says it was
A traveller journeying alone, why then,

The burden of the guilt must fall on me.
IOCASTA. But that *is* what he said, I do   820
  assure you!
He cannot take it back again! Not I
Alone, but the whole city heard him say
  it!
But even if he should revoke the tale
He told before, not even so, my lord,
Will he establish that the King was slain
According to the prophecy. For that was
  clear:
His son, and mine, should slay him.—He,
  poor thing,
Was killed himself, and never killed his
  father.
Therefore, so far as divination goes,
Or prophecy, I'll take no notice of it.   830
OEDIPUS. And that is wise.—But send a man
  to bring
The shepherd; I would not have that
  neglected.
IOCASTA. I'll send at once.—But come with
  me; for I
Would not do anything that could
  displease you.
         [*Exeunt* OEDIPUS *and* IOCASTA

Strophe 1

CHORUS. I pray that I may pass my life
(*in a steady rhythm*) In reverent holiness of
  word and deed.
For there are laws enthroned above;
Heaven created them,
Olympus was their father,
And mortal men had no part in their   840
  birth;
Nor ever shall their power pass from sight
In dull forgetfulness;
A god moves in them; he grows not old.

Antistrophe 1

Pride makes the tyrant—pride of wealth
And power, too great for wisdom and
  restraint;
For Pride will climb the topmost height;
Then is the man cast down

To uttermost destruction.
There he finds no escape, no resource.
850 But high contention for the city's good
May the gods preserve.
For me—may the gods be my defence!

Strophe 2

If there is one who walks in pride
Of word or deed, and has no fear of
  Justice,
No reverence for holy shrines—
May utter ruin fall on him!
So may his ill-starred pride be given its
  reward.
Those who seek dishonourable advantage
And lay violent hands on holy things
860 And do not shun impiety—
Who among these will secure himself
  from the wrath of God?
If deeds like these are honoured,
Why should I join in the sacred dance?

Antistrophe 2

No longer shall Apollo's shrine,
The holy centre of the Earth, receive
  my worship;
No, nor his seat at Abae, nor
The temple of Olympian Zeus,
If what the god foretold does not come
  to pass.
Mighty Zeus—if so I should address
  Thee—
870 O great Ruler of all things, look on this!
Now are thy oracles falling into
  contempt, and men
Deny Apollo's power.
Worship of the gods is passing away.

Enter IOCASTA, *attended by a girl carrying a
wreath and incense*

IOCASTA. My lords of Thebes, I have
    bethought myself
  To approach the altars of the gods, and
    lay

These wreaths on them, and burn this
    frankincense.
For every kind of terror has laid hold
On Oedipus; his judgement is distracted.
He will not read the future by the past
But yields himself to any who speaks   880
    fear.
Since then no words of mine suffice to
    calm him
I turn to Thee, Apollo—Thou art
    nearest—
Thy suppliant, with these votive offerings.
Grant us deliverance and peace, for now
Fear is on all; when we see Oedipus,
The helmsman of the ship, so terrified.

(*A reverent silence, while* IOCASTA *lays the
wreath at the altar and sets fire to the incense. The wreath will remain and the
incense smoke during the rest of the play.*)

Enter a SHEPHERD FROM CORINTH

CORINTHIAN. Might I inquire of you where
    I may find
  The royal palace of King Oedipus?
  Or, better, where himself is to be found?
CHORUS-LEADER. There is the palace;   890
    himself, Sir, is within,
  But here his wife and mother of his
    children.
CORINTHIAN. Ever may happiness attend on
    her,
  And hers, the wedded wife of such a man.
IOCASTA. May you enjoy the same; your
    gentle words
  Deserve no less.—Now, Sir, declare your
    purpose;
  With what request, what message have
    you come?
CORINTHIAN. With good news for your
    husband and his house.
IOCASTA. What news is this? And who has
    sent you here?
CORINTHIAN. I come from Corinth, and the
    news I bring
  Will give you joy, though joy be crossed   900
    with grief.
IOCASTA. What is this, with its two-fold
    influence?

CORINTHIAN. The common talk in Corinth is that they
  Will call on Oedipus to be their king.
IOCASTA. What? Does old Polybus no longer reign?
CORINTHIAN. Not now, for Death has laid him in his grave.
IOCASTA. Go quickly to your master, girl; give him
  The news.—You oracles, where are you now?
  This is the man whom Oedipus so long
  Has shunned, fearing to kill him; now he's dead,
910 And killed by Fortune, not by Oedipus.

Enter OEDIPUS, *very nervous*

OEDIPUS. My dear Iocasta, tell me, my dear wife,
  Why have you sent to fetch me from the palace?
IOCASTA. Listen to *him*, and as you hear, reflect
  What has become of all those oracles.
OEDIPUS. Who is this man?—What has he to tell me?
IOCASTA. He is from Corinth, and he brings you news
  About your father. Polybus is dead.
OEDIPUS. What say you, sir? Tell me the news yourself.
CORINTHIAN. If you would have me first report on this,
920 I tell you; death has carried him away.
OEDIPUS. By treachery? Or did sickness come to him?
CORINTHIAN. A small mischance will lay an old man low.
OEDIPUS. Poor Polybus! He died, then, of a sickness?
CORINTHIAN. That, and the measure of his many years.
OEDIPUS. Ah me! Why then, Iocasta, should a man
  Regard the Pythian house of oracles,
  Or screaming birds, on whose authority
  I was to slay my father? But he is dead;
  The earth has covered him; and here am I,

My sword undrawn—unless perchance   930
  my loss
  Has killed him; so might I be called his slayer.
  But for those oracles about my father,
  Those he has taken with him to the grave
  Wherein he lies, and they are come to nothing.
IOCASTA. Did I not say long since it would be so?
OEDIPUS. You did; but I was led astray by fear.
IOCASTA. So none of this deserves another thought.
OEDIPUS. Yet how can I not fear my mother's bed?
IOCASTA. Why should we fear, seeing that man is ruled
  By chance, and there is room for no clear   940
  forethought?
  No; live at random, live as best one can.
  So do not fear this marriage with your mother;
  Many a man has suffered this before—
  But only in his dreams. Whoever thinks
  The least of this, he lives most comfortably.
OEDIPUS. Your every word I do accept, if she
  That bore me did not live; but as she does—
  Despite your wisdom, how can I but tremble?
IOCASTA. Yet there is comfort in your father's death.
OEDIPUS. Great comfort, but still fear of her   950
  who lives.
CORINTHIAN. And who is this who makes you so afraid?
OEDIPUS. Meropê, my man, the wife of Polybus.
CORINTHIAN. And what in *her* gives cause of fear in *you*?
OEDIPUS. There was an awful warning from the gods.
CORINTHIAN. Can it be told, or must it be kept secret
OEDIPUS. No secret. Once Apollo said that I
  Was doomed to lie with my own mother, and
  Defile my own hands with my father's blood.

Wherefore has Corinth been, these many years,

960 My home no more. My fortunes have been fair.—

But it is good to see a parent's face.

CORINTHIAN. It was for fear of *this* you fled the city?

OEDIPUS. This, and the shedding of my father's blood.

CORINTHIAN. When then, my lord, since I am come in friendship,

I'll rid you here and now of that misgiving.

OEDIPUS. Be sure, your recompense would be in keeping.

CORINTHIAN. It was the chief cause of my coming here.

That your return might bring me some advantage.

OEDIPUS. Back to my parents I will never go.

970 CORINTHIAN. My son, it is clear, you know not what you do. . . .

OEDIPUS. Not know? What is this? Tell me what you mean.

CORINTHIAN. If for this reason you avoid your home.

OEDIPUS. Fearing Apollo's oracle may come true.

CORINTHIAN. And you incur pollution from your parents?

OEDIPUS. That is the thought that makes me live in terror.

CORINTHIAN. I tell you then, this fear of yours is idle.

OEDIPUS. How? Am I not their child, and they my parents?

CORINTHIAN. Because there's none of Polybus in you.

OEDIPUS. How can you say so? Was he not my father?

980 CORINTHIAN. I am your father just as much as he!

OEDIPUS. A stranger equal to the father? How?

CORINTHIAN. Neither did he beget you, nor did I.

OEDIPUS. Then for what reason did he call me son?

CORINTHIAN. He had you as a gift—from my own hands.

OEDIPUS. And showed such love to me? Me, not his own?

CORINTHIAN. Yes; his own childlessness so worked on him.

OEDIPUS. You, when you gave me: had you bought, or found me?

CORINTHIAN. I found you in the woods upon Cithaeron.

OEDIPUS. Why were you travelling in that neighbourhood?

CORINTHIAN. I tended flocks of sheep upon 990 the mountain.

OEDIPUS. You were a shepherd, then, wandering for hire?

CORINTHIAN. I was, my son; but that day, your preserver.

OEDIPUS. How so? What ailed me when you took me up?

CORINTHIAN. For that, your ankles might give evidence.

OEDIPUS. Alas! why speak of this, my life-long trouble?

CORINTHIAN. I loosed the fetters clamped upon your feet.

OEDIPUS. A pretty gift to carry from the cradle!

CORINTHIAN. It was for this they named you Oedipus.

OEDIPUS. Who did, my father or my mother? Tell me.

CORINTHIAN. I cannot; he knows more, 1000 from whom I had you.

OEDIPUS. It was another, not yourself, that found me?

CORINTHIAN. Yes, you were given me by another shepherd.

OEDIPUS. Who? Do you know him? Can you name the man?

CORINTHIAN. They said that he belonged to Laius.

OEDIPUS. What—him who once was ruler here in Thebes?

CORINTHIAN. Yes, he it was for whom this man was shepherd.

OEDIPUS. And is he still alive, that I can see him?

CORINTHIAN [*turning to the Chorus*]. You that are native here would know that best.

OEDIPUS. Has any man of you now present here
1010 Acquaintance with this shepherd, him he speaks of?
Has any seen him, here, or in the fields?
Speak; on this moment hangs discovery.
CHORUS-LEADER. It is, I think, the man that you have sent for,
The slave now in the country. But who should know
The truth of this more than Iocasta here?
OEDIPUS. The man he speaks of: do you think, Iocasta,
He is the one I have already summoned?
IOCASTA. What matters who he is? Pay no regard.—
1020 The tale is idle; it is best forgotten.
OEDIPUS. It cannot be that I should have this clue
And then not find the secret of my birth.
IOCASTA. In God's name stop, if you have any thought
For your own life! My ruin is enough.
OEDIPUS. Be not dismayed; nothing can prove you base.
Not though I find my mother thrice a slave.
IOCASTA. O, I beseech you, do not! Seek no more!
OEDIPUS. You cannot move me. I *will* know the truth.
IOCASTA. I know that what I say is for the best.
OEDIPUS. This 'best' of yours! I have no patience with it.
1030 IOCASTA. O may you never learn what man you are!
OEDIPUS. Go, someone, bring the herdsman here to me,
And leave her to enjoy her pride of birth.
IOCASTA. O man of doom! For by no other name
Can I address you now or evermore.
[*Exit* IOCASTA
CHORUS-LEADER. The Queen has fled, my lord, as if before
Some driving storm of grief. I fear that from
Her silence may break forth some great disaster.

OEDIPUS. Break forth what will! My birth, however humble,
I am resolved to find. But she, perhaps,
Is proud, as women will be; is ashamed   1040
Of my low birth. But I do rate myself
The child of Fortune, giver of all good,
And I shall not be put to shame, for I
Am born of Her; the Years who are my kinsmen
Distinguished my estate, now high, now low;
So born, I could not make me someone else,
And not do all to find my parentage.

Strophe 1

CHORUS. If I have power of prophecy,
(*animated rhythm*) If I have judgement wise and sure, Cithaeron
(I swear by Olympus),   1050
Thou shalt be honoured when the moon
Next is full, as mother and foster-nurse
And birth-place of Oedipus, with festival and dancing,
For thou hast given great blessings to our King.
To Thee, Apollo, now we raise our cry:
O grant our prayer find favour in thy sight!

Antistrophe

Who is thy mother, O my son?
Is she an ageless nymph among the mountains,
That bore thee to Pan?
Or did Apollo father thee?   1060
For dear to him are the pastures in the hills.
Or Hermes, who ruleth from the summit of Kyllene?
Or Dionysus on the mountain-tops,
Did he receive thee from thy mother's arms,
A nymph who follows him on Helicon?

OEDIPUS. If I, who never yet have met the man,

May risk conjecture, I think I see the
    herdsman
Whom we have long been seeking. In
    his age
He well accords; and more, I recognize
1070 Those who are with him as of my own
    household.
But as for knowing, you will have
    advantage
Of me, if you have seen the man before.

CHORUS-LEADER. 'Tis he, for certain—one
    of Laius' men,
One of the shepherds whom he trusted
    most.

Enter the THEBAN SHEPHERD

OEDIPUS. You first I ask, you who have
    come from Corinth:
Is that the man you mean?

CORINTHIAN.   That very man.

OEDIPUS. Come here, my man; look at me;
    asnwer me
My questions. Were you ever Laius'
    man?

THEBAN. I was; his slave—born in the
    house, not bought.

1080 OEDIPUS. What was your charge, or what
    your way of life?

THEBAN. Tending the sheep, the most part
    of my life.

OEDIPUS. And to what regions did you most
    resort?

THEBAN. Now it was Cithaeron, now the
    country round.

OEDIPUS. And was this man of your
    acquaintance there?

THEBAN. In what employment? Which is
    the man you mean?

OEDIPUS. Him yonder. Had you any
    dealings with him?

THEBAN. Not such that I can quickly call
    to mind.

CORINTHIAN. No wonder, Sir, but though
    he has forgotten
I can remind him. I am very sure,
1090 He knows the time when, round about
    Cithaeron,
He with a double flock, and I with one,
We spent together three whole summer
    seasons,
From spring until the rising of Arcturus.

Then, with the coming on of winter, I
Drove my flocks home, he his, to Laius'
    folds.
Is this the truth? or am I telling lies?

THEBAN. It is true, although it happened
    long ago.

CORINTHIAN. Then tell me: do you recollect
    a baby
You gave me once to bring up for my
    own?

THEBAN. Why this? Why are you asking
    me this question?

CORINTHIAN. My friend, *here* is the man who 1100
    was that baby!

THEBAN. O, devil take you! Cannot you
    keep silent?

OEDIPUS. Here, Sir! This man needs no
    reproof from you.
Your tongue needs chastisement much
    more than his.

THEBAN. O best of masters, how am I
    offending?

OEDIPUS. Not telling of the child of whom
    he speaks.

THEBAN. He? He knows nothing. He is
    wasting time.

OEDIPUS [*threatening*]. If you'll not speak
    from pleasure, speak from pain.

THEBAN. No, no, I pray! Not torture an
    old man!

OEDIPUS. Here, someone, quickly! Twist
    this fellow's arms!

THEBAN. Why, wretched man? What would 1110
    you know besides?

OEDIPUS. That child: you gave it him, the
    one he speaks of?

THEBAN. I did. Ah God, would I had died
    instead!

OEDIPUS. And die you shall, unless you
    speak the truth.

THEBAN. And if I do, then death is still
    more certain.

OEDIPUS. This man, I think, is trying to
    delay me.

THEBAN. Not I! I said I gave the child—
    just now.

OEDIPUS. And got it—where? Your own?
    or someone else's?

THEBAN. No, not my own. Someone had
    given it me.

OEDIPUS. Who? Which of these our citizens?
    From what house?

1120 THEBAN. No, I implore you, master! Do
    not ask!

OEDIPUS. You die if I must question you
    again.

THEBAN. Then, 'twas a child of one in
    Laius' house.

OEDIPUS. You mean a slave? Or someone
    of his kin?

THEBAN. God! I am on the verge of saying
    it.

OEDIPUS. And I of hearing it, but hear I
    must.

THEBAN. His own, or so they said. But
    she within
    Could tell you best—your wife—the
    truth of it.

OEDIPUS. What, did she give you it?

THEBAN.   She did, my lord.

OEDIPUS. With what intention?

THEBAN.   That I should destroy it.

OEDIPUS. Her own?—How could she?

1130 THEBAN.   Frightened by oracles.

OEDIPUS. What oracles?

THEBAN.   That it would kill its parents.

OEDIPUS. Why did you let it go to this
    man here?

THEBAN. I pitied it, my lord. I thought to
    send
    The child abroad, whence this man
    came. And he
    Saved it, for utter doom. For if you are
    The man he says, then you were born
    for ruin.

OEDIPUS. Ah God! Ah God! This is the
    truth, at last!
    O Sun, let me behold thee this once
    more,
    I who am proved accursed in my
    conception,

1140 And in my marriage, and in him I slew.
        [*Exeunt severally* OEDIPUS, CORINTHIAN,
                                        THEBAN

Strophe 1

CHORUS. Alas! you generations of men!

(*glyconics*) Even while you live you are next
    to nothing!
Has any man won for himself
More than the shadow of happiness,
A shadow that swiftly fades away?
Oedipus, now as I look on you,
See your ruin, how can I say that
Mortal man can be happy?

Antistrophe 1

For who won greater prosperity?
    Sovereignty and wealth beyond all   1150
        desiring?
The crooked-clawed, riddling Sphinx,
Maiden and bird, you overcame;
    You stood like a tower of strength to
        Thebes.
So you received our crown, received the
Highest honours that we could give—
King in our mighty city.

Strophe 2

Who more wretched, more afflicted now,
With cruel misery, with fell disaster,
Your life in dust and ashes?
    O noble Oedipus!   1160
    How could it be? to come again
A bridegroom of her who gave you
    birth!
How could such a monstrous thing
Endure so long, unknown?

Antistrophe 2

Time sees all, and Time, in your despite,
Disclosed and punished your unnatural
    marriage—
A child, and then a husband.
    O son of Laius,
    Would I had never looked on you!
I mourn you as one who mourns the   1170
    dead.

First you gave me back my life,
And now, that life is death.

Enter, from the palace, a MESSENGER

MESSENGER. My Lords, most honoured
  citizens of Thebes,
What deeds am I to tell of, you to see!
What heavy grief to bear, if still remains
Your native loyalty to our line of kings.
For not the Ister, no, nor Phasis' flood
Could purify this house, such things it
  hides,
Such others will it soon display to all,
1180 Evils self-sought. Of all our sufferings
Those hurt the most that we ourselves
  inflict.
CHORUS-LEADER. Sorrow enough—too
  much—in what was known
Already. What new sorrow do you bring?
MESSENGER. Quickest for me to say and you
  to hear:
It is the Queen, Iocasta—she is dead.
CHORUS-LEADER. Iocasta, dead? But how?
  What was the cause?
MESSENGER. By her own hand. Of what has
  passed, the worst
Cannot be yours: that was, to see it.
But you shall hear, so far as memory
  serves,
1190 The cruel story.—In her agony
She ran across the courtyard, snatching at
Her hair with both her hands. She made
  her way
Straight to her chamber; she barred fast
  the doors
And called on Laius, these long years
  dead,
Remembering their by-gone procreation.
'Through this did you meet death
  yourself, and leave
To me, the mother, child-bearing
  accursed
To my own child.' She cried aloud upon
The bed where she had borne a double
  brood,
1200 Husband from husband, children from a
  child.
And thereupon she died, I know not
  how;

For, groaning, Oedipus burst in, and we,
For watching him, saw not *her* agony
And how it ended. He, ranging through
  the palace,
Came up to each man calling for a
  sword,
Calling for her whom he had called his
  wife,
Asking where was she who had borne
  them all,
Himself and his own children. So he
  raved.
And then some deity showed him the
  way,
For it was none of us that stood around; 1210
He cried aloud, as if to someone who
Was leading him; he leapt upon the
  doors,
Burst from their sockets the yielding bars,
  and fell
Into the room; and there, hanged by the
  neck,
We saw his wife, held in a swinging cord.
He, when he saw it, groaned in misery
And loosed her body from the rope.
  When now
She lay upon the ground, awful to see
Was that which followed: from her dress
  he tore
The golden brooches that she had been 1220
  wearing,
Raised them, and with their points
  struck his own eyes,
Crying aloud that they should never see
What he had suffered and what he had
  done,
But in the dark henceforth they should
  behold
Those whom they ought not; nor should
  recognize
Those whom he longed to see. To such
  refrain
He smote his eyeballs with the pins, not
  once,
Nor twice; and as he smote them, blood
  ran down
His face, not dripping slowly, but there
  fell
Showers of black rain and blood-red hail 1230
  together.

Not on his head alone, but on them
   both,
Husband and wife, this common storm
   has broken.
Their ancient happiness of early days
Was happiness indeed; but now, today,
Death, ruin, lamentation, shame—of all
The ills there are, not one is wanting
   here.
CHORUS-LEADER. Now is there intermission
   in his agony?
MESSENGER. He shouts for someone to
   unbar the gates,
And to display to Thebes the parricide,
His mother's—no, I cannot speak the
   words;
For, by the doom he uttered, he will cast
Himself beyond our borders, nor remain
To be a curse at home. But he needs
   strength,
And one to guide him; for these wounds
   are greater
Than he can bear—as you shall see; for
   look!
They draw the bolts. A sight you will
   behold
To move the pity even of an enemy.

The doors open. OEDIPUS *slowly advances*

CHORUS. O horrible, dreadful sight. More
   dreadful far
(*These verses sung or chanted in a slow march-
   time.*) Than any I have yet seen. What
   cruel frenzy
Came over you? What spirit with
   superhuman leap
Came to assist your grim destiny?
Ah, most unhappy man!
But no! I cannot bear even to look at
   you,
Though there is much that I would ask
   and see and hear.
But I shudder at the very sight of you.
OEDIPUS [*sings in the dochmiac rhythm*]. Alas!
   alas! and woe for my misery!
Where are my steps taking me?
My random voice is lost in the air.
O God! how hast thou crushed me!

CHORUS-LEADER [*spoken*]. Too terribly for us   1260
   to hear or see.
OEDIPUS [*sings*]. O cloud of darkness
   abominable,
My enemy unspeakable,
In cruel onset insuperable.
Alas! alas! Assailed at once by pain
Of pin-points and of memory of crimes.
CHORUS-LEADER. In such tormenting pains
   you well may cry
A double grief and feel a double woe.
OEDIPUS [*sings*]. Ah, my friend!
Still at my side? Still steadfast?
Still can you endure me?   1270
Still care for me, a blind man?
[*speaks*] For it is you, my friend; I know
   'tis you;
Though all is darkness, yet I know your
   voice.
CHORUS-LEADER. O, to destroy your sight!
   How could you bring
Yourself to do it? What god incited you?
OEDIPUS [*sings*]. It was Apollo, friends,
   Apollo.
He decreed that I should suffer what I
   suffer;
But the hand that struck, alas! was my
   own,
And not another's.
For why should I have sight.   1280
When sight of nothing could give me
   pleasure?
CHORUS. It was even as you say.
OEDIPUS. What have I left, my friends, to
   see,
To cherish, whom to speak with, or
To listen to, with joy?
Lead me away at once, far from Thebes;
Lead me away, my friends!
I have destroyed; I am accursed, and,
   what is more,
Hateful to Heaven, as no other.
CHORUS-LEADER [*speaks*]. Unhappy your   1290
   intention, and unhappy
Your fate. O would that I had never
   known you!
OEDIPUS [*sings*]. Curses on him, whoever he
   was,
Who took the savage fetters from my feet,

1240

1250

Snatched me from death, and saved
  me.
No thanks I owe him,
For had I died that day
Less ruin had I brought on me and mine.
CHORUS. That wish is my wish too.
OEDIPUS. I had not then come and slain my
  father.
1300 Nor then would men have called me
  Husband of her that bore me.
Now am I God's enemy, child of the
  guilty,
And she that bore me has borne too my
  children;
And if there is evil surpassing evil,
  That has come to Oedipus.
CHORUS-LEADER. How can I say that you
  have counselled well?
Far better to be dead than to be blind.
OEDIPUS. That what is done was not done
  for the best
Seek not to teach me: counsel me no
  more.
1310 I know not how I could have gone to
  Hades
And with these eyes have looked upon
  my father
Or on my mother; such things have I
  done
To them, death is no worthy punishment.
Or could I look for pleasure in the sight
Of my own children, born as they were
  born?
Never! No pleasure there, for eyes of
  mine,
Nor in this city, nor its battlements
Nor sacred images. From these—ah,
  miserable!—
I, the most nobly born of any Theban
1320 Am banned for ever by my own decree
That the defiler should be driven forth,
The man accursed of Heaven and Laius'
  house.
Was I to find such taint in me, and then
With level eyes to look *them* in the face?
Nay more: if for my ears I could have
  built
Some dam to stay the flood of sound,
  that I

Might lose both sight and hearing, and
  seal up
My wretched body—that I would have
  done.
How good to dwell beyond the reach of
  pain!
  Cithaeron! Why did you accept me? 1330
  Why
Did you not take and kill me? Never
  then
Should I have come to dwell among the
  Thebans.
  O Polybus! Corinth! and that ancient
  home
I thought my father's—what a thing you
  nurtured!
How fair, how foul beneath! For I am
  found
Foul in myself and in my parentage.
  O you three ways, that in a hidden
  glen
Do meet: you narrow branching roads
  within
The forest—you, through my own hands,
  did drink
My father's blood, that was my own.— 1340
  Ah! do you
Remember what you saw me do? And
  what
I did again in Thebes? You marriages!
You did beget me: then, having begotten,
Bore the same crop again, and brought
  to light
Commingled blood of fathers, brothers,
  sons,
Brides, mothers, wives; all that there can
  be
Among the human kind most horrible!
  But that which it is foul to do, it is
Not fair to speak of. Quick as you can, I
  beg,
Banish me, hide me, slay me! Throw me 1350
  forth
Into the sea, where I may sink from
  view.
I pray you, deign to touch one so
  afflicted,
And do not fear: there is no man alive
Can bear this load of evil but myself.

CHORUS-LEADER. To listen to your prayers,
  Creon is here,
  For act or guidance opportune; for he,
  In your defection, is our champion.

Enter CREON

OEDIPUS. Alas! alas! How can I speak to
  him?
  What word of credit find? In all my
  commerce
1360 With him aforetime I am proven false.
CREON. No exultation, Oedipus, and no
  reproach
  Of injuries inflicted brings me here;
  But if the face of men moves not your
  shame,
  Then reverence show to that all-nurturing
  fire,
  The holy Sun, that he be not polluted
  By such accursèd sight, which neither
  Earth
  Nor rain from Heaven nor sunlight can
  endure.
    Take him within, and quickly: it is
    right
  His kinsmen only should behold and hear
1370 Evils that chiefly on his kinsmen fall.
OEDIPUS. In Heaven's name—since you
  cheat my expectation,
  So noble towards my baseness—grant me
  this:
  It is for you I ask it, not myself.
CREON. What is this supplication that you
  make?
OEDIPUS. Drive me at once beyond your
  bounds, where I
  Shall be alone, and no one speak to me.
CREON. I would have done it; but I first
  desired
  To ask the God what he would have me
  do.
OEDIPUS. No, his command was given in
  full, to slay
1380 Me, the polluter and the parricide.
CREON. Those were his words; but in our
  present need
  It would be wise to ask what we should
  do.

OEDIPUS. You will inquire for such a
  wretch as I?
CREON. I will; for now *you* may believe the
  god.
OEDIPUS. Yes; and on you I lay this charge
  and duty:
  Give burial, as you will, to her who lies
  Within—for she is yours, and this is
  proper;
  And, while I live, let not my father's city
  Endure to have me as a citizen.
  My home must be the mountains—on   1390
  Cithaeron,
  Which, while they lived, my parents
  chose to be
  My tomb: they wished to slay me; now
  they shall.
  For this I know: sickness can never kill
  me,
  Nor any other evil; I was not saved
  That day from death, except for some
  strange doom.
  My fate must take the course it will.—
  Now, for my sons,
  Be not concerned for them: they can,
  being men,
  Fend for themselves, wherever they may
  be:
  But my unhappy daughters, my two
  girls,
  Whose chairs were always set beside my   1400
  own
  At table—they who shared in every dish
  That was prepared for me—oh Creon!
  these
  Do I commend to you. And grant me
  this:
  To take them in my arms, and weep for
  them.
  My lord! most noble Creon! could I
  now
  But hold them in my arms, then I
  should think
  I had them as I had when I could see
  them.
  Ah! what is this?
  Ah Heaven! do I not hear my dear ones,
  sobbing?
  Has Creon, in his pity, sent to me   1410

My darling children? Has he? Is it true?
CREON. It is; they have been always your delight;
So, knowing this, I had them brought to you.
OEDIPUS. Then Heaven reward you, and for this kind service
Protect you better than it protected me!
Where are you, children? Where? O come to me!
Come, let me clasp you with a brother's arms,
These hands, which helped your father's eyes, once bright,
To look upon you as they see you now—
1420 Your father who, not seeing, nor inquiring,
Gave you for mother her who bore himself.
See you I cannot; but I weep for you,
For the unhappiness that must be yours,
And for the bitter life that you must lead.
What gathering of the citizens, what festivals,
Will you have part in? Your high celebrations
Will be to go back home, and sit in tears.
And when the time for marriage comes, what man
Will stake upon the ruin and the shame
1430 That *I* am to my parents and to you?
Nothing is wanting there: your father slew
His father, married her who gave him birth,
And then, from that same source whence he himself
Had sprung, got you.—With these things they will taunt you;
And who will take you then in marriage? —Nobody;
But you must waste, unwedded and unfruitful.
Ah, Creon! Since they have no parent now
But you—for both of us who gave them life

Have perished—suffer them not to be cast out
Homeless and beggars; for they are your   1440
kin.
Have pity on them, for they are so young,
So desolate, except for you alone.
Say 'Yes', good Creon! Let your hand confirm it.
And now, my children, for my exhortation
You are too young; but you can pray that I
May live henceforward—where I should; and you
More happily than the father who begot you.
CREON. Now make an end of tears, and go within.
OEDIPUS. Then I must go—against my will.
CREON. There is a time for everything.   1450
OEDIPUS. You know what I would have you do?
CREON. If you will tell me, I shall know.
OEDIPUS. Send me away, away from Thebes.
CREON. The God, not I, must grant you this.
OEDIPUS. The gods hate no man more than me!
CREON. Then what you ask they soon will give.
OEDIPUS. You promise this?
CREON.   Ah no! When I
Am ignorant, I do not speak.
OEDIPUS. Then lead me in; I say no more.
CREON. Release the children then, and   1460
come.
OEDIPUS. What? Take these children from me? No!
CREON. Seek not to have your way in all things:
Where you had your way before,
Your mastery broke before the end.

(*There was no doubt a short concluding utterance from the Chorus. What stands in the MSS. appears to be spurious.*)

ŒDIPUS TYRANNUS

H. D. F. Kitto

We must not hazily imagine that Sophocles was merely dramatizing the Oedipus legend and doing it rather well. Within certain obvious limits the Greek dramatists always remade the myth, to make it suit their purposes. Out of this legend Aeschylus had made a trilogy, of which only the *Seven against Thebes* has survived: it appears that in his version Laius was warned not to have a son, or it would end his race and imperil the city. Euripides, in his *Phoenissae*, implies much the same, and makes Iocasta say that Laius begat Oedipus "giving way to pleasure and heated by wine." In each case, Laius was culpable. But our affair is with Sophocles, not with "the Oedipus-myth". Therefore we will first disengage from the play the story, as Sophocles made it; then, having disengaged his raw material, so to speak, we will contemplate the dramatic structure that he built with it. Being a *poet*, a "maker", he made something; what he made, how he made it, ought to show us what ideas controlled the making.

The story, as distinct from the play, begins with Iocasta's account of his birth (vv. 711 ff.). I quote it in Jebb's careful translation: "An oracle came to Laius—I will not say from Phoebus himself, but from his ministers —that the doom should overtake him to die by the hand of his child who should spring from him and me." Jebb expounds the relative clause as meaning "whoever may be born;" an equally valid translation would be "a son (some son) born to him and me." Iocasta continues: "As for Laius, foreign brigands killed him at a branching road; and as for the child, he was not three days old when Laius clamped his feet together and had him cast over a precipice." This is the only reference in the play to the birth: so far from suggesting any defiance on the part of Laius, much less an act of lust (as Richard Lattimore has recently propounded), the text is at least compatible with the assumption that the fatal child may have been conceived already. Some scholars, anxious to find explanatory guilt, have urged that Laius incurred hybris by trying to thwart the will of god. On this, two remarks only: (i) the suggestion is never made by Sophocles, and we do not get nearer to a dramatist's thought by adding to a play bits and pieces which he neither says nor implies (nor, for that matter, do we appreciate a painter better by looking at his work through green or red spectacles). (ii) What opposite fault would we now be imputing to Laius if he had done nothing, in the face of so dire a threat? No; we must stick to the text.

Sophocles' story continues with the two shepherds who, from such natural motives, saved the child, so that it was brought up, in Corinth, by Polybus and Merope. Then comes the man who got tipsy at a banquet and opened his mouth too wide—"A remarkable incident," says Oedipus (777 ff.), "though hardly worth the attention I gave it." Polybus and Merope deny the story, indignantly; but the rumor spreads, and so rankles with Oedipus that he goes to Delphi, without telling his "parents". Now comes the second bolt from the blue: instead of answering his question, Phoebus tells him that he is to marry his mother, produce children of shame, and kill his father; to avoid which he takes the other road, resolved never to see Corinth again. There follows the affray at the Three Ways, and it is so told as to absolve Oedipus from serious guilt; a modern verdict would be Justifiable Homicide. The truculent charioteer and the old man tried to hustle Oedipus off the road; Oedipus angrily struck the charioteer, but when he was level with the chariot the old man aimed a murderous blow at his head, and if he had not been quick on the draw he would have been killed—and the prophecy would have been turned upside down. That Oedipus went on to kill (as he thought) all the others too seems unnecessary—except, obviously, for the sake of the plot; but if this is guilt, it has nothing to do with the fulfillment of the prophecies. Next, the affair of the Sphinx: Oedipus accepts the offer of the vacant throne, and of the vacant Queen also, though Sophocles has no word to say about this. One or two critics, who like their Sophocles made easy, have written that Oedipus was lured on by the prospect of glory, wealth and power: Sophocles himself is not of this company. To say this is to rewrite, not explain, the play.

Here ends the past story, embedded in the present action; this is precisely how Sophocles presents it—and what other dramatists did is not evidence. It justifies two general assertions. One is that Sophocles has avoided moralizing it. He has not made the begetting of Oedipus a crime or even culpable folly; he has not made the slaying of Laius a wanton act; he imputes no blame to Oedipus for accepting the throne and queen of Thebes. The second point is that he has made no attempt at all to make us feel the presence of some controlling Power in the background. Twice the god speaks; then, having spoken, he retires and allows things to take their course. What happens is presented as being entirely within the competence of the human agents, as a group. Laius might have destroyed the child: in fact, he thought he had. For reasons which may be obvious, but are not suggested by Sophocles, he did something that was just as good—except that it wasn't. The first shepherd happened not to be a brute; he acted, as he says, out of pity. The second was willing to bring himself to the favorable notice of his king. A man gets drunk—unhappily, a common occurrence— and blurts out a rumor which happens to be true. Polybus and Merope might have said: "Well, Oedipus, you are old enough now to be told the truth. . . ." They did not—and had no second chance, for Oedipus, in his impetuous way, went to Delphi without telling them. It may sound an odd thing to say, but the whole story, oracles apart, is so

true to life. Not of course in any naturalistic sense, I do not mean that the play might have been entitled: *Oedipus Tyrannus, or, A Typical Day in Thebes*. I mean that every single detail, barring the oracles, rings true: we know that we (like Laius) can bet on an apparent certainty and lose; that good intentions, like the shepherd's pity, can produce disastrous consequences; that people will shrink from admitting the truth, as Polybus and Merope did, and that this may prove ruinous; that coincidences do occur, like the meeting of Oedipus and Laius, and that men can be truculent, or irascible. "But," they say, "it is fantastic that all these things should happen together, to one man." And are we to suppose that Sophocles had not noticed this? He insists that no man has ever suffered as Oedipus has done—and he knew the difference between drama and reporting. The story is so fantastically untrue to life, in the literal sense, that our conclusion ought to be not that Sophocles was something of a ninny, but that we ourselves are probably on the wrong track. If we are intelligent enough to see that the play gives no balanced picture of life, we should exercise our intelligence a little further: we should reflect on the notable differences in style, texture, length between a Greek play and a novel by Dickens or Dostoievsky, which point to the conclusion that the form which these novelists used is capable of giving a balanced picture of life, while the Greek form is so incapable of giving one that presumably those who used it had no such generous ambition; that it is however remarkably well adapted to the making of one general statement about life.

Each single incident in the play, I repeat, is the sort of thing that can and does happen. Oedipus is the only man intelligent enough to answer the Sphinx's riddle, yet he goes and marries a woman old enough to be his mother. He didn't think; anyhow, he *knew* that his mother was Merope—though there had been a rumor even about that; just as Iocasta *knew* that the child had been destroyed, and that the prophecy had been belied. Sophocles does not blame these people; neither therefore must we; it is not a matter of guilt and punishment, but of how people can in fact be deceived.

So far my suggestion is this: if we can be sceptical enough to hold in suspense our own conviction, which in any case the other plays contradict, that these people are puppets dancing at the end of a divine piece of string, then the facts of the play create the impression that the god, twice, has given them a dire warning, and has left them to handle the situation. They act as their intelligence and resolution suggest, and they fail. Here we leave the matter until we have contemplated the structure which Sophocles built out of this material.

For clarity and convenience I divide the play into four main areas: (i) the opening scenes and the first ode; (ii) the two long scenes with Teiresias and Creon; (iii) from Iocasta's entry to the discovery and the self-blinding; (iv) all that follows the reappearance of Oedipus. We shall see that (ii) and (iv) both end in a way which the raw material does not in the least suggest or require, and that (iii) contains much that does not come from the myth, and is in itself rather surprising.

(i) Needs no elaborate comment. Obviously, it presents Oedipus in the sharpest possible contrast to what he will be at the end of the play; the illusion is contrasted with the reality. He is the great and devoted king (and this, at least, is not illusion); he is almost god-like in his eminence, wisdom, intelligence; he is utterly remote from the public calamity, except that he is king of the afflicted city. Next, the plague is described, once by the Priest, once by the Chorus. One odd thing about the Plague is that as the play goes on Sophocles allows us to forget it. Therefore it is not a major part of Sophocles' structure. It forces the discovery, of course— but is that all? If we listen with any care to the descriptions of it, we notice that the nature of the plague—sterility in crops, cattle, the human kind—is nicely proportioned to the

nature of the offenses—Oedipus' crimes against his parents. As at the beginning of *Hamlet*, things done contrary to Nature cause a perturbation in nature: "Foul deeds will rise . . ."—But why say "crimes", "foul deeds"? Was not Oedipus ignorant, therefore innocent—unlike Claudius? Certainly he was, but the Greek gods take no account of ignorance and innocence, being in this respect like some of the gods whom we know today: if I innocently drink some strychnine thinking it is lemonade, the god who is in charge of these things will not let me live because I did not intend suicide.

(ii) Of this part of the structure we say, truly enough, that it begins the long and stealthy process of discovery, and does it with consummate skill. Yes, but a simple question suggests itself, and deserves an answer: why should Sophocles have contrived the passage in such a way that it ends in a notable climax which does nothing to help the plot? For it ends in a violent scene in which Oedipus, virtually, commits an unpardonable and stupid crime. It is such a jangling climax that it takes a long passage of music and lyric poetry to calm things down to a point at which the detective work can be resumed; and we should notice that Oedipus at last gives way not in the least because he is convinced of error, but simply as a reluctant favor to Iocasta and the Chorus. It is a really frightening display of tyrannical hybris: why is it there? We can say: "Sophocles is showing us how irascible and violent Oedipus could be." Of course he is, but since the character of Oedipus was not a fact in natural history but the invention of Sophocles, we still want to know why he should have wanted to invent an Oedipus who could so suddenly go to the verge of a judicial murder. It is not true that it was through such a strong admixture of hybris in his character that he fulfilled the prophecy, unless we were entirely mistaken in saying that the past story is not moralized: in resenting the insolence of the charioteer and hitting him he did indeed show hot temper, but that is very different from the monstrous thing that he proposes to do here. In short, this condemnation of Creon does not explain the past, and it does not affect the future; there is of course something in common between what he does now and what he had done earlier (namely an excessive reliance on his own judgment), but it is not hybris. There is however one further point that should not pass unobserved, namely the general resemblance between the end of the present scene and the more elaborate passage in the *Antigone* (727-739) in which Haemon accuses his father of behaving like a tyrant: in each case the implication is that the King is behaving in a way that would destroy the rights of the citizen. Here, for the moment, we will leave this matter; it is something of a puzzle—especially if our minds are full of Predestination or Free Will.

(iii) When we are more or less on even keel again we have the scene in which Iocasta reassures Oedipus. She knows for certain that one oracle has failed, but in proving it she makes that mention of the Three Ways which fills Oedipus with terror.

At this point Sophocles writes an impressive ode, one which has caused much discussion. "May reverent purity in word and deed always be with me, for the Eternal Laws enjoin it. Hybris breeds the tyrant, and is always overthrown; though may the protecting god never stop that emulation which is for the city's good. He who is arrogant, irreverent, irreligious, unafraid of Dike (Justice, or Retribution), may he perish! If conduct like this is praised, why should I join in the sacred dance? If these oracles are not manifestly fulfilled, religion is at an end. Mighty Zeus! they are setting at naught the failing oracles of Laius; religion is dying."

Three questions.—Whose hybris is in question? Why, since the chorus heretofore, and again in the next ode, is entirely loyal to Oedipus, does Sophocles make it pray now for the literal fulfillment of the oracles? Finally, what sort of a mind did Sophocles have, that he should equate the verity of oracles with the validity of religion?

The hybris is commonly supposed to be that displayed in the scepticism of Iocasta. This will not do. Certainly the ode ends with a reference to it, but no audience would think of Iocasta during the first three stanzas. She did in fact carefully distinguish between the infallible god and his fallible interpreters, and if this is hybris, then the chorus itself is equally guilty, for they said exactly the same in the third stanza of their previous ode. The reference to "contention which is for the city's good" clearly points to the outstanding hybris that we have seen with our own eyes, the contention that was for nobody's good: Oedipus' treatment of Creon.

As for the second question: it is true that Sophocles normally gives a definite character to a chorus, but it is not true that he binds himself to make the chorus always speak, or rather sing, in that character. Sometimes he will use it as a purely lyrical instrument, as he notably does in the Danaeode of the *Antigone*. In the present ode he "distances" the chorus, in Aeschylean fashion; he makes it stand back somewhat, to contemplate not the immediate situation but rather one of its general implications. To this point we shall return.

In considering the third question we must distinguish. Many fifth-century Athenians undoubtedly believed implicitly in the truth of oracles, many did not. Whether Sophocles did is a biographical question, and I do not know how to determine it. What we can do— the only important thing—is to determine the significance of oracles in his dramatic thinking, and that seems quite clear: it is the dramatic expression of this faith that the universe is ultimately not chaotic but orderly: it has its general laws. What follows, I think, will prove this.

What follows is a scene which, like the condemnation of Creon, we could not possibly have predicted from our survey of the raw material. It is not "myth"; it is pure Sophocles. What makes it the more interesting, and revealing, is that the sequence that we find here is exactly the same as that in the (presumably later) *Electra*—with one challenging difference. In the *Electra*, Clytemnestra, terrified by a dream, comes out and offers prayer and sacrifice to Apollo that he will save and protect her. At once there enters a messenger with good news: Orestes is dead. She is triumphant—but not for long: the message was a false one, designed to throw her off her guard; and we recall that when Orestes had asked Apollo how he should attempt his vengeance the god had said "By guile." In the *Tyrannus*, the Queen, badly frightened, comes out and offers prayer and sacrifice to Apollo that he will deliver them. At once the man from Corinth enters with good news: Oedipus' father has just died. Iocasta is triumphant—but by the end of the scene she has gone in to hang herself. So does Apollo answer these two prayers.

The parallel is exact, except that it seems to break down at a critical point; and here, religious ideas native to us will do nothing to help us, only create confusion. For Clytemnestra's prayer is in the highest degree blasphemous. Her prayer is that the god shall maintain her in her enjoyment of the fruits of murder, adultery, usurpation and theft, and shall not suffer Orestes to live and punish her. Iocasta is praying for no more than a harmless deliverance from the horrors that menace her and Oedipus, but let us look a little further. Clytemnestra's prayer was wicked, and she deserved what she got; Iocasta is innocent: granted. (For that matter, Oedipus too was innocent.) But Iocasta is really praying that the god shall avert what the god foresaw was going to happen; she is praying that the course of things may prove to have been unpredictable, even to a god; that the universe shall be proved random, in the power of arbitrary gods.

Is this far-fetched, and aridly philosophic? See what happens. Oedipus, in his enormous relief, says "Well, so much then for oracles" —though he is still afraid of marrying his mother. But this fear too Iocasta dismisses:

Why should we fear, seeing that man is ruled
By Chance, and there is room for no clear
forethought?

No; live at random, live as best one can.
So, do not fear this marriage with your
mother . . .

Now, the whole past story shows what a part is played in human affairs by what we, not being omniscient, have to call Chance. But Iocasta goes further: she attributes everything to Chance, and therefore, logically, denies the possibility of *pronoia*, "thinking beforehand." "Live from hand to mouth; do what seems best at the moment": that is the principle that she proclaims here; law, moral law, scruple—there is no room for such; and lest I be accused of chasing abstractions and neglecting the drama, I call attention to the terrible dramatic rhetoric that Sophocles uses here: the belief that all is random, and oracles untrustworthy, leads Iocasta, the mother of Oedipus, to comfort him by saying "So, do not fear this marriage with your mother." Where will one find a more explosive fusion of philosophic thought with dramatic imagination?

Now perhaps we begin to understand why the verity of oracles and the validity of religion were equated. If not even a god can foresee, Iocasta is right: life is random, and it is useless to try to live according to any principles.

The idea of Chance is taken up again at the end of the scene. When Iocasta has gone to her death, Oedipus, once again misreading a situation that confronts him, declares that she is proud, and is afraid she may find that her husband is baseborn; but

I count myself
The child of Fortune, giver of all good,
And I shall not be put to shame, for I
Am born of her.

The chorus, taking up the theme with music and the dance, says that their King will prove to be the son of some ageless nymph and a god; whereupon the slave of Laius enters, and a short scene during which we hardly dare breathe proves Oedipus to be the son not of a god and a nymph but of Laius and Iocasta, and Oedipus *is* put to some shame.

> Why should we fear, seeing that man is ruled
> By Chance?

This is the innocent delusion which, in its results—"Live from hand to mouth"—is more ruinous even than the open wickedness of Clytemnestra. There is Chance indeed, but there is also Law, including moral law. If men are rejecting religion, the Unwritten Laws, on the grounds that all is random, they are doing it at their peril.

It may be objected that in the past story, as presented by Sophocles, neither Oedipus nor his parents have conspicuously offended against the Unwritten Laws. This is perfectly true—but one long tract of the play still remains.

(iv) Oedipus, now blind, gropes his way out of the palace. To what consummation is Sophocles going to direct his play? What could be more obvious? The god's clear injunction, Oedipus' own decree, and the prophecy of Teircsias that Oedipus will become blind, a beggar, and an exile, all point to the inevitable and dramatic ending, the perfect counterpart of the beginning: Oedipus will now depart from Thebes for ever. But the inevitable ending is not in the least inevitable, for Sophocles.

For a long time it was my experience, and therefore may be that of others, that towards the end the play lacks impetus and tautness. In explanation, one can of course use the old incantation, that the Greek tragic poets preferred to end quietly. As it happens, I have just been reading the *Electra*, and since no play known to me ends with a more shattering bang than this one, the incantation has ceased to cast any spell over me. Similarly (for this too would only be a way of avoiding observation and thought) it might be said that Sophocles avoided exiling Oedipus in this play for the sake of the *Coloneus* (written probably twenty years later), in which Oedipus, now an old man, has only recently been driven out of Thebes.—A plausible

guess, if the ending of the *Tyrannus* is in fact tentative, a kind of half-close. But is it? We must look at the dramatic facts of the case, and if it appears that the scenes that are before us do, logically and convincingly, end the *Tyrannus*, then we need not invoke the *Coloneus*.

We note, in the first place, that Sophocles is not in the least self-conscious about the matter of the exile. The Messenger (1290 f.) reports that Oedipus, to fulfill his own curse, is going to cast himself out of Thebes; twice (1340, 1410) Oedipus beseeches the chorus to drive him out; three times (1436 f., 1449 ff., 1518) he begs it of Creon—and Creon refuses. This is one dramatic fact. Another is the surprising way in which the relationship of Oedipus and Creon is handled. We remember well enough what the situation was when last we saw the two men together; now, not only has Creon been vindicated with an awful completeness, but Oedipus has been proved to have done things even worse than that which he falsely imputed to Creon. It is a *peripeteia* such as a dramatist might dream of—yet Sophocles appears to do hardly anything with it. Further, although Sophocles was so subtle in the drawing of character, our impression of Creon is at the moment rather vague: here is the opportunity, therefore, to make it sharper—to show Creon as vindictively triumphant, or nobly forgiving, or at least *something* interesting. But this master of the dramatic art, having contrived so splendid a reversal of situation, so rich in possibilities, appears to be hardly interested in it. His Creon begins:

> No exultation, Oedipus, and no reproach
> For injuries inflicted brings me here—

"but," he continues, "do not affront Thebes and pollute the sunlight by standing here, in public." Oedipus answers: "Since against my expectation you are so generous, grant me one request . . ." We realize at once that Creon can forgive and forget, but the point is made with all despatch, almost as if it were only a necessary nuisance.

What else? We have already mentioned Teiresias' prophecy about the blindness, and Oedipus' passionate explanation of why he had to do it. There remains the scene with the two children.

Of this, we can certainly say that it is a natural development of the plot: natural, though not unavoidable, for no one would feel baffled or disappointed if the two girls were not produced. We can say—and why not?—that it shows us yet another facet of Oedipus' character: it is indeed an affecting moment when we have that glimpse (1462 f.) of a past domestic happiness now turned to horror. But the burden of the long speech that Oedipus makes to the children is that through no fault of theirs their future is irretrievably blasted.

Here we may recall the two shepherds who, after the discovery, had to stumble out of the theatre as best they could before the chorus could begin its last ode. The one, the Corinthian, had found his cheerful hopes turn to dust and ashes; the other had for years lived with a dreadful secret (758–764), and now has found that what he had known was only part of the horror. Now, in the two girls, the area of disaster is further enlarged. As we underestimate *Hamlet* unless we see that Laertes, Ophelia, even Rosencrantz and Guildenstern, are Hamlet's colleagues in tragedy, so we underestimate the scope of the *Tyrannus* unless to Oedipus himself we add, as tragic victims, not only Laius and Iocasta, but also the shepherds and the children. *This* is what Life can do to us, at its worst.

Then, having brought the children before us, why should Sophocles get them off the stage in the way he does? If at the end they went out in the train of Creon or of Oedipus, with nothing said, nobody would be surprised or even interested. Why does Sophocles make such a point of causing Creon to detach them from Oedipus? Certainly not in order to represent Creon as harsh; if he meant this, he has not made it clear; what is clear is that he has not this kind of interest in Creon's character at all. We will leave this point until

we have dealt with the more important ones: the persistent denial of Oedipus' persistent demand to be driven out, and Sophocles' apparent indifference to the *peripeteia*.

If we, not being fifth-century Greeks, need a hint, we can find one in a certain verbal correspondence between this fourth part of the play and the second—which also, the reader may remember, gave us something of a puzzle. Following it up, we shall find that Sophocles does make use of his *peripeteia*, though not one which Aristotle and modern ideas about drama might have led us to expect. When Oedipus was beginning his examination of Creon, he said: "When your late King was killed, why did not that clever prophet speak out *then*?" Creon's answer was: "I don't know, and when I have no knowledge I prefer to say nothing" (569). At the very end of the play, when Oedipus for the third time has asked Creon to drive him out, the dialogue continues like this: "What you ask is in the gift of the god."—"But the gods hate no one more than me!"—"Then you will soon gain your desire."—"You promise it?" —"Ah, no; for when I have no knowledge I prefer not to speak at random." It looks as if a contrast may be intended between Creon, who recognizes the limitations imposed by ignorance, and someone else.

But why does Creon refuse? As Oedipus keeps on saying, the matter is as clear as daylight: there was the god's command, and there is his own curse. "Yes," says Creon; "I would have done it; but first I wanted to ask the god what I should do ... Yes, I know; but in our present pass it is better to ask how we should act" (1435–1443). This is another and much more important echo. In the second part of the play (603–8) Creon, accused on his life, had taken a solemn oath, had argued that the charge was on the face of it unreasonable, and finally had challenged Oedipus, unanswerably, to settle the matter by going himself to Delphi with the simple question whether Creon had correctly reported what the god had said. Oedipus brushes aside the oath, the argument, and, specifically, the challenge on the grounds that when an enemy is quick to plot one must be quick in one's reply. What the two parts of the play give us, therefore, is, if not an Aristotelian *peripeteia*, at least a striking and surely significant contrast: first, in a matter which not Creon only (608) but also the chorus (657) declares to be at least obscure, Oedipus will act, and act disastrously, on his own judgment, sweeping aside not only argument but also a challenge that would immediately decide the question; then, antistrophically, in a matter which seems abundantly clear, Creon will not act until he has found the better guidance which is available to him.

Now we can think again about "the beginnings of the discovery." These will certainly lead eventually to the truth, but first they lead Oedipus to the verge of murder. What is the idea? Reviewing the stealthy concatenation of details, as they are marshalled by Sophocles, we can see how natural it was, for the intelligent Oedipus, to piece together his clever inferences and to draw a conclusion which we can see is plausible and yet know to be entirely wrong; and on the strength of these, in unrestrained self-confidence, he proceeds to condemn Creon to death or exile. This intermediate climax, it may be, is now less of a puzzle than it was before. Now we may recall how the Priest, in his first speech, had spoken of Oedipus' intelligence (31–9): virtually, "In apprehension, how like a god." —But not *quite* a god.

We return to the children.—This, as it happens, is the play which we have all been taught, not unreasonably, to regard as the masterpiece of dramatic construction; therefore it may be that its coping-stone was not chosen at random. What is it? Creon takes the children from Oedipus' embrace, and the play ends. Not perhaps our idea of a dramatic ending, but it was Sophocles' idea, here. The last words of the play as we have it (for the final tag of the chorus is not genuine) are: "Seek not to have control (*kratein*) in everything; the control you had has not endured." (The Greek word is associated with the ideas

of power, might, force, domination.) This is the terminus at which Sophocles chose to arrive. We are not in control.

We are left looking at an immense catastrophe. Near its periphery are the minor victims, "small annexments"; near the center, Laius and Iocasta; at the center, Oedipus—all innocent. Oedipus, at the beginning, is immeasureably great; at the end, nothing, as the chorus bitterly says in its final ode. How did it happen? With divine fore-knowledge indeed, though Sophocles, to say the least, is at no pains to make us feel that it is by divine contrivance. It happened, essentially, because everybody concerned did, quite naturally, what he did and not something else; and because unforeseeable circumstances occurred, like Laius' going to Delphi on that particular day. It is a picture not of what human life is, but of what it can be; an extreme picture, of course; Sophocles was no sentimental pessimist (for pessimism can be as flabby as optimism) but a realist: life can be like this.

But if this kind of thing can happen, at the worst, *why* should it happen? If in such a world there are gods, of what kind are they, and why should we worship them? These are questions natural to us, and this is where Christian ideas, even their relics, baffle us. We can hardly think of a God without also thinking of some Divine Purpose; the Greek could, and did. His *theoi* certainly ruled the universe, or ruled *in* it, but they had not created it, and the question of a Purpose hardly arose; the universe was a fact, and so were its gods. To ask *why* the gods allow such things to happen is to ask a meaningless question. Why is our universe so contrived that if two people of incompatible bloodgroups have children, the children will die? What is the idea? There is no idea; it is simply the way in which things work; we cannot control it, but must learn to live with it. It is bigger than we are, and we are wise to recognize the fact, and to behave accordingly.

This explains the third ode, which involves

more than personal piety: it includes also "purity in word and deed", it includes modesty, restraint, a degree of humility before the gods; it condemns hybris, that wanton self-assertion and self-confidence which, as long experience proves, ends in overthrow. We are not in control; the thing is bigger than we are. We may vaunt ourselves on the power of our intelligence, and of course there is nothing amiss with intelligence; but it has its limits, for the whole thing is so complex, and it has its dangers: it may assure us that we are safe when we are not, and by increasing our self-confidence it may tempt us to folly or crime.

Sophocles, as Bernard Knox has well explained in the last chapter of his *Oedipus at Thebes*, had good reason for being serious about this: it was a time of "advanced thinking", of overconfident humanism. "The gods may or may not exist: the question is difficult, and life is short." "Man is the measure of all things." So taught the estimable Protagoras. Others, not so estimable, went much further. "Justice? Nothing but a conspiracy among the weak to defraud the strong of their natural rights. The cardinal virtues? Moonshine! Power and intelligent calculation are the guide to life. Gods? We are the masters now." Sophocles did not believe it.

Oddly enough, the best commentary on the *Tyrannus* is not Freud but a younger contemporary of the poet's, also an Athenian: Thucydides the historian, particularly, though by no means exclusively, in his Melian Dialogue and the tragic story that follows. In the Dialogue the Athenians, demanding the immediate surrender of an inoffensive neutral island, expressly set aside (according to Thucydides) all talk of justice and nonsense of that kind: Athens is powerful, and Melos is weak. The Melians, they say, must be intelligent, face facts, set aside

the delusions of hope and the idea that the gods may help them: the gods are on the side of the big battalions. Having massacred the Melians because they would not yield, the Athenians attack Sicily with a fleet of unparalleled magnificence and power, with unbounded hopes, and—says Thucydides —with a good deal of ignorance. But in the event, what with sheer mischance, a certain lack of resolution, the fact that the political situation in Sicily was not quite what they had counted on, and that by a very simple trick they had been deceived about the immense wealth which would be at their disposal in the island, hardly a man came back alive, either from this proud fleet or from a second, not inferior, which had reinforced it. In the third ode of the play the chorus execrates the man who is "unafraid of Dike": Thucydides makes the Melians ask the Athenians if they are not afraid of Retribution; "No," they reply; "we are not." Perhaps the new wisdom was not so very wise after all.

Sophocles, like Thucydides, was well aware of the power of chance, and took it into his reckoning, but he did not make the mistake that he attributes to Iocasta: chance is an inescapable part of our universe, but not the whole of it. There is much that we cannot know or foresee, but the man who does not revere the gods and scrupulously obey those of the divine laws that we do know is in the first place a fool, and in the second place will be led into the wickednesses which in their turn lead to disaster. "Then, if we behave ourselves, shall we be safe?" This is crying for the moon; this is not the way in which the gods work. But what you can be sure of is that if you give way to overconfidence, with immodesty towards that great and incalculable thing that surrounds us, you will incur disaster.

THE HEROINE AND SOCIETY

GHOSTS

Henrik Ibsen

translated by Michael Meyer

CHARACTERS

MRS. HELEN ALVING, widow of Captain Alving, late Chamberlain to the King.

OSWALD ALVING, her son, a painter.

PASTOR MANDERS.

ENGSTRAND, a carpenter.

REGINA ENGSTRAND, Mrs. Alving's maid.

The action takes place on MRS. ALVING'S *country estate by a large fjord in Western Norway.*

ACT ONE

A spacious garden-room, with a door in the left-hand wall and two doors in the right-hand wall. In the centre of the room is a round table with chairs around it; on the table are books, magazines and newspapers. Downstage left is a window, in front of which is a small sofa with a sewing-table by it. Backstage the room opens out into a slightly narrower conservatory, with walls of large panes of glass. In the right-hand wall of the conservatory is a door leading down to the garden. Through the glass wall a gloomy fjord landscape is discernible, veiled by steady rain.

ENGSTRAND, *a carpenter, is standing at the garden door. His left leg is slightly crooked; under the sole of his boot is fixed a block of wood.* REGINA, *with an empty garden syringe in her hand, bars his entry.*

REGINA (*keeping her voice low*). What do you want? Stay where you are! You're dripping wet!

ENGSTRAND. It is God's blessed rain, my child.

REGINA. The Devil's damned rain, more like.

ENGSTRAND. Why, Regina, the way you talk! (*Limps a few steps into the room.*) What I wanted to say is—

REGINA. Here, you! Don't make such a noise with that foot. The young master's asleep upstairs.

ENGSTRAND. In bed—at this hour? Why, the day's half gone.

REGINA. That's none of your business.

ENGSTRAND. I was out drinking last night—

REGINA. I'm sure.

ENGSTRAND. We are but flesh and blood, my child—

REGINA (*drily*). Quite.

ENGSTRAND. And the temptations of this world are manifold. But God is my witness; I was at my bench by half past five this morning.

REGINA. Yes, yes. Come on now, clear off. I don't want to be caught having a rendezvous with you.

ENGSTRAND. You don't what?

REGINA. I don't want anyone to see you here. Come on, go away, get out.

ENGSTRAND (*comes a few steps nearer*). Not before I've had a word with you. This afternoon I'll be through with the job down at the school house, and tonight I'm catching the steamer back to town.

REGINA (*mutters*). Bon voyage.

ENGSTRAND. Thank you, my child. They're dedicating the new Orphanage here tomorrow, and there'll be celebrations, with intoxicating liquor. And no one shall say of Jacob Engstrand that he can't turn his back on temptation. (REGINA *laughs scornfully*.) Yes, well, there'll be a lot of tip-top people coming here tomorrow. Pastor Manders is expected from town.

REGINA. He's arriving today.

ENGSTRAND. Well, there you are. And I'm damned if I'm going to risk getting into his bad books.

REGINA. Oh, so that's it.

ENGSTRAND. What do you mean?

REGINA (*looks knowingly at him*). What are you trying to fool the Pastor into this time?

ENGSTRAND. Hush! Are you mad? Me try to fool Pastor Manders? Oh no, Pastor Manders is much too good a friend to me for that. Now what I wanted to talk to you about is this. I'm going back home tonight.

REGINA. The sooner you go the better.

ENGSTRAND. Yes, but I want to take you with me, Regina.

REGINA (*her jaw drops*). You want to take *me*—? What are you talking about?

ENGSTRAND. I want to take you with me, I say.

REGINA (*scornfully*). Home with you? Not likely I won't!

ENGSTRAND. Oh, we'll see, we'll see.

REGINA. You bet your life we'll see. You expect me to go back and live with you? In that house? After Mrs. Alving's brought me up in her own home, treats me as though I was one of the family? Get out!

ENGSTRAND. What the hell's this? Are you setting yourself up against your father, my girl?

REGINA (*mutters without looking at him*). You've said often enough that I'm no concern of yours.

ENGSTRAND. Oh—you don't want to take any notice of that—

REGINA. What about all the times you've sworn at me and called me a—oh, *mon dieu*!

ENGSTRAND. May God strike me dead if I ever used such a vile word!

REGINA. Oh, I know what word you used.

ENGSTRAND. Yes, but that was only when I wasn't myself. Hm. The temptations of this world are manifold, Regina.

REGINA. Ugh!

ENGSTRAND. And when your mother was being difficult. I had to think up some way to nark her. She was always acting the fine lady. (*Mimics*.) "Let me go, Engstrand! Stop it! I've been in service for three years with Chamberlain Alving at Rosenvold, and don't you forget it!" (*Laughs*.) She never could forget the Captain had been made a Chamberlain when she was working for him.

REGINA. Poor Mother! You killed her soon enough with your bullying.

ENGSTRAND (*uncomfortably*). That's right, blame me for everything.

REGINA (*turns away and mutters beneath her breath*). Ugh! And that leg!

ENGSTRAND. What's that you said, my child?

REGINA. *Pied de mouton*!

ENGSTRAND. What's that, English?

REGINA. Yes.

ENGSTRAND. Ah, well. They've made a scholar of you out here anyway, and that'll come in handy now, Regina.

REGINA (*after a short silence*). And—what was it you wanted me for in town?

ENGSTRAND. Fancy asking such a question! What should a father want from his only child? Aren't I a lonely, forsaken widower?

REGINA. Oh, don't try to fool me with that rubbish. What do you want me up there for?

ENGSTRAND. Well, it's like this. I'm thinking of starting out on something new.

REGINA (*sniffs*). You've tried that often enough. And you've always made a mess of it.

ENGSTRAND. Yes, but this time, you'll see, Regina! God rot me if I don't—!

REGINA (*stamps her foot*). Stop swearing!

ENGSTRAND. Ssh, ssh! How right you are, my child! Now what I wanted to say was this. I've put quite a bit of money aside out of the work I've been doing at this new Orphanage.

REGINA. Have you? Good for you.

ENGSTRAND. Well, there ain't much for a man to spend his money on out here in the country, is there?

REGINA. Well? Go on.

ENGSTRAND. Yes, well, you see, so I thought I'd put the money into something that might bring me in a bit. A kind of home for sailors—

REGINA (*disgusted*). Oh, my God!

ENGSTRAND. A real smart place, you understand—not one of those low waterfront joints. No, damn it, this is going to be for captains and officers and—tip-top people, you understand.

REGINA. And I'm to—?

ENGSTRAND. You're going to help me. Just for appearance's sake, of course. You won't have to work hard, my child. You can fix your own hours.

REGINA. I see!

ENGSTRAND. Well, we've got to have a bit of skirt on show, I mean that's obvious. Got to give them a little fun in the evenings—dancing and singing and so forth. You must remember thcsc men are wandering mariners lost on the ocean of life. (*Comes closer.*) Now don't be stupid and make things difficult for yourself, Regina. What can you make of yourself out here? What good is it going to do you, all this fine education Mrs. Alving's given you? I hear you're going to look after the orphans down the road. Is that what you want to do? Are you so anxious to ruin your health for those filthy brats?

REGINA. No, if things work out the way I—Ah well, they might. They might.

ENGSTRAND. What are you talking about?

REGINA. Never you mind. This money you've managed to save out here—is it a lot?

ENGSTRAND. All told I'd say it comes to between thirty-five and forty pounds.

REGINA. Not bad.

ENGSTRAND. Enough to make a start with, my child.

REGINA. Aren't you going to give me any of it?

ENGSTRAND. Not damn likely I'm not.

REGINA. Aren't you even going to send me a new dress?

ENGSTRAND. You just come back to town and set up with me, and you'll get dresses enough.

REGINA. (*laughs scornfully*). I could do *that* on my own, if I wanted to.

ENGSTRAND. No, Regina, you need a father's hand to guide you. There's a nice house I can get in Little Harbour Street. They don't want much cash on the nail; and we could turn it into a sort of—well—sailors' mission.

REGINA. But I don't want to live with *you!* I don't want anything to do with you. Come on, get out.

ENGSTRAND. You wouldn't need to stay with me for long, my child. More's the pity. If you play your cards properly. The way you've blossomed out these last few years, you—

REGINA. Yes?

ENGSTRAND. You wouldn't have to wait long before some nice officer—perhaps even a captain—

REGINA. I don't want to marry any of them. Sailors haven't any *savoir vivre*.

ENGSTRAND. Haven't any what?

REGINA. I know sailors. There's no future in marrying them.

ENGSTRAND. All right then, don't marry them. You can do just as well without. (*Lowers his voice.*) The Englishman—him with the yacht—fifty pounds he paid out—and she wasn't any prettier than you.

REGINA (*goes towards him*). Get out!

ENGSTRAND (*shrinks*). Now, now, you wouldn't hit your own father!

REGINA. Wouldn't I? You say another word about mother, and you'll see! Get out, I tell you! (*Pushes him towards the garden door.*) And don't slam the door. Young Mr. Alving's—

ENGSTRAND. Yes, I know. He's asleep. Why do you fuss so much about him? (*More quietly.*) Ah-ha! You wouldn't be thinking of *him*, would you?

REGINA. Out, and be quick about it! You're out of your mind. No, not that way. Here's

Pastor Manders. Go out through the kitchen.

ENGSTRAND (*goes right*). All right, I'll go. But you ask *him*—his Reverence. He'll tell you what a child's duty is to its father. I am your father, you know, whatever you say. I can prove it from the parish register.

He goes out through the second door, which REGINA *has opened and closed behind him. She looks quickly at herself in the mirror, dusts herself with her handkerchief, and straightens her collar; then she begins to water the flowers.* PASTOR MANDERS, *in an overcoat and carrying an umbrella, and with a small travelling bag on a strap from his shoulder, enters through the garden door into the conservatory.*

MANDERS. Good morning, Miss Engstrand.

REGINA (*turns in surprise and delight*). Why, Pastor Manders! Has the boat come already?

MANDERS. It arrived a few minutes ago. (*Enters the garden room.*) Very tiresome this rain we're having.

REGINA (*follows him*). A blessing for the farmers, though, sir.

MANDERS. Yes, you are right. We city people tend to forget that. (*Begins to take off his overcoat.*)

REGINA. Oh, please let me help you! There. Oh, it's soaking! I'll hang it up in the hall. Oh, and the umbrella! I'll open it out to let it dry.

She takes the coat and umbrella out through the other door, right. MANDERS *takes his bag from his shoulder and puts it and his hat on a chair. Meanwhile* REGINA *comes back.*

MANDERS. Ah, it's good to be under a dry roof again. Well, I trust all is well here?

REGINA. Yes, thank you, sir.

MANDERS. Everyone very busy, I suppose, getting ready for tomorrow?

REGINA. Oh, yes, there are one or two things to be done.

MANDERS. Mrs. Alving is at home, I hope?

REGINA. Oh, dear me, yes, she's just gone upstairs to make a cup of chocolate for the young master.

MANDERS. Ah, yes. I heard when I got off the boat that Oswald had returned.

REGINA. Yes, he arrived the day before yesterday. We hadn't expected him until today.

MANDERS. In good health and spirits, I trust?

REGINA. Oh yes, thank you, I think so. He felt dreadfully tired after his journey, though. He came all the way from Paris in one go—*par rapide*. I think he's having a little sleep just now, so we'd better talk just a tiny bit quietly.

MANDERS. Ssh! We'll be like mice!

REGINA (*moves an armchair near the table*). Now sit down and make yourself comfortable, sir. (*He sits. She puts a footstool under his feet.*) There now. Are you quite comfortable?

MANDERS. Thank you, thank you; yes, very comfortable. (*Looks at her.*) Do you know, Miss Engstrand, I really believe you've grown since I last saw you.

REGINA. Do you think so? Madam says I've rounded out a bit too.

MANDERS. Rounded out? Well, yes, a little perhaps. Not too much.

Short pause.

REGINA. Shall I tell madam you've come?

MANDERS. Thank you, there's no hurry, my dear child. Er—tell me now, Regina, how is your father getting on out here?

REGINA. Thank you, Pastor, he's doing very well.

MANDERS. He came to see me when he was last in town.

REGINA. No, did he really? He's always so happy when he gets a chance to speak to you, sir.

MANDERS. And you go down and see him quite often?

REGINA. I? Oh yes, of course—whenever I get the chance—

MANDERS. Your father hasn't a very strong character, Miss Engstrand. He badly needs a hand to guide him.

REGINA. Oh—yes, I dare say you're right there.

MANDERS. He needs to have someone near him whom he is fond of, and whose judgment he respects. He admitted it quite openly the last time he visited me.

REGINA. Yes, he said something of the sort to me too. But I don't know whether Mrs. Alving will want to lose me, especially now we've the new Orphanage to look after. Besides, I'd hate to leave Mrs. Alving. She's always been so kind to me.

MANDERS. But my dear girl, a daughter's duty! Naturally we would have to obtain your mistress's permission first.

REGINA. But I don't know that it'd be right and proper for me to keep house for an unmarried man at my age.

MANDERS. What! But my dear Miss Engstrand, this is your own father we're talking about!

REGINA. Yes—but all the same—Oh yes, if it was a nice house, with a real gentleman—

MANDERS. But my dear Regina—!

REGINA. Someone I could feel affection for and look up to as a father—

MANDERS. But my dear good child—!

REGINA. Oh, I'd so love to go and live in the city. Out here it's so dreadfully lonely—and you know, don't you, sir, what it means to be all alone in the world? And I'm quick and willing—I think I can say that. Oh, Pastor Manders, don't you know of a place I could go to?

MANDERS. I? No, I'm afraid I don't know of anyone at all.

REGINA. Oh, but do please think of me if ever you should, dear, dear Pastor Manders.

MANDERS (*gets up*). Yes, yes, Miss Engstrand, I certainly will.

REGINA. You see, if only I—

MANDERS. Will you be so good as to call Mrs. Alving for me?

REGINA. Yes, sir. I'll call her at once.

She goes out left. PASTOR MANDERS *walks up and down the room a couple of times, stands for a moment upstage with his hands behind his back and looks out into the garden.*

Then he comes back to the part of the room where the table is, picks up a book and glances at its title page, starts and looks at some of the others.

MANDERS. Hm! I see!

MRS. ALVING *enters through the door left. She is followed by* REGINA, *who at once goes out through the door downstage right.*

MRS. ALVING (*holds out her hand*). Welcome to Rosenvold, Pastor.

MANDERS. Good morning, Mrs. Alving. Well, I've kept my promise.

MRS. ALVING. Punctual as always.

MANDERS. But you know it wasn't easy for me to get away. All these blessed boards and committees I sit on—

MRS. ALVING. All the kinder of you to arrive in such good time. Now we can get our business settled before lunch. But where's your luggage?

MANDERS (*quickly*). My portmanteau is down at the village store. I shall be sleeping there.

MRS. ALVING (*represses a smile*). I can't persuade you to spend a night in my house even now?

MANDERS. No, no, Mrs. Alving—it's very kind of you, but I'll sleep down there as usual. It's so convenient for when I go on board again.

MRS. ALVING. As you please. Though I really think two old people like you and me could—

MANDERS. Bless me, you're joking. But of course you must be very happy. The great day tomorrow—and you have Oswald home again.

MRS. ALVING. Yes, you can imagine how happy that makes me. It's over two years since he was home last. And now he's promised to stay with me the whole winter.

MANDERS. No, has he really? Well, that's nice of him. He knows his filial duty. I fancy life in Paris and Rome must offer altogether different attractions.

MRS. ALVING. Yes, but his home is here; and his mother. Ah, my dear boy; he loves his mother, God bless him.

MANDERS. It would be sad indeed if distance and dabbling in art and such things should blunt his natural affections.

MRS. ALVING. It certainly would. But luckily there's nothing wrong with him. I'll be amused to see whether you recognize him again. He'll be down later; he's upstairs now taking a little rest on the sofa. But please sit down, my dear Pastor.

MANDERS. Thank you. Er—you're sure this is a convenient moment—?

MRS. ALVING. Certainly.

She sits down at the table.

MANDERS. Good. Well, then— (*Goes over to the chair on which his bag is lying, takes out a sheaf of papers, sits down on the opposite side of the table and looks for a space to put down the papers.*) Well, to begin with, here are the— (*Breaks off.*) Tell me, Mrs. Alving, how do *these* books come to be here?

MRS. ALVING. Those books? I'm reading them.

MANDERS. You read writings of this kind?

MRS. ALVING. Certainly I do.

MANDERS. And does this kind of reading make you feel better or happier?

MRS. ALVING. I think they make me feel more secure.

MANDERS. How extraordinary! In what way?

MRS. ALVING. Well, they sort of explain and confirm many things that puzzle me. Yes, that's what's so strange, Pastor Manders— there isn't really anything new in these books—there's nothing in them that most people haven't already thought for them- selves. It's only that most people either haven't fully realized it, or they won't admit it.

MANDERS. Well, dear God! Do you seriously believe that most people—?

MRS. ALVING. Yes, I do.

MANDERS. But surely not in this country? Not people like us?

MRS. ALVING. Oh, yes. People like us too.

MANDERS. Well, really! I must say—!

MRS. ALVING. But what do you object to in these books?

MANDERS. Object to? You surely don't imagine I spend my time studying such publications?

MRS. ALVING. In other words, you've no idea what you're condemning?

MANDERS. I've read quite enough about these writings to disapprove of them.

MRS. ALVING. Don't you think you ought to form your own opinion—?

MANDERS. My dear Mrs. Alving, there are many occasions in life when one must rely on the judgment of others. That is the way things are and it is good that it should be so. If it were not so, what would become of society?

MRS. ALVING. Yes, yes. You may be right.

MANDERS. Of course I don't deny there may be quite a lot that is attractive about these writings. And I cannot exactly blame you for wishing to keep informed of these intellectual movements in the great world outside about which one hears so much. After all, you have allowed your son to wander there for a number of years. But—

MRS. ALVING. But—?

MANDERS (*lowers his voice*). But one does not have to talk about it, Mrs. Alving. One really does not need to account to all and sundry for what one reads and thinks within one's own four walls.

MRS. ALVING. No, of course not. I quite agree with you.

MANDERS. Remember the duty you owe to this Orphanage which you decided to found at a time when your attitude towards spiritual matters was quite differ- ent from what it is now—as far as *I* can judge.

MRS. ALVING. Yes, yes, that's perfectly true. But it was the Orphanage we were going to—

MANDERS. It was the Orphanage we were going to discuss, yes. But—be discreet, dear Mrs. Alving! And now let us turn to our business. (*Opens the packet and takes out some of the papers.*) You see these?

MRS. ALVING. Are those the deeds?

MANDERS. All of them. Ready and completed. As you can imagine, it's been no easy task to get them all through in time. I really had to get out my whip. The authorities are almost painfully conscientious when you want a decision from them. But here we have them nevertheless. (*Leafs through them.*) Here is the executed conveyance of the farmstead named Solvik in the Manor of Rosenvold, with its newly constructed buildings, schoolrooms, staff accommodation and chapel. And here is the settlement of the endowment and the trust deed of the institution. Look. (*Reads.*) Deed of trust for the Captain Alving Memorial Home.

MRS. ALVING (*stares for a long while at the paper*). So there it is.

MANDERS. I thought I'd say Captain rather than Chamberlain. Captain looks less ostentatious.

MRS. ALVING. Yes, yes, as you think best.

MANDERS. And here is the bankbook for the capital which has been placed on deposit to cover the running expenses of the Orphanage.

MRS. ALVING. Thank you; but I think it would be more convenient if you kept that, if you don't mind.

MANDERS. Certainly, certainly. I think we may as well leave the money on deposit to begin with. Admittedly the interest isn't very attractive—four per cent with six months notice of withdrawal. If we could obtain a good mortgage later—of course it would have to be a first mortgage and of unimpeachable security—we might reconsider the matter.

MRS. ALVING. Yes, well, dear Pastor Manders, you know best about all that.

MANDERS. Anyway, I'll keep my eyes open. But now there's another matter I've several times been meaning to ask you about.

MRS. ALVING. And what is that?

MANDERS. Should the buildings of the Orphanage be insured or not.

MRS. ALVING. Yes, of course they must be insured.

MANDERS. Ah, but wait a minute, Mrs. Alving. Let us consider this question a little more closely.

MRS. ALVING. Everything I have is insured—buildings, furniture, crops, livestock.

MANDERS. Naturally. On your own estate. I do the same, of course. But you see, this is quite a different matter. The Orphanage is, so to speak, to be consecrated to a higher purpose.

MRS. ALVING. Yes, but—

MANDERS. As far as I personally am concerned, I see nothing offensive in securing ourselves against all eventualities—

MRS. ALVING. Well, I certainly don't.

MANDERS. But what is the feeling among the local people out here? You can judge that better than I can.

MRS. ALVING. The feeling?

MANDERS. Are there many people with a right to an opinion—I mean, people who really have the right to hold an opinion—who might take offence?

MRS. ALVING. Well, what do you mean by people who have the right to hold an opinion?

MANDERS. Oh, I am thinking chiefly of people sufficiently independent and influential to make it impossible for one to ignore their opinions altogether.

MRS. ALVING. There are quite a few people like that who I suppose might take offence—

MANDERS. You see! In town, we have a great many such people. Followers of other denominations. People might very easily come to the conclusion that neither you nor I have sufficient trust in the ordinance of a Higher Power.

MRS. ALVING. But my dear Pastor, as long as you yourself—

MANDERS. I know, I know—my conscience is clear, that is true. But all the same, we couldn't prevent a false and unfavourable interpretation being placed on our action. And that might well adversely influence the purpose for which the Orphanage has been dedicated.

MRS. ALVING. If that were so I—

MANDERS. And I can't altogether close my eyes to the difficult—I might even say deeply embarrassing—position in which I might find myself. Among influential circles in town there is a great interest in the cause of the Orphanage. After all, it is to serve the town as well, and it is hoped that it may considerably ease the burden of the

ratepayers in respect to the poor. But since
I have acted as your adviser and been in
charge of the business side I must admit
I fear certain over-zealous persons might in
the first place direct their attacks against
me—

MRS. ALVING. Well, you mustn't lay yourself
open to that.

MANDERS. Not to speak of the attacks which
would undoubtedly be launched against me
in certain newspapers and periodicals, and
which—

MRS. ALVING. Enough, dear Pastor Manders.
That settles it.

MANDERS. Then you do not wish the Orphanage to be insured?

MRS. ALVING. No. We will forget about it.

MANDERS (*leans back in his chair*). But suppose
an accident should occur—you never can
tell—would you be able to make good the
damage?

MRS. ALVING. No, quite frankly I couldn't.

MANDERS. Well, but you know, Mrs. Alving,
this is really rather a serious responsibility
we are taking on our shoulders.

MRS. ALVING. But do you think we have any
alternative?

MANDERS. No, that's just it. I don't think
there is any real alternative. We must not
lay ourselves open to misinterpretation.
And we have no right to antagonize public
opinion.

MRS. ALVING. At any rate you, as a clergyman,
must not.

MANDERS. And I really think we must believe
that such an institution will have luck on
its side—nay, that it stands under special
protection.

MRS. ALVING. Let us hope so, Pastor Manders.

MANDERS. Shall we take the risk, then?

MRS. ALVING. Yes, let us.

MANDERS. Good. As you wish. (*Makes a note.*)
No insurance, then.

MRS. ALVING. It's strange you happened to
mention this today—

MANDERS. I've often thought of raising the
matter with you—

MRS. ALVING. Because yesterday we almost
had a fire down there.

MANDERS. What!

MRS. ALVING. Well, it was nothing much
really. Some shavings caught fire in the
carpentry shop.

MANDERS. Where Engstrand works?

MRS. ALVING. Yes. They say he's very careless
with matches.

MANDERS. He's got so many things to think
about, poor man—so many temptations.
Thank heaven I hear he has now resolved
to lead a virtuous life.

MRS. ALVING. Oh? Who says so?

MANDERS. He has assured me so himself. And
he's a good worker.

MRS. ALVING. Oh, yes—as long as he keeps
sober—

MANDERS. Yes, that is a grievous weakness!
But he is often compelled to yield to it
because of his bad leg, he says. The last
time he was in town I was quite touched.
He came to see me and thanked me so
sincerely because I had got him this job
here, so that he could be near Regina.

MRS. ALVING. I don't think he sees her very
often.

MANDERS. Oh yes, he told me himself. He
talks to her every day.

MRS. ALVING. Oh, well. Possibly.

MANDERS. He is so conscious of his need to
have someone who can restrain him when
temptation presents itself. That is what is
so lovable about Jacob Engstrand, that he
comes to one like a child and accuses himself and admits his weakness. The last time
he came up and talked to me—Tell me,
Mrs. Alving, if it were absolutely vital for
the poor man to have Regina back to live
with him again—

MRS. ALVING (*rises swiftly*). Regina!

MANDERS. You must not oppose it.

MRS. ALVING. I certainly shall. Anyway,
Regina is going to work at the Orphanage.

MANDERS. But don't forget, he is her father—

MRS. ALVING. Oh, I know very well the kind
of father he's been to her. No, I shall never
consent to her going back to him.

MANDERS (*rises*). But my dear Mrs. Alving,
you mustn't get so emotional about it. You
seem quite frightened. It's very sad the way
you misjudge this man Engstrand.

MRS. ALVING (*more quietly*). Never mind that. I have taken Regina into my house, and here she shall stay. (*Listens*) Hush now, dear Pastor Manders, let's not say anything more about it. (*Happily.*) Listen! There's Oswald coming downstairs. Now we will think of nothing but him.

OSWALD ALVING, *in a light overcoat, with his hat in his hand and smoking a big meerschaum pipe, enters through the door left.*

OSWALD (*stops in the doorway*). Oh, I'm sorry—I thought you were in the study. (*Comes closer.*) Good morning, Pastor.

MANDERS (*stares*). Why—! Most extraordinary!

MRS. ALVING. Well, Pastor Manders, what do you think of him?

MANDERS. I think—I think—! But is this really—?

OSWALD. Yes, this is the Prodigal Son, Pastor.

MANDERS. Oh, but my dear young friend—!

OSWALD. Well, the son, anyway.

MRS. ALVING. Oswald is thinking of the time when you used to be so strongly opposed to his becoming a painter.

MANDERS. Many a step which to human eyes seems dubious often turns out— (*Shakes his hand.*) Anyway, welcome, welcome! My dear Oswald—! I trust you will allow me to call you by your Christian name?

OSWALD. What else?

MANDERS. Excellent. Now, my dear Oswald, what I was going to say was this. You mustn't think I condemn the artistic profession out of hand. I presume there are many who succeed in keeping the inner man untarnished in that profession too.

OSWALD. Let us hope so.

MRS. ALVING (*happily*). I know one person who has remained pure both inwardly and outwardly. Just look at him, Pastor Manders.

OSWALD (*wanders across the room*). Yes, yes, Mother dear, please.

MANDERS. Unquestionably—there's no denying that. Besides, you have begun to acquire a name now. The newspapers often speak of you, and in most flattering terms. Well—that is to say, I don't seem to have read about you quite so much lately.

OSWALD (*by the flowers upstage*). I haven't done so much painting lately.

MRS. ALVING. Even painters have to rest now and then.

MANDERS. I suppose so. To prepare themselves and conserve their energies for some great work.

OSWALD. Yes. Mother, shall we be eating soon?

MRS. ALVING. In about half an hour. He still enjoys his food, thank heaven.

MANDERS. And his tobacco, I see.

OSWALD. I found Father's pipe upstairs in the bedroom, so I—

MANDERS. Of course!

MRS. ALVING. What do you mean?

MANDERS. When Oswald appeared in that doorway with that pipe in his mouth, it was just as though I saw his father alive again.

OSWALD. Oh? Really?

MRS. ALVING. Oh, how can you say that? Oswald takes after me.

MANDERS. Yes; but there's an expression at the corner of his mouth, something about his lips, that reminds me so vividly of Alving—at any rate now when he's smoking.

MRS. ALVING. How can you say that? Oswald has much more the mouth of a clergyman, I think.

MANDERS. True, true. Some of my colleagues have a similar expression.

MRS. ALVING. But put away that pipe, my dear boy. I don't want any smoke in here.

OSWALD (*obeys*). I'm sorry. I only wanted to try it. You see, I smoked it once when I was a child.

MRS. ALVING. What?

OSWALD. Yes. I was quite small at the time. I remember, I went upstairs to see Father in his room one evening. He was so happy and cheerful.

MRS. ALVING. Oh, you don't remember anything from that time.

OSWALD. Oh, yes, I remember very clearly, he picked me up and sat me on his knee and let me smoke his pipe. "Puff away, boy," he said, "puff hard." And I puffed as hard as I could. I felt myself go pale and the sweat broke out on my forehead in great drops. And that made him roar with laughter—

MANDERS. How very strange.

MRS. ALVING. My dear, it's just something Oswald has dreamed.

OSWALD. No, Mother, I didn't dream it. Surely you must remember—you came in and carried me back into the nursery. Then I was sick and I saw you crying. Did Father often play jokes like that?

MANDERS. In his youth he was an extremely gay young man—

OSWALD. And yet he managed to achieve so much. So much that was good and useful; although he died so young.

MANDERS. Yes, you have inherited the name of an industrious and worthy man, my dear Oswald Alving. Well, I hope this will spur you on.

OSWALD. Yes, it ought to, oughtn't it?

MANDERS. In any case it was good of you to come home and join us in honouring him.

OSWALD. It was the least I could do for Father.

MRS. ALVING. And the best thing of all is that I'm going to have him here for so long.

MANDERS. Yes, I hear you're staying the winter.

OSWALD. I am here for an indefinite period, Pastor. Oh, but it's good to be home!

MRS. ALVING (*warmly*). Yes, Oswald. It is, isn't it?

MANDERS (*looks at him sympathetically*). Yes, you went out into the world early, my dear Oswald.

OSWALD. I did. Sometimes I wonder if it wasn't too early.

MRS. ALVING. Oh, nonsense. It's good for a healthy lad; especially if he's an only child. It's bad for them to stay at home with their mother and father and be pampered.

MANDERS. That is a very debatable point, Mrs. Alving. When all is said and done, the parental home is where a child belongs.

OSWALD. I agree with you there, Pastor.

MANDERS. Take your own son. Well, it will do no harm to talk about it in his presence.

What has been the consequence for him? Here he is, twenty-six or twenty-seven years old, and he's never had the opportunity to know what a real home is like.

OSWALD. I beg your pardon, sir, but there you're quite mistaken.

MANDERS. Oh? I thought you had spent practically all your time in artistic circles.

OSWALD. I have.

MANDERS. Mostly among young artists.

OSWALD. Yes.

MANDERS. But I thought most of those people lacked the means to support a family and make a home for themselves.

OSWALD. Some of them can't afford to get married, sir.

MANDERS. Yes, that's what I'm saying.

OSWALD. But that doesn't mean they can't have a home. Several of them have; and very good and comfortable homes at that.

MRS. ALVING *listens intently and nods, but says nothing.*

MANDERS. But I'm not speaking about bachelor establishments. By a home I mean a family establishment, where a man lives with his wife and children.

OSWALD. Quite. Or with his children and their mother.

MANDERS (*starts and claps his hands together*). Merciful heavens! You don't—?

OSWALD. Yes?

MANDERS. Lives with—with the mother of his children?

OSWALD. Yes, would you rather he disowned the mother of his children?

MANDERS. So you are speaking of unlegalized relationships! These so-called free marriages!

OSWALD. I've never noticed anything particularly free about the way such people live.

MANDERS. But how is it possible that—that any reasonably well brought up man or young woman can bring themselves to live like that—openly, for everyone to see?

OSWALD. But what else can they do? A poor young artist—a poor young girl—It costs a lot of money to get married. What can they do?

MANDERS. What can they do? I'll tell you, Mr. Alving, what they can do. They should have kept away from each other in the first place—that's what they should have done.

OSWALD. That argument won't get you far with young people who are in love and have red blood in their veins.

MRS. ALVING. No, that won't get you very far.

MANDERS (*takes no notice*). And to think that the authorities tolerate such behaviour! That it is allowed to happen openly! (*Turns to* MRS. ALVING.) Wasn't I right to be so concerned about your son? In circles where immorality is practised openly and is, one might almost say, accepted—

OSWALD. Let me tell you something, sir, I have been a regular Sunday guest in one or two of these irregular households—

MANDERS. On Sundays!

OSWALD. Yes, that's the day when one's meant to enjoy oneself. But I have never heard an offensive word there, far less ever witnessed anything which could be called immoral. No; do you know when and where I have encountered immorality in artistic circles?

MANDERS. No, I don't, thank heaven.

OSWALD. Well, I shall tell you. I have encountered it when one or another of our model husbands and fathers came down there to look around a little on their own—and did the artists the honour of visiting them in their humble bistros. Then we learned a few things. Those gentlemen were able to tell us about places and things of which we had never dreamed.

MANDERS. What! Are you suggesting that honourable men from this country—!

OSWALD. Have you never, when these honourable men returned home, have you never heard them hold forth on the rampancy of immorality in foreign countries?

MANDERS. Yes, of course—

MRS. ALVING. I've heard that, too.

OSWALD. Well, you can take their word for it. Some of them are experts. (*Clasps his head.*) Oh, that beautiful life of freedom—that it should be so soiled!

MRS. ALVING. You mustn't get over-excited, Oswald. It isn't good for you.

OSWALD. No, you're right, Mother. It isn't good for my health. It's that damned tiredness, you know. Well, I'll take a little walk before dinner. I'm sorry, Pastor. I know you can't see it from my point of view. But I had to say what I felt.

He goes out through the second door on the right.

MRS. ALVING. My poor boy—!

MANDERS. Yes, you may well say that. So it's come to this.

MRS. ALVING *looks at him but remains silent.*

MANDERS (*walks up and down*). He called himself the prodigal son. Alas, alas!

MRS. ALVING *still looks at him.*

MANDERS. And what do you say to all this?

MRS. ALVING. I say that Oswald was right in every word he said.

MANDERS (*stops dead*). Right? Right! In expressing those principles!

MRS. ALVING. Here in my loneliness I have come to think like him, Pastor Manders. But I have never dared to bring up the subject. Now my son shall speak for me.

MANDERS. I feel deeply sorry for you, Mrs. Alving. But now I will have to speak to you in earnest. I am not addressing you now as your business manager and adviser, nor as your and your late husband's old friend. I stand before you now as your priest, as I did at the moment when you had strayed so far.

MRS. ALVING. And what has the priest to say to me?

MANDERS. First I wish to refresh your memory, Mrs. Alving. The occasion is appropriate. Tomorrow will be the tenth anniversary of your husband's death.

Tomorrow the memorial to him who is no longer with us is to be unveiled. Tomorrow I shall address the whole assembled flock. But today I wish to speak to you alone.

MRS. ALVING. Very well, Pastor. Speak.

MANDERS. Have you forgotten that after barely a year of marriage you stood on the very brink of the abyss? That you abandoned your house and home—that you deserted your husband—yes, Mrs. Alving, deserted, deserted—and refused to return to him, although he begged and entreated you to do so?

MRS. ALVING. Have you forgotten how desperately unhappy I was during that first year?

MANDERS. Yes, that is the sign of the rebellious spirit, to demand happiness from this earthly life. What right have we to happiness? No, Mrs. Alving, we must do our duty! And your duty was to remain with the man you had chosen, and to whom you were bound by a sacred bond.

MRS. ALVING. You know quite well the kind of life Alving led at that time; the depravities he indulged in.

MANDERS. I am only too aware of the rumours that were circulating about him; and I least of anyone approve his conduct during his youthful years, if those rumours contained the truth. But a wife is not appointed to be her husband's judge. It was your duty humbly to hear that cross which a higher will had seen fit to assign to you. But instead you rebelliously fling down that cross, abandon the erring soul you should have supported, hazard your good name, and very nearly ruin the reputations of others.

MRS. ALVING. Others? Another's, you mean?

MANDERS. It was extremely inconsiderate of you to seek refuge with me.

MRS. ALVING. With our priest? With an old friend?

MANDERS. Exactly. Well, you may thank God that I possessed the necessary firmness— that I was able to dissuade you from your frenzied intentions and that it was granted to me to lead you back on to the path of duty and home to your lawful husband.

MRS. ALVING. Yes, Pastor Manders, that was certainly your doing.

MANDERS. I was merely a humble tool in the hand of a higher purpose. And that I persuaded you to bow to the call of duty and obedience, has not that proved a blessing which will surely enrich the remainder of your days? Did I not foretell all this? Did not Alving turn from his aberrations, like a man? Did he not afterwards live a loving and blameless life with you for the remainder of his days? Did he not become a public benefactor, did he not inspire you so that in time you became his right hand in all his enterprises? And a very capable right hand—oh, yes, I know that, Mrs. Alving, I give you credit for that. But now I come to the next great error of your life.

MRS. ALVING. And what do you mean by that?

MANDERS. Once you disowned your duties as a wife. Since then, you have disowned your duties as a mother.

MRS. ALVING. Ah—!

MANDERS. All your days you have been ruled by a fatal spirit of wilfulness. You have always longed for a life unconstrained by duties and principles. You have never been willing to suffer the curb of discipline. Everything that has been troublesome in your life you have cast off ruthlessly and callously, as if it were a burden which you had the right to reject. It was no longer convenient to you to be a wife, so you left your husband. You found it tiresome to be a mother, so you put your child out to live among strangers.

MRS. ALVING. Yes, that is true. I did.

MANDERS. And in consequence you have become a stranger to him.

MRS. ALVING. No, no! That's not true!

MANDERS. It is. It must be. And how have you got him back? Think well, Mrs. Alving! You have sinned greatly against your husband. You admit that by raising the monument to him down there. Confess too, now, how you have sinned against your son. There may still be time to bring him back from the paths of wantonness.

Turn; and save what may still be saved in him. (*With raised forefinger.*) For verily, Mrs. Alving, as a mother you carry a heavy burden of guilt. This I have regarded as my duty to say to you.

Silence.

MRS. ALVING (*slow and controlled*). You have had your say, Pastor; and tomorrow you will speak publicly at my husband's ceremony. I shall not speak tomorrow. But now I shall say a few words to you, just as you have said a few words to me.

MANDERS. Of course. You wish to excuse your conduct—

MRS. ALVING. No. I simply want to tell you what happened.

MANDERS. Oh?

MRS. ALVING. Everything that you have just said about me and my husband and our life together after you, as you put it, had led me back on to the path of duty—all that is something of which you have no knowledge from your own observations. From that moment you, who used to visit us every day, never once set foot in our house.

MANDERS. You and your husband moved from town shortly afterwards.

MRS. ALVING. Yes. And you never came out here to see us while my husband was alive. It was only the business connected with the Orphanage that compelled you to visit me.

MANDERS (*quietly and uncertainly*). Helen—if this is intended as a reproach, I must beg you to consider the—

MRS. ALVING. The duty you owed to your position, yes. And then I was a wife who had run away from her husband. One can never be too careful with such unprincipled women.

MANDERS. My dear . . . Mrs. Alving, you exaggerate grotesquely.

MRS. ALVING. Yes, yes, well, let us forget it. What I wanted to say was that when you judge my conduct as a wife, you are content to base your judgment on common opinion.

MANDERS. Yes, well; what of it?

MRS. ALVING. But now, Manders, now I shall tell the truth. I have sworn to myself that one day you should know it. Only you.

MANDERS. And what is the truth?

MRS. ALVING. The truth is that my husband died just as dissolute as he had always lived.

MANDERS (*gropes for a chair*). What did you say?

MRS. ALVING. Just as dissolute, at any rate in his desires, after nineteen years of marriage, as he was before you wedded us.

MANDERS. You call these youthful escapades —these irregularities—excesses, if you like —evidence of a dissolute life!

MRS. ALVING. That is the expression our doctor used.

MANDERS. I don't understand you.

MRS. ALVING. It doesn't matter.

MANDERS. I cannot believe my ears. You mean your whole married life—all those years you shared with your husband—were nothing but a façade!

MRS. ALVING. Yes. Now you know.

MANDERS. But—but this I cannot accept! I don't understand—I cannot credit it! But how on earth is it possible—how could such a thing be kept secret?

MRS. ALVING. I had to fight, day after day, to keep it secret. After Oswald was born I thought things became a little better with Alving. But it didn't last long. And now I had to fight a double battle, fight with all my strength to prevent anyone knowing what kind of a man my child's father was. And you know what a winning personality Alving had. No one could believe anything but good of him. He was one of those people whose reputations remain untarnished by the way they live. But then, Manders—you must know this too—then came the most loathsome thing of all.

MANDERS. More loathsome than this!

MRS. ALVING. I had put up with him, although I knew well what went on secretly outside the house. But when he offended within our four walls—

MANDERS. What are you saying? Here!

MRS. ALVING. Yes, here in our own home. In

there— (*Points to the first door on the right.*) —it was in the dining-room I first found out about it. I had something to do in there and the door was standing ajar. Then I heard our maid come up from the garden to water the flowers in there.

MANDERS. Oh, yes?

MRS. ALVING. A few moments later I heard Alving enter the room. He said something to her. And then I heard— (*Gives a short laugh.*) —I still don't know whether to laugh or cry—I heard my own servant whisper: "Stop it, Mr. Alving! Let me go!"

MANDERS. What an unseemly frivolity! But it was nothing more than a frivolity, Mrs. Alving. Believe me.

MRS. ALVING. I soon found out what to believe. My husband had his way with the girl. And that relationship had consequences, Pastor Manders.

MANDERS (*petrified*). And all this took place in this house! In this house!

MRS. ALVING. I had endured much in this house. To keep him at home in the evenings—and at night—I had to make myself his companion in his secret dissipations up in his room. There I had to sit alone with him, had to clink my glass with his and drink with him, listen to his obscene and senseless drivelling, had to fight him with my fists to haul him into bed—

MANDERS (*shocked*). I don't know how you managed to endure it.

MRS. ALVING. I had to, for my little son's sake. But when the final humiliation came —when my own servant—then I swore to myself: "This must stop!" And so I took over the reins of this house; both as regards him and everything else. For now, you see, I had a weapon against him; he dared not murmur. It was then that I sent Oswald away. He was nearly seven and was beginning to notice things and ask questions, the way children do. I couldn't bear that, Manders. I thought the child could not help but be poisoned merely by breathing in this tainted home. That was why I sent him away. And so now you know why he was never allowed to set foot in his home while his father was alive. No one knows what it cost me.

MANDERS. You have indeed been sorely tried.

MRS. ALVING. I could never have borne it if I had not had my work. Yes, for I think I can say that I have worked! All the additions to the estate, all the improvements, all the useful innovations for which Alving was praised—do you imagine he had the energy to initiate any of them? He, who spent the whole day lying on the sofa reading old court circulars? No; let me tell you this too; I drove him forward when he was in his happier moods; and I had to bear the whole burden when he started again on his dissipations or collapsed in snivelling helplessness.

MANDERS. And it is to this man that you raise a memorial.

MRS. ALVING. There you see the power of a guilty conscience.

MANDERS. A guilty—? What do you mean?

MRS. ALVING. I always believed that some time, inevitably, the truth would have to come out, and that it would be believed. The Orphanage would destroy all rumours and banish all doubt.

MANDERS. You certainly made no mistake there, Mrs. Alving.

MRS. ALVING. And then I had another motive. I wanted to make sure that my own son, Oswald, should not inherit anything whatever from his father.

MANDERS. You mean it was Alving's money that—?

MRS. ALVING. Yes. The annual donations that I have made to this Orphanage add up to the sum—I have calculated it carefully— the sum which made Lieutenant Alving, in his day, "a good match."

MANDERS. I understand—

MRS. ALVING. It was the sum with which he bought me. I do not wish that money to come into Oswald's hands. My son shall inherit everything from me.

OSWALD ALVING *enters through the second door on the right; he has removed his hat and overcoat outside.*

MRS. ALVING (*goes towards him*). Are you back already? My dear, dear boy!

OSWALD. Yes; what's one to do outside in this eternal rain? But I hear we're about to have dinner. How splendid.

REGINA (*enters from the kitchen with a parcel*). A parcel has just come for you, madam. (*Hands it to her.*)

MRS. ALVING (*with a glance at* PASTOR MANDERS). Copies of the songs for tomorrow's ceremony, I suppose.

MANDERS. Hm—

REGINA. Dinner is served, madam.

MRS. ALVING. Good. We'll come presently. I just want to— (*Begins to open the parcel.*)

REGINA (*to* OSWALD). Shall it be white port or red port, Mr. Oswald?

OSWALD. Both, Miss Engstrand.

REGINA. *Bien*—very good, Mr. Oswald.

She goes into the dining-room.

OSWALD. I'd better help her open the bottles —(*Follows her into the dining-room. The door swings half open behind him.*)

MRS. ALVING. (*who has opened the parcel*). Yes, that's right. It's the copies of the songs, Pastor Manders.

MANDERS (*with folded hands*). How I am to make my address tomorrow with a clear conscience. I—!

MRS. ALVING. Oh, you'll find a way—

MANDERS (*quietly, so as not to be heard in the dining-room*). Yes, there mustn't be any scandal.

MRS. ALVING (*firmly, in a low voice*). No. But now this long, loathsome comedy is over. From the day after tomorrow, it will be as if the dead had never lived in this house. There will be no one here but my boy and his mother.

From the dining-room is heard the crash of a chair being knocked over. At the same time REGINA *says sharply, but keeping her voice low:*

REGINA. Oswald! Are you mad? Let me go!

MRS. ALVING (*starts in fear*). Ah!

She stares distraught at the half open door. OSWALD *coughs and begins to hum. A bottle is uncorked.*

MANDERS (*indignantly*). What is going on, Mrs. Alving? What was that?

MRS. ALVING (*hoarsely*). Ghosts. The couple in the conservatory—walk.

MANDERS. What are you saying! Regina—? Is she the child you—?

MRS. ALVING. Yes. Come. Not a word.

She grips PASTOR MANDERS' *arms and walks falteringly towards the door of the dining-room.*

ACT TWO

The same room. The mist still lies heavily over the landscape. PASTOR MANDERS *and* MRS. ALVING *enter from the dining-room.*

MRS. ALVING (*still in the doorway*). I'm glad you enjoyed it, Pastor Manders. (*Speaks into the dining-room.*) Aren't you joining us, Oswald?

OSWALD (*offstage*). No, thank you. I think I'll go out and take a walk.

MRS. ALVING. Yes, do. It's stopped raining now. (*Closes the door of the dining-room, goes over to the hall door and calls.*) Regina!

REGINA (*offstage*). Yes, madam.

MRS. ALVING. Go down to the wash-house and give them a hand with the garlands.

REGINA. Very good, madam.

MRS. ALVING *makes sure that* REGINA *has gone, then closes the door.*

MANDERS. He can't hear anything from in there, can he?

MRS. ALVING. Not when the door is shut. Anyway, he's going out.

MANDERS. I am still stunned. I don't understand how I managed to swallow a mouthful of that excellent meal.

MRS. ALVING (*restless but controlled, walks up and*

down). Neither do I. But what is to be done?

MANDERS. Yes, what is to be done? Upon my word, I don't know. I'm so sadly inexperienced in matters of this kind.

MRS. ALVING. I am convinced that no harm has been done yet.

MANDERS. No, heaven forbid! Nevertheless, it's a most improper situation.

MRS. ALVING. It's only a casual whim of Oswald's. You can be certain of that.

MANDERS. Well, as I said, I don't know about these things; but I'm sure—

MRS. ALVING. She must leave the house. And at once. That's obvious—

MANDERS. Yes, naturally.

MRS. ALVING. But where to? We can't just—

MANDERS. Where to? Home to her father, of course.

MRS. ALVING. To whom, did you say?

MANDERS. To her—oh, no, Engstrand isn't her—! But, dear God, Mrs. Alving, how can this be possible? Surely you must be mistaken.

MRS. ALVING. Unfortunately I know I'm not mistaken. In the end Johanna had to confess to me; and Alving couldn't deny it. So there was nothing to be done but hush the matter up.

MANDERS. Yes, I suppose that was the only thing to do.

MRS. ALVING. The girl left my service at once, and was given a considerable sum of money to keep her mouth shut. The remaining difficulties she solved for herself when she got to town. She renewed an old acquaintance with Engstrand, let it be known, I dare say, how much money she had, and spun him a story about some foreigner or other who'd been here with a yacht that summer. Then she and Engstrand got themselves married in a hurry. Well, you married them yourself.

MANDERS. But how can that be true? I remember clearly how Engstrand came to me to arrange the wedding. He was completely abject, and accused himself most bitterly of having indulged with his betrothed in a moment of weakness.

MRS. ALVING. Well, he had to take the blame on himself.

MANDERS. But to be so dishonest! And to me! I certainly would never have believed that of Jacob Engstrand. I'll speak to him seriously about this. He can be sure of that. And the immorality of it! For money! How much was it you gave the girl?

MRS. ALVING. Fifty pounds.

MANDERS. Just imagine! To go and marry a fallen woman for a paltry fifty pounds!

MRS. ALVING. What about me? I went and married a fallen man.

MANDERS. Good God Almighty, what are you saying? A fallen man!

MRS. ALVING. Do you think Alving was any purer when I accompanied him to the altar than Johanna was when Engstrand married her?

MANDERS. But the two things are utterly different—

MRS. ALVING. Not so different. Oh, yes, there was a big difference in the price. A paltry fifty pounds against an entire fortune.

MANDERS. But how can you compare two such different situations? After all, you were obeying the counsels of your heart, and of your family.

MRS. ALVING (*does not look at him*). I thought you understood the direction in which what you call my heart had strayed at that time.

MANDERS (*distantly*). If I had understood anything of the kind, I should not have been a daily guest in your husband's house.

MRS. ALVING. Anyway, I didn't follow my own counsel. That is certain.

MANDERS. Well then, you obeyed your nearest relatives. Your mother and your two aunts. As was your duty.

MRS. ALVING. Yes, that is true. The three of them worked out a balance-sheet for me. Oh, it's incredible how patly they proved that it would be utter madness for me to turn down such an offer. If my mother could look down now and see what all that promise of splendour has led to.

MANDERS. No one can be held responsible for the outcome. And this much at least is sure, that your marriage was celebrated in an orderly fashion and in full accordance with the law.

MRS. ALVING (*by the window*). All this talk about law and order. I often think that is what causes all the unhappiness in the world.

MANDERS. Mrs. Alving, now you are being sinful.

MRS. ALVING. Yes, perhaps I am. But I can't stand being bound by all these obligations and petty considerations. I can't! I must find my own way to freedom.

MANDERS. What do you mean by that?

MRS. ALVING (*taps on the window frame*). I should never have concealed the truth about Alving's life. But I dared not do otherwise—and it wasn't only for Oswald's sake. I was such a coward.

MANDERS. Coward?

MRS. ALVING. If people had known, they would have said: "Poor man, it isn't surprising he strays now and then. After all, his wife ran away from him."

MANDERS. Perhaps they would not have been altogether unjustified.

MRS. ALVING (*looks hard at him*). If I were a real mother, I would take Oswald and say to him: "Listen, my boy. Your father was a degenerate—"

MANDERS. But great heavens above—!

MRS. ALVING. And I would tell him everything I have told you. The whole story.

MANDERS. You scandalize me, Mrs. Alving.

MRS. ALVING. Yes, I know. I know! I scandalize myself. (*Comes away from the window.*) That's how cowardly I am.

MANDERS. You call it cowardice to do your simple duty! Have you forgotten that a child shall love and honour its father and mother?

MRS. ALVING. Let us not generalize so. Let us ask: "Shall Oswald love and honour Captain Alving?"

MANDERS. Is there not a voice in your mother's heart which forbids you to destroy your son's ideals?

MRS. ALVING. Yes, but what about the truth?

MANDERS. Yes, but what about the ideals?

MRS. ALVING. Oh, ideals, ideals! If only I weren't such a coward!

MANDERS. Don't despise our ideals, Mrs. Alving. Retribution will surely follow. Take Oswald in particular. He hasn't many ideals, I'm afraid. But this much I have discovered, that his father is to him an ideal.

MRS. ALVING. You are right there.

MANDERS. And you yourself have awakened and fostered these ideas of his, by your letters.

MRS. ALVING. Yes. I was bound by these obligations and considerations, so I lied to my son, year out and year in. Oh, what a coward, what a coward I have been!

MANDERS. You have established a happy illusion in your son, Mrs. Alving—and you should certainly not regard that as being of little value.

MRS. ALVING. Hm. I wonder. But I shan't allow him to use Regina as a plaything. He is not going to make that poor girl unhappy.

MANDERS. Good heavens, no! That would be dreadful.

MRS. ALVING. If I knew that he meant it seriously, and that it would make him happy—

MANDERS. Yes? What then?

MRS. ALVING. But that's impossible. Unfortunately Regina isn't that type.

MANDERS. How do you mean?

MRS. ALVING. If only I weren't such an abject coward, I'd say to him: "Marry her, or make what arrangements you please. As long as you're honest and open about it—"

MANDERS. Merciful God! You mean a legal marriage! What a terrible idea! It's absolutely unheard of—!

MRS. ALVING. Unheard of, did you say? Put your hand on your heart, Pastor Manders, and tell me—do you really believe there aren't married couples like that to be found in this country—as closely related as these two?

MANDERS. I simply don't understand you.

MRS. ALVING. Oh, yes you do.

MANDERS. You're thinking that by chance

possibly—? Yes, alas, family life is indeed not always as pure as it should be. But in that kind of case, one can never be sure—at any rate, not absolutely—But in this case—! That you, a mother, could want to allow your own—

MRS. ALVING. But I don't *want* to. I wouldn't allow it for any price in the world. That's just what I'm saying.

MANDERS. No, because you are a coward, as you put it. But if you weren't a coward—! Great God in heaven, what a shocking relationship!

MRS. ALVING. Well, we all stem from a relationship of that kind, so we are told. And who was it who arranged things like that in the world, Pastor Manders?

MANDERS. I shall not discuss such questions with you, Mrs. Alving. You are not in the right spiritual frame of mind for that. But that you dare to say that it is cowardly of you—!

MRS. ALVING. I shall tell you what I mean. I am frightened, because there is in me something ghostlike from which I can never free myself.

MANDERS. What did you call it?

MRS. ALVING. Ghostlike. When I heard Regina and Oswald in there, it was as if I saw ghosts. I almost think we are all ghosts—all of us, Pastor Manders. It isn't just what we have inherited from our father and mother that walks in us. It is all kinds of dead ideas and all sorts of old and obsolete beliefs. They are not alive in us; but they remain in us none the less, and we can never rid ourselves of them. I only have to take a newspaper and read it, and I see ghosts between the lines. There must be ghosts all over the country. They lie as thick as grains of sand. And we're all so horribly afraid of the light.

MANDERS. Aha—so there we have the fruits of your reading. Fine fruits indeed! Oh, these loathsome, rebellious, freethinking books!

MRS. ALVING. You are wrong, my dear Pastor. It was you yourself who first spurred me to think; and I thank and bless you for it.

MANDERS. I?

MRS. ALVING. Yes, when you forced me into what you called duty; when you praised as right and proper what my whole spirit rebelled against as something abominable. It was then that I began to examine the seams of your learning. I only wanted to pick at a single knot; but when I had worked it loose, the whole fabric fell apart. And then I saw that it was machine-sewn.

MANDERS (*quiet, shaken*). Is this the reward of my life's hardest struggle?

MRS. ALVING. Call it rather your life's most pitiful defeat.

MANDERS. It was my life's greatest victory, Helen. The victory over myself.

MRS. ALVING. It was a crime against us both.

MANDERS. That I besought you, saying: "Woman, go home to your lawful husband," when you came to me distraught and cried: "I am here! Take me!" Was that a crime?

MRS. ALVING. Yes, I think so.

MANDERS. We two do not understand each other.

MRS. ALVING. No; not any longer.

MANDERS. Never—never even in my most secret moments have I thought of you except as another man's wedded wife.

MRS. ALVING. Oh? I wonder.

MANDERS. Helen—

MRS. ALVING. One forgets so easily what one was like.

MANDERS. I do not. I am the same as I always was.

MRS. ALVING (*changes the subject*). Well, well, well—let's not talk any more about the past. Now you're up to your ears in commissions and committees; and I sit here fighting with ghosts, both in me and around me.

MANDERS. I will help you to bring to heel the ghosts around you. After all the dreadful things you have told me today, my conscience will not permit me to allow a young and unprotected girl to remain in your house.

MRS. ALVING. Don't you think it would be best if we could get her taken care of? I mean—well, decently married.

MANDERS. Indubitably. I think it would be desirable for her in every respect. Regina is just now at the age when—well, I don't really understand these things, but—

MRS. ALVING. Regina matured early.

MANDERS. Yes, didn't she? I seem to remember that she was noticeably well developed from a physical point of view when I prepared her for confirmation. But for the present at any rate she must go home. To her father's care—no, but of course, Engstrand isn't—! That he—that *he* could conceal the truth from me like that!

There is a knock on the door leading to the hall.

MRS. ALVING. Who can that be? Come in.

ENGSTRAND (*appears in the doorway in his Sunday suit*). Begging your pardon, madam, but—

MANDERS. Aha! Hm!

MRS. ALVING. Oh, is it you, Engstrand?

ENGSTRAND. There weren't any of the servants about, so I took the liberty of giving a little knock.

MRS. ALVING. Yes, yes. Well, come in. Do you want to speak to me about something?

ENGSTRAND (*enters*). No, thank you, ma'am. It's the Pastor I really wanted to have a word with.

MANDERS (*walks up and down*). Hm; really? You want to speak to me? Do you indeed?

ENGSTRAND. Yes, I'd be so terribly grateful if—

MANDERS (*stops in front of him*). Well! May I ask what is the nature of your question?

ENGSTRAND. Well, it's like this, Pastor. We've been paid off down there now—a thousand thanks, Mrs. Alving—and now we're ready with everything—and so I thought it'd only be right and proper if we who have worked so well together all this time—I thought we might conclude with a few prayers this evening.

MANDERS. Prayers? Down at the Orphanage?

ENGSTRAND. Well, of course, sir, if you don't think it's the right thing to do—

MANDERS. Oh yes, yes, indeed I do, but—hm—

ENGSTRAND. I've been in the habit of holding a little service myself down there of an evening—

MANDERS. Have you?

ENGSTRAND. Yes, now and then. Just a little edification, as you might say. But I'm only a poor humble man and haven't the proper gifts, God forgive me—and so I thought, seeing as Pastor Manders happens to be out here—

MANDERS. Now look here, Engstrand, first I must ask you a question. Are you in the correct frame of mind for such a meeting? Do you feel your conscience is clear and free?

ENGSTRAND. Oh, God forgive us, let's not talk about conscience, Pastor.

MANDERS. Yes, that's just what we are going to talk about. Well? What is your answer?

ENGSTRAND. Well—a man's conscience can be a bit of a beggar now and then—

MANDERS. Well, at least you admit it. But now, will you tell me the truth! What's all this about Regina?

MRS. ALVING (*quickly*). Pastor Manders!

MANDERS (*soothingly*). Leave this to me—

ENGSTRAND. Regina? Good heavens, how you frighten me! (*Looks at* MRS. ALVING.) Surely nothing's happened to Regina?

MANDERS. Let us hope not. But what I meant was, what's all this about you and Regina? You call yourself her father, don't you? Hm?

ENGSTRAND (*uncertainly*). Well—hm—you know all about me and poor Johanna.

MANDERS. Now I want no more prevarication. Your late wife told the whole truth to Mrs. Alving before she left her service.

ENGSTRAND. Well, may the—! No, did she really?

MANDERS. So now you are unmasked, Engstrand.

ENGSTRAND. And she promised and swore on the Bible that she—

MANDERS. Swore on the Bible—!

ENGSTRAND. No, she only promised, but so sincerely.

MANDERS. And all these years you have concealed the truth from me. Concealed it from *me*, who trusted you so implicitly.

ENGSTRAND. Yes, I'm afraid I have, I suppose.

MANDERS. Have I deserved this from you, Engstrand? Haven't I always been ready to assist you with help, both spiritual and material, as far as lay within my power? Answer! Haven't I?

ENGSTRAND. Things would often have looked black for me if it hadn't been for your Reverence.

MANDERS. And this is how you reward me! You cause me to enter false statements in the parish register, and withhold from me over a period of years the information which you owed both to me and to the cause of truth! Your conduct has been completely indefensible, Engstrand. From now on, I wash my hands of you.

ENGSTRAND (*with a sigh*). Yes, of course, sir. I appreciate that.

MANDERS. I mean, how could you possibly justify yourself?

ENGSTRAND. But wouldn't it have made things even worse for poor Johanna if the truth had been allowed to come out? Now just imagine if your Reverence had been in the same situation as her—

MANDERS. I!

ENGSTRAND. Oh, for heaven's sake, I don't mean exactly the same. But I mean, suppose your Reverence had something to be ashamed of in the eyes of the world, as the saying goes. We men mustn't judge a poor woman too harshly, your Reverence.

MANDERS. But I'm not. It's you I'm reproaching.

ENGSTRAND. May I ask your Reverence a tiny question?

MANDERS. Yes, yes, what is it?

ENGSTRAND. Isn't it right and proper for a man to raise up the fallen?

MANDERS. Of course it is.

ENGSTRAND. And isn't it a man's duty to stand by his word?

MANDERS. Certainly it is: but—

ENGSTRAND. That time when Johanna fell into misfortune through that Englishman—or maybe he was an American, or a Russian, as they call them—well, she came up to town. Poor creature, she'd turned up her nose at me once or twice; for she only looked at what was handsome and fine, poor thing; and of course I had this thing wrong with my leg. Well, your Reverence will remember how I'd ventured into a dancing-hall where foreign sailors were indulging in drunkenness and excess, as the saying goes. And when I tried to exhort them to start leading a better life—

MRS. ALVING (*by the window*). Hm—

MANDERS. I know, Engstrand. The ruffians threw you down the stairs. You've told me about it before. Your injury is something to be proud of.

ENGSTRAND. Oh, I take no pride in it, your Reverence. But what I was going to say was, so she came along and poured out all her troubles to me amid weeping and gnashing of teeth. I'll be frank, your Reverence; it nearly broke my heart to listen to her.

MANDERS. Did it really, Engstrand? Well, go on.

ENGSTRAND. Yes, well, so I said to her: "This American is a vagrant on the sea of life," I said. "And you, Johanna, you've committed a sin and are a fallen creature. But Jacob Engstrand," I said, "he's got both feet firmly on the ground"—speaking figuratively, you understand—

MANDERS. I understand you perfectly. Go on.

ENGSTRAND. Well, that's how I raised her up and made an honest woman of her so that people shouldn't get to know the wanton way she'd behaved with foreigners.

MANDERS. You acted very handsomely. The only thing I can't understand is how you could bring yourself to accept money—

ENGSTRAND. Money? I? Not a penny!

MANDERS (*glances questioningly at* MRS. ALVING). But—!

ENGSTRAND. Oh yes, wait a moment—now I remember. Johanna did have a few shillings with her. But I wouldn't have any of it. "Fie!" I said, "that's Mammon, that's the wages of sin. We'll throw that wretched gold—or notes, or whatever it was—back in the American's face," I said. But he'd taken his hook and disappeared across the wild sea, your Reverence.

MANDERS. Had he, my dear Engstrand?

ENGSTRAND. Oh yes. And so Johanna and I agreed that the money was to be used to bring up the child, and that's what happened; and I can account for every shilling of it.

MANDERS. But this puts quite a different face on things.

ENGSTRAND. That's the way it was, your Reverence. And I think I can say I've been a real father to Regina—as far as stood within my power—for unfortunately I'm an ailing man.

MANDERS. Now, now, my dear Engstrand—

ENGSTRAND. But this I can say, that I've brought up the child tenderly and been a loving husband to poor Johanna and ordered my household the way the good book says. But it would never have entered my head to go along to your Reverence in sinful pride and boast that for once I too had done a good deed. No, when anything of that kind happens to Jacob Engstrand, he keeps quiet about it. I don't suppose that's always the way, more's the pity. And when I do go to see Pastor Manders I've always more than enough of wickedness and weakness to talk to him about. For I said it just now and I say it again—a man's conscience can be a real beggar now and then.

MANDERS. Give me your hand, Jacob Engstrand.

ENGSTRAND. Why, good heavens, Pastor—!

MANDERS. No argument, now. (*Presses his hand.*) There!

ENGSTRAND. And if I was to go down on my bended knees and humbly to beg your Reverence's forgiveness—?

MANDERS. You? No, on the contrary. It is I who must ask your pardon—

ENGSTRAND. Oh no, really—

MANDERS. Indeed, yes. And I do so with all my heart. Forgive me that I could ever have misjudged you so. And if there is any way in which I can show the sincerity of my regrets and of my good-will towards you—

ENGSTRAND. Would your Reverence really do that?

MANDERS. Most gladly.

ENGSTRAND. Well, in that case there's a real opportunity just now. With the money I've managed to put aside through the blessed work here, I'm thinking of starting a kind of home for sailors in the city.

MANDERS. *You* are?

ENGSTRAND. Yes, a kind of refuge like the one here, in a manner of speaking. The temptations for a sailor wandering on shore are so manifold. But in this house, with me there, it'd be like them having a father to take care of them, I thought.

MANDERS. What have you to say to that, Mrs. Alving!

ENGSTRAND. My means are rather limited, God knows. But if only someone would stretch out a helping hand—

MANDERS. Yes, well, let us consider the matter more closely. Your project interests me very deeply. But go along now and get everything in order and light candles so as to make the place cheerful, and we'll have a little edification together, my dear Engstrand. For now I think you're in the right frame of mind.

ENGSTRAND. Yes, I think I am. Well, good-bye, Mrs. Alving, and thank you for everything. And take good care of Regina for me. (*Wipes a tear from his eye.*) Poor Johanna's child! Hm—it's strange, but—it's just as though she'd grown to be a part of me. It is really, yes. (*Touches his forehead and goes out through the door.*)

MANDERS. Well, what have you to say about that man now, Mrs. Alving? That was quite a different explanation we were given there.

MRS. ALVING. It was indeed.

MANDERS. You see how terribly careful one must be about condemning one's fellows. But then, again, it is a deep joy to discover that one has been mistaken. Or what do you say?

MRS. ALVING. I say: you are a great baby, Manders. And you always will be.

MANDERS. I?

MRS. ALVING (*places both her hands on his shoulders*). And I say: I'd like to throw both my arms round your neck.

MANDERS (*frees himself quickly*). No, no, bless you! Such impulses—!

MRS. ALVING (*with a smile*). Oh, you needn't be frightened of me.

MANDERS (*by the table*). You have such an extravagant way of expressing yourself sometimes. Now let me just gather these documents together and put them in my case. (*Does so.*) There! And now, *au revoir.* Keep your eyes open when Oswald comes back. I'll be with you again presently. (*Takes his hat and goes out through the hall.*)

MRS. ALVING (*sighs, looks out of the window for a moment, tidies the room a little and is about to go into the dining-room, but stops in the doorway and calls softly*). Oswald, are you still at table?

OSWALD (*offstage*). I'm just finishing my cigar.

MRS. ALVING. I thought you'd gone for a little walk.

OSWALD. In this weather?

> *There is the clink of a glass.* MRS. ALVING *leaves the door open and sits down with her sewing on the sofa by the window.*

OSWALD (*still offstage*). Wasn't that Pastor Manders who left just now?

MRS. ALVING. Yes, he's gone down to the Orphanage.

OSWALD. Hm. (*Clink of decanter and glass again.*)

MRS. ALVING (*with a worried glance*). Oswald dear, you ought to be careful with that liqueur. It's strong.

OSWALD. It keeps out the damp.

MRS. ALVING. Won't you come in and talk to me?

OSWALD. I can't smoke in there.

MRS. ALVING. You know I don't mind cigars.

OSWALD. All right, I'll come, then. Just one tiny drop more. There. (*He enters with his cigar and closes the door behind him. Short silence.*)

OSWALD. Where's the Pastor gone?

MRS. ALVING. I told you, he went down to the Orphanage.

OSWALD. Oh yes, so you did.

MRS. ALVING. You oughtn't to sit at table so long, Oswald.

OSWALD (*holding his cigar behind his back*). But I think it's so nice, Mother. (*Strokes and pats her.*) To come home, and sit at my mother's own table, in my mother's dining-room, and eat my mother's beautiful food.

MRS. ALVING. My dear, dear boy.

OSWALD (*walks and smokes a trifle impatiently*). And what else is there for me to do here? I can't work—

MRS. ALVING. Can't you?

OSWALD. In this weather? Not a glimmer of sunlight all day. (*Walks across the room.*) That's the worst thing about it—not to be able to work—

MRS. ALVING. Perhaps you shouldn't have come home.

OSWALD. Yes, Mother, I had to.

MRS. ALVING. I'd ten times rather sacrifice the happiness of having you with me than that you should—

OSWALD (*stops by the table*). Tell me, Mother. Does it really make you so happy to have me home?

MRS. ALVING. Does it make me happy?

OSWALD (*crumples a newspaper*). I think it must be almost the same for you whether I'm alive or not.

MRS. ALVING. How can you have the heart to say that to your mother, Oswald?

OSWALD. But you managed so well to live without me before.

MRS. ALVING. Yes. I have lived without you. That is true.

> *Silence. Dusk begins to gather slowly.* OSWALD *paces up and down the room. He has put down his cigar.*

OSWALD (*stops beside* MRS. ALVING). Mother, may I sit down on the sofa with you?

MRS. ALVING (*makes room for him*). Yes, of course, my dear boy.

OSWALD (*sits*). There's something I have to tell you, Mother.

MRS. ALVING (*tensely*). Yes?

OSWALD (*stares vacantly ahead of him*). I can't keep it to myself any longer.

MRS. ALVING. What? What do you mean?

OSWALD (*as before*). I couldn't bring myself to write to you about it; and since I came home I—

MRS. ALVING (*grips his arm*). Oswald, what is this?

OSWALD. Yesterday and today I've been trying to forget. To escape. But it's no good.

MRS. ALVING (*rises*). Tell me the truth, Oswald.

OSWALD (*pulls her down on to the sofa again*). Sit still and I'll try to tell you about it. I've complained so much about how tired I felt after the journey—

MRS. ALVING. Yes. Well?

OSWALD. But it isn't that that's wrong with me. It isn't any ordinary tiredness—

MRS. ALVING (*tries to rise*). You're not ill, Oswald!

OSWALD (*pulls her down again*). Sit still, Mother. Just keep calm. No, I'm not really ill; not what people usually call ill. (*Clasps his hands to his head.*) Mother, I'm spiritually broken—my will's gone—I shall never be able to work any more!

He throws himself into her lap, with his hands over his face, and sobs.

MRS. ALVING (*pale and trembling*). Oswald! Look at me! No, no, it isn't true!

OSWALD (*looks up at her despairingly*). Never to be able to work again! Never. Never. To be dead while I'm still alive. Mother, can you imagine anything so dreadful?

MRS. ALVING. My poor boy. How did this frightful thing happen to you?

OSWALD (*sits upright again*). Yes, that's just what I can't understand. I've never lived intemperately. Not in any way. You mustn't believe that of me, Mother. I've never done that.

MRS. ALVING. Of course I don't believe it, Oswald.

OSWALD. And yet it's happened to me. This dreadful thing.

MRS. ALVING. Oh, but my dear, dear boy, it'll be all right. You've just overworked. You take my word for it.

OSWALD (*heavily*). That's what I thought at first. But it isn't that.

MRS. ALVING. Tell me the whole story.

OSWALD. I shall, yes.

MRS. ALVING. When did you first notice it?

OSWALD. It was soon after the last time I'd been home, and had gone back again to Paris. I began to feel the most violent pains in my head—mostly at the back of my head, it seemed. It was as though a tight iron ring had been screwed round my neck and just above it.

MRS. ALVING. Yes?

OSWALD. At first I thought it was just the usual headaches I used to have so often while I was a child.

MRS. ALVING. Yes, yes—

OSWALD. But it wasn't. I soon realized that. I couldn't work any more. I wanted to begin on a new painting, but it was as though my powers had failed me. It was as though I was paralysed—I couldn't see anything clearly—everything went misty and began to swim in front of my eyes. Oh, it was dreadful! In the end I sent for the doctor. And he told me the truth.

MRS. ALVING. How do you mean?

OSWALD. He was one of the leading doctors down there. I had to tell him how I felt. And he began to ask me a lot of questions, which seemed to me to have absolutely nothing to do with it. I didn't understand what the man was driving at—

MRS. ALVING. Yes!

OSWALD. In the end he said: "You've been worm-eaten from birth." That was the word he used: *vermoulu.*

MRS. ALVING (*tensely*). What did he mean by that?

OSWALD. I didn't understand either, and asked him to explain more clearly. And then the old cynic said— (*Clenches his fist.*) Oh—!

MRS. ALVING. What did he say?

OSWALD. He said: "The sins of the fathers shall be visited on the children."

MRS. ALVING (*rises slowly*). The sins of the fathers—!

OSWALD. I nearly hit him in the face—

MRS. ALVING (*walks across the room*). The sins of the fathers—

OSWALD (*smiles sadly*). Yes, what do you think of that? Of course I assured him it was quite out of the question. But do you think he gave in? No, he stuck to his opinion; and it was only when I brought out your letters and translated to him all the passages that dealt with Father—

MRS. ALVING. But then he—?

OSWALD. Yes, then of course he had to admit he was on the wrong track. And then I learned the truth. The incredible truth! This wonderfully happy life with my comrades, I should have abstained from. It had been too much for my strength. In other words, I have only myself to blame.

MRS. ALVING. Oswald! Oh, no, you mustn't think that!

OSWALD. There was no other explanation possible, he said. That's the dreadful thing. Beyond cure—ruined for life—because of my own folly. Everything I wanted to accomplish in the world—not even to dare to think of it—not to be *able* to think of it. Oh, if only I could start my life over again, and undo it all!

Throws himself face down on the sofa. MRS. ALVING *wrings her hands and walks to and fro, fighting silently with herself.*

OSWALD (*after a while, looks up and remains half-leaning on his elbow*). If it had been something I'd inherited. Something I wasn't myself to blame for. But this! To have thrown away in this shameful, thoughtless, light-hearted way one's whole happiness and health, everything in the world—one's future, one's life—

MRS. ALVING. No, no, my dear, blessed boy— this is impossible! (*Leans over him.*) Things are not as desperate as you think.

OSWALD. Oh, you don't know—! (*Jumps up.*) And then, Mother, that I should cause you all this grief! I've often almost wished and hoped that you didn't care very much about me.

MRS. ALVING. I, Oswald! My only son! The only possession I have in the world—the only thing I care about!

OSWALD (*seizes both her hands and kisses them*). Yes, yes, I know. When I am at home, of course I know it. And that's one of the hardest things to bear. But now you know. And now we won't talk about it any more today. I can't bear to think about it for long. (*Walks across the room.*) Get me something to drink, Mother.

MRS. ALVING. Drink? What do you want to drink now?

OSWALD. Oh, anything. You have some cold punch in the house, haven't you?

MRS. ALVING. Yes, but, my dear Oswald—

OSWALD. Oh, Mother, don't be difficult. Be nice now! I *must* have something to help me forget these worries. (*Goes into the conservatory.*) Oh, how—how dark it is in here! (MRS. ALVING *pulls a bell-rope, right.*) And this incessant rain. It goes on week after week; sometimes for months. Never to see the sun! In all the years I've been at home I don't remember ever having seen the sun shine.

MRS. ALVING. Oswald! You are thinking of leaving me!

OSWALD. Hm— (*Sighs deeply.*) I'm not thinking about anything. I *can't* think about anything. (*Softly.*) I take good care not to.

REGINA (*enters from the dining-room*). Did you ring, madam?

MRS. ALVING. Yes, bring in the lamp.

REGINA. Yes, madam, at once. I've already lit it. (*Goes.*)

MRS. ALVING (*goes over to* OSWALD). Oswald, don't hide anything from me.

OSWALD. I'm not, Mother. (*Goes over to the table.*) Haven't I told you enough?

REGINA *enters with the lamp and puts it on the table.*

MRS. ALVING. Oh, Regina, you might bring us half a bottle of champagne.

REGINA. Very good, madam. (*Goes.*)

OSWALD (*takes* MRS. ALVING'*s head in his hands*). That's the way. I knew my Mother wouldn't let her boy go thirsty.

MRS. ALVING. My poor, dear Oswald! How could I deny you anything now?

OSWALD (*eagerly*). Is that true, Mother? Do you mean it?

MRS. ALVING. Mean what?

OSWALD. That you wouldn't deny me anything?

MRS. ALVING. But, my dear Oswald—

OSWALD. Ssh!

REGINA (*brings a tray with a half-bottle of champagne and two glasses, and puts it down on the table*). Shall I open—?

OSWALD. No, thank you, I'll do it myself.

REGINA *goes.*

MRS. ALVING (*sits down at the table*). What did you mean just now, when you said I mustn't deny you anything?

OSWALD (*busy trying to open the bottle*). Let's taste this first.

The cork jumps out. He fills one glass and is about to do likewise with the other.

MRS. ALVING (*puts her hand over it*). Thank you, not for me.

OSWALD. Well, for me, then. (*Empties the glass, refills it and empties it again. Then he sits down at the table.*)

MRS. ALVING (*tensely*). Well?

OSWALD (*not looking at her*). Tell me, Mother— I thought you and Pastor Manders looked so strange—hm—quiet—at dinner.

MRS. ALVING. Did you notice?

OSWALD. Yes—hm. (*Short silence.*) Tell me— what do you think of Regina?

MRS. ALVING. What do I think?

OSWALD. Yes, isn't she splendid?

MRS. ALVING. Oswald dear, you don't know her as well as I do—

OSWALD. Oh?

MRS. ALVING. Regina spent too much time at home, I'm afraid. I ought to have brought her here to live with me sooner.

OSWALD. Yes, but isn't she splendid to look at, Mother? (*Fills his glass.*)

MRS. ALVING. Regina has many great faults—

OSWALD. Oh, what does that matter? (*Drinks again.*)

MRS. ALVING. But I'm fond of her all the same. And I am responsible for her. I'd rather anything in the world happened than that she should come to any harm.

OSWALD (*jumps up*). Mother, Regina's my only hope!

MRS. ALVING (*rises*). What do you mean by that?

OSWALD. I can't bear all this misery alone.

MRS. ALVING. But you have your mother to bear it with you.

OSWALD. Yes, that's what I thought. And that's why I came home to you. But it won't work. I can see it; it won't work. I can't bear this life here.

MRS. ALVING. Oswald!

OSWALD. Oh, I must live differently, Mother. That's why I have to leave you. I don't want you to see.

MRS. ALVING. My poor, sick boy! Oh, but Oswald, as long as you're not well—

OSWALD. If it was just the illness, I'd stay with you, Mother. You're the best friend I have in the world.

MRS. ALVING. Yes, I am, Oswald, aren't I?

OSWALD (*walks around restlessly*). But it's all the remorse, the gnawing, the self-reproach. And then the fear! Oh—this dreadful fear!

MRS. ALVING (*follows him*). Fear? What fear? What do you mean?

OSWALD. Oh, don't ask me any more about it. I don't know. I can't describe it.

MRS. ALVING *crosses and pulls the bellrope.*

OSWALD. What do you want?

MRS. ALVING. I want my boy to be happy. He shan't sit here and brood. (*To* REGINA *who appears in the doorway.*) More champagne. A whole bottle.

REGINA *goes.*

OSWALD. Mother!

MRS. ALVING. Do you think we don't know how to live here, too?

OSWALD. Isn't she splendid to look at? The way she's made! And so healthy and strong!

MRS. ALVING (*sits at the table*). Sit down, Oswald, and let's talk calmly together.

OSWALD (*sits*). You don't know this, Mother, but I have done Regina a wrong. And I've got to put it right.

MRS. ALVING. A wrong?

OSWALD. Well, a little thoughtlessness—whatever you care to call it. Quite innocently, really. When I was home last—

MRS. ALVING. Yes?

OSWALD. She asked me so often about Paris, and I told her this and that about the life down there. And I remember, one day I happened to say: "Wouldn't you like to come there yourself?"

MRS. ALVING. Oh?

OSWALD. Well, she blushed violently, and then she said: "Yes, I'd like to very much." "Well, well," I replied, "that might be arranged"—or something of the sort.

MRS. ALVING. Yes?

OSWALD. Well, of course I forgot the whole thing. But the day before yesterday, when I asked her if she was glad that I was going to stay at home so long—

MRS. ALVING. Yes?

OSWALD. She gave me such a strange look and then she asked: "But then, what's going to become of my trip to Paris?"

MRS. ALVING. Her trip!

OSWALD. And then I got it out of her that she'd taken the whole thing seriously, that she'd been going around here thinking about me the whole time, and that she'd begun to learn French—

MRS. ALVING. I see—

OSWALD. Mother—when I saw that splendid, handsome, healthy girl standing there in front of me—well, I'd never really noticed her before—but now, when she stood there, so to speak, with open arms ready to receive me—

MRS. ALVING. Oswald!

OSWALD. Then I realized that in her I could find salvation; for I saw that she was full of the joy of life.

MRS. ALVING (*starts*). The joy of life! But how could that help?

REGINA (*enters from the dining-room with a bottle of champagne*). I'm sorry I was so long. I had to go down to the cellar— (*Puts the bottle on the table.*)

OSWALD. And fetch another glass.

REGINA (*looks at him, surprised*). There is Mrs. Alving's glass.

OSWALD. But fetch one for yourself, Regina.

REGINA *starts and throws a quick glance at* MRS. ALVING.

OSWALD. Well?

REGINA (*quietly, hesitantly*). Do you wish me to, madam?

MRS. ALVING. Fetch the glass, Regina.

REGINA *goes into the dining-room.*

OSWALD (*watches her go*). Do you see how she walks? With such purpose and gaiety!

MRS. ALVING. This must not happen, Oswald.

OSWALD. It's already decided. Surely you can see. It's no use trying to stop it.

REGINA *enters with an empty glass, which she keeps in her hand.*

OSWALD. Sit down, Regina. (*She glances questioningly at* MRS. ALVING.)

MRS. ALVING. Sit down.

REGINA *sits on a chair by the dining-room door, with the empty glass still in her hand.*

MRS. ALVING. Oswald, what was it you were saying about the joy of life?

OSWALD. Oh, yes—the joy of life, Mother—you don't know much about that here. I never feel it here.

MRS. ALVING. Not when you are with me?

OSWALD. Not when I'm at home. But you don't understand that.

MRS. ALVING. Oh, yes—I think I do now—almost.

OSWALD. The joy of life and the love of one's work. They're practically the same thing. But that you don't know anything about, either.

MRS. ALVING. No, I don't suppose we do. Oswald, tell me more about this.

OSWALD. Well, all I mean is that here people are taught to believe that work is a curse and a punishment, and that life is a misery which we do best to get out of as quickly as possible.

MRS. ALVING. A vale of tears, yes. And we do our best to make it one.

OSWALD. But out there, people don't feel like that. No one there believes in that kind of teaching any longer. They feel it's wonderful and glorious just to be alive. Mother, have you noticed how everything I've painted is concerned with the joy of life? Always, always, the joy of life. Light and sunshine and holiday—and shining, contented faces. That's what makes me afraid to be here at home with you.

MRS. ALVING. Afraid? What are you afraid of here with me?

OSWALD. I'm afraid that everything in me will degenerate into ugliness here.

MRS. ALVING (*looks hard at him*). You think that would happen?

OSWALD. I know it. Live the same life here as down there, and it wouldn't be the same life.

MRS. ALVING (*who has listened intently, rises, her eyes large and thoughtful*). Now I see.

OSWALD. What do you see?

MRS. ALVING. Now I understand for the first time. And now I can speak.

OSWALD (*rises*). Mother, I don't follow you.

REGINA (*who has also risen*). Shall I go?

MRS. ALVING. No, stay. Now I can speak. Now, my boy, you shall know everything. And then you can choose. Oswald! Regina!

OSWALD. Ssh! The Pastor—!

MANDERS (*enters from the hall*). Well, we've had a most splendid and profitable hour down there.

OSWALD. So have we.

MANDERS. We must assist Engstrand with this sailors' home. Regina must go and help him—

REGINA. No thank you, Pastor.

MANDERS (*notices her for the first time*). What! You here! And with a glass in your hand!

REGINA (*puts the glass down quickly*). Oh, pardon—

OSWALD. Regina is leaving with me, sir.

MANDERS. Leaving! With you!

OSWALD. Yes. As my wife. If she so wishes.

MANDERS. But, good heavens—!

REGINA. It isn't my doing, sir.

OSWALD. Or she will stay here, if I stay.

REGINA (*involuntarily*). Here?

MANDERS. I am petrified at you, Mrs. Alving.

MRS. ALVING. She will neither leave with you nor stay with you. Now I can speak the truth.

MANDERS. But you mustn't! No, no, no!

MRS. ALVING. I can and I will. And I shan't destroy any ideals, either.

OSWALD. Mother, what have you been hiding from me?

REGINA (*listens*). Madam! Listen! People are shouting outside!

She goes into the conservatory and looks out.

OSWALD (*at the window, left*). What's going on? Where's that light coming from?

REGINA (*cries*). The Orphanage is on fire!

MRS. ALVING (*at the window*). On fire!

MANDERS. On fire? Impossible! I've only just left it.

OSWALD. Where's my hat? Oh, never mind! Father's Orphanage—! (*Runs out through the garden door.*)

MRS. ALVING. My shawl, Regina! The whole building's alight!

MANDERS. Terrible! Mrs. Alving, there blazes the judgment of God upon this sinful house!

MRS. ALVING. Perhaps you are right. Come, Regina. (*She and* REGINA *hurry out through the hall.*)

MANDERS (*clasps his hands*). And not insured either! (*He follows them.*)

ACT THREE

*The same. All the doors are standing open.
The lamp is still burning on the table.
Outside it is dark, with only a faint glow
from the fire in the background, left.* MRS.
ALVING, *with a big shawl over her head, is
standing in the conservatory, looking out.*
REGINA, *also with a shawl round her, stands
a little behind her.*

MRS. ALVING. All burnt. Burnt to the ground.

REGINA. It's still burning in the basement.

MRS. ALVING. Why doesn't Oswald come
back? There's nothing to save.

REGINA. Would you like me to go down and
take him his hat?

MRS. ALVING. Hasn't he even got his hat?

REGINA (*points to the hall*). No, it's hanging
there.

MRS. ALVING. Let it hang. He must come up
now. I'll go and look for him myself. (*Goes
out through the garden door.*)

MANDERS (*enters from hall*). Isn't Mrs. Alving
here?

REGINA. She's just this minute gone into the
garden.

MANDERS. This is the most terrible night I
have ever experienced.

REGINA. Yes, sir, isn't it a dreadful tragedy?

MANDERS. Oh, don't talk about it! I hardly
dare even to think about it.

REGINA. But how can it have happened—?

MANDERS. Don't ask me, Miss Engstrand.
How can I know? Are you, too, going to—?
Isn't it enough that your father—?

REGINA. What's he done?

MANDERS. Oh, he's completely confused me.

ENGSTRAND (*enters from the hall*). Your Reverence—

MANDERS (*turns, alarmed*). Are you still pursuing me?

ENGSTRAND. Yes, well, God rot me if—oh,
good heavens! But this is a terrible business, your Reverence.

MANDERS (*walks up and down*). It is indeed, it
is indeed.

REGINA. What is?

ENGSTRAND. Well, you see, it all began with
this prayer service. (*Aside.*) Now we've got
him, my girl! (*Aloud.*) Fancy me being to
blame for Pastor Manders being to blame
for something like this.

MANDERS. But I assure you, Engstrand—

ENGSTRAND. But there was no one except your
Reverence mucking around with the candles down there.

MANDERS (*stops*). Yes, so you keep on saying.
But I'm sure I don't remember ever having
had a candle in my hand.

ENGSTRAND. And I saw as plain as plain
could be your Reverence take the candle
and snuff it with your fingers and throw
the wick right down among the shavings.

MANDERS. And you saw this?

ENGSTRAND. Yes, with these eyes.

MANDERS. That I cannot understand. It's not
usually my habit to snuff out candles with
my fingers.

ENGSTRAND. Yes, it looked a bit careless, I
thought. But it can't really be as bad as
you say, can it, your Reverence?

MANDERS (*paces uneasily up and down*). Oh,
don't ask me.

ENGSTRAND (*walks with him*). And of course
you haven't insured it, either?

MANDERS (*still walking*). No, no, no. I've told
you.

ENGSTRAND (*still with him*). Not insured. And
then to go straight over and set fire to it all.
Oh, good heavens, what a tragedy.

MANDERS (*wipes the sweat from his forehead*).
Yes, Engstrand, you may well say that.

ENGSTRAND. And that such a thing should
happen to a charitable institution which
was to have served the city as well as the
countryside. The newspapers won't be too
gentle with your Reverence, I'm afraid.

MANDERS. No, that's just what I'm thinking.
That's almost the worst part of it. All these
hateful attacks and accusations—! Oh, it's
frightful to think about.

MRS. ALVING (*enters from the garden*). I can't
persuade him to come away from the fire.

MANDERS. Ah, it's you, Mrs. Alving.

MRS. ALVING. Well, now you won't have to
make that speech after all, Pastor Manders.

MANDERS. Oh, I'd have been only too happy
to—

MRS. ALVING (*in a subdued voice*). It was all for
the best. Nothing good would have come
of this Orphanage.

MANDERS. You think not?

MRS. ALVING. What do you think?

MANDERS. Nevertheless, it was a terrible
tragedy.

MRS. ALVING. We'll discuss it simply as a
business matter. Are you waiting for the
Pastor, Engstrand?

ENGSTRAND (*in the doorway to the hall*). That's
right, madam.

MRS. ALVING. Well, sit down, then.

ENGSTRAND. Thank you, I'm happy standing.

MRS. ALVING (*to* MANDERS). I suppose you'll
be leaving with the steamer?

MANDERS. Yes. In an hour.

MRS. ALVING. Would you be kind enough to
take all the papers along with you? I don't
want to hear another word about this. Now
I have other things to think about—

MANDERS. Mrs. Alving—

MRS. ALVING. I'll send you a power of attorney
so that you can take any measures you
think fit.

MANDERS. I shall be only too happy to shoulder that responsibility. I fear the original
purpose of the endowment will now have
to be completely changed.

MRS. ALVING. I appreciate that.

MANDERS. Yes, I'm provisionally thinking of
arranging for the Solvik property to be
handed over to the parish. The freehold
cannot by any means be said to be without
value. It can always be put to some purpose
or other. And the interest from the capital
in the savings bank I could perhaps most
suitably employ in supporting some enterprise or other which could be said to be of
benefit to the town.

MRS. ALVING. As you please. It's a matter of
complete indifference to me.

ENGSTRAND. Remember my home for sailors,
your Reverence.

MANDERS. Yes, indeed, you have a point
there. We shall have to consider that
possibility carefully.

ENGSTRAND. Consider? To hell with—oh,
good heavens!

MANDERS (*with a sigh*). And I'm afraid I don't
know how long these matters will remain
in my hands. Public opinion may force me
to withdraw. It all depends on the outcome
of the enquiry into the cause of the fire.

MRS. ALVING. What are you saying?

MANDERS. And one cannot possibly predict
the outcome.

ENGSTRAND (*comes closer*). Oh, yes one can.
Don't I stand here, and isn't my name
Jacob Engstrand?

MANDERS. Yes, yes, but—

ENGSTRAND (*more quietly*). And Jacob Engstrand isn't the man to fail his blessed
benefactor in his time of need, as the
saying goes.

MANDERS. But, my dear man, how—?

ENGSTRAND. Jacob Engstrand can be likened
to an angel of deliverance, as you might
say, your Reverence.

MANDERS. No, no, I really cannot accept this.

ENGSTRAND. Oh, that's the way it's going to
be. I know someone who's taken the blame
for another man's wickedness once before.

MANDERS. Jacob! (*Presses his hand.*) You are
indeed a rare person. Well, you too shall
receive a helping hand. For your seamen's
home. That you can rely upon.

ENGSTRAND *wants to thank him, but is too
moved to speak.*

MANDERS (*hangs his travelling bag on his shoulder*).
Well, let's be off. We two shall go together.

ENGSTRAND (*at the dining-room door, says quietly
to* REGINA). You come with me, my girl.
You'll live as tight as the yolk in an egg.

REGINA (*tosses her head*). *Merci!* (*Goes into the
hall and fetches* MANDERS' *overcoat.*)

MANDERS. Farewell, Mrs. Alving. And may
the spirit of law and order soon enter into
this house.

MRS. ALVING. Goodbye, Manders.

She goes towards the conservatory, as she sees
OSWALD *come in through the garden door.*

ENGSTRAND (*while he and* REGINA *help* MAN-

DERS *on with his overcoat*). Goodbye, my child. And if ever you find yourself in any trouble, you know where Jacob Engstrand is to be found. (*Quietly.*) Little Harbour Street—hm—! (*To* MRS. ALVING *and* OSWALD.) And the house for wandering sailors is going to be called Captain Alving's Home. And if I am allowed to run it according to my ideas, I think I can promise you it'll be a worthy memorial to him, God rest his soul.

MANDERS (*in the doorway*). Hm—hm! Come along, my dear Engstrand. Goodbye, goodbye. (*He and* ENGSTRAND *go out through the hall.*)

OSWALD (*goes over towards the table*). What was that he was talking about?

MRS. ALVING. Some kind of home that he and Pastor Manders are going to found.

OSWALD. It'll burn down just like this one.

MRS. ALVING. Why do you say that?

OSWALD. Everything will burn. There will be nothing left to remind people of Father. I, too, am burning.

REGINA *starts and stares at him.*

MRS. ALVING. Oswald! You ought not to have stayed down there so long, my poor boy.

OSWALD (*sits down at the table*). I think you're right.

MRS. ALVING. Let me wipe your face, Oswald. It's soaking wet. (*She dries him with her handkerchief.*)

OSWALD (*stares indifferently ahead of him*). Thank you, Mother.

MRS. ALVING. Aren't you tired, Oswald? Wouldn't you like to go upstairs and sleep?

OSWALD (*frightened*). No, no, I won't sleep. I never sleep. I only pretend to. (*Heavily.*) It'll come soon enough.

MRS. ALVING (*looks worried at him*). My dear boy, you really are ill.

REGINA (*tensely*). Is Mr. Alving ill?

OSWALD (*impatiently*). And shut all the doors! Oh, this fear that haunts me—!

MRS. ALVING. Close them, Regina.

REGINA *closes the doors and remains*

standing *by the hall door.* MRS. ALVING *takes off her shawl.* REGINA *does likewise.*

MRS. ALVING (*brings a chair over to* OSWALD's *and sits down beside him*). There now. I'll sit beside you—

OSWALD. Yes, do. And Regina must stay here too. Regina must always be near me. You'll save me, Regina. Won't you?

REGINA. I don't understand—

MRS. ALVING. Save you—?

OSWALD. Yes. When the time comes.

MRS. ALVING. But Oswald, you have your mother.

OSWALD. You? (*Smiles.*) No, Mother, you wouldn't do this for me. (*Laughs heavily.*) You? Ha, ha! (*Looks earnestly at her.*) Though really you're the one who ought to. (*Violently.*) Why don't you speak to me as though I was your friend, Regina? Why don't you call me Oswald?

REGINA (*quietly*). I don't think Mrs. Alving would like it.

MRS. ALVING. You may do so presently. Come over and sit down here with us. (REGINA *sits quietly and diffidently on the other side of the table.*) And now, my poor, tormented boy, now I shall remove the burden from your mind—

OSWALD. You, Mother?

MRS. ALVING (*continues*). All this remorse and self-reproach you speak of—

OSWALD. You think you can do that?

MRS. ALVING. Yes, Oswald, now I can. You spoke of the joy of life; and that seemed to throw a new light over everything that has happened to me in my life.

OSWALD (*shakes his head*). I don't understand.

MRS. ALVING. You should have known your father when he was a young lieutenant. He was full of the joy of life, Oswald.

OSWALD. Yes, I know.

MRS. ALVING. It was like a sunny morning just to see him. And the untamed power and the vitality he had!

OSWALD. Yes?

MRS. ALVING. And this happy, carefree child —for he was like a child, then—had to live here in a little town that had no joy to offer him, only diversions. He had to live here with no purpose in life; simply a position to keep up. He could find no work into which he could throw himself heart and soul—just keeping the wheels of business turning. He hadn't a single friend capable of knowing what the joy of life means; only idlers and drinking-companions—

OSWALD. Mother—!

MRS. ALVING. And in the end the inevitable happened.

OSWALD. The inevitable?

MRS. ALVING. You said yourself this evening what would happen to you if you stayed at home.

OSWALD. You mean that Father—?

MRS. ALVING. Your poor father never found any outlet for the excess of vitality in him. And I didn't bring any sunshine into his home.

OSWALD. You didn't?

MRS. ALVING. They had taught me about duty and things like that, and I sat here for too long believing in them. In the end everything became a matter of duty—*my* duty, and *his* duty, and—I'm afraid I made his home intolerable for your poor father, Oswald.

OSWALD. Why did you never write and tell me about this?

MRS. ALVING. Until now I never saw it as something that I could tell you, because you were his son.

OSWALD. And how did you see it?

MRS. ALVING (*slowly*). I only saw that your father was a depraved man before you were born.

OSWALD (*quietly*). Ah—! (*Gets up and goes over to the window.*)

MRS. ALVING. And day in and day out I thought of only one thing, that Regina really belonged here in this house—just as much as my own son.

OSWALD (*turns swiftly*). Regina—!

REGINA (*jumps up and asks softly*). I?

MRS. ALVING. Yes, now you both know.

OSWALD. Regina!

REGINA (*to herself*). So Mother was one of them.

MRS. ALVING. Your mother was in many ways a good woman, Regina.

REGINA. Yes, but still, she was one of them. Yes, I've sometimes wondered; but—! Well, madam, if you'll allow me I think I'd better leave. At once.

MRS. ALVING. Do you really want to, Regina?

REGINA. Yes, I certainly do.

MRS. ALVING. Of course you must do as you please, but—

OSWALD (*goes over to* REGINA). Go now? But you belong here.

REGINA. *Merci*, Mr. Alving—yes, I suppose I'm allowed to say Oswald now. But it certainly isn't the way I'd hoped.

MRS. ALVING. Regina, I haven't been open with you—

REGINA. I should say not. If I'd known that Oswald was ill like this, I—Now that there can never be anything serious between us— No, I'm not going to stay out here in the country and wear myself out looking after invalids.

OSWALD. Not even for someone who is so close to you?

REGINA. I should say not. A poor girl has got to make the best of her life while she's young. Otherwise she'll be left high and dry before she knows where she is. And I've got the joy of life in me too, Mrs. Alving.

MRS. ALVING. Yes, I'm afraid you have. But don't throw yourself away, Regina.

REGINA. Oh, what will be will be. If Oswald takes after his father, I shouldn't be surprised but what I'll take after my mother. May I ask, madam, does Pastor Manders know this about me?

MRS. ALVING. Pastor Manders knows everything.

REGINA (*begins to put on her shawl*). Well then, I'd better get down to the steamer as quick as I can. The Pastor's such a nice man to get along with. And I'm sure I've as much a right to a little of that money as he has— that awful carpenter.

MRS. ALVING. I'm sure you're very welcome to it, Regina.

REGINA (*looks spitefully at her*). You might

have brought me up like the daughter of a gentleman. It'd have been more appropriate considering. (*Tosses her head.*) Oh, what the hell does it matter? (*With a bitter glance at the bottle, still unopened.*) I can still drink champagne with gentlemen.

MRS. ALVING. And if ever you need a home, Regina, come to me.

REGINA. No thank you, madam. Pastor Manders will take care of me. And if things go really wrong, I know a house where I belong.

MRS. ALVING. Where is that?

REGINA. In Captain Alving's home for sailors.

MRS. ALVING. Regina—I can see it. You will destroy yourself.

REGINA. Oh, rubbish. *Adieu!* (*Curtseys and goes out through the hall.*)

OSWALD (*stands by the window, looking out*). Has she gone?

MRS. ALVING. Yes.

OSWALD (*mumbles to himself*). I think it was wrong, all this.

MRS. ALVING (*goes over behind him and places her hands on his shoulders*). Oswald, my dear boy, has this news upset you very much?

OSWALD (*turns his face towards her*). All this about Father, you mean?

MRS. ALVING. Yes, about your poor father. I'm so afraid it may have been too much for you.

OSWALD. What on earth makes you think that? Of course it came as a great surprise to me. But I can't really feel it makes any difference.

MRS. ALVING (*takes her hands away*). No difference! That your father was so miserably unhappy!

OSWALD. I feel sorry for him of course, as I would for anyone, but—

MRS. ALVING. Nothing else? For your own father!

OSWALD (*impatiently*). Oh, Father, Father! I never knew anything about Father. I don't remember anything about him, except that once he made me sick.

MRS. ALVING. This is terrible! Surely a child

ought to love its father whatever may happen?

OSWALD. Even when a child has nothing to thank its father for? Has never known him? Do you really cling to that old superstition —you, who are otherwise so enlightened?

MRS. ALVING. Do you really think it's only a superstition—?

OSWALD. Yes, Mother, surely you realize that. It's one of those truisms people hand down to their children—

MRS. ALVING (*shudders*). Ghosts!

OSWALD (*walks across the room*). Yes, that's not a bad word for them. Ghosts.

MRS. ALVING (*emotionally*). Oswald! Then you don't love me either!

OSWALD. At least I know you—

MRS. ALVING. Know me, yes. But is that all?

OSWALD. And of course I know how fond you are of me; and for that I must be grateful to you. And you can do so much for me now that I'm ill.

MRS. ALVING. Yes, Oswald, I can, can't I? Oh, I could almost bless your sickness for bringing you home to me. I realize it now. You aren't mine. I must win you.

OSWALD (*impatiently*). Yes, yes, yes. These are just empty phrases. You must remember I'm sick, Mother. I can't be expected to bother about others. I've enough worry thinking about myself.

MRS. ALVING (*quietly*). I shall be patient and undemanding.

OSWALD. And cheerful, Mother!

MRS. ALVING. Yes, my dear boy—I know. (*Goes over to him.*) Have I freed you from all your anxiety and self-reproach now?

OSWALD. Yes, you have. But who will take away the fear?

MRS. ALVING. The fear?

OSWALD (*walks across the room*). Regina would have done it for the asking.

MRS. ALVING. I don't understand you. What's all this about fear—and Regina?

OSWALD. Is it very late, Mother?

MRS. ALVING. It's early morning. (*Looks out into the conservatory.*) The dawn's beginning to show upon the mountains. It's going to be a fine day, Oswald. In a little while you'll be able to see the sun.

OSWALD. I'll look forward to that. Oh, there's still so much for me to look forward to and live for—

MRS. ALVING. Of course there is!

OSWALD. Even if I can't work, there's—

MRS. ALVING. Oh, you'll soon be able to work again, my dear boy. You haven't all these gnawing and oppressing thoughts to brood over any longer now.

OSWALD. No, it was a good thing you managed to rid me of all those ideas. Once I've got over this one thing—! (*Sits on the sofa.*) Let's sit down and talk, Mother.

MRS. ALVING. Yes, let's. (*Moves an armchair over to the sofa, and sits close to him.*)

OSWALD. And while we talk the sun will rise. And then you'll know. And then I won't have this fear any longer.

MRS. ALVING. What will I know?

OSWALD (*not listening to her*). Mother, didn't you say earlier tonight that there wasn't anything in the world you wouldn't do for me if I asked you?

MRS. ALVING. Certainly I did.

OSWALD. And you'll keep your promise, Mother?

MRS. ALVING. Of course I will, my dearest, my only boy. I've nothing else to live for. Only you.

OSWALD. Yes, well, listen then. Mother, you're brave and strong, I know that. Now you must sit quite still while I tell you.

MRS. ALVING. But what is this dreadful thing you—?

OSWALD. You mustn't scream. You hear? Promise me that. We'll sit and talk about it quite calmly. Do you promise me that, Mother?

MRS. ALVING. Yes, yes, I promise. Only tell me.

OSWALD. Well then, all that business about being tired—and not being able to think about work—that isn't the real illness—

MRS. ALVING. What is the real illness?

OSWALD. The illness which is my inheritance —(*Points to his forehead and says quite quietly.*) That's in here.

MRS. ALVING (*almost speechless*). Oswald! No! No!

OSWALD. Don't scream. I can't bear it. Yes, Mother, it sits in here, watching and waiting. And it may break out any time; any hour.

MRS. ALVING. Oh, how horrible—!

OSWALD. Now keep calm. That's the way it is—

MRS. ALVING (*jumps up*). It isn't true, Oswald! It's impossible! It can't be true!

OSWALD. I had one attack down there. It soon passed. But when I found out what I had been like, this raging fear began to haunt me; and that's why I came back home to you as quickly as I could.

MRS. ALVING. So that's the fear—

OSWALD. Yes—it's so unspeakably repulsive, you see. Oh, if only it had been an ordinary illness that would have killed me—! Because I'm not so frightened of dying; though I'd like to live as long as I can.

MRS. ALVING. Yes, yes, Oswald, you must!

OSWALD. But this is so revolting. To be turned back into a slobbering baby; to have to be fed, to have to be—! Oh—! I can't think about it—!

MRS. ALVING. The child has its mother to nurse it.

OSWALD (*jumps up*). No, never! That's just what I won't allow! I can't bear to think that I might stay like that for years, growing old and grey. And perhaps you might die and leave me. (*Sits in* MRS. ALVING'S *chair.*) It might not mean that I'd die at once, the doctor said. He called it a softening of the brain or something. (*Smiles sadly.*) I think that sounds so beautiful. I shall always think of cherry-coloured velvet curtains—something delicious to stroke.

MRS. ALVING (*screams*). Oswald!

OSWALD (*jumps up again and walks across the room*). And now you've taken Regina from me. If only I had her! She would have saved me. I know.

MRS. ALVING (*goes over to him*). What do you mean by that, my beloved boy? Is there anything I wouldn't do to save you?

OSWALD. When I had recovered from the attack down there, the doctor told me that when it comes again—and it will come again—then there's no more hope.

MRS. ALVING. How could he be so heartless as to—?

OSWALD. I made him tell me. I told him I had arrangements to make. (*Smiles cunningly.*) And so I had. (*Takes a small box from his inside breast pocket.*) Mother, do you see this?

MRS. ALVING. What's that?

OSWALD. Morphine powders.

MRS. ALVING (*looks at him in horror*). Oswald—my boy—!

OSWALD. I've managed to collect twelve capsules—

MRS. ALVING (*tries to take it*). Give that box to me, Oswald.

OSWALD. Not yet, Mother. (*Puts it back in his pocket.*)

MRS. ALVING. I can't bear this!

OSWALD. You must bear it. If Regina had been here now, I'd have told her how things were with me—and asked her to do me this last service. I'm sure she would have helped me.

MRS. ALVING. Never!

OSWALD. When the horror was on me and she saw me lying there like a new-born baby, helpless, lost—beyond all hope—

MRS. ALVING. Regina would never have done it.

OSWALD. She would have. Regina was so splendidly carefree. And she would soon have got bored with looking after an invalid like me.

MRS. ALVING. Then thank God that Regina is not here!

OSWALD. Yes, well, so now you will have to do this last service for me, Mother.

MRS. ALVING (*screams aloud*). I?

OSWALD. Who else?

MRS. ALVING. I! Your mother!

OSWALD. Exactly.

MRS. ALVING. I, who gave you life!

OSWALD. I didn't ask you for life. And what kind of a life have you given me? I don't want it. Take it back.

MRS. ALVING. Help! Help! (*Runs out into the hall.*)

OSWALD (*goes after her*). Don't leave me! Where are you going?

MRS. ALVING (*in the hall*). To fetch the doctor, Oswald. Let me go!

OSWALD (*also offstage*). You're not going anywhere. And no one's coming here. (*A key is turned.*)

MRS. ALVING (*comes back*). Oswald! Oswald—my child!

OSWALD (*follows her*). If you have a mother's love for me, how can you see me suffer like this?

MRS. ALVING (*after a moment's silence, says in a controlled voice*). Very well. (*Takes his hand.*) I give you my word.

OSWALD. You promise?

MRS. ALVING. If it becomes necessary. But it won't be. No, no, it's impossible.

OSWALD. Yes, let us hope so. And let us live together as long as we can. Thank you, Mother.

He sits in the armchair, which MRS. ALVING *has moved over to the sofa. The day breaks. The lamp continues to burn on the table.*

MRS. ALVING (*approaches him cautiously*). Do you feel calm now?

OSWALD. Yes.

MRS. ALVING (*leans over him*). You've just imagined these dreadful things, Oswald. You've imagined it all. All this suffering has been too much for you. But now you shall rest. At home with your own mother, my own dear, blessed boy. Point at anything you want and you shall have it, just like when you were a little child. There, there. Now the attack is over. You see how easily it passed! Oh, I know it! And, Oswald, do you see what a beautiful day we're going to have? Bright sunshine. Now you can really see your home.

She goes over to the table and puts out the lamp. The sun rises. The glacier and the snow-capped peaks in the background glitter in the morning light.

OSWALD (*sits in the armchair facing downstage, motionless. Suddenly he says*). Mother, give me the sun.

MRS. ALVING (*by the table, starts and looks at him*). What did you say?

OSWALD (*repeats dully and tonelessly*). The sun. The sun.

MRS. ALVING (*goes over to him*). Oswald, how are you feeling?

> OSWALD *seems to shrink small in his chair. All his muscles go slack. His face is expressionless. His eyes stare emptily.*

MRS. ALVING (*trembles with fear*). What's this? (*Screams loudly.*) Oswald! What is it? (*Throws herself on her knees beside him and shakes him.*) Oswald! Oswald! Look at me! Don't you know me?

OSWALD (*tonelessly as before*). The sun. The sun.

MRS. ALVING (*jumps to her feet in despair, tears her hair with both hands and screams*). I can't bear this! (*Whispers as though numbed.*) I can't bear it! No! (*Suddenly.*) Where did he put them? (*Fumbles quickly across his breast.*) Here! (*Shrinks a few steps backwards and screams.*) No; no; no! Yes! No; no! (*She stands a few steps away from him with her hands twisted in her hair, speechless, and stares at him in horror.*)

OSWALD (*still motionless*). The sun. The sun.

NOTES FOR GHOSTS

Henrik Ibsen

. . . Ibsen's original draft for *Ghosts* has not been preserved, and the differences between his second draft and the final version as we know it are few and insignificant. After Ibsen's death, however, six brief sets of notes presumably relating to *Ghosts* were discovered among his papers, some (nos. 1–4) on two sheets of quarto, some (no. 5) on the back of an envelope, and some (no. 6) on a torn newspaper wrapper. They are undated, but probably belong to the winter and spring of 1881:

1. The play to be a realistic picture of life. Faith undetermined—but people daren't admit it. The "Orphanage"—for the sake of others. They want to be happy—but this, too, is only an illusion—Everything is ghosts—

   An important point: She has been a believer and a romantic—and this can't completely be eradicated by the attitude she has subsequently adopted—"Everything is ghosts."

   To marry for the wrong reasons, even though they be religious or moral, brings a Nemesis on the children.

   She, the illegitimate child, can be saved by being married to—the son—but then—?

2. He in his youth was depraved, a debauchee; then she appeared, a woman who had "seen the light"; she saved him; she was rich. He had wanted to marry a girl who was thought unworthy. His wife bore him a son; then he turned back to the girl; a daughter—

3. These modern women, misused as daughters, as sisters, as wives, not educated according to their talents, barred from their vocation, robbed of their inheritance, their minds embittered—these are the women who are to provide the mothers for the new generation. What will be the consequence?

4. She became passionately religious in her youth; partly because of this, but partly also from affection, she married him, the "bright genius," the "prodigal." They move away from town; he "gets on," eventually becomes a judge, a model public servant, a model man in every way, religious too. They had a son, then another who died young. Very early in his life the eldest was put to lodge with a clergyman, then sent to a boarding school, was seldom allowed to visit his home. The judge performed his duties for many years, much honoured and respected; she too was honoured as his "good genius," who had been worthily rewarded for her magnanimity. Then he died; a large part of the fortune into which he unexpectedly came after his marriage has been formed into a trust, and now this memorial is about to be dedicated.

   Here the play begins.

5. The main theme must be: the fine flowering of our spiritual life *via* literature, art, etc.—

and, in contrast, all mankind wandering blindly on the wrong track.

6. The perfect man is no longer a natural product, he is something cultivated like corn and fruit-trees and the Creole race and thoroughbred horses and breeds of dogs, vines, etc.—

The trouble is that mankind as a whole is a failure. If a human being demands to live and develop according to his nature as a human being, it's regarded as megalomania. All humanity, especially Christians, suffers from megalomania.

We raise monuments to the *dead*; because we feel a duty towards them; we allow lepers to marry; but their offspring—? The unborn—?

A STREETCAR NAMED DESIRE

Tennessee Williams

CHARACTERS

BLANCHE

STELLA

STANLEY

MITCH

EUNICE

STEVE

PABLO

A NEGRO WOMAN

A DOCTER

A NURSE

A YOUNG COLLECTOR

A MEXICAN WOMAN

The action of the play takes place in the spring, summer, and early fall in New Orleans.

Scene One

The exterior of a two-story corner building on a street in New Orleans which is named Elysian Fields and runs between the L & N tracks and the river. The section is poor but, unlike corresponding sections in other American cities, it has a raffish charm. The houses are mostly white frame, weathered grey, with rickety outside stairs and galleries and quaintly ornamented gables. This building contains two flats, upstairs and down. Faded white stairs ascend to the entrances of both.

It is first dark of an evening early in May. The sky that shows around the dim white building is a peculiarly tender blue, almost a turquoise, which invests the scene with a kind of lyricism and gracefully attenuates the atmosphere of decay. You can almost feel the warm breath of the brown river beyond the river warehouses with their faint redolences of bananas and coffee. A corresponding air is evoked by the music of Negro entertainers at a barroom around the corner. In this part of New Orleans you are practically always just around the corner, or a few doors down the street, from a tinny piano being played with the infatuated fluency of brown fingers. This "Blue Piano" expresses the spirit of the life which goes on here.

Two women, one white and one colored, are taking the air on the steps of the building.

The white woman is Eunice, who occupies the upstairs flat; the colored woman a neighbor, for New Orleans is a cosmopolitan city where there is a relatively warm and easy intermingling of races in the old part of town.

Above the music of the "Blue Piano" the voices of people on the street can be heard overlapping.

[*Two men come around the corner, Stanley Kowalski and Mitch. They are about twenty-eight or thirty years old, roughly dressed in blue denim work clothes. Stanley carries his bowling jacket and a red-stained package from a butcher's. They stop at the foot of the steps.*]

STANLEY [*bellowing*]. Hey, there! Stella, Baby!

[*Stella comes out on the first floor landing, a gentle young woman, about twenty-five, and of a background obviously quite different from her husband's.*]

STELLA [*mildly*]. Don't holler at me like that. Hi, Mitch.
STANLEY. Catch!
STELLA. What?
STANLEY. Meat!

[*He heaves the package at her. She cries out in protest but manages to catch it: then she laughs breathlessly. Her husband and his companion have already started back around the corner.*]

STELLA [*calling after him*]. Stanley! Where are you going?
STANLEY. Bowling!
STELLA. Can I come watch?
STANLEY. Come on. [*He goes out.*]
STELLA. Be over soon. [*To the white woman*] Hello, Eunice. How are you?
EUNICE. I'm all right. Tell Steve to get him a poor boy's sandwich 'cause nothing's left here.

[*They all laugh; the colored woman does not stop. Stella goes out.*]

COLORED WOMAN. What was that package he th'ew at 'er? [*She rises from steps, laughing louder.*]
EUNICE. You hush, now!
NEGRO WOMAN. Catch *what!*

[*She continues to laugh. Blanche comes around the corner, carrying a valise. She looks at a slip of paper, then at the building, then again at the slip and again at the building. Her expression is one of shocked disbelief. Her appearance is incongruous to this setting. She is daintily dressed in a white suit with a fluffy bodice, necklace and earrings of pearl, white gloves and hat, looking as if she were arriving at a summer tea or cocktail party in the garden district. She is about five years older than Stella. Her delicate beauty must avoid a strong light. There is something about her uncertain manner, as well as her white clothes, that suggests a moth.*]

EUNICE [*finally*]. What's the matter, honey? Are you lost?
BLANCHE [*with faintly hysterical humor*]. They told me to take a street-car named Desire, and then transfer to one called Cemeteries and ride six blocks and get off at—Elysian Fields!
EUNICE. That's where you are now.
BLANCHE. At Elysian Fields?
EUNICE. This here is Elysian Fields.
BLANCHE. They mustn't have—understood— what number I wanted . . .
EUNICE. What number you lookin' for?

[*Blanche wearily refers to the slip of paper.*]

BLANCHE. Six thirty-two.
EUNICE. You don't have to look no further.
BLANCHE [*uncomprehendingly*]. I'm looking for my sister, Stella DuBois. I mean—Mrs. Stanley Kowalski.
EUNICE. That's the party.—You just did miss her, though.
BLANCHE. This—can this be—her home?

EUNICE. She's got the downstairs here and I got the up.

BLANCHE. Oh. She's—out?

EUNICE. You noticed that bowling alley around the corner?

BLANCHE. I'm—not sure I did.

EUNICE. Well, that's where she's at, watchin' her husband bowl. [*There is a pause*] You want to leave your suitcase here an' go find her?

BLANCHE. No.

NEGRO WOMAN. I'll go tell her you come.

BLANCHE. Thanks.

NEGRO WOMAN. You welcome. [*She goes out.*]

EUNICE. She wasn't expecting you?

BLANCHE. No. No, not tonight.

EUNICE. Well, why don't you just go in and make yourself at home till they get back.

BLANCHE. How could I—do that?

EUNICE. We own this place so I can let you in.

[*She gets up and opens the downstairs door. A light goes on behind the blind, turning it light blue. Blanche slowly follows her into the downstairs flat. The surrounding areas dim out as the interior is lighted.*]

[*Two rooms can be seen, not too clearly defined. The one first entered is primarily a kitchen but contains a folding bed to be used by Blanche. The room beyond this is a bedroom. Off this room is a narrow door to a bathroom.*]

EUNICE [*defensively, noticing Blanche's look*]. It's sort of messed up right now but when it's clean it's real sweet.

BLANCHE. Is it?

EUNICE. Uh-huh, I think so. So you're Stella's sister?

BLANCHE. Yes. [*Wanting to get rid of her*] Thanks for letting me in.

EUNICE. *Por nada*, as the Mexicans say, *por nada!* Stella spoke of you.

BLANCHE. Yes?

EUNICE. I think she said you taught school.

BLANCHE. Yes.

EUNICE. And you're from Mississippi, huh?

BLANCHE. Yes.

EUNICE. She showed me a picture of your home-place, the plantation.

BLANCHE. Belle Reve?

EUNICE. A great big place with white columns.

BLANCHE. Yes . . .

EUNICE. A place like that must be awful hard to keep up.

BLANCHE. If you will excuse me, I'm just about to drop.

EUNICE. Sure, honey. Why don't you set down?

BLANCHE. What I meant was I'd like to be left alone.

EUNICE [*offended*]. Aw. I'll make myself scarce, in that case.

BLANCHE. I didn't mean to be rude, but—

EUNICE. I'll drop by the bowling alley an' hustle her up. [*She goes out the door.*]

[*Blanche sits in a chair very stiffly with her shoulders slightly hunched and her legs pressed close together and her hands tightly clutching her purse as if she were quite cold. After a while the blind look goes out of her eyes and she begins to look slowly around. A cat screeches. She catches her breath with a startled gesture. Suddenly she notices something in a half opened closet. She springs up and crosses to it, and removes a whiskey bottle. She pours a half tumbler of whiskey and tosses it down. She carefully replaces the bottle and washes out the tumbler at the sink. Then she resumes her seat in front of the table.*]

BLANCHE [*faintly to herself*]. I've got to keep hold of myself!

[*Stella comes quickly around the corner of the building and runs to the door of the downstairs flat.*]

STELLA [*calling out joyfully*]. Blanche!

[*For a moment they stare at each other. Then Blanche springs up and runs to her with a wild cry.*]

BLANCHE. Stella, oh, Stella, Stella! Stella for Star!

[*She begins to speak with feverish vivacity as if she feared for either of them to stop and think. They catch each other in a spasmodic embrace.*]

BLANCHE. Now, then, let me look at you. But don't you look at me, Stella, no, no, no, not till later, not till I've bathed and rested! And turn that over-light off! Turn that off! I won't be looked at in this merciless glare! [*Stella laughs and complies*] Come back here now! Oh, my baby! Stella! Stella for Star! [*She embraces her again*] I thought you would never come back to this horrible place! What am I saying? I didn't mean to say that. I meant to be nice about it and say—Oh, what a convenient location and such—Ha-a-ha! Precious lamb! You haven't said a *word* to me.

STELLA. You haven't given me a chance to, honey! [*She laughs, but her glance at Blanche is a little anxious.*]

BLANCHE. Well, now you talk. Open your pretty mouth and talk while I look around for some liquor! I know you must have some liquor on the place! Where could it be, I wonder? Oh, I spy, I spy!

[*She rushes to the closet and removes the bottle; she is shaking all over and panting for breath as she tries to laugh. The bottle nearly slips from her grasp.*]

STELLA [*noticing*]. Blanche, you sit down and let me pour the drinks. I don't know what we've got to mix with. Maybe a coke's in the icebox. Look'n see, honey, while I'm—

BLANCHE. No coke, honey, not with my nerves tonight! Where—where—where is—?

STELLA. Stanley? Bowling! He loves it. They're having a—found some soda!— tournament . . .

BLANCHE. Just water, baby, to chase it! Now don't get worried, your sister hasn't turned into a drunkard, she's just all shaken up and hot and tired and dirty! You sit down, now, and explain this place to me! What are you doing in a place like this?

STELLA. Now, Blanche—

BLANCHE. Oh, I'm not going to be hypocritical, I'm going to be honestly critical about it. Never, never, never in my worst dreams could I picture—Only Poe! Only Mr. Edgar Allan Poe!—could do it justice! Out there I suppose is the ghoul-haunted woodland of Weir! [*She laughs.*]

STELLA. No, honey, those are the L & N tracks.

BLANCHE. No, now seriously, putting joking aside. Why didn't you tell me, why didn't you write me, honey, why didn't you let me know?

STELLA [*carefully, pouring herself a drink*]. Tell you what, Blanche?

BLANCHE. Why, that you had to live in these conditions!

STELLA. Aren't you being a little intense about it? It's not that bad at all! New Orleans isn't like other cities.

BLANCHE. This has got nothing to do with New Orleans. You might as well say— forgive me, blessed baby! [*She suddenly stops short*] The subject is closed!

STELLA [*a little drily*]. Thanks.

[*During the pause, Blanche stares at her. She smiles at Blanche.*]

BLANCHE [*looking down at her glass, which shakes in her hand*]. You're all I've got in the world, and you're not glad to see me!

STELLA [*sincerely*]. Why, Blanche, you know that's not true.

BLANCHE. No?—I'd forgotten how quiet you were.

STELLA. You never did give me a chance to say much, Blanche. So I just got in the habit of being quiet around you.

BLANCHE [*vaguely*]. A good habit to get into . . . [*then, abruptly*] You haven't asked me how I happened to get away from the school before the spring term ended.

STELLA. Well, I thought you'd volunteer that information—if you wanted to tell me.

BLANCHE. You thought I'd been fired?

STELLA. No, I—thought you might have re-signed . . .

BLANCHE. I was so exhausted by all I'd been through my—nerves broke. [*Nervously tamping cigarette*] I was on the verge of—lunacy, almost! So Mr. Graves—Mr. Graves is the high school superintendent—he suggested I take a leave of absence. I couldn't put all those details into the wire . . . [*She drinks quickly*] Oh, this buzzes right through me and feels so *good!*

STELLA. Won't you have another?

BLANCHE. No, one's my limit.

STELLA. Sure?

BLANCHE. You haven't said a word about my appearance.

STELLA. You look just fine.

BLANCHE. God love you for a liar! Daylight never exposed so total a ruin! But you—you've put on some weight, yes, you're just as plump as a little partridge! And it's so becoming to you!

STELLA. Now, Blanche—

BLANCHE. Yes, it is, it is or I wouldn't say it! You just have to watch around the hips a little. Stand up.

STELLA. Not now.

BLANCHE. You hear me? I said stand up! [*Stella complies reluctantly*] You messy child, you, you've spilt something on that pretty white lace collar! About your hair—you ought to have it cut in a feather bob with your dainty features. Stella, you have a maid, don't you?

STELLA. No. With only two rooms it's—

BLANCHE. What? *Two* rooms, did you say?

STELLA. This one and—[*She is embarrassed.*]

BLANCHE. The other one? [*She laughs sharply. There is an embarrassed silence.*]

BLANCHE. I am going to take just one little nip more, sort of to put the stopper on, so to speak. . . . Then put the bottle away so I won't be tempted. [*She rises*] I want you to look at *my* figure! [*She turns around*] You know I haven't put on one ounce in ten years, Stella? I weigh what I weighed the summer you left Belle Reve. The summer Dad died and you left us . . .

STELLA [*a little wearily*]. It's just incredible, Blanche, how well you're looking.

BLANCHE. [*They both laugh uncomfortably*] But, Stella, there's only two rooms, I don't see where you're going to put me!

STELLA. We're going to put you in here.

BLANCHE. What kind of bed's this—one of those collapsible things? [*She sits on it.*]

STELLA. Does it feel all right?

BLANCHE [*dubiously*]. Wonderful, honey. I don't like a bed that gives much. But there's no door between the two rooms, and Stanley—will it be decent?

STELLA. Stanley is Polish, you know.

BLANCHE. Oh, yes. They're something like Irish, aren't they?

STELLA. Well—

BLANCHE. Only not so—highbrow? [*They both laugh again in the same way*] I brought some nice clothes to meet all your lovely friends in.

STELLA. I'm afraid you won't think they are lovely.

BLANCHE. What are they like?

STELLA. They're Stanley's friends.

BLANCHE. Polacks?

STELLA. They're a mixed lot, Blanche.

BLANCHE. Heterogeneous—types?

STELLA. Oh, yes. Yes, types is right!

BLANCHE. Well—anyhow—I brought nice clothes and I'll wear them. I guess you're hoping I'll say I'll put up at a hotel, but I'm not going to put up at a hotel. I want to be *near* you, got to be *with* somebody, I *can't* be *alone!* Because—as you must have noticed—I'm—*not* very *well* . . . [*Her voice drops and her look is frightened.*]

STELLA. You seem a little bit nervous or over-wrought or something.

BLANCHE. Will Stanley like me, or will I be just a visiting in-law, Stella? I couldn't stand that.

STELLA. You'll get along fine together, if you'll just try not to—well—compare him with men that we went out with at home.

BLANCHE. Is he so—different?

STELLA. Yes. A different species.

BLANCHE. In what way; what's he like?

STELLA. Oh, you can't describe someone you're in love with! Here's a picture of him! [*She hands a photograph to Blanche.*]

BLANCHE. An officer?

STELLA. A Master Sergeant in the Engineers' Corps. Those are decorations!

BLANCHE. He had those on when you met him?

STELLA. I assure you I wasn't just blinded by all the brass.

BLANCHE. That's not what I—

STELLA. But of course there were things to adjust myself to later on.

BLANCHE. Such as his civilian background! [*Stella laughs uncertainly*] How did he take it when you said I was coming?

STELLA. Oh, Stanley doesn't know yet.

BLANCHE [*frightened*]. You—haven't told him?

STELLA. He's on the road a good deal.

BLANCHE. Oh. Travels?

STELLA. Yes.

BLANCHE. Good. I mean—isn't it?

STELLA [*half to herself*]. I can hardly stand it when he is away for a night . . .

BLANCHE. Why, Stella!

STELLA. When he's away for a week I nearly go wild!

BLANCHE. Gracious!

STELLA. And when he comes back I cry on his lap like a baby . . . [*She smiles to herself.*]

BLANCHE. I guess that is what is meant by being in love . . . [*Stella looks up with a radiant smile.*] Stella—

STELLA. What?

BLANCHE [*in an uneasy rush*]. I haven't asked you the things you probably thought I was going to ask. And so I'll expect you to be understanding about what *I* have to tell *you.*

STELLA. What, Blanche? [*Her face turns anxious.*]

BLANCHE. Well, Stella—you're going to re-proach me, I know that you're bound to reproach me—but before you do—take into consideration—you left! I stayed and struggled! You came to New Orleans and looked out for yourself! *I* stayed at *Belle Reve* and tried to hold it together! I'm not meaning this in any reproachful way, but *all* the burden descended on *my* shoulders.

STELLA. The best I could do was make my own living, Blanche.

[*Blanche begins to shake again with intensity.*]

BLANCHE. I know, I know. But you are the one that abandoned Belle Reve, not I! I stayed and fought for it, bled for it, almost died for it!

STELLA. Stop this hysterical outburst and tell me what's happened? What do you mean fought and bled? What kind of—

BLANCHE. I knew you would, Stella. I knew you would take this attitude about it!

STELLA. About—what?—please!

BLANCHE [*slowly*]. The loss—the loss . . .

STELLA. Belle Reve? Lost, is it? No!

BLANCHE. Yes, Stella.

[*They stare at each other across the yellow-checked linoleum of the table. Blanche slowly nods her head and Stella looks slowly down at her hands folded on the table. The music of the "blue piano" grows louder. Blanche touches her handkerchief to her forehead.*]

STELLA. But how did it go? What happened?

BLANCHE [*springing up*]. You're a fine one to ask me how it went!

STELLA. Blanche!

BLANCHE. You're a fine one to sit there *accusing me* of it!

STELLA. *Blanche!*

BLANCHE. I, I, *I* took the blows in my face and my body! All of those deaths! The long parade to the graveyard! Father, mother! Margaret, that dreadful way! So big with it, it couldn't be put in a coffin! But had to be burned like rubbish! You just came home in time for the funerals, Stella. And funerals are pretty compared to deaths. Funerals are quiet, but deaths—not always. Sometimes their breathing is hoarse, and sometimes it rattles, and sometimes they even cry out to you, "Don't let me go!" Even the old, sometimes, say, "Don't let me go." As if you were able to stop them! But funerals are quiet, with pretty flowers. And, oh, what gorgeous boxes they pack them away in! Unless you were there at the bed when they cried out, "Hold me!" you'd never suspect there was the struggle for breath and bleeding. You didn't dream, but I saw! *Saw! Saw!* And now you sit there telling me with your eyes that I let the place go! How in hell do you think all that sickness and dying was paid for? Death is expensive, Miss Stella! And old Cousin Jessie's right after Margaret's, hers! Why, the Grim Reaper had put up his tent on our doorstep! . . . Stella. Belle Reve was his headquarters! Honey— that's how it slipped through my fingers! Which of them left us a fortune? Which of them left a cent of insurance even? Only poor Jessie—one hundred to pay for her coffin. That was all, Stella! And I with my pitiful salary at the school. Yes, accuse me! Sit there and stare at me, thinking I let the place go! *I* let the place go? Where were *you!* In bed with your—Polack!

STELLA [*springing*]. Blanche! You be still! That's enough! [*She starts out.*]

BLANCHE. Where are you going?

STELLA. I'm going into the bathroom to wash my face.

BLANCHE. Oh, Stella, Stella, you're crying!

STELLA. Does that surprise you?

BLANCHE. Forgive me—I didn't mean to—

[*The sound of men's voices is heard. Stella goes into the bathroom, closing the door behind her. When the men appear, and Blanche realizes it must be Stanley returning, she moves uncertainly from the bathroom door to the dressing table, looking apprehensively towards the front door. Stanley enters, followed by Steve and Mitch. Stanley pauses near his door, Steve by the foot of the spiral stair, and Mitch is slightly above and to the right of them, about to go out. As the men*

enter, we hear some of the following dialogue.]

STANLEY. Is that how he got it?

STEVE. Sure that's how he got it. He hit the old weather-bird for 300 bucks on a six-number-ticket.

MITCH. Don't tell him those things; he'll believe it.

[*Mitch starts out.*]

STANLEY [*restraining Mitch*]. Hey, Mitch—come back here.

[*Blanche, at the sound of voices, retires in the bedroom. She picks up Stanley's photo from dressing table, looks at it, puts it down. When Stanley enters the apartment, she darts and hides behind the screen at the head of bed.*]

STEVE [*to Stanley and Mitch*]. Hey, are we playin' poker tomorrow?

STANLEY. Sure—at Mitch's.

MITCH [*hearing this, returns quickly to the stair rail*]. No—not at my place. My mother's still sick!

STANLEY. Okay, at my place . . . [*Mitch starts out again*] But you bring the beer!

[*Mitch pretends not to hear,—calls out "Goodnight all," and goes out, singing. Eunice's voice is heard, above.*]

Break it up down there! I made the spaghetti dish and ate it myself.

STEVE [*going upstairs*]. I told you and phoned you we was playing. [*To the men*] Jax beer!

EUNICE. You never phoned me once.

STEVE. I told you at breakfast—and phoned you at lunch . . .

EUNICE. Well, never mind about that. You just get yourself home here once in a while.

STEVE. You want it in the papers?

[*More laughter and shouts of parting come from the men. Stanley throws the screen door of the kitchen open and comes in. He is of medium height, about five feet eight or nine, and strongly, compactly built. Animal joy in his being is implicit in all his movements and attitudes. Since earliest manhood the center of his life has been pleasure with women, the giving and taking of it, not with weak indulgence, dependently, but with the power and pride of a richly feathered male bird among hens. Branching out from this complete and satisfying center are all the auxiliary channels of his life, such as his heartiness with men, his appreciation of rough humor, his love of good drink and food and games, his car, his radio, everything that is his, that bears his emblem of the gaudy seed-bearer. He sizes women up at a glance, with sexual classifications, crude images flashing into his mind and determining the way he smiles at them.]*

BLANCHE [*drawing involuntarily back from his stare*]. You must be Stanley. I'm Blanche.

STANLEY. Stella's sister?

BLANCHE. Yes.

STANLEY. H'lo. Where's the little woman?

BLANCHE. In the bathroom.

STANLEY. Oh. Didn't know you were coming in town.

BLANCHE. I—uh—

STANLEY. Where you from, Blanche?

BLANCHE. Why, I—live in Laurel.

[*He has crossed to the closet and removed the whiskey bottle.*]

STANLEY. In Laurel, huh? Oh, yeah. Yeah, in Laurel, that's right. Not in my territory. Liquor goes fast in hot weather.

[*He holds the bottle to the light to observe its depletion.*]

Have a shot?

BLANCHE. No, I—rarely touch it.

STANLEY. Some people rarely touch it, but it touches them often.

BLANCHE [*faintly*]. Ha-ha.

STANLEY. My clothes're stickin' to me. Do

you mind if I make myself comfortable? [*He starts to remove his shirt.*]

BLANCHE. Please, please do.

STANLEY. Be comfortable is my motto.

BLANCHE. It's mine, too. It's hard to stay looking fresh. I haven't washed or even powdered my face and—here you are!

STANLEY. You know you can catch cold sitting around in damp things, especially when you been exercising hard like bowling is. You're a teacher, aren't you?

BLANCHE. Yes.

STANLEY. What do you teach, Blanche?

BLANCHE. English.

STANLEY. I never was a very good English student. How long you here for, Blanche?

BLANCHE. I—don't know yet.

STANLEY. You going to shack up here?

BLANCHE. I thought I would if it's not inconvenient for you all.

STANLEY. Good.

BLANCHE. Traveling wears me out.

STANLEY. Well, take it easy.

[*A cat screeches near the window. Blanche springs up.*]

BLANCHE. What's that?

STANLEY. Cats . . . Hey, Stella!

STELLA [*faintly, from the bathroom*]. Yes, Stanley.

STANLEY. Haven't fallen in, have you? [*He grins at Blanche. She tries unsuccessfully to smile back. There is a silence*] I'm afraid I'll strike you as being the unrefined type. Stella's spoke of you a good deal. You were married once, weren't you?

[*The music of the polka rises up, faint in the distance.*]

BLANCHE. Yes. When I was quite young.

STANLEY. What happened?

BLANCHE. The boy—the boy died. [*She sinks back down*] I'm afraid I'm—going to be sick!

[*Her head falls on her arms.*]

Scene Two

It is six o'clock the following evening. Blanche is bathing. Stella is completing her toilette. Blanche's dress, a flowered print, is laid out on Stella's bed.

Stanley enters the kitchen from outside, leaving the door open on the perpetual "blue piano" around the corner.

STANLEY. What's all this monkey doings?

STELLA. Oh, Stan! [*She jumps up and kisses him which he accepts with lordly composure*] I'm taking Blanche to Galatoire's for supper and then to a show, because it's your poker night.

STANLEY. How about my supper, huh? I'm not going to no Galatoire's for supper!

STELLA. I put you a cold plate on ice.

STANLEY. Well, isn't that just dandy!

STELLA. I'm going to try to keep Blanche out till the party breaks up because I don't know how she would take it. So we'll go to one of the little places in the Quarter afterwards and you'd better give me some money.

STANLEY. Where is she?

STELLA. She's soaking in a hot tub to quiet her nerves. She's terribly upset.

STANLEY. Over what?

STELLA. She's been through such an ordeal.

STANLEY. Yeah?

STELLA. Stan, we've—lost Belle Reve!

STANLEY. The place in the country?

STELLA. Yes.

STANLEY. How?

STELLA [*vaguely*]. Oh, it had to be—sacrificed or something. [*There is a pause while Stanley considers. Stella is changing into her dress*] When she comes in be sure to say something nice about her appearance. And, oh! Don't mention the baby. I haven't said anything yet, I'm waiting until she gets in a quieter condition.

STANLEY [*ominously*]. So?

STELLA. And try to understand her and be nice to her, Stan.

BLANCHE [*singing in the bathroom*]. "From the land of the sky blue water, They brought a captive maid!"

STELLA. She wasn't expecting to find us in such a small place. You see I'd try to gloss things over a little in my letters.

STANLEY. So?

STELLA. And admire her dress and tell her she's looking wonderful. That's important with Blanche. Her little weakness!

STANLEY. Yeah. I get the idea. Now let's skip back a little to where you said the country place was disposed of.

STELLA. Oh!—yes . . .

STANLEY. How about that? Let's have a few more details on that subjeck.

STELLA. It's best not to talk much about it until she's calmed down.

STANLEY. So that's the deal, huh? Sister Blanche cannot be annoyed with business details right now!

STELLA. You saw how she was last night.

STANLEY. Uh-hum, I saw how she was. Now let's have a gander at the bill of sale.

STELLA. I haven't seen any.

STANLEY. She didn't show you no papers, no deed of sale or nothing like that, huh?

STELLA. It seems like it wasn't sold.

STANLEY. Well, what in hell was it then, give away? To charity?

STELLA. Shhh! She'll hear you.

STANLEY. I don't care if she hears me. Let's see the papers!

STELLA. There weren't any papers, she didn't show any papers, I don't care about papers.

STANLEY. Have you ever heard of the Napoleonic code?

STELLA. No, Stanley, I haven't heard of the Napoleonic code and if I have, I don't see what it—

STANLEY. Let me enlighten you on a point or two, baby.

STELLA. Yes?

STANLEY. In the state of Louisiana we have the Napoleonic code according to which what belongs to the wife belongs to the husband and vice versa. For instance if I had a piece of property, or you had a piece of property—

STELLA. My head is swimming!

STANLEY. All right. I'll wait till she gets through soaking in a hot tub and then I'll inquire if *she* is acquainted with the Napoleonic code. It looks to me like you have been swindled, baby, and when you're swindled under the Napoleonic code I'm swindled *too*. And I don't like to be *swindled*.

STELLA. There's plenty of time to ask her questions later but if you do now she'll go to pieces again. I don't understand what happened to Belle Reve but you don't know how ridiculous you are being when you suggest that my sister or I or anyone of our family could have perpetrated a swindle on anyone else.

STANLEY. Then where's the money if the place was sold?

STELLA. Not sold—*lost, lost!*

[*He stalks into bedroom, and she follows him.*]

Stanley!

[*He pulls open the wardrobe trunk standing in middle of room and jerks out an armful of dresses.*]

STANLEY. Open your eyes to this stuff! You think she got them out of a teacher's pay?

STELLA. Hush!

STANLEY. Look at these feathers and furs that she come here to preen herself in! What's this here? A solid-gold dress, I believe! And this one! What is these here? Fox-pieces [*He blows on them*] Genuine fox fur-pieces, a half a mile long! Where are your fox-pieces, Stella? Bushy snow-white ones, no less! Where are your white fox-pieces?

STELLA. Those are inexpensive summer furs that Blanche has had a long time.

STANLEY. I got an acquaintance who deals in this sort of merchandise. I'll have him in

here to appraise it. I'm willing to bet you there's thousands of dollars invested in this stuff here!

STELLA. Don't be such an idiot, Stanley!

[*He hurls the furs to the daybed. Then he jerks open small drawer in the trunk and pulls up a fist-full of costume jewelry.*]

STANLEY. And what have we here? The treasure chest of a pirate!

STELLA. Oh, Stanley!

STANLEY. Pearls! Ropes of them! What is this sister of yours, a deep-sea diver? Bracelets of solid gold, too! Where are your pearls and gold bracelets?

STELLA. Shhh! Be still, Stanley!

STANLEY. And diamonds! A crown for an empress!

STELLA. A rhinestone tiara she wore to a costume ball.

STANLEY. What's rhinestone?

STELLA. Next door to glass.

STANLEY. Are you kidding? I have an acquaintance that works in a jewelry store. I'll have him in here to make an appraisal of this. Here's your plantation, or what was left of it, here!

STELLA. You have no idea how stupid and horrid you're being! Now close that trunk before she comes out of the bathroom!

[*He kicks the trunk partly closed and sits on the kitchen table.*]

STANLEY. The Kowalskis and the DuBois have different notions.

STELLA [*angrily*]. Indeed they have, thank heavens!—*I'm* going outside. [*She snatches up her white hat and gloves and crosses to the outside door*] You come out with me while Blanche is getting dressed.

STANLEY. Since when do you give me orders?

STELLA. Are you going to stay here and insult her?

STANLEY. You're damn tootin' I'm going to stay here.

[*Stella goes out to the porch. Blanche comes out of the bathroom in a red satin robe.*]

BLANCHE [*airily*]. Hello, Stanley! Here I am, all freshly bathed and scented, and feeling like a brand new human being!

[*He lights a cigarette.*]

STANLEY. That's good.

BLANCHE [*drawing the curtains at the windows*]. Excuse me while I slip on my pretty new dress!

STANLEY. Go right ahead, Blanche.

[*She closes the drapes between the rooms.*]

BLANCHE. I understand there's to be a little card party to which we ladies are cordially *not* invited!

STANLEY [*ominously*]. Yeah?

[*Blanche throws off her robe and slips into a flowered print dress.*]

BLANCHE. Where's Stella?

STANLEY. Out on the porch.

BLANCHE. I'm going to ask a favor of you in a moment.

STANLEY. What could that be, I wonder?

BLANCHE. Some buttons in back! You may enter!

[*He crosses through drapes with a smoldering look.*]

How do I look?

STANLEY. You look all right.

BLANCHE. Many thanks! Now the buttons!

STANLEY. I can't do nothing with them.

BLANCHE. You men with your big clumsy fingers. May I have a drag on your cig?

STANLEY. Have one for yourself.

BLANCHE. Why, thanks! . . . It looks like my trunk has exploded.

STANLEY. Me an' Stella were helping you unpack.

BLANCHE. Well, you certainly did a fast and thorough job of it!

STANLEY. It looks like you raided some stylish shops in Paris.

BLANCHE. Ha-ha! Yes—clothes are my passion!

STANLEY. What does it cost for a string of fur-pieces like. that?

BLANCHE. Why, those were a tribute from an admirer of mine!

STANLEY. He must have had a lot of—admiration!

BLANCHE. Oh, in my youth I excited some admiration. But look at me now! [*She smiles at him radiantly*] Would you think it possible that I was once considered to be—attractive?

STANLEY. Your looks are okay.

BLANCHE. I was fishing for a compliment, Stanley.

STANLEY. I don't go in for that stuff.

BLANCHE..What—stuff?

STANLEY. Compliments to women about their looks. I never met a woman that didn't know if she was good-looking or not without being told, and some of them give themselves credit for more than they've got. I once went out with a doll who said to me, "I am the glamorous type, I am the glamorous type!" I said, "So what?"

BLANCHE. And what did she say then?

STANLEY. She didn't say nothing. That shut her up like a clam.

BLANCHE. Did it end the romance?

STANLEY. It ended the conversation—that was all. Some men are took in by this Hollywood glamor stuff and some men are not.

BLANCHE. I'm sure you belong in the second category.

STANLEY. That's right.

BLANCHE. I cannot imagine any witch of a woman casting a spell over you.

STANLEY. That's—right.

BLANCHE. You're simple, straightforward and honest, a little bit on the primitive side I should think. To interest you a woman would have to—[*She pauses with an indefinite gesture.*]

STANLEY [*slowly*]. Lay . . . her cards on the table.

BLANCHE [*smiling*]. Well, I never cared for wishy-washy people. That was why, when you walked in here last night, I said to myself—"My sister has married a man!"— Of course that was all that I could tell about you.

STANLEY [*booming*]. Now let's cut the re-bop!

BLANCHE [*pressing hands to her ears*]. Ouuuuu!

STELLA [*calling from the steps*]. Stanley! You come out here and let Blanche finish dressing!

BLANCHE. I'm through dressing, honey.

STELLA. Well, you come out, then.

STANLEY. Your sister and I are having a little talk.

BLANCHE [*lightly*]. Honey, do me a favor. Run to the drug-store and get me a lemon-coke with plenty of chipped ice in it!—Will you do that for me, Sweetie?

STELLA [*uncertainly*]. Yes. [*She goes around the corner of the building.*]

BLANCHE. The poor little thing was out there listening to us, and I have an idea she doesn't understand you as well as I do. . . . All right; now, Mr. Kowalski, let us proceed without any more double-talk. I'm ready to answer all questions. I've nothing to hide. What is it?

STANLEY. There is such a thing in this State of Louisiana as the Napoleonic code, according to which whatever belongs to my wife is also mine—and vice versa.

BLANCHE. My, but you have an impressive judicial air!

[*She sprays herself with her atomizer; then playfully sprays him with it. He seizes the atomizer and slams it down on the dresser. She throws back her head and laughs.*]

STANLEY. If I didn't know that you was my wife's sister I'd get ideas about you!

BLANCHE. Such as what!

STANLEY. Don't play so dumb. You know what!

BLANCHE [*she puts the atomizer on the table*]. All right. Cards on the table. That suits me. [*She turns to Stanley.*] I know I fib a good deal. After all, a woman's charm is fifty per cent illusion, but when a thing is important I tell the truth, and this is the truth: I haven't cheated my sister or you or anyone else as long as I have lived.

STANLEY. Where's the papers? In the trunk?

BLANCHE. Everything that I own is in that trunk.

[*Stanley crosses to the trunk, shoves it roughly open and begins to open compartments.*]

BLANCHE. What in the name of heaven are you thinking of! What's in the back of that little boy's mind of yours? That I am absconding with something, attempting some kind of treachery on my sister?—Let me do that! It will be faster and simpler . . . [*She crosses to the trunk and takes out a box*] I keep my papers mostly in this tin box. [*She opens it.*]

STANLEY. What's them underneath? [*He indicates another sheaf of paper.*]

BLANCHE. These are love-letters, yellowing with antiquity, all from one boy. [*He snatches them up. She speaks fiercely*] Give those back to me!

STANLEY. I'll have a look at them first!

BLANCHE. The touch of your hands insults them!

STANLEY. Don't pull that stuff!

[*He rips off the ribbon and starts to examine them. Blanche snatches them from him, and they cascade to the floor.*]

BLANCHE. Now that you've touched them I'll burn them!

STANLEY [*staring, baffled*]. What in hell are they?

BLANCHE [*on the floor gathering them up*]. Poems a dead boy wrote. I hurt him the way that you would like to hurt me, but you can't! I'm not young and vulnerable any more. But my young husband was and I—never mind about that! Just give them back to me!

STANLEY. What do you mean by saying you'll have to burn them?

BLANCHE. I'm sorry, I must have lost my head for a moment. Everyone has something he won't let others touch because of their— intimate nature . . .

[*She now seems faint with exhaustion and she sits down with the strong box and puts on a pair of glasses and goes methodically through a large stack of papers.*]

Ambler & Ambler. Hmmmmm. . . . Crabtree. . . . More Ambler & Ambler.

STANLEY. What is Ambler & Ambler?

BLANCHE. A firm that made loans on the place.

STANLEY. Then it *was* lost on a mortgage?

BLANCHE [*touching her forehead*]. That must've been what happened.

STANLEY. I don't want no ifs, ands or buts! What's all the rest of them papers?

[*She hands him the entire box. He carries it to the table and starts to examine the papers.*]

BLANCHE [*picking up a large envelope containing more papers*]. There are thousands of papers, stretching back over hundreds of years, affecting Belle Reve as, piece by piece, our improvident grandfathers and father and uncles and brothers exchanged the land for their epic fornications—to put it plainly! [*She removes her glasses with an exhausted laugh*] The four-letter word deprived us of our plantation, till finally all that was left—and Stella can verify that!—was the house itself and about twenty acres of ground, including a graveyard, to which now all but Stella and I have retreated. [*She pours the contents of the envelope on the table*] Here all of them are, all papers! I hereby endow you with them! Take them, peruse them—commit them to memory, even! I think it's wonderfully fitting that Belle Reve should finally be this bunch of old papers in your big, capable hands! . . . I wonder if Stella's come back with my lemon-coke . . .

[*She leans back and closes her eyes.*]

STANLEY. I have a lawyer acquaintance who will study these out.

BLANCHE. Present them to him with a box of aspirin tablets.

STANLEY [*becoming somewhat sheepish*]. You see, under the Napoleonic code—a man has to take an interest in his wife's affairs— especially now that she's going to have a baby.

[*Blanche opens her eyes. The "blue piano" sounds louder.*]

BLANCHE. Stella? Stella going to have a baby? [*dreamily*] I didn't know she was going to have a baby!

[*She gets up and crosses to the outside door. Stella appears around the corner with a carton from the drugstore.*

[*Stanley goes into the bedroom with the envelope and the box.*

[*The inner rooms fade to darkness and the outside wall of the house is visible. Blanche meets Stella at the foot of the steps to the sidewalk.*]

BLANCHE. Stella, Stella for star! How lovely to have a baby! It's all right. Everything's all right.

STELLA. I'm sorry he did that to you.

BLANCHE. Oh, I guess he's just not the type that goes for jasmine perfume, but maybe he's what we need to mix with our blood now that we've lost Belle Reve. We thrashed it out. I feel a bit shaky, but I think I handled it nicely, I laughed and treated it all as a joke. [*Steve and Pablo appear, carrying a case of beer.*] I called him a little boy and laughed and flirted. Yes, I was flirting with your husband! [*as the men approach*] The guests are gathering for the poker party. [*The two men pass between them, and enter the house.*] Which way do we go now, Stella—this way?

STELLA. No, this way. [*She leads Blanche away.*]

BLANCHE [*laughing*]. The blind are leading the blind!

[*A tamale Vendor is heard calling.*]

VENDOR'S VOICE. Red-hot!

Scene Three

The Poker Night

There is a picture of Van Gogh's of a billiard-parlor at night. The kitchen now suggests that sort of lurid nocturnal brilliance, the raw colors of childhood's spectrum. Over the yellow linoleum of the kitchen table hangs an electric bulb with a vivid green glass shade. The poker players—Stanley, Steve, Mitch and Pablo—wear colored shirts, solid blue, a purple, a red-and-white check, a light green, and they are men at the peak of their physical manhood, as coarse and direct and powerful as the primary colors. There are vivid slices of watermelon on the table, whiskey bottles and glasses. The bedroom is relatively dim with only the light that spills between the portieres and through the wide window on the street.

For a moment, there is absorbed silence as a hand is dealt.

STEVE. Anything wild this deal?
PABLO. One-eyed jacks are wild.
STEVE. Give me two cards.
PABLO. You, Mitch?
MITCH. I'm out.
PABLO. One.
MITCH. Anyone want a shot?
STANLEY. Yeah. Me.
PABLO. Why don't somebody go to the Chinaman's and bring back a load of chop suey?
STANLEY. When I'm losing you want to eat! Ante up! Openers? Openers! Get y'r ass off the table, Mitch. Nothing belongs on a poker table but cards, chips and whiskey.

[*He lurches up and tosses some watermelon rinds to the floor.*]

MITCH. Kind of on your high horse, ain't you?
STANLEY. How many?
STEVE. Give me three.
STANLEY. One.
MITCH. I'm out again. I oughta go home pretty soon.
STANLEY. Shut up.
MITCH. I gotta sick mother. She don't go to sleep until I come in at night.
STANLEY. Then why don't you stay home with her?
MITCH. She says to go out, so I go, but I don't enjoy it. All the while I keep wondering how she is.
STANLEY. Aw, for the sake of Jesus, go home, then!
PABLO. What've you got?
STEVE. Spade flush.
MITCH. You all are married. But I'll be alone when she goes.—I'm going to the bathroom.
STANLEY. Hurry back and we'll fix you a sugar-tit.
MITCH. Aw, go rut. [*He crosses through the bedroom into the bathroom.*]
STEVE [*dealing a hand*]. Seven card stud. [*Telling his joke as he deals*] This ole farmer is out in back of his house sittin' down th'owing corn to the chickens when all at once he hears a loud cackle and this young hen comes lickety split around the side of the house with the rooster right behind her and gaining on her fast.
STANLEY [*impatient with the story*]. Deal!
STEVE. But when the rooster catches sight of the farmer th'owing the corn he puts on the brakes and lets the hen get away and starts pecking corn. And the old farmer says, "Lord God, I hopes I never gits *that* hongry!"

[*Steve and Pablo laugh. The sisters appear around the corner of the building.*]

STELLA. The game is still going on.
BLANCHE. How do I look?
STELLA. Lovely, Blanche.

BLANCHE. I feel so hot and frazzled. Wait till I powder before you open the door. Do I look done in?

STELLA. Why no. You are as fresh as a daisy.

BLANCHE. One that's been picked a few days.

[*Stella opens the door and they enter.*]

STELLA. Well, well, well. I see you boys are still at it!

STANLEY. Where you been?

STELLA. Blanche and I took in a show. Blanche, this is Mr. Gonzales and Mr. Hubbell.

BLANCHE. Please don't get up.

STANLEY. Nobody's going to get up, so don't be worried.

STELLA. How much longer is this game going to continue?

STANLEY. Till we get ready to quit.

BLANCHE. Poker is so fascinating. Could I kibitz?

STANLEY. You could not. Why don't you women go up and sit with Eunice?

STELLA. Because it is nearly two-thirty. [*Blanche crosses into the bedroom and partially closes the portieres*] Couldn't you call it quits after one more hand?

[*A chair scrapes. Stanley gives a loud whack of his hand on her thigh.*]

STELLA [*sharply*]. That's not fun, Stanley.

[*The men laugh. Stella goes into the bedroom.*]

STELLA. It makes me so mad when he does that in front of people.

BLANCHE. I think I will bathe.

STELLA. Again?

BLANCHE. My nerves are in knots. Is the bathroom occupied?

STELLA. I don't know.

[*Blanche knocks. Mitch opens the door and comes out, still wiping his hands on a towel.*]

BLANCHE. Oh!—good evening.

MITCH. Hello. [*He stares at her.*]

STELLA. Blanche, this is Harold Mitchell. My sister, Blanche DuBois.

MITCH [*with awkward courtesy*]. How do you do, Miss DuBois.

STELLA. How is your mother now, Mitch?

MITCH. About the same, thanks. She appreciated your sending over that custard.— Excuse me, please.

[*He crosses slowly back into the kitchen, glancing back at Blanche and coughing a little shyly. He realizes he still has the towel in his hands and with an embarrassed laugh hands it to Stella. Blanche looks after him with a certain interest.*]

BLANCHE. That one seems—superior to the others.

STELLA. Yes, he is.

BLANCHE. I thought he had a sort of sensitive look.

STELLA. His mother is sick.

BLANCHE. Is he married?

STELLA. No.

BLANCHE. Is he a wolf?

STELLA. Why, Blanche! [*Blanche laughs.*] I don't think he would be

BLANCHE. What does—what does he do?

[*She is unbuttoning her blouse.*]

STELLA. He's on the precision bench in the spare parts department. At the plant Stanley travels for.

BLANCHE. Is that something much?

STELLA. No. Stanley's the only one of his crowd that's likely to get anywhere.

BLANCHE. What makes you think Stanley will?

STELLA. Look at him.

BLANCHE. I've looked at him.

STELLA. Then you should know.

BLANCHE. I'm sorry, but I haven't noticed the stamp of genius even on Stanley's forehead.

[*She takes off the blouse and stands in her pink silk brassiere and white skirt in the light through the portieres. The game has continued in undertones.*]

STELLA. It isn't on his forehead and it isn't genius.

BLANCHE. Oh. Well, what is it, and where? I would like to know.

STELLA. It's a drive that he has. You're standing in the light, Blanche!

BLANCHE. Oh, am I!

[*She moves out of the yellow streak of light. Stella has removed her dress and puts on a light blue satin kimono*].

STELLA [*with girlish laughter*]. You ought to see their wives.

BLANCHE [*laughingly*]. I can imagine. Big, beefy things, I suppose.

STELLA. You know that one upstairs? [*More laughter*] One time [*laughing*] the plaster— [*laughing*] cracked—

STANLEY. You hens cut out that conversation in there!

STELLA. You can't hear us.

STANLEY. Well, you can hear me and I said to hush up!

STELLA. This is my house and I'll talk as much as I want to!

BLANCHE. Stella, don't start a row.

STELLA. He's half drunk!—I'll be out in a minute.

[*She goes into the bathroom. Blanche rises and crosses leisurely to a small white radio and turns it on.*]

STANLEY. Awright, Mitch, you in?

MITCH. What? Oh!—No, I'm out!

[*Blanche moves back into the streak of light. She raises her arms and stretches, as she moves indolently back to the chair.*]

[*Rhumba music comes over the radio. Mitch rises at the table.*]

STANLEY. Who turned that on in there?

BLANCHE. I did. Do you mind?

STANLEY. Turn it off!

STEVE. Aw, let the girls have their music.

PABLO. Sure, that's good, leave it on!

STEVE. Sounds like Xavier Cugat!

[*Stanley jumps up and, crossing to the radio, turns it off. He stops short at the sight of Blanche in the chair. She returns his look without flinching. Then he sits again at the poker table.*]

[*Two of the men have started arguing hotly.*]

STEVE. I didn't hear you name it.

PABLO. Didn't I name it, Mitch?

MITCH. I wasn't listenin'.

PABLO. What were you doing, then?

STANLEY. He was looking through them drapes. [*He jumps up and jerks roughly at curtains to close them*] Now deal the hand over again and let's play cards or quit. Some people get ants when they win.

[*Mitch rises as Stanley returns to his seat.*]

STANLEY [*yelling*]. Sit down!

MITCH. I'm going to the "head." Deal me out.

PABLO. Sure he's got ants now. Seven five-dollar bills in his pants pocket folded up tight as spitballs.

STEVE. Tomorrow you'll see him at the cashier's window getting them changed into quarters.

STANLEY. And when he goes home he'll deposit them one by one in a piggy bank his mother give him for Christmas. [*Dealing*] This game is Spit in the Ocean.

[*Mitch laughs uncomfortably and continues through the portieres. He stops just inside.*]

BLANCHE [*softly*]. Hello! The Little Boys' Room is busy right now.

MITCH. We've—been drinking beer.

BLANCHE. I hate beer.

MITCH. It's—a hot weather drink.

BLANCHE. Oh, I don't think so; it always makes me warmer. Have you got any cigs?

[*She has slipped on the dark red satin wrapper.*]

MITCH. Sure.

BLANCHE. What kind are they?

MITCH. Luckies.

BLANCHE. Oh, good. What a pretty case. Silver?

MITCH. Yes. Yes; read the inscription.

BLANCHE. Oh, is there an inscription? I can't make it out. [*He strikes a match and moves closer*] Oh! [*reading with feigned difficulty*]:
"And if God choose,
    I shall but love thee better—after—death!"
Why, that's from my favorite sonnet by Mrs. Browning!

MITCH. You know it?

BLANCHE. Certainly I do!

MITCH. There's a story connected with that inscription.

BLANCHE. It sounds like a romance.

MITCH. A pretty sad one.

BLANCHE. Oh?

MITCH. The girl's dead now.

BLANCHE [*in a tone of deep sympathy*]. *Oh!*

MITCH. She knew she was dying when she give me this. A very strange girl, very sweet—very!

BLANCHE. She must have been fond of you. Sick people have such deep, sincere attachments.

MITCH. That's right, they certainly do.

BLANCHE. Sorrow makes for sincerity, I think.

MITCH. It sure brings it out in people.

BLANCHE. The little there is belongs to people who have experienced some sorrow.

MITCH. I believe you are right about that.

BLANCHE. I'm positive that I am. Show me a person who hasn't known any sorrow and I'll show you a shuperficial—Listen to me! My tongue is a little—thick! You boys are responsible for it. The show let out at eleven and we couldn't come home on account of the poker game so we had to go somewhere and drink. I'm not accustomed to having more than one drink. Two is the limit—and *three!* [*She laughs*] Tonight I had three.

STANLEY. Mitch!

MITCH. Deal me out. I'm talking to Miss—

BLANCHE. DuBois.

MITCH. Miss DuBois?

BLANCHE. It's a French name. It means woods and Blanche means white, so the two together mean white woods. Like an orchard in spring! You can remember it by that.

MITCH. You're French?

BLANCHE. We are French by extraction. Our first American ancestors were French Huguenots.

MITCH. You are Stella's sister, are you not?

BLANCHE. Yes, Stella is my precious little sister. I call her little in spite of the fact she's somewhat older than I. Just slightly. Less than a year. Will you do something for me?

MITCH. Sure. What?

BLANCHE. I bought this adorable little colored paper lantern at a Chinese shop on Bourbon. Put it over the light bulb! Will you, please?

MITCH. Be glad to.

BLANCHE. I can't stand a naked light bulb, any more than I can a rude remark or a vulgar action.

MITCH [*adjusting the lantern*]. I guess we strike you as being a pretty rough bunch.

BLANCHE. I'm very adaptable—to circumstances.

MITCH. Well, that's a good thing to be. You are visiting Stanley and Stella?

BLANCHE. Stella hasn't been so well lately, and I came down to help her for a while. She's very run down.

MITCH. You're not—?

BLANCHE. Married? No, no. I'm an old maid schoolteacher!

MITCH. You may teach school but you're certainly not an old maid.

BLANCHE. Thank you, sir! I appreciate your gallantry!

MITCH. So you are in the teaching profession?

BLANCHE. Yes. Ah, yes . . .

MITCH. Grade school or high school or—

STANLEY [*bellowing*]. *Mitch!*

MITCH. *Coming!*

BLANCHE. Gracious, what lung-power! . . . I teach high school. In Laurel.

MITCH. What do you teach? What subject?

BLANCHE. Guess!

MITCH. I bet you teach art or music? [*Blanche

laughs delicately] Of course I could be wrong. You might teach arithmetic.

BLANCHE. Never arithmetic, sir; never arithmetic! [*with a laugh*] I don't even know my multiplication tables! No, I have the misfortune of being an English instructor. I attempt to instill a bunch of bobby-soxers and drug-store Romeos with reverence for Hawthorne and Whitman and Poe!

MITCH. I guess that some of them are more interested in other things.

BLANCHE. How very right you are! Their literary heritage is not what most of them treasure above all else! But they're sweet things! And in the spring, it's touching to notice them making their first discovery of love! As if nobody had ever known it before!

[*The bathroom door opens and Stella comes out. Blanche continues talking to Mitch.*]

Oh! Have you finished? Wait—I'll turn on the radio.

[*She turns the knobs on the radio and it begins to play "Wien, Wien, nur du allein." Blanche waltzes to the music with romantic gestures. Mitch is delighted and moves in awkward imitation like a dancing bear.*]

[*Stanley stalks fiercely through the portieres into the bedroom. He crosses to the small white radio and snatches it off the table. With a shouted oath, he tosses the instrument out the window.*]

STELLA. *Drunk—drunk—animal thing, you!* [*She rushes through to the poker table*] All of you—please go home! If any of you have one spark of decency in you—

BLANCHE [*wildly*]. Stella, watch out, he's—

[*Stanley charges after Stella.*]

MEN [*feebly*]. Take it easy, Stanley. Easy, fellow.—Let's all—

STELLA. You lay your hands on me and I'll—

[*She backs out of sight. He advances and disappears. There is the sound of a blow. Stella cries out. Blanche screams and runs into the kitchen. The men rush forward and there is grappling and cursing. Something is overturned with a crash.*]

BLANCHE [*shrilly*]. My sister is going to have a baby!

MITCH. This is terrible.

BLANCHE. Lunacy, absolute lunacy!

MITCH. Get him in here, men.

[*Stanley is forced, pinioned by the two men, into the bedroom. He nearly throws them off. Then all at once he subsides and is limp in their grasp.*]

[*They speak quietly and lovingly to him and he leans his face on one of their shoulders.*]

STELLA [*in a high, unnatural voice, out of sight*]. I want to go away, I want to go away!

MITCH. Poker shouldn't be played in a house with women.

[*Blanche rushes into the bedroom*]

BLANCHE. I want my sister's clothes! We'll go to that woman's upstairs!

MITCH. Where is the clothes?

BLANCHE [*opening the closet*]. I've got them! [*She rushes through to Stella*] Stella, Stella, precious! Dear, dear little sister, don't be afraid!

[*With her arms around Stella, Blanche guides her to the outside door and upstairs.*]

STANLEY [*dully*]. What's the matter; what's happened?

MITCH. You just blew your top, Stan.

PABLO. He's okay, now.

STEVE. Sure, my boy's okay!

MITCH. Put him on the bed and get a wet towel.

PABLO. I think coffee would do him a world of good, now.

STANLEY [*thickly*]. I want water.

MITCH. Put him under the shower!

[*The men talk quietly as they lead him to the bathroom.*]

STANLEY. Let the rut go of me, you sons of bitches!

[*Sounds of blows are heard. The water goes on full tilt.*]

STEVE. Let's get quick out of here!

[*They rush to the poker table and sweep up their winnings on their way out.*]

MITCH [*sadly but firmly*]. Poker should not be played in a house with women.

[*The door closes on them and the place is still. The Negro entertainers in the bar around the corner play "Paper Doll" slow and blue. After a moment Stanley comes out of the bathroom dripping water and still in his clinging wet polka dot drawers.*]

STANLEY. Stella! [*There is a pause*] My baby doll's left me!

[*He breaks into sobs. Then he goes to the phone and dials, still shuddering with sobs.*]

Eunice? I want my baby! [*He waits a moment; then he hangs up and dials again*] Eunice! I'll keep on ringin' until I talk with my baby!

[*An indistinguishable shrill voice is heard. He hurls phone to floor. Dissonant brass and piano sounds as the rooms dim out to darkness and the outer walls appear in the night light. The "blue piano" plays for a brief interval.*]

[*Finally, Stanley stumbles half-dressed out to the porch and down the wooden steps to the pavement before the building. There he throws back his head like a baying hound and bellows his wife's name: "Stella! Stella, sweetheart! Stella!"*]

STANLEY. Stell-*lahhhhh!*

EUNICE [*calling down from the door of her upper apartment*]. Quit that howling out there an' go back to bed!

STANLEY. I want my baby down here. Stella, Stella!

EUNICE. She ain't comin' down so you quit! Or you'll git th' law on you!

STANLEY. Stella!

EUNICE. You can't beat on a woman an' then call 'er back! She won't come! And her goin' t' have a baby! . . . You stinker! You whelp of a Polack, you! I hope they do haul you in and turn the fire hose on you, same as the last time!

STANLEY [*humbly*]. Eunice, I want my girl to come down with me!

EUNICE. Hah! [*She slams her door.*]

STANLEY [*with heaven-splitting violence*]. *STELL-LAHHHHH!*

[*The low-tone clarinet moans. The door upstairs opens again. Stella slips down the rickety stairs in her robe. Her eyes are glistening with tears and her hair loose about her throat and shoulders. They stare at each other. Then they come together with low, animal moans. He falls to his knees on the steps and presses his face to her belly, curving a little with maternity. Her eyes go blind with tenderness as she catches his head and raises him level with her. He snatches the screen door open and lifts her off her feet and bears her into the dark flat.*]

[*Blanche comes out on the upper landing in her robe and slips fearfully down the steps.*]

BLANCHE. Where is my little sister? Stella? Stella?

[*She stops before the dark entrance of her sister's flat. Then catches her breath as if struck. She rushes down to the walk before the house. She looks right and left as if for a sanctuary.*]

[*The music fades away. Mitch appears from around the corner.*]

MITCH. Miss DuBois?

BLANCHE. Oh!

MITCH. All quiet on the Potomac now?

BLANCHE. She ran downstairs and went back in there with him.

MITCH. Sure she did.

BLANCHE. I'm terrified!

MITCH. Ho-ho! There's nothing to be scared of. They're crazy about each other.

BLANCHE. I'm not used to such—

MITCH. Naw, it's a shame this had to happen when you just got here. But don't take it serious.

BLANCHE. Violence! Is so—

MITCH. Set down on the steps and have a cigarette with me.

BLANCHE. I'm not properly dressed.

MITCH. That don't make no difference in the Quarter.

BLANCHE. Such a pretty silver case.

MITCH. I showed you the inscription, didn't I?

BLANCHE. Yes. [*During the pause, she looks up at sky*] There's so much—so much confusion in the world . . . [*He coughs diffidently*] Thank you for being so kind! I need kindness now.

Scene Four

It is early the following morning. There is a confusion of street cries like a choral chant.

Stella is lying down in the bedroom. Her face is serene in the early morning sunlight. One hand rests on her belly, rounding slightly with new maternity. From the other dangles a book of colored comics. Her eyes and lips have that almost narcotized tranquility that is in the faces of Eastern idols.

The table is sloppy with remains of breakfast and the debris of the preceding night, and Stanley's gaudy pyjamas lie across the threshold of the bathroom. The outside door is slightly ajar on a sky of summer brilliance.

Blanche appears at this door. She has spent a sleepless night and her appearance entirely contrasts with Stella's. She presses her knuckles nervously to her lips as she looks through the door, before entering.

BLANCHE. Stella?

STELLA [*stirring lazily*]. Hmmh?

[*Blanche utters a moaning cry and runs into the bedroom, throwing herself down beside Stella in a rush of hysterical tenderness.*]

BLANCHE. Baby, my baby sister!

STELLA [*drawing away from her*]. Blanche, what is the matter with you?

[*Blanche straightens up slowly and stands beside the bed looking down at her sister with knuckles pressed to her lips.*]

BLANCHE. He's left?

STELLA. Stan? Yes.

BLANCHE. Will he be back?

STELLA. He's gone to get the car greased. Why?

BLANCHE. Why! I've been half crazy, Stella! When I found out you'd been insane enough to come back in here after what happened—I started to rush in after you!

STELLA. I'm glad you didn't.

BLANCHE. What were you thinking of? [*Stella makes an indefinite gesture*] Answer me! What? What?

STELLA. Please, Blanche! Sit down and stop yelling.

BLANCHE. All right, Stella. I will repeat the question quietly now. How could you come back in this place last night? Why you must have slept with him!

[*Stella gets up in a calm and leisurely way.*]

STELLA. Blanche, I'd forgotten how excitable you are. You're making much too much fuss about this.

BLANCHE. Am I?

STELLA. Yes, you are, Blanche. I know how it must have seemed to you and I'm awful sorry it had to happen, but it wasn't anything as serious as you seem to take it. In the first place, when men are drinking and playing poker anything can happen. It's always a powder-keg. He didn't know what he was doing. . . . He was as good as a lamb when I came back and he's really very, very ashamed of himself.

BLANCHE. And that—that makes it all right?

STELLA. No, it isn't all right for anybody to make such a terrible row, but—people do sometimes. Stanley's always smashed things. Why, on our wedding night—soon as we came in here—he snatched off one of my slippers and rushed about the place smashing the light-bulbs with it.

BLANCHE. He did—*what?*

STELLA. He smashed all the light-bulbs with the heel of my slipper! [*She laughs.*]

BLANCHE. And you—you *let* him? Didn't *run*, didn't *scream?*

STELLA. I was—sort of—thrilled by it. [*She waits for a moment*] Eunice and you had breakfast?

BLANCHE. Do you suppose I wanted any breakfast?

STELLA. There's some coffee left on the stove.

BLANCHE. You're so—matter of fact about it, Stella.

STELLA. What other can I be? He's taken the radio to get it fixed. It didn't land on the pavement so only one tube was smashed.

BLANCHE. And you are standing there smiling!

STELLA. What do you want me to do?

BLANCHE. Pull yourself together and face the facts.

STELLA. What are they, in your opinion?

BLANCHE. In my opinion? You're married to a madman!

STELLA. No!

BLANCHE. Yes, you are, your fix is worse than mine is! Only you're not being sensible about it. I'm going to *do* something. Get hold of myself and make myself a new life!

STELLA. Yes?

BLANCHE. But you've given in. And that isn't right, you're not old! You can get out.

STELLA [*slowly and emphatically*]. I'm not in anything I want to get out of.

BLANCHE [*incredulously*]. What—Stella?

STELLA. I said I am not in anything that I have a desire to get out of. Look at the mess in this room! And those empty bottles! They went through two cases last night! He promised this morning that he was going to quit having these poker parties, but you know how long such a promise is going to keep. Oh, well, it's his pleasure, like mine is movies and bridge. People have got to tolerate each other's habits, I guess.

BLANCHE. I don't understand you. [*Stella turns toward her*] I don't understand your indifference. Is this a Chinese philosophy you've—cultivated?

STELLA. Is what—what?

BLANCHE. This—shuffling about and mumbling—'One tube smashed—beer-bottles— mess in the kitchen!'—as if nothing out of the ordinary has happened! [*Stella laughs uncertainly and picking up the broom, twirls it in her hands.*]

BLANCHE. Are you deliberately shaking that thing in my face?

STELLA. No.

BLANCHE. Stop it. Let go of that broom. I won't have you cleaning up for him!

STELLA. Then who's going to do it? Are you?

BLANCHE. I? I!

STELLA. No, I didn't think so.

BLANCHE. Oh, let me think, if only my mind would function! We've got to get hold of some money, that's the way out!

STELLA. I guess that money is always nice to get hold of.

BLANCHE. Listen to me. I have an idea of some kind. [*Shakily she twists a cigarette into her holder*] Do you remember Shep Huntleigh? [*Stella shakes her head*] Of course you remember Shep Huntleigh. I went out with him at college and wore his pin for a while. Well—

STELLA. Well?

BLANCHE. I ran into him last winter. You know I went to Miami during the Christmas holidays?

STELLA. No.

BLANCHE. Well, I did. I took the trip as an investment, thinking I'd meet someone with a million dollars.

STELLA. Did you?

BLANCHE. Yes. I ran into Shep Huntleigh—I ran into him on Biscayne Boulevard, on Christmas Eve, about dusk . . . getting into his car—Cadillac convertible; must have been a block long!

STELLA. I should think it would have been—inconvenient in traffic!

BLANCHE. You've heard of oil-wells?

STELLA. Yes—remotely.

BLANCHE. He has them, all over Texas. Texas is literally spouting gold in his pockets.

STELLA. My, my.

BLANCHE. Y'know how indifferent I am to money. I think of money in terms of what it does for you. But he could do it, he could certainly do it!

STELLA. Do what, Blanche?

BLANCHE. Why—set us up in a—shop!

STELLA. What kind of a shop?

BLANCHE. Oh, a—shop of some kind! He could do it with half what his wife throws away at the races.

STELLA. He's married?

BLANCHE. Honey, would I be here if the man weren't married? [*Stella laughs a little. Blanche suddenly springs up and crosses to phone. She speaks shrilly*] How do I get Western Union?—Operator! Western Union!

STELLA. That's a dial phone, honey.

BLANCHE. I can't dial, I'm too—

STELLA. Just dial O.

BLANCHE. O?

STELLA. Yes, "O" for Operator! [*Blanche considers a moment; then she puts the phone down.*]

BLANCHE. Give me a pencil. Where is a slip of paper? I've got to write it down first—the message, I mean . . .

[*She goes to the dressing table, and grabs up a sheet of Kleenex and an eyebrow pencil for writing equipment.*]

Let me see now . . . [*She bites the pencil*]

'Darling Shep. Sister and I in desperate situation.'

STELLA. I beg your pardon!

BLANCHE. 'Sister and I in desperate situation. Will explain details later. Would you be interested in—?' [*She bites the pencil again*] 'Would you be—interested—in . . . '[*She smashes the pencil on the table and springs up*] You never get anywhere with direct appeals!

STELLA [*with a laugh*]. Don't be so ridiculous, darling!

BLANCHE. But I'll think of something, I've *got* to think of—some-thing! Don't, don't laugh at me, Stella! Please, please don't—I—I want you to look at the contents of my purse! Here's what's in it! [*She snatches her purse open*] Sixty-five measly cents in coin of the realm!

STELLA [*crossing to bureau*]. Stanley doesn't give me a regular allowance, he likes to pay bills himself, but—this morning he gave me ten dollars to smooth things over. You take five of it, Blanche, and I'll keep the rest.

BLANCHE. Oh, no. No, Stella.

STELLA [*insisting*]. I know how it helps your morale just having a little pocket-money on you.

BLANCHE. No, thank you—I'll take to the streets!

STELLA. Talk sense! How did you happen to get so low on funds?

BLANCHE. Money just goes—it goes places. [*She rubs her forehead*] Sometime today I've got to get hold of a bromo!

STELLA. I'll fix you one now.

BLANCHE. Not yet—I've got to keep thinking!

STELLA. I wish you'd just let things go, at least for a—while . . .

BLANCHE. Stella, I can't live with him! You can, he's your husband. But how could I stay here with him, after last night, with just those curtains between us?

STELLA. Blanche, you saw him at his worst last night.

BLANCHE. On the contrary, I saw him at his best! What such a man has to offer is animal force and he gave a wonderful ex-hibition of that! But the only way to live with such a man is to—go to bed with him! And that's your job—not mine!

STELLA. After you've rested a little, you'll see it's going to work out. You don't have to worry about anything while you're here. I mean—expenses . . .

BLANCHE. I have to plan for us both, to get us both—out!

STELLA. You take it for granted that I am in something that I want to get out of.

BLANCHE. I take it for granted that you still have sufficient memory of Belle Reve to find this place and these poker players impossible to live with.

STELLA. Well, you're taking entirely too much for granted.

BLANCHE. I can't believe you're in earnest.

STELLA. No?

BLANCHE. I understand how it happened—a little. You saw him in uniform, an officer, not here but—

STELLA. I'm not sure it would have made any difference where I saw him.

BLANCHE. Now don't say it was one of those mysterious electric things between people! If you do I'll laugh in your face.

STELLA. I am not going to say anything more at all about it!

BLANCHE. All right, then, don't!

STELLA. But there are things that happen be-tween a man and a woman in the dark—that sort of make everything else seem—unimportant. [*Pause.*]

BLANCHE. What you are talking about is brutal desire—just—Desire!—the name of that rattle-trap street-car that bangs through the Quarter, up one old narrow street and down another . . .

STELLA. Haven't you ever ridden on that street-car?

BLANCHE. It brought me here.—Where I'm not wanted and where I'm ashamed to be . . .

STELLA. Then don't you think your superior attitude is a bit out of place?

BLANCHE. I am not being or feeling at all superior, Stella. Believe me I'm not! It's

just this. This is how I look at it. A man like that is someone to go out with—once—twice—three times when the devil is in you. But live with? Have a child by?

STELLA. I have told you I love him.

BLANCHE. Then I *tremble* for you! I just—*tremble* for you. . . .

STELLA. I can't help your trembling if you insist on trembling!

[*There is a pause.*]

BLANCHE. May I—speak—*plainly?*

STELLA. Yes, do. Go ahead. As plainly as you want to.

[*Outside, a train approaches. They are silent till the noise subsides. They are both in the bedroom.*

[*Under cover of the train's noise Stanley enters from outside. He stands unseen by the women, holding some packages in his arms, and overhears their following conversation. He wears an undershirt and grease-stained seersucker pants.*]

BLANCHE. Well—if you'll forgive me—he's *common!*

STELLA. Why, yes, I suppose he is.

BLANCHE. Suppose! You can't have forgotten that much of our bringing up, Stella, that you just *suppose* that any part of a gentle-man's in his nature! *Not one particle, no!* Oh, if he was just—*ordinary!* Just *plain*—but good and wholesome, but—*no.* There's something downright—*bestial*—about him! You're hating me saying this, aren't you?

STELLA [*coldly*]. Go on and say it all, Blanche.

BLANCHE. He acts like an animal, has an animal's habits! Eats like one, moves like one, talks like one! There's even something—sub-human—something not quite to the stage of humanity yet! Yes, something—apelike about him, like one of those pic-tures I've seen in—anthropological studies! Thousands and thousands of years have passed him right by, and there he is—Stanley Kowalski—survivor of the stone age! Bearing the raw meat home from the kill in the jungle! And you—*you here—waiting* for him! Maybe he'll strike you or maybe grunt and kiss you! That is, if kisses have been discovered yet! Night falls and the other apes gather! There in the front of the cave, all grunting like him, and swilling and gnawing and hulking! His poker night!—you call it—this party of apes! Somebody growls—some creature snatches at something—the fight is on! *God!* Maybe we are a long way from being made in God's image, but Stella—my sister—there has been *some* progress since then! Such things as art—as poetry and music—such kinds of new light have come into the world since then! In some kinds of people some tenderer feelings have had some little beginning! That we have got to make *grow!* And *cling* to, and hold as our flag! In this dark march toward whatever it is we're approaching. . . . *Don't—don't hang back with the brutes!*

[*Another train passes outside. Stanley hesitates, licking his lips. Then suddenly he turns stealthily about and withdraws through front door. The women are still unaware of his presence. When the train has passed he calls through the closed front door.*]

STANLEY. Hey! Hey, Stella!
STELLA [*who has listened gravely to Blanche*]. Stanley!
BLANCHE. Stell, I—

[*But Stella has gone to the front door. Stanley enters casually with his packages.*]

STANLEY. Hiyuh, Stella. Blanche back?
STELLA. Yes, she's back.
STANLEY. Hiyuh, Blanche. [*He grins at her.*]
STELLA. You must've got under the car.
STANLEY. Them darn mechanics at Fritz's don't know their ass fr'm—*Hey!*

[*Stella has embraced him with both arms, fiercely, and full in the view of Blanche. He laughs and clasps her head to him. Over her head he grins through the curtains at Blanche.*]

[*As the lights fade away, with a lingering brightness on their embrace, the music of the "blue piano" and trumpet and drums is heard.*]

Scene Five

Blanche is seated in the bedroom fanning herself with a palm leaf as she reads over a just completed letter. Suddenly she bursts into a peal of laughter. Stella is dressing in the bedroom.

STELLA. What are you laughing at, honey?
BLANCHE. Myself, myself, for being such a liar! I'm writing a letter to Shep [*She picks up the letter*] "Darling Shep. I am spending the summer on the wing, making flying visits here and there. And who knows, perhaps I shall take a sudden notion to *swoop* down on *Dallas!* How would you feel about that? Ha-ha! [*She laughs nervously and brightly, touching her throat as if actually talking to Shep*] Forewarned is forearmed, as they say!"—How does that sound?
STELLA. Uh-huh . . .
BLANCHE [*going on nervously*]. "Most of my sister's friends go north in the summer but some have homes on the Gulf and there has been a continued round of entertainments, teas, cocktails, and luncheons—"

[*A disturbance is heard upstairs at the Hubbell's apartment.*]

STELLA. Eunice seems to be having some trouble with Steve.

[*Eunice's voice shouts in terrible wrath.*]

EUNICE. I heard about you and that blonde!
STEVE. That's a damn lie!
EUNICE. You ain't pulling the wool over my eyes! I wouldn't mind if you'd stay down at the Four Deuces, but you always going up.

STEVE. Who ever seen me up?

EUNICE. I seen you chasing her 'round the balcony—I'm gonna call the vice squad!

STEVE. Don't you throw that at me!

EUNICE [*shrieking*]. You hit me! I'm gonna call the police!

[*A clatter of aluminum striking a wall is heard, followed by a man's angry roar, shouts and overturned furniture. There is a crash; then a relative hush.*]

BLANCHE [*brightly*]. Did he *kill* her?

[*Eunice appears on the steps in daemonic disorder.*]

STELLA. No! She's coming downstairs.

EUNICE. Call the police, I'm going to call the police! [*She rushes around the corner.*]

[*They laugh lightly. Stanley comes around the corner in his green and scarlet bowling shirt. He trots up the steps and bangs into the kitchen. Blanche registers his entrance with nervous gestures.*]

STANLEY. What's a matter with Eun-uss?

STELLA. She and Steve had a row. Has she got the police?

STANLEY. Naw. She's gettin' a drink.

STELLA. That's much more practical!

[*Steve comes down nursing a bruise on his forehead and looks in the door.*]

STEVE. *She here?*

STANLEY. Naw, naw. At the Four Deuces.

STEVE. That rutting hunk! [*He looks around the corner a bit timidly, then turns with affected boldness and runs after her.*]

BLANCHE. I must jot that down in my note-book. Ha-ha! I'm compiling a notebook of quaint little words and phrases I've picked up here.

STANLEY. You won't pick up nothing here you ain't heard before.

BLANCHE. Can I count on that?

STANLEY. You can count on it up to five hundred.

BLANCHE. That's a mighty high number. [*He jerks open the bureau drawer, slams it shut and throws shoes in a corner. At each noise Blanche winces slightly. Finally she speaks*] What sign were you born under?

STANLEY [*while he is dressing*]. Sign?

BLANCHE. Astrological sign. I bet you were born under Aries. Aries people are forceful and dynamic. They dote on noise! They love to bang things around! You must have had lots of banging around in the army and now that you're out, you make up for it by treating inanimate objects with such a fury!

[*Stella has been going in and out of closet during this scene. Now she pops her head out of the closet.*]

STELLA. Stanley was born just five minutes after Christmas.

BLANCHE. Capricorn—the Goat!

STANLEY. What sign were *you* born under?

BLANCHE. Oh, my birthday's next month, the fifteenth of September; that's under Virgo.

STANLEY. What's Virgo?

BLANCHE. Virgo is the Virgin.

STANLEY [*contemptuously*]. *Hah!* [*He advances a little as he knots his tie*] Say, do you happen to know somebody named Shaw?

[*Her face expresses a faint shock. She reaches for the cologne bottle and dampens her handkerchief as she answers carefully.*]

BLANCHE. Why, everybody knows somebody named Shaw!

STANLEY. Well, this somebody named Shaw is under the impression he met you in Laurel, but I figure he must have got you mixed up with some other party because this other party is someone he met at a hotel called the Flamingo.

[*Blanche laughs breathlessly as she touches the cologne-dampened handkerchief to her temples.*]

BLANCHE. I'm afraid he does have me mixed up with this "other party." The Hotel Flamingo is not the sort of establishment I would dare to be seen in!

STANLEY. You know of it?

BLANCHE. Yes, I've seen it and smelled it.

STANLEY. You must've got pretty close if you could smell it.

BLANCHE. The odor of cheap perfume is penetrating.

STANLEY. That stuff you use is expensive?

BLANCHE. Twenty-five dollars an ounce! I'm nearly out. That's just a hint if you want to remember my birthday! [*She speaks lightly but her voice has a note of fear.*]

STANLEY. Shaw must've got you mixed up. He goes in and out of Laurel all the time so he can check on it and clear up any mistake.

[*He turns away and crosses to the portieres. Blanche closes her eyes as if faint. Her hand trembles as she lifts the handkerchief again to her forehead.*

[*Steve and Eunice come around corner. Steve's arm is around Eunice's shoulder and she is sobbing luxuriously and he is cooing love-words. There is a murmur of thunder as they go slowly upstairs in a tight embrace.*]

STANLEY [*to Stella*]. I'll wait for you at the Four Deuces!

STELLA. Hey! Don't I rate one kiss?

STANLEY. Not in front of your sister.

[*He goes out. Blanche rises from her chair. She seems faint; looks about her with an expression of almost panic.*]

BLANCHE. Stella! What have you heard about me?

STELLA. Huh?

BLANCHE. What have people been telling you about me?

STELLA. Telling?

BLANCHE. You haven't heard any—unkind—gossip about me?

STELLA. Why, no, Blanche, of course not!

BLANCHE. Honey, there was—a good deal of talk in Laurel.

STELLA. About *you*, Blanche?

BLANCHE. I wasn't so good the last two years or so, after Belle Reve had started to slip through my fingers.

STELLA. All of us do things we—

BLANCHE. I never was hard or self-sufficient enough. When people are soft—soft people have got to shimmer and glow—they've got to put on soft colors, the colors of butterfly wings, and put a—paper lantern over the light. . . . It isn't enough to be soft. You've got to be soft *and attractive*. And I—I'm fading now! I don't know how much longer I can turn the trick.

[*The afternoon has faded to dusk. Stella goes into the bedroom and turns on the light under the paper lantern. She holds a bottled soft drink in her hand.*]

BLANCHE. Have you been listening to me?

STELLA. I don't listen to you when you are being morbid! [*She advances with the bottled coke.*]

BLANCHE [*with abrupt change to gaiety*]. Is that coke for me?

STELLA. Not for anyone else!

BLANCHE. Why, you precious thing, you! Is it just coke?

STELLA [*turning*]. You mean you want a shot in it!

BLANCHE. Well, honey, a shot never does a coke any harm! Let me! You mustn't wait on me!

STELLA. I like to wait on you, Blanche. It makes it seem more like home. [*She goes into the kitchen, finds a glass and pours a shot of whiskey into it.*]

BLANCHE. I have to admit I love to be waited on . . .

[*She rushes into the bedroom. Stella goes to her with the glass. Blanche suddenly clutches Stella's free hand with a moaning sound and presses the hand to her lips. Stella is embarrassed by her show of emotion. Blanche speaks in a choked voice.*]

You're—you're—so *good* to me! And I—
STELLA. Blanche.
BLANCHE. I know, I won't! You hate me to talk sentimental! But honey, *believe* I feel things more than I *tell* you! I *won't* stay long! I won't, I *promise* I—
STELLA. Blanche!
BLANCHE [*hysterically*]. I won't, I promise, *I'll* go! Go *soon!* I will *really!* I *won't* hang around until he—throws me out . . .
STELLA. Now will you stop talking foolish?
BLANCHE. Yes, honey. Watch how you pour —that fizzy stuff foams over!

[*Blanche laughs shrilly and grabs the glass, but her hand shakes so it almost slips from her grasp. Stella pours the coke into the glass. It foams over and spills. Blanche gives a piercing cry.*]

STELLA [*shocked by the cry*]. Heavens!
BLANCHE. Right on my pretty white skirt!
STELLA. Oh . . . Use my hanky. Blot gently.
BLANCHE [*slowly recovering*]. I know—gently— gently . . .
STELLA. Did it stain?
BLANCHE. Not a bit. Ha-ha! Isn't that lucky? [*She sits down shakily, taking a grateful drink. She holds the glass in both hands and continues to laugh a little.*]
STELLA. Why did you scream like that?
BLANCHE. I don't know why I screamed! [*continuing nervously*] Mitch—Mitch is coming at seven. I guess I am just feeling nervous about our relations. [*She begins to talk rapidly and breathlessly*] He hasn't gotten a thing but a goodnight kiss, that's all I have given him, Stella. I want his respect. And men don't want anything they get too easy. But on the other hand men lose interest quickly. Especially when the girl is over—thirty. They think a girl over thirty ought to—the vulgar term is—"put out." . . . And I—I'm not "putting out." Of course he—he doesn't know—I mean I haven't informed him—of my real age!
STELLA. Why are you sensitive about your age?

BLANCHE. Because of hard knocks my vanity's been given. What I mean is—he thinks I'm sort of—prim and proper, you know! [*She laughs out sharply*] I want to *deceive* him enough to make him—want me . . .
STELLA. Blanche, do you want *him?*
BLANCHE. I want to *rest!* I want to breathe quietly again! Yes—I *want* Mitch . . . *very badly!* Just think! If it happens! I can leave here and not be anyone's problem . . .

[*Stanley comes around the corner with a drink under his belt.*]

STANLEY [*bawling*]. Hey, Steve! Hey, Eunice! Hey, Stella!

[*There are joyous calls from above. Trumpet and drums are heard from around the corner.*]

STELLA [*kissing Blanche impulsively*]. It *will* happen!
BLANCHE [*doubtfully*]. It will?
STELLA. It *will!* [*She goes across into the kitchen, looking back at Blanche.*] It will honey, it *will.* . . . But don't take another drink! [*Her voice catches as she goes out the door to meet her husband.*]

[*Blanche sinks faintly back in her chair with her drink. Eunice shrieks with laughter and runs down the steps. Steve bounds after her with goat-like screeches and chases her around corner. Stanley and Stella twine arms as they follow, laughing.*]

[*Dusk settles deeper. The music from the Four Deuces is slow and blue.*]

BLANCHE. Ah, me, ah, me, ah, me . . .

[*Her eyes fall shut and the palm leaf fan drops from her fingers. She slaps her hand on the chair arm a couple of times. There is a little glimmer of lightning about the building.*]

[*A Young Man comes along the street and rings the bell.*]

BLANCHE. Come in.

[*The Young Man appears through the portieres. She regards him with interest.*]

BLANCHE. Well, well! What can I do for *you?*

YOUNG MAN. I'm collecting for *The Evening Star.*

BLANCHE. I didn't know that stars took up collections.

YOUNG MAN. It's the paper.

BLANCHE. I know, I was joking—feebly! Will you—have a drink?

YOUNG MAN. No, ma'am. No, thank you. I can't drink on the job.

BLANCHE. Oh, well, now, let's see. . . . No, I don't have a dime! I'm not the lady of the house. I'm her sister from Mississippi. I'm one of those poor relations you've heard about.

YOUNG MAN. That's all right. I'll drop by later. [*He starts to go out. She approaches a little.*]

BLANCHE. Hey! [*He turns back shyly. She puts a cigarette in a long holder*] Could you give me a light? [*She crosses toward him. They meet at the door between the two rooms.*]

YOUNG MAN. Sure. [*He takes out a lighter*] This doesn't always work.

BLANCHE. It's temperamental? [*It flares*] Ah! —thank you. [*He starts away again*] Hey! [*He turns again, still more uncertainly. She goes close to him*] Uh—what time is it?

YOUNG MAN. Fifteen of seven, ma'am.

BLANCHE. So late? Don't you just love these long rainy afternoons in New Orleans when an hour isn't just an hour—but a little piece of eternity dropped into your hands—and who knows what to do with it? [*She touches his shoulders.*] You—uh— didn't get wet in the rain?

YOUNG MAN. No, ma'am. I stepped inside.

BLANCHE. In a drug store? And had a soda?

YOUNG MAN. Uh-huh.

BLANCHE. Chocolate?

YOUNG MAN. No, ma'am. Cherry.

BLANCHE [*laughing*]. Cherry!

YOUNG MAN. A cherry soda.

BLANCHE. You make my mouth water. [*She touches his cheek lightly, and smiles. Then she goes to the trunk.*]

YOUNG MAN. Well, I'd better be going—

BLANCHE [*stopping him*]. Young man!

[*He turns. She takes a large, gossamer scarf from the trunk and drapes it about her shoulders.*

[*In the ensuing pause, the "blue piano" is heard. It continues through the rest of this scene and the opening of the next. The young man clears his throat and looks yearningly at the door.*]

Young man! Young, young, young man! Has anyone ever told you that you look like a young Prince out of the Arabian Nights?

[*The Young Man laughs uncomfortably and stands like a bashful kid. Blanche speaks softly to him.*]

Well, you do, honey lamb! Come here. I want to kiss you, just once, softly and sweetly on your mouth!

[*Without waiting for him to accept, she crosses quickly to him and presses her lips to his.*]

Now run along, now, quickly! It would be nice to keep you, but I've got to be good— and keep my hands off children.

[*He stares at her a moment. She opens the door for him and blows a kiss at him as he goes down the steps with a dazed look. She stands there a little dreamily after he has disappeared. Then Mitch appears around the corner with a bunch of roses.*]

BLANCHE [*gaily*]. Look who's coming! My Rosenkavalier! Bow to me first . . . now present them! *Ahhhh—Merciiii!*

[*She looks at him over them, coquettishly pressing them to her lips. He beams at her self-consciously.*]

Scene Six

It is about two a.m. on the same evening. The outer wall of the building is visible. Blanche and Mitch come in. The utter exhaustion which only a neurasthenic personality can know is evident in Blanche's voice and manner. Mitch is stolid but depressed. They have probably been out to the amusement park on Lake Pontchartrain, for Mitch is bearing, upside down, a plaster statuette of Mae West, the sort of prize won at shooting-galleries and carnival games of chance.

BLANCHE [*stopping lifelessly at the steps*]. Well—

[*Mitch laughs uneasily.*]

Well . . .

MITCH. I guess it must be pretty late—and you're tired.

BLANCHE. Even the hot tamale man has deserted the street, and he hangs on till the end. [*Mitch laughs uneasily again*] How will you get home?

MITCH. I'll walk over to Bourbon and catch an owl-car.

BLANCHE [*laughing grimly*]. Is that street-car named Desire still grinding along the tracks at this hour?

MITCH [*heavily*]. I'm afraid you haven't gotten much fun out of this evening, Blanche.

BLANCHE. I spoiled it for *you*.

MITCH. No, you didn't, but I felt all the time that I wasn't giving you much—entertainment.

BLANCHE. I simply couldn't rise to the occasion. That was all. I don't think I've ever tried so hard to be gay and made such a dismal mess of it. I get ten points for trying!—I *did* try.

MITCH. Why did you try if you didn't feel like it, Blanche?

BLANCHE. I was just obeying the law of nature.

MITCH. Which law is that?

BLANCHE. The one that says the lady must entertain the gentleman—or no dice! See if you can locate my door-key in this purse. When I'm so tired my fingers are all thumbs!

MITCH [*rooting in her purse*]. This it?

BLANCHE. No, honey, that's the key to my trunk which I must soon be packing.

MITCH. You mean you are leaving here soon?

BLANCHE. I've outstayed my welcome.

MITCH. This it?

[*The music fades away.*]

BLANCHE. Eureka! Honey, you open the door while I take a last look at the sky. [*She leans on the porch rail. He opens the door and stands awkwardly behind her.*] I'm looking for the Pleiades, the Seven Sisters, but these girls are not out tonight. Oh, yes they are, there they are! God bless them! All in a bunch going home from their little bridge party. . . . Y' get the door open? Good boy! I guess you—want to go now . . .

[*He shuffles and coughs a little.*]

MITCH. Can I—uh—kiss you—goodnight?

BLANCHE. Why do you always ask me if you may?

MITCH. I don't know whether you want me to or not.

BLANCHE. Why should you be so doubtful?

MITCH. That night when we parked by the lake and I kissed you, you—

BLANCHE. Honey, it wasn't the kiss I objected to. I liked the kiss very much. It was the other little—familiarity—that I—felt obliged to—discourage. . . . I didn't resent it! Not a bit in the world! In fact, I was somewhat flattered that you—desired me! But, honey, you know as well as I do that a single girl, a girl alone in the world, has got to keep a firm hold on her emotions or she'll be lost!

MITCH [*solemnly*]. Lost?

BLANCHE. I guess you are used to girls that like to be lost. The kind that get lost immediately, on the first date!

MITCH. I like you to be exactly the way that you are, because in all my—experience—I have never known anyone like you.

[*Blanche looks at him gravely; then she bursts into laughter and then claps a hand to her mouth.*]

MITCH. Are you laughing at me?

BLANCHE. No, honey. The lord and lady of the house have not yet returned, so come in. We'll have a night-cap. Let's leave the lights off. Shall we?

MITCH. You just—do what you want to.

[*Blanche precedes him into the kitchen. The outer wall of the building disappears and the interiors of the two rooms can be dimly seen.*]

BLANCHE [*remaining in the first room*]. The other room's more comfortable—go on in. This crashing around in the dark is my search for some liquor.

MITCH. You want a drink?

BLANCHE. I want *you* to have a drink! You have been so anxious and solemn all evening, and so have I; we have both been anxious and solemn and now for these few last remaining moments of our lives together—I want to create—*joie de vivre!* I'm lighting a candle.

MITCH. That's good.

BLANCHE. We are going to be very Bohemian. We are going to pretend that we are sitting in a little artists' cafe on the Left Bank in Paris! [*She lights a candle stub and puts it in a bottle.*] *Je suis la Dame aux Camellias! Vous êtes—Armand!* Understand French?

MITCH [*heavily*]. Naw. Naw, I—

BLANCHE. *Voulez-vous couchez avec moi ce soir? Vous ne comprenez pas? Ah, quelle dommage!*— I mean it's a damned good thing. . . . I've found some liquor! Just enough for two shots without any dividends, honey . . .

MITCH [*heavily*]. That's—good.

[*She enters the bedroom with the drinks and the candle.*]

BLANCHE. Sit down! Why don't you take off your coat and loosen your collar?

MITCH. I better leave it on.

BLANCHE. No. I want you to be comfortable.

MITCH. I am ashamed of the way I perspire. My shirt is sticking to me.

BLANCHE. Perspiration is healthy. If people didn't perspire they would die in five minutes. [*She takes his coat from him*] This is a nice coat. What kind of material is it?

MITCH. They call that stuff alpaca.

BLANCHE. Oh. Alpaca.

MITCH. It's very light weight alpaca.

BLANCHE. Oh. Light weight alpaca.

MITCH. I don't like to wear a wash-coat even in summer because I sweat through it.

BLANCHE. Oh.

MITCH. And it don't look neat on me. A man with a heavy build has got to be careful of what he puts on him so he don't look too clumsy.

BLANCHE. You are not too heavy.

MITCH. You don't think I am?

BLANCHE. You are not the delicate type. You have a massive bone-structure and a very imposing physique.

MITCH. Thank you. Last Christmas I was given a membership to the New Orleans Athletic Club.

BLANCHE. Oh, good.

MITCH. It was the finest present I ever was given. I work out there with the weights and I swim and I keep myself fit. When I started there, I was getting soft in the belly but now my belly is hard. It is so hard now that a man can punch me in the belly and it don't hurt me. Punch me! Go on! See? [*She pokes lightly at him.*]

BLANCHE. Gracious. [*Her hand touches his chest.*]

MITCH. Guess how much I weigh, Blanche?

BLANCHE. Oh, I'd say in the vicinity of—one hundred and eighty?

MITCH. Guess again.

BLANCHE. Not that much?

MITCH. No. More.

BLANCHE. Well, you're a tall man and you can carry a good deal of weight without looking awkward.

MITCH. I weigh two hundred and seven pounds and I'm six feet one and one half inches tall in my bare feet—without shoes on. And that is what I weigh stripped.

BLANCHE. Oh, my goodness, me! It's awe-inspiring.

MITCH [*embarrassed*]. My weight is not a very interesting subject to talk about. [*He hesitates for a moment*] What's yours?

BLANCHE. My weight?

MITCH. Yes.

BLANCHE. Guess!

MITCH. Let me lift you.

BLANCHE. Samson! Go on; lift me. [*He comes behind her and puts his hands on her waist and raises her lightly off the ground*] Well?

MITCH. You are light as a feather.

BLANCHE. Ha-ha! [*He lowers her but keeps his hands on her waist. Blanche speaks with an affectation of demureness*] You may release me now.

MITCH. Huh?

BLANCHE [*gaily*]. I said unhand me, sir. [*He fumblingly embraces her. Her voice sounds gently reproving*] Now, Mitch. Just because Stanley and Stella aren't at home is no reason why you shouldn't behave like a gentleman.

MITCH. Just give me a slap whenever I step out of bounds.

BLANCHE. That won't be necessary. You're a natural gentleman, one of the very few that are left in the world. I don't want you to think that I am severe and old maid school-teacherish or anything like that. It's just—well—

MITCH. Huh?

BLANCHE. I guess it is just that I have—old-fashioned ideals! [*She rolls her eyes, knowing he cannot see her face. Mitch goes to the front door. There is a considerable silence between them. Blanche sighs and Mitch coughs self-consciously.*]

MITCH [*finally*]. Where's Stanley and Stella tonight?

BLANCHE. They have gone out. With Mr. and Mrs. Hubbell upstairs.

MITCH. Where did they go?

BLANCHE. I think they were planning to go to a midnight prevue at Loew's State.

MITCH. We should all go out together some night.

BLANCHE. No. That wouldn't be a good plan.

MITCH. Why not?

BLANCHE. You are an old friend of Stanley's?

MITCH. We was together in the Two-forty-first.

BLANCHE. I guess he talks to you frankly?

MITCH. Sure.

BLANCHE. Has he talked to you about me?

MITCH. Oh—not very much.

BLANCHE. The way you say that, I suspect that he has.

MITCH. No, he hasn't said much.

BLANCHE. But what he *has* said. What would you say his attitude toward me was?

MITCH. Why do you want to ask that?

BLANCHE. Well—

MITCH. Don't you get along with him?

BLANCHE. What do you think?

MITCH. I don't think he understands you.

BLANCHE. That is putting it mildly. If it weren't for Stella about to have a baby, I wouldn't be able to endure things here.

MITCH. He isn't—nice to you?

BLANCHE. He is insufferably rude. Goes out of his way to offend me.

MITCH. In what way, Blanche?

BLANCHE. Why, in every conceivable way.

MITCH. I'm surprised to hear that.

BLANCHE. Are you?

MITCH. Well, I—don't see how anybody could be rude to you.

BLANCHE. It's really a pretty frightful situation. You see, there's no privacy here. There's just these portieres between the two rooms at night. He stalks through the rooms in his underwear at night. And I have to ask him to close the bathroom door. That sort of commonness isn't necessary. You probably wonder why I don't move out. Well, I'll tell you frankly. A teacher's salary is barely sufficient for her living-expenses. I didn't save a penny last year and so I had to come here for the summer. That's why I have to put up with my sister's husband. And he has to put up with me, apparently so much against his wishes. . . . Surely he must have told you how much he hates me!

MITCH. I don't think he hates you.

BLANCHE. He hates me. Or why would he insult me? The first time I laid eyes on him I thought to myself, that man is my executioner! That man will destroy me, unless ——

MITCH. Blanche—

BLANCHE. Yes, honey?

MITCH. Can I ask you a question?

BLANCHE. Yes. What?

MITCH. How old are you?

[*She makes a nervous gesture.*]

BLANCHE. Why do you want to know?

MITCH. I talked to my mother about you and she said, "How old is Blanche?" And I wasn't able to tell her. [*There is another pause.*]

BLANCHE. You talked to your mother about me?

MITCH. Yes.

BLANCHE. Why?

MITCH. I told my mother how nice you were, and I liked you.

BLANCHE. Were you sincere about that?

MITCH. You know I was.

BLANCHE. Why did your mother want to know my age?

MITCH. Mother is sick.

BLANCHE. I'm sorry to hear it. Badly?

MITCH. She won't live long. Maybe just a few months.

BLANCHE. Oh.

MITCH. She worries because I'm not settled.

BLANCHE. Oh.

MITCH. She wants me to be settled down before she—[*His voice is hoarse and he clears his throat twice, shuffling nervously around with his hands in and out of his pockets.*]

BLANCHE. You love her very much, don't you?

MITCH. Yes.

BLANCHE. I think you have a great capacity for devotion. You will be lonely when she passes on, won't you? [*Mitch clears his throat and nods.*] I understand what that is.

MITCH. To be lonely?

BLANCHE. I loved someone, too, and the person I loved I lost.

MITCH. Dead? [*She crosses to the window and sits on the sill, looking out. She pours herself another drink.*] A man?

BLANCHE. He was a boy, just a boy, when I was a very young girl. When I was sixteen, I made the discovery—love. All at once and much, much too completely. It was like you suddenly turned a blinding light on something that had always been half in shadow, that's how it struck the world for me. But I was unlucky. Deluded. There was something different about the boy, a nervousness, a softness and tenderness which wasn't like a man's, although he wasn't the least bit effeminate looking— still—that thing was there. . . . He came to me for help. I didn't know that. I didn't find out anything till after our marriage when we'd run away and come back and all I knew was I'd failed him in some mysterious way and wasn't able to give the help he needed but couldn't speak of! He was in the quicksands and clutching at me —but I wasn't holding him out, I was slipping in with him! I didn't know that. I didn't know anything except I loved him unendurably but without being able to help him or help myself. Then I found out. In the worst of all possible ways. By coming suddenly into a room that I thought was empty—which wasn't empty, but had two people in it . . . the boy I had married and an older man who had been his friend for years . . .

[*A locomotive is heard approaching outside. She claps her hands to her ears and crouches over. The headlight of the locomotive glares into the room as it thunders past. As the noise recedes she straightens slowly and continues speaking.*]

Afterwards we pretended that nothing had been discovered. Yes, the three of us drove out to Moon Lake Casino, very drunk and laughing all the way.

[*Polka music sounds, in a minor key faint with distance.*]

We danced the Varsouviana! Suddenly in the middle of the dance the boy I had married broke away from me and ran out of the casino. A few moments later—a shot!

[*The Polka stops abruptly.*

[*Blanche rises stiffly. Then, the Polka resumes in a major key.*]

I ran out—all did!—all ran and gathered about the terrible thing at the edge of the lake! I couldn't get near for the crowding. Then somebody caught my arm. "Don't go any closer! Come back! You don't want to see!" See? See what! Then I heard voices say—Allan! Allan! The Grey boy! He'd stuck the revolver into his mouth, and fired—so that the back of his head had been—blown away!

[*She sways and covers her face.*]

It was because—on the dance-floor—unable to stop myself—I'd suddenly said—"I saw! I know! You disgust me . . ." And then the searchlight which had been turned on the world was turned off again and never for one moment since has there been any light that's stronger than this—kitchen —candle . . .

[*Mitch gets up awkwardly and moves toward her a little. The Polka music increases. Mitch stands beside her.*]

MITCH [*drawing her slowly into his arms*]. You

need somebody. And I need somebody, too. Could it be—you and me, Blanche?

[*She stares at him vacantly for a moment. Then with a soft cry huddles in his embrace. She makes a sobbing effort to speak but the words won't come. He kisses her forehead and her eyes and finally her lips. The Polka tune fades out. Her breath is drawn and released in long, grateful sobs.*]

BLANCHE. Sometimes — there's God — so quickly!

Scene Seven

It is late afternoon in mid-September.

The portieres are open and a table is set for a birthday supper, with cake and flowers.

Stella is completing the decorations as Stanley comes in.

STANLEY. What's all this stuff for?

STELLA. Honey, it's Blanche's birthday.

STANLEY. She here?

STELLA. In the bathroom.

STANLEY [*mimicking*]. "Washing out some things"?

STELLA. I reckon so.

STANLEY. How long she been in there?

STELLA. All afternoon.

STANLEY [*mimicking*]. "Soaking in a hot tub"?

STELLA. Yes.

STANLEY. Temperature 100 on the nose, and she soaks herself in a hot tub.

STELLA. She says it cools her off for the evening.

STANLEY. And you run out an' get her cokes, I suppose? And serve 'em to Her Majesty in the tub? [*Stella shrugs*] Set down here a minute.

STELLA. Stanley, I've got things to do.

STANLEY. Set down! I've got th' dope on your big sister, Stella.

STELLA. Stanley, stop picking on Blanche.

STANLEY. That girl calls *me* common!

STELLA. Lately you been doing all you can think of to rub her the wrong way, Stanley, and Blanche is sensitive and you've got to realize that Blanche and I grew up under very different circumstances than you did.

STANLEY. So I been told. And told and told and told! You know she's been feeding us a pack of lies here?

STELLA. No, I don't, and—

STANLEY. Well, she has, however. But now the cat's out of the bag! I found out some things!

STELLA. What—things?

STANLEY. Things I already suspected. But now I got proof from the most reliable sources—which I have checked on!

[*Blanche is singing in the bathroom a saccharine popular ballad which is used contrapuntally with Stanley's speech.*]

STELLA [*to Stanley*]. Lower your voice!

STANLEY. Some canary-bird, huh!

STELLA. Now please tell me quietly what you think you've found out about my sister.

STANLEY. Lie Number One: All this squeamishness she puts on! You should just know the line she's been feeding to Mitch. He thought she had never been more than kissed by a fellow! But Sister Blanche is no lily! Ha-ha! Some lily she is!

STELLA. What have you heard and who from?

STANLEY. Our supply-man down at the plant has been going through Laurel for years and he knows all about her and everybody else in the town of Laurel knows all about her. She is as famous in Laurel as if she was the President of the United States, only she is not respected by any party! This supply-man stops at a hotel called the Flamingo.

BLANCHE [*singing blithely*]. "Say, it's only a paper moon, Sailing over a cardboard sea —But it wouldn't be make-believe If you believed in me!"*

*Copyright 1933 by Harms, Inc. Used by permission. Permission for performance must be obtained from Harms, Inc.

STELLA. What about the—Flamingo?

STANLEY. She stayed there, too.

STELLA. My sister lived at Belle Reve.

STANLEY. This is after the home-place had slipped through her lily-white fingers! She moved to the Flamingo! A second-class hotel which has the advantage of not interfering in the private social life of the personalities there! The Flamingo is used to all kinds of goings-on. But even the management of the Flamingo was impressed by Dame Blanche! In fact they was so impressed by Dame Blanche that they requested her to turn in her room-key—for permanently! This happened a couple of weeks before she showed here.

BLANCHE [*singing*]. "It's a Barnum and Bailey world, Just as phony as it can be— But it wouldn't be make-believe If you believed in me!"

STELLA. What—contemptible—lies!

STANLEY. Sure, I can see how you would be upset by this. She pulled the wool over your eyes as much as Mitch's!

STELLA. It's pure invention! There's not a word of truth in it and if I were a man and this creature had dared to invent such things in my presence—

BLANCHE [*singing*]. "Without your love, It's a honky-tonk parade! Without your love, It's a melody played In a penny arcade..."

STANLEY. Honey, I told you I thoroughly checked on these stories! Now wait till I finished. The trouble with Dame Blanche was that she couldn't put on her act any more in Laurel! They got wised up after two or three dates with her and then they quit, and she goes on to another, the same old line, same old act, same old hooey! But the town was too small for this to go on forever! And as time went by she became a town character. Regarded as not just different but downright loco—nuts.

[*Stella draws back.*]

And for the last year or two she has been washed up like poison. That's why she's here this summer, visiting royalty, putting on all this act—because she's practically told by the mayor to get out of town! Yes, did you know there was an army camp near Laurel and your sister's was one of the places called "Out-of-Bounds"?

BLANCHE. "It's only a paper moon, Just as phony as it can be—
  But it wouldn't be make-believe If you believed in me!"

STANLEY. Well, so much for her being such a refined and particular type of girl. Which brings us to Lie Number Two.

STELLA. I don't want to hear any more!

STANLEY. She's not going back to teach school! In fact I am willing to bet you that she never had no idea of returning to Laurel! She didn't resign temporarily from the high school because of her nerves! No, siree, Bob! She didn't. They kicked her out of that high school before the spring term ended—and I hate to tell you the reason that step was taken! A seventeen-year-old boy—she'd gotten mixed up with!

BLANCHE. "It's a Barnum and Bailey world, Just as phony as it can be—"

[*In the bathroom the water goes on loud; little breathless cries and peals of laughter are heard as if a child were frolicking in the tub.*]

STELLA. This is making me—sick!

STANLEY. The boy's dad learned about it and got in touch with the high school superintendent. Boy, oh, boy, I'd like to have been in that office when Dame Blanche was called on the carpet! I'd like to have seen her trying to squirm out of that one! But they had her on the hook good and proper that time and she knew that the jig was all up! They told her she better move on to' some fresh territory. Yep, it was practickly a town ordinance passed against her!

[*The bathroom door is opened and Blanche thrusts her head out, holding a towel about her hair.*]

BLANCHE. Stella!

STELLA [*faintly*]. Yes, Blanche?

BLANCHE. Give me another bath-towel to dry my hair with. I've just washed it.

STELLA. Yes, Blanche. [*She crosses in a dazed way from the kitchen to the bathroom door with a towel.*]

BLANCHE. What's the matter, honey?

STELLA. Matter? Why?

BLANCHE. You have such a strange expression on your face!

STELLA. Oh—[*She tries to laugh*] I guess I'm a little tired!

BLANCHE. Why don't you bathe, too, soon as I get out?

STANLEY [*calling from the kitchen*]. How soon is that going to be?

BLANCHE. Not so terribly long! Possess your soul in patience!

STANLEY. It's not my soul, it's my kidneys I'm worried about!

[*Blanche slams the door. Stanley laughs harshly. Stella comes slowly back into the kitchen.*]

STANLEY. Well, what do you think of it?

STELLA. I don't believe all of those stories and I think your supply-man was mean and rotten to tell them. It's possible that some of the things he said are partly true. There are things about my sister I don't approve of—things that caused sorrow at home. She was always—flighty!

STANLEY. Flighty!

STELLA. But when she was young, very young, she married a boy who wrote poetry. . . . He was extremely good-looking. I think Blanche didn't just love him but she worshipped the ground he walked on! Adored him and thought him almost too fine to be human! But then she found out—

STANLEY. What?

STELLA. This beautiful and talented young man was a degenerate. Didn't your supply-man give you that information?

STANLEY. All we discussed was recent history.

That must have been a pretty long time ago.

STELLA. Yes, it was—a pretty long time ago . . .

[*Stanley comes up and takes her by the shoulders rather gently. She gently withdraws from him. Automatically she starts sticking little pink candles in the birthday cake.*]

STANLEY. How many candles you putting in that cake?

STELLA. I'll stop at twenty-five.

STANLEY. Is company expected?

STELLA. We asked Mitch to come over for cake and ice-cream.

[*Stanley looks a little uncomfortable. He lights a cigarette from the one he has just finished.*]

STANLEY. I wouldn't be expecting Mitch over tonight.

[*Stella pauses in her occupation with candles and looks slowly around at Stanley.*]

STELLA. *Why?*

STANLEY. Mitch is a buddy of mine. We were in the same outfit together—Two-forty-first Engineers. We work in the same plant and now on the same bowling team. You think I could face him if—

STELLA. Stanley Kowalski, did you—did you repeat what that—?

STANLEY. You're goddam right I told him! I'd have that on my conscience the rest of my life if I knew all that stuff and let my best friend get caught!

STELLA. Is Mitch through with her?

STANLEY. Wouldn't you be if—?

STELLA. I said, *Is Mitch through with her?*

[*Blanche's voice is lifted again, serenely as a bell. She sings "But it wouldn't be make-believe if you believed in me."*]

STANLEY. No, I don't think he's necessarily through with her—just wised up!

STELLA. Stanley, she thought Mitch was—going to—going to marry her. I was hoping so, too.

STANLEY. Well, he's not going to marry her. Maybe he *was*, but he's not going to jump in a tank with a school of sharks—now! [*He rises*] Blanche! Oh, Blanche! Can I please get in my bathroom? [*There is a pause.*]

BLANCHE. Yes, indeed, sir! Can you wait one second while I dry?

STANLEY. Having waited one hour I guess one second ought to pass in a hurry.

STELLA. And she hasn't got her job? Well, what will she do!

STANLEY. She's not stayin' here after Tuesday. You know that, don't you? Just to make sure I bought her ticket myself. A bus-ticket!

STELLA. In the first place, Blanche wouldn't go on a bus.

STANLEY. She'll go on a bus and like it.

STELLA. No, she won't, no, she won't, Stanley!

STANLEY. *She'll go!* Period. P.S. She'll go *Tuesday!*

STELLA [*slowly*]. What'll—she—do? What on earth will she—*do!*

STANLEY. Her future is mapped out for her.

STELLA. What do you mean?

[*Blanche sings.*]

STANLEY. Hey, canary bird! Toots! Get OUT of the *BATHROOM!*

[*The bathroom door flies open and Blanche emerges with a gay peal of laughter, but as Stanley crosses past her, a frightened look appears in her face, almost a look of panic. He doesn't look at her but slams the bathroom door shut as he goes in.*]

BLANCHE [*snatching up a hair-brush*]. Oh, I feel so good after my long, hot bath, I feel so good and cool and—rested!

STELLA [*sadly and doubtfully from the kitchen*]. Do you, Blanche?

BLANCHE [*brushing her hair vigorously*]. Yes, I do, so refreshed! [*She tinkles her high-ball glass.*] A hot bath and a long, cold drink always give me a brand new outlook on life! [*She looks through the portieres at Stella, standing between them, and slowly stops brushing*] Something has happened!—What is it?

STELLA [*turning away quickly*]. Why, nothing has happened, Blanche.

BLANCHE. You're lying! Something has!

[*She stares fearfully at Stella, who pretends to be busy at the table. The distant piano goes into a hectic breakdown.*]

Scene Eight

Three-quarters of an hour later.

The view through the big windows is fading gradually into a still-golden dusk. A torch of sunlight blazes on the side of a big water-tank or oil-drum across the empty lot toward the business district which is now pierced by pinpoints of lighted windows or windows reflecting the sunset.

The three people are completing a dismal birthday supper. Stanley looks sullen. Stella is embarrassed and sad.

Blanche has a tight, artificial smile on her drawn face. There is a fourth place at the table which is left vacant.

BLANCHE [*suddenly*]. Stanley, tell us a joke, tell us a funny story to make us all laugh. I don't know what's the matter, we're all so solemn. Is it because I've been stood up by my beau?

[*Stella laughs feebly.*]

It's the first time in my entire experience with men, and I've had a good deal of all sorts, that I've actually been stood up by anybody! Ha-ha! I don't know how to take it. . . . Tell us a funny little story, Stanley! Something to help us out.

STANLEY. I didn't think you liked my stories, Blanche.

BLANCHE. I like them when they're amusing but not indecent.

STANLEY. I don't know any refined enough for your taste.

BLANCHE. Then let me tell one.

STELLA. Yes, you tell one, Blanche. You used to know lots of good stories.

[*The music fades.*]

BLANCHE. Let me see, now. . . . I must run through my repertoire! Oh, yes—I love parrot stories! Do you all like parrot stories? Well, this one's about the old maid and the parrot. This old maid, she had a parrot that cursed a blue streak and knew more vulgar expressions than Mr. Kowalski!

STANLEY. Huh.

BLANCHE. And the only way to hush the parrot up was to put the cover back on its cage so it would think it was night and go back to sleep. Well, one morning the old maid had just uncovered the parrot for the day —when who should she see coming up the front walk but the preacher! Well, she rushed back to the parrot and slipped the cover back on the cage and then she let in the preacher. And the parrot was perfectly still, just as quiet as a mouse, but just as she was asking the preacher how much sugar he wanted in his coffee—the parrot broke the silence with a loud—[*She whistles*]—and said—"God *damn*, but that was a short day!"

[*She throws back her head and laughs. Stella also makes an ineffectual effort to seem amused. Stanley pays no attention to the story but reaches way over the table to spear his fork into the remaining chop which he eats with his fingers.*]

BLANCHE. Apparently Mr. Kowalski was not amused.

STELLA. Mr. Kowalski is too busy making a pig of himself to think of anything else!

STANLEY. That's right, baby.

STELLA. Your face and your fingers are disgustingly greasy. Go and wash up and then help me clear the table.

[*He hurls a plate to the floor.*]

STANLEY. That's how I'll clear the table! [*He seizes her arm*] Don't ever talk that way to me! "Pig—Polack—disgusting—vulgar—greasy!"—them kind of words have been on your tongue and your sister's too much around here! What do you two think you are? A pair of queens? Remember what Huey Long said—"Every Man is a King!" And I am the king around here, so don't forget it! [*He hurls a cup and saucer to the floor*] My place is cleared! You want me to clear your places?

[*Stella begins to cry weakly. Stanley stalks out on the porch and lights a cigarette.*

[*The Negro entertainers around the corner are heard.*]

BLANCHE. What happened while I was bathing? What did he tell you, Stella?

STELLA. Nothing, nothing, nothing!

BLANCHE. I think he told you something about Mitch and me! You know why Mitch didn't come but you won't tell me! [*Stella shakes her head helplessly*] I'm going to call him!

STELLA. I wouldn't call him, Blanche.

BLANCHE. I am, I'm going to call him on the phone.

STELLA [*miserably*]. I wish you wouldn't.

BLANCHE. I intend to be given some explanation from someone!

[*She rushes to the phone in the bedroom. Stella goes out on the porch and stares reproachfully at her husband. He grunts and turns away from her.*]

STELLA. I hope you're pleased with your doings. I never had so much trouble swallowing food in my life, looking at that girl's face and the empty chair! [*She cries quietly.*]

BLANCHE [*at the phone*]. Hello. Mr. Mitchell, please. . . . Oh. . . . I would like to leave a number if I may. Magnolia 9047. And say it's important to call. . . . Yes, very important. . . . Thank you. [*She remains by the phone with a lost, frightened look.*]

[*Stanley turns slowly back toward his wife and takes her clumsily in his arms.*]

STANLEY. Stell, it's gonna be all right after she goes and after you've had the baby. It's gonna be all right again between you and me the way that it was. You remember that way that it was? Them nights we had together? God, honey, it's gonna be sweet when we can make noise in the night the way that we used to and get the colored lights going with nobody's sister behind the curtains to hear us!

[*Their upstairs neighbors are heard in bellowing laughter at something. Stanley chuckles.*]

Steve an' Eunice. . . .

STELLA. Come on back in. [*She returns to the kitchen and starts lighting the candles on the white cake.*] Blanche?

BLANCHE. Yes. [*She returns from the bedroom to the table in the kitchen.*] Oh, those pretty, pretty little candles! Oh, don't burn them, Stella.

STELLA. I certainly will.

[*Stanley comes back in.*]

BLANCHE. You ought to save them for baby's birthdays. Oh, I hope candles are going to glow in his life and I hope that his eyes are going to be like candles, like two blue candles lighted in a white cake!

STANLEY [*sitting down*]. What poetry!

BLANCHE [*she pauses reflectively for a moment*]. I shouldn't have called him.

STELLA. There's lots of things could have happened.

BLANCHE. There's no excuse for it, Stella. I don't have to put up with insults. I won't be taken for granted.

STANLEY. Goddamn, it's hot in here with the steam from the bathroom.

BLANCHE. I've said I was sorry three times. [*The piano fades out.*] I take hot baths for my nerves. Hydro-therapy, they call it. You healthy Polack, without a nerve in your body, of course you don't know what anxiety feels like!

STANLEY. I am not a Polack. People from Poland are Poles, not Polacks. But what I am is a one hundred percent American, born and raised in the greatest country on earth and proud as hell of it, so don't ever call me a Polack.

[*The phone rings. Blanche rises expectantly.*]

BLANCHE. Oh, that's for me, I'm sure.

STANLEY. *I'm* not sure. Keep your seat. [*He crosses leisurely to phone.*] H'lo. Aw, yeh, hello, Mac.

[*He leans against wall, staring insultingly in at Blanche. She sinks back in her chair with a frightened look. Stella leans over and touches her shoulder.*]

BLANCHE. Oh, keep your hands off me, Stella. What is the matter with you? Why do you look at me with that pitying look?

STANLEY [*bawling*]. QUIET IN THERE!— We've got a noisy woman on the place.— Go on, Mac. At Riley's? No, I don't wanta bowl at Riley's. I had a little trouble with Riley last week. I'm the team-captain, ain't I? All right, then, we're not gonna bowl at Riley's, we're gonna bowl at the West Side or the Gala! All right, Mac. See you!

[*He hangs up and returns to the table. Blanche fiercely controls herself, drinking quickly from her tumbler of water. He doesn't look at her but reaches in a pocket. Then he speaks slowly and with false amiability.*]

Sister Blanche, I've got a little birthday remembrance for you.

BLANCHE. Oh, have you, Stanley? I wasn't expecting any, I—I don't know why Stella wants to observe my birthday! I'd much rather forget it—when you—reach twenty-seven! Well—age is a subject that you'd prefer to—ignore!

STANLEY. Twenty-seven?

BLANCHE [*quickly*]. What is it? Is it for *me?*

[*He is holding a little envelope toward her.*]

STANLEY. Yes, I hope you like it!

BLANCHE. Why, why—Why, it's a—

STANLEY. Ticket! Back to Laurel! On the Greyhound! Tuesday!

[*The Varsouviana music steals in softly and continues playing. Stella rises abruptly and turns her back. Blanche tries to smile. Then she tries to laugh. Then she gives both up and springs from the table and runs into the next room. She clutches her throat and then runs into the bathroom. Coughing, gagging sounds are heard.*]

Well!

STELLA. You didn't need to do that.

STANLEY. Don't forget all that I took off her.

STELLA. You needn't have been so cruel to someone alone as she is.

STANLEY. Delicate piece she is.

STELLA. She is. She was. You didn't know Blanche as a girl. Nobody, nobody, was tender and trusting as she was. But people like you abused her, and forced her to change.

[*He crosses into the bedroom, ripping off his shirt, and changes into a brilliant silk bowling shirt. She follows him.*]

Do you think you're going bowling now?

STANLEY. Sure.

STELLA. You're not going bowling. [*She catches hold of his shirt*] Why did you do this to her?

STANLEY. I done nothing to no one. Let go of my shirt. You've torn it.

STELLA. I want to know why. Tell me why.

STANLEY. When we first met, me and you, you thought I was common. How right you was, baby. I was common as dirt. You showed me the snapshot of the place with the columns. I pulled you down off them columns and how you loved it, having them colored lights going! And wasn't we happy together, wasn't it all okay till she showed here?

[*Stella makes a slight movement. Her look goes suddenly inward as if some interior voice had called her name. She begins a slow, shuffling progress from the bedroom to the kitchen, leaning and resting on the back of the chair and then on the edge of a table with a blind look and listening expression. Stanley, finishing with his shirt, is unaware of her reaction.*]

And wasn't we happy together? Wasn't it all okay? Till she showed here. Hoity-toity, describing me as an ape. [*He suddenly notices the change in Stella*] Hey, what is it, Stel? [*He crosses to her.*]

STELLA [*quietly*]. Take me to the hospital.

[*He is with her now, supporting her with his arm, murmuring indistinguishably as they go outside.*]

Scene Nine

A while later that evening. Blanche is seated in a tense hunched position in a bedroom chair that she has recovered with diagonal green and white stripes. She has on her scarlet satin robe. On the table beside chair is a bottle of liquor and a glass. The rapid, feverish polka tune, the "Varsouviana," is heard. The music is in her mind; she is drinking to escape it and the sense of disaster closing in on her, and she seems to whisper the words of the song. An electric fan is turning back and forth across her.

Mitch comes around the corner in work clothes: blue denim shirt and pants. He is unshaven. He climbs the steps to the door and rings. Blanche is startled.

BLANCHE. Who is it, please?

MITCH [*hoarsely*]. Me. Mitch.

[*The polka tune stops.*]

BLANCHE. Mitch!—Just a minute.

[*She rushes about frantically, hiding the bottle in a closet, crouching at the mirror and dabbing her face with cologne and powder. She is so excited that her breath is audible as she dashes about. At last she rushes to the door in the kitchen and lets him in.*]

Mitch!—Y'know, I really shouldn't let you in after the treatment I have received from you this evening! So utterly uncavalier! But hello, beautiful!

[*She offers him her lips. He ignores it and pushes past her into the flat. She looks fearfully after him as he stalks into the bedroom.*]

My, my, what a cold shoulder! And such uncouth apparel! Why, you haven't even shaved! The unforgivable insult to a lady! But I forgive you. I forgive you because it's such a relief to see you. You've stopped that polka tune that I had caught in my head. Have you ever had anything caught in your head? No, of course you haven't, you dumb angel-puss, you'd never get anything awful caught in your head!

[*He stares at her while she follows him while she talks. It is obvious that he has had a few drinks on the way over.*]

MITCH. Do we have to have that fan on?

BLANCHE. No!

MITCH. I don't like fans.

BLANCHE. Then let's turn it off, honey. I'm not partial to them!

[*She presses the switch and the fan nods slowly off. She clears her throat uneasily as Mitch plumps himself down on the bed in the bedroom and lights a cigarette.*]

I don't know what there is to drink. I—haven't investigated.

MITCH. I don't want Stan's liquor.

BLANCHE. It isn't Stan's. Everything here isn't Stan's. Some things on the premises are actually mine! How is your mother? Isn't your mother well?

MITCH. Why?

BLANCHE. Something's the matter tonight, but never mind. I won't cross-examine the witness. I'll just— [*She touches her forehead vaguely. The polka tune starts up again.*] —pretend I don't notice anything different about you! That—music again . . .

MITCH. What music?

BLANCHE. The "Varsouviana"! The polka tune they were playing when Allan— Wait!

[*A distant revolver shot is heard. Blanche seems relieved.*]

There now, the shot! It always stops after that.

[*The polka music dies out again.*]

Yes, now it's stopped.

MITCH. Are you boxed out of your mind?

BLANCHE. I'll go and see what I can find in the way of— [*She crosses into the closet, pretending to search for the bottle.*] Oh, by the way, excuse me for not being dressed. But I'd practically given you up! Had you forgotten your invitation to supper?

MITCH. I wasn't going to see you any more.

BLANCHE. Wait a minute. I can't hear what you're saying and you talk so little that when you do say something, I don't want to miss a single syllable of it. . . . What am I looking around here for? Oh, yes—liquor! We've had so much excitement around here this evening that I *am* boxed out of my mind! [*She pretends suddenly to find*

the bottle. *He draws his foot up on the bed and stares at her contemptuously.*] Here's something. Southern Comfort! What is that, I wonder?

MITCH. If you don't know, it must belong to Stan.

BLANCHE. Take your foot off the bed. It has a light cover on it. Of course you boys don't notice things like that. I've done so much with this place since I've been here.

MITCH. I bet you have.

BLANCHE. You saw it before I came. Well, look at it now! This room is almost—dainty! I want to keep it that way. I wonder if this stuff ought to be mixed with something? Ummm, it's sweet, so sweet! It's terribly, terribly sweet! Why, it's a *liqueur*, I believe! Yes, that's what it *is*, a liqueur! [*Mitch grunts.*] I'm afraid you won't like it, but try it, and maybe you will.

MITCH. I told you already I don't want none of his liquor and I mean it. You ought to lay off his liquor. He says you been lapping it up all summer like a wild-cat!

BLANCHE. What a fantastic statement! Fantastic of him to say it, fantastic of you to repeat it! I won't descend to the level of such cheap accusations to answer them, even!

MITCH. Huh.

BLANCHE. What's in your mind? I see something in your eyes!

MITCH [*getting up*]. It's dark in here.

BLANCHE. I like it dark. The dark is comforting to me.

MITCH. I don't think I ever seen you in the light. [*Blanche laughs breathlessly*] That's a fact!

BLANCHE. Is it?

MITCH. I've never seen you in the afternoon.

BLANCHE. Whose fault is that?

MITCH. You never want to go out in the afternoon.

BLANCHE. Why, Mitch, you're at the plant in the afternoon!

MITCH. Not Sunday afternoon. I've asked you to go out with me sometimes on Sundays but you always make an excuse.

You never want to go out till after six and then it's always some place that's not lighted much.

BLANCHE. There is some obscure meaning in this but I fail to catch it.

MITCH. What it means is I've never had a real good look at you, Blanche. Let's turn the light on here.

BLANCHE [*fearfully*]. Light? Which light? What for?

MITCH. This one with the paper thing on it. [*He tears the paper lantern off the light bulb. She utters a frightened gasp.*]

BLANCHE. What did you do that for?

MITCH. So I can take a look at you good and plain!

BLANCHE. Of course you don't really mean to be insulting!

MITCH. No, just realistic.

BLANCHE. I don't want realism. I want magic! [*Mitch laughs*] Yes, yes, magic! I try to give that to people. I misrepresent things to them. I don't tell truth, I tell what *ought* to be truth. And if that is sinful, then let me be damned for it!—*Don't turn the light on!*

[*Mitch crosses to the switch. He turns the light on and stares at her. She cries out and covers her face. He turns the light off again.*]

MITCH [*slowly and bitterly*]. I don't mind you being older than what I thought. But all the rest of it—Christ! That pitch about your ideals being so old-fashioned and all that malarkey that you've dished out all summer. Oh, I knew you weren't sixteen any more. But I was a fool enough to believe you was straight.

BLANCHE. Who told you I wasn't—'straight'? My loving brother-in-law. And you believed him.

MITCH. I called him a liar at first. And then I checked on the story. First I asked our supply-man who travels through Laurel. And then I talked directly over long-distance to this merchant.

BLANCHE. Who is this merchant?

MITCH. Kiefaber.

BLANCHE. The merchant Kiefaber of Laurel! I know the man. He whistled at me. I put him in his place. So now for revenge he makes up stories about me.

MITCH. Three people, Kiefaber, Stanley and Shaw, swore to them!

BLANCHE. Rub-a-dub-dub, three men in a tub! And such a filthy tub!

MITCH. Didn't you stay at a hotel called The Flamingo?

BLANCHE. Flamingo? No! Tarantula was the name of it! I stayed at a hotel called The Tarantula Arms!

MITCH [*stupidly*]. Tarantula?

BLANCHE. Yes, a big spider! That's where I brought my victims. [*She pours herself another drink*] Yes, I had many intimacies with strangers. After the death of Allan—intimacies with strangers was all I seemed able to fill my empty heart with.... I think it was panic, just panic, that drove me from one to another, hunting for some protection—here and there, in the most—unlikely places—even, at last, in a seventeen-year-old boy but—somebody wrote the superintendent about it—"This woman is morally unfit for her position!"

[*She throws back her head with convulsive, sobbing laughter. Then she repeats the statement, gasps, and drinks.*]

True? Yes, I suppose—unfit somehow—anyway.... So I came here. There was nowhere else I could go. I was played out. You know what played out is? My youth was suddenly gone up the water-spout, and —I met you. You said you needed somebody. Well, I needed somebody, too. I thanked God for you, because you seemed to be gentle—a cleft in the rock of the world that I could hide in! But I guess I was asking, hoping—too much! Kiefaber, Stanley and Shaw have tied an old tin can to the tail of the kite.

[*There is a pause. Mitch stares at her dumbly.*]

MITCH. You lied to me, Blanche.

BLANCHE. Don't say I lied to you.

MITCH. Lies, lies, inside and out, all lies.

BLANCHE. Never inside, I didn't lie in my heart . . .

[*A Vendor comes around the corner. She is a blind Mexican woman in a dark shawl, carrying bunches of those gaudy tin flowers that lower class Mexicans display at funerals and other festive occasions. She is calling barely audibly. Her figure is only faintly visible outside the building.*]

MEXICAN WOMAN. Flores. Flores. Flores para los muertos. Flores. Flores.

BLANCHE. What! Oh! Somebody outside . . . [*She goes to the door, opens it and stares at the Mexican Woman.*]

MEXICAN WOMAN [*she is at the door and offers Blanche some of her flowers*]. Flores? Flores para los muertos?

BLANCHE [*frightened*]. No, no! Not now! Not now!

[*She darts back into the apartment, slamming the door.*]

MEXICAN WOMAN [*she turns away and starts to move down the street.*] Flores para los muertos.

[*The polka tune fades in.*]

BLANCHE [*as if to herself*]. Crumble and fade and—regrets—recriminations . . . 'If you'd done this, it wouldn't've cost me that!'

MEXICAN WOMAN. Corones para los muertos. Corones . . .

BLANCHE. Legacies! Huh. . . . And other things such as bloodstained pillow-slips— 'Her linen needs changing'—'Yes Mother. But couldn't we get a colored girl to do it?' No, we couldn't of course. Everything gone but the—

MEXICAN WOMAN. Flores.

BLANCHE. Death—I used to sit here and she used to sit over there and death was as close as you are. . . . We didn't dare even admit we had ever heard of it!

MEXICAN WOMAN. Flores para los muertos, flores—flores . . .

BLANCHE. The opposite is desire. So do you wonder? How could you possibly wonder! Not far from Belle Reve, before we had lost Belle Reve, was a camp where they trained young soldiers. On Saturday nights they would go in town to get drunk—

MEXICAN WOMAN [*softly*]. Corones . . .

BLANCHE.—and on the way back they would stagger onto my lawn and call—'Blanche! Blanche!'—The deaf old lady remaining suspected nothing. But sometimes I slipped outside to answer their calls. . . . Later the paddy-wagon would gather them up like daisies . . . the long way home . . .

[*The Mexican Woman turns slowly and drifts back off with her soft mournful cries. Blanche goes to the dresser and leans forward on it. After a moment, Mitch rises and follows her purposefully. The polka music fades away. He places his hands on her waist and tries to turn her about.*]

BLANCHE. What do you want?

MITCH [*fumbling to embrace her*]. What I been missing all summer.

BLANCHE. Then marry me, Mitch!

MITCH. I don't think I want to marry you any more.

BLANCHE. No?

MITCH [*dropping his hands from her waist*]. You're not clean enough to bring in the house with my mother.

BLANCHE. Go away, then. [*He stares at her*] Get out of here quick before I start screaming fire! [*Her throat is tightening with hysteria*] Get out of here quick before I start screaming fire.

[*He still remains staring. She suddenly rushes to the big window with its pale blue square of the soft summer light and cries wildly.*]

Fire! Fire! Fire!

[*With a startled gasp, Mitch turns and goes out the outer door, clatters awkwardly down the steps and around the corner of the building. Blanche staggers back from the window and falls to her knees. The distant piano is slow and blue.*]

Scene Ten

It is a few hours later that night.

Blanche has been drinking fairly steadily since Mitch left. She has dragged her ward-robe trunk into the center of the bedroom. It hangs open with flowery dresses thrown across it. As the drinking and packing went on, a mood of hysterical exhilaration came into her and she has decked herself out in a somewhat soiled and crumpled white satin evening gown and a pair of scuffed silver slippers with brilliants set in their heels.

Now she is placing the rhinestone tiara on her head before the mirror of the dressing-table and murmuring excitedly as if to a group of spectral admirers.

BLANCHE. How about taking a swim, a moonlight swim at the old rock-quarry? If anyone's sober enough to drive a car! Ha-ha! Best way in the world to stop your head buzzing! Only you've got to be care-ful to dive where the deep pool is—if you hit a rock you don't come up till tomor-row . . .

[*Tremblingly she lifts the hand mirror for a closer inspection. She catches her breath and slams the mirror face down with such viol-ence that the glass cracks. She moans a little and attempts to rise.*

[*Stanley appears around the corner of the building. He still has on the vivid green silk bowling shirt. As he rounds the corner the honky-tonk music is heard. It continues softly throughout the scene.*

[*He enters the kitchen, slamming the door. As he peers in at Blanche, he gives a low*

whistle. He has had a few drinks on the way and has brought some quart beer bottles home with him.]

BLANCHE. How is my sister?
STANLEY. She is doing okay.
BLANCHE. And how is the baby?
STANLEY [*grinning amiably*]. The baby won't come before morning so they told me to go home and get a little shut-eye.
BLANCHE. Does that mean we are to be alone in here?
STANLEY. Yep. Just me and you, Blanche. Unless you got somebody hid under the bed. What've you got on those fine feathers for?
BLANCHE. Oh, that's right. You left before my wire came.
STANLEY. You got a wire?
BLANCHE. I received a telegram from an old admirer of mine.
STANLEY. Anything good?
BLANCHE. I think so. An invitation.
STANLEY. What to? A fireman's ball?
BLANCHE [*throwing back her head*]. A cruise of the Caribbean on a yacht!
STANLEY. Well, well. What do you know?
BLANCHE. I have never been so surprised in my life.
STANLEY. I guess not.
BLANCHE. It came like a bolt from the blue!
STANLEY. Who did you say it was from?
BLANCHE. An old beau of mine.
STANLEY. The one that give you the white fox-pieces?
BLANCHE. Mr. Shep Huntleigh. I wore his ATO pin my last year at college. I hadn't seen him again until last Christmas. I ran into him on Biscayne Boulevard. Then—just now—this wire—inviting me on a cruise of the Caribbean! The problem is clothes. I tore into my trunk to see what I have that's suitable for the tropics!
STANLEY. And come up with that—gor-geous—diamond—tiara?
BLANCHE. This old relic? Ha-ha! It's only rhinestones.
STANLEY. Gosh. I thought it was Tiffany diamonds. [*He unbuttons his shirt.*]

BLANCHE. Well, anyhow, I shall be entertained in style.

STANLEY. Uh-huh. It goes to show, you never know what is coming.

BLANCHE. Just when I thought my luck had begun to fail me—

STANLEY. Into the picture pops this Miami millionaire.

BLANCHE. This man is not from Miami. This man is from Dallas.

STANLEY. This man is from Dallas?

BLANCHE. Yes, this man is from Dallas where gold spouts out of the ground!

STANLEY. Well, just so he's from somewhere! [*He starts removing his shirt.*]

BLANCHE. Close the curtains before you undress any further.

STANLEY [*amiably*]. This is all I'm going to undress right now. [*He rips the sack off a quart beer-bottle*] Seen a bottle-opener?

[*She moves slowly toward the dresser, where she stands with her hands knotted together.*]

I used to have a cousin who could open a beer-bottle with his teeth. [*Pounding the bottle cap on the corner of table*] That was his only accomplishment, all he could do—he was just a human bottle-opener. And then one time, at a wedding party, he broke his front teeth off! After that he was so ashamed of himself he used t' sneak out of the house when company came . . .

[*The bottle cap pops off and a geyser of foam shoots up. Stanley laughs happily, holding up the bottle over his head.*]

Ha-ha! Rain from heaven! [*He extends the bottle toward her*] Shall we bury the hatchet and make it a loving-cup? Huh?

BLANCHE. No, thank you.

STANLEY. Well, it's a red letter night for us both. You having an oil-millionaire and me having a baby.

[*He goes to the bureau in the bedroom and crouches to remove something from the bottom drawer.*]

BLANCHE [*drawing back*]. What are you doing in here?

STANLEY. Here's something I always break out on special occasions like this. The silk pyjamas I wore on my wedding night!

BLANCHE. Oh.

STANLEY. When the telephone rings and they say, "You've got a son!" I'll tear this off and wave it like a flag! [*He shakes out a brilliant pyjama coat*] I guess we are both entitled to put on the dog. [*He goes back to the kitchen with the coat over his arm.*]

BLANCHE. When I think of how divine it is going to be to have such a thing as privacy once more—I could weep with joy!

STANLEY. This millionaire from Dallas is not going to interfere with your privacy any?

BLANCHE. It won't be the sort of thing you have in mind. This man is a gentleman and he respects me. [*Improvising feverishly*] What he wants is my companionship. Having great wealth sometimes makes people lonely! A cultivated woman, a woman of intelligence and breeding, can enrich a man's life—immeasurably! I have those things to offer, and this doesn't take them away. Physical beauty is passing. A transitory possession. But beauty of the mind and richness of the spirit and tenderness of the heart—and I have all of those things—aren't taken away, but grow! Increase with the years! How strange that I should be called a destitute woman! When I have all of those treasures locked in my heart. [*A choked sob comes from her*] I think of myself as a very, very rich woman! But I have been foolish—casting my pearls before swine!

STANLEY. Swine, huh?

BLANCHE. Yes, swine! Swine! And I'm thinking not only of you but of your friend, Mr. Mitchell. He came to see me tonight. He dared to come here in his work-clothes! And to repeat slander to me, vicious stories that he had gotten from you! I gave him his walking papers . . .

STANLEY. You did, huh?

BLANCHE. But then he came back. He returned with a box of roses to beg my forgiveness! He implored my forgiveness. But some things are not forgivable. Deliberate cruelty is not forgivable. It is the one unforgivable thing in my opinion and it is the one thing of which I have never, never been guilty. And so I told him, I said to him, "Thank you," but it was foolish of me to think that we could ever adapt ourselves to each other. Our ways of life are too different. Our attitudes and our backgrounds are incompatible. We have to be realistic about such things. So farewell, my friend! And let there be no hard feelings . . .

STANLEY. Was this before or after the telegram came from the Texas oil millionaire?

BLANCHE. What telegram? No! No, after! As a matter of fact, the wire came just as—

STANLEY. As a matter of fact there wasn't no wire at all!

BLANCHE. Oh, oh!

STANLEY. There isn't no millionaire! And Mitch didn't come back with roses 'cause I know where he is—

BLANCHE. Oh!

STANLEY. There isn't a goddam thing but imagination!

BLANCHE. Oh!

STANLEY. And lies and conceit and tricks!

BLANCHE. Oh!

STANLEY. And look at yourself! Take a look at yourself in that worn-out Mardi Gras outfit, rented for fifty cents from some rag-picker! And with the crazy crown on! What queen do you think you are?

BLANCHE. Oh—God . . .

STANLEY. I've been on to you from the start! Not once did you pull any wool over this boy's eyes! You come in here and sprinkle the place with powder and spray perfume and cover the light-bulb with a paper lantern, and lo and behold the place has turned into Egypt and you are the Queen of the Nile! Sitting on your throne and swilling down my liquor! I say—*Ha!—Ha!* Do you hear me? *Ha—ha—ha!* [*He walks into the bedroom.*]

BLANCHE. Don't come in here!

[*Lurid reflections appear on the walls around Blanche. The shadows are of a grotesque and menacing form. She catches her breath, crosses to the phone and jiggles the hook. Stanley goes into the bathroom and closes the door.*]

Operator, operator! Give me long-distance, please. . . . I want to get in touch with Mr. Shep Huntleigh of Dallas. He's so well-known he doesn't require any address. Just ask anybody who—Wait!!—No, I couldn't find it right now. . . . Please understand, I—No! No, wait! . . . One moment! Someone is—Nothing! Hold on, please!

[*She sets the phone down and crosses warily into the kitchen. The night is filled with inhuman voices like cries in a jungle.*

[*The shadows and lurid reflections move sinuously as flames along the wall spaces.*

[*Through the back wall of the rooms, which have become transparent, can be seen the sidewalk. A prostitute has rolled a drunkard. He pursues her along the walk, overtakes her and there is a struggle. A policeman's whistle breaks it up. The figures disappear.*

[*Some moments later the Negro Woman appears around the corner with a sequined bag which the prostitute had dropped on the walk. She is rooting excitedly through it.*

[*Blanche presses her knuckles to her lips and returns slowly to the phone. She speaks in a hoarse whisper.*]

BLANCHE. Operator! Operator! Never mind long-distance. Get Western Union. There isn't time to be—Western—Western Union!

[*She waits anxiously.*]

Western Union? Yes! I want to—Take down this message! "In desperate, desperate circumstances! Help me! Caught in a trap. Caught in—" *Oh!*

[*The bathroom door is thrown open and Stanley comes out in the brilliant silk pyjamas. He grins at her as he knots the tasseled sash about his waist. She gasps and backs away from the phone. He stares at her for a count of ten. Then a clicking becomes audible from the telephone, steady and rasping.*]

STANLEY. You left th' phone off th' hook.

[*He crosses to it deliberately and sets it back on the hook. After he has replaced it, he stares at her again, his mouth slowly curving into a grin, as he weaves between Blanche and the outer door.*]

[*The barely audible "blue piano" begins to drum up louder. The sound of it turns into the roar of an approaching locomotive. Blanche crouches, pressing her fists to her ears until it has gone by.*]

BLANCHE [*finally straightening*]. Let me—let me get by you!
STANLEY. Get by me? Sure. Go ahead. [*He moves back a pace in the doorway.*]
BLANCHE. You—you stand over there! [*She indicates a further position.*]
STANLEY [*grinning*]. You got plenty of room to walk by me now.
BLANCHE. Not with you there! But I've got to get out somehow!
STANLEY. You think I'll interfere with you? Ha-ha!

[*The "blue piano" goes softly. She turns confusedly and makes a faint gesture. The inhuman jungle voices rise up. He takes a step toward her, biting his tongue which protrudes between his lips.*]

STANLEY [*softly*]. Come to think of it—maybe you wouldn't be bad to—interfere with . . .

[*Blanche moves backward through the door into the bedroom.*]

BLANCHE. Stay back! Don't you come toward me another step or I'll—

STANLEY. What?
BLANCHE. Some awful thing will happen! It will!
STANLEY. What are you putting on now?

[*They are now both inside the bedroom.*]

BLANCHE. I warn you, don't, I'm in danger!

[*He takes another step. She smashes a bottle on the table and faces him, clutching the broken top.*]

STANLEY. What did you do that for?
BLANCHE. So I could twist the broken end in your face!
STANLEY. I bet you would do that!
BLANCHE. I would! I will if you—
STANLEY. Oh! So you want some rough-house! All right, let's have some rough-house!

[*He springs toward her, overturning the table. She cries out and strikes at him with the bottle top but he catches her wrist.*]

Tiger—tiger. Drop the bottle-top! Drop it! We've had this date with each other from the beginning!

[*She moans. The bottle-top falls. She sinks to her knees. He picks up her inert figure and carries her to the bed. The hot trumpet and drums from the Four Deuces sound loudly.*]

Scene Eleven

It is some weeks later. Stella is packing Blanche's things. Sound of water can be heard running in the bathroom.

The portieres are partly open on the poker players—Stanley, Steve, Mitch and Pablo—who sit around the table in the kitchen. The atmosphere of the kitchen is now the same raw, lurid one of the disastrous poker night.

The building is framed by the sky of turquoise. Stella has been crying as she arranges the flowery dresses in the open trunk.

Eunice comes down the steps from her flat above and enters the kitchen. There is an outburst from the poker table.

STANLEY. Drew to an inside straight and made it, by God.

PABLO. *Maldita sea tu suerte!*

STANLEY. Put it in English, greaseball.

PABLO. I am cursing your rutting luck.

STANLEY [*prodigiously elated*]. You know what luck is? Luck is believing you're lucky. Take at Salerno. I believed I was lucky. I figured that 4 out of 5 would not come through but I would . . . and I did. I put that down as a rule. To hold front position in this rat-race you've got to believe you are lucky.

MITCH. You . . . you . . . you. . . . Brag . . . brag . . . bull . . . bull.

[*Stella goes into the bedroom and starts folding a dress.*]

STANLEY. What's the matter with him?

EUNICE [*walking past the table*]. I always did say that men are callous things with no feelings, but this does beat anything. Making pigs of yourselves. [*She comes through the portieres into the bedroom.*]

STANLEY. What's the matter with her?

STELLA. How is my baby?

EUNICE. Sleeping like a little angel. Brought you some grapes. [*She puts them on a stool and lowers her voice.*] Blanche?

STELLA. Bathing.

EUNICE. How is she?

STELLA. She wouldn't eat anything but asked for a drink.

EUNICE. What did you tell her?

STELLA. I—just told her that—we'd made arrangements for her to rest in the country. She's got it mixed in her mind with Shep Huntleigh.

[*Blanche opens the bathroom door slightly.*]

BLANCHE. Stella.

STELLA. Yes, Blanche?

BLANCHE. If anyone calls while I'm bathing take the number and tell them I'll call right back.

STELLA. Yes.

BLANCHE. That cool yellow silk—the bouclé. See if it's crushed. If it's not too crushed I'll wear it and on the lapel that silver and turquoise pin in the shape of a seahorse. You will find them in the heart-shaped box I keep my accessories in. And Stella . . . Try and locate a bunch of artificial violets in that box, too, to pin with the seahorse on the lapel of the jacket.

[*She closes the door. Stella turns to Eunice.*]

STELLA. I don't know if I did the right thing.

EUNICE. What else could you do?

STELLA. I couldn't believe her story and go on living with Stanley.

EUNICE. Don't ever believe it. Life has got to go on. No matter what happens, you've got to keep on going.

[*The bathroom door opens a little.*]

BLANCHE [*looking out*]. Is the coast clear?

STELLA. Yes, Blanche. [*To Eunice*] Tell her how well she's looking.

BLANCHE. Please close the curtains before I come out.

STELLA. They're closed.

STANLEY. —How many for you?

PABLO. —Two.

STEVE. —Three.

[*Blanche appears in the amber light of the door. She has a tragic radiance in her red satin robe following the sculptural lines of her body. The "Varsouviana" rises audibly as Blanche enters the bedroom.*]

BLANCHE [*with faintly hysterical vivacity*]. I have just washed my hair.

STELLA. Did you?

BLANCHE. I'm not sure I got the soap out.

EUNICE. Such fine hair!

BLANCHE [*accepting the compliment*]. It's a problem. Didn't I get a call?

STELLA. Who from, Blanche?

BLANCHE. Shep Huntleigh . . .

STELLA. Why, not yet, honey!

BLANCHE. How strange! I—

[*At the sound of Blanche's voice Mitch's arm supporting his cards has sagged and his gaze is dissolved into space. Stanley slaps him on the shoulder.*]

STANLEY. Hey, Mitch, come to!

[*The sound of this new voice shocks Blanche. She makes a shocked gesture, forming his name with her lips. Stella nods and looks quickly away. Blanche stands quite still for some moments—the silverbacked mirror in her hand and a look of sorrowful perplexity as though all human experience shows on her face. Blanche finally speaks but with sudden hysteria.*]

BLANCHE. What's going on here?

[*She turns from Stella to Eunice and back to Stella. Her rising voice penetrates the concentration of the game. Mitch ducks his head lower but Stanley shoves back his chair as if about to rise. Steve places a restraining hand on his arm.*]

BLANCHE [*continuing*]. What's happened here? I want an explanation of what's happened here.

STELLA [*agonizingly*]. Hush! Hush!

EUNICE. Hush! Hush! Honey.

STELLA. Please, Blanche.

BLANCHE. Why are you looking at me like that? Is something wrong with me?

EUNICE. You look wonderful, Blanche. Don't she look wonderful?

STELLA. Yes.

EUNICE. I understand you are going on a trip.

STELLA. Yes, Blanche *is*. She's going on a vacation.

EUNICE. I'm green with envy.

BLANCHE. Help me, help me get dressed!

STELLA [*handing her dress*]. Is this what you—

BLANCHE. Yes, it will do! I'm anxious to get out of here—this place is a trap!

EUNICE. What a pretty blue jacket.

STELLA. It's lilac colored.

BLANCHE. You're both mistaken. It's Della Robbia blue. The blue of the robe in the old Madonna pictures. Are these grapes washed?

[*She fingers the bunch of grapes which Eunice had brought in.*]

EUNICE. Huh?

BLANCHE. Washed, I said. Are they washed?

EUNICE. They're from the French Market.

BLANCHE. That doesn't mean they've been washed. [*The cathedral bells chime*] Those cathedral bells—they're the only clean thing in the Quarter. Well, I'm going now. I'm ready to go.

EUNICE [*whispering*]. She's going to walk out before they get here.

STELLA. Wait, Blanche.

BLANCHE. I don't want to pass in front of those men.

EUNICE. Then wait'll the game breaks up.

STELLA. Sit down and . . .

[*Blanche turns weakly, hesitantly about. She lets them push her into a chair.*]

BLANCHE. I can smell the sea air. The rest of my time I'm going to spend on the sea. And when I die, I'm going to die on the sea. You know what I shall die of? [*She plucks a grape*] I shall die of eating an unwashed grape one day out on the ocean. I will die—with my hand in the hand of some nice-looking ship's doctor, a very young one with a small blond mustache and a big silver watch. "Poor lady," they'll say, "the quinine did her no good. That unwashed grape has transported her soul to heaven." [*The cathedral chimes are heard*] And I'll be buried at sea sewn up in a clean white sack and dropped overboard—at noon—in the blaze of summer—and into an ocean as blue as [*Chimes again*] my first lover's eyes!

[*A Doctor and a Matron have appeared around the corner of the building and climbed the steps to the porch. The gravity of their profession is exaggerated—the unmistakable aura of the state institution with its cynical detachment. The Doctor rings the doorbell. The murmur of the game is interrupted.*]

EUNICE [*whispering to Stella*]. That must be them.

[*Stella presses her fists to her lips.*]

BLANCHE [*rising slowly*]. What is it?
EUNICE [*affectedly casual*]. Excuse me while I see who's at the door.
STELLA. Yes.

[*Eunice goes into the kitchen.*]

BLANCHE [*tensely*]. I wonder if it's for me.

[*A whispered colloquy takes place at the door.*]

EUNICE [*returning, brightly*]. Someone is calling for Blanche.
BLANCHE. It *is* for me, then! [*She looks fearfully from one to the other and then to the portieres. The "Varsouviana" faintly plays*] Is it the gentleman I was expecting from Dallas?
EUNICE. I think it is, Blanche.
BLANCHE. I'm not quite ready.
STELLA. Ask him to wait outside.
BLANCHE. I . . .

[*Eunice goes back to the portieres. Drums sound very softly.*]

STELLA. Everything packed?
BLANCHE. My silver toilet articles are still out.
STELLA. Ah!
EUNICE [*returning*]. They're waiting in front of the house.

BLANCHE. They! Who's "they"?
EUNICE. There's a lady with him.
BLANCHE. I cannot imagine who this "lady" could be! How is she dressed?
EUNICE. Just—just a sort of a—plain-tailored outfit.
BLANCHE. Possibly she's—[*Her voice dies out nervously.*]
STELLA. Shall we go, Blanche?
BLANCHE. Must we go through that room?
STELLA. I will go with you.
BLANCHE. How do I look?
STELLA. Lovely.
EUNICE [*echoing*]. Lovely.

[*Blanche moves fearfully to the portieres. Eunice draws them open for her. Blanche goes into the kitchen.*]

BLANCHE [*to the men*]. Please don't get up. I'm only passing through.

[*She crosses quickly to outside door. Stella and Eunice follow. The poker players stand awkwardly at the table—all except Mitch, who remains seated, looking down at the table. Blanche steps out on a small porch at the side of the door. She stops short and catches her breath.*]

DOCTOR. How do you do?
BLANCHE. You are not the gentleman I was expecting. [*She suddenly gasps and starts back up the steps. She stops by Stella, who stands just outside the door, and speaks in a frightening whisper*] That man isn't Shep Huntleigh.

[*The "Varsouviana" is playing distantly.*

[*Stella stares back at Blanche. Eunice is holding Stella's arm. There is a moment of silence—no sound but that of Stanley steadily shuffling the cards.*

[*Blanche catches her breath again and slips back into the flat. She enters the flat with a peculiar smile, her eyes wide and brilliant. As soon as her sister goes past her, Stella closes her eyes and clenches her hands. Eunice throws her arms comfortingly about her. Then she starts up to her flat. Blanche stops just inside the door. Mitch keeps staring down at his hands on the table, but the other men look at her curiously. At last she starts around the table toward the bedroom. As she does, Stanley suddenly pushes back his chair and rises as if to block her way. The Matron follows her into the flat.]*

STANLEY. Did you forget something?

BLANCHE [*shrilly*]. Yes! Yes, I forgot something!

[She rushes past him into the bedroom. Lurid reflections appear on the walls in odd, sinuous shapes. The "Varsouviana" is filtered into a weird distortion, accompanied by the cries and noises of the jungle. Blanche seizes the back of a chair as if to defend herself.]

STANLEY [*sotto voce*]. Doc, you better go in.

DOCTOR [*sotto voce, motioning to the Matron*]. Nurse, bring her out.

[The Matron advances on one side, Stanley on the other. Divested of all the softer properties of womanhood, the Matron is a peculiarly sinister figure in her severe dress. Her voice is bold and toneless as a firebell.]

MATRON. Hello, Blanche.

[The greeting is echoed and re-echoed by other mysterious voices behind the walls, as if reverberated through a canyon of rock.]

STANLEY. She says that she forgot something.

[The echo sounds in threatening whispers.]

MATRON. That's all right.

STANLEY. What did you forget, Blanche?

BLANCHE. I— I—

MATRON. It don't matter. We can pick it up later.

STANLEY. Sure. We can send it along with the trunk.

BLANCHE [*retreating in panic*]. I don't know you—I don't know you. I want to be—left alone—please!

MATRON. Now, Blanche!

ECHOES [*rising and falling*]. Now, Blanche— now, Blanche—now, Blanche!

STANLEY. You left nothing here but spilt talcum and old empty perfume bottles— unless it's the paper lantern you want to take with you. You want the lantern?

[He crosses to dressing table and seizes the paper lantern, tearing it off the light bulb, and extends it toward her. She cries out as if the lantern was herself. The Matron steps boldly toward her. She screams and tries to break past the Matron. All the men spring to their feet. Stella runs out to the porch, with Eunice following to comfort her, simultaneously with the confused voices of the men in the kitchen. Stella rushes into Eunice's embrace on the porch.]

STELLA. Oh, my God, Eunice help me! Don't let them do that to her, don't let them hurt her! Oh, God, oh, please God, don't hurt her! What are they doing to her? What are they doing? [*She tries to break from Eunice's arms.*]

EUNICE. No, honey, no, no, honey. Stay here. Don't go back in there. Stay with me and don't look.

STELLA. What have I done to my sister? Oh, God, what have I done to my sister?

EUNICE. You done the right thing, the only thing you could do. She couldn't stay here; there wasn't no other place for her to go.

[While Stella and Eunice are speaking on the porch the voices of the men in the kitchen overlap them. Mitch has started toward the bedroom. Stanley crosses to block him. Stanley pushes him aside. Mitch lunges and strikes at Stanley. Stanley pushes Mitch back. Mitch collapses at the table, sobbing.]

[During the preceding scenes, the Matron catches hold of Blanche's arm and prevents her flight. Blanche turns wildly and scratches at the Matron. The heavy woman pinions her arms. Blanche cries out hoarsely and slips to her knees.]

MATRON. These fingernails have to be trimmed. [*The Doctor comes into the room and she looks at him.*] Jacket, Doctor?

DOCTOR. Not unless necessary.

[*He takes off his hat and now he becomes personalized. The unhuman quality goes. His voice is gentle and reassuring as he crosses to Blanche and crouches in front of her. As he speaks her name, her terror subsides a little. The lurid reflections fade from the walls, the inhuman cries and noises die out and her own hoarse crying is calmed.*]

DOCTOR. Miss DuBois.

[*She turns her face to him and stares at him with desperate pleading. He smiles; then he speaks to the Matron.*]

It won't be necessary.

BLANCHE [*faintly*]. Ask her to let go of me.

DOCTOR [*to the Matron*]. Let go.

[*The Matron releases her. Blanche extends her hands toward the Doctor. He draws her up gently and supports her with his arm and leads her through the portieres.*]

BLANCHE [*holding tight to his arm*]. Whoever you are—I have always depended on the kindness of strangers.

[*The poker players stand back as Blanche and the Doctor cross the kitchen to the front door. She allows him to lead her as if she were blind. As they go out on the porch, Stella cries out her sister's name from where she is crouched a few steps up on the stairs.*]

STELLA. Blanche! Blanche, Blanche!

[*Blanche walks on without turning, followed by the Doctor and the Matron. They go around the corner of the building.*

[*Eunice descends to Stella and places the child in her arms. It is wrapped in a pale blue blanket. Stella accepts the child, sobbingly. Eunice continues downstairs and enters the kitchen where the men, except for Stanley, are returning silently to their places about the table. Stanley has gone out on the porch and stands at the foot of the steps looking at Stella.*]

STANLEY [*a bit uncertainly*]. Stella?

[*She sobs with inhuman abandon. There is something luxurious in her complete surrender to crying now that her sister is gone.*]

STANLEY [*voluptuously, soothingly*]. Now, honey. Now, love. Now, now, love. [*He kneels beside her and his fingers find the opening of her blouse*] Now, now, love. Now, love. . . .

[*The luxurious sobbing, the sensual murmur fade away under the swelling music of the "blue piano" and the muted trumpet.*]

STEVE. This game is seven-card stud.

Curtain

DIRECTOR'S NOTEBOOK FOR A STREETCAR NAMED DESIRE

Elia Kazan

A thought—directing finally consists of turning Psychology into Behavior.

Theme—this is a message from the dark interior. This little twisted, pathetic, confused bit of light and culture puts out a cry. It is snuffed out by the crude forces of violence, insensibility and vulgarity which exist in our South—and this cry is the play.

Style—one reason a "style," a stylized production is necessary is that a subjective factor —Blanche's memories, inner life, emotions, are a real factor. We cannot really understand her behavior unless we see the effect of her past on her present behavior.

This play is a poetic tragedy. We are shown the final dissolution of a person of worth, who once had great potential, and who, even as she goes down, has worth exceeding that of the "healthy," coarse-grained figures who kill her.

Blanche is a social type, an emblem of a dying civilization, making its last curlicued and romantic exit. All her behavior patterns are those of the dying civilization she represents. In other words her behavior is *social*. Therefore find social modes! This is the source of the play's stylization and the production's style and color. Likewise Stanley's behavior is *social* too. It is the basic animal cynicism of today. "Get what's coming to you! Don't waste a day! Eat, drink, get yours!" This is the basis of his stylization, of the choice of his props. All props should be stylized: they should have a color, shape and weight that spell: style.

An effort to put poetic names on scenes to edge me into stylizations and physicalizations. Try to keep each scene in terms of Blanche.

1. Blanche comes to the last stop at the end of the line.
2. Blanche tries to make a place for herself.
3. Blanche breaks them apart, but when they come together, Blanche is more alone than ever!
4. Blanche, more desperate because more excluded, tries the direct attack and makes the enemy who will finish her.
5. Blanche finds that she is being tracked down for the kill. She must work fast.
6. Blanche suddenly finds, suddenly makes for herself, the only possible, perfect man for her.
7. Blanche comes out of the happy bathroom to find that her own doom has caught up with her.
8. Blanche fights her last fight. Breaks down. Even Stella deserts her.
9. Blanche's last desperate effort to save herself by telling the whole truth. The *truth dooms her.*
10. Blanche escapes out of this world. She is brought back by Stanley and destroyed.
11. Blanche is disposed of.

The style—the real deep style—consists of one thing only: to find behavior that's truly social, significantly typical, at each moment. It's not so much what Blanche has done—it's how she does it—with such style, grace, manners, old-world trappings and effects, props, tricks, swirls, etc., that they seem anything but vulgar.

And for the other characters, too, you face the same problem. To find the Don Quixote character for them. *This is a poetic tragedy, not a realistic or a naturalistic one. So you must find a Don Quixote scheme of things for each.*

Stylized acting and direction is to realistic acting and direction as poetry is to prose. The acting must be styled, not in the obvious sense. (Say nothing about it to the producer and actors.) But you will fail unless you find this kind of poetic realization for the behavior of these people.

BLANCHE

"Blanche is Desperate"
"This is the End of the Line of the Streetcar Named Desire"

Spine—find Protection: the tradition of the old South says that it must be through another person.

Her problem has to do with her tradition. Her notion of what a woman should be. She is stuck with this "ideal." It is her. It is her ego. Unless she lives by it, she cannot live; in fact her whole life has been for nothing. Even the Alan Gray incident as she now tells it and believes it to have been, is a necessary piece of romanticism. Essentially, in outline, she tells what happened, but it also serves the demands of her notion of herself, to make her *special* and different, out of the tradition of the romantic ladies of the past: Swinburne, Wm. Morris, Pre-Raphaelites, etc. This way it serves as an excuse for a great deal of her behavior.

Because this image of herself cannot be accomplished in reality, certainly not in the South of our day and time, it is her effort and practice to *accomplish it in fantasy.* Everything that she does in *reality* too is colored by this necessity, this compulsion to be *special.* So, in fact, *reality becomes fantasy too.* She makes it so!

The variety essential to the play, and to Blanche's playing and to Jessica Tandy's achieving the role demands that she be a "heavy" at the beginning. For instance: contemplate the inner character contradiction: bossy yet helpless, domineering yet shaky, etc. The audience at the beginning should see her bad effect on Stella, want Stanley to tell her off. He does. He exposes her and then gradually, as they see how genuinely in pain, how actually desperate she is, how warm, tender and loving she can be (the Mitch story), how freighted with need she is—then they begin to go with her. They begin to realize that they are sitting in at the death of something extraordinary... colorful, varied, passionate, lost, witty, imaginative, of her own integrity... and then they feel the tragedy. In the playing too there can be a growing sincerity and directness.

The thing about the "tradition" in the nineteenth century was that *it worked then.* It made a woman feel important, with her own secure positions and functions, her own special worth. It also made a woman at that time *one with her society.* But *today* the tradition is an anachronism which simply does not function. *It does not work.* So while Blanche must believe it because it makes her special, because it makes her sticking by Belle Reve an act of heroism, rather than an absurd romanticism, still *it does not work.* It makes Blanche feel *alone, outside of her society.* Left out, insecure, shaky. The airs the "tradition" demands isolate her further, and every once in a while, her resistance weakened by drink, she breaks down and seeks human warmth and contact where she can find it, not on her terms, on theirs; the merchant, the traveling salesman and the others . . . among whom the vulgar adolescent soldiers seem the most innocent. Since she cannot integrate these episodes, she rejects them, begins to forget them, begins to live in fantasy, begins to

rationalize and explain them to herself thus: "I never was hard or self-sufficient enough . . . men don't see women unless they are in bed with them. They don't admit their existence except when they're love-making. You've got to have your existence admitted by someone if you are going to receive someone's protection," etc. As if you had to apologize for needing human contact! Also n.b. above— the word: protection. That is what she, as a woman in the tradition, so desperately needs. That's what she comes to Stella for, Stella and her husband. Not finding it from them she tries to get it from Mitch. *Protection.* A haven, a *harbor.* She is a refugee, punch drunk, and on the ropes, making her last stand, trying to keep up a gallant front, because she is a proud person. But really if Stella doesn't provide her haven, *where is she to go.* She's a misfit, a liar, her "airs" alienate people, she must act superior to them which alienates them further. She doesn't know how to work. So she can't make a living. She's really helpless. She needs someone to help her. Protection. She's a last dying relic of the last century now adrift in our unfriendly day. From time to time, for reasons of simple human loneliness and need she goes to pieces, smashes her tradition . . . then goes back to it. This conflict has developed into a terrible crisis. All she wants is a haven: "I want to rest! I want to breathe quietly again . . . just think! If it happens! I can leave here and have a home of my own. . . ."

If this is a romantic tragedy, what is its inevitability and what is the tragic flaw? In the Aristotelian sense, the flaw is the need to be superior, special (or *her* need for protection and what it means to her), the "tradition." This creates an apartness so intense, a loneliness so gnawing that only a complete breakdown, a refusal, as it were, to contemplate what she's doing, a *binge* as it were, a destruction of all her standards, a desperate violent ride on the Streetcar Named Desire can break through the walls of her tradition. The tragic flaw creates the circumstances, inevitably, that destroy her. More later.

Try to find an entirely different character,

a self-dramatized and self-romanticized character for Blanche to play in each scene. She
is playing 11 different people. This will give
it a kind of changeable and shimmering surface it should have. And all these 11 self-
dramatized and romantic characters should
be out of the romantic tradition of the Pre-
Bellum South, etc. Example: Sc. 2 Gay Miss
Devil-may-care.

There is another, simpler and equally
terrible contradiction in her own nature. She
won't face her physical or sensual side. She
calls it "brutal desire." She thinks she sins
when she gives in to it . . . yet she does give
in to it, out of loneliness . . . but by calling it
"brutal desire," she is able to separate it
from her "real self," her "cultured," refined
self. Her tradition makes no allowance, allows
no space for this very real part of herself.
So she is constantly in conflict, not at ease,
sinning. *She's still looking for something that
doesn't exist today, a gentleman,* who will treat
her like a virgin, marry her, protect her,
defend and maintain her honor, etc. She
wants an old-fashioned wedding dressed in
white . . . and still she does things out of
"brutal desire" that make this impossible. *All
this too is tradition.*

She has worth too—she is better than
Stella. She says: "There has been some kind
of progress. . . . Such things as art—as poetry
and music—such kinds of new light have
come into the world . . . in some kinds of
people some kinds of tenderer feelings have
had some little beginning that we've got to
make *grow!* And cling to, and hold as our
flag! In this dark march toward whatever
it is we're approaching . . . don't . . . don't
hang back with the brutes!" And though the
direct psychological motivation for this is
jealousy and personal frustration, still she,
alone and abandoned in the crude society of
New Orleans back streets, is the *only voice of
light.* It is flickering and, in the course of the
play, goes out. But it is valuable because it is
unique.

Blanche is a butterfly in a jungle looking
for just a little momentary protection, doomed

to a sudden, early violent death. The more
I work on Blanche, incidentally, the less
insane she seems. She is caught in a fatal inner
contradiction, but in another society, she
would work. In Stanley's society, no!

This is like a classic tragedy. Blanche is
Medea or someone pursued by the Harpies,
being *her own nature.* Her inner sickness
pursues her like *doom* and makes it impossible
for her to attain the one thing she needs, the
only thing she needs: a safe harbor.

An effort to phrase Blanche's spine: to find
protection, to find something to hold onto,
some strength in whose protection she can
live, like a sucker shark or a parasite. The
tradition of *woman* (or all women) can only
live through the strength of someone else.
Blanche is entirely dependent. Finally the
doctor!

Blanche is an outdated creature, approaching extinction . . . like the dinosaur. She is
about to be pushed off the edge of the earth.
On the other hand she is a heightened version,
an artistic intensification of all women. That
is what makes the play universal. Blanche's
special relation to all women is that she is at
that critical point where *the one thing above all
else that she is dependent on: her attraction for men,
is beginning to go.* Blanche is like all women,
dependent on a man, looking for one to hang
onto: only *more so!*

So beyond being deeply desperate, Blanche
is in a hurry. She'll be pushed off the earth
soon. She carries her doom in her character.
Also, her past is chasing her, catching up
with her. Is it any wonder that she tries to
attract each and every man she meets. She'll
even take that protected feeling, that needed
feeling, that superior feeling, for a moment.
Because, at least for a moment, that anxiety,
the hurt and the pain will be quenched. The
sex act is the opposite of loneliness. Desire is
the opposite of Death. For a moment the
anxiety is still, for a moment the complete
desire and concentration of a man is on her.
He clings to you. He may say I love you. All
else is anxiety, loneliness and being adrift.

Compelled by her nature (she must be

special, superior) she makes it impossible with Stanley and Stella. She acts in a way that succeeds in being destructive. But the last bit of luck is with her. She finds the only man on earth whom she suits, a man who is looking for a dominant woman. For an instant she is happy. But her past catches up with her. Stanley, whom she's antagonized by her destructiveness aimed at his home, but especially by her need to be superior, uses her past, which he digs up, to destroy her. Finally she takes refuge in fantasy. She must have protection, closeness, love, safe harbor. The only place she can obtain them any longer is in her own mind. She "goes crazy."

Blanche is a stylized character, she should be played, should be dressed, should move like a stylized figure. What is the physicalization of an aristocratic woman pregnant with her own doom? . . . Behaving by a tradition that dooms her in this civilization, in this "culture"? All her behavior patterns are *old-fashioned, pure tradition.* All as if jellied in rote——

Why does the "Blues" music fit the play? The Blues is an expression of the loneliness and rejection, the exclusion and isolation of the Negro and their (opposite) longing for love and connection. Blanche too is "looking for a home," abandoned, friendless. "I don't know where I'm going, but I'm going." Thus the Blue piano catches the soul of Blanche, the miserable unusual human side of the girl which is beneath her frenetic duplicity, her trickery, lies, etc. It tells, it emotionally reminds you what all the fireworks are caused by.

Blanche—Physically. Must at all times give a single impression: her social mask is: *the High-Bred Genteel Lady in Distress.* Her past, her destiny, her falling from grace is just a surprise . . . then a tragic contradiction. But the mask never breaks down.

The only way to understand any character is through yourself. Everyone is much more alike than they willingly admit. Even as frantic and fantastic a creature as Blanche is created by things you have felt and known,

if you'll dig for them and be honest about what you see.

STELLA

Spine—hold onto Stanley (Blanche the antagonist).

One reason Stella submits to Stanley's solution at the end, is perfectly ready to, is that she has an unconscious hostility toward Blanche. Blanche is so patronizing, demanding and superior toward her . . . makes her so useless, old-fashioned and helpless . . . everything that Stanley has got her out of. Stanley has made a woman out of her. Blanche immediately returns her to the subjugation of childhood, younger-sister-ness.

Stella would have been Blanche except for Stanley. She now knows what, how much Stanley means to her health. So . . . no matter what Stanley does . . . she must cling to him, as she does to life itself. To return to Blanche would be to return to the subjugation of the tradition.

The play is a triangle. Stella is the Apex. Unconsciously, Stella wants Blanche to go to Mitch because that will take Blanche off Stella.

And there is a Terrific Conflict between Blanche and Stella, especially in Stella's feelings. Blanche in effect in Sc. 1 *Resubjugates* Stella. Stella loves her, hates her, fears her, pities her, is really through with her. Finally rejects her for Stanley.

All this of course Stella is aware of only unconsciously. It becomes a matter of conscious choice only in Sc. 11 . . . the climax of the play as it is the climax of the triangle story.

Stella is a refined girl who has found a kind of salvation or realization, *but at a terrific price.* She keeps her eyes closed, even stays in bed as much as possible so that she won't realize, won't *feel* the pain of this terrific price. She walks around as if narcotized, as if sleepy, as if in a daze. She is waiting for night. She's waiting for the dark where Stanley makes her feel *only him* and she has no reminder of the price she is paying. She wants no intrusion from the other world. She is drugged, trapped. She's in a sensual stupor. She shuts out all challenge all day long. She loafs, does her hair, her nails, fixes a dress, doesn't eat much, but prepares Stanley's dinner and waits for Stanley. She hopes for no other meaning from life. Her pregnancy just makes it more so. Stanley is in her day and night. Her entire attention is to make herself pretty and attractive for Stanley, kill time till night. In a way she is actually narcotized all day. She is buried alive in her flesh. She's half asleep. She is glazed across her eyes. She doesn't seem to see much. She laughs incessantly like a child tickled and stops abruptly as the stimuli, the tickling, stops and returns to the same condition, a pleasantly drugged child. Give her all kinds of narcotized business.

She has a paradise—a serenely limited paradise when Blanche enters—but Blanche makes her consider Stanley, judge Stanley and find him wanting, for the first time. But it is too late. In the end she returns to Stanley.

Stella is doomed too. She has sold herself out for a temporary solution. She's given up all hope, everything, just to live for Stanley's pleasures. So she is dependent on Stanley's least whim. But this can last only as long as Stanley wants her. And *secondly* and *chiefly*—Stella herself cannot live narcotized forever. There is more to her. She begins to feel, even in the sex act, *taken*, unfulfilled—not recognized . . . and besides she's deeper, needs more variety. Her only hope is her children and, like so many women, she will begin to live more and more for her children.

She tries to conceal from herself her true needs through hiding and drugging herself in a sex relationship. But her real needs, for tenderness, for the several aspects of living, for realization in terms of herself—not only in terms of Stanley, *still live . . . she can't kill them* by ignoring them. Blanche, despite apparent failure, makes her realize certain things about Stanley. She hugs Stanley in Sc. 4 out of desperation, and out of a need to silence her doubts by the violence of sexual

love (the "old reliable") . . . but Blanche has succeeded in calling Stella's attention to her own "sell-out" . . . she never sees Stanley the same again—or their relationship.

Stella, at the beginning of the play, won't face a *hostility* (concealed from herself and unrecognized) toward Stanley. She is *so* dependent on him, so compulsively compliant. She is giving up so much of herself, quieting so many voices of protest. She is Stanley's slave. She has sold out most of her life. Latent in Stella is rebellion. Blanche arouses it.

Stella is plain out of her head about Stanley. She has to keep herself from constantly touching him. She can hardly keep her hands off him. She is setting little traps all the time to conquer his act of indifference (he talks differently at night, in bed). She embarrasses him (though he is secretly proud) by following him places. They have a game where he tries to shake her all the time and she pursues him, etc. He makes her a panther in bed. He is her first man, really; he made her a woman. He fulfilled her more than she knew possible and she has to stop herself from *crawling* after him. She's utterly *blind* as to what's wrong with Stanley. She's blind to it and she doesn't care, *until* Blanche arrives. At the end of the play, her life is entirely different. It will never be the same with Stanley again.

Note from Tennessee Williams on the fourth day of rehearsal: "Gadge—I am a bit concerned over Stella in Scene One. It seems to me that she has too much vivacity, at times she is bouncing around in a way that suggests a co-ed on a benzedrine kick. I know it is impossible to be literal about the description 'narcotized tranquillity' but I do think there is an important value in suggesting it, in contrast to Blanche's rather feverish excitability. Blanche is the quick, light one. Stella is relatively slow and almost indolent. Blanche mentions her 'Chinese philosophy'—the way she sits with her little hands folded like a cherub in a choir, etc. I think her natural passivity is one of the things that makes her acceptance of Stanley acceptable. She naturally 'gives in,' accepts, lets things slide, she does not make much of an effort."

STANLEY

Spine—keep things his way (Blanche the antagonist).

The hedonist, objects, props, etc. Sucks on a cigar all day because he can't suck a teat. Fruit, food, etc. He's got it all figured out, what fits, what doesn't. The pleasure scheme. He has all the confidence of resurgent flesh.

Also with a kind of naïveté . . . even slowness . . . he means no harm. He wants to knock no one down. He only doesn't want to be taken advantage of. His code is simple and simple-minded. He is adjusted *now* . . . later, as his sexual powers die, so will he; the trouble will come later, the "problems."

But what is the chink in his armor now, the contradiction? Why does Blanche get so completely under his skin? Why does he want to bring Blanche and, before her, Stella *down to his level?* It's as if he said: "I know I haven't got much, but no one has more and no one's going to have more." It's the hoodlum aristocrat. He's deeply dissatisfied, deeply hopeless, deeply cynical . . . the physical immediate pleasures, if they come in a steady enough stream quiet this *as long as no one gets more* . . . then his bitterness comes forth and he tears down the pretender. But Blanche he can't seem to do anything with. She can't come down to his level so he levels her with his sex. He brings her right down to his level, beneath him.

One of the important things for Stanley is that Blanche *would wreck his home.* Blanche is dangerous. She is destructive. She would soon have him and Stella fighting. He's got things the way he wants them around there and he does *not* want them upset by a phony, corrupt, sick, destructive woman. *This makes Stanley right!* Are we going into the era of Stanley? He may be practical and right . . . but what the hell does it leave us? Make this a removed objective characterization for Marlon Brando.

Choose Marlon's objects . . . the things he loves and prizes: all sensuous and sensual— the shirt, the cigar, the beer (how it's poured and nursed, etc.).

The one thing that Stanley can't bear is someone who thinks that he or she is better than he. His only way of explaining himself— he thinks he stinks—is that everyone else stinks. This is symbolic. True of our National State of Cynicism. No values. There is nothing to command his loyalty. Stanley rapes Blanche because he has tried and tried to keep her down to his level. This way is the last. For a moment he succeeds. And then, in Scene 11, he has failed!

Stanley has got things his way. He fits into his environment. The culture and the civilization, even the neighborhood, etc., etc., the food, the drink, etc., are all his way. And he's got a great girl, with just enough hidden neuroticism for him—yet not enough to even threaten a real fight. Also their history is right: he conquered her. Their relationship is right: she waits up for him. Finally God and Nature gave him a fine sensory apparatus . . . he enjoys! The main thing the actor has to do in the early scenes is make the physical environment of Stanley, the *props* come to life.

Stanley is deeply indifferent. When he first meets Blanche he doesn't really seem to care if she stays or not. Stanley is interested in his own pleasures. He is completely self-absorbed to the point of fascination.

To physicalize this: he has a most annoying way of being preoccupied—or of busying himself with something else while people are talking with him, at him it becomes. Example, first couple of pages Scene 2. Stanley thinks Stella is very badly brought up. She can't do any of the ordinary things—he had a girl before this that could really cook, but she drank an awful lot. Also she, Stella, has a lot of airs, most of which he's knocked out of her by now, but which still crop up. Emphasize Stanley's love for Stella. It is rough, embarrassed and he rather truculently *won't show it.* But it is there. He's proud of her. When he's not on guard and looking at her his eyes suddenly shine. He is grateful too, proud, satisfied. But he'd never show it, demonstrate it.

Stanley is supremely indifferent to everything except his own pleasure and comfort. He is marvelously selfish, a miracle of sensuous self-centeredness. He builds a hedonist life, and fights to the death to defend it—but finally it is *not* enough to hold Stella

and

this philosophy is not successful even for him —because every once in a while the silenced, frustrated part of Stanley breaks lose in unexpected and unpredictable ways and we suddenly see, as in a burst of lightning, his real frustrated self. Usually his frustration is worked off by eating a lot, drinking a lot, gambling a lot, fornicating a lot. He's going to get very fat later. He's desperately trying to squeeze out happiness by living by *ball and jowl* . . . and it really doesn't work . . . because it simply stores up violence and stores up violence, until every *bar in the nation is full of Stanleys ready to explode*. He's desperately trying to drug his senses . . . overwhelming them with a constant round of sensation so that he will feel nothing else.

In Stanley sex goes under a disguise. Nothing is more .erotic and arousing to him than "airs" . . . she thinks she's better than me . . . I'll show her . . . . Sex equals domination . . . anything that challenges him—like calling him "common"—arouses him sexually.

In the case of Brando, the question of enjoyment is particularly important. Stanley feeds himself. His world is hedonist. But what does he enjoy? Sex equals sadism. It is his "equalizer." He conquers with his penis. But objects too—drunk. Conquest in poker, food . . . sweat. *Exercise.* But Enjoy! Not just cruel and *unpleasant* . . . but he never graduated from the baby who wants a constant nipple in his mouth. He yells when it's taken away.

As a character Stanley is most interesting in his "contradictions," his "soft" moments, his sudden pathetic little-tough-boy tenderness toward Stella. Scene 3 he cries like a baby. Somewhere in Scene 8 he almost makes

it up with Blanche. In Scene 10 he *does* try to make it up with her—and except for her doing the one thing that most arouses him, both in anger and sex, he might have.

MITCH

Spine—get away from his mother (Blanche the lever).

He wants the perfection his mother gave him . . . everything is approving, protective, *perfect for him*. Naturally no girl, today, no sensible, decent girl will give him this. But the tradition will.

Like Stella, Mitch hides from his own problem through mother-love.

Mitch is the end product of a matriarchy . . . his mother has robbed him of all daring, initiative, self-reliance. He does not face his own needs.

Mitch is Blanche's ideal in a comic form, 150 years late. He is big, tough, burly, has a rough southern voice and a manner of homespun, coarse, awkward, overgrown boy, with a heart of mush. He's like that character (who cries easy) in *Sing Out Sweet Land*. He is a little embarrassed by his strength in front of women. He is straight out of Mack Sennett comedy—but Malden has to create the reality of it, the truth behind that corny image. Against his blundering strength there is shown off the fragility and fragrance of a girl. Her delicacy. "Lennie" in *Mice and Men*.

Mitch, too, is most interesting in his basic contradictions. He doesn't want to be Mother's Boy. Goddamn it he just can't help it. He does love his Mother, but is a little embarrassed at how much. Blanche makes a man out of him, makes him important and grown-up. His Mother—he dimly realizes— keeps him eternally adolescent, forever dependent.

Violence—he's full of sperm.

energy

strength

the reason he's so clumsy with women is that he's so damn full of violent desire for them.

Mitch's Mask: He-man mama's boy. This

mask is a traditional, "corny" one in American dramatic literature. But it is true.

This play contains the crucial struggle of Mitch's life. For Mitch instinctively and even consciously, to a degree, knows what's wrong with him. He is jibed at often enough. And in his guts he knows they're right. Mitch, in his guts, hates his Mother. He loves her in a way—partially out of *early habit*, partially because she is clever—but much more fundamentally he *hates her*. It is a tragedy for him when he returns to her absolute sovereignty at the end. He will never meet another woman who will need him as much as Blanche and will need him to be a man as much as Blanche.

AVENGERS

INTRODUCTION TO THE ORESTEIA

Peter D. Arnott

AESCHYLUS AND GREEK TRAGEDY

Aeschylus lived through a crucial period in the history of Greece, and one which laid the foundations for many of that civilization's greatest achievements. In his city of Athens the rule of tyrants was superseded by an effective democracy which gave more people than ever before an active part in public affairs, and brought about a new surge of civic pride. While he was still of military age the Greek city-states, traditionally isolationist and fiercely jealous of each other, were forced to unite against the menace of Persian invasion. Persian armies twice entered Greece, and Aeschylus fought in the major battles of these campaigns. The sea-fight of Salamis, in which a small and predominantly Athenian force defeated the Persian armada, later served as background for his tragedy *The Persians*, the first Greek play that has come down to us complete. Greece emerged from the wars triumphant, though several cities had suffered great losses. This was particularly true of Athens, against which the Persians bore a special grudge. The city had to be abandoned and was twice sacked by the invading army. Athens' leadership in the resistance, however, had brought her greatly increased prestige. After the war a confederation was formed to provide against any future invasion. A number of states contributed to the maintenance of a joint fleet and treasury, with Athens eventually assuming charge of both. Little by little this confederacy was transformed into an Athenian empire, and the annual tribute of the subject states was used to rebuild the city on a more magnificent scale. Hand in hand with these territorial acquisitions went a new interest in the arts, the drama prominent among them.

Performances of tragedy had been given in Athens from about 535 B.C. as part of the great religious festivals. About the early writers and performances we know little. Tragedy appears originally to have consisted largely of choral song and pageantry. A chorus of fifty, which both sang and danced, carried the burden of the performance, assisted by a single actor who would take an occasional solo part. To Aeschylus is attributed the introduction of the second actor, which made more complex dramatic action possible and relieved the demands on the chorus. Sophocles, Aeschylus' younger contemporary and rival, introduced

Aeschylus: *The Libation Bearers*, ed. by Peter D. Arnott, copyright © 1964 AHM Publishing Corporation. Reprinted by Permission of AHM Publishing Corporation.

the third actor, an innovation which Aeschylus copied in the *Oresteia* and other later plays. Aeschylus' chorus probably still numbered fifty. It was later reduced to fifteen. Tradition associates this reduction with the performance of *The Eumenides*, whose horrific chorus of Furies threw the audience into a panic; there may well be a grain of truth in this story. In Aeschylus the chorus is still vital, and retains the dual function inherited from its origin in nondramatic performances. Its members can participate in the drama as characters—elders of Argos, slaves or Furies—or, when the playwright requires it, they can step outside the framework of the action to function as narrators or impersonal commentators, underlining a theme just stated in action or drawing a moral implication. The facility of direct address to the audience which this convention provides gave Greek tragedy, particularly in the hands of Aeschylus an enviable power and economy.

Apart from his technical innovations, Aeschylus seems to have been the first to enlarge the scope of tragedy to treat problems of significant importance. The Greeks expected drama, like all forms of art both literary and visual, to be functional, and provide some service to the state. Dramatists were regarded not merely as entertainers but as teachers, with the responsibility of filling the gap caused by the absence of any substantial body of ethical doctrine in the Greek religion. Aeschylus employs tragedy to discuss moral, social, and religious problems. Even *The Persians*, a fiercely patriotic play based on events still fresh in the mind of his audience, transcends its subject matter to investigate the whole question of the balance between the human and the divine, and the misuse of human power. The *Oresteia*, while it is consistently exciting theater, at the same time poses vital questions about man's nature and destiny, his relationship to the gods and the nature of those gods, and the progress of civilization.

Aeschylus was revered by later generations as the father of Greek tragedy. His plays were the first to be officially preserved, and it is from the transcript made for the Athenian archives that they ultimately descend to us. He was credited with introducing many of the traditional features of the Greek theater—masks, costumes, settings—though some of these we know had been in use before his time. One signal posthumous honor was awarded him. Anyone wishing to revive a play of Aeschylus for a dramatic festival instead of entering an original play of his own would automatically be granted a chorus. This veneration, however, was not completely uncritical. There were not a few who found his language ponderous and stilted, his imagery incomprehensible. Aristophanes, the Greek comic writer of the later fifth century, satirizes Aeschylus freely in *The Frogs*, and makes a number of telling points. In the fourth century, when the plays of the great dramatists were frequently revived, Sophocles and Euripides were preferred to Aeschylus, not merely because their plays were simpler to stage but because of the difficulties of language and thought in Aeschylus already mentioned. These are valid criticisms, but small in comparison to the virtues of the Aeschylean method—the monumentality of his style, the constantly fresh implications of his cosmic themes, the grandeur of his thought and diction. Aeschylus has survived both on the stage and in the study, and still poses exciting challenges to scholar, to actor, and to director alike.

THE ORESTEIA

A tragic poet wishing to compete in the annual dramatic festivals at Athens was required to submit four plays, three tragedies and one satyr play. The latter was a short burlesque of popular mythology, played as an afterpiece to give the audience some light relief. Aeschylus was considered the best writer of satyr plays of his time, and we must regret that none of his works in this genre has survived complete. The three tragedies could be completely independent of each other—a method favored by Sophocles and Euripides—or form a trilogy, in which each play, though complete in itself and capable of being performed independently, formed one act of a larger whole. This seems to have been the way in which Aeschylus preferred to work. *Seven Against Thebes* was the third play in such a sequence, *The Suppliant Women* the first; but the *Oresteia* (*Saga of Orestes*), comprising *Agamemnon*, *The Libation Bearers*, and *The Eumenides*, is the only trilogy that has survived complete.

The story on which Aeschylus bases these plays was a familiar one to Greek audiences, and furnished the plots of a number of tragedies. It was a long and complex story, beginning far earlier than the quarrel between Atreus and Thyestes which Aeschylus takes as his starting point. But a dramatist must use his material selectively, and Aeschylus restricts himself to the history of three generations. It is basically the brutal tale of a family feud, of which Greek legend contains many examples—the type of vendetta which still emerges from time to time in Greece and Sicily, and in other countries far from the Mediterranean. Atreus committed an atrocity against his brother Thyestes, for which a curse was laid upon him. Agamemnon, his son, is killed by his wife Clytemnestra and her lover Aegisthus, son of Thyestes; Clytemnestra in turn is killed by her son Orestes, honor bound to avenge his father, and Orestes himself is haunted by guilt and the fear of supernatural punishment until the curse is finally broken at the close of the trilogy. Since the tale was familiar to Aeschylus' audience, he takes us straight into the story of Agamemnon and we do not actually hear the curse recounted in full until almost the end of the first play. The primitive concept of justice embodied here was long a valid principle of Athenian law; it was not until comparatively late that the punishment of murder was taken out of the hands of the individual and entrusted to the state. It is a concept personified in the trilogy by the

Erinyes, or Furies, demonic pursuers of the wrongdoer. Their presence is constantly felt, and becomes more tangible as the action proceeds. In *Agamemnon* they are unseen, though constantly referred or appealed to. In *The Libation Bearers* they appear as hallucinations, seen by Orestes after he has murdered his mother, but not by us. In *The Eumenides* they are seen by the audience too, terrible figures with snakey hair and blazing torches, and form the chorus, hunting down Orestes for his crime.

Agamemnon is a man cursed, and so naturally susceptible to trouble in whatever form it chooses to come. If we ask why Agamemnon dies, we find not one answer but several. He has angered his wife by the sacrifice of their child Iphigeneia, and further insulted her by bringing home a concubine, the prisoner of war Cassandra, to live in his palace. He has angered the gods by his arrogance and his unnecessary destruction of their temples in Troy. Aegisthus, living embodiment of the family curse, plots to kill him in revenge for the wrong done to his father. But behind all these particular causes we see a pattern working. The curse forces Agamemnon into situations where he is compelled to make a choice, and events are so arranged that any choice he makes will be disastrous. His brother Menelaus loses his wife, Helen, to Paris, Prince of Troy. Menelaus is bound in honor to attempt to reclaim his wife, and Agamemnon is bound by family ties to support him. But this can only be achieved at the cost of alienating his people. The chorus, speaking for the population of Argos, make it clear that they consider the Trojan War a useless and frivolous expedition, one that has brought suffering and hardship to many for the sake of a wanton woman. Another choice is forced upon him as soon as war is declared. The Greek fleet is delayed at Aulis by contrary winds, and the gods can be appeased only by the sacrifice of Iphigeneia. Thus the choice becomes one between public and private good. If he sacrifices his daughter

he will alienate his family and deprive himself of a loved child. If he refuses, it will
be tantamount to deserting the army. He
chooses the public good, and thus brings
retribution on his own head.

Aeschylus brilliantly weaves together two
strains, one of triumph and one of impending
fatality. On the one hand we hear of joy
at the ending of the war and the fall of
Troy, and the triumph of the king returning
to his home victorious. But beneath this
sounds a more somber note. Argos is empty
of its men. There are only elders and boys,
dominated by the scheming Clytemnestra.
Agamemnon's supporters have been swept
away in a storm. When he enters his city
the triumph is hollow, and he is walking
into a trap that his friends are powerless to
prevent. Tempted by his wife, he enters his
home over the purple carpet, symbolic of the
arrogance of power and conquest, and is
destroyed. So the city loses its benevolent
ruler and falls under a tyranny; its only hope
is the reappearance of Orestes.

The second play is much shorter than the
first and different in mood. The joy of bloodshed has given place, in Aegisthus and Clytemnestra, to satiety and resignation. But the
pattern of the curse reasserts itself. Orestes
is faced with a choice similar to that which
confounded his father. He is bound by filial
duty to avenge his father's murder, but this
can only be achieved by the hideous crime
of murdering his mother. Once again, either
choice is bound to be wrong. He wavers,
but is finally urged to the deed; Clytemnestra and Aegisthus die, and Orestes is seen
standing over their bodies as Clytemnestra
stood in the first play. The chorus is misled
into optimism. They hope that the curse is
now worked out, and that the house may live
happily. But Orestes in turn is pursued, not
now by any mortal enemy but by the Furies.
The dreary chain of crime and punishment
is not yet at an end.

In the third play the issue transcends a
mere family feud to assume cosmic significance. The whole meaning of justice is now

involved, and the supernatural powers take
up their various stands, using the trial of
Orestes as a test case. On the one hand are
the Furies. They stand for a concept of justice
little removed from that of the jungle. If a
man has died, another must die in punishment. For them, the fact of blood-guilt is in
itself sufficient. They admit no degrees of
wrong, no extenuating circumstances. They
stand, too, for a primitive level of society in
which the only valid tie is the blood-tie.
Marriage, a social contract, has no place in
their scheme. They argue that Orestes has
killed a blood-relation, his mother, and so
must be destroyed. Clytemnestra's deed was
less reprehensible because the victim was
merely her husband. Against them are ranged
Apollo and Athena, personifications of law
and wisdom for the Greeks. Their argument
is the argument of civilization, that the bond
of marriage is as valid as that of blood-rela-
tionship; Clytemnestra was no less guilty than
Orestes. Eventually these gods, the newer
deities of a more civilized and ordered society,
triumph over the darker powers of an earlier
age, and persuade them to change their natures. The Furies become beneficent spirits;
the rule of law has conquered the spirit of
revenge, the curse has been broken and
Orestes may go free. Aeschylus deliberately
appeals to the patriotic sentiments in his
audience by setting this momentous decision
in Athens and identifying the court as the
Areopagus, the city's most venerable court of
appeal. It is Athena, the city's patron deity,
who is ultimately responsible for this victory
of light over darkness.

The *Oresteia*, then, is an allegory of civilization compressed into the story of a few
generations. Aeschylus conceives of the gods,
as well as men, as evolving from crude beginnings into something nobler and more ele-
vated. The Furies change their natures; so
does Apollo. In *Agamemnon* he appears as a
malicious and vindictive god of the Homeric
type, persecuting Cassandra because she has
dared to oppose his desires. In *The Eumenides* he has become the embodiment of har-

mony and reason, the symbol of all that the Greeks of the classical age found most admirable in their own society. This motif of change and evolution is carried through the trilogy in more subtle ways also, in the shifting significance of recurrent images and metaphors. The net, a frequent symbol, at first implies scheming and destruction—the net that Zeus fastens around Troy, the meshes woven by the Furies for Agamemnon, the net of cunning fashioned by Clytemnestra for her husband, made visible as the mantle in which she traps his body as a fisherman catches a fish. Later it becomes a symbol of hope, the net to which Orestes and Electra cling. Persuasion, the force used by Clytemnestra for harm—to lie to the chorus and the herald, and to lure her husband to his doom—in Athena's mouth becomes a weapon for good, to turn the recalcitrant Furies from their dark courses.

The text of the *Oresteia* has suffered considerable damage over the centuries. Some passages have been lost completely. Orestes' opening speech in *The Libation Bearers* is the most serious instance of this. A number of verses have disappeared, and what we have—enough, fortunately, to give the sense—has largely been reconstructed from quotations in other authors. There are several other places where a line, or several lines, have clearly been lost. Sometimes there is no clue to the original content, and the most we can achieve is an intelligent guess. Aeschylus also suffered at the hands of the copyists. His fondness for a ponderous and exotic vocabulary troubled the scribes, who, on finding themselves confronted with unfamiliar words, assumed that they must be mistakes and replaced them with more conventional words of similar sound. Nor is it always clear to which character a particular speech should be attributed. There is thus considerable disagreement between different editors and translators, and the reader must expect a number of variations, some slight, some of considerable importance, in the various versions available.

THE LIBATION BEARERS (CHOËPHORI)

Aeschylus

CHARACTERS

ORESTES, son of the late king Agamemnon and Clytemnestra
ELECTRA, his sister
CLYTEMNESTRA, Queen of Argos
AEGISTHUS, Clytemnestra's lover, now King of Argos
CILISSA, Orestes' old nurse
PYLADES, friend of Orestes
PORTER
SERVANT, of Aegisthus
CHORUS, of slavewomen

Scene: at first, by the grave of Agamemnon; later, before the door of the royal palace.

[*The grave of* AGAMEMNON. ORESTES *kneels in prayer. His friend* PYLADES *stands silent at a distance*]

ORESTES. Hermes, spirit of the underworld
And father's regent, lend to me
Your strength, and stand my champion, I pray,
For I have come home to my land again
And on this mounded tomb invoke my father
To listen and attend.

[*Laying a lock of hair upon the grave*]

1 *Hermes* messenger-god, one of whose functions was to escort the spirits of the dead to the underworld. Thus he is frequently appealed to, both in this play and *The Eumenides* as the intermediary between the living and the dead.

Aeschylus: *The Libation Bearers,* ed. by Peter D. Arnott, copyright © 1964 AHM Publishing Corporation. Reprinted by permission of AHM Publishing Corporation.

A lock of hair to Inachus, for manhood;
Its fellow here, as token for the dead;
For I was not at hand to mourn your passing,
10   My father, or salute your burial.

[*The* CHORUS *of mourning women, with* ELECTRA *among them, appear in the distance. They carry urns with libations to pour over the grave*]

But what is here now? What processional
Of women, in dignity of mourning black,
Is coming? What should I make this to mean?
A signal of new sorrow for the palace?
Or am I to suppose these women bring
Libations as late offerings to my father?
So it must be; for I think I see my sister
Electra among them, grief scored bold
Upon her face. Zeus, give me revenge
20   For my dead father; be my willing aid.
Pylades, let us give them room.
I must assure myself about this cry of women.

[ORESTES *and* PYLADES *conceal themselves as the women approach the grave*]

CHORUS. Forth from the palace gates, as I was bid,
With urns I come, with drumming hands,
Torn cheeks, the nails' fresh furrows
A talisman of red,
And in my heart old sorrow;
With rending of my robes, with fingers tearing
Wild at the linen on my breast
30   In grief of glad days gone.

For in the dead watch Fright with streaming hair

Shrilled from its cell, and to the dreaming house
Told things to come, a gust of rancor stirring
Fresh out of slumber,
Beating ironfisted on the doors
Of women. The seers swore by the gods their masters
That anger was pulsing in the grave
Against the murderers.

So in hollow office of appeasement,
Earth, O Earth, in mock of holy law,   40
She sends me forth. But there is fear
At such a word.
For who can ransom blood once spilled
On the ground? O joyless hearth,
O desolation of our house,
Sun hid his face, the pestilence
Of darkness fell thick on our palace
At the killing of our kings.
The splendor of our yesterdays, that stood
Triumphant, matchless and invincible   50
To thrill men's hearts with story, is departed
And terror comes.
Success is god, and greater than god
For mortal men. But Justice holds
Her balance attentive, coming swift
On some by day, for some waits ripening
Till evenfall, and those remaining
Are swallowed up in night.
Blood poured for mother earth to drink
Lies crusted, a living sore   60
To cry revenge. Destruction works
On the sinner, spiking him with plague
Till he is rotten through.

As once the chambers of virginity
Are forced, there is no remedy,
So all the waters of the world
Would seek to wash blood clean from guilty
Hands, and do their work in vain.

On me and on mine the gods imposed
The hard necessity of conquest   70

7 a lock of hair common votive offering, particularly in acts of mourning. *Inachus* river-god of Argos   *31 Fright with streaming hair* personification of Clytemnestra's prophetic nightmare, recounted more explicitly in vv. 555ff.

32 Shrilled from its cell the language deliberately suggests the apparatus of Apollo's oracular shrine at Delphi

And from the dwellings of my fathers
Brought me here to be a slave.
So I can do no other but approve
My masters, right or wrong—my life
Is new come in their keeping,
And I must struggle to suppress
The heart's loathing.
But still there run behind the veil
Tears for the errant destiny of kings
80 And to the secret places of my heart
Comes the cold touch of horror.

[ELECTRA *takes her place at the graveside*]

ELECTRA. You serving-maids, who set our
     house to rights,
Since you have trod this path of prayer
     with me,
Give me your counsel here. How should I
     speak
As I pour these offerings on my father's
     grave?
With what address, what sacramental
     words?
That this is love's commission to her love,
To husband from his wife—and this my
     mother?
I would not dare. Then what accompani-
     ment
90 Should herald these libations under-
     ground?
I know not. Or could I say this—
That men believe that those who send such
     wreaths
As these, deserve to be repaid in kind
With presents worthy of their merits?
Or should I pour into the thirsty earth
Without a word, without a salutation,
In manner as he died, and fling the urn
     away
As one who would be rid of it forever,
And go my way without a backward
     glance?
100 This is the question, friends. Advise me.
We share a roof, a common hate.
So do not hide your counsels out of fear
Of . . . anyone. The free man and the
     slave,

Each has his destiny. So speak;
Perhaps you know a better.
CHORUS. If you will have it so, I'll speak my
     mind
Before your father's tomb, which is for me
A sacred shrine—
EL.   Then as you reverence
My father's grave, speak to me now.
CHORUS. Pour, and call blessings on men of 110
     goodwill—
EL. And where among my friends could I
     find any
To bear that name?
CHORUS. Yourself; then anyone who hates
     Aegisthus.
EL. You, then, and me. Is that to be my
     prayer?
CHORUS. You know what I mean. But you
     must say it.
EL. Whom else shall I number in this com-
     pany?
CHORUS. Remember Orestes, banished though
     he be.
EL. That was well spoken, my good instructor.
CHORUS. And for the ones who shed this
     blood, remember—
EL. What? I am strange to this, you must 120
     dictate to me.
CHORUS. To call someone against them, from
     this world
Or from the other—
EL. To judge, or to revenge? Explain your-
     self.
CHORUS. In plain words, to take life for life.
EL. May I so pray, without offence to hea-
     ven?
CHORUS. Why not? To pay your enemy in
     kind?
EL. God of darkness, Hermes, potent mes-
     senger
Of this world and the next, I summon you
To help me now, and call
The spirits of the underworld, that watch 130
My father's house, to hear me as I pray,
And summon Earth, that brings all things
     to life
And takes her rearing to her womb again.
As I pour out these vessels to the dead,

I call upon my father. Pity me,
And light Orestes' lamp within our house,
For we are homeless now, our mother's
    chattels
With which she purchased for herself a
    man,
Aegisthus, who was partner in your
    murder.
140 I am no better than a slave; Orestes
Is banished from his rich inheritance,
While they loll back in luxury, and reap
The harvest of your labor. Thus I pray,
My father, listen close. Let fortune bring
Orestes home, and let me show myself
More modest than my mother was, my
    hand
More virtuous.
These prayers for us. This for our enemies:
Father, I charge you show us your avenger.
150 Kill them who killed you. Render them
    this justice.
And let me set against their curse
My curse, to fall on them.
Bring us blessings from the underworld;
The gods be on our side, and Earth,
And justice tiumphant.
Such is the litany to which I pour
These offerings.

[*To the* CHORUS]

            And you, as the custom is,
Must crown the prayers with your lament,
    and sing
Your hymnal to the dead.
160 CHORUS. Let fall now for the fallen lord
A watering of tears
As pitchers are upturned
On this holy mound, a bastion
Against evil, and a curse that must be laid.
Hear me, majesty; lord, as you lie dim,
Give this your mind. What champion will
    rise
To be our palace's deliverance?
What warrior to wield the backbent
Bow of Scythia, or come

169 *Bow of Scythia* the Scythians were famous archers
in antiquity

Firmhilted to the handfight?   170
EL. The earth has drunk. My father has his
    due.

[*Seeing the lock of* ORESTES' *hair*]

But here is something strange to tell,
Something for all of us.
CHORUS. Tell me what you mean.
Fear is stepping nimble in my heart.
EL. Look, on the tomb. A lock of hair.
CHORUS. Whose? Man's or woman's?
EL. Guess. Nobody could mistake it.
CHORUS. What is it? Your young years must
    teach my age.
EL. This curl could not have come from any 180
    head
But mine.
CHORUS. His nearest hate him, they would
    never
Cut hair in his mourning.
EL. But look at it—so very like—
CHORUS. Like whose hair? Tell me.
EL. My own. So like. Compare them.
CHORUS. Orestes? Has he come in secret
    To make this offering?
EL.   Yes, he has hair
    Like this.
CHORUS. He would not dare to come.   190
EL. He sent it, then; this shorn lock,
    A lovegift to his father.
CHORUS. Then I have no less cause to weep
If he will never set foot in this land again.
EL. I too. The full tide of my anger now
Has come, it is a knife to rend my heart.
The dyke is down, the tears fall from my
    eyes
Unslaked, my grief is at the flood
To see this hair. Oh, how could I imagine
That this lock could have come from any
    other
In Argos? It was not the murderess   200
That cropped her hair, my mother—what
    a name
For her, that fiend who hates her children!
But how can I say straight and clear
This glory comes from him I love the best,
Orestes—oh, I am hope's fool!
If it had wit to speak, if it could tell me,

Then I should not be torn between two minds,
But know for sure if I should cast it out
For being fathered by a head I hate
210 Or if it is one blood with mine, my sorrow's partner
To grace this grave, and reverence my father.
But on the gods we call, who know
What tempests have beset our voyaging,
And if it is ordained we come safe home,
Great trunks from little seeds may grow.

[*Seeing footprints on the ground*]

A second witness! Marks upon the ground
Like those my feet have made, the very same . . .
No, there's a double set of footprints here,
One his, and one somebody's that was with him . . .
220 The heel, the tracing of the toes; these measurements
Exactly fit with mine—I cannot bear it!
This is too much to think of!

[ORESTES *and* PYLADES *step from their hiding place*]

OR. You may inform the gods your prayers are answered.
Now pray to be as lucky in the future.
EL. Why? What favor have I won from them?
OR. You are in sight of what you prayed to see so long.
EL. The man I prayed for—what is he to you?
OR. I know how you long to see Orestes.
EL. What makes you think my prayers are answered?
230 OR. Here I am. Look no further. You will never find
A closer friend.
EL. I do not know you. Are you playing tricks on me?
OR. If so, I play a trick upon myself.
EL. Have you come here to laugh at my misfortunes?

OR. If they are your misfortunes, they are mine.
EL. Let me pretend you are Orestes, then,
And bid you—
OR.   I am Orestes,
And you do not know me when you see me.
But when you saw this hair cut off in mourning,
When you looked on the earth my feet had 240 trod,
Your mind flew on the instant to the thought
That what you saw was me.
Look, lay this lock of hair where it was cut;
It is your brother's—see, it matches yours.

[*Showing a child's garment*]

And look, the jerkin that you wove for me:
The texture, this embroidery of beasts—

[ELECTRA *is convinced, and weeps for joy*]

Control yourself, and do not let your joy
Outweigh discretion. I am well acquainted
With our dear friends, and how they hate us.
EL. Oh dearest treasure of our father's house, 250
Its hope, its future seed; how we have wept for you.
It shall be yours again. You have your father's strength
Behind you. Face that I have longed to see;
You have divided me, and made four loves from one.
One for my father—that is your name now;
One for my loving duty to my mother—
Her share is yours; to her I give my hate;
One for my sister's cruel sacrifice;
One for the brother true that I have found you,
The only one of all my family   260
To give me dignity.
So Might and Justice fight upon my side

258 *my sister's cruel sacrifice* Iphigeneia, sacrificed by Agamemnon to win the gods' favor at the outset of the Trojan War

And Zeus Almighty, greatest of them all,
To make a third.

OR. Zeus, O Zeus, look down at what has
  passed here.
Look at us both, the eagle's children,
Parentless, their father strangled
In the deadly embraces of a snake.
Their father's dead, and they must starve,
270 For they have not his art, to bring their
  catch
Home to the lair, as he did. It is myself I
  mean
And this girl, Electra. We stand here in
  your sight
Two children, fatherless, and both alike
Cast from our homes. Our father
Was lavish in his tithes to honor you.
Destroy his young, you will look hard to
  find
Another hand so generous to feast you.
If you suffer the eagle's progeny to die
Who will believe you when you manifest
  yourself
280 Hereafter? If this ministering branch
Is left to wither, when the day comes round
To serve the altar, it will not be there
To wait on you with sacrifice. Take heed:
You may uplift this house and make it
  great
Although it seems to lie in ruins now.

CHORUS. Children, saviors of your father's
  house
Be silent, or some tattletale will warn
Our overlords. I hope I live to see them
Dead, and burning in the spitting fire!

290 OR. One thing will never fail, the potent
  oracle
Of Apollo. It was he who bade me walk
This perilled way, and in the secret hours
Whispered to me a litany of horrors
To turn my blood to ice, should I neglect
To hound my father's murderers and kill
  them
As they killed him, round on them, gore
  them,
Strip them of all they have. If I should fail,

He said my own self would be forfeit; I
  should suffer
Miseries uncounted . . . he made it plain
And told how, when the dead are angry, 300
Their rancor rises as a pestilence
Up through the ground, to ride upon our
  bodies,
Creeping, feeding; cancer sets its teeth
In flesh once fair, and leaves its mark upon
Our faces, scabbed with silver scales.
He spoke of other visitations too,
Of Furies forming in the father's blood.
Dead things work by dark. Then mur-
  dered men
Come crying to their kin "Revenge!" and
  terror stalks
By night, to haunt him. Wild hallucina- 310
  tions
Come vivid on his eyes, although he screw
  them
Tight shut in the dark, and drive him forth
With barbs and scourges from the land
  that bred him.
For such an outcast there can be
No common bowl, no loving-cup,
No prayer at altars—there a sentry stands,
His father's ghost; no man will share a roof
  with him
Or take him in, till friendless and un-
  mourned
He shrivels up and dies in misery.
Such was the oracle. Could I then deny it? 320
Even if I could, the deed must still be done,
For there are many calls on me, unani-
  mous
To urge me on—the gods' commandment,
Grief for my father—there is weight in
  this—
The press of poverty, and my desire
That the marvel of the earth, my country-
  men,
Whose glorious spirit subjugated Troy
Should not bow down before this pair of
  women—
For he is woman at heart; if I am one
He soon shall learn!   330

291 Apollo god of prophecy and Orestes' patron; see
note on v. 31

[ORESTES, ELECTRA *and the* CHORUS *join
in a lament over the tomb*]

CHORUS. O you presiding Destinies
    By the will of god make ending
    In the turnabout of justice.
    Let hate cry quittance to hate once spoken.
    So Justice proclaims herself aloud, exacting
    Atonement; blood for blood
    And stroke for stroke, do and be done by;
    Thus the lesson three ages old.

OR. O terrible my father,
340   What word of mine, what act
    Can blow fair to the far shore,
    Where fast you lie, a light
    The measure of your darkness?
    And yet it has been called
    A work of grace, to tell old glories
    In mourning for the champions
    Of the house of Atreus fallen.

CHORUS. Child, when a man dies flesh is frayed
    And broken in the fire, but not his will.
350   He shows his wrath though late.
    For the dead man there is mourning,
    For the guilty man a finding,
    And the deathsong for a parent and a father
    Is a call to judgement, ranging through
    The universe disquieted
    To hunt and find.

EL. Hear me in turn, my father,
    My weeping and long sorrow.
    Here two children at your graveside
360   Raise our chant for the departed.
    Your tomb is haven
    For outcasts, and for those
    Who pray for aid. What here is good,
    What refuge from calamity?
    Can we try a fall with fate?

CHORUS. Even from such as these the god
    At will can shape a gladder strain,
    And from the lamentation at the graveside
    A song of triumph may arise
370   Within the palace, to carry home
    The well-beloved, the dear unknown.

OR. If you had only died, my father,
    At Troy, upon the field of honor,
    And struck down by a foreign hand.
    Then had you left your house
    A legacy of glory, to your children
    As they walked abroad, undying
    Regard; then had you made
    A heavy tomb upon a foreign shore
    But for your family light burden.   380

CHORUS. Welcome then would he have gone
    To those who loved him, to the nobled dead,
    And in the nether world
    Would have kept high state, in honor
    Held and majesty, first minister
    To the most mighty, to the kings of darkness.
    For he was monarch on earth, and ruled
    Those who command men's lives, who wield
    The sceptre of dominion.

EL. No, that was not a place   390
    For you to die, my father,
    Under the battlements of Troy,
    And by Scamander's ford to find
    A plot of ground among the herd,
    The reaping of the spear. Far better
    That those who killed him should have died as he did,
    And in far countries strangers to our sorrow
    Had heard tell of the manner of their passing.
CHORUS. Child, you talk of riches passing mortal,
    Of miracles, felicity   400
    They only know who live beyond the wind.
    Dreams are free. But the double scourge
    Beats louder in the land; beneath
    The earth there is a mustering
    Of forces in our aid; our lords
    Have hands unclean, and the curse is on them;
    The children's day is coming.

347 *Atreus* Agamemnon's father

393 *Scamander* river of Troy   401 *who live beyond the wind* the legendary Hyperboreans, who lived in the far north and were particular favorites of Apollo

OR. There now is a word
  To rivet the ear. O Zeus,
410 Zeus, send up from below
  The laggard punisher
  For men of wrath and guilty hand
  And let the score be settled for the parents.

CHORUS. May it be given me to raise
  A cheer at the slaying of the man,
  The woman's dying. Why should I hide
  The thought that deep within flies free?
  For in the voyage of the heart
  There is a freight of hatred, and the wind
420 Of wrath blows shrill.

EL. Zeus two-fisted come
  To smite them, yes, to smash
  Heads; let there be a place
  For faith again; where there is wrong
  I say let right be done; O hear me
  Earth, and dignities of darkness.

CHORUS. This is the law. Blood spilt upon the
    ground
  Cries out for more; the act
  Of desecration is a summons to the Fury
430 Who for the dead once fallen heaps
  Havoc on havoc, new upon the old.

OR. O potentates of darkness, see,
  See, curses that come mighty from the
    dead,
  The house of Atreus, all that is left of us,
  Helpless, driven from our rightful homes.
  Where is there aid, O Zeus?

CHORUS. And my heart too has quivered
  To hear your sorrow's utterance.
  At such a word came despair,
440 A shadow on the heart. But when
  I see you standing strong, there comes
  Hope, and lightening of sorrow
  At this fair sign.

EL. What shall our tale be then? What other
  Than sorrows suffered for our parents'
    sake?
  Fawn away, there can be no assuaging.
  Anger ravens wolfish and implacable,
  Child of the mother.

CHORUS. As in Aria the women beat their
    breasts
  Then beat I mine, and in Cissian style   450
  Made show of mourning. There was a sight
  Of drumming fists, of blood-bruised flesh,
  A dance of hands, plucking
  Higher, lower, till my sorry head
  Rang with their hammering.

EL. O ruthless, O relentless, O my mother,
  Who in forced and meagre offices
  Thought fit to bury him, a king
  Far from his folk, without
  The rites of mourning,   460
  Without a tear, your husband.

OR. In such dishonor, say you?
  But she shall pay for slighting him,
  My father, by the help
  Of the immortals, by the help
  Of these my hands.
  So let me kill her, and then die.

CHORUS. This too you must know. His limbs
    were lopped
  And travestied, upon her word
  Who ordered this his grave,   470
  Intent to lay crushing grief
  On your young life.
  So was your father slighted.

EL. As you tell it, so he died. I was not by;
  I had no rights there, I was nothing,
  Only a cur that must be locked away
  Inside, for fear she'd bite. I hid
  The welling of my grief
  Though tears came readier than smiles that
    day.
  Hear this, and write it in your memory!   480

CHORUS. Yes, write, and let the tale bore deep
  Into your heart. But bide your time
  In patience still. So stands
  The story now. You yearn

449 *Aria, Cissian style* regions in Asia Minor. The chorus
liken their reaction to Agamemnon's death to that of
professional Asiatic mourners, with the difference that
their grief was sincere.

To know the end. Steadfast
Comes fittest to the fight.

OR. Pay heed, my father. Work beside your
     own.
EL. Your weeping daughter adds her voice to
    his.
CHORUS. And so cries all this company to-
        gether.
490   Obey, and come to light; make one
       Against your enemies.

OR. Battle now match battle, right with right.
EL. O gods, bring justice and accomplish-
    ment.
CHORUS. Fear comes over me as I hear you
        pray.
        Long destiny has waited; now
        When summoned it may come.

      O curse inborn, sour song
      Of fate, the bloody chastisement.
      O hard and heavy sorrows, grief
500   That has no easy end.

      The curse is in the house, not brought
      By other hands from distant places
      But by its own, in agony and blood.
      Thus we sing unto the dark ones.

      But listen to our prayer, O blessed ones
      Below, and send your willing aid
      To these the children. Let them fight and
      conquer.

OR. Father, who died out of the royal way,
    I pray you make me master in your house.
510 EL. I ask a like gift from your hands, my
        father:
        Aegisthus' death, a husband for my
        own. . . .
OR. So when there is feasting here on earth
    May you come welcome. If not, in the
    banquet days
    When steaming meats are offered to the
    dead
    No portion shall be yours.
EL.   Let me but come
    Into my own, and on my bridal day

I'll bring gifts from the mansions of my
fathers
To pour for you, and honor this tomb
above all others.
OR. Earth, loose my father. Let him see my
    fight.
EL. Queen Persephone, give us grace and   520
    strength.
OR. Remember your laving and your death,
    my father—
EL. Remember the strange weaving that you
    wore—
OR. Hobbled in fetters forged by no man's
    hand, my father—
EL. And wrapped about in shroud of foul
    devising—
OR. Do these taunts sting you from your
    sleep, my father?
EL. And do you lift the head that we so love?
OR. Send forth your chastisement to fight
    with those
    You love, or let us turn the hold on them
    If you would change defeat to victory.
EL. And father, hear this cry, my last: 530
    See these nestlings huddled on your tomb
    And pity them, the girlchild and the boy
    together.
OR. And do not write an end to Pelops' line.
    Through them you live, though you are in
    your grave.
EL. For when a man has died, his children
    keep
    His fame alive; we are the corks upon the
    net
    That hold the skein from sinking in the
    waters.
OR. For you these tears, so give them heed.
    Reward our speech, and save yourself.
CHORUS. The tomb lacks nothing of its honor 540
        now.
        Long have you spoken, and the debt of
        tears

520 Persephone wife of the god Hades and Queen of the
Underworld   *521 your laving . . . strange weaving* Clytemnestra murdered Agamemnon in his bath, having
entangled him in his own robe. It is this robe that
Orestes displays to the chorus later in the play, vv.
1058ff.   *533 Pelops* remote ancestor of the house of
Atreus

Is paid. But if your mind is firm to act
Go on, and make experiment of fate!
OR. So be it. But there is a question still to ask
And to the point. Why did she send
These offerings? What persuaded her to
make
These late amends for sorrow long past
healing?
A miserable favor, lavished on
The dead, the mindless! What these gifts
might mean
550 I could not start to guess. How small they
weigh
Beside her sin! Spend blood, there needs
no more,
And you may spend the world to pay for it
And lose your labor. Thus the proverb
runs.
Speak, if you know. You'll find a ready ear.
CHORUS. I saw, and know, child. There was
a dream,
A horror in the night; she woke in fear
And sent these offerings in mock of piety.
OR. What did she dream? If you know, tell
all.
CHORUS. She gave birth to a snake—this was
her story.
560 OR. And then? What was the sequel to this
tale?
CHORUS. She wrapped it like a babe in cradle
clothes.
OR. What did it ask for food, this beast new-
born?
CHORUS. In the dream, she gave it her own
breast to suck.
OR. How could she, and the nipple not be
torn
By this foul thing?
CHORUS.   It sucked milk and clot-
ted blood.
OR. No riddle here. This vision means a
man—
CHORUS. Then she awoke, and screamed in
terror,
And in the dark house at the mistress' cry
The shuttered lamps began to blink their
eyes;
570 And thinking to find surgery for pain
She sent at once these offerings to the dead.

OR. I pray this earth, my father's sepulchre,
That this dream find accomplishment in
me.
Thus I interpret; it is of a piece;
The serpent came from that same place
That brought forth me; she wrapped it in
the robes
That cradled me; its mouth spread on the
breast
That suckled me, and with lifegiving milk
Drew clotted blood, and at this dreadful
thing
My mother screamed in fear; then surely 580
she
Is doomed to die, and by no gentle hand
For bringing such a fearful prodigy
Into the world, and I am made the snake
To kill her, as this dream foretells.
CHORUS. Then you are the interpreter I trust
And cry amen. Expound the rest
To your friends now, who is to work, who
wait—
OR. It can be quickly told. My sister must go
home
And see that nothing of our plan leaks out,
So they who killed by treachery a man   590
Deserving of great honor, may be caught
By treachery, and in the selfsame net
May die; for thus Apollo prophesied,
The prophet-god who never yet has lied.
Accoutred like a traveller I'll come
Before the outer gates, with this man here
Whose name is Pylades, my friend, the
bounden
Champion of men and mine. We'll both
Assume the accent of Parnassus, and talk
The way men do in Phocis. If nobody   600
Opens the gates for us and bids us welcome
Because the house is busy with its troubles,
We'll stay where we are, so anyone who
passes
Will point and say "Is Aegisthus home?
Does he know they are here? Then why
Does he bar his doors to those who ask
shelter?"

---

600 *Phocis* district on the northern shore of the Gulf of
Corinth, containing Mount *Parnassus*, traditional home
of the Muses, and *Delphi*, the shrine of Apollo

And if I gain admission at the gates
And find that man upon my father's throne
Or if he comes to look me up and down
610 And question me to my face, before he says
"Where is this stranger from?" I'll strike
  him dead,
And in the flashing of a sword he'll fall.
So the Fury, that has never yet been
  starved of slaughter,
Will drink pure blood, the third draught
  and the last.

[*To* ELECTRA]

Your part to manage everything within
The house, so all may hang together,

[*To the* CHORUS]

And yours, to keep a guard upon your
  tongue,
Speak when you should, be silent when
  you must.
And all the rest I summon this one here
620 To oversee, when I have made
All ready for the trial at arms.

[*Exeunt* ORESTES *and* PYLADES *to disguise
themselves,* ELECTRA *to the palace*]

CHORUS. Great the progeny of nature, strange
  And dreadful; in the cradle of the sea
  Lurk monsters; in the hinterland
  Of earth and heaven, fire
  Has wings to fly; and birds
  And creeping things can tell
  The malice of the stormwinds.
    But who could put to words the vaunting
630 Pride of man, the overmastering
  Selfwill of woman, bedfellow
  Of sorrows for mankind?
  For when her passion turns
  From wedlock and home, no beast
  Or man can rage as she.

619 this one here without the stage gesture which would
originally have accompanied these words, it is impossible to say who is meant. It could be Pylades, Agamemnon or Apollo

Let him who has a mind to plumb the
  depths
Of things, learn how the sad Althaea once,
Armed with prescience of fire,
Devised death for her son, and burnt
The red brand that was of an age with him 640
Since he came forth crying from his
  mother's womb,
Whose span was his, to the appointed day.

There is another written black in story,
Scylla, who dealt in death, and was
  seduced
By enemies to kill one of her nearest.
Tempted her bitch-heart was and won
By Minos' gift, the necklace wrought of
  gold,
To cut from Nisus as he heedless slept
The lock of lasting life; and from this world
  went he.

And now I have begun this bloody his- 650
  tory
Should there not be a place
For the loveless wedlock that this house
Would fain see gone? You came
In guise of enemy upon
Your husband, working on him with
Your wiles, and sly as only woman may,
On your husband armored strong in might,
And over him you prized
A house whose hearth is barren of its fire,
The heart of the man-woman. 660

Of all the evils that the world can tell

637 the chorus offer examples from mythology of
women who have been carried away by their passions.
Althaea was the mother of Meleager. When her son
was born the Fates told her that he would die when
a brand then burning in the fire was consumed. She
promptly extinguished the brand and locked it away.
When Meleager grew to manhood, he quarrelled with
his mother's brothers and killed them. In her grief and
anger Althaea rekindled the brand and Meleager died.
644 Scylla daughter of *Nisus*, king of Megara, often
confused with the sea monster of the same name. Her
father's life depended on a lock of red hair growing on
his head. *Minos*, King of Crete, who was attacking
Megara, persuaded Scylla to sever it, thus killing Nisus
and causing the surrender of the city.

Lemnos takes pride of place, a name
To fright the ear, a blasphemy,
And whatsoever dreadful thing
Shall pass, there will be one to christen it
"The crime of Lemnos." So angry were the
     gods
That from earth the race has gone dis-
     honored.
For what is evil in heaven's sight
Is so for men. Does any of these tales
670   Not fit our case?

Now stands the sword at the lifebreath
To thrust sharp home, and at the hilt
Is Justice aiding; for it is not fit
That those who trod the majesty of Zeus
Underfoot, should not be trampled
Down in their turn.

Now the anvil of Justice stands four-
     square
And Fate the swordsmith has the edge
     made keen.
For from the abyss of her mind the Fury,
680   Late come to honor, visits on the house
The child of blood shed in the former time
To make atonement.

[*The palace.* ORESTES *and* PYLADES, *disguised as travellers, come to the door and
knock*]

OR. Boy, do you hear? There's someone
     knocking!
Is anyone there? Boy, I say! Who's at
     home?
For the third time, somebody come to the
     door,
If there is still shelter to be had here
Now that Aegisthus is in charge.
PORTER [*Within*]. All right, I hear you!
     Where are you from?
OR. Go tell the masters of this house.
690   They are the ones I seek. I bring strange
     news.

And hurry; night's dark chariot comes
Apace; this is the hour
When merchants must drop anchor in a
     house
That opens up its doors to travelling men.
Send us someone in authority,
The mistress, or her man, for preference.
With women we must be polite, and talk
Around the matter. Man to man speaks
     straight
And to the point, without prevarication.

[*The door opens. Enter* CLYTEMNESTRA]

CLYTEMNESTRA. Travellers, you have only to 700
     state your needs.
Such entertainment as this house can offer
Is at your command—a warm bath, or a
     bed
To magic weariness away, and honest
Eyes to wait on you. But if
You have more weighty business to discuss,
That is the man's work, and we shall in-
     form him so.
OR. Daulis is my home. I am a traveller from
     Phocis.
I was on my way with merchandise to
     Argos
On business of my own. When I turned off
     here,
A man I had met—we were strangers to 710
     each other—
Asked my destination, and told me his.
He was Strophius the Phocian—that came
     out
In conversation—and he said to me
"Since you must go to Argos anyway,
Think to look out the parents of Orestes
And tell them he is dead. Do not forget.
Whatever his family decides to do,
Whether to bring him back, or have him
     buried
Out of his land, to lie forever among
     strangers,
Bring word accordingly, when you come 720
     back again,

---

662 *Lemnos* island off the coast of Asia Minor whose
women, according to tradition, had risen against their
husbands and killed them

712 *Strophius* friend to Argos, to whose hands the infant
Orestes had been entrusted

For we have done but this—shed proper
tears
Above his ashes, and unfolded them
In the belly of a brazen urn." That was
all he told me.
But whether I talk to those who have
Authority and interest in this business
I do not know. I think his father should be
told.
CLYT. Oh,
You tell of how the waters of our grief
Rise clear above our heads. O curse upon
our house
That ever throws disaster in our way,
730 How little slips your eyes, with what sure
aim
You send your shafts to strike down from
afar
Even the things that carefully were set
Out of your path, to strip me desolate
Of those I love. So now it is Orestes,
He who was so well schooled to tread
around
This slough of death. There was a hope
Of decency, of revel in our house;
By this we kept alive; now take that hope
And by its name write "Liar."
740 OR. I would have rather introduced myself
To entertainment so munificent
By telling of more pleasant things; for none
Could be more anxious to oblige than
travellers
Their hosts. But I should have looked upon
myself
As breaking a sacred trust, if I neglected
To carry this matter through. I gave my
promise
To Strophius, and am under obligation
To you now, as your guest.
CLYT. This changes nothing. You will be re-
ceived
750 According to your merits, and shall have
No less regard, while you are in our house.
If it had not been you who brought this
message
It would have been another. It is now
The hour when footsore travellers should
reap
The promise of their long day's march.

[*To her servants*]

Take him inside, to the guestrooms where
We lodge the menfolk, his attendants too
And fellow travellers. See that they receive
The comforts proper to a house like ours.
You have your orders. You are answerable 760
to me.
I shall go tell the master of the house
What I have heard, and with my friends
about me
Take the measure of this new disaster.

[CLYTEMNESTRA, ORESTES *and* PYLADES
go inside the palace]

CHORUS. Come friends and fellow servants all,
Is it not time for us to show
The power of our voices, and so aid
Orestes? O sovereign Earth and sovereign
Mound of the tomb, who lie upon
The body of the sealord and our king,
Now hear us, grant us aid.   770
Now is the time ripe for Persuasion
To marshal all her wiles
And for the god of the dark journey,
Hermes,
And him that dwells in night, to stand
Sentinel as the sword comes to the match.

[*Enter* CILISSA]

The harm must be afoot, the traveller is
busy—
Here is Orestes' nurse in tears.
Where are you going from the gates,
Cilissa,
With misery, the uninvited guest
Free ever of her company, to step beside 780
you?
CILISSA. Our mistress sent me hurrying to find
Aegisthus for the travellers, so he
Could talk to them man to man, and learn
The ins and outs of what they have to tell
him.
She had a wry face for her servants, but
behind

774 him that dwells in night Agamemnon

Her eyes she hid a smile that things had
worked
So well for her—but for this house
It's nothing short of tragedy—the tale
The travellers told, and that's plain
enough.
790 And it will be good news to that one
When he hears it. Oh, the pity of it!
All the troubles that we had, and never
Two alike, here in the house of Atreus,
More than a body could stand; oh, how
they vexed
This heart of mine! And yet I never
Had to endure anything like this.
The rest I got through when I set my mind
to it.
Orestes, bless him, plagued the life out of
me—
I had the rearing of him from his mother,
800 And all those times he got me up
By crying in the night—and what good did
it ever
Do me? Babes are little animals,
They can't think for themselves, you have
To guess what they want, what else can
you do?
The child in his cradle doesn't have the
words
To tell us if he's hungry, if he's thirsty,
Or wants to wet; no arguing
With young insides. I needed second sight,
And I was often wrong, believe me, and
had to be
810 His washerwoman too. Feed him, clean up
after him,
It was all the same job, and I
Doubled these offices, ever since I took
Orestes from his father's hands; and now
He's dead, they say; so much the worse for
me.
Well, I must go to find the man who
ruined
This house, and he'll be glad enough to
hear it.
CHORUS. Did she say he was to come in state?
CIL. Say that again, so I may catch your
meaning.
CHORUS. With his bodyguard, or by himself?

CIL. She told him to bring his servants 820
armed—
CHORUS. Then as you hate your master, do
not tell him this.
Say he must come alone, so his informants
May talk without constraint. Bid him
hurry
And be of good heart. It is the messenger
Who takes the crooked word and makes it
straight.
CIL. But are you happy over what I told you?
CHORUS. And if Zeus means to send a wind
To blow away foul weather?
CIL.   How?
Orestes is dead; the house has lost its hope.
CHORUS. Not yet. He would be a poor diviner 830
Who traced things so.
CIL.   What do you mean?
Do you know something we have not been
told?
CHORUS. Go with your message, do as you are
bid.
The gods will take care of their own affairs.
CIL. I'll go, and do as you have told me;
And heaven grant it turn out for the best!

[*Exit*]

CHORUS. Grant this my prayer, O Zeus
The godhead, father of Olympus,
That those who long to see
This mansion set to rights may have their 840
hope
Accomplished; what I have said
Is nothing if not just, O Zeus;
Do you enforce it.

   O Zeus, rank him who now
Is in the house above his enemies.
For if you raise him to eminence
Two and threefold will he repay you,
Zeus, and cheerfully.

   For be advised, this colt,
The orphan of a man much loved,   850
Is harnessed in the chariot
Of suffering; and you must set a measure
To the course, so we may never

See him break step, but extend himself
Full tilt across the ground.

O Zeus, rank him who now
Is in the house above his enemies.
For if you raise him to eminence
Two and threefold will he repay you,
860 Zeus, and cheerfully.

And you that haunt the inner sanctum
of the house
In pride of wealth, O gods
That think as we do, hear us.
Come, rid us of this bloody stain
Of things done in olden time.
Make manifest your justice, let
Old murder breed in the house no more.

And you who live
At the mouthpiece of the world
870 Grant to those who fell in glory
This kindness, that they may look up again
To the house of a hero, and that eyes of
love
May see it as a beacon shining, free
From enshrouding shadows.

And let the son of Maia give us fitting
aid
For he is mightiest
To give a deed fair passage
If so he will, for many a time
He deigns to make dark word plain
880 Or wraps the eyes in shadows, speaking
Riddles that no clearer come by daylight.

And you who live
At the mouthpiece of the world
Grant to those who fell in glory
This kindness, that they may look up again
To the house of a hero, and that eyes of
love
May see it as a beacon shining, free
From enshrouding shadows.

Then at last will the house be rid
Of double evil; with united voice   890
We shall speed the work, as women may,
Break out the mourning song, and sing
"The ship sails fair."
Mine, mine to reap the argosy, and wreck
Is far from my beloved.

When the time comes for doing, be
Stoutedhearted; when she calls
"My child," shout her down
With cry of "Father," and act
The sin that is grace, her murder.   900

And with Orestes' mind combine
The heart of Perseus; for your friends
On earth and under it, perform
This favor, though it sting you sore.
Let death and blood
Run wild within, and bring upon the man
Who killed, a death in punishment.

[*Enter* AEGISTHUS]

AEGISTHUS. I do but as they bid me, and am
come
In answer to the message. There are people
Lodging here, they say, who tell a tale   910
We never hoped to hear, the death
Of Orestes. This house has wounds still
raw
From bloodshed long ago; now must it take
Another burden on itself, a thing
Of running blood? What can I make of
this?
The living truth? The terrified imaginings
Of women make bubble-tales that burst
Upon the air. Can you say anything
Of this, to make me certain in my mind?
CHORUS. We heard the same. But go in to the
travelers
And let them tell you. It is better always 920
To go to the source than learn secondhand.
AEG. Yes, I should like to see this messenger
And ask if he was with him when he died

---

869 *the mouthpiece of the world* the meaning of this whole passage is obscure; probably Apollo's shrine at Delphi is meant   875 *the Son of Maia* Hermes

902 *Perseus* mythical hero who killed the Gorgon, she-monster with hair of snakes whose glance turned men to stone

Or speaks the words of groping rumor only.
The mind must have an eye for trickery.

[*Exit*]

CHORUS. Zeus, Zeus, what shall I say? And
    where begin
My prayer for the gods' aid?
How, before the ending, find
930 Words worthy of my will?
For now the bloody cutting-edge
Comes close, to rend a man.
Now in the house of Agamemnon
Will he bring ruin upon all
Or light the fire of liberty again
And in the kingdom of his father
Live rich, the honored son.
To such a wrestle must Orestes come
The challenger, by the god's advisement
940 One against two; and may he throw them!

[*A cry within*]

Ah, what is that?
What has happened in the house?
Let us stand aside till the work is finished
So there may come no blame on us all
In this foul business, for the fight
Is at an end.

[*Enter* SERVANT *from the palace*]

SERVANT. Cry desolation, for our lord is dead,
And cry again, a triple cry of sorrow!
Aegisthus is gone. Come, no delay;
950 Open the portals of the women's chambers,
Slide back the bolts; we need young
    strength
To fight for us, a man, but not for him
Who is dead and gone; no purpose there.
Ahoy, ahoy!
I call on the deaf, on those who lie
In idle slumber and do nothing. Where
Is Clytemnestra, what does she do now?
Her head is on the block, and soon
Must fall, in measure as she did to others.

[*Enter* CLYTEMNESTRA]

CLYT. What is this? What means this shout- 960
    ing in the house?
SERVANT. Listen to me. The dead are killing
    the living.
CLYT. You speak in riddles, but I read you
    well.
By sleight we killed, by sleight we are to
    die.
Come, hurry, bring an axe to kill a man.

[*Exit* SERVANT]

Let us make certain, then. It must be he
    or I,
So far have I come now in this sad history.

[*Enter* ORESTES *with a drawn sword*,
PYLADES *beside him*]

OR. You are the one I seek. His part is played.
CLYT. Are you dead, my love? Is brave Aegis-
    thus gone?
OR. You love that man? Then in one tomb
    you shall
Be buried, and be faithful after death.   970
CLYT. Hold back, my son, have pity on this
    breast
My child, where often slumbering
You lay, and suckled milk to make you
    strong.
OR. Pylades, what shall I do? How may I
    kill my mother?
PYLADES. What of the oracles still unfulfilled
Apollo spoke at Delphi? Your sworn pro-
    mise?
Better the world should hate you than the
    gods.
OR. Your word has won. You show the way
    that I must go.

[*To* CLYTEMNESTRA]

Come in, for I would kill you on his body.
In life you thought him better than my 980
    father;
Then sleep with him in death, if such you
    love
And give to him whom you should love
    your hate.

CLYT. You took my youth. May I not share your age?

OR. You killed my father. Would you share my house?

CLYT. The blame is Destiny's as well as mine.

OR. Then it is Destiny who kills you now.

CLYT. Have you no terror of a mother's curse?

OR. You bore me and then cast me out to sorrow.

CLYT. To live with friends. This was no casting out.

990 OR. I was born of a free father and you sold me.

CLYT. Then where is the price that I received for you?

OR. I could not bring myself to tell your shame.

CLYT. Tell all, but tell your father's follies too.

OR. Blame not him. He toiled, you sat at home.

CLYT. Women suffer when the man is gone, my child.

OR. Man's labor feeds the women who sit idle.

CLYT. My child, I think you mean to kill your mother.

OR. I will not kill you. You will kill yourself.

CLYT. Take care. Your mother's curse will hound you down.

1000 OR. My father's curse will find me if I fail.

CLYT. This is the serpent that I bore and fed.

OR. Indeed the terror of your dreams spoke true.

     You sinned in killing. Now be sinned against.

[ORESTES *and* PYLADES *drive* CLYTEM-NESTRA *into the house*]

CHORUS. Even for these I can find tears, and for
     Their coupled death. But since Orestes has been bold
     To top this long and bloody history
     We find it better that the light within
     The house not be extinguished utterly.
     In time there came to the sons of Priam
1010 Justice heavy in punishment

And on the house of Agamemnon came
The lions paired to battle two.
Then pressed he to the uttermost, the exile
To whom god had spoken, eager
Under heaven's admonition.

    Cry joy now for the mansions of our lords,
The end of pain, the end of rich things wasted
By two in infamy, the dark days gone.

    He came; and his part was to deceive,
To scheme and conquer. In the fight   1020
His hand was guided by the very child
Of Zeus—we mortals know her name
As Justice, and we have good cause—
She who in a blast of hate
Comes on her foes destroying.

    Cry joy now for the mansions of our lords,
The end of pain, the end of rich things wasted
By two in infamy, the dark days gone.

    As Apollo spoke from his deep-riven
Cavern on Parnassus, so   1030
Has it passed; the innocent deceit
Comes home to fight harm grown old.
Divinity has ways to keep
From going down to evil; it is fit
That we should laud the powers that reign in heaven.

    Now is there light to see, the bit
Is gone that held our house so hard.
So up, you halls, arise; for time
Too long have you lain fallen.

    Not long, and Time that brings all   1040
To pass will enter in
Our gates, when the evil presence
Is cast from our hearth, and ceremonies
Have made all clean; then chance
Will come up ever fair for those
Who take their lodging here in aftertime.

Now is there light to see, the bit
Is gone that held our house so hard.
So up, you halls, arise; for time
1050   Too long have you lain fallen.

[*The doors open.* ORESTES *is seen standing
sword in hand over the bodies of* CLYTEM-
NESTRA *and* AEGISTHUS. *He holds the robe
in which* AGAMEMNON *was killed*]

OR. See here the double lordship of this land
  Who killed my father and laid waste my
    house.
  A while they sat upon their thrones in
    state,
  And they are lovers still, as you may judge
  By what befell; their oath has kept its pro-
    mise.
  Together they swore to kill my wretched
    father
  And die together; they are not forsworn.

[*Displaying* AGAMEMNON's *robe*]

  See too, all you who look on this sad story,
  The trick they used to bind my wretched
    father,
1060   Chains for his hands, a halter for his feet.
  Come, spread it out and make a circle
    round
  To show this net to catch a man.
  So may the father see—I mean not mine,
  But he who watches every living thing
  The Sun—my mother's filthy handiwork.
  So at the judgement day, whenever it shall
    come,
  He may appear to testify
  That I had just cause to pursue the death
  Of this my mother. On Aegisthus' death
1070   I waste no words. It is written, adulterers
  Shall be punished—but she who worked so
    vile a thing
  Against her man, whose children she con-
    ceived
  And bore beneath her cincture, sweet load
    once,
  Now this you see, a curse, a thing of hate—
  What do you think her now? A water-
    snake, a viper

Who needs no fangs, whose very touch
Will rot a man, so venomous
Her mind, so quick to strike . . .
And this, what shall I call it? Has it any
  name
That one may say with decency? A snare 1080
To catch an animal, a winding sheet,
A tenting for the bath? A net, a skein
We well could say, a robe to hobble feet—
The sort of thing a cozener might use
Who lived by catching travellers and rob-
  bing them
Of money; such a trick as this
Would win him many victims, and would
  keep
His heart warm inside him. . . .
May such a woman never come to share
My home and bed; may heaven first de- 1090
  stroy me,
Before I have begotten me a child.
CHORUS. Sing sorrow for things done:
  For you a hateful death, and for the one
  Who lives, the ripening of pain.
OR. Did she do this or not? This mantle
  testifies
  That it was dyed red by Aegisthus' sword.
  Dip it and dip again, and still
  The stain of blood and its accomplice,
    Time,
  Have spoilt the work. Now I can praise
    him, now
  Make lamentation over him; and when   1100
  I speak to this, the robe that killed my
    father,
  I sorrow for the doing and the death,
  For all our race, the tainted prize
  Of this, my inconsiderable conquest.
CHORUS. No mortal man can live his life
  Through to the end untouched by suffer-
    ing.
  There is trouble here, and more to come.
OR. But hear me now; I cannot see the end;
  My chariot has run me from the course,
  My rebel senses lead me where they will, 1110
  While fear draws breath to sing within my
    heart
  And it must dance to his angry tune. While
  I

Have wits about me still, I call upon my
  friends
To hear. I killed my mother, but I say
There was some right in this; my father's
  blood
Had tainted her, she was a thing unclean
In heaven's sight.
And for the blandishments that made me
  bold
To such a deed, I cite as culpable
1120 Apollo, seer of Delphi, who proclaimed in
  oracles
That I could do this thing and still
Be innocent; but if I failed—
What then would come on me I will not
  say.
Draw bow at hazard, you would never
Come within measure of my suffering.

[*He arrays himself as a suppliant*]

See me how I go forth, with wreath
Upon my head, with branch in hand,
To the centrestone of earth, Apollo's seat
And holy shrine, that famous place
1130 Whose fire burns everlasting; I will go
Out from my own, from blood that is my
  own;
Apollo charged me that I should not turn
To any other sanctuary but his.
To all who live in Argos in the future time
I say remember how these evil things were
  done
And speak for me when Menelaus comes.
And I shall go an outcast from my land
To walk among strangers, and leave be-
  hind
In life, in death, this memory of me.
1140 CHORUS. What you did was well. Do not let
  foul speech
Harness your mouth, or turn your tongue
  to evil.
For you brought liberty to all who live
In Argos, when you came upon
This pair of snakes and cut their heads off
  clean.

1126 wreath, branch customary emblems of the suppliant *1136 Menelaus* Agamemnon's brother

[ORESTES *points and cries out*]

OR. O servants of this house, they come
  In shapes of Gorgons, clad in robes of
    black,
  Their hair a nest of snakes; I cannot stay!
CHORUS. If any man has earned a father's
  love
  You are the one; so what imaginings
  Are these, that send you reeling? Stay, 1150
  Be bold, you have good cause.
OR. I suffer, these are no imaginings
  But real; the hounding of my mother's hate.
CHORUS. It is the blood still wet on your
  hands
  That comes on you now to shake your
    senses.
OR. O Lord Apollo, are they coming yet?
  They weep, their eyes are running foul with
    blood.
CHORUS. There is one way to purify your-
  self. Apollo
  Will lay his hands on you, and make you
    free
  Of this affliction. 1160
OR. You do not see them, but I see them.
  I must go forth, I can stay here no longer.

[*Exit*]

CHORUS. Good luck go with you, then, and
  may the god
  Look kindly on you, and preserve you safe
  In fortune.
  Now for the third time
  Has storm come from the race, to blow
  Upon the palace of our kings, and passed.
  One was the child-feast,
  The grief and desolation of Thyestes. 1170
  Two was the death of kings, when the lord

1146 Gorgons Orestes sees the Furies advancing on him,
still invisible to the chorus. They were traditionally
represented as women with hair of snakes and carrying
blazing torches—thus resembling the Gorgons, to
whom Orestes compares them. See note on v. 902
1169 the child-feast Atreus, Agamemnon's father, had
killed his brother *Thyestes'* children and served them
up as a feast

Of the Achaean host was struck
Down in the bath.
Three was the coming of the savior
Or death—which shall I call it?
When will there be an ending, when
Will wrath be spent, and fate lulled to
slumber?

1177

THEMATIC IMAGERY IN THE ORESTEIA

Philip Wheelwright

THE SNAKE AND THE OMPHALOS

The action of the *Choëphori*, the middle tragedy of the *Oresteia*, hinges upon an ambiguity. Clytemnestra's supernatural solicitings, like Macbeth's, have brought her a dark prophecy which, though true in one sense, is false in another; and like Macbeth also, her failure to perceive its real import and to guard against the impending ill, leads to her doom. After murdering her royal husband Clytemnestra has been careful to placate the Furies regularly with solemn midnight offerings, and thus for a time has made good her boast on which the *Agamemnon* closed: "You and I (to Aegisthus), now masters of the house, henceforth shall govern it well." But at length, as the exiled Orestes secretly returns to his native land, she is visited by an eerie dream, which is announced by the Chorus of Bondswomen:

Clear-piercing indeed, causing the hair to rise, was the Phoibos who divines for the house in dreams, when, breathing forth wrath, he caused a shriek from the inner chamber, and terror fell heavily about the women's quarters.
(*Choe.*, 32–36)

1172 Achaean Greek

From THE BURNING FOUNTAIN: A STUDY IN THE LANGUAGE OF SYMBOLISM by Philip Wheelwright. Copyright © 1954 by Indiana University Press. Reprinted by permission of the publisher.

The description (which I have translated as literally as possible) is ingeniously duosignative. To a Greek acquainted with the manner of divination at the shrine of Apollo at Delphi such epithets as *clear-piercing*, *hair-on-end*, *Phoibos*, and *inner chamber* would carry in addition to their literal meanings a coherent allusion to the sacred Delphic mysteries. On the literal level, *phoibos* can be translated "a spectral vision," the inner chamber is a synonym for the women's quarters, and the other terms are simply descriptive. But Phoibos is also an epithet of Apollo; "inner chamber" alludes to the Inner Sanctum, the Holy of Holies, where the the clairvoyant priestess received the dread disclosures; "clear-piercing" alludes to the unearthly tones of the priestess speaking in a trance; and "hair-on-end" to the atmosphere of awe and supernatural terror which surrounded the seance. But these poetic innuendoes, although they enrich the essential drama, do not affect the overt plot. They are followed by an ambiguity which does so.

Seers, wise in the lore of dreams,
bound to speak true, do say
the dead beneath the ground
are angered sore, and wroth
at them that slew them.
(*Choe.*, 37–41)

Clytemnestra, taking the seers' reading of the drama in the likeliest sense, has sent Electra and the bondswomen with offerings to pour on Agamemnon's grave, in hope of placating his angry ghost. Later, however, in the *kommos* between Orestes and the Chorus of Bondswomen, the audience is apprised not only of the dream's content but of its real meaning.

ORESTES: From what motive did she send the libations? Why did she show such tardy regard with so paltry an offering? . . . Tell me if you know, for I am eager to learn.
CHORUS: I know, my good youth, for I was there. Because her heart quaked at dreams and

night-wandering alarms the impious woman sent these libations.

OR.: And did you learn what the dream was, so that you can describe it truly?

CHO.: She thought she gave birth to a serpent. We have it on her own word.

OR.: And what followed? What is the story's upshot?

CHO.: She dressed the creature in swaddling clothes and laid it to rest, as one would do to a child.

OR.: How did she nourish the new-born monster?

CHO.: She dreamt that she put it to her breast.

OR.: How could the teat have been unscathed by so deadly a thing?

CHO.: Scathed it was, for the creature drew curds of blood with the milk.

OR.: Ah, this is no empty apparition. It means a man.

(*Choe.*, 514–534)

In telling what the apparition signifies Orestes makes explicit one of the major symbols of the play:

OR.: So then I pray to Earth and to my father's tomb, that this dream may be a surety of my accomplishment. It plainly fits my case, as I interpret it. For if the snake issued forth from the same place as I had done, if it was wrapped in infant swaddling bands and opened its mouth to the same teat that once suckled me, if it mingled the kindly milk with curd of blood so that the pain and fear of it made her cry out, —why surely it follows that even as she nourished that monster into life, so now she must die a violent death. 'Tis I, made over into the serpent of her dream, that shall murder her.

(*Choe.*, 540–550)

Clytemnestra, whatever her vices, did not lack intelligence, but she was prevented from reading the dream aright since she still believed Orestes to be dead. On the other hand it might be remarked that Orestes was in exile, which to the ancients bore an analogy to death, and the figure of a snake issuing from the womb and taking nourishment at the breast should not have

been so very obscure to a people skilled at dream interpretation. However, we need not overstress a small implausibility which the plot required; and in any case Clytemnestra grasps the situation quickly enough when events begin to move and Aegisthus is slain.

CLYT.: What is happening? Why are you filling the house with such outcries?

SERVANT: It means that the dead are slaying the living.

CLYT.: Oho! I take the meaning of your riddle. By craft we perish even as by craft we slew.

(*Choe.*, 885–888)

And Clytemnestra completes her version of the symbolic pattern when on finding herself powerless to soften Orestes' purpose she cries:

CLYT.: Ah me! so this is that serpent which I brought forth and nourished.

(*Choe.*, 928)

In one set of connections, then, the serpent symbolizes Orestes. But in another it symbolizes Clytemnestra and the dark maternal forces that brood about her. When Orestes first sees the Furies, it is in the guise of wingless Gorgons with coils of writhing snakes, and they retain this character in the *Eumenides*, presumably up to the point of their persuasion and conversion by Athena. Aeschylus makes an effective passage to the feminine phase of serpent symbolism, by introducing it just after the Chorus has been praising Orestes for liberating the land of Argos by "deftly severing the heads of the serpents"—i.e., of Clytemnestra and Aegisthus. It is the same word—*drakon*—with which Orestes immediately after describes his horrid vision. The snake is not directly or primarily a feminine symbol—indeed, its phallic shape tends to give it an iconically masculine imputation wherever the aspect of sex is involved; but as the snake-form is a usual one for *chthonioi*, earth-spirits, to take, it enters into many associations with earth-mother symbolism—especially where, as at the end of the *Choëphori* and the beginning of the *Eumenides*, the mother-figure is also an embodiment of vengeance.

A deeper meaning of the snake-symbolism can be seen in its relation to Delphi. The action of the *Eumenides* opens in front of the temple of Apollo at Delphi, and it is there that the priestess, after praying to representative divinities of both sky and earth, discovers the snake-wreathed monsters. In the preclassical age it would appear that the worship at Delphi was purely chthonic, and that a snake was the guardian of the ancient oracle-spirit of the place. The legend of Apollo killing the Delphic snake evidently reflects the actual event of an Apollonian cult succeeding the older chthonic one in that place. Chthonian religion had grown up most naturally there, from the physical character of the grotto, within which a deep cleft gave forth vaporous exhalations that seemed to arise from the nether world. At some early period the grotto had come to be conceived as the Omphalos, the world's navel, the umbilical cord by which the children of Mother Earth retain a pristine connection with the older world of vague dark forces which affect human life with blessing or bane. At the coming of Apollonian worship the earlier notion did not disappear; it merely merged, a bit incongruously at first, with the cult of the bright Olympian sun-god, who was also, especially at Delphi, the god of prophecy and healing.

Accordingly the Pythian Priestess' description of Orestes at the Omphalos seeking expiation for his crime acquires an added dimension of significance when it is remembered that Orestes stands as suppliant at the door to the womb of mundane creation.

PRIESTESS: O horror to behold, horror even to say! . . . As I was passing into the laurelled shrine I saw at the Omphalos a man in suppliant posture, god-accursed for some deed of guilt, his hands all dripping with blood, holding a sword newly unsheathed, and the top-most branch of an olive tree decently filleted with large white tufts of spotless wool.
(*Eum.,* 34, 39–45)

The primary blood-reference is of course to Orestes' deed of matricide, for the Furies, as maternal avengers, lie sleeping about him, presently to be spurred to action by Clytemnestra's restless ghost. But the blood can also represent the bloody state of a new-born babe—which the newly unsheathed sword and the purity of spotless wool might differently indicate. If this interpretation seems lightly allowable, we have here a momentary, iconically suggested prognostic-symbol of Orestes' coming reversal of role. He has cut himself off from the mother-image by murderous violence, thus becoming an exile in more senses than one—not only geographically from the city of Argos, whence the Furies have pursued him, but psychically from all the warmth and naturalness of life which the mother-image properly connotes. The excision was needful because his own particular mother-image had become an embodiment of evil: that was part of the curse upon the royal house. But he cannot find salvation until he has placated the maternal forces of earth which are now taking vengeance upon him. The snakes with which the Furies are semi-identified represent those chthonic powers, potentially both dreadful and beneficent, with which Orestes must eventually make his spiritual peace.

The Coming of Light

CHORUS: Now is the test. Either the murderous bladepoints will leave their stain and cause the ruin of Agamemnon's house forever, or else the son, kindling fire and light for freedom, shall reëstablish the duly-ordered rule in his city and the prosperity of his fathers.
(*Choe.,* 859–865)

These words, uttered by the Chorus of Bondswomen in the *Choëphori* just before

Orestes' slaying of Aegisthus and Clytemnestra, can be taken in two senses. Paley's paraphrase indicates the surface meaning:* "Orestes will either lose all or gain all by the present stake; either he himself will be killed, or he will recover the sovereignty, and offer sacrifices for the release of the Argives from an unjust usurpation." The personal interpretation—what Orestes himself will lose or gain by the immediately forthcoming contest—is borne out by the athletic metaphor of the next four lines: "In such a wrestling match the noble Orestes, the extra contestant, is about to cope with his two adversaries." The word *ephedros*, which I have translated "extra contestant," was applied technically to the third fighter who sat by in a contest between two athletes, prepared to challenge the victor to a fresh encounter. In terms of this figure Clytemnestra has won the first bout by slaying Agamemnon, and Orestes the *ephedros* is accordingly ready to take her on, with Aegisthus as a preliminary. Paley carries out the logic of the interpretation by taking "fire" and "light" to signify the sacrificial flames which would be lighted in celebration if Orestes should prove victorious.

Now there is a deeper meaning as well—continuous with the surface meaning and even reinforcing it, but yet something more, adumbrating a tragic judgment about the nature and destiny of man in his universal condition. The state of unredeemed nature is a state of war: of ego against ego, group against group. Life on such terms is a denial of man's high destiny. Parallel to the Christian mythos of Adam's disobedience and loss of Eden stands the mythos around which Aeschylus has built the *Oresteia*: the crime of *hybris*, the curse upon the House, the

*F. A. Paley, *Aeschylus, Translated into English Prose*, 2nd ed. (Cambridge and London, 1871)

malign working out of that curse even to the third generation, and the salvation which comes down from above by divine grace in the person of Athena. Forefather Atreus' crime of serving up Thyestes' children to him as baked meats was *hybris* of so extraordinary a degree, doing such dreadful violence to the balanced course of nature (there is balance even in the natural state of war, as Heraclitus keenly perceived), that the entire family of him who committed it became more than usually vulnerable to the curse which the bereaved and outraged father invoked against it. A morality of vendetta follows, a morality of the hunter and the hunted, in which Aegisthus seeks to avenge the cannibalism practised upon his brothers, Orestes to avenge his father by slaying his slayers, and the Furies to avenge Clytemnestra by continuing the deadly pursuit against Orestes. How shall it all end, the Chorus of Bondswomen asks?

> Here, then, upon this royal House
> a third storm has blown and swept along to its end.
> First came the wretched meal of children's flesh;
> next the sad fate of our lord and king,—
> slain in the bath he perished who had led all Greece to war.
> And now a third has come—we know not whence—
> a savior? or shall I say a doom?
> O where shall fulfillment be found?
> How shall the power of guilt be lulled to rest?
>
> (*Choe.*, 1065–1076)

The tone of these words, with which the *Choëphori* closes, transcends a concern for the fate of Orestes as an individual. It points, although still darkly, toward the fundamental motif of the trilogy: the passage from a morality of vengeance and vendetta to a morality of law.

HAMLET

William Shakespeare

CHARACTERS

CLAUDIUS, King of Denmark

HAMLET, son to the late, and nephew to the present, King

POLONIUS, Lord Chamberlain

HORATIO, friend to Hamlet

LÆRTES, son to Polonius

VOLTEMAND

CORNELIUS

ROSENCRANTZ

GUILDENSTERN } courtiers

OSRIC

A GENTLEMAN

A PRIEST

MARCELLUS

BERNARDO } officers

FRANCISCO, a soldier

REYNALDO, servant to Polonius

PLAYERS

TWO CLOWNS, gravediggers

FORTINBRAS, Prince of Norway

A NORWEGIAN CAPTAIN

ENGLISH AMBASSADORS

GERTRUDE, Queen of Denmark, mother to Hamlet

OPHELIA, daughter to Polonius

GHOST OF HAMLET'S FATHER

LORDS, LADIES, OFFICERS, SOLDIERS, SAILORS, MESSENGERS, ATTENDANTS

Scene: *Elsinore*]

William Shakespeare, *Hamlet*, edited by Willard Farnham, in "The Pelican Shakespeare," General Editor: Alfred Harbage (rev. ed.; New York and Baltimore: Penguin Books Inc., 1970). Copyright © Penguin Books Inc., 1957, 1970. Reprinted by permission of Penguin Books Inc.

ACT I

Scene i

Enter Bernardo and Francisco, two sentinels.

BERNARDO. Who's there?

FRANCISCO.
Nay, answer me. Stand and unfold yourself.

BERNARDO. Long live the king!

FRANCISCO. Bernardo?

BERNARDO. He.

FRANCISCO.
You come most carefully upon your hour.

BERNARDO.
'Tis now struck twelve. Get thee to bed, Francisco.

FRANCISCO.
For this relief much thanks. 'Tis bitter cold, And I am sick at heart.

BERNARDO.
Have you had quiet guard?

FRANCISCO.   Not a mouse stirring.

BERNARDO.
Well, good night.
If you do meet Horatio and Marcellus,
The rivals of my watch, bid them make   13
haste.

Enter Horatio and Marcellus.

FRANCISCO.
I think I hear them. Stand, ho! Who is there?

HORATIO.
Friends to this ground.

MARCELLUS.   And liegemen to the Dane.   15

FRANCISCO.
Give you good night.

MARCELLUS.   O, farewell, honest soldier.
Who hath relieved you?

FRANCISCO.   Bernardo hath my place.
Give you good night.   *Exit Francisco*

MARCELLUS.   Holla, Bernardo!

I, i Elsinore Castle: a sentry-post   *13 rivals* sharers
15 Dane King of Denmark

BERNARDO. Say—
What, is Horatio there?

HORATIO. A piece of him.

BERNARDO.
Welcome, Horatio. Welcome, good Marcellus.

HORATIO.
What, has this thing appeared again tonight?

BERNARDO.
I have seen nothing.

MARCELLUS.
Horatio says 'tis but our fantasy,
And will not let belief take hold of him
Touching this dreaded sight twice seen of
us.
Therefore I have entreated him along
With us to watch the minutes of this night,
That, if again this apparition come,
29 He may approve our eyes and speak to it.

HORATIO.
Tush, tush, 'twill not appear.

BERNARDO. Sit down awhile,
And let us once again assail your ears,
That are so fortified against our story,
What we two nights have seen.

HORATIO. Well, sit we down,
And let us hear Bernardo speak of this.

BERNARDO.
Last night of all,
36 When yond same star that's westward
from the pole
Had made his course t'illume that part of
heaven
Where now it burns, Marcellus and myself,
The bell then beating one—

Enter Ghost.

MARCELLUS.
Peace, break thee off. Look where it comes
again.

BERNARDO.
In the same figure like the king that's dead.

MARCELLUS.
Thou art a scholar; speak to it, Horatio.

BERNARDO.
Looks 'a not like the king? Mark it,
Horatio.

HORATIO.
Most like. It harrows me with fear and
wonder.

BERNARDO.
It would be spoke to.

MARCELLUS. Speak to it, Horatio.

HORATIO.
What art thou that usurp'st this time of
night
Together with that fair and warlike form
In which the majesty of buried Denmark   48
Did sometimes march? By heaven I charge   49
thee, speak.

MARCELLUS.
It is offended.

BERNARDO. See, it stalks away.

HORATIO.
Stay. Speak, speak. I charge thee, speak.
Exit Ghost.

MARCELLUS.
'Tis gone and will not answer.

BERNARDO.
How now, Horatio? You tremble and look
pale.
Is not this something more than fantasy?
What think you on't?

HORATIO.
Before my God, I might not this believe
Without the sensible and true avouch
Of mine own eyes.

MARCELLUS. Is it not like the king?

HORATIO.
As thou art to thyself.
Such was the very armor he had on
When he th' ambitious Norway combated.   61
So frowned he once when, in an angry   62
parle,
He smote the sledded Polacks on the ice.
'Tis strange.

MARCELLUS.
Thus twice before, and jump at this dead   65
hour,

---

29 approve confirm   *36 pole* polestar

48 buried Denmark the buried King of Denmark   *49
sometimes* formerly   *61 Norway* King of Norway   *62
parle* parley   *65 jump* just, exactly

With martial stalk hath he gone by our
    watch.

HORATIO.

    In what particular thought to work I know
      not;
68   But, in the gross and scope of my opinion,
    This bodes some strange eruption to our
      state.

MARCELLUS.

    Good now, sit down, and tell me he that
      knows,
    Why this same strict and most observant
      watch
72   So nightly toils the subject of the land,
    And why such daily cast of brazen cannon
74   And foreign mart for implements of war,
75   Why such impress of shipwrights, whose
      sore task
    Does not divide the Sunday from the week.
77   What might be toward that this sweaty
      haste
    Doth make the night joint-laborer with the
      day?
    Who is't that can inform me?

HORATIO.   That can I.

    At least the whisper goes so. Our last king,
    Whose image even but now appeared to us,
    Was as you know by Fortinbras of
      Norway,
83   Thereto pricked on by a most emulate
      pride,
    Dared to the combat; in which our valiant
      Hamlet
    (For so this side of our known world
      esteemed him)
    Did slay this Fortinbras; who, by a sealed
      compact
87   Well ratified by law and heraldry,
    Did forfeit, with his life, all those his lands
89   Which he stood seized of to the conqueror;
90   Against the which a moiety competent
91   Was gagèd by our king, which had
      returned

To the inheritance of Fortinbras
Had he been vanquisher, as, by the same 93
    comart
And carriage of the article designed,   94
His fell to Hamlet. Now, sir, young
    Fortinbras,
Of unimprovèd mettle hot and full,   96
Hath in the skirts of Norway here and there
Sharked up a list of lawless resolutes   98
For food and diet to some enterprise
That hath a stomach in't; which is no   100
    other,
As it doth well appear unto our state,
But to recover of us by strong hand
And terms compulsatory those foresaid
    lands
So by his father lost; and this, I take it,
Is the main motive of our preparations,
The source of this our watch, and the chief 106
    head
Of this posthaste and romage in the land. 107

BERNARDO.

    I think it be no other but e'en so.
    Well may it sort that this portentous figure 109
    Comes armèd through our watch so like
      the king
    That was and is the question of these wars.

HORATIO.

    A mote it is to trouble the mind's eye.   112
    In the most high and palmy state of Rome,
    A little ere the mightiest Julius fell,
    The graves stood tenantless and the sheeted 115
      dead
    Did squeak and gibber in the Roman
      streets;
    As stars with trains of fire and dews of
      blood,
    Disasters in the sun; and the moist star   118
    Upon whose influence Neptune's empire
      stands
    Was sick almost to doomsday with eclipse.

---

68 gross and scope gross scope, general view *72 toils* makes toil; *subject* subjects *74 mart* trading *75 impress* conscription *77 toward* in preparation *83 emulate* jealously rivalling *87 law and heraldry* law of heralds regulating combat *89 seized* possessed *90 moiety competent* sufficient portion *91 gagèd* engaged, staked *93 comart* joint bargain *94 carriage* purport *96 unimprovèd* unused *98 Sharked* snatched indiscriminately as the shark takes prey; *resolutes* desperadoes *100 stomach* show of venturesomeness *106 head* fountainhead, source *107 romage* intense activity *109 sort* suit *112 mote* speck of dust *115 sheeted* in shrouds *118 Disasters* ominous signs; *moist star* moon

121 And even the like precurse of feared events,
122 As harbingers preceding still the fates
123 And prologue to the omen coming on,
Have heaven and earth together demonstrated
125 Unto our climatures and countrymen.

Enter Ghost.

But soft, behold, lo where it comes again!
127 I'll cross it, though it blast me.—Stay, illusion.

He spreads his arms.

If thou hast any sound or use of voice,
Speak to me.
If there be any good thing to be done
That may to thee do ease and grace to me,
Speak to me.
If thou art privy to thy country's fate,
134 Which happily foreknowing may avoid,
O, speak!
Or if thou hast uphoarded in thy life
Extorted treasure in the womb of earth,
For which, they say, you spirits oft walk in death,

The cock crows.

Speak of it. Stay and speak. Stop it, Marcellus.
MARCELLUS.
140 Shall I strike at it with my partisan?
HORATIO.
Do, if it will not stand.
BERNARDO.   'Tis here.
HORATIO.   'Tis here.
MARCELLUS.
'Tis gone.   [*Exit Ghost.*]
We do it wrong, being so majestical,
To offer it the show of violence,
For it is as the air invulnerable,
And our vain blows malicious mockery.

BERNARDO.
It was about to speak when the cock crew.
HORATIO.
And then it started, like a guilty thing
Upon a fearful summons. I have heard
The cock, that is the trumpet to the morn,
Doth with his lofty and shrill-sounding throat
Awake the god of day, and at his warning,
Whether in sea or fire, in earth or air,
Th' extravagant and erring spirit hies   154
To his confine; and of the truth herein
This present object made probation.   156
MARCELLUS.
It faded on the crowing of the cock.
Some say that ever 'gainst that season comes   158
Wherein our Saviour's birth is celebrated,
This bird of dawning singeth all night long,
And then, they say, no spirit dare stir abroad,
The nights are wholesome, then no planets   162
strike,
No fairy takes, nor witch hath power to   163
charm.
So hallowed and so gracious is that time.
HORATIO.
So have I heard and do in part believe it.
But look, the morn in russet mantle clad
Walks o'er the dew of yon high eastward hill.
Break we our watch up, and by my advice
Let us impart what we have seen to-night
Unto young Hamlet, for upon my life
This spirit, dumb to us, will speak to him.
Do you consent we shall acquaint him with it,
As needful in our loves, fitting our duty?
MARCELLUS.
Let's do't, I pray, and I this morning know
Where we shall find him most conveniently.
Exeunt.

*

---

121 precurse foreshadowing   *122 harbingers* forerunners; *still* constantly   *123 omen* calamity   *125 climatures* regions   *127 cross it* cross its path   *134 happily* happily, perchance   *140 partisan* pike

154 extravagant wandering beyond bounds; *erring* wandering   *156 probation* proof   *158 'gainst* just before   *162 strike* work evil by influence   *163 takes* bewitches

ACT I

Scene ii

Flourish. Enter Claudius, King of Denmark, Gertrude the Queen, Councillors, Polonius and his son Laertes, Hamlet, cum aliis [including Voltemand and Cornelius].

KING.

Though yet of Hamlet our dear brother's death
The memory be green, and that it us befitted
To bear our hearts in grief, and our whole kingdom
To be contracted in one brow of woe,
Yet so far hath discretion fought with nature
That we with wisest sorrow think on him
Together with remembrance of ourselves.
Therefore our sometime sister, now our queen,
9 Th' imperial jointress to this warlike state,
Have we, as 'twere with a defeated joy,
With an auspicious and a dropping eye,
With mirth in funeral and with dirge in marriage,
In equal scale weighing delight and dole,
14 Taken to wife. Nor have we herein barred
Your better wisdoms, which have freely gone
With this affair along. For all, our thanks.
Now follows, that you know, young Fortinbras,
Holding a weak supposal of our worth,
Or thinking by our late dear brother's death
Our state to be disjoint and out of frame,
21 Colleaguèd with this dream of his advantage,
He hath not failed to pester us with message

Importing the surrender of those lands
Lost by his father, with all bands of law,
To our most valiant brother. So much for him.
Now for ourself and for this time of meeting.
Thus much the business is: we have here writ
To Norway, uncle of young Fortinbras—
Who, impotent and bedrid, scarcely hears
Of this his nephew's purpose—to suppress
His further gait herein, in that the levies, 31
The lists, and full proportions are all made 32
Out of his subject; and we here dispatch
You, good Cornelius, and you, Voltemand,
For bearers of this greeting to old Norway,
Giving to you no further personal power
To business with the king, more than the scope
Of these delated articles allow. 38
Farewell, and let your haste commend your duty.
CORNELIUS, VOLTEMAND.
In that, and all things, will we show our duty.
KING.
We doubt it nothing. Heartily farewell.

[Exeunt Voltemand and Cornelius.]

And now, Laertes, what's the news with you?
You told us of some suit. What is't, Laertes?
You cannot speak of reason to the Dane 44
And lose your voice. What wouldst thou 45 beg, Laertes,
That shall not be my offer, not thy asking?
The head is not more native to the heart, 47
The hand more instrumental to the mouth, 48
Than is the throne of Denmark to thy father.
What wouldst thou have, Laertes?
LAERTES.   My dread lord,
Your leave and favor to return to France,
From whence though willingly I came to Denmark

I, ii Elsinore Castle: a room of state *s.d. cum aliis* with others *9 jointress* a woman who has a jointure, or joint tenancy of an estate *14 barred* excluded *21 Colleaguèd* united

31 gait going *32 proportions* amounts of forces and supplies *38 delated* detailed *44 Dane* King of Denmark *45 lose your voice* speak in vain *47 native* joined by nature *48 instrumental* serviceable

To show my duty in your coronation,
Yet now I must confess, that duty done,
My thoughts and wishes bend again toward
　France
And bow them to your gracious leave and
　pardon.

KING.
Have you your father's leave? What says
　Polonius?

POLONIUS.
He hath, my lord, wrung from me my slow
　leave
By laborsome petition, and at last
Upon his will I sealed my hard consent.
I do beseech you give him leave to go.

KING.
Take thy fair hour, Laertes. Time be thine,
And thy best graces spend it at thy will.
64　But now, my cousin Hamlet, and my son—

HAMLET. [*aside*]
65　A little more than kin, and less than kind!

KING.
How is it that the clouds still hang on you?

HAMLET.
67　Not so, my lord. I am too much in the sun.

QUEEN.
Good Hamlet, cast thy nighted color off,
And let thine eye look like a friend on
　Denmark.
70　Do not for ever with thy vailèd lids
Seek for thy noble father in the dust.
Thou know'st 'tis common. All that lives
　must die,
Passing through nature to eternity.

HAMLET.
Ay, madam, it is common.

QUEEN.　　　　　　　　If it be,
Why seems it so particular with thee?

HAMLET.
Seems, madam? Nay, it is. I know not
　'seems.'
'Tis not alone my inky cloak, good mother,
Nor customary suits of solemn black,

Nor windy suspiration of forced breath,
No, nor the fruitful river in the eye,　80
Nor the dejected havior of the visage,
Together with all forms, moods, shapes of
　grief,
That can denote me truly. These indeed
　seem,
For they are actions that a man might play,
But I have that within which passeth
　show—
These but the trappings and the suits of
　woe.

KING.
'Tis sweet and commendable in your
　nature, Hamlet,
To give these mourning duties to your
　father,
But you must know your father lost a
　father,
That father lost, lost his, and the survivor
　bound
In filial obligation for some term
To do obsequious sorrow. But to persever　92
In obstinate condolement is a course
Of impious stubbornness. 'Tis unmanly
　grief.
It shows a will most incorrect to heaven,
A heart unfortified, a mind impatient,
An understanding simple and unschooled.
For what we know must be and is as
　common
As any the most vulgar thing to sense,
Why should we in our peevish opposition　100
Take it to heart? Fie, 'tis a fault to heaven,
A fault against the dead, a fault to nature,
To reason most absurd, whose common
　theme
Is death of fathers, and who still hath cried,
From the first corse till he that died to-day,
'This must be so.' We pray you throw to
　earth
This unprevailing woe, and think of us
As of a father, for let the world take note
You are the most immediate to our throne,
And with no less nobility of love

64 cousin kinsman more distant than parent, child, brother, or sister　*65 kin* related as nephew; *kind* kindly in feeling, as by kind, or nature, a son would be to his father　*67 sun* sunshine of the king's undesired favor (with the punning additional meaning of 'place of a son')　*70 vailèd* downcast

92 obsequious proper to obsequies or funerals; *persever* persevere (accented on the second syllable, as always in Shakespeare)

Than that which dearest father bears his son
Do I impart toward you. For your intent
In going back to school in Wittenberg,
114   It is most retrograde to our desire,
And we beseech you, bend you to remain
Here in the cheer and comfort of our eye,
Our chiefest courtier, cousin, and our son.
QUEEN.
Let not thy mother lose her prayers, Hamlet.
I pray thee stay with us, go not to Wittenberg.
HAMLET.
I shall in all my best obey you, madam.
KING.
Why, 'tis a loving and a fair reply.
Be as ourself in Denmark. Madam, come.
This gentle and unforced accord of Hamlet
Sits smiling to my heart, in grace whereof
No jocund health that Denmark drinks to-day
But the great cannon to the clouds shall tell,
127   And the king's rouse the heaven shall bruit again,
Respeaking earthly thunder. Come away.

Flourish. Exeunt all but Hamlet.

HAMLET.
O that this too too sullied flesh would melt,
Thaw, and resolve itself into a dew,
Or that the Everlasting had not fixed
132   His canon 'gainst self-slaughter. O God, God,
How weary, stale, flat, and unprofitable
Seem to me all the uses of this world!
Fie on't, ah, fie, 'tis an unweeded garden
That grows to seed. Things rank and gross in nature
137   Possess it merely. That it should come to this,
But two months dead, nay, not so much, not two,
So excellent a king, that was to this

Hyperion to a satyr, so loving to my mother   140
That he might not beteem the winds of   141
heaven
Visit her face too roughly. Heaven and earth,
Must I remember? Why, she would hang on him
As if increase of appetite had grown
By what it fed on, and yet within a month—
Let me not think on't; frailty, thy name is woman—
A little month, or ere those shoes were old
With which she followed my poor father's body
Like Niobe, all tears, why she, even she—   149
O God, a beast that wants discourse of   150
reason
Would have mourned longer—married with my uncle,
My father's brother, but no more like my father
Than I to Hercules. Within a month,
Ere yet the salt of most unrighteous tears
Had left the flushing in her gallèd eyes,   155
She married. O, most wicked speed, to post
With such dexterity to incestuous sheets!
It is not nor it cannot come to good.
But break my heart, for I must hold my tongue.

Enter Horatio, Marcellus, and Bernardo.

HORATIO.
Hail to your lordship!
HAMLET.   I am glad to see you well.
Horatio—or I do forget myself.
HORATIO.
The same, my lord, and your poor servant ever.
HAMLET.
Sir, my good friend, I'll change that name with you.   163

114 *retrograde* contrary   127 *rouse* toast drunk in wine;
bruit echo   132 *canon* law   137 *merely* completely

140 *Hyperion* the sun god   141 *beteem* allow   149 *Niobe* the proud mother who boasted of having more children than Leto and was punished when they were slain by Apollo and Artemis, children of Leto; the grieving Niobe was changed by Zeus into a stone, which continually dropped tears   150 *discourse* logical power or process   155 *gallèd* irritated   163 *change* exchange

164 And what make you from Wittenberg,
    Horatio?
    Marcellus?
MARCELLUS. My good lord!
HAMLET.
    I am very glad to see you. [*to Bernardo*]
    Good even, sir.
    But what, in faith, make you from
    Wittenberg?
HORATIO.
    A truant disposition, good my lord.
HAMLET.
    I would not hear your enemy say so,
    Nor shall you do my ear that violence
    To make it truster of your own report
    Against yourself. I know you are no truant.
    But what is your affair in Elsinore?
    We'll teach you to drink deep ere you
    depart.
HORATIO.
    My lord, I came to see your father's funeral.
HAMLET.
    I prithee do not mock me, fellow student.
    I think it was to see my mother's wedding.
HORATIO.
    Indeed, my lord, it followed hard upon.
HAMLET.
    Thrift, thrift, Horatio. The funeral baked
    meats
    Did coldly furnish forth the marriage
    tables.
182 Would I had met my dearest foe in heaven
    Or ever I had seen that day, Horatio!
    My father—methinks I see my father.
HORATIO.
    Where, my lord?
HAMLET.   In my mind's eye, Horatio.
HORATIO.
    I saw him once. 'A was a goodly king.
HAMLET.
    'A was a man, take him for all in all,
    I shall not look upon his like again.
HORATIO.
    My lord, I think I saw him yesternight.
HAMLET. Saw? who?
HORATIO.
    My lord, the king your father.

HAMLET.   The king my father?
HORATIO.
    Season your admiration for a while   192
    With an attent ear till I may deliver
    Upon the witness of these gentlemen
    This marvel to you.
HAMLET.   For God's love let me hear!
HORATIO.
    Two nights together had these gentlemen,
    Marcellus and Bernardo, on their watch
    In the dead waste and middle of the night
    Been thus encountered. A figure like your
    father,
    Armèd at point exactly, cap-a-pe,   200
    Appears before them and with solemn
    march
    Goes slow and stately by them. Thrice he
    walked
    By their oppressed and fear-surprisèd eyes
    Within his truncheon's length, whilst they, 204
    distilled
    Almost to jelly with the act of fear,
    Stand dumb and speak not to him. This to
    me
    In dreadful secrecy impart they did,
    And I with them the third night kept the
    watch,
    Where, as they had delivered, both in time,
    Form of the thing, each word made true
    and good,
    The apparition comes. I knew your father.
    These hands are not more like.
HAMLET.   But where was this?
MARCELLUS.
    My lord, upon the platform where we
    watched.
HAMLET.
    Did you not speak to it?
HORATIO.   My lord, I did,
    But answer made it none. Yet once
    methought
    It lifted up its head and did address   216
    Itself to motion like as it would speak.
    But even then the morning cock crew loud,
    And at the sound it shrunk in haste away

---

164 *make* do 182 *dearest* direst, bitterest
192 *Season your admiration* control your wonder 200
at point completely; *cap-a-pe* from head to foot 204
truncheon military commander's baton *216 it* its

And vanished from our sight.

HAMLET.   'Tis very strange.

HORATIO.
As I do live, my honored lord, 'tis true,
And we did think it writ down in our duty
To let you know of it.

HAMLET.
Indeed, indeed, sirs, but this troubles me.
Hold you the watch to-night?

ALL.   We do, my lord.

HAMLET. Armed, say you?

ALL. Armed, my lord.

HAMLET.
From top to toe?

ALL.   My lord, from head to foot.

HAMLET.
Then saw you not his face?

HORATIO.
230   O, yes, my lord. He wore his beaver up.

HAMLET.
What, looked he frowningly?

HORATIO.
A countenance more in sorrow than in
   anger.

HAMLET. Pale or red?

HORATIO.
Nay, very pale.

HAMLET.   And fixed his eyes upon you?

HORATIO.
Most constantly.

HAMLET.   I would I had been there.

HORATIO.
It would have much amazed you.

HAMLET.
Very like, very like. Stayed it long?

HORATIO.
238   While one with moderate haste might tell
   a hundred.

BOTH. Longer, longer.

HORATIO.
Not when I saw't.

240 HAMLET.   His beard was grizzled, no?

HORATIO.
It was as I have seen it in his life,
242   A sable silvered.

HAMLET.   I will watch to-night.
Perchance 'twill walk again.

HORATIO.   I warr'nt it will.

HAMLET.
If it assume my noble father's person,
I'll speak to it though hell itself should gape
And bid me hold my peace. I pray you all,
If you have hitherto concealed this sight,
Let it be tenable in your silence still,   248
And whatsomever else shall hap to-night,
Give it an understanding but no tongue.
I will requite your loves. So fare you well.
Upon the platforms, 'twixt eleven and
   twelve
I'll visit you.

ALL.   Our duty to your honor.

HAMLET.
Your loves, as mine to you. Farewell.
                    Exeunt [*all but Hamlet*].
My father's spirit—in arms? All is not well.
I doubt some foul play. Would the night
   were come!
Till then sit still, my soul. Foul deeds will
   rise,
Though all the earth o'erwhelm them, to
   men's eyes.   *Exit.*

*

ACT I

Scene iii

Enter Laertes and Ophelia, his sister.

LAERTES.
My necessaries are embarked. Farewell.
And, sister, as the winds give benefit
And convoy is assistant, do not sleep,   3
But let me hear from you.

OPHELIA.   Do you doubt that?

LAERTES.
For Hamlet, and the trifling of his favor,

---

230 *beaver* visor or movable face-guard of the helmet
238 *tell* count   240 *grizzled* grey   242 *sable silvered*
black mixed with white

248 *tenable* held firmly   256 *doubt* suspect, fear
I, iii Elsinore Castle: the chambers of Polonius   3
convoy means of transport

Hold it a fashion and a toy in blood,

7 A violet in the youth of primy nature,

Forward, not permanent, sweet, not lasting,

9 The perfume and suppliance of a minute,

No more.

OPHELIA. No more but so?

LAERTES.   Think it no more.

11 For nature crescent does not grow alone

12 In thews and bulk, but as this temple waxes

The inward service of the mind and soul

Grows wide withal. Perhaps he loves you now,

15 And now no soil nor cautel doth besmirch

16 The virtue of his will, but you must fear,

17 His greatness weighed, his will is not his own.

[For he himself is subject to his birth.]

He may not, as unvalued persons do,

Carve for himself, for on his choice depends

The safety and health of this whole state,

And therefore must his choice be circumscribed

23 Unto the voice and yielding of that body

Whereof he is the head. Then if he says he loves you,

It fits your wisdom so far to believe it

As he in his particular act and place

May give his saying deed, which is no further

Than the main voice of Denmark goes withal.

Then weigh what loss your honor may sustain

30 If with too credent ear you list his songs,

Or lose your heart, or your chaste treasure open

To his unmastered importunity.

Fear it, Ophelia, fear it, my dear sister,

34 And keep you in the rear of your affection,

Out of the shot and danger of desire.

The chariest maid is prodigal enough

If she unmask her beauty to the moon.

Virtue itself scapes not calumnious strokes.

The canker galls the infants of the spring 39

Too oft before their buttons be disclosed, 40

And in the morn and liquid dew of youth

Contagious blastments are most imminent. 42

Be wary then; best safety lies in fear.

Youth to itself rebels, though none else near.

OPHELIA.

I shall the effect of this good lesson keep

As watchman to my heart, but, good my brother,

Do not as some ungracious pastors do,

Show me the steep and thorny way to heaven,

Whiles like a puffed and reckless libertine

Himself the primrose path of dalliance treads

And recks not his own rede. 51

Enter Polonius.

LAERTES.   O, fear me not.

I stay too long. But here my father comes.

A double blessing is a double grace;

Occasion smiles upon a second leave.

POLONIUS.

Yet here, Laertes? Aboard, aboard, for shame!

The wind sits in the shoulder of your sail,

And you are stayed for. There—my blessing with thee,

And these few precepts in thy memory

Look thou character. Give thy thoughts no 59 tongue,

Nor any unproportioned thought his act. 60

Be thou familiar, but by no means vulgar.

Those friends thou hast, and their adoption tried,

Grapple them unto thy soul with hoops of steel,

But do not dull thy palm with entertainment

Of each new-hatched, unfledged courage. 65 Beware

---

7 *primy* of the springtime   9 *perfume and suppliance* filling sweetness   11 *crescent* growing   12 *this temple* the body   15 *cautel* deceit   16 *will* desire   17 *greatness weighed* high position considered   23 *yielding* assent   30 *credent* credulous   34 *affection* feelings, which rashly lead forward into dangers

39 *canker* rose worm; *galls* injures   40 *buttons* buds   42 *blastments* blights   51 *recks* regards; *rede* counsel   59 *character* inscribe   60 *unproportioned* unadjusted to what is right   65 *courage* man of spirit, young blood

Of entrance to a quarrel; but being in,
Bear't that th' opposèd may beware of
    thee.
Give every man thine ear, but few thy
    voice;
69 Take each man's censure, but reserve thy
        judgment.
Costly thy habit as thy purse can buy,
But not expressed in fancy; rich, not gaudy,
For the apparel oft proclaims the man,
And they in France of the best rank and
    station
74 Are of a most select and generous chief in
        that.
Neither a borrower nor a lender be,
For loan oft loses both itself and friend,
77 And borrowing dulleth edge of husbandry.
This above all, to thine own self be true,
And it must follow as the night the day
Thou canst not then be false to any man.
81 Farewell. My blessing season this in thee!
LAERTES.
    Most humbly do I take my leave, my lord.
POLONIUS.
83 The time invites you. Go, your servants
        tend.
LAERTES.
    Farewell, Ophelia, and remember well
    What I have said to you.
OPHELIA.   'Tis in my memory locked,
    And you yourself shall keep the key of it.
LAERTES. Farewell.   *Exit Laertes.*
POLONIUS.
    What is't, Ophelia, he hath said to you?
OPHELIA.
    So please you, something touching the Lord
        Hamlet.
POLONIUS.
90 Marry, well bethought.
    'Tis told me he hath very oft of late
    Given private time to you, and you yourself
    Have of your audience been most free and
        bounteous.
    If it be so—as so 'tis put on me,
    And that in way of caution—I must tell you
    You do not understand yourself so clearly

As it behooves my daughter and your
    honor.
What is between you? Give me up the
    truth.
OPHELIA.
    He hath, my lord, of late made many   99
        tenders
    Of his affection to me.
POLONIUS.
    Affection? Pooh! You speak like a green
        girl,
    Unsifted in such perilous circumstance.   102
    Do you believe his tenders, as you call
        them?
OPHELIA.
    I do not know, my lord, what I should
        think.
POLONIUS.
    Marry, I will teach you. Think yourself a
        baby
    That you have ta'en these tenders for true 106
        pay
    Which are not sterling. Tender yourself
        more dearly,
    Or (not to crack the wind of the poor   108
        phrase,
    Running it thus) you'll tender me a fool.
OPHELIA.
    My lord, he hath importuned me with love
    In honorable fashion.
POLONIUS.
    Ay, fashion you may call it. Go to, go to. 112
OPHELIA.
    And hath given countenance to his speech,
        my lord,
    With almost all the holy vows of heaven.
POLONIUS.
    Ay, springes to catch woodcocks. I do   115
        know,

99 tenders offers   *102 Unsifted* untested   *106–09 tenders
. . . Tender . . . tender* offers . . . hold in regard . . . present (a word play going through three meanings, the
last use of the word yielding further complexity with
its valid implications that she will show herself to him
as a fool, will show him to the world as a fool, and may
go so far as to present him with a baby, which would
be a fool because 'fool' was an Elizabethan term of
endearment especially applicable to an infant as a
'little innocent')   *108 crack . . . of* make wheeze like a
horse driven too hard   *112 Go to* go away, go on
(expressing impatience)   *115 springes* snares; *wood-
cocks* birds believed foolish

69 censure judgment   *74 chief* eminence   *77 husbandry*
thriftiness   *81 season* ripen and make fruitful   *83
tend* wait   *90 Marry* by Mary

When the blood burns, how prodigal the soul
Lends the tongue vows. These blazes, daughter,
Giving more light than heat, extinct in both
Even in their promise, as it is a-making,
You must not take for fire. From this time
Be something scanter of your maiden presence.
122 Set your entreatments at a higher rate
123 Than a command to parley. For Lord Hamlet,
Believe so much in him that he is young,
And with a larger tether may he walk
Than may be given you. In few, Ophelia,
127 Do not believe his vows, for they are brokers,
128 Not of that dye which their investments show,
But mere implorators of unholy suits,
Breathing like sanctified and pious bawds,
The better to beguile. This is for all:
I would not, in plain terms, from this time forth
133 Have you so slander any moment leisure
As to give words or talk with the Lord Hamlet.
Look to't, I charge you. Come your ways.

OPHELIA.
I shall obey, my lord.   *Exeunt.*

*

ACT I

Scene iv

Enter Hamlet, Horatio, and Marcellus.

HAMLET.
1   The air bites shrewdly; it is very cold.
HORATIO.
2   It is a nipping and an eager air.

HAMLET.
What hour now?
HORATIO.   I think it lacks of twelve.
MARCELLUS. No, it is struck.
HORATIO.
Indeed? I heard it not. It then draws near the season
Wherein the spirit held his wont to walk.

A flourish of trumpets, and two pieces goes off.

What does this mean, my lord?
HAMLET.
The king doth wake to-night and takes his 8 rouse,
Keeps wassail, and the swaggering 9 upspring reels,
And as he drains his draughts of 10 Rhenish down
The kettledrum and trumpet thus bray out
The triumph of his pledge. 12
HORATIO.   Is it a custom?
HAMLET.
Ay, marry, is't,
But to my mind, though I am native here
And to the manner born, it is a custom
More honored in the breach than the 16 observance.
This heavy-headed revel east and west
Makes us traduced and taxed of other 18 nations.
They clepe us drunkards and with swinish 19 phrase
Soil our addition, and indeed it takes 20
From our achievements, though performed at height,
The pith and marrow of our attribute. 22
So oft it chances in particular men
That (for some vicious mole of nature in 24 them,
As in their birth, wherein they are not guilty,
Since nature cannot choose his origin) 26

122 *entreatments* military negotiations for surrender 123 *parley* confer with a besieger 127 *brokers* middlemen, panders 128 *investments* clothes 133 *slander* use disgracefully; *moment* momentary
I, iv The sentry-post *1 shrewdly* wickedly *2 eager* sharp

8 *rouse* carousal 9 *upspring* a German dance 10 *Rhenish* Rhine wine 12 *triumph* achievement, feat (in downing a cup of wine at one draught) 16 *More...observance* better broken than observed 18 *taxed of* censured by 19 *clepe* call 20 *addition* reputation, title added as a distinction 22 *attribute* reputation, what is attributed 24 *mole* blemish, flaw 26 *his* its

27   By the o'ergrowth of some complexion,
28   Oft breaking down the pales and forts of reason,
29   Or by some habit that too much o'erleavens
30   The form of plausive manners—that (these men
    Carrying, I say, the stamp of one defect,
32   Being nature's livery, or fortune's star)
    Their virtues else, be they as pure as grace,
    As infinite as man may undergo,
    Shall in the general censure take corruption
    From that particular fault. The dram of evil
    Doth all the noble substance of a doubt,
    To his own scandal.

      Enter Ghost.

HORATIO.   Look, my lord, it comes.
HAMLET.
    Angels and ministers of grace defend us!
40   Be thou a spirit of health or goblin damned,
    Bring with thee airs from heaven or blasts from hell,
    Be thy intents wicked or charitable,
    Thou com'st in such a questionable shape
    That I will speak to thee. I'll call thee Hamlet,
    King, father, royal Dane. O, answer me!
    Let me not burst in ignorance, but tell
47   Why thy canonized bones, hearsèd in death,
48   Have burst their cerements, why the sepulchre
    Wherein we saw thee quietly interred
    Hath oped his ponderous and marble jaws
    To cast thee up again. What may this mean
    That thou, dead corse, again in complete steel,

    Revisits thus the glimpses of the moon,
    Making night hideous, and we fools of nature   54
    So horridly to shake our disposition
    With thoughts beyond the reaches of our souls?
    Say, why is this? wherefore? what should we do?

      [Ghost] beckons.

HORATIO.
    It beckons you to go away with it,
    As if it some impartment did desire
    To you alone.
MARCELLUS.
            Look with what courteous action
    It waves you to a more removèd ground.
    But do not go with it.
HORATIO.   No, by no means.
HAMLET.
    It will not speak. Then will I follow it.
HORATIO.
    Do not, my lord.
HAMLET.   Why, what should be the fear?
    I do not set my life at a pin's fee,
    And for my soul, what can it do to that,
    Being a thing immortal as itself?
    It waves me forth again. I'll follow it.
HORATIO.
    What if it tempt you toward the flood, my lord,
    Or to the dreadful summit of the cliff
    That beetles o'er his base into the sea,   71
    And there assume some other horrible form,
    Which might deprive your sovereignty of reason   73
    And draw you into madness? Think of it.
    The very place puts toys of desperation,   75
    Without more motive, into every brain
    That looks so many fathoms to the sea
    And hears it roar beneath.
HAMLET.   It waves me still.
    Go on. I'll follow thee.

---

27 complexion part of the make-up, combination of humors *28 pales* barriers, fences *29 o'erleavens* works change throughout, as yeast ferments dough *30 plausive* pleasing *32 livery* characteristic equipment or provision; *star* make-up as formed by stellar influence *40 of health* sound, good; *goblin* fiend *47 canonized* buried with the established rites of the Church *48 cerements* waxed grave-cloths

54 fools of nature men made conscious of natural limitations by a supernatural manifestation *71 beetles* juts out *73 deprive* take away; *sovereignty of reason* state of being ruled by reason *75 toys* fancies

MARCELLUS.

You shall not go, my lord.

HAMLET. Hold off your hands.

HORATIO.

Be ruled. You shall not go.

HAMLET. My fate cries out

82 And makes each petty artere in this body

83 As hardy as the Nemean lion's nerve.

Still am I called. Unhand me, gentlemen.

85 By heaven, I'll make a ghost of him that
  lets me!

I say, away! Go on. I'll follow thee.

Exit Ghost, and Hamlet.

HORATIO.

He waxes desperate with imagination.

MARCELLUS.

Let's follow. 'Tis not fit thus to obey him.

HORATIO.

Have after. To what issue will this come?

MARCELLUS.

Something is rotten in the state of
  Denmark.

HORATIO.

Heaven will direct it.

MARCELLUS. Nay, let's follow him.

Exeunt.

*

ACT I

Scene v

Enter Ghost and Hamlet.

HAMLET.

Whither wilt thou lead me? Speak. I'll go
  no further.

GHOST.

Mark me.

HAMLET. I will.

GHOST. My hour is almost come,

When I to sulph'rous and tormenting   3
  flames

Must render up myself.

HAMLET. Alas, poor ghost!

GHOST.

Pity me not, but lend thy serious hearing

To what I shall unfold.

HAMLET. Speak. I am bound to hear.

GHOST.

So art thou to revenge, when thou shalt
  hear.

HAMLET. What?

GHOST.

I am thy father's spirit,

Doomed for a certain term to walk the
  night,

And for the day confined to fast in fires,   11

Till the foul crimes done in my days of
  nature

Are burnt and purged away. But that I am
  forbid

To tell the secrets of my prison house,

I could a tale unfold whose lightest word

Would harrow up thy soul, freeze thy
  young blood,

Make thy two eyes like stars start from   17
  their spheres,

Thy knotted and combinèd locks to part,

And each particular hair to stand an end   19

Like quills upon the fretful porpentine.   20

But this eternal blazon must not be   21

To ears of flesh and blood. List, list, O, list!

If thou didst ever thy dear father love—

HAMLET. O God!

GHOST.

Revenge his foul and most unnatural
  murder.

HAMLET. Murder?

GHOST.

Murder most foul, as in the best it is,

But this most foul, strange, and unnatural.

---

82 *artere* artery 83 *Nemean lion* a lion slain by
Hercules in the performance of one of his twelve labors;
nerve sinew 85 *lets* hinders
I, v Another part of the fortifications

3 *flames* sufferings in purgatory (not hell) 11 *fast* do
penance 17 *spheres* transparent revolving shells in
each of which, according to the Ptolemaic astronomy,
a planet or other heavenly body was placed 19 *an* on
20 *porpentine* porcupine 21 *eternal blazon* revelation of
eternity

HAMLET.
    Haste me to know't, that I, with wings as
      swift
30   As meditation or the thoughts of love,
    May sweep to my revenge.
    GHOST.   I find thee apt,
    And duller shouldst thou be than the fat
      weed
33   That roots itself in ease on Lethe wharf,
    Wouldst thou not stir in this. Now, Hamlet,
      hear.
    'Tis given out that, sleeping in my orchard,
    A serpent stung me. So the whole ear of
      Denmark
37   Is by a forgèd process of my death
    Rankly abused. But know, thou noble
      youth,
    The serpent that did sting thy father's life
    Now wears his crown.
    HAMLET.   O my prophetic soul!
    My uncle?
    GHOST.
42   Ay, that incestuous, that adulterate beast,
    With witchcraft of his wit, with traitorous
      gifts—
    O wicked wit and gifts, that have the power
    So to seduce!—won to his shameful lust
    The will of my most seeming-virtuous
      queen.
    O Hamlet, what a falling-off was there,
    From me, whose love was of that dignity
    That it went hand in hand even with the
      vow
    I made to her in marriage, and to decline
    Upon a wretch whose natural gifts were
      poor
    To those of mine!
    But virtue, as it never will be moved,
54   Though lewdness court it in a shape of
      heaven,
    So lust, though to a radiant angel linked,
    Will state itself in a celestial bed
    And prey on garbage.
    But soft, methinks I scent the morning air.

    Brief let me be. Sleeping within my
      orchard,
    My custom always of the afternoon,
    Upon my secure hour thy uncle stole   61
    With juice of cursed hebona in a vial,   62
    And in the porches of my ears did pour
    The leperous distilment, whose effect
    Holds such an enmity with blood of man
    That swift as quicksilver it courses through
    The natural gates and alleys of the body,
    And with a sudden vigor it doth posset   68
    And curd, like eager droppings into milk,   69
    The thin and wholesome blood. So did it
      mine,
    And a most instant tetter barked about   71
    Most lazar-like with vile and loathsome   72
      crust
    All my smooth body.
    Thus was I sleeping by a brother's hand
    Of life, of crown, of queen at once
      dispatched,
    Cut off even in the blossoms of my sin,
    Unhouseled, disappointed, unaneled,   77
    No reck'ning made, but sent to my
      account
    With all my imperfections on my head.
    O, horrible! O, horrible! most horrible!
    If thou hast nature in thee, bear it not.
    Let not the royal bed of Denmark be
    A couch for luxury and damnèd incest.   83
    But howsomever thou pursues this act,
    Taint not thy mind, nor let thy soul
      contrive
    Against thy mother aught. Leave her to
      heaven
    And to those thorns that in her bosom lodge
    To prick and sting her. Fare thee well at
      once.
    The glowworm shows the matin to be near 89
    And gins to pale his uneffectual fire.
    Adieu, adieu, adieu. Remember me.
                           [Exit.]

---

30 meditation thought   *33 Lethe* the river in Hades which brings forgetfulness of past life to a spirit who drinks of it   *37 forgèd process* falsified official report   *42 adulterate* adulterous   *54 shape of heaven* angelic disguise

61 secure carefree, unsuspecting   *62 hebona* some poisonous plant   *68 posset* curdle   *69 eager* sour   *71 tetter* eruption; *barked* covered as with a bark   *72 lazar-like* leper-like   *77 Unhouseled* without the Sacrament; *disappointed* unprepared spiritually; *unaneled* without extreme unction   *83 luxury* lust   *89 matin* morning

HAMLET.
O all you host of heaven! O earth! What
else?
And shall I couple hell? O fie! Hold, hold,
my heart,
And you, my sinews, grow not instant old,
But bear me stiffly up. Remember thee?
Ay, thou poor ghost, while memory holds a
seat

97 In this distracted globe. Remember thee?
98 Yea, from the table of my memory
I'll wipe away all trivial fond records,
100 All saws of books, all forms, all pressures
past
That youth and observation copied there,
And thy commandment all alone shall live
Within the book and volume of my brain,
Unmixed with baser matter. Yes, by
heaven!
O most pernicious woman!
O villain, villain, smiling, damnèd villain!
My tables—meet it is I set it down
That one may smile, and smile, and be a
villain.
At least I am sure it may be so in Denmark.

[*Writes.*]

So, uncle, there you are. Now to my word:
It is 'Adieu, adieu, remember me.'
I have sworn't.

Enter Horatio and Marcellus.

HORATIO.
My lord, my lord!
MARCELLUS. Lord Hamlet!
HORATIO. Heavens secure him!
HAMLET. So be it!
MARCELLUS.
Illo, ho, ho, my lord!
HAMLET.
115 Hillo, ho, ho, boy! Come, bird, come.
MARCELLUS.
How is't, my noble lord?

HORATIO. What news, my lord?
HAMLET. O, wonderful!
HORATIO.
Good my lord, tell it.
HAMLET. No, you will reveal it.
HORATIO.
Not I, my lord, by heaven.
MARCELLUS. Nor I, my lord.
HAMLET.
How say you then? Would heart of man
once think it?
But you'll be secret?
BOTH. Ay, by heaven, my lord.
HAMLET.
There's never a villain dwelling in all
Denmark
But he's an arrant knave.
HORATIO.
There needs no ghost, my lord, come from
the grave
To tell us this.
HAMLET. Why, right, you are in the right,
And so, without more circumstance at all, 127
I hold it fit that we shake hands and part:
You, as your business and desires shall
point you.
For every man hath business and desire
Such as it is, and for my own poor part,
Look you, I'll go pray.
HORATIO.
These are but wild and whirling words, my
lord.
HAMLET.
I am sorry they offend you, heartily;
Yes, faith, heartily.
HORATIO. There's no offense, my lord.
HAMLET.
Yes, by Saint Patrick, but there is,
Horatio,
And much offense too. Touching this vision
here,
It is an honest ghost, that let me tell you. 138
For your desire to know what is between
us,
O'ermaster't as you may. And now, good
friends,

97 *globe* head   98 *table* writing tablet, record book
100 *saws* wise sayings; *forms* mental images, concepts;
pressures impressions   115 *Illo, ho, ho* cry of the falconer
to summon his hawk

127 *circumstance* ceremony   138 *honest* genuine (not a
disguised demon)

As you are friends, scholars, and soldiers,
Give me one poor request.

HORATIO.

What is't, my lord? We will.

HAMLET.

Never make known what you have seen
   to-night.

BOTH.

My lord, we will not.

HAMLET.   Nay, but swear't.

HORATIO.   In faith,
My lord, not I.

MARCELLUS.   Nor I, my lord—in faith.

HAMLET.

147   Upon my sword.

MARCELLUS.

               We have sworn, my lord, already.

HAMLET.

Indeed, upon my sword, indeed.

Ghost cries under the stage.

GHOST. Swear.

HAMLET.

150   Ha, ha, boy, say'st thou so? Art thou there,
   truepenny?
Come on. You hear this fellow in the
   cellarage.
Consent to swear.

HORATIO.   Propose the oath, my lord.

HAMLET.

Never to speak of this that you have seen,
Swear by my sword.

GHOST. [*beneath*] Swear.

HAMLET.

156   Hic et ubique? Then we'll shift our ground.
Come hither, gentlemen,
And lay your hands again upon my
   sword.
Swear by my sword
Never to speak of this that you have heard.

GHOST. [*beneath*] Swear by his sword.

HAMLET.

Well said, old mole! Canst work i' th'
   earth so fast?

A worthy pioner! Once more remove,   163
   good friends.

HORATIO.

O day and night, but this is wondrous
   strange!

HAMLET.

And therefore as a stranger give it welcome.
There are more things in heaven and earth,
   Horatio,
Than are dreamt of in your philosophy.   167
But come:
Here as before, never, so help you mercy,
How strange or odd some'er I bear myself
(As I perchance hereafter shall think meet
To put an antic disposition on),   172
That you, at such times seeing me, never
   shall,
With arms encumb'red thus, or this head- 174
   shake,
Or by pronouncing of some doubtful
   phrase,
As 'Well, well, we know,' or 'We could, an 176
   if we would,'
Or 'If we list to speak,' or 'There be, an if
   they might,'
Or such ambiguous giving out, to note
That you know aught of me—this do swear,
So grace and mercy at your most need help
   you.

GHOST. [*beneath*] Swear.

[*They swear.*]

HAMLET.

Rest, rest, perturbèd spirit! So, gentlemen,
With all my love I do commend me to you,   183
And what so poor a man as Hamlet is
May do t' express his love and friending to
   you,
God willing, shall not lack. Let us go in
   together,
And still your fingers on your lips, I pray. 187
The time is out of joint. O cursèd spite

147 sword i.e. upon the cross formed by the sword hilt
150 truepenny honest old fellow   *156 Hic et ubique* here
and everywhere

163 pioner pioneer, miner   *167 your philosophy* this
philosophy one hears about   *172 antic* grotesque, mad
174 encumb'red folded   *176 an if* if   *183 commend*
entrust   *187 still* always

That ever I was born to set it right!
Nay, come, let's go together.   *Exeunt.*

*

ACT II

Scene i

Enter old Polonius, with his man [Reynaldo].

POLONIUS.
Give him this money and these notes,
    Reynaldo.
REYNALDO.
I will, my lord.
POLONIUS.
You shall do marvellous wisely, good
    Reynaldo,
Before you visit him, to make inquire
Of his behavior.
REYNALDO.   My lord, I did intend it.
POLONIUS.
Marry, well said, very well said. Look you,
    sir,
7   Enquire me first what Danskers are in
        Paris,
8   And how, and who, what means, and
        where they keep,
    What company, at what expense; and
        finding
10   By this encompassment and drift of
        question
    That they do know my son, come you more
        nearer
12   Than your particular demands will touch
        it.
    Take you as 'twere some distant knowledge
        of him,
    As thus, 'I know his father and his friends,
    And in part him'—do you mark this,
        Reynaldo?

REYNALDO.
Ay, very well, my lord.
POLONIUS.
'And in part him, but,' you may say, 'not
    well,
But if 't be he I mean, he's very wild
Addicted so and so.' And there put on him
What forgeries you please; marry, none so 20
    rank
As may dishonor him—take heed of that—
But, sir, such wanton, wild, and usual slips
As are companions noted and most known
To youth and liberty.
REYNALDO.   As gaming, my lord.
POLONIUS.
Ay, or drinking, fencing, swearing,
    quarrelling,
Drabbing. You may go so far.   26
REYNALDO.
My lord, that would dishonor him.
POLONIUS.
Faith, no, as you may season it in the   28
    charge.
You must not put another scandal on him,
That he is open to incontinency.   30
That's not my meaning. But breathe his   31
    faults so quaintly
That they may seem the taints of liberty,
The flash and outbreak of a fiery mind,
A savageness in unreclaimèd blood,   34
Of general assault.   35
REYNALDO.   But, my good lord—
POLONIUS.
Wherefore should you do this?
REYNALDO.   Ay, my lord,
I would know that.
POLONIUS.   Marry, sir, here's my drift,
And I believe it is a fetch of warrant.   38
You laying these slight sullies on my son
As 'twere a thing a little soiled i' th'
    working,
Mark you,
Your party in converse, him you would
    sound,

II, i The chambers of Polonius *7 Danskers* Danes *8 what means* what their wealth; *keep* dwell *10 encompassment* circling about *12 particular demands* definite questions

20 forgeries invented wrongdoings *26 Drabbing* whoring *28 season* soften *30 incontinency* extreme sensuality *31 quaintly* expertly, gracefully *34 unreclaimèd* untamed *35 Of general assault* assailing all young men *38 fetch of warrant* allowable trick

43 Having ever seen in the prenominate crimes
The youth you breathe of guilty, be assured
45 He closes with you in this consequence: 'Good sir,' or so, or 'friend,' or 'gentleman'—
47 According to the phrase or the addition
Of man and country—

REYNALDO.   Very good, my lord.

POLONIUS.
And then, sir, does 'a this— 'a does—
What was I about to say? By the mass, I was about to say something! Where did I leave?

REYNALDO. At 'closes in the consequence,' at 'friend or so,' and 'gentleman.'

POLONIUS.
At 'closes in the consequence'—Ay, marry!
He closes thus: 'I know the gentleman;
I saw him yesterday, or t' other day,
Or then, or then, with such or such, and, as you say,
58 There was 'a gaming, there o'ertook in's rouse,
59 There falling out at tennis'; or perchance, 'I saw him enter such a house of sale,'
61 Videlicet, a brothel, or so forth.
See you now—
Your bait of falsehood takes this carp of truth,
64 And thus do we of wisdom and of reach,
65 With windlasses and with assays of bias,
66 By indirections find directions out.
So, by my former lecture and advice,
Shall you my son. You have me, have you not?

REYNALDO.
My lord, I have.
69 POLONIUS.   God bye ye, fare ye well.

REYNALDO. Good my lord.

POLONIUS.
Observe his inclination in yourself.

REYNALDO. I shall, my lord.

POLONIUS.
And let him ply his music.

REYNALDO.   Well, my lord.

POLONIUS.
Farewell.   *Exit Reynaldo.*

Enter Ophelia.

How now, Ophelia, what's the matter?

OPHELIA.
O my lord, my lord, I have been so affrighted!

POLONIUS.
With what, i' th' name of God?

OPHELIA.
My lord, as I was sewing in my closet,   77
Lord Hamlet, with his doublet all   78
unbraced,
No hat upon his head, his stockings fouled,
Ungartered, and down-gyvèd to his ankle, 80
Pale as his shirt, his knees knocking each other,
And with a look so piteous in purport
As if he had been loosèd out of hell
To speak of horrors—he comes before me.

POLONIUS.
Mad for thy love?

OPHELIA.   My lord, I do not know,
But truly I do fear it.

POLONIUS.   What said he?

OPHELIA.
He took me by the wrist and held me hard.
Then goes he to the length of all his arm,
And with his other hand thus o'er his brow
He falls to such perusal of my face
As 'a would draw it. Long stayed he so.
At last, a little shaking of mine arm
And thrice his head thus waving up and down,
He raised a sigh so piteous and profound

43 *Having ever* if he has ever; *prenominate* aforementioned   45 *closes with you* follows your lead to a conclusion; *consequence* following way   47 *addition* title   58 *o'ertook* overcome with drunkenness; *rouse* carousal   59 *falling out* quarrelling   61 *Videlicet* namely   64 *reach* far-reaching comprehension   65 *windlasses* roundabout courses; *assays of bias* devious attacks   66 *directions* ways of procedure   69 *God bye ye* God be with you, good-bye

77 *closet* private living-room   78 *doublet* jacket; *unbraced* unlaced   80 *down-gyvèd* fallen down like gyves or fetters on a prisoner's legs

As it did seem to shatter all his bulk
And end his being. That done, he lets me
  go,
And with his head over his shoulder turned
He seemed to find his way without his eyes,
For out o' doors he went without their helps
And to the last bended their light on me.

POLONIUS.
Come, go with me. I will go seek the king.
102 This is the very ecstasy of love,
103 Whose violent property fordoes itself
And leads the will to desperate
  undertakings
As oft as any passion under heaven
That does afflict our natures. I am sorry.
What, have you given him any hard words
  of late?

OPHELIA.
No, my good lord; but as you did
  command
I did repel his letters and denied
His access to me.

POLONIUS.   That hath made him mad.
I am sorry that with better heed and
  judgment
112 I had not quoted him. I feared he did but
  trifle
113 And meant to wrack thee; but beshrew my
  jealousy.
By heaven, it is as proper to our age
115 To cast beyond ourselves in our opinions
As it is common for the younger sort
To lack discretion. Come, go we to the
  king.
118 This must be known, which, being kept
  close, might move
119 More grief to hide than hate to utter love.
Come.   *Exeunt.*

*

102 *ecstasy* madness 103 *property* quality; *fordoes*
destroys 112 *quoted* observed 113 *beshrew* curse
115 *cast beyond ourselves* find by calculation more
significance in something than we ought to 118
close secret; *move* cause 119 *to hide ... love* by such
hiding of love than there would be hate moved by a
revelation of it (a violently condensed putting of the
case which is a triumph of special statement for
Polonius)

ACT II

Scene ii

*Flourish. Enter King and Queen, Rosen-
crantz, and Guildenstern [with others].*

KING.
Welcome, dear Rosencrantz and
  Guildenstern.
Moreover that we much did long to see you, 2
The need we have to use you did provoke
Our hasty sending. Something have you
  heard
Of Hamlet's transformation—so call it,
Sith nor th' exterior nor the inward man   6
Resembles that it was. What it should be,
More than his father's death, that thus
  hath put him
So much from th' understanding of
  himself,
I cannot dream of. I entreat you both
That, being of so young days brought up
  with him,
And sith so neighbored to his youth and   12
  havior,
That you vouchsafe your rest here in our
  court
Some little time, so by your companies
To draw him on to pleasures, and to gather
So much as from occasion you may glean,
Whether aught to us unknown afflicts him
  thus,
That opened lies within our remedy.   18

QUEEN.
Good gentlemen, he hath much talked of
  you,
And sure I am two men there are not living
To whom he more adheres. If it will please 21
  you
To show us so much gentry and good will   22
As to expend your time with us awhile
For the supply and profit of our hope,

II, ii A chamber in the Castle *2 Moreover that* besides
the fact that *6 Sith* since *12 youth and havior* youthful
ways of life *18 opened* revealed *21 more adheres* is
more attached *22 gentry* courtesy

Your visitation shall receive such thanks
As fits a king's remembrance.

ROSENCRANTZ.   Both your majesties
Might, by the sovereign power you have of
    us,
Put your dread pleasures more into
    command
than to entreaty.

GUILDENSTERN.   But we both obey,
30   And here give up ourselves in the full bent
To lay our service freely at your feet,
To be commanded.

KING.
Thanks, Rosencrantz and gentle
    Guildenstern.

QUEEN.
Thanks, Guildenstern and gentle
    Rosencrantz.
And I beseech you instantly to visit
My too much changèd son.—Go, some of
    you,
And bring these gentlemen where Hamlet
    is.

GUILDENSTERN.
Heavens make our presence and our
    practices
Pleasant and helpful to him!

QUEEN.   Ay, amen!
Exeunt Rosencrantz and Guildenstern
[with some Attendants].

Enter Polonius.

POLONIUS.
Th' ambassadors from Norway, my good
    lord,
Are joyfully returned.

KING.
42   Thou still hast been the father of good news.

POLONIUS.
Have I, my lord? Assure you, my good
    liege,
I hold my duty as I hold my soul.
Both to my God and to my gracious king,
And I do think—or else this brain of mine
Hunts not the trail of policy so sure

As it hath used to do—that I have found
The very cause of Hamlet's lunacy.

KING.
O, speak of that! That do I long to hear.

POLONIUS.
Give first admittance to th'ambassadors.
My news shall be the fruit to that great 52
    feast.

KING.
Thyself do grace to them and bring them 53
    in.

                          [Exit Polonius.]
He tells me, my dear Gertrude, he hath
    found
The head and source of all your son's
    distemper.

QUEEN.
I doubt it is no other but the main,   56
His father's death and our o'erhasty
    marriage.

KING.
Well, we shall sift him.

Enter Ambassadors [Voltemand and Cor-
nelius, with Polonius].

                    Welcome, my good friends.
Say, Voltemand, what from our brother
    Norway?

VOLTEMAND.
Most fair return of greetings and desires.
Upon our first, he sent out to suppress   61
His nephew's levies, which to him
    appeared
To be a preparation 'gainst the Polack,
But better looked into, he truly found
It was against your highness, whereat
    grieved,
That so his sickness, age, and impotence
Was falsely borne in hand, sends out arrests 67
On Fortinbras; which he in brief obeys,
Receives rebuke from Norway, and in fine 69
Makes vow before his uncle never more
To give th' assay of arms against your   71
    majesty.

---

30 in the full bent at the limit of bending (of a bow),
to full capacity   *42 still* always

52 fruit dessert   *53 grace* honor   *56 doubt* suspect   *61*
our first our first words about the matter   *67 borne in*
hand deceived   *69 in fine* in the end   *71 assay* trial

Whereon old Norway, overcome with joy,
Gives him threescore thousand crowns in
  annual fee
And his commission to employ those
  soldiers,
So levied as before, against the Polack,
With an entreaty, herein further shown,

  [*Gives a paper.*]

That it might please you to give quiet pass
Through your dominions for this
  enterprise,
79 On such regards of safety and allowance
As therein are set down.
    KING.   It likes us well;
81 And at our more considered time we'll
    read,
Answer, and think upon this business.
Meantime we thank you for your well-took
  labor.
Go to your rest; at night we'll feast
  together.
Most welcome home! *Exeunt Ambassadors.*
POLONIUS.   This business is well ended.
86 My liege and madam, to expostulate
What majesty should be, what duty is,
Why day is day, night night, and time is
  time,
Were nothing but to waste night, day, and
  time.
90 Therefore, since brevity is the soul of wit,
And tediousness the limbs and outward
  flourishes,
I will be brief. Your noble son is mad.
Mad call I it, for, to define true madness,
What is't but to be nothing else but mad?
But let that go.
QUEEN.   More matter, with less art.
POLONIUS.
Madam, I swear I use no art at all.
That he is mad, 'tis true: 'tis true 'tis pity,
98 And pity 'tis 'tis true—a foolish figure.
But farewell it, for I will use no art.
Mad let us grant him then, and now
  remains

That we find out the cause of this effect—
Or rather say, the cause of this defect,
For this effect defective comes by cause.
Thus it remains, and the remainder thus.
Perpend.   105
I have a daughter (have while she is mine),
Who in her duty and obedience, mark,
Hath given me this. Now gather, and
  surmise.

  [*Reads the*] *letter.*

'To the celestial, and my soul's idol, the
  most beautified
Ophelia, '—
That's an ill phrase, a vile phrase;
  'beautified' is a vile phrase. But you
  shall hear. Thus:

  [*Reads.*]

'In her excellent white bosom, these, & c.'
QUEEN.
Came this from Hamlet to her?
POLONIUS.
Good madam, stay awhile. I will be faithful.

  [*Reads.*]

'Doubt thou the stars are fire;
  Doubt that the sun doth move;
Doubt truth to be a liar;   118
  But never doubt I love.
'O dear Ophelia, I am ill at these numbers. 120
I have not art to reckon my groans, but that I
love thee best, O most best, believe it. Adieu.
'Thine evermore, most dear lady,
  whilst this machine is to him, Hamlet.' 124

This in obedience hath my daughter
  shown me,
And more above hath his solicitings,   126
As they fell out by time, by means, and
  place,
All given to mine ear.

---

79 *regards* terms   81 *considered time* convenient time for
consideration   86 *expostulate* discuss   90 *wit* understanding   98 *figure* figure in rhetoric

105 *Perpend* ponder   118 *Doubt* suspect   120 *numbers*
verses   124 *machine* body; *to* attached to   126 *above*
besides

KING. But how hath she
Received his love?
POLONIUS. What do you think of me?
KING.
As of a man faithful and honorable.
POLONIUS.
I would fain prove so. But what might you
think,
When I had seen this hot love on the wing
(As I perceived it, I must tell you that,
Before my daughter told me), what might
you,
Or my dear majesty your queen here,
think,
136 If I had played the desk or table book,
137 Or given my heart a winking, mute and
dumb,
Or looked upon this love with idle sight?
139 What might you think? No, I went round
to work
And my young mistress thus I did bespeak:
141 'Lord Hamlet is a prince, out of thy star.
142 This must not be.' And then I prescripts
gave her,
That she should lock herself from his resort,
Admit no messengers, receive no tokens.
Which done, she took the fruits of my
advice,
And he, repellèd, a short tale to make,
Fell into a sadness, then into a fast,
148 Thence to a watch, thence into a weakness,
149 Thence to a lightness, and, by this
declension,
Into the madness wherein now he raves,
And all we mourn for.
KING. Do you think 'tis this?
QUEEN.
It may be, very like.
POLONIUS.
Hath there been such a time—I would fain
know that—
That I have positively said ''Tis so,'
When it proved otherwise?
KING. Not that I know.

POLONIUS. [*pointing to his head and shoulder*]
Take this from this, if this be otherwise.
If circumstances lead me, I will find
Where truth is hid, though it were hid
indeed
Within the center. 159
KING. How may we try it further?
POLONIUS.
You know sometimes he walks four hours
together
Here in the lobby.
QUEEN. So he does indeed.
POLONIUS.
At such a time I'll loose my daughter to
him.
Be you and I behind an arras then. 163
Mark the encounter. If he love her not,
And be not from his reason fallen thereon, 165
Let me be no assistant for a state
But keep a farm and carters.
KING. We will try it.

Enter Hamlet [reading on a book].

QUEEN.
But look where sadly the poor wretch
comes reading.
POLONIUS.
Away, I do beseech you both, away.
Exit King and Queen [with Attendants].
I'll board him presently. O, give me 170
leave.
How does my good Lord Hamlet?
HAMLET. Well, God-a-mercy. 172
POLONIUS. Do you know me, my lord?
HAMLET. Excellent well. You are a 174
fishmonger.
POLONIUS. Not I, my lord.
HAMLET. Then I would you were so honest a
man.
POLONIUS. Honest, my lord?

136 *desk or table book* i.e. silent receiver 137 *winking* closing of the eyes 139 *round* roundly, plainly 141 *star* condition determined by stellar influence 142 *prescripts* instructions 148 *watch* sleepless state 149 *lightness* lightheadedness

159 *center* center of the earth and also of the Ptolemaic universe 163 *arras* hanging tapestry 165 *thereon* on that account 170 *board* accost; *presently* at once 172 *God-a-mercy* thank you (literally, 'God have mercy!') 174 *fishmonger* seller of harlots, procurer (a cant term used here with a glance at the fishing Polonius is doing when he offers Ophelia as bait)

HAMLET. Ay, sir. To be honest, as this world goes, is to be one man picked out of ten thousand.

POLONIUS. That's very true, my lord.

HAMLET. For if the sun breed maggots in a
183 dead dog, being a good kissing carrion— Have you a daughter?

POLONIUS. I have, my lord.

HAMLET. Let her not walk i' th' sun. Conception is a blessing, but as your daughter may conceive, friend, look to't.

POLONIUS. [*aside*] How say you by that? Still harping on my daughter. Yet he knew me not at first. 'A said I was a fishmonger. 'A is far gone, far gone. And truly in my youth I suffered much extremity for love, very near this. I'll speak to him again.—What do you read, my lord?

HAMLET. Words, words, words.

POLONIUS. What is the matter, my lord?

198 HAMLET. Between who?

POLONIUS. I mean the matter that you read, my lord.

HAMLET. Slanders, sir, for the satirical rogue says here that old men have grey beards, that their faces are wrinkled, their eyes purging thick amber and plum-tree gum, and that they have a plentiful lack of wit, together with most weak hams. All which, sir, though I most powerfully and potently believe, yet I hold it not honesty to have it thus set down, for you yourself, sir, should be old as I am if, like a crab, you could go backward.

POLONIUS. [*aside*] Though this be madness, yet there is method in't.—Will you walk out of the air, my lord?

HAMLET. Into my grave?

POLONIUS. Indeed, that's out of the air.
217 [*aside*] How pregnant sometimes his replies
218 are! a happiness that often madness hits on, which reason and sanity could not so prosperously be delivered of. I will leave him and suddenly contrive the means of meet-

ing between him and my daughter.—My honorable lord, I will most humbly take my leave of you.

HAMLET. You cannot, sir, take from me anything that I will more willingly part withal 226
—except my life, except my life, except my life.

Enter Guildenstern and Rosencrantz.

POLONIUS. Fare you well, my lord.

HAMLET. These tedious old fools!

POLONIUS. You go to seek the Lord Hamlet. There he is.

ROSENCRANTZ. [*to Polonius*] God save you, sir!

[*Exit Polonius.*]

GUILDENSTERN. My honored lord!

ROSENCRANTZ. My most dear lord!

HAMLET. My excellent good friends! How dost thou, Guildenstern? Ah, Rosencrantz! Good lads, how do ye both?

ROSENCRANTZ.
As the indifferent children of the earth.   240

GUILDENSTERN.
Happy in that we are not over-happy.
On Fortune's cap we are not the very button.

HAMLET. Nor the soles of her shoe?

ROSENCRANTZ. Neither, my lord.

HAMLET. Then you live about her waist, or in the middle of her favors?

GUILDENSTERN. Faith, her privates we.   247

HAMLET. In the secret parts of Fortune? O, most true! she is a strumpet. What news?

ROSENCRANTZ. None, my lord, but that the world 's grown honest.

HAMLET. Then is doomsday near. But your news is not true. [Let me question more in particular. What have you, my good friends, deserved at the hands of Fortune that she sends you to prison hither?

GUILDENSTERN. Prison, my lord?

HAMLET. Denmark's a prison.

ROSENCRANTZ. Then is the world one.

183 good kissing carrion good bit of flesh for kissing *198 Between who* matter for a quarrel between what persons (Hamlet's willful misunderstanding)   *217 pregnant* full of meaning   *218 happiness* aptness of expression

226 withal with   *240 indifferent* average   *247 privates* ordinary men in private, not public, life (with obvious play upon the sexual term 'private parts')

HAMLET. A goodly one; in which there are
261 many confines, wards, and dungeons, Denmark being one o' th' worst.

ROSENCRANTZ. We think not so, my lord.

HAMLET. Why, then 'tis none to you, for there is nothing either good or bad but thinking makes it so. To me it is a prison.

ROSENCRANTZ. Why, then your ambition makes it one. 'Tis too narrow for your mind.

HAMLET. O God, I could be bounded in a nutshell and count myself a king of infinite space, were it not that I have bad dreams.

GUILDENSTERN. Which dreams indeed are ambition, for the very substance of the ambitious is merely the shadow of a dream.

HAMLET. A dream itself is but a shadow.

ROSENCRANTZ. Truly, and I hold ambition of so airy and light a quality that it is but a shadow's shadow.

280 HAMLET. Then are our beggars bodies, and
281 our monarchs and outstretched heroes the beggars' shadows. Shall we to th' court?
283 for, by my fay, I cannot reason.
284 BOTH. We'll wait upon you.

HAMLET. No such matter. I will not sort you with the rest of my servants, for, to speak to you like an honest man, I am most dreadfully attended.] But in the beaten
289 way of friendship, what make you at Elsinore?

ROSENCRANTZ. To visit you, my lord; no other occasion.

HAMLET. Beggar that I am, I am even poor in thanks, but I thank you; and sure, dear
295 friends, my thanks are too dear a halfpenny. Were you not sent for? Is it your own inclining? Is it a free visitation? Come, come, deal justly with me. Come, come. Nay, speak.

GUILDENSTERN. What should we say, my lord?

HAMLET. Why, anything—but to th' purpose. You were sent for, and there is a kind of confession in your looks, which your modesties have not craft enough to color. I know the good king and queen have sent for you.

ROSENCRANTZ. To what end, my lord?

HAMLET. That you must teach me. But let me conjure you by the rights of our fellow-
311 ship, by the consonancy of our youth, by the obligation of our ever-preserved love,
313 and by what more dear a better proposer
314 can charge you withal, be even and direct with me whether you were sent for or no.

ROSENCRANTZ. [*aside to Guildenstern*] What say you?

HAMLET. [*aside*] Nay then, I have an eye of you.—If you love me, hold not off.

GUILDENSTERN. My lord, we were sent for.

HAMLET. I will tell you why. So shall my
322 anticipation prevent your discovery, and
323 your secrecy to the king and queen moult no feather. I have of late—but wherefore I know not—lost all my mirth, forgone all custom of exercises; and indeed, it goes so heavily with my disposition that this goodly frame the earth seems to me a sterile promontory; this most excellent canopy, the air, look you, this brave o'erhanging
331 firmament, this majestical roof fretted with golden fire—why, it appeareth nothing to me but a foul and pestilent congregation of vapors. What a piece of work is a man, how noble in reason, how infinite in
336 faculties; in form and moving how express and admirable, in action how like an angel, in apprehension how like a god: the beauty of the world, the paragon of animals! And
340 yet to me what is this quintessence of dust?

261 confines places of imprisonment; *wards* cells   *280 bodies* solid substances, not shadows (because beggars lack ambition)   *281 outstretched* elongated as shadows (with a corollary implication of far-reaching with respect to the ambitions that make both heroes and monarchs into shadows)   *283 fay* faith   *284 wait upon* attend   *289 make* do   *295 a halfpenny* at a halfpenny

311 consonancy accord (in sameness of age)   *313 proposer* propounder   *314 withal* with; *even* straight   *322 prevent* forestall; *discovery* disclosure   *323 moult no feather* be left whole   *331 firmament* sky; *fretted* decorated with fretwork   *336 express* well framed   *340 quintessence* fifth or last and finest essence (an alchemical term)

Man delights not me—nor woman neither, though by your smiling you seem to say so.

ROSENCRANTZ. My lord, there was no such stuff in my thoughts.

HAMLET. Why did ye laugh then, when I said 'Man delights not me'?

ROSENCRANTZ. To think, my lord, if you
349 delight not in man, what lenten entertainment the players shall receive from you.
351 We coted them on the way, and hither are they coming to offer you service.

HAMLET. He that plays the king shall be welcome—his majesty shall have tribute of me—, the adventurous knight shall use
356 his foil and target, the lover shall not sigh
357 gratis, the humorous man shall end his part in peace, the clown shall make those laugh
359 whose lungs are tickle o' th' sere, and the lady shall say her mind freely, or the blank
361 verse shall halt for't. What players are they?

ROSENCRANTZ. Even those you were wont to take such delight in, the tragedians of the city.

HAMLET. How chances it they travel? Their
367 residence, both in reputation and profit, was better both ways.

369 ROSENCRANTZ. I think their inhibition comes
370 by the means of the late innovation.

HAMELT. Do they hold the same estimation they did when I was in the city? Are they so followed?

ROSENCRANTZ. No indeed, are they not.

[HAMLET. How comes it? Do they grow rusty?

ROSENCRANTZ. Nay, their endeavor keeps in the wonted pace, but there is, sir, an eyrie
379 of children, little eyases, that cry out on

the top of question and are most tyran- 380 nically clapped for't. These are now the fashion, and so berattle the common stages 382 (so they call them) that many wearing rapiers are afraid of goosequills and dare 384 scarce come thither.

HAMLET. What, are they children? Who maintains 'em? How are they escoted? 387 Will they pursue the quality no longer than 388 they can sing? Will they not say after- 389 wards, if they should grow themselves to common players (as it is most like, if their means are no better), their writers do them wrong to make them exclaim against their own succession?

ROSENCRANTZ. Faith, there has been much to do on both sides, and the nation holds it no sin to tarre them to controversy. There 397 was, for a while, no money bid for argu- 398 ment unless the poet and the player went to cuffs in the question.

HAMLET. Is't possible?

GUILDENSTERN. O, there has been much throwing about of brains.

HAMLET. Do the boys carry it away?

ROSENCRANTZ. Ay, that they do, my lord— Hercules and his load too.] 406

HAMLET. It is not very strange, for my uncle is King of Denmark, and those that would make mows at him while my father lived 409 give twenty, forty, fifty, a hundred ducats apiece for his picture in little. 'Sblood, 411 there is something in this more than natural, if philosophy could find it out.

A flourish.

349 lenten scanty *351 coted* overtook *356 foil and target* sword and shield *357 humorous man* eccentric character dominated by one of the humours *359 tickle o' th' sere* hair-triggered for the discharge of laughter ('sere': part of a gunlock) *361 halt* go lame *367 residence* residing at the capital *369 inhibition* impediment to acting in residence (formal prohibition?) *370 innovation* new fashion of having companies of boy actors play on the 'private' stage (?), political upheaval (?) *379 eyrie* nest; *eyases* nestling hawks

380 on the top of question above others on matter of dispute *382 berattle* berate; *common stages* 'public' theatres of the 'common' players, who were organized in companies mainly composed of adult actors (allusion being made to the 'War of the Theatres' in Shakespeare's London) *384 goosequills* pens (of satirists who made out that the London public stage showed low taste) *387 escoted* supported *388 quality* profession of acting *389 sing* i.e. with unchanged voices *397 tarre* incite *398 argument* matter of a play *406 load* i.e. the whole world (with a topical reference to the sign of the Globe Theatre, a representation of Hercules bearing the world on his shoulders) *409 mows* grimaces *411 'Sblood* by God's blood

GUILDENSTERN. There are the players.

HAMLET. Gentlemen, you are welcome to Elsinore. Your hands, come then. Th' appurtenance of welcome is fashion and ceremony. Let me comply with you in this
418 garb, lest my extent to the players (which I tell you must show fairly outwards) should more appear like entertainment than yours. You are welcome. But my uncle-father and aunt-mother are deceived.

GUILDENSTERN. In what, my dear lord?

HAMLET. I am but mad north-north-west.
425 When the wind is southerly I know a hawk from a handsaw.

Enter Polonius.

POLONIUS. Well be with you, gentlemen.

HAMLET. Hark you, Guildenstern—and you too—at each ear a hearer. That great baby you see there is not yet out of his swaddling
431 clouts.

432 ROSENCRANTZ. Happily he is the second time come to them, for they say an old man is twice a child.

HAMLET. I will prophesy he comes to tell me of the players. Mark it.—You say right, sir; a Monday morning, 'twas then indeed.

POLONIUS. My lord, I have news to tell you.

HAMLET. My lord, I have news to tell you.
440 When Roscius was an actor in Rome—

POLONIUS. The actors are come hither, my lord.

HAMLET. Buzz, buzz.

POLONIUS. Upon my honor—

HAMLET. Then came each actor on his ass—

POLONIUS. The best actors in the world, either for tragedy, comedy, history, pastoral, pastoral-comical, historical-pastoral, tragical-historical, tragical-comical-historical-
450 pastoral; scene individable, or poem un-

limited. Seneca cannot be too heavy, nor 451 Plautus too light. For the law of writ and 452 the liberty, these are the only men.

HAMLET. O Jephthah, judge of Israel, what a 454 treasure hadst thou!

POLONIUS. What treasure had he, my lord?

HAMLET. Why,
'One fair daughter, and no more,
The which he loved passing well.' 459

POLONIUS. [*aside*] Still on my daughter.

HAMLET. Am I not i' th' right, old Jephthah?

POLONIUS. If you call me Jephthah, my lord, I have a daughter that I love passing well.

HAMLET. Nay, that follows not.

POLONIUS. What follows then, my lord?

HAMLET. Why,
'As by lot, God wot,'
and then, you know,
'It came to pass, as most like it was.'
The first row of the pious chanson will show 470 you more,
for look where my abridgment comes. 472

Enter the Players.

You are welcome, masters, welcome, all.—
I am glad to see thee well.—Welcome, good friends.—O, old friend, why, thy face is valanced since I saw thee last. Com'st 476 thou to beard me in Denmark?—What, my young lady and mistress? By'r Lady, 478 your ladyship is nearer to heaven than when I saw you last by the altitude of a chopine. Pray God your voice, like a piece 481 of uncurrent gold, be not cracked within 482

418 garb fashion; *extent* showing of welcome *425 hawk* mattock or pickaxe (also called 'hack'; here used apparently with a play on 'hawk': a bird); *handsaw* carpenter's tool (apparently with a play on some corrupt form of 'hernshaw'; heron, a bird often hunted with the hawk) *431 clouts* clothes *432 Happily* haply, perhaps *440 Roscius* the greatest of Roman comic actors *450 scene individable* drama observing the unities; *poem unlimited* drama not observing the unities

451 Seneca Roman writer of tragedies; *Plautus* Roman writer of comedies *452 law of writ* orthodoxy determined by critical rules of the drama; *liberty* freedom from such orthodoxy *454 Jephthah* the compelled sacrificer of a dearly beloved daughter (Judges xi) *459 passing* surpassingly (verses are from a ballad on Jephthah) *470 row* stanza; *chanson* song *472 my abridgment* that which shortens my talk *476 valanced* fringed (with a beard) *478 young lady* boy who plays women's parts *481 chopine* women's thick-soled shoe; *uncurrent* not legal tender *482 within the ring* from the edge through the line circling the design on the coin (with a play on 'ring': a sound)

the ring.—Masters, you are all welcome.
We'll e'en to 't like French falconers, fly at
anything we see. We'll have a speech
straight. Come, give us a taste of your
quality. Come, a passionate speech.

PLAYER. What speech, my good lord?

HAMLET. I heard thee speak me a speech
once, but it was never acted, or if it was,
not above once, for the play, I remember,
492 pleased not the million; 'twas caviary to
493 the general, but it was (as I received it,
and others, whose judgments in such mat-
495 ters cried in the top of mine) an excellent
play, well digested in the scenes, set down
with as much modesty as cunning. I re-
498 member one said there were no sallets in
the lines to make the matter savory, nor
no matter in the phrase that might indict
the author of affectation, but called it an
honest method, as wholesome as sweet, and
by very much more handsome than fine.
One speech in't I chiefly loved. 'Twas
Aeneas' tale to Dido, and thereabout of it
506 especially where he speaks of Priam's
slaughter. If it live in your memory, begin
at this line—let me see, let me see:
509 'The rugged Pyrrhus, like th' Hyrcanian
beast—'
'Tis not so; it begins with Pyrrhus:
511 'The rugged Pyrrhus, he whose sable
arms,
Black as his purpose, did the night
resemble
513 When he lay couchèd in the ominous
horse,
Hath now this dread and black
complexion smeared
515 With heraldry more dismal. Head to foot
516 Now is he total gules, horridly tricked
With blood of fathers, mothers,
daughters, sons,

Baked and impasted with the parching 518
streets,
That lend a tyrannous and a damnèd
light
To their lord's murder. Roasted in wrath
and fire,
And thus o'ersizèd with coagulate gore, 521
With eyes like carbuncles, the hellish
Pyrrhus
Old grandsire Priam seeks.'
So, proceed you.

POLONIUS. Fore God, my lord, well spoken,
with good accent and good discretion.

PLAYER.   'Anon he finds him,
Striking too short at Greeks. His antique
sword,
Rebellious to his arms, lies where it falls,
Repugnant to command. Unequal
matched,
Pyrrhus at Priam drives, in rage strikes
wide,
But with the whiff and wind of his fell 532
sword
Th' unnervèd father falls. Then senseless 533
Ilium,
Seeming to feel this blow, with flaming
top
Stoops to his base, and with a hideous 535
crash
Takes prisoner Pyrrhus' ear. For lo! his
sword,
Which was declining on the milky head
Of reverend Priam, seemed i' th' air to
stick.
So as a painted tyrant Pyrrhus stood, 539
And like a neutral to his will and matter 540
Did nothing.
But as we often see, against some storm, 542
A silence in the heavens, the rack stand 543
still,
The bold winds speechless, and the orb
below

492 *caviary* caviare 493 *general* multitude 495 *in the top of* more authoritatively than 498 *sallets* salads, highly seasoned passages 506 *Priam's slaughter* i.e. at the fall of Troy (Aeneid 11, 506 ff.) 509 *Hyrcanian beast* tiger 511 *sable* black 513 *ominous* fateful; *horse* the wooden horse by which the Greeks gained entrance to Troy 515 *dismal* ill-omened 516 *gules* red (heraldic term); *tricked* decorated in color (heraldic term)

518 *parching* i.e. because Troy was burning 521 *o'ersizèd* covered as with size, a glutinous material used for filling pores of plaster, etc.; *coagulate* clotted 532 *fell* cruel 533 *senseless* without feeling 535 *his* its 539 *painted* pictured 540 *will and matter* purpose and its realization (between which he stands motionless) 542 *against* just before 543 *rack* clouds

As hush as death, anon the dreadful thunder

546 Doth rend the region, so after Pyrrhus' pause,

Arousèd vengeance sets him new awork,

548 And never did the Cyclops' hammers fall

549 On Mars' armor, forged for proof eterne,

With less remorse than Pyrrhus' bleeding sword

Now falls on Priam.

Out, out, thou strumpet Fortune! All you gods,

In general synod take away her power,

554 Break all the spokes and fellies from her wheel,

555 And bowl the round nave down the hill of heaven,

As low as to the fiends.'

POLONIUS. This is too long.

HAMLET. It shall to the barber's, with your

559 beard.—Prithee say on. He's for a jig or a tale of bawdry, or he sleeps. Say on; come to Hecuba.

PLAYER.

562 'But who (ah woe!) had seen the mobled queen—'

HAMLET. 'The mobled queen'?

POLONIUS. That's good. 'Mobled queen' is good.

PLAYER.

'Run barefoot up and down, threat'ning the flames

567 With bisson rheum; a clout upon that head

Where late the diadem stood, and for a robe,

569 About her lank and all o'erteemèd loins,

A blanket in the alarm of fear caught up—

Who this had seen, with tongue in venom steeped

'Gainst Fortune's state would treason   570 have pronounced.

But if the gods themselves did see her then,

When she saw Pyrrhus make malicious sport

In mincing with his sword her husband's limbs,

The instant burst of clamor that she made

(Unless things mortal move them not at all)

Would have made milch the burning   576 eyes of heaven

And passion in the gods.'

POLONIUS. Look, whe'r he has not turned his   578 color, and has tears in's eyes. Prithee no more.

HAMLET. 'Tis well. I'll have thee speak out the rest of this soon.—Good my lord, will you see the players well bestowed? Do you   583 hear? Let them be well used, for they are the abstract and brief chronicles of the time. After your death you were better have a bad epitaph than their ill report while you live.

POLONIUS. My lord, I will use them according to their desert.

HAMLET. God's bodkin, man, much better!   591 Use every man after his desert, and who shall scape whipping? Use them after your own honor and dignity. The less they deserve, the more merit is in your bounty. Take them in.

POLONIUS. Come, sirs.

HAMLET. Follow him, friends. We'll hear a play tomorrow. [*aside to Player*] Dost thou hear me, old friend? Can you play 'The Murder of Gonzago'?

PLAYER. Ay, my lord.

HAMLET. We'll ha't to-morrow night. You could for a need study a speech of some dozen or sixteen lines which I would set down and insert in't, could you not?

---

546 region sky *548 Cyclops* giant workmen who made armor in the smithy of Vulcan *549 proof eterne* eternal protection *554 fellies* segments of the rim *555 nave* hub *559 jig* short comic piece with singing and dancing often presented after a play *562 mobled* muffled *567 bisson rheum* blinding tears; *clout* cloth *569 o'erteemèd* overproductive of children

570 state government of worldly events *576 milch* tearful (milk-giving); *eyes* i.e. stars *578 whe'r* whether *583 bestowed* lodged *591 God's bodkin* by God's little body

PLAYER. Ay, my lord.

HAMLET. Very well. Follow that lord, and look you mock him not.—My good friends, I'll leave you till night. You are welcome to Elsinore.   *Exeunt Polonius and Players.*

ROSENCRANTZ. Good my lord.
          Exeunt [Rosencrantz and Guildenstern].

HAMLET.

Ay, so, God bye to you.—Now I am alone.

O, what a rogue and peasant slave am I!

Is it not monstrous that this player here,

But in a fiction, in a dream of passion,

617 Could force his soul so to his own conceit

That from her working all his visage wanned,

Tears in his eyes, distraction in his aspect,

620 A broken voice, and his whole function suiting

With forms to his conceit? And all for nothing,

For Hecuba!

What's Hecuba to him, or he to Hecuba,

That he should weep for her? What would he do

Had he the motive and the cue for passion

That I have? He would drown the stage with tears

And cleave the general ear with horrid speech,

Make mad the guilty and appal the free,

Confound the ignorant, and amaze indeed

The very faculties of eyes and ears.

Yet I,

632 A dull and muddy-mettled rascal, peak

633 Like John-a-dreams, unpregnant of my cause,

And can say nothing. No, not for a king,

Upon whose property and most dear life

A damned defeat was made. Am I a coward?

Who calls me villain? breaks my pate across?

Plucks off my beard and blows it in my face?

Tweaks me by the nose? gives me the lie i' th' throat

As deep as to the lungs? Who does me this?

Ha, 'swounds, I should take it, for it cannot be   641

But I am pigeon-livered and lack gall   642

To make oppression bitter, or ere this

I should ha' fatted all the region kites   644

With this slave's offal. Bloody, bawdy villain!   645

Remorseless, treacherous, lecherous, kindless villain!   646

O, vengeance!

Why, what an ass am I! This is most brave,

That I, the son of a dear father murdered,

Prompted to my revenge by heaven and hell,

Must like a whore unpack my heart with words

And fall a-cursing like a very drab,

A stallion! Fie upon't, foh! About, my brains.   653

Hum—

I have heard that guilty creatures sitting at a play

Have by the very cunning of the scene

Been struck so to the soul that presently   657

They have proclaimed their malefactions.

For murder, though it have no tongue, will speak

With most miraculous organ. I'll have these players

Play something like the murder of my father

Before mine uncle. I'll observe his looks.

I'll tent him to the quick. If 'a do blench,   663

I know my course. The spirit that I have seen

May be a devil, and the devil hath power

T'assume a pleasing shape, yea, and perhaps

Out of my weakness and my melancholy,

As he is very potent with such spirits,

Abuses me to damn me. I'll have grounds   669

---

617 *conceit* conception, idea 620 *function* action of bodily powers 632 *muddy-mettled* dull-spirited; *peak* mope 633 *John-a-dreams* a sleepy dawdler; *unpregnant* barren of realization

641 *'swounds* by God's wounds 642 *pigeon-livered* of dove-like gentleness 644 *region kites* kites of the air 645 *offal* guts 646 *kindless* unnatural 653 *stallion* prostitute (male or female) 657 *presently* immediately 663 *tent* probe; *blench* flinch 669 *Abuses* deludes

670 More relative than this. The play's the thing
Wherein I'll catch the conscience of the king.   *Exit.*

*

ACT III

Scene i

Enter King, Queen, Polonius, Ophelia, Rosencrantz, Guildenstern, Lords.

1 KING.
And can you by no drift of conference
Get from him why he puts on this confusion,
Grating so harshly all his days of quiet
With turbulent and dangerous lunacy?
ROSENCRANTZ.
He does confess he feels himself distracted,
But from what cause 'a will by no means speak.
GUILDENSTERN.
Nor do we find him forward to be sounded,
But with a crafty madness keeps aloof
When we would bring him on to some confession
Of his true state.
QUEEN.   Did he receive you well?
ROSENCRANTZ.
Most like a gentleman.
GUILDENSTERN.
But with much forcing of his disposition.
ROSENCRANTZ.
Niggard of question, but of our demands
Most free in his reply.
14 QUEEN.   Did you assay him
To any pastime?
ROSENCRANTZ.
Madam, it so fell out that certain players

We o'erraught on the way. Of these we told 17
him,
And there did seem in him a kind of joy
To hear of it. They are here about the court,
And, as I think, they have already order
This night to play before him.
POLONIUS.   'Tis most true,
And he beseeched me to entreat your majesties
To hear and see the matter.
KING.
With all my heart, and it doth much content me
To hear him so inclined.
Good gentlemen, give him a further edge 26
And drive his purpose into these delights.
ROSENCRANTZ.
We shall, my lord.
                    Exeunt Rosencrantz and Guildenstern.
KING.   Sweet Gertrude, leave us too,
For we have closely sent for Hamlet 29
hither,
That he, as 'twere by accident, may here
Affront Ophelia.   31
Her father and myself (lawful espials) 32
Will so bestow ourselves that, seeing unseen,
We may of their encounter frankly judge
And gather by him, as he is behaved,
If 't be th' affliction of his love or no
That thus he suffers for.
QUEEN.   I shall obey you.—
And for your part, Ophelia, I do wish
That your good beauties be the happy cause
Of Hamlet's wildness. So shall I hope your virtues
Will bring him to his wonted way again,
To both your honors.
OPHELIA.   Madam, I wish it may.
                    [*Exit Queen.*]
POLONIUS.
Ophelia, walk you here.—Gracious, so please you,
We will bestow ourselves.—

---

670 *relative* pertinent
III, i A chamber in the Castle *1 drift of conference*
direction of conversation *14 assay* try to win

17 *o'erraught* overtook *26 edge* keenness of desire *29*
closely privately *31 Affront* come face to face with
32 espials spies

[*To Ophelia*]   Read on this book,
45   That show of such an exercise may color
Your loneliness. We are oft to blame in this,
'Tis too much proved, that with devotion's
     visage
And pious action we do sugar o'er
The devil himself.
KING. [*aside*]   O, 'tis too true.
How smart a lash that speech doth give my
     conscience!
The harlot's cheek, beautied with plast'ring
     art,
52   Is not more ugly to the thing that helps it
Than is my deed to my most painted word.
O heavy burthen!
POLONIUS.
I hear him coming. Let's withdraw, my
     lord.   [*Exeunt King and Polonius.*]

     Enter Hamlet.

HAMLET.
To be, or not to be—that is the question:
Whether 'tis nobler in the mind to suffer
The slings and arrows of outrageous fortune
Or to take arms against a sea of troubles
And by opposing end them. To die, to
     sleep—
No more—and by a sleep to say we end
The heartache, and the thousand natural
     shocks
That flesh is heir to. 'Tis a consummation
Devoutly to be wished. To die, to sleep—
65   To sleep—perchance to dream: ay, there's
     the rub,
For in that sleep of death what dreams may
     come
67   When we have shuffled off this mortal coil,
68   Must give us pause. There's the respect
69   That makes calamity of so long life.
For who would bear the whips and scorns
     of time,

Th' oppressor's wrong, the proud man's
     contumely
The pangs of despised love, the law's delay,
The insolence of office, and the spurns
That patient merit of th' unworthy takes,
When he himself might his quietus make   75
With a bare bodkin? Who would fardels   76
     bear,
To grunt and sweat under a weary life,
But that the dread of something after death,
The undiscovered country, from whose   79
     bourn
No traveller returns, puzzles the will,
And makes us rather bear those ills we have
Than fly to others that we know not of?
Thus conscience does make cowards of us
     all,
And thus the native hue of resolution
Is sicklied o'er with the pale cast of
     thought,
And enterprises of great pitch and   86
     moment
With this regard their currents turn awry   87
And lose the name of action.—Soft you
     now,
The fair Ophelia!—Nymph, in thy orisons   89
Be all my sins remembered.
OPHELIA.   Good my lord,
How does your honor for this many a day?
HAMLET.
I humbly thank you, well, well, well.
OPHELIA.
My lord, I have remembrances of yours
That I have longèd long to re-deliver.
I pray you, now receive them.
HAMLET.   No, not I,
I never gave you aught.
OPHELIA.
My honored lord, you know right well you
     did,
And with them words of so sweet breath
     composed
As made the things more rich. Their
     perfume lost,

---

45 *exercise* religious exercise (the book being obviously one of devotion); *color* give an appearance of naturalness to 52 *to* compared to   65 *rub* obstacle (literally, obstruction encountered by a bowler's ball)   67 *shuffled off* cast off as an encumbrance; *coil* to-do, turmoil   68 *respect* consideration   69 *of so long life* so long-lived

75 *quietus* settlement (literally, release from debt)   76 *bodkin* dagger; *fardels* burdens   79 *bourn* confine, region   86 *pitch* height (of a soaring falcon's flight)   87 *regard* consideration   89 *orisons* prayers (because of the book of devotion she reads)

Take these again, for to the noble mind
Rich gifts wax poor when givers prove
    unkind.
There, my lord.

103 HAMLET. Ha, ha! Are you honest?

OPHELIA. My lord?

HAMLET. Are you fair?

OPHELIA. What means your lordship?

HAMLET. That if you be honest and fair, your
honesty should admit no discourse to your
beauty.

OPHELIA. Could beauty, my lord, have better
111 commerce than with honesty?

HAMLET. Ay, truly; for the power of beauty
will sooner transform honesty from what
it is to a bawd than the force of honesty can
translate beauty into his likeness. This was
116 sometime a paradox, but now the time
gives it proof. I did love you once.

OPHELIA. Indeed, my lord, you made me
believe so.

HAMLET. You should not have believed me,
121 for virtue cannot so inoculate our old stock
but we shall relish of it. I loved you not.

OPHELIA. I was the more deceived.

HAMLET. Get thee to a nunnery. Why wouldst
thou be a breeder of sinners? I am myself
126 indifferent honest, but yet I could accuse
me of such things that it were better my
mother had not borne me: I am very
proud, revengeful, ambitious, with more
offenses at my beck than I have thoughts
to put them in, imagination to give them
shape, or time to act them in. What should
such fellows as I do crawling between earth
and heaven? We are arrant knaves all;
believe none of us. Go thy ways to a nunnery. Where's your father?

OPHELIA. At home, my lord.

HAMLET. Let the doors be shut upon him, that
he may play the fool nowhere but in's own
house. Farewell.

OPHELIA. O, help him, you sweet heavens!

HAMLET. If thou dost marry, I'll give thee
this plague for thy dowry: be thou as
chaste as ice, as pure as snow, thou shalt
not escape calumny. Get thee to a nunnery.
Go, farewell. Or if thou wilt needs marry,
marry a fool, for wise men know well
enough what monsters you make of them. 148
To a nunnery, go, and quickly too. Farewell.

OPHELIA. O heavenly powers, restore him!

HAMLET. I have heard of your paintings too,
well enough. God hath given you one face,
and you make yourselves another. You jig,
you amble, and you lisp; you nickname
God's creatures and make your wanton- 156
ness your ignorance. Go to, I'll no more
on't; it hath made me mad. I say we will
have no more marriage. Those that are
married already—all but one—shall live.
The rest shall keep as they are. To a nunnery, go.   *Exit.*

OPHELIA.
O, what a noble mind is here o'erthrown!
The courtier's, soldier's, scholar's, eye,
    tongue, sword,
Th' expectancy and rose of the fair state,   165
The glass of fashion and the mould of form, 166
Th' observed of all observers, quite, quite
    down!
And I, of ladies most deject and wretched,
That sucked the honey of his music vows,
Now see that noble and most sovereign
    reason
Like sweet bells jangled, out of time and
    harsh,
That unmatched form and feature of blown
    youth
Blasted with ecstasy. O, woe is me   173
T' have seen what I have seen, see what I
    see!

Enter King and Polonius.

---

103 honest chaste   *111 commerce* intercourse   *116
paradox* idea contrary to common opinion   *121 inoculate* graft; *relish* have a flavor (because of original sin)
126 indifferent honest moderately respectable

148 monsters i.e., unnatural combinations of wisdom and
uxorious folly   *156 wantonness* affectation; *your ignorance* a matter for which you offer the excuse that you
don't know any better   *165 expectancy and rose* fair hope
166 glass mirror   *173 ecstasy* madness

KING.
175 Love? his affections do not that way tend,
Nor what he spake, though it lacked form
    a little,
Was not like madness. There's something
    in his soul
O'er which his melancholy sits on brood,
179 And I do doubt the hatch and the disclose
Will be some danger; which for to prevent,
I have in quick determination
Thus set it down: he shall with speed to
    England
For the demand of our neglected tribute.
Haply the seas, and countries different,
With variable objects, shall expel
186 This something-settled matter in his heart,
Whereon his brains still beating puts him
    thus
From fashion of himself. What think you
    on't?
POLONIUS.
It shall do well. But yet do I believe
The origin and commencement of his grief
Sprung from neglected love.—How now,
    Ophelia?
You need not tell us what Lord
    Hamlet said.
We heard it all.—My lord, do as you
    please,
But if you hold it fit, after the play
Let his queen mother all alone entreat him
196 To show his grief. Let her be round with
    him,
And I'll be placed, so please you, in the ear
Of all their conference. If she find him not,
To England send him, or confine him
    where
Your wisdom best shall think.
KING.   It shall be so.
Madness in great ones must not unwatched
    go.   *Exeunt.*

*

ACT III

Scene ii

Enter Hamlet and three of the Players.

HAMLET. Speak the speech, I pray you, as I
pronounced it to you, trippingly on the 2
tongue. But if you mouth it, as many of
our players do, I had as lief the town crier
spoke my lines. Nor do not saw the air too
much with your hand, thus, but use all
gently, for in the very torrent, tempest, and
(as I may say) whirlwind of your passion,
you must acquire and beget a temperance
that may give it smoothness. O, it offends
me to the soul to hear a robustious periwig- 11
pated fellow tear a passion to tatters, to 12
very rags, to split the ears of the groundl- 13
ings, who for the most part are capable of
nothing but inexplicable dumb shows and 15
noise. I would have such a fellow whipped
for o'erdoing Termagant. It out-herods 17
Herod. Pray you avoid it.
PLAYER. I warrant your honor.
HAMLET. Be not too tame neither, but let your
own discretion be your tutor. Suit the
action to the word, the word to the action,
with this special observance, that you
o'erstep not the modesty of nature. For
anything so overdone is from the purpose 25
of playing, whose end, both at the first and
now, was and is, to hold, as 'twere, the
mirror up to nature, to show virtue her own
feature, scorn her own image, and the very
age and body of the time his form and pres- 30

III, ii The hall of the Castle   *2 trippingly* easily
11 robustious boisterous   *12 periwig-pated* wig-wearing
(after the custom of actors)   *13 groundlings* spectators
who paid least and stood on the ground in the pit or
yard of the theatre   *15 dumb shows* brief actions without words, forecasting dramatic matter to follow (the
play presented later in this scene giving an old-
fashioned example)   *17 Termagant* a Saracen 'god' in
medieval romance and drama; *Herod* the raging tyrant
of old Biblical plays   *25 from* apart from   *30 pressure*
impressed or printed character; *come tardy off* brought
off slowly and badly

175 affections emotions   *179 doubt* fear   *186 something-settled* somewhat settled   *196 round* plain-
spoken

sure. Now this overdone, or come tardy off,
though it make the unskillful laugh, cannot
33 but make the judicious grieve, the censure
of the which one must in your allowance
o'erweigh a whole theatre of others. O,
there be players that I have seen play, and
heard others praise, and that highly (not to
speak it profanely), that neither having th'
accent of Christians, nor the gait of
Christian, pagan, nor man, have so
strutted and bellowed that I have thought
42 some of Nature's journeymen had made
men, and not made them well, they
imitated humanity so abominably.
45 PLAYER. I hope we have reformed that indifferently with us, sir.
HAMLET. O, reform it altogether! And let
those that play your clowns speak no more
49 than is set down for them, for there be of
them that will themselves laugh, to set on
some quantity of barren spectators to
laugh too, though in the mean time some
necessary question of the play be then to be
considered. That's villainous and shows a
most pitiful ambition in the fool that uses it.
Go make you ready.   [*Exeunt Players.*]

Enter Polonius, Guildenstern, and Rosencrantz.

How now, my lord? Will the king hear this
piece of work?
58 POLONIUS. And the queen too, and that presently.
HAMLET. Bid the players make haste.
       [*Exit Polonius.*]
Will you two help to hasten them?
ROSENCRANTZ. Ay, my lord.   *Exeunt they two.*
HAMLET. What, ho, Horatio!

Enter Horatio.

HORATIO.
Here, sweet lord, at your service.

HAMLET.
Horatio, thou art e'en as just a man
As e'er my conversation coped withal.   65
HORATIO.
O, my dear lord—
HAMLET.   Nay, do not think I flatter.
For what advancement may I hope from
thee,
That no revenue hast but thy good spirits
To feed and clothe thee? Why should the
poor be flattered?
No, let the candied tongue lick absurd
pomp,
And crook the pregnant hinges of the knee   71
Where thrift may follow fawning. Dost   72
thou hear?
Since my dear soul was mistress of her
choice
And could of men distinguish her election,
S' hath sealed thee for herself, for thou hast   75
been
As one in suff'ring all that suffers nothing,
A man that Fortune's buffets and rewards
Hast ta'en with equal thanks; and blest are
those
Whose blood and judgment are so well   79
commeddled
That they are not a pipe for Fortune's
finger
To sound what stop she please. Give me
that man
That is not passion's slave, and I will wear
him
In my heart's core, ay, in my heart of heart,
As I do thee. Something too much of this—
There is a play to-night before the king.
One scene of it comes near the circumstance
Which I have told thee, of my father's
death.
I prithee, when thou seest that act afoot,
Even with the very comment of thy soul   89
Observe my uncle. If his occulted guilt   90
Do not itself unkennel in one speech,

33 the censure of the which one the judgment of even one of whom   *42 journeymen* workmen not yet masters of their trade   *45 indifferently* fairly well   *49 of them* some of them   *58 presently* at once   *65 conversation coped withal* intercourse with men encountered   *71 pregnant* quick to move   *72 thrift* profit   *75 sealed* marked   *79 blood* passion; *commeddled* mixed together   *89 the very ... soul* thy deepest sagacity   *90 occulted* hidden

92 It is a damnèd ghost that we have seen,
And my imaginations are as foul
94 As Vulcan's stithy. Give him heedful note,
For I mine eyes will rivet to his face,
And after we will both our judgments join
97 In censure of his seeming.
HORATIO.   Well, my lord.
If 'a steal aught the while this play is
playing,
And scape detecting, I will pay the theft.

Enter Trumpets and Kettledrums, King,
Queen, Polonius, Ophelia [, Rosencrantz,
Guildenstern, and other Lords attendant].

HAMLET. They are coming to the play. I must
101 be idle. Get you a place.
102 KING. How fares our cousin Hamlet?
103 HAMLET. Excellent, i' faith, of the chameleon's
dish. I eat the air, promise-crammed. You
cannot feed capons so.
KING. I have nothing with this answer, Ham-
107 let. These words are not mine.
HAMLET. No, nor mine now. [*to Polonius*] My
lord, you played once i' th' university, you
say?
POLONIUS. That did I, my lord, and was ac-
counted a good actor.
HAMLET. What did you enact?
POLONIUS. I did enact Julius Caesar. I was
killed i' th' Capitol; Brutus killed me.
HAMLET. It was a brute part of him to kill so
capital a calf there. Be the players ready?
118 ROSENCRANTZ. Ay, my lord. They stay upon
your patience.
QUEEN. Come hither, my dear Hamlet, sit by
me.
HAMLET. No, good mother. Here's metal
more attractive.
POLONIUS. [*to the King*] Oho! do you mark
that?

HAMLET. Lady, shall I lie in your lap?

[*He lies at Ophelia's feet.*]

OPHELIA. No, my lord.
HAMLET. I mean, my head upon your lap?
OPHELIA. Ay, my lord.
HAMLET. Do you think I meant country   126
matters?
OPHELIA. I think nothing, my lord.
HAMLET. That's a fair thought to lie between
maids' legs.
OPHELIA. What is, my lord?
HAMLET. Nothing.
OPHELIA. You are merry, my lord.
HAMLET. Who, I?
OPHELIA. Ay, my lord.
HAMLET. O God, your only jig-maker! What   134
should a man do but be merry? For look
you how cheerfully my mother looks, and
my father died within's two hours.
OPHELIA. Nay, 'tis twice two months, my
lord.
HAMLET. So long? Nay then, let the devil
wear black, for I'll have a suit of sables. O 140
heavens! die two months ago, and not forgotten yet? Then there's hope a great man's
memory may outlive his life half a year.
But, by'r Lady, 'a must build churches
then, or else shall 'a suffer not thinking on,
with the hobby-horse, whose epitaph is   146
'For O, for O, the hobby-horse is forgot!'

(*The trumpets sound. Dumb show follows:*
Enter a King and a Queen [very lovingly],
the Queen embracing him, and he her. [She
kneels; and makes show of protestation unto
him.] He takes her up, and declines his head
upon her neck. He lies him down upon a bank
of flowers. She, seeing him asleep, leaves
him. Anon come in another man: takes off
his crown, kisses it, pours poison in the
sleeper's ears, and leaves him. The Queen

---

92 *damnèd ghost* evil spirit, devil (as thought of in II, ii,
664 ff.) 94 *stithy* smithy 97 *censure of* sentence upon
101 *be idle* be foolish, act the madman 102 *cousin*
nephew 103 *chameleon's dish* i.e., air (which was believed
the chameleon's food; Hamlet willfully takes *fares* in
the sense of 'feeds') 107 *not mine* not for me as the
asker of my question 118–119 *stay upon your patience*
await your indulgence

126 *country matters* rustic goings-on, barn-yard mating
(with a play upon a sexual term) 134 *jig-maker* writer
of jigs (see II, ii, 559) 140 *sables* black furs (luxurious
garb, not for mourning) 146 *hobby-horse* traditional
figure strapped round the waist of a performer in May
games and morris dances

returns, finds the King dead, makes pas-
sionate action. The poisoner, with some three
or four, come in again, seem to condole with
her. The dead body is carried away. The
poisoner woos the Queen with gifts; she
seems harsh awhile, but in the end accepts
love. [*Exeunt.*]

OPHELIA. What means this, my lord?

149 HAMLET. Marry, this is miching mallecho; it
means mischief.

OPHELIA. Belike this show imports the argument of the play.

Enter Prologue.

HAMLET. We shall know by this fellow. The
players cannot keep counsel; they'll tell
all.

OPHELIA. Will 'a tell us what this show
meant?

HAMLET. Ay, or any show that you'll show
him. Be not you ashamed to show, he'll not
shame to tell you what it means.

159 OPHELIA. You are naught, you are naught.
I'll mark the play.

PROLOGUE. For us and for our tragedy,
          Here stooping to your clemency,
          We beg your hearing patiently.
                              [*Exit.*]

164 HAMLET. Is this a prologue, or the posy of a
ring?

OPHELIA. 'Tis brief, my lord.

HAMLET. As woman's love.

Enter [two Players as] King and Queen.

KING.

167 Full thirty times hath Phoebus' cart gone
round

168 Neptune's salt wash and Tellus' orbèd
ground,

169 And thirty dozen moons with borrowed
sheen

About the world have times twelve thirties
been,

Since love our hearts, and Hymen did our 171
hands,

Unite commutual in most sacred bands.   172

QUEEN.

So many journeys may the sun and moon
Make us again count o'er ere love be done!
But woe is me, you are so sick of late,
So far from cheer and from your former
state,

That I distrust you. Yet, though I distrust, 177
Discomfort you, my lord, it nothing must.
For women fear too much, even as they
love,

And women's fear and love hold quantity, 180
In neither aught, or in extremity.

Now what my love is, proof hath made you
know,

And as my love is sized, my fear is so.
Where love is great, the littlest doubts are
fear;

Where little fears grow great, great love
grows there.

KING.

Faith, I must leave thee, love, and shortly
too;

My operant powers their functions leave to 187
do.

And thou shalt live in this fair world
behind,

Honored, beloved, and haply one as kind
For husband shalt thou—

QUEEN.   O, confound the rest!
Such love must needs be treason in my
breast.

In second husband let me be accurst!
None wed the second but who killed the
first.

HAMLET. [*aside*] That's wormwood.   194

QUEEN.

The instances that second marriage move 195
Are base respects of thrift, but none of love.
A second time I kill my husband dead

---

149 *miching mallecho* sneaking iniquity   159 *naught*
indecent   164 *posy* brief motto in rhyme ('poesy');
ring finger ring   167 *Phoebus' cart* the sun's chariot
168 *Tellus* Roman goddess of the earth   169 *borrowed*
i.e. taken from the sun

171 *Hymen* Greek god of marriage   172 *commutual*
mutually   177 *distrust you* fear for you   180 *quantity*
proportion   187 *operant powers* active bodily forces
194 *wormwood* a bitter herb   195 *instances* motives

When second husband kisses me in bed.

KING.

I do believe you think what now you speak,
But what we do determine oft we break.

201 Purpose is but the slave to memory,
202 Of violent birth, but poor validity,
Which now like fruit unripe sticks on the
tree,
But fall unshaken when they mellow be.
Most necessary 'tis that we forget
To pay ourselves what to ourselves is debt.
What to ourselves in passion we propose,
The passion ending, doth the purpose lose.
The violence of either grief or joy
210 Their own enactures with themselves
destroy.
Where joy most revels, grief doth most
lament;
Grief joys, joy grieves, on slender accident.
This world is not for aye, nor 'tis not
strange
That even our loves should with our
fortunes change,
For 'tis a question left us yet to prove,
Whether love lead fortune, or else fortune
love.
The great man down, you mark his
favorite flies,
The poor advanced makes friends of
enemies;
And hitherto doth love on fortune tend,
For who not needs shall never lack a friend,
And who in want a hollow friend doth try,
222 Directly seasons him his enemy.
But, orderly to end where I begun,
Our wills and fates do so contrary run
225 That our devices still are overthrown;
Our thoughts are ours, their ends none of
our own.
So think thou wilt no second husband wed,
But die thy thoughts when thy first lord is
dead.

QUEEN.

Nor earth to me give food, nor heaven
light,

Sport and repose lock from me day and
night,
To desperation turn my trust and hope,
An anchor's cheer in prison be my scope,   228
Each opposite that blanks the face of joy   229
Meet what I would have well, and it
destroy,
Both here and hence pursue me lasting   231
strife,
If, once a widow, ever I be wife!

HAMLET. If she should break it now!

KING.

'Tis deeply sworn. Sweet, leave me here a
while.
My spirits grow dull, and fain I would
beguile
The tedious day with sleep.

QUEEN.   Sleep rock the brain,
                                [*He sleeps.*]
And never come mischance between us
twain!   *Exit.*

HAMLET. Madam, how like you this play?

QUEEN. The lady doth protest too much,
methinks.

HAMLET. O, but she'll keep her word.

KING. Have you heard the argument? Is 241
there no offense in't?

HAMLET. No, no, they do but jest, poison in
jest; no offense i' th' world.

KING. What do you call the play?

HAMLET. 'The Mousetrap.' Marry, how?
Tropically. This play is the image of a   247
murder done in Vienna. Gonzago is the
duke's name; his wife, Baptista. You shall
see anon. 'Tis a knavish piece of work, but
what o' that? Your majesty, and we that
have free souls, it touches us not. Let the 252
galled jade winch; our withers are   253
unwrung.

Enter Lucianus.

This is one Lucianus, nephew to the king.

---

201 slave to i.e. dependent upon for life   *202 validity*
strength   *210 enactures* fulfillments   *222 seasons him*
ripens him into   *225 still* always

228 anchor's hermit's   *229 blanks* blanches, makes pale
231 hence in the next world   *241 argument* plot sum-
mary   *247 Tropically* in the way of a trope or figure
(with a play on 'trapically')   *252 free* guiltless   *253
galled* sore-backed; *jade* horse; *winch* wince; *withers*
shoulders

256 OPHELIA. You are as good as a chorus, my lord.

HAMLET. I could interpret between you and
259 your love, if I could see the puppets dallying.

OPHELIA. You are keen, my lord, you are keen.

HAMLET. It would cost you a groaning to take off my edge.

OPHELIA. Still better, and worse.

HAMLET. So you must take your husbands.—
Begin, murderer. Leave thy damnable faces and begin. Come, the croaking raven doth bellow for revenge.

LUCIANUS.
Thoughts black, hands apt, drugs fit, and time agreeing,
272 Confederate season, else no creature seeing,
Thou mixture rank, of midnight weeds collected,
274 With Hecate's ban thrice blasted, thrice infected,
Thy natural magic and dire property
On wholesome life usurps immediately.

[*Pours the poison in his ears.*]

HAMLET. 'A poisons him i' th' garden for his estate. His name 's Gonzago. The story is extant, and written in very choice Italian. You shall see anon how the murderer gets the love of Gonzago's wife.

OPHELIA. The king rises.
284 HAMLET. What, frighted with false fire?

QUEEN. How fares my lord?

POLONIUS. Give o'er the play.

KING. Give me some light. Away!

POLONIUS. Lights, lights, lights!
Exeunt all but Hamlet and Horatio.

HAMLET. Why, let the strucken deer go weep,
The hart ungallèd play.

For some must watch, while some must sleep;
Thus runs the world away.
Would not this, sir, and a forest of feathers 293
—if the rest of my fortunes turn Turk with 294
me—with two Provincial roses on my 295
razed shoes, get me a fellowship in a cry of 296
players, sir?

HORATIO. Half a share.

HAMLET. A whole one, I.
For thou dost know, O Damon dear,
This realm dismantled was
Of Jove himself; and now reigns here
A very, very—peacock.

HORATIO. You might have rhymed.

HAMLET. O good Horatio, I'll take the ghost's word for a thousand pound. Didst perceive?

HORATIO. Very well, my lord.

HAMLET. Upon the talk of the poisoning?

HORATIO. I did very well note him.

HAMLET. Aha! Come, some music! Come, the recorders! 312
For if the king like not the comedy,
Why then, belike he likes it not, perdy. 314
Come, some music!

Enter Rosencrantz and Guildenstern.

GUILDENSTERN. Good my lord, vouchsafe me a word with you.

HAMLET. Sir, a whole history.

GUILDENSTERN. The king, sir—

HAMLET. Ay, sir, what of him?

GUILDENSTERN. Is in his retirement marvellous distempered. 321

HAMLET. With drink, sir?

GUILDENSTERN. No, my lord, with choler. 323

---

256 *chorus* one in a play who explains the action   259
puppets i.e. you and your lover as in a puppet show
272 *Confederate season* the occasion being my ally   274
Hecate goddess of witchcraft and black magic; *ban* curse
284 *false fire* a firing of a gun charged with powder but
no shot, a blank-discharge

293 *feathers* plumes for actors' costumes   294 *turn
Turk* turn renegade, like a Christian turning Moham-
medan   295 *Provincial roses* ribbon rosettes   296
razed decorated with cut patterns; *cry* pack   312
recorders musical instruments of the flute class   314
perdy by God ('*par dieu*')   321 *distempered* out of temper,
vexed (twisted by Hamlet into 'deranged')   323 *choler*
anger (twisted by Hamlet into 'biliousness')

HAMLET. Your wisdom should show itself more richer to signify this to the doctor, for for me to put him to his purgation would perhaps plunge him into more choler.

GUILDENSTERN. Good my lord, put your dis- 329 course into some frame, and start not so wildly from my affair.

HAMLET. I am tame, sir; pronounce.

GUILDENSTERN. The queen, your mother, in most great affliction of spirit hath sent me to you.

HAMLET. You are welcome.

GUILDENSTERN. Nay, good my lord, this courtesy is not of the right breed. If it shall please you to make me a wholesome answer, I will do your mother's command- ment. If not, your pardon and my return shall be the end of my business.

HAMLET. Sir, I cannot.

ROSENCRANTZ. What, my lord?

HAMLET. Make you a wholesome answer; my wit's diseased. But, sir, such answer as I can make, you shall command, or rather, as you say, my mother. Therefore no more, but to the matter. My mother, you say—

ROSENCRANTZ. Then thus she says: your behavior hath struck her into amazement 351 and admiration.

HAMLET. O wonderful son, that can so stonish a mother! But is there no sequel at the heels .of this mother's admiration? Impart.

ROSENCRANTZ. She desires to speak with you 357 in her closet ere you go to bed.

HAMLET. We shall obey, were she ten times our mother. Have you any further trade with us?

ROSENCRANTZ. My lord, you once did love me.

363 HAMLET. And do still, by these pickers and stealers.

ROSENCRANTZ. Good my lord, what is your cause of distemper? You do surely bar the door upon your own liberty, if you deny your griefs to your friend.

HAMLET. Sir, I lack advancement.

ROSENCRANTZ. How can that be, when you have the voice of the king himself for your succession in Denmark?

HAMLET. Ay, sir, but 'while the grass grows' 373 —the proverb is something musty.

Enter the Player with recorders.

O, the recorders. Let me see one. To with- 375 draw with you—why do you go about to recover the wind of me, as if you would 377 drive me into a toil? 378

GUILDENSTERN. O my lord, if my duty be too bold, my love is too unmannerly. 380

HAMLET. I do not well understand that. Will you play upon this pipe?

GUILDENSTERN. My lord, I cannot.

HAMLET. I pray you.

GUILDENSTERN. Believe me, I cannot.

HAMLET. I do beseech you.

GUILDENSTERN. I know no touch of it, my lord.

HAMLET. It is as easy as lying. Govern these ventages with your fingers and thumb, give 390 it breath with your mouth, and it will dis- course most eloquent music. Look you, these are the stops.

GUILDENSTERN. But these cannot I command to any utt'rance of harmony. I have not the skill.

HAMLET. Why, look you now, how unworthy a thing you make of me! You would play upon me, you would seem to know my stops, you would pluck out the heart of my mystery, you would sound me from my lowest note to the top of my compass; and there is much music, excellent voice, in this little organ, yet cannot you make it speak. 'Sblood, do you think I am easier to be

373 *while the grass grows* (a proverb, ending: 'the horse starves') 375 *recorders* (see III, ii, 312n.); *withdraw* step aside 377 *recover the wind* come up to windward like a hunter 378 *toil* snare 380 *is too unmannerly* leads me beyond the restraint of good manners 390 *ventages* holes, vents

329 *frame* logical order 351 *admiration* wonder 357 *closet* private room 363 *pickers and stealers* i.e., hands

played on than a pipe? Call me what in-
407 strument you will, though you can fret me,
you cannot play upon me.

Enter Polonius.

God bless you, sir!
POLONIUS. My lord, the queen would speak
411 with you, and presently.
HAMLET. Do you see yonder cloud that's
almost in shape of a camel?
POLONIUS. By th' mass and 'tis, like a camel
indeed.
HAMLET. Methinks it is like a weasel.
POLONIUS. It is backed like a weasel.
HAMLET. Or like a whale.
POLONIUS. Very like a whale.
420 HAMLET. Then I will come to my mother by
and by. [*aside*] They fool me to the top of
422 my bent.—I will come by and by.
POLONIUS. I will say so.   [*Exit.*]
HAMLET. 'By and by' is easily said. Leave
me, friends.   [*Exeunt all but Hamlet.*]
'Tis now the very witching time of night,
When churchyards yawn, and hell itself
breathes out
Contagion to this world. Now could I drink
hot blood
And do such bitter business as the day
Would quake to look on. Soft, now to my
mother.
O heart, lose not thy nature; let not ever
432 The soul of Nero enter this firm bosom.
Let me be cruel, not unnatural;
I will speak daggers to her, but use none.
My tongue and soul in this be hypocrites:
436 How in my words somever she be shent,
437 To give them seals never, my soul,
consent!   *Exit.*

ACT III

Scene iii

Enter King, Rosencrantz, and Guildenstern.
KING.
I like him not, nor stands it safe with us
To let his madness range. Therefore
prepare you.
I your commission will forthwith dispatch,
And he to England shall along with you.
The terms of our estate may not endure   5
Hazard so near's as doth hourly grow
Out of his brows.   7
GUILDENSTERN. We will ourselves provide.
Most holy and religious fear it is
To keep those many many bodies safe
That live and feed upon your majesty.
ROSENCRANTZ.
The single and peculiar life is bound   11
With all the strength and armor of the
mind
To keep itself from noyance, but much   13
more
That spirit upon whose weal depends and
rests
The lives of many. The cess of majesty   15
Dies not alone, but like a gulf doth draw   16
What's near it with it; or 'tis a massy wheel
Fixed on the summit of the highest mount,
To whose huge spokes ten thousand lesser
things
Are mortised and adjoined, which when it
falls,
Each small annexment, petty consequence,
Attends the boist'rous ruin. Never alone   22
Did the king sigh, but with a general groan.
KING.
Arm you, I pray you, to this speedy voyage,   24

---

407 *fret* irritate (with a play on the fret-fingering of
certain stringed musical instruments)   411 *presently* at
once   420 *by and by* immediately   422 *bent* (see II, ii,
30n.)   432 *Nero* murderer of his mother   436 *shent*
reproved   437 *seals* authentications in actions

III, iii A chamber in the Castle   5 *terms* circumstances; *estate* royal position   7 *brows* effronteries (apparently with an implication of knitted brows)   11
peculiar individual   13 *noyance* harm   15 *cess* cessa-
tion, decease   16 *gulf* whirlpool   22 *Attends* joins in
(like a royal attendant)   24 *Arm* prepare

For we will fetters put upon this fear,
Which now goes too free-footed.
ROSENCRANTZ.   We will haste us.
                            Exeunt Gentlemen.

Enter Polonius.

POLONIUS.
  My lord, he's going to his mother's closet.
  Behind the arras I'll convey myself
29 To hear the process. I'll warrant she'll tax
     him home,
  And, as you said, and wisely was it said,
  'Tis meet that some more audience than a
     mother,
  Since nature makes them partial, should
     o'erhear
33 The speech, of vantage. Fare you well, my
     liege.
  I'll call upon you ere you go to bed
  And tell you what I know.
KING. Thanks, dear my lord. *Exit [Polonius].*
  O, my offense is rank, it smells to heaven;
37 It hath the primal eldest curse upon't,
  A brother's murder. Pray can I not,
  Though inclination be as sharp as will.
  My stronger guilt defeats my strong intent,
  And like a man to double business bound
  I stand in pause where I shall first begin,
  And both neglect. What if this cursèd hand
  Were thicker than itself with brother's
     blood,
  Is there not rain enough in the sweet
     heavens
  To wash it white as snow? Whereto serves
     mercy
47 But to confront the visage of offense?
  And what's in prayer but this twofold force,
  To be forestallèd ere we come to fall,
  Or pardoned being down? Then I'll look
     up.
  My fault is past. But, O, what form of
     prayer

Can serve my turn? 'Forgive me my foul
     murder'?
That cannot be, since I am still possessed
Of those effects for which I did the murder, 54
My crown, mine own ambition, and my
     queen.
May one be pardoned and retain th'
     offense?
In the corrupted currents of this world
Offense's gilded hand may shove by justice, 58
And oft 'tis seen the wicked prize itself
Buys out the law. But 'tis not so above.
There is no shuffling; there the action lies 61
In his true nature, and we ourselves
     compelled,
Even to the teeth and forehead of our faults, 63
To give in evidence. What then? What
     rests?
Try what repentance can. What can it not?
Yet what can it when one cannot repent?
O wretched state! O bosom black as death!
O limèd soul, that struggling to be free   68
Art more engaged! Help, angels! Make   69
     assay.
Bow, stubborn knees, and, heart with
     strings of steel,
Be soft as sinews of the new-born babe.
All may be well.

  [He kneels.]

  Enter Hamlet.

HAMLET.
  Now might I do it pat, now 'a is a-praying, 73
  And now I'll do't. And so 'a goes to heaven,
  And so am I revenged. That would be
     scanned.
  A villain kills my father, and for that
  I, his sole son, do this same villain send
  To heaven.
  Why, this is hire and salary, not revenge.

---

29 process proceedings; *tax him home* thrust home in
reprimanding him   *33 of vantage* from an advantageous position   *37 primal eldest curse* that of Cain, who
also murdered a brother   *47 offense* sin

54 effects things acquired   *58 gilded* gold-laden   *61
shuffling* sharp practice, double-dealing; *action* legal
proceeding (in heaven's court)   *63 teeth and forehead*
face-to-face recognition   *68 limèd* caught in birdlime,
a gluey material spread as a birdsnare   *69 engaged*
embedded; *assay* an attempt   *73 pat* opportunely

80 'A took my father grossly, full of bread,
81 With all his crimes broad blown, as flush as
    May;
82 And how his audit stands, who knows save
    heaven?
But in our circumstance and course of
    thought,
'Tis heavy with him; and am I then
    revenged,
To take him in the purging of his soul,
When he is fit and seasoned for his passage?
No.
88 Up, sword, and know thou a more horrid
    hent.
When he is drunk asleep, or in his rage,
Or in th' incestuous pleasure of his bed,
At game a-swearing, or about some act
92 That has no relish of salvation in't—
Then trip him, that his heels may kick at
    heaven,
And that his soul may be as damned and
    black
As hell, whereto it goes. My mother stays.
This physic but prolongs thy sickly days.
                                    Exit.

KING. [*rises*]
My words fly up, my thoughts remain
    below.
Words without thoughts never to heaven
    go.   *Exit.*

                    *

ACT III

Scene iv

Enter [Queen] Gertrude and Polonius.

POLONIUS.
1 'A will come straight. Look you lay home
    to him.

Tell him his pranks have been too broad to   2
    bear with,
And that your grace hath screened and
    stood between
Much heat and him. I'll silence me even
    here.
Pray you be round with him.   5
[HAMLET. (*within*) Mother, mother, mother!]
QUEEN. I'll warrant you; fear me not. With-
    draw; I hear him coming.
            [*Polonius hides behind the arras.*]

Enter Hamlet.

HAMLET.
    Now, mother, what's the matter?
QUEEN.
    Hamlet, thou hast thy father much
        offended.
HAMLET.
    Mother, you have my father much
        offended.
QUEEN.
    Come, come, you answer with an idle   12
        tongue.
HAMLET.
    Go, go, you question with a wicked tongue.
QUEEN.
    Why, how now, Hamlet?
HAMLET.   What's the matter now?
QUEEN.
    Have you forgot me?
HAMLET.   No, by the rood, not so! 15
    You are the queen, your husband's
        brother's wife,
    And (would it were not so) you are my
        mother.
QUEEN.
    Nay, then I'll set those to you that can
        speak.
HAMLET.
    Come, come, and sit you down. You shall
        not budge.
    You go not till I set you up a glass
    Where you may see the inmost part of you.

---

80 *grossly* in a state of gross unpreparedness; *bread* i.e.,
worldly sense gratification   81 *broad blown* fully blossomed; *flush* vigorous   82 *audit* account   88 *more horrid
hent* grasping by me on a more horrid occasion   92
relish flavor
III, iv The private chamber of the Queen   *1 lay* thrust

2 *broad* unrestrained   5 *round*   plain-spoken   12 *idle*
foolish   15 *rood* cross

QUEEN.
What wilt thou do? Thou wilt not murder
  me?
Help, ho!
POLONIUS. [*behind*] What, ho! help!
HAMLET. [*draws*]
How now? a rat? Dead for a ducat, dead!

[*Makes a pass through the arras and kills
Polonius.*]

POLONIUS. [*behind*]
O, I am slain!
QUEEN.   O me, what hast thou done?
HAMLET.
Nay, I know not. Is it the king?
QUEEN.
O, what a rash and bloody deed is this!
HAMLET.
A bloody deed—almost as bad, good
  mother,
As kill a king, and marry with his brother.
QUEEN.
As kill a king?
HAMLET.   Ay, lady, it was my word.

[*Lifts up the arras and sees Polonius.*]

Thou wretched, rash, intruding fool,
  farewell!
I took thee for thy better. Take thy fortune.
Thou find'st to be too busy is some
  danger.—
Leave wringing of your hands. Peace, sit
  you down
And let me wring your heart, for so I shall
If it be made of penetrable stuff,
38 If damnèd custom have not brazed it so
39 That it is proof and bulwark against sense.
QUEEN.
What have I done that thou dar'st wag thy
  tongue
In noise so rude against me?
HAMLET.   Such an act
That blurs the grace and blush of modesty,

38 *custom* habit; *brazed* hardened like brass   39 *proof*
armor; *sense* feeling

Calls virtue hypocrite, takes off the rose
From the fair forehead of an innocent love,
And sets a blister there, makes marriage   45
  vows
As false as dicers' oaths. O, such a deed
As from the body of contraction plucks   47
The very soul, and sweet religion makes   48
A rhapsody of words! Heaven's face does
  glow,
And this solidity and compound mass,   50
With heated visage, as against the doom,   51
Is thought-sick at the act.
QUEEN.   Ay me, what act,
That roars so loud and thunders in the
  index?   53
HAMLET.
Look here upon this picture, and on this,
The counterfeit presentment of two   55
  brothers.
See what a grace was seated on this brow:
Hyperion's curls, the front of Jove himself,   57
An eye like Mars, to threaten and
  command,
A station like the herald Mercury   59
New lighted on a heaven-kissing hill—
A combination and a form indeed
Where every god did seem to set his seal
To give the world assurance of man.
This was your husband. Look you now
  what follows.
Here is your husband, like a mildewed ear
Blasting his wholesome brother. Have you
  eyes?
Could you on this fair mountain leave to
  feed,
And batten on this moor? Ha! have you   68
  eyes?
You cannot call it love, for at your age
The heyday in the blood is tame, it's   70
  humble,

45 *blister* brand (of degradation)   47 *contraction* the
marriage contract   48 *religion* i.e. sacred marriage
vows   50 *compound mass* the earth as compounded of
the four elements   51 *against* in expectation of; *doom*
Day of Judgment   53 *index* table of contents preceding the body of a book   55 *counterfeit presentment* por-
trayed representation   57 *Hyperion* the sun god; *front*
forehead   59 *station* attitude in standing   68 *batten*
feed greedily   70 *heyday* excitement of passion

71 And waits upon the judgment, and what judgment

72 Would step from this to this? Sense sure you have,

73 Else could you not have motion, but sure that sense

74 Is apoplexed, for madness would not err,

75 Nor sense to ecstasy was ne'er so thralled

But it reserved some quantity of choice

To serve in such a difference. What devil was't

78 That thus hath cozened you at hoodman-blind?

Eyes without feeling, feeling without sight,

80 Ears without hands or eyes, smelling sans all,

Or but a sickly part of one true sense

82 Could not so mope. O shame, where is thy blush? Rebellious hell,

84 If thou canst mutine in a matron's bones, To flaming youth let virtue be as wax And melt in her own fire. Proclaim no shame

87 When the compulsive ardor gives the charge,

Since frost itself as actively doth burn,

89 And reason panders will.

QUEEN.   O Hamlet, speak no more.
Thou turn'st mine eyes into my very soul,

91 And there I see such black and grainèd spots

92 As will not leave their tinct.

HAMLET.   Nay, but to live

93 In the rank sweat of an enseamèd bed, Stewed in corruption, honeying and making love Over the nasty sty—

QUEEN.   O, speak to me no more.
These words like daggers enter in mine ears.

No more, sweet Hamlet.

HAMLET.   A murderer and a villain,
A slave that is not twentieth part the tithe 98
Of your precedent lord, a vice of kings,   99
A cutpurse of the empire and the rule,   100
That from a shelf the precious diadem stole
And put it in his pocket—

QUEEN.   No more.

Enter [the] Ghost [in his nightgown].   102

HAMLET.
A king of shreds and patches—
Save me and hover o'er me with your wings,
You heavenly guards? What would your gracious figure?

QUEEN.
Alas, he's mad.

HAMLET.
Do you not come your tardy son to chide,
That, lapsed in time and passion, lets go by   108
Th' important acting of your dread command?
O, say!

GHOST.
Do not forget. This visitation
Is but to whet thy almost blunted purpose.
But look, amazement on thy mother sits.
O, step between her and her fighting soul!
Conceit in weakest bodies strongest works.   115
Speak to her, Hamlet.

HAMLET.   How is it with you, lady?

QUEEN.
Alas, how is't with you,
That you do bend your eye on vacancy,
And with th' incorporal air do hold   119
discourse?
Forth at your eyes your spirits wildly peep,
And as the sleeping soldiers in th' alarm
Your bedded hairs like life in excrements   122
Start up and stand an end. O gentle son,   123

71 waits upon yields to *72 Sense* feeling *73 motion* desire, impulse *74 apoplexed* paralyzed *75 ecstasy* madness *78 cozened* cheated; *hoodman-blind* blindman's buff *80 sans* without *82 mope* be stupid *84 mutine* mutiny *87 compulsive* compelling; *gives the charge* delivers the attack *89 panders will* acts as procurer for desire *91 grainèd* dyed in grain *92 tinct* color *93 enseamèd* grease-laden

98 tithe tenth part *99 vice* clownish rogue (like the Vice of the morality plays) *100 cutpurse* skulking thief *102 s.d. nightgown* dressing gown *108 lapsed . . . passion* having let the moment slip and passion cool *115 Conceit* imagination *119 incorporal* bodiless *122 excrements* outgrowths *123 an* on

124 Upon the heat and flame of thy distemper
Sprinkle cool patience. Whereon do you look?

HAMLET.
On him, on him! Look you, how pale he glares!
His form and cause conjoined, preaching to stones,
128 Would make them capable.—Do not look upon me,
Lest with this piteous action you convert
130 My stern effects. Then what I have to do
Will want true color—tears perchance for blood.

QUEEN.
To whom do you speak this?

HAMLET.   Do you see nothing there?

QUEEN.
Nothing at all; yet all that is I see.

HAMLET.
Nor did you nothing hear?

QUEEN.   No, nothing but ourselves.

HAMLET.
Why, look you there! Look how it steals away!
My father, in his habit as he lived!
Look where he goes even now out at the portal!   *Exit Ghost.*

QUEEN.
This is the very coinage of your brain.
139 This bodiless creation ecstasy
Is very cunning in.

HAMLET.   Ecstasy?
My pulse as yours doth temperately keep time
And makes as healthful music. It is not madness
That I have uttered. Bring me to the test,
And I the matter will reword, which madness
145 Would gambol from. Mother, for love of grace,
146 Lay not that flattering unction to your soul,
That not your trespass but my madness speaks.

It will but skin and film the ulcerous place
Whiles rank corruption, mining all within, 149
Infects unseen. Confess yourself to heaven,
Repent what's past, avoid what is to come,
And do not spread the compost on the 152
weeds
To make them ranker. Forgive me this my virtue.
For in the fatness of these pursy times 154
Virtue itself of vice must pardon beg,
Yea, curb and woo for leave to do him 156
good.

QUEEN.
O Hamlet, thou hast cleft my heart in twain.

HAMLET.
O, throw away the worser part of it,
And live the purer with the other half.
Good night—but go not to my uncle's bed.
Assume a virtue, if you have it not.
That monster custom, who all sense doth 162
eat,
Of habits devil, is angel yet in this,
That to use of actions fair and good
He likewise gives a frock or livery 165
That aptly is put on. Refrain to-night,
And that shall lend a kind of easiness
To the next abstinence; the next more easy;
For use almost can change the stamp of 169
nature,
And either . . . the devil, or throw him out
With wondrous potency. Once more, good night,
And when you are desirous to be blest,
I'll blessing beg of you.—For this same lord,
I do repent; but heaven hath pleased it so,
To punish me with this, and this with me,
That I must be their scourge and minister.
I will bestow him and will answer well 177
The death I gave him. So again, good night.
I must be cruel only to be kind.

---

124 distemper mental disorder   *128 capable* susceptible
130 effects manifestations of emotion and purpose   *139 ecstasy* madness   *145 gambol* shy (like a startled horse)
146 unction ointment

149 mining undermining   *152 compost* fertilizing mixture   *154 fatness* gross slackness; *pursy* corpulent
156 curb bow to   *165 livery* characteristic dress (accompanying the suggestion of 'grab' in *habits*)   *169 use* habit; *stamp* impression, form   *177 bestow* stow, hide

Thus bad begins, and worse remains
180   behind.
One word more, good lady.

QUEEN.   What shall I do?

HAMLET.
Not this, by no means, that I bid you do:
183 Let the bloat king tempt you again to bed,
Pinch wanton on your cheek, call you his
    mouse,
185 And let him, for a pair of reechy kisses,
Or paddling in your neck with his damned
    fingers,
187 Make you to ravel all this matter out,
That I essentially am not in madness,
But mad in craft. 'Twere good you let him
    know,
For who that's but a queen, fair, sober,
    wise,
191 Would from a paddock, from a bat, a gib,
192 Such dear concernings hide? Who would
    do so?
No, in despite of sense and secrecy,
Unpeg the basket on the house's top,
195 Let the birds fly, and like the famous ape,
196 To try conclusions, in the basket creep
And break your own neck down.

QUEEN.
Be thou assured, if words be made of
    breath,
And breath of life, I have no life to breathe
What thou hast said to me.

HAMLET.
I must to England; you know that?

QUEEN.   Alack,
I had forgot. 'Tis so concluded on.

HAMLET.
There's letters sealed, and my two
    schoolfellows,
Whom I will trust as I will adders fanged,
205 They bear the mandate; they must sweep
    my way
And marshal me to knavery. Let it work.

For 'tis the sport to have the enginer   207
Hoist with his own petar, and 't shall go 208
    hard
But I will delve one yard below their
    mines
And blow them at the moon. O, 'tis most
    sweet
When in one line two crafts directly meet.
This man shall set me packing.   212
I'll lug the guts into the neighbor room.
Mother, good night. Indeed, this counsellor
Is now most still, most secret, and most
    grave,
Who was in life a foolish prating knave.
Come, sir, to draw toward an end with you.
Good night, mother.
            [*Exit the Queen. Then*] *exit* [*Hamlet,*
                        tugging in Polonius.]

ACT IV

Scene i

*Enter King and Queen, with Rosencrantz and
Guildenstern.*

KING.
There's matter in these sighs. These
    profound heaves
You must translate; 'tis fit we understand
    them.
Where is your son?

QUEEN.
Bestow this place on us a little while.
        [*Exeunt Rosencrantz and Guildenstern.*]
Ah, mine own lord, what have I seen
    to-night!

KING.
What, Gertrude? How does Hamlet?

---

180 *behind* to come   *183 bloat* bloated with sense
gratification   *185 reechy* filthy   *187 ravel . . . out* disent-
angle   *191 paddock* toad; *gib* tomcat   *192 dear concernings* matters of great personal significance   *195 famous
ape* (one in a story now unknown)   *196 conclusions*
experiments   *205 mandate* order

207 enginer engineer, constructor of military engines or
works   *208 Hoist* blown up; *petar* petard, bomb or mine
212 packing travelling in a hurry (with a play upon his
'packing' or shouldering of Polonius' body and also
upon his 'packing' in the sense of 'plotting' or 'contriving')
IV, i A chamber in the Castle

QUEEN.
Mad as the sea and wind when both
      contend
Which is the mightier. In his lawless fit,
Behind the arras hearing something stir,
Whips out his rapier, cries, 'A rat, a rat!'
11 And in this brainish apprehension kills
The unseen good old man.
      KING.   O heavy deed!
It had been so with us, had we been there.
His liberty is full of threats to all,
To you yourself, to us, to every one.
Alas, how shall this bloody deed be
      answered?
17 It will be laid to us, whose providence
Should have kept short, restrained, and
18   out of haunt
This mad young man. But so much was
      our love
We would not understand what was most
      fit,
But, like the owner of a foul disease,
22 To keep it from divulging, let it feed
Even on the pith of life. Where is he gone?
QUEEN.
To draw apart the body he hath killed;
25 O'er whom his very madness, like some ore
26 Among a mineral of metals base,
Shows itself pure. 'A weeps for what is done.
KING.
O Gertrude, come away!
The sun no sooner shall the mountains
      touch
But we will ship him hence, and this vile
      deed
We must with all our majesty and skill
Both countenance and excuse. Ho,
      Guildenstern!

Enter Rosencrantz and Guildenstern.

Friends both, go join you with some further
      aid.
Hamlet in madness hath Polonius slain,

And from his mother's closet hath he
      dragged him.
Go seek him out; speak fair, and bring the
      body
Into the chapel. I pray you haste in this.
            [*Exeunt Rosencrantz and Guildenstern.*]
Come, Gertrude, we'll call up our wisest
      friends
And let them know both what we mean to
      do
And what's untimely done . . .
Whose whisper o'er the world's diameter,
As level as the cannon to his blank   42
Transports his poisoned shot, may miss our
      name
And hit the woundless air. O, come away!
My soul is full of discord and dismay.
                              Exeunt.

ACT IV

Scene ii

Enter Hamlet.

HAMLET. Safely stowed.
GENTLEMEN. (*within*) Hamlet! Lord Hamlet!
HAMLET. But soft, what noise? Who calls on
      Hamlet? O, here they come.

      [*Enter*] *Rosencrantz,* [*Guildenstern,*] *and
      others.*

ROSENCRANTZ.
What have you done, my lord, with the
      dead body?
HAMLET.
Compounded it with dust, whereto 'tis kin.
ROSENCRANTZ.
Tell us where 'tis, that we may take it
      thence
And bear it to the chapel.

---

11 brainish apprehension headstrong conception   *17 pro-*
vidence foresight   *18 haunt* association with others   *22*
divulging becoming known   *25 ore* vein of gold   *26*
mineral mine

42 As level with as direct aim; *blank* mark, central white
spot on a target
IV, ii A passage in the Castle

HAMLET. Do not believe it.

ROSENCRANTZ. Believe what?

HAMLET. That I can keep your counsel and not mine own. Besides, to be demanded of
13 a sponge, what replication should be made by the son of a king?

ROSENCRANTZ. Take you me for a sponge, my lord?

HAMLET. Ay, sir, that soaks up the king's
18 countenance, his rewards, his authorities. But such officers do the king best service in the end. He keeps them, like an ape, in the corner of his jaw, first mouthed, to be last swallowed. When he needs what you have gleaned, it is but squeezing you and, sponge, you shall be dry again.

ROSENCRANTZ. I understand you not, my lord.

HAMLET. I am glad of it. A knavish speech
27 sleeps in a foolish ear.

ROSENCRANTZ. My lord, you must tell us where the body is and go with us to the king.

HAMLET. The body is with the king, but the king is not with the body. The king is a thing—

GUILDENSTERN. A thing, my lord?

35 HAMLET. Of nothing. Bring me to him. Hide fox, and all after.   *Exeunt.*

ACT IV

Scene iii

Enter King, and two or three.

KING.
I have sent to seek him and to find the body.
How dangerous is it that this man goes loose!

---

13 replication reply   *18 countenance* favor   *27 sleeps in* means nothing to   *35 Of nothing* (cf. Prayer Book, Psalm cxliv, 4, 'Man is like a thing of naught: his time passeth away like a shadow')   *35–36 Hide . . . after* (apparently well-known words from some game of hide-and-seek)
IV, iii A chamber in the Castle

Yet must not we put the strong law on him;
He's loved of the distracted multitude,   4
Who like not in their judgment, but their eyes,
And where 'tis so, th' offender's scourge is   6
weighed,
But never the offense. To bear all smooth and even,
This sudden sending him away must seem
Deliberate pause. Diseases desperate   9
grown
By desperate appliance are relieved,
Or not at all.

Enter Rosencrantz, [Guildenstern,] and all the rest.

                    How now? What hath befallen?

ROSENCRANTZ.
Where the dead body is bestowed, my lord,
We cannot get from him.

KING.   But where is he?

ROSENCRANTZ.
Without, my lord; guarded, to know your pleasure.

KING.
Bring him before us.

ROSENCRANTZ.   Ho! Bring in the lord.

They enter [with Hamlet].

KING. Now, Hamlet, where's Polonius?

HAMLET. At supper.

KING. At supper? Where?

HAMLET. Not where he eats, but where 'a is eaten. A certain convocation of politic   20
worms are e'en at him. Your worm is your only emperor for diet. We fat all creatures   22
else to fat us, and we fat ourselves for maggots. Your fat king and your lean beggar is but variable service—two dishes, but to one   25
table. That's the end.

---

4 distracted confused   *6 scourge* punishment   *9 Deliberate pause* something done with much deliberation   *20 politic worms* political and craftily scheming worms (such as Polonius might well attract)   *22 diet* food and drink (perhaps with a play upon a famous 'convocation,' the Diet of Worms opened by the Emperor Charles V on January 28, 1521, before which Luther appeared)   *25 variable service* different servings of one food

KING. Alas, alas!

HAMLET. A man may fish with the worm that hath eat of a king, and eat of the fish that hath fed of that worm.

KING. What dost thou mean by this?

HAMLET. Nothing but to show you how a
33 king may go a progress through the guts of a beggar.

KING. Where is Polonius?

HAMLET. In heaven. Send thither to see. If your messenger find him not there, seek him i' th' other place yourself. But if indeed you find him not within this month, you shall nose him as you go up the stairs into the lobby.

KING. [*to Attendants*] Go seek him there.

HAMLET. 'A will stay till you come.

[*Exeunt Attendants.*]

KING.
Hamlet, this deed, for thine especial safety,
45 Which we do tender as we dearly grieve
For that which thou hast done, must send thee hence
With fiery quickness. Therefore prepare thyself.
The bark is ready and the wind at help,
49 Th' associates tend, and everything is bent
For England.

HAMLET.   For England?

KING.   Ay, Hamlet.

HAMLET.   Good.

KING.
So is it, if thou knew'st our purposes.
52 HAMLET. I see a cherub that sees them. But come, for England! Farewell, dear mother.

KING. Thy loving father, Hamlet.

HAMLET. My mother—father and mother is man and wife, man and wife is one flesh, and so, my mother. Come, for England!

Exit.

KING.
58 Follow him at foot; tempt him with speed aboard.
Delay it not; I'll have him hence to-night.

Away! for everything is sealed and done
That else leans on th' affair. Pray you make 61
haste.   [*Exeunt all but the King.*]
And, England, if my love thou hold'st at 62
aught—
As my great power thereof may give thee sense,
Since yet thy cicatrice looks raw and red
After the Danish sword, and thy free awe 65
Pays homage to us—thou mayst not coldly set 66
Our sovereign process, which imports at 67
full
By letters congruing to that effect 68
The present death of Hamlet. Do it, 69
England,
For like the hectic in my blood he rages, 70
And thou must cure me. Till I know 'tis done,
Howe'er my haps, my joys were n'er begun. 72
Exit.

ACT IV

Scene iv

Enter Fortinbras with his Army over the stage.

FORTINBRAS.
Go, captain, from me greet the Danish king.
Tell him that by his license Fortinbras
Craves the conveyance of a promised 3
march
Over his kingdom. You know the rendezvous.
If that his majesty would aught with us,
We shall express our duty in his eye; 6
And let him know so.

33 *progress* royal journey of state   45 *tender* hold dear; *dearly* intensely   49 *tend* wait; *bent* set in readiness (like a bent bow)   52 *cherub* one of the cherubim (angels with a distinctive quality of knowledge)   58 *at foot* at heel, close

61 *leans on* is connected with   62 *England* King of England   65 *free awe* voluntary show of respect   66 *set* esteem   67 *process* formal command   68 *congruing* agreeing   69 *present* instant   70 *hectic* a continuous fever   72 *haps* fortunes
IV, iv A coastal highway   3 *conveyance* escort   6 *eye* presence

CAPTAIN.   I will do't, my lord.

FORTINBRAS.

8   Go softly on.   [*Exeunt all but the Captain.*]

*Enter Hamlet, Rosencrantz, [Guildenstern,]
and others.*

HAMLET.

9   Good sir, whose powers are these?

CAPTAIN

They are of Norway, sir.

HAMLET.

How purposed, sir, I pray you?

CAPTAIN.

Against some part of Poland.

HAMLET.

Who commands them, sir?

CAPTAIN.

The nephew to old Norway, Fortinbras.

HAMLET.

15   Goes it against the main of Poland, sir,
Or for some frontier?

CAPTAIN.

17   Truly to speak, and with no addition,
We go to gain a little patch of ground
That hath in it no profit but the name.

20   To pay five ducats, five, I would not farm
it,
Nor will it yield to Norway or the Pole

22   A ranker rate, should it be sold in fee.

HAMLET.

Why, then the Polack never will defend it.

CAPTAIN.

Yes, it is already garrisoned.

HAMLET.

Two thousand souls and twenty thousand
ducats
Will not debate the question of this straw.

27   This is th' imposthume of much wealth and
peace,
That inward breaks, and shows no cause
without
Why the man dies. I humbly thank you,
sir.

CAPTAIN.

God bye you, sir.   [*Exit.*]

ROSENCRANTZ. Will't please you go, my lord?

HAMLET.

I'll be with you straight. Go a little before.
[*Exeunt all but Hamlet.*]

How all occasions do inform against me   32
And spur my dull revenge! What is a man,
If his chief good and market of his time   34
Be but to sleep and feed? A beast, no more.
Sure he that made us with such large
discourse,   36
Looking before and after, gave us not
That capability and godlike reason
To fust in us unused. Now, whether it be   39
Bestial oblivion, or some craven scruple   40
Of thinking too precisely on th' event—   41
A thought which, quartered, hath but one
part wisdom
And ever three parts coward—I do not
know
Why yet I live to say, 'This thing 's to do,'
Sith I have cause, and will, and strength,
and means
To do't. Examples gross as earth exhort me.   46
Witness this army of such mass and charge,   47
Led by a delicate and tender prince,
Whose spirit, with divine ambition puffed,
Makes mouths at the invisible event,   50
Exposing what is mortal and unsure
To all that fortune, death, and danger dare,
Even for an eggshell. Rightly to be great
Is not to stir without great argument,
But greatly to find quarrel in a straw   55
When honor 's at the stake. How stand I
then,
That have a father killed, a mother
stained,
Excitements of my reason and my blood,
And let all sleep, while to my shame I see
The imminent death of twenty thousand
men

32 inform take shape   *34 market of* compensation for
36 discourse power of thought   *39 fust* grow mouldy
40 oblivion forgetfulness   *41 event* outcome (as also in
l. 50)   *46 gross* large and evident   *47 charge* expense
50 Makes mouths makes faces scornfully   *55 greatly . . .
straw* to recognize the great argument even in some
small matter

8 softly slowly   *9 powers* forces   *15 main* main body
17 addition exaggeration   *20 To pay* i.e. for a yearly
rental of   *22 ranker* more abundant; *in fee* outright
27 imposthume abscess

61 That for a fantasy and trick of fame
   Go to their graves like beds, fight for a plot
63 Whereon the numbers cannot try the
      cause,
64 Which is not tomb enough and continent
   To hide the slain? O, from this time forth,
   My thoughts be bloody, or be nothing
      worth! *Exit.*

ACT IV

Scene v

*Enter Horatio, [Queen] Gertrude, and a
Gentleman.*

QUEEN.
   I will not speak with her.
GENTLEMAN.
2 She is importunate, indeed distract.
   Her mood will needs be pitied.
QUEEN. What would she have?
GENTLEMAN.
   She speaks much of her father, says she
      hears
5 There's tricks i' th' world, and hems, and
      beats her heart,
6 Spurns enviously at straws, speaks things in
      doubt
   That carry but half sense. Her speech is
      nothing,
8 Yet the unshapèd use of it doth move
9 The hearers to collection; they aim at it,
10 And botch the words up fit to their own
      thoughts,
   Which, as her winks and nods and gestures
      yield them,
   Indeed would make one think there might
      be thought,

61 *fantasy* fanciful image; *trick* toy   63 *try the cause* find
space in which to settle the issue by battle   64 *continent*
receptacle
IV, v A chamber in the Castle   2 *distract* insane   5
tricks deceits   6 *Spurns enviously* kicks spitefully, takes
offense; *straws* trifles   8 *unshapèd use* disordered manner   9 *collection* attempts at shaping meaning; *aim*
guess   10 *botch* patch

Though nothing sure, yet much unhappily.
HORATIO.
   'Twere good she were spoken with, for she
      may strew
   Dangerous conjectures in all-breeding
      minds.
QUEEN.
   Let her come in. *[Exit Gentleman.]*

   [Aside]

   To my sick soul (as sin's true nature is)
   Each toy seems prologue to some great   18
      amiss.
   So full of artless jealousy is guilt   19
   It spills itself in fearing to be spilt.   20

   Enter Ophelia [distracted.]

OPHELIA.
   Where is the beauteous majesty of
      Denmark?
QUEEN. How now, Ophelia?
OPHELIA.
   She sings. How should I your true-love
      know
         From another one?
   By his cockle hat and staff   25
         And his sandal shoon.   26
QUEEN.
   Alas, sweet lady, what imports this song?
OPHELIA. Say you? Nay, pray you mark.
         Song.
      He is dead and gone, lady,
         He is dead and gone;
      At his head a grass-green turf,
         At his heels a stone.
   O, ho!
QUEEN. Nay, but Ophelia—
OPHELIA. Pray you mark.
   [Sings] White his shroud as the mountain
      snow—

   Enter King.

18 *toy* trifle; *amiss* calamity   19 *artless* unskillfully
managed; *jealousy* suspicion   20 *spills* destroys   25
cockle hat hat bearing a cockle shell, worn by a pilgrim
who had been to the shrine of St James of Compostela
26 *shoon* shoes

QUEEN. Alas, look here, my lord.

OPHELIA.   *Song.*

38   Larded all with sweet flowers;
            Which bewept to the grave did
                not go
            With true-love showers.

KING. How do you, pretty lady?

42 OPHELIA. Well, God dild you! They say the
    owl was a baker's daughter. Lord, we
    know what we are, but know not what we
    may be. God be at your table!

46 KING. Conceit upon her father.

OPHELIA. Pray let's have no words of this, but
    when they ask you what it means, say you
    this:

                    Song.
            To-morrow is Saint Valentine's
                day.
51   All in the morning betime,
            And I a maid at your window,
                To be your Valentine.
            Then up he rose and donned his
                clo'es
55   And dupped the chamber
                door,
            Let in the maid, that out a maid
                Never departed more.

KING. Pretty Ophelia!

OPHELIA. Indeed, la, without an oath, I'll
    make an end on't:

61 [*Sings*] By Gis and by Saint Charity,
            Alack, and fie for shame!
            Young men will do't if they come
                to't.
64   By Cock, they are to blame.
            Quoth she, 'Before you tumbled
                me,
            You promised me to wed.'

He answers:

'So would I' a' done, by yonder
    sun,
    And thou hadst not come to my
        bed.'

KING. How long hath she been thus?

OPHELIA. I hope all will be well. We must be
    patient, but I cannot choose but weep to
    think they would lay him i' th' cold ground.
    My brother shall know of it; and so I thank
    you for your good counsel. Come, my
    coach! Good night, ladies, good night.
    Sweet ladies, good night, good night.

                                [*Exit.*]

KING.
    Follow her close; give her good watch, I
        pray you.   [*Exit Horatio.*]
    O, this is the poison of deep grief; it springs
    All from her father's death—and now
        behold!
    O Gertrude, Gertrude,
    When sorrows come, they come not single
        spies,
    But in battalions: first, her father slain;
    Next, your son gone, and he most violent
        author
    Of his own just remove; the people
        muddied,   85
    Thick and unwholesome in their thoughts
        and whispers
    For good Polonius' death, and we have
        done but greenly   87
    In hugger-mugger to inter him; poor   88
        Ophelia
    Divided from herself and her fair judgment,
    Without the which we are pictures or mere
        beasts;
    Last, and as much containing as all these,
    Her brother is in secret come from France,
    Feeds on his wonder, keeps himself in
        clouds,   93
    And wants not buzzers to infect his ear   94
    With pestilent speeches of his father's
        death,

---

38 *Larded* garnished   *42 dild* yield, repay; *the owl* an
owl into which, according to a folk-tale, a baker's
daughter was transformed because of her failure to
show whole-hearted generosity when Christ asked for
bread in the baker's shop   *46 Conceit* thought   *51
betime* early   *55 dupped* opened   *61 Gis* Jesus   *64 Cock*
God (with a perversion of the name not uncommon
in oaths)

85 *muddied* stirred up and confused   *87 greenly* foolishly
88 *hugger-mugger* secrecy and disorder   *93 clouds*
obscurity   *94 wants* lacks; *buzzers* whispering tale-
bearers

96 Wherein necessity, of matter beggared,
97 Will nothing stick our person to arraign
    In ear and ear. O my dear Gertrude, this,
99 Like to a murd'ring piece, in many places
    Gives me superfluous death.

A noise within.

Enter a Messenger.

QUEEN.   Alack, what noise is this?
KING.
102 Attend, where are my Switzers? Let them
      guard the door.
    What is the matter?
MESSENGER.   Save yourself, my lord.
104 The ocean, overpeering of his list,
105 Eats not the flats with more impiteous haste
106 Than young Laertes, in a riotous head,
    O'erbears your officers. The rabble call
      him lord,
    And, as the world were now but to begin,
    Antiquity forgot, custom not known,
110 The ratifiers and props of every word,
    They cry, 'Choose we! Laertes shall be
      king!'
    Caps, hands, and tongues applaud it to the
      clouds,
    'Laertes shall be king! Laertes king!'

A noise within.

QUEEN.
    How cheerfully on the false trail they cry!
115 O, this is counter, you false Danish dogs!
KING.
    The doors are broke.

Enter Laertes with others.

LAERTES.
    Where is this king?—Sirs, stand you all
      without.

ALL.
    No, let's come in.
LAERTES.   I pray you give me leave.
ALL. We will, we will.
LAERTES.
    I thank you. Keep the door.
                        [*Exeunt his Followers.*]
                        O thou vile king,
    Give me my father.
QUEEN.   Calmly, good Laertes.
LAERTES.
    That drop of blood that's calm proclaims
      me bastard,
    Cries cuckold to my father, brands the
      harlot
    Even here between the chaste unsmirchèd
      brows
    Of my true mother.
KING.   What is the cause, Laertes,
    That thy rebellion looks so giant-like?
    Let him go, Gertrude. Do not fear our   127
      person.
    There's such divinity doth hedge a king
    That treason can but peep to what it   129
      would,
    Acts little of his will. Tell me, Laertes,
    Why thou art thus incensed. Let him go,
      Gertrude.
    Speak, man.
LAERTES.
    Where is my father?
KING.   Dead.
QUEEN.   But not by him.
KING.
    Let him demand his fill.
LAERTES.
    How came he dead? I'll not be juggled
      with.
    To hell allegiance, vows to the blackest
      devil,
    Conscience and grace to the profoundest
      pit!
    I dare damnation. To this point I stand,
    That both the worlds I give to negligence,   139

96 *of matter beggared* unprovided with facts 97 *nothing*
stick in no way hesitate; *arraign* accuse 99 *murd'ring*
piece cannon loaded with shot meant to scatter 102
Switzers hired Swiss guards 104 *overpeering of* rising
to look over and pass beyond; *list* boundary 105
impiteous pitiless 106 *head* armed force 110 *word*
promise 115 *counter* hunting backward on the trail

127 *fear* fear for 129 *peep to* i.e. through the barrier
139 *both the worlds* whatever may result in this world
or the next; *give to negligence* disregard

Let come what comes, only I'll be
   revenged
141 Most throughly for my father.
KING.   Who shall stay you?
LAERTES.
My will, not all the world's.
And for my means, I'll husband them so
   well
They shall go far with little.
KING.   Good Laertes,
If you desire to know the certainty
Of your dear father, is't writ in your
   revenge
147 That swoopstake you will draw both friend
   and foe,
Winner and loser?
LAERTES.
None but his enemies.
KING.   Will you know them then?
LAERTES.
To his good friends thus wide I'll ope my
   arms
151 And like the kind life-rend'ring pelican
Repast them with my blood.
KING.   Why, now you speak
Like a good child and a true gentleman.
That I am guiltless of your father's death,
155 And am most sensibly in grief for it,
156 It shall as level to your judgment 'pear
As day does to your eye.

A noise within: 'Let her come in.'

LAERTES.
How now? What noise is that?

Enter Ophelia.

O heat, dry up my brains; tears seven
   times salt
Burn out the sense and virtue of mine eye!
By heaven, thy madness shall be paid by
   weight

Till our scale turn the beam. O rose of   162
   May,
Dear maid, kind sister, sweet Ophelia!
O heavens, is't possible a young maid's wits
Should be as mortal as an old man's life?
[Nature is fine in love, and where 'tis fine, 166
It sends some precious instance of itself   167
After the thing it loves.]
OPHELIA.   *Song.*
They bore him barefaced on the bier
   [Hey non nony, nony, hey nony]
And in his grave rained many a tear—
Fare you well, my dove!
LAERTES.
Hadst thou thy wits, and didst persuade
   revenge,
It could not move thus.
OPHELIA. You must sing 'A-down a-down,
and you call him a-down-a.' O, how the
wheel becomes it! It is the false steward, 177
that stole his master's daughter.
LAERTES. This nothing 's more than matter. 179
OPHELIA. There's rosemary, that's for re-
membrance. Pray you, love, remember.
And there is pansies, that's for thoughts.
LAERTES. A document in madness, thoughts 183
and remembrance fitted.
OPHELIA. There's fennel for you, and colum- 185
bines. There's rue for you, and here's some 186
for me. We may call it herb of grace o'
Sundays. O, you must wear your rue with
a difference. There's a daisy. I would give 189
you some violets, but they withered all 190
when my father died. They say 'a made a
good end.
[*Sings*] For bonny sweet Robin is all my
       joy.
LAERTES.
Thought and affliction, passion, hell itself,
She turns to favor and to prettiness.   195
OPHELIA.   *Song.*

141 **throughly** thoroughly   147 *swoopstake* sweepstake, taking all stakes on the gambling table   *151 life-rend'ring* life-yielding (because the mother pelican supposedly took blood from her breast with her bill to feed her young)   *155 sensibly* feelingly   *156 level* plain

162 beam bar of a balance   *166 fine* refined to purity *167 instance* token   *177 wheel* burden, refrain   *179 more than matter* more meaningful than sane speech *183 document* lesson   *185 fennel* symbol of flattery; *columbines* symbol of thanklessness (?)   *186 rue* symbol of repentance   *189 daisy* symbol of dissembling *190 violets* symbol of faithfulness   *195 favor* charm

And will 'a not come again?
And will 'a not come again?
  No, no, he is dead;
  Go to thy deathbed;
He never will come again.
His beard was as white as snow,

202   All flaxen was his poll.
  He is gone, he is gone,
  And we cast away moan.
God 'a' mercy on his soul!

206 And of all Christian souls, I pray God. God
  bye you.   [*Exit.*]

LAERTES.
Do you see this, O God?

KING.
Laertes, I must commune with your grief,
Or you deny me right. Go but apart,
Make choice of whom your wisest friends
  you will,
And they shall hear and judge 'twixt you
  and me.

213 If by direct or by collateral hand
214 They find us touched, we will our kingdom
  give,
Our crown, our life, and all that we call
  ours,
To you in satisfaction; but if not,
Be you content to lend your patience to us,
And we shall jointly labor with your soul
To give it due content.

LAERTES.   Let this be so.
His means of death, his obscure funeral—

221 No trophy, sword, nor hatchment o'er his
  bones,
222 No noble rite nor formal ostentation—
Cry to be heard, as 'twere from heaven to
  earth,
224 That I must call't in question.

KING.   So you shall;
And where th' offense is, let the great axe
  fall.
I pray you go with me.   *Exeunt.*

ACT IV

Scene vi

Enter Horatio and others.

HORATIO. What are they that would speak
  with me?
GENTLEMAN. Seafaring men, sir. They say
  they have letters for you.
HORATIO. Let them come in. [*Exit Attendant.*]
  I do not know from what part of the world
  I should be greeted, if not from Lord
  Hamlet.

Enter Sailors.

SAILOR. God bless you, sir.
HORATIO. Let him bless thee too.
SAILOR. 'A shall, sir, an't please him. There's
  a letter for you, sir—it came from th'
  ambassador that was bound for England—
  if your name be Horatio, as I am let to
  know it is.
HORATIO. [*reads the letter*] 'Horatio, when
  thou shalt have overlooked this, give these 15
  fellows some means to the king. They have
  letters for him. Ere we were two days old
  at sea, a pirate of very warlike appointment 18
  gave us chase. Finding ourselves too slow
  of sail, we put on a compelled valor, and in
  the grapple I boarded them. On the instant they got clear of our ship; so I alone
  became their prisoner. They have dealt
  with me like thieves of mercy, but they 24
  knew what they did: I am to do a good
  turn for them. Let the king have the letters
  I have sent, and repair thou to me with as
  much speed as thou wouldest fly death. I
  have words to speak in thine ear will make
  thee dumb; yet are they much too light
  for the bore of the matter. These good fel- 31
  lows will bring thee where I am. Rosen-

---

202 poll head   *206 of* on   *213 collateral* indirect   *214 touched* i.e., with the crime   *221 trophy* memorial; *hatchment* coat of arms   *222 ostentation* ceremony   *224 That* so that

IV, vi A chamber in the Castle   *15 overlooked* surveyed, scanned; *means* i.e., of access   *18 appointment* equipment   *24 thieves of mercy* merciful thieves   *31 bore* caliber (as of a gun)

crantz and Guildenstern hold their course
for England. Of them I have much to tell
thee. Farewell.
        'He that thou knowest thine, Hamlet.'

Come, I will give you way for these your
    letters,
And do't the speedier that you may direct
    me
To him from whom you brought them.
                                            Exeunt.

ACT IV

Scene vii

Enter King and Laertes.

KING.
    Now must your conscience my
        acquittance seal,
    And you must put me in your heart for
        friend,
    Sith you have heard, and with a
        knowing ear,
    That he which hath your noble father
        slain
    Pursued my life.
LAERTES.   It well appears. But tell me
6   Why you proceeded not against these feats
7   So crimeful and so capital in nature,
    As by your safety, wisdom, all things else,
9   You mainly were stirred up.
KING.   O, for two special reasons,
    Which may to you perhaps seem much
        unsinewed,
    But yet to me they're strong. The queen his
        mother
    Lives almost by his looks, and for myself—
    My virtue or my plague, be it either
        which—
14 She is so conjunctive to my life and soul
    That, as the star moves not but in his
        sphere,

I could not but by her. The other motive
Why to a public count I might not go   17
Is the great love the general gender bear 18
    him,
Who, dipping all his faults in their
    affection,
Would, like the spring that turneth wood
    to stone,
Convert his gyves to graces; so that my   21
    arrows,
Too slightly timbered for so loud a wind,
Would have reverted to my bow again,
And not where I had aimed them.
LAERTES.
    And so have I a noble father lost,
    A sister driven into desp'rate terms,   26
    Whose worth, if praises may go back again, 27
    Stood challenger on mount of all the age   28
    For her perfections. But my revenge will
        come.
KING.
    Break not your sleeps for that. You must
        not think
    That we are made of stuff so flat and dull
    That we can let our beard be shook with
        danger,
    And think it pastime. You shortly shall hear
        more.
    I loved your father, and we love ourself,
    And that, I hope, will teach you to
        imagine—

Enter a Messenger with letters.

[How now? What news?]
MESSENGER.
            [Letters, my lord, from Hamlet:]
    These to your majesty, this to the queen.
KING.
    From Hamlet? Who brought them?
MESSENGER.
    Sailors, my lord, they say; I saw them not.
    They were given me by Claudio; he
        received them

IV, vii A chamber in the Castle   *6 feats* deeds   *7
capital* punishable by death   *9 mainly* powerfully   *14
conjunctive* closely united

17 count trial, accounting   *18 general gender* common
people   *21 gyves* fetters   *26 terms* circumstances   *27
back again* i.e., to her better circumstances   *28 on mount*
on a height

Of him that brought them.

KING.   Laertes, you shall hear them.—
Leave us.   [*Exit Messenger.*]
[*Reads*] 'High and mighty, you shall know
43   I am set naked on your kingdom. Tomorrow shall I beg leave to see your kingly
eyes; when I shall (first asking your pardon
thereunto) recount the occasion of my sudden and more strange return.   Hamlet.'
What should this mean? Are all the rest
come back?
49   Or is it some abuse, and no such thing?

LAERTES.
Know you the hand?
50   KING.   'Tis Hamlet's character. 'Naked'!
And in a postscript here, he says 'alone.'
52   Can you devise me?

LAERTES.
I am lost in it, my lord. But let him come.
It warms the very sickness in my heart
That I shall live and tell him to his teeth,
'Thus diddest thou.'

KING.   If it be so, Laertes,
(As how should it be so? how otherwise?)
Will you be ruled by me?

LAERTES.   Ay, my lord,
So you will not o'errule me to a peace.

KING.·
To thine own peace. If he be now
returned,
61   As checking at his voyage, and that he
means
No more to undertake it, I will work him
To an exploit now ripe in my device,
Under the which he shall not choose but
fall;
And for his death no wind of blame shall
breathe,
66   But even his mother shall uncharge the
practice
And call it accident.

LAERTES.   My lord, I will be ruled;
The rather if you could devise it so
69   That I might be the organ.

43 *naked* destitute   49 *abuse* imposture   50 *character*
handwriting   52 *devise* explain to   61 *checking at*
turning aside from (like a falcon turning from its quarry
for other prey)   66 *uncharge the practice* acquit the
stratagem of being a plot   69 *organ* instrument

KING.   It falls right.
You have been talked of since your travel
much,
And that in Hamlet's hearing, for a quality
Wherein they say you shine. Your sum of
parts
Did not together pluck such envy from him
As did that one, and that, in my regard,
Of the unworthiest siege.   75

LAERTES.   What part is that, my lord?
KING.
A very riband in the cap of youth,   76
Yet needful too, for youth no less becomes
The light and careless livery that it wears   78
Than settled age his sables and his weeds,   79
Importing health and graveness. Two   80
months since
Here was a gentleman of Normandy.
I have seen myself, and served against, the
French,
And they can well on horseback, but this   83
gallant
Had witchcraft in't. He grew unto his seat,
And to such wondrous doing brought his
horse
As had he been incorpsed and   86
demi-natured
With the brave beast. So far he topped my   87
thought
That I, in forgery of shapes and tricks,   88
Come short of what he did.

LAERTES.   A Norman was't?
KING. A Norman.
LAERTES.
Upon my life, Lamord.
KING.   The very same.
LAERTES.
I know him well. He is the brooch indeed   92
And gem of all the nation.

75 *siege* seat, rank   76 *riband* decoration   78 *livery*
distinctive attire   79 *sables* dignified robes richly
furred with sable; *weeds* distinctive garments   80 *health*
welfare, prosperity   83 *can well* can perform well   86
incorpsed made one body; *demi-natured* made sharer of
nature half and half (as man shares with horse in
the centaur)   87 *topped* excelled; *thought* imagination
of possibilities   88 *forgery* invention   92 *brooch* orna-
ment

KING.
94   He made confession of you,
      And gave you such a masterly report
      For art and exercise in your defense,
      And for your rapier most especial,
      That he cried out 'twould be a sight indeed
99   If one could match you. The scrimers of
          their nation
      He swore had neither motion, guard, nor
          eye,
      If you opposed them. Sir, this report of his
      Did Hamlet so envenom with his envy
      That he could nothing do but wish and beg
      Your sudden coming o'er to play with you.
      Now, out of this—
LAERTES.   What out of this, my lord?
KING.
      Laertes, was your father dear to you?
      Or are you like the painting of a sorrow,
      A face without a heart?
LAERTES.   Why ask you this?
KING.
      Not that I think you did not love your
          father,
      But that I know love is begun by time,
111   And that I see, in passages of proof,
112   Time qualifies the spark and fire of it.
      There lives within the very flame of love
114   A kind of wick or snuff that will abate it,
115   And nothing is at a like goodness still,
116   For goodness, growing to a plurisy,
      Dies in his own too-much. That we would
          do
      We should do when we would, for this
          'would' changes,
      And hath abatements and delays as many
      As there are tongues, are hands, are
          accidents,
      And then this 'should' is like a spendthrift
          sigh,
122   That hurts by easing. But to the quick o'
          th' ulcer—

Hamlet comes back; what would you
    undertake
To show yourself your father's son in deed
More than in words?
LAERTES.   To cut his throat i' th' church!
KING.
No place indeed should murder   126
    sanctuarize;
Revenge should have no bounds. But, good
    Laertes,
Will you do this? Keep close within your
    chamber.
Hamlet returned shall know you are come
    home.
We'll put on those shall praise your   130
    excellence
And set a double varnish on the fame
The Frenchman gave you, bring you in fine 132
    together
And wager on your heads. He, being
    remiss,   133
Most generous, and free from all
    contriving,
Will not peruse the foils, so that with ease, 135
Or with a little shuffling, you may choose
A sword unbated, and, in a pass of practice, 137
Requite him for your father.
LAERTES.   I will do't,
And for that purpose I'll anoint my sword.
I bought an unction of a mountebank,   140
So mortal that, but dip a knife in it,
Where it draws blood no cataplasm so rare,   142
Collected from all simples that have virtue 143
Under the moon, can save the thing from
    death
That is but scratched withal. I'll touch my 145
    point
With this contagion, that, if I gall him   146
    slightly,
It may be death.
KING.   Let's further think of this,
Weigh what convenience both of time and
    means

---

94 *made confession* admitted the rival accomplishments
99 *scrimers* fencers   *111 passages of proof* incidents of
experience   *112 qualifies* weakens   *114 snuff* uncon-
sumed portion of the burned wick   *115 still* always
116 plurisy excess   *122 hurts* i.e. shortens life by drawing blood from the heart (as was believed); *quick*
sensitive flesh

126 sanctuarize protect from punishment, give sanctuary to   *130 put on* instigate   *132 in fine* finally   *133
remiss* negligent   *135 peruse* scan   *137 unbated* not
blunted; *pass of practice* thrust made effective by
trickery   *140 unction* ointment; *mountebank* quack-
doctor   *142 cataplasm* poultice   *143 simples* herbs
145 withal with it   *146 gall* scratch

149   May fit us to our shape. If this should fail,
150   And that our drift look through our bad
        performance,
     'Twere better not assayed. Therefore this
        project
     Should have a back or second, that might
        hold
153   If this did blast in proof. Soft, let me see.
     We'll make a solemn wager on your
        cunnings—
     I ha't!
     When in your motion you are hot and
        dry—
     As make your bouts more violent to that
        end—
     And that he calls for drink, I'll have
158   preferred him
159   A chalice for the nonce, whereon but
        sipping,
160   If he by chance escape your venomed stuck,
     Our purpose may hold there.—But stay,
        what noise?

     Enter Queen.

QUEEN.
     One woe doth tread upon another's heel,
     So fast they follow. Your sister 's drowned,
        Laertes.
LAERTES. Drowned! O, where?
QUEEN.
165   There is a willow grows askant the brook,
166   That shows his hoar leaves in the glassy
        stream.
     Therewith fantastic garlands did she make
     Of crowflowers, nettles, daisies, and long
        purples,
169   That liberal shepherds give a grosser name,
     But our cold maids do dead men's fingers
        call them.
171   There on the pendent boughs her crownet
        weeds
     Clamb'ring to hang, an envious sliver
        broke,
     When down her weedy trophies and herself

Fell in the weeping brook. Her clothes
   spread wide,
And mermaid-like a while they bore her
   up,
Which time she chanted snatches of old
   lauds,   176
As one incapable of her own distress,   177
Or like a creature native and indued   178
Unto that element. But long it could not be
Till that her garments, heavy with their
   drink,
Pulled the poor wretch from her melodious
   lay
To muddy death.
LAERTES.   Alas, then she is drowned?
QUEEN. Drowned, drowned.
LAERTES.
     Too much of water hast thou, poor
        Ophelia,
     And therefore I forbid my tears; but yet
     It is our trick; nature her custom holds,   186
     Let shame say what it will. When these are
        gone,
     The woman will be out. Adieu, my lord.   188
     I have a speech o' fire, that fain would
        blaze
     But that this folly drowns it.   *Exit.*
KING.   Let's follow, Gertrude.
     How much I had to do to calm his rage!
     Now fear I this will give it start again;
     Therefore let's follow.   *Exeunt.*

                 *

ACT V

Scene i

Enter two Clowns.

CLOWN. Is she to be buried in Christian 1
burial when she willfully seeks her own
   salvation?

---

149 shape plan   *150 drift* intention; *look* show   *153 blast in proof* burst during trial (like a faulty cannon)   *158 preferred* offered   *159 nonce* occasion   *160 stuck* thrust   *165 askant* alongside   *166 hoar* grey   *169 liberal* free-spoken, licentious   *171 crownet* coronet

176 lauds hymns   *177 incapable of* insensible to   *178 indued* endowed   *186 trick* way (i.e. to shed tears when sorrowful)   *188 woman* unmanly part of nature.
V, i A churchyard   *s.d. Clowns* rustics   *1 in Christian burial* in consecrated ground with the prescribed service of the Church (a burial denied to suicides)

OTHER. I tell thee she is. Therefore make her
5   grave straight. The crowner hath sate on
her, and finds it Christian burial.

CLOWN. How can that be, unless she drowned
herself in her own defense?

OTHER. Why, 'tis found so.

10 CLOWN. It must be *se offendendo*; it cannot be
else. For here lies the point: if I drown
myself wittingly, it argues an act, and an
act hath three branches—it is to act, to do,
14   and to perform. Argal, she drowned herself wittingly.

OTHER. Nay, but hear you, Goodman
17   Delver.

CLOWN. Give me leave. Here lies the water—
good. Here stands the man—good. If the
man go to this water and drown himself, it
21   is, will he nill he, he goes, mark you that.
But if the water come to him and drown
him, he drowns not himself. Argal, he that
is not guilty of his own death shortens not
his own life.

OTHER. But is this law?

27 CLOWN. Ay marry, is't—crowner's quest law.

OTHER. Will you ha' the truth on't? If this
had not been a gentlewoman, she should
have been buried out o' Christian burial.

31 CLOWN. Why, there thou say'st. And the
more pity that great folk should have
33   count'nance in this world to drown or hang
34   themselves more than their even-Christen.
Come, my spade. There is no ancient
gentlemen but gard'ners, ditchers, and
grave-makers. They hold up Adam's
profession.

OTHER. Was he a gentleman?

CLOWN. 'A was the first that ever bore arms.

41 [OTHER. Why, he had none.

CLOWN. What, art a heathen? How dost thou
understand the Scripture? The Scripture
says Adam digged. Could he dig without
arms?] I'll put another question to thee. If

thou answerest me not to the purpose,
confess thyself—

OTHER. Go to.

CLOWN. What is he that builds stronger than
either the mason, the shipwright, or the
carpenter?

OTHER. The gallows-maker, for that frame
outlives a thousand tenants.

CLOWN. I like thy wit well, in good faith. The
gallows does well. But how does it well? It
does well to those that do ill. Now thou
dost ill to say the gallows is built stronger
than the church. Argal, the gallows may
do well to thee. To't again, come.

OTHER. Who builds stronger than a mason, a
shipwright, or a carpenter?

CLOWN. Ay, tell me that, and unyoke.   62

OTHER. Marry, now I can tell.

CLOWN. To't.

OTHER. Mass, I cannot tell.   65

CLOWN. Cudgel thy brains no more about it,
for your dull ass will not mend his pace
with beating. And when you are asked this
question next, say 'a grave-maker.' The
houses he makes last till doomsday. Go,
get thee in, and fetch me a stoup of liquor. 71
                    [*Exit Other Clown.*]

Enter Hamlet and Horatio [*as Clown digs
and sings*].

                Song.
In youth when I did love, did love,
    Methought it was very sweet
To contract—O—the time for—a—my
    behove,   74
    O, methought there—a—was nothing—
    a—meet.

HAMLET. Has this fellow no feeling of his
business, that 'a sings at grave-making?

HORATIO. Custom hath made it in him a
property of easiness.   79

HAMLET. 'Tis e'en so. The hand of little
employment hath the daintier sense.   81

---

5 straight straightway, at once; *crowner* coroner   *10*
se offendendo a clownish transformation of '*se defen-
dendo*,' 'in self-defense'   *14 Argal* for '*ergo*,' 'therefore'
17 Delver Digger   *21 will he nill he* willy-nilly   *27*
quest inquest   *31 thou say'st* you have it right   *33*
count'nance privilege   *34 even-Christen* fellow Christian
41 had none i.e. had no gentleman's coat of arms

62 unyoke i.e., unharness your powers of thought after
a good day's work   *65 Mass* by the Mass   *71 stoup*
large mug   *74 behove* behoof, benefit   *79 property*
peculiarity; *easiness* easy acceptability   *81 daintier*
sense more delicate feeling (because the hand is less
calloused)

CLOWN.   *Song.*
> But age with his stealing steps
>   Hath clawed me in his clutch,
84   And hath shipped me intil the land,
>   As if I had never been such.

[*Throws up a skull.*]

HAMLET. That skull had a tongue in it, and
87   could sing once. How the knave jowls it to
the ground, as if 'twere Cain's jawbone,
that did the first murder! This might be
90   the pate of a politician, which this ass now
o'erreaches; one that would circumvent
God, might it not?

HORATIO. It might, my lord.

HAMLET. Or of a courtier, which could say
'Good morrow, sweet lord! How dost thou,
sweet lord?' This might be my Lord Such-
a-one, that praised my Lord Such-a-one's
horse when 'a meant to beg it, might it
not?

HORATIO. Ay, my lord.

HAMLET. Why, e'en so, and now my Lady
102 Worm's, chapless, and knocked about the
103 mazzard with a sexton's spade. Here's fine
revolution, an we had the trick to see't.
Did these bones cost no more the breeding
106 but to play at loggets with 'em? Mine ache
to think on't.

CLOWN.   *Song.*
> A pickaxe and a spade, a spade,
109   For and a shrouding sheet;
> O, a pit of clay for to be made
>   For such a guest is meet.

[*Throws up another skull.*]

HAMLET. There's another. Why may not that
be the skull of a lawyer? Where be his
114 quiddities now, his quillities, his cases, his

tenures, and his tricks? Why does he suffer 115
this mad knave now to knock him about
the sconce with a dirty shovel, and will not 117
tell him of his action of battery? Hum!
This fellow might be in's time a great buyer
of land, with his statutes, his recognizances, 120
his fines, his double vouchers, his recoveries. [Is this the fine of his fines, and the 122
recovery of his recoveries,] to have his fine
pate full of fine dirt? Will his vouchers
vouch him no more of his purchases, and
double ones too, than the length and
breadth of a pair of indentures? The very 127
conveyances of his lands will scarcely lie in
this box, and must th' inheritor himself
have no more, ha?

HORATIO. Not a jot more, my lord.

HAMLET. Is not parchment made of sheep-
skins?

HORATIO. Ay, my lord, and of calveskins too.

HAMLET. They are sheep and calves which
seek out assurance in that. I will speak to
this fellow. Whose grave's this, sirrah?

CLOWN. Mine, sir.
> [*Sings*]   O, a pit of clay for to be made
>   For such a guest is meet.

HAMLET. I think it be thine indeed, for thou
liest in't.

CLOWN. You lie out on't, sir, and therefore
'tis not yours. For my part, I do not lie in't,
yet it is mine.

HAMLET. Thou dost lie in't, to be in't and
say it is thine. 'Tis for the dead, not for the
quick; therefore thou liest. 147

CLOWN. 'Tis a quick lie, sir; 'twill away again
from me to you.

HAMLET. What man dost thou dig it for?

CLOWN. For no man, sir.

HAMLET. What woman then?

CLOWN. For none neither.

HAMLET. Who is to be buried in't?

---

84 intil into   *87 jowls* hurls   *90 politician* crafty schemer; *o'erreaches* gets the better of (with a play upon the literal meaning)   *102 chapless* lacking the lower chap or jaw   *103 mazzard* head   *106 loggets* small pieces of wood thrown in a game   *109 For and* and *114 quiddities* subtleties (from scholastic '*quidditas*,' meaning the distinctive nature of anything); *quillities* nice distinctions

115 tenures holdings of property   *117 sconce* head   *120 statutes, recognizances* legal documents or bonds acknowledging debt   *122 fines, recoveries* modes of converting estate tail into fee simple; *vouchers* persons vouched or called on to warrant a title; *fine* end (introducing a word play involving four meanings of 'fine')   *127 pair of indentures* deed or legal agreement in duplicate; *conveyances* deeds   *147 quick* living

CLOWN. One that was a woman, sir; but, rest her soul, she's dead.

157 HAMLET. How absolute the knave is! We
158 must speak by the card, or equivocation will undo us. By the Lord, Horatio, this three years I have taken note of it, the age
161 is grown so picked that the toe of the peasant comes so near the heel of the courtier
163 he galls his kibe.—How long hast thou been a grave-maker?

CLOWN. Of all the days i' th' year, I came to't that day that our last king Hamlet overcame Fortinbras.

HAMLET. How long is that since?

CLOWN. Cannot you tell that? Every fool can tell that. It was the very day that young Hamlet was born—he that is mad, and sent into England.

HAMLET. Ay, marry, why was he sent into England?

CLOWN. Why, because 'a was mad. 'A shall recover his wits there; or, if 'a do not, 'tis no great matter there.

HAMLET. Why?

CLOWN. 'Twill not be seen in him there. There the men are as mad as he.

HAMLET. How came he mad?

CLOWN. Very strangely, they say.

HAMLET. How strangely?

CLOWN. Faith, e'en with losing his wits.

HAMLET. Upon what ground?

CLOWN. Why, here in Denmark. I have been sexton here, man and boy, thirty years.

HAMLET. How long will a man lie i' th' earth ere he rot?

CLOWN. Faith, if 'a be not rotten before 'a die
191 (as we have many pocky corses now-a-days that will scarce hold the laying in), 'a will last you some eight year or nine year. A tanner will last you nine year.

HAMLET. Why he more than another?

CLOWN. Why, sir, his hide is so tanned with his trade that 'a will keep out water a great

while, and your water is a sore decayer of your whoreson dead body. Here's a skull now hath lien you i' th' earth three-and-twenty years.

HAMLET. Whose was it?

CLOWN. A whoreson mad fellow's it was. Whose do you think it was?

HAMLET. Nay, I know not.

CLOWN. A pestilence on him for a mad rogue! 'A poured a flagon of Rhenish on 207 my head once. This same skull, sir, was—sir—Yorick's skull, the king's jester.

HAMLET. This?

CLOWN. E'en that.

HAMLET. Let me see. [*Takes the skull.*] Alas, poor Yorick! I knew him, Horatio, a fellow of infinite jest, of most excellent fancy. He hath borne me on his back a thousand times. And now how abhorred in my imagination it is! My gorge rises at it. Here hung those lips that I have kissed I know not how oft. Where be your gibes now? Your gambols, your songs, your flashes of merriment that were wont to set the table on a roar? Not one now to mock your own grinning? Quite chapfall'n? Now get you 223 to my lady's chamber, and tell her, let her paint an inch thick, to this favor she must 225 come. Make her laugh at that. Prithee, Horatio, tell me one thing.

HORATIO. What's that, my lord?

HAMLET. Dost thou think Alexander looked o' this fashion i' th' earth?

HORATIO. E'en so.

HAMLET. And smelt so? Pah!

[Puts down the skull.]

HORATIO. E'en so, my lord.

HAMLET. To what base uses we may return, Horatio! Why may not imagination trace the noble dust of Alexander till 'a find it stopping a dunghole?

HORATIO. 'Twere to consider too curiously, 238 to consider so.

---

157 *absolute* positive 158 *by the card* by the card on which the points of the mariner's compass are marked, absolutely to the point; *equivocation* ambiguity 161 *picked* refined, spruce 163 *galls* chafes; *kibe* chilblain 191 *pocky* rotten (literally, corrupted by pox, or syphilis)

207 *Rhenish* Rhine wine 223 *chapfall'n* lacking the lower shap, or jaw (with a play on the sense 'down in the mouth,' 'dejected') 225 *favor* countenance, aspect 238 *curiously* minutely

HAMLET. No, faith, not a jot, but to follow
240 him thither with modesty enough, and
likelihood to lead it; as thus: Alexander
died, Alexander was buried, Alexander re-
turneth to dust; the dust is earth; of earth
we make loam; and why of that loam
whereto he was converted might they not
stop a beer barrel?
247 Imperious Caesar, dead and turned to
clay,
Might stop a hole to keep the wind away.
O, that that earth which kept the world in
awe
Should patch a wall t' expel the winter's
250 flaw!
But soft, but soft awhile! Here comes the
king—

Enter King, Queen, Laertes, and the Corse
[with Lords attendant and a Doctor of
Divinity as Priest].

The queen, the courtiers. Who is this they
follow?
And with such maimèd rites? This doth
betoken
The corse they follow did with desp'rate
hand
255 Fordo it own life. 'Twas of some estate.
256 Couch we awhile, and mark.

[Retires with Horatio.]

LAERTES.
What ceremony else?
HAMLET.   That is Laertes,
A very noble youth. Mark.
LAERTES.
What ceremony else?
DOCTOR.
Her obsequies have been as far enlarged
As we have warranty. Her death was
doubtful,
And, but that great command o'ersways
the order,

She should in ground unsanctified have
lodged
Till the last trumpet. For charitable
prayers,
Shards, flints, and pebbles should be   265
thrown on her.
Yet here she is allowed her virgin crants,   266
Her maiden strewments, and the bringing 267
home
Of bell and burial.
LAERTES.
Must there no more be done?
DOCTOR.   No more be done.
We should profane the service of the dead
To sing a requiem and such rest to her
As to peace-parted souls.
LAERTES.   Lay her i' th' earth,
And from her fair and unpolluted flesh
May violets spring! I tell thee, churlish
priest,
A minist'ring angel shall my sister be
When thou liest howling.
HAMLET.   What, the fair Ophelia?
QUEEN.
Sweets to the sweet! Farewell.

[Scatters flowers.]

I hoped thou shouldst have been my
Hamlet's wife.
I thought thy bride-bed to have decked,
sweet maid,
And not have strewed thy grave.
LAERTES.   O, treble woe
Fall ten times treble on that cursèd head
Whose wicked deed thy most ingenious   282
sense
Deprived thee of! Hold off the earth awhile,
Till I have caught her once more in mine
arms.

[Leaps in the grave.]

Now pile your dust upon the quick and
dead

240 *modesty* moderation 247 *Imperious* imperial 250
flaw gust of wind 255 *Fordo* destroy; *it* its; *estate*
rank 256 *Couch* hide

265 *Shards* broken pieces of pottery 266 *crants* garland
267 *strewments* strewings of the grave with flowers;
bringing home laying to rest 282 *most ingenious* of
quickest apprehension

Till of this flat a mountain you have made
287   T' o'ertop old Pelion or the skyish head
Of blue Olympus.
   HAMLET. [*coming forward*] What is he whose grief
Bears such an emphasis? whose phrase of sorrow
290 Conjures the wand'ring stars, and makes them stand
Like wonder-wounded hearers? This is I, Hamlet the Dane.

[*Leaps in after Laertes.*]

LAERTES.   The devil take thy soul!

[*Grapples with him.*]

HAMLET.
Thou pray'st not well.
I prithee take thy fingers from my throat,
295 For, though I am not splenitive and rash,
Yet have I in me something dangerous,
Which let thy wisdom fear. Hold off thy hand.
KING.
Pluck them asunder.
QUEEN.   Hamlet, Hamlet!
ALL.
Gentlemen!
HORATIO.   Good my lord, be quiet.

[*Attendants part them, and they come out of the grave.*]

HAMLET.
Why, I will fight with him upon this theme
Until my eyelids will no longer wag.
QUEEN.

O my son, what theme?
HAMLET.
I loved Ophelia. Forty thousand brothers
Could not with all their quantity of love
Make up my sum. What wilt thou do for her?
KING.
O, he is mad, Laertes.
QUEEN.
For love of God, forbear him.
HAMLET.
'Swounds, show me what thou't do.
Woo't weep? woo't fight? woo't fast?   309
  woo't tear thyself?
Woo't drink up esill? eat a crocodile?   310
I'll do't. Dost thou come here to whine?
To outface me with leaping in her grave?
Be buried quick with her, and so will I.   313
And if thou prate of mountains, let them throw
Millions of acres on us, till our ground,
Singeing his pate against the burning zone,
Make Ossa like a wart! Nay, an thou'lt mouth,
I'll rant as well as thou.
QUEEN.   This is mere madness; 318
And thus a while the fit will work on him.
Anon, as patient as the female dove
When that her golden couplets are   321
  disclosed,
His silence will sit drooping.
HAMLET.   Hear you, sir.
What is the reason that you use me thus?
I loved you ever. But it is no matter.
Let Hercules himself do what he may,
The cat will mew, and dog will have his day.
KING.
I pray thee, good Horatio, wait upon him.
        Exit Hamlet and Horatio.

[*To Laertes*]

---

287 *Pelion* a mountain in Thessaly, like Olympus and also Ossa (the allusion being to the war in which the Titans fought the gods and attempted to heap Ossa and Olympus on Pelion, or Pelion and Ossa on Olympus, in order to scale heaven) 290 *Conjures* charms, puts a spell upon; *wand'ring stars* planets 295 *splenitive* of fiery temper (the spleen being considered the seat of anger)

309 *Woo't* wilt (thou) 310 *esill* vinegar 313 *quick* alive 318 *mere* absolute 321 *couplets* pair of fledglings; *disclosed* hatched

328 Strengthen your patience in our last night's
speech.

329 We'll put the matter to the present push.—
Good Gertrude, set some watch over your
son.—
This grave shall have a living monument.
An hour of quiet shortly shall we see;
Till then in patience our proceeding be.
Exeunt.

*

ACT V

Scene ii

Enter Hamlet and Horatio.

HAMLET.
So much for this, sir; now shall you see the
other.
You do remember all the circumstance?

HORATIO.
Remember it, my lord!

HAMLET.
Sir, in my heart there was a kind of
fighting
That would not let me sleep. Methought I
lay

6 Worse than the mutines in the bilboes.
Rashly,
And praised by rashness for it—let us
know,
Our indiscretion sometime serves us well

9 When our deep plots do pall, and that
should learn us
There's a divinity that shapes our ends,

11 Rough-hew them how we will—

HORATIO. That is most certain.

HAMLET.
Up from my cabin,

My sea-gown scarfed about me, in the dark
Groped I to find out them, had my desire,
Fingered their packet, and in fine withdrew 15
To mine own room again, making so bold,
My fears forgetting manners, to unseal
Their grand commission; where I found,
Horatio—
Ah, royal knavery!—an exact command,
Larded with many several sorts of reasons, 20
Importing Denmark's health, and 21
England's too,
With, ho! such bugs and goblins in my life, 22
That on the supervise, no leisure bated, 23
No, not to stay the grinding of the axe,
My head should be struck off.

HORATIO. Is't possible?

HAMLET.
Here's the commission; read it at more
leisure.
But wilt thou hear me how I did proceed?

HORATIO. I beseech you.

HAMLET.
Being thus benetted round with villainies,
Or I could make a prologue to my brains, 30
They had begun the play. I sat me down,
Devised a new commission, wrote it fair.
I once did hold it, as our statists do, 33
A baseness to write fair, and labored much 34
How to forget that learning, but, sir, now
It did me yeoman's service. Wilt thou know 36
Th' effect of what I wrote? 37

HORATIO. Ay, good my lord.

HAMLET.
An earnest conjuration from the king,
As England was his faithful tributary,
As love between them like the palm might
flourish,
As peace should still her wheaten garland 41
wear

---

328 *in* by calling to mind   329 *present push* immediate
trial
V, ii The hall of the Castle   6 *mutines* mutineers;
bilboes fetters   9 *pall* fail   11 *Rough-hew* shape roughly
in trial form

15 *Fingered* filched; *in fine* finally   20 *Larded* enriched
21 *Importing* relating to   22 *bugs* bugbears; *in my life*
to be encountered as dangers if I should be allowed
to live   23 *supervise* perusal; *bated* deducted, allowed
30 *Or* ere   33 *statists* statesmen   34 *fair* with professional clarity (like a clerk or a scrivener, not like a
gentleman)   36 *yeoman's service* stout service such as
yeomen footsoldiers gave as archers   37 *effect* purport
41 *wheaten garland* adornment of fruitful agriculture

42 And stand a comma 'tween their amities,
43 And many such-like as's of great charge,
    That on the view and knowing of these
      contents,
    Without debatement further, more or less,
    He should the bearers put to sudden death,
47 Not shriving time allowed.
    HORATIO.   How was this sealed?
    HAMLET.
48 Why, even in that was heaven ordinant.
    I had my father's signet in my purse,
50 Which was the model of that Danish seal,
    Folded the writ up in the form of th' other,
52 Subscribed it, gave't th' impression, placed
      it safely,
    The changeling never known. Now, the
      next day
    Was our sea-fight, and what to this was
54   sequent
    Thou know'st already.
    HORATIO.
    So Guildenstern and Rosencrantz go to't.
    HAMLET.
    [Why, man, they did make love to this
      employment.]
    They are not near my conscience; their
      defeat
59 Does by their own insinuation grow.
    'Tis dangerous when the baser nature
      comes
61 Between the pass and fell incensèd points
    Of mighty opposites.
    HORATIO.   Why, what a king is this!
    HAMLET.
63 Does it not, think thee, stand me now
      upon—
    He that hath killed my king, and whored
      my mother,
65 Popped in between th' election and my
      hopes,

Thrown out his angle for my proper life,   66
And with such coz'nage—is't not perfect   67
  conscience
[To quit him with this arm? And is't not to 68
  be damned
To let this canker of our nature come   69
In further evil?
HORATIO.
It must be shortly known to him from
  England
What is the issue of the business there.
HAMLET.
It will be short; the interim is mine,
And a man's life 's no more than to say
  'one.'
But I am very sorry, good Horatio,
That to Laertes I forgot myself,
For by the image of my cause I see
The portraiture of his. I'll court his favors.
But sure the bravery of his grief did put me 79
Into a tow'ring passion.
HORATIO.   Peace, who comes here?]

Enter [Osric,] a courtier.

OSRIC. Your lordship is right welcome back
  to Denmark.
HAMLET. I humbly thank you, sir. [*aside to
  Horatio*] Dost know this waterfly?
HORATIO. [*aside to Hamlet*] No, my good lord.
HAMLET. [*aside to Horatio*] Thy state is the
  more gracious, for 'tis a vice to know him.
  He hath much land, and fertile. Let a beast
  be lord of beasts, and his crib shall stand at
  the king's mess. 'Tis a chough, but, as I say, 90
  spacious in the possession of dirt.
OSRIC. Sweet lord, if your lordship were at
  leisure, I should impart a thing to you from
  his majesty.
HAMLET. I will receive it, sir, with all dili-
  gence of spirit. Put your bonnet to his
  right use. 'Tis for the head.
OSRIC. I thank your lordship, it is very hot.
HAMLET. No, believe me, 'tis very cold; the
  wind is northerly.

---

42 *comma* connective (because it indicates continuity of thought in a sentence)   43 *charge* burden (with a double meaning to fit a play that makes *as*'s into 'asses')   47 *shriving time* time for confession and absolution   48 *ordinant* controlling   50 *model* counterpart   52 *impression* i.e. of the signet   54 *sequent* subsequent   59 *insinuation* intrusion   61 *pass* thrust; *fell* fierce   63 *stand* rest incumbent   65 *election* i.e. to the kingship (the Danish kingship being elective)

66 *angle* fishing line; *proper* own   67 *coz'nage* cozenage, trickery   68 *quit* repay   69 *canker* cancer, ulcer   79 *bravery* ostentatious display   90 *mess* table; *chough* jackdaw, chatterer

101 OSRIC. It is indifferent cold, my lord, indeed.

HAMLET. But yet methinks it is very sultry
103 and hot for my complexion.

OSRIC. Exceedingly, my lord; it is very sultry,
as 'twere—I cannot tell how. But, my lord,
his majesty bade me signify to you that 'a
has laid a great wager on your head. Sir,
this is the matter—

109 HAMLET. I beseech you remember.

[Hamlet moves him to put on his hat.]

110 OSRIC. Nay, good my lord; for mine ease, in
good faith. Sir, here is newly come to court
Laertes—believe me, an absolute gentle-
113 man, full of most excellent differences, of
114 very soft society and great showing. In-
115 deed, to speak feelingly of him, he is the
card or calendar of gentry; for you shall
117 find in him the continent of what part a
gentleman would see.

119 HAMLET. Sir, his definement suffers no perdition in you, though, I know, to divide him
121 inventorially would dozy th' arithmetic of
122 memory, and yet but yaw neither in
respect of his quick sail. But, in the verity
of extolment, I take him to be a soul of
125 great article, and his infusion of such
126 dearth and rareness as, to make true dic-
127 tion of him, his semblable is his mirror, and
128 who else would trace him, his umbrage,
nothing more.

OSRIC. Your lordship speaks most infallibly of
him.

HAMLET. The concernancy, sir? Why do we 132
wrap the gentleman in our more rawer 133
breath?

OSRIC. Sir?

HORATIO. Is't not possible to understand in
another tongue? You will to't, sir, really. 137

HAMLET. What imports the nomination of 138
this gentleman?

OSRIC. Of Laertes?

HORATIO. *[aside to Hamlet]* His purse is empty
already. All's golden words are spent.

HAMLET. Of him, sir.

OSRIC. I know you are not ignorant—

HAMLET. I would you did, sir; yet, in faith,
if you did, it would not much approve me. 146
Well, sir?

OSRIC. You are not ignorant of what excellence Laertes is—

HAMLET. I dare not confess that, lest I should
compare with him in excellence; but to 151
know a man well were to know himself.

OSRIC. I mean, sir, for his weapon; but in the
imputation laid on him by them, in his
meed he's unfellowed. 155

HAMLET. What's his weapon?

OSRIC. Rapier and dagger.

HAMLET. That's two of his weapons—but
well.

OSRIC. The king, sir, hath wagered with him
six Barbary horses, against the which he
has impawned, as I take it, six French 162
rapiers and poniards, with their assigns, as 163
girdle, hangers, and so. Three of the car- 164
riages, in faith, are very dear to fancy, very 165
responsive to the hilts, most delicate carriages, and of very liberal conceit. 167

HAMLET. What call you the carriages?

HORATIO. *[aside to Hamlet]* I knew you must
be edified by the margent ere you had 170
done.

101 indifferent somewhat *103 complexion* temperament
109 remember i.e., remember you have done all that
courtesy demands *110 for mine ease* i.e., I keep my hat
off just for comfort (a conventional polite phrase)
113 differences differentiating characteristics, special
qualities *114 soft society* gentle manners; *great showing*
noble appearance *115 feelingly* appropriately; *card*
map; *calendar* guide; *gentry* gentlemanliness *117*
continent all-containing embodiment (with an implication of geographical continent to go with *card*) *119*
definement definition; *perdition* loss *121 dozy* dizzy,
stagger *122 yaw* hold to a course unsteadily like a
ship that steers wild; *neither* for all that *122–23 in*
respect of in comparison with *125 article* scope, importance; *infusion* essence *126 dearth* scarcity *127*
semblable likeness (i.e., only true likeness); *trace* follow
128 umbrage shadow

132 concernancy relevance *133 rawer breath* cruder
speech *137 to't* i.e., get to an understanding *138*
nomination mention *146 approve me* be to my credit
151 compare compete *155 meed* worth *162 impawned*
staked *163 assigns* appurtenances *164 hangers* straps
by which the sword hangs from the belt *165 dear to*
fancy finely designed; *responsive* corresponding closely
167 liberal conceit tasteful design, refined conception *170*
margent margin (i.e., explanatory notes there printed)

OSRIC. The carriages, sir, are the hangers.

HAMLET. The phrase would be more germane to the matter if we could carry a cannon by our sides. I would it might be hangers till then. But on! Six Barbary horses against six French swords, their assigns, and three liberal-conceited carriages—that's the French bet against the Danish. Why is this all impawned, as you call it?

OSRIC. The king, sir, hath laid, sir, that in a dozen passes between yourself and him he shall not exceed you three hits; he hath laid on twelve for nine, and it would come to immediate trial if your lordship would vouchsafe the answer.

HAMLET. How if I answer no?

OSRIC. I mean, my lord, the opposition of your person in trial.

191 HAMLET. Sir, I will walk here in the hall. If it please his majesty, it is the breathing time of day with me. Let the foils be brought, the gentleman willing, and the king hold his purpose, I will win for him
195 an I can; if not, I will gain nothing but my shame and the odd hits.

OSRIC. Shall I redeliver you e'en so?

HAMLET. To this effect, sir, after what flourish your nature will.

OSRIC. I commend my duty to your lordship.

HAMLET. Yours, yours. [*Exit Osric.*] He does well to commend it himself; there are no tongues else for's turn.

204 HORATIO. This lapwing runs away with the shell on his head.

206 HAMLET. 'A did comply, sir, with his dug before 'a sucked it. Thus has he, and many
208 more of the same bevy that I know the
209 drossy age dotes on, only got the tune of the time and, out of an habit of encounter, a kind of yeasty collection, which carries
212 them through and through the most fanned and winnowed opinions; and do but blow them to their trial, the bubbles are out.

Enter a Lord.

191 breathing time exercise hour   *195 an* if   *204 lapwing* a bird reputed to be so precocious as to run as soon as hatched   *206 comply* observe formalities of courtesy; *dug* mother's nipple   *208 bevy* company   *209 drossy* frivolous   *212 fanned and winnowed* select and refined

LORD. My lord, his majesty commended him to you by young Osric, who brings back to him that you attend him in the hall. He sends to know if your pleasure hold to play with Laertes, or that you will take longer time.

HAMLET. I am constant to my purposes; they follow the king's pleasure. If his fitness speaks, mine is ready; now or whensoever, provided I be so able as now.

LORD. The king and queen and all are coming down.

HAMLET. In happy time. 227

LORD. The queen desires you to use some gentle entertainment to Laertes before you 229 fall to play.

HAMLET. She well instructs me. [*Exit Lord.*]

HORATIO. You will lose this wager, my lord.

HAMLET. I do not think so. Since he went into France I have been in continual practice. I shall win at the odds. But thou wouldst not think how ill all's here about my heart. But it is no matter.

HORATIO. Nay, good my lord—

HAMLET. It is but foolery, but it is such a kind of gain-giving as would perhaps trouble a 240 woman.

HORATIO. If your mind dislike anything, obey it. I will forestall their repair hither and say you are not fit.

HAMLET. Not a whit, we defy augury. There is special providence in the fall of a sparrow. If it be now, 'tis not to come; if it be not to come, it will be now; if it be not now, yet it will come. The readiness is all. 249 Since no man of aught he leaves knows, what is't to leave betimes? Let be.

A table prepared. [Enter] Trumpets, Drums, and Officers with cushions; King, Queen, [Osric,] and all the State, [with] foils, daggers, [and stoups of wine borne in;] and Laertes.

KING.
Come, Hamlet, come, and take this hand from me.

227 In happy time I am happy (a polite response)   *229 entertainment* words of reception or greeting   *240 gain-giving* misgiving   *249 all* all that matters

[*The King puts Laertes' hand into Hamlet's.*]

HAMLET.
Give me your pardon, sir. I have done you wrong,
But pardon't, as you are a gentleman.
255 This presence knows, and you must needs have heard,
How I am punished with a sore distraction.
What I have done
That might your nature, honor, and
258 exception
Roughly awake, I here proclaim was madness.
Was't Hamlet wronged Laertes? Never Hamlet.
If Hamlet from himself be ta'en away,
And when he's not himself does wrong Laertes,
Then Hamlet does it not, Hamlet denies it.
Who does it then? His madness. If't be so,
265 Hamlet is of the faction that is wronged;
His madness is poor Hamlet's enemy.
Sir, in this audience,
Let my disclaiming from a purposed evil
Free me so far in your most generous thoughts
That I have shot my arrow o'er the house
And hurt my brother.
271 LAERTES.   I am satisfied in nature,
Whose motive in this case should stir me most
273 To my revenge. But in my terms of honor
I stand aloof, and will no reconcilement
Till by some elder masters of known honor
276 I have a voice and precedent of peace
277 To keep my name ungored. But till that time
I do receive your offered love like love,
And will not wrong it.
HAMLET.   I embrace it freely,
And will this brother's wager frankly play.
Give us the foils. Come on.
LAERTES.   Come, one for me.

HAMLET.
I'll be your foil, Laertes. In mine ignorance   282
Your skill shall, like a star i' th' darkest night,
Stick fiery off indeed.   284
LAERTES.   You mock me, sir.
HAMLET.
No, by this hand.
KING.
Give them the foils, young Osric. Cousin Hamlet,
You know the wager?
HAMLET.   Very well, my lord.
Your grace has laid the odds o' th' weaker side.
KING.
I do not fear it, I have seen you both;
But since he is bettered, we have therefore odds.
LAERTES.
This is too heavy; let me see another.
HAMLET.
This likes me well. These foils have all a length?

[*Prepare to play.*]

OSRIC.
Ay, my good lord.
KING.
Set me the stoups of wine upon that table.
If Hamlet give the first or second hit,
Or quit in answer of the third exchange,   296
Let all the battlements their ordnance fire.
The king shall drink to Hamlet's better breath,
And in the cup an union shall he throw   299
Richer than that which four successive kings
In Denmark's crown have worn. Give me the cups,
And let the kettle to the trumpet speak,   302
The trumpet to the cannoneer without,
The cannons to the heavens, the heaven to earth,

---

255 *presence* assembly   258 *exception* disapproval   265 *faction* body of persons taking a side in a contention   271 *nature* natural feeling as a person   273 *terms of honor* position as a man of honor   276 *voice* authoritative statement   277 *ungored* uninjured

282 *foil* setting that displays a jewel advantageously (with a play upon the meaning 'weapon')   284 *Stick fiery off* show in brilliant relief   296 *quit* repay by a hit   299 *union* pearl   302 *kettle* kettledrum

'Now the king drinks to Hamlet.' Come, begin.

Trumpets the while.

And you, the judges, bear a wary eye.
HAMLET.
Come on, sir.
LAERTES.   Come, my lord.

[They play.]

HAMLET.   One.
LAERTES.   No.
HAMLET.   Judgment?
OSRIC.
A hit, a very palpable hit.

Drum, trumpets, and shot. Flourish; a piece goes off.

LAERTES.   Well, again.
KING.
Stay, give me drink. Hamlet, this pearl is thine.
Here's to thy health. Give him the cup.
HAMLET.
I'll play this bout first; set it by awhile.
Come. *[They play.]* Another hit. What say you?
LAERTES.
A touch, a touch; I do confess't.
KING.
Our son shall win.
314 QUEEN.   He's fat, and scant of breath.
315 Here, Hamlet, take my napkin, rub thy brows.
316 The queen carouses to thy fortune, Hamlet.
HAMLET.
Good madam!
KING.   Gertrude, do not drink.
QUEEN.
I will, my lord; I pray you pardon me.

[Drinks.]

KING. *[aside]*
It is the poisoned cup; it is too late.
HAMLET.
I dare not drink yet, madam—by and by.
QUEEN.
Come, let me wipe thy face.
LAERTES.
My lord, I'll hit him now.
KING.   I do not think't.
LAERTES. *[aside]*
And yet it is almost against my conscience.
HAMLET.
Come for the third, Laertes. You but dally.
I pray you pass with your best violence;
I am afeard you make a wanton of me.   326
LAERTES.
Say you so? Come on.

[They play.]

OSRIC.
Nothing neither way.
LAERTES.
Have at you now!

[In scuffling they change rapiers, and both are wounded with the poisoned weapon.]

KING.   Part them. They are incensed.
HAMLET.
Nay, come—again!

[The Queen falls.]

OSRIC.   Look to the queen there, ho!
HORATIO.
They bleed on both sides. How is it, my lord?
OSRIC.
How is't, Laertes?
LAERTES.
Why, as a woodcock to mine own springe, 333 Osric.
I am justly killed with mine own treachery.
HAMLET.
How does the queen?

314 *fat* not physically fit, out of training   315 *napkin* handkerchief   316 *carouses* drinks a toast

326 *wanton* pampered child   333 *woodcock* a bird reputed to be stupid and easily trapped; *springe* trap

335 KING.   She sounds to see them bleed.

QUEEN.

  No, no, the drink, the drink! O my dear
    Hamlet!
  The drink, the drink! I am poisoned.

      [Dies.]

HAMLET.

  O villainy! Ho! let the door be locked.
  Treachery! Seek it out.

      [Laertes falls.]

LAERTES.

  It is here, Hamlet. Hamlet, thou art slain;
  No med'cine in the world can do thee good.
  In thee there is not half an hour's life.
  The treacherous instrument is in thy hand,
344 Unbated and envenomed. The foul
    practice
  Hath turned itself on me. Lo, here I lie,
  Never to rise again. Thy mother 's
    poisoned.
  I can no more. The king, the king 's to
    blame.

HAMLET.

  The point envenomed too?
  Then venom, to thy work.

      [Hurts the King.]

ALL. Treason! treason!

KING.

  O, yet defend me, friends. I am but hurt.

HAMLET.

  Here, thou incestuous, murd'rous,
    damnèd Dane,
  Drink off this potion. Is thy union here?
  Follow my mother.

      [King dies.]

LAERTES.   He is justly served.

355 It is a poison tempered by himself.
  Exchange forgiveness with me, noble
    Hamlet.

  Mine and my father's death come not upon
    thee,
  Nor thine on me!

      [Dies.]

HAMLET.

  Heaven make thee free of it! I follow thee.
  I am dead, Horatio. Wretched queen,
    adieu!
  You that look pale and tremble at this
    chance,
  That are but mutes or audience to this act, 362
  Had I but time—as this fell sergeant,   363
    Death,
  Is strict in his arrest—O, I could tell you—
  But let it be. Horatio, I am dead;
  Thou livest; report me and my cause aright
  To the unsatisfied.

HORATIO.   Never believe it.

  I am more an antique Roman than a Dane.
  Here's yet some liquor left.

HAMLET.   As th'art a man,

  Give me the cup. Let go. By heaven, I'll
    ha't!
  O God, Horatio, what a wounded name,
  Things standing thus unknown, shall live
    behind me!
  If thou didst ever hold me in thy heart,
  Absent thee from felicity awhile,
  And in this harsh world draw thy breath in
    pain,
  To tell my story.

      A march afar off.

               What warlike noise is this?

OSRIC.

  Young Fortinbras, with conquest come
    from Poland,
  To the ambassadors of England gives
  This warlike volley.

HAMLET.   O, I die, Horatio!

  The potent poison quite o'ercrows my   380
    spirit.
  I cannot live to hear the news from
    England,

---

335 sounds swoons   *344 Unbated* unblunted; *practice*
stratagem   *355 tempered* mixed

362 mutes actors in a play who speak no lines   *363
sergeant* sheriff's officer   *380 o'ercrows* triumphs over
(like a victor in a cockfight)

382 But I do prophesy th' election lights
383 On Fortinbras. He has my dying voice.
384 So tell him, with th' occurrents, more and
     less,
385 Which have solicited—the rest is silence.

[*Dies.*]

HORATIO.
    Now cracks a noble heart. Good night,
        sweet prince,
    And flights of angels sing thee to thy rest!

[*March within.*]

Why does the drum come hither?

*Enter Fortinbras, with the Ambassadors
[and with his train of Drum, Colors, and
Attendants].*

FORTINBRAS.
    Where is this sight?
HORATIO.   What is it you would see?
    If aught of woe or wonder, cease your
        search.
FORTINBRAS.
391 This quarry cries on havoc. O proud
     Death,
392 What feast is toward in thine eternal cell
    That thou so many princes at a shot
    So bloodily hast struck?
AMBASSADOR.   The sight is dismal;
    And our affairs from England come too
        late.
    The ears are senseless that should give us
        hearing
    To tell him his commandment is fulfilled,
    That Rosencrantz and Guildenstern are
        dead.
    Where should we have our thanks?
HORATIO.   Not from his mouth,

Had it th'ability of life to thank you.
He never gave commandment for their
    death.
But since, so jump upon this bloody   402
    question,
You from the Polack wars, and you from
    England,
Are here arrived, give order that these
    bodies
High on a stage be placèd to the view,   405
And let me speak to th'yet unknowing
    world
How these things came about. So shall you
    hear
Of carnal, bloody, and unnatural acts,
Of accidental judgments, casual slaughters, 409
Of deaths put on by cunning and forced   410
    cause,
And, in this upshot, purposes mistook
Fall'n on th' inventors' heads. All this can I
Truly deliver.
FORTINBRAS. Let us haste to hear it,
And call the noblest to the audience.
For me, with sorrow I embrace my
    fortune.
I have some rights of memory in this   416
    kingdom,
Which now to claim my vantage doth   417
    invite me.
HORATIO.
Of that I shall have also cause to speak,
And from his mouth whose voice will draw
    on more.   419
But let this same be presently performed,   420
Even while men's minds are wild, lest
    more mischance
On plots and errors happen.   422
FORTINBRAS.   Let four captains
Bear Hamlet like a soldier to the stage,
For he was likely, had he been put on,   424
To have proved most royal; and for his   425
    passage

382 *election* i.e., to the throne   383 *voice* vote   384 *occurrents* occurrences   385 *solicited* incited, provoked   391 *quarry* pile of dead (literally, of dead deer gathered after the hunt); *cries on* proclaims loudly; *havoc* indiscriminate killing and destruction such as would follow the order 'havoc,' or 'pillage,' given to an army   392 *toward* forthcoming   402 *jump* precisely   405 *stage* platform   409 *judgments* retributions; *casual* not humanly planned (reinforcing *accidental*)   410 *put on* instigated   416 *of memory* traditional and kept in mind   417 *vantage* advantageous opportunity   419 *more* i.e., more voices, or votes, for the kingship   420 *presently* immediately   422 *On* on the basis of   424 *put on* set to perform in office   425 *passage* death

The soldiers' music and the rites of war
Speak loudly for him.
Take up the bodies. Such a sight as this
Becomes the field, but here shows much
  amiss.
Go, bid the soldiers shoot.

> Exeunt [*marching; after the which
> a peal of ordinance are shot off*].

HAMLET AND GREEK DRAMA

H. D. F. Kitto

'There is an old saying that high prosperity, when it reaches its peak, dies not childless, but has offspring; out of good fortune is born misery without end. But my thought takes a lonely path of its own. It is wickedness that begets a numerous offspring, resembling its parents; but in the house that pursues Justice, prosperity breeds fair fortune. Among the wicked, old sin breeds new sin, and a wicked spirit of recklessness, with black ruin for the family.'[1] *Hamlet* might serve as an illustration of this Aeschylean text. Claudius, the 'limed soul', in struggling to be free, is still more engaged, and in his struggle he smears others with the same deadly concoction in which he himself is held fast.

To begin with, there are the consequences, to Claudius, of the death of Polonius. No fewer than three times does he speak of the danger in which this involves him:

> *O heavy deed!*
> *It had been so with us, had we been there . . .*
> *Alas, how shall this bloody deed be answered?*
> *It will be laid to us, whose providence*
> *Should have kept short, restrain'd, and out of*
>   *haunt*
> *This mad young man.*

H. D. F. Kitto, "*Hamlet* and Greek Drama," *Form and Meaning in Drama* (London: Methuen, 1960), pp. 317–337. Reprinted by permission of Methuen & Co., Ltd.
[1]*Agamemnon* 751–771, paraphrased.

Again:

> *So, haply, slander—*
> *Whose whisper o'er the world's diameter*
> *As level as the cannon to its blank*
> *Transports his poisoned shot—may miss our*
>   *name*
> *And hit the woundless air.*

Again:

> *How dangerous is it that this man goes loose!*
> *Yet must not we put the strong law on him:*
> *He's loved of the distracted multitude . . .*

Therefore, as we now learn, the King will add another treacherous crime to his tally: Hamlet is to be murdered in England:

> *Till I know 'tis done,*
> *Howe'er my haps, my joys were ne'er begun.*

This evil intention is frustrated, and the failure of the King's plot is presented by Shakespeare in a way that must be carefully observed. Unlike the Greek dramatists, Shakespeare did not work in a convention that permitted him to use the gods in his theatre; nevertheless, references to Providence now become very frequent, and perhaps we should not dismiss them too lightly. For instance, if we remain with our feet firmly planted on the most prosaic level we can find, secure in the knowledge that at least we can fall no lower, we shall have to say, when the pirate-ship turns up, that the magnificent Shakespeare is condescending to a stale contrivance that would discredit a second-rate melodrama; and having said this we shall for very shame begin to cast about for excuses or explanations, like the prosaic critics who do not understand why Aeschylus freezes the Strymon.

We will go back to the point where Hamlet is being sent to England. He has his suspicions, and the way in which they are conveyed to us is worth noting:

HAMLET: *For England!*
KING: *Aye, Hamlet.*

HAMLET: *Good.*
KING: *So 'tis, if thou knew'st our purposes.*
HAMLET: *I see a cherub that sees them.*

One of the older editors explains: Hamlet means that he divines them, or has an inkling of them. That is indeed what he means, but what he says is: 'I see a cherub that sees them', and the phrase is not idly chosen.

But before he puts Hamlet on board ship, Shakespeare contrives, in a rough and ready way, that he shall meet the Norwegian Captain, and in an even rougher and readier way, he clears the stage for a final soliloquy. At first sight this soliloquy is not easy to understand. But the meaning of the whole passage becomes plain when we see that it is a parallel to the Pyrrhus-Hecuba passage. Superficially, each of them is superfluous—proof enough that Shakespeare thought them necessary. Each ends with a soliloquy, and each soliloquy with an important declaration. Naturally, to these formal resemblances an inner one corresponds, as is clear from the fact that each soliloquy asks the same torturing question: Why cannot I act? But how far, or how deep, does the resemblance go?

In each case Hamlet is contrasted with someone who *can* act. The earlier passage showed us that Hamlet, by no means deficient in passion, cannot give rein to it, like the Player. Now he is set over against Fortinbras, and the theme is Honour.

> *How all occasions do inform against me*
> *And spur my dull revenge! What is a man*
> *If his chief good and market of his time*
> *Be but to sleep and feed? A beast, no more.*
> *Sure, He that made us with such large discouse,*
> *Looking before and after, gave us not*
> *That capability and godlike reason*
> *To fust in us unused . . .*

If any man has 'that capability and godlike reason' it is Hamlet himself; no one could be more of a man, less of a beast that only sleeps and feeds. So that when, a moment later, he again asks himself the baffling question

> *Why yet I live to say* This thing's to do,

we know that the answer is not 'bestial oblivion.' Nor is it cowardice. The answer is hidden from Hamlet, but it would indeed be a strange play if it were also hidden from us. First he was held back by a sense of evil that paralysed him—an evil that he came to think barely credible. The paralysis disappeared; he convinced his reason, and was ready to do it—not out of passion but as a necessary act of justice. Yet it was precisely his reasoning that betrayed him: if only he had known what Claudius knew so well at that moment, Claudius would have been dead. To follow Reason is godlike, but can be perilous to such as are not gods.

Now he is confronted with something which seems to him to deny all reason:

> *Why then, the Polack never will defend it.*

He has before him men who are following a different guide to conduct—twenty thousand men going to their graves like beds, all for so miserable plot of ground,

> *Led by a delicate and tender prince*
> *Whose spirit with divine ambition puffed*
> *Makes mouths at the invisible event*
> *Exposing what is mortal and unsure*
> *To all that fortune, death and danger dare*
> *Even for an eggshell.*

True greatness, he reflects, is to demand indeed great argument before acting, but to find that argument even in a straw, 'when honour's at the stake.' 'How stand I then?'

Inspired by this example, Hamlet decides: he must follow where Honour beckons. But we must observe how the speech ends, for the end illuminates much:

> *O from this time forth*
> *My thoughts be bloody, or be nothing worth.*

To Fortinbras, following Honour is—we must not say easy, but at least simple; to Hamlet, placed as he is, it is not. We must not sentimentalise him. He was ready to 'make a ghost of him that lets me,' and he has little compunction in sending Rosencrantz and Guildenstern to their death; nevertheless, he has already told us, twice, what he thinks of this business. Shakespeare makes it quite plain what is happening to him—that he feels himself being inexorably dragged down, as on a 'massy wheel,' to actions which, being free, he would condemn. 'Hell itself breathes out contagion to this world,' and he is affected by it. The same thought he repeats to Gertrude:

> *They must sweep my way*
> *And marshal me to knavery.*

The path of honour, to Fortinbras, is straightforward; in Denmark, Hamlet's fineness must necessarily suffer corruption.

It has been the burden of all Hamlet's self-questionings hitherto, that he is losing his honour.

> *Who calls me villain? breaks my pate across,*
> *Plucks off my beard, and blows it in my face?*

Now, having surmounted his paralysis, having convinced his reason, having reconciled himself to 'knavery,' he becomes resolute. But by now it is dangerously late; Claudius is fully warned and deeply committed. Indeed, the question is whether the villain Claudius will not destroy Hamlet, and triumph. In the event, villainy does triumph, to the extent that it destroys Hamlet; but we can hardly fail to notice how often, in what remains of the play, Shakespeare reminds us that there is an overruling Providence which, though it will not intervene to save Hamlet, does intervene to defeat Claudius, and does guide events to a consummation in which evil frustrates itself, even though it destroys the innocent by the way.

We may not follow Hamlet's fortunes yet without distorting the structure; for Shakespeare now engages our interest in other events, and these are not merely contemporaneous with those but are also complementary to them, cohering with them in the wide design of the play. As in the first six scenes, we must be prepared for significant juxtaposition.

What we are to be concerned with is the madness and then the death of Ophelia, the return of Laertes, the willingness of 'the false Danish dogs' to rebel against Claudius, the failure of his present plot against Hamlet, and the hatching of the new double plot by Claudius and Laertes together. If we try to take, as the essence of the play, the duel between Hamlet and Claudius, or the indecision of Hamlet, or any other theme which is only a part, not the whole, of the play, then much of this act is only peripheral; but everything coheres closely and organically when we see that the central theme is the disastrous growth of evil.

How, for instance, does Shakespeare introduce the madness of Ophelia? In a very arresting way indeed:

> *I will not speak with her.*

These few words reveal much. We last saw Gertrude utterly contrite at the sins which Hamlet had revealed to her. She has received a straight hint that she is living with her husband's murderer; she has seen Polonius killed, and his daughter crazed—all this the direct or indirect consequence of the villainy in which she has been a partner. No wonder that she would avoid being confronted with this latest disaster: 'I will not speak with her.'

But Horatio tells her that she must, lest worse happen:

> *'Twere good she were spoken with, for she may strew*
> *Dangerous conjectures in ill-breeding minds.*

She gives way, hoping to make the best of it

> *Let her come in.—*
> *To my sick soul, as sin's true nature is,*
> *Each toy seems prelude to some great amiss.*
> *So full of artless jealousy is guilt,*
> *It spills itself in fearing to be spilt.*

She is frightened by her knowledge of her own guilt, but against this she sets the thought that too great consciousness of guilt, and too great circumspection in hiding it, may of themselves reveal that guilt to the world. It is one of the themes that run through the play, that sin breaks through every attempt to keep it secret: 'Foul deeds will rise.' The oath of the cellarage-scene was sworn in vain.

After this it is the King's turn to show what offspring his own sins are breeding for him, and what he says does but repeat, more urgently, what he has said before.[2]

> *When sorrows come, they come not single spies,*
> *But in battalions.*

Polonius is dead, Hamlet gone, the people mudded—

> *and we have done but greenly*
> *In hugger-mugger to inter him—*

and Laertes has come secretly from France, to hear 'pestilent speeches of his father's death.'

> *O my dear Gertrude, this,*
> *Like to a murdering-piece, in many places*
> *Gives me superfluous death.*

Immediately upon this comes Laertes, at the head of an incipient rebellion. The Court may be subservient and complaisant, but among the people Claudius commands little respect:

> *Thick and unwholesome in their thoughts and*
> *   whispers*
> *For good Polonius' death,*

and bearing 'great love' for the exiled Prince. Claudius has given a handle to any enemy he may have, and the people are willing to take from him the crown which he has done so much to win. But he is equal to the occasion; Hamlet has gone to his death, and Laertes can be talked over.

[2]In Act III, Scene 5.

With Laertes he has little trouble:

LAERTES: *And so have I a noble father lost;*
A sister driven into desperate terms,
Whose worth, if praises may go
*   back again,*
Stood challenger on mount of all the
*   age.*

KING: *Break not your sleeps for that: you*
*   must not think*
That we are made of stuff so flat and
*   dull,*
That we can let our beard be shook
*   with danger,*
And think it pastime. You shortly
*   shall hear more:*
I loved your father, and we love
*   ourself;*
And that, I hope, will teach you to
*   imagine—*
*   Enter a Messenger.*

Sophocles too used Messengers in this way. Claudius is confronted with news which we have briefly learned already. His plot has failed; Hamlet is back in Denmark. To Claudius it is incredible:

> *How should it be? how otherwise?*

The full story of his escape we are still to learn, but we may suspect that there was indeed a cherub that saw the King's purposes. But for the plot that has failed he substitutes another, since he 'loves himself.' Laertes consents—like two other men, now dead—to serve Claudius:

KING: *Will you be ruled by me?*
LAERTES: *I will, my lord,*
So you will not o'errule me to a peace.
KING: *To thine own peace.*

But hardly so, since it involves Laertes first in treachery, then in death.

Again a Messenger interrupts the King:

KING: *. . . wherein but sipping,*
If he by chance escape your venomed
*   stuck,*

Our purpose may hold there.—
        Enter the Queen.
                How now, sweet Queen?
QUEEN: *One woe doth tread upon another's*
        heel,
        So fast they follow.—Your sister's
        drowned, Laertes.

Death has struck again. It is the fitting climax to this part of the play. Since it began, with the Queen's vain declaration: 'I will not speak with her,' our thoughts have not been encouraged to stray very far from the idea of evil breeding evil, and leading to ruin. Each toy *is* prelude to some great amiss. The present one reaches its consummation in the scene that follows; and the horrible spectacle of Hamlet and Laertes struggling with each other beside the grave[3] points the way to the end. Sophocles, in the *Electra*, has a vivid image of the irresistible advance of Vengeance on the criminals:

See how Ares (Violence) advances, breathing
    implacable slaughter

except that the word which I have translated 'advances' really means 'grazes its way forward,' as a flock will slowly and deliberately eat its way across a pasture, in a way which nothing but satiety will stop. The same feeling of inevitability prevails here.

At the end of the Churchyard-scene we are told what happened on the North Sea. We last saw Hamlet being sent away, under guard, for 'instant death.' It looked as if Claudius might triumph. But Hamlet is home again. All we know of the manner of his escape is what we have learned from his letter to Horatio; everything turned on the veriest accident—seconded by Hamlet's own impetuous valour. Shakespeare now chooses to amplify the story; and the colour he gives it is surely a definite and significant one, and

___

[3]Not *in* the grave. To what Granville Barker has to say about this (*Introduction to Hamlet*, 162f.) add that Ophelia's body is not coffined—or how could Laertes say: 'Hold off the earth awhile, Till I have caught her once more in mine arms'?

entirely harmonious with the colours of the whole play.

Sir, in my heart there was a kind of fighting
That would not let me sleep.

This time, as when he killed Polonius, and as always henceforth, Hamlet yields to the prompting of the occasion:

HAMLET: *Rashly—*
        And praised be rashness for it: let
        us know
        Our indiscretion sometimes serves us
        well
        When our deep plots do pall; and
        that should teach us
        There's a divinity that shapes our
        ends
        Rough-hew them how we will,—
HORATIO: *That is most certain.*
HAMLET: *Up from my cabin . . .*

This is a very different Hamlet from the one who sought confirmation—or disproof—of what the Ghost had told him, and who sought more than mere death for Claudius. It is the Hamlet who did the 'rash and bloody deed' on Polonius, where also 'rashness' serves the ends of Providence.

As for what Hamlet did to Rosencrantz and Guildenstern, we must be on our guard against seeing the obvious and missing what is significant. There is no irrelevant reproof in Horatio's brief comment:

So Rosencrantz and Guildenstern go to 't.

Hamlet continues:

Why, man, they did make love to this employ-
    ment.
They are not on my conscience; their defeat
Doth by their own insinuation grow.
'Tis dangerous when the baser nature comes
Between the pass and fell incensèd points
Of mighty opposites.

This is not Hamlet trying to exculpate himself. Shakespeare is not interested in that kind of thing here. He is saying: 'This is what happens in life, when foolish men allow themselves to be used by such as Claudius, and to get themselves involved in desperate affairs like these.' To prove that this is what he meant, we may once more reflect what Horatio might have said, and then listen to what he does say:

Why, what a King is this!

How could Shakespeare more decisively draw our attention away from a nice and private appraisal of Hamlet's character, as expressed in this affair, and direct it to the philosophic or 'religious' framework in which it is set? Horatio says just what Laertes says later: 'The King! the King's to blame.'

It was a lucky chance, though not an unlikely one, that Hamlet had his father's signet in his purse; but this is how Hamlet puts it:

Why, even in this was Heaven ordinant.

It was also a lucky chance that the pirate ship caught up with them at this time; and our natural response is: Here too Heaven was ordinant. But it was no lucky chance that Hamlet (with his well-known indecision) was the first and only man to board the pirate.

Once more, the English tragic poet recalls the Greek. In the *Agamemnon* 'some god' took the helm of the King's ship, saved it from the storm, and brought it to land, that Agamemnon might suffer what Justice demanded. Hamlet is a hero very different from Agamemnon, but he too is brought safely back from the sea by Providence; it is no part of the universal design that villainy should triumph. And further: it is through the actions of men that the designs of Providence are fulfilled—through the reckless courage of Hamlet, through the valour and intelligence of the Greeks, in the *Persae*, through the resolution of Electra and Orestes in Sophocles' play. The gods and men are 'partners,' μεταίτιοι. This is not to say that the religion or philosophy of Shakespeare was the same as that of Aeschylus and Sophocles, nor that

his drama was influenced by theirs, either directly or indirectly; only that they were all tragic poets, grappling with the same fundamental realities, and expressing themselves in what is recognisably the same dramatic language.

Once more Hamlet and Claudius confront each other, and Claudius, we know, has another deadly plot ready. Horatio warns Hamlet that the time is short; but Hamlet replies 'The interim is mine.'

But there is no interim at all; the tide has run out, and Hamlet seems to feel it: 'If his fitness speaks, mine is ready.' That Claudius is fit for death is plain enough; but what of Hamlet? 'I will forstall their repair hither,' says Horatio, 'and say you are not fit.' Every word in this dialogue makes us feel that the tragic action is at last poised, ready for the catastrophe. Hamlet has his 'gaingiving,' but he defies augury: 'Mine is ready.' Even more forcibly we are made to feel that Providence is working in the events; an eternal Law is being exemplified: 'There is a special providence in the fall of a sparrow.' But if Providence is working, what is the catastrophe intended to reveal?

The significant design of the catastrophe is unmistakeable. The action of the play began with poison, and it ends with a double poison, that of Claudius and that of Laertes. Gertrude, left to Heaven as the Ghost had commanded, drinks Claudius's poison literally as she had once done metaphorically. Claudius is killed by both, for Hamlet first runs him through with Laertes' poisoned sword, and then makes him drink his own poisoned cup. Laertes himself confesses: 'I am most justly slain by my own treachery'; and in his dying reconciliation with Hamlet he accepts, in effect, what Hamlet had said to him earlier in his own defence:

Hamlet does it not, Hamlet denies it.
Who does it then? His madness. If 't be so,
Hamlet is of the faction that is wronged.

For Hamlet's 'madness' was but the reflection of the evil with which he found himself surrounded, of which Claudius was the most prolific source. So Laertes declares: 'The King! The King's to blame.' Hamlet's death shall not come on Laertes, nor the death of Polonius on Hamlet, but both on Claudius. Horatio, on the other hand, is forcibly prevented from sharing in this common death. He has stood outside the action; he has not been tainted. What is taking place is something like the working-out of Dikê, and in this there is no place for heroic suicide. Hamlet is destroyed not because evil works mechanically, but because his nature was such that he could not confront it until too late.

> *Fie, 'tis an unweeded garden,*
> *That grows to seed; things rank and gross in*
> *nature*
> *Possess it merely.*

Weeds can choke flowers. These weeds have choked Ophelia, and at last they choke Hamlet, because he could not do the coarse work of eradicating them. First, his comprehensive awareness of evil, reversing every habit of his mind, left him prostrate in anguish and apathy; then, the desire for vengeance being aroused, he missed everything by trying to encompass too much; finally, pursuing Honour when it was nearly too late, he found it, but only in his own death. So finely poised, so brittle a nature as Hamlet's, is especially vulnerable to the destructive power of evil.

In the first act, the sinister Claudius drank to Hamlet's health, and guns proclaimed to Heaven and Earth the 'heavy-headed revel.' Now in the last scene the guns roar again: Claudius is drinking to Hamlet's death. The action has completed its circle. The guns remind us of what Hamlet said when first they spoke: some vicious mole of nature, like their birth, wherein they are not guilty; the overgrowth of some complexion that breaks down the pales and forts of reason; some habit that o'erleavens, or works too strongly for, plausive manners—all these bring corruption to a man whose virtues else may be 'pure as grace, as infinite as man may undergo.' All this we see fulfilled in Hamlet. Gertrude's sin, his 'birth,'

has worked in his mind to spoil it; his philosophic 'complexion,' too absolute, was overthrown and turned to 'madness'; his habit of 'godlike reason' betrayed him at the great crisis.

But does Hamlet 'in the general censure take corruption'? This is a question which Shakespeare answers by letting off guns for a third time.

> *Let four captains*
> *Bear Hamlet, like a soldier, to the stage;*
> *For he was likely, had he been put on,*
> *T' have proved most royally: and for his*
> *passage*
> *The soldiers' music and the rites of war*
> *Speak loudly for him.*

This time the guns proclaim neither swinish coarseness nor black treachery, but Honour.

This examination of *Hamlet* has been based on the same assumptions as our examination of certain Greek plays: that the dramatist said exactly what he meant, through the medium of his art, and means therefore exactly what he has said. We have tried therefore to observe what in fact he has said, considering every scene and every considerable passage (as one would in analysing a picture, for example, or a piece of music), not passing over this or that because it did not happen to interest us, or illustrate our point; nor being too ready to disregard a passage on the grounds that it was put there for some extraneous reason; remembering too that a dramatist can 'say' things by means other than words. I do not so flatter myself as to suppose that anything new has been brought to light. Nevertheless, if this general account of the play is acceptable, if its structure has been made to appear purposeful, in details big and small, such that the interpretation (blunders excepted) carries some measure of authority, then the critical method and the assumptions on which it is based may be held to be sound. It seems to me that this may be true.

As we said at the outset, the first thing that strikes us, or should strike us, when we contemplate the play is that it ends in the complete destruction of the two houses that are concerned. The character of Hamlet and the inner experience that he undergoes are indeed drawn at length and with great subtlety, and we must not overlook the fact; nevertheless, the architectonic pattern just indicated is so vast as to suggest at once that what we are dealing with is no individual tragedy of character, however profound, but something more like religious drama; and this means that unless we are ready, at every step, to relate the dramatic situation to its religious or philosophical background—in other words, to look at the play from a point of view to which more recent drama has not accustomed us—then we may not see either the structure or the meaning of the play as Shakespeare thought them.

Why do Rosencrantz and Guildenstern die, and Ophelia, and Laertes? Are these disasters casual by-products of 'the tragedy of a man who could not make up his mind'? Or are they necessary parts of a firm structure? Each of these disasters we can refer to something that Hamlet has done or failed to do, and we can say that each reveals something more of Hamlet's character; but if we see no more than this we are short-sighted, and are neglecting Shakespeare's plain directions in favour of our own. We are told much more than this when we hear Horatio, and then Laertes, cry 'Why, what a King is this!', 'The King, the King's to blame'; also when Guildenstern says, with a deep and unconscious irony 'We here give up ourselves . . .,' and when Laertes talks of 'contagious blastments.' Shakespeare puts before us a group of young people, friends or lovers, none of them wicked, one of them at least entirely virtuous, all surrounded by the poisonous air of Denmark (which also Shakespeare brings frequently and vividly before our minds), all of them brought to death because of its evil influences. Time after time, either in some significant patterning or with some phrase pregnant with irony, he makes us see that these people are partners in disaster, all of them borne down on the 'massy wheel' to 'boisterous ruin.'

In this, the natural working-out of sin, there is nothing mechanical. That is the philosophic reason why character and situation must be drawn vividly. Neither here nor in Greek drama have we anything to do with characters who are puppets in the hands of Fate. In both, we see something of the power of the gods, or the designs of Providence; but these no more override or reduce to unimportance the natural working of individual character than the existence, in the physical world, of universal laws overrides the natural behaviour of natural bodies. It is indeed precisely in the natural behaviour of men, and its natural results, in given circumstances, that the operation of the divine laws can be discerned. In *Hamlet*, Shakespeare draws a complete character, not for the comparatively barren purpose of 'creating' a Hamlet for our admiration, but in order to show how he, like the others, is inevitably engulfed by the evil that has been set in motion, and how he himself becomes the cause of further ruin. The conception which unites these eight persons in one coherent catastrophe may be said to be this: evil, once started on its course, will so work as to attack and overthrow impartially the good and the bad; and if the dramatist makes us feel, as he does, that a Providence is ordinant in all this, that, as with the Greeks, is his way of universalising the particular event.

Claudius, the arch-villain, driven by crime into further crime, meets at last what is manifestly divine justice. 'If his fitness speaks . . .' says Hamlet; the 'fitness' of Claudius has been speaking for a long time. At the opposite pole stands Ophelia, exposed to corruption through uncorrupted, but pitifully destroyed as the chain of evil uncoils itself. Then Gertrude, one of Shakespeare's most tragic characters: she is the first, as Laertes is the last, to be tainted by Claudius; but while he dies in forgiveness and reconciliation, no such gentle influence alleviates her end. In the bedchamber scene Hamlet had pointed out to her the hard road to amendment; has she tried to follow it? On this, Shakespeare is silent; but her last grim experience of life is to find that 'O my dear Hamlet, the drink, the drink! I am poisoned'— poisoned, as she must realise, by the cup that her new husband had prepared for the son whom she loved so tenderly. After her own sin, and as a direct consequence of it, everything that she holds dear is blasted. Her part in this tragedy is indeed a frightening one. She is no Claudius, recklessly given to crime, devoid of any pure or disinterested motive. Her love for her son shines through every line she speaks; this, and her affection for Ophelia, show us the Gertrude that might have been, if a mad passion had not swept her into the arms of Claudius. By this one sin she condemned herself to endure, and, still worse, to understand, all its devastating consequences: her son driven 'mad,' killing Polonius, denouncing herself and her crime in cruel terms that she cannot rebut, Ophelia driven out of her senses and into her grave— nearly a criminal's grave; all her hopes irretrievably ruined. One tragic little detail, just before the end, shows how deeply Shakespeare must have pondered on his Gertrude. We know that she has seen the wild struggle in the graveyard between Laertes and Hamlet. When the Lord enters, to invite Hamlet to the fencing-match, he says: 'The Queen desires you to use some gentle entertainment to Laertes before you fall to play.' 'She well instructs me,' says Hamlet. What can this mean, except that she has vague fears of Laertes' anger, and a pathetic hope that Hamlet might appease it, by talk more courteous than he had used in the graveyard? It recalls her equally pathetic wish that Ophelia's beauty and virtue might 'bring him to his wonted ways again.' The mischief is always much greater than her worst fears. We soon see how Hamlet's gentle entertainment is received by Laertes; and she, in the blinding flash in which she dies, learns how great a treachery had been prepared against her Hamlet.

We cannot think of Gertrude's death, and the manner of it, without recalling what the Ghost had said: Leave her to Heaven. But if we are to see the hand of Providence—

whatever that may signify—in her death, can we do other with the death of Polonius? A 'casual slaughter'? A 'rash and bloody deed'? Certainly; and let us by all means blame Hamlet for it, as also for the callousness with which he sends Rosencrantz and Guildenstern to their doom; but if we suppose that Shakespeare contrived these things only to show us what Hamlet was like, we shall be treating as secular drama what Shakespeare designed as something bigger. In fact, Hamlet was *not* like this, any more than he was, by nature, hesitant or dilatory; any more than Ophelia was habitually mad. This is what he has become. The dramatist does indeed direct us to regard the killing of Polonius in two aspects at once: it is a sudden, unpremeditated attack made by Hamlet, 'mad,' on one who he hopes will prove to be Claudius; and at the same time it is the will of Heaven:

> *For this same lord*
> *I do repent; but Heaven hath pleased it so*
> *To punish me with this and this with me,*
> *That I must be their scourge and minister.*

Surely this is exactly the same dramaturgy that we meet in Sophocles' *Electra*. When Orestes comes out from killing his mother, Electra asks him how things are. 'In the *palace*,'[4] he says, 'all is well—if Apollo's oracle was well.' Perhaps it was a 'rash and bloody deed'; it seems to bring Orestes little joy. We may think of it what we like; Sophocles does not invite us to approve, and if we suppose that he does, we have not understood his play, or his gods. Apollo approves, and Orestes, though he acts for his own reasons, is the gods' 'scourge and minister.' Polonius, no unworthy Counsellor of this King, a mean and crafty man whose soul is mirrored in his language no less than in his acts, meets a violent death while spying; and that such a man should so be killed is, in a large sense, right. Hamlet may 'repent'; Orestes may feel

---

[4] I italicise this word in order to represent Sophocles' untranslateable μέν, which suggests a coming antithesis that in fact is not expressed.

remorse at a dreadful act, but in each case Heaven was ordinant.

The death of Laertes too is a coherent part of this same pattern. To this friend of Hamlet's we can attribute one fault; nor are we taken by surprise when we meet it, for Shakespeare has made his preparations. Laertes is a noble and generous youth, but his sense of honour has no very secure foundations—and Polonius' farewell speech to him makes the fact easy to understand. His natural and unguarded virtue, assailed at once by his anger, his incomplete understanding of the facts, and the evil suggestions of Claudius, gives way; he falls into treachery, and through it, as he comes to see, he is 'most justly killed.'

Of Rosencrantz and Guildenstern, two agreeable though undistinguished young men, flattered and suborned and cruelly destroyed, there is no more to be said; but there remains Hamlet, last and greatest of the eight. Why must he be destroyed? It would be true to say that he is destroyed simply because he has failed to destroy Claudius first; but this is 'truth' as it is understood between police-inspectors, on duty. The dramatic truth must be something which, taking this in its stride, goes much deeper; and we are justified in saying 'must be' since this catastrophe too is presented as being directed by Providence, and therefore inevitable and 'right.' If 'there is a special providence in the fall of a sparrow,' there surely is in the fall of a Hamlet.

Of the eight victims, we have placed Claudius at one pole and Ophelia at the other; Hamlet, plainly, stands near Ophelia. In both Hamlet and Ophelia we can no doubt detect faults: she ought to have been able to see through Polonius, and he should not have hesitated. But to think like this is to behave like a judge, one who must stand outside the drama and sum up from a neutral point of view; the critic who tries to do this would be better employed in a police-court than in criticism. We must remain within the play, not try to peer at the characters through a window of our own constructing. If we do remain within the play, we observe that what

Shakespeare puts before us, all the time, is not faults that we can attribute to Ophelia and Hamlet, but their virtues; and when he does make Hamlet do things deserving of blame, he also makes it evident on whom the blame should be laid. The impression with which he leaves us is not the tragedy that one so fine as Hamlet should be ruined by one fault; it is the tragedy that one so fine should be drawn down into the gulf; and, beyond this, that the poison let loose in Denmark should destroy indiscriminately the good, the bad and the indifferent. Good and bad, Hamlet and Claudius, are coupled in the one sentence 'If his fitness speaks, mine is ready.' That Claudius is 'fit and seasoned for his passage' is plain enough; is it not just as plain that Hamlet is equally 'ready'? What has he been telling us, throughout the play, but that life can henceforth have no meaning or value to him? Confronted by what he sees in Denmark, he, the man of action, has been reduced to impotence; the man of reason has gone 'mad'; the man of religion has been dragged down to 'knavery,' and has felt the contagions of Hell. There is room, though not very much, for subtle and judicious appraisal of his character and conduct; the core of his tragedy is not here, but in the fact that such surpassing excellence is, like the beauty and virtue of Ophelia, brought to nothing by evil. Through all the members of these two doomed houses the evil goes on working, in a concatenation

Of carnal, bloody and unnatural acts,
Of accidental judgments, casual slaughters,
Of deaths put on by cunning and forced cause,

until none are left, and the slate is wiped clean.

The structure of *Hamlet*, then, suggests that we should treat it as religious drama, and when we do, it certainly does not lose either in significance or in artistic integrity. As we have seen more than once, it has fundamental things in common with Greek religious drama —yet in other respects it is very different, being so complex in form and texture. It may be worth while to enquire, briefly, why this should be so.

One naturally compares it with the two Greek revenge-tragedies, the *Choephori* and Sophocles' *Electra*, but whether we do this, or extend the comparison to other Greek religious tragedies like the *Agamemnon* or *Oedipus Tyrannus* or *Antigone*, we find one difference which is obviously pertinent to our enquiry: in the Greek plays the sin, crime or error which is the mainspring of the action is specific, while in Hamlet it is something more general, a quality rather than a single act. Thus, although there are crimes enough in the *Oresteia*, what we are really concerned with, throughout the trilogy, is the problem of avenging or punishing crime. The *Agamemnon* is full of hybris, blind folly, blood-lust, adultery, treachery; but what humanity is suffering from, in the play, is not these sins in themselves, but a primitive conception of Justice, one which uses, and can be made to justify, these crimes, and leads to chaos; and the trilogy ends not in any form of reconciliation or forgiveness among those who have injured each other, nor in any purging of sin, or acceptance of punishment, but in the resolution of the dilemma.

Hamlet resembles the *Choephori* in this, that the murder of a King, and adultery, or something like it, are the crimes which have to be avenged; also that these can be avenged only through another crime, though perhaps a sinless one; but the differences are deep and far-reaching. They are not merely that Orestes kills, and Hamlet shrinks from killing. We may say that both in the Greek trilogy and in Shakespeare's play the Tragic Hero, ultimately, is humanity itself; and what humanity is suffering from in *Hamlet* is not a specific evil, but Evil itself. The murder is only the chief of many manifestations of it, the particular case which is the mainspring of the tragic action.

This seems to be typical. In the *Antigone* a whole house is brought down in ruin, and, again, the cause is quite a specific one. It is

nothing like the comprehensive wickedness of Iago, or the devouring ambition of Macbeth, or the consuming and all-excluding love of Antony and Cleopatra. It is, quite precisely, that Creon makes, and repeats, a certain error of judgment, ἁμαρτία; and I use the phrase 'error of judgment' meaning not that it is venial, nor that it is purely intellectual, but that it is specific. It is not a trivial nor a purely intellectual mistake if a man, in certain circumstances, rejects the promptings of humanity, and thinks that the gods will approve; but this is what Creon does, and the tragedy springs from this and from nothing else. He is not a wicked man—not lecherous or envious or ambitious or vindictive. All this is irrelevant. He is simply the man to make and maintain this one specific and disastrous error.

This contrast between the specific and the general obviously has a close connexion with the contrast between the singleness of the normal Greek tragic structure and the complexity of *Hamlet*. In the first place, since Shakespeare's real theme is not the moral or theological or social problem of crime and vengeance, still less its effect on a single mind and soul, but the corroding power of sin, he will present it not as a single 'error of judgment' but as a hydra with many heads. We have shown, let us hope, how this explains, or helps to explain, such features of the play as, so to speak, the simultaneous presentation of three Creons: Claudius, Gertrude and Polonius, each of them, in his own degree, an embodiment of the general evil. Hence too the richer character-drawing. Claudius is a drunkard, and the fact makes its own contribution to the complete structure; if Sophocles had made Creon a drunkard, it would have been an excrescence on the play. Hence too the frequent changes of scene in the first part of the play; also the style of speech invented for Polonius and Osric. The general enemy is the rottenness that pervades Denmark; therefore it is shown in many persons and many guises.

Then, not only are the sources of the corruption diverse, but so are its ramifications too. We are to see how it spreads, whether from Claudius or from Gertrude or from Polonius, and how it involves one after another, destroying as it goes. To be sure, Greek tragedy shows us something similar—but it is not the same. For example, the condemnation of Antigone leads to the death of Haemon, and that to the death of Eurydice; in the *Oresteia* too there is a long succession of crime. In fact, we remarked above that Claudius recalls the *Agamemnon* and its πρώταρχος ἄτη, the crime that sets crime in motion. So he does; but there is a big difference. Both in *Hamlet* and in the Greek plays crime leads to crime, or disaster to disaster, in this linear fashion, but in *Hamlet* it spreads in another way too, one which is not Greek: it spreads from soul to soul, as a contagion, as when Laertes is tempted by Claudius, or, most notably, when, by his mother's example and Polonius' basely inspired interference, Hamlet's love is corrupted into lewdness, or when he turns against his two compromised friends and pitilessly sends them to death.

Extension of evil in this fashion is, I think, foreign to Greek tragedy. Clearly, it involves a dramatic form which is complexive, not linear and single, like the Greek. Of his successive victims, Sophocles does not even mention Haemon until the middle of the play, and Eurydice not until the end; and the effect is most dramatic. In *Hamlet* there are eight victims, all of whom we have to watch, from time to time, as they become more and more deeply involved.

Further, not only are more people involved at the same time in this more generalised Tragic Flaw, but they are involved more intimately, which again makes for a richer dramatic texture. We may compare Hamlet with Orestes. Externally, they are in a similar position. But when Aeschylus has shown us that Orestes is an avenger pure in heart, and that his dilemma is from every point of view an intolerable one, it is not far wrong to say that his interest in Orestes, as a character, is exhausted; anything more would be unneces-

sary. Hamlet exists in a different kind of tragedy, one which requires that we should see how the contagion gradually spreads over his whole spirit and all his conduct.

The same contrast exists between Hamlet and Sophocles' Orestes and Electra. She, one might say, is drawn much more intimately than the Orestes of Aeschylus. True; but still she is drawn, so to speak, all at once: There is the situation, here is Electra, and this is the way in which it makes her act. It is not Sophocles' conception to show how her mother's continuing crime gradually warps her mind, by a stealthy growth of evil. If she is warped, it has all happened already. His dramatic interest in the characters of the avengers is focussed on this, that they, being what they are, and being affected by Clytemnestra's crime in this way, will naturally act as they do.

It is, in short, a general statement which I think will bear examination, that Greek tragedy presents sudden and complete disaster, or one disaster linked to another in linear fashion, while Shakespearean tragedy presents the complexive, menacing spread of ruin; and that at least one explanation of this is that the Greek poets thought of the tragic error as the breaking of a divine law (or sometimes, in Aeschylus, as the breaking down of a temporary divine law), while Shakespeare saw it as an evil quality which, once it has broken loose, will feed on itself and on anything else that it can find until it reaches its natural end. So, for example in *Macbeth:* in 'noble Macbeth,' ambition is stimulated, and is not controlled by reason or religion; it meets with a stronger response from Lady Macbeth, and grows insanely into a monstrous passion that threatens a whole kingdom. It is a tragic conception which is essentially dynamic, and demands the very unhellenic fluidity and expansiveness of expression which the Elizabethan theatre afforded. Whether this is a reflection of some profound difference between Greek and Christian thought is a question which I am not competent to discuss.

A VIEW FROM THE BRIDGE
A Play in Two Acts

Arthur Miller

CHARACTERS

LOUIS

MIKE

ALFIERI

EDDIE

CATHERINE

BEATRICE

MARCO

TONY

RODOLPHO

FIRST IMMIGRATION OFFICER

SECOND IMMIGRATION OFFICER

MR. LIPARI

MRS. LIPARI

TWO "SUBMARINES"

NEIGHBORS

ACT ONE

The street and house front of a tenement building. The front is skeletal entirely.

The main acting area is the living room-dining room of EDDIE's *apartment. It is a worker's flat, clean, sparse, homely. There is a rocker down front; a round dining table at center, with chairs; and a portable phonograph.*

At back are a bedroom door and an opening to the kitchen; none of these interiors are seen.

At the right, forestage, a desk. This is MR. ALFIERI's *law office. There is also a telephone booth. This is not used until the last scenes, so it may be covered or left in view.*

A stairway leads up to the apartment, and then farther up to the next story, which is not seen.

Ramps, representing the street, run upstage and off to right and left.

As the curtain rises, LOUIS *and* MIKE, *longshoremen, are pitching coins against the building at left.*

A distant foghorn blows.

Enter ALFIERI, *a lawyer in his fifties turning gray; he is portly, good-humored, and thoughtful. The two pitchers nod to him as he passes. He crosses the stage to his desk, removes his hat, runs his fingers through his hair, and grinning, speaks to the audience.*

ALFIERI. You wouldn't have known it, but something amusing has just happened. You see how uneasily they nod to me? That's because I am a lawyer. In this neighborhood to meet a lawyer or a priest on the street is unlucky. We're only thought of in connection with disasters, and they'd rather not get too close.

I often think that behind that suspicious little nod of theirs lie three thousand years of distrust. A lawyer means the law, and in Sicily, from where their fathers came, the law has not been a friendly idea since the Greeks were beaten.

I am inclined to notice the ruins in things, perhaps because I was born in Italy. . . . I only came here when I was twenty-five. In those days, Al Capone, the greatest Carthaginian of all, was learning his trade on these pavements, and Frankie Yale himself was cut precisely in half by a machine gun on the corner of Union Street, two blocks away. Oh, there were many here who were justly shot by unjust men. Justice is very important here.

But this is Red Hook, not Sicily. This is the slum that faces the bay on the seaward side of Brooklyn Bridge. This is the gullet of New York swallowing the tonnage of the world. And now we are quite civilized, quite American. Now we settle for half, and I like it better. I no longer keep a pistol in my filing cabinet.

And my practice is entirely unromantic.

My wife has warned me, so have my friends; they tell me the people in this neighborhood lack elegance, glamour. After all, who have I dealt with in my life? Longshoremen and their wives, and fathers and grandfathers, compensation cases, evictions, family squabbles—the petty troubles of the poor—and yet . . . every few years there is still a case, and as the parties tell me what the trouble is, the flat air in my office suddenly washes in with the green scent of the sea, the dust in this air is blown away and the thought comes that in some Caesar's year, in Calabria perhaps or on the cliff at Syracuse, another lawyer, quite differently dressed, heard the same complaint and set there as powerless as I, and watched it run its bloody course.

[EDDIE *has appeared and has been pitching coins with the men and is highlighted among them. He is forty—a husky, slightly overweight longshoreman.*]

This one's name was Eddie Carbone, a longshoreman working the docks from Brooklyn Bridge to the breakwater where the open sea begins.

[ALFIERI *walks into darkness.*]

EDDIE. [*Moving up steps into doorway.*] Well, I'll see ya, fellas.

[CATHERINE *enters from kitchen, crosses down to window, looks out.*]

LOUIS. You workin' tomorrow?
EDDIE. Yeah, there's another day yet on that ship. See ya, Louis. [EDDIE *goes into the house, as light rises in the apartment.*]

[CATHERINE *is waving to* LOUIS *from the window and turns to him.*]

CATHERINE. Hi, Eddie!

[EDDIE *is pleased and therefore shy about it; he hangs up his cap and jacket.*]

EDDIE. Where you goin' all dressed up?
CATHERINE. [*Running her hands over her skirt.*] I just got it. You like it?
EDDIE. Yeah, it's nice. And what happened to your hair?
CATHERINE. You like it? I fixed it different. [*Calling to kitchen.*] He's here, B.!
EDDIE. Beautiful. Turn around, lemme see in the back. [*She turns for him.*] Oh, if your mother was alive to see you now! She wouldn't believe it.
CATHERINE. You like it, huh?
EDDIE. You look like one of them girls that went to college. Where you goin'?
CATHERINE. [*Taking his arm.*] Wait'll B. comes in, I'll tell you something. Here, sit down. [*She is walking him to the armchair. Calling offstage.*] Hurry up, will you, B.?
EDDIE. [*Sitting.*] What's goin' on?
CATHERINE. I'll get you a beer, all right?
EDDIE. Well, tell me what happened. Come over here, talk to me.
CATHERINE. I want to wait till B. comes in. [*She sits on her heels beside him.*] Guess how much we paid for the skirt.
EDDIE. I think it's too short, ain't it?

CATHERINE. [*Standing.*] No! not when I stand up.

EDDIE. Yeah, but you gotta sit down sometimes.

CATHERINE. Eddie, it's the style now. [*She walks to show him.*] I mean, if you see me walkin' down the street—

EDDIE. Listen, you been givin' me the willies the way you walk down the street, I mean it.

CATHERINE. Why?

EDDIE. Catherine, I don't want to be a pest, but I'm tellin' you you're walkin' wavy.

CATHERINE. I'm walkin' wavy?

EDDIE. Now don't aggravate me, Katie, you are walkin' wavy! I don't like the looks they're givin' you in the candy store. And with them new high heels on the sidewalk —clack, clack, clack. The heads are turnin' like windmills.

CATHERINE. But those guys look at all the girls, you know that.

EDDIE. You ain't "all the girls."

CATHERINE. [*Almost in tears because he disapproves.*] What do you want me to do? You want me to—

EDDIE. Now don't get mad, kid.

CATHERINE. Well, I don't know what you want from me.

EDDIE. Katie, I promised your mother on her deathbed. I'm responsible for you. You're a baby, you don't understand these things. I mean like when you stand here by the window, wavin' outside.

CATHERINE. I was wavin' to Louis!

EDDIE. Listen, I could tell you things about Louis which you wouldn't wave to him no more.

CATHERINE. [*Trying to joke him out of his warning.*] Eddie, I wish there was one guy you couldn't tell me things about!

EDDIE. Catherine, do me a favor, will you? You're gettin' to be a big girl now, you gotta keep yourself more, you can't be so friendly, kid. [*Calls.*] Hey, B., what're you doin' in there? [*To* CATHERINE.] Get her in here, will you? I got news for her.

CATHERINE. [*Starting out.*] What?

EDDIE. Her cousins landed.

CATHERINE. [*Clapping her hands together.*] No! [*She turns instantly and starts for the kitchen.*] B.! Your cousins!

[BEATRICE *enters, wiping her hands with a towel.*]

BEATRICE. [*In the face of* CATHERINE's *shout.*] What?

CATHERINE. Your cousins got in!

BEATRICE. [*Astounded, turns to* EDDIE.] What are you talkin' about? Where?

EDDIE. I was just knockin' off work before and Tony Bereli come over to me; he says the ship is in the North River.

BEATRICE. [*Her hands are clasped at her breast; she seems half in fear, half in unutterable joy.*] They're all right?

EDDIE. He didn't see them yet, they're still on board. But as soon as they get off he'll meet them. He figures about ten o'clock they'll be here.

BEATRICE. [*Sits, almost weak from tension.*] And they'll let them off the ship all right? That's fixed, heh?

EDDIE. Sure, they give them regular seamen papers and they walk off with the crew. Don't worry about it, B., there's nothin' to it. Couple of hours they'll be here.

BEATRICE. What happened? They wasn't supposed to be till next Thursday.

EDDIE. I don't know; they put them on any ship they can get them out on. Maybe the other ship they was supposed to take there was some danger— What you cryin' about?

BEATRICE. [*Astounded and afraid.*] I'm—I just—I can't believe it! I didn't even buy a new tablecloth; I was gonna wash the walls—

EDDIE. Listen, they'll think it's a millionaire's house compared to the way they live. Don't worry about the walls. They'll be thankful. [*To* CATHERINE.] Whyn't you run down buy a tablecloth. Go ahead, here. [*He is reaching into his pocket.*]

CATHERINE. There's no stores open now.

EDDIE. [*To* BEATRICE.] You was gonna put a new cover on the chair.

BEATRICE. I know—well, I thought it was gonna be next week! I was gonna clean the walls, I was gonna wax the floors. [*She stands disturbed.*]

CATHERINE. [*Pointing upward.*] Maybe Mrs. Dondero upstairs—

BEATRICE. [*Of the tablecloth.*] No, hers is worse than this one. [*Suddenly.*] My God, I don't even have nothin' to eat for them! [*She starts for the kitchen.*]

EDDIE. [*Reaching out and grabbing her arm.*] Hey, hey! Take it easy.

BEATRICE. No, I'm just nervous, that's all. [*To* CATHERINE.] I'll make the fish.

EDDIE. You're savin' their lives, what're you worryin' about the tablecloth? They probably didn't see a tablecloth in their whole life where they come from.

BEATRICE. [*Looking into his eyes.*] I'm just worried about you, that's all I'm worried.

EDDIE. Listen, as long as they know where they're gonna sleep.

BEATRICE. I told them in the letters. They're sleepin' on the floor.

EDDIE. Beatrice, all I'm worried about is you got such a heart that I'll end up on the floor with you, and they'll be in our bed.

BEATRICE. All right, stop it.

EDDIE. Because as soon as you see a tired relative, I end up on the floor.

BEATRICE. When did you end up on the floor?

EDDIE. When your father's house burned down I didn't end up on the floor?

BEATRICE. Well, their house burned down!

EDDIE. Yeah, but it didn't keep burnin' for two weeks!

BEATRICE. All right, look, I'll tell them to go someplace else. [*She starts into the kitchen.*]

EDDIE. Now wait a minute, Beatrice! [*She halts. He goes to her.*] I just don't want you bein' pushed around, that's all. You got too big a heart. [*He touches her hand.*] What're you so touchy?

BEATRICE. I'm just afraid if it don't turn out good you'll be mad at me.

EDDIE. Listen, if everybody keeps his mouth shut, nothin' can happen. They'll pay for their board.

BEATRICE. Oh, I told them.

EDDIE. Then what the hell. [*Pauses. He moves.*] It's an honor, B. I mean it. I was just thinkin' before, comin' home, suppose my father didn't come to this country, and I was starvin' like them over there . . . and I had people in America could keep me a couple of months? The man would be honored to lend me a place to sleep.

BEATRICE. [*There are tears in her eyes. She turns to* CATHERINE.] You see what he is? [*She turns and grabs* EDDIE's *face in her hands.*] Mmm! You're an angel! God'll bless you. [*He is gratefully smiling.*] You'll see, you'll get a blessing for this!

EDDIE. [*Laughing.*] I'll settle for my own bed.

BEATRICE. Go, Baby, set the table.

CATHERINE. We didn't tell him about me yet.

BEATRICE. Let him eat first, then we'll tell him. Bring everything in. [*She hurries* CATHERINE *out.*]

EDDIE. [*Sitting at the table.*] What's all that about? Where's she goin'?

BEATRICE. Noplace. It's very good news, Eddie. I want you to be happy.

EDDIE. What's goin' on?

[CATHERINE *enters with plates, forks.*]

BEATRICE. She's got a job. [*Pause.* EDDIE *looks at* CATHERINE, *then back to* BEATRICE.]

EDDIE. What job? She's gonna finish school.

CATHERINE. Eddie, you won't believe it—

EDDIE. No—no, you gonna finish school. What kinda job, what do you mean? All of a sudden you—

CATHERINE. Listen a minute, it's wonderful.

EDDIE. It's not wonderful. You'll never get nowheres unless you finish school. You can't take no job. Why didn't you ask me before you take a job?

BEATRICE. She's askin' you now, she didn't take nothin' yet.

CATHERINE. Listen a minute! I came to school this morning and the principal called me out of the class, see? To go to his office.

EDDIE. Yeah?

CATHERINE. So I went in and he says to me he's got my records, y'know? And there's a company wants a girl right away. It ain't exactly a secretary, it's a stenographer first, but pretty soon you get to be secretary. And he says to me that I'm the best student in the whole class—

BEATRICE. You hear that?

EDDIE. Well why not? Sure she's the best.

CATHERINE. I'm the best student, he says, and if I want, I should take the job and the end of the year he'll let me take the examination and he'll give me the certificate. So I'll save practically a year!

EDDIE. [*Strangely nervous.*] Where's the job? What company?

CATHERINE. It's a big plumbing company over Nostrand Avenue.

EDDIE. Nostrand Avenue and where?

CATHERINE. It's someplace by the Navy Yard.

BEATRICE. Fifty dollars a week, Eddie.

EDDIE. [*To* CATHERINE, *surprised.*] Fifty?

CATHERINE. I swear.

[*Pause.*]

EDDIE. What about all the stuff you wouldn't learn this year, though?

CATHERINE. There's nothin' more to learn, Eddie, I just gotta practice from now on. I know all the symbols and I know the keyboard. I'll just get faster, that's all. And when I'm workin' I'll keep gettin' better and better, you see?

BEATRICE. Work is the best practice anyway.

EDDIE. That ain't what I wanted, though.

CATHERINE. Why! It's a great big company—

EDDIE. I don't like that neighborhood over there.

CATHERINE. It's a block and half from the subway, he says.

EDDIE. Near the Navy Yard plenty can happen in a block and a half. And a plumbin' company! That's one step over the water front. They're practically longshoremen.

BEATRICE. Yeah, but she'll be in the office, Eddie.

EDDIE. I know she'll be in the office, but that ain't what I had in mind.

BEATRICE. Listen, she's gotta go to work sometime.

EDDIE. Listen, B., she'll be with a lotta plumbers? And sailors up and down the street? So what did she go to school for?

CATHERINE. But it's fifty a week, Eddie.

EDDIE. Look, did I ask you for money? I supported you this long I support you a little more. Please, do me a favor, will ya? I want you to be with different kind of people. I want you to be in a nice office. Maybe a lawyer's office someplace in New York in one of them nice buildings. I mean if you're gonna get outa here then get out; don't go practically in the same kind of neighborhood.

[*Pause.* CATHERINE *lowers her eyes.*]

BEATRICE. Go, Baby, bring in the supper. [CATHERINE *goes out.*] Think about it a little bit, Eddie. Please. She's crazy to start work. It's not a little shop, it's a big company. Some day she could be a secretary. They picked her out of the whole class. [*He is silent, staring down at the tablecloth, fingering the pattern.*] What are you worried about? She could take care of herself. She'll get out of the subway and be in the office in two minutes.

EDDIE. [*Somehow sickened.*] I know that neighborhood, B., I don't like it.

BEATRICE. Listen, if nothin' happened to her in this neighborhood it ain't gonna happen noplace else. [*She turns his face to her.*] Look, you gotta get used to it, she's no baby no more. Tell her to take it. [*He turns his head away.*] You hear me? [*She is angering.*] I don't understand you; she's seventeen years old, you gonna keep her in the house all her life?

EDDIE. [*Insulted.*] What kinda remark is that?

BEATRICE. [*With sympathy but insistent force.*] Well, I don't understand when it ends. First it was gonna be when she graduated high school, so she graduated high school. Then it was gonna be when she learned stenographer, so she learned stenographer. So what're we gonna wait for now? I mean it, Eddie, sometimes I don't understand you; they picked her out of the whole class, it's an honor for her.

[CATHERINE *enters with food, which she silently sets on the table. After a moment of watching her face,* EDDIE *breaks into a smile, but it almost seems that tears will form in his eyes.*]

EDDIE. With your hair that way you look like a madonna, you know that? You're the madonna type. [*She doesn't look at him but continues ladling out food onto the plates.*] You wanna go to work, heh, Madonna?

CATHERINE. [*Softly.*] Yeah.

EDDIE. [*With a sense of her childhood, her babyhood, and the years.*] All right, go to work. [*She looks at him, then rushes and hugs him.*] Hey, hey! Take it easy! [*He holds her face away from him to look at her.*] What're you cryin' about? [*He is affected by her, but smiles his emotion away.*]

CATHERINE. [*Sitting at her place.*] I just— [*Bursting out.*] I'm gonna buy all new dishes with my first pay! [*They laugh warmly.*] I mean it. I'll fix up the whole house! I'll buy a rug!

EDDIE. And then you'll move away.

CATHERINE. No, Eddie!

EDDIE. [*Grinning.*] Why not? That's life. And you'll come visit on Sundays, then once a month, then Christmas and New Year's, finally.

CATHERINE. [*Grasping his arm to reassure him and to erase the accusation.*] No, please!

EDDIE. [*Smiling but hurt.*] I only ask you one thing—don't trust nobody. You got a good aunt but she's got too big a heart, you learned bad from her. Believe me.

BEATRICE. Be the way you are, Katie, don't listen to him.

EDDIE. [*To* BEATRICE—*strangely and quickly resentful.*] You lived in a house all your life, what do you know about it? You never worked in your life.

BEATRICE. She likes people. What's wrong with that?

EDDIE. Because most people ain't people. She's goin' to work; plumbers; they'll chew her to pieces if she don't watch out. [*To* CATHERINE.] Believe me, Katie, the less you trust, the less you be sorry.

[EDDIE *crosses himself and the women do the same, and they eat.*]

CATHERINE. First thing I'll buy is a rug, heh, B.?

BEATRICE. I don't mind. [*To* EDDIE.] I smelled coffee all day today. You unloadin' coffee today?

EDDIE. Yeah, a Brazil ship.

CATHERINE. I smelled it too. It smelled all over the neighborhood.

EDDIE. That's one time, boy, to be a longshoreman is a pleasure. I could work coffee ships twenty hours a day. You go down in the hold, y'know? It's like flowers, that smell. We'll bust a bag tomorrow, I'll bring you some.

BEATRICE. Just be sure there's no spiders in it, will ya? I mean it. [*She directs this to* CATHERINE, *rolling her eyes upward.*] I still remember that spider coming out of that bag he brung home. I nearly died.

EDDIE. You call that a spider? You oughta see what comes outa the bananas sometimes.

BEATRICE. Don't talk about it!

EDDIE. I see spiders could stop a Buick.

BEATRICE. [*Clapping her hands over her ears.*] All right, shut up!

EDDIE. [*Laughing and taking a watch out of his pocket.*] Well, who started with spiders?

BEATRICE. All right, I'm sorry, I didn't mean it. Just don't bring none home again. What time is it?

EDDIE. Quarter nine. [*Puts watch back in his pocket.*]

[*They continue eating in silence.*]

CATHERINE. He's bringin' them ten o'clock, Tony?

EDDIE. Around, yeah. [*He eats.*]

CATHERINE. Eddie, suppose somebody asks if they're livin' here. [*He looks at her as though already she had divulged something publicly. Defensively.*] I mean if they ask.

EDDIE. Now look, Baby, I can see we're gettin' mixed up again here.

CATHERINE. No, I just mean . . . people'll see them goin' in and out.

EDDIE. I don't care who sees them goin' in and out as long as you don't see them goin' in and out. And this goes for you too, B. You don't see nothin' and you don't know nothin'.

BEATRICE. What do you mean? I understand.

EDDIE. You don't understand; you still think you can talk about this to somebody just a little bit. Now lemme say it once and for all, because you're makin' me nervous again, both of you. I don't care if somebody comes in the house and sees them sleepin' on the floor, it never comes out of your mouth who they are or what they're doin' here.

BEATRICE. Yeah, but my mother'll know—

EDDIE. Sure she'll know, but just don't you be the one who told her, that's all. This is the United States government you're playin' with now, this is the Immigration Bureau. If you said it you knew it, if you didn't say it you didn't know it.

CATHERINE. Yeah, but Eddie, suppose somebody—

EDDIE. I don't care what question it is. You—don't—know—nothin'. They got stool pigeons all over this neighborhood they're payin' them every week for information, and you don't know who they are. It could be your best friend. You hear? [*To* BEATRICE.] Like Vinny Bolzano, remember Vinny?

BEATRICE. Oh, yeah. God forbid.

EDDIE. Tell her about Vinny. [*To* CATHERINE.] You think I'm blowin' steam here? [*To* BEATRICE.] Go ahead, tell her. [*To* CATHERINE.] You was a baby then. There was a family lived next door to her mother, he was about sixteen—

BEATRICE. No, he was no more than fourteen, cause I was to his confirmation in Saint Agnes. But the family had a uncle that they were hidin' in the house, and he snitched to the Immigration.

CATHERINE. The kid snitched?

EDDIE. On his own uncle!

CATHERINE. What, was he crazy?

EDDIE. He was crazy after, I tell you that, boy.

BEATRICE. Oh, it was terrible. He had five brothers and the old father. And they grabbed him in the kitchen and pulled him down the stairs—three flights his head was bouncin' like a coconut. And they spit on him in the street, his own father and his brothers. The whole neighborhood was cryin'.

CATHERINE. Ts! So what happened to him?

BEATRICE. I think he went away. [*To* EDDIE.] I never seen him again, did you?

EDDIE. [*Rises during this, taking out his watch.*] Him? You'll never see him no more, a guy do a thing like that? How's he gonna show his face? [*To* CATHERINE, *as he gets up uneasily.*] Just remember, kid, you can quicker get back a million dollars that was stole than a word that you gave away. [*He is standing now, stretching his back.*]

CATHERINE. Okay, I won't say a word to nobody, I swear.

EDDIE. Gonna rain tomorrow. We'll be slidin' all over the decks. Maybe you oughta put something on for them, they be here soon.

BEATRICE. I only got fish, I hate to spoil it if they ate already. I'll wait, it only takes a few minutes; I could broil it.

CATHERINE. What happens, Eddie, when that ship pulls out and they ain't on it, though? Don't the captain say nothin'?

EDDIE. [*Slicing an apple with his pocket knife.*] Captain's pieced off, what do you mean?

CATHERINE. Even the captain?

EDDIE. What's the matter, the captain don't have to live? Captain gets a piece, maybe one of the mates, piece for the guy in Italy who fixed the papers for them, Tony here'll get a little bite. . . .

BEATRICE. I just hope they get work here, that's all I hope.

EDDIE. Oh, the syndicate'll fix jobs for them; till they pay 'em off they'll get them work every day. It's after the pay-off, then they'll have to scramble like the rest of us.

BEATRICE. Well, it be better than they got there.

EDDIE. Oh sure, well, listen. So you gonna start Monday, heh, Madonna?

CATHERINE. [*Embarrassed.*] I'm supposed to, yeah.

[EDDIE *is standing facing the two seated women. First* BEATRICE *smiles, then* CATHERINE, *for a powerful emotion is on him, a childish one and a knowing fear, and the tears show in his eyes—and they are shy before the avowal.*]

EDDIE. [*Sadly smiling, yet somehow proud of her.*] Well . . . I hope you have good luck. I wish you the best. You know that, kid.

CATHERINE. [*Rising, trying to laugh.*] You sound like I'm goin' a million miles!

EDDIE. I know: I guess I just never figured on one thing.

CATHERINE. [*Smiling.*] What?

EDDIE. That you would ever grow up. [*He utters a soundless laugh at himself, feeling his breast pocket of his shirt.*] I left a cigar in my other coat, I think. [*He starts for the bedroom.*]

CATHERINE. Stay there! I'll get it for you.

[*She hurries out. There is a slight pause, and* EDDIE *turns to* BEATRICE, *who has been avoiding his gaze.*]

EDDIE. What are you mad at me lately?

BEATRICE. Who's mad. [*She gets up, clearing the dishes.*] I'm not mad. [*She picks up the dishes and turns to him.*] You're the one is mad. [*She turns and goes into the kitchen as* CATHERINE *enters from the bedroom with a cigar and a pack of matches.*]

CATHERINE. Here! I'll light it for you! [*She strikes a match and holds it to his cigar.*

He puffs. Quietly.] Don't worry about me, Eddie, heh?

EDDIE. Don't burn yourself. [*Just in time she blows out the match.*] You better go in help her with the dishes.

CATHERINE. [*Turns quickly to the table, and, seeing the table cleared, she says, almost guiltily.* Oh! [*She hurries into the kitchen, and as she exits there.*] I'll do the dishes, B.!

[*Alone,* EDDIE *stands looking toward the kitchen for a moment. Then he takes out watch, glances at it, replaces it in his pocket, sits in the armchair, and stares at the smoke flowing out of his mouth.*

The lights go down, then come up on ALFIERI, *who has moved onto the forestage.*]

ALFIERI. He was as good a man as he had to be in a life that was hard and even. He worked on the piers when there was work, he brought home his pay, and he lived. And toward ten o'clock of that night, after they had eaten, the cousins came.

[*The lights fade on* ALFIERI *and rise on the street.*

Enter TONY, *escorting* MARCO *and* RODOLPHO, *each with a valise.* TONY *halts, indicates the house. They stand for a moment looking at it.*]

MARCO. [*He is a square-built peasant of thirty-two, suspicious, tender, and quiet-voiced.*] Thank you.

TONY. You're on your own now. Just be careful, that's all. Ground floor.

MARCO. Thank you.

TONY. [*Indicating the house.*] I'll see you on the pier tomorrow. You'll go to work.

[MARCO *nods.* TONY *continues on walking down the street.*]

RODOLPHO. This will be the first house I ever walked into in America! Imagine! She said they were poor!

MARCO. Ssh! Come. [*They go to door.*]

[MARCO *knocks. The lights rise in the room.* EDDIE *goes and opens the door. Enter* MARCO *and* RODOLPHO, *removing their caps.* BEATRICE *and* CATHERINE *enter from the kitchen. The lights fade in the street.*]

EDDIE. You Marco?

MARCO. Marco.

EDDIE. Come on in! [*He shakes* MARCO'S *hand.*]

BEATRICE. Here, take the bags!

MARCO. [*Nods, looks to the women and fixes on* BEATRICE. *Crosses to* BEATRICE.] Are you my cousin?

[*She nods. He kisses her hand.*]

BEATRICE. [*Above the table, touching her chest with her hand.*] Beatrice. This is my husband, Eddie. [*All nod.*] Catherine, my sister Nancy's daughter. [*The brothers nod.*]

MARCO. [*Indicating* RODOLPHO.] My brother. Rodolpho. [RODOLPHO *nods.* MARCO *comes with a certain formal stiffness to* EDDIE.] I want to tell you now Eddie—when you say go, we will go.

EDDIE. Oh, no . . . [*Takes* MARCO'S *bag.*]

MARCO. I see it's a small house, but soon, maybe, we can have our own house.

EDDIE. You're welcome, Marco, we got plenty of room here. Katie, give them supper, heh? [*Exits into bedroom with their bags.*]

CATHERINE. Come here, sit down. I'll get you some soup.

MARCO. [*As they go to the table.*] We ate on the ship. Thank you. [*To* EDDIE, *calling off to bedroom.*] Thank you.

BEATRICE. Get some coffee. We'll all have coffee. Come sit down.

[RODOLPHO *and* MARCO *sit, at the table.*]

CATHERINE. [*Wondrously.*] How come he's so dark and you're so light, Rodolpho?

RODOLPHO. [*Ready to laugh.*] I don't know. A thousand years ago, they say, the Danes invaded Sicily.

[BEATRICE *kisses* RODOLPHO. *They laugh as* EDDIE *enters.*]

CATHERINE. [*To* BEATRICE.] He's practically blond!

EDDIE. How's the coffee doin'?

CATHERINE. [*Brought up.*] I'm gettin' it. [*She hurries out to kitchen.*]

EDDIE. [*Sits on his rocker.*] Yiz have a nice trip?

MARCO. The ocean is always rough. But we are good sailors.

EDDIE. No trouble gettin' here?

MARCO. No. The man brought us. Very nice man.

RODOLPHO. [*To* EDDIE.] He says we start to work tomorrow. Is he honest?

EDDIE. [*Laughing.*] No. But as long as you owe them money, they'll get you plenty of work. [*To* MARCO.] Yiz ever work on the piers in Italy?

MARCO. Piers? Ts!—no.

RODOLPHO. [*Smiling at the smallness of his town.*] In our town there are no piers, only the beach, and little fishing boats.

BEATRICE. So what kinda work did yiz do?

MARCO. [*Shrugging shyly, even embarrassed.*] Whatever there is, anything.

RODOLPHO. Sometimes they build a house, or if they fix the bridge—Marco is a mason and I bring him the cement. [*He laughs.*] In harvest time we work in the fields . . . if there is work. Anything.

EDDIE. Still bad there, heh?

MARCO. Bad, yes.

RODOLPHO. [*Laughing.*] It's terrible! We stand around all day in the piazza listening to the fountain like birds. Everybody waits only for the train.

BEATRICE. What's on the train?

RODOLPHO. Nothing. But if there are many passengers and you're lucky you make a few lire to push the taxi up the hill.

[*Enter* CATHERINE; *she listens.*]

BEATRICE. You gotta push a taxi?

RODOLPHO. [*Laughing.*] Oh, sure! It's a feature in our town. The horses in our town are skinnier than goats. So if there are too many passengers we help to push the carriages up to the hotel. [*He laughs.*] In our town the horses are only for show.

CATHERINE. Why don't they have automobile taxis?

RODOLPHO. There is one. We push that too. [*They laugh*]. Everything in our town, you gotta push!

BEATRICE. [*To* EDDIE.] How do you like that!

EDDIE. [*To* MARCO.] So what're you wanna do, you gonna stay here in this country or you wanna go back?

MARCO. [*Surprised.*] Go back?

EDDIE. Well, you're married, ain't you?

MARCO. Yes. I have three children.

BEATRICE. Three! I thought only one.

MARCO. Oh, no. I have three now. Four years, five years, six years.

BEATRICE. Ah . . . I bet they're cryin' for you already, heh?

MARCO. What can I do? The older one is sick in his chest. My wife—she feeds them from her own mouth. I tell you the truth, if I stay there they will never grow up. They eat the sunshine.

BEATRICE. My God. So how long you want to stay?

MARCO. With your permission, we will stay maybe a—

EDDIE. She don't mean in this house, she means in the country.

MARCO. Oh. Maybe four, five, six years, I think.

RODOLPHO. [*Smiling.*] He trusts his wife.

BEATRICE. Yeah, but maybe you'll get enough, you'll be able to go back quicker.

MARCO. I hope. I don't know. [*To* EDDIE.] I understand it's not so good here either.

EDDIE. Oh, you guys'll be all right—till you pay them off, anyway. After that, you'll have to scramble, that's all. But you'll make better here than you could there.

RODOLPHO. How much? We hear all kinds of figures. How much can a man make? We work hard, we'll work all day, all night—

[MARCO *raises a hand to hush him.*]

EDDIE. [*He is coming more and more to address* MARCO *only.*] On the average a whole year? Maybe—well, it's hard to say, see. Sometimes we lay off, there's no ships three four weeks.

MARCO. Three, four weeks!—Ts!

EDDIE. But I think you could probably—thirty, forty a week, over the whole twelve months of the year.

MARCO. [*Rises, crosses to* EDDIE.] Dollars.

EDDIE. Sure dollars.

[MARCO *puts an arm round* RODOLPHO *and they laugh.*]

MARCO. If we can stay here a few months, Beatrice—

BEATRICE. Listen, you're welcome, Marco—

MARCO. Because I could send them a little more if I stay here.

BEATRICE. As long as you want, we got plenty a room.

MARCO. [*His eyes showing tears.*] My wife— [*To* EDDIE.] My wife—I want to send right away maybe twenty dollars—

EDDIE. You could send them something next week already.

MARCO. [*He is near tears.*] Eduardo . . . [*He goes to* EDDIE, *offering his hand.*]

EDDIE. Don't thank me. Listen, what the hell, it's no skin off me. [*To* CATHERINE.] What happened to the coffee?

CATHERINE. I got it on. [*To* RODOLPHO.] You married too? No.

RODOLPHO. [*Rises.*] Oh, no . . .

BEATRICE. [*To* CATHERINE.] I told you he—

CATHERINE. I know, I just thought maybe he got married recently.

RODOLPHO. I have no money to get married. I have a nice face, but no money. [*He laughs.*]

CATHERINE. [*To* BEATRICE.] He's a real blond!

BEATRICE. [*To* RODOLPHO.] You want to stay here too, heh? For good?

RODOLPHO. Me? Yes, forever! Me, I want to be an American. And then I want to go back to Italy when I am rich, and I will buy a motorcycle. [*He smiles.* MARCO *shakes him affectionately.*]

CATHERINE. A motorcycle!

RODOLPHO. With a motorcycle in Italy you will never starve any more.

BEATRICE. I'll get you coffee. [*She exits to the kitchen.*]

EDDIE. What you do with a motorcycle?

MARCO. He dreams, he dreams.

RODOLPHO. [*To* MARCO.] Why? [*To* EDDIE.] Messages! The rich people in the hotel always need someone who will carry a message. But quickly, and with a great noise. With a blue motorcycle I would station myself in the courtyard of the hotel, and in a little while I would have messages.

MARCO. When you have no wife you have dreams.

EDDIE. Why can't you just walk, or take a trolley or sump'm?

[*Enter* BEATRICE *with coffee.*]

RODOLPHO. Oh, no, the machine, the machine is necessary. A man comes into a great hotel and says, I am a messenger. Who is this man? He disappears walking, there is no noise, nothing. Maybe he will never come back, maybe he will never deliver the message. But a man who rides up on a great machine, this man is responsible, this man exists. He will be given messages. [*He helps* BEATRICE *set out the coffee things.*] I am also a singer, though.

EDDIE. You mean a regular—?

RODOLPHO: Oh, yes. One night last year Andreola got sick. Baritone. And I took his place in the garden of the hotel. Three arias I sang without a mistake! Thousand-lire notes they threw from the tables, money was falling like a storm in the treasury. It was magnificent. We lived six months on that night, eh, Marco?

[MARCO *nods doubtfully.*]

MARCO. Two months.

[EDDIE *laughs.*]

BEATRICE. Can't you get a job in that place?

RODOLPHO. Andreola got better. He's a baritone, very strong.

[BEATRICE *laughs.*]

MARCO. [*Regretfully, to* BEATRICE.] He sang too loud.

RODOLPHO. Why too loud?

MARCO. Too loud. The guests in that hotel are all Englishmen. They don't like too loud.

RODOLPHO. [*To* CATHERINE.] Nobody ever said it was too loud!

MARCO. I say. It was too loud. [*To* BEATRICE.] I knew it as soon as he started to sing. Too loud.

RODOLPHO. Then why did they throw so much money?

MARCO. They paid for your courage. The English like courage. But once is enough.

RODOLPHO. [*To all but* MARCO.] I never heard anybody say it was too loud.

CATHERINE. Did you ever hear of jazz?

RODOLPHO. Oh, sure! I *sing* jazz.

CATHERINE. [*Rises.*] You could sing jazz?

RODOLPHO. Oh, I sing Napolidan, jazz, bel canto—I sing "Paper Doll," you like "Paper Doll"?

CATHERINE. Oh, sure, I'm crazy for "Paper Doll." Go ahead, sing it.

RODOLPHO. [*Takes his stance after getting a nod of permission from* MARCO, *and with a high tenor voice begins singing.*]

I'll tell you boys it's tough to be alone,
And it's tough to love a doll that's not your own.
I'm through with all of them,
I'll never fall again,
Hey, boy, what you gonna do?
I'm gonna buy a paper doll that I can call my own,
A doll that other fellows cannot steal.

[EDDIE *rises and moves upstage.*]

And then those flirty, flirty guys
With their flirty, flirty eyes
Will have to flirt with dollies that are real—

EDDIE. Hey, kid—hey, wait a minute—

CATHERINE. [*Enthralled.*] Leave him finish, it's beautiful! [*To* BEATRICE.] He's terrific! It's terrific, Rodolpho.

EDDIE. Look, kid; you don't want to be picked up, do ya?

MARCO. No—no! [*He rises.*]

EDDIE. [*Indicating the rest of the building.*] Because we never had no singers here . . . and all of a sudden there's a singer in the house, y'know what I mean?

MARCO. Yes, yes. You'll be quiet, Rodolpho.

EDDIE. [*He is flushed.*] They got guys all over the place, Marco. I mean.

MARCO. Yes. He'll be quiet. [*To* RODOLPHO.] You'll be quiet.

[RODOLPHO *nods.* EDDIE *has risen, with iron control, even a smile. He moves to* CATHERINE.]

EDDIE. What's the high heels for, Garbo?

CATHERINE. I figured for tonight—

EDDIE. Do me a favor, will you? Go ahead.

[*Embarrassed now, angered,* CATHERINE *goes out into the bedroom.* BEATRICE *watches her go and gets up; in passing, she gives* EDDIE *a cold look, restrained only by the strangers, and goes to the table to pour coffee.*]

EDDIE. [*Striving to laugh, and to* MARCO, *but directed as much to* BEATRICE.] All actresses they want to be around here.

RODOLPHO. [*Happy about it.*] In Italy too! All the girls.

[CATHERINE *emerges from the bedroom in low-heel shoes, comes to the table.* RODOLPHO *is lifting a cup.*]

EDDIE. [*He is sizing up* RODOLPHO, *and there is a concealed suspicion.*] Yeah, heh?

RODOLPHO. Yes! [*Laughs, indicating* CATHERINE.] Especially when they are so beautiful!

CATHERINE. You like sugar?

RODOLPHO. Sugar? Yes! I like sugar very much!

[EDDIE *is downstage, watching as she pours a spoonful of sugar into his cup, his face puffed with trouble, and the room dies.*]

[*Lights rise on* ALFIERI.]

ALFIERI. Who can ever know what will be discovered? Eddie Carbone had never expected to have a destiny. A man works, raises his family, goes bowling, eats, gets old, and then he dies. Now, as the weeks passed, there was a future, there was a trouble that would not go away.

[*The lights fade on* ALFIERI, *then rise on* EDDIE *standing at the doorway of the house.* BEATRICE *enters on the street. She sees* EDDIE, *smiles at him. He looks away. She starts to enter the house when* EDDIE *speaks.*]

EDDIE. It's after eight.

BEATRICE. Well, it's a long show at the Paramount.

EDDIE. They must've seen every picture in Brooklyn by now. He's supposed to stay in the house when he ain't working. He ain't supposed to go advertising himself.

BEATRICE. Well that's his trouble, what do you care? If they pick him up they pick him up, that's all. Come in the house.

EDDIE. What happened to the stenography? I don't see her practice no more.

BEATRICE. She'll get back to it. She's excited, Eddie.

EDDIE. She tell you anything?

BEATRICE. [*Comes to him, now the subject is opened.*] What's the matter with you? He's nice kid, what do you want from him?

EDDIE. That's a nice kid? He gives me the heeby-jeebies.

BEATRICE. [*Smiling.*] Ah, go on, you're just jealous.

EDDIE. Of *him?* Boy, you don't think much of me.

BEATRICE. I don't understand you. What's so terrible about him?

EDDIE. You mean it's all right with you? That's gonna be her husband?

BEATRICE. Why? He's a nice fella, hard workin', he's a good-lookin' fella.

EDDIE. He sings on the ships, didja know that?

BEATRICE. What do you mean, he sings?

EDDIE. Just what I said, he sings. Right on the deck, all of a sudden, a whole song comes out of his mouth—with motions. You know what they're callin' him now? Paper Doll they're callin' him, Canary. He's like a weird. He comes out on the pier, one-two-three, it's a regular free show.

BEATRICE. Well, he's a kid; he don't know how to behave himself yet.

EDDIE. And with that wacky hair; he's like a chorus girl or sump'm.

BEATRICE. So he's blond, so—

EDDIE. I just hope that's his regular hair, that's all I hope.

BEATRICE. You crazy or sump'm? [*She tries to turn him to her.*]

EDDIE. [*He keeps his head turned away.*] What's so crazy? I don't like his whole way.

BEATRICE. Listen, you never seen a blond guy in your life? What about Whitey Balso?

EDDIE. [*Turning to her victoriously.*] Sure, but Whitey don't sing; he don't do like that on the ships.

BEATRICE. Well, maybe that's the way they do in Italy.

EDDIE. Then why don't his brother sing? Marco goes around like a man; nobody kids Marco. [*He moves from her, halts. She realizes there is a campaign solidified in him.*] I tell you the truth I'm surprised I have to tell you all this. I mean I'm surprised, B.

BEATRICE. [*She goes to him with purpose now.*] Listen, you ain't gonna start nothin' here.

EDDIE. I ain't startin' nothin', but I ain't gonna stand around lookin' at that. For that character I didn't bring her up. I swear, B., I'm surprised at you; I sit there waitin' for you to wake up but everything is great with you.

BEATRICE. No, everything ain't great with me.

EDDIE. No?

BEATRICE. No. I got other worries.

EDDIE. Yeah. [*He is already weakening.*]

BEATRICE. Yeah, you want me to tell you?

EDDIE. [*In retreat.*] Why? What worries you got?

BEATRICE. When am I gonna be a wife again, Eddie?

EDDIE. I ain't been feelin' good. They bother me since they came.

BEATRICE. It's almost three months you don't feel good; they're only here a couple of weeks. It's three months, Eddie.

EDDIE. I don't know, B. I don't want to talk about it.

BEATRICE. What's the matter, Eddie, you don't like me, heh?

EDDIE. What do you mean, I don't like you? I said I don't feel good, that's all.

BEATRICE. Well, tell me, am I doing something wrong? Talk to me.

EDDIE. [*Pause. He can't speak, then.*] I can't. I can't talk about it.

BEATRICE. Well tell me what—

EDDIE. I got nothin' to say about it!

[*She stands for a moment; he is looking off; she turns to go into the house.*]

EDDIE. I'll be all right, B.; just lay off me, will ya? I'm worried about her.

BEATRICE. The girl is gonna be eighteen years old, it's time already.

EDDIE. B., he's taking her for a ride!

BEATRICE. All right, that's her ride. What're you gonna stand over her till she's forty? Eddie, I want you to cut it out now, you hear me? I don't like it! Now come in the house.

EDDIE. I want to take a walk, I'll be in right away.

BEATRICE. They ain't goin' to come any quicker if you stand in the street. It ain't nice, Eddie.

EDDIE. I'll be in right away. Go ahead. [*He walks off.*]

[*She goes into the house.* EDDIE *glances up the street, sees* LOUIS *and* MIKE *coming, and sits on an iron railing.* LOUIS *and* MIKE *enter.*]

LOUIS. Wanna go bowlin' tonight?

EDDIE. I'm too tired. Goin' to sleep.

LOUIS. How's your two submarines?

EDDIE. They're okay.

LOUIS. I see they're gettin' work allatime.

EDDIE. Oh yeah, they're doin' all right.

MIKE. That's what we oughta do. We oughta leave the country and come in under the water. Then we get work.

EDDIE. You ain't kiddin'.

LOUIS. Well, what the hell. Y'know?

EDDIE. Sure.

LOUIS. [*Sits on railing beside* EDDIE.] Believe me, Eddie, you got a lotta credit comin' to you.

EDDIE. Aah, they don't bother me, don't cost me nutt'n.

MIKE. That older one, boy, he's a regular bull. I seen him the other day liftin' coffee bags over the Matson Line. They leave him alone he woulda load the whole ship by himself.

EDDIE. Yeah, he's strong guy, that guy. Their father was a regular giant, supposed to be.

LOUIS. Yeah, you could see. He's a regular slave.

MIKE. [*Grinning.*] That blond one, though— [EDDIE *looks at him.*] He's got a sense of humor. [LOUIS *snickers.*]

EDDIE. [*Searchingly.*] Yeah. He's funny—

MIKE. [*Starting to laugh.*] Well he ain't exackly funny, but he's always like makin' remarks like, y'know? He comes around, everybody's laughin'. [LOUIS *laughs.*]

EDDIE. [*Uncomfortably, grinning.*] Yeah, well ... he's got a sense of humor.

MIKE. [*Laughing.*] Yeah, I mean, he's always makin' like remarks, like, y'know?

EDDIE. Yeah, I know. But he's a kid yet, y'know? He—he's just a kid, that's all.

MIKE. [*Getting hysterical with* LOUIS.] I know. You take one look at him—everybody's happy. [LOUIS *laughs.*] I worked one day with him last week over the Moore-MacCormack Line, I'm tellin' you they

was all hysterical. [LOUIS *and he explode in laughter.*]

EDDIE. Why? What'd he do?

MIKE. I don't know ... he was just humorous. You never can remember what he says, y'know? But it's the way he says it. I mean he gives you a look sometimes and you start laughin'!

EDDIE. Yeah. [*Troubled.*] He's got a sense of humor.

MIKE. [*Gasping.*] Yeah.

LOUIS. [*Rising.*] Well, we see ya, Eddie.

EDDIE. Take it easy.

LOUIS. Yeah. See ya.

MIKE. If you wanna come bowlin' later we're goin' Flatbush Avenue.

[*Laughing, they move to exit, meeting* RODOLPHO *and* CATHERINE *entering on the street. Their laughter rises as they see.* RODOLPHO, *who does not understand but joins in.* EDDIE *moves to enter the house as* LOUIS *and* MIKE *exit.* CATHERINE *stops him at the door.*]

CATHERINE. Hey, Eddie—what a picture we saw! Did we laugh!

EDDIE. [*He can't help smiling at sight of her.*] Where'd you go?

CATHERINE. Paramount. It was with those two guys, y'know? That—

EDDIE. Brooklyn Paramount?

CATHERINE. [*With an edge of anger, embarrassed before* RODOLPHO.] Sure, the Brooklyn Paramount. I told you we wasn't goin' to New York.

EDDIE. [*Retreating before the threat of her anger.*] All right, I only asked you. [*To* RODOLPHO.] I just don't want her hangin' around Times Square, see? It's full of tramps over there.

RODOLPHO. I would like to go to Broadway once, Eddie. I would like to walk with her once where the theaters are and the opera. Since I was a boy I see pictures of those lights.

EDDIE. [*His little patience waning.*] I want to talk to her a minute, Rodolpho. Go inside, will you?

RODOLPHO. Eddie, we only walk together in the streets. She teaches me.

CATHERINE. You know what he can't get over? That there's no fountains in Brooklyn!

EDDIE. [*Smiling unwillingly.*] Fountains? [RODOLPHO *smiles at his own naïveté.*]

CATHERINE. In Italy he says, every town's got fountains, and they meet there. And you know what? They got oranges on the trees where he comes from, and lemons. Imagine—on the trees? I mean it's interesting. But he's crazy for New York.

RODOLPHO. [*Attempting familiarity.*] Eddie, why can't we go once to Broadway—?

EDDIE. Look, I gotta tell her something—

RODOLPHO. Maybe you can come too. I want to see all those lights. [*He sees no response in* EDDIE's *face. He glances at* CATHERINE.] I'll walk by the river before I go to sleep. [*He walks off down the street.*]

CATHERINE. Why don't you talk to him, Eddie? He blesses you, and you don't talk to him hardly.

EDDIE. [*Enveloping her with his eyes.*] I bless you and you don't talk to me. [*He tries to smile.*]

CATHERINE. *I* don't talk to you? [*She hits his arm.*] What do you mean?

EDDIE. I don't see you no more. I come home you're runnin' around someplace—

CATHERINE. Well, he wants to see everything, that's all, so we go. . . . You mad at me?

EDDIE. No. [*He moves from her, smiling sadly.*] It's just I used to come home, you was always there. Now, I turn around, you're a big girl. I don't know how to talk to you.

CATHERINE. Why?

EDDIE. I don't know, you're runnin', you're runnin', Katie. I don't think you listening any more to me.

CATHERINE. [*Going to him.*] Ah, Eddie, sure I am. What's the matter? You don't like him?

[*Slight pause.*]

EDDIE. [*Turns to her.*] *You* like him, Katie?

CATHERINE. [*With a blush but holding her ground.*] Yeah. I like him.

EDDIE. —[*His smile goes.*] You like him.

CATHERINE. [*Looking down.*] Yeah. [*Now she looks at him for the consequences, smiling but tense. He looks at her like a lost boy.*] What're you got against him? I don't understand. He only blesses you.

EDDIE. [*Turns away.*] He don't bless me, Katie.

CATHERINE. He does! You're like a father to him!

EDDIE. [*Turns to her.*] Katie.

CATHERINE. What, Eddie?

EDDIE. You gonna marry him?

CATHERINE. I don't know. We just been . . . goin' around, that's all. [*Turns to him.*] What're you got against him, Eddie? Please, tell me. What?

EDDIE. He don't respect you.

CATHERINE. Why?

EDDIE. Katie . . . if you wasn't an orphan, wouldn't he ask your father's permission before he run around with you like this?

CATHERINE. Oh, well, he didn't think you'd mind.

EDDIE. He knows I mind, but it don't bother him if I mind, don't you see that?

CATHERINE. No, Eddie, he's got all kinds of respect for me. And you too! We walk across the street he takes my arm—he almost bows to me! You got him all wrong, Eddie; I mean it, you—

EDDIE. Katie, he's only bowin' to his passport.

CATHERINE. His passport!

EDDIE. That's right. He marries you he's got the right to be an American citizen. That's what's goin' on here. [*She is puzzled and surprised.*] You understand what I'm tellin' you? The guy is lookin' for his break, that's all he's lookin' for.

CATHERINE. [*Pained.*] Oh, no, Eddie, I don't think so.

EDDIE. You don't think so! Katie, you're gonna make me cry here. Is that a workin' man? What does he do with his first money? A snappy new jacket he buys, records, a pointy pair new shoes and his brother's kids are starvin' over there with tuberculosis? That's a hit-and-run guy, baby, he's got bright lights in his head, Broadway. Them guys don't think of nobody but theirself! You marry him and the next time you see him it'll be for divorce!

CATHERINE. [*Steps toward him.*] Eddie, he never said a word about his papers or—

EDDIE. You mean he's supposed to tell you that?

CATHERINE. I don't think he's even thinking about it.

EDDIE. What's better for him to think about! He could be picked up any day here and he's back pushin' taxis up the hill!

CATHERINE. No, I don't believe it.

EDDIE. Katie, don't break my heart, listen to me.

CATHERINE. I don't want to hear it.

EDDIE. Katie, listen . . .

CATHERINE. He loves me!

EDDIE. [*With deep alarm.*] Don't say that, for God's sake! This is the oldest racket in the country—

CATHERINE. [*Desperately, as though he had made his imprint.*] I don't believe it! [*She rushes to the house.*]

EDDIE. [*Following her.*] They been pullin' this since the Immigration Law was put in! They grab a green kid that don't know nothin' and they—

CATHERINE. [*Sobbing.*] I don't believe it and I wish to hell you'd stop it!

EDDIE. Katie!

[*They enter the apartment. The lights in the living room have risen and* BEATRICE *is there. She looks past the sobbing* CATHERINE *at* EDDIE, *who in the presence of his wife, makes an awkward gesture of eroded command, indicating* CATHERINE.]

EDDIE. Why don't you straighten her out?

BEATRICE. [*Inwardly angered at his flowing emotion, which in itself alarms her.*] When are you going to leave her alone?

EDDIE. B., the guy is no good!

BEATRICE. [*Suddenly, with open fright and fury.*] You going to leave her alone? Or you gonna drive me crazy? [*He turns, striving to retain his dignity, but nevertheless in guilt walks out of the house, into the street and away.* CATHERINE *starts into a bedroom.*] Listen, Catherine. [CATHERINE *halts, turns to her sheepishly.*] What are you going to do with yourself?

CATHERINE. I don't know.

BEATRICE. Don't tell me you don't know; you're not a baby any more, what are you going to do with yourself?

CATHERINE. He won't listen to me.

BEATRICE. I don't understand this. He's not your father, Catherine. I don't understand what's going on here.

CATHERINE. [*As one who herself is trying to rationalize a buried impulse.*] What am I going to do, just kick him in the face with it?

BEATRICE. Look, honey, you wanna get married, or don't you wanna get married? What are you worried about, Katie?

CATHERINE. [*Quietly, trembling.*] I don't know B. It just seems wrong if he's against it so much.

BEATRICE. [*Never losing her aroused alarm.*] Sit down, honey, I want to tell you something. Here, sit down. Was there ever any fella he liked for you? There wasn't, was there?

CATHERINE. But he says Rodolpho's just after his papers.

BEATRICE. Look, he'll say anything. What does he care what he says? If it was a prince came here for you it would be no different. You know that, don't you?

CATHERINE. Yeah, I guess.

BEATRICE. So what does that mean?

CATHERINE. [*Slowly turns her head to* BEATRICE.] What?

BEATRICE. It means you gotta be your own self more. You still think you're a little girl, honey. But nobody else can make up your mind for you any more, you understand? You gotta give him to understand that he can't give you orders no more.

CATHERINE. Yeah, but how am I going to do that? He thinks I'm a baby.

BEATRICE. Because *you* think you're a baby.

I told you fifty times already, you can't act the way you act. You still walk around in front of him in your slip—

CATHERINE. Well I forgot.

BEATRICE. Well you can't do it. Or like you sit on the edge of the bathtub talkin' to him when he's shavin' in his underwear.

CATHERINE. When'd I do that?

BEATRICE. I seen you in there this morning.

CATHERINE. Oh . . . well, I wanted to tell him something and I—

BEATRICE. I know, honey. But if you act like a baby and he be treatin' you like a baby. Like when he comes home sometimes you throw yourself at him like when you was twelve years old.

CATHERINE. Well I like to see him and I'm happy so I—

BEATRICE. Look, I'm not tellin' you what to do honey, but—

CATHERINE. No, you could tell me, B.! Gee, I'm all mixed up. See, I—He looks so sad now and it hurts me.

BEATRICE. Well look Katie, if it's goin' to hurt you so much you're gonna end up an old maid here.

CATHERINE. No!

BEATRICE. I'm tellin' you, I'm not makin' a joke. I tried to tell you a couple of times in the last year or so. That's why I was so happy you were going to go out and get work, you wouldn't be here so much, you'd be a little more independent. I mean it. It's wonderful for a whole family to love each other, but you're a grown woman and you're in the same house with a grown man. So you'll act different now, heh?

CATHERINE. Yeah, I will. I'll remember.

BEATRICE. Because it ain't only up to him, Katie, you understand? I told him the same thing already.

CATHERINE. [*Quickly.*] What?

BEATRICE. That he should let you go. But, you see, if only I tell him, he thinks I'm just bawlin' him out, or maybe I'm jealous or somethin', you know?

CATHERINE. [*Astonished.*] He said you was jealous?

BEATRICE. No, I'm just sayin' maybe that's what he think. [*She reaches over to* CATHERINE'S *hand; with a strained smile.*] You think I'm jealous of you, honey?

CATHERINE. No! It's the first I thought of it.

BEATRICE. [*With a quiet sad laugh.*] Well you should have thought of it before . . . but I'm not. We'll be all right. Just give him to understand; you don't have to fight, you're just— You're a woman, that's all, and you got a nice boy, and now the time came when you said good-by. All right?

CATHERINE. [*Strangely moved at the prospect.*] All right. . . . If I can.

BEATRICE. Honey . . . you gotta. [CATHERINE, *sensing now an imperious demand, turns with some fear, with a discovery, to* BEATRICE. *She is at the edge of tears, as though a familiar world had shattered.*]

CATHERINE. Okay.

[*Lights out on them and up on* ALFIERI, *seated behind his desk.*]

ALFIERI. It was at this time that he first came to me. I had represented his father in an accident case some years before, and I was acquainted with the family in a casual way. I remember him now as he walked through my doorway—

[*Enter* EDDIE *down right ramp.*]

His eyes were like tunnels; my first thought was that he had committed a crime, [EDDIE *sits beside the desk, cap in hand, looking out.*] but soon I saw it was only a passion that had moved into his body, like a stranger. [ALFIERI *pauses, looks down at his desk, then to* EDDIE *as though he were continuing a conversation with him.*] I don't quite understand what I can do for you. Is there a question of law somewhere?

EDDIE. That's what I want to ask you.

ALFIERI. Because there's nothing illegal about a girl falling in love with an immigrant.

EDDIE. Yeah, but what about it if the only reason for it is to get his papers?

ALFIERI. First of all you don't know that.

EDDIE. I see it in his eyes; he's laughin' at her and he's laughin' at me.

ALFIERI. Eddie, I'm a lawyer. I can only deal in what's provable. You understand that, don't you? Can you prove that?

EDDIE. *I know what's in his mind, Mr. Alfieri!*

ALFIERI. Eddie, even if you could prove that—

EDDIE. Listen . . . will you listen to me a minute? My father always said you was a smart man. I want you to listen to me.

ALFIERI. I'm only a lawyer, Eddie.

EDDIE. Will you listen a minute? I'm talkin' about the law. Lemme just bring out what I mean. A man, which he comes into the country illegal, don't it stand to reason he's gonna take every penny and put it in the sock? Because they don't know from one day to another, right?

ALFIERI. All right.

EDDIE. He's spendin'. Records he buys now. Shoes. Jackets. Y'understand me? This guy ain't worried. This guy is *here*. So it must be that he's got it all laid out in his mind already—he's stayin'. Right?

ALFIERI. Well? What about it?

EDDIE. All right. [*He glances at* ALFIERI, *then down to the floor.*] I'm talking to you confidential, ain't I?

ALFIERI. Certainly.

EDDIE. I mean it don't go no place but here. Because I don't like to say this about anybody. Even my wife I didn't exactly say this.

ALFIERI. What is it?

EDDIE. [*Takes a breath and glances briefly over each shoulder.*] The guy ain't right, Mr. Alfieri.

ALFIERI. What do you mean?

EDDIE. I mean he ain't right.

ALFIERI. I don't get you.

EDDIE. [*Shifts to another position in the chair.*] Dja ever get a look at him?

ALFIERI. Not that I know of, no.

EDDIE. He's a blond guy. Like . . . platinum. You know what I mean?

ALFIERI. No.

EDDIE. I mean if you close the paper fast— you could blow him over.

ALFIERI. Well that doesn't mean—

EDDIE. Wait a minute, I'm tellin' you sump'm. He sings, see. Which is—I mean it's all right, but sometimes he hits a note, see. I turn around. I mean—high. You know what I mean?

ALFIERI. Well, that's a tenor.

EDDIE. I know a tenor, Mr. Alfieri. This ain't no tenor. I mean if you came in the house and you didn't know who was singin', you wouldn't be lookin' for him you be lookin' for her.

ALFIERI. Yes, but that's not—

EDDIE. I'm tellin' you sump'm, wait a minute. Please, Mr. Alfieri. I'm tryin' to bring out my thoughts here. Couple of nights ago my niece brings out a dress which it's too small for her, because she shot up like a light this last year. He takes the dress, lays it on the table, he cuts it up; one-two-three, he makes a new dress. I mean he looked so sweet there, like an angel—you could kiss him he was so sweet.

ALFIERI. Now look, Eddie—

EDDIE. Mr. Alfieri, they're laughin' at him on the piers. I'm ashamed. Paper Doll they call him. Blondie now. His brother thinks it's because he's got a sense of humor, see—which he's got—but that ain't what they're laughin'. Which they're not goin' to come out with it because they know he's my relative, which they have to see me if they make a crack, y'know? But I know what they're laughin' at, and when I think of that guy layin' his hands on her I could—I mean it's eatin' me out, Mr. Alfieri, because I struggled for that girl. And now he comes in my house and—

ALFIERI. Eddie, look—I have my own children. I understand you. But the law is very specific. The law does not . . .

EDDIE. [*With a fuller flow of indignation.*] You mean to tell me that there's no law that a guy which he ain't right can go to work and marry a girl and—?

ALFIERI. You have no recourse in the law, Eddie.

EDDIE. Yeah, but if he ain't right, Mr. Alfieri, you mean to tell me—

ALFIERI. There is nothing you can do, Eddie, believe me.

EDDIE. Nothin'.

ALFIERI. Nothing at all. There's only one legal question here.

EDDIE. What?

ALFIERI. The manner in which they entered the country. But I don't think you want to do anything about that, do you?

EDDIE. You mean—?

ALFIERI. Well, they entered illegally.

EDDIE. Oh, Jesus, no, I wouldn't do nothin' about that, I mean—

ALFIERI. All right, then, let me talk now, eh?

EDDIE. Mr. Alfieri, I can't believe what you tell me. I mean there must be some kinda law which—

ALFIERI. Eddie, I want you to listen to me. [*Pause.*] You know, sometimes God mixes up the people. We all love somebody, the wife, the kids—every man's got somebody that he loves, heh? But sometimes . . . there's too much. You know? There's too much, and it goes where it mustn't. A man works hard, he brings up a child, sometimes it's a niece, sometimes even a daughter, and he never realizes it, but through the years—there is too much love for the daughter, there is too much love for the niece. Do you understand what I'm saying to you?

EDDIE. [*Sardonically.*] What do you mean, I shouldn't look out for her good?

ALFIERI. Yes, but these things have to end, Eddie, that's all. The child has to grow up and go away, and the man has to learn to forget. Because after all, Eddie—what other way can it end? [*Pause.*] Let her go. That's my advice. You did your job, now it's her life; wish her luck, and let her go. [*Pause.*] Will you do that? Because there's no law, Eddie; make up your mind to it; the law is not interested in this.

EDDIE. You mean to tell me, even if he's a punk? If he's—

ALFIERI. There's nothing you can do.

[EDDIE *stands.*]

EDDIE. Well, all right, thanks. Thanks very much.

ALFIERI. What are you going to do?

EDDIE. [*With a helpless but ironic gesture.*] What can I do? I'm a patsy, what can a patsy do? I worked like a dog twenty years so a punk could have her, so that's what I done. I mean, in the worst times, in the worst, when there wasn't a ship comin' in the harbor, I didn't stand around lookin' for relief—I hustled. When there was empty piers in Brooklyn I went to Hoboken, Staten Island, the West Side, Jersey, all over—because I made a promise. I took out of my own mouth to give to her. I took out of my wife's mouth. I walked hungry plenty days in this city! [*It begins to break through.*] And now I gotta sit in my own house and look at a son-of-a-bitch punk like that—which he came out of nowhere! I give him my house to sleep! I take the blankets off my bed for him, and he takes and puts his dirty filthy hands on her like a goddam thief!

ALFIERI. [*Rising.*] But, Eddie, she's a woman now.

EDDIE. He's stealing from me!

ALFIERI. She wants to get married, Eddie. She can't marry you, can she?

EDDIE. [*Furiously.*] What're you talkin' about, marry me! I don't know what the hell you're talkin' about!

[*Pause.*]

ALFIERI. I gave you my advice, Eddie. That's it. [EDDIE *gathers himself. A pause.*]

EDDIE. Well, thanks. Thanks very much. It just—it's breakin' my heart, y'know. I—

ALFIERI. I understand. Put it out of your mind. Can you do that?

EDDIE. I'm—[*He feels the threat of sobs, and with a helpless wave.*] I'll see you around. [*He goes out up the right ramp.*]

ALFIERI. [*Sits on desk.*] There are times when

you want to spread an alarm, but nothing has happened. I knew, I knew then and there—I could have finished the whole story that afternoon. It wasn't as though there was a mystery to unravel. I could see every step coming, step after step, like a dark figure walking down a hall toward a certain door. I knew where he was heading for, I knew where he was going to end. And I sat here many afternoons asking myself why, being an intelligent man, I was so powerless to stop it. I even went to a certain old lady in the neighborhood, a very wise old woman, and I told her, and she only nodded, and said, "Pray for him . . ." And so I—waited here.

[*As lights go out on* ALFIERI, *they rise in the apartment where all are finishing dinner.* BEATRICE *and* CATHERINE *are clearing the table.*]

CATHERINE. You know where they went?

BEATRICE. Where?

CATHERINE. They went to Africa once. On a fishing boat. [EDDIE *glances at her.*] It's true, Eddie.

[BEATRICE *exits into the kitchen with dishes.*]

EDDIE. I didn't say nothin'. [*He goes to his rocker, picks up a newspaper.*]

CATHERINE. And I was never even in Staten Island.

EDDIE. [*Sitting with the paper.*] You didn't miss nothin'. [*Pause.* CATHERINE *takes dishes out.*] How long that take you, Marco—to get to Africa?

MARCO. [*Rising.*] Oh . . . two days. We go all over.

RODOLPHO. [*Rising.*] Once we went to Yugoslavia.

EDDIE. [*To* MARCO.] They pay all right on them boats?

[BEATRICE *enters. She and* RODOLPHO *stack the remaining dishes.*]

MARCO. If they catch fish they pay all right. [*Sits on a stool.*]

RODOLPHO. They're family boats, though. And nobody in our family owned one. So we only worked when one of the families was sick.

BEATRICE. Y'know, Marco, what I don't understand—there's an ocean full of fish and yiz are all starvin'.

EDDIE. They gotta have boats, nets, you need money.

[CATHERINE *enters.*]

BEATRICE. Yeah, but couldn't they like fish from the beach? You see them down Coney Island—

MARCO. Sardines.

EDDIE. Sure. [*Laughing.*] How you gonna catch sardines on a hook?

BEATRICE. Oh, I didn't know they're sardines. [*To* CATHERINE.] They're sardines!

CATHERINE. Yeah, they follow them all over the ocean, Africa, Yugoslavia . . . [*She sits and begins to look through a movie magazine.* RODOLPHO *joins her.*]

BEATRICE. [*To* EDDIE.] It's funny, y'know. You never think of it, that sardines are swimming in the ocean! [*She exits to kitchen with dishes.*]

CATHERINE. I know. It's like oranges and lemons on a tree. [*To* EDDIE.] I mean you ever think of oranges and lemons on a tree?

EDDIE. Yeah, I know. It's funny. [*To* MARCO.] I heard that they paint the oranges to make them look orange.

[BEATRICE *enters.*]

MARCO. [*He has been reading a letter.*] Paint?

EDDIE. Yeah, I heard that they grow like green.

MARCO. No, in Italy the oranges are orange.

RODOLPHO. Lemons are green.

EDDIE. [*Resenting his instruction.*] I know lemons are green, for Christ's sake, you see them in the store they're green sometimes. I said oranges they paint, I didn't say nothin' about lemons.

BEATRICE. [*Sitting; diverting their attention.*] Your wife is gettin' the money all right, Marco?

MARCO. Oh, yes. She bought medicine for my boy.

BEATRICE. That's wonderful. You feel better, heh?

MARCO. Oh, yes! But I'm lonesome.

BEATRICE. I just hope you ain't gonna do like some of them around here. They're here twenty-five years, some men, and they didn't get enough together to go back twice.

MARCO. Oh, I know. We have many families in our town, the children never saw the father. But I will go home. Three, four years, I think.

BEATRICE. Maybe you should keep more here. Because maybe she thinks it comes so easy you'll never get ahead of yourself.

MARCO. Oh, no, she saves. I send everything. My wife is very lonesome. [*He smiles shyly.*]

BEATRICE. She must be nice. She pretty? I bet, heh?

MARCO. [*Blushing.*] No, but she understand everything.

RODOLPHO. Oh, he's got a clever wife!

EDDIE. I betcha there's plenty surprises sometimes when those guys get back there, heh?

MARCO. Surprises?

EDDIE. [*Laughing.*] I mean, you know—they count the kids and there's a couple extra than when they left?

MARCO. No—no . . . The women wait, Eddie. Most. Most. Very few surprises.

RODOLPHO. It's more strict in our town. [EDDIE *looks at him now.*] It's not so free.

EDDIE. [*Rises, paces up and down.*] It ain't so free here either, Rodolpho, like you think. I seen greenhorns sometimes get in trouble that way—they think just because a girl don't go around with a shawl over her head that she ain't strict, y'know? Girl don't have to wear black dress to be strict. Know what I mean?

RODOLPHO. Well, I always have respect—

EDDIE. I know, but in your town you wouldn't just drag off some girl without permission, I mean. [*He turns.*] You know what I mean, Marco? It ain't that much different here.

MARCO. [*Cautiously.*] Yes.

BEATRICE. Well, he didn't exactly drag her off though, Eddie.

EDDIE. I know, but I seen some of them get the wrong idea sometimes. [*To* RODOLPHO.] I mean it might be a little more free here but it's just as strict.

RODOLPHO. I have respect for her, Eddie. I do anything wrong?

EDDIE. Look, kid, I ain't her father, I'm only her uncle—

BEATRICE. Well then, be an uncle then. [EDDIE *looks at her, aware of her criticizing force.*] I *mean.*

MARCO. No, Beatrice, if he does wrong you must tell him. [*To* EDDIE.] What does he do wrong?

EDDIE. Well, Marco, till he came here she was never out on the street twelve o'clock at night.

MARCO. [*To* RODOLPHO.] You come home early now.

BEATRICE. [*To* CATHERINE.] Well, you said the movie ended late, didn't you?

CATHERINE. Yeah.

BEATRICE. Well, tell him, honey. [*To* EDDIE.] The movie ended late.

EDDIE. Look, B., I'm just sayin'—he thinks she always stayed out like that.

MARCO. You come home early now, Rodolpho.

RODOLPHO. [*Embarrassed.*] All right, sure. But I can't stay in the house all the time, Eddie.

EDDIE. Look, kid, I'm not only talkin' about her. The more you run around like that the more chance you're takin'. [*To* BEATRICE.] I mean suppose he gets hit by a car or something. [*To* MARCO.] Where's his papers, who is he? Know what I mean?

BEATRICE. Yeah, but who is he in the daytime, though? It's the same chance in the daytime.

EDDIE. [*Holding back a voice full of anger.*] Yeah, but he don't have to go lookin' for it, Beatrice. If he's here to work, then he should work; if he's here for a good time then he could fool around! [*To* MARCO.] But I understood, Marco, that you was both comin' to make a livin' for your family. You understand me, don't you, Marco? [*He goes to his rocker.*]

MARCO. I beg your pardon, Eddie.

EDDIE. I mean, that's what I understood in the first place, see.

MARCO. Yes. That's why we came.

EDDIE. [*Sits on his rocker.*] Well, that's all I'm askin'. [EDDIE *reads his paper. There is a pause, an awkwardness. Now* CATHERINE *gets up and puts a record on the phonograph—* "*Paper Doll.*"]

CATHERINE. [*Flushed with revolt.*] You wanna dance, Rodolpho?

[EDDIE *freezes.*]

RODOLPHO. [*In deference to Eddie.*] No, I— I'm tired.

BEATRICE. Go ahead, dance, Rodolpho.

CATHERINE. Ah, come on. They got a beautiful quartet, these guys. Come. [*She has taken his hand and he stiffly rises, feeling* EDDIE'S *eyes on his back, and they dance.*]

EDDIE. [*To* CATHERINE.] What's that, a new record?

CATHERINE. It's the same one. We bought it the other day.

BEATRICE. [*To* EDDIE.] They only bought three records. [*She watches them dance;* EDDIE *turns his head away.* MARCO *just sits there, waiting. Now* BEATRICE *turns to* EDDIE.] Must be nice to go all over in one of them fishin' boats. I would like that myself. See all them other countries?

EDDIE. Yeah.

BEATRICE. [*To* MARCO.] But the women don't go along, I bet.

MARCO. No, not on the boats. Hard work.

BEATRICE. What're you got, a regular kitchen and everything?

MARCO. Yes, we eat very good on the boats—especially when Rodolpho comes along; everybody gets fat.

BEATRICE. Oh, he cooks?

MARCO. Sure, very good cook. Rice, pasta, fish, everything.

[EDDIE *lowers his paper.*]

EDDIE. He's a cook, too! [*Looking at* RODOLPHO.] He sings, he cooks . . .

[RODOLPHO *smiles thankfully.*]

BEATRICE. Well it's good, he could always make a living.

EDDIE. It's wonderful. He sings, he cooks, he could make dresses . . .

CATHERINE. They get some high pay, them guys. The head chefs in all the big hotels are men. You read about them.

EDDIE. That's what I'm sayin'.

[CATHERINE *and* RODOLPHO *continue dancing.*]

CATHERINE. Yeah, well, I mean.

EDDIE. [*To* BEATRICE.] He's lucky, believe me. [*Slight pause. He looks away, then back to* BEATRICE.] That's why the water front is no place for him. [*They stop dancing.* RODOLPHO *turns off phonograph.*] I mean like me—I can't cook, I can't sing, I can't make dresses, so I'm on the water front. But if I could cook, if I could sing, if I could make dresses, I wouldn't be on the water front. [*He has been unconsciously twisting the newspaper into a tight roll. They are all regarding him now; he senses he is exposing the issue and he is driven on.*] I would be someplace else. I would be like in a dress store. [*He has bent the rolled paper and it suddenly tears in two. He suddenly gets up and pulls his pants up over his belly and goes to* MARCO.] What do you say, Marco, we go to the bouts next Saturday night. You never seen a fight, did you?

MARCO. [*Uneasily.*] Only in the moving pictures.

EDDIE. [*Going to* RODOLPHO.] I'll treat yiz. What do you say, Danish? You wanna come along? I'll buy the tickets.

RODOLPHO. Sure. I like to go.

CATHERINE. [*Goes to* EDDIE; *nervously happy now.*] I'll make some coffee, all right?

EDDIE. Go ahead, make some! Make it nice and strong. [*Mystified, she smiles and exits to kitchen. He is weirdly elated, rubbing*

his fists into his palms. He strides to MARCO.]
You wait, Marco, you see some real fights
here. You ever do any boxing?

MARCO. No, I never.

EDDIE. [*To* RODOLPHO.] Betcha you have
done some, heh?

RODOLPHO. No.

EDDIE. Well, come on, I'll teach you.

BEATRICE. What's he got to learn that for?

EDDIE. Ya can't tell, one a these days
somebody's liable to step on his foot or
sump'm. Come on, Rodolpho, I show you
a couple a passes. [*He stands below table.*]

BEATRICE. Go ahead, Rodolpho. He's a good
boxer, he could teach you.

RODOLPHO. [*Embarrassed.*] Well, I don't know
how to—[*He moves down to* EDDIE.]

EDDIE. Just put your hands up. Like this,
see? That's right. That's very good, keep
your left up, because you lead with the left,
see, like this. [*He gently moves his left into*
RODOLPHO's *face.*] See? Now what you gotta
do is you gotta block me, so when I come
in like that you—[RODOLPHO *parries his
left.*] Hey, that's very good! [RODOLPHO
laughs.] All right, now come into me. Come
on.

RODOLPHO. I don't want to hit you, Eddie.

EDDIE. Don't pity me, come on. Throw
it, I'll show you how to block it. [RODOLPHO
jabs at him, laughing. The others join.]
'At's it. Come on again. For the jaw right
here. [RODOLPHO *jabs with more assurance.*]
Very good!

BEATRICE. [*To Marco.*] He's very good!

[EDDIE *crosses directly upstage of* RO-
DOLPHO.]

EDDIE. Sure, he's great! Come on, kid, put
sump'm behind it, you can't hurt me.
[RODOLPHO, *more seriously, jabs at* EDDIE's
jaw and grazes it.] Attaboy.

[CATHERINE *comes from the kitchen,
watches.*]

Now I'm gonna hit you, so block me, see?

CATHERINE. [*With beginning alarm.*] What are
they doin'?

[*They are lightly boxing now.*]

BEATRICE. [*She senses only the comradeship in
it now.*] He's teachin' him; he's very good!

EDDIE. Sure, he's terrific! Look at him go!
[RODOLPHO *lands a blow.*] 'At's it! Now,
watch out, here I come, Danish! [*He feints
with his left hand and lands with his right.
It mildly staggers* RODOLPHO. MARCO *rises.*]

CATHERINE. [*Rushing to* RODOLPHO.] Eddie!

EDDIE. Why? I didn't hurt him. Did I
hurt you, kid? [*He rubs the back of his hand
across his mouth.*]

RODOLPHO. No, no, he didn't hurt me.
[*To* EDDIE *with a certain gleam and a smile.*]
I was only surprised.

BEATRICE. [*Pulling* EDDIE *down into the
rocker.*] That's enough, Eddie; he did pretty
good, though.

EDDIE. Yeah. [*Rubbing his fists together.*] He
could be very good, Marco. I'll teach him
again.

[MARCO *nods at him dubiously.*]

RODOLPHO. Dance, Catherine. Come. [*He
takes her hand; they go to phonograph and
start it. It plays "Paper Doll."* RODOLPHO
takes her in his arms. They dance. EDDIE
in thought sits in his chair, and MARCO *takes
a chair, places it in front of* EDDIE, *and looks
down at it.* BEATRICE *and* EDDIE *watch him.*]

MARCO. Can you lift this chair?

EDDIE. What do you mean?

MARCO. From here. [*He gets on one knee with
one hand behind his back, and grasps the
bottom of one of the chair legs but does not
raise it.*]

EDDIE. Sure, why not? [*He comes to the
chair, kneels, grasps the leg, raises the chair
one inch, but it leans over to the floor.*] Gee,
that's hard, I never knew that. [*He tries
again, and again fails.*] It's on an angle,
that's why, heh?

MARCO. Here. [*He kneels, grasps, and with
strain slowly raises the chair higher and
higher, getting to his feet now.* RODOLPHO
and CATHERINE *have stopped dancing as*
MARCO *raises the chair over his head.* MARCO

is face to face with EDDIE, *a strained tension gripping his eyes and jaw, his neck stiff, the chair raised like a weapon over* EDDIE's *head— and he transforms what might appear like a glare of warning into a smile of triumph, and* EDDIE's *grin vanishes as he absorbs his look.*]

CURTAIN

ACT TWO

Light rises on ALFIERI *at his desk.*

ALFIERI. On the twenty-third of that December a case of Scotch whisky slipped from a net while being unloaded—as a case of Scotch whisky is inclined to do on the twenty-third of December on Pier Forty-one. There was no snow, but it was cold, his wife was out shopping. Marco was still at work. The boy had not been hired that day; Catherine told me later that this was the first time they had been alone together in the house.

[*Light is rising on* CATHERINE *in the apartment.* RODOLPHO *is watching as she arranges a paper pattern on cloth spread on the table.*]

CATHERINE. You hungry?

RODOLPHO. Not for anything to eat. [*Pause.*] I have nearly three hundred dollars. Catherine?

CATHERINE. I heard you.

RODOLPHO. You don't like to talk about it any more?

CATHERINE. Sure, I don't mind talkin' about it.

RODOLPHO. What worries you, Catherine?

CATHERINE. I been wantin' to ask you about something. Could I?

RODOLPHO. All the answers are in my eyes, Catherine. But you don't look in my eyes lately. You're full of secrets. [*She looks at him. She seems withdrawn.*] What is the question?

CATHERINE. Suppose I wanted to live in Italy.

RODOLPHO. [*Smiling at the incongruity.*] You going to marry somebody rich?

CATHERINE. No, I mean live there—you and me.

RODOLPHO. [*His smile vanishing.*] When?

CATHERINE. Well . . . when we get married.

RODOLPHO. [*Astonished.*] You want to be an Italian?

CATHERINE. No, but I could live there without being Italian. Americans live there.

RODOLPHO. Forever?

CATHERINE. Yeah.

RODOLPHO. [*Crosses to rocker.*] You're fooling.

CATHERINE. No, I mean it.

RODOLPHO. Where do you get such an idea?

CATHERINE. Well, you're always saying it's so beautiful there, with the mountains and the ocean and all the—

RODOLPHO. You're fooling me.

CATHERINE. I mean it.

RODOLPHO. [*Goes to her slowly.*] Catherine, if I ever brought you home with no money, no business, nothing, they would call the priest and the doctor and they would say Rodolpho is crazy.

CATHERINE. I know, but I think we would be happier there.

RODOLPHO. Happier! What would you eat? You can't cook the view!

CATHERINE. Maybe you could be a singer, like in Rome or—

RODOLPHO. Rome! Rome is full of singers.

CATHERINE. Well, I could work then.

RODOLPHO. Where?

CATHERINE. God, there must be jobs somewhere!

RODOLPHO. There's nothing! Nothing, nothing, nothing. Now tell me what you're talking about. How can I bring you from a rich country to suffer in a poor country? What are you talking about? [*She searches for words.*] I would be a criminal stealing your face. In two years you would have an old, hungry face. When my brother's babies cry they give them water, water that boiled a bone. Don't you believe that?

CATHERINE. [*Quietly.*] I'm afraid of Eddie here.

[*Slight pause.*]

RODOLPHO. [*Steps closer to her.*] We wouldn't live here. Once I am a citizen I could work anywhere and I would find better jobs and we would have a house, Catherine. If I were not afraid to be arrested I would start to be something wonderful here!

CATHERINE. [*Steeling herself*]. Tell me something. I mean just tell me, Rodolpho —would you still want to do it if it turned out we had to go live in Italy? I mean just if it turned out that way.

RODOLPHO. This is your question or his question?

CATHERINE. I would like to know, Rodolpho. I mean it.

RODOLPHO. To go there with nothing.

CATHERINE. Yeah.

RODOLPHO. No. [*She looks at him wide-eyed.*] No.

CATHERINE. You wouldn't?

RODOLPHO. No; I will not marry you to live in Italy. I want you to be my wife, and I want to be a citizen. Tell him that, or I will. Yes. [*He moves about angrily.*] And tell him also, and tell yourself, please, that I am not a beggar, and you are not a horse, a gift, a favor for a poor immigrant.

CATHERINE. Well, don't get mad!

RODOLPHO. I am furious! [*Goes to her.*] Do you think I am so desperate? My brother is desperate, not me. You think I would carry on my back the rest of my life a woman I didn't love just to be an American? It's so wonderful? You think we have no tall buildings in Italy? Electric lights? No wide streets? No flags? No automobiles? Only work we don't have. I want to be an American so I can work, that is the only wonder here—work! How can you insult me, Catherine?

CATHERINE. I didn't mean that—

RODOLPHO. My heart dies to look at you. Why are you so afraid of him?

CATHERINE. [*Near tears.*] I don't know!

RODOLPHO. Do you trust me, Catherine? You?

CATHERINE. It's only that I— He was good to me, Rodolpho. You don't know him; he was always the sweetest guy to me. Good. He razzes me all the time but he don't mean it. I know. I would—just feel ashamed if I made him sad. 'Cause I always dreamt that when I got married he would be happy at the wedding, and laughin'— and now he's—mad all the time and nasty—[*She is weeping.*] Tell him you'd live in Italy—just tell him, and maybe he would start to trust you a little, see? Because I want him to be happy; I mean— I like him, Rodolpho—and I can't stand it!

RODOLPHO. Oh, Catherine—oh, little girl.

CATHERINE. I love you, Rodolpho, I love you.

RODOLPHO. Then why are you afraid? That he'll spank you?

CATHERINE. Don't, don't laugh at me! I've been here all my life. . . . Every day I saw him when he left in the morning and when he came home at night. You think it's so easy to turn around and say to a man he's nothin' to you no more?

RODOLPHO. I know, but—

CATHERINE. You don't know; nobody knows! I'm not a baby, I know a lot more than people think I know. Beatrice says to be a woman, but—

RODOLPHO. Yes.

CATHERINE. Then why don't she be a woman? If I was a wife I would make a man happy instead of goin' at him all the time. I can tell a block away when he's blue in his mind and just wants to talk to somebody quiet and nice. . . . I can tell when he's hungry or wants a beer before he even says anything. I know when his feet hurt him, I mean I *know* him and now I'm supposed to turn around and make a stranger out of him? I don't know why I have to do that, I mean.

RODOLPHO. Catherine. If I take in my hands a little bird. And she grows and wishes to fly. But I will not let her out of my hands because I love her so much, is that right for me to do? I don't say you must hate him; but anyway you must go, mustn't you? Catherine?

CATHERINE. [*Softly.*] Hold me.

RODOLPHO. [*Clasping her to him.*] Oh, my little girl.

CATHERINE. Teach me. [*She is weeping.*] I don't know anything, teach me, Rodolpho, hold me.

RODOLPHO. There's nobody here now. Come inside. Come. [*He is leading her toward the bedrooms.*] And don't cry any more.

[*Light rises on the street. In a moment* EDDIE *appears. He is unsteady, drunk. He mounts the stairs. He enters the apartment, looks around, takes out a bottle from one pocket, puts it on the table. Then another bottle from another pocket, and a third from an inside pocket. He sees the pattern and cloth, goes over to it and touches it, and turns toward upstage.*]

EDDIE. Beatrice? [*He goes to the open kitchen door and looks in.*] Beatrice? Beatrice?

[CATHERINE *enters from bedroom; under his gaze she adjusts her dress.*]

CATHERINE. You got home early.

EDDIE. Knocked off for Christmas early. [*Indicating the pattern.*] Rodolpho makin' you a dress?

CATHERINE. No. I'm makin' a blouse.

[RODOLPHO *appears in the bedroom doorway.* EDDIE *sees him and his arm jerks slightly in shock.* RODOLPHO *nods to him testingly.*]

RODOLPHO. Beatrice went to buy presents for her mother.

[*Pause.*]

EDDIE. Pack it up. Go ahead. Get your stuff and get outa here. [CATHERINE

instantly turns and walks toward the bedroom, and EDDIE *grabs her arm.*] Where you goin'?

CATHERINE. [*Trembling with fright.*] I think I have to get out of here, Eddie.

EDDIE. No, you ain't goin' nowheres, he's the one.

CATHERINE. I think I can't stay here no more. [*She frees her arm, steps back toward the bedroom.*] I'm sorry, Eddie. [*She sees the tears in his eyes.*] Well, don't cry. I'll be around the neighborhood; I'll see you. I just can't stay here no more. You know I can't. [*Her sobs of pity and love for him break her composure.*] Don't you know I can't? You know that, don't you? [*She goes to him.*] Wish me luck. [*She clasps her hands prayerfully.*] Oh, Eddie, don't be like that!

EDDIE. You ain't goin' nowheres.

CATHERINE. Eddie, I'm not gonna be a baby any more! You—

[*He reaches out suddenly, draws her to him, and as she strives to free herself he kisses her on the mouth.*]

RODOLPHO. Don't! [*He pulls on* EDDIE's *arm.*] Stop that! Have respect for her!

EDDIE. [*Spun round by* RODOLPHO.] You want something?

RODOLPHO. Yes! She'll be my wife. That is what I want. My wife!

EDDIE. But what're you gonna be?

RODOLPHO. I show you what I be!

CATHERINE. Wait outside; don't argue with him!

EDDIE. Come on, show me! What're you gonna be? Show me!

RODOLPHO. [*With tears of rage.*] Don't say that to me! [RODOLPHO *flies at him in attack.* EDDIE *pins his arms, laughing, and suddenly kisses him.*]

CATHERINE. Eddie! Let go, ya hear me! I'll kill you! Leggo of him! [*She tears at* EDDIE's *face and* EDDIE *releases* RODOLPHO. EDDIE *stands there with tears rolling down his face as he laughs mockingly at* RODOLPHO. *She is staring at him in horror.* RODOLPHO *is rigid. They are like animals that have torn at one another and broken up without a decision, each waiting for the other's mood.*]

EDDIE. [*To* CATHERINE.] You see? [*To* RODOLPHO.] I give you till tomorrow, kid. Get outa here. Alone. You hear me? Alone.

CATHERINE. I'm going with him, Eddie. [*She starts toward* RODOLPHO.]

EDDIE. [*Indicating* RODOLPHO *with his head.*] Not with that. [*She halts, frightened. He sits, still panting for breath, and they watch him helplessly as he leans toward them over the table.*] Don't make me do nuttin', Catherine. Watch your step, submarine. By rights they oughta throw you back in the water. But I got pity for you. [*He moves unsteadily toward the door, always facing* RODOLPHO.] Just get outa here and don't lay another hand on her unless you wanna go out feet first. [*He goes out of the apartment.*]

[*The lights go down, as they rise on* ALFIERI.]

ALFIERI. On December twenty-seventh I saw him next. I normally go home well before six, but that day I sat around looking out my window at the bay, and when I saw him walking through my doorway, I knew why I had waited. And if I seem to tell this like a dream, it was that way. Several moments arrived in the course of the two talks we had when it occurred to me how—almost transfixed I had come to feel. I had lost my strength somewhere. [EDDIE *enters, removing his cap, sits in the chair, looks thoughtfully out.*] I looked in his eyes more than I listened—in fact, I can hardly remember the conversation. But I will never forget how dark the room became when he looked at me; his eyes were like tunnels. I kept wanting to call the police, but nothing had happened. Nothing at all had really happened. [*He breaks off and looks down at the desk. Then he turns to* EDDIE.] So in other words, he won't leave?

EDDIE. My wife is talkin' about renting a room upstairs for them. An old lady on the top floor is got an empty room.

ALFIERI. What does Marco say?

EDDIE. He just sits there. Marco don't say much.

ALFIERI. I guess they didn't tell him, heh? What happened?

EDDIE. I don't know; Marco don't say much.

ALFIERI. What does your wife say?

EDDIE. [*Unwilling to pursue this.*] Nobody's talkin' much in the house. So what about that?

ALFIERI. But you didn't prove anything about him. It sounds like he just wasn't strong enough to break your grip.

EDDIE. I'm tellin' you I know—he ain't right. Somebody that don't want it can break it. Even a mouse, if you catch a teeny mouse and you hold it in your hand, that mouse can give you the right kind of fight. He didn't give me the right kind of fight, I know it, Mr. Alfieri, the guy ain't right.

ALFIERI. What did you do that for, Eddie?

EDDIE. To show her what he is! So she would see, once and for all! Her mother'll turn over in the grave! [*He gathers himself almost peremptorily.*] So what do I gotta do now? Tell me what to do.

ALFIERI. She actually said she's marrying him?

EDDIE. She told me, yeah. So what do I do?

[*Slight pause.*]

ALFIERI. This is my last word, Eddie, take it or not, that's your business. Morally and legally you have no rights, you cannot stop it; she is a free agent.

EDDIE. [*Angering.*] Didn't you hear what I told you?

ALFIERI. [*With a tougher tone.*] I heard what you told me, and I'm telling you what the answer is. I'm not only telling you now, I'm warning you—the law is nature. The law is only a word for what has a right to happen. When the law is wrong it's because it's unnatural, but in this case it is natural and a river will drown you if you buck it now. Let her go. And bless her. [*A phone booth begins to glow on the opposite side of the stage; a faint, lonely blue.* EDDIE *stands up, jaws clenched.*] Somebody had to come for her, Eddie, sooner or later. [EDDIE *starts turning to go and* ALFIERI *rises with new anxiety.*] You won't have a friend in the world, Eddie! Even those who understand will turn against you, even the ones who feel the same will despise you! [EDDIE *moves off.*] Put it out of your mind! Eddie! [*He follows into the darkness, calling desperately.*]

[EDDIE *is gone. The phone is glowing in light now. Light is out on* ALFIERI. EDDIE *has at the same time appeared beside the phone.*]

EDDIE. Give me the number of the Immigration Bureau. Thanks. [*He dials.*] I want to report something. Illegal immigrants. Two of them. That's right. Four-forty-one Saxon Street, Brooklyn, yeah. Ground floor. Heh? [*With greater difficulty.*] I'm just around the neighborhood, that's all. Heh? [*Evidently he is being questioned further, and he slowly hangs up. He leaves the phone just as* LOUIS *and* MIKE *come down the street.*]

LOUIS. Go bowlin', Eddie?

EDDIE. No, I'm due home.

LOUIS. Well, take it easy.

EDDIE. I'll see yiz.

[*They leave him, exiting right, and he watches them go. He glances about, then goes up into the house. The lights go on in the apartment.* BEATRICE *is taking down Christmas decorations and packing them in a box.*]

EDDIE. Where is everybody? [BEATRICE *does not answer.*] I says where is everybody?

BEATRICE. [*Looking up at him, wearied with it, and concealing a fear of him.*] I decided to move them upstairs with Mrs. Dondero.

EDDIE. Oh, they're all moved up there already?

BEATRICE. Yeah.

EDDIE. Where's Catherine? She up there?

BEATRICE. Only to bring pillow cases.

EDDIE. She ain't movin' in with them.

BEATRICE. Look, I'm sick and tired of it. I'm sick and tired of it!

EDDIE. All right, all right, take it easy.

BEATRICE. I don't wanna hear no more about it, you understand? Nothin'!

EDDIE. What're you blowin' off about? Who brought them in here?

BEATRICE. All right, I'm sorry; I wish I'd drop dead before I told them to come. In the ground I wish I was.

EDDIE. Don't drop dead, just keep in mind who brought them in here, that's all. [*He moves about restlessly.*] I mean I got a couple of rights here. [*He moves, wanting to beat down her evident disapproval of him.*] This is my house here not their house.

BEATRICE. What do you want from me? They're moved out; what do you want now?

EDDIE. I want my respect!

BEATRICE. So I moved them out, what more do you want? You got your house now, you got your respect.

EDDIE. [*He moves about biting his lip.*] I don't like the way you talk to me, Beatrice.

BEATRICE. I'm just tellin' you I done what you want!

EDDIE. I don't like it! The way you talk to me and the way you look at me. This is my house. And she is my niece and I'm responsible for her.

BEATRICE. So that's why you done that to him?

EDDIE. I done what to him?

BEATRICE. What you done to him in front of her; you know what I'm talkin' about. She goes around shakin' all the time, she can't go to sleep! That's what you call responsible for her?

EDDIE. [*Quietly.*] The guy ain't right, Beatrice. [*She is silent.*] Did you hear what I said?

BEATRICE. Look, I'm finished with it. That's all. [*She resumes her work.*]

EDDIE. [*Helping her to pack the tinsel.*] I'm gonna have it out with you one of these days, Beatrice.

BEATRICE. Nothin' to have out with me, it's all settled. Now we gonna be like it never happened, that's all.

EDDIE. I want my respect, Beatrice, and you know what I'm talkin' about.

BEATRICE. What?

[*Pause.*]

EDDIE. [*Finally his resolution hardens.*] What I feel like doin' in the bed and what I don't feel like doin'. I don't want no—

BEATRICE. When'd I say anything about that?

EDDIE. You said, you said, I ain't deaf. I don't want no more conversations about that, Beatrice. I do what I feel like doin' or what I don't feel like doin'.

BEATRICE. Okay.

[*Pause.*]

EDDIE. You used to be different, Beatrice. You had a whole different way.

BEATRICE. *I'm* no different.

EDDIE. You didn't used to jump me all the time about everything. The last year or two I come in the house I don't know what's gonna hit me. It's a shootin' gallery in here and I'm the pigeon.

BEATRICE. Okay, okay.

EDDIE. Don't tell me okay, okay, I'm tellin' you the truth. A wife is supposed to believe the husband. If I tell you that guy ain't right don't tell me he is right.

BEATRICE. But how do you know?

EDDIE. Because I know. I don't go around makin' accusations. He give me the heeby-jeebies the first minute I seen him. And I don't like you sayin' I don't want her marryin' anybody. I broke my back payin' her stenography lessons so she could go out and meet a better class of people. Would I do that if I didn't want her to get married? Sometimes you talk like I was a crazy man or sump'm.

BEATRICE. But she likes him.

EDDIE. Beatrice, she's a baby, how is she gonna know what she likes?

BEATRICE. Well, you kept her a baby, you wouldn't let her go out. I told you a hundred times.

[*Pause.*]

EDDIE. All right. Let her go out, then.

BEATRICE. She don't wanna go out now. It's too late, Eddie.

[*Pause.*]

EDDIE. Suppose I told her to go out. Suppose I—

BEATRICE. They're going to get married next week, Eddie.

EDDIE. [*His head jerks around to her.*] She said that?

BEATRICE. Eddie, if you want my advice, go to her and tell her good luck. I think maybe now that you had it out you learned better.

EDDIE. What's the hurry next week?

BEATRICE. Well, she's been worried about him bein' picked up; this way he could start to be a citizen. She loves him, Eddie. [*He gets up, moves about uneasily, restlessly.*] Why don't you give her a good word? Because I still think she would like you to be a friend, y'know? [*He is standing, looking at the floor.*] I mean like if you told her you'd go to the wedding.

EDDIE. She asked you that?

BEATRICE. I know she would like it. I'd like to make a party here for her. I mean there oughta be some kinda send-off. Heh? I mean she'll have trouble enough in her life, let's start it off happy. What do you say? Cause in her heart she still loves you, Eddie. I know it. [*He presses his fingers against his eyes.*] What're you, cryin'? [*She goes to him, holds his face.*] Go...whyn't you go tell her you're sorry? [CATHERINE *is seen on the upper landing of the stairway, and they hear her descending.*] There...she's comin' down. Come on, shake hands with her.

EDDIE. [*Moving with suppressed suddenness.*] No, I can't, I can't talk to her.

BEATRICE. Eddie, give her a break; a wedding should be happy!

EDDIE. I'm goin', I'm goin' for a walk. [*He goes upstage for his jacket.* CATHERINE *enters and starts for the bedroom door.*]

BEATRICE. Katie? . . . Eddie, don't go, wait a minute. [*She embraces* EDDIE's *arm with warmth.*] Ask him, Katie. Come on, honey.

EDDIE. It's all right, I'm—[*He starts to go and she holds him.*]

BEATRICE. No, she wants to ask you. Come on, Katie, ask him. We'll have a party! What're we gonna do, hate each other? Come on!

CATHERINE. I'm gonna get married, Eddie. So if you wanna come, the wedding be on Saturday.

[*Pause.*]

EDDIE. Okay. I only wanted the best for you, Katie. I hope you know that.

CATHERINE. Okay. [*She starts out again.*]

EDDIE. Catherine? [*She turns to him.*] I was just tellin' Beatrice . . . if you wanna go out, like . . . I mean I realize maybe I kept you home too much. Because he's the first guy you ever knew, y'know? I mean now that you got a job, you might meet some fellas, and you get a different idea, y'know? I mean you could always come back to him, you're still only kids, the both of yiz. What's the hurry? Maybe you'll get around a little bit, you grow up a little more, maybe you'll see different in a couple of months. I mean you be surprised, it don't have to be him.

CATHERINE. No, we made it up already.

EDDIE. [*With increasing anxiety.*] Katie, wait a minute.

CATHERINE. No, I made up my mind.

EDDIE. But you never knew no other fella, Katie! How could you make up your mind?

CATHERINE. Cause I did. I don't want nobody else.

EDDIE. But, Katie, suppose he gets picked up.

CATHERINE. That's why we gonna do it

right away. Soon as we finish the wedding he's goin' right over and start to be a citizen. I made up my mind, Eddie. I'm sorry. [*To* BEATRICE.] Could I take two more pillow cases for the other guys?

BEATRICE. Sure, go ahead. Only don't let her forget where they came from.

[CATHERINE *goes into a bedroom.*]

EDDIE. She's got other boarders up there?

BEATRICE. Yeah, there's two guys that just came over.

EDDIE. What do you mean, came over?

BEATRICE. From Italy. Lipari the butcher—his nephew. They come from Bari, they just got here yesterday. I didn't even know till Marco and Rodolpho moved up there before. [CATHERINE *enters, going toward exit with two pillow cases.*] It'll be nice, they could all talk together.

EDDIE. Catherine! [*She halts near the exit door. He takes in* BEATRICE *too.*] What're you, got no brains? You put them up there with two other submarines?

CATHERINE. Why?

EDDIE. [*In a driving fright and anger.*] Why! How do you know they're not trackin' these guys? They'll come up for them and find Marco and Rodolpho! Get them out of the house!

BEATRICE. But they been here so long already—

EDDIE. How do you know what enemies Lipari's got? Which they'd love to stab him in the back?

CATHERINE. Well what'll I do with them?

EDDIE. The neighborhood is full of rooms. Can't you stand to live a couple of blocks away from him? Get them out of the house!

CATHERINE. Well maybe tomorrow night I'll—

EDDIE. Not tomorrow, do it now. Catherine, you never mix yourself with somebody else's family! These guys get picked up, Lipari's liable to blame you or me and we got his whole family on our head. They got a temper, that family.

[*Two men in overcoats appear outside, start into the house.*]

CATHERINE. How'm I gonna find a place tonight?

EDDIE. Will you stop arguin' with me and get them out! You think I'm always tryin' to fool you or sump'm? What's the matter with you, don't you believe I could think of your good? Did I ever ask sump'm for myself? You think I got no feelin's? I never told you nothin' in my life that wasn't for your good. Nothin'! And look at the way you talk to me! Like I was an enemy! Like I—[*A knock on the door. His head swerves. They all stand motionless. Another knock.* EDDIE, *in a whisper, pointing upstage.*] Go up the fire escape, get them out over the back fence.

[CATHERINE *stands motionless, uncomprehending.*]

FIRST OFFICER. [*In the hall.*] Immigration! Open up in there!

EDDIE. Go, go. Hurry up! [*She stands a moment staring at him in a realized horror.*] Well, what're you lookin' at!

FIRST OFFICER. Open up!

EDDIE. [*Calling toward door.*] Who's that there?

FIRST OFFICER. Immigration, open up.

[EDDIE *turns, looks at* BEATRICE. *She sits. Then he looks at* CATHERINE. *With a sob of fury* CATHERINE *streaks into a bedroom. Knock is repeated.*]

EDDIE. All right, take it easy, take it easy. [*He goes and opens the door. The* OFFICER *steps inside.*] What's all this?

FIRST OFFICER. Where are they?

[SECOND OFFICER *sweeps past and, glancing about, goes into the kitchen.*]

EDDIE. Where's who?

FIRST OFFICER. Come on, come on, where are they? [*He hurries into the bedrooms.*]

EDDIE. Who? We got nobody here. [*He*

looks at BEATRICE, *who turns her head away. Pugnaciously, furious, he steps toward* BEATRICE.] What's the matter with *you*?

[FIRST OFFICER *enters from the bedroom, calls to the kitchen.*]

FIRST OFFICER. Dominick?

[*Enter* SECOND OFFICER *from kitchen.*]

SECOND OFFICER. Maybe it's a different apartment.

FIRST OFFICER. There's only two more floors up there. I'll take front, you go up the fire escape. I'll let you in. Watch your step up there.

SECOND OFFICER. Okay, right, Charley. [FIRST OFFICER *goes out apartment door and runs up the stairs.*] This is Four-forty-one, isn't it?

EDDIE. That's right. [SECOND OFFICER *goes out into the kitchen.* EDDIE *turns to* BEATRICE. *She looks at him now and sees his terror.*]

BEATRICE. [*Weakened with fear.*] Oh, Jesus, Eddie.

EDDIE. What's the matter with *you*?

BEATRICE. [*Pressing her palms against her face.*] Oh, my God, my God.

EDDIE. What're you, accusin' me?

BEATRICE. [*Her final thrust is to turn toward him instead of running from him.*] My God, what did you do?

[*Many steps on the outer stair draw his attention. We see the* FIRST OFFICER *descending, with* MARCO, *behind him* RODOLPHO, *and* CATHERINE *and the two strange immigrants, followed by* SECOND OFFICER. BEATRICE *hurries to door.*]

CATHERINE. [*Backing down stairs, fighting with* FIRST OFFICER; *as they appear on the stairs.*] What do yiz want from them? They work, that's all. They're boarders upstairs, they work on the piers.

BEATRICE. [*To* FIRST OFFICER.] Ah, mister, what do you want from them, who do they hurt?

CATHERINE. [*Pointing to* RODOLPHO.] They ain't no submarines, he was born in Philadelphia.

FIRST OFFICER. Step aside, lady.

CATHERINE. What do you mean? You can't just come in a house and—

FIRST OFFICER. All right, take it easy. [*To* RODOLPHO.] What street were you born in Philadelphia?

CATHERINE. What do you mean, what street? Could you tell me what street you were born?

FIRST OFFICER. Sure. Four blocks away One-eleven Union Street. Let's go fellas.

CATHERINE. [*Fending him off* RODOLPHO.] No, you can't! Now, get outa here!

FIRST OFFICER. Look, girlie, if they're all right they'll be out tomorrow. If they're illegal they go back where they came from. If you want, get yourself a lawyer, although I'm tellin' you now you're wasting your money. Let's get them in the car, Dom. [*To the men.*] Andiamo, Andiamo, let's go. [*The men start, but* MARCO *hangs back.*]

BEATRICE. [*From doorway.*] Who're they hurtin', for God's sake, what do you want from them? They're starvin' over there, what do you want! Marco!

[MARCO *suddenly breaks from the group and dashes into the room and faces* EDDIE; BEATRICE *and* FIRST OFFICER *rush in as* MARCO *spits into* EDDIE's *face.* CATHERINE *runs into hallway and throws herself into* RODOLPHO's *arms.* EDDIE, *with an enraged cry, lunges for* MARCO.]

EDDIE. Oh, you mother's—!

[FIRST OFFICER *quickly intercedes and pushes* EDDIE *from* MARCO, *who stands there accusingly.*]

FIRST OFFICER. [*Between them, pushing* EDDIE *from* MARCO.] Cut it out!

EDDIE. [*Over the* FIRST OFFICER's *shoulder, to* MARCO.] I'll kill you for that, you son of a bitch!

FIRST OFFICER. Hey! [*Shakes him.*] Stay in here now, don't come out, don't bother him. You hear me? Don't come out, fella. [*For an instant there is silence. Then* FIRST OFFICER *turns and takes* MARCO's *arm and then gives a last, informative look at* EDDIE. *As he and* MARCO *are going out into the hall,* EDDIE *erupts.*]

EDDIE. I don't forget that, Marco! You hear what I'm sayin'?

[*Out in the hall,* FIRST OFFICER *and* MARCO *go down the stairs. Now, in the street,* LOUIS, MIKE, *and several neighbors including the butcher,* LIPARI—*a stout, intense, middle-aged man—are gathering around the stoop.* LIPARI, *the butcher, walks over to the two strange men and kisses them. His wife, keening, goes and kisses their hands.* EDDIE *is emerging from the house shouting after* MARCO. BEATRICE *is trying to restrain him.*]

EDDIE. That's the thanks I get? Which I took the blankets off my bed for yiz? You gonna apologize to me, Marco! *Marco!*

FIRST OFFICER. [*In the doorway with* MARCO.] All right, lady, let them go. Get in the car, fellas, it's over there.

[RODOLPHO *is almost carrying the sobbing* CATHERINE *off up the street, left.*]

CATHERINE. He was born in Philadelphia! What do you want from him?

FIRST OFFICER. Step aside, lady, come on now . . .

[*The* SECOND OFFICER *has moved off with the two strange men.* MARCO, *taking advantage of the* FIRST OFFICER's *being occupied with* CATHERINE, *suddenly frees himself and points back at* EDDIE.]

MARCO. That one! I accuse that one!

[EDDIE *brushes* BEATRICE *aside and rushes out to the stoop.*]

FIRST OFFICER. [*Grabbing him and moving him quickly off up the left street.*] Come on!

MARCO. [*As he is taken off, pointing back at* EDDIE.] That one! He killed my children! That one stole the food from my children!

[MARCO *is gone. The crowd has turned to* EDDIE.]

EDDIE. [*To* LIPARI *and wife.*] He's crazy! I give them the blankets off my bed. Six months I kept them like my own brothers!

[LIPARI, *the butcher, turns and starts up left with his arm around his wife.*]

EDDIE. Lipari! [*He follows* LIPARI *up left.*] For Christ's sake, I kept them, I give them the blankets off my bed!

[LIPARI *and wife exit.* EDDIE *turns and starts crossing down right to* LOUIS *and* MIKE.]

EDDIE. Louis! *Louis!*

[LOUIS *barely turns, then walks off and exits down right with* MIKE. *Only* BEATRICE *is left on the stoop.* CATHERINE *now returns, blank-eyed, from offstage and the car.* EDDIE *calls after* LOUIS *and* MIKE.]

EDDIE. He's gonna take that back. He's gonna take that back or I'll kill him! You hear me? I'll kill him! I'll kill him! [*He exits up street calling.*]

[*There is a pause of darkness before the lights rise, on the reception room of a prison.* MARCO *is seated;* ALFIERI, CATHERINE, *and* RODOLPHO *standing.*]

ALFIERI. I'm waiting, Marco, what do you say?

RODOLPHO. Marco never hurt anybody.

ALFIERI. I can bail you out until your hearing comes up. But I'm not going to do it, you understand me? Unless I have your promise. You're an honorable man,

I will believe your promise. Now what do you say?

MARCO. In my country he would be dead now. He would not live this long.

ALFIERI. All right, Rodolpho—you come with me now.

RODOLPHO. No! Please, Mister. Marco— promise the man. Please, I want you to watch the wedding. How can I be married and you're in here? Please, you're not going to do anything; you know you're not.

[MARCO *is silent.*]

CATHERINE. [*Kneeling left of* MARCO.] Marco, don't you understand? He can't bail you out if you're gonna do something bad. To hell with Eddie. Nobody is gonna talk to him again if he lives to a hundred. Everybody knows you spit in his face, that's enough, isn't it? Give me the satisfaction—I want you at the wedding. You got a wife and kids, Marco. You could be workin' till the hearing comes up, instead of layin' around here.

MARCO. [*To* ALFIERI.] I have no chance?

ALFIERI. [*Crosses to behind* MARCO.] No, Marco. You're going back. The hearing is a formality, that's all.

MARCO. But him? There is a chance, eh?

ALFIERI. When she marries him he can start to become an American. They permit that, if the wife is born here.

MARCO. [*Looking at* RODOLPHO.] Well— we did something. [*He lays a palm on* RODOLPHO's *arm and* RODOLPHO *covers it.*]

RODOLPHO. Marco, tell the man.

MARCO. [*Pulling his hand away.*] What will I tell him? He knows such a promise is dishonorable.

ALFIERI. To promise not to kill is not dishonorable.

MARCO. [*Looking at* ALFIERI.] No?

ALFIERI. No.

MARCO. [*Gesturing with his head—this is a new idea.*] Then what is done with such a man?

ALFIERI. Nothing. If he obeys the law, he lives. That's all.

MARCO. [*Rises, turns to* ALFIERI.] The law? All the law is not in a book.

ALFIERI. Yes. In a book. There is no other law.

MARCO. [*His anger rising.*] He degraded my brother. My blood. He robbed my children, he mocks my work. I work to come here, mister!

ALFIERI. I know, Marco—

MARCO. There is no law for that? Where is the law for that?

ALFIERI. There is none.

MARCO. [*Shaking his head, sitting.*] I don't understand this country.

ALFIERI. Well? What is your answer? You have five or six weeks you could work. Or else you sit here. What do you say to me?

MARCO. [*Lowers his eyes. It almost seems he is ashamed.*] All right.

ALFIERI. You won't touch him. This is your promise.

[*Slight pause.*]

MARCO. Maybe he wants to apologize to me. [MARCO *is staring away.* ALFIERI *takes one of his hands.*]

ALFIERI. This is not God, Marco. You hear? Only God makes justice.

MARCO. All right.

ALFIERI. [*Nodding, not with assurance.*] Good! Catherine, Rodolpho, Marco, let us go.

[CATHERINE *kisses* RODOLPHO *and* MARCO, *then kisses* ALFIERI'S *hand.*]

CATHERINE. I'll get Beatrice and meet you at the church. [*She leaves quickly.*]

[MARCO *rises.* RODOLPHO *suddenly embraces him.* MARCO *pats him on the back and* RODOLPHO *exits after* CATHERINE. MARCO *faces* ALFIERI.]

ALFIERI. Only God, Marco.

[MARCO *turns and walks out.* ALFIERI *with a certain processional tread leaves the stage. The lights dim out.*]

The lights rise in the apartment. EDDIE *is alone in the rocker, rocking back and forth in little surges. Pause. Now* BEATRICE *emerges from a bedroom. She is in her best clothes, wearing a hat.*]

BEATRICE. [*With fear, going to* EDDIE.] I'll be back in about an hour, Eddie. All right?

EDDIE. [*Quietly, almost inaudibly, as though drained.*] What, have I been talkin' to myself?

BEATRICE. Eddie, for God's sake, it's her wedding.

EDDIE. Didn't you hear what I told you? You walk out that door to that wedding you ain't comin' back here, Beatrice.

BEATRICE. Why! What do you want?

EDDIE. I want my respect. Didn't you ever hear of that? From my wife?

[CATHERINE *enters from bedroom.*]

CATHERINE. It's after three; we're supposed to be there already, Beatrice. The priest won't wait.

BEATRICE. Eddie. It's her wedding. There'll be nobody there from her family. For my sister let me go. I'm going for my sister.

EDDIE. [*As though hurt.*] Look, I been arguin' with you all day already, Beatrice, and I said what I'm gonna say. He's gonna come here and apologize to me or nobody from this house is goin' into that church today. Now if that's more to you than I am, then go. But don't come back. You be on my side or on their side, that's all.

CATHERINE. [*Suddenly.*] Who the hell do you think you are?

BEATRICE. Sssh!

CATHERINE. You got no more right to tell nobody nothin'! Nobody! The rest of your life, nobody!

BEATRICE. Shut up, Katie! [*She turns* CATHERINE *around.*]

CATHERINE. You're gonna come with me!

BEATRICE. I can't Katie, I can't . . .

CATHERINE. How can you listen to him? This rat!

BEATRICE. [*Shaking* CATHERINE.] Don't you call him that!

CATHERINE. [*Clearing from* BEATRICE.] What're you scared of? He's a rat! He belongs in the sewer!

BEATRICE. Stop it!

CATHERINE. [*Weeping.*] He bites people when they sleep! He comes when nobody's lookin' and poisons decent people. In the garbage he belongs!

[EDDIE *seems about to pick up the table and fling it at her.*]

BEATRICE. No, Eddie! Eddie! [*To* CATHERINE.] Then we all belong in the garbage. You, and me too. Don't say that. Whatever happened we all done it, and don't you ever forget it, Catherine. [*She goes to* CATHERINE.] Now go, go to your wedding, Katie, I'll stay home. Go. God bless you, God bless your children.

[*Enter* RODOLPHO.]

RODOLPHO. Eddie?

EDDIE. Who said you could come in here? Get outa here!

RODOLPHO. Marco is coming, Eddie. [*Pause.* BEATRICE *raises her hands in terror.*] He's praying in the church. You understand? [*Pause.* RODOLPHO *advances into the room.*] Catherine, I think it is better we go. Come with me.

CATHERINE. Eddie, go away, please.

BEATRICE. [*Quietly.*] Eddie. Let's go someplace. Come. You and me. [*He has not moved.*] I don't want you to be here when he comes. I'll get your coat.

EDDIE. Where? Where am I goin'? This is my house.

BEATRICE. [*Crying out.*] What's the use of it! He's crazy now, you know the way they get, what good is it! You got nothin' against Marco, you always liked Marco!

EDDIE. I got nothin' against Marco? Which he called me a rat in front of the whole neighborhood? Which he said I killed his children! Where you been?

RODOLPHO. [*Quite suddenly, stepping up to* EDDIE.] It is my fault, Eddie. Everything. I wish to apologize. It was wrong that I do not ask your permission. I kiss your hand. [*He reaches for* EDDIE's *hand, but* EDDIE *snaps it away from him.*]

BEATRICE. Eddie, he's apologizing!

RODOLPHO. I have made all our troubles. But you have insult me too. Maybe God understand why you did that to me. Maybe you did not mean to insult me at all—

BEATRICE. Listen to him! Eddie, listen what he's tellin' you!

RODOLPHO. I think, maybe when Marco comes, if we can tell him we are comrades now, and we have no more argument between us. Then maybe Marco will not—

EDDIE. Now, listen—

CATHERINE. Eddie, give him a chance!

BEATRICE. What do you want! Eddie, what do you want!

EDDIE. I want my name! He didn't take my name; he's only a punk. Marco's got my name—[*To* RODOLPHO.] and you can run tell him, kid, that he's gonna give it back to me in front of this neighborhood, or we have it out. [*Hoisting up his pants.*] Come on, where is he? Take me to him.

BEATRICE. Eddie, listen—

EDDIE. I heard enough! Come on, let's go!

BEATRICE. Only blood is good? He kissed your hand!

EDDIE. What he does don't mean nothin' to nobody! [*To* RODOLPHO.] Come on!

BEATRICE. [*Barring his way to the stairs.*] What's gonna mean somethin'? Eddie, listen to me. Who could give you your name? Listen to me, I love you, I'm talkin' to you, I love you; if Marco'll kiss your hand outside, if he goes on his knees, what is he got to give you? That's not what you want.

EDDIE. Don't bother me!

BEATRICE. You want somethin' else, Eddie, and you can never have her!

CATHERINE. [*In horror.*] B.!

EDDIE. [*Shocked, horrified, his fists clenching.*] Beatrice.

[MARCO *appears outside, walking toward the door from a distant point.*]

BEATRICE. [*Crying out, weeping.*] The truth is not as bad as blood, Eddie! I'm tellin' you the truth—tell her good-by forever!

EDDIE. [*Crying out in agony.*] That's what you think of me—that I would have such a thought? [*His fists clench his head as though it will burst.*]

MARCO. [*Calling near the door outside.*] Eddie Carbone!

[EDDIE *swerves about; all stand transfixed for an instant. People appear outside.*]

EDDIE. [*As though flinging his challenge.*] Yeah, Marco! Eddie Carbone. Eddie Carbone. Eddie Carbone. [*He goes up the stairs and emerges from the apartment.* RODOLPHO *streaks up and out past him and runs to* MARCO.]

RODOLPHO. No, Marco, please! Eddie, please, he has children! You will kill a family!

BEATRICE. Go in the house! Eddie, go in the house!

EDDIE. [*He gradually comes to address the people.*] Maybe he came to apologize to me. Heh, Marco? For what you said about me in front of the neighborhood? [*He is incensing himself and little bits of laughter even escape him as his eyes are murderous and he cracks his knuckles in his hands with a strange sort of relaxation.*] He knows that ain't right. To do like that? To a man? Which I put my roof over their head and my food in their mouth? Like in the Bible? Strangers I never seen in my whole life? To come out of the water and grab a girl for a passport? To go and take from your own family like from the stable—and never a word to me? And now accusations in the bargain! [*Directly to* MARCO.] Wipin' the neighborhood with my name like a dirty rag! I want my name, Marco. [*He is moving now, carefully, toward* MARCO.] Now gimme my name and we go together to the wedding.

BEATRICE *and* CATHERINE. [*Keening.*] Eddie! Eddie, don't! Eddie!

EDDIE. No, Marco knows what's right from wrong. Tell the people, Marco, tell them what a liar you are! [*He has his arms spread and* MARCO *is spreading his.*] Come on, liar, you know what you done! [*He lunges for* MARCO *as a great hushed shout goes up from the people.* MARCO *strikes* EDDIE *beside the neck.*]

MARCO. Animal! You go on your knees to me!

[EDDIE *goes down with the blow and* MARCO *starts to raise a foot to stomp him when* EDDIE *springs a knife into his hand and* MARCO *steps back.* LOUIS *rushes in toward* EDDIE.]

LOUIS. Eddie, for Christ's sake!

[EDDIE *raises the knife and* LOUIS *halts and steps back.*]

EDDIE. You lied about me, Marco. Now say it. Come on now, say it!

MARCO. Anima-a-a-l!

[EDDIE *lunges with the knife.* MARCO *grabs his arm, turning the blade inward and pressing it home as the women and* LOUIS *and* MIKE *rush in and separate them, and* EDDIE, *the knife still in his hand, falls to his knees before* MARCO. *The two women support him for a moment, calling his name again and again.*]

CATHERINE. Eddie I never meant to do nothing bad to you.

EDDIE. Then why—Oh, B.!

BEATRICE. Yes, yes!

EDDIE. My B.! [*He dies in her arms, and* BEATRICE *covers him with her body.* ALFIERI, *who is in the crowd, turns out to the audience. The lights have gone down, leaving him in a glow, while behind him the dull prayers of the people and the keening of the women continue.*]

ALFIERI. Most of the time now we settle for half and I like it better. But the truth is holy, and even as I know how wrong he was, and his death useless, I tremble, for I confess that something perversely pure calls to me from his memory—not purely good, but himself purely, for he allowed himself to be wholly known and for that I think I will love him more than all my sensible clients. And yet, it is better to settle for half, it must be! And so I mourn him—I admit it—with a certain . . . alarm.

CURTAIN

INTRODUCTION TO THE TWO-ACT VERSION OF A VIEW FROM THE BRIDGE

Arthur Miller

A play is rarely given a second chance. Unlike a novel, which may be received initially with less than enthusiasm, and then as time goes by hailed by a large public, a play usually makes its mark right off or it vanishes into oblivion. Two of mine, *The Crucible* and *A View from the Bridge*, failed to find large audiences with their original Broadway productions. Both were regarded as rather cold plays at first. However, after a couple of years *The Crucible* was produced again off Broadway and ran two years, without a line being changed from the original. With McCarthy dead it was once again possible to feel warmly toward the play, whereas during his time of power it was suspected of being a special plea, a concoction and unaesthetic. On its second time around its humanity emerged and it could be enjoyed as drama.

At this writing I have not yet permitted a second New York production of *A View from the Bridge* principally because I have not had the desire to see it through the mill a second time. However, a year or so after its first production it was done with great success

in London and then in Paris, where it ran two years. It is done everywhere in this country without any apparent difficulty in reaching the emotions of the audience. This play, however, unlike *The Crucible*, I have revised, and it was the revision which London and Paris saw. The nature of the revisions bears directly upon the questions of form and style which interest students and theater workers.

The original play produced on Broadway (Viking, 1955) was in one act. It was a hard, telegraphic, unadorned drama. Nothing was permitted which did not advance the progress of Eddie's catastrophe in a most direct way. In a Note to the published play, I wrote: "What struck me first about this tale when I heard it one night in my neighborhood was how directly, with what breathtaking simplicity, it did evolve. It seemed to me, finally, that its very bareness, its absolutely unswerving path, its exposed skeleton, so to speak, was its wisdom and even its charm and must not be tampered with. . . . These *qualities* of the events themselves, their texture, seemed to me more psychologically telling than a conventional investigation in width which would necessarily relax that clear, clean line of his catastrophe."

The explanation for this point of view lies in great part in the atmosphere of the time in which the play was written. It seemed to me then that the theater was retreating into an area of psycho-sexual romanticism, and this at the very moment when great events both at home and abroad cried out for recognition and analytic inspection. In a word, I was tired of mere sympathy in the theater. The spectacle of still another misunderstood victim left me impatient. The tender emotions, I felt, were being overworked. I wanted to write in a way that would call up the faculties of knowing as well as feeling. To bathe the audience in tears, to grip people by the age-old methods of suspense, to theatricalize life, in a word, seemed faintly absurd to me if not disgusting.

In *The Crucible* I had taken a step, I felt, toward a more self-aware drama. The Puritan not only felt, but constantly referred his feelings to concepts, to codes and ideas of social and ethical importance. Feeling, it seemed to me, had to be made of importance; the dramatic victory had to be more than a triumph over the audience's indifference. It must call up a concept, a new awareness.

I had known the story of *A View from the Bridge* for a long time. A water-front worker who had known Eddie's prototype told it to me. I had never thought to make a play of it because it was too complete, there was nothing I could add. And then a time came when its very completeness became appealing. It suddenly seemed to me that I ought to deliver it onto the stage as fact; that interpretation was inherent in the very existence of the tale in the first place. I saw that the reason I had not written it was that as a whole its meaning escaped me. I could not fit it into myself. It existed apart from me and seemed not to express anything within me. Yet it refused to disappear.

I wrote it in a mood of experiment—to see what it might mean. I kept to the *tale*, trying not to change its original shape. I wanted the audience to feel toward it as I had on hearing it for the first time—not so much with heart-wringing sympathy as with wonder. For when it was told to me I knew its ending a few minutes after the teller had begun to speak. I wanted to create suspense but not by withholding information. It must be suspenseful because one knew too well how it would come out, so that the basic feeling would be the desire to stop this man and tell him what he was really doing to his life. Thus, by knowing more than the hero, the audience would rather automatically see his life through conceptualized feelings.

As a consequence of this viewpoint, the characters were not permitted to talk about this and that before getting down to their functions in the tale; when a character entered he proceeded directly to serve the catastrophe. Thus, normal naturalistic acting techniques had to be modified. Excessive and arbitrary gestures were eliminated; the set itself was shorn of every adorn-

ment. An atmosphere was attempted in which nothing existed but the purpose of the tale.

The trouble was that neither the director, the actors, nor I had had any experience with this kind of staging. It was difficult to know how far to go. We were all aware that a strange style was called for which we were unsure how to provide.

About a year later in London new conditions created new solutions. Seemingly inconsequential details suggested these solutions at times. For one, the British actors could not reproduce the Brooklyn argot and had to create one that was never heard on heaven or earth. Already naturalism was evaporated by this much: the characters were slightly strange beings in a world of their own. Also, the pay scales of the London theater made it possible to do what I could not do in New York—hire a crowd.

These seemingly mundane facts had important consequences. The mind of Eddie Carbone is not comprehensible apart from its relation to his neighborhood, his fellow workers, his social situation. His self-esteem depends upon their estimate of him, and his value is created largely by his fidelity to the code of his culture. In New York we could have only four strategically placed actors to represent the community. In London there were at least twenty men and women surrounding the main action. Peter Brook, the British director, could then proceed to design a set which soared to the roof with fire escapes, passage-ways, suggested apartments, so that one sensed that Eddie was living out his horror in the midst of a certain normality, and that, invisibly and without having to speak of it, he was getting ready to invoke upon himself the wrath of his tribe. A certain size accrued to him as a result. The importance of his interior psychological dilemma was magnified to the size it would have in life. What had seemed like a mere aberration had now risen to a fatal violation of an ancient law. By the presence of his neighbors alone the play and Eddie were made more humanly understandable and moving. There was also the fact that the British cast, accustomed to playing Shakespeare, could incorporate into a seemingly realistic style the conception of the play— they moved easily into the larger-than-life attitude which the play demanded, and without the self-conscious awkwardness, the uncertain stylishness which hounds many actors without classic training.

As a consequence of not having to work at making the play seem as factual, as bare as I had conceived it, I felt now that it could afford to include elements of simple human motivation which I had rigorously excluded before—specifically, the viewpoint of Eddie's wife, and *her* dilemma in relation to him. This, in fact, accounts for almost all the added material which made it necessary to break the play in the middle for an intermission. In other words, once Eddie had been placed squarely in his social context, among his people, the mythlike feeling of the story emerged of itself, and he could be made more human and less a figure, a force. It thus seemed quite in keeping that certain details of realism should be allowed; a Christmas tree and decorations in the living room, for one, and a realistic make-up, which had been avoided in New York, where the actor was always much cleaner than a longshoreman ever is. In a word, the nature of the British actor and of the production there made it possible to concentrate more upon realistic characterization while the universality of Eddie's type was strengthened at the same time.

But it was not only external additions, such as a new kind of actor, sets, and so forth, which led to the expansion of the play. As I have said, the original was written in the hope that I would understand what it meant to me. It was only during the latter part of its run in New York that, while watching a performance one afternoon, I saw my own involvement in this story. Quite suddenly the play seemed to be "mine" and not merely a story I had heard. The revisions subsequently made were in part the result of that new awareness.

In general, then, I think it can be said that by the addition of significant psychological and behavioral detail the play became not only more human, warmer and less remote, but also a clearer statement. Eddie is still not a man to weep over; the play does not attempt to swamp an audience in tears. But it is more possible now to relate his actions to our own and thus to understand ourselves a little better not only as isolated psychological entities, but as we connect to our fellows and our long past together.

MARCH 1960

PART TWO

COMEDY

In tragedy there are no temporal solutions, but in comedy, in the comic norm, problems are solved, sometimes just as we would like them to be and sometimes with more realistic irony than we would desire. Instead of tragedy's inevitability and necessity, what is discovered in comedy's recognition is something we find more customary and natural; the laws of natural and reasonable attitudes usually prevail as all the complications and improbabilities of the plot are resolved in the resolution of the comic norm. That the resolution does not have to seem probable to seem appropriate is another way of saying with Northrop Frye that "happy endings do not impress us as true, but as desirable." Our desire creates assent for the appropriateness of even some highly manipulated resolutions.

The sensible view of nature, central to the comic vision, must include much that is strange, grotesque, and even tragic from a particular perspective because all things are found in nature, but comedy's perspective is continuous. Time, which in tragedy produces closed inevitabilities, ripens the older generation in comedy and replaces them with young lovers. The comic norm shows us "the ways of wisdom and folly" in Susanne Langer's phrase, but the comic contest shows us life as opportunity, its vital rhythm "a brainy opportunism in the face of an essentially dreadful universe."

THE CON GAME

The hero of Roman comedy used deception and disguise to counteract the actions of blocking figures, usually fathers, opposing his union with a girl who did not appear on stage. The characters on stage—with the exception of an occasional maid, mother, or courtesan—were men. They either aided the hero or attempted to block his union with the girl, and the contest of one con game against another became an essential feature of comedy from those early times. The fathers and other miserly blocking figures in the small, artificial, invented world of that comedy represented all that is rigid, unspontaneous and life-denying in the experience of the audience. The hero's deception of them seemed justified in the audience's emotions in the name of all that is natural and liberating. Through the sexual union of the lovers, life could be renewed. It was a contest between a conventional "humorous" society and a well-intentioned hero. But the audience's interest was less in the lovers than in the plot of deception that stripped the blocking figures of power against them.

In *Tartuffe*, a prime example of the comic con game in the French neo-classical style, Molière employs the chief characters of the Roman plot—the lovers, the blocking father, and the witty servant—but it is chiefly Tartuffe as the con man who overreaches himself, the deceiver self-deceived, whose action gives shape to the plot. Had Tartuffe been content to exploit the gullibility and religiosity of Orgon, he might have succeeded because Tartuffe, neither religious nor a convincing imposter, had an easy prey in Orgon. In the comic norm the success of a deception depends on the self-deception of the one deceived. Tartuffe is caught only when, blind with self-assurance, he attempts to seduce Elmire and is exposed by the natural, undeceived characters of the play. The deceiver, whether hero or villain, and the self-deceived, whether villain, lover, madman, or fool, are comedy's basic characters.

As comedy became increasingly realistic and ironic, deception and recognition remained the basis of its plot, and the cleverness of the situation, the characters, and the dialogue the basis of the audience's interest. The masters of comedy became masters of the depiction of fools, clever villains, and lovers. The exposure of the villains and fools may have seemed to be the moral, but the audience watched life resolved, as they have always wanted life to be resolved, in favor of the well-intentioned. The more inventive and expert the villain, the greater the interest in his ingenuity and the greater the satisfaction in the defeat of his bad intentions. The con man was always of more interest than the lover unless the lover was himself a master of the game.

Comedy, which merges into irony on one extreme and into romance at the other, has as its dramatic base farce, fantasy, and exaggeration in style. It may satirize society or human absurdity or both, but usually it celebrates, as *The Love of Don Perlimplín* and *The Playboy of the Western World* do, the value of love, wit, and good intentions. As it moves toward irony the worth of intentions becomes ambiguous and the value of wit no longer measurable in an existential world, and as the "essentially dreadful universe" comes into perspective as in Pinter's tragicomedy *The Dumb Waiter*, we see absurd men using their wits to survive in a world as mysterious and unreasonable, as absurd, to them as our own

is in some moods to us. At the opposite extreme, that of romance, the value of wit and good intentions is clear, and love, as the farcical and fantastic story of Don Perlimplín suggests, is worth dying for. At his death, with survival no longer the issue, we may question whether we are still in the realm of the comic. While that question is certainly worth discussing, the farcical elements in the costumes, the dialogue and texture of the interactions in that play make it clear that Lorca's intention was to write a comedy, but one of a special kind, a comedy with an unhappy ending.

As an example of the con game, the play of *Perlimplín* achieves some sort of ultimate audacity. Perlimplín, as con man, must outwit the blocking figure—in this case, his own pathetic body. (In the slang of Spanish children, the word *perlimplín* means small penis.) In moving from the play's beginning to its end, the childish old man, through Lorca's theatrical quicksilver, traverses back and forth between protagonist and antagonist: the protagonist is Perlimplín's spirit, the antagonist his flesh.

But Perlimplín is a figure of comedy in that he insists upon the flesh. Because of this choice, he takes us from the unthinking laughter of farce, through agony, and into moral serenity. The same course is run in the play's style. Lorca first shows us his actors as figures out of a comic book. The *aleluya* of the subtitle refers to a Spanish custom of distributing decorated papers, something like our valentines, except that Lorca, when he is his most explicit, is sometimes, like Perlimplín, most devious. Even at the moment when the love of Perlimplín begins to take a sinister turn, when he realizes that his bride has betrayed him on their wedding night, the playwright shows us a flight of black paper birds as if to reassure us that it is all still a game. It ends in agony, an agony which is also a triumph. Lorca has said that, to him, the best sort of comedy is that in which the audience can exercise its own choice between laughter and tears.

THE LOVERS

Comedy's perspective is the point of view of the world, and the hero, whether his intentions are good or ill, is in a contest with the world for the means of survival, as Susanne Langer's definition describes. We watch the success of his ingenuity with some satisfaction, but we keep our emotions at some distance from him because, knowing the world, we see the contrivance of the plot. We are ready for exaggeration, surprise, audacious attempts, disappointments overtaken by new good fortunes, reunions, reconciliations, and a triumph over all that is foolish, mean in spirit, and corrupt—even over evil itself. Such comedy gives us the world as we would like it. It may have also a satirical or corrective function. It may expose those "humors," follies, self-deceptions, and obsessions that we know to be universally a part of the world. It may arouse our moral indignation, as *Tartuffe* does, and provoke what Meredith called "thoughtful laughter." But the center of the essential cosmic spirit is the young lovers whose union can provide for the survival of the race and the possible reformation of society. Susanne Langer observes that "Comedy abstracts, and reincarnates for our perception. . . ." Viewed abstractly, the young lovers are nature's agents in a contest with a society that they will renew and possibly reform.

The lovers in *Major Barbara* illustrate Shaw's belief in creative evolution; he gives us lovers, superior in mind and spirit, who cooperate in a larger process for the betterment of mankind. They reason with one another, and they admire reasonableness and "character," by which they mean independence of mind and spirit. Socially responsible, they are never slaves to conventional morality but always moralists for larger creative purposes. "Let God's will be done for its own sake," says Barbara (passionately?) as she agrees to marry Cousins. The reasonable, well-educated lovers of Shaw's *Major Barbara* may be contrasted

to the passionate, country lovers of Synge's *The Playboy of the Western World*, whose lyrical language defies both reason and responsibility in its joyous celebration of life. Working with the ribald ingredients of folk tales and the "popular imagination that is fiery and magnificent" referred to in the Preface, Synge's play communicates his joy in life and language that is "rich and loving." It invites us to suspend our moral indignation at a man who has killed his father, to admire at normal comic distance his audacity, to celebrate his acceptance of love and life, and to see in Pegeen's rejection of him a compromise, one we all know something of, with society's expectations.

That we can suspend our moral indignation in *Playboy of the Western World*, with what Bergson called "a momentary anesthesia of the heart," is an achievement of Synge's style. There is no single characteristic that marks a style as comic. This book has examples of four entirely different comic styles, but wit and surprise are common to both the reasonable styles of Molière and Shaw and the passionate styles of Synge and Lorca. Wit and the reversal of expectation that so much wit is based on is essential not just for laughter but for the comic contest itself, which shows humans using their wits to survive. In the great comedies people are quicker with their wits and words than we are, and we laugh with what Santayana called a "little triumph" of the mind when it receives an illumination.

Synge and Lorca, Shaw's contemporaries, wrote poetic drama while the realistic drama was on the ascendency around them. Even as Synge argued that his language was realistic, merely an artistic rendering of language to be heard in certain parts of Ireland, he was willing to call *The Playboy of the Western World* "an extravaganza," a term that might apply as well to Lorca's *The Love of Don Perlimplín*. Both Synge, working from a language he heard, and Lorca, working from an inherited Spanish tradition, wrote comedies that develop surprising twists on the comic norm. These variations are not so much the result of characterization as of the total conception. The final reversed expectations are something inherent in the whole—the style and wit and inner logic—not the result of characterization so completely realized that we feel, as we do in tragedy, that the individual could not have done other than he did.

THE CON GAME

TARTUFFE

Molière

translated by Richard Wilbur

CHARACTERS

MME PERNELLE, Orgon's mother

ORGON, Elmire's husband

ELMIRE, Orgon's wife

DAMIS, Orgon's son, Elmire's stepson

MARIANE, Orgon's daughter, Elmire's step-daughter, in love with Valère

VALERE, in love with Mariane

CLEANTE, Orgon's brother-in-law

TARTUFFE, a hypocrite

DORINE, Mariane's lady's-maid

M. LOYAL, a bailiff

A POLICE OFFICER

FLIPOTE, Mme Pernelle's maid

The scene throughout: Orgon's house in Paris

ACT I

Scene One

MADAME PERNELLE *and* FLIPOTE, *her maid*, ELMIRE, MARIANE, DORINE, DAMIS, CLÉANTE

MADAME PERNELLE

Come, come, Flipote; it's time I left this place.

ELMIRE

I can't keep up, you walk at such a pace.

MADAME PERNELLE

Don't trouble, child; no need to show me out.
It's not your manners I'm concerned about.

ELMIRE

We merely pay you the respect we owe.
But, Mother, why this hurry? Must you go?

MADAME PERNELLE

I must. This house appals me. No one in it
Will pay attention for a single minute.
Children, I take my leave much vexed in
   spirit.
I offer good advice, but you won't hear it.
You all break in and chatter on and on.
It's like a madhouse with the keeper gone.

DORINE

If . . .

MADAME PERNELLE

   Girl, you talk too much, and I'm afraid
You're far too saucy for a lady's-maid.
You push in everywhere and have your say.

DAMIS

But . . .

MADAME PERNELLE

   You, boy, grow more foolish every day.
To think my grandson should be such a
   dunce!
I've said a hundred times, if I've said it once,
That if you keep the course on which you've
   started,
You'll leave your worthy father broken-
   hearted.

MARIANE

I think . . .

MADAME PERNELLE

   And you, his sister, seem so pure,
So shy, so innocent, and so demure.
But you know what they say about still
   waters.
I pity parents with secretive daughters.

ELMIRE

Now, Mother . . .

MADAME PERNELLE

   And as for you, child, let me add
That your behavior is extremely bad,
And a poor example for these children, too.
Their dear, dead mother did far better than
   you.
You're much too free with money, and I'm
   distressed
To see you so elaborately dressed.
When it's one's husband that one aims to
   please,
One has no need of costly fripperies.

CLÉANTE

Oh, Madam, really . . .

MADAME PERNELLE

   You are her brother, Sir,
And I respect and love you; yet if I were
My son, this lady's good and pious spouse,
I wouldn't make you welcome in my house.
You're full of worldly counsels which, I fear,
Aren't suitable for decent folk to hear.
I've spoken bluntly, Sir; but it behooves us
Not to mince words when righteous fervor
   moves us.

DAMIS

Your man Tartuffe is full of holy speeches . . .

MADAME PERNELLE

And practises precisely what he preaches.
He's a fine man, and should be listened to.
I will not hear him mocked by fools like you.

DAMIS

Good God! Do you expect me to submit
To the tyranny of that carping hypocrite?
Must we forgo all joys and satisfactions
Because that bigot censures all our actions?

DORINE

To hear him talk—and he talks all the time—
There's nothing one can do that's not a crime.
He rails at everything, your dear Tartuffe.

MADAME PERNELLE

Whatever he reproves deserves reproof.
He's out to save your souls, and all of you
Must love him, as my son would have you do.

DAMIS

Ah no, Grandmother, I could never take
To such a rascal, even for my father's sake.
That's how I feel, and I shall not dissemble.
His every action makes me seethe and tremble
With helpless anger, and I have no doubt
That he and I will shortly have it out.

DORINE

Surely it is a shame and a disgrace
To see this man usurp the master's place—
To see this beggar who, when first he came,
Had not a shoe or shoestring to his name
So far forget himself that he behaves
As if the house were his, and we his slaves.

MADAME PERNELLE

Well, mark my words, your souls would fare
   far better
If you obeyed his precepts to the letter.

DORINE

You see him as a saint. I'm far less awed;
In fact, I see right through him. He's a fraud.

MADAME PERNELLE

Nonsense!

DORINE

   His man Laurent's the same, or worse;
I'd not trust either with a penny purse.

MADAME PERNELLE

I can't say what his servant's morals may be;
His own great goodness I can guarantee.
You all regard him with distaste and fear
Because he tells you what you're loath to
   hear,
Condemns your sins, points out your moral
   flaws,

And humbly strives to further Heaven's
   cause.

DORINE

If sin is all that bothers him, why is it
He's so upset when folk drop in to visit?
Is Heaven so outraged by a social call
That he must prophesy against us all?
I'll tell you what I think: if you ask me,
He's jealous of my mistress' company.

MADAME PERNELLE

Rubbish! (*To Elmire:*) He's not alone, child,
   in complaining
Of all your promiscuous entertaining.
Why, the whole neighborhood's upset, I
   know,
By all these carriages that come and go,
With crowds of guests parading in and out
And noisy servants loitering about.
In all of this, I'm sure there's nothing vicious;
But why give people cause to be suspicious?

CLÉANTE

They need no cause; they'll talk in any case.
Madam, this world would be a joyless place
If, fearing what malicious tongues might say,
We locked our doors and turned our friends
   away.
And even if one did so dreary a thing,
D'you think those tongues would cease their
   chattering?
One can't fight slander; it's a losing battle;
Let us instead ignore their tittle-tattle.
Let's strive to live by conscience' clear
   decrees,
And let the gossips gossip as they please.

DORINE

If there is talk against us, I know the source:
It's Daphne and her little husband, of course.
Those who have greatest cause for guilt and
   shame
Are quickest to besmirch a neighbor's name.
When there's a chance for libel, they never
   miss it;

When something can be made to seem illicit
They're off at once to spread the joyous news,
Adding to fact what fantasies they choose.
By talking up their neighbor's indiscretions
They seek to camouflage their own trans-
    gressions,
Hoping that others' innocent affairs
Will lend a hue of innocence to theirs,
Or that their own black guilt will come to
    seem
Part of a general shady color-scheme.

MADAME PERNELLE

All that is quite irrelevant. I doubt
That anyone's more virtuous and devout
Than dear Orante; and I'm informed that
    she
Condemns your mode of life most vehe-
    mently.

DORINE

Oh, yes, she's strict, devout, and has no
    taint
Of worldliness; in short, she seems a saint.
But it was time which taught her that dis-
    guise;
She's thus because she can't be otherwise.
So long as her attractions could enthrall,
She flounced and flirted and enjoyed it all,
But now that they're no longer what they
    were
She quits a world which fast is quitting her,
And wears a veil of virtue to conceal
Her bankrupt beauty and her lost appeal.
That's what becomes of old coquettes today:
Distressed when all their lovers fall away,
They see no recourse but to play the prude,
And so confer a style on solitude.
Thereafter, they're severe with everyone,
Condemning all our actions, pardoning
    none,
And claiming to be pure, austere, and
    zealous
When, if the truth were known, they're
    merely jealous,
And cannot bear to see another know
The pleasures time has forced them to forgo.

MADAME PERNELLE (*Initially to Elmire:*)

That sort of talk is what you like to hear;
Therefore you'd have us all keep still, my
    dear,
While Madam rattles on the livelong day.
Nevertheless, I mean to have my say.
I tell you that your're blest to have Tartuffe
Dwelling, as my son's guest, beneath this
    roof;
That Heaven has sent him to forestall its
    wrath
By leading you, once more, to the true path;
That all he reprehends its reprehensible,
And that you'd better heed him, and be
    sensible.
These visits, balls, and parties in which you
    revel
Are nothing but inventions of the Devil.
One never hears a word that's edifying:
Nothing but chaff and foolishness and lying,
As well as vicious gossip in which one's
    neighbor
Is cut to bits with epee, foil, and saber.
People of sense are driven half-insane
At such affairs, where noise and folly reign
And reputations perish thick and fast.
As a wise preacher said on Sunday last,
Parties are Towers of Babylon, because
The guests all babble on with never a
    pause;
And then he told a story which, I think . . .

(*To Cléante:*)

I heard that laugh, Sir, and I saw that
    wink!
Go find your silly friends and laugh some
    more!
Enough; I'm going; don't show me to the
    door.
I leave this household much dismayed and
    vexed;
I cannot say when I shall see you next.

(*Slapping Flipote:*)

Wake up, don't stand there gaping into
    space!

I'll slap some sense into that stupid face.
Move, move, you slut.

Scene Two

CLÉANTE, DORINE

CLÉANTE

      I think I'll stay behind;
I want no further pieces of her mind.
How that old lady . . .

DORINE

      Oh, what wouldn't she say
If she could hear you speak of her that way!
She'd thank you for the *lady*, but I'm sure
She'd find the *old* a little premature.

CLÉANTE

My, what a scene she made, and what a din!
And how this man Tartuffe has taken her
   in!

DORINE

Yes, but her son is even worse deceived;
His folly must be seen to be believed.
In the late troubles, he played an able part
And served his king with wise and loyal
   heart,
But he's quite lost his senses since he fell
Beneath Tartuffe's infatuating spell.
He calls him brother, and loves him as his
   life,
Preferring him to mother, child, or wife.
In him and him alone will he confide;
He's made him his confessor and his guide;
He pets and pampers him with love more
   tender
Than any pretty mistress could engender,
Gives him the place of honor when they
   dine,
Delights to see him gorging like a swine,
Stuffs him with dainties till his guts distend,
And when he belches, cries "God bless you,
   friend!"

In short, he's mad; he worships him; he
   dotes;
His deeds he marvels at, his words he quotes,
Thinking each act a miracle, each word
Oracular as those that Moses heard.
Tartuffe, much pleased to find so easy a
   victim,
Has in a hundred ways beguiled and tricked
   him,
Milked him of money, and with his
   permission
Established here a sort of Inquisition.
Even Laurent, his lackey, dares to give
Us arrogant advice on how to live;
He sermonizes us in thundering tones
And confiscates our ribbons and colognes.
Last week he tore a kerchief into pieces
Because he found it pressed in a *Life of Jesus*:
He said it was a sin to juxtapose
Unholy vanities and holy prose.

Scene Three

ELMIRE, MARIANE, DAMIS, CLÉANTE,
DORINE

ELMIRE (*To Cléante:*)

You did well not to follow; she stood in the
   door
And said *verbatim* all she'd said before.
I saw my husband coming. I think I'd best
Go upstairs now, and take a little rest.

CLÉANTE

I'll wait and greet him here; then I must
   go.
I've really only time to say hello.

DAMIS

Sound him about my sister's wedding,
   please.
I think Tartuffe's against it, and that he's
Been urging Father to withdraw his blessing.
As you well know, I'd find that most
   distressing.

Unless my sister and Valère can marry,
My hopes to wed *his* sister will miscarry,
And I'm determined . . .

DORINE

He's coming.

Scene Four

ORGON, CLÉANTE, DORINE

ORGON

Ah, Brother, good-day.

CLÉANTE

Well, welcome back. I'm sorry I can't stay.
How was the country? Blooming, I trust, and
green?

ORGON

Excuse me, Brother; just one moment.

(To Dorine:)

Dorine . . .

(To Cléante:)

To put my mind at rest, I always learn
The household news the moment I return.

(To Dorine:)

Has all been well, these two days I've been
gone?
How are the family? What's been going on?

DORINE

Your wife, two days ago, had a bad fever,
And a fierce headache which refused to leave
her.

ORGON

Ah. And Tartuffe?

DORINE

Tartuffe? Why, he's round and red,
Bursting with health, and excellently fed.

ORGON

Poor fellow!

DORINE

That night, the mistress was unable
To take a single bite at the dinner-table.
Her headache-pains, she said, were simply
hellish.

ORGON

Ah. And Tartuffe?

DORINE

He ate his meal with relish,
And zealously devoured in her presence
A leg of mutton and a brace of pheasants.

ORGON

Poor fellow!

DORINE

Well, the pains continued strong,
And so she tossed and tossed the whole night
long,
Now icy-cold, now burning like a flame.
We sat beside her bed till morning came.

ORGON

Ah. And Tartuffe?

DORINE

Why, having eaten, he rose
And sought his room, already in a doze,
Got into his warm bed, and snored away
In perfect peace until the break of day.

ORGON

Poor fellow!

DORINE

After much ado, we talked her
Into dispatching someone for the doctor.
He bled her, and the fever quickly fell.

ORGON

Ah. And Tartuffe?

DORINE

He bore it very well.
To keep his cheerfulness at any cost,
And make up for the blood *Madame* had lost,
He drank, at lunch, four beakers full of port.

ORGON

Poor fellow!

DORINE

Both are doing well, in short.
I'll go and tell *Madame* that you've expressed
Keen sympathy and anxious interest.

Scene Five

ORGON, CLÉANTE

CLÉANTE

That girl was laughing in your face, and
    though
I've no wish to offend you, even so
I'm bound to say that she had some excuse.
How can you possibly be such a goose?
Are you so dazed by this man's hocus-pocus
That all the world, save him, is out of focus?
You've given him clothing, shelter, food, and
    care;
Why must you also . . .

ORGON

Brother, stop right there.
You do not know the man of whom you
    speak.

CLÉANTE

I grant you that. But my judgment's not so
    weak
That I can't tell, by his effect on others . . .

ORGON

Ah, when you meet him, you two will be like
    brothers!
There's been no loftier soul since time began.
He is a man who . . . a man who . . . an
    excellent man.
To keep his precepts is to be reborn,
And view this dunghill of a world with
    scorn.
Yes, thanks to him I'm a changed man
    indeed.
Under his tutelage my soul's been freed
From earthly loves, and every human tie:
My mother, children, brother, and wife
    could die,
And I'd not feel a single moment's pain.

CLÉANTE

That's a fine sentiment, Brother; most
    humane.

ORGON

Oh, had you seen Tartuffe as I first knew
    him,
Your heart, like mine, would have
    surrendered to him.
He used to come into our church each day
And humbly kneel nearby, and start to pray.
He'd draw the eyes of everybody there
By the deep fervor of his heartfelt prayer;
He'd sigh and weep, and sometimes with a
    sound
Of rapture he would bend and kiss the
    ground;
And when I rose to go, he'd run before
To offer me holy-water at the door.
His serving-man, no less devout than he,
Informed me of his master's poverty;
I gave him gifts, but in his humbleness
He'd beg me every time to give him less.
"Oh, that's too much," he'd cry, "too much
    by twice!"

I don't deserve it. The half, Sir, would
   suffice."
And when I wouldn't take it back, he'd
   share
Half of it with the poor, right then and
   there.
At length, Heaven prompted me to take
   him in
To dwell with us, and free our souls from sin.
He guides our lives, and to protect my honor
Stays by my wife, and keeps an eye upon her;
He tells me whom she sees, and all she does,
And seems more jealous than I ever was!
And how austere he is! Why, he can detect
A mortal sin where you would least suspect;
In smallest trifles, he's extremely strict.
Last week, his conscience was severely
   pricked
Because, while praying, he had caught a flea
And killed it, so he felt, too wrathfully.

CLÉANTE

Good God, man! Have you lost your
   common sense—
Or is this all some joke at my expense?
How can you stand there and in all
   sobriety . . .

ORGON

Brother, your language savors of impiety.
Too much free-thinking's made your faith
   unsteady,
And as I've warned you many times already,
'Twill get you into trouble before you're
   through.

CLÉANTE

So I've been told before by dupes like you:
Being blind, you'd have all others blind as
   well;
The clear-eyed man you call an infidel,
And he who sees through humbug and
   pretense
Is charged, by you, with want of reverence.
Spare me your warnings, Brother; I have
   no fear
Of speaking out, for you and Heaven to
   hear,

Against affected zeal and pious knavery.
There's true and false in piety, as in bravery,
And just as those whose courage shines the
   most
In battle, are the least inclined to boast,
So those whose hearts are truly pure and
   lowly
Don't make a flashy show of being holy.
There's a vast difference, so it seems to me,
Between true piety and hypocrisy:
How do you fail to see it, may I ask?
Is not a face quite different from a mask?
Cannot sincerity and cunning art,
Reality and semblance, be told apart?
Are scarecrows just like men, and do you
   hold
That a false coin is just as good as gold?
Ah, Brother, man's a strangely fashioned
   creature
Who seldom is content to follow Nature,
But recklessly pursues his inclination
Beyond the narrow bounds of moderation,
And often, by transgressing Reason's laws,
Perverts a lofty aim or noble cause.
A passing observation, but it applies.

ORGON

I see, dear Brother, that you're profoundly
   wise;
You harbor all the insight of the age.
You are our one clear mind, our only sage,
The era's oracle, its Cato too,
And all mankind are fools compared to you.

CLÉANTE

Brother, I don't pretend to be a sage,
Nor have I all the wisdom of the age.
There's just one insight I would dare to
   claim:
I know that true and false are not the same;
And just as there is nothing I more revere
Than a soul whose faith is steadfast and
   sincere,
Nothing that I more cherish and admire
Than honest zeal and true religious fire,
So there is nothing that I find more base
Than specious piety's dishonest face—
Than these bold mountebanks, these histrios

Whose impious mummeries and hollow
   shows
Exploit our love of Heaven, and make a jest
Of all that men think holiest and best;
These calculating souls who offer prayers
Not to their Maker, but as public wares,
And seek to buy respect and reputation
With lifted eyes and sighs of exaltation;
These charlatans, I say, whose pilgrim souls
Proceed, by way of Heaven, toward earthly
   goals,
Who weep and pray and swindle and extort,
Who preach the monkish life, but haunt
   the court,
Who make their zeal the partner of their
   vice—
Such men are vengeful, sly, and cold as ice,
And when there is an enemy to defame
They cloak their spite in fair religion's name,
Their private spleen and malice being made
To seem a high and virtuous crusade,
Until, to mankind's reverent applause,
They crucify their foe in Heaven's cause.
Such knaves are all too common; yet, for
   the wise,
True piety isn't hard to recognize,
And, happily, these present times provide us
With bright examples to instruct and guide
   us.
Consider Ariston and Périandre;
Look at Oronte, Alcidamas, Clitandre;
Their virtue is acknowledged; who could
   doubt it?
But you won't hear them beat the drum
   about it.
They're never ostentatious, never vain,
And their religion's moderate and humane;
It's not their way to criticize and chide:
They think censoriousness a mark of pride,
And therefore, letting others preach and
   rave,
They show, by deeds, how Christians should
   behave.
They think no evil of their fellow man,
But judge of him as kindly as they can.
They don't intrigue and wangle and
   conspire;
To lead a good life is their one desire;

The sinner wakes no rancorous hate in
   them;
It is the sin alone which they condemn;
Nor do they try to show a fiercer zeal
For Heaven's cause than Heaven itself
   could feel.
These men I honor, these men I advocate
As models for us all to emulate.
Your man is not their sort at all, I fear:
And, while your praise of him is quite
   sincere,
I think that you've been dreadfully deluded.

ORGON

Now then, dear Brother, is your speech
   concluded?

CLÉANTE

Why, yes.

ORGON

      Your servant, Sir. (*He turns to go.*)

CLÉANTE

                              No, Brother; wait.
There's one more matter. You agreed of
   late
That young Valère might have your
   daughter's hand.

ORGON

I did.

CLÉANTE

   And set the date, I understand.

ORGON

Quite so.

CLÉANTE

   You've now postponed it; it that true?

ORGON

No doubt.

CLÉANTE

The match no longer pleases you?

ORGON

Who knows?

CLÉANTE

D'you mean to go back on your word?

ORGON

I won't say that.

CLÉANTE

Has anything occurred
Which might entitle you to break your
pledge?

ORGON

Perhaps.

CLÉANTE

Why must you hem, and haw, and hedge?
The boy asked me to sound you in this
affair . . .

ORGON

It's been a pleasure.

CLÉANTE

But what shall I tell Valère?

ORGON

Whatever you like.

CLÉANTE

But what have you decided?
What are your plans?

ORGON

I plan, Sir, to be guided
By Heaven's will.

CLÉANTE

Come, Brother, don't talk rot.
You've given Valère your word; will you
keep it, or not?

ORGON

Good day.

CLÉANTE

This looks like poor Valère's undoing;
I'll go and warn him that there's trouble
brewing.

ACT II

Scene One

ORGON, MARIANE

ORGON

Mariane.

MARIANE

Yes, Father?

ORGON

A word with you; come here.

MARIANE

What are you looking for?

ORGON (*Peering into a small closet:*)

Eavesdroppers, dear.
I'm making sure we shan't be overheard.
Someone in there could catch our every
word.
Ah, good, we're safe. Now, Mariane, my
child,
You're a sweet girl who's tractable and mild,
Whom I hold dear, and think most highly of.

MARIANE

I'm deeply grateful, Father, for your love.

ORGON

That's well said, Daughter; and you can repay me
If, in all things, you'll cheerfully obey me.

MARIANE

To please you, Sir, is what delights me best.

ORGON

Good, good. Now, what d'you think of Tartuffe, our guest?

MARIANE

I, Sir?

ORGON

Yes. Weigh your answer; think it through.

MARIANE

Oh, dear. I'll say whatever you wish me to.

ORGON

That's wisely said, my Daughter. Say of him, then,
That he's the very worthiest of men,
And that you're fond of him, and would rejoice
In being his wife, if that should be my choice.
Well?

MARIANE

What?

ORGON

What's that?

MARIANE

I . . .

ORGON

Well?

MARIANE

Forgive me, pray.

ORGON

Did you not hear me?

MARIANE

Of *whom*, Sir, must I say
That I am fond of him, and would rejoice
In being his wife, if that should be your choice?

ORGON

Why, of Tartuffe.

MARIANE

But, Father, that's false, you know.
Why would you have me say what isn't so?

ORGON

Because I am resolved it shall be true.
That it's my wish should be enough for you.

MARIANE

You can't mean, Father . . .

ORGON

Yes, Tartuffe shall be
Allied by marriage to this family,
And he's to be your husband, is that clear?
It's a father's privilege . . .

Scene Two

DORINE, ORGON, MARIANE

ORGON (*To Dorine:*)

What are you doing in here?
Is curiosity so fierce a passion

With you, that you must eavesdrop in this
    fashion?

ORGON

How dare you talk that way?

DORINE

There's lately been a rumor going about—
Based on some hunch or chance remark, no
    doubt—
That you mean Mariane to wed Tartuffe.
I've laughed it off, of course, as just a spoof.

DORINE

All right, then: we believe you, sad to say.
But how a man like you, who looks so wise
And wears a moustache of such splendid size,
Can be so foolish as to . . .

ORGON

You find it so incredible?

ORGON

                    Silence, please!
My girl, you take too many liberties.
I'm master here, as you must not forget.

DORINE

                    Yes, I do.
I won't accept that story, even from you.

DORINE

Do let's discuss this calmly; don't be upset.
You can't be serious, Sir, about this plan.
What should that bigot want with Mariane?
Praying and fasting ought to keep him busy.
And then, in terms of wealth and rank,
    what is he?
Why should a man of property like you
Pick out a beggar son-in-law?

ORGON

Well, you'll believe it when the thing is
    done.

DORINE

Yes, yes, of course. Go on and have your
    fun.

ORGON

I've never been more serious in my life.

ORGON

                    That will do.
Speak of his poverty with reverence.
His is a pure and saintly indigence
Which far transcends all worldly pride and
    pelf.
He lost his fortune, as he says himself,
Because he cared for Heaven alone, and so
Was careless of his interests here below.
I mean to get him out of his present straits
And help him to recover his estates—
Which, in his part of the world, have no
    small fame.
Poor though he is, he's a gentleman just
    the same.

DORINE

Ha!

ORGON

Daughter, I mean it; you're to be his wife.

DORINE

No, don't believe your father; it's all a hoax.

ORGON

See here, young woman . . .

DORINE

                    Come, Sir, no more jokes;
You can't fool us.

DORINE

Yes, so he tells us; and, Sir, it seems to me
Such pride goes very ill with piety.
A man whose spirit spurns this dungy earth
Ought not to brag of lands and noble birth;

Such worldly arrogance will hardly square
With meek devotion and the life of prayer.
. . . But this approach, I see, has drawn a
blank;
Let's speak, then, of his person, not his
rank.
Doesn't it seem to you a trifle grim
To give a girl like her to a man like him?
When two are so ill-suited, can't you see
What the sad consequence is bound to be?
A young girl's virtue is imperilled, Sir,
When such a marriage is imposed on her;
For if one's bridegroom isn't to one's taste,
It's hardly an inducement to be chaste,
And many a man with horns upon his brow
Has made his wife the thing that she is now.
It's hard to be a faithful wife, in short,
To certain husbands of a certain sort,
And he who gives his daughter to a man
she hates
Must answer for her sins at Heaven's gates.
Think, Sir, before you play so risky a role.

ORGON

This servant-girl presumes to save my soul!

DORINE

You would do well to ponder what I've
said.

ORGON

Daughter, we'll disregard this dunderhead.
Just trust your father's judgment. Oh, I'm
aware
That I once promised you to young Valère;
But now I hear he gambles, which greatly
shocks me;
What's more, I've doubts about his
orthodoxy.
His visits to church, I note, are very few.

DORINE

Would you have him go at the same hours
as you,
And kneel nearby, to be sure of being seen?

ORGON

I can dispense with such remarks, Dorine.

(*To Mariane:*)

Tartuffe, however, is sure of Heaven's
blessing,
And that's the only treasure worth possessing.
This match will bring you joys beyond all
measure;
Your cup will overflow with every pleasure;
You two will interchange your faithful loves
Like two sweet cherubs, or two turtle-doves.
No harsh word shall be heard, no frown be
seen,
And he shall make you happy as a queen.

DORINE

And she'll make him a cuckold, just wait
and see.

ORGON

What language!

DORINE

　　　　　Oh, he's a man of destiny;
He's *made* for horns, and what the stars
demand
Your daughter's virtue surely can't
withstand.

ORGON

Don't interrupt me further. Why can't you
learn
That certain things are none of your
concern?

DORINE

It's for your own sake that I interfere.

(*She repeatedly interrupts Orgon just as he
is turning to speak to his daughter:*)

ORGON

Most kind of you. Now, hold your tongue,
d'you hear?

DORINE

If I didn't love you . . .

ORGON

Spare me your affection.

DORINE

I'll love you, Sir, in spite of your objection.

ORGON

Blast!

DORINE

I can't bear, Sir, for your honor's sake,
To let you make this ludicrous mistake.

ORGON

You mean to go on talking?

DORINE

If I didn't protest
This sinful marriage, my conscience couldn't
rest.

ORGON

If you don't hold your tongue, you little
shrew . . .

DORINE

What, lost your temper? A pious man like
you?

ORGON

Yes! Yes! You talk and talk. I'm maddened
by it.
Once and for all, I tell you to be quiet.

DORINE

Well, I'll be quiet. But I'll be thinking hard.

ORGON

Think all you like, but you had better
guard
That saucy tongue of yours, or I'll . . .

(*Turning back to Mariane:*)

Now, child,
I've weighed this matter fully.

DORINE (*Aside:*)

It drives me wild
That I can't speak.

(*Orgon turns his head, and she is silent.*)

ORGON

Tartuffe is no young dandy,
But, still, his person . . .

DORINE (*Aside:*)

Is as sweet as candy.

ORGON

Is such that, even if you shouldn't care
For his other merits . . .

(*He turns and stands facing Dorine, arms crossed.*)

DORINE (*Aside:*)

They'll make a lovely pair.
If I were she, no man would marry me
Against my inclination, and go scot-free.
He'd learn, before the wedding-day was
over,
How readily a wife can find a lover.

ORGON (*To Dorine:*)

It seems you treat my orders as a joke.

DORINE

Why, what's the matter? 'Twas not to you
I spoke.

ORGON

What *were* you doing?

DORINE

Talking to myself, that's all.

ORGON

Ah! (*Aside:*) One more bit of impudence
 and gall,
And I shall give her a good slap in the face.

(*He puts himself in position to slap her;
Dorine, whenever he glances at her, stands
immobile and silent:*)

Daughter, you shall accept, and with good
 grace,
The husband I've selected . . . Your
 wedding-day . . .

(*To Dorine:*)

Why don't you talk to yourself?

DORINE

I've nothing to say.

ORGON

Come, just one word.

DORINE

No thank you, Sir. I pass.

ORGON

Come, speak; I'm waiting.

DORINE

I'd not be such an ass.

ORGON (*Turning to Mariane:*)

In short, dear Daughter, I mean to be
 obeyed,
And you must bow to the sound choice I've
 made.

DORINE (*Moving away:*)

I'd not wed such a monster, even in jest.

(*Orgon attempts to slap her, but misses.*)

ORGON

Daughter, that maid of yours is a thorough
 pest;
She makes me sinfully annoyed and nettled.
I can't speak further; my nerves are too
 unsettled.
She's so upset me by her insolent talk,
I'll calm myself by going for a walk.

Scene Three

DORINE, MARIANE

DORINE (*Returning:*)

Well, have you lost your tongue, girl? Must
 I play
Your part, and say the lines you ought to
 say?
Faced with a fate so hideous and absurd,
Can you not utter one dissenting word?

MARIANE

What good would it do? A father's power is
 great.

DORINE

Resist him now, or it will be too late.

MARIANE

But . . .

DORINE

Tell him one cannot love at a father's whim;
That you shall marry for yourself, not him;
That since it's you who are to be the bride,
It's you, not he, who must be satisfied;
And that if his Tartuffe is so sublime,
He's free to marry him at any time.

MARIANE

I've bowed so long to Father's strict control,
I couldn't oppose him now, to save my soul.

DORINE

Come, come, Mariane. Do listen to reason,
  won't you?
Valère has asked your hand. Do you love
  him, or don't you?

MARIANE

Oh, how unjust of you! What can you
  mean
By asking such a question, dear Dorine?
You know the depth of my affection for
  him;
I've told you a hundred times how I adore
  him.

DORINE

I don't believe in everything I hear;
Who knows if your professions were sincere?

MARIANE

They were, Dorine, and you do me wrong to
  doubt it;
Heaven knows that I've been all too frank
  about it.

DORINE

You love him, then?

MARIANE

        Oh, more than I can express.

DORINE

And he, I take it, cares for you no less?

MARINE

I think so.

DORINE

        And you both, with equal fire,
Burn to be married?

MARIANE

        That is our one desire.

DORINE

What of Tartuffe, then? What of your
  father's plan?

MARIANE

I'll kill myself, if I'm forced to wed that
  man.

DORINE

I hadn't thought of that recourse. How
  splendid!
Just die, and all your troubles will be ended!
A fine solution. Oh, it maddens me
To hear you talk in that self-pitying key.

MARIANE

Dorine, how harsh you are! It's most unfair.
You have no sympathy for my despair.

DORINE

I've none at all for people who talk drivel
And, faced with difficulties, whine and snivel.

MARIANE

No doubt I'm timid, but it would be
  wrong . . .

DORINE

True love requires a heart that's firm and
  strong.

MARIANE

I'm strong in my affection for Valère,
But coping with my father is his affair.

DORINE

But if your father's brain has grown so
  cracked
Over his dear Tartuffe that he can retract
His blessing, though your wedding-day was
  named,
It's surely not Valère who's to be blamed.

MARIANE

If I defied my father, as you suggest,
Would it not seem unmaidenly, at best?

Shall I defend my love at the expense
Of brazenness and disobedience?
Shall I parade my heart's desires, and
    flaunt . . .

DORINE

No, I ask nothing of you. Clearly you want
To be Madame Tartuffe, and I feel bound
Not to oppose a wish so very sound.
What right have I to criticize the match?
Indeed, my dear, the man's a brilliant catch.
Monsieur Tartuffe! Now, there's a man of
    weight!
Yes, yes, Monsieur Tartuffe, I'm bound to
    state,
Is quite a person; that's not to be denied;
'Twill be no little thing to be his bride.
The world already rings with his renown;
He's a great noble—in his native town;
His ears are red, he has a pink complexion,
And all in all, he'll suit you to perfection.

MARIANE

Dear God!

DORINE

            Oh, how triumphant you will feel
At having caught a husband so ideal!

MARIANE

Oh, do stop teasing, and use your cleverness
To get me out of this appalling mess.
Advise me, and I'll do whatever you say.

DORINE

Ah no, a dutiful daughter must obey
Her father, even if he weds her to an ape.
You've a bright future; why struggle to
    escape?
Tartuffe will take you back where his family
    lives,
To a small town aswarm with relatives—
Uncles and cousins whom you'll be charmed
    to meet.
You'll be received at once by the elite,
Calling upon the bailiff's wife, no less—
Even, perhaps, upon the mayoress,

Who'll sit you down in the *best* kitchen chair.
Then, once a year, you'll dance at the village
    fair
To the drone of bagpipes—two of them,
    in fact—
And see a puppet-show, or an animal act.
Your husband . . .

MARIANE

            Oh, you turn my blood to ice!
Stop torturing me, and give me your advice.

DORINE (*Threatening to go:*)

Your servant, Madam.

MARIANE

            Dorine, I beg of you . . .

DORINE

No, you deserve it; this marriage must go
    through.

MARIANE

Dorine!

DORINE

        No.

MARIANE

Not Tartuffe! You know I think him . . .

DORINE

Tartuffe's your cup of tea, and you shall
    drink him.

MARIANE

I've always told you everything, and
    relied . . .

DORINE

No. You deserve to be tartuffified.

MARIANE

Well, since you mock me and refuse to care,

I'll henceforth seek my solace in despair:
Despair shall be my counsellor and friend,
And help me bring my sorrows to an end.

(*She starts to leave.*)

DORINE

There now, come back; my anger has
  subsided.
You do deserve some pity, I've decided.

MARIANE

Dorine, if Father makes me undergo
This dreadful martyrdom, I'll die, I know.

DORINE

Don't fret; it won't be difficult to discover
Some plan of action . . . But here's Valère,
  your lover.

Scene Four

VALÈRE, MARIANE, DORINE

VALÈRE

Madam, I've just received some wondrous
  news
Regarding which I'd like to hear your
  views.

MARIANE

What news?

VALÈRE

You're marrying Tartuffe.

MARIANE

I find
That Father does have such a match in
  mind.

VALÈRE

Your father, Madam . . .

MARIANE

. . . has just this minute said
That it's Tartuffe he wishes me to wed.

VALÈRE

Can he be serious?

MARIANE

Oh, indeed he can;
He's clearly set his heart upon the plan.

VALÈRE

And what position do you propose to take,
Madam?

MARIANE

Why—I don't know.

VALÈRE

For heaven's sake—
You don't know?

MARIANE

No.

VALÈRE

Well, well!

MARIANE

Advise me, do.

VALÈRE

Marry the man. That's my advice to you.

MARIANE

That's your advice?

VALÈRE

Yes.

MARIANE

Truly?

VALÈRE

Oh, absolutely.
You couldn't choose more wisely, more
astutely.

MARIANE

Thanks for this counsel; I'll follow it, of
course.

VALÈRE

Do, do; I'm sure 'twill cost you no remorse.

MARIANE

To give it didn't cause your heart to break.

VALÈRE

I gave it, Madam, only for your sake.

MARIANE

And it's for your sake that I take it, Sir.

DORINE (*Withdrawing to the rear of the
stage:*)

Let's see which fool will prove the
stubborner.

VALÈRE

So! I am nothing to you, and it was flat
Deception when you . . .

MARIANE

Please, enough of that.
You've told me plainly that I should agree
To wed the man my father's chosen for me,
And since you've deigned to counsel me so
wisely,
I promise, Sir, to do as you advise me.

VALÈRE

Ah, no, 'twas not by me that you were
swayed.
No, your decision was already made;
Though now, to save appearances, you
protest
That you're betraying me at my behest.

MARIANE

Just as you say.

VALÈRE

Quite so. And I now see
That you were never truly in love with me.

MARIANE

Alas, you're free to think so if you choose.

VALÈRE

I choose to think so, and here's a bit of
news:
You've spurned my hand, but I know
where to turn
For kinder treatment, as you shall quickly
learn.

MARIANE

I'm sure you do. Your noble qualities
Inspire affection . . .

VALÈRE

Forget my qualities, please.
They don't inspire you overmuch, I find.
But there's another lady I have in mind
Whose sweet and generous nature will not
scorn
To compensate me for the loss I've borne.

MARIANE

I'm no great loss, and I'm sure that you'll
transfer
Your heart quite painlessly from me to her.

VALÈRE

I'll do my best to take it in my stride.
The pain I feel at being cast aside
Time and forgetfulness may put an end to.
Or if I can't forget, I shall pretend to.
No self-respecting person is expected
To go on loving once he's been rejected.

MARIANE

Now, that's a fine, high-minded sentiment.

VALÈRE

One to which any sane man would assent.
Would you prefer it if I pined away
In hopeless passion till my dying day?
Am I to yield you to a rival's arms
And not console myself with other charms?

MARIANE

Go then: console yourself; don't hesitate.
I wish you to; indeed, I cannot wait.

VALÈRE

You wish me to?

MARIANE

Yes.

VALÈRE

That's the final straw.
Madam, farewell. Your wish shall be my
  law.

*(He starts to leave, and then returns: this
repeatedly:)*

MARIANE

Splendid.

VALÈRE *(Coming back again:)*

This breach, remember, is of your making;
It's you who've driven me to the step I'm
  taking.

MARIANE

Of course.

VALÈRE *(Coming back again:)*

Remember, too, that I am merely
Following your example.

MARIANE

I see that clearly.

VALÈRE

Enough. I'll go and do your bidding, then.

MARIANE

Good.

VALÈRE *(Coming back again:)*

You shall never see my face again.

MARIANE

Excellent.

VALÈRE *(Walking to the door, then turning
about:)*

Yes?

MARIANE

What?

VALÈRE

What's that? What did you say?

MARIANE

Nothing. You're dreaming.

VALÈRE

Ah. Well, I'm on my way.
Farewell, *Madame.*

(He moves slowly away.)

MARIANE

Farewell.

DORINE *(To Mariane:)*

If you ask me,
Both of you are as mad as mad can be.
Do stop this nonsense, now. I've only let you
Squabble so long to see where it would get
  you.
Whoa there, Monsieure Valère!

*(She goes and seizes Valère by the arm; he
makes a great show of resistance.)*

VALÈRE

What's this, Dorine?

DORINE

Come here.

VALÈRE

No, no, my heart's too full of spleen.
Don't hold me back; her wish must be
   obeyed.

DORINE

Stop!

VALÈRE

It's too late now; my decision's made.

DORINE

Oh, pooh!

MARIANE (*Aside:*)

He hates the sight of me, that's plain.
I'll go, and so deliver him from pain.

DORINE (*Leaving Valère, running after
Mariane:*)

And now *you* run away! Come back.

MARIANE

                                  No, no.
Nothing you say will keep me here. Let go!

VALÈRE (*Aside:*)

She cannot bear my presence, I perceive.
To spare her further torment, I shall leave.

DORINE (*Leaving Mariane, running after
Valère:*)

Again! You'll not escape, Sir; don't you
   try it.
Come here, you two. Stop fussing, and be
   quiet.

(*She takes Valère by the hand, then Mariane,
and draws them together.*)

VALÈRE (*To Dorine:*)

What do you want of me?

MARIANE (*To Dorine:*)

                          What is the point of this?

DORINE

We're going to have a little armistice.

(*To Valère:*)

Now, weren't you silly to get so overheated?

VALÈRE

Didn't you see how badly I was treated?

DORINE (*To Mariane:*)

Aren't you a simpleton, to have lost your
   head?

MARIANE

Didn't you hear the hateful things he said?

DORINE (*To Valère:*)

You're both great fools. Her sole desire,
   Valère,
Is to be yours in marriage. To that I'll
   swear.

(*To Mariane:*)

He loves you only, and he wants no wife
But you, Mariane. On that I'll stake my life.

MARIANE (*To Valère:*)

Then why you advised me so, I cannot see.

VALÈRE (*To Mariane:*)

On such a question, why ask advice of *me?*

DORINE

Oh, you're impossible. Give me your hands,
you two.

(*To Valère:*)

Yours first.

VALÈRE (*Giving Dorine his hand:*)

But why?

DORINE (*To Mariane:*)

And now a hand from you.

MARIANE (*Also giving Dorine her hand:*)

What are you doing?

DORINE

There: a perfect fit.
You suit each other better than you'll admit.

(*Valère and Mariane hold hands for some
time without looking at each other.*)

VALÈRE (*Turning toward Mariane:*)

Ah, come, don't be so haughty. Give a man
A look of kindness, won't you, Mariane?

(*Mariane turns toward Valère and smiles.*)

DORINE

I tell you, lovers are completely mad!

VALÈRE (*To Mariane:*)

Now come, confess that you were very bad
To hurt my feelings as you did just now.
I have a just complaint, you must allow.

MARIANE

You must allow that you were most
unpleasant . . .

DORINE

Let's table that discussion for the present;
Your father has a plan which must be
stopped.

MARIANE

Advise us, then; what means must we
adopt?

DORINE

We'll use all manner of means, and all at
once.

(*To Mariane:*)

Your father's addled; he's acting like a
dunce.
Therefore you'd better humor the old fossil.
Pretend to yield to him, be sweet and docile,
And then postpone, as often as necessary,
The day on which you have agreed to
marry.
You'll thus gain time, and time will turn
the trick.
Sometimes, for instance, you'll be taken
sick,
And that will seem good reason for delay;
Or some bad omen will make you change
the day—
You'll dream of muddy water, or you'll pass
A dead man's hearse, or break a looking-glass.
If all else fails, no man can marry you
Unless you take his ring and say "I do."
But now, let's separate. If they should find
Us talking here, our plot might be divined.

(*To Valère:*)

Go to your friends, and tell them what's
occurred,
And have them urge her father to keep his
word.
Meanwhile, we'll stir her brother into
action,
And get Elmire, as well, to join our faction.
Good-bye.

VALÈRE (*To Mariane:*)

        Though each of us will do his best,
It's your true heart on which my hopes shall
    rest.

MARIANE (*To Valère:*)

Regardless of what Father may decide,
None but Valère shall claim me as his bride.

VALÈRE

Oh, how those words content me! Come
    what will . . .

DORINE

Oh, lovers, lovers! Their tongues are never
    still.
Be off, now.

VALÈRE (*Turning to go, then turning back:*)
    One last word . . .

DORINE

            No time to chat:
You leave by this door; and *you* leave by
    that.

(*Dorine pushes them, by the shoulders,
toward opposing doors.*)

ACT III

Scene One

DAMIS, DORINE

DAMIS

May lightning strike me even as I speak,
May all men call me cowardly and weak,
If any fear or scruple holds me back
From settling things, at once, with that
    great quack!

DORINE

Now, don't give way to violent emotion.
Your father's merely talked about this
    notion,
And words and deeds are far from being
    one.
Much that is talked about is left undone.

DAMIS

No, I must stop that scoundrel's
    machinations;
I'll go and tell him off; I'm out of patience.

DORINE

Do calm down and be practical. I had
    rather
My mistress dealt with him—and with your
    father.
She has some influence with Tartuffe, I've
    noted.
He hangs upon her words, seems most
    devoted,
And may, indeed, be smitten by her charm.
Pray Heaven it's true! 'Twould do our
    cause no harm.
She sent for him, just now, to sound him
    out
On this affair you're so incensed about;
She'll find out where he stands, and tell
    him, too,
What dreadful strife and trouble will ensue
If he lends countenance to your father's
    plan.
I couldn't get in to see him, but his man
Says that he's almost finished with his
    prayers.
Go, now. I'll catch him when he comes
    downstairs.

DAMIS

I want to hear this conference, and I will.

DORINE

No, they must be alone.

DAMIS

Oh, I'll keep still.

DORINE

Not you. I know your temper. You'd start
  a brawl,
And shout and stamp your foot and spoil it
  all.
Go on.

DAMIS

I won't; I have a perfect right . . .

DORINE

Lord, you're a nuisance! He's coming; get
  out of sight.

(*Damis conceals himself in a closet at the
rear of the stage.*)

Scene Two

TARTUFFE, DORINE

TARTUFFE (*Observing Dorine, and calling
to his manservant offstage:*)

Hang up my hair-shirt, put my scourge in
  place,
And pray, Laurent, for Heaven's perpetual
  grace.
I'm going to the prison now, to share
My last few coins with the poor wretches
  there.

DORINE (*Aside:*)

Dear God, what affectation! What a fake!

TARTUFFE

You wished to see me?

DORINE

Yes . . .

TARTUFFE (*Taking a handkerchief from
his pocket:*)

For mercy's sake,
Please take this handkerchief, before you
  speak.

DORINE

What?

TARTUFFE

Cover that bosom, girl. The flesh is weak,
And unclean thoughts are difficult to
  control.
Such sights as that can undermine the soul.

DORINE

Your soul, it seems, has very poor defenses,
And flesh makes quite an impact on your
  senses.
It's strange that you're so easily excited;
My own desires are not so soon ignited,
And if I saw you naked as a beast,
Not all your hide would tempt me in the
  least.

TARTUFFE

Girl, speak more modestly; unless you do,
I shall be forced to take my leave of you.

DORINE

Oh, no, it's I who must be on my way;
I've just one little message to convey.
Madame is coming down, and begs you, Sir,
To wait and have a word or two with her.

TARTUFFE

Gladly.

DORINE (*Aside:*)

That had a softening effect!
I think my guess about him was correct.

TARTUFFE

Will she be long?

DORINE

No: that's her step I hear.
Ah, here she is, and I shall disappear.

Scene Three

ELMIRE, TARTUFFE

TARTUFFE

May Heaven, whose infinite goodness we
  adore,
Preserve your body and soul forevermore,
And bless your days, and answer thus the
  plea
Of one who is its humblest votary.

ELMIRE

I thank you for that pious wish. But please,
Do take a chair and let's be more at ease.

(*They sit down.*)

TARTUFFE

I trust that you are once more well and
  strong?

ELMIRE

Oh, yes: the fever didn't last for long.

TARTUFFE

My prayers are too unworthy, I am sure,
To have gained from Heaven this most
  gracious cure;
But lately, Madam, my every supplication
Has had for object your recuperation.

ELMIRE

You shouldn't have troubled so. I don't
  deserve it.

TARTUFFE

Your health is priceless, Madam, and to
  preserve it
I'd gladly give my own, in all sincerity.

ELMIRE

Sir, you outdo us all in Christian charity.
You've been most kind. I count myself
  your debtor.

TARTUFFE

'Twas nothing, Madam. I long to serve
  you better.

ELMIRE

There's a private matter I'm anxious to
  discuss.
I'm glad there's no one here to hinder us.

TARTUFFE

I too am glad; it floods my heart with bliss
To find myself alone with you like this.
For just this chance I've prayed with all
  my power—
But prayed in vain, until this happy hour.

ELMIRE

This won't take long, Sir, and I hope you'll
  be
Entirely frank and unconstrained with me.

TARTUFFE

Indeed, there's nothing I had rather do
Than bare my inmost heart and soul to
  you.
First, let me say that what remarks I've
  made
About the constant visits you are paid
Were prompted not by any mean emotion,
But rather by a pure and deep devotion,
A fervent zeal . . .

ELMIRE

No need for explanation.
Your sole concern, I'm sure, was my
  salvation.

TARTUFFE (*Taking Elmire's hand and
pressing her fingertips:*)

Quite so; and such great fervor do I feel . . .

ELMIRE

Ooh! Please! You're pinching!

TARTUFFE

'Twas from excess of zeal.
I never meant to cause you pain, I swear.
I'd rather . . .

(*He places his hand on Elmire's knee.*)

ELMIRE

What can your hand be doing there?

TARTUFFE

Feeling your gown; what soft, fine-woven
stuff!

ELMIRE

Please, I'm extremely ticklish. That's enough.

(*She draws her chair away; Tartuffe pulls
his after her.*)

TARTUFFE (*Fondling the lace collar of her gown:*)
My, my, what lovely lacework on your
dress!
The workmanship's miraculous, no less.
I've not seen anything to equal it.

ELMIRE

Yes, quite. But let's talk business for a bit.
They say my husband means to break his
word
And give his daughter to you, Sir. Had you
heard?

TARTUFFE

He did once mention it. But I confess
I dream of quite a different happiness.
It's elsewhere, Madam, that my eyes
discern
The promise of that bliss for which I yearn.

ELMIRE

I see: you care for nothing here below.

TARTUFFE

Ah, well—my heart's not made of stone,
you know.

ELMIRE

All your desires mount heavenward, I'm
sure,
In scorn of all that's earthly and impure.

TARTUFFE

A love of heavenly beauty does not preclude
A proper love for earthly pulchritude;
Our senses are quite rightly captivated
By perfect works our Maker has created.
Some glory clings to all that Heaven has
made;
In you, all Heaven's marvels are displayed.
On that fair face, such beauties have been
lavished,
The eyes are dazzled and the heart is
ravished;
How could I look on you, O flawless
creature,
And not adore the Author of all Nature,
Feeling a love both passionate and pure
For you, his triumph of self-portraiture?
At first, I trembled lest that love should be
A subtle snare that Hell had laid for me;
I vowed to flee the sight of you, eschewing
A rapture that might prove my soul's
undoing;
But soon, fair being, I became aware
That my deep passion could be made to
square
With rectitude, and with my bounden duty.
I thereupon surrendered to your beauty.
It is, I know, presumptuous on my part
To bring you this poor offering of my heart,
And it is not my merit, Heaven knows,
But your compassion on which my hopes
repose.
You are my peace, my solace, my salvation;
On you depends my bliss—or desolation;
I bide your judgment and, as you think
best,
I shall be either miserable or blest.

ELMIRE

Your declaration is most gallant, Sir,
But don't you think it's out of character?
You'd have done better to restrain your
    passion
And think before you spoke in such a
    fashion.
It ill becomes a pious man like you . . .

TARTUFFE

I may be pious, but I'm human too:
With your celestial charms before his eyes,
A man has not the power to be wise.
I know such words sound strangely, coming
    from me,
But I'm no angel, nor was meant to be,
And if you blame my passion, you must
    needs
Reproach as well the charms on which it
    feeds.
Your loveliness I had no sooner seen
Than you became my soul's unrivalled
    queen;
Before your seraph glance, divinely sweet,
My heart's defenses crumbled in defeat,
And nothing fasting, prayer, or tears might
    do
Could stay my spirit from adoring you.
My eyes, my sighs have told you in the past
What now my lips make bold to say at last,
And if, in your great goodness, you will
    deign
To look upon your slave, and ease his
    pain,—
If, in compassion for my soul's distress,
You'll stoop to comfort my unworthiness,
I'll raise to you, in thanks for that sweet
    manna,
An endless hymn, an infinite hosanna.
With me, of course, there need be no
    anxiety,
No fear of scandal or of notoriety.
These young court gallants, whom all the
    ladies fancy,
Are vain in speech, in action rash and
    chancy;

When they succeed in love, the world soon
    knows it;
No favor's granted them but they disclose it
And by the looseness of their tongues
    profane
The very altar where their hearts have lain.
Men of my sort, however, love discreetly,
And one may trust our reticence completely.
My keen concern for my good name insures
The absolute security of yours;
In short, I offer you, my dear Elmire,
Love without scandal, pleasure without
    fear.

ELMIRE

I've heard your well-turned speeches to the
    end,
And what you urge I clearly apprehend.
Aren't you afraid that I may take a notion
To tell my husband of your warm devotion,
And that, supposing he were duly told,
His feelings toward you might grow rather
    cold?

TARTUFFE

I know, dear lady, that your exceeding
    charity
Will lead your heart to pardon my temerity;
That you'll excuse my violent affection
As human weakness, human imperfection;
And that—O fairest!—you will bear in mind
That I'm but flesh and blood, and am not
    blind.

ELMIRE

Some women might do otherwise, perhaps,
But I shall be discreet about your lapse;
I'll tell my husband nothing of what's
    occurred
If, in return, you'll give your solemn word
To advocate as forcefully as you can
The marriage of Valère and Mariane,
Renouncing all desire to dispossess
Another of his rightful happiness,
And . . .

Scene Four

DAMIS, ELMIRE, TARTUFFE

DAMIS (*Emerging from the closet where he has been hiding:*)

No! We'll not hush up this vile affair;
I heard it all inside that closet there,
Where Heaven, in order to confound the
  pride
Of this great rascal, prompted me to hide.
Ah, now I have my long-awaited chance
To punish his deceit and arrogance,
And give my father clear and shocking
  proof
Of the black character of his dear Tartuffe.

ELMIRE

Ah no, Damis; I'll be content if he
Will study to deserve my leniency.
I've promised silence—don't make me
  break my word;
To make a scandal would be too absurd.
Good wives laugh off such trifles, and forget
  them;
Why should they tell their husbands, and
  upset them?

DAMIS

You have your reasons for taking such a
  course,
And I have reasons, too, of equal force.
To spare him now would be insanely wrong.
I've swallowed my just wrath for far too
  long
And watched this insolent bigot bringing
  strife
And bitterness into our family life.
Too long he's meddled in my father's affairs,
Thwarting my marriage-hopes, and poor
  Valère's.
It's high time that my father was undeceived,
And now I've proof that can't be
  disbelieved—

Proof that was furnished me by Heaven
  above.
It's too good not to take advantage of.
This is my chance, and I deserve to lose it
If, for one moment, I hesitate to use it.

ELMIRE

Damis . . .

DAMIS

No, I must do what I think right.
Madam, my heart is bursting with delight,
And, say whatever you will, I'll not consent
To lose the sweet revenge on which I'm
  bent.
I'll settle matters without more ado;
And here, most opportunely, is my cue.

Scene Five

ORGON, DAMIS, TARTUFFE, ELMIRE

DAMIS

Father, I'm glad you've joined us. Let us
  advise you
Of some fresh news which doubtless will
  surprise you.
You've just now been repaid with interest
For all your loving-kindness to our guest.
He's proved his warm and grateful feelings
  toward you;
It's with a pair of horns he would reward
  you.
Yes, I surprised him with your wife, and
  heard
His whole adulterous offer, every word.
She, with her all too gentle disposition,
Would not have told you of his proposition;
But I shall not make terms with brazen
  lechery,
And feel that not to tell you would be
  treachery.

ELMIRE

And I hold that one's husband's peace of
    mind
Should not be spoilt by tattle of this kind.
One's honor doesn't require it: to be
    proficient
In keeping men at bay is quite sufficient.
These are my sentiments, and I wish,
    Damis,
That you had heeded me and held your
    peace.

Scene Six

ORGON, DAMIS, TARTUFFE

ORGON

Can it be true, this dreadful thing I hear?

TARTUFFE

Yes, Brother, I'm a wicked man, I fear:
A wretched sinner, all depraved and twisted,
The greatest villain that has ever existed.
My life's one heap of crimes, which grows
    each minute;
There's naught but foulness and corruption
    in it;
And I perceive that Heaven, outraged by
    me,
Has chosen this occasion to mortify me.
Charge me with any deed you wish to
    name;
I'll not defend myself, but take the blame.
Believe what you are told, and drive
    Tartuffe
Like some base criminal from beneath your
    roof;
Yes, drive me hence, and with a parting
    curse:
I shan't protest, for I deserve far worse.

ORGON (*To Damis:*)

Ah, you deceitful boy, how dare you try
To stain his purity with so foul a lie?

DAMIS

What! Are you taken in by such a bluff?
Did you not hear . . . ?

ORGON

Enough, you rogue, enough!

TARTUFFE

Ah, Brother, let him speak: you're being
    unjust.
Believe his story; the boy deserves your
    trust.
Why, after all, should you have faith in me?
How can you know what I might do, or be?
Is it on my good actions that you base
Your favor? Do you trust my pious face?
Ah, no, don't be deceived by hollow shows;
I'm far, alas, from being what men suppose;
Though the world takes me for a man of
    worth,
I'm truly the most worthless man on earth.

(*To Damis:*)

Yes, my dear son, speak out now: call me
    the chief
Of sinners, a wretch, a murderer, a thief;
Load me with all the names most abhor;
I'll not complain; I've earned them all, and
    more;
I'll kneel here while you pour them on my
    head
As a just punishment for the life I've led.

ORGON (*To Tartuffe:*)

This is too much, dear Brother.

(*To Damis:*)

                    Have you no heart?

DAMIS

Are you so hoodwinked by this rascal's
    art . . . ?

ORGON

Be still, you monster.

(To Tartuffe:)

Brother, I pray you, rise.

(To Damis:)

Villain!

DAMIS

But . . .

ORGON

Silence!

DAMIS

Can't you realize . . . ?

ORGON

Just one word more, and I'll tear you limb
from limb.

TARTUFFE

In God's name, Brother, don't be harsh
with him.
I'd rather far be tortured at the stake
Than see him bear one scratch for my poor
sake.

ORGON *(To Damis:)*

Ingrate!

TARTUFFE

If I must beg you, on bended knee,
To pardon him . . .

ORGON *(Falling to his knees, addressing
Tartuffe:)*

Such goodness cannot be!

(To Damis:)

Now, *there's* true charity!

DAMIS

What, you . . . ?

ORGON

Villain, be still!
I know your motives; I know you wish him
ill:
Yes, all of you—wife, children, servants,
all—
Conspire against him and desire his fall,
Employing every shameful trick you can
To alienate me from this saintly man.
Ah, but the more you seek to drive him
away,
The more I'll do to keep him. Without
delay,
I'll spite this household and confound its
pride
By giving him my daughter as his bride.

DAMIS

You're going to force her to accept his
hand?

ORGON

Yes, and this very night, d'you understand?
I shall defy you all, and make it clear
That I'm the one who gives the orders here.
Come, wretch, kneel down and clasp his
blessed feet,
And ask his pardon for your black deceit.

DAMIS

I ask that swindler's pardon? Why, I'd
rather . . .

ORGON

So! You insult him, and defy your father!
A stick! A stick! *(To Tartuffe:)* No, no—
release me, do.

(To Damis:)

Out of my house this minute! Be off with
you,
And never dare set foot in it again.

DAMIS

Well, I shall go, but . . .

ORGON

                    Well, go quickly, then.
I disinherit you; an empty purse
Is all you'll get from me—except my curse!

Scene Seven

ORGON, TARTUFFE

ORGON

How he blasphemed your goodness! What
  a son!

TARTUFFE

Forgive him, Lord, as I've already done.

(*To Orgon:*)

You can't know how it hurts when someone
  tries
To blacken me in my dear Brother's eyes.

ORGON

Ahh!

TARTUFFE

    The mere thought of such ingratitude
Plunges my soul into so dark a mood . . .
Such horror grips my heart . . . I gasp for
  breath,
And cannot speak, and feel myself near
  death.

ORGON

(*He runs, in tears, to the door through which
he has just driven his son.*)

You blackguard! Why did I spare you?
  Why did I not
Break you in little pieces on the spot?
Compose yourself, and don't be hurt, dear
  friend.

TARTUFFE

These scenes, these dreadful quarrels, have
  got to end.
I've much upset your household, and I
  perceive
That the best thing will be for me to leave.

ORGON

What are you saying!

TARTUFFE

                    They're all against me here;
They'd have you think me false and
  insincere.

ORGON

Ah, what of that? Have I ceased believing
  in you?

TARTUFFE

Their adverse talk will certainly continue,
And charges which you now repudiate
You may find credible at a later date.

ORGON

No, Brother, never.

TARTUFFE

                    Brother, a wife can sway
Her husband's mind in many a subtle way.

ORGON

No, no.

TARTUFFE

    To leave at once is the solution;
Thus only can I end their persecution.

ORGON

No, no, I'll not allow it; you shall remain.

TARTUFFE

Ah, well; 'twill mean much martyrdom
  and pain,
But if you wish it . . .

ORGON

Ah!

TARTUFFE

Enough; so be it.
But one thing must be settled, as I see it.
For your dear honor, and for our
friendship's sake,
There's one precaution I feel bound to take.
I shall avoid your wife, and keep away . . .

ORGON

No, you shall not, whatever they may say.
It pleases me to vex them, and for spite
I'd have them see you with her day and
night.
What's more, I'm going to drive them to
despair
By making you my only son and heir;
This very day, I'll give to you alone
Clear deed and title to everything I own.
A dear, good friend and son-in-law-to-be
Is more than wife, or child, or kin to me.
Will you accept my offer, dearest son?

TARTUFFE

In all things, let the will of Heaven be done.

ORGON

Poor fellow! Come, we'll go draw up the
deed.
Then let them burst with disappointed
greed!

ACT IV

Scene One

CLÉANTE, TARTUFFE

CLÉANTE

Yes, all the town's discussing it, and truly,
Their comments do not flatter you unduly.

I'm glad we've met, Sir, and I'll give my
view
Of this sad matter in a word or two.
As for who's guilty, that I shan't discuss;
Let's say it was Damis who caused the fuss;
Assuming, then, that you have been ill-used
By young Damis, and groundlessly accused,
Ought not a Christian to forgive, and ought
He not to stifle every vengeful thought?
Should you stand by and watch a father
make
His only son an exile for your sake?
Again I tell you frankly, be advised:
The whole town, high and low, is
scandalized;
This quarrel must be mended, and my
advice is
Not to push matters to a further crisis.
No, sacrifice your wrath to God above,
And help Damis regain his father's love.

TARTUFFE

Alas, for my part I should take great joy
In doing so. I've nothing against the boy.
I pardon all, I harbor no resentment;
To serve him would afford me much
contentment.
But Heaven's interest will not have it so:
If he comes back, then I shall have to go.
After his conduct—so extreme, so vicious—
Our further intercourse would look
suspicious.
God knows what people would think! Why,
they'd describe
My goodness to him as a sort of bribe;
They'd say that out of guilt I made pretense
Of loving-kindness and benevolence—
That, fearing my accuser's tongue, I strove
To buy his silence with a show of love.

CLÉANTE

Your reasoning is badly warped and
stretched,
And these excuses, Sir, are most far-fetched.
Why put yourself in charge of Heaven's
cause?
Does Heaven need our help to enforce its
laws?

Leave vengeance to the Lord, Sir; while
    we live,
Our duty's not to punish, but forgive;
And what the Lord commands, we should
    obey
Without regard to what the world may say.
What! Shall the fear of being misunderstood
Prevent our doing what is right and good?
No, no; let's simply do what Heaven
    ordains,
And let no other thoughts perplex our
    brains.

TARTUFFE

Again, Sir, let me say that I've forgiven
Damis, and thus obeyed the laws of Heaven;
But I am not commanded by the Bible
To live with one who smears my name
    with libel.

CLÉANTE

Were you commanded, Sir, to indulge the
    whim
Of poor Orgon, and to encourage him
In suddenly transferring to your name
A large estate to which you have no claim?

TARTUFFE

'Twould never occur to those who know me
    best
To think I acted from self-interest.
The treasures of this world I quite despise;
Their specious glitter does not charm my
    eyes;
And if I have resigned myself to taking
The gift which my dear Brother insists on
    making,
I do so only, as he well understands,
Lest so much wealth fall into wicked hands,
Lest those to whom it might descend in
    time
Turn it to purposes of sin and crime,
And not, as I shall do, make use of it
For Heaven's glory and mankind's benefit.

CLÉANTE

Forget these trumped-up fears. Your
    argument

Is one the rightful heir might well resent;
It *is* a moral burden to inherit
Such wealth, but give Damis a chance to
    bear it.
And would it not be worse to be accused
Of swindling, than to see that wealth
    misused?
I'm shocked that you allowed Orgon to
    broach
This matter, and that you feel no
    self-reproach;
Does true religion teach that lawful heirs
May freely be deprived of what is theirs?
And if the Lord has told you in your heart
That you and young Damis must dwell
    apart,
Would it not be the decent thing to beat
A generous and honorable retreat,
Rather than let the son of the house be sent,
For your convenience, into banishment?
Sir, if you wish to prove the honesty
Of your intentions . . .

TARTUFFE

              Sir, it is half-past three.
I've certain pious duties to attend to,
And hope my prompt departure won't
    offend you.

CLÉANTE (*Alone:*)

Damn.

Scene Two

ELMIRE, MARIANE, CLÉANTE, DORINE

DORINE

    Stay, Sir, and help Mariane,
    for Heaven's sake!
She's suffering so, I fear her heart will break.
Her father's plan to marry her off tonight
Has put the poor child in a desperate plight.
I hear him coming. Let's stand together,
    now,
And see if we can't change his mind,
    somehow,
About this match we all deplore and fear.

Scene Three

ORGON, ELMIRE, MARIANE, CLÉANTE, DORINE

ORGON

Hah! Glad to find you all assembled here.

(*To Mariane:*)

This contract, child, contains your
    happiness,
And what it says I think your heart can
    guess.

MARIANE (*Falling to her knees:*)

Sir, by that Heaven which sees me here
    distressed,
And by whatever else can move your breast,
Do not employ a father's power, I pray you,
To crush my heart and force it to obey you,
Nor by your harsh commands oppress me so
That I'll begrudge the duty which I owe—
And do not so embitter and enslave me
That I shall hate the very life you gave me.
If my sweet hopes must perish, if you refuse
To give me to the one I've dared to choose,
Spare me at least—I beg you, I implore—
The pain of wedding one whom I abhor;
And do not, by a heartless use of force,
Drive me to contemplate some desperate
    course.

ORGON (*Feeling himself touched by her:*)

Be firm, my soul. No human weakness, now.

MARIANE

I don't resent your love for him. Allow
Your heart free rein, Sir; give him your
    property,
And if that's not enough, take mine from
    me;
He's welcome to my money; take it, do,
But don't, I pray, include my person too.
Spare me, I beg you; and let me end the
    tale
Of my sad days behind a convent veil.

ORGON

A convent! Hah! When crossed in their
    amours,
All lovesick girls have the same thought as
    yours.
Get up! The more you loathe the man, and
    dread him,
The more ennobling it will be to wed him.
Marry Tartuffe, and mortify your flesh!
Enough; don't start that whimpering afresh.

DORINE

But why . . . ?

ORGON

  Be still, there. Speak when you're spoken to.
Not one more bit of impudence out of you.

CLÉANTE

If I may offer a word of counsel here . . .

ORGON

Brother, in counseling you have no peer;
All your advice is forceful, sound, and
    clever;
I don't propose to follow it, however.

ELMIRE (*To Orgon:*)

I am amazed, and don't know what to say;
Your blindness simply takes my breath
    away.
You are indeed bewitched, to take no
    warning
From our account of what occurred this
    morning.

ORGON

Madam, I know a few plain facts, and one
Is that you're partial to my rascal son;
Hence, when he sought to make Tartuffe
    the victim
Of a base lie, you dared not contradict him.
Ah, but you underplayed your part, my pet;
You should have looked more angry, more
    upset.

ELMIRE

When men make overtures, must we reply
With righteous anger and a battle-cry?
Must we turn back their amorous advances
With sharp reproaches and with fiery
    glances?
Myself, I find such offers merely amusing,
And make no scenes and fusses in refusing;
My taste is for good-natured rectitude,
And I dislike the savage sort of prude
Who guards her virtue with her teeth and
    claws,
And tears men's eyes out for the slightest
    cause:
The Lord preserve me from such honor as
    that,
Which bites and scratches like an alley-cat!
I've found that a polite and cool rebuff
Discourages a lover quite enough.

ORGON

I know the facts, and I shall not be shaken.

ELMIRE

I marvel at your power to be mistaken.
Would it, I wonder, carry weight with you
If I could *show* you that our tale was true?

ORGON

Show me?

ELMIRE

    Yes.

ORGON

    Rot.

ELMIRE

        Come, what if I found a way
To make you see the facts as plain as day?

ORGON

Nonsense.

ELMIRE

    Do answer me; don't be absurd.
I'm not now asking you to trust our word.
Suppose that from some hiding-place in here
You learned the whole sad truth by eye
    and ear—
What would you say of your good friend,
    after that?

ORGON

Why, I'd say . . . nothing, by Jehoshaphat!
It can't be true.

ELMIRE

        You've been too long deceived,
And I'm quite tired of being disbelieved.
Come now: let's put my statements to the
    test,
And you shall see the truth made manifest.

ORGON

I'll take that challenge. Now do your
    uttermost.
We'll see how you make good your empty
    boast.

ELMIRE (*To Dorine:*)

Send him to me.

DORINE

        He's crafty; it may be hard
To catch the cunning scoundrel off his
    guard.

ELMIRE

No, amorous men are gullible. Their conceit
So blinds them that they're never hard to
    cheat.
Have him come down (*To Cléante &
Mariane:*) Please leave us, for a bit.

Scene Four

ELMIRE, ORGON

ELMIRE

Pull up this table, and get under it.

ORGON

What?

ELMIRE

It's essential that you be well-hidden.

ORGON

Why there?

ELMIRE

Oh, Heavens! Just do as you are bidden.
I have my plans; we'll soon see how they
   fare.
Under the table, now; and once you're
   there,
Take care that you are neither seen nor
   heard.

ORGON

Well, I'll indulge you, since I gave my word
To see you through this infantile charade.

ELMIRE

Once it is over, you'll be glad we played.

   (*To her husband, who is now under the
   table:*)

I'm going to act quite strangely, now, and
   you
Must not be shocked at anything I do.
Whatever I may say, you must excuse
As part of that deceit I'm forced to use.
I shall employ sweet speeches in the task
Of making that imposter drop his mask;
I'll give encouragement to his bold desires,
And furnish fuel to his amorous fires.
Since it's for your sake, and for his
   destruction,

That I shall seem to yield to his seduction,
I'll gladly stop whenever you decide
That all your doubts are fully satisfied.
I'll count on you, as soon as you have seen
What sort of man he is, to intervene,
And not expose me to his odious lust
One moment longer than you feel you must.
Remember: you're to save me from my
   plight
Whenever . . . He's coming! Hush! Keep
   out of sight!

Scene Five

TARTUFFE, ELMIRE, ORGON

TARTUFFE

You wish to have a word with me, I'm told.

ELMIRE

Yes. I've a little secret to unfold.
Before I speak, however, it would be wise
To close that door, and look about for spies.

   (*Tartuffe goes to the door, closes it, and
   returns.*)

The very last thing that must happen now
Is a repetition of this morning's row.
I've never been so badly caught off guard.
Oh, how I feared for you! You saw how
   hard
I tried to make that troublesome Damis
Control his dreadful temper, and hold his
   peace.
In my confusion, I didn't have the sense
Simply to contradict his evidence;
But as it happened, that was for the best,
And all has worked out in our interest.
This storm has only bettered your position;
My husband doesn't have the least suspicion,
And now, in mockery of those who do,
He bids me be continually with you.
And that is why, quite fearless of reproof,
I now can be alone with my Tartuffe,

And why my heart—perhaps too quick to
yield—
Feels free to let its passion be revealed.

TARTUFFE

Madam, your words confuse me. Not long
ago,
You spoke in quite a different style, you
know.

ELMIRE

Ah, Sir, if that refusal made you smart,
It's little that you know of woman's heart,
Or what that heart is trying to convey
When it resists in such a feeble way!
Always, at first, our modesty prevents
The frank avowal of tender sentiments;
However high the passion which inflames
us,
Still, to confess its power somehow shames
us.
Thus we reluct, at first, yet in a tone
Which tells you that our heart is overthrown,
That what our lips deny, our pulse confesses,
And that, in time, all noes will turn to yesses.
I fear my words are all too frank and free,
And a poor proof of woman's modesty;
But since I'm started, tell me, if you will—
Would I have tried to make Damis be still,
Would I have listened, calm and unoffended,
Until your lengthy offer of love was ended,
And been so very mild in my reaction,
Had your sweet words not given me
satisfaction?
And when I tried to force you to undo
The marriage-plans my husband has in
view,
What did my urgent pleading signify
If not that I admired you, and that I
Deplored the thought that someone else
might own
Part of a heart I wished for mine alone?

TARTUFFE

Madam, no happiness is so complete
As when, from lips we love, come words so
sweet;

Their nectar floods my every sense, and
drains
In honeyed rivulets through all my veins.
To please you is my joy, my only goal;
Your love is the restorer of my soul;
And yet I must beg leave, now, to confess
Some lingering doubts as to my happiness.
Might this not be a trick? Might not the
catch
Be that you wish me to break off the match
With Mariane, and so have feigned to love
me?
I shan't quite trust your fond opinion of me
Until the feelings you've expressed so
sweetly
Are demonstrated somewhat more concretely,
And you have shown, by certain kind
concessions,
That I may put my faith in your professions.

ELMIRE (*She coughs, to warn her husband.*)

Why be in such a hurry? Must my heart
Exhaust its bounty at the very start?
To make that sweet admission cost me dear,
But you'll not be content, it would appear,
Unless my store of favors is disbursed
To the last farthing, and at the very first.

TARTUFFE

The less we merit, the less we dare to hope,
And with our doubts, mere words can never
cope.
We trust no promised bliss till we receive it;
Not till a joy is ours can we believe it.
I, who so little merit your esteem,
Can't credit this fulfillment of my dream,
And shan't believe it, Madam, until I savor
Some palpable assurance of your favor.

ELMIRE

My, how tyrannical your love can be,
And how it flusters and perplexes me!
How furiously you take one's heart in hand,
And make your every wish a fierce
command!
Come, must you hound and harry me to
death?

Will you not give me time to catch my
   breath?
Can it be right to press me with such force,
Give me no quarter, show me no remorse,
And take advantage, by your stern
   insistence,
Of the fond feelings which weaken my
   resistance?

TARTUFFE

Well, if you look with favor upon my love,
Why, then, begrudge me some clear proof
   thereof?

ELMIRE

But how can I consent without offense
To Heaven, toward which you feel such
   reverence?

TARTUFFE

If Heaven is all that holds you back, don't
   worry.
I can remove that hindrance in a hurry.
Nothing of that sort need obstruct our path.

ELMIRE

Must one not be afraid of Heaven's wrath?

TARTUFFE

Madam, forget such fears, and be my pupil,
And I shall teach you how to conquer
   scruple.
Some joys, it's true, are wrong in Heaven's
   eyes;
Yet Heaven is not averse to compromise;
There is a science, lately formulated,
Whereby one's conscience may be liberated,
And any wrongful act you care to mention
May be redeemed by purity of intention.
I'll teach you, Madam, the secrets of that
   science;
Meanwhile, just place on me your full
   reliance.
Assuage my keen desires, and feel no dread:
The sin, if any, shall be on my head.

(*Elmire coughs, this time more loudly.*)

You've a bad cough.

ELMIRE

   Yes, yes. It's bad indeed.

TARTUFFE (*Producing a little paper bag:*)

A bit of licorice may be what you need.

ELMIRE

No, I've a stubborn cold, it seems. I'm
   sure it
Will take much more than licorice to cure it.

TARTUFFE

How aggravating.

ELMIRE

   Oh, more than I can say.

TARTUFFE

If you're still troubled, think of things this
   way:
No one shall know our joys, save us alone,
And there's no evil till the act is known;
It's scandal, Madam, which makes it an
   offense,
And it's no sin to sin in confidence.

ELMIRE (*Having coughed once more:*)

Well, clearly I must do as you require,
And yield to your importunate desire.
It is apparent, now, that nothing less
Will satisfy you, and so I acquiesce.
To go so far is much against my will;
I'm vexed that it should come to this; but
   still,
Since you are so determined on it, since you
Will not allow mere language to convince
   you,
And since you ask for concrete evidence, I
See nothing for it, now, but to comply.
If this is sinful, if I'm wrong to do it,

So much the worse for him who drove me
   to it.
The fault can surely not be charged to me.

TARTUFFE

Madam, the fault is mine, if fault there be,
And . . .

ELMIRE

       Open the door a little, and peek out;
I wouldn't want my husband poking about.

TARTUFFE

Why worry about the man? Each day he
   grows
More gullible; one can lead him by the
   nose.
To find us here would fill him with delight,
And if he saw the worst, he'd doubt his
   sight.

ELMIRE

Nevertheless, do step out for a minute
Into the hall, and see that no one's in it.

Scene Six

ORGON, ELMIRE

ORGON (*Coming out from under the table :*)

That man's a perfect monster, I must admit!
I'm simply stunned. I can't get over it.

ELMIRE

What, coming out so soon? How premature!
Get back in hiding, and wait until you're
   sure.
Stay till the end, and be convinced
   completely;
We mustn't stop till things are proved
   concretely.

ORGON

Hell never harbored anything so vicious!

ELMIRE

Tut, don't be hasty. Try to be judicious.
Wait, and be certain that there's no mistake.
No jumping to conclusions, for Heaven's
   sake!

     (*She places Orgon behind her, as Tartuffe
re-enters.*)

Scene Seven

TARTUFFE, ELMIRE, ORGON

TARTUFFE (*Not seeing Orgon :*)

Madam, all things have worked out to
   perfection;
I've given the neighboring rooms a full
   inspection;
No one's about; and now I may at last . . .

ORGON (*Intercepting him :*)

Hold on, my passionate fellow, not so fast!
I should advise a little more restraint.
Well, so you thought you'd fool me, my
   dear saint!
How soon you wearied of the saintly life—
Wedding my daughter, and coveting my
   wife!
I've long suspected you, and had a feeling
That soon I'd catch you at your
   double-dealing.
Just now, you've given me evidence galore;
It's quite enough; I have no wish for more.

ELMIRE (*To Tartuffe :*)

I'm sorry to have treated you so slyly,
But circumstances forced me to be wily.

TARTUFFE

Brother, you can't think . . .

ORGON

No more talk from you;
Just leave this household, without more
ado.

TARTUFFE

What I intended . . .

ORGON

That seems fairly clear.
Spare me your falsehoods and get out of
here.

TARTUFFE

No, I'm the master, and you're the one to
go!
This house belongs to me, I'll have you
know,
And I shall show you that you can't hurt *me*
By this contemptible conspiracy,
That those who cross me know not what
they do,
And that I've means to expose and punish
you,
Avenge offended Heaven, and make you
grieve
That ever you dared order me to leave.

Scene Eight

ELMIRE, ORGON

ELMIRE

What was the point of all that angry
chatter?

ORGON

Dear God, I'm worried. This is no laughing
matter.

ELMIRE

How so?

ORGON

I fear I understood his drift.
I'm much disturbed about that deed of gift.

ELMIRE

You gave him . . . ?

ORGON

Yes, it's all been drawn and signed.
But one thing more is weighing on my mind.

ELMIRE

What's that?

ORGON

I'll tell you; but first let's see if there's
A certain strong-box in his room upstairs.

ACT V

Scene One

ORGON, CLÉANTE

CLÉANTE

Where are you going so fast?

ORGON

God knows!

CLÉANTE

Then wait;
Let's have a conference, and deliberate
On how this situation's to be met.

ORGON

That strong-box has me utterly upset;
This is the worst of many, many shocks.

CLÉANTE

Is there some fearful mystery in that box?

ORGON

My poor friend Argas brought that box to
    me
With his own hands, in utmost secrecy;
'Twas on the very morning of his flight.
It's full of papers which, if they came to
    light,
Would ruin him—or such is my impression.

CLÉANTE

Then why did you let it out of your
    possession?

ORGON

Those papers vexed my conscience, and it
    seemed best
To ask the counsel of my pious guest.
The cunning scoundrel got me to agree
To leave the strong-box in his custody,
So that, in case of an investigation,
I could employ a slight equivocation
And swear I didn't have it, and thereby,
At no expense to conscience, tell a lie.

CLÉANTE

It looks to me as if you're out on a limb.
Trusting him with that box, and offering
    him
That deed of gift, were actions of a kind
Which scarcely indicate a prudent mind.
With two such weapons, he has the upper
    hand,
And since you're vulnerable, as matters
    stand,
You erred once more in bringing him to
    bay.
You should have acted in some subtler way.

ORGON

Just think of it: behind that fervent face,
A heart so wicked, and a soul so base!
I took him in, a hungry beggar, and then . . .
Enough, by God! I'm through with pious
    men:
Henceforth I'll hate the whole false
    brotherhood,

And persecute them worse than Satan
    could.

CLÉANTE

Ah, there you go—extravagant as ever!
Why can you not be rational? You never
Manage to take the middle course, it seems,
But jump, instead, between absurd
    extremes.
You've recognized your recent grave mistake
In falling victim to a pious fake;
Now, to correct that error, must you embrace
An even greater error in its place,
And judge our worthy neighbors as a
    whole
By what you've learned of one corrupted
    soul?
Come, just because one rascal made you
    swallow
A show of zeal which turned out to be
    hollow,
Shall you conclude that all men are
    deceivers,
And that, today, there are no true believers?
Let atheists make that foolish inference;
Learn to distinguish virtue from pretense,
Be cautious in bestowing admiration,
And cultivate a sober moderation.
Don't humor fraud, but also don't asperse
True piety; the latter fault is worse,
And it is best to err, if err one must,
As you have done, upon the side of trust.

Scene Two

DAMIS, ORGON, CLÉANTE

DAMIS

Father, I hear that scoundrel's uttered
    threats
Against you; that he pridefully forgets
How, in his need, he was befriended by
    you,
And means to use your gifts to crucify you.

ORGON

It's true, my boy. I'm too distressed for
    tears.

DAMIS ˉ

Leave it to me, Sir; let me trim his ears.
Faced with such insolence, we must not
    waver.
I shall rejoice in doing you the favor
Of cutting short his life, and your distress.

CLÉANTE

What a display of young hotheadedness!
Do learn to moderate your fits of rage.
In this just kingdom, this enlightened age,
One does not settle things by violence.

Scene Three

MADAME PERNELLE, MARIANE, ELMIRE,
DORINE, DAMIS, ORGON, CLÉANTE

MADAME PERNELLE

I hear strange tales of very strange events.

ORGON

Yes, strange events which these two eyes
    beheld.
The man's ingratitude is unparalleled.
I save a wretched pauper from starvation,
House him, and treat him like a blood
    relation,
Shower him every day with my largesse,
Give him my daughter, and all that I
    possess;
And meanwhile the unconscionable knave
Tries to induce my wife to misbehave;
And not content with such extreme
    rascality,
Now threatens me with my own liberality,
And aims, by taking base advantage of
The gifts I gave him out of Christian love,
To drive me from my house, a ruined man,
And make me end a pauper, as he began.

DORINE

Poor fellow!

MADAME PERNELLE

        No, my son, I'll never bring
Myself to think him guilty of such a thing.

ORGON

How's that?

MADAME PERNELLE

    The righteous always were maligned.

ORGON

Speak clearly, Mother. Say what's on your
    mind.

MADAME PERNELLE

I mean that I can smell a rat, my dear.
You know how everybody hates him, here.

ORGON

That has no bearing on the case at all.

MADAME PERNELLE

I told you a hundred times, when you
    were small,
That virtue in this world is hated ever;
Malicious men may die, but malice never.

ORGON

No doubt that's true, but how does it apply?

MADAME PERNELLE

They've turned you against him by a clever
    lie.

ORGON

I've told you, I was there and saw it done.

MADAME PERNELLE

Ah, slanderers will stop at nothing, Son.

ORGON

Mother, I'll lose my temper . . . For the
   last time,
I tell you I was witness to the crime.

MADAME PERNELLE

The tongues of spite are busy night and
   noon,
And to their venom no man is immune.

ORGON

You're talking nonsense. Can't you realize
I saw it; saw it; saw it with my eyes?
Saw, do you understand me? Must I shout
   it
Into your ears before you'll cease to doubt
   it?

MADAME PERNELLE

Appearances can deceive, my son. Dear me,
We cannot always judge by what we see.

ORGON

Drat! Drat!

MADAME PERNELLE

            One often interprets things awry;
Good can seem evil to a suspicious eye.

ORGON

Was I to see his pawing at Elmire
As an act of charity?

MADAME PERNELLE

               Till his guilt is clear,
A man deserves the benefit of the doubt.
You should have waited, to see how things
   turned out.

ORGON

Great God in Heaven, what more proof did
   I need?
Was I to sit there, watching, until he'd . . .
You drive me to the brink of impropriety.

MADAME PERNELLE

No, no, a man of such surpassing piety
Could not do such a thing. You cannot
   shake me.
I don't believe it, and you shall not make
   me.

ORGON

You vex me so that, if you weren't my
   mother,
I'd say to you . . . some dreadful thing or
   other.

DORINE

It's your turn now, Sir, not to be listened
   to;
You'd not trust us, and now she won't
   trust you.

CLÉANTE

My friends, we're wasting time which
   should be spent
In facing up to our predicament.
I fear that scoundrel's threats weren't made
   in sport.

DAMIS

Do you think he'd have the nerve to go to
   court?

ELMIRE

I'm sure he won't: they'd find it all too
   crude
A case of swindling and ingratitude.

CLÉANTE

Don't be too sure. He won't be at a loss
To give his claims a high and righteous
   gloss;
And clever rogues with far less valid cause
Have trapped their victims in a web of laws.
I say again that to antagonize
A man so strongly armed was most unwise.

ORGON

I know it; but the man's appalling cheek

Outraged me so, I couldn't control my
pique.

CLÉANTE

I wish to Heaven that we could devise
Some truce between you, or some
compromise.

ELMIRE

If I had known what cards he held, I'd not
Have roused his anger by my little plot.

ORGON (*To Dorine, as M. Loyal enters:*)

What is that fellow looking for? Who is he?
Go talk to him—and tell him that I'm busy.

Scene Four

MONSIEUR LOYAL, MADAME PERNELLE,
ORGON, DAMIS, MARIANE, DORINE,
ELMIRE, CLÉANTE

MONSIEUR LOYAL

Good day, dear sister. Kindly let me see
Your master.

DORINE

He's involved with company,
And cannot be disturbed just now, I fear.

MONSIEUR LOYAL

I hate to intrude; but what has brought
me here
Will not disturb your master, in any event.
Indeed, my news will make him most
content.

DORINE

Your name?

MONSIEUR LOYAL

Just say that I bring greetings from
Monsieur Tartuffe, on whose behalf I've
come.

DORINE (*To Orgon:*)

Sir, he's a very gracious man, and bears
A message from Tartuffe, which, he declares,
Will make you most content.

CLÉANTE

Upon my word,
I think this man had best be seen, and
heard.

ORGON

Perhaps he has some settlement to suggest.
How shall I treat him? What manner
would be best?

CLÉANTE

Control your anger, and if he should
mention
Some fair adjustment, give him your full
attention.

MONSIEUR LOYAL

Good health to you, good Sir. May Heaven
confound
Your enemies, and may your joys abound.

ORGON (*Aside, to Cléante:*)

A gentle salutation: it confirms
My guess that he is here to offer terms.

MONSIEUR LOYAL

I've always held your family most dear;
I served your father, Sir, for many a year.

ORGON

Sir, I must ask your pardon; to my shame,
I cannot now recall your face or name.

MONSIEUR LOYAL

Loyal's my name; I come from Normandy,
And I'm a bailiff, in all modesty.
For forty years, praise God, it's been my
boast
To serve with honor in that vital post,

And I am here, Sir, if you will permit
The liberty, to serve you with this writ . . .

ORGON

To—*what?*

MONSIEUR LOYAL

Now, please, Sir, let us have no friction:
It's nothing but an order of eviction.
You are to move your goods and family out
And make way for new occupants, without
Deferment or delay, and give the keys . . .

ORGON

I? Leave this house?

MONSIEUR LOYAL

Why yes, Sir, if you please.
This house, Sir, from the cellar to the roof,
Belongs now to the good Monsieur Tartuffe,
And he is lord and master of your estate
By virtue of a deed of present date,
Drawn in due form, with clearest legal
    phrasing . . .

DAMIS

Your insolence is utterly amazing!

MONSIEUR LOYAL

Young man, my business here is not with
    you,
But with your wise and temperate father,
    who,
Like every worthy citizen, stands in awe
Of justice, and would never obstruct the
    law.

ORGON

But . . .

MONSIEUR LOYAL

Not for a million, Sir, would you rebel
Against authority; I know that well.
You'll not make trouble, Sir, or interfere
With the execution of my duties here.

DAMIS

Someone may execute a smart tattoo
On that black jacket of yours, before you're
    through.

MONSIEUR LOYAL

Sir, bid your son be silent. I'd much regret
Having to mention such a nasty threat
Of violence, in writing my report.

DORINE (*Aside:*)

This man Loyal's a most disloyal sort!

MONSIEUR LOYAL

I love all men of upright character,
And when I agreed to serve these papers,
    Sir,
It was your feelings that I had in mind.
I couldn't bear to see the case assigned
To someone else, who might esteem you
    less
And so subject you to unpleasantness.

ORGON

What's more unpleasant than telling a man
    to leave
His house and home?

MONSIEUR LOYAL

You'd like a short reprieve?
If you desire it, Sir, I shall not press you,
But wait until tomorrow to dispossess you.
Splendid. I'll come and spend the night
    here, then,
Most quietly, with half a score of men.
For form's sake, you might bring me, just
    before
You go to bed, the keys to the front door.
My men, I promise, will be on their best
Behavior, and will not disturb your rest.
But bright and early, Sir, you must be
    quick
And move out all your furniture, every
    stick:
The men I've chosen are both young and
    strong,

And with their help it shouldn't take you
   long.
In short, I'll make things pleasant and
   convenient,
And since I'm being so extremely lenient,
Please show me, Sir, a like consideration,
And give me your entire cooperation.

ORGON (*Aside:*)

I may be all but bankrupt, but I vow
I'd give a hundred louis, here and now,
Just for the pleasure of landing one good
   clout
Right on the end of that complacent snout.

CLÉANTE

Careful; don't make things worse.

DAMIS

              My bootsole itches
To give that beggar a good kick in the
   breeches.

DORINE

Monsieur Loyal, I'd love to hear the whack
Of a stout stick across your fine broad back.

MONSIEUR LOYAL

Take care: a woman too may go to jail if
She uses threatening language to a bailiff.

CLÉANTE

Enough, enough, Sir. This must not go on.
Give me that paper, please, and then
   begone.

MONSIEUR LOYAL

Well, *au revoir*. God give you all good cheer!

ORGON

May God confound you, and him who sent
   you here!

Scene Five

ORGON, CLÉANTE, MARIANE, ELMIRE,
MADAME PERNELLE, DORINE, DAMIS

ORGON

Now, Mother, was I right or not? This writ
Should change your notion of Tartuffe a bit.
Do you perceive his villainy at last?

MADAME PERNELLE

I'm thunderstruck. I'm utterly aghast.

DORINE

Oh, come, be fair. You mustn't take offense
At this new proof of his benevolence.
He's acting out of selfless love, I know.
Material things enslave the soul, and so
He kindly has arranged your liberation
From all that might endanger your
   salvation.

ORGON

Will you not ever hold your tongue, you
   dunce?

CLÉANTE

Come, you must take some action, and at
   once.

ELMIRE

Go tell the world of the low trick he's tried.
The deed of gift is surely nullified
By such behavior, and public rage will not
Permit the wretch to carry out his plot.

Scene Six

VALÈRE, ORGON, CLÉANTE, ELMIRE,
MARIANE, MADAME PERNELLE,
DAMIS, DORINE

VALÈRE

Sir, though I hate to bring you more bad
   news,

Such is the danger that I cannot choose.
A friend who is extremely close to me
And knows my interest in your family
Has, for my sake, presumed to violate
The secrecy that's due to things of state,
And sends me word that you are in a plight
From which your one salvation lies in flight.
That scoundrel who's imposed upon you so
Denounced you to the King an hour ago
And, as supporting evidence, displayed
The strong-box of a certain renegade
Whose secret papers, so he testified,
You had disloyally agreed to hide.
I don't know just what charges may be
  pressed,
But there's a warrant out for your arrest;
Tartuffe has been instructed, furthermore,
To guide the arresting officer to your door.

CLÉANTE

He's clearly done this to facilitate
His seizure of your house and your estate.

ORGON

That man, I must say, is a vicious beast!

VALÈRE

Quick, Sir; you mustn't tarry in the least.
My carriage is outside, to take you hence;
This thousand louis should cover all expense.
Let's lose no time, or you shall be undone;
The sole defense, in this case, is to run.
I shall go with you all the way, and place
  you
In a safe refuge to which they'll never trace
  you.

ORGON

Alas, dear boy, I wish that I could show
  you
My gratitude for everything I owe you.
But now is not the time; I pray the Lord
That I may live to give you your reward.
Farewell, my dears; be careful . . .

CLÉANTE

                                Brother, hurry.
We shall take care of things; you needn't
  worry.

Scene Seven

THE OFFICER, TARTUFFE, VALÈRE, ORGON,
ELMIRE, MARIANE, MADAME PERNELLE,
DORINE, CLÉANTE, DAMIS

TARTUFFE

Gently, Sir, gently; stay right where you
  are.
No need for haste; your lodging isn't far.
You're off to prison, by order of the Prince.

ORGON

This is the crowning blow, you wretch;
  and since
It means my total ruin and defeat,
Your villainy is now at last complete.

TARTUFFE

You needn't try to provoke me; it's no use.
Those who serve Heaven must expect
  abuse.

CLÉANTE

You are indeed most patient, sweet, and
  blameless.

DORINE

How he exploits the name of Heaven! It's
  shameless.

TARTUFFE

Your taunts and mockeries are all for
  naught;
To do my duty is my only thought.

MARIANE

Your love of duty is most meritorious,
And what you've done is little short of
glorious.

TARTUFFE

All deeds are glorious, Madam, which obey
The sovereign prince who sent me here
today.

ORGON

I rescued you when you were destitute;
Have you forgotten that, you thankless
brute?

TARTUFFE

No, no, I well remember everything;
But my first duty is to serve my King.
That obligation is so paramount
That other claims, beside it, do not count;
And for it I would sacrifice my wife,
My family, my friend, or my own life.

ELMIRE

Hypocrite!

DORINE

All that we most revere, he uses
To cloak his plots and camouflage his ruses.

CLÉANTE

If it is true that you are animated
By pure and loyal zeal, as you have stated,
Why was this zeal not roused until you'd
sought
To make Orgon a cuckold, and been
caught?
Why weren't you moved to give your
evidence
Until your outraged host had driven you
hence?
I shan't say that the gift of all his treasure
Ought to have damped your zeal in any
measure;

But if he is a traitor, as you declare,
How could you condescend to be his heir?

TARTUFFE (*To the Officer:*)

Sir, spare me all this clamor; it's growing
shrill.
Please carry out your orders, if you will.

OFFICER

Yes, I've delayed too long, Sir. Thank you
kindly.
You're just the proper person to remind me.
Come, you are off to join the other boarders
In the King's prison, according to his
orders.

TARTUFFE

Who? I, Sir?

OFFICER

Yes.

TARTUFFE

To prison? This can't be true!

OFFICER

I owe an explanation, but not to you.

(*To Orgon:*)

Sir, all is well; rest easy, and be grateful.
We serve a Prince to whom all sham is
hateful,
A Prince who sees into our inmost hearts,
And can't be fooled by any trickster's arts.
His royal soul, though generous and human,
Views all things with discernment and
acumen;
His sovereign reason is not lightly swayed,
And all his judgments are discreetly
weighed.
He honors righteous men of every kind,
And yet his zeal for virtue is not blind,

Nor does his love of piety numb his wits
And make him tolerant of hypocrites.
'Twas hardly likely that this man could
    cozen
A King who's foiled such liars by the dozen.
With one keen glance, the King perceived
    the whole
Perverseness and corruption of his soul,
And thus high Heaven's justice was
    displayed:
Betraying you, the rogue stood self-betrayed.
The King soon recognized Tartuffe as one
Notorious by another name, who'd done
So many vicious crimes that one could fill
Ten volumes with them, and be writing still.
But to be brief: our sovereign was appalled
By this man's treachery toward you, which
    he called
The last, worst villainy of a vile career,
And bade me follow the impostor here
To see how gross his impudence could be,
And force him to restore your property.
Your private papers, by the King's
    command,
I hereby seize and give into your hand.
The King, by royal order, invalidates
The deed which gave this rascal your
    estates,
And pardons, furthermore, your grave
    offense
In harboring an exile's documents.
By these decrees, our Prince rewards you for
Your loyal deeds in the late civil war,
And shows how heartfelt is his satisfaction
In recompensing any worthy action,
How much he prizes merit, and how he
    makes
More of men's virtues than of their mistakes.

DORINE

Heaven be praised!

MADAME PERNELLE

          I breathe again, at last.

ELMIRE

We're safe.

MARIANE

I can't believe the danger's past.

ORGON (*To Tartuffe:*)

Well, traitor, now you see . . .

CLÉANTE

                    Ah, Brother, please,
Let's not descend to such indignities.
Leave the poor wretch to his unhappy fate,
And don't say anything to aggravate
His present woes; but rather hope that he
Will soon embrace an honest piety,
And mend his ways, and by a true
    repentance
Move our just King to moderate his
    sentence.
Meanwhile, go kneel before your sovereign's
    throne
And thank him for the mercies he has
    shown.

ORGON

Well said: let's go at once and, gladly
    kneeling,
Express the gratitude which all are feeling.
Then, when that first great duty has been
    done,
We'll turn with pleasure to a second one,
And give Valère, whose love has proven so
    true,
The wedded happiness which is his due.

INTRODUCTION
Richard Wilbur

There may be people who deny comedy
the right to be serious, and think it improper
for any but trivial themes to consort with

Introduction to Molière's *Tartuffe* translated by
Richard Wilbur, © 1961, 1962, 1963, by Richard
Wilbur. Reprinted by permission of Harcourt Brace
Jovanovich, Inc.

laughter. It would take people of that kind to find in *Tartuffe* anything offensive to religion. The warped characters of the play express an obviously warped religious attitude, which is corrected by the reasonable orthodoxy of Cléante, the wholesomeness of Dorine, and the entire testimony of the action. The play is not a satire on religion, as those held who kept it off the boards for five years. Is it, then, a satire on religious hypocrisy, as Molière claimed in his polemical preface of 1669?

The play speaks often of religious hypocrisy, displays it in action, and sometimes seems to be gesturing toward its practitioners in seventeenth-century French society. Tartuffe is made to recommend, more than once, those Jesuitical techniques for easing the conscience which Pascal attacked in the *Provincial Letters*. Cléante makes a long speech against people who feign piety for the sake of preferment or political advantage. And yet no one in the play can be said to be a religious hypocrite in any representative sense. Tartuffe may at times suggest or symbolize the slippery casuist, or the sort of hypocrite denounced by Cléante, but he is not himself such a person. He is a versatile parasite or confidence man, with a very long criminal record, and to pose as a holy man is not his only *modus operandi*: we see him, in the last act, shifting easily from the role of saint to that of hundred-percenter. As for the other major characters who might qualify, Madame Pernelle is simply a nasty bigot, while the religious attitudes of her son Orgon are, for all their underlying corruption, quite sincere.

Tartuffe is only incidentally satiric; what we experience in reading or seeing it, as several modern critics have argued, is not a satire but a "deep" comedy in which (1) a knave tries to control life by cold chicanery, (2) a fool tries to oppress life by unconscious misuse of the highest values, and (3) life, happily, will not have it.

Orgon, the central character of the play, is a rich bourgeois of middle age, with two grown children by his first wife. His second wife, Elmire, is attractive, young, and socially clever. We gather from the maid Dorine that Orgon has until lately seemed a good and sensible man, but the Orgon whom we meet in Act I, Scene 4 has become a fool. What has happened to him? It appears that he, like many another middle-aged man, has been alarmed by a sense of failing powers and failing authority, and that he has compensated by adopting an extreme religious severity. In this he is comparable to the aging coquette described by Dorine, who "quits a world which fast is quitting her," and saves face by becoming a censorious prude.

Orgon's resort to bigotry has coincided with his discovery of Tartuffe, a wily opportunist who imposes upon him by a pretense of sanctity, and is soon established in Orgon's house as honored guest, spiritual guide, and moral censor. Tartuffe's attitude toward Orgon is perfectly simple: he regards his benefactor as a dupe, and proposes to swindle him as badly as he can. Orgon's attitude toward Tartuffe is more complex and far less conscious. It consists, in part, of an unnatural fondness or "crush" about which the clear-sighted Dorine is explicit:

*He pets and pampers him with love more tender
Than any pretty mistress could engender. . . .*

It also involves, in the strict sense of the word, idolatry: Orgon's febrile religious emotions are all related to Tartuffe and appear to terminate in him. Finally, and least consciously, Orgon cherishes Tartuffe because, with the sanction of the latter's austere precepts, he can tyrannize over his family and punish them for possessing what he feels himself to be losing: youth, gaiety, strong natural desires. This punitive motive comes to the surface, looking like plain sadism, when Orgon orders his daughter to

Marry Tartuffe, and mortify your flesh!

Orgon is thus both Tartuffe's victim and his unconscious exploiter; once we apprehend this, we can better understand Orgon's stubborn refusal to see Tartuffe for the fraud that he is.

When Orgon say to Cléante,

My mother, children, brother and wife could die,
And I'd not feel a single moment's pain,

he is parodying or perverting a Christian idea which derives from the Gospels and rings out purely in Luther's "A Mighty Fortress is Our God":

Let goods and kindred go,
This mortal life also. . . .

The trouble with Orgon's high spirituality is that one cannot obey the first commandment without obeying the second also. Orgon has withdrawn all proper feeling from those about him, and his vicious fatuity creates an atmosphere which is the comic equivalent of *King Lear*'s. All natural bonds of love and trust are strained or broken; evil is taken for good; truth must to kennel. Cleante's reasonings, the rebellious protests of Damis, the entreaties of Mariane, and the mockeries of Dorine are ineffectual against Orgon's folly; he must see Tartuffe paw at his wife, and hear Tartuffe speak contemptuously of him, before he is willing to part with the sponsor of his spiteful piety. How little "religion" there has been in Orgon's behavior, how much it has arisen from infatuation and bitterness, we may judge by his indiscriminate outburst in the fifth act:

Enough, by God! I'm through with pious men!
Henceforth I'll hate the whole false brotherhood,
And persecute them worse than Satan could.

By the time Orgon is made to see Tartuffe's duplicity, the latter has accomplished his swindle, and is in a position to bring about Orgon's material ruin. It takes Louis

XIV himself to save the day, in a conclusion which may seem both forced and flattering, but which serves to contrast a judicious, humane and forgiving ruler with the domestic tyrant Orgon. The King's moral insight is Tartuffe's final undoing; nevertheless there is an earlier scene in which we are given better assurance of the invincibility of the natural and sane. I refer to Tartuffe's first conversation with Elmire, in which passion compels the hypocrite recklessly to abandon his role. What comes out of Tartuffe in that scene is an expression of helpless lust, couched in an appalling mixture of the languages of gallantry and devotion. It is not attractive; and yet one is profoundly satisfied to discover that, as W. G. Moore puts it, "Tartuffe's human nature escapes his calculation." To be flawlessly monstrous is, thank heaven, not easy.

In translating *Tartuffe* I have tried, as with *The Misanthrope* some years ago, to reproduce with all possible fidelity both Molière's words and his poetic form. The necessity of keeping verse and rhyme, in plays as these, was argued at some length in an introduction to the earlier translation, and I shall not repeat all those arguments here. It is true that *Tartuffe* presents an upper-bourgeois rather than a courtly milieu; there is less deliberate wit and elegance than in the dialogue of *The Misanthrope*, and consequently there is less call for the couplet as a conveyor of epigrammatic effects. Yet there are such effects in *Tartuffe*, and rhyme and verse are required here for other good reasons: to pay out the long speeches with clarifying emphasis, and at an assimilable rate; to couple farcical sequences to passages of greater weight and resonance; and to give a purely formal pleasure, as when balancing verse-patterns support the "ballet" movement of the close of Act II. My convictions being what they are, I am happy to report what a number of productions of the *Misanthrope* translation have shown: that contemporary audiences are quite willing to put up with rhymed verse on the stage.

THE LOVE OF DON PERLIMPLÍN AND BELISA IN THE GARDEN
AN EROTIC ALELUYA
IN FOUR SCENES
CHAMBER VERSION

Federico García Lorca

translated by James Graham-Luján and Richard O'Connell

CHARACTERS

DON PERLIMPLIN

BELISA

MARCOLFA

MOTHER OF BELISA

FIRST SPRITE

SECOND SPRITE

PROLOGUE

House of Don Perlimplín. Green walls; chairs and furniture painted black. At the rear, a deep window with balcony through which Belisa's balcony may be seen. A sonata is heard. Perlimplín wears a green cassock and a white wig full of curls. Marcolfa, the servant, wears the classic striped dress.

PERLIMPLÍN. Yes?

MARCOLFA. Yes.

PERLIMPLÍN. But why "yes"?

MARCOLFA. Just because yes.

PERLIMPLÍN. And if I should say no?

MARCOLFA, *acidly.* No?

PERLIMPLÍN. No.

MARCOLFA. Tell me, Master, the reason for that "no."

Federico García Lorca, FIVE PLAYS, translated by James Graham-Luján and Richard O'Connell. Copyright 1941 by Charles Scribner's Sons, © 1963 by New Directions Publishing Corporation. Reprinted by permission of New Directions Publishing Corporation.

PERLIMPLÍN. You tell me, you persevering domestic, the reasons for that "yes."

Pause.

MARCOLFA. Twenty and twenty are forty . . .

PERLIMPLÍN, *listening.* Proceed.

MARCOLFA. And ten, fifty.

PERLIMPLÍN. Go ahead.

MARCOLFA. At fifty years one is no longer a child.

PERLIMPLÍN. Of course!

MARCOLFA. I may die any minute.

PERLIMPLÍN. Good Lord!

MARCOLFA, *weeping.* And what will happen to you all alone in the world?

PERLIMPLÍN. What will happen?

MARCOLFA. That's why you have to marry.

PERLIMPLÍN, *distracted.* Yes?

MARCOLFA, *sternly.* Yes.

PERLIMPLÍN, *miserably.* But Marcolfa . . . why "yes"? When I was a child a woman strangled her husband. He was a shoemaker. I can't forget it. I've always said I wouldn't marry. My books are enough for me. What good will marriage do me?

MARCOLFA. Marriage holds great charms, Master. It isn't what it appears on the outside. It's full of hidden things . . . things which it would not be becoming for a servant to mention. You see that . . .

PERLIMPLÍN. That what?

MARCOLFA. That I have blushed.

Pause. A piano is heard.

VOICE OF BELISA, *within, singing.*
Ah love, ah love.
Tight in my thighs imprisoned
There swims like a fish the sun.
Warm water in the rushes.
Ah love.
Morning cock, the night is going!
Don't let it vanish, no!

MARCOLFA. My master will see the reason I have.

PERLIMPLÍN, *scratching his head.* She sings prettily.

MARCOLFA. She is the woman for my master. The fair Belisa.

PERLIMPLÍN. Belisa . . . but wouldn't it be better . . . ?

MARCOLFA. No. Now come.

She takes him by the hand and goes toward the balcony.

Say, "Belisa."

PERLIMPLÍN. Belisa . . .

MARCOLFA. Louder.

PERLIMPLÍN. Belisa!

The balcony of the house opposite opens and Belisa appears, resplendent in her loveliness. She is half naked.

BELISA. Who calls?

Marcolfa hides behind the window curtains.

MARCOLFA. Answer!

PERLIMPLÍN, *trembling.* I was calling.

BELISA. Yes?

PERLIMPLÍN. Yes.

BELISA. But why, "yes"?

PERLIMPLÍN. Just because yes.

BELISA. And if I should say no?

PERLIMPLÍN. I would be sorry, because . . . we have decided that I want to marry.

BELISA, *laughs.* Marry whom?

PERLIMPLÍN. You.

BELISA, *serious.* But . . .

Calling.

Mamá! Mamá-á-á!

MARCOLFA. This is going well.

Enter the Mother wearing a great eighteenth-century wig full of birds, ribbons and glass beads.

BELISA. Don Perlimplín wants to marry me. What must I do?

MOTHER. The very best of afternoons to you, my charming little neighbor. I always said to my poor little girl that you have the grace and elegance of that great lady who was your mother, whom I did not have the pleasure of knowing.

PERLIMPLÍN. Thank you.

MARCOLFA, *furiously, from behind the curtain.* I have decided that we are going . . .

PERLIMPLÍN. We have decided that we are going . . .

MOTHER. To contract matrimony. Is that not so?

PERLIMPLÍN. That is so.

BELISA. But, Mamá, what about me?

MOTHER. You are agreeable, naturally. Don Perlimplín is a fascinating husband.

PERLIMPLÍN. I hope to be one, madam.

MARCOLFA, *calling to Don Perlimplín.* This is almost settled.

PERLIMPLÍN. Do you think so?

They whisper together.

MOTHER, *to Belisa.* Don Perlimplín has many lands. On these are many geese and sheep. The sheep are taken to market. At the market they give money for them. Money produces beauty . . . and beauty is sought after by all men.

PERLIMPLÍN. Then . . .

MOTHER. Ever so thrilled . . . Belisa . . . go inside. It isn't well for a maiden to hear certain conversations.

BELISA. Until later.

She leaves.

MOTHER. She is a lily. You've seen her face?

Lowering her voice.

But if you should see further! Just like sugar. But, pardon. I need not call these things to the attention of a person as modern and competent as you. . . .

PERLIMPLÍN. Yes?

MOTHER. Why, yes. I said it without irony.

PERLIMPLÍN. I don't know how to express our gratitude.

MOTHER. Oh, "our gratitude." What extraordinary delicacy! The gratitude of your heart and yourself . . . I have sensed it. I have sensed it . . . in spite of the fact that it is twenty years since I have had relations with a man.

MARCOLFA, *aside.* The wedding.

PERLIMPLÍN. The wedding . . .

MOTHER. Whenever you wish. Though . . .

She brings out a handkerchief and weeps.

. . . to every mother . . . until later!

Leaves.

MARCOLFA. At last!

PERLIMPLÍN. Oh, Marcolfa, Marcolfa! Into what world are you going to thrust me?

MARCOLFA. Into the world of matrimony.

PERLIMPLÍN. And if I should be frank, I would say that I feel thirsty. Why don't you bring me some water?

Marcolfa approaches him and whispers in his ear.

Who could believe it?

The piano is heard. The stage is in darkness. Belisa opens the curtains of her balcony, almost naked, singing languidly.

BELISA.
　Ah love, ah love.
　Tight in my warm thighs imprisoned,
　There swims like a fish the sun.

MARCOLFA. Beautiful maiden.

PERLIMPLÍN. Like sugar . . . white inside. Will she be capable of strangling me?

MARCOLFA. Woman is weak if frightened in time.

BELISA.
　Ah love, ah love.
　Morning cock, the night is going!
　Don't let it vanish, no!

PERLIMPLÍN. What does she mean, Marcolfa? What does she mean?

Marcolfa laughs.

What is happening to me? What is it?

The piano goes on playing. Past the balcony flies a band of black paper birds.

CURTAIN

Scene 1

Don Perimplín's room. At the center there is a great bed topped by a canopy with plume ornaments. In the back wall there are six doors. The first one on the right serves as entrance and exit for Don Perlimplín. It is the wedding night.

Marcolfa, with a candelabrum in her hand, speaks at the first door on the left side.

MARCOLFA. Good night.

BELISA, *offstage.* Good night, Marcolfa.

Don Perlimplín enters, magnificently dressed.

MARCOLFA. May my master have a good wedding night.

PERLIMPLÍN. Good night, Marcolfa.

Marcolfa leaves. Perlimplín tiptoes toward the room in front and looks from the door.

Belisa, in all that froth of lace you look like a wave, and you give me the same fear of the sea that I had as a child. Since you came from the church my house is full of secret whispers, and the water grows warm by itself in the glasses. Oh! Perlimplín . . . Where are you, Perlimplín?

Leaves on tiptoe. Belisa appears, dressed in a great sleeping garment adorned with lace. She wears an enormous headdress which launches cascades of needlework and lace down to her feet. Her hair is loose and her arms bare.

BELISA. The maid perfumed this room with thyme and not with mint as I ordered. . . .

Goes toward the bed.

Nor did she put on the fine linen which Marcolfa has.

At this moment there is a soft music of guitars. Belisa crosses her hands over her breast.

Ah! Whoever seeks me ardently will find me. My thirst is never quenched, just as the thirst of the gargoyles who spurt water in the fountains is never quenched.

The music continues.

Oh, what music! Heavens, what music! Like the soft warm downy feathers of a swan! Oh! Is it I? Or is it the music?

She throws a great cape of red velvet over her shoulders and walks about the room. The music is silent and five whistles are heard.

BELISA. Five of them!

Perlimplín appears.

PERLIMPLÍN. Do I disturb you?
BELISA. How could that be possible?
PERLIMPLÍN. Are you sleepy?
BELISA, *ironically.* Sleepy?
PERLIMPLÍN. The night has become a little chilly.

Rubs his hands. Pause.

BELISA, *with decision.* Perlimplín.
PERLIMPLÍN, *trembling.* What do you want?
BELISA, *vaguely.* It's a pretty name, "Perlimplín."
PERLIMPLÍN. Yours is prettier, Belisa.
BELISA, *laughing.* Oh! Thank you!

Short pause.

PERLIMPLÍN. I wanted to tell you something.
BELISA. And that is?
PERLIMPLÍN. I have been late in deciding . . . but . . .
BELISA. Say it.
PERLIMPLÍN. Belisa, I love you.
BELISA. Oh, you little gentleman! That's your duty.
PERLIMPLÍN. Yes?
BELISA. Yes.
PERLIMPLÍN. But why "yes"?
BELISA, *coyly.* Because.
PERLIMPLÍN. No.
BELISA. Perlimplín!
PERLIMPLÍN. No, Belisa, before I married you, I didn't love you.
BELISA, *jokingly.* What are you saying?
PERLIMPLÍN. I married . . . for whatever reason, but I didn't love you. I couldn't have imagined your body until I saw it through the keyhole when you were putting on your wedding dress. And then it was that I felt love come to me. Then! Like the deep thrust of a lancet in my throat.
BELISA, *intrigued.* But, the other women?
PERLIMPLÍN. What women?
BELISA. Those you knew before.
PERLIMPLÍN. But are there other women?
BELISA, *getting up.* You astonish me!
PERLIMPLÍN. The first to be astonished was I.

Pause. The five whistles are heard.

What's that?
BELISA. The clock.
PERLIMPLÍN. Is it five?
BELISA. Bedtime.
PERLIMPLÍN. Do I have your permission to remove my coat?
BELISA. Of course,

Yawning.

little husband. And put out the light, if that is your wish.

Perlimplín puts out the light.

PERLIMPLÍN, *in a low voice.* Belisa.

BELISA, *loudly.* What, child?

PERLIMPLÍN, *whispering.* I've put the light out.

BELISA, *jokingly.* I see that.

PERLIMPLÍN, *in a much lower voice.* Belisa . . .

BELISA, *in a loud voice.* What, enchanter?

PERLIMPLÍN. I adore you!

•The five whistles are heard much louder and the bed is uncovered. Two Sprites, entering from opposite sides of the stage, run a curtain of misty gray. The theater is left in darkness. Flutes sound with a sweet, sleepy tone. The Sprites should be two children. They sit on the prompt box facing the audience.

FIRST SPRITE. And how goes it with you in this tiny darkness?

SECOND SPRITE. Neither well nor badly, little friend.

FIRST SPRITE. Here we are.

SECOND SPRITE. And how do you like it? It's always nice to cover other people's failings . . .

FIRST SPRITE. And then to let the audience take care of uncovering them.

SECOND SPRITE. Because if things are not covered up with all possible precautions . . .

FIRST SPRITE. They would never be discovered.

SECOND SPRITE. And without this covering and uncovering . . .

FIRST SPRITE. What would the poor people do?

SECOND SPRITE, *looking at the curtain.* There must not even be a slit.

FIRST SPRITE. For the slits of today are darkness tomorrow.

They laugh.

SECOND SPRITE. When things are quite evident . . .

FIRST SPRITE. Man figures that he has no need to discover them . . . in them secrets he already knew.

SECOND SPRITE. And he goes to dark things to discover them . . . in them secrets he already knew.

FIRST SPRITE. But that's what we're here for. We Sprites!

SECOND SPRITE. Did you know Perlimplín?

FIRST SPRITE. Since he was a child.

SECOND SPRITE. And Belisa?

FIRST SPRITE. Very well. Her room exhaled such intense perfume that I once fell asleep and awoke between her cat's claws.

They laugh.

SECOND SPRITE. This affair was . . .

FIRST SPRITE. Oh, of course!

SECOND SPRITE. All the world thought so.

FIRST SPRITE. And the gossip must have turned then to more mysterious things.

SECOND SPRITE. That's why our efficient and most sociable screen should not be opened yet.

FIRST SPRITE. No, don't let them find out.

SECOND SPRITE. The soul of Perlimplín, tiny and frightened like a newborn duckling, becomes enriched and sublime at these moments.

They laugh.

FIRST SPRITE. The audience is impatient.

SECOND SPRITE. And with reason. Shall we go?

FIRST SPRITE. Let's go. I feel a fresh breeze on my back already.

SECOND SPRITE. Five cool camellias of the dawn have opened in the walls of the bedroom.

FIRST SPRITE. Five balconies upon the city.

They rise and throw on some great blue hoods.

SECOND SPRITE. Don Perlimplín, do we help or hinder you?

FIRST SPRITE. Help: because it is not fair to place before the eyes of the audience the misfortune of a good man.

SECOND SPRITE. That's true, little friend, for it's not the same to say: "I have seen," as "It is said."

FIRST SPRITE. Tomorrow the whole world will know about it.

SECOND SPRITE. And that's what we wish.

FIRST SPRITE. One word of gossip and the whole world knows.

SECOND SPRITE. Sh . . .

Flutes begin to sound.

FIRST SPRITE. Shall we go through this tiny darkness?

SECOND SPRITE. Let us go now, little friend.

FIRST SPRITE. Now?

SECOND SPRITE. Now.

They open the curtain. Don Perlimplín appears on the bed, with two enormous gilded horns. Belisa is at his side. The five balconies at the back of the stage are wide open, and through them the white light of dawn enters.

PERLIMPLÍN, *awakening.* Belisa! Belisa! Answer me!

BELISA, *pretending to awaken.* Perlimplinpinito . . . what do you want?

PERLIMPLÍN. Tell me quickly.

BELISA. What do you want me to tell you? I fell asleep long before you did.

PERLIMPLÍN, *leaps from the bed. He has on his cassock.* Why are the balconies open?

BELISA. Because this night the wind has blown as never before.

PERLIMPLÍN. Why do the balconies have five ladders that reach to the ground?

BELISA. Because that is the custom in my mother's country.

PERLIMPLÍN. And whose are those five hats which I see under the balconies?

BELISA, *leaping from the bed.* The little drunkards who come and go. Perlimplinillo! Love!

Perlimplín looks at her, staring stupefied.

PERLIMPLÍN. Belisa! Belisa! And why not? You explain everything so well. I am satisfied. Why couldn't it have been like that?

BELISA, *coyly.* I'm not a little fibber.

PERLIMPLÍN. And I love you more every minute!

BELISA. That's the way I like it.

PERLIMPLÍN. For the first time in my life I am happy!

He approaches and embraces her, but, in that instant, turns brusquely from her.

Belisa, who has kissed you? Don't lie, for I know!

BELISA, *gathering her hair and throwing it over her shoulder.* Of course you know! What a playful little husband I have!

In a low voice.

You! You have kissed me!

PERLIMPLÍN. Yes. I have kissed you . . . but . . . if someone else had kissed you . . . if someone else had kissed you . . . do you love me?

BELISA, *lifting a naked arm.* Yes, little Perlimplín.

PERLIMPLÍN. Then, what do I care?

He turns and embraces her.

Are you Belisa?

BELISA, *coyly, and in a low voice.* Yes! Yes! Yes!

PERLIMPLÍN. It almost seems like a dream!

BELISA, *recovering.* Look, Perlimplín, close the balconies because before long people will be getting up.

PERLIMPLÍN. What for? Since we have both slept enough, we shall see the dawn. Don't you like that?

BELISA. Yes, but . . .

She sits on the bed.

PERLIMPLÍN. I have never seen the sunrise.

Belisa, exhausted, falls on the pillows of the bed.

It is a spectacle which . . . this may seem an untruth . . . thrills me! Don't you like it?

Goes toward the bed.

Belisa, are you asleep?

BELISA, *in her dreams.* Yes.

Perlimplín tiptoes over and covers her with the red cape. An intense golden light enters through the balconies. Bands of paper birds cross them amidst the ringing of the morning bells. Perlimplín has seated himself on the edge of the bed.

PERLIMPLÍN.
   Love, love
   that here lies wounded.
   So wounded by love's going;
   so wounded,
   dying of love.
   Tell every one that it was just
   the nightingale.
   A surgeon's knife with four sharp edges;
   the bleeding throat—forgetfulness.
   Take me by the hands, my love,
   for I come quite badly wounded,
   so wounded by love's going.
   So wounded!
   Dying of love!

CURTAIN

Scene 2

Perlimplín's dining room. The perspectives are deliciously wrong. All the objects on the table are painted as in a primitive Last Supper.

PERLIMPLÍN. Then you will do as I say?

MARCOLFA, *crying.* Don't worry, master.

PERLIMPLÍN. Marcolfa, why do you keep on crying?

MARCOLFA. Your Grace knows. On your wedding night five men entered your bedroom through the balconies. Five! Representatives of the five races of the earth. The European, with his beard—the Indian—the Negro—the Yellow Man—and the American. And you unaware of it all.

PERLIMPLÍN. That is of no importance.

MARCOLFA. Just imagine: yesterday I saw her with another one.

PERLIMPLÍN, *intrigued.* Really?

MARCOLFA. And she didn't even hide from me.

PERLIMPLÍN. But I am happy, Marcolfa.

MARCOLFA. The master astonishes me.

PERLIMPLÍN. You have no idea how happy I am. I have learned many things and above all I can imagine many others.

MARCOLFA. My master loves her too much.

PERLIMPLÍN. Not as much as she deserves.

MARCOLFA. Here she comes.

PERLIMPLÍN. Please leave.

Marcolfa leaves and Perlimplín hides in a corner. Enter Belisa dressed in a red dress of eighteenth-century style. The skirt, at the back, is slit, allowing silk stockings to be seen. She wears huge earrings and a red hat trimmed with big ostrich plumes.

BELISA. Again I have failed to see him. In my walk through the park they were all behind me except him. His skin must be dark, and his kisses must perfume and burn at the same time—like saffron and cloves. Sometimes he passes underneath my balconies and moves his hand slowly in a greeting that makes my breasts tremble.

PERLIMPLÍN. Ahem!

BELISA, *turning.* Oh! What a fright you gave me.

PERLIMPLÍN, *approaching her affectionately.* I observe you were speaking to yourself.

BELISA, *distastefully.* Go away!

PERLIMPLÍN. Shall we take a walk?

BELISA. No.

PERLIMPLÍN. Shall we go to the confectioner's?

BELISA. I said no!

PERLIMPLÍN. Pardon.

A letter rolled about a stone falls through the balcony. Perlimplín picks it up.

BELISA. Give that to me.

PERLIMPLÍN. Why?

BELISA. Because it's for me.

PERLIMPLÍN, *jokingly*. And who told you that?

BELISA. Perlimplín! Don't read it!

PERLIMPLÍN, *jokingly severe*. What are you trying to say?

BELISA, *weeping*. Give me that letter!

PERLIMPLÍN, *approaching her*. Poor Belisa! Because I understand your feelings I give you this paper which means so much to you.

Belisa takes the note and hides it in her bosom.

I can see things. And even though it wounds me deeply, I understand you live a drama.

BELISA, *tenderly*. Perlimplín!

PERLIMPLÍN. I know that you are faithful to me, and that you will continue to be so.

BELISA, *fondly*. I've never known any man other than my Perlimplinillo.

PERLIMPLÍN. That's why I want to help you as any good husband should when his wife is a model of virtue. . . . Look.

He closes the door and adopts a mysterious air.

I know everything! I realized immediately. You are young and I am old . . . what can we do about it! But I understand perfectly.

Pause. In a low voice.

Has he come by here today?

BELISA. Twice.

PERLIMPLÍN. And has he signaled to you?

BELISA. Yes . . . but in a manner that's a little disdainful . . . and that hurts me!

PERLIMPLÍN. Don't be afraid. Two weeks ago I saw that young man for the first time. I can tell you with all sincerity that his beauty dazzled me. I have never seen another man in whom manliness and delicacy meet in a more harmonious fashion. Without knowing why, I thought of you.

BELISA. I haven't seen his face . . . but . . .

PERLIMPLÍN. Don't be afraid to speak to me. I know you love him . . . and I love you now as if I were your father. I am far from that foolishness; therefore . . .

BELISA. He writes me letters.

PERLIMPLÍN. I know that.

BELISA. But he doesn't let me see him.

PERLIMPLÍN. That's strange.

BELISA. And it even seems . . . as though he scorns me.

PERLIMPLÍN. How innocent you are!

BELISA. But there's no doubt he loves me as I wish. . . .

PERLIMPLÍN, *intrigued*. How is that?

BELISA. The letters I have received from other men . . . and which I didn't answer because I had my little husband, spoke to me of ideal lands—of dreams and wounded hearts. But these letters from him . . . they . . .

PERLIMPLÍN. Speak without fear.

BELISA. They speak about me . . . about my body . . .

PERLIMPLÍN, *stroking her hair*. About your body!

BELISA. "What do I want your soul for?" he tells me. "The soul is the patrimony of the weak, of crippled heroes and sickly people. Beautiful souls are at death's door, leaning upon whitest hairs and lean hands. Belisa, it is not your soul that I desire, but your white and soft trembling body."

PERLIMPLÍN. Who could that beautiful youth be?

BELISA. No one knows.

PERLIMPLÍN, *inquisitive*. No one?

BELISA. I have asked all my friends.

PERLIMPLÍN, *inscrutably and decisively*. And if I should tell you I know him?

BELISA. Is that possible?

PERLIMPLÍN. Wait.

Goes to the balcony.

Here he is.

BELISA, *running*. Yes?

PERLIMPLÍN. He has just turned the corner.

BELISA, *choked*. Oh!

PERLIMPLÍN. Since I am an old man, I want

to sacrifice myself for you. This that I do no one ever did before. But I am already beyond the world and the ridiculous morals of its people. Good-by.

BELISA. Where are you going?

PERLIMPLÍN, *at the door, grandiosely.* Later you will know everything. Later.

CURTAIN

Scene 3

A grove of cypresses and orange trees. When the curtain rises, Marcolfa and Perlimplín appear in the garden.

MARCOLFA. Is it time yet?

PERLIMPLÍN. No, it isn't time yet.

MARCOLFA. But what has my master thought?

PERLIMPLÍN. Everything he hadn't thought before.

MARCOLFA, *weeping.* It's my fault!

PERLIMPLÍN. Oh, if you only knew what gratitude there is in my heart for you!

MARCOLFA. Before this, everything went smoothly. In the morning, I would take my master his coffee and milk and grapes. . . .

PERLIMPLÍN. Yes . . . the grapes! The grapes! But . . . I? It seems to me that a hundred years have passed. Before, I could not think of the extraordinary things the world holds. I was merely on the threshold. On the other hand . . . today! Belisa's love has given me a precious wealth that I ignored before . . . don't you see? Now I can close my eyes and . . . I can see what I want. For example, my mother, when she was visited by the elves. Oh, you know how elves are . . . tiny. It's marvelous! They can dance upon my little finger.

MARCOLFA. Yes, yes, the elves, the elves, but . . . how about this other?

PERLIMPLÍN. The other? Ah!

With satisfaction.

What did you tell my wife?

MARCOLFA. Even though I'm not very good at these things, I told her what the master had instructed me to say . . . that that young man . . . would come tonight at ten o'clock sharp to the garden, wrapped, as usual, in his red cape.

PERLIMPLÍN. And she?

MARCOLFA. She became as red as a geranium, put her hands to her heart, and kissed her lovely braids passionately.

PERLIMPLÍN, *enthusiastic.* So she got red as a geranium, eh? And, what did she say?

MARCOLFA. She just sighed; that's all. But, oh! such a sigh!

PERLIMPLÍN. Oh, yes! As no woman ever sighed before! Isn't that so?

MARCOLFA. Her love must border on madness.

PERLIMPLÍN, *vibrantly.* That's it! What I need is for her to love that youth more than her own body. And there is no doubt that she loves him.

MARCOLFA, *weeping.* It frightens me to hear you . . . but how is it possible? Don Perlimplín, how is it possible that you yourself should encourage your wife in the worst of sins?

PERLIMPLÍN. Because Perlimplín has no honor and wants to amuse himself! Now do you see? Tonight the new and unknown lover of my lady Belisa will come. What should I do but sing?

Singing.

Don Perlimplín has no honor! Has no honor!

MARCOLFA. Let my master know that from this moment on I consider myself dismissed from his service. We servants also have a sense of shame.

PERLIMPLÍN. Oh, innocent Marcolfa! Tomorrow you will be as free as a bird. Wait until tomorrow. Now go and perform your duty. You will do what I have told you?

MARCOLFA, *leaving, drying her tears.* What else is there for me to do? What else?

PERLIMPLÍN. Good, that's how I like it.

A sweet serenade begins to sound. Don Perlimplín hides behind some rosebushes.

VOICES.
Upon the banks of the river
the passing night has paused to bathe.
The passing night has paused to bathe.
And on the breasts of Belisa
the flowers languish of their love.
The flowers languish of their love.
PERLIMPLÍN.
The flowers languish of their love.
VOICES.
The naked night stands there singing,
singing on the bridge of March.
Singing on the bridge of March.
Belisa, too, bathes her body
with briny water and spikenard.
With briny water and spikenard.
PERLIMPLÍN.
The flowers languish of their love!
VOICES.
The night of anise and silver
on all the roofs glows and shines.
On all the roofs glows and shines.
The silver of streams and of mirrors
and anise white of your thighs.
And anise white of your thighs.
PERLIMPLÍN. The flowers languish of their
love!

Belisa appears in the garden splendidly dressed. The moon lights the stage.

BELISA. What voices fill with sweet harmony
the air of this fragment of the night? I
have felt your warmth and your weight,
delicious youth of my soul. Oh! The
branches are moving . . .

A man dressed in a red cape appears and crosses the garden cautiously.

BELISA. Sh! Here! Here!

The man signals with his hand that he will return immediately.

Oh! Yes . . . come back my love! Like a

jasmine floating and without roots, the
sky will fall over my moistening shoulders. Night! My night of mint and lapis
lazuli . . .

Perlimplín appears.

PERLIMPLÍN, *surprised.* What are you doing
here?
BELISA. I was walking.
PERLIMPLÍN. Only that?
BELISA. In the clear night.
PERLIMPLÍN, *severely.* What were you doing
here?
BELISA, *surprised.* Don't you know?
PERLIMPLÍN. I don't know anything.
BELISA. You sent me the message.
PERLIMPLÍN, *with ardent desire.* Belisa . . . are
you still waiting for him?
BELISA. With more ardor than ever.
PERLIMPLÍN, *severely.* Why?
BELISA. Because I love him.
PERLIMPLÍN. Well, he will come.
BELISA. The perfume of his flesh passes
beyond his clothes. I love him! Perlim-
plín, I love him! It seems to me that I
am another woman!
PERLIMPLÍN. That is my triumph.
BELISA. What triumph?
PERLIMPLÍN. The triumph of my imagination.
BELISA. It's true that you helped me love
him.
PERLIMPLÍN. As now I will help you mourn
him.
BELISA, *puzzled.* Perlimplín! What are you
saying?

The clock sounds ten. A nightingale sings.

PERLIMPLÍN. It is the hour.
BELISA. He should be here this instant.
PERLIMPLÍN. He's leaping the walls of my
garden.
BELISA. Wrapped in his red cape.
PERLIMPLÍN, *drawing a dagger.* Red as his
blood.
BELISA, *holding him.* What are you going to do?
PERLIMPLÍN, *embracing her.* Belisa, do you love
him?

BELISA, *forcefully*. Yes!

PERLIMPLÍN. Well, since you love him so much, I don't want him ever to leave you. And in order that he should be completely yours, it has come to me that the best thing would be to stick this dagger in his gallant heart. Would you like that?

BELISA. For God's sake, Perlimplín!

PERLIMPLÍN. Then, dead, you will be able to caress him in your bed—so handsome and well groomed—without the fear that he should cease to love you. He will love you with the infinite love of the dead, and I will be free of this dark little nightmare of your magnificent body.

Embracing her.

Your body . . . that I will never decipher!

Looking into the garden.

Look where he comes.. Let go, Belisa. Let go!

He exits running.

BELISA, *desperately*. Marcolfa! Bring me the sword from the dining room; I am going to run my husband's throat through.

Calling.

> Don Perlimplín
> Evil husband!
> If you kill him,
> I'll kill you!

A man wrapped in a large red cape appears among the branches. He is wounded and stumbling.

BELISA. My love! . . . Who has wounded you in the breast?

The man hides his face in his cape. The cape must be enormous and cover him to the feet. She embraces him.

Who opened your veins so that you fill my garden with blood? Love, let me look at your face for an instant. Oh! Who has killed you . . . Who?

PERLIMPLÍN, *uncovering himself*. Your husband has just killed me with this emerald dagger.

He shows the dagger stuck in his chest.

BELISA, *frightened*. Perlimplín!

PERLIMPLÍN. He ran away through the fields and you will never see him again. He killed me because he knew I loved you as no one else. . . . While he wounded me he shouted: "Belisa has a soul now!" Come near.

He has stretched out on the bench.

BELISA. Why is this? And you are truly wounded.

PERLIMPLÍN. Perlimplín killed me. . . . Ah, Don Perlimplín! Youngish old man, manikin without strength, you couldn't enjoy the body of Belisa . . . the body of Belisa was for younger muscles and warm lips. . . . I, on the other hand, loved your body only . . . your body! But he has killed me . . . with this glowing branch of stones.

BELISA. What have you done?

PERLIMPLÍN, *near death*. Don't you understand? I am my soul and you are your body. Allow me this last moment, since you have loved me so much, to die embracing it.

Belisa, half naked, draws near and embraces him.

BELISA. Yes . . . but the young man? Why have you deceived me?

PERLIMPLÍN. The young man?

Closes his eyes. The stage is left in magical light. Marcolfa enters.

MARCOLFA. Madam . . .

BELISA, *weeping*. Don Perlimplín is dead!

MARCOLFA. I knew it! Now his shroud will be the youthful red suit in which he used to walk under his own balconies.

BELISA, *weeping.* I never thought he was so devious.

MARCOLFA. You have found out too late. I shall make him a crown of flowers like the noonday sun.

BELISA, *confused, as if in another world.* Perlimplín, what have you done, Perlimplín?

MARCOLFA. Belisa, now you are another woman. You are dressed in the most glorious blood of my master.

BELISA. But who was this man? Who was he?

MARCOLFA. The beautiful adolescent whose face you never will see.

BELISA. Yes, yes, Marcolfa—I love him—I love him with all the strength of my flesh and my soul—but where is the young man in the red cape? Dear God, where is he?

MARCOLFA. Don Perlimplín, sleep peacefully. . . . Do you hear? Don Perlimplín. . . . Do you hear her?

The bells sound.

CURTAIN

DON PERLIMPLÍN: LORCA'S THEATER-POETRY

Francis Fergusson

For something like forty years poets in English-speaking countries have been trying to write poetic drama for the modern stage. This movement, if something so scattered and diverse may be called a movement, stems largely from Yeats and Eliot. Their plays are still the best modern poetic drama we have, and their theories still define the prevailing conception of poetic drama. But no one is quite satisfied with the results. We still lack a

From *The Human Image in Dramatic Literature.* New York: Doubleday Anchor, 1957. Reprinted by the permission of the author.

poetic theater-form comparable to those of more fortunate ages, or to the "unpoetic" convention of modern realism.

Federico García Lorca wrote poetic drama . . . which lives naturally on the modern stage. Lorca did very little theorizing, but he found, at a very early age, in pre-Franco Spain, singularly direct ways to use the stage for the purposes of poetry. It is true that he is not a creature of the commercial theater. Madrid in his time had a theater corresponding to Broadway, but Lorca was always in more or less hidden opposition to it. He was the director of "La Barraca," a group of University players which was subsidized by the government and toured the provincial towns and cities of Spain with a repertory of classics. It is evident that his own plays owe a great deal to this experience. La Barraca found an "off-Broadway" audience in Spain, and since then Lorca's plays have found audiences in France, Switzerland, Germany, Mexico, South America, and college towns all over this country. No one has succeeded in producing him successfully on Broadway, but in being rejected by the timid snobbery of Times Square he is in excellent company. And there is no doubt that he can by-pass the taboos of the market, and reach a wide contemporary audience in free Europe and the Americas.

Lorca's theater-poetry fulfills many of the prescriptions of Yeats and Eliot, but it is strongly marked by his unique genius, his rare combination of talents. And it is nourished by the Spanish tradition, which was showing new vitality just before Franco put out the light. These matters are already clear in his early play, *The Love of Don Perlimplín for Belisa, in His Garden. Don Perlimplín* is a romantic farce, slighter and lighter than his most famous pieces, *Blood Wedding* and *The House of Bernarda Alba*, but it is a small masterpiece. When he wrote it he was already in control of his difficult art.

The story is old, lewd and rather savage: that of the old man married to a lusty young wife, one of the standard situations of neo-classic farce. But Lorca, without losing sight of the farce, lifts it to poetry also, and poetry of power and freshness. This he accomplishes in four swift scenes; and to understand his art it is necessary to think over this sequence in some detail.

In the first scene we see Don Perlimplín, a studious type on the dark side of middle age, dressed in a white wig and dressing gown, in his study. His old servant Marcolfa is telling him that it's time he got married, so that when she dies he will have a wife to take care of him. Marriage, says Marcolfa, has great charm, hidden delights; and at that moment we hear Belisa offstage singing a song of shameless childish eroticism. Marcolfa leads Don Perlimplín upstage to the window; we look out with him, and see Belisa on her balcony across the way, very lightly clad. Don Perlimplín gets the point of this vision: Belisa is white inside, like sugar, he says; would she strangle me? Belisa's mother appears, and between her and Marcolfa Don Perlimplín finds himself betrothed to Belisa. The mother is one of those terrible cold-hearted eighteenth-century duennas; she reminds her daughter with speed and clarity that money is the foundation of happiness, and Don Perlimplín has money. The scene ends with Don Perlimplín firmly committed, and trembling with a mixture of terror and delight, like a boy when the possibilities of sex first touch him.

The second scene shows Don Perlimplín's bedroom on the wedding night. In the middle of the stage is a huge ornate bed, and there are six doors, one to the rest of the house, the others giving on to five balconies. First we see Don Perlimplín, magnificently dressed, receiving final instructions from Marcolfa. They disappear and Belisa enters in ruffled negligee, singing to offstage guitar music. After a brief scene between her and Don Perlimplín—who says that she is like a wave of the sea—two sprites draw a gray curtain across the stage, concealing Don Perlimplín, Belisa, and the bed. These sprites giggle and chatter with the inhuman merriment of little girls of twelve or thirteen, say—bright-eyed, heartless, knowing little creatures, as children are when they are full of shrewd curiosity but not yet seasoned by any human experience. Presently they open the curtain and depart. Stage and bed are flooded with bright sunlight coming through the five opened doors to the balconies, the iron church bells of the city are banging for matins, and Don Perlimplín is sitting up in bed beside the sleeping Belisa, with a great pair of horns on his head, decorated with flowers. Belisa, when she lazily wakes, admits nothing, but Don Perlimplín sees five hats under the five balconies which show that five men have visited her during the night. Lorca has thus exaggerated the farcical situation of the old man and his young wife; but the combination of bright light, loud iron bells, and big ornate horns adds pity and terror to the scene. When Belisa wanders off to get dressed, Don Perlimplín is left sitting alone on the edge of the bed, and he sings a beautiful lyric on the theme that love has mortally wounded him.

The third scene shows Don Perlimplín and Marcolfa. Marcolfa is deeply ashamed for her master, and moreover she reports that Belisa has already become infatuated with a sixth man. Don Perlimplín is delighted to hear it. He tells the weeping Marcolfa that she understands nothing, and brusquely sends her away. Belisa enters dreamily, mulling over the new young man, whom she has seen, from whom she has received letters, but whom she has never talked to. Don Perlimplín catches her in this daydreaming, tells her that he understands everything, that (being old) he is beyond mortal life and its ridiculous customs, and that he will sacrifice himself for her and her new love.

The final scene is Belisa's rendezvous with the young man, in the garden, at night. First we see Don Perlimplín and Marcolfa, she more grieved than ever, Don Perlimplín more crazily inspired. He tells Marcolfa that tomorrow she will be free, and that then she will understand everything; this bit feels like a farewell. When they go we hear offstage singing, and Belisa enters in her most glamorous finery. She sings a serenade in alternation with the offstage voices. Don Perlimplín meets her, and assures himself that she loves the young man better than she has ever loved before, better than her own body. He tells her that in order that she may have the young man forever, he will kill him—and he runs off, drawing his dagger. Belisa yells for a sword to kill Don Perlimplín: but at that moment the young man, his head wrapped in a scarlet cape, a dagger in his breast, staggers in mortally wounded. Belisa pulls off the cape, revealing Don Perlimplín, who dies. He has just time to explain that this was the triumph of his imagination; he had made Belisa fall in love with the lover he invented. So he gave her a new and deeper knowledge of love, made a new woman of her, as Marcolfa explains at the end: gave a human soul, at last, to the beautiful body. It is Belisa's initiation into love's mystery, corresponding to Don Perlimplín's initiation in the first scene.

The poetic effect of this sequence is intense and direct, but Lorca gets it out of a combination of very old and traditional elements.

Thus there is the basic situation of the old man and the young wife, which in baroque Continental comedy, or on the Restoration stage in England, is usually treated in the hearty, simple-minded mode of broad farce. Cervantes wrote a brilliant interlude of this kind called *The Jealous Old Man*, in which the fun is based on the disharmonies of human physiology, and the audience is expected to sympathize solely with the triumphant wife. Lorca expects us to remember that worldly old theme, and he emphasizes both its theatricality and its ancient, classic quality in the characters, their language, and their costumes. Don Perlimplín in his white wig and scholarly dressing gown; Marcolfa in the striped dress of the stage servant; Belisa's mother with her great wig full of beads and ribbons and stuffed birds; and Belisa herself, the sharp essence of the amoral female: this cast of characters is made to seem as old as nightmare, almost eternal.

But just because the farce and its people seem so ancient, it strikes us as not only farcical but also sinister. Lorca, while keeping the cynical old tale, with its neoclassic stagy glitter, also views it in the perspective of a later, gloomier, and more romantic age; he transposes it to bring out also the love-death theme. That theme also is traditional in European literature, as Denis de Rougemont explained in his book, *Love in the Western World*. He traces the terrible aspiration beyond physical love to some of the Provençal poets, and he thinks that the love-death theme which re-echoes through the nineteenth-century literature obscurely revives the heretical cult of the Cathari. Lorca certainly seems to echo the theme here with a full sense of its deep roots, especially in Don Perlimplín's lyric on the mortal wound of love, and in the final scene in the garden, which has the ceremoniousness of the dark old erotic rite.

It is an extravagant notion to combine farce and *Liebestod*, but Lorca knew that it was extravagant. It is by means of the *style* of the piece that he makes an acceptable fusion of such disparate elements; for a knowing style implies the limitations of mood and viewpoint which the author has accepted in advance, and thus makes them acceptable and comprehensible to the audience. Lorca indicates the style of his play in its subtitle: "An Erotic Alleluya." An alleluya is something like a valentine: a love poem decorated with pictures, gilt cutouts, lace paper, and the like; something heroic, overdone, absurd: an *extravagant* offering to the beloved. All the elements of the production, music, sets, costumes, acting, should obey the requirements of this style. And one must remember that it is a Spanish style, akin perhaps to those drawings and paintings of Goya's— wounded cavaliers, frightening mustachioed old women, greedy young women in discreet mantillas—in which the remains of eighteenth-century elegance are seen in a somber light.

Though this play is so unlike anything in English, it is a species of poetic drama. And it achieves much that Yeats and Eliot sought with only partial success. They were both lyric poets first and dramatists second; and both tended in their early efforts to approach poetic drama as though it were an overgrown type of lyric. Yeats's early plays have the Yeatsian lyric melody, but lack the tensions, the contrasts, and the varied movement of drama. Eliot's *Murder in the Cathedral* and *Family Reunion* sound like his lyrics considerably diluted. Eliot felt that himself, as he has explained; but his usual diagnosis of the trouble is that he has not discovered the right verse form for the stage. He proposes to solve the problem by working out the proper versification. To Eliot's experiments, and to his immense authority, we owe the notion that the problem of poetic drama in our time is simply that of finding a type of verse which will work onstage. And many young poets proceed as though drama could somehow be deduced from the lyric by further exploration of the properties of verse.

Lorca also was a lyric poet before he succeeded on the stage, and his lyric verse shows (like that of Yeats and Eliot) the all-pervasive *symboliste* influence. He is an authentic poet, even by the exigent standards of our masters. But from the first he drew also upon the resources of the old and popular Spanish tradition of balladry: his first collection is entitled *Romancero Gitano*, "Gypsy Balladier." And the ballad is a far more promising clue to drama than the "pure" *symboliste* lyric, precisely because it typically suggests a story: a situation, contrasted characters, a significant event. The *symboliste* lyric, on the other hand, owes its purity to its source in the single feeling of the isolated poet. It is very difficult to derive from it the sense of separate but interacting lives; the movement of real change; the significance of a deed or an event: in short, the objectivity of drama, which is founded (however indirectly) upon sympathy and perception. We must simply recognize, I think, that the inspiration, the poetic point, of the *symboliste* lyric is not dramatic, while that of the ballad is.

It is clear that the whole conception of *Don Perlimplín*—the gentle, absurd, heroic old man; the animal-beauty and her mother; the weepy servant, the struggle with love's cruelty—struck Lorca as poetic. The narrative sequence is itself poetic, like that of the ballads we know. One can conceive a ballad version of *Don Perlimplín*, but not a *symboliste* lyric which would really capture the theme. Thus in trying to get the poetry of the play one must consider not only the passages in verse, beautiful though they are, but the movement of the play as a whole. The poetry is in the characters and their relationships, in the conception of each of the four scenes, and especially in the sharp but quickly resolved contrasts between them. Cocteau's formula applies exactly to *Don Perlimplín:* "The action of my play is in images, while the text is not: I attempt to substitute a 'poetry of the theater' for 'poetry in the theater.' Poetry in the theater is a piece of lace which it is impossible to see at a distance. Poetry of the theater would be coarse lace; a lace of ropes, a ship at sea. . . . The scenes are integrated like the words of a poem." Thus the poetic effect of *Don Perlimplín* strikes us most sharply in the transitions from one scene to another: from Don Perlimplín's study to the glamour and music of the wedding night; from the childish chatter of the sprites to Don Perlimplín's humiliation in the morning. And as soon as we feel the poetry in the whole sequence, Lorca's prose has its poetic effect as well as his music and his visual scheme. Lorca is such a virtuoso of the theater that he can use and control all of its resources to present his poetic vision.

If the story is not strictly a myth, it has the qualities our poets seek in myth: it seems much older and much more generally significant than any history which is literally true; yet Lorca does not seem to have thought it up, but rather to have perceived it, or heard it, in the most intimate chamber of his sensibility. In embodying it on the stage he is careful to preserve this oft-told feeling, like song, or a tale told by a grandmother. This he does with the utmost confidence and simplicity. He is sustained by the knowledge that he is talking about things which other artists have seen before in his Spanish tradition; for Don Perlimplín seems to come from the same world—which we now see is still alive—as Don Quixote and Goya's frightening people.

Because the story has this "mythic" quality, its basic form is quite naturally that of ritual or traditional ceremony. The first scene is a betrothal, and we are made to feel that it has been celebrated countless times before, and will be endlessly again: it is the first stage of the initiation into love's cruel mystery; for the old man is as virginal as a boy. The second scene (a kind of interlude in the movement of the piece) is not a ritual; but the third scene, a wedding night with all the pomp of music and costume, is conceived as a sinister epithalamion, moving with decorum toward its predestined pathos. The final scene in the garden, with its serenade in antiphonal form, its symbolic suicide, its cult of love as death, is the place where Lorca's feeling for the ancient heretical love rites that De Rougemont studies is most unmistakable. It is there that Belisa, in her turn, is "initiated." I do not know how consciously Lorca worked all this out; he has the authentic artist's sophistication of feeling combined with philosophical reticence. But I am sure that the ceremonious quality of these scenes (like a duel or a bullfight) must be carefully observed in production, for it is their decorum which gives the underlying passion its cutting edge.

The House of Bernarda Alba, the play which Mr. Sánchez regards as the best dramatically, is interesting in this connection. Mr. Sánchez thinks it a powerful picture of contemporary Spanish provincial life, with the qualities of the best modern realistic drama. Lorca himself calls it a photograph; and according to people who know the country, he has achieved a surface accuracy comparable to Ibsen's or Chekhov's. But it would be a mistake to take its realism too straight: the label "photograph," like the label "alleluya" on *Don Perlimplín*, indicates the very self-conscious style, which alludes to a whole context of meaning. *Bernarda Alba* is a period piece like the others; it utilizes the conventions of nineteenth-century realism with the

same kind of sophisticated intention as that with which *Don Perlimplín* utilizes its more ancient conventions. The blankness of the photograph is part of the composition which includes the severe character of Bernarda herself, and the deathly white walls within which she strives to hold her myopic vision steady.

In this problem of Lorca's restaging of Spanish art we must remember the analogies between forms of art and forms of human life. They are most evident in old countries with whose art and literature we are familiar. One may feel it even on revisiting New England: the white clapboards, the old ladies, the slender elms still seem to be "right out of the pages" of Whittier or Hawthorne. The Paris taxi drivers still argue à la Molière; the hardbitten concierges in cheap hotels are still imitating Balzac. And the Spanish mark on art and character is one of the deepest. I have never been to Spain, but I have seen Sancho Panza and his burro in northern New Mexico, and the faces of old people reflecting (even at a distance of thousands of miles and many generations) the subtle faces in Spanish painting. Perhaps the natural role of the artist in a living culture is to make these forms, with the changes which time brings, visible and significant again.

But Lorca was unusually fortunate in being able to work with such fertility within his native culture; it is a commentary on our rootless state, in which all the familiar forms of life and art begin to seem vague and irrelevant, that his riches should seem somehow against the rules. It is growing harder and harder in our time for a writer to stay within one traditional culture. Yeats was hardly content with his Irish revival beyond youth. Our own Southern writers hesitate painfully between the South, where their roots are, and the national scene in which they are obliged to live, almost as ill-defined as the rest of us.

The deeply Spanish nature of Lorca's art does not prevent it from speaking to us. His sense of history—"the masquerades which time resumes"—is very modern; in his ability to mingle the most contradictory perspectives in one composition, and to shift with sureness from the pathetic to the farcical-frightening, he is in the class of our favorite poets. And he writes poetry of the theater as our poets would like to do. We cannot use his Spanish language, or the symbolic language of the moral and esthetic forms of his tradition. But we can learn to read it, and to discover thereby an authentic modern poetic drama.

THE LOVERS

MAJOR BARBARA

Bernard Shaw

CHARACTERS

LADY BRITOMART UNDERSHAFT

STEPHEN UNDERSHAFT

MORRISON

BARBARA UNDERSHAFT

SARAH UNDERSHAFT

CHARLES LOMAX

ADOLPHUS CUSINS

ANDREW UNDERSHAFT

RUMMY MITCHENS

SNOBBY PRICE

JENNY HILL

PETER SHIRLEY

BILL WALKER

MRS BAINES

BILTON

Period—Three successive days in January 1906

ACT I *The Library in Lady Britomart Undershaft's House in Wilton Crescent, London*

ACT II *The West Ham Shelter of the Salvation Army*

ACT III Scene 1: *The Library at Wilton Crescent*

Scene 2: *Among the High-explosive Sheds at the Arsenal of Messrs Undershaft and Lazarus, near the Model Town of Perivale St Andrews*

N.B. The Euripidean verses in the second act of Major Barbara are not by me, nor even directly by Euripides. They are by Professor Gilbert Murray, whose English version of The Bacchæ came into our dramatic literature with all the impulsive power of an original work shortly before Major Barbara was begun. The play, indeed, stands indebted to him in more ways than one.

G. B. S.

ACT I

It is after dinner in January 1906, in the library in Lady Britomart Undershaft's house in Wilton Crescent. A large and comfortable settee is in the middle of the room, upholstered in dark leather. A person sitting on it (it is vacant at present) would have, on his right, Lady Britomart's writing table, with the lady herself busy at it; a smaller writing table behind him on his left; the door behind him on Lady Britomart's side; and a window with a window seat directly on his left. Near the window is an armchair.

Lady Britomart is a woman of fifty or thereabouts, well dressed and yet careless of her dress, well bred and quite reckless of her breeding, well mannered and yet appallingly outspoken and indifferent to the opinion of her interlocutors, amiable and yet peremptory, arbitrary, and high-tempered to the last bearable degree, and withal a very typical managing matron of the upper class, treated as a naughty child until she grew into a scolding mother, and finally settling down with plenty of practical ability and worldly experience, limited in the oddest way with domestic and class limitations, conceiving the universe exactly as if it were a large house in Wilton Crescent, though handling her corner of it very effectively on that assumption, and being quite enlightened and liberal as to the books in the library, the pictures on the walls, the music in the portfolios, and the articles in the papers.

Her son, Stephen, comes in. He is a gravely correct young man under 25, taking himself very seriously, but still in some awe of his mother, from childish habit and bachelor shyness rather than from any weakness of character.

STEPHEN. Whats the matter?

LADY BRITOMART. Presently, Stephen.

Stephen submissively walks to the settee and sits down. He takes up a Liberal weekly called The Speaker.

LADY BRITOMART. Dont begin to read, Stephen. I shall require all your attention.

STEPHEN. It was only while I was waiting—

LADY BRITOMART. Dont make excuses, Stephen. [*He puts down The Speaker*]. Now! [*She finishes her writing; rises; comes to the settee*]. I have not kept you waiting very long, I think.

STEPHEN. Not at all, mother.

LADY BRITOMART. Bring me my cushion.

[*He takes the cushion from the chair at the desk and arranges it for her as she sits down on the settee*]. Sit down. [*He sits down and fingers his tie nervously*]. Dont fiddle with your tie, Stephen: there is nothing the matter with it.

STEPHEN. I beg your pardon. [*He fiddles with his watch chain instead*].

LADY BRITOMART. Now are you attending to me, Stephen?

STEPHEN. Of course, mother.

LADY BRITOMART. No: it's not of course. I want something much more than your everyday matter-of-course attention. I am going to speak to you very seriously, Stephen. I wish you would let that chain alone.

STEPHEN [*hastily relinquishing the chain*] Have I done anything to annoy you, mother? If so, it was quite unintentional.

LADY BRITOMART [*astonished*] Nonsense! [*With some remorse*] My poor boy, did you think I was angry with you?

STEPHEN. What is it, then, mother? You are making me very uneasy.

LADY BRITOMART [*squaring herself at him rather aggressively*] Stephen: may I ask how soon you intend to realize that you are a grown-up man, and that I am only a woman?

STEPHEN [*amazed*] Only a—

LADY BRITOMART. Dont repeat my words, please: it is a most aggravating habit. You must learn to face life seriously, Stephen. I really cannot bear the whole burden of our family affairs any longer. You must advise me: you must assume the responsibility.

STEPHEN. I!

LADY BRITOMART. Yes, you, of course. You were 24 last June. Youve been at Harrow and Cambridge. Youve been to India and Japan. You must know a lot of things, now; unless you have wasted your time most scandalously. Well, advise me.

STEPHEN [*much perplexed*] You know I have never interfered in the household—

LADY BRITOMART. No: I should think not. I dont want you to order the dinner.

STEPHEN. I mean in our family affairs.

LADY BRITOMART. Well, you must interfere now; for they are getting quite beyond me.

STEPHEN [*troubled*] I have thought sometimes that perhaps I ought; but really, mother, I know so little about them; and what I do know is so painful! it is so impossible to mention some things to you— [*he stops, ashamed*].

LADY BRITOMART. I suppose you mean your father.

STEPHEN [*almost inaudibly*] Yes.

LADY BRITOMART. My dear: we cant go on all our lives not mentioning him. Of course you were quite right not to open the subject until I asked you to; but you are old enough now to be taken into my confidence, and to help me to deal with him about the girls.

STEPHEN. But the girls are all right. They are engaged.

LADY BRITOMART [*complacently*] Yes: I have made a very good match for Sarah. Charles Lomax will be a millionaire at 35. But that is ten years ahead; and in the meantime his trustees cannot under the terms of his father's will allow him more than £800 a year.

STEPHEN. But the will says also that if he increases his income by his own exertions, they may double the increase.

LADY BRITOMART. Charles Lomax's exertions are much more likely to decrease his income than to increase it. Sarah will have to find at least another £800 a year for the next ten years; and even then they will be as poor as church mice. And what about Barbara? I thought Barbara was going to make the most brilliant career of all of you. And what does she do? Joins the Salvation Army; discharges her maid; lives on a pound a week; and walks in one evening with a professor of Greek whom she has picked up in the street, and who pretends to be a Salvationist, and actually plays the big drum for her in public because he has fallen head over ears in love with her.

STEPHEN. I was certainly rather taken aback when I heard they were engaged. Cusins is a very nice fellow, certainly: nobody would ever guess that he was born in Australia; but—

LADY BRITOMART. Oh, Adolphus Cusins will make a very good husband. After all, nobody can say a word against Greek; it stamps a man at once as an educated gentleman. And my family, thank Heaven, is not a pig-headed Tory one. We are Whigs, and believe in liberty. Let snobbish people say what they please: Barbara shall marry, not the man they like, but the man *I* like.

STEPHEN. Of course I was thinking only of his income. However, he is not likely to be extravagant.

LADY BRITOMART. Dont be too sure of that, Stephen. I know your quiet, simple, refined, poetic people like Adolphus: quite content with the best of everything! They cost more than your extravagant people, who are always as mean as they are second rate. No: Barbara will need at least £2000 a year. You see it means two additional households. Besides, my dear, you must marry soon. I dont approve of the present fashion of philandering bachelors and late marriages; and I am trying to arrange something for you.

STEPHEN. It's very good of you, mother; but perhaps I had better arrange that for myself.

LADY BRITOMART. Nonsense! you are much too young to begin matchmaking: you would be taken in by some pretty little nobody. Of course I dont mean that you are not to be consulted: you know that as well as I do. [*Stephen closes his lips and is silent*]. Now dont sulk, Stephen.

STEPHEN. I am not sulking, mother. What has all this got to do with—with—with my father?

LADY BRITOMART. My dear Stephen: where is the money to come from? It is easy enough for you and the other children to live on my income as long as we are in the same house; but I cant keep four families in four separate houses. You know how poor my father is: he has barely seven thousand a year now; and really, if he were not the Earl of Stevenage, he would have to give up society. He can do nothing for us. He says, naturally enough, that it is absurd that he should be asked to provide for the children of a man who is rolling in money. You see, Stephen, your father must be fabulously wealthy, because there is always a war going on somewhere.

STEPHEN. You need not remind me of that, mother. I have hardly ever opened a newspaper in my life without seeing our name in it. The Undershaft torpedo! The Undershaft quick firers! The Undershaft ten inch! the Undershaft disappearing rampart gun! the Undershaft submarine! and now the Undershaft aerial battleship! At Harrow they called me the Woolwich Infant. At Cambridge it was the same. A little brute at King's who was always trying to get up revivals, spoilt my Bible—your first birthday present to me—by writing under my name, "Son and heir to Undershaft and Lazarus, Death and Destruction Dealers: address, Christendom and Judea." But that was not so bad as the way I was kowtowed to everywhere because my father was making millions by selling cannons.

LADY BRITOMART. It is not only the cannons, but the war loans that Lazarus arranges under cover of giving credit for the cannons. You know, Stephen, it's perfectly scandalous. Those two men, Andrew Undershaft and Lazarus, positively have Europe under their thumbs. That is why your father is able to behave as he does. He is above the law. Do you think Bismarck or Gladstone or Disraeli could have openly defied every social and moral obligation all their lives as your father has? They simply wouldn't have dared. I asked Gladstone to take it up. I asked The Times to take it up. I asked the Lord Chamberlain to take it up. But it was just like asking them to declare war on the Sultan. They wouldn't. They said they couldn't touch him. I believe they were afraid.

STEPHEN. What could they do? He does not actually break the law.

LADY BRITOMART. Not break the law! He is always breaking the law. He broke the law when he was born: his parents were not married.

STEPHEN. Mother! Is that true?

LADY BRITOMART. Of course it's true: that was why we separated.

STEPHEN. He married without letting you know this!

LADY BRITOMART [*rather taken aback by this inference*] Oh no. To do Andrew justice, that was not the sort of thing he did. Besides, you know the Undershaft motto: Unashamed. Everbody knew.

STEPHEN. But you said that was why you separated.

LADY BRITOMART. Yes, because he was not content with being a foundling himself: he wanted to disinherit you for another foundling. That was what I couldn't stand.

STEPHEN [*ashamed*] Do you mean for—for—for—

LADY BRITOMART. Dont stammer, Stephen. Speak distinctly.

STEPHEN. But this is so frightful to me, mother. To have to speak to you about such things!

LADY BRITOMART. It's not pleasant for me, either, especially if you are still so childish that you must make it worse by a display of embarrassment. It is only in the middle classes, Stephen, that people get into a state of dumb helpless horror when they find that there are wicked people in the world. In our class, we have to decide what is to be done with wicked people; and nothing should disturb our self-possession. Now ask your question properly.

STEPHEN. Mother: have you no consideration for me? For Heaven's sake either treat me as a child, as you always do, and tell me nothing at all; or tell me everything and let me take it as best I can.

LADY BRITOMART. Treat you as a child! What do you mean? It is most unkind and ungrateful of you to say such a thing. You know I have never treated any of you as children. I have always made you my companions and friends, and allowed you perfect freedom to do and say whatever you liked, so long as you like what I could approve of.

STEPHEN [*desperately*] I daresay we have been the very imperfect children of a very perfect mother; but I do beg you to let me alone for once, and tell me about this horrible business of my father wanting to set me aside for another son.

LADY BRITOMART [*amazed*] Another son! I never said anything of the kind. I never dreamt of such a thing. This is what comes of interrupting me.

STEPHEN. But you said—

LADY BRITOMART [*cutting him short*] Now be a good boy, Stephen, and listen to me patiently. The Undershafts are descended from a foundling in the parish of St. Andrew Undershaft in the city. That was long ago, in the reign of James the First. Well, this foundling was adopted by an armorer and gun-maker. In the course of time the foundling succeeded to the business; and from some notion of gratitude, or some vow or something, he adopted another foundling, and left the business to him. And that foundling did the same. Ever since that, the cannon business has always been left to an adopted foundling named Andrew Undershaft.

STEPHEN. But did they never marry? Were there no legitimate sons?

LADY BRITOMART. Oh yes: they married just as your father did; and they were rich enough to buy land for their own children and leave them well provided for. But they always adopted and trained some foundling to succeed them in the business; and of course they always quarrelled with their wives furiously over it. Your father was adopted in that way; and he pretends to consider himself bound to keep up the tradition and adopt somebody to leave the business to. Of course I was not going to stand that. There may have been some reason for it when the Undershafts could only marry women in their own class, whose sons were not fit to govern great estates. But there could be no excuse for passing over my son.

STEPHEN [*dubiously*] I am afraid I should make a poor hand of managing a cannon foundry.

LADY BRITOMART. Nonsense! you could easily get a manager and pay him a salary.

STEPHEN. My father evidently had no great opinion of my capacity.

LADY BRITOMART. Stuff, child! you were only a baby: it had nothing to do with your capacity. Andrew did it on principle, just as he did every perverse and wicked thing on principle. When my father remonstrated, Andrew actually told him to his face that history tells us of only two successful institutions: one the Undershaft firm, and the other the Roman Empire under the Antonines. That was because the Antonine emperors all adopted their successors. Such rubbish! The Stevenages are as good as the Antonines, I hope; and you are a Stevenage. But that was Andrew all over. There you have the man! Always clever and unanswerable when he was defending nonsense and wickedness: always awkward and sullen when he had to behave sensibly and decently!

STEPHEN. Then it was on my account that your home life was broken up, mother. I am sorry.

LADY BRITOMART. Well, dear, there were other differences. I really cannot bear an immoral man. I am not a Pharisee, I hope; and I should not have minded his merely doing wrong things: we are none of us perfect. But your father didn't exactly do wrong things: he said them and thought them: that was what was so dreadful. He really had a sort of religion of wrongness. Just as one doesnt mind men practising immorality so long as they own that they are in the wrong by preaching morality; so I couldnt forgive Andrew for preaching immorality while he practised morality. You would all have grown up without principles, without any knowledge of right and wrong, if he had been in the house. You know, my dear, your father was a very attractive man in some ways. Children did not dislike him; and he took advantage of it to put the wickedest ideas into their heads, and make them quite unmanageable. I did not dislike him myself: very far from it; but nothing can bridge over moral disagreement.

STEPHEN. All this simply bewilders me, mother. People may differ about matters of opinion, or even about religion; but how can they differ about right and wrong? Right is right; and wrong is wrong; and if a man cannot distinguish them properly, he is either a fool or a rascal: thats all.

LADY BRITOMART [*touched*] Thats my own boy [*she pats his cheek*]! Your father never could answer that: he used to laugh and get out of it under cover of some affectionate nonsense. And now that you understand the situation, what do you advise me to do?

STEPHEN. Well, what can you do?

LADY BRITOMART. I must get the money somehow.

STEPHEN. We cannot take money from him. I had rather go and live in some cheap place like Bedford Square or even Hampstead than take a farthing of his money.

LADY BRITOMART. But after all, Stephen, our present income comes from Andrew.

STEPHEN [*shocked*] I never knew that.

LADY BRITOMART. Well, you surely didnt suppose your grandfather had anything to give me. The Stevenages could not do everything for you. We gave you social position. Andrew had to contribute something. He had a very good bargain, I think.

STEPHEN [*bitterly*] We are utterly dependent on him and his cannons, then?

LADY BRITOMART. Certainly not: the money is settled. But he provided it. So you see it is not a question of taking money from him or not: it is simply a question of how much. I dont want any more for myself.

STEPHEN. Nor do I.

LADY BRITOMART. But Sarah does; and Bar-bara does. That is, Charles Lomax and Adolphus Cusins will cost them more. So I must put my pride in my pocket and ask for it, I suppose. That is your advice, Stephen, is it not?

STEPHEN. No.

LADY BRITOMART [*sharply*] Stephen!

STEPHEN. Of course if you are determined—

LADY BRITOMART. I am not determined: I ask your advice; and I am waiting for it. I will not have all the responsibility thrown on my shoulders.

STEPHEN [*obstinately*] I would die sooner than ask him for another penny.

LADY BRITOMART [*resignedly*] You mean that *I* must ask him. Very well, Stephen: it shall be as you wish. You will be glad to know that your grandfather concurs. But he thinks I ought to ask Andrew to come here and see the girls. After all, he must have some natural affection for them.

STEPHEN. Ask him here!!!

LADY BRITOMART. Do not repeat my words, Stephen. Where else can I ask him?

STEPHEN. I never expected you to ask him at all.

LADY BRITOMART. Now dont tease, Stephen. Come! you see that it is necessary that he should pay us a visit, dont you?

STEPHEN [*reluctantly*] I suppose so, if the girls cannot do without his money.

LADY BRITOMART. Thank you, Stephen: I knew you would give me the right advice when it was properly explained to you. I have asked your father to come this evening. [*Stephen bounds from his seat*] Dont jump, Stephen: it fidgets me.

STEPHEN [*in utter consternation*] Do you mean to say that my father is coming here tonight—that he may be here at any moment?

LADY BRITOMART [*looking at her warch*] I said nine. [*He gasps. She rises.*] Ring the bell, please. [*Stephen goes to the smaller writing table; presses a button on it; and sits at it with his elbows on the table and his head in his hands, outwitted and overwhelmed*]. It is ten minutes to nine yet: and I have to prepare the girls. I asked Charles Lomax and Adolphus to dinner on purpose that they might be here. Andrew had better see them in case he should cherish any delusions as to their being capable of supporting their wives. [*The butler enters: Lady Britomart goes behind the settee to speak to him*]. Morrison: go up to the drawing room and tell everybody to come down here at once. [*Morrison withdraws. Lady Britomart turns to Stephen*]. Now remember, Stephen: I shall need all your countenance and authority. [*He rises and tries to recover some vestige of these attributes.*] Give me a chair, dear. [*He pushes a chair forward from the wall to where she stands, near the smaller writing table. She sits down; and he goes to the armchair, into which he throws himself*]. I dont know how Barbara will take it. Ever since they made her a major in the Salvation Army she has developed a propensity to have her own way and order people about which quite cows me sometimes. It's not ladylike: I'm sure I dont know where she picked it up. Anyhow, Barbara shant bully me; but still it's just as well that your father should be here before she has time to refuse to meet him or make a fuss. Dont look nervous, Stephen: it will only encourage Barbara to make difficulties. *I* am nervous enough, goodness knows: but I dont shew it.

Sarah and Barbara come in with their respective young men, Charles Lomax and Adolphus Cusins. Sarah is slender, bored, and mundane. Barbara is robuster, jollier, much more energetic. Sarah is fashionably dressed: Barbara is in Salvation Army uniform. Lomax, a young man about town, is like many other young men about town. He is afflicted with a frivolous sense of humor which plunges him at the most inopportune moments into paroxysms of imperfectly suppressed laughter. Cusins is a spectacled student, slight, thin haired, and sweet voiced, with a more complex form of Lomax's complaint. His sense of humor is intellectual and subtle, and is complicated by an appalling temper. The lifelong struggle

of a benevolent temperament and a high conscience against impulses of inhuman ridicule and fierce impatience has set up a chronic strain which has visibly wrecked his constitution. He is a most implacable, determined, tenacious, intolerant person who by mere force of character presents himself as—and indeed actually is—considerate, gentle, explanatory, even mild and apologetic, capable possibly of murder, but not of cruelty or coarseness. By the operation of some instinct which is not merciful enough to blind him with the illusions of love, he is obstinately bent on marrying Barbara. Lomax likes Sarah and thinks it will be rather a lark to marry her. Consequently he has not attempted to resist Lady Britomart's arrangements to that end.

All four look as if they had been having a good deal of fun in the drawing room. The girls enter first, leaving the swains outside. Sarah comes to the settee. Barbara comes in after her and stops at the door.

BARBARA. Are Cholly and Dolly to come in?

LADY BRITOMART. [*forcibly*] Barbara: I will not have Charles called Cholly: the vulgarity of it positively makes me ill.

BARBARA. It's all right, mother: Cholly is quite correct nowadays. Are they to come in?

LADY BRITOMART. Yes, if they will behave themselves.

BARBARA [*through the door*] Come in, Dolly; and behave yourself.

Barbara comes to her mother's writing table. Cusins enters smiling, and wanders towards Lady Britomart.

SARAH [*calling*] Come in, Cholly. [*Lomax enters, controlling his features very imperfectly, and places himself vaguely between Sarah and Barbara*].

LADY BRITOMART [*peremptorily*] Sit down, all of you. [*They sit. Cusins crosses to the window and seats himself there. Lomax takes a chair. Barbara sits at the writing table and Sarah on the settee*]. I dont in the least know what you are laughing at, Adolphus. I am surprised at you, though I expected nothing better from Charles Lomax.

CUSINS [*in a remarkably gentle voice*] Barbara has been trying to teach me the West Ham Salvation March.

LADY BRITOMART. I see nothing to laugh at in that; nor should you if you are really converted.

CUSINS [*sweetly*] You were not present. It was really funny, I believe.

LOMAX. Ripping.

LADY BRITOMART. Be quiet, Charles. Now listen to me, children. Your father is coming here this evening.

General stupefaction. Lomax, Sarah, and Barbara rise; Sarah scared, and Barbara amused and expectant.

LOMAX [*remonstrating*] Oh I say!

LADY BRITOMART. You are not called on to say anything, Charles.

SARAH. Are you serious, mother?

LADY BRITOMART. Of course I am serious. It is on your account, Sarah, and also on Charles's. [*Silence. Sarah sits, with a shrug. Charles looks painfully unworthy*]. I hope you are not going to object, Barbara.

BARBARA. I! why should I? My father has a soul to be saved like anybody else. He's quite welcome as far as I am concerned. [*She sits on the table, and softly whistles 'Onward Christian Soldiers'*].

LOMAX [*still remonstrant*] But really, dont you know! Oh I say!

LADY BRITOMART [*frigidly*] What do you wish to convey, Charles?

LOMAX. Well, you must admit that this is a bit thick.

LADY BRITOMART [*turning with ominous suavity to Cusins*] Adolphus: you are a professor of Greek. Can you translate Charles Lomax's remarks into reputable English for us?

CUSINS [*cautiously*] If I may say so, Lady Brit, I think Charles has rather happily expressed what we all feel. Homer,

speaking of Autolycus, uses the same phrase. πυκινὸν δόμον ἐλθεῖν means a bit thick.

LOMAX [*handsomely*] Not that I mind, you know, if Sarah dont. [*He sits*].

LADY BRITOMART [*crushingly*] Thank you. Have I your permission, Adolphus, to invite my own husband to my own house?

CUSINS [*gallantly*] You have my unhesitating support in everything you do.

LADY BRITOMART. Tush! Sarah: have you nothing to say?

SARAH. Do you mean that he is coming regularly to live here?

LADY BRITOMART. Certainly not. The spare room is ready for him if he likes to stay for a day or two and see a little more of you; but there are limits.

SARAH. Well, he cant eat us, I suppose. *I* dont mind.

LOMAX [*chuckling*] I wonder how the old man will take it.

LADY BRITOMART. Much as the old woman will, no doubt, Charles.

LOMAX [*abashed*] I didnt mean—at least—

LADY BRITOMART. You didnt think, Charles. You never do; and the result is, you never mean anything. And now please attend to me, children. Your father will be quite a stranger to us.

LOMAX. I suppose he hasnt seen Sarah since she was a little kid.

LADY BRITOMART. Not since she was a little kid, Charles, as you express it with that elegance of diction and refinement of thought that seem never to desert you. Accordingly—er—[*impatiently*] Now I have forgotten what I was going to say. That comes of your provoking me to be sarcastic, Charles. Adolphus: you will kindly tell me where I was.

CUSINS [*sweetly*] You were saying that as Mr Undershaft has not seen his children since they were babies, he will form his opinion of the way you have brought them up from their behavior tonight, and that therefore you wish us all to be particularly careful to conduct ourselves well, especially Charles.

LADY BRITOMART [*with emphatic approval*] Precisely.

LOMAX. Look here, Dolly: Lady Brit didnt say that.

LADY BRITOMART [*vehemently*] I did, Charles. Adolphus's recollection is perfectly correct. It is most important that you should be good; and I do beg you for once not to pair off into opposite corners and giggle and whisper while I am speaking to your father.

BARBARA. All right, mother. We'll do you credit. [*She comes off the table, and sits in her chair with ladylike elegance*].

LADY BRITOMART. Remember, Charles, that Sarah will want to feel proud of you instead of ashamed of you.

LOMAX. Oh I say! theres nothing to be exactly proud of, dont you know.

LADY BRITOMART. Well, try and look as if there was.

Morrison, pale and dismayed, breaks into the room in unconcealed disorder.

MORRISON. Might I speak a word to you, my lady?

LADY BRITOMART. Nonsense! Shew him up.

MORRISON. Yes, my lady. [*He goes*].

LOMAX. Does Morrison know who it is?

LADY BRITOMART. Of course. Morrison has always been with us.

LOMAX. It must be a regular corker for him, dont you know.

LADY BRITOMART. Is this a moment to get on my nerves, Charles, with your outrageous expressions?

LOMAX. But this is something out of the ordinary, really—

MORRISON [*at the door*] The—er—Mr Undershaft. [*He retreats in confusion*].

Andrew Undershaft comes in. All rise. Lady Britomart meets him in the middle of the room behind the settee.

Andrew is, on the surface, a stoutish, easygoing elderly man, with kindly patient manners, and an engaging simplicity of character. But he has a watchful, deliberate, waiting, listening face, and formidable reserves of power, both bodily and mental, in his capacious chest and long head. His gentleness is partly that of a strong man who has learnt by experience that his natural grip hurts ordinary people unless he handles them very carefully, and partly the mellowness of age and success. He is also a little shy in his present very delicate situation.

LADY BRITOMART. Good evening, Andrew.

UNDERSHAFT. How d'ye do, my dear.

LADY BRITOMART. You look a good deal older.

UNDERSHAFT [*apologetically*] I am somewhat older. [*Taking her hand with a touch of courtship*] Time has stood still with you.

LADY BRITOMART [*throwing away his hand*] Rubbish! This is your family.

UNDERSHAFT [*surprised*] Is it so large? I am sorry to say my memory is failing very badly in some things. [*He offers his hand with paternal kindness to Lomax*].

LOMAX [*jerkily shaking his hand*] Ahdedoo.

UNDERSHAFT. I can see you are my eldest. I am very glad to meet you again, my boy.

LOMAX [*remonstrating*] No, but look here don't you know—[*Overcome*] Oh I say!

LADY BRITOMART [*recovering from momentary speechlessness*] Andrew: do you mean to say that you dont remember how many children you have?

UNDERSHAFT. Well, I am afraid I—. They have grown so much—er. Am I making any ridiculous mistake? I may as well confess: I recollect only one son. But so many things have happened since, of course—er—

LADY BRITOMART [*decisively*] Andrew: you are talking nonsense. Of course you have only one son.

UNDERSHAFT. Perhaps you will be good enough to introduce me, my dear.

LADY BRITOMART. That is Charles Lomax, who is engaged to Sarah.

UNDERSHAFT. My dear sir, I beg your pardon.

LOMAX. Notatall. Delighted, I assure you.

LADY BRITOMART. This is Stephen.

UNDERSHAFT [*bowing*] Happy to make your acquaintance, Mr. Stephen. Then [*going to Cusins*] you must be my son. [*Taking Cusins' hands in his*] How are you, my young friend? [*To Lady Britomart*] He is very like you, my love.

CUSINS. You flatter me, Mr Undershaft, My name is Cusins: engaged to Barbara. [*Very explicitly*] That is Major Barbara Undershaft, of the Salvation Army. That is Sarah, your second daughter. This is Stephen Undershaft, your son.

UNDERSHAFT. My dear Stephen, I beg your pardon.

STEPHEN. Not at all.

UNDERSHAFT. Mr Cusins: I am much indebted to you for explaining so precisely. [*Turning to Sarah*] Barbara, my dear—

SARAH [*prompting him*] Sarah.

UNDERSHAFT. Sarah, of course. [*They shake hands. He goes over to Barbara*] Barbara—I am right this time, I hope?

BARBARA. Quite right. [*They shake hands*].

LADY BRITOMART [*resuming command*] Sit down, all of you. Sit down, Andrew. [*She comes forward and sits on the settee. Cusins also brings his chair forward on her left. Barbara and Stephen resume their seats. Lomax gives his chair to Sarah and goes for another*].

UNDERSHAFT. Thank you, my love.

LOMAX [*conversationally, as he brings a chair forward between the writing table and the settee, and offers it to Undershaft*] Takes you some time to find out exactly where you are, dont it?

UNDERSHAFT [*accepting the chair, but remaining standing*] That is not what embarrasses me, Mr Lomax. My difficulty is that if I play the part of a father, I shall produce the effect of an intrusive stranger; and if I play the part of a discreet stranger, I may appear a callous father.

LADY BRITOMART. There is no need for you to play any part at all, Andrew. You had much better be sincere and natural.

UNDERSHAFT [*submissively*] Yes, my dear: I daresay that will be best. [*He sits down comfortably*]. Well, here I am. Now what can I do for you all?

LADY BRITOMART. You need not do anything, Andrew. You are one of the family. You can sit with us and enjoy yourself.

A painfully conscious pause. Barbara makes a face at Lomax, whose too long suppressed mirth immediately explodes in agonized neighings.

LADY BRITOMART [*outraged*] Charles Lomax: if you can behave yourself, behave yourself. If not, leave the room.

LOMAX. I'm awfully sorry, Lady Brit; but really you know, upon my soul! [*He sits on the settee between Lady Britomart and Undershaft, quite overcome*].

BARBARA. Why dont you laugh if you want to, Cholly? It's good for your inside.

LADY BRITOMART. Barbara: you have had the education of a lady. Please let your father see that; and dont talk like a street girl.

UNDERSHAFT. Never mind me, my dear. As you know, I am not a gentleman; and I was never educated.

LOMAX [*encouragingly*] Nobody'd know it, I assure you. You look all right, you know.

CUSINS. Let me advise you to study Greek, Mr Undershaft. Greek scholars are privileged men. Few of them know Greek; and none of them know anything else; but their position is unchallengeable. Other languages are the qualifications of waiters and commercial travellers: Greek is to a man of position what the hallmark is to silver.

BARBARA. Dolly: dont be insincere. Cholly: fetch your concertina and play something for us.

LOMAX [*jumps up eagerly, but checks himself to remark doubtfully to Undershaft*] Perhaps that sort of thing isnt in your line, eh?

UNDERSHAFT. I am particularly fond of music.

LOMAX [*delighted*] Are you? Then I'll get it. [*He goes upstairs for the instrument*].

UNDERSHAFT. Do you play, Barbara?

BARBARA. Only the tambourine. But Cholly's teaching me the concertina.

UNDERSHAFT. Is Cholly also a member of the Salvation Army?

BARBARA. No: he says it's bad form to be a dissenter. But I dont despair of Cholly. I made him come yesterday to a meeting at the dock gates, and take the collection in his hat.

UNDERSHAFT [*looks whimsically at his wife*]!!

LADY BRITOMART. It is not my doing, Andrew. Barbara is old enough to take her own way. She has no father to advise her.

BARBARA. Oh yes she has. There are no orphans in the Salvation Army.

UNDERSHAFT. Your father there has a great many children and plenty of experience, eh?

BARBARA [*looking at him with quick interest and nodding*] Just so. How did you come to understand that? [*Lomax is heard at the door trying the concertina*].

LADY BRITOMART. Come in, Charles. Play us something at once.

LOMAX. Righto! [*He sits down in his former place, and preludes*].

UNDERSHAFT. One moment, Mr Lomax. I am rather interested in the Salvation Army. Its motto might be my own: Blood and Fire.

LOMAX [*shocked*] But not your sort of blood and fire, you know.

UNDERSHAFT. My sort of blood cleanses: my sort of fire purifies.

BARBARA. So do ours. Come down tomorrow to my shelter—the West Ham shelter—and see what we're doing. We're going to march to a great meeting in the Assembly Hall at Mile End. Come and see the shelter and then march with us: it will do you a lot of good. Can you play anything?

UNDERSHAFT. In my youth I earned pennies, and even shillings occasionally, in the streets and in public parlors by my natural talent for stepdancing. Later on, I became a member of the Undershaft orchestral society, and performed passably on the tenor trombone.

LOMAX [*scandalized—putting down the concertina*] Oh I say!

BARBARA. Many a sinner has played himself into heaven on the trombone, thanks to the Army.

LOMAX [*to Barbara, still rather shocked*] Yes; but what about the cannon business, dont you know? [*To Undershaft*] Getting into heaven is not exactly in your line, is it?

LADY BRITOMART. Charles!!!

LOMAX. Well; but it stands to reason, dont it? The cannon business may be necessary and all that: we cant get on without cannons; but it isnt right, you know. On the other hand, there may be a certain amount of tosh about the Salvation Army—I belong to the Established Church myself—but still you cant deny that it's religion; and you cant go against religion, can you? At least unless youre downright immoral, dont you know.

UNDERSHAFT. You hardly appreciate my position, Mr Lomax—

LOMAX [*hastily*] I'm not saying anything against you personally—

UNDERSHAFT. Quite so, quite so. But consider for a moment. Here I am, a profiteer in mutilation and murder. I find myself in a specially amiable humor just now because, this morning, down at the foundry, we blew twenty-seven dummy soldiers into fragments with a gun which formerly destroyed only thirteen.

LOMAX [*leniently*] Well, the more destructive war becomes, the sooner it will be abolished, eh?

UNDERSHAFT. Not at all. The more destructive war becomes the more fascinating we find it. No, Mr Lomax: I am obliged to you for making the usual excuse for my trade; but I am not ashamed of it. I am not one of those men who keep their morals and their business in water-tight compartments. All the spare money my trade rivals spend on hospitals, cathedrals, and other receptacles for conscience money, I devote to experiments and researches in improved methods of destroying life and property. I have always done so; and I always shall. Therefore your Christmas card moralities of peace on earth and goodwill among men are of no use to me. Your Christianity, which enjoins you to resist not evil, and to turn the other cheek, would make me a bankrupt. My morality—my religion—must have a place for cannons and torpedoes in it.

STEPHEN [*coldly—almost sullenly*] You speak as if there were half a dozen moralities and religions to choose from, instead of one true morality and one true religion.

UNDERSHAFT. For me there is only one true morality; but it might not fit you, as you do not manufacture aerial battleships. There is only one true morality for every man; but every man has not the same true morality.

LOMAX [*overtaxed*] Would you mind saying that again? I didnt quite follow it.

CUSINS. It's quite simple. As Euripides says, one man's meat is another man's poison morally as well as physically.

UNDERSHAFT. Precisely.

LOMAX. Oh, that! Yes, yes, yes. True. True.

STEPHEN. In other words, some men are honest and some are scoundrels.

BARBARA. Bosh! There are no scoundrels.

UNDERSHAFT. Indeed? Are there any good men?

BARBARA. No. Not one. There are neither good men nor scoundrels: there are just children of one Father; and the sooner they stop calling one another names the better. You neednt talk to me: I know them. Ive had scores of them through my hands: scoundrels, criminals, infidels, philanthropists, missionaries, county councillors, all sorts. Theyre all just the same sort of sinner; and theres the same salvation ready for them all.

UNDERSHAFT. May I ask have you ever saved a maker of cannons?

BARBARA. No. Will you let me try?

UNDERSHAFT. Well, I will make a bargain with you. If I go to see you tomorrow in your Salvation Shelter, will you come the day after to see me in my cannon works?

BARBARA. Take care. It may end in your giving up the cannons for the sake of the Salvation Army.

UNDERSHAFT. Are you sure it will not end in your giving up the Salvation Army for the sake of the cannons?

BARBARA. I will take my chance of that.

UNDERSHAFT. And I will take my chance of the other. [*They shake hands on it*]. Where is your shelter?

BARBARA. In West Ham. At the sign of the cross. Ask anybody in Canning Town. Where are your works?

UNDERSHAFT. In Perivale St Andrews. At the sign of the sword. Ask anybody in Europe.

LOMAX. Hadnt I better play something?

BARBARA. Yes. Give us Onward, Christian Soldiers.

LOMAX. Well, thats rather a strong order to begin with, dont you know. Suppose I sing Thou'rt passing hence, my brother. It's much the same tune.

BARBARA. It's too melancholy. You get saved, Cholly; and youll pass hence, my brother, without making such a fuss about it.

LADY BRITOMART. Really, Barbara, you go on as if religion were a pleasant subject. Do have some sense of propriety.

UNDERSHAFT. I do not find it an unpleasant subject, my dear. It is the only one that capable people really care for.

LADY BRITOMART [*looking at her watch*] Well, if you are determined to have it, I insist on having it in a proper and respectable way. Charles: ring for prayers.

General amazement. Stephen rises in dismay.

LOMAX [*rising*] Oh I say!

UNDERSHAFT [*rising*] I am afraid I must be going.

LADY BRITOMART. You cannot go now, Andrew: it would be most improper. Sit down. What will the servants think?

UNDERSHAFT. My dear: I have conscientious scruples. May I suggest a compromise? If Barbara will conduct a little service in the drawing room, with Mr Lomax as organist, I will attend it willingly. I will even take part, if a trombone can be procured.

LADY BRITOMART. Dont mock, Andrew.

UNDERSHAFT [*shocked—to Barbara*] You dont think I am mocking, my love, I hope.

BARBARA. No, of course not; and it wouldnt matter if you were: half the Army came to their first meeting for a lark. [*Rising*] Come along. [*She throws her arm round her father and sweeps him out, calling to the others from the threshold*] Come, Dolly. Come, Cholly. [*Cusins rises*].

LADY BRITOMART. I will not be disobeyed by everybody. Adolphus: sit down. [*He does not*]. Charles: you may go. You are not fit for prayers: you cannot keep your countenance.

LOMAX. Oh I say! [*He goes out*].

LADY BRITOMART [*continuing*] But you, Adolphus, can behave yourself if you choose to. I insist on your staying.

CUSINS. My dear Lady Brit: there are things in the family prayer book that I couldnt bear to hear you say.

LADY BRITOMART. What things, pray?

CUSINS. Well, you would have to say before all the servants that we have done things we ought not to have done, and left undone things we ought to have done, and that there is no health in us. I cannot bear to hear you doing yourself such an injustice, and Barbara such an injustice. As for myself, I flatly deny it: I have done my best. I shouldnt dare to marry Barbara—I couldnt look you in the face—if it were true. So I must go to the drawing room.

LADY BRITOMART [*offended*] Well, go. [*He starts for the door*]. And remember this, Adolphus [*he turns to listen*]: I have a very strong suspicion that you went to the Salvation Army to worship Barbara and nothing else. And I quite appreciate the very clever way in which you systematically

humbug me. I have found you out. Take care Barbara doesnt. Thats all.

CUSINS [*with unruffled sweetness*] Dont tell on me. [*He steals out*].

LADY BRITOMART. Sarah: if you want to go, go. Anything's better than to sit there as if you wished you were a thousand miles away.

SARAH [*languidly*] Very well, mamma. [*She goes*].

Lady Britomart, with a sudden flounce, gives way to a little gust of tears.

STEPHEN [*going to her*] Mother: whats the matter?

LADY BRITOMART [*swishing away her tears with her handkerchief*] Nothing! Foolishness. You can go with him, too, if you like, and leave me with the servants.

STEPHEN. Oh, you mustnt think that, mother. I—I dont like him.

LADY BRITOMART. The others do. That is the injustice of a woman's lot. A woman has to bring up her children; and that means to restrain them, to deny them things they want, to set them tasks, to punish them when they do wrong, to do all the unpleasant things. And the father, who has nothing to do but pet them and spoil them, comes in when all her work is done and steals their affection from her.

STEPHEN. He has not stolen our affection from you. It is only curiosity.

LADY BRITOMART [*violently*] I wont be consoled, Stephen. There is nothing the matter with me. [*She rises and goes towards the door*].

STEPHEN. Where are you going, mother?

LADY BRITOMART. To the drawing room, of course [*She goes out. Onward, Christian Soldiers, on the concertina, with tambourine accompaniment, is heard when the door opens*]. Are you coming, Stephen?

STEPHEN. No. Certainly not. [*She goes. He sits down on the settee, with compressed lips and an expression of strong dislike*].

ACT II

The yard of the West Ham shelter of the Salvation Army is a cold place on a January morning. The building itself, an old warehouse, is newly whitewashed. Its gabled end projects into the yard in the middle, with a door on the ground floor, and another in the loft above it without any balcony or ladder, but with a pulley rigged over it for hoisting sacks. Those who come from this central gable end into the yard have the gateway leading to the street on their left, with a stone horse-trough just beyond it, and, on the right, a penthouse shielding a table from the weather. There are forms at the table; and on them are seated a man and a woman, both much down on their luck, finishing a meal of bread (one thick slice each, with margarine and golden syrup) and diluted milk.

The man, a workman out of employment, is young, agile, a talker, a poser, sharp enough to be capable of anything in reason except honesty or altruistic considerations of any kind. The woman is a commonplace old bundle of poverty and hard-worn humanity. She looks sixty and is probably forty-five. If they were rich people, gloved and muffed and well wrapped up in furs and overcoats, they would be numbed and miserable; for it is a grindingly cold raw January day; and a glance at the background of grimy warehouses and leaden sky visible over the whitewashed walls of the yard would drive any idle rich person straight to the Mediterranean. But these two, being no more troubled with visions of the Mediterranean than of the moon, and being compelled to keep more of their clothes in the pawnshop, and less on their persons, in winter than in summer, are not depressed by the cold: rather are they stung into vivacity, to which their meal has just now given an almost jolly turn. The man takes a pull at his mug, and then gets up and moves about the yard with his hands deep in his pockets, occasionally breaking into a stepdance.

THE WOMAN. Feel better arter your meal, sir?

THE MAN. No. Call that a meal! Good enough for you, praps; but wot is it to me, an intelligent workin man.

THE WOMAN. Workin man! Wot are you?

THE MAN. Painter.

THE WOMAN [*sceptically*] Yus, I dessay.

THE MAN. Yus, you dessay! I know. Every loafer that cant do nothink calls isself a painter. Well, I'm a real painter: grainer, finisher, thirty-eight bob a week when I can get it.

THE WOMAN. Then why dont you go and get it?

THE MAN. I'll tell you why. Fust: I'm intelligent—fffff! it's rotten cold here [*he dances a step or two*]—yes: intelligent beyond the station o life into which it has pleased the capitalists to call me; and they dont like a man that sees through em. Second, an intelligent bein needs a doo share of appiness; so I drink somethink cruel when I get the chawnce. Third, I stand by my class and do as little as I can so's to leave arf the job for me fellow workers. Fourth, I'm fly enough to know wots inside the law and wots outside it; and inside it I do as the capitalists do: pinch wot I can lay me ands on. In a proper state of society I am sober, industrious and honest: in Rome, so to speak, I do as the Romans do. Wots the consequence? When trade is bad—and it's rotten bad just now—and the employers az to sack arf their men, they generally start on me.

THE WOMAN. Whats your name?

THE MAN. Price. Bronterre O'Brien Price. Usually called Snobby Price, for short.

THE WOMAN. Snobby's a carpenter, aint it? You said you was a painter.

PRICE. Not that kind of snob, but the genteel sort. I'm too uppish, owing to my intelligence, and my father being a Chartist and a reading, thinking man: a stationer, too. I'm none of your common hewers of wood and drawers of water; and dont you forget it. [*He returns to his seat at the table, and takes up his mug*]. Wots your name?

THE WOMAN. Rummy Mitchens, sir.

PRICE [*quaffing the remains of his milk to her*] Your elth, Miss Mitchens.

RUMMY [*correcting him*] Missis Mitchens.

PRICE. Wot! Oh Rummy, Rummy! Respectable married woman, Rummy, gittin rescued by the Salvation Army by pretendin to be a bad un. Same old game!

RUMMY. What am I to do? I cant starve. Them Salvation lasses is dear good girls; but the better you are, the worse they likes to think you were before they rescued you. Why shouldnt they av a bit o credit, poor loves? theyre worn to rags by their work. And where would they get the money to rescue us if we was to let on we're no worse than other people? You know what ladies and gentlemen are.

PRICE. Thievin swine! Wish I ad their job, Rummy, all the same. Wot does Rummy stand for? Pet name praps?

RUMMY. Short for Romola.

PRICE. For wot!?

RUMMY. Romola. It was out of a new book. Somebody me mother wanted me to grow up like.

PRICE. We're companions in misfortune, Rummy. Both on us got names that nobody cawnt pronounce. Consequently I'm Snobby and youre Rummy because Bill and Sally wasnt good enough for our parents. Such is life!

RUMMY. Who saved you, Mr Price? Was it Major Barbara?

PRICE. No: I come here on my own. I'm going to be Bronterre O'Brien Price, the converted painter. I know wot they like. I'll tell em how I blasphemed and gambled and wopped my poor old mother—

RUMMY [*shocked*] Used you to beat your mother?

PRICE. Not likely. She used to beat me. No matter: you come and listen to the converted painter, and youll hear how she was a pious woman that taught me me prayers at er knee, an how I used to come home drunk and drag her out o bed be er snow white airs, an lam into er with the poker.

RUMMY. Thats whats so unfair to us women. Your confessions is just as big lies as ours: you dont tell what you really done no more than us; but you men can tell your lies right out at the meetins and be made much of for it; while the sort o confessions we az to make az to be wispered to one lady at a time. It aint right, spite of all their piety.

PRICE. Right! Do you spose the Army'd be allowed if it went and did right? Not much. It combs our air and makes us good little blokes to be robbed and put upon. But I'll play the game as good as any of em. I'll see somebody struck by lightnin, or hear a voice sayin "Snobby Price: where will you spend eternity?" I'll av a time of it, I tell you.

RUMMY. You wont be let drink, though.

PRICE. I'll take it out in gorspellin, then. I dont want to drink if I can get fun enough any other way.

Jenny Hill, a pale, overwrought, pretty Salvation lass of 18, comes in through the yard gate, leading Peter Shirley, a half hardened, half worn-out elderly man, weak with hunger.

JENNY [*supporting him*] Come! pluck up. I'll get you something to eat. Youll be all right then.

PRICE [*rising and hurrying officiously to take the old man off Jenny's hands*] Poor old man! Cheer up, brother: youll find rest and peace and appiness ere. Hurry up with the food, miss: e's fair done. [*Jenny hurries into the shelter*]. Ere, buck up, daddy! she's fetchin y'a thick slice o breadn treacle, an a mug o skyblue. [*He seats him at the corner of the table*].

RUMMY [*gaily*] Keep up your old art! Never say die!

SHIRLEY. I'm not an old man. I'm only 46. I'm as good as ever I was. The grey patch come in my hair before I was thirty. All it wants is three pennorth o hair dye: am I to be turned on the streets to starve for it? Holy God! Ive worked ten to twelve hours a day since I was thirteen, and paid my way all through; and now am I to be thrown into the gutter and my job given to a young man that can do it no better than me because Ive black hair that goes white at the first change?

PRICE [*cheerfully*] No good jawrin about it. Youre ony a jumped-up, jerked-off, orspittle-turned-out incurable of an ole workin man: who cares about you? Eh? Make the thievin swine give you a meal: theyve stole many a one from you. Get a bit o your own back. [*Jenny returns with the usual meal*]. There you are, brother. Awsk a blessin an tuck that into you.

SHIRLEY [*looking at it ravenously but not touching it, and crying like a child*] I never took anything before.

JENNY [*petting him*] Come, come! the Lord sends it to you: he wasnt above taking bread from his friends; and why should you be? Besides, when we find you a job you can pay us for it if you like.

SHIRLEY [*eagerly*] Yes, yes: thats true. I can pay you back: it's only a loan. [*Shivering*] Oh Lord! oh Lord! [*He turns to the table and attacks the meal ravenously*].

JENNY. Well, Rummy, are you more comfortable now?

RUMMY. God bless you, lovey! youve fed my body and saved my soul, havnt you? [*Jenny, touched, kisses her*]. Sit down and rest a bit: you must be ready to drop.

JENNY. Ive been going hard since morning. But theres more work than we can do. I mustnt stop.

RUMMY. Try a prayer for just two minutes. Youll work all the better after.

JENNY [*her eyes lighting up*] Oh isnt it wonderful how a few minutes prayer revives you! I was quite lightheaded at twelve o'clock, I was so tired; but Major Barbara just sent me to pray for five minutes; and I was able to go on as if I had only just begun. [*To Price*] Did you have a piece of bread?

PRICE [*with unction*] Yes, miss; but Ive got the piece that I value more; and thats the peace that passeth hall hannerstennin.

RUMMY [*fervently*] Glory Hallelujah!

Bill Walker, a rough customer of about 25, appears at the yard gate and looks malevolently at Jenny.

JENNY. That makes me so happy. When you say that, I feel wicked for loitering here. I must get to work again.

She is hurrying to the shelter, when the new-comer moves quickly up to the door and intercepts her. His manner is so threatening that she retreats as he comes at her truculently, driving her down the yard.

BILL. Aw knaow you. Youre the one that took awy maw girl. Youre the one that set er agen me. Well, I'm gowin to ev er aht. Not that Aw care a carse for er or you: see? Bat Aw'll let er knaow; and Aw'll let you knaow. Aw'm gowing to give her a doin thatll teach er to cat awy from me. Nah in wiv you and tell er to cam aht afore Aw can in and kick er aht. Tell er Bill Walker wants er. She'll knaow wot thet means; and if she keeps me witin itll be worse. You stop to jawr beck at me; and Aw'll stawt on you: d'ye eah? Theres your wy. In you gow. [*He takes her by the arm and slings her towards the door of the shelter. She falls on her hand and knee. Rummy helps her up again*].

PRICE [*rising, and venturing irresolutely towards Bill*] Easy there, mate. She aint doin you no arm.

BILL. Oo are you callin mite? [*Standing over him threateningly*] Youre gowin to stend ap for er, aw yer? Put ap your ends.

RUMMY [*running indignantly to scold him*] Oh, you great brute—[*He instantly swings his left hand back against her face. She screams and reels back to the trough, where she sits down, covering her bruised face with her hands and rocking herself and moaning with pain*]

JENNY [*going to her*] Oh, God forgive you! How could you strike an old woman like that?

BILL [*seizing her by the hair so violently that she also screams, and tearing her away from the old woman*] You Gawd forgimme again an Aw'll Gawd forgive you one on the jawr thetll stop you pryin for a week. [*Holding her and turning fiercely on Price*] Ev you ennything to sy agen it?

PRICE [*intimidated*] No, matey: she aint anything to do with me.

BILL. Good job for you! Aw'd pat two meals into you and fawt you with one finger arter, you stawved cur. [*To Jenny*] Nah are you gowin to fetch aht Mog Ebbijem; or em Aw to knock your fice off you and fetch her meself?

JENNY [*writhing in his grasp*] Oh please someone go in and tell Major Barbara— [*she screams again as he wrenches her head down; and Price and Rummy flee into the shelter*].

BILL. You want to gow in and tell your Mijor of me, do you?

JENNY. Oh please dont drag my hair. Let me go.

BILL. Do you or downt you? [*She stifles a scream*]. Yus or nao?

JENNY. God give me strength—

BILL [*striking her with his fist in the face*] Gow an shaow her thet, and tell her if she wants one lawk it to cam and interfere with me. [*Jenny, crying with pain, goes into the shed. He goes to the form and addresses the old man*]. Eah: finish your mess; an git aht o maw wy.

SHIRLEY [*springing up and facing him fiercely, with the mug in his hand*] You take a liberty with me, and I'll smash you over the face with the mug and cut your eye out. Aint you satisfied—young whelps like you—with takin the bread out o the mouths of your elders that have brought you up and slaved for you, but you must come shovin and cheekin and bullyin in here, where the bread of charity is sickenin in our stummicks?

BILL [*contemptuously, but backing a little*] Wot good are you, you aold palsy mag? Wot good are you?

SHIRLEY. As good as you and better. I'll do a day's work agen you or any fat young soaker of your age. Go and take my job at Horrockses, where I worked for ten year. They want young men there: they cant afford to keep men over forty-five. Theyre very sorry—give you a character and happy to help you to get anything suited to your years—sure a steady man wont be long out of a job. Well, let em try you. Theyll find the differ. What do you know? Not as much as how to beeyave yourself—layin your dirty fist across the mouth of a respectable woman!

BILL. Downt provowk me to ly it acrost yours: d'ye eah?

SHIRLEY [*with blighting contempt*] Yes: you like an old man to hit, dont you, when youve finished with the women. I aint seen you hit a young one yet.

BILL [*stung*] You loy, you aold soupkitchener, you. There was a yang menn eah. Did Aw offer to itt him or did Aw not?

SHIRLEY. Was he starvin or was he not? Was he a man or only a crosseyed thief an a loafer? Would you hit my son-in-law's brother?

BILL. Oo's ee?

SHIRLEY. Todger Fairmile o Balls Pond. Him that won £20 off the Japanese wrastler at the music hall by standin out 17 minutes 4 seconds agen him.

BILL [*sullenly*] Aw'm nao music awl wrastler. Ken he box?

SHIRLEY. Yes: an you cant.

BILL. Wot! Aw cawnt, cawnt Aw? Wots thet you sy [*threatening him*]?

SHIRLEY [*not budging an inch*] Will you box Todger Fairmile if I put him on to you? Say the word.

BILL [*subsiding with a slouch*] Aw'll stend ap to enny menn alawv, if he was ten Todger Fairmawls. But Aw dont set ap to be a perfeshnal.

SHIRLEY [*looking down on him with unfathomable disdain*] You box! Slap an old woman with the back o your hand! You hadnt even the sense to hit her where a magistrate couldnt see the mark of it, you silly young lump of conceit and ignorance. Hit a girl in the jaw and ony make her cry! If Todger Fairmile'd done it, she wouldnt a got up inside o ten minutes, no more than you would if he got on to you. Yah! I'd set about you myself if I had a week's feedin in me instead o two month's starvation. [*He turns his back on him and sits down moodily at the table*].

BILL [*following him and stooping over him to drive the taunt in*] You loy! youve the bread and treacle in you that you cam eah to beg.

SHIRLEY [*bursting into tears*] Oh God! it's true: I'm only an old pauper on the scrap heap. [*Furiously*] But youll come to it yourself; and then youll know. Youll come to it sooner than a teetotaller like me, fillin yourself with gin at this hour o the mornin!

BILL. Aw'm nao gin drinker, you oald lawr; bat wen Aw want to give my girl a bloomin good awdin Aw lawk to ev a bit o devil in me: see? An eah Aw emm, talkin to a rotten aold blawter like you sted o givin her wot for. [*Working himself into a rage*] Aw'm gowin in there to fetch her aht. [*Her makes vengefully for the shelter door*].

SHIRLEY. Youre goin to the station on a stretcher, more likely; and theyll take the gin and the devil out of you there when they get you inside. You mind what youre about: the major here is the Earl o Stevenage's granddaughter.

BILL [*checked*] Garn!

SHIRLEY. Youll see.

BILL [*his resolution oozing*] Well, Aw aint dan nathin to er.

SHIRLEY. Spose she said you did! who'd believe you?

BILL [*very uneasy, skulking back to the corner of the penthouse*] Gawd! theres no jastice in this cantry. To think wot them people can do! Aw'm as good as er.

SHIRLEY. Tell her so. It's just what a fool like you would do.

Barbara, brisk and businesslike, comes from the shelter with a note book, and addresses herself to Shirley. Bill, cowed, sits down in the corner on a form, and turns his back on them.

BARBARA. Good morning.

SHIRLEY [*standing up and taking off his hat*] Good morning, miss.

BARBARA. Sit down: make yourself at home. [*He hesitates; but she puts a friendly hand on his shoulder and makes him obey.*] Now then! since youve made friends with us, we want to know all about you. Names and addresses and trades.

SHIRLEY. Peter Shirley. Fitter. Chucked out two months ago because I was too old.

BARBARA [*not at all surprised*] Youd pass still. Why didnt you dye your hair?

SHIRLEY. I did. Me age come out at a coroner's inquest on me daughter.

BARBARA. Steady?

SHIRLEY. Teetotaller. Never out of a job before. Good worker. And sent to the knackers like an old horse!

BARBARA. No matter: if you did your part God will do his.

SHIRLEY [*suddenly stubborn*] My religion's no concern of anybody but myself.

BARBARA [*guessing*] I know. Secularist?

SHIRLEY [*hotly*] Did I offer to deny it?

BARBARA. Why should you? My own father's a Secularist, I think. Our Father—yours and mine—fulfils himself in many ways; and I daresay he knew what he was about when he made a Secularist of you. So buck up, Peter! we can always find a job for a steady man like you. [*Shirley, disarmed and a little bewildered, touches his hat. She turns from him to Bill*]. Whats your name?

BILL [*insolently*] Wots thet to you?

BARBARA [*calmly making a note*] Afraid to give his name. Any trade?

BILL. Oo's afride to give is nime? [*Doggedly, with a sense of heroically defying the House of Lords in the person of Lord Stevenage*] If you want to bring a chawge agen me, bring it. [*She waits, unruffled*]. Moy nime's Bill Walker.

BARBARA [*as if the name were familiar: trying to

remember how] Bill Walker? [*Recollecting*] Oh, I know: youre the man that Jenny Hill was praying for inside just now. [*She enters his name in her note book*].

BILL. Oo's Jenny Ill? And wot call as she to pry for me?

BARBARA. I dont know. Perhaps it was you that cut her lip.

BILL [*defiantly*] Yus, it was me that cat her lip. Aw aint afride o you.

BARBARA. How could you be, since youre not afraid of God? Youre a brave man, Mr Walker. It takes some pluck to do our work here; but none of us dare lift our hand against a girl like that, for fear of her father in heaven.

BILL [*sullenly*] I want nan o your kentin jawr. I spowse you think Aw cam eah to beg from you, like this demmiged lot eah. Not me. Aw downt want your bread and scripe and ketlep. Aw dont blieve in your Gawd, no more than you do yourself.

BARBARA [*sunnily apologetic and ladylike, as on a new footing with him*] Oh, I beg your pardon for putting your name down, Mr Walker. I didnt understand. I'll strike it out.

BILL [*taking this as a slight, and deeply wounded by it*] Eah! you let maw nime alown. Aint it good enaff to be in your book?

BARBABA [*considering*] Well, you see, theres no use putting down your name unless I can do something for you, is there? Whats your trade?

BILL [*still smarting*] Thets nao concern o yours.

BARBARA. Just so. [*Very businesslike*] I'll put you down as [*writing*] the man who— struck—poor little Jenny Hill—in the mouth.

BILL [*rising threateningly*] See eah. Awve ed enaff o this.

BARBARA [*quite sunny and fearless*] What did you come to us for?

BILL. Aw cam for maw gel, see? Aw cam to tike her aht o this and to brike er jawr for er.

BARBARA [*complacently*] You see I was right about your trade. [*Bill, on the point of

retorting furiously, finds himself, to his great shame and terror, in danger of crying instead. He sits down again suddenly*]. Whats her name?

BILL [*dogged*] Er nime's Mog Ebbijem: thets wot her nime is.

BARBARA. Mog Habbijam! Oh, she's gone to Canning Town, to our barracks there.

BILL [*fortified by his resentment of Mog's perfidy*] Is she? [*Vindictively*] Then Aw'm gowin to Kennintahn arter her. [*He crosses to the gate; hesitates; finally comes back at Barbara*]. Are you loyin to me to git shat o me?

BARBARA. I dont want to get shut of you. I want to keep you here and save your soul. Youd better stay: youre going to have a bad time today, Bill.

BILL. Oo's gowing to give it to me? You, preps?

BARBARA. Someone you dont believe in. But youll be glad afterwards.

BILL [*slinking off*] Aw'll gow to Kennintahn to be aht o reach o your tangue. [*Suddenly turning on her with intense malice*] And if Aw downt fawnd Mog there, Aw'll cam beck and do two years for you, selp me Gawd if Aw downt!

BARBARA [*a shade kindlier, if possible*] It's no use, Bill. She's got another bloke.

BILL. Wot!

BARBARA. One of her own converts. He fell in love with her when he saw her with her soul saved, and her face clean, and her hair washed.

BILL [*surprised*] Wottud she wash it for, the carroty slat? It's red.

BARBARA. It's quite lovely now, because she wears a new look in her eyes with it. It's a pity youre too late. The new bloke has put your nose out of joint, Bill.

BILL. Aw'll put his nowse aht o joint for him. Not that Aw care a carse for er, mawnd thet. But Aw'll teach her to drop me as if Aw was dirt. And Aw'll teach him to meddle with maw judy. Wots iz bleedin nime?

BARBARA. Sergeant Toder Fairmile.

SHIRLEY [*rising with grim joy*] I'll go with him, miss. I want to see them two meet. I'll take him to the infirmary when it's over.

BILL [*to Shirley, with undissembled misgiving*] Is thet im you was speakin on?

SHIRLEY. Thats him.

BILL. Im that wrastled in the music awl?

SHIRLEY. The competitions at the National Sportin Club was worth nigh a hundred a year to him. He's gev em up now for religion; so he's a bit fresh for want of the exercise he was accustomed to. He'll be glad to see you. Come along.

BILL. Wots is wight?

SHIRLEY. Thirteen four. [*Bill's last hope expires*].

BARBARA. Go and talk to him, Bill. He'll convert you.

SHIRLEY. He'll convert your head into a mashed potato.

BILL [*sullenly*] Aw aint afride of im. Aw aint afride of ennybody Bat e can lick me. She's dan me. [*He sits down moodily on the edge of the horse trough*].

SHIRLEY. You aint goin. I thought not. [*He resumes his seat*].

BARBARA [*calling*] Jenny!

JENNY [*appearing at the shelter door with a plaster on the corner of her mouth*] Yes, Major.

BARBARA. Send Rummy Mitchens out to clear away here.

JENNY. I think she's afraid.

BARBARA [*her resemblance to her mother flashing out for a moment*] Nonsense! she must do as she's told.

JENNY [*calling into the shelter*] Rummy: the Major says you must come.

Jenny comes to Barbara, purposely keeping on the side next Bill, lest he should suppose that she shrank from him or bore malice.

BARBARA. Poor little Jenny! Are you tired? [*Looking at the wounded cheek*] Does it hurt?

JENNY. No: it's all right now. It was nothing.

BARBARA [*critically*] It was as hard as he could hit, I expect. Poor Bill! You dont feel angry with him, do you?

JENNY. Oh no, no, no: indeed I dont, Major, bless his poor heart! [*Barbara kisses her; and she runs away merrily into the shelter. Bill writhes with an agonizing return of his new and alarming symptoms, but says nothing. Rummy Mitchens comes from the shelter*].

BARBARA [*going to meet Rummy*] Now Rummy, bustle. Take in those mugs and plates to be washed; and throw the crumbs about for the birds.

Rummy takes the three plates and mugs; but Shirley takes back his mug from her, as there is still some milk left in it.

RUMMY. There aint any crumbs. This aint a time to waste good bread on birds.

PRICE [*appearing at the shelter door*] Gentleman come to see the shelter, Major. Says he's your father.

BARBARA. All right. Coming [*Snobby goes back into the shelter, followed by Barbara*].

RUMMY [*stealing across to Bill and addressing him in a subdued voice, but with intense conviction*] I'd av the lor of you, you flat eared pignosed potwalloper, if she's let me. Youre no gentleman, to hit a lady in the face. [*Bill, with greater things moving in him, takes no notice*].

SHIRLEY [*following her*] Here! in with you and dont get yourself into more trouble by talking.

RUMMY [*with hauteur*] I aint ad the pleasure o being hintroduced to you, as I can remember. [*She goes into the shelter with the plates*].

SHIRLEY. Thats the—

BILL [*savagely*] Downt you talk to me, d'ye eah? You lea me alown, or Aw'll do you a mischief. Aw'm not dirt under your feet, ennywy.

SHIRLEY [*calmly*] Dont you be afeerd. You aint such prime company that you need expect to be sought after. [*He is about to go into the shelter when Barbara comes out, with Undershaft on her right*].

BARBARA. Oh, there you are, Mr Shirley!

[*Between them*] This is my father: I told you he was a Secularist, didnt I? Perhaps youll be able to comfort one another.

UNDERSHAFT [*startled*] A Secularist! Not the least in the world: on the contrary, a confirmed mystic.

BARBARA. Sorry, I'm sure. By the way, papa, what is your religion? in case I have to introduce you again.

UNDERSHAFT. My religion? Well, my dear, I am a Millionaire. That is my religion.

BARBARA. Then I'm afraid you and Mr Shirley wont be able to comfort one another after all. Youre not a Millionaire, are you, Peter?

SHIRLEY. No; and proud of it.

UNDERSHAFT [*gravely*] Poverty, my friend, is not a thing to be proud of.

SHIRLEY [*angrily*] Who made your millions for you? Me and my like. Whats kep us poor? Keepin you rich. I wouldnt have your conscience, not for all your income.

UNDERSHAFT. I wouldnt have your income, not for all your conscience, Mr Shirley. [*He goes to the penthouse and sits down on a form*].

BARBARA [*stopping Shirley adroitly as he is about to retort*] You wouldnt think he was my father, would you, Peter? Will you go into the shelter and lend the lasses a hand for a while: we're worked off our feet.

SHIRLEY [*bitterly*] Yes: I'm in their debt for a meal, aint I?

BARBARA. Oh, not because youre in their debt, but for love of them, Peter, for love of them. [*He cannot understand, and is rather scandalized*] There! dont stare at me. In with you; and give that conscience of yours a holiday [*bustling him into the shelter*].

SHIRLEY [*as he goes in*] Ah! it's a pity you never was trained to use your reason, miss. Youd have been a very taking lecturer on Secularism.

Barbara turns to her father.

UNDERSHAFT. Never mind me, my dear. Go about your work; and let me watch it for a while.

BARBARA. All right.

UNDERSHAFT. For instance, whats the matter with that outpatient over there?

BARBARA [*looking at Bill, whose attitude has never changed, and whose expression of brooding wrath has deepened*] Oh, we shall cure him in no time. Just watch [*She goes over to Bill and waits. He glances up at her and casts his eyes down again, uneasy, but grimmer than ever*]. It would be nice to just stamp on Mog Habbijam's face, wouldnt it, Bill?

BILL [*starting up from the trough in consternation*] It's a loy: Aw never said so. [*She shakes her head*]. Oo taold you wot was in moy mawnd?

BARBARA. Only your new friend.

BILL. Wot new friend?

BARBARA. The devil, Bill. When he gets round people they get miserable, just like you.

BILL [*with a heartbreaking attempt at devil-may-care cheerfulness*] Aw aint miserable. [*He sits down again, and stretches his legs in an attempt to seem indifferent*].

BARBARA. Well, if youre happy, why dont you look happy, as we do?

BILL [*his legs curling back in spite of him*] Aw'm eppy enaff, Aw tell you. Woy cawnt you lea me alown? Wot ev I dan to you? Aw aint smashed your fice, ev Aw?

BARBARA [*softly: wooing his soul*] It's not me thats getting at you, Bill.

BILL. Oo else is it?

BARBARA. Somebody that doesnt intend you to smash women's faces, I suppose. Somebody or something that wants to make a man of you.

BILL [*blustering*] Mike a menn o me. Aint Aw a menn? eh? Oo sez Aw'm not a menn?

BARBARA. Theres a man in you somewhere, I suppose. But why did he let you hit poor little Jenny Hill? That wasnt very manly of him, was it?

BILL [*tormented*] Ev dan wiv it, Aw tell you. Chack it. Aw'm sick o your Jenny Ill and er silly little fice.

BARBARA. Then why do you keep thinking about it? Why does it keep coming up against you in your mind? Youre not getting converted, are you?

BILL [*with conviction*] Not ME. Not lawkly.

BARBARA. Thats right, Bill. Hold out against it. Put out your strength. Dont lets get you cheap. Todger Fairmile said he wrestled for three nights against his salvation harder than he ever wrestled with the Jap at the music hall. He gave in to the Jap when his arm was going to break. But he didnt give in to his salvation until his heart was going to break. Perhaps youll escape that. You havnt any heart, have you?

BILL. Wot d'ye mean? Woy aint Aw got a awt the sime as ennybody else?

BARBARA. A man with a heart wouldnt have bashed poor little Jenny's face, would he?

BILL [*almost crying*] Ow, will you lea me alown? Ev Aw ever offered to meddle with you, that you cam neggin and provowkin me lawk this? [*He writhes convulsively from his eyes to his toes*].

BARBARA [*with a steady soothing hand on his arm and a gentle voice that never lets him go*] It's your soul thats hurting you, Bill, and not me. Weve been through it all ourselves. Come with us, Bill. [*He looks wildly round*]. To brave manhood on earth and eternal glory in heaven. [*He is on the point of breaking down*]. Come. [*A drum is heard in the shelter; and Bill, with a gasp, escapes from the spell as Barbara turns quickly. Adolphus enters from the shelter with a big drum.*] Oh! there you are, Dolly. Let me introduce a new friend of mine, Mr Bill Walker. This is my bloke, Bill: Mr Cusins. [*Cusins salutes with his drumstick*].

BILL. Gowin to merry im?

BARBARA. Yes.

BILL [*fervently*] Gawd elp im! Gaw-aw-aw-awd elp im!

BARBARA. Why? Do you think he wont be happy with me?

BILL. Awve aony ed to stend it for a mawnin: e'll ev to stend it for a lawftawm.

CUSINS. That is a frightful reflection, Mr Walker. But I cant tear myself away from her.

BILL. Well, Aw ken. [*To Barbara*] Eah! do you knaow where Aw'm gowin to, and wot Aw'm gowin to do?

BARBARA. Yes: youre going to heaven; and youre coming back here before the week's out to tell me so.

BILL. You loy. Aw'm gowin to Kennintahn, to spit in Todger Fairmawl's eye. Aw beshed Jenny Ill's fice; an nar Aw'll git me aown fice beshed and cam beck and shaow it to er. Ee'll itt me ardern Aw itt er. Thatll mike us square. [*To Adolphus*] Is thet fair or is it not? Youre a genlmn: you oughter knaow.

BARBARA. Two black eyes wont make one white one, Bill.

BILL. Aw didnt awst you. Cawnt you never keep your mahth shat? Oy awst the genlmn.

CUSINS [*reflectively*] Yes: I think youre right, Mr Walker. Yes: I should do it. It's curious: it's exactly what an ancient Greek would have done.

BARBARA. But what good will it do?

CUSINS. Well, it will give Mr Fairmile some exercise; and it will satisfy Mr Walker's soul.

BILL. Rot! there aint nao such a thing as a saoul. Ah kin you tell wevver Awve a saoul or not? You never seen it.

BARBARA. Ive seen it hurting you when you went against it.

BILL [*with compressed aggravation*] If you was maw gel and took the word aht o me mahth lawk thet, Aw'd give you sathink youd feel urtin, Aw would. [*To Adolphus*] You tike maw tip, mite. Stop er jawr; or youll doy afoah your tawm [*With intense expression*] Wore aht: thets wot youll be: wore aht. [*He goes away through the gate*].

CUSINS [*looking after him*] I wonder!

BARBARA. Dolly! [*indignant, in her mother's manner*].

CUSINS. Yes, my dear, it's very wearing to be in love with you. If it lasts, I quite think I shall die young.

BARBARA. Should you mind?

CUSINS. Not at all. [*He is suddenly softened, and kisses her over the drum, evidently not for the first time, as people cannot kiss over a big drum without practice. Undershaft coughs*].

BARBARA. It's all right, papa, weve not forgotten you. Dolly: explain the place to papa: I havnt time. [*She goes busily into the shelter*].

Undershaft and Adolphus now have the yard to themselves. Undershaft, seated on a form, and still keenly attentive, looks hard at Adolphus. Adolphus looks hard at him.

UNDERSHAFT. I fancy you guess something of what is in my mind, Mr Cusins. [*Cusins flourishes his drumsticks as if in the act of beating a lively rataplan, but makes no sound.* Exactly so. But suppose Barbara finds you out!

CUSINS. You know, I do not admit that I am imposing on Barbara. I am quite genuinely interested in the views of the Salvation Army. The fact is, I am a sort of collector of religions; and the curious thing is that I find I can believe them all. By the way, have you any religion?

UNDERSHAFT. Yes.

CUSINS. Anything out of the common?

UNDERSHAFT. Only that there are two things necessary to Salvation.

CUSINS [*disappointed, but polite*] Ah, the Church Catechism. Charles Lomax also belongs to the Established Church.

UNDERSHAFT. The two things are—

CUSINS. Baptism and—

UNDERSHAFT. No. Money and gunpowder.

CUSINS [*surprised, but interested*] That is the general opinion of our governing classes. The novelty is in hearing any man confess it.

UNDERSHAFT. Just so.

CUSINS. Excuse me: is there any place in your religion for honor, justice, truth, love, mercy and so forth?

UNDERSHAFT. Yes: they are the graces and luxuries of a rich, strong, and safe life.

CUSINS. Suppose one is forced to choose between them and money or gunpowder?

UNDERSHAFT. Choose money and gunpowder; for without enough of both you cannot afford the others.

CUSINS. That is your religion?

UNDERSHAFT. Yes.

The cadence of this reply makes a full close in the conversation. Cusins twists his face dubiously and contemplates Undershaft. Undershaft contemplates him.

CUSINS. Barbara wont stand that. You will have to choose between your religion and Barbara.

UNDERSHAFT. So will you, my friend. She will find out that that drum of yours is hollow.

CUSINS. Father Undershaft: you are mistaken: I am a sincere Salvationist. You do not understand the Salvation Army. It is the army of joy, of love, of courage: it has banished the fear and remorse and despair of the old hell-ridden evangelical sects: it marches to fight the devil with trumpet and drum, with music and dancing, with banner and palm, as becomes a sally from heaven by its happy garrison. It picks the waster out of the public house and makes a man of him: it finds a worm wriggling in a back kitchen, and lo! a woman! Men and women of rank too, sons and daughters of the Highest. It takes the poor professor of Greek, the most artificial and self-suppressed of human creatures, from his meal of roots, and lets loose the rhapsodist in him; reveals the true worship of Dionysos to him; sends him down the public street drumming dithyrambs [*he plays a thundering flourish on the drum*].

UNDERSHAFT. You will alarm the shelter.

CUSINS. Oh, they are accustomed to these sudden ecstasies. However, if the drum worries you—[*he pockets the drumsticks; unhooks the drum; and stands it on the ground opposite the gateway*].

UNDERSHAFT. Thank you.

CUSINS. You remember what Euripides says about your money and gunpowder?

UNDERSHAFT. No.

CUSINS [*declaiming*]

One and another
In money and guns may outpass his brother;
And men in their millions float and flow
And seethe with a million hopes as leaven;
And they win their will; or they miss their
will;
And their hopes are dead or are pined for still;
But who'er can know
As the long days go
That to live is happy, has found his heaven.

My translation: what do you think of it?

UNDERSHAFT. I think, my friend, that if you wish to know, as the long days go, that to live is happy, you must first acquire money enough for a decent life, and power enough to be your own master.

CUSINS. You are damnably discouraging. [*He resumes his declamation*].

Is it so hard a thing to see
That the spirit of God—whate'er it be—
The law that abides and changes not, ages
long,
The Eternal and Nature-born: these things be
strong?
What else is Wisdom? What of Man's
endeavor,
Or God's high grace so lovely and so great?
To stand from fear set free? to breathe and
wait?
To hold a hand uplifted over Fate?
And shall not Barbara be loved for ever?

UNDERSHAFT. Euripides mentions Barbara, does he?

CUSINS. It is a fair translation. The word means Loveliness.

UNDERSHAFT. May I ask—as Barbara's father—how much a year she is to be loved for ever on?

CUSINS. As Barbara's father, that is more your affair than mine. I can feed her by teaching Greek: that is about all.

UNDERSHAFT. Do you consider it a good match for her?

CUSINS [*with polite obstinacy*] Mr Undershaft: I am in many ways a weak, timid, ineffectual person; and my health is far from satisfactory. But whenever I feel that I

must have anything, I get it, sooner or later. I feel that way about Barbara. I dont like marriage: I feel intensely afraid of it; and I dont know what I shall do with Barbara or what she will do with me. But I feel that I and nobody else must marry her. Please regard that as settled.— Not that I wish to be arbitrary; but why should I waste your time in discussing what is inevitable?

UNDERSHAFT. You mean that you will stick at nothing: not even the conversion of the Salvation Army to the worship of Dionysos.

CUSINS. The business of the Salvation Army is to save, not to wrangle about the name of the pathfinder. Dionysos or another: what does it matter?

UNDERSHAFT [*rising and approaching him*] Professor Cusins: you are a young man after my own heart.

CUSINS. Mr Undershaft: you are, as far as I am able to gather, a most infernal old rascal; but you appeal very strongly to my sense of ironic humor.

Undershaft mutely offers his hand. They shake.

UNDERSHAFT [*suddenly concentrating himself*] And now to business.

CUSINS. Pardon me. We are discussing religion. Why go back to such an uninteresting and unimportant subject as business?

UNDERSHAFT. Religion is our business at present, because it is through religion alone that we can win Barbara.

CUSINS. Have you, too, fallen in love with Barbara?

UNDERSHAFT. Yes, with a father's love.

CUSINS. A father's love for a grown-up daughter is the most dangerous of all infatuations. I apologize for mentioning my own pale, coy, mistrustful fancy in the same breath with it.

UNDERSHAFT. Keep to the point, We have to win her; and we are neither of us Methodists.

CUSINS. That doesnt matter. The power Barbara wields here—the power that wields Barbara herself—is not Calvinism, not Presbyterianism, not Methodism—

UNDERSHAFT. Not Greek Paganism either, eh?

CUSINS. I admit that. Barbara is quite original in her religion.

UNDERSHAFT [*triumphantly*] Aha! Barbara Undershaft would be. Her inspiration comes from within herself.

CUSINS. How do you suppose it got here?

UNDERSHAFT [*in towering excitement*] It is the Undershaft inheritance. I shall hand on my torch to my daughter. She shall make my converts and preach my gospel—

CUSINS. What! Money and gunpowder!

UNDERSHAFT. Yes, money and gunpowder. Freedom and power. Command of life and command of death.

CUSINS [*urbanely: trying to bring him down to earth*] This is extremely interesting, Mr Undershaft. Of course you know that you are mad.

UNDERSHAFT [*with redoubled force*] And you?

CUSINS. Oh, mad as a hatter. You are welcome to my secret since I have discovered yours. But I am astonished. Can a madman make cannons?

UNDERSHAFT. Would anyone else than a madman make them? And now [*with surging energy*] question for question. Can a sane man translate Euripides?

CUSINS. No.

UNDERSHAFT [*seizing him by the shoulder*] Can a sane woman make a man of a waster or a woman of a worm?

CUSINS [*reeling before the storm*] Father Colossus—Mammoth Millionaire—

UNDERSHAFT [*pressing him*] Are there two mad people or three in this Salvation shelter today?

CUSINS. You mean Barbara is as mad as we are?

UNDERSHAFT [*pushing him lightly off and resuming his equanimity suddenly and completely*] Pooh, Professor! let us call things by their proper names. I am a millionaire; you are a poet; Barbara is a savior of souls. What have we three to do with the common mob of slaves and idolaters? [*He sits down again with a shrug of contempt for the mob*].

CUSINS. Take care! Barbara is in love with the common people. So am I. Have you never felt the romance of that love?

UNDERSHAFT [*cold and sardonic*] Have you ever been in love with Poverty, like St Francis? Have you ever been in love with Dirt, like St Simeon! Have you ever been in love with disease and suffering, like our nurses and philanthropists? Such passions are not virtues, but the most unnatural of all the vices. This love of the common people may please an earl's granddaughter and a university professor; but I have been a common man and a poor man; and it has no romance for me. Leave it to the poor to pretend that poverty is a blessing: leave it to the coward to make a religion of his cowardice by preaching humility: we know better than that. We three must stand together above the common people: how else can we help their children to climb up beside us? Barbara must belong to us, not to the Salvation Army.

CUSINS. Well, I can only say that if you think you will get her away from the Salvation Army by talking to her as you have been talking to me, you dont know Barbara.

UNDERSHAFT. My friend: I never ask for what I can buy.

CUSINS [*in a white fury*] Do I understand you to imply that you can buy Barbara?

UNDERSHAFT. No; but I can buy the Salvation Army.

CUSINS. Quite impossible.

UNDERSHAFT. You shall see. All religious organizations exist by selling themselves to the rich.

CUSINS. Not the Army. That is the Church of the poor.

UNDERSHAFT. All the more reason for buying it.

CUSINS. I dont think you quite know what the Army does for the poor.

UNDERSHAFT. Oh yes I do. It draws their teeth: that is enough for me as a man of business.

CUSINS. Nonsense! It makes them sober—

UNDERSHAFT. I prefer sober workmen. The profits are larger.

CUSINS—honest—

UNDERSHAFT. Honest workmen are the most economical.

CUSINS—attached to their homes—

UNDERSHAFT. So much the better: they will put up with anything sooner than change their shop.

CUSINS—happy—

UNDERSHAFT. An invaluable safeguard against revolution.

CUSINS—unselfish—

UNDERSHAFT. Indifferent to their own interests, which suits me exactly.

CUSINS—with their thoughts on heavenly things—

UNDERSHAFT [*rising*] And not on Trade Unionism nor Socialism. Excellent.

CUSINS [*revolted*] You really are an infernal old rascal.

UNDERSHAFT [*indicating Peter Shirley, who has just come from the shelter and strolled dejectedly down the yard between them*] And this is an honest man!

SHIRLEY. Yes; and what av I got by it? [*he passes on bitterly and sits on the form, in the corner of the penthouse*].

Snobby Price, beaming sanctimoniously, and Jenny Hill, with a tambourine full of coppers, come from the shelter and go to the drum, on which Jenny begins to count the money.

UNDERSHAFT [*replying to Shirley*] Oh, your employers must have got a good deal by it from first to last. [*He sits on the table, with one foot on the side form. Cusins, overwhelmed, sits down on the same form nearer the shelter. Barbara comes from the shelter to the middle of the yard. She is excited and a little overwrought.*]

BARBARA. Weve just had a splendid experi-
ence meeting at the other gate in Cripps's lane. Ive hardly ever seen them so much moved as they were by your confession, Mr Price.

PRICE. I could almost be glad of my past wickedness if I could believe that it would elp to keep hathers stright.

BARBARA. So it will, Snobby. How much, Jenny?

JENNY. Four and tenpence, Major.

BARBARA. Oh Snobby, if you had given your poor mother just one more kick, we should have got the whole five shillings!

PRICE. If she heard you say that, miss, she'd be sorry I didnt. But I'm glad. Oh what a joy it will be to her when she hears I'm saved!

UNDERSHAFT. Shall I contribute the odd twopence, Barbara? The millionaire's mite, eh? [*He takes a couple of pennies from his pocket*].

BARBARA. How did you make that twopence?

UNDERSHAFT. As usual. By selling cannons, torpedoes, submarines, and my new patent Grand Duke hand grenade.

BARBARA. Put it back in your pocket. You cant buy your salvation here for twopence: you must work it out.

UNDERSHAFT. Is twopence not enough? I can afford little more, if you press me.

BARBARA. Two million millions would not be enough. There is bad blood on your hands; and nothing but good blood can cleanse them. Money is no use. Take it away. [*She turns to Cusins*]. Dolly: you must write another letter for me to the papers. [*He makes a wry face*]. Yes: I know you dont like it; but it must be done. The starvation this winter is beating us: everybody is unemployed. The General says we must close this shelter if we cant get more money. I force the collections at the meetings until I am ashamed: dont I, Snobby?

PRICE. It's a fair treat to see you work it, miss. The way you got them up from three-and-six to four-and-ten with that hymn, penny by penny and verse by verse, was a caution. Not a Cheap Jack on Mile End Waste could touch you at it.

BARBARA. Yes; but I wish we could do without it. I am getting at last to think more of the collection than of the people's souls. And what are those hatfuls of pence and halfpence? We want thousands! tens of thousands! hundreds of thousands! I want to convert people, not to be always begging for the Army in a way I'd die sooner than beg for myself.

UNDERSHAFT [*in profound irony*] Genuine unselfishness is capable of anything, my dear.

BARBARA [*unsuspectingly, as she turns away to take the money from the drum and put it in a cashbag she carries*] Yes, isnt it? [*Undershaft looks sardonically at Cusins*].

CUSINS [*aside to Undershaft*] Mephistopheles! Machiavelli!

BARBARA [*tears coming into her eyes as she ties the bag and pockets it*] How are we to feed them? I cant talk religion to a man with bodily hunger in his eyes. [*Almost breaking down*] It's frightful.

JENNY [*running to her*] Major, dear—

BARBARA [*rebounding*] No: dont comfort me. It will be all right. We shall get the money.

UNDERSHAFT. How?

JENNY. By praying for it, of course. Mrs Baines says she prayed for it last night; and she has never prayed for it in vain: never once. [*She goes to the gate and looks out into the street*].

BARBARA [*who has dried her eyes and regained her composure*] By the way, dad, Mrs Baines has come to march with us to our big meeting this afternoon; and she is very anxious to meet you, for some reason or other. Perhaps she'll convert you.

UNDERSHAFT. I shall be delighted, my dear.

JENNY [*at the gate: excitedly*] Major! Major! heres that man back again.

BARBARA. What man?

JENNY. The man that hit me. Oh, I hope he's coming back to join us.

Bill Walker, with frost on his jacket, comes through the gate, his hands deep in his pockets and his chin sunk between his shoulders, like a cleaned-out gambler. He halts between Barbara and the drum.

BARBARA. Hullo, Bill! Back already!

BILL [*nagging at her*] Bin talkin ever sence, ev you?

BARBARA. Pretty nearly. Well, has Todger paid you out for poor Jenny's jaw?

BILL. Nao e aint.

BARBARA. I thought your jacket looked a bit snowy.

BILL. Sao it is snaowy. You want to knaow where the snaow cam from, downt you?

BARBARA. Yes.

BILL. Well, it cam from orf the grahnd in Pawkinses Corner in Kennintahn. It got rabbed orf be maw shaoulders: see?

BARBARA. Pity you didnt rub some off with your knees, Bill! That would have done you a lot of good.

BILL [*with sour mirthless humor*] Aw was sivin anather menn's knees at the tawm. E was kneelin on moy ed, e was.

JENNY. Who was kneeling on your head?

BILL. Todger was. E was pryin for me: pryin camfortable wiv me as a cawpet. Sow was Mog. Sao was the aol bloomin meetin. Mog she sez "Ow Lawd brike is stabborn sperrit; bat downt urt is dear art." Thet was wot she said. "Downt urt is dear art"! An er blowk—thirteen stun four!—kneelin wiv all is wight on me. Fanny, aint it?

JENNY. Oh no. We're so sorry, Mr Walker.

BARBARA [*enjoying it frankly*] Nonsense! of course it's funny. Served you right, Bill! You must have done something to him first.

BILL [*doggedly*] Aw did wot Aw said Aw'd do. Aw spit in is eye. E looks ap at the skoy and sez, "Ow that Aw should be fahnd worthy to be spit upon for the gospel's sike!" e sez; an Mog sez "Glaory Allelloolier!"; an then e called me Braddher, an dahned me as if Aw was a kid and e was me mather worshin me a Setterda nawt. Aw ednt jast nao shaow wiv im at all. Arf the street pryed; an the tather arf larfed fit to split theirselves. [*To Barbara*] There! are you settisfawd nah?

BARBARA [*her eyes dancing*] Wish I'd been there, Bill.

BILL. Yus: youd a got in a hextra bit o talk on me, wouldnt you?

JENNY. I'm so sorry, Mr Walker.

BILL [*fiercely*] Downt you gow bein sorry for me: youve no call. Listen eah. Aw browk your jawr.

JENNY. No, it didnt hurt me: indeed it didnt, except for a moment. It was only that I was frightened.

BILL. Aw downt want to be forgive be you, or be ennybody. Wot Aw did Aw'll py for. Aw trawd to gat me aown jawr browk to settisfaw you—

JENNY [*distressed*] Oh no—

BILL [*impatiently*] Tell y' Aw did: cawnt you listen to wots bein taold you? All Aw got be it was bein mide a sawt of in the pablic street for me pines. Well, if Aw cawnt settisfaw you one wy, Aw ken another. Listen eah! Aw ed two quid sived agen the frost; an Awve a pahnd of it left. A mite o mawn last week ed words with the judy e's gowin to merry. E give er wot-for; an e's bin fawnd fifteen bob. E ed a rawt to itt er cause they was gowin to be merrid; but Aw ednt nao rawt to itt you; sao put anather fawv bob on an call it a pahnd's worth. [*He produces a sovereign*]. Eahs the manney. Tike it; and lets ev no more o your forgivin an pryin and your Mijor jawrin me. Let wot Aw dan be dan an pide for; and let there be a end of it.

JENNY. Oh, I couldnt take it, Mr Walker. But if you would give a shilling or two to poor Rummy Mitchens! you really did hurt her; and she's old.

BILL [*contemptuously*] Not lawkly. Aw'd give her anather as soon as look at er. Let her ev the lawr o me as she threatened! She aint forgiven me: not mach. Wot Aw

dan to er is not on me mawnd—wot she [*indicating Barbara*] mawt call on me conscience—no more than stickin a pig. It's this Christian gime o yours that Aw wownt ev plyed agen me: this bloomin forgivin an negging an jawrin that mikes a menn thet sore that iz lawf's a burdn to im. Aw wownt ev it, Aw tell you; sao tike your manney and stop thraowin your silly beshed fice hap agen me.

JENNY. Major: may I take a little of it for the Army?

BARBARA. No: the Army is not to be bought. We want your soul, Bill; and we'll take nothing less.

BILL [*bitterly*] Aw knaow. Me an maw few shillins is not good enaff for you. Youre a earl's grendorter, you are. Nathink less than a anderd pahnd for you.

UNDERSHAFT. Come, Barbara! you could do a great deal of good with a hundred pounds. If you will set this gentleman's mind at ease by taking his pound, I will give the other ninety-nine.

Bill, dazed by such opulence, instinctively touches his cap.

BARBARA. Oh, youre too extravagant, papa. Bill offers twenty pieces of silver. All you need offer is the other ten. That will make the standard price to buy anybody who's for sale. I'm not; and the Army's not. [*To Bill*] Youll never have another quiet moment, Bill, until you come round to us. You cant stand out against your salvation.

BILL [*sullenly*] Aw cawnt stend aht agen music awl wrastlers and awtful tangued women. Awve offered to py. Aw can do no more. Tike it or leave it. There it is. [*He throws the sovereign on the drum, and sits down on the horse-trough. The coin fascinates Snobby Price, who takes an early opportunity of dropping his cap on it*].

Mrs Baines comes from the shelter. She is dressed as a Salvation Army Commissioner.

She is an earnest looking woman of about 40, *with a caressing, urgent voice, and an appealing manner.*

BARBARA. This is my father, Mrs Baines. [*Undershaft comes from the table, taking off his hat with marked civility*]. Try what you can do with him. He wont listen to me, because he remembers what a fool I was when I was a baby. [*She leaves them together and chats with Jenny*].

MRS BAINES. Have you been shewn over the shelter, Mr Undershaft? You know the work we're doing, of course.

UNDERSHAFT [*very civilly*] The whole nation knows it, Mrs Baines.

MRS BAINES. No, sir: the whole nation does not know it, or we should not be crippled as we are for want of money to carry our work through the length and breadth of the land. Let me tell you that there would have been rioting this winter in London but for us.

UNDERSHAFT. You really think so?

MRS BAINES. I know it. I remember 1886, when you rich gentlemen hardened your hearts against the cry of the poor. They broke the windows of your clubs in Pall Mall.

UNDERSHAFT [*gleaming with approval of their method*] And the Mansion House Fund went up next day from thirty thousand pounds to seventy-nine thousand! I remember quite well.

MRS BAINES. Well, wont you help me to get at the people? They wont break windows then. Come here, Price. Let me shew you to this gentleman [*Price comes to be inspected*]. Do you remember the window breaking?

PRICE. My ole father thought it was the revolution, maam.

MRS BAINES. Would you break windows now?

PRICE. Oh no, maam. The windows of eaven av bin opened to me. I know now that the rich man is a sinner like myself.

RUMMY [*appearing above at the loft door*] Snobby Price!

SNOBBY. Wot is it?

RUMMY. Your mother's askin for you at the other gate in Cripps's Lane. She's heard about your confession [*Price turns pale*].

MRS BAINES. Go, Mr Price; and pray with her.

JENNY. You can go through the shelter, Snobby.

PRICE [*to Mrs Baines*] I couldnt face her now, maam, with all the weight of my sins fresh on me. Tell her she'll find her son at ome, waitin for her in prayer. [*He skulks off through the gate, incidentally stealing the sovereign on his way out by picking up his cap from the drum*].

MRS BAINES [*with swimming eyes*] You see how we take the anger and the bitterness against you out of their hearts, Mr Undershaft.

UNDERSHAFT. It is certainly most convenient and gratifying to all large employers of labor, Mrs Baines.

MRS BAINES. Barbara: Jenny: I have good news: most wonderful news. [*Jenny runs to her*]. My prayers have been answered. I told you they would, Jenny, didnt I?

JENNY. Yes, yes.

BARBARA [*moving nearer to the drum*] Have we got money enough to keep the shelter open?

MRS BAINES. I hope we shall have enough to keep all the shelters open. Lord Saxmundham has promised us five thousand pounds—

BARBARA. Hooray!

JENNY. Glory!

MRS BAINES.—if—

BARBARA. "If!" If what?

MRS BAINES.—if five other gentlemen will give a thousand each to make it up to ten thousand.

BARBARA. Who is Lord Saxmundham? I never heard of him.

UNDERSHAFT [*who has pricked up his ears at the peer's name, and is now watching Barbara curiously*] A new creation, my dear. You have heard of Sir Horace Bodger?

BARBARA. Bodger! Do you mean the distiller? Bodger's whisky!

UNDERSHAFT. That is the man. He is one of

the greatest of our public benefactors. He restored the cathedral at Hakington. They made him a baronet for that. He gave half a million to the funds of his party: they made him a baron for that.

SHIRLEY. What will they give him for the five thousand?

UNDERSHAFT. There is nothing left to give him. So the five thousand, I should think, is to save his soul.

MRS BAINES. Heaven grant it may! Oh Mr Undershaft, you have some very rich friends. Cant you help us towards the other five thousand? We are going to hold a great meeting this afternoon at the Assembly Hall in the Mile End Road. If I could only announce that one gentleman had come forward to support Lord Sax-mundham, others would follow. Dont you know somebody? couldnt you? wouldnt you? [*her eyes fill with tears*] oh, think of those poor people, Mr Undershaft: think of how much it means to them, and how little to a great man like you.

UNDERSHAFT [*sardonically gallant*] Mrs Baines: you are irresistible. I cant disappoint you; and I cant deny myself the satisfaction of making Bodger pay up. You shall have your five thousand pounds.

MRS BAINES. Thank God!

UNDERSHAFT. You dont thank me?

MRS BAINES. Oh sir, dont try to be cynical: dont be ashamed of being a good man. The Lord will bless you abundantly; and our prayers will be like a strong fortification round you all the days of your life. [*With a touch of caution*] You will let me have the cheque to shew at the the meeting, wont you? Jenny: go in and fetch a pen and ink. [*Jenny runs to the shelter door*].

UNDERSHAFT. Do not disturb Miss Hill: I have a fountain pen [*Jenny halts. He sits at the table and writes the cheque. Cusins rises to make room for him. They all watch him silently*].

BILL [*cynically, aside to Barbara, his voice and accent horribly debased*] Wot prawce selvytion nah?

BARBARA. Stop. [*Undershaft stops writing:*

they all turn to her in surprise]. Mrs Baines: are you really going to take this money?

MRS BAINS [*astonished*] Why not, dear?

BARBARA. Why not! Do you know what my father is? Have you forgotten that Lord Saxmundham is Bodger the whisky man? Do you remember how we implored the County Council to stop him from writing Bodger's Whisky in letters of fire against the sky; so that the poor drink-ruined creatures on the Embankment could not wake up from their snatches of sleep without being reminded of their deadly thirst by that wicked sky sign? Do you know that the worst thing I have had to fight here is not the devil, but Bodger, Bodger, Bodger, with his whisky, his distilleries, and his tied houses? Are you going to make our shelter another tied house for him, and ask me to keep it?

BILL. Rotten dranken whisky it is too.

MRS BAINES. Dear Barbara: Lord Saxmundham has a soul to be saved like any of us. If heaven has found the way to make a good use of his money, are we to set ourselves up against the answer to our prayers?

BARBARA. I know he has a soul to be saved. Let him come down here; and I'll do my best to help him to his salvation. But he wants to send his cheque down to buy us, and go on being as wicked as ever.

UNDERSHAFT [*with a reasonableness which Cusins alone perceives to be ironical*] My dear Barbara: alcohol is a very necessary article. It heals the sick—

BARBARA. It does nothing of the sort.

UNDERSHAFT. Well, it assists the doctor: that is perhaps a less questionable way of putting it. It makes life bearable to millions of people who could not endure their existence if they were quite sober. It enables Parliament to do things at eleven at night that no sane person would do at eleven in the morning. Is it Bodger's fault that this inestimable gift is deplorably abused by less than one per cent of the poor? [*He turns again to the table; signs the cheque; and crosses it*].

MRS BAINES. Barbara: will there be less drinking or more if all those poor souls we are saving come tomorrow and find the doors of our shelters shut in their faces? Lord Saxmundham gives us the money to stop drinking—to take his own business from him.

CUSINS [*impishly*] Pure self-sacrifice on Bodger's part, clearly! Bless dear Bodger! [*Barbara almost breaks down as Adolphus, too, fails her*].

UNDERSHAFT [*tearing out the cheque and pocketing the book as he rises and goes past Cusins to Mrs Baines*] I also, Mrs Baines, may claim a little disinterestedness. Think of my business! think of the widows and orphans! the men and lads torn to pieces with shrapnel and poisoned with lyddite! [*Mrs Baines shrinks; but he goes on remorselessly*] the oceans of blood, not one drop of which is shed in a really just cause! the ravaged crops! the peaceful peasants forced, women and men, to till their fields under the fire of opposing armies on pain of starvation! the bad blood of the fierce little cowards at home who egg on others to fight for the gratification of their national vanity! All this makes money for me: I am never richer, never busier than when the papers are full of it. Well, it is your work to preach peace on earth and goodwill to men. [*Mrs Baines's face lights up again*]. Every convert you make is a vote against war. [*Her lips move in prayer*]. Yet I give you this money to help you to hasten my own commercial ruin. [*He gives her the cheque*].

CUSINS [*mounting the form in an ecstasy of mischief*] The millenium will be inaugurated by the unselfishness of Undershaft and Bodger. Oh be joyful! [*He takes the drum-sticks from his pocket and flourishes them*].

MRS BAINES [*taking the cheque*] The longer I live the more proof I see that there is an Infinite Goodness that turns everything to the work of salvation sooner or later. Who would have thought that any good could have come out of war and drink? And yet their profits are brought today to the feet of salvation to do its blessed work. [*She is affected to tears*].

JENNY [*running to Mrs Baines and throwing her arms around her*] Oh dear! how blessed, how glorious it all is!

CUSINS [*in a convulsion of irony*] Let us seize this unspeakable moment. Let us march to the great meeting at once. Excuse me just an instant. [*He rushes into the shelter. Jenny takes her tambourine from the drum head*].

MRS BAINES. Mr Undershaft: have you ever seen a thousand people fall on their knees with one impulse and pray? Come with us to the meeting. Barbara shall tell them that the Army is saved, and saved through you.

CUSINS [*returning impetuously from the shelter with a flag and a trombone, and coming between Mrs Baines and Undershaft*] You shall carry the flag down the first street, Mrs Baines [*he gives her the flag*]. Mr Undershaft is a gifted trombonist: he shall intone an Olympian diapason to the West Ham Salvation March. [*Aside to Undershaft, as he forces the trombone on him*] Blow, Machiavelli, blow.

UNDERSHAFT [*aside to him, as he takes the trombone*] The trumpet in Zion! [*Cusins rushes to the drum, which he takes up and puts on. Undershaft continues, aloud*] I will do my best. I could vamp a bass if I knew the tune.

CUSINS. It is a wedding chorus from one of Donizetti's operas; but we have converted it. We convert everything to good here, including Bodger. You remember the chorus. "For thee immense rejoicing—immenso giubilo—immenso giubilo." [*With drum obbligato*] Rum tum ti tum tum, tum tum ti ta—

BARBARA. Dolly: you are breaking my heart.

CUSINS. What is a broken heart more or less here? Dionysos Undershaft has descended. I am possessed.

MRS BAINES. Come, Barbara: I must have my dear Major to carry the flag with me.

JENNY. Yes, yes, Major darling.

CUSINS [*snatches the tambourine out of Jenny's hand and mutely offers it to Barbara*].

BARBARA [*coming forward a little as she puts the offer behind her with a shudder, whilst Cusins recklessly tosses the tambourine back to Jenny and goes to the gate*] I cant come.

JENNY. Not come!

MRS BAINES [*with tears in her eyes*] Barbara: do you think I am wrong to take the money?

BARBARA [*impulsively going to her and kissing her*] No, no: God help you, dear, you must; you are saving the Army. Go; and may you have a great meeting!

JENNY. But arnt you coming?

BARBARA. No. [*She begins taking off the silver S brooch from her collar*].

MRS BAINES. Barbara: what are you doing?

JENNY. Why are you taking your badge off? You cant be going to leave us, Major.

BARBARA [*quietly*] Father: come here.

UNDERSHAFT [*coming to her*] My dear! [*Seeing that she is going to pin the badge on his collar, he retreats to the penthouse in some alarm*].

BARBARA [*following him*] Dont be frightened. [*She pins the badge on and steps back towards the table, shewing him to the others*] There! It's not much for £5000, is it?

MRS BAINES. Barbara: if you wont come and pray with us, promise me you will pray for us.

BARBARA. I cant pray now. Perhaps I shall never pray again.

MRS BAINES. Barbara!

JENNY. Major!

BARBARA [*almost delirious*] I cant bear any more. Quick march!

CUSINS [*calling to the procession in the street outside*] Off we go. Play up, there! Immenso giubilo. [*He gives the time with his drum; and the band strikes up the march, which rapidly becomes more distant as the procession moves briskly away*].

MRS BAINES. I must go, dear. Youre overworked: you will be all right tomorrow. We'll never lose you. Now Jenny: step out with the old flag. Blood and Fire! [*She marches out through the gate with her flag*].

JENNY. Glory Hallelujah! [*flourishing her tambourine and marching*].

UNDERSHAFT [*to Cusins, as he marches out past him easing the slide of his trombone*] "My ducats and my daughter"!

CUSINS [*following him out*] Money and gunpowder!

BARBARA. Drunkenness and Murder! My God: why hast thou forsaken me?

She sinks on the form with her face buried in her hands. The march passes away into silence. Bill Walker steals across to her.

BILL [*taunting*] Wot prawce selvytion nah?

SHIRLEY. Dont you hit her when she's down.

BILL. She itt me wen aw wiz dahn. Waw shouldnt Aw git a bit o me aown beck?

BARBARA [*raising her head*] I didnt take your money, Bill. [*She crosses the yard to the gate and turns her back on the two men to hide her face from them*].

BILL [*sneering after her*] Naow, it warnt enaff for you. [*Turning to the drum, he misses the money*] Ellow! If you aint took it sammun else ez. Weres it gorn? Bly me if Jenny Ill didnt tike it arter all!

RUMMY [*screaming at him from the loft*] You lie, you dirty blackguard! Snobby Price pinched it off the drum when he took up his cap. I was up here all the time an see im do it.

BILL. Wot! Stowl maw manney! Waw didnt you call thief on him, you silly aold macker you?

RUMMY. To serve you aht for ittin me acrost the fice. It's cost y'pahnd, that az. [*Raising a pæan of squalid triumph*] I done you. I'm even with you. Ive ad it aht o y—[*Bill snatches up Shirley's mug and hurls it at her. She slams the loft door and vanishes. The mug smashes against the door and falls in fragments*].

BILL [*beginning to chuckle*] Tell us, aol menn, wot o'clock this mawnin was it wen im as they call Snobby Prawce was sived?

BARBARA [*turning to him more composedly, and*

with unspoiled sweetness] About half past twelve, Bill. And he pinched your pound at a quarter to two. *I* know. Well, you cant afford to lose it. I'll send it to you.

BILL [*his voice and accent suddenly improving*] Not if Aw wiz to stawve for it. Aw aint to be bought.

SHIRLEY. Aint you? Youd sell yourself to the devil for a pint o beer; ony there aint no devil to make the offer.

BILL [*unshamed*] Sao Aw would, mite, and often ev, cheerful. But she cawnt baw me. [*Approaching Barbara*] You wanted maw saoul, did you? Well, you aint got it.

BARBARA. I nearly got it, Bill. But weve sold it back to you for ten thousand pounds.

SHIRLEY. And dear at the money!

BARBARA. No, Peter: it was worth more than money.

BILL [*salvationproof*] It's nao good: you cawnt get rahnd me nah. Aw downt blieve in it; and Awve seen tody that Aw was rawt. [*Going*] Sao long, aol soupkitchener! Ta, ta, Mijor Earl's Grendorter! [*Turning at the gate*] Wot prawce selvytion nah? Snobby Prawce! Ha! ha!

BARBARA [*offering her hand*] Goodbye, Bill.

BILL [*taken aback, half plucks his cap off; then shoves it on again defiantly*] Git aht. [*Barbara drops her hand, discouraged. He has a twinge of remorse*]. But thets aw rawt, you knaow. Nathink pasnl. Naow mellice. Sao long, Judy. [*He goes*].

BARBARA. No malice. So long, Bill.

SHIRLEY [*shaking his head*] You make too much of him, miss, in your innocence.

BARBARA [*going to him*] Peter: I'm like you now. Cleaned out, and lost my job.

SHIRLEY. Youve youth an hope. Thats two better than me.

BARBARA. I'll get you a job, Peter. Thats hope for you: the youth will have to be enough for me. [*She counts her money*]. I have just enough left for two teas at Lockharts, a Rowton doss for you, and my tram and bus home. [*He frowns and rises with offended pride. She takes his arm*]. Dont be proud, Peter: it's sharing between friends. And promise me youll talk to me and not let me cry. [*She draws him towards the gate*].

SHIRLEY. Well, I'm not accustomed to talk to the like of you—

BARBARA [*urgently*] Yes, yes: you must talk to me. Tell me about Tom Paine's books and Bradlaugh's lectures. Come along.

SHIRLEY. Ah, if you would only read Tom Paine in the proper spirit, miss! [*They go out through the gate together*].

ACT III

Next day after lunch Lady Britomart is writing in the library in Wilton Crescent. Sarah is reading in the armchair near the window. Barbara, in ordinary fashionable dress, pale and brooding, is on the settee. Charles Lomax enters. He starts on seeing Barbara fashionably attired and in low spirits.

LOMAX. Youve left off your uniform!

Barbara says nothing; but an expression of pain passes over her face.

LADY BRITOMART [*warning him in low tones to be careful*] Charles!

LOMAX [*much concerned, coming behind the settee and bending sympathetically over Barbara*] I'm awfully sorry, Barbara. You know I helped you all I could with the concertina and so forth. [*Momentously*] Still, I have never shut my eyes to the fact that there is a certain amount of tosh about the Salvation Army. Now the claims of the Church of England—

LADY BRITOMART. Thats enough, Charles. Speak of something suited to your mental capacity.

LOMAX. But surely the Church of England is suited to all our capacities.

BARBARA [*pressing his hand*] Thank you for your sympathy, Cholly. Now go and spoon with Sarah.

LOMAX [*dragging a chair from the writing table and seating himself affectionately by Sarah's side*] How is my ownest today?

SARAH. I wish you wouldnt tell Cholly to do things, Barbara. He always comes straight and does them. Cholly: we're going to the works this afternoon.

LOMAX. What works?

SARAH. The cannon works.

LOMAX. What? your governor's shop!

SARAH. Yes.

LOMAX. Oh I say!

Cusins enters in poor condition. He also starts visibly when he sees Barbara without her uniform.

BARBARA. I expected you this morning, Dolly. Didnt you guess that?

CUSINS [*sitting down beside her*] I'm sorry. I have only just breakfasted.

SARAH. But weve just finished lunch.

BARBARA. Have you had one of your bad nights?

CUSINS. No: I had rather a good night: in fact, one of the most remarkable nights I have ever passed.

BARBARA. The meeting?

CUSINS. No: after the meeting.

LADY BRITOMART. You should have gone to bed after the meeting. What were you doing?

CUSINS. Drinking.

LADY BRITOMART.⎫ ⎧Adolphus!
SARAH.   ⎬ ⎨Dolly!
BARBARA.   ⎪ ⎪Dolly!
LOMAX.   ⎭ ⎩Oh I say!

LADY BRITOMART. What were you drinking, may I ask?

CUSINS. A most devilish kind of Spanish burgundy, warranted free from added alcohol: a Temperance burgundy in fact. Its richness in natural alcohol made any addition superfluous.

BARBARA. Are you joking, Dolly?

CUSINS [*patiently*] No. I have been making a night of it with the nominal head of this household: that is all.

LADY BRITOMART. Andrew made you drunk!

CUSINS. No: he only provided the wine. I think it was Dionysos who made me drunk. [*To Barbara*] I told you I was possessed.

LADY BRITOMART. Youre not sober yet. Go home to bed at once.

CUSINS. I have never before ventured to reproach you, Lady Brit; but how could you marry the Prince of Darkness?

LADY BRITOMART. It was much more excusable to marry him than to get drunk with him. That is a new accomplishment of Andrew's, by the way. He usent to drink.

CUSINS. He doesnt now. He only sat there and completed the wreck of my moral basis, the rout of my convictions, the purchase of my soul. He cares for you, Barbara. That is what makes him so dangerous to me.

BARBARA. That has nothing to do with it, Dolly. There are larger loves and diviner dreams than the fireside ones. You know that, dont you?

CUSINS. Yes: that is our understanding. I know it. I hold to it. Unless he can win me on that holier ground he may amuse me for a while; but he can get no deeper hold, strong as he is.

BARBARA. Keep to that; and the end will be right. Now tell me what happened at the meeting?

CUSINS. It was an amazing meeting. Mrs Baines almost died of emotion. Jenny Hill simply gibbered with hysteria. The Prince of Darkness played his trombone like a madman: its brazen roarings were like the laughter of the damned. 117 conversions took place then and there. They prayed with the most touching sincerity and gratitude for Bodger, and for the anonymous donor of the £5000. Your father would not let his name be given.

LOMAX. That was rather fine of the old man, you know. Most chaps would have wanted the advertisement.

CUSINS. He said all the charitable institutions would be down on him like kites on a battle-field if he gave his name.

LADY BRITOMART. Thats Andrew all over.

He never does a proper thing without giving an improper reason for it.

CUSINS. He convinced me that I have all my life been doing improper things for proper reasons.

LADY BRITOMART. Adolphus: now that Barbara has left the Salvation Army, you had better leave it too. I will not have you playing that drum in the streets.

CUSINS. Your orders are already obeyed, Lady Brit.

BARBARA. Dolly: were you ever really in earnest about it? Would you have joined if you had never seen me?

CUSINS [*disingenuously*] Well—er—well, possibly, as a collector of religions—

LOMAX [*cunningly*] Not as a drummer, though, you know. You are a very clearheaded brainy chap, Dolly; and it must have been apparent to you that there is a certain amount of tosh about—

LADY BRITOMART. Charles: if you must drivel, drivel like a grown-up man and not like a schoolboy.

LOMAX [*out of countenance*] Well, drivel is drivel, dont you know, whatever a man's age.

LADY BRITOMART. In good society in England, Charles, men drivel at all ages by repeating silly formulas with an air of wisdom. Schoolboys make their own formulas out of slang, like you. When they reach your age, and get political private secretaryships and things of that sort, they drop slang and get their formulas out of The Spectator or The Times. You had better confine yourself to The Times. You will find that there is a certain amount of tosh about The Times; but at least its language is reputable.

LOMAX [*overwhelmed*] You are so awfully strongminded, Lady Brit—

LADY BRITOMART. Rubbish! [*Morrison comes in*]. What is it?

MORRISON. If you please, my lady, Mr Undershaft has just drove up to the door.

LADY BRITOMART. Well, let him in. [*Morrison hesitates*]. Whats the matter with you?

MORRISON. Shall I announce him, my lady; or is he at home here, so to speak, my lady?

LADY BRITOMART. Announce him.

MORRISON. Thank you, my lady. You wont mind my asking, I hope. The occasion is in a manner of speaking new to me.

LADY BRITOMART. Quite right. Go and let him in.

MORRISON. Thank you, my lady. [*He withdraws*].

LADY BRITOMART. Children: go and get ready. [*Sarah and Barbara go upstairs for their out-of-door wraps*]. Charles: go and tell Stephen to come down here in five minutes: you will find him in the drawing room. [*Charles goes*]. Adolphus: tell them to send round the carriage in about fifteen minutes. [*Adolphus goes*].

MORRISON [*at the door*] Mr Undershaft.

Undershaft comes in. Morrison goes out.

UNDERSHAFT. Alone! How fortunate!

LADY BRITOMART [*rising*] Dont be sentimental, Andrew. Sit down. [*She sits on the settee: he sits beside her, on her left. She comes to the point before he has time to breathe*]. Sarah must have £800 a year until Charles Lomax comes into his property. Barbara will need more, and need it permanently, because Adolphus hasnt any property.

UNDERSHAFT [*resignedly*] Yes, my dear: I will see to it. Anything else? for yourself, for instance?

LADY BRITOMART. I want to talk to you about Stephen.

UNDERSHAFT [*rather wearily*] Dont, my dear. Stephen doesnt interest me.

LADY BRITOMART. He does interest me. He is our son.

UNDERSHAFT. Do you really think so? He has induced us to bring him into the world; but he chose his parents very incongruously, I think. I see nothing of myself in him, and less of you.

LADY BRITOMART. Andrew: Stephen is an excellent son, and a most steady, capable, highminded young man. You are simply trying to find an excuse for disinheriting him.

UNDERSHAFT. My dear Biddy: the Undershaft tradition disinherits him. It would be dishonest of me to leave the cannon foundry to my son.

LADY BRITOMART. It would be most unnatural and improper of you to leave it to anyone else, Andrew. Do you suppose this wicked and immoral tradition can be kept up for ever? Do you pretend that Stephen could not carry on the foundry just as well as all the other sons of the big business houses?

UNDERSHAFT. Yes: he could learn the office routine without understanding the business, like all the other sons; and the firm would go on by its own momentum until the real Undershaft—probably an Italian or a German—would invent a new method and cut him out.

LADY BRITOMART. There is nothing that any Italian or German could do that Stephen could not do. And Stephen at least has breeding.

UNDERSHAFT. The son of a foundling! Nonsense!

LADY BRITOMART. My son, Andrew! And even you may have good blood in your veins for all you know.

UNDERSHAFT. True. Probably I have. That is another argument in favor of a foundling.

LADY BRITOMART. Andrew: dont be aggravating. And dont be wicked. At present you are both.

UNDERSHAFT. This conversation is part of the Undershaft tradition, Biddy. Every Undershaft's wife has treated him to it ever since the house was founded. It is mere waste of breath. If the tradition be ever broken it will be for an abler man than Stephen.

LADY BRITOMART [*pouting*] Then go away.

UNDERSHAFT [*deprecatory*] Go away!

LADY BRITOMART. Yes: go away. If you will do nothing for Stephen, you are not wanted here. Go to your foundling, whoever he is; and look after him.

UNDERSHAFT. The fact is, Biddy—

LADY BRITOMART. Dont call me Biddy. I dont call you Andy.

UNDERSHAFT. I will not call my wife Britomart: it is not good sense. Seriously, my love, the Undershaft tradition has landed me in a difficulty. I am getting on in years; and my partner Lazarus has at last made a stand and insisted that the succession must be settled one way or the other; and of course he is quite right. You see, I havnt found a fit successor yet.

LADY BRITOMART [*obstinately*] There is Stephen.

UNDERSHAFT. Thats just it: all the foundlings I can find are exactly like Stephen.

LADY BRITOMART. Andrew!!

UNDERSHAFT. I want a man with no relations and no schooling: that is, a man who would be out of the running altogether if he were not a strong man. And I cant find him. Every blessed foundling nowadays is snapped up in his infancy by Barnardo homes, or School Board Officers, or Boards of Guardians; and if he shews the least ability he is fastened on by schoolmasters; trained to win scholarships like a racehorse; crammed with secondhand ideas; drilled and disciplined in docility and what they call good taste; and lamed for life so that he is fit for nothing but teaching. If you want to keep the foundry in the family, you had better find an eligible foundling and marry him to Barbara.

LADY BRITOMART. Ah! Barbara! Your pet! You would sacrifice Stephen to Barbara.

UNDERSHAFT. Cheerfully. And you, my dear, would boil Barbara to make soup for Stephen.

LADY BRITOMART. Andrew: this is not a question of our likings and dislikings: it is a question of duty. It is your duty to make Stephen your successor.

UNDERSHAFT. Just as much as it is your duty to submit to your husband. Come, Biddy! these tricks of the governing class are of no use with me. I am one of the governing class myself; and it is waste of time giving tracts to a missionary. I have the power in this matter; and I am not to be humbugged into using it for your purposes.

LADY BRITOMART. Andrew: you can talk my head off; but you cant change wrong into right. And your tie is all on one side. Put it straight.

UNDERSHAFT [*disconcerted*] It wont stay unless it's pinned [*he fumbles at it with childish grimaces*]—

Stephen comes in.

STEPHEN [*at the door*] I beg your pardon [*about to retire*].

LADY BRITOMART. No: come in, Stephen. [*Stephen comes forward to his mother's writing table*].

UNDERSHAFT [*not very cordially*] Good afternoon.

STEPHEN [*coldly*] Good afternoon.

UNDERSHAFT [*to Lady Britomart*] He knows all about the tradition, I suppose?

LADY BRITOMART. Yes. [*To Stephen*] It is what I told you last night, Stephen.

UNDERSHAFT [*sulkily*] I understand you want to come into the cannon business.

STEPHEN. *I* go into trade! Certainly not.

UNDERSHAFT [*opening his eyes, greatly eased in mind and manner*] Oh! in that case—

LADY BRITOMART. Cannons are not trade, Stephen. They are enterprise.

STEPHEN. I have no intention of becoming a man of business in any sense. I have no capacity for business and no taste for it. I intend to devote myself to politics.

UNDERSHAFT [*rising*] My dear boy: this is an immense relief to me. And I trust it may prove an equally good thing for the country. I was afraid you would consider yourself disparaged and slighted [*He moves towards Stephen as if to shake hands with him*].

LADY BRITOMART [*rising and interposing*] Stephen: I cannot allow you to throw away an enormous property like this.

STEPHEN [*stiffly*] Mother: there must be an end of treating me as a child, if you please. [*Lady Britomart recoils, deeply wounded by his tone*]. Until last night I did not take your attitude seriously, because I did not think you meant it seriously. But I find now that

you left me in the dark as to matters which you should have explained to me years ago. I am extremely hurt and offended. Any further discussion of my intentions had better take place with my father, as between one man and another.

LADY BRITOMART. Stephen! [*She sits down again, her eyes filling with tears*].

UNDERSHAFT [*with grave compassion*] You see, my dear, it is only the big men who can be treated as children.

STEPHEN. I am sorry, mother, that you have forced me—

UNDERSHAFT [*stopping him*] Yes, yes, yes, yes: thats all right, Stephen. She wont interfere with you any more: your independence is achieved: you have won your latchkey. Dont rub it in; and above all, dont apologize. [*He resumes his seat*]. Now what about your future, as between one man and another—I beg your pardon, Biddy: as between two men and a woman.

LADY BRITOMART [*who has pulled herself together strongly*] I quite understand, Stephen. By all means go your own way if you feel strong enough. [*Stephen sits down magisterially in the chair at the writing table with an air of affirming his majority*].

UNDERSHAFT. It is settled that you do not ask for the succession to the cannon business.

STEPHEN. I hope it is settled that I repudiate the cannon business.

UNDERSHAFT. Come, come! dont be so devilishly sulky: it's boyish. Freedom should be generous. Besides, I owe you a fair start in life in exchange for disinheriting you. You cant become prime minister all at once. Havnt you a turn for something? What about literature, art, and so forth?

STEPHEN. I have nothing of the artist about me, either in faculty or character, thank Heaven.

UNDERSHAFT. A philosopher, perhaps? Eh?

STEPHEN. I make no such ridiculous pretension.

UNDERSHAFT. Just so. Well, there is the

army, the navy, the Church, the Bar. The Bar requires some ability. What about the Bar?

STEPHEN. I have not studied law. And I am afraid I have not the necessary push—I believe that is the name barristers give to their vulgarity—for success in pleading.

UNDERSHAFT. Rather a difficult case, Stephen. Hardly anything left but the stage, is there? [*Stephen makes an impatient movement*]. Well, come! is there anything you know or care for?

STEPHEN [*rising and looking at him steadily*] I know the difference between right and wrong.

UNDERSHAFT [*hugely tickled*] You dont say so! What! no capacity for business, no knowledge of law, no sympathy with art, no pretension to philosophy; only a simple knowledge of the secret that has puzzled all the philosophers, baffled all the lawyers, muddled all the men of business, and ruined most of the artists: the secret of right and wrong. Why, man, youre a genius, a master of masters, a god! At twentyfour, too!

STEPHEN [*keeping his temper with difficulty*] You are pleased to be facetious. I pretend to nothing more than any honourable English gentleman claims as his birthright [*he sits down angrily*].

UNDERSHAFT. Oh, thats everybody's birthright. Look at poor little Jenny Hill, the Salvation lassie! she would think you were laughing at her if you asked her to stand up in the street and teach grammar or geography or mathematics or even drawing room dancing; but it never occurs to her to doubt that she can teach morals and religion. You are all alike, you respectable people. You cant tell me the bursting strain of a ten-inch gun, which is a very simple matter; but you all think you can tell me the bursting strain of a man under temptation. You darent handle high explosives; but youre all ready to handle honesty and truth and justice and the whole duty of man, and

kill one another at that game. What a country! What a world!

LADY BRITOMART [*uneasily*] What do you think he had better do, Andrew?

UNDERSHAFT. Oh, just what he wants to do. He knows nothing and he thinks he knows everything. That points clearly to a political career. Get him a private secretaryship to someone who can get him an Under Secretaryship; and then leave him alone. He will find his natural and proper place in the end on the Treasury Bench.

STEPHEN [*springing up again*] I am sorry, sir, that you force me to forget the respect due to you as my father. I am an Englishman and I will not hear the Government of my country insulted. [*He thrusts his hands in his pockets, and walks angrily across to the window*].

UNDERSHAFT [*with a touch of brutality*] The government of your country! *I* am the government of your country: I, and Lazarus. Do you suppose that you and half a dozen amateurs like you, sitting in a row in that foolish gabble shop, can govern Undershaft and Lazarus? No, my friend: you will do what pays us. You will make war when it suits us, and keep peace when it doesnt. You will find out that trade requires certain measures when we have decided on those measures. When I want anything to keep my dividends up, you will discover that my want is a national need. When other people want something to keep my dividends down, you will call out the police and military. And in return you shall have the support and applause of my newspapers, and the delight of imagining that you are a great statesman. Government of your country! Be off with you, my boy, and play with your caucuses and leading articles and historic· parties and great leaders and burning questions and the rest of your toys. *I* am going back to my counting-house to pay the piper and call the tune.

STEPHEN [*actually smiling, and putting his hand on his father's shoulder with indulgent patronage*]

Really, my dear father, it is impossible to be angry with you. You dont know how absurd all this sounds to me. You are properly proud of having been industrious enough to make money; and it is greatly to your credit that you have made so much of it. But it has kept you in circles where you are valued for your money and deferred to for it, instead of in the doubtless very old-fashioned and behind-the-times public school and university where I formed my habits of mind. It is natural for you to think that money governs England; but you must allow me to think I know better.

UNDERSHAFT. And what does govern England, pray?

STEPHEN. Character, father, character.

UNDERSHAFT. Whose character? Yours or mine?

STEPHEN. Neither yours nor mine, father, but the best elements in the English national character.

UNDERSHAFT. Stephen: Ive found your profession for you. Youre a born journalist. I'll start you with a high-toned weekly review. There!

Before Stephen can reply Sarah, Barbara, Lomax, and Cusins come in ready for walking. Barbara crosses the room to the window and looks out. Cusins drifts amiably to the armchair. Lomax remains near the door, whilst Sarah comes to her mother.

Stephen goes to the smaller writing table and busies himself with his letters.

SARAH. Go and get ready, mamma: the carriage is waiting. [*Lady Britomart leaves the room*].

UNDERSHAFT [*to Sarah*] Good day, my dear. Good afternoon, Mr Lomax.

LOMAX [*vaguely*] Ahdedoo.

UNDERSHAFT [*to Cusins*] Quite well after last night, Euripides, eh?

CUSINS. As well as can be expected.

UNDERSHAFT. Thats right. [*To Barbara*] So you are coming to see my death and devastation factory, Barbara?

BARBARA [*at the window*] You came yesterday to see my salvation factory. I promised you a return visit.

LOMAX [*coming forward between Sarah and Undershaft*] Youll find it awfully interesting. Ive been through the Woolwich Arsenal; and it gives you a ripping feeling of security, you know, to think of the lot of beggars we could kill if it came to fighting. [*To Undershaft, with sudden solemnity*] Still, it must be rather an awful reflection for you, from the religious point of view as it were. Youre getting on, you know, and all that.

SARAH. You dont mind Cholly's imbecility, papa, do you?

LOMAX [*much taken aback*] Oh I say!

UNDERSHAFT. Mr Lomax looks at the matter in a very proper spirit, my dear.

LOMAX. Just so. Thats all I meant, I assure you.

SARAH. Are you coming, Stephen?

STEPHEN. Well, I am rather busy—er— [*Magnanimously*] Oh well, yes: I'll come. That is, if there is room for me.

UNDERSHAFT. I can take two with me in a little motor I am experimenting with for field use. You wont mind its being rather unfashionable. It's not painted yet; but it's bullet proof.

LOMAX [*appalled at the prospect of confronting Wilton Crescent in an unpainted motor*] Oh I say!

SARAH. The carriage for me, thank you. Barbara doesnt mind what she's seen in.

LOMAX. I say, Dolly, old chap: do you really mind the car being a guy? Because of course if you do I'll go in it. Still—

CUSINS. I prefer it.

LOMAX. Thanks awfully, old man. Come, my ownest. [*He hurries out to secure his seat in the carriage. Sarah follows him*].

CUSINS [*moodily walking across to Lady Britomart's writing table*] Why are we two coming to this Works Department of Hell? that is what I ask myself.

BARBARA. I have always thought of it as

a sort of pit where lost creatures with blackened faces stirred up smoky fires and were driven and tormented by my father? Is it like that, dad?

UNDERSHAFT [*scandalized*] My dear! It is a spotlessly clean and beautiful hillside town.

CUSINS. With a Methodist chapel? Oh do say theres a Methodist chapel.

UNDERSHAFT. There are two: a Primitive one and a sophisticated one. There is even an Ethical Society; but it is not much patronized, as my men are all strongly religious. In the High Explosives Sheds they object to the presence of Agnostics as unsafe.

CUSINS. And yet they dont object to you!

BARBARA. Do they obey all your orders?

UNDERSHAFT. I never give them any orders. When I speak to one of them it is "Well, Jones, is baby doing well? and has Mrs Jones made a good recovery?" "Nicely, thank you, sir." And thats all.

CUSINS. But Jones has to be kept in order. How do you maintain discipline among your men?

UNDERSHAFT. I dont. They do. You see, the one thing Jones wont stand is any rebellion from the man under him, or any assertion of social equality between the wife of the man with 4 shillings a week less than himself, and Mrs Jones! Of course they all rebel against me, theoretically. Practically, every man of them keeps the man just below him in his place. I never meddle with them. I never bully them. I dont even bully Lazarus. I say that certain things are to be done; but I dont order anybody to do them. I dont say, mind you, that there is no ordering about and snubbing and even bullying. The men snub the boys and order them about; the carmen snub the sweepers; the artisans snub the unskilled laborers; the foremen drive and bully both the laborers and artisans; the assistant engineers find fault with the foremen; the chief engineers drop on the assistants; the departmental managers worry the chiefs; and the clerks have tall hats and hymnbooks and keep up the social tone by refusing to associate on equal terms with anybody. The result is a colossal profit, which comes to me.

CUSINS [*revolted*] You really are a—well, what I was saying yesterday.

BARBARA. What was he saying yesterday?

UNDERSHAFT. Never mind, my dear. He thinks I have made you unhappy. Have I?

BARBARA. Do you think I can be happy in this vulgar silly dress? I! who have worn the uniform. Do you understand what you have done to me? Yesterday I had a man's soul in my hand. I set him in the way of life with his face to salvation. But when we took your money he turned back to drunkenness and derision. [*With intense conviction*] I will never forgive you that. If I had a child, and you destroyed its body with your explosives—if you murdered Dolly with your horrible guns—I could forgive you if my forgiveness would open the gates of heaven to you. But to take a human soul from me, and turn it into the soul of a wolf! that is worse than any murder.

UNDERSHAFT. Does my daughter despair so easily? Can you strike a man to the heart and leave no mark on him?

BARBARA [*her face lighting up*] Oh, you are right: he can never be lost now: where was my faith?

CUSINS. Oh, clever clever devil!

BARBARA. You may be a devil; but God speaks through you sometimes. [*She takes her father's hands and kisses them*]. You have given me back my happiness: I feel it deep down now, though my spirit is troubled.

UNDERSHAFT. You have learnt something. That always feels at first as if you had lost something.

BARBARA. Well, take me to the factory of death; and let me learn something more. There must be some truth or other behind all this frightful irony. Come, Dolly. [*She goes out*].

CUSINS. My guardian angel! [*To Undershaft*] Avaunt! [*He follows Barbara*].

STEPHEN [*quietly, at the writing table*] You must not mind Cusins, father. He is a very amiable good fellow; but he is a Greek scholar and naturally a little eccentric.

UNDERSHAFT. Ah, quite so. Thank you, Stephen. Thank you. [*He goes out*].

Stephen smiles patronizingly; buttons his coat responsibly; and crosses the room to the the door. Lady Britomart, dressed for out-of-doors, opens it before he reaches it. She looks round for the others; looks at Stephen; and turns to go without a word.

STEPHEN [*embarrassed*] Mother—

LADY BRITOMART. Dont be apologetic, Stephen. And dont forget that you have outgrown your mother. [*She goes out*].

Perivale St Andrews lies between two Middlesex hills, half climbing the northern one. It is an almost smokeless town of white walls, roofs of narrow green slates or red tiles, tall trees, domes, campaniles, and slender chimney shafts, beautifully situated and beautiful in itself. The best view of it is obtained from the crest of a slope about half a mile to the east, where the high explosives are dealt with. The foundry lies hidden in the depths between, the tops of its chimneys sprouting like huge skittles into the middle distance. Across the crest runs on emplacement of concrete, with a firestep, and a parapet which suggests a fortification, because there is a huge cannon of the obsolete Woolwich Infant pattern peering across it at the town. The cannon is mounted on an experimental gun carriage: possibly the original model of the Undershaft disappearing rampart gun alluded to by Stephen. The firestep, being a convenient place to sit, is furnished here and there with straw disc cushions; and at one place there is the additional luxury of a fur rug.

Barbara is standing on the firestep, looking over the parapet towards the town. On her right is the cannon; on her left the end of a shed raised on piles, with a ladder of three or four steps up to the door, which opens outwards and has a little wooden landing at the threshold, with a fire bucket in the corner of the landing. Several dummy soldiers more or less mutilated, with straw protruding from their gashes, have been shoved out of the way under the landing. A few others are nearly upright against the shed; and one has fallen forward and lies, like a grotesque corpse, on the emplacement. The parapet stops short of the shed, leaving a gap which is the beginning of the path down the hill through the foundry to the town. The rug is on the firestep near this gap. Down on the emplacement behind the cannon is a trolley carrying a huge conical bombshell with a red band painted on it. Further to the right is the door of an office, which, like the sheds, is of the lightest possible construction.

Cusins arrives by the path from the town.

BARBARA. Well?

CUSINS. Not a ray of hope. Everything perfect! wonderful! real! It only needs a cathedral to be a heavenly city instead of a hellish one.

BARBARA. Have you found out whether they have done anything for old Peter Shirley?

CUSINS. They have found him a job as gatekeeper and timekeeper. He's frightfully miserable. He calls the time-keeping brain-work, and says he isnt used to it; and his gate lodge is so splendid that he's ashamed to use the rooms, and skulks in the scullery.

BARBARA. Poor Peter!

Stephen arrives from the town. He carries a fieldglass.

STEPHEN [*enthusiastically*] Have you two seen the place? Why did you leave us?

CUSINS. I wanted to see everything I was not intended to see; and Barbara wanted to make the men talk.

STEPHEN. Have you found anything discreditable?

CUSINS. No. They call him Dandy Andy and are proud of his being a cunning old rascal; but it's all horribly, frightfully, immorally, unanswerably perfect.

Sarah arrives.

SARAH. Heavens! what a place! [*She crosses to the trolley*]. Did you see the nursing home!? [*She sits down on the shell*].

STEPHEN. Did you see the libraries and schools!?

SARAH. Did you see the ball room and the banqueting chamber in the Town Hall!?

STEPHEN. Have you gone into the insurance fund, the pension fund, the building society, the various applications of co-operation!?

Undershaft comes from the office, with a sheaf of telegrams in his hand.

UNDERSHAFT. Well, have you seen everything! I'm sorry I was called away. [*Indicating the telegrams*] Good news from Manchuria.

STEPHEN. Another Japanese victory?

UNDERSHAFT. Oh, I dont know. Which side wins does not concern us here. No: the good news is that the aerial battleship is a tremendous success. At the first trial it has wiped out a fort with three hundred soldiers in it.

CUSINS [*from the platform*] Dummy soldiers?

UNDERSHAFT [*striding across to Stephen and kicking the prostrate dummy brutally out of his way*] No: the real thing.

Cusins and Barbara exchange glances. Then Cusins sits on the step and buries his face in his hands. Barbara gravely lays her hand on his shoulder. He looks up at her in whimsical desperation.

UNDERSHAFT. Well, Stephen, what do you think of the place?

STEPHEN. Oh, magnificent. A perfect triumph of modern industry. Frankly, my dear father, I have been a fool: I had no idea of what it all meant: of the wonderful forethought, the power of organization, the administrative capacity, the financial genius, the colossal capital it represents. I have been repeating to myself as I came through your streets "Peace hath her victories no less renowned than War." I have only one misgiving about it all.

UNDERSHAFT. Out with it.

STEPHEN. Well, I cannot help thinking that all this provision for every want of your workmen may sap their independence and weaken their sense of responsibility. And greatly as we enjoyed our tea at that splendid restaurant—how they gave us all that luxury and cake and jam and cream for threepence I really cannot imagine!—still you must remember that restaurants break up home life. Look at the continent, for instance! Are you sure so much pampering is really good for the men's characters?

UNDERSHAFT. Well you see, my dear boy, when you are organizing civilization you have to make up your mind whether trouble and anxiety are good things or not. If you decide that they are, then, I take it, you simply dont organize civilization; and there you are, with trouble and anxiety enough to make us all angels! But if you decide the other way, you may as well go through with it. However, Stephen, our characters are safe here. A sufficient dose of anxiety is always provided by the fact that we may be blown to smithereens at any moment.

SARAH. By the way, papa, where do you make the explosives?

UNDERSHAFT. In separate little sheds, like that one. When one of them blows up, it costs very little; and only the people quite close to it are killed.

Stephen, who is quite close to it, looks at it rather scaredly, and moves away quickly to the cannon. At the same moment the door of the shed is thrown abruptly open; and a foreman in overalls and list slippers comes out on the little landing and holds the door for Lomax, who appears in the doorway.

LOMAX [*with studied coolness*] My good fellow: you neednt get into a state of nerves.

Nothing's going to happen to you; and I suppose it wouldnt be the end of the world if anything did. A little bit of British pluck is what you want, old chap. [*He descends and strolls across to Sarah*].

UNDERSHAFT [*to the foreman*] Anything wrong, Bilton?

BILTON [*with ironic calm*] Gentleman walked into the high explosives shed and lit a cigaret, sir: thats all.

UNDERSHAFT. Ah, quite so. [*Going over to Lomax*] Do you happen to remember what you did with the match?

LOMAX. Oh come! I'm not a fool. I took jolly good care to blow it out before I chucked it away.

BILTON. The top of it was red hot inside, sir.

LOMAX. Well, suppose it was! I didn't chuck it into any of your messes.

UNDERSHAFT. Think no more of it, Mr Lomax. By the way, would you mind lending me your matches.

LOMAX [*offering his box*] Certainly.

UNDERSHAFT. Thanks. [*He pockets the matches*].

LOMAX [*lecturing to the company generally*] You know, these high explosives dont go off like gunpowder, except when theyre in a gun. When theyre spread loose, you can put a match to them without the least risk; they just burn quietly like a bit of paper. [*Warming to the scientific interest of the subject*] Did you know that, Undershaft? Have you ever tried?

UNDERSHAFT. Not on a large scale, Mr Lomax. Bilton will give you a sample of gun cotton when you are leaving if you ask him. You can experiment with it at home. [*Bilton looks puzzled*].

SARAH. Bilton will do nothing of the sort, papa. I suppose it's your busines to blow up the Russians and Japs; but you might really stop short of blowing up poor Cholly. [*Bilton gives it up and retires into the shed*].

LOMAX. My ownest, there is no danger. [*He sits beside her on the shell*].

Lady Britomart arrives from the town with a bouquet.

LADY BRITOMART [*impetuously*] Andrew: you shouldnt have let me see this place.

UNDERSHAFT. Why, my dear?

LADY BRITOMART. Never mind why: you shouldnt have: thats all. To think of all that [*indicating the town*] being yours! and that you have kept it to yourself all these years!

UNDERSHAFT. It does not belong to me. I belong to it. It is the Undershaft inheritance.

LADY BRITOMART. It is not. Your ridiculous cannons and that noisy banging foundry may be the Undershaft inheritance; but all that plate and linen, all that furniture and those houses and orchards and gardens belong to us. They belong to me: they are not a man's business. I wont give them up. You must be out of your senses to throw them all away; and if you persist in such folly, I will call in a doctor.

UNDERSHAFT [*stooping to smell the bouquet*] Where did you get the flowers, my dear?

LADY BRITOMART. Your men presented them to me in your William Morris Labor Church.

CUSINS. Oh! It needed only that. A Labor Church! [*he mounts the firestep distractedly, and leans with his elbows on the parapet, turning his back to them*].

LADY BRITOMART. Yes, with Morris's words in mosaic letters ten feet high round the dome. NO MAN IS GOOD ENOUGH TO BE ANOTHER MAN'S MASTER. The cynicism of it!

UNDERSHAFT. It shocked the men at first, I am afraid. But now they take no more notice of it than of the ten commandments in church.

LADY BRITOMART. Andrew: you are trying to put me off the subject of the inheritance by profane jokes. Well, you shant. I dont ask it any longer for Stephen: he has inherited far too much of your perversity to be fit for it. But Barbara has rights as well as Stephen. Why should not Adolphus succeed to the inheritance? I could manage the town for him; and he can look after the cannons, if they are really necessary.

UNDERSHAFT. I should ask nothing better if Adolphus were a foundling. He is exactly the sort of new blood that is wanted in English business. But he's not a foundling; and theres an end of it. [*He makes for the office door*].

CUSINS [*turning to them*] Not quite. [*They all turn and stare at him*]. I think—Mind! I am not committing myself in any way as to my future course—but I think the foundling difficulty can be got over. [*He jumps down to the emplacement*].

UNDERSHAFT [*coming back to him*] What do you mean?

CUSINS. Well, I have something to say which is in the nature of a confession.

SARAH.
LADY BRITOMART.
BARBARA.
STEPHEN.
} Confession!

LOMAX. Oh I say!

CUSINS. Yes, a confession. Listen, all. Until I met Barbara I thought myself in the main an honorable, truthful man, because I wanted the approval of my conscience more than I wanted anything else. But the moment I saw Barbara, I wanted her far more than the approval of my conscience.

LADY BRITOMART. Adolphus!

CUSINS. It is true. You accused me yourself, Lady Brit, of joining the Army to worship Barbara; and so I did. She bought my soul like a flower at a street corner; but she bought it for herself.

UNDERSHAFT. What! Not for Dionysos or another?

CUSINS. Dionysos and all the others are in herself. I adored what was divine in her, and was therefore a true worshipper. But I was romantic about her too. I thought she was a woman of the people, and that a marriage with a professor of Greek would be far beyond the wildest social ambition of her rank.

LADY BRITOMART. Adolphus!!

LOMAX. Oh I say!!!

CUSINS. When I learnt the horrible truth—

LADY BRITOMART. What do you mean by the horrible truth, pray?

CUSINS. That she was enormously rich; that her grandfather was an earl; that her father was the Prince of Darkness—

UNDERSHAFT. Chut!

CUSINS.—and that I was only an adventurer trying to catch a rich wife, then I stooped to deceive her about my birth.

BARBARA [*rising*] Dolly!

LADY BRITOMART. Your birth! Now Adolphus, dont dare to make up a wicked story for the sake of these wretched cannons. Remember: I have seen photographs of your parents; and the Agent General for South Western Australia knows them personally and has assured me that they are most respectable married people.

CUSINS. So they are in Australia; but here they are outcasts. Their marriage is legal in Australia, but not in England. My mother is my father's deceased wife's sister; and in this island I am consequently a foundling. [*Sensation*].

BARBARA. Silly! [*She climbs to the cannon, and leans, listening, in the angle it makes with the parapet*].

CUSINS. Is the subterfuge good enough, Machiavelli?

UNDERSHAFT [*thoughtfully*] Biddy: this may be a way out of the difficulty.

LADY BRITOMART. Stuff! A man cant make cannons any the better for being his own cousin instead of his proper self [*she sits down on the rug with a bounce that expresses her downright contempt for their casuistry*].

UNDERSHAFT [*to Cusins*] You are an educated man. That is against the tradition.

CUSINS. Once in ten thousand times it happens that the schoolboy is a born master of what they try to teach him. Greek has not destroyed my mind: it has nourished it. Besides, I did not learn it at an English public school.

UNDERSHAFT. Hm! Well, I cannot afford to be too particular: you have cornered the foundling market. Let it pass. You are eligible, Euripides: you are eligible.

BARBARA. Dolly: yesterday morning, when Stephen told us all about the tradition, you became very silent; and you have been strange and excited ever since. Were you thinking of your birth then?

CUSINS. When the finger of Destiny suddenly points at a man in the middle of his breakfast, it makes him thoughtful.

UNDERSHAFT. Aha! You have had your eye on the business, my young friend, have you?

CUSINS. Take care! There is an abyss of moral horror between me and your accursed aerial battleships.

UNDERSHAFT. Never mind the abyss for the present. Let us settle the practical details and leave your final decision open. You know that you will have to change your name. Do you object to that?

CUSINS. Would any man named Adolphus—any man called Dolly!—object to be called something else?

UNDERSHAFT. Good. Now, as to money! I propose to treat you handsomely from the beginning. You shall start at a thousand a year.

CUSINS [*with sudden heat, his spectacles twinkling with mischief*] A thousand! You dare offer a miserable thousand to the son-in-law of a millionaire! No, by Heavens, Machiavelli! you shall not cheat me. You cannot do without me; and I can do without you. I must have two thousand five hundred a year for two years. At the end of that time, if I am a failure, I go. But if I am a success, and stay on, you must give me the other five thousand.

UNDERSHAFT. What other five thousand?

CUSINS. To make the two years up to five thousand a year. The two thousand five hundred is only half pay in case I should turn out a failure. The third year I must have ten per cent on the profits.

UNDERSHAFT [*taken aback*] Ten per cent! Why, man, do you know what my profits are?

CUSINS. Enormous, I hope: otherwise I shall require twentyfive per cent.

UNDERSHAFT. But, Mr Cusins, this is a serious matter of business. You are not bringing any capital into the concern.

CUSINS. What! no capital! Is my mastery of Greek no capital? Is my access to the subtlest thought, the loftiest poetry yet attained by humanity, no capital? My character! my intellect! my life! my career! what Barbara calls my soul! are these no capital? Say another word; and I double my salary.

UNDERSHAFT. Be reasonable—

CUSINS [*peremptorily*] Mr Undershaft: you have my terms. Take them or leave them.

UNDERSHAFT [*recovering himself*] Very well. I note your terms; and I offer you half.

CUSINS [*disgusted*] Half!

UNDERSHAFT [*firmly*] Half.

CUSINS. You call yourself a gentleman; and you offer me half!!

UNDERSHAFT. I do not call myself a gentleman; but I offer you half.

CUSINS. This to your future partner! your successor! your son-in-law!

BARBARA. You are selling your own soul, Dolly, not mine. Leave me out of the bargain, please.

UNDERSHAFT. Come! I will go a step further for Barbara's sake. I will give you three fifths; but that is my last word.

CUSINS. Done!

LOMAX. Done in the eye! Why, *I* get only eight hundred, you know.

CUSINS. By the way, Mac, I am a classical scholar, not an arithmetical one. Is three fifths more than half or less?

UNDERSHAFT. More, of course.

CUSINS. I would have taken two hundred and fifty. How you can succeed in business when you are willing to pay all that money to a University don who is obviously not worth a junior clerk's wages!—well! What will Lazarus say?

UNDERSHAFT. Lazarus is a gentle romantic Jew who cares for nothing but string quartets and stalls at fashionable theatres. He will be blamed for your rapacity in money matters, poor fellow! as he has hitherto been blamed for mine. You are a shark of the first order, Euripides. So much the better for the firm!

BARBARA. Is the bargain closed, Dolly? Does your soul belong to him now?

CUSINS. No: the price is settled: that is all. The real tug of war is still to come. What about the moral question?

LADY BRITOMART. There is no moral question in the matter at all, Adolphus. You must simply sell cannons and weapons to people whose cause is right and just, and refuse them to foreigners and criminals.

UNDERSHAFT [*determinedly*] No: none of that. You must keep the true faith of an Armorer, or you dont come in here.

CUSINS. What on earth is the true faith of an Armorer?

UNDERSHAFT. To give arms to all men who offer an honest price for them, without respect of persons or principles: to aristocrat and republican, to Nihilist and Tsar, to Capitalist and Socialist, to Protestant and Catholic, to burglar and policeman, to black man, white man and yellow man, to all sorts and conditions, all nationalities, all faiths, all follies, all causes and all crimes. The first Undershaft wrote up in his shop IF GOD GAVE THE HAND, LET NOT MAN WITHHOLD THE SWORD. The second wrote up ALL HAVE THE RIGHT TO FIGHT: NONE HAVE THE RIGHT TO JUDGE. The third wrote up TO MAN THE WEAPON: TO HEAVEN THE VICTORY. The fourth had no literary turn; so he did not write up anything; but he sold cannons to Napoleon under the nose of George the Third. The fifth wrote up PEACE SHALL NOT PREVAIL SAVE WITH A SWORD IN HER HAND. The sixth, my master, was the best of all. He wrote up NOTHING IS EVER DONE IN THIS WORLD UNTIL MEN ARE PREPARED TO KILL ONE ANOTHER IF IT IS NOT DONE. After that, there was nothing left for the seventh to say. So he wrote up, simply, UNASHAMED.

CUSINS. My good Machiavelli, I shall certainly write something up on the wall; only, as I shall write it in Greek, you wont be able to read it. But as to your Armorer's faith, if I take my neck out of the noose of my own morality I am not going to put it into the noose of yours. I shall sell cannons to whom I please and refuse them to whom I please. So there!

UNDERSHAFT. From the moment when you become Andrew Undershaft, you will never do as you please again. Dont come here lusting for power, young man.

CUSINS. If power were my aim I should not come here for it. You have no power.

UNDERSHAFT. None of my own, certainly.

CUSINS. I have more power than you, more will. You do not drive this place: it drives you. And what drives the place?

UNDERSHAFT [*enigmatically*] A will of which I am a part.

BARBARA [*startled*] Father! Do you know what you are saying; or are you laying a snare for my soul?

CUSINS. Dont listen to his metaphysics, Barbara. The place is driven by the most rascally part of society, the money hunters, the pleasure hunters, the military promotion hunters; and he is their slave.

UNDERSHAFT. Not necessarily. Remember the Armorer's Faith. I will take an order from a good man as cheerfully as from a bad one. If you good people prefer preaching and shirking to buying my weapons and fighting the rascals, dont blame me. I can make cannons: I cannot make courage and conviction. Bah! you tire me, Euripides, with your morality mongering. Ask Barbara: she understands. [*He suddenly reaches up and takes Barbara's hands, looking powerfully into her eyes*] Tell him, my love, what power really means.

BARBARA. [*hypnotized*] Before I joined the Salvation Army, I was in my own power; and the consequence was that I never knew what to do with myself. When I joined it, I had not time enough for all the things I had to do.

UNDERSHAFT [*approvingly*] Just so. And why was that, do you suppose?

BARBARA. Yesterday I should have said,

because I was in the power of God. [*She resumes her self-possession, withdrawing her hands from his with a power equal to his own*]. But you came and shewed me that I was in the power of Bodger and Undershaft. Today I feel—oh! how can I put it into words? Sarah: do you remember the earthquake at Cannes, when we were little children?—how little the surprise of the first shock mattered compared to the dread and horror of waiting for the second? That is how I feel in this place today. I stood on the rock I thought eternal: and without a word of warning it reeled and crumbled under me. I was safe with an infinite wisdom watching me, an army marching to Salvation with me; and in a moment, at a stroke of your pen in a cheque book, I stood alone; and the heavens were empty. That was the first shock of the earthquake: I am waiting for the second.

UNDERSHAFT. Come, come, my daughter! dont make too much of your little tinpot tragedy. What do we do here when we spend years of work and thought and thousands of pounds of solid cash on a new gun or an aerial battleship that turns out just a hairsbreadth wrong after all? Scrap it. Scrap it without wasting another hour or another pound on it. Well, you have made for yourself something that you call a morality or a religion or what not. It doesnt fit the facts. Well, scrap it. Scrap it and get one that does fit. That is what is wrong with the world at present. It scraps its obsolete steam engines and dynamos; but it wont scrap its old prejudices and its old moralities and its old religions and its old political constitutions. Whats the result? In machinery it does very well; but in morals and religion and politics it is working at a loss that brings it nearer bankruptcy every year. Dont persist in that folly. If your old religion broke down yesterday, get a newer and a better one for tomorrow.

BARBARA. Oh how gladly I would take a better one to my soul! But you offer me a worse one. [*Turning on him with sudden vehemence*]. Justify yourself: shew me some light through the darkness of this dreadful place, with its beautifully clean workshops, and respectable workmen, and model homes.

UNDERSHAFT. Cleanliness and respectability do not need justification, Barbara: they justify themselves. I see no darkness here, no dreadfulness. In your Salvation shelter I saw poverty, misery, cold and hunger. You gave them bread and treacle and dreams of heaven. I give from thirty shillings a week to twelve thousand a year. They find their own dreams; but I look after the drainage.

BARBARA. And their souls?

UNDERSHAFT. I save their souls just as I saved yours.

BARBARA [*revolted*] You saved my soul! What do you mean?

UNDERSHAFT. I fed you and clothed you and housed you. I took care that you should have money enough to live handsomely—more than enough; so that you could be wasteful, careless, generous. That saved your soul from the seven deadly sins.

BARBARA [*bewildered*] The seven deadly sins!

UNDERSHAFT. Yes, the deadly seven. [*Counting on his fingers*] Food, clothing, firing, rent, taxes, respectability and children. Nothing can lift those seven millstones from Man's neck but money; and the spirit cannot soar until the millstones are lifted. I lifted them from your spirit. I enabled Barbara to become Major Barbara; and I saved her from the crime of poverty.

CUSINS. Do you call poverty a crime?

UNDERSHAFT. The worst of crimes. All the other crimes are virtues beside it: all the other dishonors are chivalry itself by comparison. Poverty blights whole cities; spreads horrible pestilences; strikes dead the very souls of all who come within sight, sound, or smell of it. What you call crime is nothing: a murder here and a theft there, a blow now and a curse then: what do they matter? they are only the accidents and illnesses of life: there are not fifty geniune professional criminals in London. But there are millions of poor people, abject people, dirty people, ill fed, ill clothed people. They poison us morally and physically: they kill the happiness of society: they force us to do away with our own liberties and to organize unnatural cruelties for fear they should rise against us and drag us down into their abyss. Only fools fear crime: we all fear poverty. Pah! [*turning on Barbara*] you talk of your half-saved ruffian in West Ham: you accuse me of dragging his soul back to perdition. Well, bring him to me here; and I will drag his soul back again to salvation for you. Not by words and dreams; but by thirtyeight shillings a week, a sound house in a handsome street, and a permanent job. In three weeks he will have a fancy waistcoat; in three months a tall hat and a chapel sitting; before the end of the year he will shake hands with a duchess at a Primrose League meeting, and join the Conservative Party.

BARBARA. And will he be the better for that?

UNDERSHAFT. You know he will. Dont be a hypocrite, Barbara. He will be better fed, better housed, better clothed, better behaved; and his children will be pounds heavier and bigger. That will be better than an American cloth mattress in a shelter, chopping firewood, eating bread and treacle, and being forced to kneel down from time to time to thank heaven for it: knee drill, I think you call it. It is cheap work converting starving men with a Bible in one hand and a slice of bread in the other. I will undertake to convert West Ham to Mahometanism on the same terms. Try your hand on my men: their souls are hungry because their bodies are full.

BARBARA. And leave the east end to starve?

UNDERSHAFT [*his energetic tone dropping into one of bitter and brooding remembrance*] I was an east ender. I moralized and starved until one day I swore that I would be a full-fed free man at all costs; that nothing should stop me except a bullet, neither reason nor morals nor the lives of other men. I said "Thou shalt starve ere I starve"; and with that word I became free and great. I was a dangerous man until I had my will: now I am a useful, beneficent, kindly person. That is the history of most self-made millionaires, I fancy. When it is the history of every Englishman we shall have an England worth living in.

LADY BRITOMART. Stop making speeches, Andrew. This is not the place for them.

UNDERSHAFT [*punctured*] My dear: I have no other means of conveying my ideas.

LADY BRITOMART. Your ideas are nonsense. You got on because you were selfish and unscrupulous.

UNDERSHAFT. Not at all. I had the strongest scruples about poverty and starvation. Your moralists are quite unscrupulous about both: they make virtues of them. I had rather be a thief than a pauper. I had rather be a murderer than a slave. I dont want to be either; but if you force the alternative on me, then, by Heaven, I'll choose the braver and more moral one. I hate poverty and slavery worse than any other crimes whatsoever. And let me tell you this. Poverty and slavery have stood up for centuries to your sermons and leading articles: they will not stand up to my machine guns. Dont preach at them: dont reason with them. Kill them.

BARBARA. Killing. Is that your remedy for everything?

UNDERSHAFT. It is the final test of conviction, the only lever strong enough to overturn a social system, the only way of saying Must. Let six hundred and seventy fools loose in the streets; and three policemen can scatter them. But huddle them together in a certain house in Westminster; and let them go through certain ceremonies and call themselves certain names until at last they get the courage to kill; and your six hundred and seventy fools become a government. Your pious mob fills up ballot papers and imagines it is governing its masters; but the ballot paper that really governs is the paper that has a bullet wrapped up in it.

CUSINS. That is perhaps why, like most intelligent people, I never vote.

UNDERSHAFT. Vote! Bah! When you vote, you only change the names of the cabinet. When you shoot, you pull down governments, inaugurate new epochs, abolish old orders and set up new. Is that historically true, Mr Learned Man, or is it not?

CUSINS. It is historically true. I loathe having to admit it. I repudiate your sentiments. I abhor your nature. I defy you in every possible way. Still, it is true. But it ought not to be true.

UNDERSHAFT. Ought! ought! ought! ought! ought! Are you going to spend your life saying ought, like the rest of our moralists? Turn your oughts into shalls, man. Come and make explosives with me. Whatever can blow men up can blow society up. The history of the world is the history of those who had courage enough to embrace this truth. Have you the courage to embrace it, Barbara?

LADY BRITOMART. Barbara: I positively forbid you to listen to your father's abominable wickedness. And you, Adolphus, ought to know better than to go about saying that wrong things are true. What does it matter whether they are true if they are wrong?

UNDERSHAFT. What does it matter whether they are wrong if they are true?

LADY BRITOMART [*rising*] Children: come home instantly. Andrew: I am exceedingly sorry I allowed you to call on us. You are wickeder than ever. Come at once.

BARBARA [*shaking her head*] It's no use running away from wicked people, mamma.

LADY BRITOMART. It is every use. It shews your disapprobation of them.

BARBARA. It does not save them.

LADY BRITOMART. I can see that you are going to disobey me. Sarah: are you coming home or are you not?

SARAH. I daresay it's very wicked of papa to make cannons; but I dont think I shall cut him on that account.

LOMAX [*pouring oil on the troubled waters*] The fact is, you know, there is a certain amount of tosh about this notion of wickedness. It doesnt work. You must look at facts. Not that I would say a word in favor of anything wrong; but then, you see, all sorts of chaps are always doing all sorts of things; and we have to fit them in somehow, dont you know. What I mean is that you cant go cutting everybody; and thats about what it comes to. [*Their rapt attention to his eloquence makes him nervous*]. Perhaps I dont make myself clear.

LADY BRITOMART. You are lucidity itself, Charles. Because Andrew is successful and has plenty of money to give to Sarah, you will flatter him and encourage him in his wickedness.

LOMAX [*unruffled*] Well, where the carcase is, there will the eagles be gathered, dont you know. [*To Undershaft*] Eh? What?

UNDERSHAFT. Precisely. By the way, may I call you Charles?

LOMAX. Delighted. Cholly is the usual ticket.

UNDERSHAFT [*to Lady Britomart*] Biddy—

LADY BRITOMART [*violently*] Dont dare call me Biddy. Charles Lomax: you are a fool. Adolphus Cusins: you are a Jesuit. Stephen: you are a prig. Barbara: you are a lunatic. Andrew: you are a vulgar tradesman. Now you all know my opinion; and my conscience is clear, at all events [*she sits down with a vehemence that the rug fortunately softens*].

UNDERSHAFT. My dear: you are the incarnation of morality. [*She snorts*]. Your conscience is clear and your duty done when you have called everybody names. Come, Euripides! it is getting late; and we all want to go home. Make up your mind.

CUSINS. Understand this, you old demon—

LADY BRITOMART. Adolphus!

UNDERSHAFT. Let him alone, Biddy. Proceed, Euripides.

CUSINS. You have me in a horrible dilemma. I want Barbara.

UNDERSHAFT. Like all young men, you greatly exaggerate the difference between one young woman and another.

BARBARA. Quite true, Dolly.

CUSINS. I also want to avoid being a rascal.

UNDERSHAFT [*with biting contempt*] You lust for personal righteousness, for self-approval, for what you call a good conscience, for what Barbara calls salvation, for what I call patronizing people who are not so lucky as yourself.

CUSINS. I do not: all the poet in me recoils from being a good man. But there are things in me that I must reckon with. Pity—

UNDERSHAFT. Pity! The scavenger of misery.

CUSINS. Well, love.

UNDERSHAFT. I know. You love the needy and the outcast: you love the oppressed races, the negro, the Indian ryot, the underdog everywhere. Do you love the Japanese? Do you love the French? Do you love the English?

CUSINS. No. Every true Englishman detests the English. We are the wickedest nation on earth; and our success is a moral horror.

UNDERSHAFT. That is what comes of your gospel of love, is it?

CUSINS. May I not love even my father-in-law?

UNDERSHAFT. Who wants your love, man? By what right do you take the liberty of offering it to me? I will have your due heed and respect, or I will kill you. But your love! Damn your impertinence!

CUSINS [*grinning*] I may not be able to control my affections, Mac.

UNDERSHAFT. You are fencing, Euripides. You are weakening: your grip is slipping. Come! try your last weapon. Pity and love have broken in your hand: forgiveness is still left.

CUSINS. No: forgiveness is a beggar's refuge. I am with you there: we must pay our debts.

UNDERSHAFT. Well said. Come! you will suit me. Remember the words of Plato.

CUSINS [*starting*] Plato! You dare quote Plato to me!

UNDERSHAFT. Plato says, my friend, that society cannot be saved until either the Professors of Greek take to making gunpowder, or else the makers of gunpowder become Professors of Greek.

CUSINS. Oh, tempter, cunning tempter!

UNDERSHAFT. Come! choose, man, choose.

CUSINS. But perhaps Barbara will not marry me if I make the wrong choice.

BARBARA. Perhaps not.

CUSINS [*desperately perplexed*] You hear!

BARBARA. Father: do you love nobody?

UNDERSHAFT. I love my best friend.

LADY BRITOMART. And who is that, pray?

UNDERSHAFT. My bravest enemy. That is the man who keeps me up to the mark.

CUSINS. You know, the creature is really a sort of poet in his way. Suppose he is a great man, after all!

UNDERSHAFT. Suppose you stop talking and make up your mind, my young friend.

CUSINS. But you are driving me against my nature. I hate war.

UNDERSHAFT. Hatred is the coward's revenge for being intimidated. Dare you make war on war? Here are the means: my friend Mr Lomax is sitting on them.

LOMAX [*springing up*] Oh I say! You dont mean that this thing is loaded, do you? My ownest: come off it.

SARAH [*sitting placidly on the shell*] If I am to be blown up, the more thoroughly it is done the better. Dont fuss, Cholly.

LOMAX [*to Undershaft, strongly remonstrant*] Your own daughter, you know!

UNDERSHAFT. So I see. [*To Cusins*] Well, my friend, may we expect you here at six tomorrow morning?

CUSINS [*firmly*] Not on any account. I will see the whole establishment blown up with its own dynamite before I will get up at five. My hours are healthy, rational hours: eleven to five.

UNDERSHAFT. Come when you please: before a week you will come at six and stay until I turn you out for the sake of your health. [*Calling*] Bilton! [*He turns to Lady Britomart, who rises*]. My dear: let us leave these two young people to themselves for a moment.

[*Bilton comes from the shed*]. I am going to take you through the gun cotton shed.

BILTON [*Barring the way*] You cant take anything explosive in here, sir.

LADY BRITOMART. What do you mean? Are you alluding to me?

BILTON [*unmoved*] No, maam. Mr Undershaft has the other gentleman's matches in his pocket.

LADY BRITOMART [*abruptly*] Oh! I beg your pardon. [*She goes into the shed*].

UNDERSHAFT. Quite right, Bilton, quite right: here you are. [*He gives Bilton the box of matches*]. Come, Stephen. Come, Charles, Bring Sarah. [*He passes into the shed*].

Bilton opens the box and deliberately drops the matches into the fire-bucket.

LOMAX. Oh! I say [*Bilton hands him the empty box*]. Infernal nonsense! Pure scientific ignorance! [*He goes in*].

SARAH. Am I all right, Bilton?

BILTON. Youll have to put on list slippers, miss: thats all. Weve got em inside. [*She goes in*].

STEPHEN [*very seriously to Cusins*] Dolly, old fellow, think. Think before you decide. Do you feel that you are a sufficiently practical man? It is a huge undertaking, an enormous responsibility. All this mass of business will be Greek to you.

CUSINS. Oh, I think it will be much less difficult than Greek.

STEPHEN. Well, I just want to say this before I leave you to yourselves. Dont let anything I have said about right and wrong prejudice you against this great chance in life. I have satisfied myself that the business is one of the highest character and a credit to our country. [*Emotionally*] I am very proud of my father. I—[*Unable to proceed, he presses Cusins' hand and goes hastily into the shed, followed by Bilton*].

Barbara and Cusins, left alone together, look at one another silently.

CUSINS. Barbara: I am going to accept this offer.

BARBARA. I thought you would.

CUSINS. You understand, dont you, that I had to decide without consulting you. If I had thrown the burden of the choice on you, you would sooner or later have despised me for it.

BARBARA. Yes: I did not want you to sell your soul for me any more than for this inheritance.

CUSINS. It is not the sale of my soul that troubles me: I have sold it too often to care about that. I have sold it for a professorship. I have sold it for an income. I have sold it to escape being imprisoned for refusing to pay taxes for hangmen's ropes and unjust wars and things that I abhor. What is all human conduct but the daily and hourly sale of our souls for trifles? What I am now selling it for is neither money nor position nor comfort, but for reality and for power.

BARBARA. You know that you will have no power, and that he has none.

CUSINS. I know. It is not for myself alone. I want to make power for the world.

BARBARA. I want to make power for the world too; but it must be spiritual power.

CUSINS. I think all power is spiritual: these cannons will not go off by themselves. I have tried to make spiritual power by teaching Greek. But the world can never be really touched by a dead language and a dead civilization. The people must have power: and the people cannot have Greek. Now the power that is made here can be wielded by all men.

BARBARA. Power to burn women's houses down and kill their sons and tear their husbands to pieces.

CUSINS. You cannot have power for good without having power for evil too. Even mother's milk nourishes murderers as well as heroes. This power which only tears men's bodies to pieces has never been so horribly abused as the intellectual power, the imaginative power, the poetic, religious power that can enslave men's souls. As a teacher of Greek I gave the intellectual man weapons against the common man. I now want to give the common man weapons against the intellectual man. I love the common people. I want to arm them against the lawyers, the doctors, the priests, the literary men, the professors, the artists, and the politicians, who, once in authority, are more disastrous and tyrannical than all the fools, rascals, and imposters. I want a power simple enough for common men to use, yet strong enough to force the intellectual oligarchy to use its genius for the general good.

BARBARA. Is there no higher power than that [*pointing to the shell*]?

CUSINS. Yes: but that power can destroy the higher powers just as a tiger can destroy a man: there Man must master that power first. I admitted this when the Turks and Greeks were last at war. My best pupil went out to fight for Hellas. My parting gift to him was not a copy of Plato's Republic, but a revolver and a hundred Undershaft cartridges. The blood of every Turk he shot—if he shot any—is on my head as well as on Undershaft's. That act committed me to this place for ever. Your father's challenge has beaten me. Dare I make war on war? I dare. I must. I will. And now, is it all over between us?

BARBARA [*touched by his evident dread of her answer*] Silly baby Dolly! How could it be!

CUSINS [*overjoyed*] Then you—you—you—Oh for my drum! [*He flourishes imaginary drumsticks*].

BARBARA [*angered by his levity*] Take care, Dolly, take care. Oh, if only I could get away from you and from father and from it all! if I could have the wings of a dove and fly away to heaven!

CUSINS. And leave me!

BARBARA. Yes, you, and all the other naughty mischievous children of men. But I cant. I was happy in the Salvation Army for a moment. I escaped from the world into a paradise of enthusiasm and prayer and soul saving; but the moment our money ran short, it all came back to

Bodger: it was he who saved our people: he, and the Prince of Darkness, my papa. Undershaft and Bodger: their hands stretch everywhere: when we feed a starving fellow creature, it is with their bread, because there is no other bread; when we tend the sick, it is in the hospitals they endow; if we turn from the churches they build, we must kneel on the stones of the streets they pave. As long as that lasts, there is no getting away from them. Turning our backs on Bodger and Undershaft is turning our backs on life.

CUSINS. I thought you were determined to turn your back on the wicked side of life.

BARBARA. There is no wicked side: life is all one. And I never wanted to shirk my share in whatever evil must be endured, whether it be sin or suffering. I wish I could cure you of middle-class ideas, Dolly.

CUSINS [*gasping*] Middle cl—! A snub! A social snub to me! from the daughter of a foundling!

BARBARA. That is why I have no class, Dolly: I come straight out of the heart of the whole people. If I were middle-class I should turn my back on my father's business; and we should both live in an artistic drawing room, with you reading the reviews in one corner, and I in the other at the piano, playing Schumann: both very superior persons, and neither of us a bit of use. Sooner than that, I would sweep out the guncotton shed, or be one of Bodger's barmaids. Do you know what would have happened if you had refused papa's offer?

CUSINS. I wonder!

BARBARA. I should have given you up and married the man who accepted it. After all, my dear old mother has more sense than any of you. I felt like her when I saw this place—felt that I must have it— that never, never, never could I let it go; only she thought it was the houses and the kitchen ranges and the linen and china, when it was really all the human souls to be saved: not weak souls in starved bodies, sobbing with gratitude for a scrap of bread and treacle, but fulfilled, quarrelsome, snobbish, uppish creatures, all standing on their little rights and dignities, and thinking that my father ought to be greatly obliged to them for making so much money for him—and so he ought. That is where salvation is really wanted. My father shall never throw it in my teeth again that my converts were bribed with bread. [*She is transfigured*]. I have got rid of the bribe of bread. I have got rid of the bribe of heaven. Let God's work be done for its own sake: the work he had to create us to do because it cannot be done except by living men and women. When I die, let him be in my debt, not I in his; and let me forgive him as becomes a woman of my rank.

CUSINS. Then the way of life lies through the factory of death?

BARBARA. Yes, through the raising of hell to heaven and of man to God, through the unveiling of an eternal light in the Valley of The Shadow. [*Seizing him with both hands*] Oh, did you think my courage would never come back? did you believe that I was a deserter? that I, who have stood in the streets, and taken my people to my heart, and talked of the holiest and greatest things with them, could ever turn back and chatter foolishly to fashionable people about nothing in a drawing room? Never, never, never, never: Major Barbara will die with the colors. Oh! and I have my dear little Dolly boy still; and he has found me my place and my work. Glory Hallelujah! [*She kisses him*].

CUSINS. My dearest: consider my delicate health. I cannot stand as much happiness as you can.

BARBARA. Yes: it is not easy work being in love with me, is it? But it's good for you. [*She runs to the shed, and calls, childlike*] Mamma! Mamma! [*Bilton comes out of the shed, followed by Undershaft*]. I want Mamma.

UNDERSHAFT. She is taking off her list slippers, dear. [*He passes on to Cusins*]. Well? What does she say?

CUSINS. She has gone right up into the skies.

LADY BRITOMART [*coming from the shed and stopping on the steps, obstructing Sarah, who follows with Lomax. Barbara clutches like a baby at her mother's skirt*] Barbara: when will you learn to be independent and to act and think for yourself? I know as well as possible what that cry of "Mamma, Mamma," means. Always running to me!

SARAH [*touching Lady Britomart's ribs with finger tips and imitating a bicycle horn*] Pip! pip!

LADY BRITOMART [*highly indignant*] How dare you say Pip! pip! to me, Sarah? You are both very naughty children. What do you want, Barbara?

BARBARA. I want a house in the village to live in with Dolly. [*Dragging at the skirt*] Come and tell me which one to take.

UNDERSHAFT [*to Cusins*] Six o'clock tomorrow morning, Euripides.

PREFACE
Bernard Shaw

FIRST AID TO CRITICS

Before dealing with the deeper aspects of Major Barbara, let me, for the credit of English literature, make a protest against an unpatriotic habit into which many of my critics have fallen. Whenever my view strikes them as being at all outside the range of, say, an ordinary suburban churchwarden, they conclude that I am echoing Schopenhauer, Nietzsche, Ibsen, Strindberg, Tolstoy, or some other heresiarch in northern or eastern Europe.

I confess there is something flattering in this simple faith in my accomplishment as a linguist and my erudition as a philosopher. But I cannot countenance the assumption that life and literature are so poor in these islands that we must go abroad for all dramatic material that is not common and all ideas that are not superficial. I therefore venture to put my critics in possession of certain facts concerning my contact with modern ideas.

About half a century ago, an Irish novelist, Charles Lever, wrote a story entitled A Day's Ride: A Life's Romance. It was published by Charles Dickens in Household Words, and proved so strange to the public taste that Dickens pressed Lever to make short work of it. I read scraps of this novel when I was a child; and it made an enduring impression on me. The hero was a very romantic hero, trying to live bravely, chivalrously, and powerfully by dint of mere romance-fed imagination, without courage, without means, without knowledge, without skill, without anything real except his bodily appetites. Even in my childhood I found in this poor devil's unsuccessful encounters with the facts of life, a poignant quality that romantic fiction lacked. The book, in spite of its first failure, is not dead: I saw its title the other day in the catalogue of Tauchnitz.

Now why is it that when I also deal in the tragicomic irony of the conflict between real life and the romantic imagination, critics never affiliate me to my countryman and immediate forerunner, Charles Lever, whilst they confidently derive me from a Norwegian author of whose language I do not know three words, and of whom I knew nothing until years after the Shavian *Anschauung* was already unequivocally declared in books full of what came, ten years later, to be perfunctorily labelled Ibsenism? I was not Ibsenist even at second hand; for Lever, though he may have read Henri Beyle, *alias* Stendhal, certainly never read Ibsen. Of the books that made Lever popular, such as Charles O'Malley and Harry Lorrequer, I know nothing but the names and some of the illustrations. But the story of the day's ride and life's romance of Potts (claiming alliance with Pozzo di Borgo) caught me and fascinated me as something strange and significant, though I already knew all about Alnaschar and Don Quixote and Simon Tappertit and many another romantic hero mocked by reality. From the plays of Aris-

tophanes to the tales of Stevenson that mockery has been made familiar to all who are properly saturated with letters.

Where, then, was the novelty in Lever's tale? Partly, I think, in a new seriousness in dealing with Potts's disease. Formerly, the contrast between madness and sanity was deemed comic: Hogarth shews us how fashionable people went in parties to Bedlam to laugh at the lunatics. I myself have had a village idiot exhibited to me as something irresistibly funny. On the stage the madman was once a regular comic figure: that was how Hamlet got his opportunity before Shakespear touched him. The originality of Shakespear's version lay in his taking the lunatic sympathetically and seriously, and thereby making an advance towards the eastern consciousness of the fact that lunacy may be inspiration in disguise, since a man who has more brains than his fellows necessarily appears as mad to them as one who has less. But Shakespear did not do for Pistol and Parolles what he did for Hamlet. The particular sort of madman they represented, the romantic make-believer, lay outside the pale of sympathy in literature: he was pitilessly despised and ridiculed here as he was in the east under the name of Alnaschar, and was doomed to be, centuries later, under the name of Simon Tappertit. When Cervantes relented over Don Quixote, and Dickens relented over Pickwick, they did not become impartial: they simply changed sides, and became friends and apologists where they had formerly been mockers.

In Lever's story there is a real change of attitude. There is no relenting towards Potts: he never gains our affections like Don Quixote and Pickwick: he has not even the infatuate courage of Tappertit. But we dare not laugh at him, because, somehow, we recognize ourselves in Potts. We may, some of us, have enough nerve, enough muscle, enough luck, enough tact or skill or address or knowledge to carry things off better than he did; to impose on the people who saw through him; to fascinate Katinka (who cut Potts so ruthlessly at the end of the story);

but for all that, we know that Potts plays an enormous part in ourselves and in the world, and that the social problem is not a problem of story-book heroes of the older pattern, but a problem of Pottses, and of how to make men of them. To fall back on my old phrase, we have the feeling—one that Alnaschar, Pistol, Parolles, and Tappertit never gave us—that Potts is a piece of really scientific natural history as distinguished from funny story telling. His author is not throwing a stone at a creature of another and inferior order, but making a confession, with the effect that the stone hits each of us full in the conscience and causes our self-esteem to smart very sorely. Hence the failure of Lever's book to please the readers of Household Words. That pain in the self-esteem nowadays causes critics to raise a cry of Ibsenism. I therefore assure them that the sensation first came to me from Lever and may have come to him from Beyle, or at least out of the Stendhalian atmosphere. I exclude the hypothesis of complete originality on Lever's part, because a man can no more be completely original in that sense than a tree can grow out of air.

Another mistake as to my literary ancestry is made whenever I violate the romantic convention that all women are angels when they are not devils; that they are better looking than men; that their part in courtship is entirely passive; and that the human female form is the most beautiful object in nature. Schopenhauer wrote a splenetic essay which, as it is neither polite nor profound, was probably intended to knock this nonsense violently on the head. A sentence denouncing the idolized form as ugly has been largely quoted. The English critics have read that sentence; and I must here affirm, with as much gentleness as the implication will bear, that it has yet to be proved that they have dipped any deeper. At all events, whenever an English playwright represents a young and marriageable woman as being anything but a romantic heroine, he is disposed of without further thought as an echo of Schopenhauer. My own case is a specially hard one, because, when I implore the critics

who are obsessed with the Schopenhauerian formula to remember that playwrights, like sculptors, study their figures from life, and not from philosophic essays, they reply passionately that I am not a playwright and that my stage figures do not live. But even so, I may and do ask them why, if they must give the credit of my plays to a philosopher, they do not give it to an English philosopher? Long before I ever read a word by Schopenhauer, or even knew whether he was a philosopher or a chemist, the Socialist revival of the eighteen-eighties brought me into contact, both literary and personal, with Ernest Belfort Bax, an English Socialist and philosophic essayist, whose handling of modern feminism would provoke romantic protests from Schopenhauer himself, or even Strindberg. As a matter of fact I hardly noticed Schopenhauer's disparagements of women when they came under my notice later on, so thoroughly had Bax familiarized me with the homoist attitude, and forced me to recognize the extent to which public opinion, and consequently legislation and jurisprudence, is corrupted by feminist sentiment.

Belfort Bax's essays were not confined to the Feminist question. He was a ruthless critic of current morality. Other writers have gained sympathy for dramatic criminals by eliciting the alleged "soul of goodness in things evil"; but Bax would propound some quite undramatic and apparently shabby violation of our commercial law and morality, and not merely defend it with the most disconcerting ingenuity, but actually prove it to be a positive duty that nothing but the certainty of police persecution should prevent every right-minded man from at once doing on principle. The Socialists were naturally shocked, being for the most part morbidly moral people; but at all events they were saved later on from the delusion that nobody but Nietzsche had ever challenged our mercanto-Christian morality. I first heard the name of Nietzsche from a German mathematician, Miss Borchardt, who had read my Quintessence of Ibsenism, and told me that she saw what I had been reading: namely, Nietzsche's Jenseits von Gut und Böse. Which I protest I had never seen, and could not have read with any comfort, for want of the necessary German, if I had seen it.

Nietzsche, like Schopenhauer, is the victim in England of a single much quoted sentence containing the phrase "big blonde beast." On the strength of this alliteration it is assumed that Nietzsche gained his European reputation by a senseless glorification of selfish bullying as the rule of life, just as it is assumed, on the strength of the single word Superman (Übermensch) borrowed by me from Nietzsche, that I look for the salvation of society to the despotism of a single Napoleonic Superman, in spite of my careful demonstration of the folly of that outworn infatuation. But even the less recklessly superficial critics seem to believe that the modern objection to Christianity as a pernicious slave-morality was first put forward by Nietzsche. It was familiar to me before I ever heard of Nietzsche. The late Captain Wilson, author of several queer pamphlets, propagandist of a metaphysical system called Comprehensionism, and inventor of the term "Crosstianity" to distinguish the retrograde element in Christendom, was wont thirty years ago, in the discussions of the Dialectical Society, to protest earnestly against the beatitudes of the Sermon on the Mount as excuses for cowardice and servility, as destructive of our will, and consequently of our honor and manhood. Now it is true that Captain Wilson's moral criticism of Christianity was not a historical theory of it, like Nietzsche's; but this objection cannot be made to Stuart-Glennie, the successor of Buckle as a philosophic historian, who devoted his life to the elaboration and propagation of his theory that Christianity is part of an epoch (or rather an aberration, since it began as recently as 6000 B.C. and is already collapsing) produced by the necessity in which the numerically inferior white races found themselves to impose their domination on the colored races by priestcraft, making a virtue and a popular religion of drudgery and

submissiveness in this world not only as a means of achieving saintliness of character but of securing a reward in heaven. Here was the slave-morality view formulated by a Scotch philosopher of my acquaintance long before we all began chattering about Nietzsche.

As Stuart-Glennie traced the evolution of society to the conflict of races, his theory made some sensation among Socialists— that is, among the only people who were seriously thinking about historical evolution at all—by its collision with the class-conflict theory of Karl Marx. Nietzsche, as I gather, regarded the slave-morality as having been invented and imposed on the world by slaves making a virtue of necessity and a religion of their servitude. Stuart-Glennie regarded the slave-morality as an invention of the superior white race to subjugate the minds of the inferior races whom they wished to exploit, and who would have destroyed them by force of numbers if their minds had not been subjugated. As this process is in operation still, and can be studied at first hand not only in our Church schools and in the struggle between our modern proprietary classes and the proletariat, but in the part played by Christian missionaries in reconciling the black races of Africa to their subjugation by European Capitalism, we can judge for ourselves whether the initiative came from above or below. My object here is not to argue the historical point, but simply to make our theatre critics ashamed of their habit of treating Britain as an intellectual void, and assuming that every philosophical idea, every historic theory, every criticism of our moral, religious and juridical institutions, must necessarily be either a foreign import, or else a fantastic sally (in rather questionable taste) totally unrelated to the existing body of thought. I urge them to remember that this body of thought is the slowest of growths and the rarest of blossomings, and that if there be such a thing on the philosophic plane as a matter of course, it is that no individual can make more than a minute contribution to it. In fact, their conception of clever persons parthenogenetically bringing forth complete original cosmogonies by dint of sheer "brilliancy" is part of that ignorant credulity which is the despair of the honest philosopher, and the opportunity of the religious imposter.

The Gospel of St Andrew Undershaft

It is this credulity that drives me to help my critics out with Major Barbara by telling them what to say about it. In the millionaire Undershaft I have represented a man who has become intellectually and spiritually as well as practically conscious of the irresistible natural truth which we all abhor and repudiate: to wit, that the greatest of our evils, and the worst of our crimes is poverty, and that our first duty, to which every other consideration should be sacrificed, is not to be poor. "Poor but honest," "the respectable poor," and such phrases are as intolerable and as immoral as "drunken but amiable," "fraudulent but a good after-dinner speaker," "splendidly criminal," or the like. Security, the chief pretence of civilization, cannot exist where the worst of dangers, the danger of poverty, hangs over everyone's head, and where the alleged protection of our persons from violence is only an accidental result of the existence of a police force whose real business is to force the poor man to see his children starve whilst idle people overfeed pet dogs with the money that might feed and clothe them.

It is exceedingly difficult to make people realize that an evil is an evil. For instance, we seize a man and deliberately do him a malicious injury: say, imprison him for years. One would not suppose that it needed any exceptional clearness of wit to recognize in this an act of diabolical cruelty. But in England such a recognition provokes a stare of surprise, followed by an explanation that the outrage is punishment or justice or something else that is all right, or perhaps by a heated attempt to argue that we should all

be robbed and murdered in our beds if such stupid villainies as sentences of imprisonment were not committed daily. It is useless to argue that even if this were true, which it is not, the alternative to adding crimes of our own to the crimes from which we suffer is not helpless submission. Chickenpox is an evil; but if I were to declare that we must either submit to it or else repress it sternly by seizing everyone who suffers from it and punishing them by inoculation with smallpox, I should be laughed at; for though nobody could deny that the result would be to prevent chickenpox to some extent by making people avoid it much more carefully, and to effect a further apparent prevention by making them conceal it very anxiously, yet people would have sense enough to see that the deliberate propagation of smallpox was a creation of evil, and must therefore be ruled out in favor of purely humane and hygienic measures. Yet in the precisely parallel case of a man breaking into my house and stealing my wife's diamonds I am expected as a matter of course to steal ten years of his life, torturing him all the time. If he tries to defeat that monstrous retaliation by shooting me, my survivors hang him. The net result suggested by the police statistics is that we inflict atrocious injuries on the burglars we catch in order to make the rest take effectual precautions against detection; so that instead of saving our wives' diamonds from burglary we only greatly decrease our chances of ever getting them back, and increase our chances of being shot by the robber if we are unlucky enough to disturb him at his work.

But the thoughtless wickedness with which we scatter sentences of imprisonment, torture in the solitary cell and on the plank bed, and flogging, on moral invalids and energetic rebels, is as nothing compared to the silly levity with which we tolerate poverty as if it were either a wholesome tonic for lazy people or else a virtue to be embraced as St Francis embraced it. If a man is indolent, let him be poor. If he is drunken, let him be poor. If he is not a gentleman, let him be poor. If he is addicted to the fine arts or to pure science instead of to trade and finance, let him be poor. If he chooses to spend his urban eighteen shillings a week or his agricultural thirteen shillings a week on his beer and his family instead of saving it up for his old age, let him be poor. Let nothing be done for "the undeserving": let him be poor. Serve him right! Also—somewhat inconsistently—blessed are the poor!

Now what does this Let Him Be Poor mean? It means let him be weak. Let him be ignorant. Let him become a nucleus of disease. Let him be a standing exhibition and example of ugliness and dirt. Let him have rickety children. Let him be cheap, and drag his fellows down to his own price by selling himself to do their work. Let his habitations turn our cities into poisonous congeries of slums. Let his daughters infect our young men with the diseases of the streets, and his sons revenge him by turning the nation's manhood into scrofula, cowardice, cruelty, hypocrisy, political imbecility, and all the other fruits of oppression and malnutrition. Let the undeserving become still less deserving; and let the deserving lay up for himself, not treasures in heaven, but horrors in hell upon earth. This being so, is it really wise to let him be poor? Would he not do ten times less harm as a prosperous burglar, incendiary, ravisher or murderer, to the utmost limits of humanity's comparatively negligible impulses in these directions? Suppose we were to abolish all penalties for such activities, and decide that poverty is the one thing we will not tolerate—that every adult with less than, say, £365 a year, shall be painlessly but inexorably killed, and every hungry half naked child forcibly fattened and clothed, would not that be an enormous improvement on our existing system, which has already destroyed so many civilizations, and is visibly destroying ours in the same way?

Is there any radicle of such legislation in our parliamentary system? Well, there are two measures just sprouting in the political soil, which may conceivably grow to something valuable. One is the institution of a Legal Minimum Wage. The other, Old Age Pensions. But there is a better plan than either of these. Some time ago I mentioned the subject of Universal Old Age Pensions to my fellow Socialist Cobden-Sanderson, famous as an artist-craftsman in book-binding and printing. "Why not Universal Pensions for Life?" said Cobden-Sanderson. In saying this, he solved the industrial problem at a stroke. At present we say callously to each citizen "If you want money, earn it" as if his having or not having it were a matter that concerned himself alone. We do not even secure for him the opportunity of earning it: on the contrary, we allow our industry to be organized in open dependence on the maintenance of "a reserve army of unemployed" for the sake of "elasticity." The sensible course would be Cobden-Sanderson's: that is, to give every man enough to live well on, so as to guarantee the community against the possibility of a case of the malignant disease of poverty, and then (necessarily) to see that he earned it.

Undershaft, the hero of Major Barbara, is simply a man who, having grasped the fact that poverty is a crime, knows that when society offered him the alternative of poverty or a lucrative trade in death and destruction, it offered him, not a choice between opulent villainy and humble virtue, but between energetic enterprise and cowardly infamy. His conduct stands the Kantian test, which Peter Shirley's does not. Peter Shirley is what we call the honest poor man. Undershaft is what we call the wicked rich one: Shirley is Lazarus, Undershaft Dives. Well, the misery of the world is due to the fact that the great mass of men act and believe as Peter Shirley acts and believes. If they acted and believed as Undershaft acts and believes, the immediate result would be a revolution of incalculable beneficence. To be wealthy, says Undershaft, is with me a point of honor for which I am prepared to kill at the risk of my own life. This preparedness is, as he says, the final test of sincerity. Like Froissart's medieval hero, who saw that "to rob and pill was a good life" he is not the dupe of that public sentiment against killing which is propagated and endowed by people who would otherwise be killed themselves, or of the mouth-honor paid to poverty and obedience by rich and insubordinate do-nothings who want to rob the poor without courage and command them without superiority. Froissart's knight, in placing the achievement of a good life before all the other duties —which indeed are not duties at all when they conflict with it, but plain wickednesses— behaved bravely, admirably, and, in the final analysis, public-spiritedly. Medieval society, on the other hand, behaved very badly indeed in organizing itself so stupidly that a good life could be achieved by robbing and pilling. If the knight's contemporaries had been all as resolute as he, robbing and pilling would have been the shortest way to the gallows, just as, if we were all as resolute and clear-sighted as Undershaft, an attempt to live by means of what is called "an independent income" would be the shortest way to the lethal chamber. But as, thanks to our political imbecility and personal cowardice (fruits of poverty, both), the best imitation of a good life now procurable is life on an independent income, all sensible people aim at securing such an income, and are, of course, careful to legalize and moralize both it and all the actions and sentiments which lead to it and support it as an institution. What else can they do? They know, of course, that they are rich because others are poor. But they cannot help that: it is for the poor to repudiate poverty when they have had enough of it. The thing can be done easily enough: the demonstrations to the contrary made by the economists, jurists, moralists and sentimentalists hired by the rich to defend them, or even doing the work gratuitously out of sheer folly and abjectness, impose only on those who want to be imposed on.

The reason why the independent income-tax payers are not solid in defence of their position is that since we are not medieval rovers through a sparsely populated country, the poverty of those we rob prevents our having the good life for which we sacrifice them. Rich men or aristocrats with a developed sense of life—men like Ruskin and William Morris and Kropotkin—have enormous social appeties and very fastidious personal ones. They are not content with handsome houses: they want handsome cities. They are not content with bediamonded wives and blooming daughters: they complain because the charwoman is badly dressed, because the laundress smells of gin, because the sempstress is anemic, because every man they meet is not a friend and every woman not a romance. They turn up their noses at their neighbor's drains, and are made ill by the architecture of their neighbor's houses. Trade patterns made to suit vulgar people do not please them (and they can get nothing else): they cannot sleep nor sit at ease upon "slaughtered" cabinet makers' furniture. The very air is not good enough for them: there is too much factory smoke in it. They even demand abstract conditions: justice, honor, a noble moral atmosphere, a mystic nexus to replace the cash nexus. Finally they declare that though to rob and pill with your own hand on horseback and in steel coat may have been a good life, to rob and pill by the hands of the policeman, the bailiff, and the soldier, and to underpay them meanly for doing it, is not a good life, but rather fatal to all possibility of even a tolerable one. They call on the poor to revolt, and, finding the poor shocked at their ungentlemanliness, despairingly revile the proletariat for its "damned wantlessness" (*verdammte Bedürfnislosigkeit*).

So far, however, their attack on society has lacked simplicity. The poor do not share their tastes nor understand their art-criticisms. They do not want the simple life, nor the esthetic life; on the contrary, they want very much to wallow in all the costly vulgarities from which the elect souls among the rich turn away with loathing. It is by surfeit and not by abstinence that they will be cured of their hankering after unwholesome sweets. What they do dislike and despise and are ashamed of is poverty. To ask them to fight for the difference between the Christmas number of the Illustrated London News and the Kelmscott Chaucer is silly: they prefer the News. The difference between a stockbroker's cheap and dirty starched white shirt and collar and the comparatively costly and carefully dyed blue shirt of William Morris is a difference so disgraceful to Morris in their eyes that if they fought on the subject at all, they would fight in defence of the starch. "Cease to be slaves, in order that you may become cranks" is not a very inspiring call to arms; nor is it really improved by substituting saints for cranks. Both terms denote men of genius; and the common man does not want to live the life of a man of genius: he would much rather live the life of a pet collie if that were the only alternative. But he does want more money. Whatever else he may be vague about, he is clear about that. He may or may not prefer Major Barbara to the Drury Lane pantomime; but he always prefers five hundred pounds to five hundred shillings.

Now to deplore this preference as sordid, and teach children that it is sinful to desire money, is to strain towards the extreme possible limit of impudence in lying and corruption in hypocrisy. The universal regard for money is the one hopeful fact in our civilization, the one sound spot in our social conscience. Money is the most important thing in the world. It represents health, strength, honor, generosity and beauty as conspicuously and undeniably as the want of it represents illness, weakness, disgrace, meanness and ugliness. Not the least of its virtues is that it destroys base people as certainly as it fortifies and dignifies noble people. It is only when it is cheapened to worthlessness for some and made impossibly dear to others, that it becomes a curse. In short, it is a curse only in such foolish social conditions that life itself is a curse. For the two things are inseparable: money is the counter that enables life to be distributed socially: it *is* life as truly as sovereigns and bank notes are money. The first duty of every citizen is to insist on having money on reasonable terms;

and this demand is not complied with by giving four men three shillings each for ten or twelve hours' drudgery and one man a thousand pounds for nothing. The crying need of the nation is not for better morals, cheaper bread, temperance, liberty, culture, redemption of fallen sisters and erring brothers, nor the grace, love and fellowship of the Trinity, but simply for enough money. And the evil to be attacked is not sin, suffering, greed, priestcraft, kingcraft, demagogy, monopoly, ignorance, drink, war, pestilence, nor any other of the scapegoats which reformers sacrifice, but simply poverty.

Once take your eyes from the ends of the earth and fix them on this truth just under your nose; and Andrew Undershaft's views will not perplex you in the least. Unless indeed his constant sense that he is only the instrument of a Will or Life Force which uses him for purposes wider than his own, may puzzle you. If so, that is because you are walking either in artificial Darwinian darkness, or in mere stupidity. All genuinely religious people have that consciousness. To them Undershaft the Mystic will be quite intelligible, and his perfect comprehension of his daughter the Salvationist and her lover the Euripidean republican natural and inevitable. That, however, is not new, even on the stage. What is new, as far as I know, is that article in Undershaft's religion which recognizes in Money the first need and in poverty the vilest sin of man and society.

This dramatic conception has not, of course, been attained *per saltum*. Nor has it been borrowed from Nietzsche or from any man born beyond the Channel. The late Samuel Butler, in his own department the greatest English writer of the latter half of the XIX century, steadily inculcated the necessity and morality of a conscientious Laodiceanism in religion and of an earnest and constant sense of the importance of money. It drives one almost to despair of English literature when one sees so extraordinary a study of English life as Butler's posthumous Way of All Flesh making so little impression that when, some years later,

I produce plays in which Butler's extraordinarily fresh, free and future-piercing suggestions have an obvious share, I am met with nothing but vague cacklings about Ibsen and Nietzsche, and am only too thankful that they are not about Alfred de Musset and Georges Sand. Really, the English do not deserve to have great men. They allowed Butler to die practically unknown, whilst I, a comparatively insignificant Irish journalist, was leading them by the nose into an advertisement of me which has made my own life a burden. In Sicily there is a Via Samuele Butler. When an English tourist sees it, he either asks "Who the devil was Samuele Butler?" or wonders why the Sicilians should perpetuate the memory of the author of Hudibras.

Well, it cannot be denied that the English are only too anxious to recognize a man of genius if somebody will kindly point him out to them. Having pointed myself out in this manner with some success, I now point out Samuel Butler, and trust that in consequence I shall hear a little less in future of the novelty and foreign origin of the ideas which are now making their way into the English theatre through plays written by Socialists. There are living men whose originality and powers are as obvious as Butler's and when they die that fact will be discovered. Meanwhile I recommend them to insist on their own merits as an important part of their own business.

THE SALVATION ARMY

When Major Barbara was produced in London, the second act was reported in an important northern newspaper as a withering attack on the Salvation Army, and the despairing ejaculation of Barbara deplored by a London daily as a tasteless blasphemy. And they were set right, not by the professed critics of the theatre, but by religious and philosophical publicists like Sir Oliver Lodge and Dr Stanton Coit, and strenuous Nonconformist journalists like William Stead, who not only understood the act as well as the Salvationists themselves, but also saw it in its relation to the religious life of the nation, a life which seems to lie not only outside the sympathy of many of our theatre critics, but actually outside their knowledge of society. Indeed nothing could be more ironically curious than the confrontation Major Barbara effected of the theatre enthusiasts with the religious enthusiasts. On the one hand was the playgoer, always seeking pleasure, paying exorbitantly for it, suffering unbearable discomforts for it, and hardly ever getting it. On the other hand was the Salvationist, repudiating gaiety and courting effort and sacrifice, yet always in the wildest spirits, laughing, joking, singing, rejoicing, drumming, and tambourining: his life flying by in a flash of excitement, and his death arriving as a climax of triumph. And, if you please, the playgoer despising the Salvationist as a joyless person, shut out from the heaven of the theatre, self-condemned to a life of hideous gloom; and the Salvationist mourning over the playgoer as over a prodigal with vine leaves in his hair, careering outrageously to hell amid the popping of champagne corks and the ribald laughter of sirens! Could misunderstanding be more complete, or sympathy worse misplaced?

Fortunately, the Salvationists are more accessible to the religious character of the drama than the playgoers to the gay energy and artistic fertility of religion. They can see, when it is pointed out to them, that a theatre, as a place where two or three are gathered together, takes from that divine presence an inalienable sanctity of which the grossest and profanest farce can no more deprive it than a hypocritical sermon by a snobbish bishop can desecrate Westminster Abbey. But in our professional playgoers this indispensable preliminary conception of sanctity seems wanting. They talk of actors as mimes and mummers, and, I fear, think of dramatic authors as liars and pandars, whose main business is the voluptuous soothing of the tired city speculator when what he calls the serious business of the day is over. Passion, the life of drama, means nothing to them but primitive sexual excitement: such phrases as "impassioned poetry" or "passionate love of truth" have fallen quite out of their vocabulary and been replaced by "passional crime" and the like. They assume, as far as I can gather, that people in whom passion has a larger scope are passionless and therefore uninteresting. Consequently they come to think of religious people as people who are not interesting and not amusing. And so, when Barbara cuts the regular Salvation Army jokes, and snatches a kiss from her lover across his drum, the devotees of the theatre think they ought to appear shocked, and conclude that the whole play is an elaborate mockery of the Army. And then either hypocritically rebuke me for mocking, or foolishly take part in the supposed mockery!

Even the handful of mentally competent critics got into difficulties over my demonstration of the economic deadlock in which the Salvation Army finds itself. Some of them thought that the Army would not have taken money from a distiller and a cannon founder: others thought it should not have taken it: all assumed more or less definitely that it reduced itself to absurdity or hypocrisy by taking it. On the first point the reply of the Army itself was prompt and conclusive. As one of its officers said, they would take money from the devil himself and be only too glad to get it out of his hands and into God's. They gratefully acknowledged that publicans not only give them money but allow them to collect it in the bar—sometimes even when there is a Salvation meeting outside preaching teetotalism. In fact, they questioned the verisimilitude of the play, not because Mrs Baines took the money, but because Barbara refused it.

On the point that the Army ought not to take such money, its justification is obvious. It must take the money because it cannot exist without money, and there is no other money to be had. Practically all the spare money in the country consists of a mass of rent, interest, and profit, every penny of which is bound up with crime, drink, prostitution, disease, and all the evil fruits of poverty, as inextricably as with enterprise, wealth, commercial probity, and national prosperity. The notion that you can earmark certain coins as tainted is an unpractical individualist superstition. None the less the fact that all our money is tainted gives a very severe shock to earnest young souls when some dramatic instance of the taint first makes them conscious of it. When an enthusiastic young clergyman of the Established Church first realizes that the Ecclesiastical Commissioners receive the rents of sporting public houses, brothels, and sweating dens; or that the most generous contributor at his last charity sermon was an employer trading in female labor cheapened by prostitution as unscrupulously as a hotel keeper trades in waiters' labor cheapened by tips, or commissionaires' labor cheapened by pensions; or that the only patron who can afford to rebuild his church or his schools or give his boys' brigade a gymnasium or a library is the son-in-law of a Chicago meat King, that young clergyman has, like Barbara, a very bad quarter hour. But he cannot help himself by refusing to accept money from anybody except sweet old ladies with independent incomes and gentle and lovely ways of life. He has only to follow up the income of the sweet ladies to its industrial source, and there he will find Mrs Warren's profession and the poisonous canned meat and all the rest of it. His own stipend has the same root. He must either share the world's guilt or go to another planet. He must save the world's honor if he is to save his own. That is what all the Churches find just as the Salvation Army and Barbara find it in the play. Her discovery that she is her father's accomplice; that the Salvation Army is the accomplice of the distiller and the dynamite maker; that they can no more escape one another than they can escape the air they breathe; that there is no salvation for them through personal righteousness, but only through the redemption of the whole nation from its vicious, lazy, competitive anarchy: this discovery has been made by everyone except the Pharisees and (apparently) the professional playgoers, who still wear their Tom Hood shirts and underpay their washerwomen without the slightest misgiving as to the elevation of their private characters, the purity of their private atmospheres, and their right to repudiate as foreign to themselves the coarse depravity of the garret and the slum. Not that they mean any harm: they only desire to be, in their little private way, what they call gentlemen. They do not understand Barbara's lesson because they have not, like her, learnt it by taking their part in the larger life of the nation.

BARBARA'S RETURN TO THE COLORS

Barbara's return to the colors may yet provide a subject for the dramatic historian of the future. To go back to the Salvation Army with the knowledge that even the Salvationists themselves are not saved yet; that poverty is not blessed, but a most damnable sin; and that when General Booth chose Blood and Fire for the emblem of Salvation instead of the Cross, he was perhaps better inspired than he knew: such knowledge, for the daughter of Andrew Undershaft, will clearly lead to something hopefuller than distributing bread and treacle at the expense of Bodger.

It is a very significant thing, this instinctive choice of the military form of organization, this substitution of the drum for the organ, by the Salvation Army. Does it not suggest that the Salvationists divine that they must actually fight the devil instead of merely praying at him? At present, it is true, they have not quite ascertained his correct address. When they do, they may give a very rude shock to that sense of security which he has gained from his experience of the fact that hard words, even when uttered by eloquent essayists and lecturers, or carried unanimously at enthusiastic public meetings on the motion of eminent reformers, break no bones. It has been said that the French Revolution was the work of Voltaire, Rousseau and the Encyclopedists. It seems to me to have been the work of men who had observed that virtuous indignation, caustic criticism, conclusive argument and instructive pamphleteering, even when done by the most earnest and witty literary geniuses, were as useless as praying, things going steadily from bad to worse whilst the Social Contract and the pamphlets of Voltaire were at the height of their vogue. Eventually, as we know, perfectly respectable citizens and earnest philanthropists connived at the September massacres because hard experience had convinced them that if they contented themselves with appeals to humanity and patriotism, the aristocracy, though it would read their appeals with the greatest enjoyment and appreciation, flattering and admiring the writers, would none the less continue to conspire with foreign monarchists to undo the revolution and restore the old system with every circumstance of savage vengeance and ruthless repression of popular liberties.

The nineteenth century saw the same lesson repeated in England. It had its Utilitarians, its Christian Socialists, its Fabians (still extant): it had Bentham, Mill, Dickens, Ruskin, Carlyle, Butler, Henry George, and Morris. And the end of all their efforts is the Chicago described by Mr Upton Sinclair and the London in which the people who pay to be amused by my dramatic representation of Peter Shirley turned out to starve at forty because there are younger slaves to be had for his wages, do not take, and have not the slightest intention of taking, any effective step to organize society in such a way as to make that everyday infamy impossible. I, who have preached and pamphleteered like any Encyclopedist, have to confess that my methods are no use, and would be no use if I were Voltaire, Rousseau, Bentham, Marx, Mill, Dickens, Carlyle, Ruskin, Butler, and

Morris all rolled into one, with Euripides, More, Montaigne, Molière, Beaumarchais, Swift, Goethe, Ibsen, Tolstoy, Jesus and the prophets all thrown in (as indeed in some sort I actually am, standing as I do on all their shoulders). The problem being to make heroes out of cowards, we paper apostles and artist-magicians have succeeded only in giving cowards all the sensations of heroes whilst they tolerate every abomination, accept every plunder, and submit to every oppression. Christianity, in making a merit of such submission, has marked only that depth in the abyss at which the very sense of shame is lost. The Christian has been like Dickens' doctor in the debtor's prison, who tells the newcomer of its ineffable peace and security: no duns; no tyrannical collector of rates, taxes, and rent; no importunate hopes nor exacting duties; nothing but the rest and safety of having no farther to fall.

Yet in the poorest corner of this soul-destroying Christendom vitality suddenly begins to germinate again. Joyousness, a sacred gift long dethroned by the hellish laughter of derision and obscenity, rises like a flood miraculously out of the fetid dust and mud of the slums; rousing marches and impetuous dithyrambs rise to the heavens from people among whom the depressing noise called "sacred music" is a standing joke; a flag with Blood and Fire on it is unfurled, not in murderous rancor, but because fire is beautiful and blood a vital and splendid red; Fear, which we flatter by calling Self, vanishes; and transfigured men and women carry their gospel through a transfigured world, calling their leader General, themselves captains and brigadiers, and their whole body an Army: praying, but praying only for refreshment, for strength to fight, and for needful MONEY (a notable sign, that) preaching, but not preaching submission; daring ill-usage and abuse, but not putting up with more of it than is inevitable; and practising what the world will let them practise, including soap and water, color and music. There is danger in such activity; and where there is danger there is hope. Our present

security is nothing, and can be nothing, but evil made irresistible.

WEAKNESSES OF THE SALVATION ARMY

For the present, however, it is not my business to flatter the Salvation Army. Rather must I point out to it that it has almost as many weaknesses as the Church of England itself. It is building up a business organization which will compel it eventually to see that its present staff of enthusiast-commanders shall be succeeded by a bureaucracy of men of business who will be no better than bishops, and perhaps a good deal more unscrupulous. That has always happened sooner or later to great orders founded by saints; and the order founded by St William Booth is not exempt from the same danger. It is even more dependent than the Church on rich people who would cut off supplies at once if it began to preach that indispensable revolt against poverty which must also be a revolt against riches. It is hampered by a heavy contingent of pious elders who are not really Salvationists at all, but Evangelicals of the old school. It still, as Commissioner Howard affirms, "sticks to Moses," which is flat nonsense at this time of day if the Commissioner means, as I am afraid he does, that the Book of Genesis contains a trustworthy scientific account of the origin of species, and that the god to whom Jephthah sacrificed his daughter is any less obviously a tribal idol than Dagon or Chemosh.

Further, there is still too much other-worldliness about the Army. Like Frederick's grenadier, the Salvationist wants to live for ever (the most monstrous way of crying for the moon); and though it is evident to anyone who has ever heard General Booth and his best officers that they would work as hard for human salvation as they do at present if they believed that death would be the end of them individually, they and their followers have a bad habit of talking as if the Salvationists were heroically enduring a very bad time on earth as an investment which will bring them in dividends later on in the form, not of a better life to come for the whole world, but of an eternity spent by themselves personally in a sort of bliss which would bore any active person to a second death. Surely the truth is that the Salvationists are unusually happy people. And is it not the very diagnostic of true salvation that it shall overcome the fear of death? Now the man who has come to believe that there is no such thing as death, the change so called being merely the transition to an exquisitely happy and utterly careless life, has not overcome the fear of death at all: on the contrary, it has overcome him so completely that he refuses to die on any terms whatever. I do not call a Salvationist really saved until he is ready to lie down cheerfully on the scrap heap, having paid scot and lot and something over, and let his eternal life pass on to renew its youth in the battalions of the future.

Then there is the nasty lying habit called confession, which the Army encourages because it lends itself to dramatic oratory, with plenty of thrilling incident. For my part, when I hear a convert relating the violences and oaths and blasphemies he was guilty of before he was saved, making out that he was a very terrible fellow then and is the most contrite and chastened of Christians now, I believe him no more than I believe the millionaire who says he came up to London or Chicago as a boy with only three halfpence in his pocket. Salvationists have said to me that Barbara in my play would never have been taken in by so transparent a humbug as Snobby Price; and certainly I do not think Snobby could have taken in any experienced Salvationist on a point on which the Salvationist did not wish to be taken in. But on the point of conversion all Salvationists wish to be taken in; for the more obvious the sinner the more obvious the miracle of his conversion. When you advertize a converted burglar or reclaimed drunkard as one of the attractions at an experience meeting, your burglar can hardly have been too burglarious or your drunkard too drunken. As long as such attractions are relied on, you will have your Snobbies claiming to have beaten their mothers when they were as a matter of prosaic fact habitually beaten by them, and your Rummies of the tamest respectability pretending to a past of reckless and dazzling vice. Even when confessions are sincerely autobiographic we should beware of assuming that the impulse to make them was pious or that the interest of the hearers is wholesome. As well might we assume that the poor people who insist on shewing disgusting ulcers to district visitors are convinced hygienists, or that the curiosity which sometimes welcomes such exhibitions is a pleasant and creditable one. One is often tempted to suggest that those who pester our police superintendents with confessions of murder might very wisely be taken at their word and executed, except in the few cases in which a real murderer is seeking to be relieved of his guilt by confession and expiation. For though I am not, I hope, an unmerciful person, I do not think that the inexorability of the deed once done should be disguised by any ritual, whether in the confessional or on the scaffold.

And here my disagreement with the Salvation Army, and with all propagandists of the Cross (which I loathe as I loathe all gibbets) becomes deep indeed. Forgiveness, absolution, atonement, are figments: punishment is only a pretence of cancelling one crime by another; and you can no more have forgiveness without vindictiveness than you can have a cure without a disease. You will never get a high morality from people who conceive that their misdeeds are revocable and pardonable, or in a society where absolution and expiation are officially provided for us all. The demand may be very real; but the supply is spurious. Thus Bill Walker, in my play, having assaulted the Salvation Lass, presently finds himself overwhelmed with an intolerable conviction of sin under the skilled treatment of Barbara. Straightway he begins to try to unassault the lass and deruffianize his deed, first by getting punished for it in kind, and, when that relief is denied him, by fining himself a pound to compensate the girl. He is foiled both ways. He finds the Salvation Army as inexorable as fact itself. It will not punish him: it will not take his money. It will not tolerate a redeemed ruffian: it leaves him no means of salvation except ceasing to be a ruffian. In doing this, the Salvation Army instinctively grasps the central truth of Christianity and discards its central superstition: that central truth being the vanity of revenge and punishment, and that central superstition the salvation of the world by the gibbet.

For, be it noted, Bill has assaulted an old and starving woman also; and for this worse offence he feels no remorse whatever, because she makes it clear that her malice is as great as his own. "Let her have the law of me, as she said she would," says Bill: "what I done to her is no more on what you might call my conscience than sticking a pig." This shews a perfectly natural and wholesome state of mind on his part. The old woman, like the law she threatens him with, is perfectly ready to play the game of retaliation with him: to rob him if he steals, to flog him if he strikes, to murder him if he kills. By example and precept the law and public opinion teach him to impose his will on others by anger, violence, and cruelty, and to wipe off the moral score by punishment. That is sound Crosstianity. But this Crosstianity has got entangled with something which Barbara calls Christianity, and which unexpectedly causes her to refuse to play the hangman's game of Satan casting out Satan. She refuses to prosecute a drunken ruffian; she converses on equal terms with a blackguard to whom no lady should be seen speaking in the public street: in short she imitates Christ. Bill's conscience reacts to this just as naturally as it does to the old woman's threats. He is placed in a position of unbearable moral inferiority, and strives by every means in his power to escape from it, whilst he is still quite ready to meet the abuse of the old woman by attempting to smash a mug on her face. And that is the triumphant justification of Barbara's Christianity as against our system of judicial punishment and the vindic-tive villain-thrashings and "poetic justice" of the romantic stage.

For the credit of literature it must be pointed out that the situation is only partly novel. Victor Hugo long ago gave us the epic of the convict and the bishop's candlesticks, of the Crosstian policeman annihilated by his encounter with the Christian Valjean. But Bill Walker is not, like Valjean, romantically changed from a demon into an angel. There are millions of Bill Walkers in all classes of society today; and the point which I, as a professor of natural psychology, desire to demonstrate, is that Bill, without any change in his character or circumstances whatsoever, will react one way to one sort of treatment and another way to another.

In proof I might point to the sensational object lesson provided by our commercial millionaires today. They begin as brigands: merciless, unscrupulous, dealing out ruin and death and slavery to their competitors and employees, and facing desperately the worst that their competitors can do to them. The history of the English factories, the American Trusts, the exploitation of African gold, diamonds, ivory and rubber, outdoes in villainy the worst that has ever been imagined of the buccaneers of the Spanish Main. Captain Kidd would have marooned a modern Trust magnate for conduct unworthy of a gentleman of fortune. The law every day seizes on unsuccessful scoundrels of this type and punishes them with a cruelty worse than their own, with the result that they come out of the torture house more dangerous than they went in, and renew their evil doing (nobody will employ them at anything else) until they are again seized, again tormented, and again let loose, with the same result.

But the successful scoundrel is dealt with very differently, and very Christianly. He is not only forgiven: he is idolized, respected, made much of, all but worshipped. Society returns him good for evil in the most extravagant overmeasure. And with what result? He begins to idolize himself, to respect himself, to live up to the treatment he receives. He preaches sermons; he writes books of the most edifying advice to young men, and actually persuades himself that he got on by taking his own advice; he endows educational institutions; he supports charities; he dies finally in the odor of sanctity, leaving a will which is a monument of public spirit and bounty. And all this without any change in his character. The spots of the leopard and the stripes of the tiger are as brilliant as ever; but the conduct of the world towards him has changed; and his conduct has changed accordingly. You have only to reverse your attitude towards him—to lay hands on his property, revile him, assault him, and he will be a brigand again in a moment, as ready to crush you as you are to crush him, and quite as full of pretentious moral reasons for doing it.

In short, when Major Barbara says that there are no scoundrels, she is right: there are no absolute scoundrels, though there are impracticable people of whom I shall treat presently. Every reasonable man (and woman) is a potential scoundrel and a potential good citizen. What a man is depends on his character; but what he does, and what we think of what he does, depends on his circumstances. The characteristics that ruin a man in one class make him eminent in another. The characters that behave differently in different circumstances behave alike in similar circumstances. Take a common English character like that of Bill Walker. We meet Bill everywhere: on the judicial bench, on the episcopal bench, in the Privy Council, at the War Office and Admiralty, as well as in the Old Bailey dock or in the ranks of casual unskilled labor. And the morality of Bill's characteristics varies with these various circumstances. The faults of the burglar are the qualities of the financier: the manners and habits of a duke would cost a city clerk his situation. In short, though character is independent of circumstances, conduct is not; and our moral judgments of character are not: both are circumstantial. Take any condition of life in which the circumstances are for a mass of men practically alike: felony, the House of Lords, the factory,

the stables, the gipsy encampment or where you please! In spite of diversity of character and temperament, the conduct and morals of the individuals in each group are as predictable and as alike in the main as if they were a flock of sheep, morals being mostly only social habits and circumstantial necessities. Strong people know this and count upon it. In nothing have the masterminds of the world been distinguished from the ordinary suburban season-ticket holder more than in their straightforward perception of the fact that mankind is practically a single species, and not a menagerie of gentlemen and bounders, villains and heroes, cowards and daredevils, peers and peasants, grocers and aristocrats, artisans and laborers, washerwomen and duchesses, in which all the grades of income and caste represent distinct animals who must not be introduced to one another or intermarry. Napoleon constructing a galaxy of generals and courtiers, and even of monarchs, out of his collection of social nobodies: Julius Cæsar appointing as governor of Egypt the son of a freedman—one who but a short time before would have been legally disqualified for the post even of a private soldier in the Roman army; Louis XI making his barber his privy councillor: all these had in their different ways a firm hold of the scientific fact of human equality, expressed by Barbara in the Christian formula that all men are children of one father. A man who believes that men are naturally divided into upper and lower and middle classes morally is making exactly the same mistake as the man who believes that they are naturally divided in the same way socially. And just as our persistent attempts to found political institutions on a basis of social inequality have always produced long periods of destructive friction relieved from time to time by violent explosions of revolution; so the attempt—will Americans please note—to found moral institutions on a basis of moral inequality can lead to nothing but unnatural Reigns of the Saints relieved by licentious Restorations; to Americans who have made divorce a public institution turning the face of Europe into one huge sardonic smile by refusing to stay in the same hotel with a Russian man of genius who has changed wives without the sanction of South Dakota; to grotesque hypocrisy, cruel persecution, and final utter confusion of conventions and compliances with benevolence and respectability. It is quite useless to declare that all men are born free if you deny that they are born good. Guarantee a man's goodness and his liberty will take care of itself. To guarantee his freedom on condition that you approve of his moral character is formally to abolish all freedom whatsoever, as every man's liberty is at the mercy of a moral indictment which any fool can trump up against everyone who violates custom, whether as a prophet or as a rascal. This is the lesson Democracy has to learn before it can become anything but the most oppressive of all the priesthoods.

Let us now return to Bill Walker and his case of conscience against the Salvation Army. Major Barbara, not being a modern Tetzel, or the treasurer of a hospital, refuses to sell absolution to Bill for a sovereign. Unfortunately, what the Army can afford to refuse in the case of Bill Walker, it cannot refuse in the case of Bodger. Bodger is master of the situation because he holds the purse strings. "Strive as you will," says Bodger, in effect: "me you cannot do without. You cannot save Bill Walker without my money." And the Army answers, quite rightly under the circumstances, "We will take money from the devil himself sooner than abandon the work of Salvation." So Bodger pays his conscience-money and gets the absolution that is refused to Bill. In real life Bill would perhaps never know this. But I, the dramatist whose business it is to shew the connexion between things that seem apart and unrelated in the haphazard order of events in real life, have contrived to make it known to Bill, with the result that the Salvation Army loses its hold of him at once.

But Bill may not be lost, for all that. He is still in the grip of the facts and of his own conscience, and may find his taste for black-

guardism permanently spoiled. Still, I cannot guarantee that happy ending. Walk through the poorer quarters of our cities on Sunday when the men are not working, but resting and chewing the cud of their reflections. You will find one expression common to every mature face: the expression of cynicism. The discovery made by Bill Walker about the Salvation Army has been made by everyone there. They have found that every man has his price; and they have been foolishly or corruptly taught to mistrust and despise him for that necessary and salutary condition of social existence. When they learn that General Booth, too, has his price, they do not admire him because it is a high one, and admit the need of organizing society so that he shall get it in an honorable way: they conclude that his character is unsound and that all religious men are hypocrites and allies of their sweaters and oppressors. They know that the large subscriptions which help to support the Army are endowments, not of religion, but of the wicked doctrine of docility in poverty and humility under oppression; and they are rent by the most agonizing of all the doubts of the soul, the doubt whether their true salvation must not come from their most abhorrent passions, from murder, envy, greed, stubbornness, rage, and terrorism, rather than from public spirit, reasonableness, humanity, generosity, tenderness, delicacy, pity and kindness. The confirmation of that doubt, at which our newspapers have been working so hard for years past, is the morality of militarism; and the justification of militarism is that circumstances may at any time make it the true morality of the moment. It is by producing such moments that we produce violent and sanguinary revolutions, such as the one now in progress in Russia and the one which Capitalism in England and America is daily and diligently provoking.

At such moments it becomes the duty of the Churches to evoke all the powers of destruction against the existing order. But if they do this, the existing order must forcibly suppress them. Churches are suffered to exist only on condition that they preach submission to the State as at present capitalistically organized. The Church of England itself is compelled to add to the thirtysix articles in which it formulates its religious tenets, three more in which it apologetically protests that the moment any of these articles comes in conflict with the State it is to be entirely renounced, abjured, violated, abrogated and abhorred, the policeman being a much more important person than any of the Persons of the Trinity. And this is why no tolerated Church nor Salvation Army can ever win the entire confidence of the poor. It must be on the side of the police and the military, no matter what it believes or disbelieves; and as the police and the military are the instruments by which the rich rob and oppress the poor (on legal and moral principles made for the purpose), it is not possible to be on the side of the poor and of the police at the same time. Indeed the religious bodies, as the almoners of the rich, become a sort of auxiliary police, taking off the insurrectionary edge of poverty with coals and blankets, bread and treacle, and soothing and cheering the victims with hopes of immense and inexpensive happiness in another world when the process of working them to premature death in the service of the rich is complete in this.

CHRISTIANITY AND ANARCHISM

Such is the false position from which neither the Salvation Army nor the Church of England nor any other religious organization whatever can escape except through a reconstitution of society. Nor can they merely endure the State passively, washing their hands of its sins. The State is constantly forcing the consciences of men by violence and cruelty. Not content with exacting money from us for the maintenance of its soldiers and policemen, its gaolers and executioners, it forces us to take an active personal part in its proceedings on pain of becoming ourselves the victims of its violence. As I write these lines, a sensational example is given to the world. A royal marriage has been celebrated,

first by sacrament in a cathedral, and then by a bullfight having for its main amusement the spectacle of horses gored and disembowelled by the bull, after which, when the bull is so exhausted as to be no longer dangerous, he is killed by a cautious matador. But the ironic contrast between the bullfight and the sacrament of marriage does not move anyone. Another contrast—that between the splendor, the happiness, the atmosphere of kindly admiration surrounding the young couple, and the price paid for it under our abominable social arrangements in the misery, squalor and degradation of millions of other young couples—is drawn at the same moment by a novelist, Mr Upton Sinclair, who chips a corner of the veneering from the huge meat packing industries of Chicago, and shews it to us as a sample of what is going on all over the world underneath the top layer of prosperous plutocracy. One man is sufficiently moved by that contrast to pay his own life as the price of one terrible blow at the responsible parties. His poverty has left him ignorant enough to be duped by the pretence that the innocent young bride and bridegroom, put forth and crowned by plutocracy as the heads of a State in which they have less personal power than any policeman, and less influence than any Chairman of a Trust, are responsible. At them accordingly he launches his sixpennorth of fulminate, missing his mark, but scattering the bowels of as many horses as any bull in the arena, and slaying twentythree persons, besides wounding ninetynine. And of all these, the horses alone are innocent of the guilt he is avenging: had he blown all Madrid to atoms with every adult person in it, not one could have escaped the charge of being an accessory, before, at, and after the fact, to poverty and prostitution, to such wholesale massacre of infants as Herod never dreamt of, to plague, pestilence and famine, battle, murder and lingering death—perhaps not one who had not helped, through example, precept, connivance, and even clamor, to teach the dynamiter his well-learnt gospel of hatred and vengeance, by approving every day of sentences of years of imprisonment so infernal in their unnatural stupidity and panicstricken cruelty, that their advocates can disavow neither the dagger nor the bomb without stripping the mask of justice and humanity from themselves also.

Be it noted that at this very moment there appears the biography of one of our dukes, who, being a Scot, could argue about politics, and therefore stood out as a great brain among our aristocrats. And what, if you please, was his grace's favorite historical episode, which he declared he never read without intense satisfaction? Why, the young General Bonapart's pounding of the Paris mob to pieces in 1795, called in playful approval by our respectable classes "the whiff of grapeshot," though Napoleon, to do him justice, took a deeper view of it, and would fain have had it forgotten. And since the Duke of Argyll was not a demon, but a man of like passions with ourselves, by no means rancorous or cruel as men go, who can doubt that all over the world proletarians of the ducal kidney are now revelling in "the whiff of dynamite" (the flavor of the joke seems to evaporate a little, does it not?) because it was aimed at the class they hate even as our argute duke hated what he called the mob.

In such an atmosphere there can be only one sequel to the Madrid explosion. All Europe burns to emulate it. Vengeance! More blood! Tear "the Anarchist beast" to shreds. Drag him to the scaffold. Imprison him for life. Let all civilized States band together to drive his like off the face of the earth; and if any State refuses to join, make war on it. This time the leading London newspaper, anti-Liberal and therefore anti-Russian in politics, does not say "Serve you right" to the victims, as it did, in effect, when Bobrikoff, and De Plehve, and Grand Duke Sergius, were in the same manner unofficially fulminated into fragments. No: fulminate our rivals in Asia by all means, ye brave Russian revolutionaries; but to aim at an English princess! monstrous! hideous! hound down the wretch to his doom; and observe, please, that we are a civilized and merciful

people, and, however much we may regret it, must not treat him as Ravaillac and Damiens were treated. And meanwhile, since we have not yet caught him, let us soothe our quivering nerves with the bullfight, and comment in a courtly way on the unfailing tact and good taste of the ladies of our royal houses, who, though presumably of full normal natural tenderness, have been so effectually broken in to fashionable routine that they can be taken to see the horses slaughtered as helplessly as they could no doubt be taken to a gladiator show, if that happened to be the mode just now.

Strangely enough, in the midst of this raging fire of malice, the one man who still has faith in the kindness and intelligence of human nature is the fulminator, now a hunted wretch, with nothing, apparently, to secure his triumph over all the prisons and scaffolds of infuriate Europe except the revolver in his pocket and his readiness to discharge it at a moment's notice into his own or any other head. Think of him setting out to find a gentleman and a Christian in the multitude of human wolves howling for his blood. Think also of this: that at the very first essay he finds what he seeks, a veritable grandee of Spain, a noble, high-thinking, unterrified, malice-void soul, in the guise— of all masquerades in the world!—of a modern editor. The Anarchist wolf, flying from the wolves of plutocracy, throws himself on the honor of the man. The man, not being a wolf (nor a London editor), and therefore not having enough sympathy with his exploit to be made bloodthirsty by it, does not throw him back to the pursuing wolves—gives him, instead, what help he can to escape, and sends him off acquainted at last with a force that goes deeper than dynamite, though you cannot buy so much of it for sixpence. That righteous and honorable high human deed is not wasted on Europe, let us hope, though it benefits the fugitive wolf only for a moment. The plutocratic wolves presently smell him out. The fugitive shoots the unlucky wolf whose nose is nearest; shoots himself; and then convinces the world, by his photograph, that he was no monstrous freak of reversion to the tiger, but a good looking young man with nothing abnormal about him except his appalling courage and resolution (that is why the terrified shriek Coward at him): one to whom murdering a happy young couple on their wedding morning would have been an unthinkably unnatural abomination under rational and kindly human circumstances.

Then comes the climax of irony and blind stupidity. The wolves, balked of their meal of fellow-wolf, turn on the man, and proceed to torture him, after their manner, by imprisonment, for refusing to fasten his teeth in the throat of the dynamiter and hold him down until they came to finish him.

Thus, you see, a man may not be a gentleman nowadays even if he wishes to. As to being a Christian, he is allowed some latitude in that matter, because, I repeat, Christianity has two faces. Popular Christianity has for its emblem a gibbet, for its chief sensation a sanguinary execution after torture, for its central mystery an insane vengeance bought off by a trumpery expiation. But there is a nobler and profounder Christianity which affirms the sacred mystery of Equality, and forbids the glaring futility and folly of vengeance, often politely called punishment or justice. The gibbet part of Christianity is tolerated. The other is criminal felony. Connoisseurs in irony are well aware of the fact that the only editor in England who denounces punishment as radically wrong, also repudiates Christianity; calls his paper The Freethinker; and has been imprisoned for "bad taste" under the law against blasphemy.

SANE CONCLUSIONS

And now I must ask the excited reader not to lose his head on one side or the other, but to draw a sane moral from these grim absurdities. It is not good sense to propose that laws against crime should apply to principals only and not to accessories whose consent, counsel,

or silence may secure impunity to the principal. If you institute punishment as part of the law, you must punish people for refusing to punish. If you have a police, part of its duty must be to compel everybody to assist the police. No doubt if your laws are unjust, and your policemen agents of oppression, the result will be an unbearable violation of the private consciences of citizens. But that cannot be helped: the remedy is, not to license everybody to thwart the law if they please, but to make laws that will command the public assent, and not to deal cruelly and stupidly with law-breakers. Everybody disapproves of burglars; but the modern burglar, when caught and overpowered by a householder, usually appeals, and often, let us hope, with success, to his captor not to deliver him over to the useless horrors of penal servitude. In other cases the lawbreaker escapes because those who could give him up do not consider his breach of the law a guilty action. Sometimes, even, private tribunals are formed in opposition to the official tribunals; and these private tribunals employ assassins as executioners, as was done, for example, by Mahomet before he had established his power officially, and by the Ribbon lodges of Ireland in their long struggle with the landlords. Under such circumstances, the assassin goes free although everybody in the district knows who he is and what he has done. They do not betray him, partly because they justify him exactly as the regular Government justifies its official executioner, and partly because they would themselves be assassinated if they betrayed him: another method learnt from the official government. Given a tribunal, employing a slayer who has no personal quarrel with the slain; and there is clearly no moral difference between official and unofficial killing.

In short, all men are anarchists with regard to laws which are against their consciences, either in the preamble or in the penalty. In London our worst anarchists are the magistrates, because many of them are so old and ignorant that when they are called upon to administer any law that is based on ideas or knowledge less than half a century old, they disagree with it, and being mere ordinary homebred private Englishmen without any respect for law in the abstract, naïvely set the example of violating it. In this instance the man lags behind the law; but when the law lags behind the man, he becomes equally an anarchist. When some huge change in social conditions, such as the industrial revolution of the eighteenth and nineteenth centuries, throws our legal and industrial institutions out of date, Anarchism becomes almost a religion. The whole force of the most energetic geniuses of the time in philosophy, economics, and art, concentrates itself on demonstrations and reminders that morality and law are only conventions, fallible and continually obsolescing. Tragedies in which the heroes are bandits, and comedies in which law-abiding and conventionally moral folk are compelled to satirize themselves by outraging the conscience of the spectators every time they do their duty, appear simultaneously with economic treatises entitled "What is Property? Theft!" and with histories of "The Conflict between Religion and Science."

Now this is not a healthy state of things. The advantages of living in society are proportionate, not to the freedom of the individual from a code, but to the complexity and subtlety of the code he is prepared not only to accept but to uphold as a matter of such vital importance that a lawbreaker at large is hardly to be tolerated on any plea. Such an attitude becomes impossible when the only men who can make themselves heard and remembered throughout the world spend all their energy in raising our gorge against current law, current morality, current respectability, and legal property. The ordinary man, uneducated in social theory even when he is schooled in Latin verse, cannot be set against all the laws of his country and yet persuaded to regard law in the abstract as vitally necessary to society. Once he is brought to repudiate the laws and institutions he knows, he will repudiate the very conception of law and the very groundwork of institutions, ridiculing human rights, ex-

tolling brainless methods as "historical," and tolerating nothing except pure empiricism in conduct, with dynamite as the basis of politics and vivisection as the basis of science. That is hideous; but what is to be done? Here am I, for instance, by class a respectable man, by common sense a hater of waste and disorder, by intellectual constitution legally minded to the verge of pedantry, and by temperament apprehensive and economically disposed to the limit of old-maidishness; yet I am, and have always been, and shall now always be, a revolutionary writer, because our laws make law impossible; our liberties destroy all freedom; our property is organized robbery; our morality is an impudent hypocrisy; our wisdom is administered by inexperienced or malexperienced dupes, our power wielded by cowards and weaklings, and our honor false in all its points. I am an enemy of the existing order for good reasons; but that does not make my attacks any less encouraging or helpful to people who are its enemies for bad reasons. The existing order may shriek that if I tell the truth about it, some foolish person may drive it to become still worse by trying to assassinate it. I cannot help that, even if I could see what worse it could do than it is already doing. And the disadvantage of that worst even from its own point of view is that society, with all its prisons and bayonets and whips and ostracisms and starvations, is powerless in the face of the Anarchist who is prepared to sacrifice his own life in the battle with it. Our natural safety from the cheap and devastating explosives which every Russian student can make, and every Russian grenadier has learnt to handle in Manchuria, lies in the fact that brave and resolute men, when they are rascals, will not risk their skins for the good of humanity, and, when they are not, are sympathetic enough to care for humanity, abhorring murder, and never committing it until their consciences are outraged beyond endurance. The remedy is, then, simply not to outrage their consciences.

Do not be afraid that they will not make allowances. All men make very large allowances indeed before they stake their own lives in a war to the death with society. Nobody demands or expects the millennium. But there are two things that must be set right, or we shall perish, like Rome, of soul atrophy disguised as empire.

The first is, that the daily ceremony of dividing the wealth of the country among its inhabitants shall be so conducted that no crumb shall, save as a criminal's ration, go to any able-bodied adults who are not producing by their personal exertions not only a full equivalent for what they take, but a surplus sufficient to provide for their superannuation and pay back the debt due for their nurture.

The second is that the deliberate infliction of malicious injuries which now goes on under the name of punishment be abandoned; so that the thief, the ruffian, the gambler, and the beggar, may without inhumanity be handed over to the law, and made to understand that a State which is too humane to punish will also be too thrifty to waste the life of honest men in watching or restraining dishonest ones. That is why we do not imprison dogs. We even take our chance of their first bite. But if a dog delights to bark and bite, it goes to the lethal chamber. That seems to me sensible. To allow the dog to expiate his bite by a period of torment, and then·let him loose in a much more savage condition (for the chain makes a dog savage) to bite again and expiate again, having meanwhile spent a great deal of human life and happiness. in the task of chaining and feeding and tormenting him, seems to me idiotic and superstitious. Yet that is what we do to men who bark and bite and steal. It would be far more sensible to put up with their vices, as we put up with their illnesses, until they give more trouble than they are worth, at which point we should, with many apologies and expressions of sympathy, and some generosity in complying with their last wishes, place them in the lethal chamber and get rid of them. Under no circumstances should they be allowed to expiate their misdeeds by a manufactured penalty, to subscribe to a charity, or to compensate the victims. If there is to be no punishment there can be no forgiveness. We shall never have real moral responsibility until everyone knows that his deeds are irrevocable, and that his life depends on his usefulness. Hitherto, alas! humanity has never dared face these hard facts. We frantically scatter conscience money and invent systems of conscience banking, with expiatory penalties, atonements, redemptions, salvations, hospital subscription lists and what not, to enable us to contract-out of the moral code. Not content with the old scapegoat and sacrificial lamb, we deify human saviors, and pray to miraculous virgin intercessors. We attribute mercy to the inexorable; soothe our consciences after committing murder by throwing ourselves on the bosom of divine love; and shrink even from our own gallows because we are forced to admit that it, at least, is irrevocable—as if one hour of imprisonment were not as irrevocable as any execution!

If a man cannot look evil in the face without illusion, he will never know what it really is, or combat it effectually. The few men who have been able (relatively) to do this have been called cynics, and have sometimes had an abnormal share of evil in themselves, corresponding to the abnormal strength of their minds; but they have never done mischief unless they intended to do it. That is why great scoundrels have been beneficent rulers whilst amiable and privately harmless monarchs have ruined their countries by trusting to the hocus-pocus of innocence and guilt, reward and punishment, virtuous indignation and pardon, instead of standing up to the facts without either malice or mercy. Major Barbara stands up to Bill Walker in that way, with the result that the ruffian who cannot get hated, had to hate himself. To relieve this agony he tries to get punished; but the Salvationist whom he tries to provoke is as merciless as Barbara, and only prays for him. Then he tries to pay, but can get nobody to take his money. His doom is the doom of Cain, who, failing to find either a savior, a policeman, or an almoner to help him to pretend that his brother's blood no longer cried from the ground, had to live and die a murderer. Cain took care not to commit another murder, unlike our railway shareholders (I am one) who kill and maim shunters by hundreds to save the cost of automatic couplings, and make atonement by annual subscriptions to deserving charities. Had Cain been allowed to pay off his score, he might possibly have killed Adam and Eve for the mere sake of a second luxurious reconciliation with God afterwards. Bodger, you may depend on it, will go on to the end of his life poisoning people with bad whisky, because he can always depend on the Salvation Army or the Church of England to negotiate a redemption for him in consideration of a trifling percentage of his profits.

There is a third condition too, which must be fulfilled before the great teachers of the world will cease to scoff at its religions. Creeds must become intellectually honest. At present there is not a single credible established religion in the world. That is perhaps the most stupendous fact in the whole world-situation. This play of mine, Major Barbara, is, I hope, both true and inspired; but whoever says that it all happened, and that faith in it and understanding of it consist in believing that it is a record of an actual occurrence, is, to speak according to Scripture, a fool and a liar, and is hereby solemnly denounced and cursed as such by me, the author, to all posterity.

London, June 1906

POSTSCRIPT 1933. In spite of the emphasis laid both in this preface and in the play on the fact that poverty is an infectious pestilence to be prevented at all costs, the lazy habit still prevails of tolerating it not only as an inevitable misfortune to be charitably patronized and relieved, but as a useful punishment for all sorts of misconduct and inefficiency that are not expressly punishable by law. Until we have a general vital hatred of poverty, and a determination to "liquidate" the underfed either by feeding them or killing them, we shall not tackle the poverty question seriously. Long ago I proposed to eradicate the dangerous disease of hunger among children by placing good bread on public supply like drinking water. No Government nor municipality has yet taken up that very sensible proposal.

THE PLAYBOY OF THE WESTERN WORLD
John Millington Synge

CHARACTERS

CHRISTOPHER MAHON
OLD MAHON, his father, a squatter
MICHAEL JAMES FLAHERTY (called MICHAEL JAMES), a publican
MARGARET FLAHERTY (called PEGEEN MIKE), his daughter
WIDOW QUIN, a woman of about thirty
SHAWN KEOGH, her [second] cousin, a young farmer
PHILLY CULLEN and JIMMY FARRELL, small farmers[1]
SARA TANSEY, SUSAN BRADY and HONOR BLAKE [and NELLY], village girls
A BELLMAN
SOME PEASANTS

The action takes place near a village, on a wild coast of Mayo. The First Act passes on an evening of autumn, the other two Acts on the following day.

ACT I

SCENE: *Country public house or shebeen, very rough and untidy. There is a sort of*

1 small farmers poor farmers

counter on the right with shelves, holding many bottles and jugs, just seen above it. Empty barrels stand near the counter. At back, a little to left of counter, there is a door into the open air, then, more to the left, there is a settle with shelves above it, with more jugs, and a table beneath a window. At the left there is a large open fireplace, with turf fire, and a small door into inner room. PEGEEN, a wild-looking but fine girl, of about twenty, is writing at table. She is dressed in the usual peasant dress.

PEGEEN (*slowly as she writes*). Six yards of stuff for to make a yellow gown. A pair of lace boots with lengthy heels on them and brassy eyes. A hat is suited for a wedding day. A fine tooth comb. To be sent with three barrels of porter in Jimmy Farrell's creel cart[1] on the evening of the coming Fair[2] to Mister Michael James Flaherty. With the best compliments of this season. Margaret Flaherty.

SHAWN KEOGH (*a fat and fair young man comes in as she signs, looks round awkwardly, when he sees she is alone*). Where's himself?[3]

PEGEEN (*without looking at him*). He's coming. (*She directs letter.*) To Mister Sheamus Mulroy, Wine and Spirit Dealer, Castlebar.[4]

SHAWN (*uneasily*). I didn't see him on the road.

PEGEEN. How would you see him (*licks stamp and puts it on letter*) and it dark night this half hour gone by?

SHAWN (*turning towards door again*). I stood a while outside wondering would I have a right to pass on or to walk in and see you, Pegeen Mike (*comes to fire*), and I could hear the cows breathing, and sighing in the stillness of the air, and not a step moving any place from this gate to the bridge.

PEGEEN (*putting letter in envelope*). It's above at the cross-roads he is meeting Philly Cullen; and a couple more are going along with him to Kate Cassidy's wake.[5]

SHAWN (*looking at her blankly*). And he's going that length in the dark night?

PEGEEN (*impatiently*). He is surely, and leaving me lonesome on the scruff of the hill. (*She gets up and puts envelope on dresser, then winds clock.*) Isn't it long the nights are now, Shawn Keogh, to be leaving a poor girl with her own self counting the hours to the dawn of day?

SHAWN (*with awkward humour*). If it is, when we're wedded in a short while you'll have no call[6] to complain, for I've little will to be walking off to wakes or weddings in the darkness of the night.

PEGEEN (*with rather scornful good humour*). You're making mighty certain, Shaneen,[7] that I'll wed you now.

SHAWN. Aren't we after making a good bargain,[8] the way we're only waiting these days on Father Reilly's dispensation[9] from the bishops, or the Court of Rome.

PEGEEN (*looking at him teasingly, washing up at dresser*). It's a wonder, Shaneen, the Holy Father'd be taking notice of the likes of you; for if I was him I wouldn't bother with this place where you'll meet none but Red Linahan, has a squint in his eye, and Patcheen is lame in his heel, or the mad Mulrannies were driven from California and they lost in their wits. We're a queer lot these times to go troubling the Holy Father on his sacred seat.

SHAWN (*scandalized*). If we are, we're as good this place as another, maybe, and as good these times as we were for ever.

PEGEEN (*with scorn*). As good, is it? Where now will you meet the like of Daneen Sullivan knocked the eye from a peeler,[10] or Marcus Quin, God rest him, got six months for maiming ewes, and he a great

---

1 creel cart cart with open, barred, or grated sides used to carry turf, sheep, pigs, etc.   *2 Fair* the high day for talk and commerce in livestock, held in the middle of the month   *3 himself* the master of the house, Michael James   *4 Castlebar* a principal city of East Mayo

5 wake the watching of the dead, once an occasion for riot and drunkenness   *6 no call* no need   *7 Shaneen* little Shawn   *8 bargain* Shawn's fair day view of marriage   *9 dispensation* to marry his *second* cousin   *10 peeler* policeman, so-called after Sir Robert Peel

warrant[11] to tell stories of holy Ireland till he'd have the old women shedding down tears about their feet. Where will you find the like of them, I'm saying?

SHAWN (*timidly*). If you don't, it's a good job, maybe; for (*with peculiar emphasis on the words*) Father Reilly has small conceit[12] to have that kind walking around and talking to the girls.

PEGEEN (*impatiently, throwing water from basin out of the door*). Stop tormenting me with Father Reilly (*imitating his voice*) when I'm asking only what way[13] I'll pass these twelve hours of dark, and not take my death with the fear.

(*Looking out of door*)

SHAWN (*timidly*). Would I fetch you the Widow Quin, maybe?

PEGEEN. Is it the like of that murderer? You'll not, surely.

SHAWN (*going to her, soothingly*). Then I'm thinking himself will stop along with you when he sees you taking on, for it'll be a long night-time with great darkness, and I'm after feeling a kind of fellow above in the furzy ditch, groaning wicked like a maddening dog, the way[14] it's good cause you have, maybe, to be fearing now.

PEGEEN (*turning on him sharply*). What's that? Is it a man you seen?

SHAWN (*retreating*). I couldn't see him at all; but I heard him groaning out, and breaking his heart. It should have been a young man from his words speaking.

PEGEEN (*going after him*). And you never went near to see was he hurted or what ailed him at all?

SHAWN. I did not, Pegeen Mike. It was a dark lonesome place to be hearing the like of him.

PEGEEN. Well, you're a daring fellow, and if they find his corpse stretched above in the dews of dawn, what'll you say then to the peelers, or the Justice of the Peace?

SHAWN (*thunderstruck*). I wasn't thinking of that. For the love of God, Pegeen Mike, don't let on[15] I was speaking of him. Don't tell your father and the men is coming above; for if they heard that story, they'd have great blabbing this night at the wake.

PEGEEN. I'll maybe tell them, and I'll maybe not.

SHAWN. They are coming at the door. Will you whisht,[16] I'm saying?

PEGEEN. Whisht yourself.

(*She goes behind counter.* MICHAEL JAMES, *fat jovial publican, comes in followed by* PHILLY CULLEN, *who is thin and mistrusting, and* JIMMY FARRELL, *who is fat and amorous, about forty-five.*)

MEN (*together*). God bless you. The blessing of God on this place.

PEGEEN. God bless you kindly.[17]

MICHAEL (*to men who go to the counter*). Sit down now, and take your rest. (*Crosses to* SHAWN *at the fire*) And how is it you are, Shawn Keogh? Are you coming over the sands to Kate Cassidy's wake?

SHAWN. I am not, Michael James. I'm going home the short cut to my bed.

PEGEEN (*speaking across the counter*). He's right too, and have you no shame, Michael James, to be quitting off for the whole night, and leaving myself lonesome in the shop?

MICHAEL (*good-humouredly*). Isn't it the same whether I go for the whole night or a part only? and I'm thinking it's a queer daughter you are if you'd have me crossing backward through the Stooks[18] of the Dead Women, with a drop taken.[19]

PEGEEN. If I am a queer daughter, it's a queer father'd be leaving me lonesome these twelve hours of dark, and I piling the turf with the dogs barking, and the calves

---

11 *a great warrant* a great gift for, a great hand at 12 *conceit* a liking, a fancy for 13 *what way* how 14 *the way* so that

15 *let on* don't admit 16 *whisht* be quiet, shut up 17 *God bless you kindly* Irish ritual blessing on entering a house 18 *Stooks* rocks or low dunes along the sea-shore, shaped like *stooks*, shocks of corn generally containing 12 sheaves 19 *drop taken* drunk

mooing, and my own teeth rattling with the fear.

JIMMY (*flatteringly*). What is there to hurt you, and you a fine, hardy girl would knock the head of any two men in the place?

PEGEEN (*working herself up*). Isn't there the harvest boys[20] with their tongues red for drink, and the ten tinkers[21] is camped in the east glen, and the thousand militia[22]—bad cess[23] to them!—walking idle through the land. There's lots surely to hurt me, and I won't stop alone in it, let himself do what he will.

MICHAEL. If you're that afeard,[24] let Shawn Keogh stop along with you. It's the will of God, I'm thinking, himself should be seeing to you now.

(*They all turn on* SHAWN.)

SHAWN (*in horrified confusion*). I would and welcome,[25] Michael James, but I'm afeard of Father Reilly; and what at all would the Holy Father and the Cardinals of Rome be saying if they heard I did the like of that?

MICHAEL (*with contempt*). God help you! Can't you sit in by the hearth with the light lit and herself[26] beyond in the room? You'll do that surely, for I've heard tell there's a queer fellow above, going mad or getting his death, maybe, in the gripe[27] of the ditch, so she'd be safer this night with a person here.

SHAWN (*with plaintive despair*). I'm afeard of Father Reilly, I'm saying. Let you not be tempting me, and we near married itself.

PHILLY (*with cold contempt*). Lock him in the west room. He'll stay then and have no sin to be telling to the priest.

MICHAEL (*to* SHAWN, *getting between him and the door*). Go up now.[28]

20 *harvest boys* workers who migrated to Scotland and England to help with the harvest and who returned in late autumn with a few pounds to help survive the winter 21 *tinkers* the gypsies of the Irish roads 22 *militia* part of the military garrison that once numbered over 35,000 in Ireland and no friend to the people 23 *bad cess* bad luck 24 *afeard* afraid 25 *would and welcome* gladly 26 *and herself* while Pegeen is 27 *gripe* the hollow, the trench 28 *Go up now* get back to the hearth

SHAWN (*at the top of his voice*). Don't stop me, Michael James. Let me out of the door, I'm saying, for the love of the Almighty God. Let me out (*trying to dodge past him*). Let me out of it, and may God grant you His indulgence in the hour of need.

MICHAEL (*loudly*). Stop your noising, and sit down by the hearth.

(*Gives him a push and goes to counter laughing*)

SHAWN (*turning back, wringing his hands*). Oh, Father Reilly and the saints of God, where will I hide myself today? Oh, St. Joseph and St. Patrick and St. Brigid, and St. James, have mercy on me now!

(SHAWN *turns round, sees door clear, and makes a rush for it.*)

MICHAEL (*catching him by the coat-tail*). You'd be going, is it?

SHAWN (*screaming*). Leave me go, Michael James, leave me go, you old Pagan, leave me go, or I'll get the curse of the priests on you, and of the scarlet-coated bishops of the courts of Rome.

(*With a sudden movement he pulls himself out of his coat, and disappears out of the door, leaving his coat in* MICHAEL's *hands.*)

MICHAEL (*turning round, and holding up coat*). Well, there's the coat of a Christian man. Oh, there's sainted glory this day in the lonesome west; and by the will of God I've got you a decent man, Pegeen, you'll have no call to be spying after if you've a score of young girls, maybe, weeding in your fields.

PEGEEN (*taking up the defence of her property*). What right have you to be making game of a poor fellow for minding the priest, when it's your own the fault is, not paying a penny pot-boy[29] to stand along with me and give me courage in the doing of my work?

29 *pot-boy* a menial in a public house

(She snaps the coat away from him, and goes behind counter with it.)

MICHAEL *(taken aback)*. Where would I get a potboy? Would you have me send the bellman screaming in the streets of Castlebar?

SHAWN *(opening the door a chink and putting in his head, in a small voice)*. Michael James!

MICHAEL *(imitating him)*. What ails you?

SHAWN. The queer dying fellow's beyond looking over the ditch. He's come up, I'm thinking, stealing your hens. *(Looks over his shoulder)* God help me, he's following me now *(he runs into room)*, and if he's heard what I said, he'll be having my life, and I going home lonesome in the darkness of the night.

(For a perceptible moment they watch the door with curiosity. Someone coughs outside. Then CHRISTY MAHON, a slight young man, comes in very tired and frightened and dirty.)

CHRISTY *(in a small voice)*. God save all here!

MEN. God save you kindly.

CHRISTY *(going to the counter)*. I'd trouble you for a glass of porter, woman of the house.

(He puts down coin.)

PEGEEN *(serving him)*. You're one of the tinkers, young fellow, is beyond camped in the glen?

CHRISTY. I am not; but I'm destroyed walking.

MICHAEL *(patronizingly)*. Let you come up then to the fire. You're looking famished with the cold.

CHRISTY. God reward you. *(He takes up his glass and goes a little way across to the left, then stops and looks about him.)* Is it often the polis[30] do be coming into this place, master of the house?

MICHAEL. If you'd come in better hours, you'd have seen "Licensed for the sale of Beer and Spirits, to be consumed on the premises," written in white letters above the door, and what would the polis want spying on me, and not a decent house within four miles, the way every living Christian is a bona fide,[31] saving one widow alone?

CHRISTY *(with relief)*. It's a safe house, so.

(He goes over to the fire, sighing and moaning. Then he sits down putting his glass beside him and begins gnawing a turnip, too miserable to feel the others staring at him with curiosity.)

MICHAEL *(going after him)*. Is it yourself is fearing the polis? You're wanting,[32] maybe?

CHRISTY. There's many wanting.

MICHAEL. Many surely, with the broken harvest and the ended wars.[33] *(He picks up some stockings, etc., that are near the fire, and carries them away furtively.)* It should be larceny, I'm thinking?

CHRISTY *(dolefully)*. I had it in my mind it was a different word and a bigger.

PEGEEN. There's a queer lad. Were you never slapped in school, young fellow, that you don't know the name of your deed?

CHRISTY *(bashfully)*. I'm slow at learning, a middling scholar only.

MICHAEL. If you're a dunce itself, you'd have a right to know that larceny's robbing and stealing. Is it for the like of that you're wanting?

CHRISTY *(with a flash of family pride)*. And I the son of a strong farmer[34] *(with a sudden qualm)*, God rest his soul, could have bought up the whole of your old house a while since, from the butt of his tailpocket,[35] and not have missed the weight of it gone.

MICHAEL *(impressed)*. If it's not stealing, it's maybe something big.

CHRISTY *(flattered)*. Aye; it's maybe something big.

---

30 polis police

31 bona fide a genuine traveler, i.e., one who having traveled four or more miles could be served after licensing hours   *32 wanting* wanted by police   *33 ended wars* perhaps both the Land Wars (1879–82) and the Boer War (1899–1902)   *34 strong farmer* a well-to-do farmer with a large farm and much cattle   *35 tailpocket* of the old-fashioned swallow-tailed coat

JIMMY. He's a wicked-looking young fellow. Maybe he followed after a young woman on a lonesome night.

CHRISTY (*shocked*). Oh, the saints forbid, mister; I was all times a decent lad.

PHILLY (*turning on* JIMMY). You're a silly man, Jimmy Farrell. He said his father was a farmer a while since, and there's himself now in a poor state. Maybe the land was grabbed[36] from him, and he did what any decent man would do.

MICHAEL (*to* CHRISTY, *mysteriously*). Was it bailiffs?[37]

CHRISTY. The divil a one.[38]

MICHAEL. Agents?[39]

CHRISTY. The divil a one.

MICHAEL. Landlords?

CHRISTY (*peevishly*). Ah, not at all, I'm saying. You'd see the like of them stories on any little paper of a Munster[40] town. But I'm not calling to mind any person, gentle, simple, judge or jury, did the like of me.

(*They all draw nearer with delighted curiosity.*)

PHILLY. Well, that lad's a puzzle-the-world.

JIMMY. He'd beat Dan Davies' circus, or the holy missioners making sermons on the villainy of man. Try him again, Philly.

PHILLY. Did you strike golden guineas[41] out of solder, young fellow, or shilling coins itself?

CHRISTY. I did not mister, not sixpence nor a farthing[42] coin.

JIMMY. Did you marry three wives maybe?

I'm told there's a sprinkling have done that among the holy Luthers[43] of the preaching north.

CHRISTY (*shyly*). I never married with one, let alone with a couple or three.

PHILLY. Maybe he went fighting for the Boers,[44] the like of the man beyond, was judged to be hanged, quartered and drawn. Were you off east, young fellow, fighting bloody wars for Kruger[45] and the freedom of the Boers?

CHRISTY. I never left my own parish till Tuesday was a week.[46]

PEGEEN (*coming from counter*). He's done nothing, so. (*To* CHRISTY) If you didn't commit murder or a bad, nasty thing, or false coining, or robbery, or butchery, or the like of them, there isn't anything that would be worth your troubling for to run from now. You did nothing at all.

CHRISTY (*his feelings hurt*). That's an unkindly thing to be saying to a poor orphaned traveller, has a prison behind him, and hanging before, and hell's gap gaping below.

PEGEEN (*with a sign to the men to be quiet*). You're only saying it. You did nothing at all. A soft lad the like of you wouldn't slit the windpipe of a screeching sow.

CHRISTY (*offended*). You're not speaking the truth.

PEGEEN (*in mock rage*). Not speaking the truth, is it? Would you have me knock the head of you with the butt of the broom?

CHRISTY (*twisting round on her with a sharp cry of horror*). Don't strike me. I killed my poor father, Tuesday was a week, for doing the like of that.

PEGEEN (*with blank amazement*). Is it killed your father?

CHRISTY (*subsiding*). With the help of God I did surely, and that the Holy Immaculate Mother may intercede for his soul.

---

36 *land was grabbed* the common landlord practice of seizing tenant's land and evicting him for failing to pay the "rack-rent;" an action often attended with the most inhuman cruelty, rapine, and murder   37 *bailiffs* district officials charged with collecting the tax   38 *divil a one* strong negative   39 *Agents* landlord representatives serving process on tenants failing to pay "the rent." The reference is to what Chesterfield called "the deputy of deputy of deputy system of land tenure."   40 *Munster* South-Western province of Ireland including Kerry   41 *golden guineas* old English coin once worth 21 shillings   42 *farthing* coin worth one-quarter of English penny

43 *holy Luthers* Presbyterians   44 *Boers* South African War (1899–1902); the Boers had a number of Irish Brigades fighting the British   45 *Kruger* Stephen, J. P. (1825–1904), South African statesman and leader of 1880 Boer Rebellion   46 *till Tuesday was a week* a week ago Tuesday

PHILLY (*retreating with* JIMMY). There's a daring fellow.

JIMMY. Oh, glory be to God!

MICHAEL (*with great respect*). That was a hanging crime, mister honey. You should have had good reason for doing the like of that.

CHRISTY (*in a very reasonable tone*). He was a dirty man, God forgive him, and he getting old and crusty, the way I couldn't put up with him at all.

PEGEEN. And you shot him dead?

CHRISTY (*shaking his head*). I never used weapons. I've no licence, and I'm a law-fearing man.

MICHAEL. It was with a hilted knife maybe? I'm told, in the big world, it's bloody knives they use.

CHRISTY (*loudly, scandalized*). Do you take me for a slaughter-boy?

PEGEEN. You never hanged him, the way Jimmy Farrell hanged his dog from the licence,[47] and had it screeching and wriggling three hours at the butt of a string, and himself swearing it was a dead dog, and the peelers swearing it had life?

CHRISTY. I did not then. I just riz[48] the loy[49] and let fall the edge of it on the ridge of his skull, and he went down at my feet like an empty sack, and never let a grunt or groan from him at all.

MICHAEL (*making a sign to* PEGEEN *to fill* CHRISTY'S *glass*). And what way weren't you hanged, mister? Did you bury him then?

CHRISTY (*considering*). Aye. I buried him then. Wasn't I digging spuds in the field?

MICHAEL. And the peelers never followed after you the eleven days that you're out?

CHRISTY (*shaking his head*). Never a one of them, and I walking forward facing hog, dog, or divil on the highway of the road.

PHILLY (*nodding wisely*). It's only with a common week-day kind of a murderer them lads would be trusting their carcase, and

that man should be a great terror when his temper's roused.

MICHAEL. He should then. (*To* CHRISTY) And where was it, mister honey, that you did the deed?

CHRISTY (*looking at him with suspicion*). Oh, a distant place, master of the house, a windy corner of high distant hills.

PHILLY (*nodding with approval*). He's a close man,[50] and he's right surely.

PEGEEN. That'd be a lad with the sense of Solomon to have for a pot-boy, Michael James, if it's the truth you're seeking one at all.

PHILLY. The peelers is fearing him, and if you'd that lad in the house there isn't one of them would come smelling around if the dogs itself were lapping poteen[51] from the dung-pit of the yard.

JIMMY. Bravery's a treasure in a lonesome place, and a lad would kill his father, I'm thinking, would face a foxy divil with a pitchpike[52] on the flags of hell.

PEGEEN. It's the truth they're saying, and if I'd that lad in the house, I wouldn't be fearing the loosèd kharki cut-throats,[53] or the walking dead.

CHRISTY (*swelling with surprise and triumph*). Well, glory be to God!

MICHAEL (*with deference*). Would you think well to stop here and be pot-boy, mister honey, if we gave you good wages, and didn't destroy you with the weight of work?

SHAWN (*coming forward uneasily*). That'd be a queer kind to bring into a decent quiet household with the like of Pegeen Mike.

PEGEEN (*very sharply*). Will you wisht? Who's speaking to you?

SHAWN (*retreating*). A bloody-handed murderer the like of . . .

PEGEEN (*snapping at him*). Whisht I am saying; we'll take no fooling from your like at all. (*To* CHRISTY *with a honeyed voice*) And you, young fellow, you'd have a right to stop,

---

47 *from the licence* on account of the dog licence fee which he either would not or could not pay　48 *riz* raised; an example of strong inflection preferred by the Irish　49 *loy* a long narrow spade

50 *close man* a tight-lipped man　51 *poteen* illicit whiskey　52 *pitchpike* pitchfork　53 *loosèd kharki cut-throats* the English Garrison

I'm thinking, for we'd do our all and utmost to content your needs.

CHRISTY (*overcome with wonder*). And I'd be safe this place from the searching law?

MICHAEL. You would, surely. If they're not fearing you, itself, the peelers in this place is decent droughty[54] poor fellows, wouldn't touch a cur dog and not give warning in the dead of night.

PEGEEN (*very kindly and persuasively*). Let you stop a short while anyhow. Aren't you destroyed walking with your feet in bleeding blisters, and your whole skin needing washing like a Wicklow sheep.

CHRISTY (*looking round with satisfaction*). It's a nice room, and if it's not humbugging me you are, I'm thinking that I'll surely stay.

JIMMY (*jumps up*). Now, by the grace of God, herself[55] will be safe this night, with a man killed his father holding danger from the door, and let you come on, Michael James, or they'll have the best stuff drunk at the wake.

MICHAEL (*going to the door with men*). And begging your pardon, mister, what name will we call you, for we'd like to know?

CHRISTY. Christopher Mahon.

MICHAEL. Well, God bless you, Christy, and a good rest till we meet again when the sun'll be rising to the noon of day.

CHRISTY. God bless you all.

MEN. God bless you.

(*They go out except* SHAWN, *who lingers at door.*)

SHAWN (*to* PEGEEN). Are you wanting me to stop along with you and keep you from harm?

PEGEEN (*gruffly*). Didn't you say you were fearing Father Reilly?

SHAWN. There'd be no harm staying now, I'm thinking, and himself in it[56] too.

PEGEEN. You wouldn't stay when there was need for you, and let you step off nimble this time when there's none.

SHAWN. Didn't I say it was Father Reilly . . .

PEGEEN. Go on, then, to Father Reilly (*in a jeering tone*), and let him put you in the holy brotherhoods,[57] and leave that lad to me.

SHAWN. If I meet the Widow Quin . . .

PEGEEN. Go on, I'm saying, and don't be waking this place with your noise. (*She hustles him out and bolts door.*) That lad would wear the spirits from the saints of peace. (*Bustles about, then takes off her apron and pins it up in the window as a blind.* CHRISTY *watching her timidly. Then she comes to him and speaks with bland good-humour.*) Let you stretch out now by the fire, young fellow. You should be destroyed travelling.

CHRISTY (*shyly again, drawing off his boots*). I'm tired surely, walking wild eleven days, and waking fearful in the night.

(*He holds up one of his feet, feeling his blisters, and looking at them with compassion.*)

PEGEEN (*standing beside him, watching him with delight*). You should have had great people in your family, I'm thinking, with the little, small feet you have, and you with a kind of a quality name,[58] the like of what you'd find on the great powers and potentates of France and Spain.

CHRISTY (*with pride*). We were great surely, with wide and windy acres of rich Munster land.

PEGEEN. Wasn't I telling you, and you a fine, handsome young fellow with a noble brow?

CHRISTY (*with a flash of delighted surprise*). Is it me?

PEGEEN. Aye. Did you never hear that from the young girls where you come from in the west or south?

CHRISTY (*with venom*). I did not then. Oh, they're bloody[59] liars in the naked parish where I grew a man.

---

54 *droughty* thirsty   55 *herself* Pegeen   56 *himself in it* Christy here

57 *holy brotherhoods* religious groups of men with vows of poverty, chastity, and obedience   58 *quality name* a gentry name, an aristocrat   59 *bloody* in the West a mild expletive like beastly or bloomin'. Recall the furor over Shaw's use of it in *Pygmalion*

PEGEEN. If they are itself, you've heard it these days, I'm thinking, and you walking the world telling out your story to young girls or old.

CHRISTY. I've told my story no place till this night, Pegeen Mike, and it's foolish I was here, maybe, to be talking free, but you're decent people, I'm thinking, and yourself a kindly woman, the way I wasn't fearing you at all.

PEGEEN (*filling a sack with straw*). You've said the like of that, maybe, in every cot[60] and cabin where you've met a young girl on your way.

CHRISTY (*going over to her, gradually raising his voice*). I've said it nowhere till this night, I'm telling you, for I've seen none the like of you the eleven long days I am walking the world, looking over a low ditch or a high ditch on my north or south, into stony scattered fields, or scribes[61] of bog, where you'd see young, limber girls, and fine prancing women making laughter with the men.

PEGEEN. If you weren't destroyed travelling, you'd have as much talk and streeleen,[62] I'm thinking, as Owen Roe O'Sullivan[63] or the poets of the Dingle Bay,[64] and I've heard all times it's the poets are your like, fine fiery fellows with great rages when their temper's roused.

CHRISTY (*drawing a little nearer to her*). You've a power[65] of rings, God bless you, and would there be any offence if I was asking are you single now?

PEGEEN. What would I want wedding so young?

CHRISTY (*with relief*). We're alike, so.

PEGEEN (*she puts sack on settle and beats it up*). I never killed my father. I'd be afeard to do that, except I was the like of yourself with blind rages tearing me within, for I'm thinking you should have had great tussling when the end was come.

CHRISTY (*expanding with delight at the first confidential talk he has ever had with a woman*). We had not then. It was a hard woman[66] was come over the hill, and if he was always a crusty kind when he'd a hard woman setting him on, not the divil himself or his four fathers[67] could put up with him at all.

PEGEEN (*with curiosity*). And isn't it a great wonder that one wasn't fearing you?

CHRISTY (*very confidentially*). Up to the day I killed my father, there wasn't a person in Ireland knew the kind I was, and I there drinking, waking, eating, sleeping, a quiet, simple poor fellow with no man giving me heed.

PEGEEN (*getting a quilt out of cupboard and putting it on the sack*). It was the girls were giving you heed maybe, and I'm thinking it's most conceit you'd have to be gaming[68] with their like.

CHRISTY (*shaking his head, with simplicity*). Not the girls itself, and I won't tell you a lie. There wasn't anyone heeding me in that place saving only the dumb beasts of the field.   (*He sits down at fire.*)

PEGEEN (*with disappointment*). And I thinking you should have been living the like of a king of Norway or the eastern world.[69]

(*She comes and sits beside him after placing bread and mug of milk on the table.*)

CHRISTY (*laughing piteously*). The like of a king, is it? And I after toiling, moiling,[70] digging, dodging[71] from the dawn till dusk with never a sight of joy or sport saving only when I'd be abroad in the dark night poaching rabbits on hills, for I was a divil to poach, God forgive me, (*very naively*) and I near got six months for going with a dung fork and stabbing a fish.

PEGEEN. And it's that you'd call sport, is it, to be abroad in the darkness with yourself alone?

CHRISTY. I did, God help me, and there I'd

---

60 *cot* a small cabin or cottage   61 *scribes* long and narrow strips of arable land   62 *streeleen* chatter   63 *Owen Roe O'Sullivan* 18th century Kerry poet, something of a playboy himself   64 *Dingle Bay* a large inlet of the Kerry coast   65 *a power* a large quantity

66 *hard woman* dreadful woman   67 *four fathers* whole family   68 *gaming* fooling   69 *eastern world* a sort of wonderland in Irish folktales   70 *moiling* working hard   71 *dodging* going at a slow pace over a small job

be as happy as the sunshine of St. Martin's Day,[72] watching the light passing the north or the patches of fog, till I'd hear a rabbit starting to screech and I'd go running in the furze. Then when I'd my full share I'd come walking down where you'd see the ducks and geese stretched sleeping on the highway of the road, and before I'd pass the dunghill, I'd hear himself snoring out, a loud lonesome snore he'd be making all times, the while he was sleeping, and he a man'd be raging all times, the while he was waking, like a gaudy officer you'd hear cursing and damning and swearing oaths.

PEGEEN. Providence and Mercy, spare us all!

CHRISTY. It's that you'd say surely if you seen him and he after drinking for weeks, rising up in the red dawn, or before it maybe, and going out into the yard as naked as an ash tree in the moon of May, and shying clods against the visage of the stars till he'd put the fear of death into the banbhs[73] and the screeching sows.

PEGEEN. I'd be well-nigh afeard of that lad myself, I'm thinking. And there was no one in it but the two of you alone?

CHRISTY. The divil a one, though he'd sons and daughters walking all great states and territories of the world, and not a one of them, to this day, but would say their seven curses on him, and they rousing up to let a cough or sneeze, maybe, in the deadness of the night.

PEGEEN (*nodding her head*). Well, you should have been a queer lot. I never cursed my father the like of that, though I'm twenty and more years of age.

CHRISTY. Then you'd have cursed mine. I'm telling you, and he a man never gave peace to any, saving when he'd get two months or three, or be locked in the asylums for battering peelers or assaulting men, (*with depression*) the way it was a bitter life he led me till I did up a Tuesday and halve his skull.

PEGEEN (*putting her hand on his shoulder*). Well, you'll have peace in this place, Christy Mahon, and none to trouble you, and it's near time a fine lad like you should have your good share of the earth.

CHRISTY. It's time surely, and I a seemly fellow with great strength in me and bravery of . . .

(*Some one knocks*)

CHRISTY (*clinging to* PEGEEN). Oh, glory! it's late for knocking, and this last while I'm in terror of the peelers, and the walking dead.

(*Knocking again.*)

PEGEEN. Who's there?

VOICE (*outside*). Me.

PEGEEN. Who's me?

VOICE. The Widow Quin.

PEGEEN (*jumping up and giving him the bread and milk*). Go on now with your supper, and let on[74] to be sleepy, for if she found you were such a warrant to talk, she'd be stringing gabble till the dawn of day.

(*He takes bread and sits shyly with his back to the door.*)

PEGEEN (*opening door, with temper*). What ails you, or what is it you're wanting at this hour of the night?

WIDOW QUIN (*coming in a step and peering at* CHRISTY). I'm after meeting Shawn Keogh and Father Reilly below, who told me of your curiosity man, and they fearing by this time he was maybe roaring, romping on your hands with drink.

PEGEEN (*pointing to* CHRISTY). Look now is he roaring, and he stretched out drowsy with his supper and his mug of milk. Walk down and tell that to Father Reilly and to Shaneen Keogh.

WIDOW QUIN (*coming forward*). I'll not see them again, for I've their word[75] to lead that lad forward for to lodge with me.

---

72 *St. Martin's Day* November 11th   73 *banbhs* young pigs

74 *let on* pretend   75 *word* their orders

PEGEEN (*in blank amazement*). This night, is it?

WIDOW QUIN (*going over*). This night. "It isn't fitting," says the priesteen,[76] "to have his likeness lodging with an orphaned girl." (*To* CHRISTY) God save you, mister!

CHRISTY (*shyly*). God save you kindly.

WIDOW QUIN (*looking at him with half-amused curiosity*). Well, aren't you a little smiling fellow? It should have been great and bitter torments did rouse your spirits to a deed of blood.

CHRISTY (*doubtfully*). It should, maybe.

WIDOW QUIN. It's more than "maybe" I'm saying, and it'd soften my heart to see you sitting so simple with your cup and cake, and you fitter to be saying your catechism than slaying your da.[77]

PEGEEN (*at counter, washing glasses*). There's talking[78] when any'd see he's fit to be holding his head high with the wonders of the world. Walk on from this, for I'll not have him tormented and he destroyed travelling since Tuesday was a week.

WIDOW QUIN (*peaceably*). We'll be walking surely when his supper's done, and you'll find we're great company, young fellow, when it's of the like of you and me you'd hear the penny poets[79] singing in an August Fair.

CHRISTY (*innocently*). Did you kill your father?

PEGEEN (*contemptuously*). She did not. She hit himself[80] with a worn pick, and the rusted poison did corrode his blood the way he never overed it,[81] and died after. That was a sneaky kind of murder did win small glory with the boys itself.

(*She crosses to* CHRISTY's *left.*)

WIDOW QUIN (*with good-humour*). If it didn't, maybe all knows a widow woman has buried her children and destroyed her man is a wiser comrade for a young lad than a girl, the like of you, who'd go helter-skeltering after any man would let you a wink upon the road.

PEGEEN (*breaking out into wild rage*). And you'll say that, Widow Quin, and you gasping with the rage you had racing the hill beyond to look on his face.

WIDOW QUIN (*laughing derisively*). Me, is it? Well, Father Reilly has cuteness[82] to divide you now. (*She pulls* CHRISTY *up.*) There's great temptation in a man did slay his da, and we'd best be going, young fellow; so rise up and come with me.

PEGEEN (*seizing his arm*). He'll not stir. He's pot-boy in this place, and I'll not have him stolen off and kidnapped while himself's abroad.

WIDOW QUIN. It'd be a crazy pot-boy'd lodge him in the shebeen[83] where he works by day, so you'd have a right to come on, young fellow, till you see my little houseen,[84] a perch off on the rising hill.

PEGEEN. Wait till morning, Christy Mahon. Wait till you lay eyes on her leaky thatch is growing more pasture[85] for her buck goat than her square of fields, and she without a tramp itself to keep in order her place at all.

WIDOW QUIN. When you see me contriving in my little gardens, Christy Mahon, you'll swear the Lord God formed me to be living lone, and that there isn't my match in Mayo for thatching, or mowing, or shearing a sheep.

PEGEEN (*with noisy scorn*). It's true the Lord God formed you to contrive indeed. Doesn't the world know you reared a black ram at your own breast, so that the Lord Bishop of Connaught felt the elements of a Christian, and he eating it after in a kidney stew? Doesn't the world know you've been shaving the foxy skipper from France[86] for a threepenny bit and a sop of grass tobacco would wring the liver from

---

76 *priesteen* little priest, used contemptuously   77 *da* father   78 *There's talking* ironically—grand talk, great talk   79 *penny poets* ballad-singers   80 *himself* her husband   81 *overed it* recovered

82 *cuteness* sharpness or ingenuity   83 *shebeen* an unlicensed place where intoxicating liquors are sold   84 *houseen* little house   85 *pasture* her thatch roof has been up so long that grass has taken root there   86 *skipper from France* from French trawlers fishing off the coast

a mountain goat you'd meet leaping the hills?

WIDOW QUIN (*with amusement*). Do you hear her now, young fellow? Do you hear the way she'll be rating at your own self when a week is by?

PEGEEN (*to* CHRISTY). Don't heed her. Tell her to go on into her pigsty and not plague us here.

WIDOW QUIN. I'm going; but he'll come with me.

PEGEEN (*shaking him*). Are you dumb, young fellow?

CHRISTY (*timidly, to* WIDOW QUIN). God increase you;[87] but I'm pot-boy in this place, and it's here I'd liefer[88] stay.

PEGEEN (*triumphantly*). Now you have heard him, and go on from this.

WIDOW QUIN (*looking round the room*). It's lonesome this hour crossing the hill, and if he won't come along with me, I'd have a right maybe to stop this night with yourselves. Let me stretch out on the settle, Pegeen Mike; and himself can lie by the hearth.

PEGEEN (*short and fiercely*). Faith,[89] I won't. Quit off[90] or I will send you now.

WIDOW QUIN (*gathering her shawl up*). Well, it's a terror to be aged a score. (*To* CHRISTY) God bless you now, young fellow, and let you be wary, or there's right torment will await you here if you go romancing with her like, and she waiting only, as they bade me say, on a sheepskin parchment[91] to be wed with Shawn Keogh of Killakeen.

CHRISTY (*going to* PEGEEN *as she bolts door*). What's that she's after saying?

PEGEEN. Lies and blather, you've no call to mind. Well, isn't Shawn Keogh an impudent fellow to send up spying on me? Wait till I lay hands on him. Let him wait, I'm saying.

CHRISTY. And you're not wedding him at all?

PEGEEN. I wouldn't wed him if a bishop came walking for to join us here.

CHRISTY. That God in glory may be thanked for that.

PEGEEN. There's your bed now. I've put a quilt upon you I'm after quilting a while since[92] with my own two hands, and you'd best stretch out now for your sleep, and may God give you a good rest till I call you in the morning when the cocks will crow.

CHRISTY (*as she goes to inner room*). May God and Mary and St. Patrick bless you and reward you, for your kindly talk. (*She shuts the door behind her. He settles his bed slowly, feeling the quilt with immense satisfaction.*) Well, it's a clean bed and soft with it,[93] and it's great luck and company I've won me in the end of time—two fine women fighting for the likes of me—till I'm thinking this night wasn't I a foolish fellow not to kill my father in the years gone by.

CURTAIN

ACT II

SCENE: *As before. Brilliant morning light.* CHRISTY, *looking bright and cheerful, is cleaning a girl's boots.*

CHRISTY (*to himself, counting jugs on dresser*). Half a hundred beyond. Ten there. A score that's above. Eighty jugs. Six cups and a broken one. Two plates. A power of glasses. Bottles, a schoolmaster'd be hard set to count, and enough in them, I'm thinking, to drunken all the wealth and wisdom of the County Clare.[1] (*He puts down the boot carefully.*) There's her boots now, nice and decent for her evening use, and isn't it grand brushes she has? (*He puts them down and goes by degrees to the looking-glass.*) Well,

---

87 *God increase you* meaning your substance, an Irish blessing 88 *liefer* rather 89 *Faith* in faith, not to be used lightly 90 *Quit off* get out 91 *sheepskin parchment* the dispensation

92 *a while since* a while ago 93 *soft with it* soft too
1 *County Clare* Western county bordering the Atlantic between Galway and Kerry

this'd be a fine place to be my whole life talking out with swearing Christians, in place of my old dogs and cat, and I stalking around, smoking my pipe and drinking my fill, and never a day's work but drawing a cork an odd time, or wiping a glass, or rinsing out a shiny tumbler for a decent man. (*He takes the looking-glass from the wall and puts it on the back of a chair; then sits down in front of it and begins washing his face.*) Didn't I know rightly I was handsome, though it was the divil's own mirror we had beyond, would twist a squint across an angel's brow, and I'll be growing fine from this day, the way I'll have a soft lovely skin on me and won't be the like of the clumsy young fellows do be ploughing all times in the earth and dung. (*He starts.*) Is she coming again? (*He looks out.*) Stranger girls. God help me, where'll I hide myself away and my long neck naked to the world? (*He looks out.*) I'd best go to the room maybe till I'm dressed again.

(*He gathers up his coat and the looking-glass, and runs into the inner room. The door is pushed open, and* SUSAN BRADY *looks in, and knocks on door.*)

SUSAN. There's nobody in it. (*Knocks again*)
NELLY (*pushing her in and following her, with* HONOR BLAKE *and* SARA TANSEY). It'd be early for them both to be out walking the hill.
SUSAN. I'm thinking Shawn Keogh was making game of us and there's no such man in it at all.
HONOR (*pointing to straw and quilt*). Look at that. He's been sleeping there in the night. Well, it'll be a hard case[2] if he's gone off now, the way we'll never set our eyes on a man killed his father, and we after rising early and destroying ourselves running fast on the hill.
NELLY. Are you thinking them's his boots?
SARA (*taking them up*). If they are, there should be his father's track on them. Did you

never read in the papers the way murdered men do bleed and drip?
SUSAN. Is that blood there, Sara Tansey?
SARA (*smelling it*). That's bog water, I'm thinking, but it's his own they are surely, for I never seen the like of them for whitely mud, and red mud, and turf on them, and the fine sands. of the sea. That man's been walking, I'm telling you.

(*She goes down right, putting on one of his boots.*)

SUSAN (*going to window*). Maybe he's stolen off to Belmullet[3] with the boots of Michael James, and you'd have a right so to follow after him, Sara Tansey, and you the one yoked the ass cart and drove ten miles to set your eyes on the man bit the yellow lady's nostril on the northern shore.
                                   (*She looks out.*)
SARA (*running to window, with one boot on*). Don't be talking, and we fooled to-day. (*Putting on the other boot*) There's a pair do fit me well, and I'll be keeping them for walking to the priest, when you'd be ashamed this place, going up winter and summer with nothing worth while to confess at all.
HONOR (*who has been listening at door*). Whisht! there's some one inside the room. (*She pushes door a chink open.*) It's a man.

(*Sara kicks off boots and puts them where they were. They all stand in a line looking through chink.*)

SARA. I'll call him. Mister! Mister! (*He puts in his head.*) Is Pegeen within?
CHRISTY (*coming in as meek as a mouse, with the looking-glass held behind his back*). She's above on the cnuceen,[4] seeking the nanny goats, the way she'd have a sup of goat's milk for to colour my tea.
SARA. And asking your pardon, is it you's the man killed his father?

2 *a hard case* a sad state of affairs

3 *Belmullet* small seaport on Mullet peninsula 4 *cnuceen* Irish for little hill

CHRISTY (*sidling toward the nail where the glass was hanging*). I am, God help me!

SARA (*taking eggs she has brought*). Then my thousand welcomes to you, and I've run up with a brace of duck's eggs for your food to-day. Pegeen's ducks is no use, but these are the real rich sort. Hold out your hand and you'll see it's no lie I'm telling you.

CHRISTY (*coming forward shyly, and holding out his left hand*). They're a great and weighty size.

SUSAN. And I run up with a pat of butter, for it'd be a poor thing to have you eating your spuds dry, and you after running a great way since you did destroy your da.

CHRISTY. Thank you kindly.

HONOR. And I brought you a little cut of a cake, for you should have a thin stomach on you, and you that length walking the world.

NELLY. And I brought you a little laying pullet—boiled and all she is—was crushed at the fall of night by the curate's car. Feel the fat of that breast, Mister.

CHRISTY. It's bursting, surely.

(*He feels it with the back of his hand, in which he holds the presents.*)

SARA. Will you pinch it? Is your right hand too sacred for to use at all? (*She slips round behind him.*) It's a glass he has. Well, I never seen to this day a man with a looking-glass held to his back. Them that kills their fathers is a vain lot surely. (GIRLS *giggle.*)

CHRISTY (*smiling innocently and piling presents on glass*). I'm very thankful to you all to-day. . . .

WIDOW QUIN (*coming in quickly, at door.*) Sara Tansey, Susan Brady, Honor Blake! What in glory has you here at this hour of day?

GIRLS (*giggling*). That's the man killed his father.

WIDOW QUIN (*coming to them*). I know well it's the man; and I'm after putting him down in the sports below for racing, leaping, pitching, and the Lord knows what.

SARA (*exuberantly*). That's right, Widow Quin.

I'll bet my dowry that he'll lick the world.

WIDOW QUIN. If you will, you'd have a right to have him fresh and nourished in place of nursing a feast. (*Taking presents*) Are you fasting or fed, young fellow?

CHRISTY. Fasting, if you please.

WIDOW QUIN (*loudly*). Well, you're the lot. Stir up now and give him his breakfast. (*To* CHRISTY) Come here to me (*she puts him on bench beside her while the girls make tea and get his breakfast*) and let you tell us your story before Pegeen will come, in place of grinning your ears off like the moon of May.

CHRISTY (*beginning to be pleased*). It's a long story; you'd be destroyed listening.

WIDOW QUIN. Don't be letting on to be shy, a fine, gamey,[5] treacherous lad the like of you. Was it in your house beyond you cracked his skull?

CHRISTY (*shy but flattered*). It was not. We were digging spuds in his cold, sloping, stony, divil's patch of a field.

WIDOW QUIN. And you went asking money of him, or making talk of getting a wife would drive him from his farm?

CHRISTY. I did not, then; but there I was, digging and digging, and "You squinting idiot," says he, "let you walk down now and tell the priest you'll wed the Widow Casey in a score of days."

WIDOW QUIN. And what kind was she?

CHRISTY (*with horror*). A walking terror from beyond the hills, and she two score and five years, and two hundredweights and five pounds in the weighing scales, with a limping leg on her, and a blinded eye, and she a woman of noted misbehaviour with the old and young.

GIRLS (*clustering round him, serving him*). Glory be.

WIDOW QUIN. And what did he want driving you to wed her?

(*She takes a bit of the chicken.*)

CHRISTY (*eating with growing satisfaction*). He was letting on I was wanting a protector

5 *gamey* merry

from the harshness of the world, and he without a thought the whole while but how he'd have her hut to live in and her gold to drink.

WIDOW QUIN. There's maybe worse than a dry hearth and a widow woman and your glass at night. So you hit him then?

CHRISTY (*getting almost excited*). I did not. "I won't wed her," says I, "when all know she did suckle me for six weeks when I came into the world, and she a hag this day with a tongue on her has the crows and seabirds scattered, the way they wouldn't cast a shadow on her garden with the dread of her curse."

WIDOW QUIN (*teasingly*). That one should be right company.

SARA (*eagerly*). Don't mind her. Did you kill him then?

CHRISTY. "She's too good for the like of you," says he, "and go on now or I'll flatten you out like a crawling beast has passed under a dray."[6] "You will not if I can help it," says I. "Go on," says he, "or I'll have the divil making garters of your limbs tonight." "You will not if I can help it," says I. (*He sits up, brandishing his mug.*)

SARA. You were right surely.

CHRISTY (*impressively*). With that the sun came out between the cloud and the hill, and it shining green in my face. "God have mercy on your soul," says he, lifting a scythe; "or on your own," says I, raising the loy.

SUSAN. That's a grand story.

HONOR. He tells it lovely.

CHRISTY (*flattered and confident, waving bone*). He gave a drive with the scythe, and I gave a lep[7] to the east. Then I turned around with my back to the north, and I hit a blow on the ridge of his skull, laid him stretched out, and he split to the knob of his gullet.

(*He raises the chicken bone to his Adam's apple.*)

GIRLS (*together*). Well, you're a marvel! Oh, God bless you! You're the lad surely!

SUSAN. I'm thinking the Lord God sent him this road to make a second husband to the Widow Quin, and she with a great yearning to be wedded, though all dread her here. Lift him on her knee, Sara Tansey.

WIDOW QUIN. Don't tease him.

SARA (*going over to dresser and counter very quickly, and getting two glasses and porter*). You're heroes surely, and let you drink a supeen[8] with your arms linked like the outlandish lovers in the sailor's song. (*She links their arms and gives them the glasses.*) There now. Drink a health to the wonders of the western world,[9] the pirates, preachers, poteen-makers, with the jobbing jockies;[10] parching peelers, and the juries fill their stomachs selling judgments of the English law.

(*Brandishing the bottle*)

WIDOW QUIN. That's a right toast, Sara Tansey. Now Christy.

(*They drink with their arms linked, he drinking with his left hand, she with her right. As they are drinking, PEGEEN MIKE comes in with a milk can and stands aghast. They all spring away from CHRISTY. He goes down left. WIDOW QUIN remains seated.*)

PEGEEN (*angrily to SARA*). What is it you're wanting?

SARA (*twisting her apron*). An ounce of tobacco.

PEGEEN. Have you tuppence?[11]

SARA. I've forgotten my purse.

PEGEEN. Then you'd best be getting it and not be fooling us here. (*To the WIDOW QUIN, with more elaborate scorn*) And what is it you're wanting, Widow Quin?

WIDOW QUIN (*insolently*). A penn'orth[12] of starch.

PEGEEN (*breaking out*). And you without a white shift[13] or a shirt in your whole family

---

6 *dray* a little cart with or without wheels   7 *lep* a leap

8 *supeen* a little sup   9 *western world* western Ireland
10 *jobbing jockies* men who go round breaking in horses
11 *tuppence* two pence   12 *penn'orth* penny worth   13
shift a woman's slip

since the drying of the flood. I've no starch for the like of you, and let you walk on now to Killamuck.

WIDOW QUIN (*turning to* CHRISTY, *as she goes out with the girls*). Well, you're mighty huffy this day, Pegeen Mike, and, you young fellow, let you not forget the sports and racing when the noon is by.

(*They go out.*)

PEGEEN (*imperiously*). Fling out that rubbish and put them cups away. (CHRISTY *tidies away in great haste.*) Shove in the bench by the wall. (*He does so.*) And hang that glass[14] on the nail. What disturbed it at all?

CHRISTY (*very meekly*). I was making myself decent only, and this a fine country for young lovely girls.

PEGEEN (*sharply*). Whisht your talking of girls.

(*Goes to counter on right*)

CHRISTY. Wouldn't any wish to be decent in a place . . .

PEGEEN. Whisht I'm saying.

CHRISTY (*looks at her face for a moment with great misgivings, then as a last effort, takes up a loy, and goes towards her, with feigned assurance*). It was with a loy the like of that I killed my father.

PEGEEN (*still sharply*). You've told me that story six times since the dawn of day.

CHRISTY (*reproachfully*). It's a queer thing you wouldn't care to be hearing it and them girls after walking four miles to be listening to me now.

PEGEEN (*turning round astonished*). Four miles?

CHRISTY (*apologetically*). Didn't himself say there were only bona fides[15] living in the place?

PEGEEN. It's bona fides by the road they are, but that lot came over the river lepping[16] the stones. It's not three perches when you go like that, and I was down this morning looking on the papers the post-boy does have in his bag. (*With meaning and emphasis*) For there was great news this day, Christopher Mahon.

(*She goes into room on left.*)

CHRISTY (*suspiciously*). Is it news of my murder?

PEGEEN (*inside*). Murder, indeed.

CHRISTY (*loudly*). A murdered da?

PEGEEN (*coming in again and crossing right*). There was not, but a story filled half a page of the hanging of a man. Ah, that should be a fearful end, young fellow, and it worst of all for a man destroyed his da, for the like of him would get small mercies, and when it's dead he is, they'd put him in a narrow grave, with cheap sacking wraping him round, and pour down quicklime on his head, the way you'd see a woman pouring any frish-frash[17] from a cup.

CHRISTY (*very miserably*). Oh, God help me. Are you thinking I'm safe? You were saying at the fall of night, I was shut of[18] jeopardy and I here with yourselves.

PEGEEN (*severely*). You'll be shut of jeopardy no place if you go talking with a pack of wild girls the like of them do be walking abroad with the peelers, talking whispers at the fall of night.

CHRISTY (*with terror*). And you're thinking they'd tell?

PEGEEN (*with mock sympathy*). Who knows, God help you?

CHRISTY (*loudly*). What joy would they have to bring hanging to the likes of me?

PEGEEN. It's queer joys they have, and who knows the thing they'd do, if it'd make the green stones cry itself to think of you swaying and swiggling at the butt of a rope, and you with a fine, stout neck, God bless you! the way you'd be a half an hour, in great anguish, getting your death.

CHRISTY (*getting his boots and putting them on*). If there's that terror of them, it'd be best,

14 *glass* the mirror   15 *bona fides* earlier Michael James had reassured Christy that no one except a widow lived within four miles of his public house so that anyone coming at any hour could *bona fide* call for a drink and be served without prejudice to the licensing laws   16 *lepping* leaping

17 *frish-frash* a kind of Indian meal and raw cabbage boiled down as thin as gruel   18 *shut of* to be rid of

maybe, I went on wandering like Esau[19] or Cain and Abel[20] on the sides of Neifin[21] or the Erris plain.[22]

PEGEEN (*beginning to play with him*). It would, maybe, for I've heard the Circuit Judges this place is a heartless crew.

CHRISTY (*bitterly*). It's more than Judges this place is a heartless crew. (*Looking up at her*) And isn't it a poor thing to be starting again and I a lonesome fellow will be looking out on women and girls the way the needy fallen spirits do be looking on the Lord?

PEGEEN. What call[23] have you to be that lonesome when there's poor girls walking Mayo in their thousands now?

CHRISTY (*grimly*). It's well you know what call I have. It's well you know it's a lonesome thing to be passing small towns with the lights shining sideways when the night is down, or going in strange places with a dog noising before you and a dog noising behind, or drawn to the cities where you'd hear a voice kissing and talking deep love in every shadow of the ditch, and you passing on with an empty, hungry stomach failing from your heart.

PEGEEN. I'm thinking you're an odd man, Christy Mahon. The oddest walking fellow I ever set my eyes on to this hour to-day.

CHRISTY. What would any be but odd men and they living lonesome in the world?

PEGEEN. I'm not odd, and I'm my whole life with my father only.

CHRISTY (*with infinite admiration*). How would a lovely handsome woman the like of you be lonesome when all men should be thronging around to hear the sweetness of your voice, and the little infant children should be pestering your steps I'm thinking, and you walking the roads.

PEGEEN. I'm hard set to know what way a coaxing fellow the like of yourself should be lonesome either.

CHRISTY. Coaxing?

PEGEEN. Would you have me think a man never talked with the girls would have the words you've spoken to-day? It's only letting on you are to be lonesome, the way you'd get around me now.

CHRISTY. I wish to God I was letting on; but I was lonesome all times, and born lonesome, I'm thinking, as the moon of dawn. (*Going to door*)

PEGEEN (*puzzled by his talk*). Well, it's a story I'm not understanding at all why you'd be worse than another, Christy Mahon, and you a fine lad with the great savagery to destroy your da.

CHRISTY. It's little I'm understanding myself, saving only that my heart's scalded this day, and I going off stretching out the earth between us, the way I'll not be waking near you another dawn of the year till the two of us do arise to hope or judgment with the saints of God, and now I'd best be going with my wattle[24] in my hand, for hanging is a poor thing (*turning to go*), and it's little welcome only is left me in this house to-day.

PEGEEN (*sharply*). Christy! (*He turns round.*) Come here to me. (*He goes towards her.*) Lay down that switch and throw some sods on the fire. You're pot-boy in this place, and I'll not have you mitch off[25] from us now.

CHRISTY. You were saying I'd be hanged if I stay.

PEGEEN (*quite kindly at last*). I'm after going down and reading the fearful crimes of Ireland for two weeks or three, and there wasn't a word of your murder. (*Getting up and going over to the counter*) They've likely not found the body. You're safe so[26] with ourselves.

CHRISTY (*astonished, slowly*). It's making game of me you were (*following her with fearful joy*), and I can stay so, working at your

---

19 *Esau* elder son of Isaac and Rebekah and brother of Jacob. Christy, like Esau, has lost his birthright—the right to inherit Old Mahon's "divil's patch," and so must provide for himself 20 *Cain and Abel* Christy like Cain is guilty of murder and now shares the curse of Cain to be a wanderer and a fugitive on the face of the earth 21 *Neifin* Mayo's Mount Nephin (Irish, *Néifin*) just west of Lough Conn 22 *Erris plain* the plain of North Mayo 23 *What call* what right

24 *wattle* a short thick stick 25 *mitch off* to sneak away, to play truant 26 *safe so* in that case

side, and I not lonesome from this mortal day.

PEGEEN. What's to hinder you staying, except the widow woman or the young girls would inveigle[27] you off?

CHRISTY (*with rapture*). And I'll have your words from this day filling my ears, and that look is come upon you meeting my two eyes, and I watching you loafing around in the warm sun, or rinsing your ankles when the night is come.

PEGEEN (*kindly, but a little embarrassed*). I'm thinking you'll be a loyal young lad to have working around, and if you vexed me a while since with your leaguing[28] with the girls, I wouldn't give a thraneen[29] for a lad hadn't a mighty spirit in him and a gamey heart.

(SHAWN KEOGH *runs in carrying a cleeve[30] on his back, followed by the* WIDOW QUIN.)

SHAWN (*to* PEGEEN). I was passing below, and I seen your mountainy sheep eating cabbages in Jimmy's field. Run up or they'll be bursting surely.

PEGEEN. Oh, God mend them![31]

(*She puts a shawl over her head and runs out.*)

CHRISTY (*looking from one to the other. Still in high spirits*). I'd best go to her aid maybe. I'm handy with ewes.

WIDOW QUIN (*closing the door*). She can do that much, and there is Shaneen has long speeches for to tell you now. (*She sits down with an amused smile.*)

SHAWN (*taking something from his pocket and offering it to* CHRISTY). Do you see that, mister?

CHRISTY (*looking at it*). The half of a ticket to the Western States![32]

SHAWN (*trembling with anxiety*). I'll give it to you and my new hat (*pulling it out of hamper*); and my breeches with the double seat (*pulling it out*); and my new coat is woven from the blackest shearings for three miles around (*giving him the coat*); I'll give you the whole of them, and my blessing, and the blessing of Father Reilly itself, maybe, if you'll quit from this and leave us in the peace we had till last night at the fall of dark.

CHRISTY (*with a new arrogance*). And for what is it you're wanting to get shut of me?

SHAWN (*looking to the* WIDOW *for help*). I'm a poor scholar with middling faculties to coin a lie, so I'll tell you the truth, Christy Mahon. I'm wedding with Pegeen beyond, and I don't think well of having a clever fearless man the like of you dwelling in her house.

CHRISTY (*almost pugnaciously*). And you'd be using bribery for to banish me?

SHAWN (*in an imploring voice*). Let you not take it badly, mister honey, isn't beyond the best place for you where you'll have golden chains and shiny coats and you riding upon hunters with the ladies of the land.

(*He makes an eager sign to the* WIDOW QUIN *to come to help him.*)

WIDOW QUIN (*coming over*). It's true for him, and you'd best quit off and not have that poor girl setting her mind on you, for there's Shaneen thinks she wouldn't suit you though all is saying that she'll wed you now.

(CHRISTY *beams with delight.*)

SHAWN (*in terrified earnest*). She wouldn't suit you, and she with the divil's own temper the way you'd be strangling one another in a score of days. (*He makes the movement of strangling with his hands.*) It's the like of me only that she's fit for, a quiet simple fellow wouldn't raise a hand upon her if she scratched itself.

WIDOW QUIN (*putting* SHAWN's *hat on* CHRISTY). Fit them clothes on you anyhow, young fellow, and he'd maybe loan

27 *inveigle* lure 28 *leaguing* mixing with 29 *thraneen* a straw, a withered stalk of meadow grass 30 *cleeve* a basket, a creel 31 *God mend them* serve them right 32 *half . . . States* one-way ticket to America

them to you for the sports. (*Pushing him towards inner door*) Fit them on and you can give your answer when you have them tried.

CHRISTY (*beaming, delighted with the clothes*). I will then. I'd like herself to see me in them tweeds and hat.

(*He goes into room and shuts the door.*)

SHAWN (*in great anxiety*). He'd like herself to see them. He'll not leave us, Widow Quin. He's a score of divils in him the way it's well nigh certain he will wed Pegeen.

WIDOW QUIN (*jeeringly*). It's true all girls are fond of courage and do hate the like of you.

SHAWN (*walking about in desperation*). Oh, Widow Quin, what'll I be doing now? I'd inform again him,[33] but he'd burst from Kilmainham[34] and he'd be sure and certain to destroy me. If I wasn't so God-fearing, I'd near have courage to come behind him and run a pike[35] into his side. Oh, it's a hard case to be an orphan and not to have your father that you're used to, and you'd easy kill and make yourself a hero in the sight of all. (*Coming up to her*) Oh, Widow Quin, will you find me some contrivance when I've promised you a ewe?

WIDOW QUIN. A ewe's a small thing, but what would you give me if I did wed him and did save you so?

SHAWN (*with astonishment*). You?

WIDOW QUIN. Aye. Would you give me the red cow you have and the mountainy ram, and the right of way across your rye path, and a load of dung at Michaelmas,[36] and turbary[37] upon the western hill?

SHAWN (*radiant with hope*). I would surely, and I'd give you the wedding-ring I have, and the loan of a new suit, the way you'd have him decent on the wedding-day. I'd give you two kids for your dinner, and a gallon

of poteen, and I'd call the piper on the long car[38] to your wedding from Crossmolina[39] or from Ballina.[40] I'd give you . . .

WIDOW QUIN. That'll do, so, and let you whisht, for he's coming now again.

(CHRISTY *comes in very natty in the new clothes.* WIDOW QUIN *goes to him admiringly.*)

WIDOW QUIN. If you seen yourself now, I'm thinking you'd be too proud to speak to us at all, and it'd be a pity surely to have your like sailing from Mayo to the Western World.[41]

CHRISTY (*as proud as a peacock*). I'm not going. If this is a poor place itself, I'll make myself contented to be lodging here.

(WIDOW QUIN *makes a sign to* SHAWN *to leave them.*)

SHAWN. Well, I'm going measuring the racecourse while the tide is low, so I'll leave you the garments and my blessing for the sports to-day. God bless you!

(*He wriggles out.*)

WIDOW QUIN (*admiring* CHRISTY). Well, you're mighty spruce, young fellow. Sit down now while you're quiet till you talk with me.

CHRISTY (*swaggering*). I'm going abroad on the hillside for to seek Pegeen.

WIDOW QUIN. You'll have time and plenty for to seek Pegeen, and you heard me saying at the fall of night the two of us should be great company.

CHRISTY. From this out I'll have no want of company when all sorts is bringing me their food and clothing (*he swaggers to the door, tightening his belt*), the way they'd set their eyes upon a gallant orphan cleft his father with one blow to the breeches belt. (*He opens door, then staggers back.*) Saints of

---

33 *again him* against him   34 *Kilmainham* once notorious Dublin jail   35 *pike* pitchfork   36 *Michaelmas* feast of St. Michael and All Angels, September 29th   37 *turbary* right to cut turf (peat)

38 *long car* an enlarged, four-wheeled, jaunting car   39 *Crossmolina* a small market town of North-East Mayo   40 *Ballina* market town and small seaport of North Mayo   41 *Western World* America

glory! Holy angels from the throne of light!

WIDOW QUIN (*going over*). What ails you?

CHRISTY. It's the walking spirit of my murdered da!

WIDOW QUIN (*looking out*). Is it that tramper?

CHRISTY (*wildly*). Where'll I hide my poor body from that ghost of hell?

(*The door is pushed open, and* OLD MAHON *appears on threshold.* CHRISTY *darts in behind door.*)

WIDOW QUIN (*in great amusement*). God save you, my poor man.

MAHON (*gruffly*). Did you see a young lad passing this way in the early morning or the fall of night?

WIDOW QUIN. You're a queer kind to walk in not saluting at all.

MAHON. Did you see the young lad?

WIDOW QUIN (*stiffly*). What kind was he?

MAHON. An ugly young streeler[42] with a murderous gob[43] on him, and a little switch in his hand. I met a tramper seen him coming this way at the fall of night.

WIDOW QUIN. There's harvest hundreds do be passing these days for the Sligo[44] boat. For what is it you're wanting him, my poor man?

MAHON. I want to destroy him for breaking the head on me with the clout of a loy. (*He takes off a big hat, and shows his head in a mass of bandages and plaster, with some pride.*) It was he did that, and amn't I a great wonder to think I've traced him ten days with that rent in my crown?

WIDOW QUIN (*taking his head in both hands and examining it with extreme delight*). That was a great blow. And who hit you? A robber maybe?

MAHON. It was my own son hit me, and he the divil a robber, or anything else, but a dirty, stuttering lout.

WIDOW QUIN (*letting go his skull and wiping her hands in her apron*). You'd best be wary of a mortified scalp, I think they call it, lepping around with that wound in the splendour of the sun. It was a bad blow surely, and you should have vexed him fearful to make him strike that gash in his da.

MAHON. Is it me?

WIDOW QUIN (*amusing herself*). Aye. And isn't it a great shame when the old and hardened do torment the young?

MAHON (*raging*). Torment him is it? And I after holding out with the patience of a martyred saint till there's nothing but destruction on, and I'm driven out in my old age with none to aid me.

WIDOW QUIN (*greatly amused*). It's a sacred wonder the way that wickedness will spoil a man.

MAHON. My wickedness, is it? Amn't I after saying it is himself has me destroyed, and he a liar on walls,[45] a talker of folly, a man you'd see stretched the half of the day in the brown ferns with his belly to the sun.

WIDOW QUIN. Not working at all?

MAHON. The divil a work, or if he did itself, you'd see him raising up a haystack like the stalk of a rush, or driving our last cow till he broke her leg at the hip, and when he wasn't at that he'd be fooling over little birds he had—finches and felts[46]—or making mugs at his own self in the bit of a glass we had hung on the wall.

WIDOW QUIN (*looking at* CHRISTY). What way was he so foolish? It was running wild after the girls maybe?

MAHON (*with a shout of derision*). Running wild, is it? If he seen a red petticoat coming swinging over the hill, he'd be off to hide in the sticks, and you'd see him shooting out his sheep's eyes between the little twigs and the leaves, and his two ears rising like a hare looking out through a gap. Girls, indeed!

WIDOW QUIN. It was drink maybe?

MAHON. And he a poor fellow would get drunk on the smell of a pint. He'd a queer

---

42 *streeler* an idle, slovenly person   43 *gob* mouth   44 *Sligo* large town and seaport north of Mayo. Seasonal migrants sailed from Sligo for Scotland and England to seek work as harvesters and, with their meagre earnings, to return to pay the rents on their tiny holdings

45 *liar on walls* perhaps of the gossiping and boasting of men leaning against field walls   46 *felts* fieldfares

rotten stomach, I'm telling you, and when I gave him three pulls from my pipe a while since, he was taken with contortions till I had to send him in the ass cart to the females' nurse.

WIDOW QUIN (*clasping her hands*). Well, I never till this day heard tell of a man the like of that!

MAHON. I'd take a mighty oath you didn't surely, and wasn't he the laughing joke of every female woman where four baronies meet, the way the girls would stop their weeding if they seen him coming the road to let a roar at him, and call him the looney[47] of Mahon's.

WIDOW QUIN. I'd give the world and all to see the like of him. What kind was he?

MAHON. A small low fellow.

WIDOW QUIN. And dark?

MAHON. Dark and dirty.

WIDOW QUIN (*considering*). I'm thinking I seen him.

MAHON (*eagerly*). An ugly young black-guard.[48]

WIDOW QUIN. A hideous, fearful villain, and the spit of you.

MAHON. What way is he fled?

WIDOW QUIN. Gone over the hills to catch a coasting steamer to the north or south.

MAHON. Could I pull up on him now?

WIDOW QUIN. If you'll cross the sands below where the tide is out, you'll be in it as soon as himself, for he had to go round ten miles by the top of the bay. (*She points to the door.*) Strike down by the head beyond and then follow on the roadway to the north and east.

(MAHON *goes abruptly.*)

WIDOW QUIN (*shouting after him*). Let you give him a good vengeance when you come up with him, but don't put yourself in the power of the law, for it'd be a poor thing to see a judge in his black cap reading out his sentence on a civil warrior the like of you.

(*She swings the door to and looks at* CHRISTY, *who is cowering in terror, for a moment, then she bursts into a laugh.*)

WIDOW QUIN. Well, you're the walking play-boy of the western world, and that's the poor man you had divided to his breeches belt.

CHRISTY (*looking out: then, to her*). What'll Pegeen say when she hears that story? What'll she be saying to me now?

WIDOW QUIN. She'll knock the head of you, I'm thinking, and drive you from the door. God help her to be taking you for a wonder, and you a little schemer making up a story you destroyed your da.

CHRISTY (*turning to the door, nearly speechless with rage, half to himself*). To be letting on he was dead, and coming back to his life, and following after me like an old weasel tracing a rat, and coming in here laying desolation between my own self and the fine women of Ireland, and he a kind of carcase that you'd fling upon the sea.[49] . . .

WIDOW QUIN (*more soberly*). There's talking[50] for a man's one only son.

CHRISTY (*breaking out*). His one son, is it? May I meet him with one tooth and it aching, and one eye to be seeing seven and seventy divils in the twists of the road, and one old timber leg on him to limp into the scalding grave. (*Looking out*) There he is now crossing the strands, and that the Lord God would send a high wave to wash him from the world.

WIDOW QUIN (*scandalised*). Have you no shame? (*putting her hand on his shoulder and turning him round*) What ails you? Near crying, is it?

CHRISTY (*in despair and grief*). Amn't I after seeing the love-light of the star of knowledge[51] shining from her brow, and hearing words would put you thinking on the holy

47 *looney* idle, stupid fellow   48 *blackguard* a scoundrel

49 *carcase . . . sea* dead sheep and cattle are pushed over the cliffs into the ocean   50 *There's talking* ironically, that's a fine thing to be saying   51 *star of knowledge* conventional Irish love-image

Brigid[52] speaking to the infant saints, and now she'll be turning again, and speaking hard words to me, like an old woman with a spavindy ass[53] she'd have, urging on a hill.

WIDOW QUIN. There's poetry talk for a girl you'd see itching and scratching, and she with a stale stink of poteen on her from selling in the shop.

CHRISTY (*impatiently*). It's her like is fitted to be handling merchandise in the heavens above, and what'll I be doing now, I ask you, and I a kind of wonder was jilted by the heavens when a day was by.

(*There is a distant noise of girls' voices.* WIDOW QUIN *looks from window and comes to him, hurriedly.*)

WIDOW QUIN. You'll be doing like myself, I'm thinking, when I did destroy my man, for I'm above many's the day, odd times in great spirits, abroad in the sunshine, darning a stocking or stitching a shift, and odd times again looking out on the schooners, hookers,[54] trawlers is sailing the sea, and I thinking on the gallant hairy fellows are drifting beyond, and myself long years living alone.

CHRISTY (*interested*). You're like me, so.

WIDOW QUIN. I am your like, and it's for that I'm taking a fancy to you, and I with my little houseen above where there'd be myself to tend you, and none to ask were you a murderer or what at all.

CHRISTY. And what would I be doing if I left Pegeen?

WIDOW QUIN. I've nice jobs you could be doing, gathering shells to make a whitewash for our hut within, building up a little goose-house, or stretching a new skin on an old curragh[55] I have, and if my hut is far

from all sides, it's there you'll meet the wisest old men, I tell you, at the corner of my wheel,[56] and it's there yourself and me will have great times whispering and hugging. . . .

VOICES (*outside, calling far away*). Christy! Christy Mahon! Christy!

CHRISTY. Is it Pegeen Mike?

WIDOW QUIN. It's the young girls, I'm thinking, coming to bring you to the sports below, and what is it you'll have me to tell them now?

CHRISTY. Aid me for to win Pegeen. It's herself only that I'm seeking now. (WIDOW QUIN *gets up and goes to window.*) Aid me for to win her, and I'll be asking God to stretch a hand to you in the hour of death, and lead you short cuts through the Meadows of Ease, and up the floor of Heaven to the Footstool of the Virgin's Son.

WIDOW QUIN. There's praying!

VOICES (*nearer*). Christy! Christy Mahon!

CHRISTY (*with agitation*). They're coming. Will you swear to aid and save me for the love of Christ?

WIDOW QUIN (*looks at him for a moment*). If I aid you, will you swear to give me a right of way I want, and a mountainy ram, and a load of dung at Michaelmas, the time that you'll be master here?

CHRISTY. I will, by the elements and stars of night.

WIDOW QUIN. Then we'll not say a word of the old fellow, the way Pegeen won't know your story till the end of time.

CHRISTY. And if he chances to return again?

WIDOW QUIN. We'll swear he's a maniac and not your da. I could take an oath I seen him raving on the sands to-day.

(GIRLS *run in.*)

SUSAN. Come on to the sports below. Pegeen says you're to come.

SARA TANSEY. The lepping's beginning, and we've a jockey's suit to fit upon you for the mule race on the sands below.

HONOR. Come on, will you?

---

52 *Brigid* St. Brigid, or Bride (*ca.* 451–525), Abbess of Kildare, and, after St. Patrick greatest and most venerated of Irish saints   53 *spavindy ass* an ass lame with spavin, a disease of the hock   54 *hookers* a one-masted fishing-smack   55 *curragh* (or curagh) a light, open boat made of a frame-work of lath covered formerly with hide or leather but now with tarred canvas

56 *wheel* spinning wheel

CHRISTY. I will then if Pegeen's beyond.

SARA. She's in the boreen[57] making game of Shaneen Keogh.

CHRISTY. Then I'll be going to her now.

(He runs out followed by the girls.)

WIDOW QUIN. Well, if the worst comes in the end of all, it'll be great game to see there's none to pity him but a widow woman, the like of me, has buried her children and destroyed her man.

(She goes out.)

CURTAIN

ACT III

SCENE: *As before. Later in the day.* JIMMY *comes in, slightly drunk.*

JIMMY *(calls).* Pegeen! *(Crosses to inner door)* Pegeen Mike! *(Comes back again into the room)* Pegeen! *(*PHILLY *comes in in the same state.)* (To* PHILLY*)* Did you see herself?

PHILLY. I did not; but I sent Shawn Keogh with the ass cart for to bear him home. *(Trying cupboards which are locked)* Well, isn't he a nasty man to get into such staggers at a morning wake? and isn't herself the divil's daughter for locking, and she so fussy after that young gaffer,[1] you might take your death with drought and none to heed you?

JIMMY. It's little wonder she'd be fussy, and he after bringing bankrupt ruin on the roulette man, and the trick-o'-the-loop[2] man, and breaking the nose of the cockshot-man,[3] and winning all in the sports below, racing, lepping, dancing, and the Lord

knows what! He's right luck, I'm telling you.

PHILLY. If he has, he'll be rightly hobbled[4] yet, and he not able to say ten words without making a brag of the way he killed his father, and the great blow he hit with the loy.

JIMMY. A man can't hang by his own informing, and his father should be rotten by now.

*(*OLD MAHON *passes window slowly.)*

PHILLY. Supposing a man's digging spuds in that field with a long spade, and supposing he flings up the two halves of that skull, what'll be said then in the papers and the courts of law?

JIMMY. They'd say it was an old Dane,[5] maybe, was drowned in the flood. *(*OLD MAHON *comes in and sits down near door listening.)* Did you never hear tell of the skulls they have in the city of Dublin, ranged out like blue jugs in a cabin of Connaught?

PHILLY. And you believe that?

JIMMY *(pugnaciously).* Didn't a lad see them and he after coming from harvesting in the Liverpool boat? "They have them there," says he, "making a show of the great people there was one time walking the world. White skulls and black skulls and yellow skulls, and some with full teeth, and some haven't only but one."

PHILLY. It was no lie, maybe, for when I was a young lad, there was a graveyard beyond the house with the remnants of a man who had thighs as long as your arm. He was a horrid man, I'm telling you, and there was many a fine Sunday I'd put him together for fun, and he with shiny bones, you wouldn't meet the like of these days in the cities of the world.

MAHON *(getting up).* You wouldn't is it? Lay your eyes on that skull, and tell me where and when there was another the like of it, is splintered only from the blow of a loy.

57 *boreen* a narrow road, a lane
    1 gaffer a young chap   *2 trick-o'-the-loop* to guess the center loop in a little leather belt   *3 cockshot-man* a man with his face blackened, except one cheek and eye, standing shots of a wooden ball behind a board with a large hole in the middle

4 hobbled legs tied together like an animal   *5 Dane* Vikings raided Irish coast from the 9th to the 12th centuries

PHILLY. Glory be to God! And who hit you at all?

MAHON (*triumphantly*). It was my own son hit me. Would you believe that?

JIMMY. Well, there's wonders hidden in the heart of man!

PHILLY (*suspiciously*). And what way was it done?

MAHON (*wandering about the room*). I'm after walking hundreds and long scores of miles, winning clean beds and the fill of my belly four times in the day, and I doing nothing but telling stories of that naked truth. (*He comes to them a little aggressively.*) Give me a supeen and I'll tell you now.

(WIDOW QUIN *comes in and stands aghast behind him. He is facing* JIMMY *and* PHILLY, *who are on the left.*)

JIMMY. Ask herself beyond. She's the stuff hidden in her shawl.

WIDOW QUIN (*coming to* MAHON *quickly*). You here, is it? You didn't go far at all?

MAHON. I seen the coasting steamer passing, and I got a drought upon me and a cramping leg, so I said, "The divil go along with him," and turned again. (*Looking under her shawl*) And let you give me a supeen, for I'm destroyed travelling since Tuesday was a week.

WIDOW QUIN (*getting a glass, in a cajoling tone*). Sit down then by the fire and take your ease for a space. You've a right to be destroyed indeed, with your walking, and fighting, and facing the sun (*giving him poteen from a stone jar she has brought in*). There now is a drink for you, and may it be to your happiness and length of life.

MAHON (*taking glass greedily, and sitting down by fire*). God increase you!

WIDOW QUIN (*taking men to the right stealthily*). Do you know what? That man's raving from his wound to-day, for I met him a while since telling a rambling tale of a tinker had him destroyed. Then he heard of Christy's deed, and he up and says it was his son had cracked his skull. O isn't madness a fright, for he'll go killing some-one yet, and he thinking it's the man has struck him so?

JIMMY (*entirely convinced*). It's a fright surely. I knew a party was kicked in the head by a red mare, and he went killing horses a great while, till he eat the insides of a clock and died after.

PHILLY (*with suspicion*). Did he see Christy?

WIDOW QUIN. He didn't. (*With a warning gesture*) Let you not be putting him in mind of him, or you'll be likely summoned if there's murder done. (*Looking round at* MAHON) Whisht! He's listening. Wait now till you hear me taking him easy and unravelling all. (*She goes to* MAHON.) And what way are you feeling, mister? Are you in contentment now?

MAHON (*slightly emotional from his drink*). I'm poorly only, for it's a hard story the way I'm left to-day, when it was I did tend him from his hour of birth, and he a dunce never reached his second book, the way he'd come from school, many's the day, with his legs lamed under him, and he blackened with his beatings like a tinker's ass. It's a hard story, I'm saying, the way some do have their next and nighest raising up a hand of murder on them, and some is lonesome getting their death with lamentation in the dead of night.

WIDOW QUIN (*not knowing what to say*). To hear you talking so quiet, who'd know you were the same fellow we seen pass to-day?

MAHON. I'm the same surely. The wrack and ruin of threescore years; and it's a terror to live that length, I tell you, and to have your sons going to the dogs against you, and you wore out scolding them, and skelping[6] them, and God knows what.

PHILLY (*to* JIMMY). He's not raving. (*To* WIDOW QUIN) Will you ask him what kind was his son?

WIDOW QUIN (*to* MAHON, *with a peculiar look*). Was your son that hit you a lad of one year and a score maybe, a great hand at racing and lepping and licking the world?

MAHON (*turning on her with a roar of rage*).

6 *skelping* hitting

Didn't you hear me say he was the fool of men, the way from this out he'll know the orphan's lot with old and young making game of him and they swearing, raging, kicking at him like a mangy cur.

(*A great burst of cheering outside, some way off*)

MAHON (*putting his hands to his ears*). What in the name of God do they want roaring below?

WIDOW QUIN (*with the shade of a smile*). They're cheering a young lad, the champion playboy of the Western World. (*More cheering*)

MAHON (*going to window*). It'd split my heart to hear them, and I with pulses in my brain-pan[7] for a week gone by. Is it racing they are?

JIMMY (*looking from door*). It is then. They are mounting him for the mule race will be run upon the sands. That's the playboy on the winkered[8] mule.

MAHON (*puzzled*). That lad, is it? If you said it was a fool he was, I'd have laid a mighty oath he was the likeness of my wandering son (*uneasily, putting his hand to his head*). Faith, I'm thinking I'll go walking for to view the race.

WIDOW QUIN (*stopping him, sharply*). You will not. You'd best take the road to Belmullet, and not be dillydallying in this place where there isn't a spot you could sleep.

PHILLY (*coming forward*). Don't mind her. Mount there on the bench and you'll have a view of the whole. They're hurrying before the tide will rise, and it'd be near over if you went down the pathway through the crags below.

MAHON (*mounts on bench,* WIDOW QUIN *beside him*). That's a right view again the edge of the sea. They're coming now from the point. He's leading. Who is he at all?

WIDOW QUIN. He's the champion of the world, I tell you, and there isn't a hap'orth[9] isn't falling lucky to his hands to-day.

PHILLY (*looking out, interested in the race*). Look at that. They're pressing him now.

JIMMY. He'll win it yet.

PHILLY. Take you time, Jimmy Farrell. It's too soon to say.

WIDOW QUIN (*shouting*). Watch him taking the gate. There's riding.

JIMMY (*cheering*). More power to the young lad!

MAHON. He's passing the third.

JIMMY. He'll lick them yet!

WIDOW QUIN. He'd lick them if he was running races with a score itself.

MAHON. Look at the mule he has, kicking the stars.

WIDOW QUIN. There was a lep! (*Catching hold of* MAHON *in her excitement*) He's fallen! He's mounted again! Faith, he's passing them all!

JIMMY. Look at him skelping her!

PHILLY. And the mountain girls hooshing[10] him on!

JIMMY. It's the last turn! The post's cleared for them now!

MAHON. Look at the narrow place. He'll be into the bogs! (*With a yell.*) Good rider! He's through it again!

JIMMY. He's neck and neck!

MAHON. Good boy[11] to him! Flames, but he's in!

(*Great cheering, in which all join*)

MAHON (*with hesitation*). What's that? They're raising him up. They're coming this way. (*With a roar of rage and astonishment*) It's Christy! by the stars of God! I'd know his way of spitting and he astride the moon.

(*He jumps down and makes a run for the door, but* WIDOW QUIN *catches him and pulls him back.*)

WIDOW QUIN. Stay quiet, will you? That's not your son. (*To* JIMMY) Stop him, or you'll get a month for the abetting of manslaughter and be fined as well.

---

7 *brain-pan* the skull 8 *winkered* wearing blinkers 9 *hap'orth* a halfpenny worth

10 *hooshing* a cry used to scare or drive away fowls, pigs
11 *Good boy* brave and tough

JIMMY. I'll hold him.

MAHON (*struggling*). Let me out! Let me out, the lot of you! till I have my vengeance on his head to-day.

WIDOW QUIN (*shaking him, vehemently*). That's not your son. That's a man is going to make a marriage with the daughter of this house, a place with fine trade, with a licence, and with poteen too.

MAHON (*amazed*). That man marrying a decent and a moneyed[12] girl! Is it mad yous are? Is it in a crazy-house for females that I'm landed now?

WIDOW QUIN. It's mad yourself is with the blow upon your head. That lad is the wonder of the Western World.

MAHON. I seen it's my son.

WIDOW QUIN. You seen that you're mad. (*Cheering outside*) Do you hear them cheering him in the zigzags of the road? Aren't you after saying that your son's a fool, and how would they be cheering a true idiot born?

MAHON (*getting distressed*). It's maybe out of reason[13] that that man's himself. (*Cheering again*) There's none surely will go cheering him. Oh, I'm raving with a madness that would fright the world! (*He sits down with his hand to his head.*) There was one time I seen ten scarlet divils letting on they'd cork my spirit in a gallon can; and one time I seen rats as big as badgers sucking the life-blood from the butt of my lug;[14] but I never till this day confused that dribbling idiot with a likely man. I'm destroyed surely.

WIDOW QUIN. And who'd wonder when it's your brain-pan that is gaping now?

MAHON. Then the blight of the sacred drought upon myself and him, for I never went mad to this day, and I not three weeks with the Limerick[15] girls drinking myself silly, and parlatic[16] from the dusk to dawn. (*To* WIDOW QUIN, *suddenly*) Is my visage astray?

WIDOW QUIN. It is then. You're a sniggering maniac, a child could see.

MAHON (*getting up more cheerfully*). Then I'd best be going to the union[17] beyond, and there'll be a welcome before me, I tell you (*with great pride*), and I a terrible and fearful case, the way that there I was one time, screeching in a straightened waist-coat, with seven doctors writing out my sayings in a printed book. Would you believe that?

WIDOW QUIN. If you're a wonder itself, you'd best be hasty, for them lads caught a maniac one time and pelted the poor creature till he ran out, raving and foaming, and was drowned in the sea.

MAHON (*with philosophy*). It's true mankind is the divil when your head's astray. Let me out now and I'll slip down the boreen, and not see them so.

WIDOW QUIN (*showing him out*). That's it. Run to the right, and not a one will see. (*He runs off.*)

PHILLY (*wisely*). You're at some gaming, Widow Quin; but I'll walk after him and give him his dinner and a time to rest, and I'll see then if he's raving or as sane as you.

WIDOW QUIN (*annoyed*). If you go near that lad, let you be wary of your head, I'm saying. Didn't you hear him telling he was crazed at times?

PHILLY. I heard him telling a power; and I'm thinking we'll have right sport, before night will fall. (*He goes out.*)

JIMMY. Well, Philly's a conceited and foolish man. How could that madman have his senses and his brain-pan slit? I'll go after them and see him turn on Philly now.

(*He goes;* WIDOW QUIN *hides poteen behind counter. Then hubbub outside*)

VOICES. There you are! Good jumper! Grand lepper! Darlint boy! He's the racer! Bear him on, will you!

---

12 *moneyed* publicans are usually wealthy   13 *out of reason* mad to think   14 *lug* ear   15 *Limerick* one of the six counties of Munster whose capital city, Limerick, is situated at the head of the Shannon estuary   16 *parlatic* paralytic

17 *union* poorhouse, a concomitant of Irish landlord-ism, used to give shelter to tramps, the destitute and the imbecile

(CHRISTY *comes in, in jockey's dress, with* PEGEEN MIKE, SARA, *and other girls, and men.*)

PEGEEN (*to crowd*). Go on now and don't destroy him and he drenching with sweat. Go along, I'm saying, and have your tug-of-warring till he's dried his skin.

CROWD. Here's his prizes! A bagpipes! A fiddle was played in a poet in the years gone by! A flat and three-thorned black-thorn[18] would lick the scholars out of Dublin town!

CHRISTY (*taking prizes from the men*). Thank you kindly, the lot of you. But you'd say it was little only I did this day if you'd seen me a while since striking my one single blow.

TOWN CRIER (*outside, ringing a bell*). Take notice, last event of this day! Tug-of-warring on the green below! Come on, the lot of you! Great achievements for all Mayo men!

PEGEEN. Go on, and leave him for to rest and dry. Go on, I tell you, for he'll do no more. (*She hustles crowd out;* WIDOW QUIN *following them.*)

MEN (*going*). Come on then. Good luck for the while!

PEGEEN (*radiantly, wiping his face with her shawl*). Well, you're the lad, and you'll have great times from this out when you could win that wealth of prizes, and you sweating in the heat of noon!

CHRISTY (*looking at her with delight*). I'll have great times if I win the crowning prize I'm seeking now, and that's your promise that you'll wed me in a fortnight, when our banns[19] is called.

PEGEEN (*backing away from him*). You've right daring to go ask me that, when all knows you'll be starting to some girl in your own townland, when your father's rotten in four months, or five.

CHRISTY (*indignantly*). Starting from you, is it? (*He follows her.*) I will not, then, and

when the airs is warming in four months, or five, it's then yourself and me should be pacing Neifin[20] in the dews of night, the times sweet smells do be rising, and you'd see a little, shiny new moon, maybe, sinking on the hills.

PEGEEN (*looking at him playfully*). And it's that kind of a poacher's love you'd make, Christy Mahon, on the sides of Neifin, when the night is down?

CHRISTY. It's little you'll think if my love's a poacher's, or an earl's itself, when you'll feel my two hands stretched around you, and I squeezing kisses on your puckered lips, till I'd feel a kind of pity for the Lord God is all ages sitting lonesome in his golden chair.

PEGEEN. That'll be right fun, Christy Mahon, and any girl would walk her heart out before she'd meet a young man was your like for eloquence, or talk, at all.

CHRISTY (*encouraged*). Let you wait, to hear me talking, till we're astray in Erris,[21] when Good Friday's[22] by, drinking a sup from a well, and making mighty kisses with our wetted mouths, or gaming in a gap of sunshine, with yourself stretched back unto your necklace, in the flowers of the earth.

PEGEEN (*in a lower voice, moved by his tone*). I'd be nice so, is it?

CHRISTY (*with rapture*). If the mitred bishops seen you that time, they'd be the like of the holy prophets, I'm thinking, do be straining the bars of Paradise to lay eyes on the Lady Helen of Troy, and she abroad, pacing back and forward, with a nosegay in her golden shawl.

PEGEEN (*with real tenderness*). And what is it I have, Christy Mahon, to make me fitting entertainment for the like of you, that has such poet's talking, and such bravery of heart?

CHRISTY (*in a low voice*). Isn't there the light of seven heavens in your heart alone, the way you'll be an angel's lamp to me from

---

18 *blackthorn* a shillelagh   19 *banns* public announcement in church of a proposed marriage   20 *Neifin* Mount Nephin. Its name belongs to the popular Irish love song of Connaught "The Brow of Néfin"   21 *Erris* a barony of North-West Mayo   22 *Good Friday's* when spring has come

this out, and I abroad in the darkness, spearing salmons in the Owen, or the Carrowmore?[23]

PEGEEN. If I was your wife, I'd be along with you those nights, Christy Mahon, the way you'd see I was a great hand at coaxing bailiffs, or coining funny nicknames for the stars of night.

CHRISTY. You, is it? Taking your death in the hailstones, or in the fogs of dawn.

PEGEEN. Yourself and me would shelter easy in a narrow bush, (*with a qualm of dread*) but we're only talking, maybe, for this would be a poor, thatched place to hold a fine lad is the like of you.

CHRISTY (*putting his arm round her*). If I wasn't a good Christian, it's on my naked knees I'd be saying my prayers and paters[24] to every jackstraw you have roofing your head, and every stony pebble is paving the laneway to your door.

PEGEEN (*radiantly*). If that's the truth, I'll be burning candles[25] from this out to the miracles of God that have brought you from the south to-day, and I, with my gowns bought ready, the way that I can wed you, and not wait at all.

CHRISTY. It's miracles, and that's the truth. Me there toiling a long while, and walking a long while, not knowing at all I was drawing all times nearer to this holy day.

PEGEEN. And myself, a girl, was tempted often to go sailing the seas till I'd marry a Jew-man, with ten kegs of gold, and I not knowing at all there was the like of you drawing nearer, like the stars of God.

CHRISTY. And to think I'm long years hearing women talking that talk, to all bloody fools, and this the first time I've heard the like of your voice talking sweetly for my own delight.

PEGEEN. And to think it's me is talking sweetly, Christy Mahon, and I the fright of seven townlands for my biting tongue. Well, the heart's a wonder; and, I'm thinking, there won't be our like in Mayo, for gallant lovers from this hour, to-day. (*Drunken singing is heard outside.*) There's my father coming from the wake, and when he's had his sleep we'll tell him, for he's peaceful then. (*They separate.*)

MICHAEL (*singing outside*)—
The jailor and the turnkey
    They quickly ran us down,
And brought us back as prisoners
    Once more to Cavan town.

(*He comes in supported by* SHAWN.)

There we lay bewailing
    All in a prison bound. . . .

(*He sees* CHRISTY. *Goes and shakes him drunkenly by the hand, while* PEGEEN *and* SHAWN *talk on the left.*)

MICHAEL (*to* CHRISTY). The blessing of God and the holy angels on your head, young fellow. I hear tell you're after winning all in the sports below; and wasn't it a shame I didn't bear you along with me to Kate Cassidy's wake, a fine, stout lad, the like of you, for you'd never see the match of it for flows of drink, the way when we sunk her bones at noonday in her narrow grave, there were five men, aye, and six men, stretched out retching speechless on the holy stones.

CHRISTY (*uneasily, watching* PEGEEN). Is that the truth?

MICHAEL. It is then, and aren't you a louty[26] schemer to go burying your poor father unbeknownst[27] when you'd a right to throw him on the crupper[28] of a Kerry mule and drive him westwards, like holy Joseph[29] in the days gone by, the way we could have given him a decent burial, and not have him rotting beyond, and not a Christian drinking a smart drop to the glory of his soul?

---

23 *Owen . . . Carrowmore* Owen River and Lough Carrowmore of North-West Mayo   24 *paters* paternosters   25 *burning candles* votive lights

26 *louty* stupid   27 *unbeknownst* in secret   28 *crupper* rump   29 *Joseph* reference to the great and elaborate funeral Joseph gave to his father Jacob. *Genesis* L.1-14

CHRISTY (*gruffly*). It's well enough he's lying, for the likes of him.

MICHAEL (*slapping him on the back*). Well, aren't you a hardened slayer? It'll be a poor thing for the household man where you go sniffing for a female wife; and (*pointing to Shawn*) look beyond at that shy and decent Christian I have chosen for my daughter's hand, and I after getting the gilded dispensation this day for to wed them now.

CHRISTY. And you'll be wedding them this day, is it?

MICHAEL (*drawing himself up*). Aye. Are you thinking, if I'm drunk itself, I'd leave my daughter living single with a little frisky rascal is the like of you?

PEGEEN (*breaking away from* SHAWN). Is it the truth the dispensation's come?

MICHAEL (*triumphantly*). Father Reilly's after reading it in gallous[30] Latin, and "It's come in the nick of time," says he; "so I'll wed them in a hurry, dreading that young gaffer who'd capsize the stars."

PEGEEN (*fiercely*). He's missed his nick of time, for it's that lad, Christy Mahon, that I'm wedding now.

MICHAEL (*loudly with horror*). You'd be making him a son to me, and he wet and crusted with his father's blood?

PEGEEN. Aye. Wouldn't it be a bitter thing for a girl to go marrying the like of Shaneen, and he a middling kind of a scarecrow, with no savagery or fine words in him at all?

MICHAEL (*gasping and sinking on a chair*). Oh, aren't you a heathen daughter to go shaking the fat of my heart, and I swamped and drownded with the weight of drink? Would you have them turning on me the way that I'd be roaring to the dawn of day with the wind upon my heart? Have you not a word to aid me, Shaneen? Are you not jealous at all?

SHAWN (*in great misery*). I'd be afeard to be jealous of a man did slay his da.

PEGEEN. Well, it'd be a poor thing to go marrying your like. I'm seeing there's a world of peril for an orphan girl, and isn't it a great blessing I didn't wed you, before himself came walking from the west or south?

SHAWN. It's a queer story you'd go picking a dirty tramp up from the highways of the world.

PEGEEN (*playfully*). And you think you're a likely beau to go straying along with, the shiny Sundays of the opening year, when it's sooner on a bullock's liver you'd put a poor girl thinking than on the lily or the rose?

SHAWN. And have you no mind of my weight of passion, and the holy dispensation, and the drift[31] of heifers I am giving, and the golden ring?

PEGEEN. I'm thinking you're too fine for the like of me, Shawn Keogh of Killakeen, and let you go off till you'd find a radiant lady with droves of bullocks on the plains of Meath,[32] and herself bedizened[33] in the diamond jewelleries of Pharaoh's ma. That'd be your match, Shaneen. So God save you now!

(*She retreats behind* CHRISTY.)

SHAWN. Won't you hear me telling you . . . ?

CHRISTY (*with ferocity*). Take yourself from this, young fellow, or I'll maybe add a murder to my deeds to-day.

MICHAEL (*springing up with a shriek*). Murder is it? Is it mad yous are? Would you go making murder in this place, and it piled with poteen for our drink to-night? Go on to the foreshore if it's fighting you want, where the rising tide will wash all traces from the memory of man.

(*Pushing* SHAWN *towards* CHRISTY)

SHAWN (*shaking himself free, and getting behind* MICHAEL). I'll not fight him, Michael James. I'd liefer live a bachelor, simmering in passions to the end of time, than face

---

30 *gallous* fine   31 *drift* herd   32 *Meath* County Meath in the midlands where the land is exceptionally fertile   33 *bedizened* dressed in vulgar finery

a lepping savage the like of him has descended from the Lord knows where. Strike him yourself, Michael James, or you'll lose my drift of heifers and my blue bull from Sneem.

MICHAEL. Is it me fight him, when it's father-slaying he's bred to now? (*Pushing* SHAWN) Go on you fool and fight him now.

SHAWN (*coming forward a little*). Will I strike him with my hand?

MICHAEL. Take the loy is on your western side.

SHAWN. I'd be afeard of the gallows if I struck with that.

CHRISTY (*taking up the loy*). Then I'll make you face the gallows or quit off[34] from this.

(SHAWN *flies out of the door.*)

CHRISTY. Well, fine weather be after him, (*going to* MICHAEL, *coaxingly*) and I'm thinking you wouldn't wish to have that quaking blackguard in your house at all. Let you give us your blessing and hear her swear her faith to me, for I'm mounted on the springtide of the stars of luck, the way it'll be good for any to have me in the house.

PEGEEN (*at the other side of* MICHAEL). Bless us now, for I swear to God I'll wed him, and I'll not renege.

MICHAEL (*standing up in the centre, holding on to both of them*). It's the will of God, I'm thinking, that all should win an easy or a cruel end, and it's the will of God that all should rear up lengthy families for the nurture of the earth. What's a single man, I ask you, eating a bit in one house and drinking a sup in another, and he with no place of his own, like an old braying jackass strayed upon the rocks? (*To* CHRISTY) It's many would be in dread to bring your like into their house for to end them, maybe, with a sudden end; but I'm a decent man of Ireland, and I liefer face the grave untimely and I seeing a score of grandsons growing up little gallant swearers by the name of

God, than go peopling my bedside with puny weeds the like of what you'd breed, I'm thinking, out of Shaneen Keogh. (*He joins their hands.*) A daring fellow is the jewel of the world, and a man did split his father's middle with a single clout, should have the bravery of ten, so may God and Mary and St. Patrick bless you, and increase you from this mortal day.

CHRISTY and PEGEEN. Amen, O Lord!

(*Hubbub outside*)

(OLD MAHON *rushes in, followed by all the crowd, and* WIDOW QUIN. *He makes a rush at* CHRISTY, *knocks him down, and begins to beat him.*)

PEGEEN (*dragging back his arm*). Stop that, will you? Who are you at all?

MAHON. His father, God forgive me!

PEGEEN (*drawing back*). Is it rose from the dead?

MAHON. Do you think I look so easy quenched with the tap of a loy?

(*Beats* CHRISTY *again*)

PEGEEN (*glaring at* CHRISTY). And it's lies you told, letting on you had him slitted, and you nothing at all.

CHRISTY (*catching* MAHON's *stick*). He's not my father. He's a raving maniac would scare the world. (*Pointing to* WIDOW QUIN) Herself knows it is true.

CROWD. You're fooling Pegeen! The Widow Quin seen him this day, and you likely knew! You're a liar!

CHRISTY (*dumbfounded*). It's himself was a liar, lying stretched out with an open head on him, letting on he was dead.

MAHON. Weren't you off racing the hills before I got my breath with the start I had seeing you turn on me at all?

PEGEEN. And to think of the coaxing glory we had given him, and he after doing nothing but hitting a soft blow and chasing northward in a sweat of fear. Quit off from this.

CHRISTY (*piteously*). You've seen my doings this day, and let you save me from the old man; for why would you be in such a

34 *quit off* get out

scorch of haste to spur me to destruction now?

PEGEEN. It's there your treachery is spurring me, till I'm hard set to think you're the one I'm after lacing in my heart-strings half an hour gone by. (*To* MAHON) Take him on from this, for I think bad the world should see me raging for a Munster liar, and the fool of men.

MAHON. Rise up now to retribution, and come on with me.

CROWD (*jeeringly*). There's the playboy! There's the lad thought he'd rule the roost in Mayo. Slate[35] him now, mister.

CHRISTY (*getting up in shy terror*). What is it drives you to torment me here, when I'd asked the thunders of the might of God to blast me if I ever did hurt to any saving only that one single blow.

MAHON (*loudly*). If you didn't, you're a poor good-for-nothing, and isn't it by the like of you the sins of the whole world are committed?

CHRISTY (*raising his hands*). In the name of the Almighty God. . . .

MAHON. Leave troubling the Lord God. Would you have Him sending down droughts, and fevers, and the old hen[36] and the cholera morbus?[37]

CHRISTY (*to* WIDOW QUIN). Will you come between us and protect me now?

WIDOW QUIN. I've tried a lot, God help me, and my share is done.

CHRISTY (*looking round in desperation*). And I must go back into my torment is it, or run off like a vagabond straying through the Unions with the dusts of August making mudstains in the gullet of my throat, or the winds of March blowing on me till I'd take an oath I felt them making whistles of my ribs within?

SARA. Ask Pegeen to aid you. Her like does often change.

CHRISTY. I will not then, for there's torment in the splendour of her like, and she a girl any moon of midnight would take pride to

meet, facing southwards on the heaths of Keel.[38] But what did I want crawling forward to scorch my understanding at her flaming brow?

PEGEEN (*to* MAHON, *vehemently, fearing she will break into tears*). Take him on from this or I'll set the young lads to destroy him here.

MAHON (*going to him, shaking his stick*). Come on now if you wouldn't have the company to see you skelped.

PEGEEN (*half laughing, through her tears*). That's it, now the world will see him pandied,[39] and he an ugly liar was playing off the hero, and the fright of men.

CHRISTY (*to* MAHON, *very sharply*). Leave me go!

CROWD. That's it. Now Christy. If them two set fighting, it will lick the world.

MAHON (*making a grab at* CHRISTY). Come here to me.

CHRISTY (*more threateningly*). Leave me go, I'm saying.

MAHON. I will maybe, when your legs is limping, and your back is blue.

CROWD. Keep it up, the two of you. I'll back the old one. Now the playboy.

CHRISTY (*in low and intense voice*). Shut your yelling, for if you're after making a mighty man of me this day by the power of a lie, you're setting me now to think if it's a poor thing to be lonesome, it's worse maybe go mixing with the fools of earth.

(MAHON *makes a movement towards him.*)

CHRISTY (*almost shouting*). Keep off . . . lest I do show a blow unto the lot of you would set the guardian angels winking in the clouds above.

(*He swings round with a sudden rapid movement and picks up a loy.*)

CROWD (*half frightened, half amused*). He's going mad! Mind yourselves! Run from the idiot!

---

35 *slate* thrash   36 *old hen* influenza   37 *cholera morbus* cholera plague

38 *Keel* village on Achill Island   39 *pandied* flogged on the extended plam with a cane or ruler, a punishment to schoolboys

CHRISTY. If I am an idiot, I'm after hearing my voice this day saying words would raise the topknot[40] on a poet in a merchant's town.[41] I've won your racing, and your lepping, and . . .

MAHON. Shut your gullet and come on with me.

CHRISTY. I'm going, but I'll stretch you first.

(*He runs at* OLD MAHON *with the loy, chases him out of the door, followed by crowd and* WIDOW QUIN. *There is a great noise outside, then a yell, and dead silence for a moment.* CHRISTY *comes in, half dazed, and goes to fire.*)

WIDOW QUIN (*coming in, hurriedly, and going to him*). They're turning again you. Come on, or you'll be hanged, indeed.

CHRISTY. I'm thinking, from this out, Pegeen'll be giving me praises, the same as in the hours gone by.

WIDOW QUIN (*impatiently*). Come by the back door. I'd think bad to have you stifled on the gallows tree.

CHRISTY (*indignantly*). I will not, then. What good'd be my lifetime, if I left Pegeen?

WIDOW QUIN. Come on, and you'll be no worse than you were last night; and you with a double murder this time to be telling to the girls.

CHRISTY. I'll not leave Pegeen Mike.

WIDOW QUIN (*impatiently*). Isn't there the match of her in every parish public,[42] from Binghamstown[43] unto the plain of Meath? Come on, I tell you, and I'll find you finer sweethearts at each waning moon.

CHRISTY. It's Pegeen I'm seeking only, and what'd I care if you brought me a drift of chosen females, standing in their shifts itself, maybe, from this place to the Eastern World?

SARA (*runs in, pulling off one of her petticoats*). They're going to hang him. (*Holding out petticoat and shawl*) Fit these upon him, and let him run off to the east.

WIDOW QUIN. He's raving now; but we'll fit them on him, and I'll take him, in the ferry, to the Achill[44] boat.

CHRISTY (*struggling feebly*). Leave me go, will you? when I'm thinking of my luck to-day, for she will wed me surely, and I a proven hero in the end of all. (*They try to fasten petticoat round him.*)

WIDOW QUIN. Take his left hand, and we'll pull him now. Come on, young fellow.

CHRISTY (*suddenly starting up*). You'll be taking me from her? You're jealous, is it, of her wedding me? Go on from this.

(*He snatches up a stool, and threatens them with it.*)

WIDOW QUIN (*going*). It's in the madhouse they should put him, not in jail, at all. We'll go by the back door, to call the doctor, and we'll save him so.

(*She goes out, with* SARA, *through inner room. Men crowd in the doorway.* CHRISTY *sits down again by the fire.*)

MICHAEL (*in a terrified whisper*). Is the old lad killed surely?

PHILLY. I'm after feeling the last gasps quitting his heart.

(*They peer in at* CHRISTY.)

MICHAEL (*with a rope*). Look at the way he is. Twist a hangman's knot on it, and slip it over his head, while he's not minding at all.

PHILLY. Let you take it, Shaneen. You're the soberest of all that's here.

SHAWN. Is it me to go near him, and he the wickedest and worst with me? Let you take it, Pegeen Mike.

PEGEEN. Come on, so.

(*She goes forward with the others, and they drop the double hitch over his head.*)

CHRISTY. What ails you?

---

40 *topknot* pompon   41 *merchant's town* poets gathered at fairs in merchant towns   42 *parish public* public-house   43 *Binghamston* a village on the Mullet

44 *Achill* large island on the Mayo coast

SHAWN (*triumphantly, as they pull the rope tight on his arms*). Come on to the peelers, till they stretch you now.

CHRISTY. Me!

MICHAEL. If we took pity on you, the Lord God would, maybe, bring us ruin from the law[45] to-day, so you'd best come easy, for hanging is an easy and a speedy end.

CHRISTY. I'll not stir. (*To* PEGEEN) And what is it you'll say to me, and I after doing it this time in the face of all?

PEGEEN. I'll say, a strange man is a marvel, with his mighty talk; but what's a squabble in your back yard, and the blow of a loy, have taught me that there's a great gap between a gallous story and a dirty deed. (*To men*) Take him on from this, or the lot of us will be likely put on trial for his deed to-day.

CHRISTY (*with horror in his voice*). And it's yourself will send me off, to have a horny-fingered hangman hitching his bloody slip-knots at the butt of my ear.

MEN (*pulling rope*). Come on, will you?

(*He is pulled down on the floor.*)

CHRISTY (*twisting his legs round the table*). Cut the rope, Pegeen, and I'll quit the lot of you, and live from this out, like the madmen[46] of Keel, eating muck and green weeds, on the faces of the cliffs.

PEGEEN. And leave us to hang, is it, for a saucy liar, the like of you? (*To men*) Take him on, out from this.

SHAWN. Pull a twist on his neck, and squeeze him so.

PHILLY. Twist yourself. Sure he cannot hurt you, if you keep your distance from his teeth alone.

SHAWN. I'm afeard of him (*To* PEGEEN) Lift a lighted sod, will you, and scorch his leg.

PEGEEN (*blowing the fire with a bellows*). Leave go now, young fellow, or I'll scorch your shins.

CHRISTY. You're blowing for to torture me? (*His voice rising and growing stronger*) That's your kind, is it? Then let the lot of you be

wary, for, if I've to face the gallows, I'll have a gay march down, I tell you, and shed the blood of some of you before I die.

SHAWN (*in terror*). Keep a good hold, Philly. Be wary, for the love of God. For I'm thinking he would liefest[47] wreak his pains on me.

CHRISTY (*almost gaily*). If I do lay my hands on you, it's the way you'll be at the fall of night, hanging as a scarecrow for the fowls of hell. Ah, you'll have a gallous jaunt I'm saying, coaching out through Limbo with my father's ghost.

SHAWN (*to* PEGEEN). Make haste, will you? Oh, isn't he a holy terror, and isn't it true for Father Reilly, that all drink's a curse that has the lot of you so shaky and uncertain now?

CHRISTY. If I can wring a neck among you, I'll have a royal judgment looking on the trembling jury in the courts of law. And won't there be crying out in Mayo the day I'm stretched upon the rope with ladies in their silks and satins snivelling in their lacy kerchiefs, and they rhyming songs and ballads on the terror of my fate?

(*He squirms round on the floor and bites* SHAWN's *leg.*)

SHAWN (*shrieking*). My leg's bit on me. He's the like of a mad dog, I'm thinking, the way that I will surely die.

CHRISTY (*delighted with himself*). You will then, the way you can shake out hell's flags of welcome for my coming in two weeks or three, for I'm thinking Satan hasn't many have killed their da in Kerry, and in Mayo too. (OLD MAHON *comes in behind on all fours and looks on unnoticed.*)

MEN (*to* PEGEEN). Bring the sod, will you?

PEGEEN (*coming over*). God help him so. (*Burns his leg*)

CHRISTY (*kicking and screaming*). O, glory be to God!

(*He kicks loose from the table, and they all drag him towards the door.*)

45 *ruin . . . law* because of the poteen   46 *madmen* gone mad from hunger in the famine days

47 *liefest* most willingly

JIMMY (*seeing* OLD MAHON). Will you look what's come in?

(*They all drop* CHRISTY *and run left.*)

CHRISTY (*scrambling on his knees face to face with* OLD MAHON). Are you coming to be killed a third time, or what ails you now?

MAHON. For what is it they have you tied?

CHRISTY. They're taking me to the peelers to have me hanged for slaying you.

MICHAEL (*apologetically*). It is the will of God that all should guard their little cabins from the treachery of law, and what would my daughter be doing if I was ruined or was hanged itself?

MAHON (*grimly, loosening* CHRISTY). It's little I care if you put a bag on her back, and went picking cockles till the hour of death; but my son and myself will be going our own way, and we'll have great times from this out telling stories of the villainy of Mayo, and the fools is here. (*To* CHRISTY, *who is freed*) Come on now.

CHRISTY. Go with you, is it? I will then, like a gallant captain with his heathen slave. Go on now and I'll see you from this day stewing my oatmeal and washing my spuds, for I'm master of all fights from now. (*Pushing* MAHON) Go on, I'm saying.

MAHON. Is it me?

CHRISTY. Not a word out of you. Go on from this.

MAHON (*walking out and looking back at* CHRISTY *over his shoulder*). Glory be to God! (*With a broad smile*) I am crazy again!
(*Goes*)

CHRISTY. Ten thousand blessings upon all that's here, for you've turned me a likely gaffer in the end of all, the way I'll go romancing through a romping lifetime from this hour to the dawning of the judgment day.   (*He goes out.*)

MICHAEL. By the will of God, we'll have peace now for our drinks. Will you draw the porter, Pegeen?

SHAWN (*going up to her*). It's a miracle Father Reilly can wed us in the end of all, and we'll have none to trouble us when his vicious bite is healed.

PEGEEN (*hitting him a box on the ear*). Quit my sight. (*Putting her shawl over her head and breaking out into wild lamentations*) Oh my grief, I've lost him surely. I've lost the only playboy of the Western World.

CURTAIN

PREFACE TO THE PLAYBOY OF THE WESTERN WORLD

John Millington Synge

In writing THE PLAYBOY OF THE WESTERN WORLD, as in my other plays, I have used one or two words only that I have not heard among the country people of Ireland, or spoken in my own nursery before I could read the newspapers. A certain number of the phrases I employ I have heard also from herds and fishermen along the coast from Kerry to Mayo, or from beggar-women and ballad-singers nearer Dublin; and I am glad to acknowledge how much I owe to the folk-imagination of these fine people. Anyone who has lived in real intimacy with the Irish peasantry will know that the wildest sayings and ideas in this play are tame indeed, compared with the fancies one may hear in any little hillside cabin in Geesala, or Carraroe, or Dingle Bay. All art is a collaboration; and there is little doubt that in the happy ages of literature, striking and beautiful phrases were as ready to the storyteller's or the playwright's hand, as the rich cloaks and dresses of his time. It is probable that when the Elizabethan dramatist took his ink-horn and sat down to his work he used many phrases that he had just heard, as he sat at dinner, from his mother or his children. In Ireland, those of us who know the people have the same privilege. When I was writing *The Shadow of the Glen*, some years ago, I got more aid than any learning could have given me from a chink in the floor of the old Wicklow house where I was staying, that let me hear what was being said by the servant girls in the kitchen. This matter, I think, is of importance, for in countries where the imagination of the people, and the language they use, is rich and living, it is possible for a writer to be rich and copious in his words, and at the same time to give the reality, which is the root of all poetry, in a comprehensive and natural form. In the modern literature of towns, however, richness is found only in sonnets, or prose poems, or in one or two elaborate books that are far away from the profound and common interests of life. One has, on one side, Mallarmé and Huysmans producing this literature; and on the other, Ibsen and Zola dealing with the reality of life in joyless and pallid words. On the stage one must have reality, and one must have joy; and that is why the intellectual modern drama has failed, and people have grown sick of the false joy of the musical comedy, that has been given them in place of the rich joy found only in what is superb and wild in reality. In a good play every speech should be as fully flavoured as a nut or apple, and such speeches cannot be written by anyone who works among people who have shut their lips on poetry. In Ireland, for a few years more, we have a popular imagination that is fiery and magnificent, and tender; so that those of us who wish to write start with a chance that is not given to writers in places where the springtime of the local life has been forgotten, and the harvest is a memory only, and the straw has been turned into bricks.

J.M.S.

January 21st, 1907.

INTRODUCTION TO THE PLAYBOY OF THE WESTERN WORLD

William E. Hart, M.S.

The Background of the Play. Standing like three stone fortresses guarding the mouth of Galway Bay from the fury of the open Atlantic are the Aran Islands. On the middle island, Inishmaan, in the early summer of 1898, J. M. Synge heard the story "about a Connaught man who killed his father with the blow of a spade when he was in passion," and then fled to Inishmaan where, despite police and bounty, the islanders hid him until he escaped to America. This well-known story, recorded by Synge in *The Aran Islands*, provided him not only with the prototype of the Playboy but also with the wild fantasy of a primitive community protecting a criminal from the law.

Through at least five titles, ten complete drafts and a score of scenarios, Synge reworked the material of that Inishmaan story for seven years. As with every play he wrote, it was a long process of acute observation, careful selection, and sensitive creation. Scenes were sketched and abandoned; characters grew in stature and importance, changed names and roles, and often in the interest of theme and design were completely discarded. Among the manuscripts found after Synge's death were seven complete versions of Act I, eight of Act II, and ten of Act III. These manuscripts reveal the playwright's great concern for the orchestral harmony of word, image, mood, rhythm, and gesture in the total design of the play. They also show that the dramatic structure Synge sought to create was less like a regular development to a crisis followed by a resolution than an irregular movement of changing moods in a work which still maintained its organic unity.[1]

To appreciate better both the way in which Synge refashioned the Inishmaan story and the aesthetics of his astonishing craftsmanship, three principles of his literary criticism must be cited. Not everyone, perhaps not most, will agree with his ideas, but for an understanding of his work it is necessary to know his guiding principles. There is

[1]For this information I am indebted to Dr. Ann Saddlemyer, Oxford University Press editor of Synge's *Plays, Collected Works,* and associate professor of English at the University of Victoria, British Columbia.

no systematic theory, but at various times and places he gave expression to these principles.

1. "All art is a collaboration."
2. "The drama, like the symphony, does not teach or prove anything."
3. "No personal originality is enough to make a rich work unique, unless it has also the characteristic of a particular time and locality and the life that is in it."

Although in theory the principles are three, actually they are one, for by collaboration Synge meant the artist's attempt to fuse fancy and fact, to wed reality to the ideal, to combine a criticism of things as they are with an aspiration toward things as they can be. He sought to present reality by going to a given people in a given time and place for the subject matter, living speech, psychic moods, attitudes, and emotions of a drama whose purpose was to excite the imagination, relax tensions, and free the spirit.

Thus Synge took as his starting point a primitive community's readiness to hide a criminal who had killed his father with a blow of a spade. This he fashioned into the story of Christy Mahon, a lonely, weak-willed Kerry farm boy who on a dark evening in autumn comes upon an isolated public house along a wild coast of Mayo and admits to being on the run eleven days for having, as he thought, killed his father with "a blow on the ridge of his skull, laid him stretched out, and he split to the knob of his gullet." For what the natives, according to Synge, regard as the courage and passion of his deed, Christy is hailed a hero and a marvel. The men fear him; the publican's lively daughter Pegeen Mike rejects her fiance Shawn Keogh for him; the lonely Widow Quin desires him; the young girls go wild over him, and to be rid of him Shawn offers him "The half of a ticket to the Western States!" Under the admiration of the Mayo folk Christy blossoms from the shy, lonely "loony of Mahon's" to the champion playboy of the West. Then at the moment of Christy's supreme triumph in

sports, in love, and in poetic speech, his father appears on the scene very much alive, revealing Christy to be nothing but a garrulous impostor and destroying his Mayo status as poet and champion. Yet with an even greater irony, that same reversal helps to transform Christy into the very poet and champion the people first considered him, but now they want no part of him. Praise a boy and he will prosper, says an Irish proverb. Christy is praised and he does prosper but not without some tragic consequence as the play's romantic and Rabelaisian notes come to a climax in this thoroughly Irish comedy.

As Ireland was always Connaught to Yeats's imagination, so Connaught was always Mayo to Synge's. If there was a particular Irish time and locality with a psychic state rich enough to make *The Playboy* dramatically viable and imaginatively acceptable, it was late 19th-century Mayo. As his notebooks and essays on the Congested Districts reveal, Synge knew Connaught well, and from this knowledge he drew much of folk character, mood, incident, imagination, and expression to collaborate with the life of Mayo, that lonely desolate land of the West "that the Lord created last." Here nature and history conspired to form "a half-savage temperament" of traditional rebellion—a temperament made melancholy by the dank weather and desolate isolation, brutalized by the violence of cruel evictions and the Land Wars (1879-1882), restrained at times by faith, anesthetized with poteen, and aroused by any stranger with a wild song or story.

The "particular time" of *The Playboy* is late 19th century Ireland. The "characteristic" of that time is violence bred of earlier famine and fever—a violence engendered by Moonlighters, Agrarian Reform, Land Wars, hanging judges and venal juries, evictions, land grabbing, the Boer War and the "loosèd kharki cut-throats."

The "particular locality" is the isolated district of Ballycroy along the road from Bangor to Malaranny on the North-West coast of Mayo. "Characteristic" of that locality is the wild remoteness to which Synge gives lyric expression not only in his nature descriptions but also in his presentation of the natives' belief that they are a race beyond the ridge of the world.

Synge makes the life of the place itself— "the life that is in it"—a life of drunken talk about violence, brutality, wars, drink, and the grotesqueries of death, hangings, skulls, and a dead man's bones. It is a life whose harsh drudgery is broken by fairs, sports, wakes and weddings; a life whose wild loneliness is forgotten in the thrill of poteen-making, poaching, and the fantasy of the walking dead. It is a life whose spirit is so scarred with the memory of "the treachery of law" and the ordinary violence of "a common week-day kind of murderer" that the coming of a lad with a marvelous tale of fantastic crime and fierce passion is enough to excite the starved imagination of an entire countryside to an equally fantastic exaltation of a father-slayer. The "characteristic of the life in it" is the wildness and unpredictability of the Irish peasantry and their common need to escape the harsh realities, to "have peace now for our drinks."

The Language. To that realistically conceived and artistically controlled setting Synge added the distinction of his dramatic speech founded on Western Ireland's Anglo-Irish dialect. This was the dialect used by persons accustomed to speaking Gaelic who when speaking English still thought in Gaelic, literally translating Irish idioms into English expressions. Thus Anglo-Irish takes most of its vocabulary from English, but its habit of thought and idiom come from Irish.

Synge's Anglo-Irish dialect is distinctive for its Irish imagery in descriptions of nature and love and for its lilting rhythms. What Synge did with that dialect was to fashion it into a dramatically functional poetic speech that defines, intensifies, and extends setting, character, and action. Although his language has often been attacked as too violent and too ornate, and too artificial in its striving for rhythm, it cannot be denied that there is in his speech a fundamental realism, a

living quality that is highly effective. As an illustration of this, read aloud the opening lines of the play, the famous love scene in Act III, and Christy's fiery speeches toward the end of the play. Synge's dialogue may have its limitations, but it should be considered that, except for comic relief, dialect had rarely been used in the English theatre; Synge and his fellow Abbey dramatists proved that the Irish peasantry and their habits of speech could be the substance and the medium of sublime tragedy and fine comedy.

Synge's language is not difficult. In *The Playboy* there are only about twelve words of strictly Irish origin; the relatively few archaic or Tudor forms of English words that appear are easily understood. Some of the more common Anglo-Irish constructions in the play are the following: the pleonastic infinitive form **for to** in place of the usual English **to**: "Six yards of stuff **for to** make a yellow gown"; the use of **after** with a form of the verb **to be** to express an action just completed: "**Aren't** we **after** making a good bargain"; the use of **and** in place of such conjunctions as **when, while, since, although** to introduce various subordinate clauses: "How would you see him **and** it dark night this half hour gone by"; "he'll be having my life, **and** I going home"; a marked preference for using the present participle with the infinitive **to be,** and the use of **do be** to express habit or frequency: "It was a dark lonesome place **to be hearing** the like of him"; "Is it often the polis **do be coming** into this place, master of the house?" Other Anglo-Irish expressions which Synge frequently uses are **the way** to indicate result, **the way** and **what way** to mean **how** or **why,** and **in it** to mean **present**: "Aren't we after making a good bargain, **the way** we're only waiting these days"; "And **what way** weren't you hanged, mister?"; "There'd be no harm staying now, I'm thinking, and himself **in it** too." Another peculiarity is the use of **itself** meaning **even**: "If you're a dunce **itself,** you'd have a right to know . . ."

Synge and Irish Humor. Synge's humor in its matter and manner is thoroughly Irish.

Like the medieval bards and the poets of the 17th and 18th centuries Synge used the common subjects of popular humor: the "made match" that wed May to December and haggled over the size of dowries, the clergy, the self-glorification over the saints of the race, and the people's tendency to lose themselves in imagination, blinding themselves to actuality. Especially in these two latter objects of comedy Synge anticipates the work of Joyce, O'Casey, O'Flaherty, O'Connor, and Behan. The Irish quality of Synge's humor is evidenced in such scenes as the girls idolizing Christy, Christy biting Shawn, and Pegeen burning Christy in retaliation. Irish is the macabre and grotesque humor, born of the peasants' ambivalent a titude toward life and death, expressed in the drunken riot attending Kate Cassidy's wake and by the men "stretched out retching speechless on the holy stones." Again macabre and grotesque is the talk of skulls "ranged out like blue jugs in a cabin of Connaught" and Philly's remark about the graveyard "remnants of a man who had thighs as long as your arm" which he would put together "for fun" many a fine Sunday. Typical of Irish humor is the verbal irony of such passages as "Marcus Quin, God rest him, got six months for maiming ewes, and he a great warrant [with a great gift] to tell stories of holy Ireland" and Christy's reply to the question did he kill his father: "With the help of God I did surely, and that the Holy Immaculate Mother may intercede for his soul." Perhaps what is most Irish in Synge's humor is the comic practice of developing to an extreme point the implications of a situation so that no aspect of life is too sacred to be spared the mockery of laughter. It is the atavistic play-spirit, a regression to the pagan half-belief that refuses to take either mortals or immortals too seriously. In the play nothing escapes this humor—neither life nor death, God nor the Angels, saints nor devils, prophets nor Pope, Cardinals nor priests, neither "the preaching north" nor the Erris plain, romance nor hatred, neither the intrigue of poaching nor the escape of poteen.

The personal distinction of Synge's humor is his irony. It is an attitude of half-cynical factitious hope born of his own lonely agnostic vision. He thought sardonic laughter the healthy attitude for one convinced that the only resolution of life's problem is the grave "with worms eternally." Yeats referred to this skeptical attitude when he wrote of "the astringent joy and hardness" in all Synge did. Again it was Synge's ironic view of life Yeats spoke of when he said that "the strength that made him delight in setting the hard virtues by the soft, the bitter by the sweet, salt by mercury, the stone by the elixir, gave him a hunger for harsh facts, for ugly surprising things, for all that defies our hope." In *The Playboy* irony is everywhere: in the title which may be freely rendered "The World's Champion Impostor," and in the plot as illusion creates a hero from an awkward boy while reality, destroying the illusion, makes him an even greater hero. In the play's protrayal of every man's need to be a hero, if only to himself, and everyone's need to have a hero, if only for sacrifice, here again is the frozen laugh at the folly of men.

PART THREE

MODERN TRAGICOMEDY AND IRONY

Between the comic and the tragic lies a middle ground of plays in which both tragic and comic effects are achieved and neither completely predominates. Such plays tend either to the tragic or the comic, and different productions will emphasize the one or the other, but every new modern play that has employed the mixture has puzzled at least part of its audience. Impressed by the seriousness of the situation enacted, some tend to laugh uncomfortably at its comic treatment. Sometimes, failing to see that a play imitates the incongruities and ambiguities of their own lives, others may feel ambivalent and confused, especially at the end of an absurdist play where the world without meaning, the world without tradition and belief, is expressed in the structure and style as well as in the attitudes of characters. But tragicomedy has become, particularly in ironic and absurdist forms, more important in recent modern drama than either tragedy or comedy. Its recent importance is a natural development of modern realism to move away from both tragic heroism and comic artificiality to some mixture of tragic and comic effects that seems closer to life as we experience it.

MODERN TRAGICOMEDY

Tragicomedy is the term most commonly used to classify plays that mix tragedy and comedy. It is not applied to *Hamlet*, which is clearly a tragedy, even though Hamlet's wit makes audiences laugh, and it is not applied to *Tartuffe*, even though some people lament the bad fortune of poor Tartuffe. But for plays that are neither comedies nor tragedies, even though they mix the effects of each, it is the most convenient term. In tragedy reversal and recognition reveal what Langer calls "closed inevitabilities"; in modern tragicomedy recognition, without necessarily any reversal, reveals things-as-they-are as not much different from how everyone feared things were, as in Chekhov and Beckett; or the reversal may conclude the play in a surprising and inconclusive way as in Pinter. The vision of modern realistic tragicomedy is essentially double; it reveals the reality and the irony. The human condition is comic or tragic according to our perspective and our mood, but as spectators of others we can often see it both ways at once. Some tragicomedies have a strong social purpose as Brecht's "Theatre for Pleasure or Theatre for Instruction" explains for his own drama, but more commonly in the best modern plays the satire exposes only a part of the reality revealed in the general analysis of our human condition.

In general we can say that modern tragicomedy is the realm of what Northrop Frye calls the "all too human," the hero as victim, the immature hero, the anti-hero, or the ineffectual hero, but even when the "all too human" is stressed in the characterization, we can find in some plays heroic figures who display an exceptional ability to endure, sustain others, and survive. The concerns of tragicomedy are those common to all drama —justice and injustice, truth and hypocrisy, order (cosmic, natural, and social) and disorder, self-knowledge and self-deception, love and hate, but chiefly the gulf between actuality and desire. While tragedy isolates the individual in the cosmos and reveals inevitabilities the hero could not have foreseen, tragicomedy isolates the individual in society and reveals social and psychological actualities that mock his desire. The boundary between tragedy and tragicomedy is not clearly defined; it is arbitrary according to particular definitions of tragedy, but the tragicomic mixture is based on something in experience reflected in the nature of the plays we have to classify.

IRONY

One solution to the problem of describing the particular quality of a large group of tragicomedies is Northrop Frye's description of the ironic mode. Frye uses the term mode to distinguish the essential actions of tragedy, romance, comedy, and irony. Rather than seeing tragedy and comedy as merging into each other, he identifies an area between them in which the action has particular characteristics.

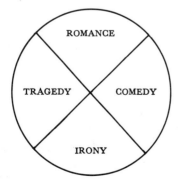

Tragedy and comedy do not blend into each other; they are opposites and they blend into either irony or romance. Irony and romance are opposites, and the structure of an ironic play is a parody of romance. While romance gives form to the ideal, the ironic play gives form to "the shifting ambiguities and complexities of unidealized existence." The ironic mode is the realm of realism in which the protagonist's power of choice is most limited and human activity, smothered by social and psychological pressures, tends to isolation, stasis, and silence. Not all tragicomic plays can be classified as ironic, particularly not Renaissance tragicomedies that end happily and affirm traditional values, but for much modern tragicomedy, both realistic and absurdist, Frye's ironic mode provides a useful classification.

There are many kinds of irony in drama, all drama, that result from the audience looking on as spectators; they can see ironies that the participants on stage miss. Dramatic irony is something felt by the spectator whenever he knows something a character on stage does not know. Structural irony is merely another way of describing the reversal the plot is based on, but it is especially ironic when, as Aristotle insisted, the tragic hero participates in turning events against himself—or the comic hero succeeds despite himself. Verbal irony occurs in the language of drama when characters say things truer than they or others realize. But in the ironic mode the ironic attitude in the total effect prevails over tragic and comic elements and interludes. As tragedy becomes ironic it becomes increasingly unheroic, "the tragedy always conditioned by the relentless banality of life," in the phrase of Joyce Carol Oates. As comedy moves to irony good intentions become futile gestures, the self-deceived remain unenlightened, good fortune becomes random chance, and discontinuity replaces the continuity symbolized by the union of the lovers.

Modern absurdist plays are the most recent development of a particularly ironic form of the tragicomic mixture. The term *theatre of* the absurd is used to include the practice of playwrights as different as Beckett, Pinter, Genet, Albee, Ionesco, Stoppard, and others, many of whom may not be entirely happy to find their work lumped together with others whose forms and attitudes are quite different from theirs. But there are similarities among them in both the absurdity of the human condition imitated and in the non-realistic theatrical means employed. Many absurdist techniques are traced by Joyce Carol Oates back to Chekhov in the essay "Chekhov and the Theater of the Absurd." The absurdist plays in this book, *The Dumb Waiter* and *All That Fall*, illustrate Martin Esslin's claim that absurdists can represent both external reality and *internal* reality— the fantasies, fears, and bewilderment of humankind. *The Dumb Waiter* does not represent a particular fear that people might have but is a particularized image, as nightmare is a particularized image, of a common hostility and sense of powerlessness. *All That Fall* enacts a universal sense of dissolution. It does not show life to be only dissolution, but it does structure a dense cluster of images of dissolution and evoke the audience's recognition that such images are structured that way in the suppressed reality of their fears. Just as science explores the unknown in physical reality, these dramatists explore human internal reality, a universal sense of mystification and uncertainty, in forms that have given new vitality to the theatre.

The Human Condition

Of the plays classified here as tragicomedy and irony, all of them illustrating Northrop Frye's ironic form, *The Cherry Orchard* and *All That Fall* present the human condition from the different perspectives of Chekhov's realism and Beckett's absurdist techniques. The tone of both swings between extremes of frivolity and seriousness, and a common theme is change and loss. But in Chekhov we see daily human necessities created by others and by an imprisoning self. Chekhov

wrote what he called "a comedy; almost a farce" in which the characters, no matter how pathetic we may see them to be, are, in Robert Corrigan's phrase, "comedians by some inner necessity." In Beckett's metaphysical tragicomedy the necessities of the human condition seem to come from beyond any human source. Maddy and Dan, like aged minor figures left behind in a tragedy, confront a cosmic mystery and greet with "wild laughter" the title reference to a benevolent divinity for which they can see no evidence. The human condition in *All That Fall* is to stumble in the dark without "kindly light."

The Ironic Con Game

Mother Courage plays the ironic con game. In the world of her play the game requires a ruthless personal dehumanization and a constant wary suspicion of all good fortune and the good intentions of others. The rules of the ironic con game are that the stakes may very well be life and death and that no amount of skill will guarantee that choices will produce results either predictable or desirable. Brecht's is a social drama, but it is not a simple contest between the powerful and the powerless. The price of survival for the powerless is the dehumanization Courage tries in vain to teach her children. The play develops the irony that the powerful may be resistible but not if the powerless have learned the lesson of survival so well that they feed on one another. The terrible price of survival is to have learned the rules of the game too well and to live in jeopardy: "Let all of you who still survive/Get out of bed and look alive," is the couplet that ends the play. Brecht's ironic form is designed to serve the social purpose he describes in the prose pieces in this book.

Pinter's is not a social drama like Brecht's but an absurdist drama like Beckett's with a structure of events that parodies the certainties of romance. The con game in Pinter's *The Dumb Waiter* is played by players who are totally mystified at every turn of events.

Even what they think they know turns out to be mistaken. Their mystification generates fear; afraid they become hostile. Pinter presents, with all the ambiguity that is part of events, the unreasonableness and heartlessness with which his characters attempt to deal with their hostilities, their isolation, and their need for approval and dominance. In *Mother Courage*, an anti-war play that uses war as an instance, the social structure creates the inhumanity; in *The Dumb Waiter* the frustrations and hostilities in the relationship between Gus and Ben show the source of inhumanity to be deep in human nature.

OUTSIDERS

The reunion of lovers, families, and social groups is replaced by the process of separation when comedy becomes ironic. In one phase of the ironic mode families divide, individuals grow apart, and outsiders struggle alone to survive, to discover meaning and identity, and to reestablish communication with others. The concentration is on particular aspects of the human condition: aloneness in a society that seems at best distant, alien, and indifferent; precariousness in a world that can be confronted only with tentative and probing actions; and uncertainty that necessitates illusions. *Mother Courage* and *The Dumb Waiter* examine from different perspectives the process of separation and isolation; *Hughie* and *A Son, Come Home* show individuals as outsiders to the society making tentative attempts to communicate with others. Each of the four plays examines different aspects of the causes and effects of individual isolations, and each employs an innovative technique for its examination.

Eugene O'Neill's *Hughie* reflects his interest in "a big kind of comedy that doesn't stay funny very long." Though he was most successful with a realistic style, he was a restless experimenter. One half of *Hughie* is the realistic dialogue of two outsiders; the other half is the night clerk's fantasies of the violent world outside. Doris Alexander argues convincingly that these fantasies should be presented to the audience by some film technique. The sounds that enter from outside intensify the isolation that Erie and the night clerk feel, and the images of the night clerk's fantasy depict his imagined revenge—the city that has rejected him will burn down. But O'Neill, at the end of his life, left the problem of what images should be projected to inventive producers and student readers.

Ed Bullins' *A Son, Come Home* employs a different innovative technique to solve a problem that every dramatist encounters: how to present events that occurred prior to the play's action. The presentation of this prior action, usually called the exposition, is often concentrated in the first act where the situation to be resolved is defined. Just as we can see the past of our own lives to have a determining effect on our present, dramatists show the past to have a varying relevance to the situations and motivations of characters. In *The Libation Bearers* and *Hamlet* past crimes must be avenged. But first the audience must be informed about past events. Ed Bullins' *A Son, Come Home* offers a new solution to the problem. Dividing his stage into two parts, one for the past and one for the present, he achieves a fluid and objective method for presenting the past, not as simply determining and ethnic but as it is present in the awareness of his characters.

THE HUMAN CONDITION

THE CHERRY ORCHARD

Anton Chekhov

translated by Robert W. Corrigan

CHARACTERS

LYUBOV ANDREYEVNA RANEVSKY, owner of the cherry orchard

ANYA, her daughter, age 17

VARYA, her adopted daughter, age 24

LEONID ANDREYEVICH GAEV, Lyubov's brother

YERMOLAY ALEXEYEVICH LOPAHIN, a business man

PYOTR SERGEYEVICH TROFIMOV, a student

BORIS BORISOVICH SEMYONOV-PISHCHIK, a landowner

CHARLOTTA IVANOVNA, a governess

SEMYON PANTALEYEVICH EPIHODOV, a clerk on the Ranevsky estate

DUNYASHA, a maid

FEERS, an old servant, age 87

YASHA, a young servant

A TRAMP

THE STATION MASTER

A POST-OFFICE CLERK

GUESTS and SERVANTS

The action takes place on the estate of Madame Ranevsky.

ACT I

A room which used to be the children's room and is still called the nursery. Several doors, one leading into ANYA's *room. It is early in the morning and the sun is rising. It is early in May, but there is a morning frost. The windows are closed but through them can be seen the blossoming cherry trees. Enter* DUNYASHA, *carrying a candle, and* LOPAHIN *with a book in his hand.*

LOPAHIN. The train's arrived, thank God. What time is it?

DUNYASHA. It's nearly two. (*Blows out the candle.*) It's daylight already.

LOPAHIN. The train must have been at least two hours late. (*Yawns and stretches.*) And what a fool I am! I make a special trip out here to meet them at the station, and then I fall asleep. . . . Just sat down in the chair and dropped off. What a nuisance. Why didn't you wake me up?

DUNYASHA. I thought you'd gone. (*Listens.*) I think they're coming.

LOPAHIN (*also listens*). No . . . I should've been there to help them with their luggage and other things . . . (*Pause.*) Lyubov Andreyevna has been abroad for five years. I wonder what she's like now. She used to be such a kind and good person. So easy to get along with and always considerate. Why, I remember when I was fifteen, my father—he had a store in town then—hit me in the face and it made my nose bleed. . . . We'd come out here for something or other, and he was drunk. Oh, I remember it as if it happened yesterday. . . . She was so young and beautiful . . . Lyubov Andreyevna brought me into this very room—the nursery, and she fixed my nose and she said to me, "Don't cry, little peasant, it'll be better by the time you get married" . . . (*Pause.*) "Little peasant" . . . She was right, my father was a peasant. And look at me now—going about in a white waistcoat and brown shoes, like a crow in peacock's feathers. Oh, I am rich all right, I've got lots of money, but when you think about it, I'm still just a peasant. (*Turning over pages of the book.*) Here, I've been reading this book, and couldn't understand a word of it. Fell asleep reading it. (*Pause.*)

DUNYASHA. The dogs have been awake all night: they know their mistress is coming.

LOPAHIN. Why, what's the matter with you, Dunyasha?

DUNYASHA. My hands are shaking. I think I'm going to faint.

LOPAHIN. You've become too delicate and refined, Dunyasha. You get yourself all dressed up like a lady, and you fix your hair like one, too. You shouldn't do that, you know. You must remember your place.

Enter EPIHODOV *with a bouquet of flowers; he wears a jacket and brightly polished high boots which squeak loudly. As he enters he drops the flowers.*

EPIHODOV (*picks up the flowers*). The gardener sent these. He says they're to go in the dining room. (*Hands the flowers to* DUNYASHA.)

LOPAHIN. And bring me some kvass.

DUNYASHA. All right.

EPIHODOV. It's chilly outside this morning, three degrees of frost, and here the cherry trees are all in bloom. I can't say much for this climate of ours, you know. (*Sighs.*) No, I really can't. It doesn't contribute to—well, you know, things . . . And what do you think, Yermolay Alexeyevich, the day before yesterday I bought myself a pair of boots and they squeak so much . . . well, I mean to say, they're impossible. . . . What can I use to fix them?

LOPAHIN. Oh, be quiet! And don't bother me!

EPIHODOV. Every day something unpleasant happens to me. But I don't complain; I'm used to it, why I even laugh. (*Enter* DUNYASHA: *she serves* LOPAHIN *with kvass.*) Well, I have to be going. (*Bumps into a chair which falls over.*) There, you see! (*Triumphantly.*) You can see for yourself what I mean,

you see . . . so to speak . . . It's absolutely amazing! (*Goes out.*)

DUNYASHA. I must tell you a secret, Yermolay Alexeyevich. Epihodov proposed to me.

LOPAHIN. Really!

DUNYASHA. I don't know what to do. . . . He's a quiet man, but then sometimes he starts talking, and then you can't understand a word he says. It sounds nice, and he says it with so much feeling, but it doesn't make any sense. I think I like him a little, and he's madly in love with me. But the poor man, he's sort of unlucky! Do you know, something unpleasant seems to happen to him every day. That's why they tease him and call him "two-and-twenty misfortunes."

LOPAHIN (*listens*). I think I hear them coming. . . .

DUNYASHA. Coming! . . . Oh, what's the matter with me. . . . I feel cold all over.

LOPAHIN. Yes, they're really coming! Let's go and meet them at the door. I wonder if she'll recognize me? We haven't seen each other for five years.

DUNYASHA (*agitated*). I'm going to faint . . . Oh, I'm going to faint! . . .

The sound of two carriages driving up to the house can be heard. LOPAHIN *and* DUNYASHA *hurry out. The stage is empty. Then there are sounds of people arriving in the next room.* FEERS, *who has gone to meet the train, enters the room leaning on a cane. He crosses the stage as rapidly as he can. He is dressed in an old-fashioned livery coat and a top hat and is muttering to himself, though it is impossible to make out what he is saying. The noises off-stage become louder.*

VOICE (*off-stage*). Let's go through here.

Enter LYUBOV ANDREYEVNA, ANYA, *and* CHARLOTTA IVANOVNA, *leading a small dog, all in traveling clothes,* VARYA, *wearing an overcoat and a kerchief over her head,* GAEV, SEMYONOV-PISHCHIK, LOPAHIN, DUNYASHA, *carrying a bundle and parasol and other servants with luggage.*

ANYA. Let's go through here. Do you remember what room this is, Mamma?

LYUBOV (*joyfully, through her tears*). The nursery!

VARYA. How cold it is! My hands are numb. (*To* LYUBOV.) Your rooms are the same as always, Mamma dear, the white one, and the lavender one.

LYUBOV. The nursery, my dear, beautiful room! . . . I used to sleep here when I was little. (*Cries.*) And here I am again, like a little child . . . (*She kisses her brother, then* VARYA, *then her brother again.*) And Varya hasn't changed a bit, looking like a nun. And I recognized Dunyasha, too. (*Kisses* DUNYASHA.)

GAEV. The train was two hours late. Just think of it! Such efficiency!

CHARLOTTA (*to* PISHCHIK). And my dog eats nuts, too.

PISHCHIK (*astonished*). Think of that!

They all go out except ANYA *and* DUNYASHA.

DUNYASHA. We've waited and waited for you . . . (*Helps* ANYA *to take off her hat and coat.*)

ANYA. I haven't slept for four nights . . . I'm freezing.

DUNYASHA. It was Lent when you left, and it was snowing and freezing; but it's spring now. Darling! (*She laughs and kisses her.*) Oh, how I've missed you! I could hardly stand it. My pet, my precious . . . But I must tell you . . . I can't wait another minute . . .

ANYA (*without enthusiasm*). What time is it? . . .

DUNYASHA. Epihodov, the clerk, proposed to me right after Easter.

ANYA. You never talk about anything else. . . (*Tidies her hair.*) I've lost all my hairpins. . . . (*She's so tired she can hardly keep on her feet.*)

DUNYASHA. I really don't know what to think. He loves me . . . he loves me very much!

ANYA (*looking through the door into her room, tenderly*). My own room, my own windows, just as if I'd never left them! I'm home again! Tomorrow I'm going to get up and run right to the garden! Oh, if only I could fall asleep! I couldn't sleep all the way back, I've been so worried.

DUNYASHA. Pyotr Sergeyevich came the day before yesterday.

ANYA (*joyfully*). Pyeta!

DUNYASHA. We put him in the bathhouse, he's probably asleep now. He said he didn't want to inconvenience you. (*Looks at her watch.*) I should have gotten him up, but Varya told me not to. "Don't you dare get him up," she said.

Enter VARYA *with a bunch of keys at her waist.*

VARYA. Dunyasha, get some coffee, and hurry! Mamma wants some.

DUNYASHA. I'll get it right away. (*Goes out*).

VARYA. Thank God, you're back! You're home again. (*Embracing her.*) My little darling's come home! How are you, my precious?

ANYA. If you only knew what I've had to put up with!

VARYA. I can just imagine . . .

ANYA. You remember, I left just before Easter and it was cold then. And Charlotta never stopped talking the whole time, talking and those silly tricks of hers. Why did you make me take Charlotta?

VARYA. But you couldn't go all alone, darling. At seventeen!

ANYA. When we got to Paris it was cold and snowing. My French was terrible. Mamma was living on the fifth floor, and the place was filled with people—some French ladies, and an old priest with a little book, and the room was full of cigarette smoke. It was so unpleasant. All of a sudden I felt so sorry for Mamma that I put my arms around her neck and hugged her and wouldn't let go I was so upset. Later Mamma cried and was very kind.

VARYA (*tearfully*). I can't stand to hear it! . . .

ANYA. She had already sold her villa at Mentone, and she had nothing left, not a thing.

And I didn't have any money left either, not a penny. In fact, I barely had enough to get to Paris. And Mamma didn't understand it at all. On the way, we'd eat at the best restaurants and she'd order the most expensive dishes and tip the waiters a rouble each. Charlotta's the same way. And Yasha expected a full-course dinner for himself; it was horrible. You know, Yasha is Mamma's valet, now, we brought him with us.

VARYA. Yes, I've seen the scoundrel.

ANYA. Well, how's everything here? Have you paid the interest on the mortgage?

VARYA. With what?

ANYA. Oh dear! Oh dear!

VARYA. The time runs out in August, and then it will be up for sale.

ANYA. Oh dear!

LOPAHIN (*puts his head through the door and moos like a cow*). Moo-o. . . . (*Disappears.*)

VARYA (*tearfully*). I'd like to hit him . . . (*Clenches her fist.*)

ANYA (*her arms round* VARYA, *dropping her voice*). Varya, has he proposed to you? (VARYA *shakes her head.*) But he loves you. . . . Why don't you talk to him, what are you waiting for?

VARYA. Nothing will come of it. He's too busy to have time to think of me . . . He doesn't notice me at all. It's easier when he isn't around, it makes me miserable just to see him. Everybody talks of our wedding and congratulates me, but in fact there's nothing to it, it's all a dream. (*In a different tone.*) You've got a new pin, it looks like a bee.

ANYA (*sadly*). Mamma bought it for me. (*She goes into her room and then with childlike gaiety.*) Did you know that in Paris I went up in a balloon?

VARYA. My darling's home again! My precious one's home. (DUNYASHA *returns with a coffeepot and prepares coffee. Standing by* ANYA's *door.*) You know, all day long, as I go about the house doing my work, I'm always dreaming. If only we could marry you to some rich man, I'd be more at peace. Then they could go away; first I'd

go to the cloisters, and then I'd go on a pilgrimage to Kiev, and then Moscow . . . I'd spend my life just walking from one holy place to another. On and on. Oh, what a wonderful life that would be!

ANYA. The birds are singing in the garden. What time is it?

VARYA. It must be nearly three. Time you went to bed, darling. (*Goes into* ANYA's *room.*) Oh, what a wonderful life!

Enter YASHA, *with a blanket and a small bag.*

YASHA (*crossing the stage, in an affectedly genteel voice*). May I go through here?

DUNYASHA. My, how you've changed since you've been abroad, Yasha. I hardly recognized you.

YASHA. Hm! And who are you?

DUNYASHA. When you went away, I was no bigger than this . . . (*Shows her height from the floor.*) I'm Dunyasha, Fyodor's daughter. You don't remember me!

YASHA. Hm! You're quite a little peach! (*Looks around and embraces her; she screams and drops a saucer.* YASHA *goes out quickly.*)

VARYA (*in the doorway, crossly*). What's happening in here?

DUNYASHA (*tearfully*). I've broken a saucer.

VARYA. That's good luck.

ANYA (*coming out of her room*). We ought to warn Mamma that Petya's here.

VARYA. I gave strict orders not to wake him up.

ANYA (*pensively*). Six years ago father died, and then a month later Grisha was drowned in the river. He was such a beautiful little boy—and only seven! Mamma couldn't stand it so she went away . . . and never looked back. (*Shivers.*) How well I understand her! If she only knew! (*Pause.*) And, Petya was Grisha's tutor, he might remind her . . .

Enter FEERS, *wearing a jacket and a white waistcoat.*

FEERS (*goes over and is busy with the samovar*). The mistress will have her coffee in here.

(*Puts on white gloves.*) Is it ready? (*To* DUNYASHA, *severely.*) Where's the cream?

DUNYASHA. Oh, I forgot! (*Goes out quickly.*)

FEERS (*fussing around the coffeepot*). That girl's hopeless. . . . (*Mutters.*) They've come from Paris . . . Years ago the master used to go to Paris . . . Used to go by carriage . . . (*Laughs.*)

VARYA. Feers, what are you laughing at?

FEERS. What would you like? (*Happily.*) The mistress has come home! Home at last! I don't mind if I die now . . . (*Weeps with joy.*)

Enter LYUBOV, LOPAHIN, GAEV *and* SEMYONOV-PISHCHIK, *the latter in a long peasant coat of fine cloth and full trousers tucked inside high boots.* GAEV, *as he comes in, moves his arms and body as if he were playing billiards.*

LYUBOV. How does it go now? Let me think . . . The red off the side and into the middle pocket!

GAEV. That's right! Then I put the white into the corner pocket! . . . Years ago we used to sleep in this room, and now I'm fifty-one, strange as it may seem.

LOPAHIN. Yes, time flies.

GAEV. What?

LOPAHIN. Time flies, I say.

GAEV. This place smells of patchouli . . .

ANYA. I'm going to bed. Goodnight, Mamma. (*Kisses her.*)

LYUBOV. My precious child! (*Kisses her hands.*) Are you glad you're home? I still can't get used to it.

ANYA. Goodnight, Uncle.

GAEV (*kisses her face and hands*). God bless you. You're so much like your mother! (*To his sister.*) You looked exactly like her at her age, Lyuba.

ANYA *shakes hands with* LOPAHIN *and* PISHCHIK, *goes out and shuts the door after her.*

LYUBOV. She's very tired.

PISHCHIK. It's been a long trip for her.

VARYA (*to* LOPAHIN *and* PISHCHIK). Well, gentlemen? It's nearly three o'clock, time to say good-bye.

LYUBOV (*laughs*). You haven't changed a bit, Varya. (*Draws* VARYA *to her and kisses her.*) Let me have some coffee, then we'll all turn in. (FEERS *places a cushion under her feet.*) Thank you, my dear. I've got into the habit of drinking coffee. I drink it day and night. Thank you, my dear old friend. (*Kisses* FEERS.)

VARYA. I'd better see if they brought all the luggage in. (*Goes out.*)

LYUBOV. Is it really me sitting here? (*Laughing.*) I'd like to dance and wave my arms about. (*Covering her face with her hands.*) But am I just dreaming? God, how I love it here—my own country! Oh, I love it so much, I could hardly see anything from the train, I was crying so hard. (*Through tears.*) Here, but I must drink my coffee. Thank you, Feers, thank you, my dear old friend. I'm so glad you're still alive.

FEERS. The day before yesterday.

GAEV. He doesn't hear very well.

LOPAHIN. I've got to leave for Kharkov a little after four. What a nuisance! It's so good just to see you, and I want to talk with you . . . You look as lovely as ever.

PISHCHIK (*breathing heavily*). Prettier. In her fancy Parisian clothes . . . She's simply ravishing!

LOPAHIN. Your brother here—Leonid Andreyevich—says that I'm nothing but a hick from the country, a tight-fisted peasant, but it doesn't bother me. Let him say what he likes. All I want is that you trust me as you always have. Merciful God! My father was your father's serf, and your grandfather's, too, but you've done so much for me that I've forgotten all that. I love you as if you were my own sister . . . more than that even.

LYUBOV. I just can't sit still, I can't for the life of me! (*She jumps up and walks about in great excitement.*) I'm so happy, it's too much for me. It's all right, you can laugh at me. I know I'm being silly . . . My wonderful old bookcase! (*Kisses bookcase.*) And my little table!

GAEV. You know, the old Nurse died while you were away.

LYUBOV (*sits down and drinks coffee*). Yes, you wrote to me about it. May she rest in peace.

GAEV. Anastasy died, too. And Petrushka quit and is working in town for the chief of police. (*Takes a box of gumdrops out of his pocket and puts one in his mouth.*)

PISHCHIK. My daughter, Dashenka, sends you her greetings.

LOPAHIN. I feel like telling you some good news, something to cheer you up. (*Looks at his watch.*) I'll have to leave in a minute, so there's not much time to talk. But briefly it's this. As you know, the cherry orchard is going to be sold to pay your debts. They've set August 22nd as the date for the auction, but you can sleep in peace and not worry about it; there's a way out. Here's my plan, so please pay close attention. Your estate is only twenty miles from town, and the railroad is close by. Now, if the cherry orchard and the land along the river were subdivided and leased for the building of summer cottages, you'd have a yearly income of at least twenty-five thousand roubles.

GAEV. Such nonsense!

LYUBOV. I'm afraid I don't quite understand, Yermolay Alexeyevich.

LOPAHIN. You'd divide the land into one acre lots and rent them for at least twenty-five roubles a year. I'll bet you, that if you advertise it now there won't be a lot left by the fall; they'll be snapped up almost at once. You see, you're saved! And really, I must congratulate you; it's a perfect setup. The location is marvelous and the river's deep enough for swimming. Of course, the land will have to be cleared and cleaned up a bit. For instance, all those old buildings will have to be torn down . . . And this house, too . . . but then it's not really good for anything any more. . . . And then, the old cherry orchard will have to be cut down . . .

LYUBOV. Cut down? My good man, forgive me, but you don't seem to understand. If there's one thing that's interesting and really valuable in this whole part of the country, it's our cherry orchard.

LOPAHIN. The only valuable thing about it is that it's very large. It only produces a crop every other year and then who wants to buy it?

GAEV. Why, this orchard is even mentioned in the Encyclopedia.

LOPAHIN (*looking at his watch*). If you don't decide now, and do something about it before August, the cherry orchard as well as the estate will be auctioned off. So make up your minds! There's no other way out, I promise you. There's no other way.

FEERS. In the old days, forty or fifty years ago, the cherries were dried, preserved, pickled, made into jam, and sometimes. . . .

GAEV. Be quiet, Feers.

FEERS. And sometimes, whole wagon-loads of dried cherries were shipped to Moscow and Kharkov. We used to make a lot of money on them then! And the dried cherries used to be soft, juicy, sweet, and very good . . . They knew how to do it then . . . they had a way of cooking them . . .

LYUBOV. And where is that recipe now?

FEERS. They've forgotten it. Nobody can remember it.

PISHCHIK (*to* LYUBOV). What's it like in Paris? Did you eat frogs?

LYUBOV. I ate crocodiles.

PISHCHIK. Well, will you imagine that!

LOPAHIN. Until recently only rich people and peasants lived in the country, but now lots of people come out for the summer. Almost every town, even the small ones, is surrounded with summer places. And probably within the next twenty years there'll be more and more of these people. Right now, all they do is sit on the porch and drink tea, but later on they might begin to grow a few things, and then your cherry orchard would be full of life again . . . rich and prosperous.

GAEV (*indignantly*). Such a lot of nonsense!

Enter VARYA *and* YASHA.

VARYA. There were two telegrams for you,

Mamma dear. (*Takes out the keys and opens the old bookcase, making a great deal of noise.*) Here they are.

LYUBOV. They're from Paris. (*Tears them up without reading them.*) I'm through with Paris.

GAEV. Do you know, Lyuba, how old this bookcase is? Last week I pulled out the bottom drawer, and I found the date it was made burned in the wood. Just think, it's exactly a hundred years old. What do you think of that, eh? We ought to celebrate its anniversary. I know it's an inanimate object, but still—it's a bookcase!

PISHCHIK (*astonished*). A hundred years! Can you imagine that!

GAEV. Yes . . . That's quite something. (*Feeling round the bookcase with his hands.*) Dear, most honored bookcase! I salute you! For one hundred years you have served the highest ideals of goodness and justice. For one hundred years you have made us aware of the need for creative work; several generations of our family have had their courage sustained and their faith in a brighter future fortified by your silent call; you have fostered in us the ideals of public service and social consciousness. (*Pause.*)

LOPAHIN. Yes . . .

LYUBOV. You haven't changed a bit, Leonia.

GAEV (*slightly embarrassed*). I shoot it off the corner into the middle pocket! . . .

LOPAHIN (*looks at his watch*). Well, I've got to go.

YASHA (*brings medicine to* LYUBOV). Would you like to take your pills now; it's time.

PISHCHIK. You shouldn't take medicine, my dear . . . they don't do you any good . . . or harm either. Let me have them. (*Takes the box from her, pours the pills into the palm of his hand, blows on them, puts them all into his mouth and drinks them down with kvass.*) There!

LYUBOV (*alarmed*). You're out of your mind!

PISHCHIK. I took all the pills.

LOPAHIN. What a stomach! (*All laugh.*)

FEERS. His honor was here during Holy Week, and he ate half a bucket of pickles. (*Mutters.*)

LYUBOV. What's he saying?

VARYA. He's been muttering like that for three years now. We're used to it.

YASHA. It's his age. . . .

CHARLOTTA IVANOVNA, *very thin, and tightly laced in a white dress, with a lorgnette at her waist, passes across the stage.*

LOPAHIN. Excuse me, Charlotta Ivanovna, for not greeting you. I didn't have a chance. (*Tries to kiss her hand.*)

CHARLOTTA (*withdrawing her hand*). If I let you kiss my hand, then you'd want to kiss my elbow next, and then my shoulder.

LOPAHIN. This just isn't my lucky day. (*All laugh.*) Charlotta Ivanovna, do a trick for us.

CHARLOTTA. Not now. I want to go to bed. (*Goes out.*)

LOPAHIN. I'll be back in three weeks. (*Kisses* LYUBOV's *hand.*) It's time I'm going so I'll say good-bye. (*To* GAEV.) Au revoir. (*Embraces* PISHCHIK.) Au revoir. (*Shakes hands with* VARYA, *then with* FEERS *and* YASHA.) I don't want to go, really. (*To* LYUBOV.) Think over the idea of the summer cottages and if you decide anything, let me know, and I'll get you a loan of at least fifty thousand. So think it over seriously.

VARYA (*crossly.*) Won't you ever go?

LOPAHIN. I'm going, I'm going. (*Goes out.*)

GAEV. What a boor! I beg your pardon . . . Varya's going to marry him, he's Varya's fiancé.

VARYA. Please don't talk like that, Uncle.

LYUBOV. Well, Varya, I'd be delighted. He's a good man.

PISHCHIK. He's a man . . . you have to say that . . . a most worthy fellow . . . My Dashenka says so too . . . she says all sorts of things. . . . (*He drops asleep and snores, but wakes up again at once.*) By the way, my dear, will you lend me two hundred and forty roubles? I've got to pay the interest on the mortgage tomorrow . . .

VARYA (*in alarm*). We haven't got it, really we haven't!

LYUBOV. It's true, I haven't got a thing.

PISHCHIK. It'll turn up. (*Laughs.*) I never lose hope. There are times when I think everything's lost, I'm ruined, and then—suddenly!—a railroad is built across my land, and they pay me for it! Something's bound to happen, if not today, then tomorrow, or the next day. Perhaps Dashenka will win two hundred thousand—she's got a lottery ticket.

LYUBOV. Well, we've finished our coffee; now we can go to bed.

FEERS (*brushing* GAEV, *admonishing him*). You've got on those trousers again! What am I going to do with you?

VARYA (*in a low voice*). Anya's asleep. (*Quietly opens a window.*) The sun's rising and see how wonderful the trees are! And the air smells so fragrant! The birds are beginning to sing.

GAEV (*coming to the window*). The orchard is all white. You haven't forgotten, Lyuba? How straight that lane is . . . just like a ribbon. And how it shines on moonlight nights. Do you remember? You haven't forgotten, have you?

LYUBOV (*looks through the window at the orchard*). Oh, my childhood, my innocent childhood! I used to sleep here, and I'd look out at the orchard and every morning when I woke up I was so happy. The orchard was exactly the same, nothing's changed. (*Laughs happily.*). All, all white! Oh, my orchard! After the dark, gloomy autumn and the cold winter, you are young again and full of joy; the angels have not deserted you! If only this burden could be taken from me, if only I could forget my past!

GAEV. Yes, and now the orchard's going to be sold to pay our debts, how strange it all is.

LYUBOV. Look, there's Mother walking through the orchard . . . dressed all in white! (*Laughs happily.*) It is Mother!

GAEV. Where?

VARYA. Oh, please, Mamma dear!

LYUBOV. You're right, it's no one, I only imagined it. Over there, you see, on the right, by the path that goes to the arbor; there's a small white tree that's bending so it looks just like a woman.

Enter TROFIMOV. *He is dressed in a shabby student's uniform, and wears glasses.*

What a wonderful orchard! Masses of white blossoms, the blue sky . . .

TROFIMOV. Lyubov Andreyevna! (*She turns to him.*) I'll just say hello and leave at once. (*Kisses her hand warmly.*) They told me to wait until morning, but I couldn't wait any longer. (LYUBOV *looks at him, puzzled.*)

VARYA (*through tears*). This is Petya Trofimov.

TROFIMOV. Petya Trofimov, I was Grisha's tutor. Have I changed that much?

LYUBOV *puts her arms round him and weeps quietly.*

GAEV (*embarrassed*). Now, now, Lyuba . . .

VARYA (*weeps*). Didn't I tell you to wait until tomorrow, Petya?

LYUBOV. My Grisha . . . my little boy . . . Oh, Grisha . . . my son . . .

VARYA. Don't cry, Mamma darling. There's nothing we can do, it was God's will.

TROFIMOV (*gently, with emotion*). Don't, don't . . . please.

LYUBOV (*weeping quietly*). My little boy was lost . . . drowned . . . Why? Why, my friend? (*More quietly.*) Anya's asleep in there, and here I'm crying and making a scene. But tell me, Petya, what's happened to your good looks? You've aged so.

TROFIMOV. A peasant woman on the train called me "that moth-eaten man."

LYUBOV. You used to be such an attractive boy, a typical young student. But now your hair is thin and you wear glasses. Are you still a student? (*She walks to the door.*)

TROFIMOV. I expect I'll be a student as long as I live.

LYUBOV (*kisses her brother, then* VARYA). Well, go to bed now. You have aged, too, Leonid.

PISHCHIK (*following her*). Yes, I suppose it's time to get to bed. Oh, my gout! I'd better spend the night here, and in the morning, Lyubov Andreyevna, my dear, I'd like to borrow the two hundred and forty roubles.

GAEV. Don't you ever stop?

PISHCHIK. Just two hundred and forty roubles . . . To pay the interest on my mortgage.

LYUBOV. I haven't any money, my friend.

PISHCHIK. Oh, I'll pay you back, my dear. It's not much, after all.

LYUBOV. Oh, all right. Leonid will give it to you. You give him the money, Leonid.

GAEV. Why, of course; glad to. As much as he wants!

LYUBOV. What else can we do? He needs it. He'll pay it back.

LYUBOV, TROFIMOV, PISHCHIK *and* FEERS *go out.* GAEV, VARYA *and* YASHA *remain.*

GAEV. My sister hasn't lost her habit of throwing money away. (*To* YASHA.) Get out of the way, you smell like a barnyard.

YASHA (*with a sneer*). And you haven't changed either, have you Leonid Andreyevich?

GAEV. What's that? (*To* VARYA.) What did he say?

VARYA (*to* YASHA). Your mother came out from town yesterday to see you, and she's been waiting out in the servants' quarters ever since.

YASHA. I wish she wouldn't bother me.

VARYA. Oh, you ought to be ashamed of yourself.

YASHA. What's she in such a hurry for? She could have come tomorrow. (YASHA *goes out.*)

VARYA. Mamma hasn't changed a bit. She'd give away everything we had, if she could.

GAEV. Yes . . . You know, when many things are prescribed to cure a disease, that means it's incurable. I've been wracking my brains to find an answer, and I've come up with several solutions, plenty of them— which means there aren't any. It would be wonderful if we could inherit some money, or if our Anya were to marry some very rich man, or if one of us went to Yaroslavl and tried our luck with our old aunt, the Countess. You know she's very rich.

VARYA (*weeping*). If only God would help us.

GAEV. Oh, stop blubbering! The Countess is very rich, but she doesn't like us . . . To begin with, my sister married a lawyer, and not a nobleman . . . (ANYA *appears in the doorway.*) She married a commoner . . .

and since then no one can say she's behaved in the most virtuous way possible. She's good, kind, and lovable, and I love her very much, but no matter how much you may allow for extenuating circumstances, you've got to admit that her morals have not been beyond reproach. You can sense it in everything she does . . .

VARYA (*in a whisper*). Anya's standing in the doorway.

GAEV. What? (*A pause.*) Isn't that strange, something's gotten into my right eye . . . I'm having a terrible time seeing. And last Thursday, when I was in the District Court . . . (ANYA *comes in.*)

VARYA. Anya, why aren't you asleep?

ANYA. I don't feel like sleeping. I just can't.

GAEV. My dear little girl! (*Kisses* ANYA's *face and hands.*) My child! (*Tearfully.*) You're not just my niece, you're an angel, my whole world. Please believe me, believe . . .

ANYA. I believe you, Uncle. Everyone loves you, respects you . . . but, dear Uncle, you shouldn't talk so much, just try to keep quiet. What were you saying just now about mother, about your own sister? What made you say that?

GAEV. Yes, yes! (*He takes her hand and puts it over his face.*) You're quite right, it was a horrible thing to say! My God! My God! And that speech I made to the bookcase . . . so stupid! As soon as I finished it, I realized how stupid it was.

VARYA. It's true, Uncle dear, you oughtn't to talk so much. Just keep quiet, that's all.

ANYA. If you keep quiet, you'll find life is more peaceful.

GAEV. I'll be quiet. (*Kisses* ANYA's *and* VARYA's *hands.*) I'll be quiet. But I must tell you something about all this business, it's important. Last Thursday I went to the District Court, and I got talking with some friends, and from what they said it looks as if it might be possible to get a second mortgage so we can pay the interest to the bank.

VARYA. If only God would help us!

GAEV. I'm going again on Tuesday to talk with them some more. (*To* VARYA.) Oh, stop crying. (*To* ANYA.) Your mother's going to talk with Lopahin, and he certainly won't refuse her. And after you've had a little rest, you can go to Yaroslavl to see your grandmother, the Countess. You see, we'll attack the problem from three sides, and—it's as good as solved! We'll pay the interest, I'm sure of it. (*He eats a gumdrop.*) On my honor, on anything you like, I swear the estate'll not be sold! (*Excited.*) I'll bet my happiness on it! Here's my hand, you can call me a worthless liar if I allow the auction to take place. I swear it with all my soul!

ANYA (*calmer, with an air of happiness*). How good you are, Uncle, and how sensible! (*Embracing him.*) I'm not afraid anymore. I feel so happy and at peace.

Enter FEERS.

FEERS (*reproachfully*). Leonid Andreyevich, aren't you ashamed of yourself? When are you going to bed?

GAEV. In a minute. Now you go away, Feers. I can get ready for bed myself. Come along, children, time for bed. We'll talk about it some more tomorrow, you must go to bed now. (*Kisses* ANYA *and* VARYA.) You know, I'm a man of the 'eighties. People don't think much of that period these days, but still I can say that I've suffered a great deal in my lifetime because of my convictions. There's a reason why the peasants love me. You have to know the peasants! You have to know . . .

ANYA. You're beginning again, Uncle!

VARYA. Yes, you'd better keep quiet, Uncle dear.

FEERS (*sternly*). Leonid Andreyevich!

GAEV. I'm coming, I'm coming! Go to bed now! Bank the white into the side pocket. There's a shot for you . . . (*Goes out;* FEERS *hobbles after him.*)

ANYA. I feel better now, although I don't want to go to Yaroslavl, I don't like the Countess at all, but then, thanks to Uncle, we really don't have to worry at all. (*She sits down.*)

VARYA. I've got to get some sleep. I'm going. Oh, by the way, we had a terrible scene while you were gone. You know, there are only a few old servants left out in the servants' quarters: just Yefmushka, Polya, Yevstignay, and Karp. Well, they let some tramp sleep out there, and at first I didn't say anything about it. But then later, I heard people saying that I had given orders to feed them nothing but beans. Because I was stingy, you see . . . Yevstignay was the cause of it all. "Well," I think to myself, "if that's how things are, just you wait!" So I called Yevstignay in. (*Yawns.*) So he came. "What's all this, Yevstignay," I said to him, "you're such a fool." (*She walks up to* ANYA. Anichka! (*A pause.*) She's asleep! . . . (*Takes her arm.*) Let's go to bed! Come! (*Leads her away.*) My darling's fallen asleep! Come . . . (*They go towards the door. The sound of a shepherd's pipe is heard from far away, beyond the orchard.* TROFIMOV *crosses the stage, but, seeing* VARYA *and* ANYA, *stops.*) Sh-sh! She's asleep . . . asleep . . . Come along, come along.

ANYA (*softly, half-asleep*). I'm so tired. . . . I can hear the bells ringing all the time . . . Uncle . . . dear . . . Mamma and Uncle. . . .

VARYA. Come, darling, come. . . . (*They go into* ANYA's *room.*)

TROFIMOV (*deeply moved*). Oh, Anya . . . my sunshine! My spring!

Curtain

ACT II

An old abandoned chapel in field. Beside it are a well, an old bench, and some tombstones. A road leads to the Ranevsky estate. On one side a row of poplars casts a shadow; at that point the cherry orchard begins. In the distance, a line of telegraph poles can be seen, and beyond them, on the horizon is the outline of a large town, visible only in very clear weather. It's nearly sunset. CHARLOTTA, YASHA *and* DUNYASHA *are sitting on the bench;* EPIHODOV *is standing near by, playing a guitar; everyone is lost in thought.* CHARLOTTA *is wearing an old hunting cap; she has taken a shotgun off her shoulder and is adjusting the buckle on the strap.*

CHARLOTTA (*thoughtfully*). I don't know how old I am. For you see, I haven't got a passport . . . but I keep pretending that I'm still very young. When I was a little girl, my father and mother traveled from fair to fair giving performances—oh, very good ones. And I used to do the "*salto-mortale*" and all sorts of other tricks, too. When Papa and Mamma died, a German lady took me to live with her and sent me to school. So when I grew up I became a governess. But where I come from and who I am, I don't know. Who my parents were —perhaps they weren't even married—I don't know. (*Taking a cucumber from her pocket and beginning to eat it.*) I don't know anything. (*Pause.*) I'm longing to talk to someone, but there isn't anybody. I haven't anybody . . .

EPIHODOV (*plays the guitar and sings*). "What care I for the noisy world? . . . What care I for friends and foes?" How pleasant it is to play the mandolin!

DUNYASHA. That's a guitar, not a mandolin. (*She looks at herself in a little mirror and powders her face.*)

EPIHODOV. To a man who's madly in love this is a mandolin. (*Sings quietly.*) "If only my heart were warmed by the fire of love requited.". . . (YASHA *joins in.*)

CHARLOTTA. How dreadfully these people sing! . . . Ach! Like a bunch of jackals.

DUNYASHA (*to* YASHA). You're so lucky to have been abroad!

YASHA. Of course I am. Naturally. (*Yawns, then lights a cigar.*)

EPIHODOV. Stands to reason. Abroad everything's reached its maturity . . . I mean to say, everything's been going on for such a long time.

YASHA. Obviously.

EPIHODOV. Now, I'm a cultured man, I read all kinds of extraordinary books, you know, but somehow I can't seem to figure out where I'm going, what it is I really want, I mean to say—whether to live or to shoot myself. Nevertheless, I always carry a revolver on me. Here it is. (*Shows the revolver.*)

CHARLOTTA. That's finished, so now I'm going. (*Slips the strap of the gun over her shoulder.*) Yes, Epihodov, you are a very clever man, and frightening, too; the women must be wild about you! Brrr! (*Walks off.*) All these clever people are so stupid, I haven't anyone to talk to. I'm so lonely, always alone, I have nobody and . . . and who I am and what I'm here for, nobody knows . . . (*Wanders out.*)

EPIHODOV. Frankly, and I want to keep to the point, I have to admit that Fate, so to speak, treats me absolutely without mercy, like a small ship is buffeted by the storm, as it were. I mean to say, suppose I'm mistaken, then why for instance should I wake up this morning and suddenly see a gigantic spider sitting on my chest? Like this . . . (*Showing the size with both hands.*) Or if I pick up a jug to have a drink of kvass, there's sure to be something horrible, like a cockroach, inside it. (*Pause.*) Have you read Buckle? (*Pause.*) May I trouble you for a moment, Dunyasha? I'd like to speak with you.

DUNYASHA. Well, go ahead.

EPIHODOV. I'd very much like to speak with you alone. (*Sighs.*)

DUNYASHA (*embarrassed*). Oh, all right . . . But first bring me my little cape . . . It's hanging by the cupboard. It's getting terribly chilly . . .

EPIHODOV. Very well, I'll get it. . . . Now I know what to do with my revolver. (*Takes his guitar and goes off playing it.*)

YASHA. Two-and-twenty misfortunes! Just between you and me, he's a stupid fool. (*Yawns.*)

DUNYASHA. I hope to God he doesn't shoot himself. (*Pause.*) He makes me so nervous and I'm always worrying about him. I came to live here when I was still a little girl. Now I no longer know how to live a simple life, and my hands are as white . . . as white as a lady's. I've become such a delicate and sensitive creature. I'm afraid of everything . . . so frightened. If you deceive me, Yasha, I don't know what will happen to my nerves.

YASHA (*kisses her*). You sweet little peach! Just remember, a girl must always control herself. Personally I think nothing is worse than a girl who doesn't behave herself.

DUNYASHA. I love you so much, so passionately! You're so intelligent, you can talk about anything. (*Pause.*)

YASHA (*yawns*). Yes, I suppose so . . . In my opinion, it's like this; if a girl loves someone it means she's immoral. (*Pause.*) I enjoy smoking a cigar in the fresh air . . . (*Listens.*) Someone's coming. It's the ladies and gentlemen. . . . (DUNYASHA *impulsively embraces him.*) Go to the house now, as though you'd been swimming down at the river. No, this way or they'll see you. I wouldn't want them to think I was interested in you.

DUNYASHA (*coughing softly*). That cigar has given me such a headache . . . (*Goes out.*)

YASHA *remains sitting by the shrine. Enter* LYUBOV, GAEV *and* LOPAHIN.

LOPAHIN. You've got to make up your minds once and for all; there's no time to lose. After all, it's a simple matter. Will you lease your land for the cottages, or won't you? You can answer in one word: yes or no? Just one word!

LYUBOV. Who's been smoking such wretched cigars? (*Sits down.*)

GAEV. How very convenient everything is with the railroad nearby. (*Sits down.*) Well, here we are—we've been to town, had lunch and we're home already. I put the red into the middle pocket! I'd like to go in . . . just for one game. . . .

LYUBOV. You've got lots of time.

LOPAHIN. Just one word! (*Beseechingly.*) Please give me an answer!

GAEV (*yawns*). What did you say?

LYUBOV (*looking into her purse*). Yesterday I had lots of money, but today there's practically none left. My poor Varya feeds us all milk soups to economize; the old servants in the kitchen have nothing but dried peas, and here I am wasting money senselessly, I just don't understand it. . . . (*She drops her purse, scattering gold coins.*) Now I've dropped it again. . . . (*Annoyed.*)

YASHA. Allow me, madam, I'll pick them right up. (*Picks up the money.*)

LYUBOV. Thank you, Yasha . . . And why did we go out for lunch today? And that restaurant of yours . . . the food was vile, the music ghastly, and the tablecloths smelled of soap. And Leonia, why do you drink so much? And eat so much? And talk so much? Today at the restaurant you were at it again, and it was all so pointless. About the seventies, and the decadents. And to whom? Really, talking to the waiters about the decadents!

LOPAHIN. Yes, that's too much.

GAEV (*waving his hand*). I know I'm hopeless. (*To* YASHA, *irritably.*) Why are you always bustling about in front of me?

YASHA (*laughs*). The minute you open your mouth I start laughing.

GAEV (*to his sister*). Either he goes, or I do. . . .

LYUBOV. Get along, Yasha, you'd better leave us now.

YASHA (*hands the purse to* LYUBOV). I'm going. (*He can hardly restrain his laughter.*) Right this minute. . . . (*Goes out.*)

LOPAHIN. You know, that rich merchant Deriganov is thinking of buying your estate. They say he's coming to the auction himself.

LYUBOV. Where did you hear that?

LOPAHIN. That's what they say in town.

GAEV. Our Aunt in Yaroslavl has promised to send us some money, but when and how much we don't know.

LOPAHIN. How much will she send? A hundred thousand? Two hundred?

LYUBOV. Well, hardly . . . Ten or fifteen thousand, perhaps. And we should be thankful for that.

LOPAHIN. Forgive me for saying it, but really, in my whole life I've never met such unrealistic, unbusinesslike, queer people as you. You're told in plain language that your estate's going to be sold, and you don't seem to understand it at all.

LYUBOV. But what are we to do? Please, tell us.

LOPAHIN. I keep on telling you. Every day I tell you the same thing. You must lease the cherry orchard and the rest of the land for summer cottages, and you must do it now, as quickly as possible. It's almost time for the auction. Please, try to understand! Once you definitely decide to lease it for the cottages, you'll be able to borrow as much money as you like, and you'll be saved.

LYUBOV. Summer cottages and vacationers! Forgive me, but it's so vulgar.

GAEV. I agree with you entirely.

LOPAHIN. Honestly, I'm going to burst into tears, or scream, or faint. I can't stand it any more! It's more than I can take! (*To* GAEV.) And you're an old woman!

GAEV. What did you say?

LOPAHIN. I said, you're an old woman!

LYUBOV (*alarmed*). No, don't go, please stay. I beg you! Perhaps we can think of something.

LOPAHIN. What's there to think of?

LYUBOV. Please don't go! I feel so much more cheerful when you're here. (*Pause.*) I keep expecting something horrible to happen ... as though the house were going to collapse on top of us.

GAEV (*in deep thought*). I bank it off the cushions, and then into the middle pocket. . . .

LYUBOV. We've sinned too much. . . .

LOPAHIN. Sinned! What sins have you . . .

GAEV (*putting a gumdrop into his mouth*). They say I've eaten up my fortune in gumdrops. (*Laughs.*)

LYUBOV. Oh, my sins! Look at the way I've always wasted money. It's madness. And then I married a man who had nothing but debts. And he was a terrible drinker . . . Champagne killed him! And then, as if I hadn't enough misery, I fell in love with someone else. We went off together, and just at that time—it was my first punishment, a blow that broke my heart—my little boy was drowned right here in this river . . . so I went abroad. I went away for good, never to return, never to see this river again . . . I just shut my eyes and ran away in a frenzy of grief, but *he* . . . he followed me. It was so cruel and brutal of him! I bought a villa near Mentone because he fell ill there, and for three years, day and night, I never had any rest. He was very sick, and he completely exhausted me; my soul dried up completely. Then, last year when the villa had to be sold to pay the debts, I went to Paris, and there he robbed me of everything I had and left me for another woman. . . . I tried to poison myself. . . . It was all so stupid, so shameful! And then suddenly I felt an urge to come back to Russia, to my own country, to my little girl . . . (*Dries her tears.*) Oh, Lord, Lord, be merciful, forgive my sins! Don't punish me any more! (*Takes a telegram out of her pocket.*) This came from Paris today. He's asking my forgiveness, he's begging me to return. (*Tears up the telegram.*) Sounds like music somewhere. (*Listens.*)

GAEV. That's our famous Jewish orchestra. Don't you remember, four violins, a flute, and a bass?

LYUBOV. Are they still playing? Sometime we should have a dance and they could play for us.

LOPAHIN (*listens*). I can't hear anything . . . (*Sings quietly.*) "And the Germans, if you pay, will turn Russians into Frenchmen, so they say" . . . (*Laughs.*) I saw a wonderful play last night. It was so funny.

LYUBOV. It probably wasn't funny at all. Instead of going to plays, you should take a good look at yourself. Just think how dull your life is, and how much nonsense you talk!

LOPAHIN. That's true, I admit it! Our lives are stupid . . . (*Pause.*) My father was a peasant, an idiot. He knew nothing and he taught me nothing. He only beat me when he was drunk, and always with a stick. And as a matter of fact, I'm just as much an idiot myself. I don't know anything and my handwriting's awful. I'm ashamed for people to see it—it's like a pig's.

LYUBOV. You ought to get married, my friend.

LOPAHIN. Yes . . . That's true.

LYUBOV. You ought to marry our Varya. She's a fine girl.

LOPAHIN. Yes.

LYUBOV. She comes from simple people, and she works hard all day long without stopping. But the main thing is she loves you, and you've liked her for a long time yourself.

LOPAHIN. Well. . . . I think it's a fine idea . . . She's a nice girl. (*Pause.*)

GAEV. I've been offered a job at the bank. Six thousand a year. Did I tell you?

LYUBOV. Yes, you did. You'd better stay where you are.

FEERS enters, bringing an overcoat.

FEERS (*to* GAEV). Please put it on, sir, you might catch cold.

GAEV (*puts on the overcoat*). Oh, you *are* a nuisance.

FEERS. You must stop this! You went off this morning without letting me know. (*Looks him over.*)

LYUBOV. How you've aged, Feers!

FEERS. What can I do for you, Madam?

LOPAHIN. She says you've aged a lot.

FEERS. I've lived for a long time. They were planning to marry me before your father was born. (*Laughs.*) Why, I was already head butler at the time of the emancipation, but I wouldn't take my freedom, I stayed on with the master and mistress. . . . (*Pause.*) I remember everyone was happy at the time, but what they were happy about, they didn't know themselves.

LOPAHIN. That was the good life all right! All the peasants were flogged!

FEERS (*not having heard him*). That's right! The peasants belonged to their masters, and the masters belonged to the peasants; but now everything's all confused and people don't know what to make of it.

GAEV. Be quiet, Feers. Tomorrow I've got to go to town. I've been promised an introduction to some general or other who might lend us some money for the mortgage.

LOPAHIN. Nothing will come of it. And how would you pay the interest, anyway?

LYUBOV. He's talking nonsense again. There aren't any generals.

Enter TROFIMOV, ANYA *and* VARYA.

GAEV. Here come the children.

ANYA. There's Mamma.

LYUBOV. Come here, my dears. Oh, my darling children. . . . (*Embraces* ANYA *and* VARYA.) If you only knew how much I love you! Here now, sit down beside me. (*All sit down.*)

LOPAHIN. Our perennial student is always with the girls.

TROFIMOV. It's none of your business.

LOPAHIN. He'll soon be fifty, and he's still a student.

TROFIMOV. Oh, stop your stupid jokes.

LOPAHIN. What's bothering you? My, you *are* a strange fellow!

TROFIMOV. Why do you keep pestering me?

LOPAHIN (*laughs*). Just let me ask you one question: what's your opinion of me?

TROFIMOV. My opinion of you, Yermolay Alexeyevich, is this: you're a rich man, and soon you'll be a millionaire. For the same reason that wild beasts are necessary to maintain nature's economic laws, you are necessary, too—each of you devours everything that gets in his way. (*Everybody laughs.*)

VARYA. You'd better talk about the planets, Petya.

LYUBOV. No, let's go on with the conversation we had yesterday.

TROFIMOV. What was that?

GAEV. About pride.

TROFIMOV. We talked for a long time yesterday, but we didn't agree on anything. The proud man, the way you use the word, has some mysterious quality about him. Perhaps you're right in a way, but if we look at it simply, without trying to be too subtle, you have to ask yourself why should we be proud at all? Why be proud when you realize that Man, as a species, is poorly constructed physiologically, and is usually coarse, stupid, and profoundly unhappy, too? We ought to put an end to such vanity and just go to work. That's right, we ought to work.

GAEV. You'll die just the same, no matter what you do.

TROFIMOV. Who knows? And anyway, what does it mean—to die? It could be that man has a hundred senses, and when he dies only the five that are known perish, while the other ninety-five go on living.

LYUBOV. How clever you are, Petya!

LOPAHIN (*ironically*). Oh, very clever!

TROFIMOV. Humanity is continually advancing, is continually seeking to perfect its powers. Someday all the things which we can't understand now, will be made clear. But if this is to happen, we've got to work, work with all our might to help those who are searching for truth. Up until now, here in Russia only a few have begun to work. Nearly all of the intelligentsia that I know have no commitment, they don't do anything, and are as yet incapable of work. They call themselves "the intelligentsia," but they still run roughshod over their servants, and they treat the peasants like animals, they study without achieving anything, they read only childish drivel, and they don't do a thing. As for their knowledge of science, it's only jargon, and they have no appreciation of art either. They are all so serious, and they go about with solemn looks on their faces; they philosophize and talk about important matters; and yet before our very eyes our workers are poorly fed, they live in the worst kind of squalor, sleeping not on beds, but on the floor thirty to forty in a room—with roaches, odors, dampness, and depravity everywhere. It's perfectly clear that all our moralizing is intended to deceive not only ourselves, but others as well. Tell me, where are the nursery schools we're always talking about, where are the libraries? We only write about them in novels, but in actuality there aren't any. There's nothing but dirt, vulgarity, and decadent Orientalism. . . . I'm afraid of those serious faces, I don't like them; I'm afraid of serious talk. It would be better if we'd just keep quiet.

LOPAHIN. Well, let me tell you that *I'm* up before five every morning, and I work from morning till night. I always have money, my own and other people's, and I have lots of opportunities to see what the people around me are like. You only have to start doing something to realize how few honest, decent people there are. Sometimes, when I can't sleep, I start thinking about it. God's given us immense forests, and wide-open fields, and unlimited horizons—living in such a world we ought to be giants!

LYUBOV. But why do you want giants? They're all right in fairy tales, anywhere else they're terrifying.

EPIHODOV crosses the stage in the background, playing his guitar.

LYUBOV (*pensively*). There goes Epihodov. . . .

ANYA (*pensively*). There goes Epihodov. . . .

GAEV. The sun's gone down, my friends.

TROFIMOV. Yes.

GAEV (*in a subdued voice, as if reciting a poem*). Oh, glorious Nature, shining with eternal light, so beautiful, yet so indifferent to our fate . . . you, whom we call Mother, the wellspring of Life and Death, you live and you destroy. . . .

VARYA (*imploringly*). Uncle, please!

ANYA. You're doing it again, Uncle!

TROFIMOV. You'd better bank the red into middle pocket.

GAEV. All right, I'll keep quiet.

They all sit deep in thought; the only thing that can be heard is the muttering of FEERS. *Suddenly there is a sound in the distance, as if out of the sky, like the sound of a harp string breaking, gradually and sadly dying away.*

LYUBOV. What was that?

LOPAHIN. I don't know. Sounded like a cable broke in one of the mines. But it must've been a long way off.

GAEV. Perhaps it was a bird . . . a heron, maybe.

TROFIMOV. Or an owl. . . .

LYUBOV (*shudders*). Whatever it was, it sounded unpleasant . . . (*A pause.*)

FEERS. It was the same way before the disaster: the owl hooted and the samovar was humming.

GAEV. What disaster?

FEERS. Before they freed us. (*A pause.*)

LYUBOV. We'd better get started, my friends. It's getting dark and we should get home. (*To* ANYA.) You're crying, my darling! What's wrong? (*She embraces her.*)

ANYA. Nothing, Mamma. It's nothing.

TROFIMOV. Someone's coming.

Enter A TRAMP *in a battered white hunting cap and an overcoat; he's slightly drunk.*

TRAMP. Excuse me, but can I get to the station through here?

GAEV. Yes, just follow the road.

TRAMP. Much obliged to you, sir. (*Coughs.*) It's a beautiful day today. (*Declaiming.*) "Oh, my brother, my suffering brother!. . . Come to the Volga, whose groans . . ." (*To* VARYA.) Mademoiselle, could a poor starving Russian trouble you for just enough to . . . (VARYA *cries out, frightened.*)

LOPAHIN (*angrily*). Really, this is too much!

LYUBOV (*at a loss what to do*). Here, take this . . . here you are. (*Looks in her purse.*) I haven't any silver . . . but that's all right, here's a gold one. . . .

TRAMP. Thank you very much! (*Goes off. Laughter.*)

VARYA (*frightened*). I'm going. . . . I'm going . . . Oh, Mamma, you know there's not even enough to eat in the house, and you gave him all that!

LYUBOV. Well, what can you do with a silly woman like me? I'll give you everything I've got as soon as we get home. Yermolay Alexeyevich, you'll lend me some more, won't you?

LOPAHIN. Why of course I will.

LYUBOV. Come, it's time to go now. By the way, Varya, we've just about arranged your marriage. Congratulations!

VARYA (*through her tears*). Don't joke about things like that, Mother!

LOPAHIN. Go to a nunnery, Okhmelia! . . .

GAEV. Look at how my hands are trembling: I haven't had a game for so long.

LOPAHIN. Okhmelia, nymph, remember me in your prayers!

LYUBOV. Come along, everybody. It's almost supper time.

VARYA. That man frightened me so. My heart's still pounding.

LOPAHIN. My friends, just one thing, please just a word: the cherry orchard's to be sold on the 22nd of August. Remember that! Think of what. . . .

All go out except TROFIMOV *and* ANYA.

ANYA (*laughs*). We can thank the tramp for a chance to be alone! He frightened Varya so.

TROFIMOV. Varya's afraid—she's afraid we might fall in love—so she follows us about all day long. She's so narrow-minded, she can't understand that we're above falling in love. To free ourselves of all that's petty and ephemeral, all that prevents us from being free and happy, that's the whole aim and meaning of our life. Forward! We march forward irresistibly towards that bright star shining there in the distance! Forward! Don't fall behind, friends!

ANYA (*raising her hands*). How beautifully you talk! (*A pause.*) It's wonderful here today.

TROFIMOV. Yes, the weather's marvelous.

ANYA. What have you done to me, Petya? Why don't I love the cherry orchard like I used to? I used to love it so very much, I used to think that there wasn't a better place in all the world than our orchard.

TROFIMOV. The whole of Russia is our orchard. The earth is great and beautiful and there are many wonderful places in it. (*A pause.*) Just think, Anya: Your grandfather, and your great grandfather, and all your ancestors were serf owners—they owned living souls. Don't you see human beings staring at you from every tree in the orchard, from every leaf and every trunk? Don't you hear their voices? ... They owned living souls—and it has made you all different persons, those who came before you, and you who are living now, so that your mother, your uncle and you yourself don't even notice that you're living on credit, at the expense of other people, people you don't admit any further than your kitchen. We're at least two hundred years behind the times; we have no real values, no sense of our past, we just philosophize and complain of how depressed we feel, and drink vodka. Yet it's obvious that if we're ever to live in the present, we must first atone for our past and make a clean break with it, and we can only atone for it by suffering, by extraordinary, unceasing work. You've got to understand that, Anya.

ANYA. The house we live in hasn't really been ours for a long time. I'll leave it, I promise you.

TROFIMOV. Yes, leave it, and throw away the keys. Be free as the wind.

ANYA (*in rapture*). How beautifully you say things.

TROFIMOV. You must believe me, Anya, you must. I'm not thirty yet, I'm young, and I'm still a student, but I've suffered so much already. As soon as winter comes, I'll be hungry and sick and nervous, poor as a beggar. Fate has driven me everywhere! And yet, my soul is always—every moment of every day and every night—it's always full of such marvelous hopes and visions. I have a premonition of happiness, Anya, I can sense its coming. . . .

ANYA (*pensively*). The moon's coming up.

EPIHODOV is heard playing the same melancholy tune on his guitar. The moon comes

up. Somewhere near the poplars VARYA *is looking for* ANYA *and calling.*

VARYA (*off-stage*). Anya! Where are you?

TROFIMOV. Yes, the moon is rising. (*A pause.*) There it is—happiness—it's coming nearer and nearer. Already, I can hear its footsteps. And if we never see it, if we never know it, what does it matter? Others will see it!

VARYA'S VOICE. Anya! Where are you?

TROFIMOV. It's Varya again! (*Angrily.*) It's disgusting!

ANYA. Well? Let's go to the river. It's lovely there.

TROFIMOV. Yes, let's. (TROFIMOV *and* ANYA *go out.*)

VARYA'S VOICE. Anya! Anya!

Curtain.

ACT III

The drawing room separated by an arch from the ballroom. The same Jewish orchestra that was mentioned in Act II, is playing off-stage. The chandelier is lighted. It is evening. In the ballroom they are dancing the Grand-rond. SEMYONOV-PISHCHIK *is heard calling: "Promenade à une paire!" Then they all enter the drawing room.* PISHCHIK *and* CHARLOTTA IVANOVNA *are the first couple, followed by* TROFIMOV *and* LYUBOV, ANYA *and a* POST-OFFICE CLERK, VARYA *and* THE STATION MASTER, *etc.* VARYA *is crying softly and wipes away her tears as she dances.* DUNYASHA *is in the last couple.* PISHCHIK *shouts: "Grand-rond balancez!" and "Les cavaliers à genoux et remerciez vos dames!"* FEERS, *wearing a dress coat, crosses the room with soda water on a tray.* PISHCHIK *and* TROFIMOV *come back into the drawing room.*

PISHCHIK. I've got this high blood-pressure— I've had two strokes already, you know—

and it makes dancing hard work for me; but, as they say, if you're one of a pack, you wag your tail, whether you bark or not. Actually I'm as strong as a horse. My dear father—may he rest in peace—had a little joke. He used to say that the ancient line of Semyonov-Pishchik was descended from the very same horse that Caligula made a member of the Senate. (*Sitting down.*) But my trouble is, I haven't any money. A starving dog can think of nothing but food... (*Starts to snore, but wakes up almost at once.*) That's just like me—I can't think of anything but money...

TROFIMOV. You know, you're right, there *is* something horsy about you.

PISHCHIK. Well, a horse is a fine animal, you can sell a horse....

The sound of someone playing billiards is heard in the next room. VARYA *appears under the arch to the ballroom.*

TROFIMOV (*teasing her*). Madam Lopahin! Madame Lopahin!

VARYA (*angrily*). The "moth-eaten man"!

TROFIMOV. Yes, I am a moth-eaten man, and I'm proud of it.

VARYA (*thinking bitterly*). Now we've hired an orchestra—but how are we going to pay for it? (*Goes out.*)

TROFIMOV (*to PISHCHIK*). If all the energy you've spent during your life looking for money to pay the interest on your debts had been used for something useful, you'd have probably turned the world upside down by now.

PISHCHIK. The philosopher Nietzsche, the greatest, the most famous—a man of the greatest intelligence, in fact—says it's quite all right to counterfeit.

TROFIMOV. Oh, you've read Nietzsche?

PISHCHIK. Of course not, Dashenka told me. But right now I'm in such an impossible position that I could forge a few notes. The day after tomorrow I've got to pay 310 roubles. I've borrowed 130 already.... (*Feels in his pockets, in alarm.*) The money's

gone! I've lost the money. (*Tearfully.*) Where's the money? (*Joyfully.*) Oh, here it is, inside the lining! I'm so upset, I'm sweating all over!...

Enter LYUBOV *and* CHARLOTTA.

LYUBOV (*humming the "Lezginka"*). What's taking Leonid so long? What's he doing in town? (*To DUNYASHA.*) Dunyasha, offer the musicians some tea.

TROFIMOV. The auction was probably postponed.

LYUBOV. The orchestra came at the wrong time, and the party started at the wrong time...Oh, well...never mind... (*She sits down and hums quietly.*)

CHARLOTTA (*hands a deck of cards to PISHCHIK*). Here's a deck of cards—think of any card.

PISHCHIK. I've thought of one.

CHARLOTTA. Now shuffle the deck. That's right. Now give it to me, my dear Monsieur Pishchik. "*Ein, zwei, drei!*" Why look! There it is, in your coat pocket.

PISHCHIK (*takes the card out of his coat pocket*). The eight of spades, that's right! (*In astonishment.*) Isn't that amazing!

CHARLOTTA (*holding the deck of cards on the palm of her hand, to TROFIMOV*). Quickly, which card's on the top?

TROFIMOV. Well...ahh...the queen of spades.

CHARLOTTA. You're right, here it is! Now, which card?

PISHCHIK. The ace of hearts.

CHARLOTTA. Right again! (*She claps her hand over the pack of cards, which disappears.*) What beautiful weather we're having today! (*A woman's voice, as if coming from underneath the floor, answers her.*)

VOICE. Oh yes, indeed, the weather's perfectly marvelous!

CHARLOTTA (*addressing the voice*). How charming you are! I'm fond of you!

VOICE. And I like you very much, too.

STATION MASTER (*applauding*). Bravo, Madame ventriloquist! Bravo!

PISHCHIK (*astonished*). Isn't that amazing!

Charlotta Ivanovna, you're absolutely wonderful! I'm completely in love with you!

CHARLOTTA (*shrugging her shoulders*). In love? What do you know about love? *"Guter Mensch, aber schlechter Musikant."*

TROFIMOV (*slaps* PISHCHIK *on the shoulder*). He's just an old horse, he is!

CHARLOTTA. Your attention please! Here's one more trick. (*She takes a shawl from a chair.*) Now there's this very nice shawl . . . (*Shakes it out.*) Who'd like to buy it?

PISHCHIK (*amazed*). Imagine that!

CHARLOTTA. *"Ein, zwei, drei!"*

She lifts up the shawl and ANYA *is standing behind it;* ANYA *curtsies, runs to her mother, gives her a hug, and runs back to the ballroom. Everybody's delighted.*

LYUBOV (*clapping*). Bravo, bravo!

CHARLOTTA. Once more. *"Ein, zwei, drei!"*

Lifts the shawl again; behind it is VARYA. *who bows.*

PISHCHIK (*amazed*). Isn't that amazing!

CHARLOTTA. It's all over! (*She throws the shawl over* PISHCHIK, *curtsies, and runs into the ballroom.*)

PISHCHIK (*going after her*). You little rascal! . . . Have you ever seen anything like her? What a girl . . . (*Goes out.*)

LYUBOV. Leonid's still not here. I can't understand what's keeping him all this time in town. Anyway, by now everything's been settled; either the estate's been sold or the auction didn't take place. Why does he wait so long to let us know?

VARYA (*trying to comfort her*). Uncle's bought it, I'm sure he did.

TROFIMOV (*sarcastically*). Why of course he did!

VARYA. Our great-aunt sent him power of attorney to buy it in her name, and transfer the mortgage to her. She's done it for Anya's sake . . . God will look after us, I'm sure of it—Uncle will buy the estate.

LYUBOV. Your great-aunt sent us fifteen thousand to buy the estate in her name—she doesn't trust us—but that's not enough to even pay the interest. (*She covers her face with her hands.*) My fate is being decided today, my fate. . . .

TROFIMOV (*to* VARYA, *teasingly*). Madame Lopahin!

VARYA (*crossly*). The perpetual student! Why, you've been thrown out of the University twice already!

LYUBOV. But why get so cross, Varya? He's only teasing you about Lopahin, there's no harm in that, is there? If you want to, why don't you marry him; he's a fine man, and he's interesting, too. Of course, if you don't want to, don't. No one's trying to force you, darling.

VARYA. I'm very serious about this, Mother . . . and I want to be frank with you . . . he's a good man and I like him.

LYUBOV. Then marry him. What are you waiting for? I don't understand you at all.

VARYA. But, Mother, I can't propose to him myself, can I? It's been two years now since everybody began talking to me about him, and everybody's talking, but he doesn't say a word, or when he does, he just jokes with me. I understand, of course. He's getting rich and his mind's busy with other things, and he hasn't any time for me. If only I had some money, even a little, just a hundred roubles, I'd leave everything and go away, the farther the better. I'd go into a convent.

TROFIMOV. How beautiful!

VARYA (*to* TROFIMOV). Of course, a student like you has to be so intelligent! (*Quietly and tearfully.*) How ugly you've become, Petya, how much older you look! (*To* LYUBOV, *her tearfulness gone.*) The only thing I can't stand, Mother, is not having any work to do. I've got to stay busy.

Enter YASHA.

YASHA (*with difficulty restraining his laughter*). Epihodov's broken a cue! . . . (*Goes out.*)

VARYA. But what's Epihodov doing here? Who let him play billiards? I don't understand these people. . . . (*Goes out.*)

LYUBOV. Please don't tease her, Petya. Don't you see she's upset already?

TROFIMOV. Oh, she's such a busy-body—always sticking her nose into other people's business. She hasn't left Anya and me alone all summer. She's afraid we might fall in love. What difference should it make to her? Besides, I didn't give her any reason to think so. I don't believe in such trivialities. We're above love!

LYUBOV. And I suppose I'm below love. (*Uneasily.*) Why isn't Leonid back? If only I knew whether the estate's been sold or not. It's such an incredible calamity that for some reason I don't know what to think, I feel so helpless. I think I'm going to scream this very minute . . . I'll do something silly. Help me, Petya. Talk to me, say something!

TROFIMOV. What difference does it make whether the estate's sold today or not? It was gone a long time ago. You can't turn back, the path's lost. You mustn't worry, and above all you mustn't deceive yourself. For once in your life you must look the truth straight in the face.

LYUBOV. What truth? *You* know what truth is and what it isn't, but I've lost such visionary powers. I don't see anything. You're able to solve all your problems so decisively—but, tell me, my dear boy, isn't that because you're young, because life is still hidden from your young eyes, because you can't believe anything horrible will ever happen to you and you don't expect it to? Oh, yes, you're more courageous and honest and serious than we are, but put yourself in our position, try to be generous—if only a little bit—and have pity on me. I was born here, you know, and my father and mother lived here, and my grandfather, too, and I love this house—I can't conceive of life without the cherry orchard, and if it really has to be sold, then sell me with it . . . (*Embraces* TROFIMOV, *kisses him on the forehead.*) You know, my little boy was drowned here. . . . (*Weeps.*) Have pity on me, my dear, kind friend.

TROFIMOV. You know that I sympathize with you from the bottom of my heart.

LYUBOV. But you should say it differently . . . differently. (*Takes out her handkerchief and a telegram falls on to the floor.*) There's so much on my mind today, you can't imagine. It's so noisy around here that my soul trembles with every sound, and I'm shaking all over—yet I can't go to my room because the silence of being alone frightens me. . . . Don't blame me, Petya. . . . I love you as if you were my own son. I'd gladly let Anya marry you, honestly I would, but, my dear boy, you must study, you've got to graduate. You don't do anything, Fate tosses you from one place to another—it's so strange—Well, it is, isn't it? Isn't it? And you should do something about your beard, make it grow somehow. . . . (*Laughs.*) You look so funny!

TROFIMOV (*picks up the telegram*). I don't care how I look. That's so superficial.

LYUBOV. This telegram's from Paris. I get one every day . . . Yesterday, today. That beast is sick again, and everything's going wrong for him. . . . He wants me to forgive him, he begs me to return, and really, I suppose I should go to Paris and stay with him for a while. You're looking very stern, Petya, but what am I to do, my dear boy, what am I to do? He's sick, and lonely, and unhappy, and who'll take care of him, who'll stop him from making a fool of himself, and give him his medicine at the right time? And anyway, why should I hide it, or keep quiet about it? I love him; yes, I love him. I do, I do. . . . He's a stone around my neck, and I'm sinking to the bottom with him—but I love him and I can't live without him. (*She presses* TROFIMOV's *hand.*) Don't think I'm evil, Petya, don't say anything, please don't. . . .

TROFIMOV (*with strong emotion*). Please—forgive my frankness, but that man's swindling you!

LYUBOV. No, no, no, you mustn't talk like that. . . . (*Puts her hands over her ears.*)

TROFIMOV. But he's a scoundrel, and you're the only one who doesn't know it! He's a despicable, worthless scoundrel. . . .

LYUBOV (*angry, but in control of herself*). You're twenty-six or twenty-seven years old, but you're talking like a schoolboy!

TROFIMOV. Say whatever you want!

LYUBOV. You should be a man at your age, you ought to understand what it means to be in love. And you should be in love. . . . Tell me, why haven't you fallen in love! (*Angrily.*) Yes, yes! Oh, you're not so "pure," your purity is a perversion, you're nothing but a ridiculous prude, a freak. . . .

TROFIMOV (*horrified*). What is she saying?

LYUBOV. "I'm above love!" You're not above love, you're useless, as Feers would say. Imagine not having a mistress at your age! . . .

TROFIMOV (*horrified*). This is terrible! What's she saying? (*Goes quickly toward the ballroom, clutching his head between his hands.*) This is dreadful. . . . I can't stand it, I'm going. . . . (*Goes out, but returns at once.*) Everything's over between us! (*Goes out through the door into the hall.*)

LYUBOV (*calls after him*). Petya, wait! You funny boy, I was only joking! Petya!

Someone can be heard running quickly downstairs and suddenly falling down with a crash. ANYA *and* VARYA *scream, and then begin laughing.*

What's happened?

ANYA *runs in.*

ANYA (*laughing*). Petya fell down the stairs. (*Runs out.*)

LYUBOV. What a strange boy he is!

The STATION MASTER *stands in the middle of the ballroom and begins to recite "The Sinner" by Alexey Tolstoy. The others listen to him, but he's hardly had time to recite more than a little bit when a waltz is played, and he stops. Everyone dances.* TROFIMOV, ANYA, VARYA *come in from the hall.*

Poor Petya . . . there, my dear boy . . . Please forgive me . . . Come, let's dance . . .

She dances with PETYA. ANYA *and* VARYA *dance. Enter* FEERS, *then* YASHA. FEERS *leans on his cane by the side door.* YASHA *looks at the dancers from the drawing room.*

YASHA. How are you, old boy?

FEERS. Not too well . . . We used to have generals, barons, and admirals at our parties . . . long ago, but now we send for the post-office clerk and the station master, and even they don't want to come it seems. I seem to be getting weaker somehow . . . My old master, the mistress' grandfather, used to make everyone take sealing wax no matter what was wrong with them. I've been taking it every day for the last twenty years, maybe even longer. Perhaps that's why I'm still alive.

YASHA. How you bore me, old man! (*Yawns.*) Why don't you just go away and die . . . It's about time.

FEERS. Eh, you! . . . You're useless . . . (*Mutters.*)

TROFIMOV *and* LYUBOV *dancing, come into the drawing room.*

LYUBOV. Thank you. I think I'll sit down for a bit. (*Sits down.*) I'm tired.

Enter ANYA.

ANYA (*agitated*). There's a man in the kitchen who's been saying that the cherry orchard was sold today.

LYUBOV. Sold? To whom?

ANYA. He didn't say. He's gone.

She and TROFIMOV *dance into the ballroom.*

YASHA. There was some old man gossiping there. A stranger.

FEERS. Leonid Andreyevich isn't back yet, he hasn't come yet. And he's only got his light overcoat on; he'll probably catch a cold. Oh, these youngsters!

LYUBOV. I've got to know, or I think I'll die. Yasha, go and find out who bought it.

YASHA. But the old guy went away a long time ago. (*Laughs.*)

LYUBOV (*with a touch of annoyance*). What are you laughing at? What's so humorous?

YASHA. Epihodov's so funny—he's so stupid. Two-and-twenty misfortunes!

LYUBOV. Feers, if the estate's sold, where will you go?

FEERS. I'll go wherever you tell me to go.

LYUBOV. Why are you looking like that? Aren't you well? You ought to be in bed.

FEERS. Yes . . . (*With a faint smile.*) But if I went to bed, who'd take care of the guests and keep things going? There's no one in the house but me.

YASHA (*to* LYUBOV). Lyubov Andreyevna! I want to ask you something! If you go back to Paris, will you please take me with you? I couldn't stand staying here. (*Looking round and speaking in a low voice.*) I don't have to say it, you can see for youself how uncivilized everything is here. The people are immoral, it's frightfully dull, and the food is terrible. And then there's that Feers walking about the place and muttering all sorts of stupid things. Take me with you please!

Enter PISHCHIK.

PISHCHIK. May I have this dance, beautiful lady . . . (LYUBOV *gets up to dance.*) I'll have that 180 roubles from you yet, you enchantress . . . Yes, I will . . . (*Dances.*) Just 180 roubles, that's all . . . (*They go into the ballroom.*)

YASHA (*sings quietly*). "Don't you understand the passion in my soul? . . ."

In the ballroom a woman in a grey top hat and check trousers starts jumping and throwing her arms about; shouts of: "Bravo, Charlotta Ivanovna!"

DUNYASHA (*stops to powder her face*). Anya told me to dance: there are so many men and not enough ladies; but I get so dizzy from dancing and it makes my heart beat so fast. Feers Nikolayevich, the post-office clerk said something to me just now that completely took my breath away. (*The music stops.*)

FEERS. What did he say?

DUNYASHA. You're like a flower, he said.

YASHA (*yawns*). What ignorance! . . . (*Goes out.*)

DUNYASHA. Like a flower . . . I'm so sensitive, I love it when people say beautiful things to me.

FEERS. You'll be having your head turned if you're not careful.

Enter EPIHODOV.

EPIHODOV. Avdotya Fyodorovna, you act as if you don't want to see me . . . as if I were some kind of insect. (*Sighs.*) Such is life!

DUNYASHA. What do you want?

EPIHODOV. But then, you may be right. (*Sighs.*) Of course, if one looks at it from a certain point of view—if I may so express myself, and please excuse my frankness, you've driven me into such a state . . . Oh, I know what my fate is; every day some misfortune's sure to happen to me, but I've long since been accustomed to that, so I look at life with a smile. You gave me your word, and though I . . .

DUNYASHA. Please, let's talk later, just let me alone now. I'm lost in a dream. (*Plays with her fan.*)

EPIHODOV. Some misfortune happens to me every day, but I—how should I put it— I just smile, I even laugh.

VARYA *enters from the ballroom.*

VARYA. Are you still here, Semyon? Your manners are abominable, really! (*To* DUNYASHA.) You'd better go now, Dunyasha. (*To* EPIHODOV.) First you play billiards and break a cue, and now you're going about the drawing room, like one of the guests.

EPIHODOV. Permit me to inform you, but you have no right to attack me like this.

VARYA. I'm not attacking, I'm telling you. You just wander from one place to another, instead of doing your work. We've hired a clerk, but why no one knows.

EPIHODOV (*offended*). Whether I work, wander, eat, or play billiards, the only people who are entitled to judge my actions are those who are older than me and have some idea of what they're talking about.

VARYA. How dare you say that to me? (*Beside herself in anger.*) You dare to say that? Are you suggesting that I don't know what I'm talking about? Get out of here! Right now!

EPIHODOV (*cowed*). I wish you'd express yourself more delicately.

VARYA (*beside herself*). Get out this minute! Get out! (*He goes to the door, she follows him.*) Two-and-twenty misfortunes! Get out of here! I don't want ever to see you again!

EPIHODOV (*goes out; his voice is heard from outside the door*). I'm going to complain.

VARYA. Oh, you're coming back, are you? (*She seizes the stick which* FEERS *left by the door.*) Well, come along, come in . . . I'll show you! So, you're coming back . . . are you? There, take that . . . (*Swings the stick, and at that moment* LOPAHIN *comes in.*)

LOPAHIN (*whom the stick did not, in fact, touch*). Thank you very much!

VARYA (*angry and ironically*). I'm sorry!

LOPAHIN. Don't mention it. I'm much obliged to you for the kind reception.

VARYA. That's quite all right. (*Walks away and then looks around and asks gently.*) I haven't hurt you, have I?

LOPAHIN. No, not at all. . . . But there's going to be a huge bump, though.

VOICES (*in the ballroom*). Lopahin's here! Yermolay Alexeyevich!

PISHCHIK. There he is! You can see him, do you hear him? . . . (*Embraces* LOPAHIN.) You smell of cognac, my good fellow! . . . Well we're having a party here, too.

Enter LYUBOV.

LYUBOV. It's you, Yermolay Alexeyevich? What's taken you so long? Where's Leonid?

LOPAHIN. Leonid Andreyevich's here, he'll be along in a minute.

LYUBOV (*agitated*). Well, what happened? Was there an auction? Tell me!

LOPAHIN (*embarrassed, afraid of betraying his joy*). The auction was over by four o'clock . . . We missed our train and had to wait until nine-thirty. (*Sighs heavily.*) Ugh! I feel a little dizzy . . .

Enter GAEV; *he carries packages in his right hand and wipes away his tears with his left.*

LYUBOV. Leonia, what happened? Leonia? (*Impatiently, with tears.*) Tell me quickly, for God's sake! . . .

GAEV (*doesn't answer, but waves his hand*). (*To* FEERS, *crying.*) Here, take these . . . it's some anchovies and Kerch herrings . . . I haven't eaten all day . . . What I've been through!

Through the open door leading to the ballroom a game of billiards can be heard and YASHA's *voice is heard.*

YASHA. Seven and eighteen.

GAEV (*his expression changes and he stops crying*). I'm very tired. Come, Feers, I want to change my things. (*Goes out through the ballroom, followed by* FEERS.)

PISHCHIK. Well, what happened at the auction? Come on, tell us!

LYUBOV. Has the cherry orchard been sold?

LOPAHIN. It has.

LYUBOV. Who bought it?

LOPAHIN. I did.

A pause. LYUBOV *is overcome; only the fact that she is standing beside a table and a chair keeps her from falling.* VARYA *takes the keys from her belt, throws them on the floor in the middle of the room and goes out.*

I bought it. Wait a moment, ladies and gentlemen, please. I'm so mixed up, I don't quite know what to say . . . (*Laughs.*) When we got to the auction, Deriganov was already there. Leonid had only fifteen thousand roubles, and immediately Deriganov bid thirty thousand over and above the mortgage. I saw how things were so I stepped in and raised it to forty. He bid forty-five, I went to fifty-five; he kept on raising five thousand and I raised it ten thousand. Well, finally it ended—I bid ninety thousand over and above the mortgage, and it went to me. The cherry orchard's mine now! All right, tell me I'm drunk, tell me I'm crazy and that I'm just imagining all this. . . . (*Stamps his feet.*) Don't laugh at me! If only my father and grandfather could rise from their graves and see all that's happened . . . how their Yermolay, their ignorant, beaten Yermolay, the little boy that ran around in his bare feet in the winter . . . if only they could see that he's bought this estate, the most beautiful place in the world! Yes, he's bought the very estate where his father and grandfather were slaves and where they weren't even admitted to the kitchen! I must be asleep, I'm dreaming, it only seems to be true . . . it's all just my imagination, my imagination must be confused . . . (*Picks up the keys, smiling gently.*) She threw these down because she wanted to show that she's not the mistress here anymore. (*Jingles the keys.*) Well, never mind. (*The orchestra is heard tuning up.*) Hey there! you musicians, play something for us! I want some music! My friends, come along and soon you'll see Yermolay Lopahin take an axe to the cherry orchard, you'll see the trees come crashing to the ground! We're going to build hundreds of summer cottages, and our children and our grandchildren will see a whole new world growing up here . . . So play, let's have some music!

The band plays. LYUBOV *has sunk into a chair and is crying bitterly. Reproachfully.*

Why, why didn't you listen to me? My poor, dear lady, you'll never get it back now. (*With tears.*) Oh, if only all this could be over soon, if only we could change this unhappy and disjointed life of ours somehow!

PISHCHIK (*taking his arm, in a low voice*). She's crying. Come into the ballroom, let her be by herself . . . Come on . . . (*Takes his arm and leads him away to the ballroom.*)

LOPAHIN. What's the matter! Where's the music? Come on, play! Play! Everything will be as *I* want it now. (*Ironically.*) Here comes the new owner, here comes the owner of the cherry orchard! (*He tips over a little table accidentally and nearly upsets the candelabra.*) Don't worry about it, I can pay for everything! (*Goes out with* PISHCHIK.)

> *There is no one left in the ballroom or drawing room, but* LYUBOV, *who sits huddled up in a chair, crying bitterly. The orchestra continues to play quietly.* ANYA *and* TROFIMOV *enter quickly;* ANYA *goes up to her mother and kneels beside her,* TROFIMOV *remains at the entrance to the ballroom.*

ANYA. Mamma! . . . Mamma, you're crying. Dear, kind, good Mamma, my precious one, I love you! God bless you, Mamma! The cherry orchard's sold, that's true, it's gone, but don't cry, Mamma, you still have your life ahead of you, you still have your good, innocent heart. You must come with me, Mamma, away from here! We'll plant a new orchard, even more wonderful than this one—and when you see it, you'll understand everything, and your heart will be filled with joy, like the sun in the evening; and then you'll smile again, Mamma! Come, dearest one, come with me! . . .

> *Curtain.*

ACT IV

The same setting as for Act I. There are no pictures on the walls or curtains at the windows; most of the furniture is gone and the few remaining pieces are stacked in a corner, as if for sale. There is a sense of desolation. Beside the door, suitcases and other luggage have been piled together. The voices of VARYA *and* ANYA *can be heard through the door on the left, which is open.* LOPAHIN *stands waiting;* YASHA *is holding a tray with glasses of champagne. In the hall* EPIHODOV *is tying up a large box. Off-stage there is a low hum of voices; the peasants have called to say good-bye.* GAEV's *voice from off-stage.*

GAEV. Thank you, friends, thank you.

YASHA. The peasants have come to say good-bye. In my opinion, Yermolay Alexeyevich, they're good people, but they don't know much.

The hum subsides. LYUBOV *and* GAEV *enter from the hall;* LYUBOV *is not crying but her face is pale and it quivers. She is unable to speak.*

GAEV. You gave them everything you had, Lyuba. You shouldn't have done that. You really shouldn't.

LYUBOV. I couldn't help it! I couldn't help it! (*Both go out.*)

LOPAHIN (*calls after them through the door*). Please, have some champagne, please do! Just a little glass before you go. I didn't think to bring some from town, and at the station I could find only this one bottle. Please have some. (*A pause.*) You don't want any, my friends? (*Walks away from the door.*) If I'd known that, I wouldn't have brought it. . . . Well, then I won't have any either. (YASHA *carefully puts the tray on a chair.*) Have a drink, Yasha, nobody else wants any.

YASHA. To the travelers! And to those staying behind. (*Drinks.*) This champagne isn't the real thing, believe me.

LOPAHIN. What do you mean, eight roubles a bottle. (*A pause.*) God, it's cold in here.

YASHA. The stoves weren't lit today. What difference does it make since we're leaving? (*Laughs.*)

LOPAHIN. Why are you laughing?

YASHA. Because I feel good.

LOPAHIN. It's October already, but it's still sunny and clear, just like summer. Good building weather. (*Looks at his watch, then at the door.*) Ladies and gentlemen, the train leaves in forty-seven minutes. We've got to start in twenty minutes. So hurry up.

TROFIMOV, *wearing an overcoat, comes in from outdoors.*

TROFIMOV. It's time we get started. The horses are ready. God knows where my goloshes are, they've disappeared. (*Calls through the door.*) Anya, my goloshes aren't here; I can't find them.

LOPAHIN. I've got to go to Kharkov. I'm taking the same train. I'll be spending the winter in Kharkov: I've stayed around here too long, and it drives me crazy having nothing to do. I can't be without work: I just don't know what to do with my hands; they hang there, as if they didn't belong to me.

TROFIMOV. We'll be gone soon, then you can start making money again.

LOPAHIN. Have a drink.

TROFIMOV. No, thanks.

LOPAHIN. So, you're going to Moscow?

TROFIMOV. Yes, I'll go with them to town, and then, tomorrow I'll leave for Moscow.

LOPAHIN. I suppose the professors are waiting for you to come before they begin classes.

TROFIMOV. That's none of your business.

LOPAHIN. How many years have you been studying at the university?

TROFIMOV. Can't you say something new for a change, that's getting pretty old. (*Looks for his galoshes.*) By the way, since we probably won't see each other again, let me give you a bit of advice, as we say good-bye: stop waving your arms! Try to get rid of that habit of making wide, sweeping gestures. And another thing, all this talk about building estates, these calculations about summer tourists that are going to buy property, all these predictions—they're all sweeping gestures, too. . . . You know, in spite of everything, I like you. You've got beautiful delicate fingers, like an artist's, you've a fine, sensitive soul. . . .

LOPAHIN (*embraces him*). Good-bye, my friend. Thanks for everything. I can give you some money for your trip, if you need it.

TROFIMOV. What for? I don't need it.

LOPAHIN. But you haven't got any!

TROFIMOV. Yes, I have, thank you. I got some money for a translation. Here it is, in my pocket. (*Anxiously.*) But I can't find my goloshes.

VARYA (*from the other room*). Here, take the nasty things! (*She throws a pair of rubber galoshes into the room.*)

TROFIMOV. What are you so angry about, Varya? Hm . . . but these aren't my goloshes!

LOPAHIN. I sowed three thousand acres of poppies last spring, and I've made forty thousand on it. And when they were in bloom, what a picture it was! What I mean to say is that I've made the forty thousand, so now I can lend you some money. Why be so stuck up? So I'm a peasant . . . I speak right out.

TROFIMOV. Your father was a peasant, mine was a druggist. What's that got to do with it? (LOPAHIN *takes out his wallet.*) Forget it, put it away . . . Even if you offered me two hundred thousand, I wouldn't take it. I'm a free man. And all that you rich men —and poor men too—all that you value so highly doesn't have the slightest power over me—it's all just so much fluff floating about in the air. I'm strong and I'm proud! I can get along without you, I can pass you by. Humanity is advancing towards the highest truth, the greatest happiness that it's possible to achieve on earth, and I'm one of the avant-garde!

LOPAHIN. Will you get there?

TROFIMOV. Yes. (*A pause.*) I'll get there myself, or show others the way to get there.

The sound of an axe hitting a tree is heard in the distance.

LOPAHIN. Well, my friend, it's time to go.

Good-bye. We show off in front of one another, and all the time life is slipping by. When I work all day long, without resting, I'm happier and sometimes I even think I know why I exist. But how many people there are in Russia, my friend, who exist for no reason· at all. But, never mind, it doesn't matter. They say Leonid Andreyevich has a job at the bank, at six thousand a year. That won't last long; he's too lazy. . . .

ANYA (*in the doorway*). Mamma begs you not to let them cut down the orchard until we've left.

TROFIMOV. Really, haven't you got any tact? (*Goes out through the hall.*)

LOPAHIN. All right, I'll take care of it. . . . These people! (*Follows* TROFIMOV.)

ANYA. Has Feers been taken to the hospital?

YASHA. I told them to take him this morning. He's gone, I think.

ANYA (*to* EPIHODOV, *who passes through the ballroom*). Semyon Pantaleyevich, will you please find out whether Feers has been taken to the hospital?

YASHA (*offended*). I told Yegor this morning. Why ask a dozen times?

EPIHODOV. That old Feers—frankly speaking, I mean—he's beyond repair, it's time he joined his ancestors. As for me, I can only envy him. (*He places a suitcase on top of a cardboard hatbox and squashes it.*) There you are, you see! . . . I might have known it! (*Goes out.*)

YASHA (*sardonically*). Two-and-twenty misfortunes!

VARYA (*from behind the door*). Has Feers been taken to the hospital?

ANYA. Yes.

VARYA. Why wasn't the letter to the doctor taken then?

ANYA. I'll send someone after them with it . . . (*Goes out.*)

VARYA (*from the adjoining room*). Where's Yasha? Tell him his mother is here and wants to say good-bye to him.

YASHA (*waves his hand*). This is too much! I'll lose my patience.

While the foregoing action has been taking place, DUNYASHA *has been busy with the luggage; now that* YASHA *is alone, she comes up to him.*

DUNYASHA. If only you'd look at me just once, Yasha! You're going . . . you're leaving me! . . . (*She cries and throws her arms around his neck.*)

YASHA. What are you crying for? (*Drinks champagne.*) In a week I'll be in Paris again. Tomorrow we'll get on the train—and off we'll go—gone! I can't believe it. "*Vive la France!*" I can't stand it here and could never live here—nothing ever happens. I've seen enough of all this ignorance. I've had enough of it. (*Drinks.*) What are you crying for? Behave yourself properly, then you won't cry.

DUNYASHA (*looking into a handmirror and powdering her nose*). Please write to me from Paris. You know how much I've loved you, Yasha. Oh, I've loved you so much! I'm very sensitive, Yasha!

YASHA. Sshh, someone's coming. (*Pretends to be busy with a suitcase, humming quietly.*)

Enter LYUBOV ANDREYEVNA, GAEV, ANYA *and* CHARLOTTA IVANOVNA.

GAEV. We've got to leave soon. There isn't much time left. (*Looks at* YASHA.) What a smell! Who's been eating herring?

LYUBOV. We'll have to leave in the carriage in ten minutes. (*Looks about the room.*) Goodbye, dear house, the home of our fathers. Winter will pass and spring will come again, and then you won't be here any more, you'll be torn down. How much these walls have seen! (*Kisses her daughter passionately.*) My little treasure, how radiant you look, your eyes are shining like diamonds. Are you glad? Very glad?

ANYA. Oh, yes, very glad, Mamma! Our new life is just beginning!

GAEV (*gaily*). Really, everything's all right now. Before the cherry orchard was sold we were all worried and upset, but as soon as things were settled once and for all, we all calmed down and even felt quite cheerful. I'm working in a bank now, a real financier. . . . The red into the side pocket . . . And say what you like, Lyuba, you're looking much better. No doubt about it.

LYUBOV. Yes, that's true, my nerves are better. (*Someone helps her on with her hat and coat.*) I'm sleeping better, too. Take out my things, Yasha, it's time. (*To* ANYA.) My little darling, we'll be seeing each other again soon. I'm going to Paris—I'll live on the money which your Grandmother sent us to buy the estate—God bless Grandmamma!—but that money won't last very long either.

ANYA. You'll come back soon, Mamma . . . won't you? I'll study and pass my exams and then I'll work and help you. We'll read together, Mamma . . . all sorts of things . . . won't we? (*She kisses her mother's hands.*) We'll read during the long autumn evenings. We'll read lots of books, and a new wonderful world will open up before us . . . (*Dreamily.*) Mamma, come back soon . . .

LYUBOV. I'll come back, my precious. (*Embraces her.*)

Enter LOPAHIN. CHARLOTTA *quietly sings to herself.*

GAEV. Happy Charlotta! She's singing.

CHARLOTTA (*picks up a bundle that looks like a baby in a blanket*). Bye-bye, little baby. (*A sound like a baby crying is heard.*) Hush, be quiet, my darling, be a good little boy. (*The "crying" continues.*) Oh, my baby, you poor thing! (*Throws the bundle down.*) Are you going to find me another job? If you don't mind, I've got to have one.

LOPAHIN. We'll find you one, Charlotta Ivanovna, don't worry.

GAEV. Everybody's leaving us, Varya's going away . . . all of a sudden nobody wants us.

CHARLOTTA. There's no place for me to live in town. I'll have to go. (*Hums.*) Oh, well, what do I care. (*Enter* PISHCHIK.)

LOPAHIN. Look what's here!

PISHCHIK (*gasping for breath*). Oohhh, let me get my breath . . . I'm worn out . . . My good friends. . . . Give me some water . . .

GAEV. I suppose you want to borrow some money? I'm going . . . Excuse me . . . (*Goes out.*)

PISHCHIK. I haven't seen you for a long time . . . my beautiful lady . . . (*To* LOPAHIN.) You're here, too . . . glad to see you . . . you're a man of great intelligence . . . here . . . take this . . . (*Gives money to* LOPAHIN.) Four hundred roubles . . . I still owe you eight hundred and forty. . . .

LOPAHIN (*shrugging his shoulders in amazement*). It's like a dream . . . Where did you get it?

PISHCHIK. Wait a minute . . . I'm so hot . . . A most extraordinary thing happened. Some Englishmen came along and discovered some kind of white clay on my land. . . . (*To* LYUBOV.) Here's four hundred for you also, my dear . . . enchantress . . . (*Gives her the money.*) You'll get the rest later. (*Takes a drink of water.*) A young man on the train was just telling me that some great philosopher advises people to jump off roofs. You just jump off, he says, and that settles the whole problem. (*Amazed at what he has just said.*) Imagine that! More water, please.

LOPAHIN. What Englishmen?

PISHCHIK. I leased the land to them for twenty-four years. . . . And now you must excuse me, I'm in a hurry and have to get on. I'm going to Znoikov's, then to Kardamonov's . . . I owe then all money. (*Drinks.*) Your health. I'll come again on Thursday . . .

LYUBOV. We're just leaving for town, and tomorrow I'm going abroad.

PISHCHIK. What's that? (*In agitation.*) Why to town? Oh, I see . . . this furniture and the suitcases. . . . Well, never mind . . . (*Tearfully.*) What difference does it make. . . . These Englishmen, you know, they're very intelligent . . . Never mind. . . . I wish you all the best, God bless you. Never mind, everything comes to an end eventually. (*Kisses* LYUBOV's *hand.*) And when you hear that my end has come, just think of a horse, and say: "There used to be a man like that once . . . his name was Semyonov-Pishchik—God bless him!" Wonderful weather we're having. Yes . . . (*Goes out embarrassed, but returns at once and stands in the doorway.*) Dashenka sends her greetings. (*Goes out.*)

LYUBOV. Well, we can get started now. I'm leaving with two worries on my mind. One is Feers—he's sick. (*Glances at her watch.*) We've still got five minutes. . . .

ANYA. Mamma, Feers has been taken to the hospital. Yasha sent him this morning.

LYUBOV. The other is Varya. She's used to getting up early and working, and now, with nothing to do, she's like a fish out of water. She's gotten so thin and pale, and she cries a lot, the poor dear. (*A pause.*) You know very well, Yermolay Alexeyevich, that I've been hoping you two would get married . . . and everything pointed to it. (*Whispers to* ANYA *and motions to* CHARLOTTA, *and they both go out.*) She loves you, and you're fond of her, too . . . I just don't know, I don't know why you seem to avoid each other. I don't understand it.

LOPAHIN. Neither do I, I admit it. The whole thing's so strange. . . . If there's still time, I'm ready to. . . . Let's settle it at once— and get it over with! Without you here, I don't feel I'll ever propose to her.

LYUBOV. That's an excellent idea! You won't need more than a minute. I'll call her at once.

LOPAHIN. And there's champagne here, too, we'll celebrate. (*Looks at the glasses.*) They're empty, someone's drunk it all. (YASHA *coughs.*) They must have poured it down.

LYUBOV (*with animation*). Oh, I'm so glad. I'll call her, and we'll leave you alone. Yasha, "*allez!*" (*Through the door.*) Varya, come here for a minute, leave what you're doing and come here! Varya! (*Goes out with* YASHA.)

LOPAHIN (*looking at his watch*). Yes. . . .

A pause. Whispering and suppressed laughter are heard behind the door, then VARYA *comes in and starts fussing with the luggage. At last she says:*

VARYA. That's strange, I can't find it. . . .

LOPAHIN. What are you looking for?

VARYA. I packed it myself, and I can't remember . . . (*A pause.*)

LOPAHIN. Where are you going to now, Varvara Mihailovna?

VARYA. I? To the Rogulins. I've taken a job as their housekeeper.

LOPAHIN. That's in Yashnevo, isn't it? Almost seventy miles from here. (*A pause.*) So this is the end of life in this house. . . .

VARYA (*still fussing with the luggage*). Where could it be? Perhaps I put it in the trunk? Yes, life in this house has come to an end . . . there won't be any more. . . .

LOPAHIN. And I'm going to Kharkov. . . . On the next train. I've got a lot of work to do there. I'm leaving Epihodov here. . . . I've hired him.

VARYA. Really! . . .

LOPAHIN. Remember, last year at this time it was snowing already, but now it's still so bright and sunny. Though it's cold . . . Three degrees of frost.

VARYA. I haven't looked. (*A pause.*) Besides, our thermometer's broken. . . .

A pause. A voice is heard from outside the door.

VOICE. Yermolay Alexeyevich!

LOPAHIN (*as if he had been waiting for it*). I'm coming! Right away! (*Goes out quickly.*)

VARYA *sits on the floor, with her head on a bundle of clothes, crying quietly. The door opens,* LYUBOV *enters hesitantly.*

LYUBOV. Well? (*A pause.*) We must be going.

VARYA (*stops crying and wipes her eyes*). Yes, Mamma, it's time we got started. I'll just have time to get to the Rogulins today, if we don't miss the train.

LYUBOV (*calls through the door*). Anya, put your things on.

Enter ANYA, *followed by* GAEV *and* CHARLOTTA. GAEV *wears a heavy overcoat with a hood. Servants and coachmen come into the room.* EPIHODOV *is picking up the luggage.*

Now we can begin our journey!

ANYA (*joyfully*). Our journey!

GAEV. My friends, my dear, beloved friends! As I leave this house forever, how can I be silent, how can I refrain from expressing to you, as I say good-bye for the last time, the feelings which now overwhelm me. . . .

ANYA (*begging*). Uncle!

VARYA. Uncle, please don't!

GAEV (*downcast*). I put the red into the corner and then . . . I'll keep quiet.

Enter TROFIMOV *and* LOPAHIN.

TROFIMOV. Well, ladies and gentlemen, it's time we get started.

LOPAHIN. Epihodov, my coat!

LYUBOV. I'll just stay for one more minute. It seems as if I'd never seen the walls and ceilings of this house before, and now I look at them with such longing, such love. . . .

GAEV. I remember when I was six—it was Trinity Sunday . . . I was sitting here at this window watching father on his way to church. . . .

LYUBOV. Have they taken everything out?

LOPAHIN. It looks like it. (*To* EPIHODOV, *as he puts on his coat.*) Be sure to take care of everything, Epihodov.

EPIHODOV (*in a husky voice*). Don't worry, Yermolay Alexeyevich!

LOPAHIN. What is wrong with your voice?

EPIHODOV. I just had some water, and it went down the wrong throat.

YASHA (*with contempt*). What a fool!

LYUBOV. After we leave, there won't be a soul here. . . .

LOPAHIN. Not until spring.

VARYA (*pulls an umbrella from a bundle of clothes;* LOPAHIN *pretends to be afraid*). What are you doing that for? . . . I didn't mean to. . . .

TROFIMOV. Ladies and gentlemen, hurry up, it's time. The train will be here soon.

VARYA Petya, here are your goloshes beside the suitcase. (*Tearfully.*) How dirty and old they are! . . .

TROFIMOV (*puts them on*). Hurry up, ladies and gentlemen!

GAEV (*greatly embarrassed, afraid of breaking into tears*). The train, the station . . . The red off the white into the middle pocket. . . .

LYUBOV. Let us go!

LOPAHIN. Are we all here? No one left? (*Locks the door on the left.*) There are some things stored in there, best to keep it locked up. Come along!

ANYA. Good-bye, old house! Good-bye, old life!

TROFIMOV. Welcome to the new life! . . . (*Goes out with* ANYA.)

VARYA *looks around the room and goes out slowly.* YASHA *and* CHARLOTTA, *with her little dog, follow.*

LOPAHIN. And so, until the spring. Come, my friends. . . . Au revoir! (*Goes out.*)

LYUBOV *and* GAEV *alone. They seem to have been waiting for this moment, and now they embrace each other and cry quietly, with restraint, so as not to be heard.*

GAEV (*in despair*). Sister, my sister. . . .

LYUBOV. Oh, my orchard, my beloved, my beautiful orchard! My life, my youth, my happiness . . . good-bye! . . . Good-bye!

ANYA (*off-stage, calling gaily*). Mama! . . .

TROFIMOV (*off-stage, gaily and excitedly*). Yoo-hoo! . . .

LYUBOV. Just one last time—to look at these walls, these windows. . . . Mother loved to walk in this room. . . .

GAEV. Sister, my sister . . .

ANYA (*off-stage*). Mamma!

TROFIMOV (*off-stage*). Yoo-hoo!

LYUBOV. We're coming . . . (*They go out.*)

The stage is empty. The sound of doors being locked and then of carriages driving off. Silence. In the stillness the dull sounds of an axe striking on a tree can be heard. They sound mournful and sad. Footsteps are heard and from the door on the right FEERS *enters. He is dressed, as usual, in a coat and white waistcoat, and is wearing slippers. He is ill.*

FEERS (*walks up to the middle door and tries the handle*). Locked. They've gone . . . (*Sits down on a sofa.*) They've forgotten me. Never mind. . . . I'll sit here for a bit. I don't suppose Leonid Andreyevich put on his fur coat, he probably wore his light one. (*Sighs, preoccupied.*) I didn't take care of it . . . These young people! . . . (*Mutters something unintelligible.*) My life's slipped by as if I'd never lived. . . . (*Lies down.*) I'll lie down a bit. You haven't got any strength left, nothing's left, nothing. . . . Oh, you . . . you old good-for-nothing! . . . (*Lies motionless.*)

A distant sound that seems to come out of the sky, like a breaking harp string, slowly and sadly dying away. Then all is silent, except for the sound of an axe striking a tree in the orchard far away.

Curtain.

THREE LETTERS

Anton Chekhov

TO A. S. SOUVORIN, MOSCOW: OCTOBER 27, 1888

In conversation with my literary colleagues I always insist that it is not the artist's business to solve problems that require a specialist's knowledge. It is a bad thing if a writer tackles a subject he does not understand. We have specialists for dealing with special ques-

Reprinted from LETTERS OF ANTON CHEKHOV translated by Constance Garnett. Reprinted by permission of Mr. David Garnett and Chatto & Windus.

tions: it is their business to judge of the commune, of the future, of capitalism, of the evils of drunkenness, of boots, of the diseases of women. An artist must judge only of what he understands, his field is just as limited as that of any other specialist—I repeat this and insist on it always. That in his sphere there are no questions, but only answers, can be maintained only by those who have never written and have had no experience of thinking in images. An artist observes, selects, guesses, combines—and this in itself presupposes a problem: unless he had set himself a problem from the very first there would be nothing to conjecture and nothing to select. To put it briefly, I will end by using the language of psychiatry: if one denies that creative work involves problems and purposes, one must admit that an artist creates without premeditation or intention, in a state of aberration; therefore, if an author boasted to me of having written a novel without a preconceived design, under a sudden inspiration, I should call him mad.

You are right in demanding that an artist should take an intelligent attitude to his work, but you confuse two things: *solving a problem and stating a problem correctly*. It is only the second that is obligatory for the artist. In *Anna Karenina* and *Evgeni Onegin* not a single problem is solved, but they satisfy you completely because all the problems in these works are correctly stated. It is the business of the judge to put the right questions, but the answers must be given by the jury according to their own lights.

TO KONSTANTIN STANISLAVSKI, YALTA:
OCTOBER 30, 1903

Thank you very much for the letter and for the telegram. Letters are always very precious to me because, one, I am here all alone, and two, I sent the play off three weeks ago and your letter came only yesterday; if it were not for my wife, I would have been entirely in the dark and would have imagined any old thing that might have crept into my head. When I

worked on the part of Lopahin, I thought it might be for you. If for some reason it doesn't appeal to you, take Gayev. Lopahin, of course, is only a merchant, but he is a decent person in every sense, should conduct himself with complete decorum, like a cultivated man, without pettiness or trickery, and it did seem to me that you will be brilliant in this part, which is central for the play. (If you do decide to play Gayev, let Vishnevski play Lopahin. He won't make an artistic Lopahin but still he won't be a petty one. Lujski would be a cold-blooded foreigner in this part and Leonidov would play it like a little kulak. You mustn't lose sight of the fact that Varya, an earnest, devout young girl is in love with Lopahin; she wouldn't love a little kulak.)

I want so much to go to Moscow but I don't know how I can get away from here. It is turning cold and I hardly ever leave the house; I am not used to fresh air and am coughing. I do not fear Moscow, or the trip itself, but I am afraid of having to stay in Sevastopol from two to eight, and in the most tedious company.

Write me what role you are taking for yourself. My wife wrote that Moskvin wants to play Epihodov. Why not, it would be a very good idea, and the play would gain from it.

My deepest compliments and regards to Maria Petrovna, and may I wish her and you all the best. Keep well and gay.

You know, I haven't yet seen *The Lower Depths* or *Julius Caesar*. I would so much like to see them.

TO VLADIMIR NEMIROVICH-DANCHENKO,
YALTA: NOVEMBER 2, 1903

Two letters from you in one day, thanks a lot! I don't drink beer, the last time I drank any was in July; and I cannot eat honey, as it gives me a stomach ache. Now as to the play.

1. Anya can be played by any actress you'd like, even an utter unknown, if only she is young and looks like a young girl, and

talks in a young, resonant voice. This role is not one of the important ones.

2. Varya's part is more on the serious side, if only Maria Petrovna would take it. If she doesn't the part will turn out rather flat and coarse, and I would have to do it over and soften it. M.P. won't repeat herself because, firstly, she is a gifted actress, and secondly, because Varya does not resemble Sonya or Natasha; she is a figure in a black dress, a little nun-like creature, somewhat simple-minded, plaintive and so forth and so on.

3. Gayev and Lopahin—have Stanislavski try these parts and make his choice. If he takes Lopahin and feels at home in the part, the play is bound to be a success. Certainly if Lopahin is a pallid figure, played by a pallid actor, both the part and the play will fail.

4. Pishchik—the part for Gribunin. God have mercy on you if you assign the part to Vishnevski.

5. Charlotta—a big part. It would of course be impossible to give the part to Pomyalova; Muratova might be good, perhaps, but not funny. This is the part for Mme. Knipper.

6. Epihodov—if Moskvin wants the part let him have it. He'll be a superb Epihodov. . . .

7. Firs—the role for Artem.

8. Dunyasha—for Khalutina.

9. Yasha. If it is the Alexandrov you wrote about, the one that is assistant to your producer, let him have it. Moskvin would make a splendid Yasha. And I haven't anything against Leonidov for the part.

10. The passer-by—Gromov.

11. The stationmaster who reads "The Sinner" in Act III should have a bass voice.

Charlotta speaks with a good accent, not broken Russian, except that once in a while she gives a soft sound to a consonant at the end of a word rather than the hard sound that is proper, and she mixes masculine and feminine adjectives. Pishchik is an old Russian fellow broken down with gout, old age and satiety, plump, dressed in a long Russian coat (à la Simov) and boots without heels.

Lopahin wears a white vest and tan shoes, flails his arms when he is in motion, takes long strides, is lost in thought when he moves about and walks in a straight line. He doesn't cut his hair short and so he frequently tosses his head back; in reflection he strokes his beard back and forth, i.e., from his neck to his lips. I think Trofimov is clearly sketched. Varya wears a black dress and wide belt.

I have been intending to write *The Cherry Orchard* these past three years and for three years have been telling you to hire an actress who could play a part like Lyubov Andreyevna. This long waiting game never pays.

I have got into the stupidest position: I am here alone and don't know why. But you are unjust in saying that despite your work it is "Stanislavski's theatre." You are the one that people speak about and write about while they do nothing but criticize Stanislavski for his performance of Brutus. If you leave the theatre, so will I. Gorki is younger than we and has his own life to lead. As to the Nizhni-Novgorod theatre, this is only an episode in his life; Gorki will try it, sniff at it and cast it aside. I may say in this connection that people's theatres and people's literature are plain foolishness, something to sweeten up the people. Gogol shouldn't be pulled down to the people, but the people raised to Gogol's level.

I would like so much to visit the Hermitage Restaurant, eat some sturgeon and drink a bottle of wine. Once I drank a bottle of champagne solo and didn't get drunk, then I had some cognac and didn't get drunk either.

I'll write you again and in the meantime send my humble greetings and thanks. Was it Lujski's father that died? I read about it in the paper today.

Why does Maria Petrovna insist on playing Anya? And why does Maria Fyodorovna think she is too aristocratic to play Varya? Isn't she playing in *The Lower Depths*, after all? Well, the devil take them. I embrace you, keep well.

Translated by Constance Garnett

ALL THAT FALL

Samuel Beckett

Characters

MRS. ROONEY (MADDY), a lady in her seventies

CHRISTY, a carter

MR. TYLER, a retired bill-broker

MR. SLOCUM, Clerk of the Racecourse

TOMMY, a porter

MR. BARRELL, a station-master

MISS FITT, a lady in her thirties

A FEMALE VOICE

DOLLY, a small girl

MR. ROONEY (DAN), husband of Mrs. Rooney, blind

JERRY, a small boy

Rural sounds. Sheep, bird, cow, cock, severally, then together.

Silence.

Mrs. Rooney advances along country road towards railway-station. Sound of her dragging feet.

Music faint from house by way. "Death and the Maiden." Then steps slow down, stop.

MRS. ROONEY. Poor woman. All alone in that ruinous old house.

Music louder. Silence but for music playing.

The steps resume. Music dies. Mrs. Rooney murmurs melody. Her murmur dies.

Sound of approaching cartwheels. The cart stops. The steps slow down, stop.

MRS. ROONEY. Is that you, Christy?

CHRISTY. It is, Ma'am.

MRS. ROONEY. I thought the hinny was familiar. How is your poor wife?

CHRISTY. No better, Ma'am.

MRS. ROONEY. Your daughter then?

CHRISTY. No worse, Ma'am.

Silence.

MRS. ROONEY. Why do you halt? (*Pause.*) But why do I halt?

Silence.

CHRISTY. Nice day for the races, Ma'am.

MRS. ROONEY. No doubt it is. (*Pause.*) But will it hold up? (*Pause. With emotion.*) Will it hold up?

Silence.

CHRISTY. I suppose you wouldn't—

MRS. ROONEY. Hist! (*Pause.*) Surely to goodness that cannot be the up mail I hear already?

Silence. The hinny neighs. Silence.

CHRISTY. Damn the mail.

MRS. ROONEY. Oh thank God for that! I could have sworn I heard it, thundering up the track in the far distance. (*Pause.*) So hinnies whinny. Well, it is not surprising.

CHRISTY. I suppose you wouldn't be in need of a small load of dung?

MRS. ROONEY. Dung? What class of dung?

CHRISTY. Stydung.

MRS. ROONEY. Stydung . . . I like your frankness, Christy. (*Pause.*) I'll ask the master. (*Pause.*) Christy.

CHRISTY. Yes, Ma'am.

MRS. ROONEY. Do you find anything . . . bizarre about my way of speaking? (*Pause.*) I do not mean the voice. (*Pause.*) No, I mean the words. (*Pause. More to herself.*) I use none but the simplest words, I hope, and yet I sometimes find my way of speaking very . . . bizarre. (*Pause.*) Mercy! What was that?

CHRISTY. Never mind her, Ma'am, she's very fresh in herself to-day.

Silence.

MRS. ROONEY. Dung? What would we want with dung, at our time of life? (*Pause.*) Why are you on your feet down on the road? Why do you not climb up on the crest of your manure and let yourself be carried along? Is it that you have no head for heights?

Silence.

CHRISTY (*to the hinny*). Yep! (*Pause. Louder.*) Yep wiyya to hell owwa that!

Silence.

MRS. ROONEY. She does not move a muscle. (*Pause.*) I too should be getting along, if I do not wish to arrive late at the station. (*Pause.*) But a moment ago she neighed and pawed the ground. And now she refuses to advance. Give her a good welt on the rump. (*Sound of welt. Pause.*) Harder! (*Sound of welt. Pause.*) Well! If someone were to do that for me I should not dally. (*Pause.*) How she gazes at me to be sure, with her great moist cleg-tormented eyes! Perhaps if I were to move on, down the road, out of her field of vision . . . (*Sound of welt.*) No, no, enough! Take her by the snaffle and pull her eyes away from me. Oh this is awful! (*She moves on. Sound of her dragging feet.*) What have I done to deserve all this, what, what? (*Dragging feet.*) So long ago . . . No! No! (*Dragging feet. Quotes.*) "Sigh out a something something tale of things, Done long ago and ill done." (*She halts.*) How can I go on, I cannot. Oh let me just flop down flat on the road like a big fat jelly out of a bowl and never move again! A great big slop thick with grit and dust and flies, they would have to scoop me up with a shovel. (*Pause.*) Heavens, there

is that up mail again, what will become of me! (*The dragging steps resume.*) Oh I am just a hysterical old hag I know, destroyed with sorrow and pining and gentility and church-going and fat and rheumatism and childlessness. (*Pause. Brokenly.*) Minnie! Little Minnie! (*Pause.*) Love, that is all I asked, a little love, daily, twice daily, fifty years of twice daily love like a Paris horse-butcher's regular, what normal woman wants affection? A peck on the jaw at morning, near the ear, and another at evening, peck, peck, till you grow whiskers on you. There is that lovely laburnum again.

Dragging feet. Sound of bicycle-bell. It is old Mr. Tyler coming up behind her on his bicycle, on his way to the station. Squeak of brakes. He slows down and rides abreast of her.

MR. TYLER. Mrs. Rooney! Pardon me if I do not doff my cap, I'd fall off. Divine day for the meeting.

MRS. ROONEY. Oh, Mr. Tyler, you startled the life out of me stealing up behind me like that like a deer-stalker! Oh!

MR. TYLER (*playfully*). I rang my bell, Mrs. Rooney, the moment I sighted you I started tinkling my bell, now don't you deny it.

MRS. ROONEY. Your bell is one thing, Mr. Tyler, and you are another. What news of your daughter?

MR. TYLER. Fair, fair. They removed everything, you know, the whole . . . er . . . bag of tricks. Now I am grandchildless.

Dragging feet.

MRS. ROONEY. Gracious how you wobble! Dismount, for mercy's sake, or ride on.

MR. TYLER. Perhaps if I were to lay my hand lightly on your shoulder, Mrs. Rooney, how would that be? (*Pause.*) Would you permit that?

MRS. ROONEY. No, Mr. Rooney, Mr. Tyler I mean, I am tired of light old hands on my shoulders and other senseless places, sick and tired of them. Heavens, here comes Connolly's van! (*She halts. Sound of motor-van. It approaches, passes with thunderous rattle, recedes.*) Are you all right, Mr. Tyler? (*Pause.*) Where is he? (*Pause.*) Ah there you are! (*The dragging steps resume.*) That was a narrow squeak.

MR. TYLER. I alit in the nick of time.

MRS. ROONEY. It is suicide to be abroad. But what is it to be at home, Mr. Tyler, what is it to be at home? A lingering dissolution. Now we are white with dust from head to foot. I beg your pardon?

MR. TYLER. Nothing, Mrs. Rooney, nothing, I was merely cursing, under my breath, God and man, under my breath, and the wet Saturday afternoon of my conception. My back tire has gone down again. I pumped it hard as iron before I set out. And now I am on the rim.

MRS. ROONEY. Oh what a shame!

MR. TYLER. Now if it were the front I should not so much mind. But the back. The back! The chain! The oil! The grease! The hub! The brakes! The gear! No! It is too much!

Dragging feet.

MRS. ROONEY. Are we very late, Mr. Tyler, I have not the courage to look at my watch.

MR. TYLER (*bitterly*). Late! I on my bicycle as I bowled along was already late. Now therefore we are doubly late, trebly, quadrupedly late. Would I had shot by you, without a word.

Dragging feet.

MRS. ROONEY. Whom are you meeting, Mr. Tyler?

MR. TYLER. Hardy. (*Pause.*) We used to climb together. (*Pause.*) I saved his life once. (*Pause.*) I have not forgotten it.

Dragging feet. They stop.

MRS. ROONEY. Let us a halt a moment and this vile dust fall back upon the viler worms.

Silence. Rural sounds.

MR. TYLER. What sky! What light! Ah in spite of all it is a blessed thing to be alive in such weather, and out of hospital.

MRS. ROONEY. Alive?

MR. TYLER. Well half alive shall we say?

MRS. ROONEY. Speak for yourself, Mr. Tyler. I am not half alive nor anything approaching it. (*Pause.*) What are we standing here for? This dust will not settle in our time. And when it does some great roaring machine will come and whirl it all skyhigh again.

MR. TYLER. Well, shall we be getting along in that case?

MRS. ROONEY. No.

MR. TYLER. Come, Mrs. Rooney—

MRS. ROONEY. Go, Mr. Tyler, go on and leave me, listening to the cooing of the ringdoves. (*Cooing.*) If you see my poor blind Dan tell him I was on my way to meet him when it all came over me again, like a flood. Say to him, Your poor wife, she told me to tell you it all came flooding over her again and . . . (*the voice breaks*) . . . she simply went back home . . . straight back home . . .

MR. TYLER. Come, Mrs. Rooney, come, the mail has not yet gone up, just take my free arm and we'll be there with time and to spare.

MRS. ROONEY (*sobbing*). What? What's all this now? (*Calmer.*) Can't you see I'm in trouble? (*With anger.*) Have you no respect for misery? (*Sobbing.*) Minnie! Little Minnie!

MR. TYLER. Come, Mrs. Rooney, come, the mail has not yet gone up, just take my free arm and we'll be there with time and to spare.

MRS. ROONEY (*brokenly*). In her forties now she'd be, I don't know, fifty, girding up her lovely little loins, getting ready for the change . . .

MR. TYLER. Come, Mrs. Rooney, come, the mail—

MRS. ROONEY (*exploding*). Will you get along with you, Mr. Rooney, Mr. Tyler I mean, will you get along with you now and cease molesting me? What kind of a country is this where a woman can't weep her heart out on the highways and byways without being tormented by retired bill-brokers! (*Mr. Tyler prepares to mount his bicycle.*) Heavens, you're not going to ride her flat! (*Mr. Tyler mounts.*) You'll tear your tube to ribbons! (*Mr. Tyler rides off. Receding sound of bumping bicycle. Silence. Cooing.*) Venus birds! Billing in the woods all the long summer long. (*Pause.*) Oh cursed corset! If I could let it out, without indecent exposure. Mr. Tyler! Mr. Tyler! Come back and unlace me behind the hedge! (*She laughs wildly, ceases.*) What's wrong with me, what's wrong with me, never tranquil, seething out of my dirty old pelt, out of my skull, oh to be in atoms, in atoms! (*Frenziedly.*) ATOMS! (*Silence. Cooing. Faintly.*) Jesus! (*Pause.*) Jesus!

Sound of car coming up behind her. It slows down and draws up beside her, engine running. It is Mr. Slocum, the Clerk of the Racecourse.

MR. SLOCUM. Is anything wrong, Mrs. Rooney? You are bent all double. Have you a pain in the stomach?

Silence. Mrs. Rooney laughs wildly.

Finally.

MRS. ROONEY. Well, if it isn't my old admirer, the Clerk of the Course, in his limousine.

MR. SLOCUM. May I offer you a lift, Mrs. Rooney? Are you going in my direction?

MRS. ROONEY. I am, Mr. Slocum, we all are. (*Pause.*) How is your poor mother?

MR. SLOCUM. Thank you, she is fairly comfortable. We manage to keep her out of pain. That is the great thing, Mrs. Rooney, is it not?

MRS. ROONEY. Yes, indeed, Mr. Slocum, that is the great thing, I don't know how you do it. (*Pause. She slaps her cheek violently.*) Ah these wasps!

MR. SLOCUM (*coolly*). May I then offer you a seat, Madam?

MRS. ROONEY (*with exaggerated enthusiasm*). Oh that would be heavenly, Mr. Slocum, just simply heavenly. (*Dubiously.*) But would I ever get in, you look very high off the ground to-day, these new balloon tires, I presume. (*Sound of door opening and Mrs. Rooney trying to get in.*) Does this roof never come off? No? (*Efforts of Mrs. Rooney.*) No . . . I'll never do it . . . you'll have to get down, Mr. Slocum, and help me from the rear. (*Pause.*) What was that? (*Pause. Aggrieved.*) This is all your suggestion, Mr. Slocum, not mine. Drive on, Sir, drive on.

MR. SLOCUM (*switching off the engine*). I'm coming, Mrs. Rooney, I'm coming, give me time, I'm as stiff as yourself.

Sound of Mr. Slocum extracting himself from driver's seat.

MRS. ROONEY. Stiff! Well I like that! And me heaving all over back and front. (*To herself.*) The dry old reprobate!

MR. SLOCUM (*in position behind her*). Now, Mrs. Rooney, how shall we do this?

MRS. ROONEY. As if I were a bale, Mr. Slocum, don't be afraid. (*Pause. Sounds of effort.*) That's the way! (*Effort.*) Lower! (*Effort.*) Wait! (*Pause.*) No, don't let go! (*Pause.*) Suppose I do get up, will I ever get down?

MR. SLOCUM (*breathing hard*). You'll get down, Mrs. Rooney, you'll get down. We may not get you up, but I warrant you we'll get you down.

He resumes his efforts. Sound of these.

MRS. ROONEY. Oh! . . Lower! . . Don't be afraid! . . We're past the age when . . . There! . . Now! . . Get your shoulder under it . . . Oh! . . (*Giggles.*) Oh glory! . . Up! Up! . . Ah! . . I'm in! (*Panting of Mr. Slocum. He slams the door. In a scream.*) My frock! You've nipped my frock! (*Mr. Slocum opens the door. Mrs. Rooney frees her frock. Mr. Slocum slams the door. His violent *unintelligible muttering as he walks round to the other door. Tearfully.*) My nice frock! Look what you've done to my nice frock! (*Mr. Slocum gets into his seat, slams driver's door, presses starter. The engine does not start. He releases starter.*) What will Dan say when he sees me?

MR. SLOCUM. Has he then recovered his sight?

MRS. ROONEY. No, I mean when he knows, what will he say when he feels the hole? (*Mr. Slocum presses starter. As before. Silence.*) What are you doing, Mr. Slocum?

MR. SLOCUM. Gazing straight before me, Mrs. Rooney, through the windscreen, into the void.

MRS. ROONEY. Start her up, I beseech you, and let us be off. This is awful!

MR. SLOCUM (*dreamily*). All morning she went like a dream and now she is dead. That is what you get for a good deed. (*Pause. Hopefully.*) Perhaps if I were to choke her. (*He does so, presses the starter. The engine roars. Roaring to make himself heard.*) She was getting too much air!

He throttles down, grinds in his first gear, moves off, changes up in a grinding of gears.

MRS. ROONEY (*in anguish*). Mind the hen! (*Scream of brakes. Squawk of hen.*) Oh mother, you have squashed her, drive on, drive on! (*The car accelerates. Pause.*) What a death! One minute picking happy at the dung, on the road, in the sun, with now and then a dust bath, and then—bang!—all her troubles over. (*Pause.*) All the laying and the hatching. (*Pause.*) Just one great squawk and then . . . peace. (*Pause.*) They would have slit her weasand in any case. (*Pause.*) Here we are, let me down. (*The car slows down, stops, engine running. Mr. Slocum blows his horn. Pause. Louder. Pause.*) What are you up to now, Mr. Slocum? We are at a standstill, all danger is past and you blow your horn. Now if instead of blowing it now you had blown it at that unfortunate—

Horn violently. Tommy the porter appears at top of station steps.

MR. SLOCUM (*calling*). Will you come down, Tommy, and help this lady out, she's stuck. (*Tommy descends the steps.*) Open the door, Tommy, and ease her out.

Tommy opens the door.

TOMMY. Certainly, Sir. Nice day for the races, Sir. What would you fancy for—

MRS. ROONEY. Don't mind me. Don't take any notice of me. I do not exist. The fact is well known.

MR. SLOCUM. Do as you're asked, Tommy, for the love of God.

TOMMY. Yessir. Now, Mrs. Rooney.

He starts pulling her out.

MRS. ROONEY. Wait, Tommy, wait now, don't bustle me, just let me wheel round and get my feet to the ground. (*Her efforts to achieve this.*) Now.

TOMMY (*pulling her out*). Mind your feather, Ma'am. (*Sounds of effort.*) Easy now, easy.

MRS. ROONEY. Wait, for God's sake, you'll have me beheaded.

TOMMY. Crouch down, Mrs. Rooney, crouch down, and get your head in the open.

MRS. ROONEY. Crouch down! At my time of life! This is lunacy!

TOMMY. Press her down, Sir.

Sounds of combined efforts.

MRS. ROONEY. Merde!

TOMMY. Now! She's coming! Straighten up, Ma'am! There!

Mr. Slocum slams the door.

MRS. ROONEY. Am I out?

The voice of Mr. Barrell, the station-master, raised in anger.

MR. BARRELL. Tommy! Tommy! Where the hell is he?

Mr. Slocum grinds in his gear.

TOMMY. (*hurriedly*). You wouldn't have something for the Ladies Plate, Sir, I was given Flash Harry.

MR. SLOCUM (*scornfully*). Flash Harry! That carthorse!

MR. BARRELL (*at top of steps, roaring*). Tommy! Blast your bleeding bloody—(*He sees Mrs. Rooney.*) Oh, Mrs. Rooney . . . (*Mr. Slocum drives away in a grinding of gears.*) Who's that crucifying his gearbox, Tommy?

TOMMY. Old Cissy Slocum.

MRS. ROONEY. Cissy Slocum! That's a nice way to refer to your betters. Cissy Slocum! And you an orphan!

MR. BARRELL (*angrily to Tommy*). What are you doing stravaging down here on the public road? This is no place for you at all! Nip up there on the platform now and whip out the truck! Won't the twelve thirty be on top of us before we can turn round?

TOMMY (*bitterly*). And that's the thanks you get for a Christian act.

MR. BARRELL (*violently*). Get on with you now before I report you! (*Slow feet of Tommy climbing steps.*) Do you want me to come down to you with the shovel? (*The feet quicken, recede, cease.*) Ah, God forgive me, it's a hard life. (*Pause.*) Well, Mrs. Rooney, it's nice to see you up and about again. You were laid up there a long time.

MRS. ROONEY. Not long enough, Mr. Barrell. (*Pause.*) Would I were still in bed, Mr. Barrell. (*Pause.*) Would I were lying stretched out in my comfortable bed, Mr. Barrell, just wasting slowly painlessly away, keeping up my strength with arrowroot and calves-foot jelly, till in the end you wouldn't see me under the blankets any more than a board. (*Pause.*) Oh no coughing or spitting or bleeding or vomiting, just drifting gently down into the higher life, and remembering, remembering . . . (*the voice breaks*) . . . all the silly unhappiness . . . as though . . . it had never happened . . . what did I do with that handkerchief? (*Sound of handkerchief loudly ap-*

plied.) How long have you been master of this station now, Mr. Barrell?

MR. BARRELL. Don't ask me, Mrs. Rooney, don't ask me.

MRS. ROONEY. You stepped into your father's shoes, I believe, when he took them off.

MR. BARRELL. Poor Pappy! (*Reverent pause.*) He didn't live long to enjoy his ease.

MRS. ROONEY. I remember him clearly. A small ferrety purple-faced widower, deaf as a doornail, very testy and snappy. (*Pause.*) I suppose you'll be retiring soon yourself, Mr. Barrell, and growing your roses. (*Pause.*) Did I understand you to say the twelve thirty would soon be upon us?

MR. BARRELL. Those were my words.

MRS. ROONEY. But according to my watch, which is more or less right—or was—by the eight o'clock news, the time is now coming up to twelve . . . (*pause as she consults her watch*) . . . thirty-six. (*Pause.*) And yet upon the other hand the up mail has not yet gone through. (*Pause.*) Or has it sped by unbeknown to me? (*Pause.*) For there was a moment there, I remember now, I was so plunged in sorrow I wouldn't have heard a steam roller go over me. (*Pause. Mr. Barrell turns to go.*) Don't go, Mr. Barrell! (*Mr. Barrell goes. Loud.*) Mr. Barrell! (*Pause. Louder.*) Mr. Barrell!

Mr. Barrell comes back.

MR. BARRELL (*testily*). What is it, Mrs. Rooney, I have my work to do.

Silence. Sound of wind.

MRS. ROONEY. The wind is getting up. (*Pause. Wind.*) The best of the day is over. (*Pause. Wind. Dreamily.*) Soon the rain will begin to fall and go on falling, all afternoon. (*Mr. Barrell goes.*) Then at evening the clouds will part, the setting sun will shine an instant, then sink, behind the hills. (*She realizes Mr. Barrell has gone.*) Mr. Barrell! Mr. Barrell! (*Silence.*) I estrange them all. They come towards me, uninvited, bygones bygones, full of kindness, anxious to help . . . (*the voice breaks*) . . .

genuinely pleased . . . to see me again . . . looking so well . . . (*Handkerchief.*) A few simple words . . . from my heart . . . and I am all alone . . . once more . . . (*Handkerchief. Vehemently.*) I should not be out at all! I should never leave the grounds! (*Pause.*) Oh there is that Fitt woman, I wonder will she bow to me. (*Sound of Miss Fitt approaching, humming a hymn. She starts climbing the steps.*) Miss Fitt! (*Miss Fitt halts, stops humming.*) Am I then invisible, Miss Fitt? Is this cretonne so becoming to me that I merge into the masonry? (*Miss Fitt descends a step.*) That is right, Miss Fitt, look closely and you will finally distinguish a once female shape.

MISS FITT. Mrs. Rooney! I saw you, but I did not know you.

MRS. ROONEY. Last Sunday we worshipped together. We knelt side by side at the same altar. We drank from the same chalice. Have I so changed since then?

MISS FITT (*shocked*). Oh but in church, Mrs. Rooney, in church I am alone with my Maker. Are not you? (*Pause.*) Why, even the sexton himself, you know, when he takes up the collection, knows it is useless to pause before me. I simply do not see the plate, or bag, whatever it is they use, how could I? (*Pause.*) Why even when all is over and I go out into the sweet fresh air, why even then for the first furlong or so I stumble in a kind of daze as you might say, oblivious to my co-religionists. And they are very kind, I must admit—the vast majority—very kind and understanding. They know me now and take no umbrage. There she goes, they say, there goes the dark Miss Fitt, alone with her Maker, take no notice of her. And they step down off the path to avoid my running into them. (*Pause.*) Ah yes, I am distray, very distray, even on week-days. Ask Mother, if you do not believe me. Hetty, she says, when I start eating my doily instead of the thin bread and butter, Hetty, how can you be so distray? (*Sighs.*) I suppose the truth is I am not there, Mrs. Rooney, just not really there at all. I see, hear, smell, and so on,

I go through the usual motions, but my heart is not in it, Mrs. Rooney, but heart is in none of it. Left to myself, with no one to check me, I would soon be flown . . . home. (*Pause.*) So if you think I cut you just now, Mrs. Rooney, you do me an injustice. All I saw was a big pale blur, just another big pale blur. (*Pause.*) Is anything amiss, Mrs. Rooney, you do not look normal somehow. So bowed and bent.

MRS. ROONEY (*ruefully*). Maddy Rooney, née Dunne, the big pale blur. (*Pause.*) You have piercing sight, Miss Fitt, if you only knew it, literally piercing.

Pause.

MISS FITT. Well . . . is there anything I can do, now that I am here?

MRS. ROONEY. If you would help me up the face of this cliff, Miss Fitt, I have little doubt your Maker would requite you, if no one else.

MISS FITT. Now now, Mrs. Rooney, don't put your teeth in me. Requite! I make these sacrifices for nothing—or not at all. (*Pause. Sound of her descending steps.*) I take it you want to lean on me, Mrs. Rooney.

MRS. ROONEY. I asked Mr. Barrell to give me his arm, just give me his arm. (*Pause.*) He turned on his heel and strode away.

MISS FITT. Is it my arm you want then? (*Pause. Impatiently.*) Is it my arm you want, Mrs. Rooney, or what is it?

MRS. ROONEY (*exploding*). Your arm! Any arm! A helping hand! For five seconds! Christ, what a planet!

MISS FITT. Really . . . Do you know what it is, Mrs. Rooney, I do not think it is wise of you to be going about at all.

MRS. ROONEY (*violently*). Come down here, Miss Fitt, and give me your arm, before I scream down the parish!

Pause. Wind. Sound of Miss Fitt descending last steps.

MISS FITT (*resignedly*). Well, I suppose it is the Protestant thing to do.

MRS. ROONEY. Pismires do it for one another. (*Pause.*) I have seen slugs do it. (*Miss Fitt proffers her arm.*) No, the other side, my dear, if it's all the same to you, I'm left-handed on top of everything else. (*She takes Miss Fitt's right arm.*) Heavens, child, you're just a bag of bones, you need building up. (*Sound of her toiling up steps on Miss Fitt's arm.*) This is worse than the Matterhorn, were you ever up the Matterhorn, Miss Fitt, great honeymoon resort. (*Sound of toiling.*) Why don't they have a handrail? (*Panting.*) Wait till I get some air. (*Pause.*) Don't let me go! (*Miss Fitt hums her hymn. After a moment Mrs. Rooney joins in with the words.*) . . . the encircling gloo-oom (*Miss Fitt stops humming*) . . . tum tum me on. (*Forte.*) The night is dark and I am far from ho-ome, tum tum—

MISS FITT (*hysterically*). Stop it, Mrs. Rooney, stop it, or I'll drop you!

MRS. ROONEY. Wasn't it that they sung on the Lusitania? Or Rock of Ages? Most touching it must have been. Or was it the Titanic?

Attracted by the noise a group, including Mr. Tyler, Mr. Barrell and Tommy, gathers at top of steps.

MR. BARRELL. What the—

Silence.

MR. TYLER. Lovely day for the fixture.

Loud titter from Tommy cut short by Mr. Barrell with backhanded blow in the stomach. Appropriate noise from Tommy.

FEMALE VOICE (*shrill*). Oh look, Dolly, look!

DOLLY. What, Mamma?

FEMALE VOICE. They are stuck! (*Cackling laugh.*) They are stuck!

MRS. ROONEY. Now we are the laughing-stock of the twenty-six counties. Or is it thirty-six?

MR. TYLER. That is a nice way to treat your defenceless subordinates, Mr. Barrell, hitting them without warning in the pit of the stomach.

MISS FITT. Has anybody seen my mother?

MR. BARRELL. Who is that?

TOMMY. The dark Miss Fitt.

MR. BARRELL. Where is her face?

MRS. ROONEY. Now, deary, I am ready if you are. (*They toil up remaining steps.*) Stand back, you cads!

Shuffle of feet.

FEMALE VOICE. Mind yourself, Dolly!

MRS. ROONEY. Thank you, Miss Fitt, thank you, that will do, just prop me up against the wall like a roll of tarpaulin and that will be all, for the moment. (*Pause.*) I am sorry for all this ramdam, Miss Fitt, had I known you were looking for your mother I should not have importuned you, I know what it is.

MR. TYLER (*in marvelling aside*). Ramdam!

FEMALE VOICE. Come, Dolly darling, let us take up our stand before the first-class smokers. Give me your hand and hold me tight, one can be sucked under.

MR. TYLER. You have lost your mother, Miss Fitt?

MISS FITT. Good-morning, Mr. Tyler.

MR. TYLER. Good-morning, Miss Fitt.

MR. BARRELL. Good-morning, Miss Fitt.

MISS FITT. Good-morning, Mr. Barrell.

MR. TYLER. You have lost your mother, Miss Fitt?

MISS FITT. She said she would be on the last train.

MRS. ROONEY. Do not imagine, because I am silent, that I am not present, and alive, to all that is going on.

MR. TYLER (*to Miss Fitt*). When you say the last train—

MRS. ROONEY. Do not flatter yourselves for one moment, because I hold aloof, that my sufferings have ceased. No. The entire scene, the hills, the plain, the racecourse with its miles and miles of white rails and three red stands, the pretty little wayside station, even you yourselves, yes, I mean it, and over all the clouding blue, I see it all, I stand here and see it all with eyes . . . (*the voice breaks*) . . . through eyes . . . oh, if you had my eyes . . . you would understand . . . the things they have seen . . . and not looked away . . . this is nothing . . . nothing . . . what did I do with that handkerchief?

Pause.

MR. TYLER (*to Miss Fitt*). When you say the last train—(*Mrs. Rooney blows her nose violently and long*)—when you say the last train, Miss Fitt, I take it you mean the twelve thirty.

MISS FITT. What else could I mean, Mr. Tyler, what else could I *conceivably* mean?

MR. TYLER. Then you have no cause for anxiety, Miss Fitt, for the twelve thirty has not yet arrived. Look. (*Miss Fitt looks.*) No, up the line. (*Miss Fitt looks. Patiently.*) No, Miss Fitt, follow the direction of my index. (*Miss Fitt looks.*) There. You see now. The signal. At the bawdy hour of nine. (*In rueful afterthought.*) Or three alas! (*Mr. Barrell stifles a guffaw.*) Thank you, Mr. Barrell.

MISS FITT. But the time is now getting on for—

MR. TYLER (*patiently*). We all know, Miss Fitt, we all know only too well what the time is now getting on for, and yet the cruel fact remains that the twelve thirty has not yet arrived.

MISS FITT. Not an accident, I trust! (*Pause.*) Do not tell me she has left the track! (*Pause.*) Oh darling mother! With the fresh sole for lunch!

Loud titter from Tommy, checked as before by Mr. Barrell.

MR. BARRELL. That's enough old guff out of you. Nip up to the box now and see has Mr. Case anything for me.

Tommy goes.

MRS. ROONEY (*sadly*). Poor Dan!

MISS FITT (*in anguish*). What terrible thing has happened?

MR. TYLER. Now now, Miss Fitt, do not—

MRS. ROONEY (*with vehement sadness*). Poor Dan!

MR. TYLER. Now now, Miss Fitt, do not give way . . . to despair, all will come right . . . in the end. (*Aside to Mr. Barrell.*) What *is* the situation, Mr. Barrell? Not a collision surely?

MRS. ROONEY (*enthusiastically*). A collision! Oh that would be wonderful!

MISS FITT (*horrified*). A collision! I knew it!

MR. TYLER. Come, Miss Fitt, let us move a little up the platform.

MRS. ROONEY. Yes, let us all do that. (*Pause.*) No? (*Pause.*) You have changed your mind? (*Pause.*) I quite agree, we are better here, in the shadow of the waiting-room.

MR. BARRELL. Excuse me a moment.

MRS. ROONEY. Before you slink away, Mr. Barrell, please, a statement of some kind, I insist. Even the slowest train on this brief line is not ten minutes and more behind its scheduled time without good cause, one imagines. (*Pause.*) We all know your station is the best kept of the entire network, but there are times when that is not enough, just not enough. (*Pause.*) Now, Mr. Barrell, leave off chewing your whiskers, we are waiting to hear from you —we the unfortunate ticket-holders' nearest if not dearest.

Pause.

MR. TYLER (*reasonably*). I do think we are owed some kind of explanation, Mr. Barrell, if only to set our minds at rest.

MR. BARRELL. I know nothing. All I know is there has been a hitch. All traffic is retarded.

MRS. ROONEY (*derisively*). Retarded! A hitch! Ah these celibates! Here we are eating our hearts out with anxiety for our loved ones and he calls that a hitch! Those of us like myself with heart and kidney trouble may collapse at any moment and he calls that

a hitch! In our ovens the Saturday roast is
burning to a shrivel and he calls that—

MR. TYLER. Here comes Tommy, running! I
am glad I have been spared to see this.

TOMMY (*excitedly, in the distance*). She's coming.
(*Pause. Nearer.*) She's at the level-crossing!

*Immediately exaggerated station sounds. Fall-
ing signals. Bells. Whistles. Crescendo of
train whistle approaching. Sound of train
rushing through station.*

MRS. ROONEY (*above rush of train*). The up mail!
The up mail! (*The up mail recedes, the down
train approaches, enters the station, pulls up with
great hissing of steam and clashing of couplings.
Noise of passengers descending, doors banging,
Mr. Barrell shouting "Boghill! Boghill!," etc.
Piercingly.*) Dan!..Are you all right?..
Where is he?..Dan!..Did you see my
husband?..Dan!..(*Noise of station empty-
ing. Guard's whistle. Train departing, receding.
Silence.*) He isn't on it! The misery I have
endured, to get here, and he isn't on it!..
Mr. Barrell!..Was he not on it? (*Pause.*)
Is anything the matter, you look as if you
had seen a ghost. (*Pause.*) Tommy!..Did
you see the master?

TOMMY. He'll be along, Ma'am, Jerry is
minding him.

*Mr. Rooney suddenly appears on platform,
advancing on small boy Jerry's arm. He is
blind, thumps the ground with his stick and
pants incessantly.*

MRS. ROONEY. Oh, Dan! There you are! (*Her
dragging feet as she hastens towards him. She
reaches him. They halt.*) Where in the world
were you?

MR. ROONEY (*coolly*). Maddy.

MRS. ROONEY. Where were you all this time?

MR. ROONEY. In the men's.

MRS. ROONEY. Kiss me!

MR. ROONEY. Kiss you? In public? On the
platform? Before the boy? Have you taken
leave of your senses?

MRS. ROONEY. Jerry wouldn't mind. Would
you, Jerry?

JERRY. No, Ma'am.

MRS. ROONEY. How is your poor father?

JERRY. They took him away, Ma'am.

MRS. ROONEY. Then you are all alone?

JERRY. Yes, Ma'am.

MR. ROONEY. Why are you here? You did not
notify me.

MRS. ROONEY. I wanted to give you a surprise.
For your birthday.

MR. ROONEY. My birthday?

MRS. ROONEY. Don't you remember? I wished
you your happy returns in the bathroom.

MR. ROONEY. I did not hear you.

MRS. ROONEY. But I gave you a tie! You have
it on!

Pause.

MR. ROONEY. How old am I now?

MRS. ROONEY. Now never mind about that.
Come.

MR. ROONEY. Why did you not cancel the
boy? Now we shall have to give him a
penny.

MRS. ROONEY (*miserably*). I forgot! I had such
a time getting here! Such horrid nasty
people! (*Pause. Pleading.*) Be nice to me,
Dan, be nice to me today!

MR. ROONEY. Give the boy a penny.

MRS. ROONEY. Here are two halfpennies,
Jerry. Run along now and buy yourself a
nice gobstopper.

JERRY. Yes, Ma'am.

MR. ROONEY. Come for me on Monday, if I
am still alive.

JERRY. Yessir.

He runs off.

MR. ROONEY. We could have saved sixpence.
We have saved fivepence. (*Pause.*) But at
what cost?

*They move off along platform arm in arm.
Dragging feet, panting, thudding stick.*

MRS. ROONEY. Are you not well?

They halt, on Mr. Rooney's initiative.

MR. ROONEY. Once and for all, do not ask me to speak and move at the same time. I shall not say this in this life again.

They move off. Dragging feet, etc. They halt at top of steps.

MRS. ROONEY. Are you not—

MR. ROONEY. Let us get this precipice over.

MRS. ROONEY. Put your arm round me.

MR. ROONEY. Have you been drinking again? (*Pause.*) You are quivering like a blancmange. (*Pause.*) Are you in a condition to lead me? (*Pause.*) We shall fall into the ditch.

MRS. ROONEY. Oh, Dan! It will be like old times!

MR. ROONEY. Pull yourself together or I shall send Tommy for the cab. Then, instead of having saved sixpence, no, fivepence, we shall have lost . . . (*calculating mumble*) . . . two and three less six one and no plus one one and no plus three one and nine and one ten and three two and one . . . (*normal voice*) two and one, we shall be the poorer to the tune of two and one. (*Pause.*) Curse that sun, it has gone in. What is the day doing?

Wind.

MRS. ROONEY. Shrouding, shrouding, the best of it is past. (*Pause.*) Soon the first great drops will fall splashing in the dust.

MR. ROONEY. And yet the glass was firm. (*Pause.*) Let us hasten home and sit before the fire. We shall draw the blinds. You will read to me. I think Effie is going to commit adultery with the Major. (*Brief drag of feet.*) Wait! (*Feet cease. Stick tapping at steps.*) I have been up and down these steps five thousand times and still I do not know how many there are. When I think there are six there are four or five or seven or eight and when I remember there are five there are three or four or six or seven and when finally I realize there are seven there are five or six or eight or nine. Sometimes I wonder if they do not change them in the night. (*Pause. Irritably.*) Well? How many do you make them to-day?

MRS. ROONEY. Do not ask me to count, Dan, not now.

MR. ROONEY. Not count! One of the few satisfactions in life?

MRS. ROONEY. Not steps, Dan, please, I always get them wrong. Then you might fall on your wound and I would have that on my manure-heap on top of everything else. No, just cling to me and all will be well.

Confused noise of their descent. Panting, stumbling, ejaculations, curses. Silence.

MR. ROONEY. Well! That is what you call well!

MRS. ROONEY. We are down. And little the worse (*Silence. A donkey brays. Silence.*) That was a true donkey. Its father and mother were donkeys.

Silence.

MR. ROONEY. Do you know what it is, I think I shall retire.

MRS. ROONEY (*appalled*). Retire! And live at home? On your grant!

MR. ROONEY. Never tread these cursed steps again. Trudge this hellish road for the last time. Sit at home on the remnants of my bottom counting the hours—till the next meal. (*Pause.*) The very thought puts life in me! Forward, before it dies!

They move on. Dragging feet, panting, thudding stick.

MRS. ROONEY. Now mind, here is the path . . . Up! . . Well done! Now we are in safety and a straight run home.

MR. ROONEY (*without halting, between gasps*). A straight . . . run! . . She calls that . . . a straight . . . run! . .

MRS. ROONEY. Hush! do not speak as you go along, you know it is not good for your coronary. (*Dragging steps, etc.*) Just concentrate on putting one foot before the next or whatever the expression is. (*Dragging feet, etc.*) That is the way, now we are doing nicely. (*Dragging feet, etc. They suddenly halt, on Mrs. Rooney's initiative.*) Heavens! I knew there was something! With all the excitement! I forgot!

MR. ROONEY (*quietly*). Good God.

MRS. ROONEY. But you must know, Dan, of course, you were on it. What ever happened? Tell me!

MR. ROONEY. I have never known anything to happen.

MRS. ROONEY. But you must—

MR. ROONEY (*violently*). All this stopping and starting again is devilish, devilish! I get a little way on me and begin to be carried along when suddenly you stop dead! Two hundred pounds of unhealthy fat! What possessed you to come out at all? Let go of me!

MRS. ROONEY (*in great agitation*). No, I must know, we won't stir from here till you tell me. Fifteen minutes late! On a thirty minute run! It's unheard of!

MR. ROONEY. I know nothing. Let go of me before I shake you off.

MRS. ROONEY. But you must know! You were on it! Was it at the terminus? Did you leave on time? Or was it on the line? (*Pause.*) Did something happen on the line? (*Pause.*) Dan! (*Brokenly.*) Why won't you tell me!

Silence. They move off. Dragging feet, etc. They halt. Pause.

MR. ROONEY. Poor Maddy! (*Pause. Children's cries.*) What was that?

Pause for Mrs. Rooney to ascertain.

MRS. ROONEY. The Lynch twins jeering at us.

Cries.

MR. ROONEY. Will they pelt us with mud today, do you suppose?

Cries.

MRS. ROONEY. Let us turn and face them.

(*Cries. They turn. Silence.*) Threaten them with your stick. (*Silence.*) They have run away.

Pause.

MR. ROONEY. Did you ever wish to kill a child? (*Pause.*) Nip some young doom in the bud. (*Pause.*) Many a time at night, in winter, on the black road home, I nearly attacked the boy. (*Pause.*) Poor Jerry! (*Pause.*) What restrained me then? (*Pause.*) Not fear of man. (*Pause.*) Shall we go on backwards now a little?

MRS. ROONEY. Backwards?

MR. ROONEY. Yes. Or you forwards and I backwards. The perfect pair. Like Dante's damned, with their faces arsy-versy. Our tears will water our bottoms.

MRS. ROONEY. What is the matter, Dan? Are you not well?

MR. ROONEY. Well! Did you ever know me to be well? The day you met me I should have been in bed. The day you proposed to me the doctors gave me up. You knew that, did you not? The night you married me they came for me with an ambulance. You have not forgotten that, I suppose? (*Pause.*) No, I cannot be said to be well. But I am no worse. Indeed I am better than I was. The loss of my sight was a great fillip. If I could go deaf and dumb I think I might pant on to be a hundred. Or have I done so? (*Pause.*) Was I a hundred to-day? (*Pause.*) Am I a hundred, Maddy?

Silence.

MRS. ROONEY. All is still. No living soul in sight. There is no one to ask. The world is feeding. The wind—(*brief wind*)—scarcely stirs the leaves and the birds—(*brief chirp*) —are tired singing. The cows—(*brief moo*) —and sheep—(*brief baa*)—ruminate in silence. The dogs—(*brief bark*)—are hushed and the hens—(*brief cackle*)—sprawl torpid in the dust. We are alone. There is no one to ask.

Silence.

MR. ROONEY (*clearing his throat, narrative tone*). We drew out on the tick of time, I can vouch for that. I was—

MRS. ROONEY. How can you vouch for it?

MR. ROONEY (*normal tone, angrily*). I can vouch for it, I tell you! Do you want my relation or don't you? (*Pause. Narrative tone.*) On the tick of time. I had the compartment to myself, as usual. At least I hope so, for I made no attempt to restrain myself. My mind—(*Normal tone.*) But why do we not sit down somewhere? Are we afraid we should never rise again?

MRS. ROONEY. Sit down on what?

MR. ROONEY. On a bench, for example.

MRS. ROONEY. There is no bench.

MR. ROONEY. Then on a bank, let us sink down upon a bank.

MRS. ROONEY. There is no bank.

MR. ROONEY. Then we cannot. (*Pause.*) I dream of other roads, in other lands. Of another home, another—(*he hesitates*)—another home. (*Pause.*) What was I trying to say?

MRS. ROONEY. Something about your mind.

MR. ROONEY (*startled*). My mind? Are you sure? (*Pause. Incredulous.*) My mind?.. (*Pause.*) Ah yes. (*Narrative tone.*) Alone in the compartment my mind began to work, as so often after office hours, on the way home, in the train, to the lilt of the bogeys. Your season-ticket, I said, costs you twelve pounds a year and you earn, on an average, seven and six a day, that is to say barely enough to keep you alive and twitching with the help of food, drink, tobacco and periodicals until you finally reach home and fall into bed. Add to this—or subtract from it—rent, stationery, various subscriptions, tramfares to and fro, light and heat, permits and licences, hairtrims and shaves, tips to escorts, upkeep of premises and appearances, and a thousand unspecifiable sundries, and it is clear that by lying at home in bed, day and night, winter and summer, with a change of pyjamas once a fortnight, you would add very considerably to your income. Business, I said—(*A cry. Pause. Again. Normal tone.*) Did I hear a cry?

MRS. ROONEY. Mrs. Tully, I fancy. Her poor husband is in constant pain and beats her unmercifully.

Silence.

MR. ROONEY. That was a short knock. (*Pause.*) What was I trying to get at?

MRS. ROONEY. Business.

MR. ROONEY. Ah yes, business. (*Narrative tone.*) Business, old man, I said, retire from business, it has retired from you. (*Normal tone.*) One has these moments of lucidity.

MRS. ROONEY. I feel very cold and weak.

MR. ROONEY (*narrative tone*). On the other hand, I said, there are the horrors of home life, the dusting, sweeping, airing, scrubbing, waxing, waning, washing, mangling, drying, mowing, clipping, raking, rolling, scuffling, shovelling, grinding, tearing, pounding, banging and slamming. And the brats, the happy little hearty little howling neighbours' brats. Of all this and much more the week-end, the Saturday intermission and then the day of rest, have given you some idea. But what must it be like on a working-day? A Wednesday? A Friday! What must it be like on a Friday! And I fell to thinking of my silent, backstreet, basement office, with its obliterated plate, rest-couch and velvet hangings, and what it means to be buried there alive, if only from ten to five, with convenient to the one hand a bottle of light pale ale and to the other a long ice-cold fillet of hake. Nothing, I said, not even fully certified death, can ever take the place of that. It was then I noticed we were at a standstill. (*Pause. Normal tone. Irritably.*) Why are you hanging out of me like that? Have you swooned away?

MRS. ROONEY. I feel very cold and faint. The wind—(*whistling wind*)—is whistling through my summer frock as if I had nothing on over my bloomers. I have had no solid food since my elevenses.

MR. ROONEY. You have ceased to care. I speak —and you listen to the wind.

MRS. ROONEY. No no, I am agog, tell me all,

then we shall press on and never pause, never pause, till we come safe to haven.

Pause.

MR. ROONEY. Never pause . . . safe to haven . . . Do you know, Maddy, sometimes one would think you were struggling with a dead language.

MRS. ROONEY. Yes indeed, Dan, I know full well what you mean, I often have that feeling, it is unspeakably excruciating.

MR. ROONEY. I confess I have it sometimes myself, when I happen to overhear what I am saying.

MRS. ROONEY. Well, you know, it will be dead in time, just like our own poor dear Gaelic, there is that to be said.

Urgent baa.

MR. ROONEY (*startled*). Good God!

MRS. ROONEY. Oh, the pretty little woolly lamb, crying to suck its mother! Theirs has not changed, since Arcady.

Pause.

MR. ROONEY. Where was I in my composition?

MRS. ROONEY. At a standstill.

MR. ROONEY. Ah yes. (*Clears his throat. Narrative tone.*) I concluded naturally that we had entered a station and would soon be on our way again, and I sat on, without misgiving. Not a sound. Things are very dull to-day, I said, nobody getting down, nobody getting on. Then as time flew by and nothing happened I realized my error. We had not entered a station.

MRS. ROONEY. Did you not spring up and poke your head out of the window?

MR. ROONEY. What good would that have done me?

MRS. ROONEY. Why to call out to be told what was amiss.

MR. ROONEY. I did not care what was amiss. No, I just sat on, saying, If this train were never to move again I should not greatly mind. Then gradually a—how shall I say— a growing desire to—er—you know—

welled up within me. Nervous probably. In fact now I am sure. You know, the feeling of being confined.

MRS. ROONEY. Yes yes, I have been through that.

MR. ROONEY. If we sit here much longer, I said, I really do not know what I shall do. I got up and paced to and fro between the seats, like a caged beast.

MRS. ROONEY. That is a help sometimes.

MR. ROONEY. After what seemed an eternity we simply moved off. And the next thing was Barrell bawling the abhorred name. I got down and Jerry led me to the men's, or Fir as they call it now, from Vir Viris I suppose, the *V* becoming *F*, in accordance with Grimm's Law. (*Pause.*) The rest you know. (*Pause.*) You say nothing? (*Pause.*) Say something, Maddy. Say you believe me.

MRS. ROONEY. I remember once attending a lecture by one of these new mind doctors, I forget what you call them. He spoke—

MR. ROONEY. A lunatic specialist?

MRS. ROONEY. No no, just the troubled mind, I was hoping he might shed a little light on my lifelong preoccupation with horses' buttocks.

MR. ROONEY. A neurologist.

MRS. ROONEY. No no, just mental distress, the name will come back to me in the night. I remember his telling us the story of a little girl, very strange and unhappy in her ways, and how he treated her unsuccessfully over a period of years and was finally obliged to give up the case. He could find nothing wrong with her, he said. The only thing wrong with her as far as he could see was that she was dying. And she did in fact die, shortly after he washed his hands of her.

MR. ROONEY. Well? What is there so wonderful about that?

MRS. ROONEY. No, it was just something he said, and the way he said it, that have haunted me ever since.

MR. ROONEY. You lie awake at night, tossing to and fro and brooding on it.

MRS. ROONEY. On it and other . . . wretchedness. (*Pause.*) When he had done with the little girl he stood there motionless for some time, quite two minutes I should say, looking down at his table. Then he suddenly raised his head and exclaimed, as if he had a revelation, The trouble with her was she had never been really born! (*Pause.*) He spoke throughout without notes. (*Pause.*) I left before the end.

MR. ROONEY. Nothing about your buttocks? (*Mrs. Rooney weeps. In affectionate remonstrance.*) Maddy!

MRS. ROONEY. There is nothing to be done for those people!

MR. ROONEY. For which is there? (*Pause.*) That does not sound right somehow. (*Pause.*) What way am I facing?

MRS. ROONEY. What?

MR. ROONEY. I have forgotten what way I am facing.

MRS. ROONEY. You have turned aside and are bowed down over the ditch.

MR. ROONEY. There is a dead dog down there.

MRS. ROONEY. No no, just the rotting leaves.

MR. ROONEY. In June? Rotting leaves in June?

MRS. ROONEY. Yes dear, from last year, and from the year before last, and from the year before that again. (*Silence. Rainy wind. They move on. Dragging steps, etc.*) There is that lovely laburnum again. Poor thing, it is losing all its tassels. (*Dragging steps, etc.*) There are the first drops. (*Rain. Dragging feet, etc.*) Golden drizzle. (*Dragging steps, etc.*) Do not mind me, dear, I am just talking to myself. (*Rain heavier. Dragging steps, etc.*) Can hinnies procreate, I wonder.

They halt, on Mr. Rooney's initiative.

MR. ROONEY. Say that again.

MRS. ROONEY. Come on, dear, don't mind me, we are getting drenched.

MR. ROONEY (*forcibly*). Can what what?

MRS. ROONEY. Hinnies procreate. (*Silence.*) You know, hinnies, or is it jinnies, aren't they barren, or sterile, or whatever it is? (*Pause.*) It wasn't an ass's colt at all, you know, I asked the Regius Professor.

Pause.

MR. ROONEY. He should know.

MRS. ROONEY. Yes, it was a hinny, he rode into Jerusalem or wherever it was on a hinny. (*Pause.*) That must mean something. (*Pause.*) It's like the sparrows, than many of which we are of more value, they weren't sparrows at all.

MR. ROONEY. Than many of which . . . You exaggerate, Maddy.

MRS. ROONEY (*with emotion*). They weren't sparrows at all!

MR. ROONEY. Does that put our price up?

Silence. They move on. Wind and rain. Dragging feet, etc. They halt.

MRS. ROONEY. Do you want some dung? (*Silence. They move on. Wind and rain, etc. They halt.*) Why do you stop? Do you want to say something?

MR. ROONEY. No.

MRS. ROONEY. Then why do you stop?

MR. ROONEY. It is easier.

MRS. ROONEY. Are you very wet?

MR. ROONEY. To the buff.

MRS. ROONEY. The buff?

MR. ROONEY. The buff. From buffalo.

MRS. ROONEY. We shall hang up all our things in the hot-cupboard and get into our dressing-gowns. (*Pause.*) Put your arm round me. (*Pause.*) Be nice to me! (*Pause. Gratefully.*) Ah Dan! (*They move on. Wind and rain. Dragging feet, etc. Faintly same music as before. They halt. Music clearer. Silence but for music playing. Music dies.*) All day the same old record. All alone in that great empty house. She must be a very old woman now.

MR. RONNEY (*indistinctly*). Death and the Maiden.

Silence.

MRS. ROONEY. You are crying. (*Pause.*) Are you crying?

MR. ROONEY (*violently*). Yes! (*They move on. Wind and rain. Dragging feet, etc. They halt. They move on. Wind and rain. Dragging feet, etc. They halt.*) Who is the preacher tomorrow? The incumbent?

MRS. ROONEY. No.

MR. ROONEY. Thank God for that. Who?

MRS. ROONEY. Hardy.

MR. ROONEY. "How to be Happy though Married"?

MRS. ROONEY. No no, he died, you remember. No connexion.

MR. ROONEY. Has he announced the text?

MRS. ROONEY. "The Lord upholdeth all that fall and raiseth up all those that be bowed down." (*Silence. They join in wild laughter. They move on. Wind and rain. Dragging feet, etc.*) Hold me tighter, Dan! (*Pause.*) Oh yes!

They halt.

MR. ROONEY. I hear something behind us.

Pause.

MRS. ROONEY. It looks like Jerry. (*Pause.*) It is Jerry.

Sound of Jerry's running steps approaching. He halts beside them, panting.

JERRY (*panting*). You dropped—

MRS. ROONEY. Take your time, my little man, you will burst a bloodvessel.

JERRY (*panting*). You dropped something, Sir, Mr. Barrell told me to run after you.

MRS. ROONEY. Show. (*She takes the object.*) What is it? (*She examines it.*) What is this thing, Dan?

MR. ROONEY. Perhaps it is not mine at all.

JERRY. Mr. Barrell said it was, Sir.

MRS. ROONEY. It looks like a kind of ball. And yet it is not a ball.

MR. ROONEY. Give it to me.

MRS. ROONEY (*giving it*). What *is* it, Dan?

MR. ROONEY. It is a thing I carry about with me.

MRS. ROONEY. Yes, but what—

MR. ROONEY (*violently*). It is a thing I carry about with me!

Silence. Mrs. Rooney looks for a penny.

MRS. ROONEY. I have no small money. Have you?

MR. ROONEY. I have none of any kind.

MRS. ROONEY. We are out of change, Jerry. Remind Mr. Rooney on Monday and he will give you a penny for your pains.

JERRY. Yes, Ma'am.

MR. ROONEY. If I am alive.

JERRY. Yessir.

Jerry starts running back towards the station.

MRS. ROONEY. Jerry! (*Jerry halts.*) Did you hear what the hitch was? (*Pause.*) Did you hear what kept the train so late?

MR. ROONEY. How would he have heard? Come on.

MRS. ROONEY. What was it, Jerry?

JERRY. It was a—

MR. ROONEY. Leave the boy alone, he knows nothing! Come on!

MRS. ROONEY. What was it, Jerry?

JERRY. It was a little child, Ma'am.

Mr. Rooney groans.

MRS. ROONEY. What do you mean, it was a litle child?

JERRY. It was a little child fell out of the carriage. On to the line, Ma'am. (*Pause.*) Under the wheels, Ma'am.

Silence. Jerry runs off. His steps die away. Tempest of wind and rain. It abates. They move on. Dragging steps, etc. They halt. Tempest of wind and rain.

A GLOSSARY FOR ALL THAT FALL
Joan Bogar

Beckett's *All That Fall* is a play written for the radio; as Hugh Kenner points out, an essential fact about this medium is that there is nothing to see. There is no stage, no speaker, to reassure us of the continued existence of place and person; there is only sound coming out of silence, existing for a moment, then fading back into silence again, leaving nothing to confirm the impression that the

Reprinted by permission of the author.

source of the sound continues to exist. Thus when Maddy, irrepressibly alive in spite of her "sorrow and pining and gentility and church-going and fat and rheumatism and childlessness," states, after a few moments of silence, "Do not imagine, because I am silent, that I am not present, and alive, to all that is going on," it is not only an assertion of her own personality and existence, but also, as Kenner notes, a statement about the nature of the play itself, in which what is unheard appears to have no existence.[1]

This is not to say, however, that what we do not hear is not important. The silences and pauses, of which the reader who does not actually hear the play performed must be particularly aware, may be as crucial as the words and sounds themselves. What is not said—the responses not given, the questions not answered—may be as important as any statement. The pauses and silences, however, are not the only unheard messages; the various allusions in the play are also a source of unspoken information. The reader who comes to the play with an understanding of these references will come away with a fuller experience of its complex pattern and texture. The following glossary explains allusions in the order in which they occur in the text.

All That Fall: from Psalm 145:14, "The Lord upholdeth all that fall, and raiseth up all those that be bowed down." The verse from which the title is taken, the only complete Biblical reference given in the play, is not quoted in full until the play is almost over. We do, however, hear echoes of it earlier. Miss Fitt finds Maddy looking "bowed and bent," and Dan later finds himself actually "bowed down over the ditch." The ubiquitous sound of Maddy's dragging feet and the thud of Dan's stick remind us quite literally of the imminent danger of falling. And throughout the play we have seen that, in a world where support is often

needed, whatever lifting and upholding we can visualize is provided by other mortals at least potentially as helpless as those they support: like Maddy, just recovered from a long illness and barely able to guide her blind husband home, upholding is often a case of the halt leading the blind. Nor is help always given graciously. Although Mr. Slocum, Maddy's old admirer, willingly offers her a "lift," Maddy must threaten to "shout down the parish" before Miss Fitt can be persuaded to help her up the stairs, and the boy who usually guides Dan home must be paid for his services. It is not surprising, then, that when the complete Biblical quotation is given as the text for the next day's sermon, Dan and Maddy "join in wild laughter."

Death and the Maiden: a poem by Claudius, set to music by Franz Schubert. The music comes from a lonely old woman's "ruinous old house," which Maddy must pass on her way to and from the station. We hear it shortly after the play opens, before we hear any human voice, and again near the close of the play when Maddy and Dan are returning home. It links the end of the play with the beginning and reminds us that the journey has been a movement forwards and then back again, a "repetition in retrograde," as Louise Cleveland calls it.[2] Like the Biblical text from which the play's title comes, the song is not positively identified until almost the end of the play, when Dan mumbles its title.

The words of the song, not quoted in the play, are spoken by both the Maiden and Death, the Maiden speaking first. Having recognized Death, she protests his coming for her:

> Forbear me, ah, forbear me,
> Thou bony man so wan!
> I yet am young, oh spare me!
> I pray thee, now begone,
> I pray thee, now begone!

[1]Hugh Kenner, *Samuel Beckett: A Critical Study* (Berkeley and Los Angeles: University of California Press, 1968), pp. 167–69.

[2]Louise O. Cleveland, "Trials in the Soundscape: The Radio Plays of Samuel Beckett," *Modern Drama,* XI (December 1968), p. 271.

Death replies, in the soothing accents of a lover:

> Give me thy hand, thou fair and tender maid,
> Thy friend am I, nor will I harm thee;
> I am not wild; be not afraid!
> Sweet sleep within my arms shall charm thee.

There is no further reply from the Maiden, whom Death will win in time. The music suggests a major theme of the play before a word is spoken, for, like the very sounds which make up the play itself, human life is transient: maidens die and old people degenerate. No one is exempt from the ravages of time and no place is safe: as Maddy remarks to Mr. Slocum, everyone is going in the same direction, and as she says to Mr. Tyler, "It is suicide to be abroad," but to remain at home is "a lingering dissolution." We hear of the ailments of a number of people: Christy's mother and daughter, Mr. Tyler's daughter, Mr. Slocum's mother, and Maddy herself. However, it is not the old, as we would expect, but the young who are dying: the Maiden of the song, Maddy's daughter, the child who falls under the train wheels, and the young girl whom the mind doctor could not save because "she had never been really born." Death before birth, in a very literal sense, is a crucial motif in the play—the young die before procreating, and only the old, who can no longer reproduce, remain.

hinny: the offspring of a stallion and a female donkey, similar to the mule, which is the offspring of a male donkey and a horse mare. Both animals are sterile hybrids, thus the answer to the question Maddy ponders, "Can a hinny procreate, I wonder?" is of course "No." The hinny which Christy is driving might just as appropriately have been a donkey, a common and inexpensive work animal still used in Ireland today, but it is the hinny Beckett chooses, for it introduces another important motif in the play—sterility. Although there are some images of successful procreation in the animal world, the possibility of reproduction is not realized by any of the women in the play except for the prostitute on the station platform, who is apparently training her daughter, Dolly, to follow the same profession. Maddy's only child, little Minnie, apparently died young, and even if she were alive, Maddy notes, she would be "getting ready for the change" (menopause), thus becoming barren. Mr. Tyler, we learn, is to be forever grandchildless, since his daughter has just had a hysterectomy. It is a hen, not a rooster, that is killed by Mr. Slocum's car; as Maddy points out, "All the laying and the hatching" is over. Miss Fitt, who is still of childbearing age, is concerned not with having a child but with caring for her aged mother. Like the hinny, nearly all of the women in *All That Fall* are somehow incapable of reproduction; their chance for the only kind of immortality of which we can be certain—children—has been lost. They and their line, like their voices, will be obliterated in time.

ringdoves (Venus birds): closely related to the turtle doves of legend and literature; like them (and all doves) monogamous, thus a symbol of connubial love and constancy. In Greek mythology the dove is sacred to Venus and is often depicted drawing her chariot. Its prolific breeding ability and its conspicuous courtship ritual, of which the cooing is an important part, may also account for its association with the goddess of sexual love. The dove has other associations as well— peace, purity, the Holy Spirit, even death and mourning—but it is the courtship and mating ritual, signified by the cooing, which Maddy notices, imagining the birds "billing in the woods all the long summer long." The image reflects her own carnal desires for "a little love, daily, twice daily, fifty years of twice daily love like a Paris horse-butcher's regular." She would like to fall into the ditch with Dan and to allow Mr. Tyler to unlace her "cursed corset" behind the hedge. The scene in which she is hoisted up into Mr. Slocum's car is the broadest of sexual innuendo—Louise Cleveland calls it "a *tour de force* in audial pornography."[3]

amid th'encircling gloom: words from the first line of a poem by John Henry Cardinal Newman, which, when set to music by John B. Dyke, became a well-known hymn. Significantly, the first words of the line, which also comprise the title of the hymn, "Lead, Kindly Light," are omitted. The first verse of the hymn is as follows:

> Lead, kindly light, amid th'encircling gloom,
> Lead Thou me on!
> The night is dark, and I am far from home;
> Lead Thou me on!
> Keep Thou my feet, I do not ask to see
> The distant scene; one step enough for me.

Maddy wonders if it was this hymn or "Rock of Ages" which the passengers of the *Lusitania* or perhaps the *Titanic*, she cannot remember which, sang when the ship was sinking. She is certain of neither the identity of the ship nor the name of the hymn, but in any case singing a hymn did not prevent the passengers from drowning. Maddy articulates only fragments of the hymn, omitting all references to the "kindly light" which might lead man safely to some eternal home; what she remembers of it is only what her experience supports, "th'encircling gloom" which surrounds her. It is she who leads her blind husband home from the station; to the best of our knowledge she and the boy are the only guides he has. The fragments of a once effectual creed, represented by the fragments of a great old hymn, can no longer provide her comfort, safety, or certain knowledge of her eventual destiny.

arsy-versy: a reference to Dante's *Inferno*, Canto XX. Dante and his guide Vergil see the sorcerers and diviners of classical mythology, doomed forever to walk backwards

because their heads are twisted about upon their bodies and they can only see behind them. As they weep for their fate, their tears run down the clefts of their buttocks. This is their punishment for trying to see "the distant scene," that is, for predicting the future. As Vergil says of one of the seers, Amphiarus of Argos:

> Mark how the shoulders now his bosom make.
> Because he wished too far before to see
> He looks behind and ever goeth back. (11. 37–39)

This reversal of anatomical features is an image of the impossibility of distinguishing forwards from backwards. Like Dan's suggestion that they "go on backwards now a little," the image raises doubts about the progress of forward motion. Dan's reference to himself and Maddy as "the perfect pair" may be an allusion to an image in Plato's *Symposium* of the two sexes originally existing in one being with two faces, four arms, and four feet, so that when one went backwards the other went forwards. This is another image suggesting that the idea of progress is deceptive. Also, the movement of the play itself is merely a back and forth motion, from home to the station and then back again. If there is no destination but death, direction does not matter: one might as well go backwards as forwards. Similarly, making choices becomes pointless, since whatever action man takes will lead him to the same end. Dan considers retirement, but cannot decide which is worse, the arduous journey to and from his office, with its "cursed steps" and "hellish road," or the "horrors of home life," the "dusting, sweeping, airing, scrubbing, waxing," which merge into destructive images of "grinding, tearing, pounding, banging, and slamming." Dan is invigorated by the reduction of his faculties instead of being further debilitated, because losing his eyesight reduces the number of choices he must make.

[3]Cleveland, "Trials in the Soundscape," p. 273.

relation-composition: Dan's own terms for his explanation of the events of the train trip, which he relates in a "narrative tone" as if it were a speech prepared for the occasion rather than an answer to a question. The most important event in the narrative as he tells it is his growing need to urinate; if he knew the cause of the delay or was responsible for it he gives no indication. He is like an artist whose creation may include or eliminate whatever he wishes: as Hugh Kenner points out, "We can only know what Mr. Rooney chooses to tell us, which may in turn be the fiction he chooses to entertain himself with . . ."[4] Maddy does not reply to his passionate plea, "Say you believe me," with any direct answer, for the response to a composition, or a work of art, is not a matter of belief or disbelief. She responds instead with a narrative of her own which appears to be about an entirely different enigma, the child who died without ever having been really born. Both compositions are concerned with the mystery of a child's death, but whether Dan knows that the train was delayed because a child fell under the wheels or whether he was in any way responsible for the child's death is an enigma also.

sparrows: from the Biblical texts Matthew 10:29–31 and Luke 12:6–7, in which Jesus, preaching to the multitude, assures them that each person is of great value in the eyes of God, who notes the fall of even a sparrow. He tells the crowd, "Fear ye not, therefore, ye are of more value than many sparrows" (Matt. 10:31). In attempting to recall the passage Maddy tangles the syntax so that the message is distorted, and man seems to be of more value than only certain of the sparrows. Maddy's concern about whether the birds were actually sparrows is like her concern about whether the animal Christ rode into Jerusalem was really a hinny rather than an ass's colt. As Dan's remark implies, these are not the important questions, and in his opinion being able to prove that they are not sparrows would not "put our price up."

[4]Kenner, *Samuel Beckett*, p. 173.

Grimm's Law: a theory formulated by Jacob Grimm to explain changes in consonant sounds which took place in the proto-Germanic language that was the ancestor of English, also known as the first Germanic consonant shift. The essential change, which took place in stages over a long period of time, was from voiced to voiceless consonants; three voiced stops, the Indo-European bh, dh, and gh, were eventually lost from the language.

It is characteristic of Dan that when he speaks of language he speaks of laws and rules, which, like the mathematical computation that he finds "one of the few satisfactions in life," appear to provide some certainty. Ironically, however, Dan is in error about Grimm's law; it is not the v but the p which became f. Not only does he fail to recall accurately the laws of language, but his computational ability also fails him: he cannot determine his own age and, what is of more practical importance, cannot arrive at an accurate count of the number of stairs to the station platform. Because of human error, even mathematics fails to produce accurate answers. It is also appropriate that Dan should refer to a linguistic change from voiced to voiceless sounds, a sequence in which the next logical step is to silence. Because man's ability to express complex ideas through language is pointless if there is nothing certain to express, all languages, like "our poor dear Gaelic," might as well dwindle into silence.

a little child: occurs in several well-known Biblical passages, particularly Isaiah 11: 6–9 and in the Gospels, Matthew 11: 1–6 and Luke 18:16–17. The Isaiah allusion is an ironic comment upon the possible circumstances of the child's death. It predicts Jesus' coming and anticipates an earthly paradise in which man and nature will live in harmony and there will even be peace between beasts which are natural enemies: "The wolf also shall dwell with the lamb and the leopard shall lie down with the kid . . . and a little child shall lead them" (Isaiah 11: 6). In the Gospel passages Jesus calls a little child to him to demonstrate to his disciples that only those who "become as little children" (Matt. 18:3), that is, humble, innocent, and trusting, shall enter the kingdom of heaven. The Matthew passage continues:

> But whoso shall offend one of these little ones which believe in me, it were better for him that a millstone were hanged about his neck, and that he were drowned in the depth of the sea.
> (Matt. 18:6)

There are clues which point to Dan as someone who has "offended" a little child: he confesses that he has often wanted to "nip some young doom in the bud," he pleads for Maddy to believe his "relation," and the object "like a ball" which Jerry returns to him may be evidence that the child who fell from the train had been in his compartment. But none of these clues provide certain evidence of Dan's connection with or even his knowledge of the child's fall under the train wheels. Dan may have simply sat by listening to the child enter the compartment and open the exterior door without attempting to prevent him from falling. Or, since Dan is blind and the train in motion would have been noisy, the child could have entered Dan's compartment from the aisle, opened the outside door, and fallen without Dan's noticing. It is also quite possible that the child was never in Dan's compartment at all. Furthermore, we do not know that the object which resembles a ball either belonged to the child or has ever been in Dan's possession, although Dan does say that it is something he carries about with him. Nor do we know exactly what this object is: Maddy says, "It looks like a kind of ball. And yet it is not a ball." The evidence is inconclusive, and this ambiguity is deliberate. Because we can see nothing for ourselves in this radio play, and Dan, the only possible witness, is blind, we know only that a child fell under the wheels and delayed the train. We learn this fact only at the close of the play, and not even the usually loquacious Maddy can find words to cope with it. Factual questions, like metaphysical questions, are presented enigmatically, left unresolved, and followed by silence.

THE IRONIC CON GAME

MOTHER COURAGE AND HER CHILDREN

Bertolt Brecht

English Version by Eric Bentley

CHARACTERS

MOTHER COURAGE

KATTRIN, her dumb daughter

EILIF, her elder son

SWISS CHEESE, her younger son

RECRUITING OFFICER

SERGEANT

COOK

SWEDISH COMMANDER

CHAPLAIN

ORDNANCE OFFICER

YVETTE POTTIER

MAN WITH THE BANDAGE

ANOTHER SERGEANT

OLD COLONEL

CLERK

YOUNG SOLDIER

OLDER SOLDIER

PEASANT
PEASANT WOMAN
YOUNG MAN
OLD MAN
ANOTHER PEASANT
ANOTHER PEASANT WOMAN
YOUNG PEASANT
LIEUTENANT
VOICE

1

Spring, 1624. In Dalarna, the Swedish Commander Oxenstierna is recruiting for the campaign in Poland. The canteen woman Anna Fierling, commonly known as Mother Courage, loses a son.

Highway outside a town. A SERGEANT *and a* RECRUITING OFFICER *stand shivering.*

RECRUITING OFFICER. How the hell can you line up a squadron in a place like this? You know what I keep thinking about, Sergeant? Suicide. I'm supposed to knock four platoons together by the twelfth—four platoons the Chief's asking for! And they're so friendly around here, I'm scared to go to sleep at night. Suppose I do get my hands on some character and squint at him so I don't notice he's pigeon-chested and has varicose veins. I get him drunk and relaxed, he signs on the dotted line. I pay for the drinks, he steps outside for a minute, I have a hunch I should follow him to the door, and am I right? Off he's shot like a louse from a scratch. You can't take a man's word any more, Sergeant. There's no loyalty left in the world, no trust, no faith, no sense of honor. I'm losing my confidence in mankind, Sergeant.

SERGEANT. What they could use around here is a good war. What else can you expect with peace running wild all over the place? You know what the trouble with peace is? No organization. And when do you get organization? In a war. Peace is one big

waste of equipment. Anything goes, no one gives a damn. See the way they eat? Cheese on pumpernickel, bacon on the cheese? Disgusting! How many horses have they got in this town? How many young men? Nobody knows! They haven't bothered to count 'em! That's peace for you! I've been in places where they haven't had a war for seventy years and you know what? The people haven't even been given names! They don't know who they are! It takes a war to fix that. In a war, everyone registers, everyone's name's on a list. Their shoes are stacked, their corn's in the bag, you count it all up—cattle, men, *et cetera*—and you take it away! That's the story: no organization, no war!

RECRUITING OFFICER. It's the God's truth.

SERGEANT. Of course, a war's like any good deal: hard to get going. But when it does get moving, it's a pisser, and they're all scared of peace, like a dice player who can't stop—'cause when peace comes they have to pay up. Of course, *until* it gets going, they're just as scared of war, it's such a novelty!

RECRUITING OFFICER. Hey, look, here's a canteen wagon. Two women and a couple of fellows. Stop the old lady, Sergeant. And if there's nothing doing this time, you won't catch me freezing my ass in the April wind any longer.

A harmonica is heard. A canteen wagon rolls on, drawn by two young fellows. MOTHER COURAGE *is sitting on it with her dumb daughter,* KATTRIN.

MOTHER COURAGE. A good day to you, Sergeant!

SERGEANT (*barring the way*). Good day to *you!* Who d'you think *you* are?

MOTHER COURAGE. Tradespeople.

She sings.

Stop all the troops: here's Mother Courage!
Hey, Captain, let them come and buy!
For they can get from Mother Courage

Boots they will march in till they die!
Your marching men do not adore you
(Packs on their backs, lice in their hair)
But it's to death they're marching for you
And so they need good boots to wear!
    Christians, awake! Winter is gone!
    The snows depart! Dead men sleep on!
    Let all of you who still survive
    Get out of bed and look alive!

Your men will walk till they are dead, sir,
But cannot fight unless they eat.
The blood they spill for you is red, sir,
What fires that blood is my red meat.
Cannon is rough on empty bellies:
First with my meat they should be crammed.
Then let them go and find where hell is
And give my greetings to the damned!
    Christians, awake! Winter is gone!
    The snows depart! Dead men sleep on!
    Let all of you who still survive
    Get out of bed and look alive!

SERGEANT. Halt! Where are you from, riff-raff?

EILIF. Second Finnish Regiment!

SERGEANT. Where are your papers?

MOTHER COURAGE. Papers?

SWISS CHEESE. But this is Mother Courage!

SERGEANT. Never heard of her. Where'd she get a name like that?

MOTHER COURAGE. They call me Mother Courage 'cause I was afraid I'd be ruined, so I drove through the bombardment of Riga like a madwoman, with fifty loaves of bread in my cart. They were going moldy, what else could I do?

SERGEANT. No funny business! Where are your papers?

MOTHER COURAGE (*rummaging among papers in a tin box and clambering down from her wagon*). Here, Sergeant! Here's a missal—I got it in Altötting to wrap my cucumbers in. Here's a map of Moravia—God knows if I'll ever get there—the birds can have it if I don't. And here's a document saying my horse hasn't got hoof and mouth disease—pity he died on us, he cost fifteen guilders,

thank God I didn't pay it. Is that enough paper?

SERGEANT. Are you pulling my leg? Well, you've got another guess coming. You need a license and you know it.

MOTHER COURAGE. Show a little respect for a lady and don't go telling these grown children of mine I'm pulling anything of yours. What would I want with you? My license in the Second Protestant Regiment is an honest face. If *you* wouldn't know how to read it, that's not my fault, I want no rubber stamp on it anyhow.

RECRUITING OFFICER. Sergeant, we have a case of insubordination on our hands. Do you know what we need in the army? Discipline!

MOTHER COURAGE. I was going to say sausages.

SERGEANT. Name?

MOTHER COURAGE. Anna Fierling.

SERGEANT. So you're all Fierlings.

MOTHER COURAGE. I was talking about me.

SERGEANT. And I was talking about your children.

MOTHER COURAGE. Must they all have the same name? (*Pointing to the elder son.*) This fellow, for instance, I call him Eilif Noyocki. Why? He got the name from his father who told me he was called Koyocki. Or was it Moyocki? Anyhow, the lad remembers him to this day. Only the man he remembers is someone else, a Frenchman with a pointed beard. But he certainly has his father's brains—that man could whip the breeches off a farmer's backside before he could turn around. So we all have our own names.

SERGEANT. You're all called something different?

MOTHER COURAGE. Are you pretending you don't understand?

SERGEANT (*pointing at the younger son*). He's Chinese, I suppose.

MOTHER COURAGE. Wrong again. Swiss.

SERGEANT. After the Frenchman?

MOTHER COURAGE. Frenchman? What Frenchman? Don't confuse the issue, Sergeant, or we'll be here all day. He's Swiss, but he happens to be called Feyos, a name that has nothing to do with his father, who was called something else—a military engineer, if you please, and a drunkard.

SWISS CHEESE *nods, beaming; even* KATTRIN *smiles.*

SERGEANT. Then how come his name's Feyos?

MOTHER COURAGE. Oh, Sergeant, you have no imagination. *Of course* he's called Feyos: when he came, I was with a Hungarian. He didn't mind. He had a floating kidney, though he never touched a drop. He was a very *honest* man. The boy takes after him.

SERGEANT. But that wasn't his father!

MOTHER COURAGE. I said: he took after him. I call him Swiss Cheese. Why? Because he's good at pulling wagons. (*Pointing to her daughter.*) And that is Kattrin Haupt, she's half German.

SERGEANT. A nice family, I must say!

MOTHER COURAGE. And we've seen the whole wide world together—this wagonload and me.

SERGEANT. We'll need all that in writing. (*He writes.*) You're from Bamberg in Bavaria. What are you doing *here?*

MOTHER COURAGE. I can't wait till the war is good enough to come to Bamberg.

RECRUITING OFFICER. And you two oxen pull the cart. Jacob Ox and Esau Ox! D'you ever get out of harness?

EILIF. Mother! May I smack him in the puss? I'd like to.

MOTHER COURAGE. I'd like *you* to stay where you are. And now, gentlemen, what about a brace of pistols? Or a belt? Sergeant? Yours is worn clean through.

SERGEANT. It's something else *I'm* looking for. These lads of yours are straight as birch trees, strong limbs, massive chests. . . . What are such fine specimens doing out of the army?

MOTHER COURAGE (*quickly*). A soldier's life is not for sons of mine!

RECRUITING OFFICER. Why not? It means money. It means fame. Peddling shoes is

woman's work. (*To* EILIF.) Step this way and let's see if that's muscle or chicken fat.

MOTHER COURAGE. It's chicken fat. Give him a good hard look, and he'll fall right over.

RECRUITING OFFICER. Yes, and kill a calf in the falling! (*He tries to hustle* EILIF *away.*)

MOTHER COURAGE. Let him alone! He's not for you!

RECRUITING OFFICER. He called my face a puss. That is an insult. The two of us will now go and settle the affair on the field of honor.

EILIF. Don't worry, Mother, I can handle him.

MOTHER COURAGE. Stay here. You're never happy till you're in a fight. He has a knife in his boot and he knows how to use it.

RECRUITING OFFICER. I'll draw it out of him like a milk tooth. Come on, young fellow!

MOTHER COURAGE. Officer, I'll report you to the Colonel, and he'll throw you in jail. His lieutenant is courting my daughter.

SERGEANT. Go easy. (*To* MOTHER COURAGE.) What have you got against the service, wasn't his own father a soldier? Didn't you say he died a soldier's death?

MOTHER COURAGE. This one's just a baby. You'll lead him like a lamb to the slaughter. I know you, you'll get five guilders for him.

RECRUITING OFFICER (*to* EILIF). First thing you know, you'll have a lovely cap and high boots, how about it?

EILIF. Not from you.

MOTHER COURAGE. "Let's you and me go fishing," said the angler to the worm. (*To* SWISS CHEESE.) Run and tell everybody they're trying to steal your brother! (*She draws a knife.*) Yes, just you try, and I'll cut you down like dogs! We sell cloth, we sell ham, we are peaceful people!

SERGEANT. You're peaceful all right: your knife proves that. Why, you should be ashamed of yourself. Give me that knife, you hag! You admit you live off the war, what else *could* you live off? Now tell me, how can we have a war without soldiers?

MOTHER COURAGE. Do they have to be mine?

SERGEANT. So that's the trouble. The war

should swallow the peach stone and spit out the peach, hm? Your brood should get fat off the war, but the poor war must ask nothing in return, it can look after itself, can it? Call yourself Mother Courage and then get scared of the war, your bread-winner? Your sons aren't scared, I know that much.

EILIF. Takes more than a war to scare me.

SERGEANT. Correct! Take me. The soldier's life hasn't done *me* any harm, has it? I enlisted at seventeen.

MOTHER COURAGE. You haven't reached seventy.

SERGEANT. I will, though.

MOTHER COURAGE. Above ground?

SERGEANT. Are you trying to rile me, telling me I'll die?

MOTHER COURAGE. Suppose it's the truth? Suppose I see it's your fate? Suppose I *know* you're just a corpse on furlough?

SWISS CHEESE. She can look into the future. Everyone says so.

RECRUITING OFFICER. Then by all means look into the sergeant's future. It might amuse him.

SERGEANT. I don't believe in that stuff.

MOTHER COURAGE. Helmet!

The SERGEANT *gives her his helmet.*

SERGEANT. It means less than a crap in the grass. Anything for a laugh.

MOTHER COURAGE (*taking a sheet of parchment and tearing it in two*). Eilif, Swiss Cheese, Kattrin! So shall we all be torn in two if we let ourselves get too deep into this war! (*To the* SERGEANT.) I'll give you the bargain rate, and do it free. Watch! Death is black, so I draw a black cross.

SWISS CHEESE. And the other she leaves blank, see?

MOTHER COURAGE. I fold them, put them in the helmet, and mix 'em up together, the way we're all mixed up together from our mother's womb on. Now draw!

The SERGEANT *hesitates.*

RECRUITING OFFICER (*to* EILIF). I don't take just anybody. I'm choosy. And you've got guts, I like that.

SERGEANT (*fishing around in the helmet*). It's silly. Means as much as blowing your nose.

SWISS CHEESE. The black cross! Oh, his number's up!

RECRUITING OFFICER. Don't let them get under your skin. There aren't enough bullets to go around.

SERGEANT (*hoarsely*). You cheated me!

MOTHER COURAGE. You cheated yourself the day you enlisted. And now we must drive on. There isn't a war every day in the week, we must get to work.

SERGEANT. Hell, you're not getting away with this! We're taking that bastard of yours with *us!*

EILIF. I'd like that, Mother.

MOTHER COURAGE. Quiet—you Finnish devil, you!

EILIF. And Swiss Cheese wants to be a soldier, too.

MOTHER COURAGE. That's news to me. I see I'll have to draw lots for all three of you. (*She goes to the back to draw the crosses on bits of paper.*)

RECRUITING OFFICER (*to* EILIF). People've been saying the Swedish soldier is religious. That kind of loose talk has hurt us a lot. One verse of a hymn every Sunday—and then only if you have a voice . . .

MOTHER COURAGE (*returning with the slips and putting them in the* SERGEANT's *helmet*). So they'd desert their old mother, would they, the scoundrels? They take to war like a cat to cream. But I'll consult these slips, and they'll see the world's no promised land, with a "Join up, son, you're officer material!" Sergeant, I'm afraid for them, very afraid they won't get through this war. They have terrible qualities, all three. (*She holds the helmet out to* EILIF.) There. Draw your lot. (EILIF *fishes in the helmet, unfolds a slip. She snatches it from him.*) There you have it: a cross. Unhappy mother that I am, rich only in a mother's sorrows! He dies. In the springtime of his life, he must go. If he's a soldier, he must bite the dust, that's clear. He's too brave, like his father. And if he doesn't use his head, he'll go the way of all flesh, the slip proves it. (*Hectoring him.*) Will you use your head?

EILIF. Why not?

MOTHER COURAGE. It's using your head to stay with your mother. And when they make fun of you and call you a chicken, just laugh.

RECRUITING OFFICER. If you're going to wet your pants, I'll try your brother.

MOTHER COURAGE. I told you to laugh. Laugh! Now it's your turn, Swiss Cheese. You should be a better bet, you're honest. (*He fishes in the helmet.*) Why are you giving that slip such a funny look? You've drawn a blank for sure. It can't be there's a cross on it. It can't be I'm going to lose *you*. (*She takes the slip.*) A cross? Him too! Could it be 'cause he's so simple? Oh, Swiss Cheese, you'll be a goner too, if you aren't honest, honest, honest the whole time, the way I always brought you up to be, the way you always bring me all the change when you buy me a loaf. It's the only way you can save yourself. Look, Sergeant, if it isn't a black cross!

SERGEANT. It's a cross! I don't understand how *I* got one. I always stay well in the rear. (*To the* OFFICER.) But it can't be a trick: it gets *her* children too.

SWISS CHEESE. It gets me too. But I don't accept it!

MOTHER COURAGE (*to* KATTRIN). And now all I have left for certain is you, you're a cross in yourself, you have a good heart. (*She holds the helmet up high toward the wagon but takes the slip out herself.*) Oh, I could give up in despair! There must be some mistake, I didn't mix them right. Don't be too kind, Kattrin, just don't, there's a cross in your path too. Always be very quiet, it can't be hard, you can't speak. Well, so now you know, all of you: be careful, you'll need to be. Now let's climb on the wagon and move on. (*She returns the helmet to the* SERGEANT *and climbs on the wagon.*)

RECRUITING OFFICER (*to the* SERGEANT). Do something!

SERGEANT. I don't feel very well.

RECRUITING OFFICER. Maybe you caught a chill when you handed over your helmet in this wind. Get her involved in a business transaction! (*Aloud.*) That belt, Sergeant, you could at least take a look at it. These good people live by trade, don't they? Hey, all of you, the sergeant wants to buy the belt!

MOTHER COURAGE. Half a guilder. A belt like that is worth two guilders. (*She clambers down again from the wagon.*)

SERGEANT. It isn't new. But there's too much wind here. I'll go and look at it behind the wagon. (*He does so.*)

MOTHER COURAGE. I don't find it windy.

SERGEANT. Maybe it's worth half a guilder at that. There's silver on it.

MOTHER COURAGE (*following him behind the wagon*). A solid six ounces worth!

RECRUITING OFFICER (*to* EILIF). And we can have a drink, just us men. I'll advance you some money to cover it. Let's go.

EILIF *stands undecided.*

MOTHER COURAGE. Half a guilder, then.

SERGEANT. I don't understand it. I always stay in the rear. There's no safer spot for a sergeant to be. You can send the others on ahead in quest of fame. My appetite is ruined. I can tell you right now: I won't be able to get anything down.

MOTHER COURAGE. You shouldn't take on so, just because you can't eat. Just stay in the rear. Here, take a slug of brandy, man. (*She gives him brandy.*)

RECRUITING OFFICER (*taking* EILIF *by the arm and making off toward the back*). Ten guilders in advance and you're a soldier of the king and a stout fellow and the women will be mad about you. And you can give me a smack in the puss for insulting you.

Both leave.

Dumb KATTRIN *jumps down from the wagon and lets out harsh cries.*

MOTHER COURAGE. Coming, Kattrin, coming! The sergeant's just paying up. (*She bites the half guilder.*) I'm suspicious of all money, I've been badly burned, Sergeant. But this money's good. And now we'll be going. Where's Eilif?

SWISS CHEESE. Gone with the recruiting officer.

MOTHER COURAGE (*standing quite still, then*). Oh, you simpleton! (*To* KATTRIN.) You *can't* speak, I know. You are innocent.

SERGEANT. That's life. Take a slug yourself, Mother. Being a soldier isn't the worst that could happen. You want to live off war and keep you and yours out of it, do you?

MOTHER COURAGE. You must help your brother now, Kattrin.

Brother and sister get into harness together and pull the wagon. MOTHER COURAGE *walks at their side. The wagon gets under way.*

SERGEANT (*looking after them*).
When a war gives you all you earn
One day it may claim something in return!

2

In the years 1625 and 1626 Mother Courage journeys through Poland in the baggage train of the Swedish army. She meets her son again before the fortified town of Wallhof.—Of the successful sale of a capon and great days for the brave son.

Tent of the SWEDISH COMMANDER. *Kitchen next to it. Thunder of cannon. The* COOK *is quarreling with* MOTHER COURAGE, *who is trying to sell him a capon.*

COOK. Sixty hellers for that miserable bird?

MOTHER COURAGE. Miserable bird? This fat fowl? Your Commander is a glutton. Woe betide you if you've nothing for him to eat. This capon is worth sixty hellers to you.

COOK. They're ten hellers a dozen on every corner.

MOTHER COURAGE. A capon like this on every corner! With a siege going on and people all skin and bones? Maybe you can get a field rat! I said maybe. Because we're all out of *them* too. Don't you see the soldiers running five deep after one hungry little field rat? All right then, in a siege, my price for a giant capon is fifty hellers.

COOK. But we're not "in a siege," we're doing the besieging, it's the other side that's "in a siege," when will you get this into your head?

MOTHER COURAGE. A fat lot of difference that makes, *we* haven't got a thing to eat either. They took everything into the town with them before all this started, and now they've nothing to do but eat and drink, I hear. It's us I'm worried about. Look at the farmers around here, they haven't a thing.

COOK. Certainly they have. They hide it.

MOTHER COURAGE (*triumphant*). They have not! They're ruined, that's what. They're so hungry I've seen 'em digging up roots to eat. I could boil your leather belt and make their mouths water with it. That's how things are around here. And I'm expected to let a capon go for forty hellers!

COOK. Thirty. Not forty. I said thirty hellers.

MOTHER COURAGE. I say this is no ordinary capon. It was a talented animal, so I hear. It would only feed to music—one march in particular was its favorite. It was so intelligent it could count. Forty hellers is too much for all this? I know *your* problem: if you don't find something to eat and quick, the Chief will—cut—your—fat—head—off!

COOK. All right, just watch. (*He takes a piece of beef and lays his knife on it.*) Here's a piece of beef, I'm going to roast it. I give you one more chance.

MOTHER COURAGE. Roast it, go ahead, it's only one year old.

COOK. One *day* old! Yesterday it was a cow. I saw it running around.

MOTHER COURAGE. In that case it must have started stinking before it died.

COOK. I don't care if I have to cook it for five hours. We'll see if it's still hard after that. (*He cuts into it.*)

MOTHER COURAGE. Put plenty of pepper in, so the Commander won't smell the smell.

The SWEDISH COMMANDER, *a* CHAPLAIN, *and* EILIF *enter the tent.*

COMMANDER (*clapping* EILIF *on the shoulder*). In the Commander's tent with you, my son! Sit at my right hand, you happy warrior! You've played a hero's part, you've served the Lord in his own Holy War, *that's* the thing! And you'll get a gold bracelet out of it when we take the town if *I* have any say in the matter! We come to save their souls and what do they do, the filthy, shameless peasant pigs? Drive their cattle away from *us*, while they stuff their priests with beef at both ends! But you showed 'em. So here's a can of red wine for you, we'll drink together! (*They do so.*) The chaplain gets the dregs, he's pious. Now what would you like for dinner, my hearty?

EILIF. How about a slice of meat?

COOK. Nothing to eat, so he brings company to eat it!

MOTHER COURAGE *makes him stop talking; she wants to listen.*

EILIF. Tires you out, skinning peasants. Gives you an appetite.

MOTHER COURAGE. Dear God, it's my Eilif!

COOK. Who?

MOTHER COURAGE. My eldest. It's two years since I saw him, he was stolen from me in the street. He must be in high favor if the Commander's invited him to dinner. And what do you have to eat? Nothing. You hear what the Commander's guest wants? Meat! Better take my advice, buy the capon. The price is one guilder.

The COMMANDER *has sat down with* EILIF *and the* CHAPLAIN.

COMMANDER (*roaring*). Cook! Dinner, you pig, or I'll have your head!

COOK. This is blackmail. Give me the damn thing!

MOTHER COURAGE. A miserable bird like this?

COOK. You were right. Give it here. It's highway robbery, fifty hellers.

MOTHER COURAGE. I said one guilder. Nothing's too high for my eldest, the Commander's guest of honor.

COOK (*giving her the money*). Well, you might at least pluck it till I have a fire going.

MOTHER COURAGE (*sitting down to pluck the capon*). I can't wait to see his face when he sees me. This is my brave and clever son. I have a stupid one as well but he's honest. The daughter is nothing. At least, she doesn't talk: we must be thankful for small mercies.

COMMANDER. Have another can, my son, it's my favorite Falernian. There's only one cask left—two at the most—but it's worth it to meet a soldier that still believes in God! The shepherd of our flock here just looks on, he only preaches, he hasn't a clue how anything gets done. So now, Eilif, my son, give us the details: tell us how you fixed the peasants and grabbed the twenty bullocks. And let's hope they'll soon be here.

EILIF. In one day's time. Two at the most.

MOTHER COURAGE. Now that's considerate of Eilif—to bring the oxen tomorrow—otherwise my capon wouldn't have been so welcome today.

EILIF. Well, it was like this. I found out that the peasants had hidden their oxen and—on the sly and chiefly at night—had driven them into a certain wood. The people from the town were to pick them up there. I let them get their oxen in peace—they ought to know better than me where they are, I said to myself. Meanwhile I made my men crazy for meat. Their rations were short and I made sure they got shorter. Their mouths'd water at the sound of any word beginning with MEA . . . , like measles.

COMMANDER. Smart fella.

EILIF. Not bad. The rest was a snap. Only the

peasants had clubs and outnumbered us three to one and made a murderous attack on us. Four of them drove me into a clump of trees, knocked my good sword from my hand, and yelled, "Surrender!" What now, I said to myself, they'll make mincemeat of me.

COMMANDER. What did you do?

EILIF. I laughed.

COMMANDER. You what?

EILIF. I laughed. And so we got to talking. I came right down to business and said: "Twenty guilders an ox is too much, I bid fifteen." Like I wanted to buy. That foxed 'em. So while they were scratching their heads, I reached for my good sword and cut 'em to pieces. Necessity knows no law, huh?

COMMANDER. What do *you* say, shepherd of the flock?

CHAPLAIN. Strictly speaking, that saying is not in the Bible. Our Lord made five hundred loaves out of five so that no such necessity would arise. When he told men to love their neighbors, their bellies were full. Things have changed since his day.

COMMANDER (*laughing*). Things have changed! A swallow of wine for those wise words, you pharisee! (*To* EILIF.) You cut 'em to pieces in a good cause, our fellows were hungry and you gave 'em to eat. Doesn't it say in the Bible "Whatsoever thou doest for the least of these my children, thou doest for me?" And what *did* you do for 'em? You got 'em the best steak dinner they ever tasted. Moldy bread is not what they're used to. They always ate white bread, and drank wine in their helmets, before going out to fight for God.

EILIF. I reached for my good sword and cut 'em to pieces.

COMMANDER. You have the makings of a Julius Caesar, why, you should be presented to the King!

EILIF. I've seen him—from a distance of course. He seemed to shed a light all around. I must try to be like him!

COMMANDER. I think you're succeeding, my boy! Oh, Eilif, you don't know how I value

a brave soldier like you! I treat such a chap as my very own son. (*He takes him to the map.*) Take a look at our position, Eilif, it isn't all it might be, is it?

MOTHER COURAGE *has been listening and is now plucking angrily at her capon.*

MOTHER COURAGE. He must be a very bad Commander.

COOK. Just a gluttonous one. Why bad?

MOTHER COURAGE. Because he needs *brave* soldiers, that's why. If his plan of campaign was any good, why would he need *brave* soldiers, wouldn't plain, ordinary soldiers do? Whenever there are great virtues, it's a sure sign something's wrong.

COOK. You mean, it's a sure sign something's right.

MOTHER COURAGE. I mean what I say. Why? When a general or a king is stupid and leads his soldiers into a trap, they need this virtue of courage. When he's tightfisted and hasn't enough soldiers, the few he does have need the herosim of Hercules—another virtue. And if he's slovenly and doesn't give a damn about anything, they have to be as wise as serpents or they're finished. Loyalty's another virtue and you need plenty of it if the king's always asking too much of you. All virtues which a well-regulated country with a good king or a good general wouldn't need. In a good country virtues wouldn't be necessary. Everybody could be quite ordinary, middling, and, for all I care, cowards.

COMMANDER. I bet your father was a soldier.

EILIF. I've heard he was a great soldier. My mother warned me. I know a song about that.

COMMANDER. Sing it to us. (*Roaring.*) Bring that meat!

EILIF. It's called The Song of the Wise Woman and the Soldier.

He sings and at the same time does a war dance with his saber:

A shotgun will shoot and a jackknife will knife,

If you wade in the water, it will drown you,
Keep away from the ice, if you want my advice,
Said the wise woman to the soldier.

But that young soldier, he loaded his gun,
And he reached for his knife, and he started to run:
For marching never could hurt him!
From the north to the south he will march through the land
With his knife at his side and his gun in his hand:
That's what the soldiers told the wise woman.

Woe to him who defies the advice of the wise!
If you wade in the water, it will drown you!
Don't ignore what I say or you'll rue it one day,
Said the wise woman to the soldier.

But that young soldier, his knife at his side
And his gun in his hand, he steps into the tide:
For water never could hurt him!
When the new moon is shining on yonder church tower
We are all coming back: go and pray for that hour:
That's what the soldiers told the wise woman.

MOTHER COURAGE (*continues the song from her kitchen, beating on a pan with a spoon*).
Then the wise woman spoke: you will vanish like smoke
Leaving nothing but cold air behind you!
Just watch the smoke fly! Oh God, don't let him die!
Said the wise woman to the soldier.
EILIF. What's that?
MOTHER COURAGE (*singing on*).

And the lad who defied the wise woman's advice,
When the new moon shone, floated down with the ice:
He waded in the water and it drowned him.

The wise woman spoke, and they vanished like smoke,
And their glorious deeds did not warm us.
Your glorious deeds do not warm us!

COMMANDER. What a kitchen I've got! There's no end to the liberties they take!

EILIF *has entered the kitchen and embraced his mother.*

EILIF. To see you again! Where are the others?
MOTHER COURAGE (*in his arms*). Happy as ducks in a pond. Swiss Cheese is paymaster with the Second Regiment, so at least he isn't in the fighting. I couldn't keep him out altogether.
EILIF. Are your feet holding up?
MOTHER COURAGE. I've a bit of trouble getting my shoes on in the morning.

The COMMANDER *has come over.*

COMMANDER. So you're his mother! I hope you have more sons for me like this fellow.
EILIF. If I'm not the lucky one: to be feasted by the Commander while you sit listening in the kitchen!
MOTHER COURAGE. Yes. I heard all right. (*She gives him a box on the ear.*)
EILIF (*his hand on his cheek*). Because I took the oxen?
MOTHER COURAGE. No. Because you didn't surrender when the four peasants let fly at you and tried to make mincemeat of you! Didn't I teach you to take care of yourself? You Finnish devil, you!

The COMMANDER *and the* CHAPLAIN *stand laughing in the doorway.*

3

Three years pass and Mother Courage, with parts of a Finnish regiment, is taken prisoner. Her daughter is saved, her wagon likewise, but her honest son dies.

A camp. The regimental flag is flying from a pole. Afternoon. All sorts of wares hanging on the wagon. MOTHER COURAGE'*s clothesline is tied to the wagon at one end, to a cannon at the other. She and* KATTRIN *are folding the washing on the cannon. At the same time she is bargaining with an* ORD- NANCE OFFICER *over a bag of bullets.* SWISS CHEESE, *in paymaster's uniform now, looks on.* YVETTE POTTIER, *a very good-looking young person, is sewing at a colored hat, a glass of brandy before her. She is in stocking feet. Her red boots are near by.*

OFFICER. I'm letting you have the bullets for two guilders. Dirt cheap. 'Cause I need the money. The Colonel's been drinking with the officers for three days and we're out of liquor.

MOTHER COURAGE. They're army property. If they find 'em on me, I'll be court-martialed. You sell your bullets, you bastards, and send your men out to fight with nothing to shoot with.

OFFICER. Oh, come on, you scratch my back, and I'll scratch yours.

MOTHER COURAGE. I won't take army stuff. Not at *that* price.

OFFICER. You can resell 'em for five guilders, maybe eight, to the Ordnance Officer of the Fourth Regiment. All you have to do is give him a receipt for twelve. He hasn't a bullet left.

MOTHER COURAGE. Why don't you do it yourself?

OFFICER. I don't trust him. We're friends.

MOTHER COURAGE (*taking the bag*). Give it here. (*To* KATTRIN.) Take it around to the back and pay him a guilder and a half. (*As the* OFFICER *protests.*) I said a guilder and a half! (KATTRIN *drags the bag away. The*

OFFICER *follows.* MOTHER COURAGE *speaks to* SWISS CHEESE.) Here's your underwear back, take care of it; it's October now, autumn may come at any time; I purposely don't say it must come, I've learned from experience there's nothing that must come, not even the seasons. But your books *must* balance now you're the regimental paymaster. *Do* they balance?

SWISS CHEESE. Yes, Mother.

MOTHER COURAGE. Don't forget they made you paymaster because you're honest and so simple you'd never think of running off with the cash. Don't lose that underwear.

SWISS CHEESE. No, mother. I'll put it under the mattress. (*He starts to go.*)

OFFICER. I'll go with you, paymaster.

MOTHER COURAGE. Don't teach him any monkey business.

Without a good-by the OFFICER *leaves with* SWISS CHEESE.

YVETTE (*waving to him*). You might at least say good-by!

MOTHER COURAGE (*to* YVETTE). I don't like that. *He's* no sort of company for my Swiss Cheese. But the war's not making a bad start. Before all the different countries get into it, four or five years'll have gone by like nothing. If I look ahead and make no mistakes, business will be good. Don't you know you shouldn't drink in the morning with your illness?

YVETTE. Who says I'm ill? That's libel!

MOTHER COURAGE. They all say so.

YVETTE. They're all liars. I'm desperate, Mother Courage. They all avoid me like a stinking fish. Because of those lies. So what am I arranging my hat for? (*She throws it down.*) That's why I drink in the morning. I never used to, it gives you crow's feet. But what's the difference? Every man in the regiment knows me. I should have stayed at home when my first was unfaithful. But pride isn't for the likes of us, you eat dirt or down you go.

MOTHER COURAGE. Now don't you start again

with your friend Peter and how it all happened—in front of my innocent daughter.

YVETTE. She's the one that should hear it.
So she'll get hardened against love.

MOTHER COURAGE. That's something no one
ever gets hardened against.

YVETTE. I'll tell you about it, and get it off
my chest. I grew up in Flanders' fields,
that's where it starts, or I'd never even
have caught sight of him and I wouldn't
be here in Poland today. He was an army
cook, blond, a Dutchman, but thin. Kattrin, beware of thin men! I didn't. I
didn't even know he'd had another girl
before me and she called him Peter Piper
because he never took his pipe out of his
mouth the whole time, it meant so little to
him.

She sings "The Fraternization Song."

When I was almost seventeen
The foe came to our land
And laying aside his saber
He took me gently by the hand.

First came the May Day Rite
Then came the May Day night.
The pipes played and the drums did
    beat.
The foe paraded down the street.
And then with us they took their ease
And fraternized behind the trees.

Our foes they came in plenty.
A cook was my own foe.
I hated him by daylight
But in the dark I loved him so.

First comes the May Day Rite
Then comes the May Day night.
The pipes play and the drums do beat.
The foe parades down every street.
And then with us they take their ease
And fraternize behind the trees.

The heavens seemed to open
Such passion did I feel.
But my people never understood
The love I felt was real.

One day the sun rose slow
On all my pain and woe.
My loved one, with the other men,
Presented arms and stood at ease
Then marched away past all those
    trees
And never did come back again.

I made the mistake of running after him,
I never found him. It's five years ago now.
(*With swaying gait she goes behind the
wagon.*)

MOTHER COURAGE. You've left your hat.

YVETTE. For the birds.

MOTHER COURAGE. Let this be a lesson to you,
Kattrin, never start anything with a soldier. The heavens do seem to open, so
watch out! Even with men who're not in
the army life's no honeypot. He tells you
he'd like to kiss the ground under your
feet—did you wash 'em yesterday, while
we're on the subject?—and then if you
don't look out, your number's up, you're
his slave for life. Be glad you're dumb,
Kattrin: you'll never contradict yourself,
you'll never want to bite your tongue off
because you spoke out of turn. Dumbness
is a gift from God. Here comes the Commander's cook, what's bothering *him*?

Enter the COOK *and the* CHAPLAIN.

CHAPLAIN. I bring a message from your son
Eilif. The cook came with me. You've
made, ahem, an impression on him.

COOK. I thought I'd get a little whiff of the
balmy breeze.

MOTHER COURAGE. You're welcome to that if
you behave yourself, and even if you don't
I think I can handle you. But what does
Eilif want? I don't have any money.

CHAPLAIN. Actually, I have something to tell
his brother, the paymaster.

MOTHER COURAGE. He isn't here. And he isn't
anywhere else either. He's not his brother's
paymaster, and I won't have him led into
temptation. Let Eilif try it on with someone else! (*She takes money from the purse at her
belt.*) Give him this. It's a sin. He's speculat-

ing in mother love, he ought to be ashamed of himself.

COOK. Not for long. He has to go with his regiment now—to his death maybe. Send some more money, or you'll be sorry. You women are hard—and sorry afterward. A glass of brandy wouldn't cost very much, but you refuse to provide it, and six feet under goes your man and you can't dig him up again.

CHAPLAIN. All very touching, my dear cook, but to fall in this war is not a misfortune, it's a blessing. This is a war of religion. Not just any old war but a special one, a religious one, and therefore pleasing unto God.

COOK. Correct. In one sense it's a war because there's fleecing, bribing, plundering, not to mention a little raping, but it's different from all other wars because it's a war of religion. That's clear. All the same, it makes you thirsty.

CHAPLAIN (*to* MOTHER COURAGE, *pointing at the* COOK). I tried to hold him off but he said you'd bewitched him. He dreams about you.

COOK (*lighting a clay pipe*). Brandy from the fair hand of a lady, that's for me. And don't embarrass me any more: the stories the chaplain was telling me on the way over still have me blushing.

MOTHER COURAGE. A man of his cloth! I must get you both something to drink or you'll be making improper advances out of sheer boredom.

CHAPLAIN. That is indeed a temptation, said the court chaplain, and gave way to it. (*Turning toward* KATTRIN *as he walks.*) And who is this captivating young person?

MOTHER COURAGE. She's not a captivating young person, she's a respectable young person.

The CHAPLAIN *and the* COOK *go with* MOTHER COURAGE *behind the cart, and one hears them talk politics.*

MOTHER COURAGE. The trouble here in Poland is that the Poles *would* keep meddling. It's true our King moved in on them with man, beast, and wagon, but instead of keeping the peace the Poles attacked the Swedish King when he was in the act of peacefully withdrawing. So they were guilty of a breach of the peace and their blood is on their own heads.

CHAPLAIN. Anyway, our King was thinking of nothing but freedom. The Kaiser enslaved them all, Poles and Germans alike, so our King *had* to liberate them.

COOK. Just what *I* think. Your health! Your brandy is first-rate, I'm never mistaken in a face.

> KATTRIN *looks after them, leaves the washing, goes to the hat, picks it up, sits down, and takes up the red boots.*

And the war is a war of religion. (*Singing while* KATTRIN *puts the boots on.*) "A mighty fortress is our God . . ." (*He sings a verse or so of Luther's hymn.*) And talking of King Gustavus, this freedom he tried to bring to Germany cost him a pretty penny. Back in Sweden he had to levy a salt tax, the poorer folks didn't like it a bit. Then, too, he had to lock up the Germans and even cut their heads off, they clung so to slavery and their Kaiser. Of course, if no one had *wanted* to be free, the King would have got quite mad. First it was just Poland he tried to protect from bad men, especially the Kaiser, then his appetite grew with eating, and he ended up protecting Germany too. Now Germany put up a pretty decent fight. So the good King had nothing but worries in return for his outlay and his goodness, and of course he had to get his money back with taxes, which made bad blood, but he didn't shrink even from that. For he had one thing in his favor anyway, God's Holy Word, which was all to the good, because otherwise they could have said he did it for profit. That's how he kept his conscience clear. He always put conscience first.

MOTHER COURAGE. It's plain you're no Swede, or you'd speak differently of the Hero King.

CHAPLAIN. What's more, you eat his bread.

COOK. I don't eat his bread. I bake his bread.

MOTHER COURAGE. He's unbeatable. Why? His men believe in him. (*Earnestly.*) To hear the big fellows talk, they wage war from fear of God and for all things bright and beautiful, but just look into it, and you'll see they're not so silly: they want a good profit out of it, or else the little fellows like you and me wouldn't back'em up.

COOK. That's right.

CHAPLAIN. And as a Dutchman you'd do well to see which flag's flying here before you express an opinion!

MOTHER COURAGE. All good Protestants forever!

COOK. A health!

KATTRIN *has begun to strut about with* YVETTE'S *hat on, copying* YVETTE'S *sexy walk. Suddenly cannon and shots. Drums.* MOTHER COURAGE, *the* COOK, *and the* CHAPLAIN *rush around to the front of the cart, the last two with glasses in their hands. The* ORDNANCE OFFICER *and a* SOLDIER *come running to the cannon and try to push it along.*

MOTHER COURAGE. What's the matter? Let me get my washing off that gun, you slobs! (*She tries to do so.*)

OFFICER. The Catholics! Surprise attack! We don't know if we can get away! (*To the* SOLDIER.) Get that gun! (*He runs off.*)

COOK. For heaven's sake! I must go to the Commander. Mother Courage, I'll be back in a day or two—for a short conversation. (*He rushes off.*)

MOTHER COURAGE. Hey, you've left your pipe!

COOK (*off*). Keep it for me, I'll need it!

MOTHER COURAGE. This *would* happen just when we were making money.

CHAPLAIN. Well, I must be going too. Yes, if the enemy's so close, it can be dangerous. "Blessed are the peacemakers," a good slogan in war time! If only I had a cloak.

MOTHER COURAGE. I'm lending no cloaks. Not even to save a life, I'm not. I've had experience in that line.

CHAPLAIN. But I'm in special danger. Because of my religion.

MOTHER COURAGE (*bringing him a cloak*). It's against my better judgment. Now run!

CHAPLAIN. I thank you, you're very generous, but maybe I'd better stay and sit here. If I run, I might attract the enemy's attention, I might arouse suspicion.

MOTHER COURAGE (*to the* SOLDIER). Let it alone, you dolt, who's going to pay you for this? It'll cost you your life, let me hold it for you.

SOLDIER (*running away*). You're my witness: I tried!

MOTHER COURAGE. I'll swear to it! (*Seeing* KATTRIN *with the hat.*) What on earth are you up to—with a whore's hat! Take if off this minute! Are you mad? With the enemy coming? (*She tears the hat off her head.*) Do you want them to find you and make a whore of you? And she has the boots on too, straight from Babylon. I'll soon fix that. (*She tries to get them off.*) Oh, God, Chaplain, help me with these boots, I'll be right back. (*She runs to the wagon.*)

YVETTE (*entering and powdering her face*). What's that you say: the Catholics are coming? Where's my hat? Who's been trampling on it? I can't run around in that, what will they think of me? And I don't even have a mirror. (*To the* CHAPLAIN.) How do I look—too much powder?

CHAPLAIN. Just, er, right.

YVETTE. And where are my red boots? (*She can't find them because* KATTRIN *is hiding her feet under her skirt.*) I left them here! Now I've got to go barefoot to my tent, it's a scandal! (*Exit.*)

SWISS CHEESE *comes running in carrying a cash box.* MOTHER COURAGE *enters with her hands covered with ashes.*

MOTHER COURAGE (*to* KATTRIN). Ashes! (*To* SWISS CHEESE.) What have you got there?

SWISS CHEESE. The regimental cash box.

MOTHER COURAGE. Throw it away! Your pay-mastering days are over!

SWISS CHEESE. It's a trust! (*He goes to the back.*)

MOTHER COURAGE (*to the* CHAPLAIN). Off with your pastor's cloak, Chaplain, or they'll recognize you, cloak or no cloak. (*She is rubbing ashes into* KATTRIN'*s face.*) Keep still. A little dirt, and you're safe. A calamity! The sentries were drunk. Well, one must hide one's light under a bushel, as they say. When a soldier sees a clean face, there's one more whore in the world. Especially a Catholic soldier. For weeks on end, no grub. Then, when the plundering starts and they steal some, they jump on top of the women-folk. That should do. Let me look at you. Not bad. Looks like you've been rolling in muck. Don't tremble. Nothing can happen to you now. (*To* SWISS CHEESE.) Where've you left the cash box?

SWISS CHEESE. I thought I'd just put it in the wagon.

MOTHER COURAGE (*horrified*). What! In my wagon? God punish you for a prize idiot! If I just look away for a moment! They'll hang all three of us!

SWISS CHEESE. Then I'll put it somewhere else. Or escape with it.

MOTHER COURAGE. You'll stay where you are. It's too late.

CHAPLAIN (*still changing his clothes*). For heaven's sake: the flag!

MOTHER COURAGE (*taking down the flag*). God in heaven! I don't notice it any more. I've had it twenty-five years.

The thunder of cannon grows.

Three days later. Morning. The cannon is gone. MOTHER COURAGE, KATTRIN, *the* CHAPLAIN, *and* SWISS CHEESE *sit anxiously eating.*

SWISS CHEESE. This is the third day I've been sitting here doing nothing, and the Sergeant, who's always been patient with me, may be slowly beginning to ask, "Where on earth is Swiss Cheese with that cash box?"

MOTHER COURAGE. Be glad they're not on the trail.

CHAPLAIN. What about me? I can't hold a service here or I'll be in hot water. It is written, "Out of the abundance of the heart, the tongue speaketh." But woe is me if *my* tongue speaketh!

MOTHER COURAGE. That's how it is. Here you sit—one with his religion, the other with his cash box, I don't know which is more dangerous.

CHAPLAIN. We're in God's hands now!

MOTHER COURAGE. I hope we're not *that* desperate, but it *is* hard to sleep nights. 'Course it'd be easier if *you* weren't here, Swiss Cheese, all the same I've not done badly. I told them I was against the Antichrist, who's a Swede with horns on his head. I told them I noticed his left horn's a bit threadbare. When they cross-examined me, I always asked where I could buy holy candles a bit cheaper. I know these things because Swiss Cheese's father was a Catholic and made jokes about it. They didn't quite believe me but they needed a canteen, so they turned a blind eye. Maybe it's all for the best. We're prisoners. But so are lice in fur.

CHAPLAIN. The milk is good. As far as quantity goes, we may have to reduce our Swedish appetites somewhat. We are defeated.

MOTHER COURAGE. Who's defeated? The defeats and victories of the fellows at the top aren't always defeats and victories for the fellows at the bottom. Not at all. There've been cases where a defeat is a victory for the fellows at the bottom, it's only their honor that's lost, nothing serious. In Livonia once, our Chief took such a knock from the enemy, in the confusion I got a fine gray mare out of the baggage train, it pulled my wagon seven months—till we won and there was an inventory. But in general both defeat and victory are a costly business for us that haven't got much. The best thing is for politics to get stuck in the mud. (*To* SWISS CHEESE.) Eat!

SWISS CHEESE. I don't like it. How will the sergeant pay his men?

MOTHER COURAGE. Soldiers in flight don't get paid.

SWISS CHEESE. Well, they could claim to be. No pay, no flight. They can refuse to budge.

MOTHER COURAGE. Swiss Cheese, your sense of duty worries me. I've brought you up to be honest because you're not very bright. But don't overdo it. And now I'm going with the chaplain to buy a Catholic flag and some meat. There's no one can hunt out meat like him, sure as a sleepwalker. He can tell a good piece of meat from the way his mouth waters. A good thing they let me stay in the business. In business you ask what price, not what religion. And Protestant trousers keep you just as warm.

CHAPLAIN. As the mendicant monk said when there was talk of the Lutherans turning the whole world upside down: Beggars will *always* be needed. (MOTHER COURAGE *disappears into the wagon.*) She's worried about the cash box. Up to now they've ignored us—as if we were part of the wagon—but can it last?

SWISS CHEESE. I can get rid of it.

CHAPLAIN. That's almost *more* dangerous. Suppose you're seen. They have spies. Yesterday morning one jumped out of the very hole I was relieving myself in. I was so scared I almost broke out in prayer— *that* would have given me away all right! I believe their favorite way of finding a Protestant is smelling his excrement. The spy was a little brute with a bandage over one eye.

MOTHER COURAGE (*clambering out of the wagon with a basket*). I've found you out, you shameless hussy! (*She holds up* YVETTE's *red boots in triumph.*) Yvette's red boots! She just swiped them—because you went and told her she was a captivating person. (*She lays them in the basket.*) Stealing Yvette's boots! But *she* disgraces herself for money, *you* do it for nothing—for pleasure! I told

you, you must wait for the peace. No soldiers! Save your proud peacock ways for peacetime!

CHAPLAIN. I don't find her proud.

MOTHER COURAGE. Prouder than she can afford to be. I like her when people say "I never noticed the poor thing." I like her when she's a stone in Dalarna, where there's nothing but stones. (*To* SWISS CHEESE.) Leave the cash box where it is, do you hear? And pay attention to your sister, she needs it. Between the two of you, you'll be the death of me yet. I'd rather take care of a bag of fleas.

She leaves with the CHAPLAIN. KATTRIN *clears the dishes away.*

SWISS CHEESE. Not many days more when you can sit in the sun in your shirtsleeves. (KATTRIN *points to a tree.*) Yes, the leaves are yellow already. (*With gestures,* KATTRIN *asks if he wants a drink.*) I'm not drinking, I'm thinking. (*Pause.*) She says she can't sleep. So I *should* take the cash box away. I've found a place for it. I'll keep it in the mole hole by the river till the time comes. I might get it tonight before sunrise and take it to the regiment. How far can they have fled in three days? The Sergeant's eyes'll pop out of his head. "I give you the cash box to take care of, and what do you do," he'll say, "but hand it right back to me: you've disappointed me most pleasantly, Swiss Cheese." Yes, Kattrin, I *will* have a glass now!

When KATTRIN *reappears behind the wagon two men confront her. One of them is a* SERGEANT. *The other doffs his hat and flourishes it in a showy greeting. He has a bandage over one eye.*

MAN WITH THE BANDAGE. Good morning, young lady. Have you seen a man from the Second Protestant Regiment?

Terrified, KATTRIN *runs away, spilling her brandy. The two men look at each other and then withdraw after seeing* SWISS CHEESE.

SWISS CHEESE (*starting up from his reflection*). You're spilling it! What's the matter with you, have you hurt your eye? I don't understand. Yes, and I must be going, too. I've decided it's the thing to do. (*He stands up. She does all she can to make him aware of the danger he is in. He only pushes her away.*) I'd like to know what you mean. I know you mean well, poor thing, you just can't get it out. And don't trouble yourself about the brandy, I'll live to drink so much of it, what's one glass? (*He takes the cash box out of the wagon and puts it under his coat.*) I'll be back right away. But don't hold me up or I'll have to scold you. Yes, I know you mean well. If you could only speak!

When she tries to hold him back he kisses her and pulls himself free. Exit. She is desperate and runs up and down, emitting little sounds. MOTHER COURAGE *and the* CHAPLAIN *return.* KATTRIN *rushes at her mother.*

MOTHER COURAGE. What *is* it, what *is* it, Kattrin? Control yourself! Has someone done something to you? Where is Swiss Cheese? (*To the* CHAPLAIN.) Don't stand around, get that Catholic flag up! (*She takes a Catholic flag out of her basket and the* CHAPLAIN *runs it up the pole.*)
CHAPLAIN (*bitterly*). All good Catholics forever!
MOTHER COURAGE. Now, Kattrin, calm down and tell all about it, your mother understands you. What, that little bastard of mine's taken the cash box away? I'll box his ears for him, the rascal! Now take your time and don't try to talk, use your hands. I don't like it when you howl like a dog, what'll the chaplain think of you? You're giving him the creeps. A man with one eye was here?
CHAPLAIN. That fellow with one eye is an informer! Have they caught Swiss Cheese? (KATTRIN *shakes her head, shrugs her shoulders.*) This is the end.

Voices off. The two men bring in SWISS CHEESE.

SWISS CHEESE. Let me go. I've nothing on me. You're breaking my shoulder! I am innocent.
SERGEANT. This is where he comes from. These are his friends.
MOTHER COURAGE. Us? Since when?
SWISS CHEESE. I don't even know 'em. I was just getting my lunch here. Ten hellers it cost me. Maybe you saw me sitting on that bench. It was too salty.
SERGEANT. Who *are* you people, anyway?
MOTHER COURAGE. Law-abiding citizens! It's true what he says. He bought his lunch here. And it was too salty.
SERGEANT. Are you pretending you don't know him?
MOTHER COURAGE. I can't know all of them, can I? *I* don't ask, "What's your name and are you a heathen?" If they pay up, they're not heathens to me. Are you a heathen?
SWISS CHEESE. Oh, no!
CHAPLAIN. He sat there like a law-abiding fellow and never once opened his mouth. Except to eat. Which is necessary.
SERGEANT. Who do you think *you* are?
MOTHER COURAGE. Oh, he's my barman. And you're thirsty, I'll bring you a glass of brandy. You must be footsore and weary!
SERGEANT. No brandy on duty. (*To* SWISS CHEESE.) You were carrying something. You must have hidden it by the river. We saw the bulge in your shirt.
MOTHER COURAGE. Sure it was him?
SWISS CHEESE. I think you mean another fellow. There *was* a fellow with something under his shirt, I saw him. I'm the wrong man.
MOTHER COURAGE. I think so too. It's a misunderstanding. Could happen to anyone. Oh, I know what people are like, I'm Mother Courage, you've heard of me, everyone knows about me, and I can tell you this: he looks honest.
SERGEANT. We're after the regimental cash box. And we know what the man looks like who's been keeping it. We've been looking for him two days. It's you.
SWISS CHEESE. No, it's not!

SERGEANT. And if you don't shell out, you're dead, see? Where is it?

MOTHER COURAGE (*urgently*). 'Course he'd give it to you to save his life. He'd up and say, *I've* got it, here it is, you're stronger than me. He's not *that* stupid. Speak, little stupid, the sergeant's giving you a chance!

SWISS CHEESE. What if I haven't got it?

SERGEANT. Come with us. We'll get it out of you. (*They take him off.*)

MOTHER COURAGE (*shouting after them*). He'd tell you! He's not *that* stupid! And don't you break his shoulder! (*She runs after them.*)

The same evening. The CHAPLAIN *and* KATTRIN *are rinsing glasses and polishing knives.*

CHAPLAIN. Cases of people getting caught like this are by no means unknown in the history of religion. I am reminded of the Passion of Our Lord and Savior. There's an old song about it.

He sings "The Song of the Hours."

In the first hour of the day
Simple Jesus Christ was
Presented as a murderer
To the heathen Pilate.

Pilate found no fault in him
No cause to condemn him
So he sent the Lord away.
Let King Herod see him!

Hour the third: the Son of God
Was with scourges beaten
And they set a crown of thorns
On the head of Jesus.

And they dressed him as a king
Joked and jested at him
And the cross to die upon
He himself must carry.

Six: they stripped Lord Jesus bare.
To the cross they nailed him.
When the blood came gushing, he
Prayed and loud lamented.

Each upon his cross, two thieves
Mocked him like the others.
And the bright sun crept away
Not to see such doings.

Nine: Lord Jesus cried aloud
That he was forsaken!
In a sponge upon a pole
Vinegar was fed him.

Then the Lord gave up the ghost
And the earth did tremble.
Temple curtains split in twain.
Cliffs fell in the ocean.

Evening: they broke the bones
Of the malefactors.
Then they took a spear and pierced
The side of gentle Jesus.

And the blood and water ran
And they laughed at Jesus.
Of this simple son of man
Such and more they tell us.

MOTHER COURAGE (*entering, excited*). It's life and death. But the Sergeant will still listen to us. The only thing is, he musn't know it's our Swiss Cheese, or they'll say we helped him. It's only a matter of money, but where can *we* get money? Isn't Yvette here yet? I talked to her on the way over. She's picked up a Colonel who may be willing to buy her a canteen business.

CHAPLAIN. You'd sell the wagon, everything?

MOTHER COURAGE. Where else would I get the money for the Sergeant?

CHAPLAIN. What are you to live off?

MOTHER COURAGE. That's just it.

Enter YVETTE *with a hoary old* COLONEL.

YVETTE (*embracing* MOTHER COURAGE). *Dear* Mistress Courage, we meet again. (*Whispering.*) He didn't say no. (*Aloud.*) This is my friend, my, um, business adviser. I happened to hear you might sell your wagon. Due to special circumstances, I'd like to think about it.

MOTHER COURAGE. I want to pawn it, not sell it. And nothing hasty. In war time you don't find another wagon like that so easy.

YVETTE (*disappointed*). Only pawn it? I thought you wanted to sell. I don't know if I'm interested. (*To the* COLONEL.) What do *you* think, my dear?

COLONEL. I quite agree with you, bunny.

MOTHER COURAGE. It's only for pawn.

YVETTE. I thought you *had* to have the money.

MOTHER COURAGE (*firmly*). I do have to have it. But I'd rather wear my feet off looking for an offer than just sell. Why? We live off the wagon. It's an opportunity for you, Yvette. Who knows when you'll have another such? Who knows when you'll find another business adviser?

COLONEL. Take it, take it!

YVETTE. My friend thinks I should go ahead, but I'm not sure, if it's only for pawn. You think we should buy it outright, don't you?

COLONEL. I do, bunny, I do!

MOTHER COURAGE. Then you must go and find something that's for sale. Maybe you'll find it—if you have the time, and your friend goes with you, let's say in about a week, or two weeks, you may find the right thing.

YVETTE. Yes, we can certainly look around for something. I love going around looking, I love going around with you, Poldy . . .

COLONEL. Really? Do you?

YVETTE. Oh, it's lovely! I could take two weeks of it!

COLONEL. Really, could you?

YVETTE. If you get the money, when are you thinking of paying it back?

MOTHER COURAGE. In two weeks. Maybe one.

YVETTE. I can't make up my mind. Poldy, advise me, *chéri*! (*She takes the* COLONEL *to one side.*) She'll *have* to sell, don't worry. That Lieutenant—the blond one, you know the one I mean—he'll lend me the money. He's *mad* about me, he says I remind him of someone. What do you advise?

COLONEL. Oh, I have to warn you against *him*. He's no good. He'll exploit the situation. I told you, bunny, I told you *I'd*

buy you something, didn't I tell you that?

YVETTE. I simply can't let you!

COLONEL. Oh, please, please!

YVETTE. Well, if you think the Lieutenant might exploit the situation I *will* let you!

COLONEL. I do think so.

YVETTE. So you advise me to?

COLONEL. I do, bunny, I do!

YVETTE (*returning to* MOTHER COURAGE). My friend says all right. Write me out a receipt saying the wagon's mine when the two weeks are up—with everything in it. I'll just run through it all now, the two hundred guilders can wait. (*To the* COLONEL.) You go ahead to the camp, I'll follow, I must go over all this so nothing'll be missing later from *my* wagon!

COLONEL. Wait, I'll help you up! (*He does so.*) Come soon, honey bun! (*Exit.*)

MOTHER COURAGE. Yvette, Yvette!

YVETTE. There aren't many boots left!

MOTHER COURAGE. Yvette, this is no time to go through the wagon, yours or not yours. You promised you'd talk to the Sergeant about Swiss Cheese. There isn't a minute to lose. He's up before the court-martial one hour from now.

YVETTE. I just want to count these shirts again.

MOTHER COURAGE (*dragging her down the steps by the skirt*). You hyena, Swiss Cheese's life's at stake! And don't say who the money comes from. Pretend he's your sweetheart, for heaven's sake, or we'll all get it for helping him.

YVETTE. I've arranged to meet One Eye in the bushes. He must be there by now.

CHAPLAIN. And don't hand over all two hundred, a hundred and fifty's sure to be enough.

MOTHER COURAGE. Is it your money? I'll thank you to keep your nose out of this, I'm not doing *you* out of your porridge. Now run, and no haggling, remember his life's at stake. (*She pushes* YVETTE *off.*)

CHAPLAIN. I didn't want to talk you into anything, but what are we going to live on? You have an unemployable daughter around your neck.

MOTHER COURAGE. I'm counting on that cash box, smart aleck. They'll pay his expenses out of it.

CHAPLAIN. You think she can work it?

MOTHER COURAGE. It's in her own interest: I pay the two hundred and she gets the wagon. She knows what she's doing, she won't have her Colonel on the string forever. Kattrin, go and clean the knives, use pumice stone. And don't *you* stand around like Jesus in Gethsemane. Get a move on, wash those glasses. There'll be over fifty cavalrymen here tonight, and you'll be saying you're not used to being on your feet. "Oh my poor feet, in church I never had to run around like this!" I think they'll let us have him. Thanks be to God they're corruptible. They're not wolves, they're human and after money. God is merciful, and men are bribable, that's how His will is done on earth as it is in Heaven. Corruption is our only hope. As long as there's corruption, there'll be merciful judges and even the innocent may get off.

YVETTE comes in panting.

YVETTE. They'll do it for two hundred if you make it snappy—these things change from one minute to the next. I'd better take One Eye to my Colonel at once. He confessed he had the cash box, they put the thumbscrews on him. But he threw it in the river when he noticed them coming up behind him. So it's gone. Shall I run and get the money from my Colonel?

MOTHER COURAGE. The cash box gone? How'll I ever get my two hundred back?

YVETTE. So you thought you could get it from the cash box? I *would* have been sunk. Not a hope, Mother Courage. If you want your Swiss Cheese, you'll have to pay. Or should I let the whole thing drop, so you can keep your wagon?

MOTHER COURAGE. I wasn't figuring on this. But you needn't hound me, you'll get the wagon, it's yours already, and it's been mine seventeen years. I need a minute to think it over, it's all so sudden. What can I

do? I *can't* pay two hundred. You *should* have haggled with them. I must hold on to something, or any passer-by can kick me in the ditch. Go and say I'll pay a hundred and twenty or the deal's off. Even then I lose the wagon.

YVETTE. They won't do it. And anyway, One Eye's in a hurry. He keeps looking over his shoulder all the time, he's so worked up. Hadn't I better give them the whole two hundred?

MOTHER COURAGE (*desperate*). I can't pay it! I've been working thirty years. She's twenty-five and still no husband. I have her to think of. So leave me alone. I know what I'm doing. A hundred and twenty or no deal.

YVETTE. You know best. (*She runs off.*)

MOTHER COURAGE *turns away and slowly walks a few paces to the rear. Then she turns around, looks neither at the* CHAPLAIN *nor her daughter, and sits down to help* KATTRIN *polish the knives.*

MOTHER COURAGE. Don't break the glasses, they're not ours. Watch what you're doing, you're cutting yourself. Swiss Cheese will be back, I'll give two hundred, if I have to. You'll get your brother back. With eighty guilders we could pack a hamper with goods and begin again. It wouldn't be the end of the world.

CHAPLAIN. The Bible says: the Lord will provide.

MOTHER COURAGE. Rub them dry, I said.

They clean the knives in silence.

They say the war will stop soon. How would it? I ask. And no one can answer me. (*Slowly.*) The King and the Pope are mortal enemies, their Faith is different. They must go for each other till one of them drops dead, neither of them can relax till then. Even so they can't get on with it. Why not? The Emperor is in the way, and they both have something against him. They're not going to fight each other to the death with the Emperor lurking about till they're half dead so he can fall on both of 'em! No, they're banding together against the Emperor so he'll drop dead first and they can go for each other.

Suddenly KATTRIN *runs sobbing behind the wagon.*

Someone once offered me five hundred guilders for the wagon. I didn't take it. My Eilif, wherever he may be, thought I'd taken it and cried all night.

YVETTE *comes running in.*

YVETTE. They won't do it. I warned you. One Eye was going to drop it then and there. There's no point, he said. He said the drums would roll any second now and that's the sign a verdict has been reached. I offered a hundred and fifty, he didn't even shrug. I could hardly get him to stay there while I came here.

MOTHER COURAGE. Tell him I'll pay two hundred. Run!

YVETTE *runs.* MOTHER COURAGE *sits, silent. The* CHAPLAIN *has stopped doing the glasses.*

I believe—I've haggled too long.

In the distance, a roll of drums. The CHAPLAIN *stands up and walks toward the rear.* MOTHER COURAGE *remains seated. It grows dark. It gets light again.* MOTHER COURAGE *has not moved.* YVETTE *appears, pale.*

YVETTE. Now you've done it—with your haggling. You can keep the wagon now. He got eleven bullets in him. I don't know why I still bother about you, you don't deserve it, but I just happened to learn they don't think the cash box is really in the river. They suspect it's here, they think you're connected with him. I think they're going to bring him here to see if you'll give yourself away when you see him. You'd

better not know him or we're in for it. And I'd better tell you straight, they're just behind me. Shall I keep Kattrin away? (MOTHER COURAGE *shakes her head.*) Does she know? Maybe she never heard the drums or didn't understand.

MOTHER COURAGE. She knows. Bring her.

YVETTE *brings* KATTRIN, *who walks over to her mother and stands by her.* MOTHER COURAGE *takes her hand. Two men come on with a stretcher; there is a sheet on it and something underneath. Beside them, the* SERGEANT. *They put the stretcher down.*

SERGEANT. Here's a man we can't identify. But he has to be registered to keep the records straight. He bought a meal from you. Look at him, see if you know him. (*He pulls back the sheet.*) Do you know him? (MOTHER COURAGE *shakes her head.*) What? You never saw him before he took that meal? (MOTHER COURAGE *shakes her head.*) Lift him up. Throw him in the carrion pit. He has no one that knows him.

They carry him off.

4

Mother Courage sings "The Song of the Great Capitulation."

Outside an officer's tent. MOTHER COURAGE *waits. A* CLERK *looks out of the tent.*

CLERK. I know you. You had a Protestant paymaster with you, he was hiding out with you. Better make no complaint.

MOTHER COURAGE. But I'm innocent and if I give up it'll look as if I have a bad conscience. They cut everything in my wagon to ribbons with their sabers and then claimed a fine of five thalers for nothing and less than nothing.

CLERK. For you own good, keep your trap shut. We haven't many canteens, so we let you stay in business, especially if you've a bad conscience and have to pay a fine now and then.

MOTHER COURAGE. I'm going to file a complaint.

CLERK. As you wish. Wait here till the Captain has time. (*He withdraws into the tent.*)

A YOUNG SOLDIER *comes storming in.*

YOUNG SOLDIER. Screw the Captain! Where *is* the son of a bitch? Swiping my reward, spending it on brandy for his whores, I'll rip his belly open!

AN OLDER SOLDIER (*coming after him*). Shut your hole, you'll wind up in the stocks.

YOUNG SOLDIER. Come out, you thief, I'll make lamb chops out of you! I was the only one in the squad who swam the river and *he* grabs my money, I can't even buy myself a beer. Come on out! And let me slice you up!

OLDER SOLDIER. Holy Christ, he'll destroy himself!

YOUNG SOLDIER. Let me go or I'll run *you* down too. This has got to be settled!

OLDER SOLDIER. Saved the Colonel's horse and didn't get the reward. He's young, he hasn't been at it long.

MOTHER COURAGE. Let him go. He doesn't have to be chained, he's not a dog. Very reasonable to want a reward. Why else should he want to shine?

YOUNG SOLDIER. He's in there pouring it down! You're all nice. I've done something special, I want the reward!

MOTHER COURAGE. Young man, don't scream at *me*, I have my own troubles. And go easy with your voice, you may need it when the Captain comes. The Captain'll come and you'll be hoarse and can't make a sound, so he'll have to deny himself the pleasure of sticking you in the stocks till you pass out. The screamers don't scream long, only half an hour, after which they have to be sung to sleep, they're all in.

YOUNG SOLDIER. I'm not all in, and sleep's out of the question. I'm hungry. They're making their bread out of acorns and hempseed, and not even much of that. He's whoring on my money, and I'm hungry. I'll murder him!

MOTHER COURAGE. I understand: you're hungry. Last year your Commander ordered you people out of the streets and into the fields. So the crops got trampled down. I could have got ten guilders for boots, if anyone'd had ten guilders, and if I'd had any boots. He didn't expect to be around this year, but he is, and there's famine. I understand: you're angry.

YOUNG SOLDIER. It's no use your talking. I won't stand for injustice!

MOTHER COURAGE. You're quite right. But how long? How long won't you stand for injustice? One hour? Or two? You haven't asked yourself that, have you? And yet it's the main thing. It's pure misery to sit in the stocks. Especially if you leave it till then to decide you do stand for injustice.

YOUNG SOLDIER. I don't know why I listen to you. Screw that Captain! Where is he?

MOTHER COURAGE. You listen because you know I'm right. Your rage has calmed down already. It was a short one and you'd need a long one. But where would you find it?

YOUNG SOLDIER. Are you trying to say it's not right to ask for the money?

MOTHER COURAGE. Just the opposite. I only say, your rage won't last. You'll get nowhere with it, it's a pity. If your rage was a long one, I'd urge you on. Slice him up, I'd advise you. But what's the use if you *don't* slice him up because you can feel your tail between your legs? You stand there and the Captain lets you have it.

OLDER SOLDIER. You're quite right, he's crazy.

YOUNG SOLDIER. All right, we'll see whether I slice him up or not. (*He draws his sword.*) When he comes out, I slice him up!

CLERK (*looking out*). The Captain will be out in a minute. (*In the tone of military command.*) Be seated!

The YOUNG SOLDIER *sits.*

MOTHER COURAGE. And he *is* seated. What

did I tell you? You are seated. They know us through and through. They know how they must work it. Be seated! And we sit. And in sitting there's no revolt. Better not stand up again—not the way you did before—don't stand up again. And don't be embarrassed in front of me, I'm no better, not a scrap. They've drawn our teeth, haven't they? If we say boo, it's bad for business. Let me tell you about the great capitulation.

She sings "The Song of the Great Capitulation."

Long ago when I was a green beginner
I believed I was a special case.

(None of your ordinary run of the mill girls, with my looks and my talent, and my love of the higher things in life!)

And if I picked a hair out of my dinner
I would put the cook right in his place.

(All or nothing. Anyhow, never the second best, I am the master of my Fate. I'll take no orders from no one.)

Then a little bird whispered in my ear:
"That's all very well, but wait a year
And you will join the big brass band
And with your trumpet in your hand
You'll march in lockstep with the rest.
Then one day, look! The battalions wheel!
The whole thing swings from east to west!
And falling on your knees, you'll squeal:
The Lord God, He knows best!
(But don't give *me* that!)"

And a month or two before that year was over
I had learned to drink their cup of tea.

(Two children round your neck, and the price of bread and what all!)

And the day soon came when I was to discover
They had me just where they wanted me.

(You must get in good with people. If you scratch my back, I'll scratch yours. Don't stick your neck out.)

And that little bird whispered in my ear:
"You didn't even take a year!
And you have joined the big brass band
And with your trumpet in your hand
You marched in lockstep with the rest.
But one day, look! The battalions wheeled!
The whole thing swung from east to west!
And falling on your knees, you squealed:
The Lord God, He knows best!
(But don't give *me* that!)"

Yes, our hopes are high, our plans colossal!
And we hitch our wagon to a star!

(Where there's a will there's a way. One can't hold a good man down.)

We can move mountains, says St. Paul the great Apostle

And yet: how heavy one cigar!

(We must cut our coat according to our cloth.)

For that little bird whispers in your ear:
"That's all very well but wait a year
And we will join the big brass band
And with our trumpet in our hand
We march in lockstep with the rest.
But one day, look! The battalions wheel!
The whole thing swings from east to west!
And falling on our knees, we squeal:
The Lord God, He knows best!
(But don't give *me* that!)"

And so I think you should stay here with

your sword drawn if you're set on it and your anger is big enough. You have good cause, I admit. But if your anger is a short one, you'd better go.

YOUNG SOLDIER. Kiss my ass. (*He stumbles off, the other* SOLDIER *following him.*)

CLERK (*sticking his head out*). The Captain is ready now. You can file your complaint.

MOTHER COURAGE. I've thought better of it. I'm not complaining. (*Exit.*)

The CLERK *looks after her, shaking his head.*

5

Two years have passed. The war covers wider and wider territory. Forever on the move, the little wagon crosses Poland, Moravia, Bavaria, Italy, and again Bavaria. 1631. Tilly's victory at Magdeburg costs Mother Courage four officers' shirts.

The wagon stands in a war-ravaged village. Faint military music from the distance. Two SOLDIERS *are being served at a counter by* KATTRIN *and* MOTHER COURAGE. *One of them has a woman's fur coat about his shoulders.*

MOTHER COURAGE. What, you can't pay? No money, no brandy! They can play victory marches, they should pay their men.

FIRST SOLDIER. I want my brandy! I arrived too late for plunder. The Chief allowed one hour to plunder the town, it's a swindle. He's not inhuman, he says. So I suppose they bought him off.

CHAPLAIN (*staggering in*). There are more in the farmhouse. A family of peasants. Help me someone. I need linen!

The second SOLDIER *goes with him.* KAT-TRIN *is getting very excited. She tries to get her mother to bring linen out.*

MOTHER COURAGE. I have none. I sold all my bandages to the regiment. I'm not tearing up my officers' shirts for these people.

CHAPLAIN (*calling over his shoulder*). I said I need linen!

MOTHER COURAGE (*stopping* KATTRIN *from entering the wagon*). Not a thing! They can't pay, and why? They have nothing and they pay nothing!

CHAPLAIN (*to a* WOMAN *he is carrying in*). Why did you stay out there in the line of fire?

WOMAN. Our farm—

MOTHER COURAGE. Think they'd ever let go of *anything?* And now I'm supposed to pay. Well, I won't!

FIRST SOLDIER. They're Protestants, why should they be Protestants?

MOTHER COURAGE. Protestant, Catholic, what do *they* care? Their farm's gone, that's what.

SECOND SOLDIER. They're not Protestants anyway, they're Catholics.

FIRST SOLDIER. In a bombardment we can't pick and choose.

A PEASANT (*brought on by the* CHAPLAIN). My arm's gone.

CHAPLAIN. Where's that linen?

All look at MOTHER COURAGE, *who does not budge.*

MOTHER COURAGE. I can't give you any. With all I have to pay out—taxes, duties, bribes. . . . (KATTRIN *takes up a board and threatens her mother with it, emitting gurgling sounds.*) Are you out of your mind? Put that board down or I'll let you have one, you lunatic! I'm giving nothing, I don't dare, I have myself to think of. (*The* CHAPLAIN *lifts her bodily off the steps of the wagon and sets her down on the ground. He takes out shirts from the wagon and tears them in strips.*) My shirts, my officers' shirts!

From the house comes the cry of a child in pain.

PEASANT. The child's still in there.

KATTRIN *runs in.*

CHAPLAIN (*to the* WOMAN). Stay where you are. She's getting it for you.

MOTHER COURAGE. Hold her back, the roof may fall in!

CHAPLAIN. I'm not going back in there!

MOTHER COURAGE (*pulled in both directions*). Go easy on my expensive linen.

The SECOND SOLDIER *holds her back.* KATTRIN *brings a baby out of the ruins.*

MOTHER COURAGE. Another baby to drag around, you must be pleased with yourself. Give it to its mother this minute! Or do I have to fight you again for hours till I get it from you? Are you deaf? (*To the* SECOND SOLDIER.) Don't stand about gawking, go back there and tell 'em to stop that music, I can see their victory without it. I have nothing but losses from your victory!

CHAPLAIN (*bandaging*). The blood's coming through.

KATTRIN *is rocking the child and half humming a lullaby.*

MOTHER COURAGE. There she sits, happy as a lark in all this misery. Give the baby back, the mother is coming to! (*She sees the* FIRST SOLDIER. *He had been handling the drinks, and is now trying to make off with the bottle.*) God's truth! You beast! You want another victory, do you? Then pay for it!

FIRST SOLDIER. I have nothing.

MOTHER COURAGE (*snatching the fur coat back*). Then leave this coat, it's stolen goods anyhow.

CHAPLAIN. There's still someone in there.

6

Before the city of Ingolstadt in Bavaria Mother Courage is present at the funeral of the fallen commander, Tilly. Conversations take place about war heroes and the duration of the war. The Chaplain complains that his talents are lying fallow and Kattrin gets the red boots. The year is 1632.

The inside of a canteen tent. The inner side of a counter at the rear. Rain. In the distance, drums and funeral music. The CHAPLAIN *and the regimental* CLERK *are playing draughts.* MOTHER COURAGE *and her daughter are taking an inventory.*

CHAPLAIN. The funeral procession is just starting out.

MOTHER COURAGE. Pity about the Chief—twenty-two pairs of socks—getting killed that way. They say it was an accident. There was a fog over the fields that morning, and the fog was to blame. The Chief called up another regiment, told 'em to fight to the death, rode back again, missed his way in the fog, went forward instead of back, and ran smack into a bullet in the thick of battle—only four lanterns left. (*A whistle from the rear. She goes to the counter. To a* SOLDIER.) It's a disgrace the way you're all skipping your Commander's funeral! (*She pours a drink.*)

CLERK. They shouldn't have handed the money out before the funeral. Now the men are all getting drunk instead of going to it.

CHAPLAIN (*to the* CLERK). Don't you have to be there?

CLERK. I stayed away because of the rain.

MOTHER COURAGE. It's different for you, the rain might spoil your uniform. I hear they wanted to ring the bells for his funeral, which is natural, but it came out that the churches had been shot up by his orders, so the poor Commander won't be hearing any bells when they lower him in his grave. Instead, they'll fire off three shots so the occasion won't be *too* sober—sixteen leather belts.

A VOICE FROM THE COUNTER. Service! One brandy!

MOTHER COURAGE. Your money first. No, you *can't* come inside the tent, not with those boots on. You can drink outside, rain or no rain. I only let officers in here. (*To the*

CLERK.) The Chief had his troubles lately, I hear. There was unrest in the Second Regiment because he didn't pay 'em. He said it was a war of religion and they must fight it free of charge.

Funeral march. All look toward the rear.

CHAPLAIN. Now they're filing past the body.

MOTHER COURAGE. I feel sorry for a Commander or an Emperor like that—when he might have had something special in mind, something they'd talk about in times to come, something they'd raise a statue to him for. The conquest of the world now, *that's* a goal for a Commander, he wouldn't know any better. . . . Lord, worms have got into the biscuits. . . . In short, he works his hands to the bone and then it's all spoiled by the common riffraff that only wants a jug of beer or a bit of company, not the higher things in life. The finest plans have always been spoiled by the littleness of them that should carry them out. Even Emperors can't do it all by themselves. They count on support from their soldiers and the people round about. Am I right?

CHAPLAIN (*laughing*). You're right, Mother Courage, till you come to the soldiers. They do what they can. Those fellows outside, for example, drinking their brandy in the rain, I'd trust 'em to fight a hundred years, one war after another, two at a time if necessary. And I wasn't trained as a commander.

MOTHER COURAGE. . . . Seventeen leather belts. . . . Then you don't think the war might end?

CHAPLAIN. Because a commander's dead? Don't be childish, they grow on trees. There are always heroes.

MOTHER COURAGE. Well, I wasn't asking for the sake of argument. I was wondering if I should buy up a lot of supplies. They happen to be cheap just now. But if the war ended, I might just as well throw them away.

CHAPLAIN. I realize you are serious, Mother Courage. Well, there've always been peo-

ple going around saying some day the war will end. I say, you can't be sure the war will *ever* end. Of course it may have to pause occasionally—for breath, as it were—it can even meet with an accident—nothing on this earth is perfect—a war of which we could say it left nothing to be desired will probably never exist. A war can come to a sudden halt—from unforeseen causes—you can't think of everything—a little oversight, and the war's in the hole, and someone's got to pull it out again! The someone is the Emperor or the King or the Pope. They're such friends in need, the war has really nothing to worry about, it can look forward to a prosperous future.

A SOLDIER (*singing at the counter*).

> One schnapps, mine host, make haste!
> We have no time to waste:
> We must be shooting, shooting, shooting
> Our Emperor's foes uprooting!

Make it a double. This is a holiday.

MOTHER COURAGE. If I was sure you're right . . .

CHAPLAIN. Think it out for yourself: how *could* the war end?

SOLDIER (*off-stage*).

> Two breasts, mine host, make haste!
> We have no time to waste:
> We must be hating, hating, hating
> We cannot keep our Emperor waiting!

CLERK (*suddenly*). What about peace? Yes, peace. I'm from Bohemia. I'd like to get home once in a while.

CHAPLAIN. Oh, you would, would you? Dear old peace! What happens to the hole when the cheese is gone?

SOLDIER (*off-stage*).

> Your blessing, priest, make haste!
> For we have no time to waste:
> We must be dying, dying, dying
> Our Emperor's greatness glorifying!

CLERK. In the long run you can't live without peace!

CHAPLAIN. Well, I'd say there's peace even in war, war has its islands of peace. For war satisfies *all* needs, even those of peace, yes, they're provided for, or the war couldn't keep going. In war—as in the very thick of peace—you can take a crap, and between one battle and the next there's always a beer, and even on the march you can snatch a nap—on your elbow maybe, in a gutter—something can always be managed. Of course you can't play cards during an attack, but neither can you while ploughing the fields in peace time: it's when the victory's won that there are possibilities. You have your leg shot off, and at first you raise quite an outcry as if it *was* something, but soon you calm down or take a swig of brandy, and you end up hopping about, and the war is none the worse for your little misadventure. And can't you be fruitful and multiply in the thick of slaughter—behind a barn or somewhere? Nothing can keep you from it very long in any event. And so the war has your offspring and can carry on. War is like love, it always finds a way. Why *should* it end?

KATTRIN *has stopped working. She stares at the* CHAPLAIN.

MOTHER COURAGE. Then I *will* buy those supplies, I'll rely on you. (KATTRIN *suddenly bangs a basket of glasses down on the ground and runs out.* MOTHER COURAGE *laughs.*) Kattrin! Lord, Kattrin's still going to wait for peace. I promised her she'll get a husband —when it's peace. (*She runs after her.*)
CLERK (*standing up*). I win. You were talking. You pay.
MOTHER COURAGE (*returning with* KATTRIN). Be sensible, the war'll go on a bit longer, and we'll make a bit more money, then peace'll be all the nicer. Now you go into the town, it's not ten minutes walk, and bring the things from the Golden Lion, just the more expensive ones, we can get the rest later in the wagon. It's all arranged, the clerk will go with you, most of the

soldiers are at the Commander's funeral, nothing can happen to you. Do a good job, don't lose anything, Kattrin, think of your trousseau!

KATTRIN *ties a cloth around her head and leaves with the* CLERK.

CHAPLAIN. You don't mind her going with the clerk?
MOTHER COURAGE. She's not so pretty anyone would want to ruin her.
CHAPLAIN. The way you run your business and always come through is highly commendable, Mother Courage—I see how you got your name.
MOTHER COURAGE. The poor need courage. Why? They're lost. That they even get up in the morning is something—in *their* plight. Or that they plough a field—in war time. Even their bringing children into the world shows they have courage, for they have no prospects. They have to hang each other one by one and slaughter each other in the lump, so if they want to look each other in the face once in a while, well, it takes courage. That they put up with an Emperor and a Pope, that takes an unnatural amount of courage, for *they* cost you your life. (*She sits, takes a small pipe from her pocket and smokes it.*) You might chop me a bit of firewood.
CHAPLAIN (*reluctantly taking his coat off and preparing to chop wood*). Properly speaking, I'm a pastor of souls, not a woodcutter.
MOTHER COURAGE. But I don't have a soul. And I do need wood.
CHAPLAIN. What's that little pipe you've got there?
MOTHER COURAGE. Just a pipe.
CHAPLAIN. I think it's a very particular pipe.
MOTHER COURAGE. Oh?
CHAPLAIN. The cook's pipe in fact. The cook from the Oxenstierna Regiment.
MOTHER COURAGE. If you know, why beat about the bush?
CHAPLAIN. Because I don't know if you've been *aware* that's what you've been smoking. It was possible you just rummaged

among your belongings and your fingers just lit on a pipe and you just took it. In pure absent-mindedness.

MOTHER COURAGE. How do you know that's not it?

CHAPLAIN. It isn't. You *are* aware of it. (*He brings the ax down on the block with a crash.*)

MOTHER COURAGE. What if I was?

CHAPLAIN. I must give you a warning, Mother Courage, it's my duty. You are unlikely to see the gentleman again but that's no pity, you're in luck. Mother Courage, he did not impress me as trustworthy. On the contrary.

MOTHER COURAGE. Really? He was such a nice man.

CHAPLAIN. Well! So that's what you call a nice man. I do not. (*The ax falls again.*) Far be it from me to wish him ill, but I cannot—cannot—describe him as nice. No, no, he's a Don Juan, a cunning Don Juan. Just look at that pipe if you don't believe me. You must admit it tells all.

MOTHER COURAGE. I see nothing special in it. It's been used, of course.

CHAPLAIN. It's bitten halfway through! He's a man of great violence! It is the pipe of a man of great violence, you can see *that* if you've any judgment left (*He deals the block a tremendous blow.*)

MOTHER COURAGE. Don't bite my chopping block halfway through!

CHAPLAIN. I told you I had no training as a woodcutter. The care of souls was my field. Around here my gifts and capabilities are grossly misused. In physical labor my God-given talents find no—um—adequate expression—which is a sin. You haven't heard me preach. Why, I can put such spirit into a regiment with a single sermon that the enemy's a mere flock of sheep to them and their own lives no more than smelly old shoes to be thrown away at the thought of final victory! God has given me the gift of tongues. I can preach you out of your senses!

MOTHER COURAGE. I need my senses. What would I do without them?

CHAPLAIN. Mother Courage, I have often thought that—under a veil of plain speech —you conceal a heart. You are human, you need warmth.

MOTHER COURAGE. The best way of warming this tent is to chop plenty of firewood.

CHAPLAIN. You're changing the subject. Seriously, my dear Courage, I sometimes ask myself how it would be if our relationship should be somewhat more firmly cemented. I mean, now the wild wind of war has whirled us so strangely together.

MOTHER COURAGE. The cement's pretty firm already. I cook your meals. And you lend a hand—at chopping firewood, for instance.

CHAPLAIN (*going over to her, gesturing with the ax*). You know what I mean by a close relationship. It has nothing to do with eating and woodcutting and such base necessities. Let your heart speak!

MOTHER COURAGE. Don't come at me like that with your ax, that'd be *too* close a relationship!

CHAPLAIN. This is no laughing matter, I am in earnest. I've thought it all over.

MOTHER COURAGE. Dear Chaplain, be a sensible fellow. I like you, and I don't want to heap coals of fire on your head. All I want is to bring me and my children through in that wagon. It isn't just mine, the wagon, and anyway I've no mind to start any adventures. At the moment I'm taking quite a risk buying these things when the Commander's fallen and there's all this talk of peace. Where would you go, if I was ruined? See? You don't even know. Now chop some firewood and it'll be warm of an evening, which is quite a lot in times like these. What was that? (*She stands up.* KATTRIN *enters, breathless, with a wound across the eye and forehead. She is dragging all sorts of articles, parcels, leather goods, a drum, etc.*) What is it, were you attacked? On the way back? She was attacked on the way back! I'll bet it was that soldier who got drunk on my liquor. I should never have let you go. Dump all that stuff! It's not bad, the wound is only a flesh wound. I'll bandage it for you, it'll all be healed up in a week. They're worse than animals. (*She bandages the wound.*)

CHAPLAIN. I reproach them with nothing. At home they never did these shameful things. The men who start the wars are responsible, they bring out the worst in people.

MOTHER COURAGE. Didn't the clerk walk you back home? That's because you're a respectable girl, he thought they'd leave you alone. The wound's not at all deep, it will never show. There: all bandaged up. Now, I've got something for you, rest easy. I've been keeping them secret. (*She digs* YVETTE's *red boots out of a bag.*) Well, what do you see? You always wanted them. Now you have them. (*She helps her to put the boots on.*) Put them on quick, before I change my mind. It will never show, though it wouldn't bother *me* if it did. The ones they like fare worst. They drag them around till they're finished. Those they don't care for they leave alone. I've seen so many girls, pretty as they come in the beginning, then all of a sudden they're so ugly they'd scare a wolf. They can't even go behind a tree on the street without having something to fear from it. They lead a frightful life. Like with trees: the tall, straight ones are cut down for roof timber, and the crooked ones can enjoy life. So this wound here is really a piece of luck. The boots have kept well. I gave them a good cleaning before I put them away.

KATTRIN *leaves the boots and creeps into the wagon.*

CHAPLAIN (*when she's gone*). I hope she won't be disfigured?

MOTHER COURAGE. There'll be a scar. She needn't wait for peace now.

CHAPLAIN. She didn't let them get any of the stuff.

MOTHER COURAGE. Maybe I shouldn't have made such a point of it. If only I ever knew what went on inside her head. Once she stayed out all night, once in all the years. Afterward she seemed much the same, except that she worked harder. I

could never get out of her what happened. I worried about it for quite a while. (*She picks up the things* KATTRIN *spilled and sorts them angrily.*) This is a war. A nice source of income, I must say!

Cannon shots.

CHAPLAIN. Now they're lowering the Commander into his grave! A historic moment.

MOTHER COURAGE. It's a historic moment to me when they hit my daughter over the eye. She's all but finished now, she'll never get a husband, and she's so mad about children! Even her dumbness comes from the war. A soldier stuck something in her mouth when she was little. I'll never see Swiss Cheese again, and where my Eilif is the Good Lord knows. Curse the war!

7

Mother Courage at the height of her business career.

A highway. The CHAPLAIN, MOTHER COURAGE, *and her daughter* KATTRIN *pull the wagon, and new wares are hanging from it.* MOTHER COURAGE *wears a necklace of silver coins.*

MOTHER COURAGE. I won't let you spoil my war for me. Destroys the weak, does it? Well, what does peace do for 'em huh? War feeds its people better.

She sings.

If war don't suit your disposition
When victory comes, you will be dead.
War is a business proposition:
But not with cheese, with steel instead!
    Christians, awake! Winter is gone!
    The snows depart! Dead men sleep on!
    Let all of you who still survive
    Get out of bed and look alive!

And staying in one place won't help either.
Those who stay at home are the first to go.

She sings.

> Too many seek a bed to sleep in:
> Each ditch is taken, and each cave
> And he who digs a hole to creep in
> Finds he has dug an early grave.
> And many a man spends many a
>   minute
> In hurrying toward some resting place.
> You wonder, when at last he's in it
> Just why the fellow forced the pace.

The wagon proceeds.

8

*1632. In this same year Gustavus Adolphus
fell in the battle of Lützen. Then peace
threatens Mother Courage with ruin. Her
brave son performs one heroic deed too many
and comes to a shameful end.*

*A camp. A summer morning. In front of the
wagon, an* OLD WOMAN *and her son. The
son is dragging a large bag of bedding.*

MOTHER COURAGE (*from inside the wagon*).
Must you come at the crack of dawn?

YOUNG MAN. We've been walking all night,
twenty miles it was, we have to be back
today.

MOTHER COURAGE (*still inside*). What do I
want with bed feathers? People don't even
have houses.

YOUNG MAN. At least wait till you see 'em.

OLD WOMAN. Nothing doing here either, let's
go.

YOUNG MAN. And let 'em sign away the roof
over our heads for taxes? Maybe she'll pay
three guilders if you throw in that bracelet.
(*Bells start ringing.*) You hear, mother?

VOICES (*from the rear*). It's peace! The King
of Sweden's been killed!

MOTHER COURAGE *sticks her head out of
the wagon. She hasn't done her hair yet.*

MOTHER COURAGE. Bells! What are the bells
for, middle of the week?

CHAPLAIN (*crawling out from under the wagon*).
What's that they're shouting?

YOUNG MAN. It's peace.

CHAPLAIN. Peace!

MOTHER COURAGE. Don't tell me peace has
broken out—when I've just gone and
bought all these supplies!

CHAPLAIN (*calling, toward the rear*). Is it
peace?

VOICE (*from a distance*). They say the war
stopped three weeks ago. I've only just
heard.

CHAPLAIN (*to* MOTHER COURAGE). Or why
would they ring the bells?

VOICE. A great crowd of Lutherans have
just arrived with wagons—they brought
the news.

YOUNG MAN. It's peace, mother. (*The* OLD
WOMAN *collapses.*) What's the matter?

MOTHER COURAGE (*back in the wagon*). Kattrin,
it's peace! Put on your black dress, we're
going to church, we owe it to Swiss
Cheese! Can it be true?

YOUNG MAN. The people here say so too, the
war's over. Can you stand up? (*The* OLD
WOMAN *stands up, dazed.*) I'll get the har-
ness shop going again now, I promise you.
Everything'll be all right, father will get
his bed back. . . . Can you walk? (*To the*
CHAPLAIN.) She felt ill, it was the news.
She didn't believe there'd ever be peace
again. Father always said there would.
We're going home. (*They leave.*)

MOTHER COURAGE (*off*). Give her some
brandy.

CHAPLAIN. They've left already.

MOTHER COURAGE (*still off*). What's going on
in the camp over there?

CHAPLAIN. They're all getting together. I
think I'll go over. Shall I put my pastor's
coat on again?

MOTHER COURAGE. Better get the exact news
first, and not risk being taken for the Anti-

christ. I'm glad about the peace even though I'm ruined. At least I've got two of my children through the war. Now I'll see my Eilif again.

CHAPLAIN. And who may this be coming down from the camp? Well, if it isn't our Swedish Commander's cook!

COOK (*somewhat bedraggled, carrying a bundle*). Who's here? The chaplain!

CHAPLAIN. Mother Courage, a visitor!

MOTHER COURAGE *clambers out.*

COOK. Well, I promised I'd come over for a brief conversation as soon as I had time. I didn't forget your brandy, Mrs. Fierling.

MOTHER COURAGE. Jesus, the Commander's cook! After all these years! Where is Eilif, my eldest?

COOK. Isn't he here yet? He went on ahead yesterday, he was on his way over.

CHAPLAIN. I *will* put my pastor's coat on. I'll be back. (*He goes behind the wagon.*)

MOTHER COURAGE. He may be here any minute then. (*She calls toward the wagon.*) Kattrin, Eilif's coming! Bring a glass of brandy for the cook, Kattrin! (KATTRIN *doesn't come.*) Just pull your hair over it. Mr. Lamb is no stranger. (*She gets the brandy herself.*) She won't come out. Peace is nothing to her, it was too long coming. They hit her right over the eye. You can hardly see it now. But she thinks people stare at her.

COOK. Ah yes, war! (*He and* MOTHER COURAGE *sit.*)

MOTHER COURAGE. Cook, you come at a bad time: I'm ruined.

COOK. What? That's terrible!

MOTHER COURAGE. The peace has broken my neck. On the chaplain's advice I've gone and bought a lot of supplies. Now everybody's leaving and I'm holding the baby.

COOK. How could you listen to the chaplain? If I'd had time—but the Catholics were too quick for me—I'd have warned you against him. He's a windbag. Well, so now he's the big man round here!

MOTHER COURAGE. He's been doing the dishes for me and helping with the wagon.

COOK. With the wagon—him! And I'll bet he's told you a few of his jokes. He has a most unhealthy attitude to women. I tried to influence him but it was no good. He isn't sound.

MOTHER COURAGE. Are you sound?

COOK. If I'm nothing else, I'm sound. Your health!

MOTHER COURAGE. Sound! Only one person around here was ever sound, and I never had to slave as I did then. He sold the blankets off the children's beds in the spring, and he called my harmonica unchristian. You aren't recommending yourself if you *admit* you're sound.

COOK. You fight tooth and nail, don't you? I like that.

MOTHER COURAGE. Don't tell me you've been dreaming of my teeth and nails.

COOK. Well, here we sit, while the bells of peace do ring, and you pouring your famous brandy as only you know how!

MOTHER COURAGE. I don't think much of the bells of peace at the moment. I don't see how they can hand out all this pay that's in arrears. And then where shall I be with my famous brandy? Have you all been paid?

COOK (*hesitating*). Not exactly. That's why we disbanded. In the circumstances, I thought, why stay? For the time being, I'll look up a couple of friends. So here I sit—with you.

MOTHER COURAGE. In other words, you're broke.

COOK (*annoyed by the bells*). It's about time they stopped that racket! I'd like to set myself up in some business. I'm fed up with being their cook. I'm supposed to make do with tree roots and shoe leather, and then they throw my hot soup in my face! Being a cook nowadays is a dog's life. I'd sooner be a soldier, but of course, it's peace now. (*As the* CHAPLAIN *turns up, wearing his old coat.*) We'll talk it over later.

CHAPLAIN. The coat's pretty good. Just a few moth holes.

COOK. I don't know why you take the trouble.

You won't find another pulpit. Who could you incite now to earn an honest living or risk his life for a cause? Besides, I have a bone to pick with you.

CHAPLAIN. Have you?

COOK. I have. You advised a lady to buy superfluous goods on the pretext that the war would never end.

CHAPLAIN (*hotly*). I'd like to know what business it is of yours?

COOK. It's unprincipled behavior! How can you give unwanted advice? And interfere with the conduct of other people's business?

CHAPLAIN. Who's interfering now, I'd like to know? (*To* MOTHER COURAGE.) I had no idea you were such a close friend of this gentleman and had to account to *him* for everything.

MOTHER COURAGE. Now don't get excited. The cook's giving his personal opinion. You can't deny your war was a flop.

CHAPLAIN. You have no respect for peace, Courage. You're a hyena of the battlefield!

MOTHER COURAGE. A what?

COOK. Who insults my girl friend insults me!

CHAPLAIN. I am *not* speaking to you, your intentions are only too transparent! (*To* MOTHER COURAGE.) But when I see *you* take peace between finger and thumb like a snotty old hanky, my humanity rebels! It shows that you want war, not peace, for what you get out of it. But don't forget the proverb: he who sups with the devil must use a long spoon!

MOTHER COURAGE. Remember what one fox said to another that was caught in a trap? "If you stay there, you're just asking for trouble!" There isn't much love lost between me and the war. And when it comes to calling me a hyena, you and I part company.

CHAPLAIN. Then why all this grumbling about the peace just as everyone's heaving a sigh of relief? Is it for the junk in your wagon?

MOTHER COURAGE. My goods are not junk. I live off them. *You've* been living off them.

CHAPLAIN. You live off war. Exactly.

COOK (*to the* CHAPLAIN). As a grown man, you should know better than to go around advising people. (*To* MOTHER COURAGE.) Now, in your situation you'd be smart to get rid of certain goods at once—before the prices sink to nothing. Get ready and get going, there isn't a moment to lose!

MOTHER COURAGE. That's sensible advice, I think I'll take it.

CHAPLAIN. Because the cook says so.

MOTHER COURAGE. Why didn't *you* say so? He's right, I must get to the market. (*She climbs into the wagon.*)

COOK. One up for me, Chaplain. You have no presence of mind. You should have said, "*I* gave you advice? Why, I was just talking politics!" And you shouldn't take me on as a rival. Cockfights are not becoming to your cloth.

CHAPLAIN. If you don't shut your trap, I'll murder you, cloth or no cloth!

COOK (*taking his boots off and unwinding the wrappings on his feet*). If you hadn't degenerated into a godless tramp, you could easily get yourself a parsonage, now its peace. Cooks won't be needed, there's nothing to cook, but there's still plenty to believe, and people will go right on believing it.

CHAPLAIN. Mr. Lamb, please don't drive me out! Since I became a tramp, I'm a somewhat better man. I couldn't preach to 'em any more.

YVETTE POTTIER *enters, decked out in black, with a stick. She is much older, fatter, and heavily powdered. Behind her, a* SERVANT.

YVETTE. Hullo, everybody! Is this Mother Courage's establishment?

CHAPLAIN. Quite right. And with whom have we the pleasure?

YVETTE. I am Madame Colonel Starhemberg, good people. Where's Mother Courage?

CHAPLAIN (*calling to the wagon*). Madame Colonel Starhemberg wants to speak to you!

MOTHER COURAGE (*from inside*). Coming!

YVETTE (*calling*). It's Yvette!

MOTHER COURAGE (*inside*). Yvette!

YVETTE. Just to see how you're getting on! (*As the* COOK *turns around in horror.*) Peter!

COOK. Yvette!

YVETTE. Of all things! How did *you* get here?

COOK. On a cart.

CHAPLAIN. Well! You know each other? Intimately?

YVETTE. I'll say. (*Scrutinizing the* COOK.) You're fat.

COOK. For that matter, *you're* no beanpole.

YVETTE. Anyway, it's lucky we've met, tramp. Now I can tell you what I think of you.

CHAPLAIN. Do so, tell him all, but wait till Mother Courage comes out.

COOK. Now don't make a scene . . .

MOTHER COURAGE (*coming out, laden with goods*). Yvette! (*They embrace.*) But why are you in mourning?

YVETTE. Doesn't it suit me? My husband, the colonel, died several years ago.

MOTHER COURAGE. The old fellow that nearly bought my wagon?

YVETTE. His elder brother.

MOTHER COURAGE. So you're not doing badly. Good to see one person who got somewhere in the war.

YVETTE. I've had my ups and downs.

MOTHER COURAGE. Don't let's speak ill of colonels. They make money like hay.

CHAPLAIN (*to the* COOK). If I were you, I'd put my shoes on again. (*To* YVETTE.) You promised to give us your opinion of this gentleman.

COOK. Now, Yvette, don't make a stink!

MOTHER COURAGE. He's a friend of mine, Yvette.

YVETTE. He's—Peter Piper, that's who.

MOTHER COURAGE. What!

COOK. Cut the nicknames. My name's Lamb.

MOTHER COURAGE (*laughing*). Peter Piper? Who turned the women's heads? And I've been keeping your pipe for you.

CHAPLAIN. And smoking it.

YVETTE. Lucky I can warn you against him. He's a bad lot. You won't find worse on the whole coast of Flanders. He got more girls in trouble than . . .

COOK. That's a long time ago, it isn't true any more.

YVETTE. Stand up when you talk to a lady! Oh, how I loved that man; and all the time he was having a little bowlegged brunette. He got *her* into trouble too, of course.

COOK. I seem to have brought *you* luck!

YVETTE. Shut your trap, you hoary ruin! And you take care, Mother Courage, this type is still dangerous even in decay.

MOTHER COURAGE (*to* YVETTE). Come with me, I must get rid of this stuff before the prices fall.

YVETTE (*concentrating on the* COOK). Miserable cur!

MOTHER COURAGE. Maybe you can help me at army headquarters, you have contacts.

YVETTE. Seducer!

MOTHER COURAGE (*shouting into the wagon*). Kattrin, church is all off, I'm going to market!

YVETTE. Whore hunter!

MOTHER COURAGE (*still to* KATTRIN). When Eilif comes, give him something to drink!

YVETTE. That a man like him should have been able to turn me from the straight and narrow! I have my own star to thank that I rose none the less to the heights! But I've put an end to your tricks, Peter Piper, and one day—in a better life than this—the Lord God will reward me! Come, Mother Courage! (*She leaves with* MOTHER COURAGE.)

CHAPLAIN. As our text this morning let us take the saying: the mills of God grind slowly. And you complain of my jokes!

COOK. I never have any luck. I'll be frank, I was hoping for a good hot dinner, I'm starving. And now they'll be talking about me, and she'll get a completely wrong picture. I think I should go before she comes back.

CHAPLAIN. I think so too.

COOK. Chaplain, peace makes me sick. Mankind must perish by fire and sword, we're born and bred in sin! Oh, how I wish I was roasting a great fat capon for the Commander—God knows where *he's* got to—

with mustard sauce and those little yellow carrots . . .

CHAPLAIN. Red cabbage—with capon, red cabbage.

COOK. You're right. But he always wanted yellow carrots.

CHAPLAIN. He never understood a thing.

COOK. You always put plenty away.

CHAPLAIN. Under protest.

COOK. Anyway, you must admit, those were the days.

CHAPLAIN. Yes, that I might admit.

COOK. Now you've called her a hyena, there's not much future for you here either. What are you staring at?

CHAPLAIN. It's Eilif!

Followed by two soldiers with halberds, EILIF *enters. His hands are fettered. He is white as chalk.*

CHAPLAIN. What's happened to you?

EILIF. Where's mother?

CHAPLAIN. Gone to town.

EILIF. They said she was here. I was allowed a last visit.

COOK (*to the* SOLDIERS). Where are you taking him?

A SOLDIER. For a ride.

The other SOLDIER *makes the gesture of throat cutting.*

CHAPLAIN. What has he done?

SOLDIER. He broke in on a peasant. The wife is dead.

CHAPLAIN. Eilif, how could you?

EILIF. It's no different. It's what I did before.

COOK. That was in war time.

EILIF. Shut your hole. Can I sit down till she comes?

SOLDIER. No.

CHAPLAIN. It's true. In war time they honored him for it. He sat at the Commander's right hand. It was bravery. Couldn't we speak with the military police?

SOLDIER. What's the use? Stealing cattle from a peasant, what's brave about that?

COOK. It was just stupid.

EILIF. If I'd been stupid, I'd have starved, smarty.

COOK. So you were bright and paid for it.

CHAPLAIN. At least we must bring Kattrin out.

EILIF. Let her alone. Just give me some brandy.

SOLDIER. No.

CHAPLAIN. What shall we tell your mother?

EILIF. Tell her it was no different. Tell her it was the same. Oh, tell her nothing.

The SOLDIERS *take him away.*

CHAPLAIN. I'll come with you, I'll . . .

EILIF. I don't need a priest!

CHAPLAIN. You don't know—yet. (*He follows him.*)

COOK (*calling after him*). I'll have to tell her, she'll want to see him!

CHAPLAIN. Better tell her nothing, Or maybe just that he was here, and he'll return, maybe tomorrow. Meantime I'll be back and can break the news. (*He leaves quickly.*)

The COOK *looks after him, shakes his head, then walks about uneasily. Finally, he approaches the wagon.*

COOK. Hello! Won't you come out? You want to sneak away from the peace, don't you? Well, so do I! I'm the Swedish Commander's cook, remember me? I was wondering if you've got anything to eat in there—while we're waiting for your mother. I wouldn't mind a bit of bacon— or even bread—just to pass the time. (*He looks in.*) She's got a blanket over her head.

The thunder of cannon.

MOTHER COURAGE *runs in, out of breath, still carrying the goods.*

MOTHER COURAGE. Cook, the peace is over, the war's on again, has been for three days! I didn't get rid of this stuff after all, thank God! There's a shooting match in the town already—with the Lutherans. We must get away with the wagon. Pack, Kattrin!

What's on *your* mind? Something the matter?

COOK. Nothing.

MOTHER COURAGE. But there is. I see it in your face.

COOK. Because the war's on again, most likely. May it last till tomorrow evening, so I can get something in my belly!

MOTHER COURAGE. You're not telling me.

COOK. Eilif was here. Only he had to go away again.

MOTHER COURAGE. He was here? Then we'll see him on the march. I'll be with our side this time. How'd he look?

COOK. The same.

MOTHER COURAGE. He'll *never* change. And the war couldn't get *him*, he's bright. Help me with the packing. (*She starts it.*) Did he tell you anything? Is he well in with the Provost? Did he tell you about his heroic deeds?

COOK (*darkly*). He's done one of them again.

MOTHER COURAGE. Tell me about it later. (KATTRIN *appears.*) Kattrin, the peace is over, we're on the move again. (*To the* COOK.) What *is* the matter with you?

COOK. I'll enlist.

MOTHER COURAGE. A good idea. Where's the Chaplain?

COOK. In the town. With Eilif.

MOTHER COURAGE. Stay with us a while, Lamb, I need a bit of help.

COOK. This matter of Yvette . . .

MOTHER COURAGE. Hasn't done you any harm at all in my eyes. Just the opposite. Where there's smoke, there's fire, they say. You'll come?

COOK. I may as well.

MOTHER COURAGE. The Twelfth Regiment's under way. Into harness with you! Maybe I'll see Eilif before the day is out, just think! That's what I like best. Well, it wasn't such a long peace, we can't grumble. Let's go!

The COOK *and* KATTRIN *are in harness.*
MOTHER COURAGE *sings.*

From Ulm to Metz, past dome and steeple

My wagon always moves ahead.
The war can care for all its people
So long as there is steel and lead.
Though steel and lead are stout supporters
A war needs human beings too.
Report today to your headquarters!
If it's to last, this war needs you!

9

The great war of religion has lasted sixteen years and Germany has lost half its inhabitants. Those who are spared in battle die by plague. Over once blooming countryside hunger rages. Towns are burned down. Wolves prowl the empty streets. In the autumn of 1634 we find Mother Courage in the Fichtelgebirge not far from the road the Swedish army is taking. Winter has come early and is hard. Business is bad. Only begging remains. The cook receives a letter from Utrecht and is sent packing.

In front of a half-ruined parsonage. Early winter. A gray morning. Gusts of wind. MOTHER COURAGE *and the* COOK *at the wagon in shabby clothes.*

COOK. There are no lights on. No one's up.

MOTHER COURAGE. But it's a parsonage. The parson'll have to leave his feather bed and ring the bells. Then he'll have some hot soup.

COOK. Where'll he get it from? The whole village is starving.

MOTHER COURAGE. The house is lived in. There was a dog barking.

COOK. If the parson has anything, he'll hang on to it.

MOTHER COURAGE. Maybe if we sang him something . . .

COOK. I've had enough. (*Suddenly.*) I didn't tell you, a letter came from Utrecht. My mother's died of cholera, the inn is mine. There's the letter, if you don't believe me. I'll show it to you, though my aunt's railing about me and my ups and downs is none of your business.

MOTHER COURAGE (*reading*). Lamb, I'm tired of wandering, too. I feel like a butcher's dog taking meat to my customers and getting none myself. I've nothing more to sell and people have nothing to pay with. In Saxony someone tried to force a chestful of books on me in return for two eggs. And in Württemberg they would have let me have their plough for a bag of salt. Nothing grows any more, only thorn bushes. In Pomerania I hear the villagers have been eating their younger children. Nuns have been caught committing robbery.

COOK. The world's dying out.

MOTHER COURAGE. Sometimes I see myself driving through hell with this wagon and selling brimstone. And sometimes I'm driving through heaven handing our provisions to wandering souls! If only we could find a place where there's no shooting, me and my children—what's left of 'em—we might rest a while.

COOK. We could open this inn together. Think about it, Courage. *My* mind's made up. With or without you, I'm leaving for Utrecht. And today too.

MOTHER COURAGE. I must talk to Kattrin, it's a bit sudden, and I don't like to make my decisions in the cold on an empty stomach. (KATTRIN *emerges from the wagon.*) Kattrin, I've something to tell you. The cook and I want to go to Utrecht, he's been left an inn. You'd be able to stay put and get to know some people. Many a man'd be prepared to take on a girl with a position. Looks aren't everything. I like the idea. I get on well with the cook. I'll say this for him: he has a head for business. We'd be sure of our dinner, that would be all right, wouldn't it? You'd have your own bed, what do you think of *that*? In the long run, this is no life, on the road. You might be killed any time. You're eaten up with lice as it is. And we must decide now, because otherwise we go north with the Swedes. They must be over there somewhere. (*She points left.*) I think we'll decide to go, Kattrin.

COOK. Anna, I must have a word with you alone.

MOTHER COURAGE. Go back inside, Kattrin.

KATTRIN *does so.*

COOK. I'm interrupting because there's a misunderstanding, Anna. I thought I wouldn't have to say it right out, but I see I must. If you're bringing *her*, it's all off. Do we understand each other?

KATTRIN *has her head out of the back of the wagon and is listening.*

MOTHER COURAGE. You mean I leave Kattrin behind?

COOK. What do you think? There's no room in the inn, it isn't one of those places with three counters. If the two of us look lively we can earn a living, but three's too many. Let Kattrin keep your wagon.

MOTHER COURAGE. I was thinking we might find her a husband in Utrecht.

COOK. Don't make me laugh. With that scar? And old as she is? And dumb?

MOTHER COURAGE. Not so loud!

COOK. Loud or soft, what is, is. That's another reason I can't have her in the inn. Customers don't like having something like that always before their eyes. You can't blame them.

MOTHER COURAGE. Shut up. I told you not to talk so loud.

COOK. There's a light in the parsonage, we can sing now!

MOTHER COURAGE. Cook, how could she pull the wagon by herself? The war frightens her. She can't bear it. She has terrible dreams. I hear her groan at night, especially after battles. What she sees in her dreams I don't know. She suffers from sheer pity. The other day I found her with a hedgehog that we'd run over.

COOK. The inn's too small. (*Calling.*) Worthy Sir, menials, and all within! We now present the song of Solomon, Julius Caesar, and other great souls who came to no good, so you can see we're law-abiding folk too, and have a hard time getting by, especially in winter.

He sings "The Song of the Great Souls of this Earth."

King Solomon was very wise,
So what's his history?
He came to view this life with scorn,
Yes, he came to regret he ever had been born
Declaring: all is vanity.
King Solomon was very wise,
But long before the day was out
The consequence was clear, alas:
His wisdom 'twas that brought him to this pass.
A man is better off without.

For the virtues are dangerous in this world, as our fine song tells. You're better off without, you have a nice life, breakfast included—some good hot soup maybe . . . I'm an example of a man who's not had any, and I'd like some. I'm a soldier, but what good did my bravery do me in all those battles? None at all. I might just as well have wet my pants like a poltroon and stayed at home. For why?

Old Julius Caesar, he was brave.
His fame shall never cease.
He sat like a god on an altar piece.
Yet they tore brave old Julius limb from valiant limb
And Brutus helped to slaughter him.
Old Julius was very brave
But long before the day was out
The consequence was clear, alas:
His bravery 'twas that brought him to this pass.
A man is better off without.

(*Under his breath.*) They don't even look out. (*Aloud.*) Worthy Sir, menials, and all within! You could say, no, courage isn't the thing to fill a man's belly, try honesty, that should be worth a dinner, at any rate it must have *some* effect. Let's see.

You all know honest Socrates
Who always spoke the truth.
They owed him thanks for that, you'd think,
But what happened? Why, they put hemlock in his drink
And swore that he misled the youth.
How honest was this Socrates!
Yet long before the day was out
The consequence was clear, alas:
His honesty had brought him to this pass.
A man is better off without.

Yes, we're told to be unselfish and share what we have, but what if we have nothing? And those who do share it don't have an easy time either, for what's left when you're through sharing? Unselfishness is a very rare virtue—it doesn't pay.

Unselfish Martin could not bear
His fellow creatures' woes.
He met a poor man in the snows
And he gave this poor fellow half his cloak to wear:
So both of them fell down and froze.
His brothers' woes he could not bear,
So long before the day was out
The consequence was clear, alas:
Unselfishness had brought him to this pass.
A man is better off without.

That's how it is with us. We're law-abiding folk, we keep to ourselves, don't steal, don't kill, don't burn the place down. And in this way we sink lower and lower and the song proves true and there's no soup going. And if we were different, if we were thieves and killers, maybe we could eat our fill! For virtues bring no reward, only vices. Such is the world, need it be so?

God's ten commandments we have kept
And acted as we should.
It has not done us any good.
All you people who sit beside a roaring fire

O help us in our need so dire!
The ten commandments we have kept
And long before the day was out
The consequence was clear, alas:
Our godliness has brought us to this
    pass.
A man is better off without.

VOICE (*from above*). You there! Come up!
There's some soup here for you!
MOTHER COURAGE. Lamb, I couldn't swallow
a thing. I don't say what you said is un-
reasonable, but was it your last word?
We've always understood each other.
COOK. Yes, Anna. Think it over.
MOTHER COURAGE. There's nothing to think
over. I'm not leaving her here.
COOK. You're going to be silly, but what can
I do? I'm not inhuman, it's just that the
inn's a small one. And now we must go
up, or there'll be nothing doing here too,
and we've been singing in the cold for
nothing.
MOTHER COURAGE. I'll fetch Kattrin.
COOK. Better stick something in your pocket
for her. If there are three of us, they'll
get a shock.

Exeunt.

KATTRIN *clambers out of the wagon with a
bundle. She makes sure they are both gone.
Then, on a wagon wheel, she lays out a
skirt of her mother's and a pair of the cook's
trousers side by side and easy to see. She has
just finished, and has picked up her bundle,
when* MOTHER COURAGE *returns.*

MOTHER COURAGE (*with a plate of soup*).
Kattrin! Stay where you are, Kattrin!
Where do you think you're going with
that bundle? (*She examines the bundle.*)
She's packed her things. Were you listening? I told him there was nothing doing,
he can *have* Utrecht and his lousy inn,
what would we want with a lousy inn?
(*She sees the skirt and trousers.*) Oh, you're a
stupid girl, Kattrin, what if I'd seen that
and you gone? (*She takes hold of* KATTRIN

who is trying to leave.) And don't think I've
sent him packing on your account. It was
the wagon. You can't part us, I'm too used
to it, it was the wagon. Now we're leaving
and we'll put the cook's things here where
he'll find 'em, the stupid man. (*She clambers
up and throws a couple of things down to go
with the trousers.*) There! He's fired. The last
man I'll take into *this* business! Now let's
be going, you and me. This winter'll pass,
like all the others. Get into harness, it
looks like snow.

*They harness themselves to the wagon, turn
it around, and start out. A gust of wind.
Enter the* COOK, *still chewing. He sees his
things.*

10

*During the whole of 1635 Mother Courage
and Kattrin pull the wagon along the roads
of central Germany in the wake of the ever
more tattered armies.*
On the highway. MOTHER COURAGE *and*
KATTRIN *are pulling the wagon. They come
to a prosperous farmhouse. Someone inside
is singing.*

VOICE.

In March a bush we planted
To make the garden gay.
In June we were enchanted:
A lovely rose was blooming
The balmy air perfuming!
Blest are they
Who have gardens gay!
In June we were enchanted.

When snow falls helter-skelter
And loudly blows the storm
Our farmhouse gives us shelter.
The winter's in a hurry
But we've no cause to worry.
We are warm
In the midst of the storm!
Our farmhouse gives us shelter.

MOTHER COURAGE *and* KATTRIN *have stopped to listen. Then they start out again.*

11

January, 1636. Catholic troops threaten the Protestant town of Halle. The stone begins to speak. Mother Courage loses her daughter and journeys onward alone. The war is not yet near its end.

The wagon, very far gone now, stands near a farmhouse with a straw roof. It is night. Out of the woods come a LIEUTENANT *and three* SOLDIERS *in full armor.*

LIEUTENANT. And there mustn't be a sound. If anyone yells, cut him down.

FIRST SOLDIER. But we'll have to knock—if we want a guide.

LIEUTENANT. Knocking's a natural noise, it's all right, could be a cow hitting the wall of the cowshed.

The SOLDIERS *knock at the farmhouse door. An* OLD PEASANT WOMAN *opens. A hand is clapped over her mouth. Two* SOLDIERS *enter.*

A MAN'S VOICE. What is it?

The SOLDIERS *bring out an* OLD PEASANT *and his son.*

LIEUTENANT (*pointing to the wagon on which* KATTRIN *has appeared*). There's one. (*A* SOLDIER *pulls her out.*) Is this everybody that lives here?

PEASANTS (*alternating*). That's our son. And that's a girl that can't talk. Her mother's in town buying up stocks because the shopkeepers are running away and selling cheap. They're canteen people.

LIEUTENANT. I'm warning you. Keep quiet. One sound and we'll crack you over the head with a pike. And I need someone to show us the path to the town. (*He points to the* YOUNG PEASANT.) You! Come here!

YOUNG PEASANT. I don't know any path!

SECOND SOLDIER (*grinning*). He don't know any path!

YOUNG PEASANT. I don't help Catholics.

LIEUTENANT (*to the* SECOND SOLDIER). Let him feel your pike in his side.

YOUNG PEASANT (*forced to his knees, the pike at his throat*). I'd rather die!

SECOND SOLDIER (*again mimicking*). He'd rather die!

FIRST SOLDIER. I know how to change his mind. (*He walks over to the cowshed.*) Two cows and a bull. Listen, you. If you aren't going to be reasonable, I'll saber your cattle.

YOUNG PEASANT. Not the cattle!

PEASANT WOMAN (*weeping*). Spare the cattle, Captain, or we'll starve!

LIEUTENANT. If he must be pigheaded!

FIRST SOLDIER. I think I'll start with the bull.

YOUNG PEASANT (*to the old one*). Do I have to? (*The older one nods.*) I'll do it.

PEASANT WOMAN. Thank you, thank you, Captain, for sparing us, for ever and ever, Amen.

The OLD MAN *stops her going on thanking him.*

FIRST SOLDIER. I knew the bull came first all right!

Led by the YOUNG PEASANT, *the* LIEUTENANT *and the* SOLDIERS *go on their way.*

OLD PEASANT. I wish we knew what it was. Nothing good, I suppose.

PEASANT WOMAN. Maybe they're just scouts. What are you doing?

OLD PEASANT (*setting a ladder against the roof and climbing up*). I'm seeing if they're alone. (*On the roof.*) Things are moving—all over. I can see armor. And cannon. There must be more than a regiment. God have mercy on the town and all within!

PEASANT WOMAN. Are there lights in the town?

OLD PEASANT. No, they're all asleep. (*He

climbs down.) There'll be an attack, and they'll all be slaughtered in their beds.

PEASANT WOMAN. The watchman'll give warning.

OLD PEASANT. They must have killed the watchman in the tower on the hill or he'd have sounded his horn before this.

PEASANT WOMAN. If there were more of us . . .

OLD PEASANT. But being that we're alone with that cripple . . .

PEASANT WOMAN. There's nothing we can do, is there?

OLD PEASANT. Nothing.

PEASANT WOMAN. We can't get down there. In the dark.

OLD PEASANT. The whole hillside's swarming with 'em.

PEASANT WOMAN. We could give a sign?

OLD PEASANT. And be cut down for it?

PEASANT WOMAN. No, there's nothing we can do. (*To* KATTRIN.) Pray, poor thing, pray! There's nothing we can do to stop this bloodshed, so even if you can't talk, at least pray! He hears, if no one else does. I'll help you. (*All kneel,* KATTRIN *behind.*) Our Father, which art in Heaven, hear our prayer, let not the town perish with all that lie therein asleep and fearing nothing. Wake them, that they rise and go to the walls and see the foe that comes with fire and sword in the night down the hill and across the fields. (*Back to* KATTRIN.) God protect our mother and make the watchman not sleep but wake ere it's too late. And save our son-in-law, too, O God, he's there with his four children, let them not perish, they're innocent, they know nothing—(*To* KATTRIN, *who groans.*)—one of them's not two years old, the eldest is seven. (KATTRIN *rises, troubled.*) Heavenly Father, hear us, only Thou canst help us or we die, for we are weak and have no sword nor nothing; we cannot trust our own strength but only Thine, O Lord; we are in Thy hands, our cattle, our farm, and the town too, we're all in Thy hands, and the foe is nigh unto the walls with all his power.

KATTRIN, *unperceived, has crept off to the wagon, has taken something out of it, put it under her apron, and has climbed up the ladder to the roof.*

Be mindful of the children in danger, especially the little ones, be mindful of the old folk who cannot move, and of all Christian souls, O Lord.

OLD PEASANT. And forgive us our trespasses as we forgive them that trespass against us. Amen.

Sitting on the roof, KATTRIN *takes a drum from under her apron and starts to beat it.*

PEASANT WOMAN. Heavens, what's she doing?

OLD PEASANT. She's out of her mind!

PEASANT WOMAN. Get her down, quick.

The OLD PEASANT *runs to the ladder but* KATTRIN *pulls it up on the roof.*

She'll get us in trouble.

OLD PEASANT. Stop it this minute, you silly cripple!

PEASANT WOMAN. The soldiers'll come!

OLD PEASANT (*looking for stones*). I'll stone you!

PEASANT WOMAN. Have you no pity, have you no heart? We have relations there too, four grandchildren, but there's nothing we can do. If they find us now, it's the end, they'll stab us to death!

KATTRIN *is staring into the far distance, toward the town. She goes on drumming.*

PEASANT WOMAN (*to the* PEASANT). I told you not to let that riffraff on your farm. What do *they* care if we lose our cattle?

LIEUTENANT (*running back with* SOLDIERS *and the* YOUNG PEASANT). I'll cut you all to bits!

PEASANT WOMAN. We're innocent, sir, there's nothing we can do. She did it, a stranger!

LIEUTENANT. Where's the ladder?

OLD PEASANT. On the roof.

LIEUTENANT (*calling*). Throw down the drum.

I order you! (KATTRIN *goes on drumming.*) You're all in this, but you won't live to tell the tale.

OLD PEASANT. They've been cutting down fir trees around here. If we bring a tall enough trunk we can knock her off the roof . . .

FIRST SOLDIER (*to the* LIEUTENANT). I beg leave to make a suggestion. (*He whispers something to the* LIEUTENANT, *who nods.*) Listen, you! We have an idea—for your own good. Come down and go with us to the town. Show us your mother and we'll spare her.

KATTRIN goes on drumming.

LIEUTENANT (*pushing him away*). She doesn't trust you, no wonder with your face. (*He calls up to* KATTRIN:) Hey, you! Suppose I give you my word? I'm an officer, my word's my bond!

KATTRIN drums harder.

Nothing is sacred to her.

YOUNG PEASANT. Sir, it's not just because of her mother!

FIRST SOLDIER. This can't go on, they'll hear it in the town as sure as hell.

LIEUTENANT. We must make another noise with something. Louder than that drum. What can we make a noise with?

FIRST SOLDIER. But we musn't make a noise!

LIEUTENANT. A harmless noise, fool, a peace-time noise!

OLD PEASANT. I could start chopping wood.

LIEUTENANT. That's it! (*The* PEASANT *brings his ax and chops away.*) Chop! Chop harder! Chop for your life!

KATTRIN has been listening, beating the drum less hard. Very upset, and peering around, she now goes on drumming.

It's not enough. (*To the* FIRST SOLDIER.) You chop too!

OLD PEASANT. I've only one ax. (*He stops chopping.*)

LIEUTENANT. We must set fire to the farm. Smoke her out.

OLD PEASANT. That's no good, Captain. When they see fire from the town, they'll know everything.

During the drumming KATTRIN *has been listening again. Now she laughs.*

LIEUTENANT. She's laughing at us, that's too much, I'll have her guts if it's the last thing I do. Bring a musket!

Two SOLDIERS *off.* KATTRIN *goes on drumming.*

PEASANT WOMAN. I have it, Captain. That's their wagon over there, Captain. If we smash that, she'll stop. It's all they have, Captain.

LIEUTENANT (*to the* YOUNG PEASANT). Smash it! (*Calling.*) If you don't stop that noise, we'll smash your wagon!

The YOUNG PEASANT *deals the wagon a couple of feeble blows with a board.*

PEASANT WOMAN (*to* KATTRIN). Stop, you little beast!

KATTRIN stares at the wagon and pauses. Noises of distress come out of her. But she goes on drumming.

LIEUTENANT. Where are those sons of bitches with that gun?

FIRST SOLDIER. They can't have heard anything in the town or we'd hear their cannon.

LIEUTENANT (*calling*). They don't hear you. And now we're going to shoot you. I'll give you one more chance: throw down that drum!

YOUNG PEASANT (*dropping the board, screaming to* KATTRIN). Don't stop now! Or they're all done for. Go on, go on, go on . . .

The SOLDIER *knocks him down and beats him with his pike.* KATTRIN *starts crying but goes on drumming.*

PEASANT WOMAN. Not in the back, you're killing him!

The SOLDIERS *arrive with the musket.*

SECOND SOLDIER. The Colonel's foaming at the mouth. We'll be court-martialed.
LIEUTENANT. Set it up! Set it up! (*Calling while the musket is set up on forks.*) Once and for all: stop that drumming!

Still crying, KATTRIN *is drumming as hard as she can.*

Fire!

The SOLDIERS *fire.* KATTRIN *is hit. She gives the drum another feeble beat or two, then slowly collapses.*

LIEUTENANT. That's an end to the noise.

But the last beats of the drum are lost in the din of cannon from the town. Mingled with the thunder of cannon, alarm bells are heard in the distance.

FIRST SOLDIER. She made it.

12

Toward morning. The drums and pipes of troops on the march, receding. In front of the wagon MOTHER COURAGE *sits by KATTRIN's body. The* PEASANTS *of the last scene are standing near.*

PEASANTS. You must leave, woman. There's only one regiment to go. You can never get away by yourself.
MOTHER COURAGE. Maybe she's fallen asleep.

She sings.

Lullaby, baby, what's that in the hay?
The neighbor's kids cry but mine are gay.

The neighbor's kids are dressed in dirt:
Your silks are cut from an angel's skirt.
They are all starving: you have a pie.
If it's too stale, you need only cry.
Lullaby, baby, what's rustling there?
One lad fell in Poland. The other is—
    where?

You shouldn't have told her about the children.
PEASANTS. If you hadn't gone off to the town to get your cut, maybe it wouldn't have happened.
MOTHER COURAGE. She's asleep now.
PEASANTS. She's not asleep, it's time you realized. She's gone. You must get away. There are wolves in these parts. And the bandits are worse.
MOTHER COURAGE. That's right. (*She goes and fetches a cloth from the wagon to cover up the body.*)
PEASANT WOMAN. Have you no one now? Someone you can go to?
MOTHER COURAGE. There's one. My Eilif.
PEASANT (*while* MOTHER COURAGE *covers the body*). Find him then. Leave *her* to us. We'll give her a proper burial. You needn't worry.
MOTHER COURAGE. Here's money for the expenses.

She pays the PEASANT. *The* PEASANT *and his son shake her hand and carry* KATTRIN *away.*

PEASANT WOMAN (*also taking her hand, and bowing, as she goes away*). Hurry!
MOTHER COURAGE (*harnessing herself to the wagon*). I hope I can pull the wagon by myself. Yes, I'll manage, there's not much in it now. I must get back into business.

Another regiment passes at the rear with pipe and drum.

MOTHER COURAGE *starts pulling the wagon.*

MOTHER COURAGE. Hey! Take me with you!

Soldiers are heard singing.

Dangers, surprises, devastations!
The war moves on, but will not quit.
And though it last three generations,
We shall get nothing out of it.
Starvation, filth, and cold enslave us.
The army robs us of our pay.

But God may yet come down and save
    us:
His holy war won't end today.
    Christians, awake! Winter is gone!
    The snows depart! Dead men sleep on!
    Let all of you who still survive
    Get out of bed and look alive!

DIRECTOR'S NOTES TO MOTHER COURAGE AND HER CHILDREN, SCENES XI AND XII

Bertolt Brecht

translated by Eric Bentley and Hugo Schmidt

ELEVENTH SCENE

Dumb Kattrin Saves the City of Halle

The city of Halle is to be taken by surprise. Soldiers force a young peasant to show them the way. A peasant and his wife ask Kattrin to pray with them for the city of Halle. The dumb girl climbs onto the roof of the stable and beats the drum in order to awaken the city of Halle. Neither the offer to spare her mother in the city, nor the threat to smash the wagon keep Kattrin from going on drumming. Dumb Kattrin's death.

BASIC ARRANGEMENT

The city of Halle is to be taken by surprise. Soldiers force a young peasant to show them the way. A Lieutenant and two soldiers enter a farm during the night. They fetch the drowsy peasants, and Kattrin from her wagon. By threatening to cut down the only ox, they force the young peasant to guide them. (They

Reprinted by permission of Stefan S. Brecht and Eric Bentley and Hugo Schmidt from *Encore* (London), May-June, 1965.

lead him to the back, all exit to the right.)

Peasant and wife ask Kattrin to pray with them for the city of Halle. The peasant props a ladder against the stable (right), climbs up, and sees that the woods are teeming with soldiers. Climbing down, he and his wife say that they must not endanger themselves by an attempt to warn the city. The woman goes up to Kattrin (downstage right), asks her to beg God to help the city; and they and the peasant kneel down to pray.

The dumb girl climbs onto the roof of the stable and beats the drum in order to awaken the city of Halle. From the peasant woman's prayer Kattrin learns that the children of the city of Halle are in danger. Stealthily she fetches a drum from the wagon, the same one that she had brought back when she was disfigured, and climbs onto the stable roof with it. She starts drumming. In vain the peasants try to keep her quiet.

Neither the offer to spare her mother in the city, nor the threat to smash the wagon keeps Kattrin from going on drumming. Upon hearing the drum, the Lieutenant and the soldiers come running back with the young peasant; the soldiers post themselves in front of the wagon; and the Lieutenant threatens the peasants with his sword. One of the soldiers steps into the middle of the stage in order to make promises to the drumming girl; and after him the Lieutenant. The peasant runs up to a tree (downstage left) and hits it with an axe, in order to drown the noise of the drum. Kattrin emerges victorious from this competition in noise. The Lieutenant wants to enter the house to set it on fire; the peasant woman points to the wagon. One of the soldiers forces the young peasant to deal blows to the wagon by kicking him. The other soldier is sent to get a musket. He sets it up, and the Lieutenant orders him to fire.

Death of Dumb Kattrin. Kattrin falls forward, the drumsticks in her faltering hands strike one more blow and a weaker afterblow. For a moment the Lieutenant triumphs; then the guns of Halle answer, taking up the rhythm of the drum beats of Dumb Kattrin.

BAD COMEDIANS ALWAYS LAUGH, BAD TRAGEDIANS ALWAYS CRY

In playing funny as well as sad scenes, everything depends on a blending of precision and casualness, on the assurance of a nimble wrist in handling the story within the arrangement. The actors take their places and form their groups very much in the manner in which marbles, scattered, fall into hollowed-out parts of wooden trays in some roulette-like toys. In such a game, it is not predetermined which marble will fall into which hole, whereas in theatrical arrangement it only *seems* not to be predetermined. The rigidity and heaviness which generally prevails during sad scenes in Germany stems from the fact that for no good reason *the human body is forgotten*. The actors seem to be seized with a muscle cramp. What nonsense!

THE TWO FEARS OF DUMB KATTRIN

Her dumbness does not help Kattrin one bit—war holds out a drum to her. With the unsold drum, she has to climb to the stable roof to save the children of the city of Halle.

It is necessary to steer free of the heroic cliché. Two fears fill Dumb Kattrin: for the city of Halle, and for herself.

"THE DRAMATIC SCENE"

The drum scene excited the audience in a special manner. This was sometimes explained by the fact that this is the most dramatic scene of the play, and that the audience preferred the dramatic to the epic. Actually, Epic Theater is able to present much more than agitated events, clashes, complots, mental tortures, etc., but it is also able to represent these. Spectators may identify themselves with Dumb Kattrin in this scene; they may project their personality into this creature; and may happily feel that such forces are present in them, too. They will, however, not have been able to project in this manner throughout every bit of the play; hardly, e.g., in the first scenes.

ALIENATION

If one wants to keep the scene free from wild excitement on the stage—excitement that spells destruction to whatever is remarkable in the scene—one must carry out certain "alienations" especially carefully.

E.g., the conversation of the peasants about the surprise attack is in danger of being simply sympathized with, if it is part of a general turmoil. It would not show how they justify their doing nothing and assure each other of the necessity of doing nothing—so that the only "action" possible is prayer.

Therefore the actors were told, during rehearsals, to add after their lines "said the man," "said the woman." As follows:

" 'The watchman will give warning,' said the woman."

" 'They must have killed the watchman,' said the man."

" 'If only there were more of us,' said the woman."

" 'But being that we are alone with that cripple,' said the man."

" 'There is nothing we can do, is there?' said the woman."

" 'Nothing,' said the man." Etc.

DUMB KATTRIN'S DRUMMING

The drumming is interrupted since Kattrin always keeps an eye on the events in the farm. The interruptions come in after:

"Heavens, what is she doing?"

"I'll cut you all to bits."

"Listen you! We have an idea—for your own good."

"No wonder with your face!"

"We must set fire to the farm."

DETAILS DURING STORMY SCENES

Scenes like the one in which the peasant tries to drown Kattrin's drumming by chopping wood must be acted out fully. While drumming, Kattrin must look down at the peasant and must take up the challenge. A certain persistency in directing is needed to make such pantomimes last long enough in stormy scenes.

A DETAIL

Hurwicz showed increasing exhaustion while drumming.

CEREMONIAL CHARACTER OF DESPAIR

The lamentations of the peasant woman whose son the soldiers take away and whose farm they threaten must sound somewhat hackneyed. They must be somewhat of a "generally accepted form of reaction" at the time when Dumb Kattrin begins her act of waking and drumming. The war has lasted a long time. Lamenting, begging and informing have become rigid forms: this is the way to behave when the soldiery appears.

It pays to forego the "immediate impression" of the apparently unique, actual horror in order to reach more subtle strata of horror where frequent, ever repeated misfortune has forced man to formalize his defensive gestures—though of course, he cannot substitute these gestures for real fear. Fear must show through the ceremony in this scene.

TO ACT OLD AGE

During a tour, a very young actress had the opportunity to play the peasant woman of the 11th scene—who is at least forty, but probably prematurely aged, as befits her class. In such cases one usually tries (wrongly) to produce from the start the image of old age by changing one's voice and gestures. Instead, one should assume that the lines and attitudes are those of a forty-year-old woman in the text and one should simply work out, from the text, one sound after the next and one gesture after the next, and should be assured that the image of a forty-year-old will eventually emerge by virtue of this inductive method. The "age" of the peasant woman was created through the disfigurings and rapes that she was exposed to, the miscarriages and processions behind the coffins of little children, hard labor during childhood,

physical abuse from parents and husband, psychic abuse from clergy, the necessity of boot-licking and snivelling, etc. This way only, by being herself raped and informed on, could she turn into an informer and opportunist. On account of the actress's youth it was difficult for her during rehearsals to hit the mark in kneeling down to pray in that wretchedly routine fashion, or in kneeling down to whimper for mercy. To her, whining and kneeling down were one thing, but the peasant woman had first to kneel down, and then whine—the whole action being a deliberate production put on regularly. While praying, she had to strike a pose that was to her as comfortable as possible—putting one knee on the ground first (careful not to chafe it), then the other one, and then the hands folded over her belly. Besides, it must be an act of leading in prayer. The peasant woman is teaching the stranger how to pray. In doing this, the actress had a very good thought that made her "older" than an artificial change of voice could have made her. After the treacherous little dialogue in which the peasant and his wife assure each other that they could do nothing for the threatened city, she saw Dumb Kattrin standing there, motionless. She shuffled up to her, looking reproachfully at her: "Pray, poor wretch, pray!"—as if she accused the stranger of an unforgivable omission, of an unwillingness to do anything. The act of prayer consisted of the usual vapid bleating: the soothing sound of one's own voice, the cadence learned from clergymen, which express submission to all heavenly decrees . . . But, when describing the enemies moving toward the city, she made it clear that she well realized what was going on— thereby making her indifference all the more a crime—and toward the end of the prayer she almost prayed "genuinely": praying, so to speak, made her more pious. All this is usually not within the scope of young people, but the actress managed to age visibly and gradually by absorbing the reality of her lines and gestures. Or rather, she allowed herself *to be aged*. Of course, the director has to judge

objectively and honestly the final result of
such methods, and, in case the necessary age
has not been reached, must recast the role
without delay.

When Regine Lutz played the camp whore
Yvette Pottier, who marries the colonel, it
was also a matter of having the age of the
colonel's widow emerge from the story, as a
very special kind of age. She showed Yvette
as a creature whom war has turned into a
whore, and whom whoring has made a rich
colonel's wife. She showed how much the
rise cost. She has aged prematurely, way
ahead of her years. Stuffing herself and giving
orders are the only pleasures she has left.
These pleasures have disfigured her completely. She waddles and carries her belly
before her as a sight for sore eyes. Her contemptuously drawn mouth (corners pulled
down) reveal the degree of her besottedness:
she gasps for air like a codfish on dry land.
With the urge for revenge that is typical of
old unhappy people she barks at the Cook.
But even now, this grotesquely deformed person lets us guess the bygone charm of the
camp whore.

In the same fashion the young Käthe
Reichel tried the role of the tradeswoman
who, together with her son, tries to sell house-
wares to Courage in the 8th scene. Since this
scene describes the reaction of several people
to the news that peace has been concluded,
she solved her problem within the short space
of this scene by showing the somewhat slow
reactions of an elderly person. When the call
"Peace" sounded from far away, she pushed
her kerchief from one ear with her hand. This
gave the impression not so much of deafness
as of a mental seclusion from the world
around her, such as one finds with old people.
Her head followed with jerky movements the
words of the people around her, as if she were
trying to form an opinion from their opinions.

She comprehends the fact that there is
peace, and she faints with joy. But she hurries
to regain her composure so as to be able to go
home quickly. She leaves, short as she is, taking long strides, the way elderly people walk
who have to economize on energy.

THE LIEUTENANT IN THE NEW PRODUCTION
was the kicking soldier of the 4th scene.
Courage's lesson and several other lessons
seem to have been effective: the great capitulation has turned this man into a void, cold,
and brutal officer. He can be recognized
(from his old role), if at all, through his words
"I am an officer, I give you my word," which
at one time had read "I've done something
special, I want my reward."

Dumb Kattrin wears him out completely.
In his desperation, he stops yelling at his men,
and begs them for advice instead. When the
cannons of the city that has been awakened
by the drum start roaring he sits down and
beats the ground with his fists like a child.

THE SOLDIERS IN THE NEW PRODUCTION
show complete apathy. They leave excitement over the escapade to the officer. The
action of Dumb Kattrin makes an impression
on them, too. They relish the defeat of their
officer; they grin when he is not looking. The
soldier who has to fetch the musket trots with
the well-known kind of tardiness that cannot
be proven. Nevertheless, he fires. These
soldiers do not resemble the Chinese volun-
teers in Korea about whom the West German
Spiegel wrote: "The Chinese dashed into the
mine fields of the Americans. The soldiers of
the first waves let themselves be torn to bits
by the exploding mines so that those behind
them could break through. Bunches of dead
or dying Chinese hung on the American
barbed wire. The flabbergasted GI's thought
the attackers had been doped. (They were all
sober, as examinations of prisoners revealed.)"

TWELFTH SCENE

Courage Moves On

*The peasants have to convince Courage that Kattrin
is dead. Kattrin's lullaby. Mother Courage pays
for Kattrin's funeral and receives the expressions of
sympathy of the peasants. Mother Courage harnesses herself to her empty covered wagon. Still hoping to get back into business, she follows the tattered army.*

BASIC ARRANGEMENT

The wagon stands on the empty stage. Mother Courage holds dead Kattrin's head in her lap. The peasants stand at the foot of the dead girl, huddled together and hostile. Courage talks as if her daughter were only sleeping, and deliberately overhears the reproach of the peasants that she was to blame for Kattrin's death.

Kattrin's lullaby. The mother's face is bent low over the face of the daughter. The song does not conciliate those who listen.

Mother Courage pays for Kattrin's funeral and receives expressions of sympathy from the peasants. After she has realized that her last child is dead, Courage gets up laboriously and hobbles around the corpse (right), along the footlights, behind the wagon. She returns with a tent cloth, and answers over her shoulder the peasant's question whether she had no one to turn to: "Oh yes, one. Eilif." And places the cloth over the body, with her back toward the footlights. At the head of the corpse, she pulls the cloth all the way over the face, then again takes her place behind the corpse. The peasant and his son shake hands with her and bow ceremoniously before carrying the body out (to the right). The peasant woman, too, shakes hands with Courage, walks to the right and stops once more, undecided. The two women exchange a few words, then the peasant woman exits.

Mother Courage harnesses herself to her empty covered wagon. Still hoping to get back into business, she follows the tattered army. Slowly, the old woman walks to the wagon, rolls up the rope which Dumb Kattrin had been pulling to this point, takes a stick, looks at it, slips it through the sling of the second rope, tucks the stick under her arm, and starts pulling. The turntable begins to move, and Courage circles the stage once. The curtain closes when she is upstage right for the second time.

THE PEASANTS

The attitude of the peasants toward Courage is hostile. She got them into difficulties,

and they will be saddled with her if she does not catch up with the regiments. Besides, she is to blame for the accident herself, in their opinion. And moreover the canteen woman is not part of the resident population, and now, in time of war, she belongs to the fleecers, cutthroats, and marauders in the wake of the armies. When they condole with her by shaking her hand, they merely follow custom.

THE BOW

During this entire scene, Weigel, as Courage, showed an almost animal indifference. All the more beautiful was the deep bow that she made when the body was carried away.

THE LULLABY

The lullaby must be sung without sentimentality and without the desire to arouse sentimentality. Otherwise, its significance does not get across. The thought that is the basis of this song is a murderous one: the child of this mother was supposed to be better off than other children of other mothers. Through a slight stress on the "you," Weigel revealed the treacherous hope of Courage to get her child, and perhaps only hers, through the war alive. The child to whom the most common things were denied was promised the uncommon.

PAYING FOR THE FUNERAL

Even when paying for the funeral, Weigel gave another hint at the character of Courage. She fished a few coins from her leather purse, put one back, and gave the rest to the peasant. The overpowering impression she gave of having been destroyed was not in the least diminished by this.

THE LAST VERSE

While Courage slowly harnessed herself to her wagon, the last verse of her song was sung from the box in which the band had been placed. It expresses one more time her undestroyed hope to get something out of war anyway. It becomes more impressive in that it does not aim at the illusion that the song is actually sung by army units moving past in the distance.

Giehse in the role of courage

When covering up the body, Giehse put her head under the cloth, looking at her daughter one more time, before finally dropping it over her face.

Before she began pulling away her covered wagon—another beautiful variant—she looked into the distance, to figure out where to go, and before she started pulling, she blew her nose with her index finger.

Take your time

At the end of the play it is necessary that one see the wagon roll away. Naturally, the audience gets the idea when the wagon starts. If the movement is extended, a moment of irritation arises ("that's long enough, now"). If it is prolonged even further, deeper understanding sets in.

Pulling the wagon in the last scene

For the 12th scene, farm house and stable with roof (of the 11th scene) were cleared away, and only the wagon and Dumb Kattrin's body were left. The act of dragging the wagon off—the large letters "Saxony" were pulled up (out of sight) when the music begins—took place on a completely empty stage: whereby one remembered the setting of the first scene. Courage and her wagon moved in a complete circle on the revolving stage. She passed the footlights once more. As usual, the stage was bathed in light.

Discoveries of the realists

Wherein lies the effectiveness of Weigel's gesture when she mechanically puts one coin back into her purse, after having fished her money out, as she hands the peasant the funeral money for dead Kattrin? She shows that this tradeswoman, in all her grief, does not completely forget to count, since money is so hard to come by. And she shows this as a discovery about human nature that is shaped by certain conditions. This little feature has the power and the suddenness of a discovery. The art of the realists consists of digging out the truth from under the rubble of the evident, of connecting the particular with the general, of pinning down the unique within the larger process.

A change of text

After "I'll manage, there isn't much in it now," Courage added, in the Munich and then also in the Berlin production: "I must start up again in business."

Mother Courage learns nothing

In the last scene, Weigel's Courage appeared like an eighty-year-old woman. And she comprehends nothing. She reacts only to the statements that are connected with war, such as that one must not remain behind. She overhears the crude reproach of the peasants that Kattrin's death was her fault.

Courage's inability to learn from the unproductiveness of war was a prophecy in the year 1938 when the play was written. At the Berlin production in 1948 the desire was voiced that Courage should at least come to a realization in the play. To make it possible for the spectator to get something out of this realistic play, i.e., to make the spectator learn a lesson, theaters have to arrive at an acting style that does not seek an identification of the spectator with the protagonist.

Judging on the basis of reports of spectators and newspaper reviews, the Zurich world premiere—although artistically on a high level—presented only the image of war as a natural catastrophe and an inevitable fate, and thereby it underscored to the middle-class spectator in the orchestra his own indestructibility, his ability to survive. But even to the likewise middle-class Courage, the decision "Join in or don't join in" was always left open in the play. The production, it seems, must also have presented Courage's business dealings, profiteering, willingness to take risks, as quite natural, "eternally human" behavior, so that she had no other choice. Today, it is true, the man of the middle class can no longer stay out of war, as Courage could have. To him, a production of the play can probably teach nothing but a real hatred of war, and a certain insight into the fact that the big deals of which war consists are not made by the little people. In that sense, the play is more of a lesson than reality is, because here in the play the situation of war is more of an experimental situation, made for the sake of insights. I.e., the spectator attains the attitude of a student— as long as the acting style is correct. The part of the audience that belongs to the proletariat, i.e., the class that actually can struggle against and overcome war, should be given insight into the connection between business and war (again provided the acting style is correct): the proletariat as a class can do away with war by doing away with capitalism. Of course, as far as the proletarian part of the audience is concerned, one must also take into consideration the fact that this class is busy drawing its own conclusions—inside as well as outside the theater.

The epic element

The Epic element was certainly visible in the production at the *Deutsches Theater*—in the arrangement, in the presentation of the characters, in the minute execution of details, and in the pacing of the entire play. Also, contradictory elements were not eliminated but stressed, and the parts, visible as such, made a convincing whole. However, the goal of Epic Theater was not reached. Much became clear, but clarification was in the end absent. Only in a few recasting-rehearsals did it clearly emerge, for then the actors were only "pretending," i.e., they only showed to the newly-added colleague the positions and intonations, and then the whole thing received that preciously loose, unlabored, non-urgent element that incites the spectator to have his own independent thoughts and feelings.

That the production did not have an Epic foundation was never remarked, however: which was probably the reason the actors did not dare provide one.

Concerning the notes themselves

We hope that the present notes, offering various explanations and inventions essential to the production of a play, will not have an air of spurious seriousness. It is admittedly hard to establish the lightness and casualness that are of the essence of theater. The arts, even when they are instructive, are forms of amusement.

THE DUMB WAITER

Harold Pinter

Characters

BEN
GUS

Scene: A basement room. Two beds, flat against the back wall. A serving hatch, closed, between the beds. A door to the kitchen and lavatory, left. A door to a passage, right.

BEN *is lying on a bed, left, reading a paper.* GUS *is sitting on a bed, right, tying his shoelaces, with difficulty. Both are dressed in shirts, trousers and braces.*

Silence.

GUS *ties his laces, rises, yawns and begins to walk slowly to the door, left. He stops, looks down, and shakes his foot.*

BEN *lowers his paper and watches him.* GUS *kneels and unties his shoe-lace and slowly takes off the shoe. He looks inside it and brings out a flattened matchbox. He shakes it and examines it. Their eyes meet.* BEN *rattles his paper and reads.* GUS *puts the matchbox in his pocket and bends down to put on his shoe. He ties his lace, with difficulty.* BEN *lowers his paper and watches him.* GUS *walks to the door, left, stops, and shakes the other foot. He kneels, unties his shoe-lace, and slowly takes off the shoe. He looks inside it and brings out a flattened cigarette packet. He shakes it and examines it. Their eyes meet.* BEN *rattles his paper and reads.* GUS *puts the packet in his pocket, bends down, puts on his shoe and ties the lace.*

He wanders off, left.

BEN *slams the paper down on the bed and glares after him. He picks up the paper and lies on his back, reading.*

Silence.

A lavatory chain is pulled twice off left, but the lavatory does not flush.

Silence.

GUS *re-enters, left, and halts at the door, scratching his head.*

BEN *slams down the paper.*

BEN. Kaw!

He picks up the paper.

What about this? Listen to this!

He refers to the paper.

A man of eighty-seven wanted to cross the road. But there was a lot of traffic, see? He couldn't see how he was going to squeeze through. So he crawled under a lorry.

GUS. He what?

BEN. He crawled under a lorry. A stationary lorry.

GUS. No?

BEN. The lorry started and ran over him.

GUS. Go on!

BEN. That's what it says here.

GUS. Get away.

BEN. It's enough to make you want to puke, isn't it?

GUS. Who advised him to do a thing like that?

BEN. A man of eighty-seven crawling under a lorry!

GUS. It's unbelievable.

BEN. It's down here in black and white.

GUS. Incredible.

Silence.

GUS *shakes his head and exits.* BEN *lies back and reads.*

The lavatory chain is pulled once off left, but the lavatory does not flush.

BEN *whistles at an item in the paper.*

GUS *re-enters.*

I want to ask you something.

BEN. What are you doing out there?

GUS. Well, I was just—

BEN. What about the tea?

GUS. I'm just going to make it.

BEN. Well, go on, make it.

GUS. Yes, I will. (*He sits in a chair. Ruminatively.*) He's laid on some very nice crockery this time, I'll say that. It's sort of striped. There's a white stripe.

BEN *reads.*

It's very nice. I'll say that.

BEN *turns the page.*

You know, sort of round the cup. Round the rim. All the rest of it's black, you see. Then the saucer's black, except for right in the middle, where the cup goes, where it's white.

BEN *reads.*

Then the plates are the same, you see. Only they've got a black stripe—the plates —right across the middle. Yes, I'm quite taken with the crockery.

BEN (*still reading*). What do you want plates for? You're not going to eat.

GUS. I've brought a few biscuits.

BEN. Well, you'd better eat them quick.

GUS. I always bring a few biscuits. Or a pie. You know I can't drink tea without anything to eat.

BEN. Well, make the tea then, will you? Time's getting on.

GUS *brings out the flattened cigarette packet and examines it.*

GUS. You got any cigarettes? I think I've run out.

He throws the packet high up and leans forward to catch it.

I hope it won't be a long job, this one.

Aiming carefully, he flips the packet under his bed.

Oh, I wanted to ask you something.

BEN (*slamming his paper down*). Kaw!

GUS. What's that?

BEN. A child of eight killed a cat!

GUS. Get away.

BEN. It's a fact. What about that, eh? A child of eight killing a cat!

GUS. How did he do it?

BEN. It was a girl.

GUS. How did she do it?

BEN. She—

He picks up the paper and studies it.

It doesn't say.

GUS. Why not?

BEN. Wait a minute. It just says—Her brother, aged eleven, viewed the incident from the toolshed.

GUS. Go on!

BEN. That's bloody ridiculous.

Pause.

GUS. I bet he did it.

BEN.. Who?

GUS. The brother.

BEN. I think you're right.

Pause.

(*Slamming down the paper.*) What about that, eh? A kid of eleven killing a cat and blaming it on his little sister of eight! It's enough to—

He breaks off in disgust and seizes the paper.
GUS *rises.*

GUS. What time is he getting in touch?

BEN *reads.*

What time is he getting in touch?

BEN. What's the matter with you? It could be any time. Any time.

GUS (*moves to the foot of* BEN's *bed*). Well, I was going to ask you something.

BEN. What?

GUS. Have you noticed the time that tank takes to fill?

BEN. What tank?

GUS. In the lavatory.

BEN. No. Does it?

GUS. Terrible.

BEN. Well, what about it?

GUS. What do you think's the matter with it?

BEN. Nothing.

GUS. Nothing?

BEN. It's got a deficient ballcock, that's all.

GUS. A deficient what?

BEN. Ballcock.

GUS. No? Really?

BEN. That's what I should say.

GUS. Go on! That didn't occur to me.

GUS *wanders to his bed and presses the mattress.*

I didn't have a very restful sleep today, did you? It's not much of a bed. I could have done with another blanket too. (*He catches sight of a picture on the wall.*) Hello, what's this? (*Peering at it.*) "The First Eleven." Cricketers. You seen this, Ben?

BEN (*reading*). What?

GUS. The first eleven.

BEN. What?

GUS. There's a photo here of the first eleven.

BEN. What first eleven?

GUS (*studying the photo*). It doesn't say.

BEN. What about that tea?

GUS. They all look a bit old to me.

GUS *wanders downstage, looks out front, then all about the room.*

I wouldn't like to live in this dump. I wouldn't mind if you had a window, you could see what it looked like outside.

BEN. What do you want a window for?

GUS. Well, I like to have a bit of a view, Ben. It whiles away the time.

He walks about the room.

I mean, you come into a place when it's still dark, you come into a room you've never seen before, you sleep all day, you do your job, and then you go away in the night again.

Pause.

I like to get a look at the scenery. You never get the chance in this job.

BEN. You get your holidays, don't you?

GUS. Only a fortnight.

BEN (*lowering the paper*). You kill me. Anyone would think you're working every day. How often do we do a job? Once a week? What are you complaining about?

GUS. Yes, but we've got to be on tap though, haven't we? You can't move out of the house in case a call comes.

BEN. You know what your trouble is?

GUS. What?

BEN. You haven't got any interests.

GUS. I've got interests.

BEN. What? Tell me one of your interests.

Pause.

GUS. I've got interests.

BEN. Look at me. What have I got?

GUS. I don't know. What?

BEN. I've got my woodwork. I've got my model boats. Have you ever seen me idle? I'm never idle. I know how to occupy my time, to its best advantage. Then when a call comes, I'm ready.

GUS. Don't you ever get a bit fed up?

BEN. Fed up? What with?

Silence.

BEN *reads.* GUS *feels in the pocket of his jacket, which hangs on the bed.*

GUS. You got any cigarettes? I've run out.

The lavatory flushes off left.

There she goes.

GUS *sits on his bed.*

No, I mean, I say the crockery's good. It is. It's very nice. But that's about all I can say for this place. It's worse than the last one. Remember that last place we were in? Last time, where was it? At least there was a wireless there. No, honest. He doesn't seem to bother much about our comfort these days.

BEN. When are you going to stop jabbering?

GUS. You'd get rheumatism in a place like this, if you stay long.

BEN. We're not staying long. Make the tea, will you? We'll be on the job in a minute.

GUS *picks up a small bag by his bed and brings out a packet of tea. He examines it and looks up.*

GUS. Eh, I've been meaning to ask you.

BEN. What the hell is it now?

GUS. Why did you stop the car this morning, in the middle of that road?

BEN (*lowering the paper*). I thought you were asleep.

GUS. I was, but I woke up when you stopped. You did stop, didn't you?

Pause.

In the middle of that road. It was still dark, don't you remember? I looked out. It was all misty. I thought perhaps you wanted to kip, but you were sitting up dead straight, like you were waiting for something.

BEN. I wasn't waiting for anything.

GUS. I must have fallen asleep again. What was all that about then? Why did you stop?

BEN (*picking up the paper*). We were too early.

GUS. Early? (*He rises.*) What do you mean? We got the call, didn't we, saying we were to start right away. We did. We shoved out on the dot. So how could we be too early?

BEN (*quietly*). Who took the call, me or you?

GUS. You.

BEN. We were too early.

GUS. Too early for what?

Pause.

You mean someone had to get out before we got in?

He examines the bedclothes.

I thought these sheets didn't look too bright. I thought they ponged a bit. I was too tired to notice when I got in this morning. Eh, that's taking a bit of a liberty, isn't it? I don't want to share my bed-sheets. I told you things were going down the drain. I mean, we've always had clean sheets laid on up till now. I've noticed it.

BEN. How do you know those sheets weren't clean?

GUS. What do you mean?

BEN. How do you know they weren't clean? You've spent the whole day in them, haven't you?

GUS. What, you mean it might be my pong? (*He sniffs sheets.*) Yes. (*He sits slowly on bed.*) It could be my pong, I suppose. It's difficult to tell. I don't really know what I pong like, that's the trouble.

BEN (*referring to the paper*). Kaw!

GUS. Eh, Ben.

BEN. Kaw!

GUS. Ben.

BEN. What?

GUS. What town are we in? I've forgotten.

BEN. I've told you. Birmingham.

GUS. Go on!

He looks with interest about the room.

That's in the Midlands. The second biggest city in Great Britain. I'd never have guessed.

He snaps his fingers.

Eh, it's Friday today, isn't it? It'll be Saturday tomorrow.

BEN. What about it?

GUS (*excited*). We could go and watch the Villa.

BEN. They're playing away.

GUS. No, are they? Caarr! What a pity.

BEN. Anyway, there's no time. We've got to get straight back.

GUS. Well, we have done in the past, haven't we? Stayed over and watched a game, haven't we? For a bit of relaxation.

BEN. Things have tightened up, mate. They've tightened up.

GUS *chuckles to himself.*

GUS. I saw the Villa get beat in a cup tie once. Who was it against now? White shirts. It was one-all at half-time. I'll never forget it. Their opponents won by a penalty. Talk about drama. Yes, it was a disputed penalty. Disputed. They got beat two-one, anyway, because of it. You were there yourself.

BEN. Not me.

GUS. Yes, you were there. Don't you remember that disputed penalty?

BEN. No.

GUS. He went down just inside the area. Then they said he was just acting. I didn't think the other bloke touched him myself. But the referee had the ball on the spot.

BEN. Didn't touch him! What are you talking about? He laid him out flat!

GUS. Not the Villa. The Villa don't play that sort of game.

BEN. Get out of it.

Pause.

GUS. Eh, that must have been here, in Birmingham.

BEN. What must?

GUS. The Villa. That must have been here.

BEN. They were playing away.

GUS. Because you know who the other team was? It was the Spurs. It was Tottenham Hotspur.

BEN. Well, what about it?

GUS. We've never done a job in Tottenham.

BEN. How do you know?

GUS. I'd remember Tottenham.

BEN *turns on his bed to look at him.*

BEN. Don't make me laugh, will you?

BEN turns back and reads. GUS *yawns and speaks through his yawn.*

GUS. When's he going to get in touch?

Pause.

Yes, I'd like to see another football match. I've always been an ardent football fan. Here, what about coming to see the Spurs tomorrow?

BEN (*tonelessly*). They're playing away.

GUS. Who are?

BEN. The Spurs.

GUS. Then they might be playing here.

BEN. Don't be silly.

GUS. If they're playing away they might be playing here. They might be playing the Villa.

BEN (*tonelessly*). But the Villa are playing away.

Pause. An envelope slides under the door, right. GUS *sees it. He stands, looking at it.*

GUS. Ben.

BEN. Away. They're all playing away.

GUS. Ben, look here.

BEN. What?

GUS. Look.

BEN turns his head and sees the envelope. He stands.

BEN. What's that?

GUS. I don't know.

BEN. Where did it come from?

GUS. Under the door.

BEN. Well, what is it?

GUS. I don't know.

They stare at it.

BEN. Pick it up.

GUS. What do you mean?

BEN. Pick it up!

GUS *slowly moves towards it, bends and picks it up.*

What is it?

GUS. An envelope.

BEN. Is there anything on it?

GUS. No.

BEN. Is it sealed?

GUS. Yes.

BEN. Open it.

GUS. What?

BEN. Open it!

GUS opens it and looks inside.

What's in it?

GUS empties twelve matches into his hand.

GUS. Matches.

BEN. Matches?

GUS. Yes.

BEN. Show it to me.

GUS passes the envelope. BEN *examines it.*

Nothing on it. Not a word.

GUS. That's funny, isn't it?

BEN. It came under the door?

GUS. Must have done.

BEN. Well, go on.

GUS. Go on where?

BEN. Open the door and see if you can catch anyone outside.

GUS. Who, me?

BEN. Go on!

GUS stares at him, puts the matches in his pocket, goes to his bed and brings a revolver from under the pillow. He goes to the door, opens it, looks out and shuts it.

GUS. No one.

He replaces the revolver.

BEN. What did you see?

GUS. Nothing.

BEN. They must have been pretty quick.

GUS takes the matches from pocket and looks at them.

GUS. Well, they'll come in handy.

BEN. Yes.

GUS. Won't they?

BEN. Yes, you're always running out, aren't you?

GUS. All the time.

BEN. Well, they'll come in handy then.

GUS. Yes.

BEN. Won't they?

GUS. Yes, I could do with them. I could do with them too.

BEN. You could, eh?

GUS. Yes.

BEN. Why?

GUS. We haven't got any.

BEN. Well, you've got some now, haven't you?

GUS. I can light the kettle now.

BEN. Yes, you're always cadging matches. How many have you got there?

GUS. About a dozen.

BEN. Well, don't lose them. Red too. You don't even need a box.

GUS probes his ear with a match.

(*Slapping his hand*). Don't waste them! Go and light it.

GUS. Eh?

BEN. Go and light it.

GUS. Light what?

BEN. The kettle.

GUS. You mean the gas.

BEN. Who does?

GUS. You do.

BEN (*his eyes narrowing*). What do you mean, I mean the gas?

GUS. Well, that's what you mean, don't you? The gas.

BEN (*powerfully*). If I say go and light the kettle I mean go and light the kettle.

GUS. How can you light a kettle?

BEN. It's a figure of speech! Light the kettle. It's a figure of speech!

GUS. I've never heard it.

BEN. Light the kettle! It's common usage!

GUS. I think you've got it wrong.

BEN (*menacing*). What do you mean?

GUS. They say put on the kettle.

BEN (*taut*). Who says?

They stare at each other, breathing hard.

(*Deliberately.*) I have never in all my life heard anyone say put on the kettle.

GUS. I bet my mother used to say it.

BEN. Your mother? When did you last see your mother?

GUS. I don't know, about—

BEN. Well, what are you talking about your mother for?

They stare.

Gus, I'm not trying to be unreasonable. I'm just trying to point out something to you.

GUS. Yes, but—

BEN. Who's the senior partner here, me or you?

GUS. You.

BEN. I'm only looking after your interests, Gus. You've got to learn, mate.

GUS. Yes, but I've never heard—

BEN (*vehemently*). Nobody says light the gas! What does the gas light?

GUS. What does the gas—?

BEN (*grabbing him with two hands by the throat, at arm's length*). THE KETTLE, YOU FOOL!

GUS takes the hands from his throat.

GUS. All right, all right.

Pause.

BEN. Well, what are you waiting for?

GUS. I want to see if they light.

BEN. What?

GUS. The matches.

He takes out the flattened box and tries to strike.

No.

He throws the box under the bed.
BEN *stares at him.*
GUS *raises his foot.*

Shall I try it on here?

BEN *stares.* GUS *strikes a match on his shoe.*
It lights.

Here we are.
BEN (*wearily*). Put on the bloody kettle, for
Christ's sake.

BEN *goes to his bed, but, realising what he*
has said, stops and half turns. They look at
each other. GUS *slowly exits, left.* BEN *slams*
his paper down on the bed and sits on it,
head in hands.

GUS (*entering*). It's going.
BEN. What?
GUS. The stove.

GUS *goes to his bed and sits.*

I wonder who it'll be tonight.

Silence.

Eh, I've been wanting to ask you something.
BEN (*putting his legs on the bed*). Oh, for Christ's
sake.
GUS. No. I was going to ask you something.

He rises and sits on BEN's *bed.*

BEN. What are you sitting on my bed for?

GUS *sits.*

What's the matter with you? You're always asking me questions. What's the
matter with you?
GUS. Nothing.
BEN. You never used to ask me so many
damn questions. What's come over you?

GUS. No, I was just wondering.
BEN. Stop wondering. You've got a job to do.
Why don't you just do it and shut up?
GUS. That's what I was wondering about.
BEN. What?
GUS. The job.
BEN. What job?
GUS (*tentatively*). I thought perhaps you might
know something.

BEN *looks at him.*

I thought perhaps you—I mean—have
you got any idea—who it's going to be
tonight?
BEN. Who what's going to be?

They look at each other.

GUS (*at length*). Who it's going to be.

Silence.

BEN. Are you feeling all right?
GUS. Sure.
BEN. Go and make the tea.
GUS. Yes, sure.

GUS *exits, left,* BEN *looks after him. He*
then takes his revolver from under the pillow
and checks it for ammunition. GUS *re-enters.*

The gas has gone out.
BEN. Well, what about it?
GUS. There's a meter.
BEN. I haven't got any money.
GUS. Nor have I.
BEN. You'll have to wait.
GUS. What for?
BEN. For Wilson.
GUS. He might not come. He might just send
a message. He doesn't always come.
BEN. Well, you'll have to do without it, won't
you?
GUS. Blimey.
BEN. You'll have a cup of tea afterwards.
What's the matter with you?
GUS. I like to have one before.

BEN *holds the revolver up to the light and polishes it.*

BEN. You'd better get ready anyway.
GUS. Well, I don't know, that's a bit much, you know, for my money.

He picks up a packet of tea from the bed and throws it into the bag.

I hope he's got a shilling, anyway, if he comes. He's entitled to have. After all, it's his place, he could have seen there was enough gas for a cup of tea.
BEN. What do you mean, it's his place?
GUS. Well, isn't it?
BEN. He's probably only rented it. It doesn't have to be his place.
GUS. I know it's his place. I bet the whole house is. He's not even laying on any gas now either.

GUS *sits on his bed.*

It's his place all right. Look at all the other places. You go to this address, there's a key there, there's a teapot, there's never a soul in sight—(*He pauses.*) Eh, nobody ever hears a thing, have you ever thought of that? We never get any complaints, do we, too much noise or anything like that? You never see a soul, do you?—except the bloke who comes. You ever noticed that? I wonder if the walls are sound-proof. (*He touches the wall above his bed.*) Can't tell. All you do is wait, eh? Half the time he doesn't even bother to put in an appearance, Wilson.
BEN. Why should he? He's a busy man.
GUS (*thoughtfully*). I find him hard to talk to, Wilson. Do you know that, Ben?
BEN. Scrub round it, will you?

Pause.

GUS. There are a number of things I want to ask him. But I can never get round to it, when I see him.

Pause.

I've been thinking about the last one.
BEN. What last one?
GUS. That girl.

BEN *grabs the paper, which he reads.*

(*Rising, looking down at* BEN). How many times have you read that paper?

BEN *slams the paper down and rises.*

BEN (*angrily*). What do you mean?
GUS. I was just wondering how many times you'd—
BEN. What are you doing, criticising me?
GUS. No, I was just—
BEN. You'll get a swipe round your earhole if you don't watch your step.
GUS. Now look here, Ben—
BEN. I'm not looking anywhere! (*He addresses the room.*) How many times have I—! A bloody liberty!
GUS. I didn't mean that.
BEN. You just get on with it, mate. Get on with it, that's all.

BEN *gets back on the bed.*

GUS. I was just thinking about that girl, that's all.

GUS *sits on his bed.*

She wasn't much to look at, I know, but still. It was a mess though, wasn't it? What a mess. Honest, I can't remember a mess like that one. They don't seem to hold together like men, women. A looser texture, like. Didn't she spread, eh? She didn't half spread. Kaw! But I've been meaning to ask you.

BEN *sits up and clenches his eyes.*

Who clears up after we've gone? I'm curious about that. Who does the clearing up? Maybe they don't clear up. Maybe they just leave them there, eh? What do you think? How many jobs have we done?

Blimey, I can't count them. What if they never clear anything up after we've gone.

BEN (*pityingly*). You mutt. Do you think we're the only branch of this organisation? Have a bit of common. They got departments for everything.

GUS. What cleaners and all?

BEN. You birk!

GUS. No, it was that girl made me start to think—

There is a loud clatter and racket in the bulge of wall between the beds, of something descending. They grab their revolvers, jump up and face the wall. The noise comes to a stop. Silence. They look at each other. BEN *gestures sharply towards the wall.* GUS *approaches the wall slowly. He bangs it with his revolver. It is hollow.* BEN *moves to the head of his bed, his revolver cocked.* GUS *puts his revolver on his bed and pats along the bottom of the center panel. He finds a rim. He lifts the panel. Disclosed is a serving-hatch, a "dumb waiter". A wide box is held by pulleys.* GUS *peers into the box. He brings out a piece of paper.*

BEN. What is it?

GUS. You have a look at it.

BEN. Read it.

GUS (*reading*). Two braised steak and chips. Two sago puddings. Two teas without sugar.

BEN. Let me see that. (*He takes the paper.*)

GUS (*to himself*). Two teas without sugar.

BEN. Mmnn.

GUS. What do you think of that?

BEN. Well—

The box goes up. BEN *levels his revolver.*

GUS. Give us a chance! They're in a hurry, aren't they?

BEN *re-reads the note.* GUS *looks over his shoulder.*

That's a bit—that's a bit funny, isn't it?

BEN (*quickly*). No. It's not funny. It probably used to be a café here, that's all. Upstairs. These places change hands very quickly.

GUS. A café?

BEN. Yes.

GUS. What, you mean this was the kitchen, down here?

BEN. Yes, they change hands overnight, these places. Go into liquidation. The people who run it, you know, they don't find it a going concern, they move out.

GUS. You mean the people who ran this place didn't find it a going concern and moved out?

BEN. Sure.

GUS. WELL, WHO'S GOT IT NOW?

Silence.

BEN. What do you mean, who's got it now?

GUS. Who's got it now? If they moved out, who moved in?

BEN. Well, that all depends—

The box descends with a clatter and bang. BEN *levels his revolver.* GUS *goes to the box and brings out a piece of paper.*

GUS (*reading*). Soup of the day. Liver and onions. Jam tart.

A pause. GUS *looks at* BEN. BEN *takes the note and reads it. He walks slowly to the hatch.* GUS *follows.* BEN *looks into the hatch but not up it.* GUS *puts his hand on* BEN'S *shoulder.* BEN *throws it off.* GUS *puts his finger to his mouth. He leans on the hatch and swiftly looks up it.* BEN *flings him away in alarm.* BEN *looks at the note. He throws his revolver on the bed and speaks with decision.*

BEN. We'd better send something up.

GUS. Eh?

BEN. We'd better send something up.

GUS. Oh! Yes. Yes. Maybe you're right.

They are both relieved at the decision.

BEN (*purposefully*). Quick! What have you got in that bag?

GUS. Not much.

GUS goes to the hatch and shouts up it.

Wait a minute!

BEN. Don't do that!

GUS examines the contents of the bag and brings them out, one by one.

GUS. Biscuits. A bar of chocolate. Half a pint of milk.

BEN. That all?

GUS. Packet of tea.

BEN. Good.

GUS. We can't send the tea. That's all the tea we've got.

BEN. Well, there's no gas. You can't do anything with it, can you?

GUS. Maybe they can send us down a bob.

BEN. What else is there?

GUS (*reaching into bag*). One Eccles cake.

BEN. One Eccles cake?

GUS. Yes.

BEN. You never told me you had an Eccles cake.

GUS. Didn't I?

BEN. Why only one? Didn't you bring one for me?

GUS. I didn't think you'd be keen.

BEN. Well, you can't send up one Eccles cake, anyway.

GUS. Why not?

BEN. Fetch one of those plates.

GUS. All right.

GUS goes towards the door, left, and stops.

Do you mean I can keep the Eccles cake then?

BEN. Keep it?

GUS. Well, they don't know we've got it, do they?

BEN. That's not the point.

GUS. Can't I keep it?

BEN. No, you can't. Get the plate.

GUS exits, left. BEN *looks in the bag. He brings out a packet of crisps. Enter* GUS *with a plate.*

(*Accusingly, holding up the crisps*). Where did these come from?

GUS. What?

BEN. Where did these crisps come from?

GUS. Where did you find them?

BEN (*hitting him on the shoulder*). You're playing a dirty game, my lad!

GUS. I only eat those with beer!

BEN. Well, where were you going to get the beer?

GUS. I was saving them till I did.

BEN. I'll remember this. Put everything on the plate.

They pile everything on to the plate. The box goes up without the plate.

Wait a minute!

They stand.

GUS. It's gone up.

BEN. It's all your stupid fault, playing about!

GUS. What do we do now?

BEN. We'll have to wait till it comes down.

BEN *puts the plate on the bed, puts on his shoulder holster, and starts to put on his tie.*

You'd better get ready.

GUS goes to his bed, puts on his tie, and starts to fix his holster.

GUS. Hey, Ben.

BEN. What?

GUS. What's going on here?

Pause.

BEN. What do you mean?

GUS. How can this be a café?

BEN. It used to be a café.

GUS. Have you seen the gas stove?

BEN. What about it?

GUS. It's only got three rings.

BEN. So what?

GUS. Well, you couldn't cook much on three rings, not for a busy place like this.

BEN (*irritably*). That's why the service is slow!

BEN *puts on his waistcoat.*

GUS. Yes, but what happens when we're not here? What do they do then? All these menus coming down and nothing going up. It might have been going on like this for years.

BEN *brushes his jacket.*

What happens when we go?

BEN *puts on his jacket.*

They can't do much business.

The box descends. They turn about. GUS *goes to the hatch and brings out a note.*

GUS (*reading*). Macaroni Pastitsio. Ormitha Macarounada.

BEN. What was that?

GUS. Macaroni Pastitsio. Ormitha Macarounada.

BEN. Greek dishes.

GUS. No.

BEN. That's right.

GUS. That's pretty high class.

BEN. Quick before it goes up.

GUS *puts the plate in the box.*

GUS (*calling up the hatch*). Three McVitie and Price! One Lyons Red Label! One Smith's Crisps! One Eccles cake! One Fruit and Nut!

BEN. Cadbury's.

GUS (*up the hatch*). Cadbury's!

BEN (*handing the milk*). One bottle of milk.

GUS (*up the hatch*). One bottle of milk! Half a pint! (*He looks at the label.*) Express Dairy! (*He puts the bottle in the box.*)

The box goes up.

Just did it.

BEN. You shouldn't shout like that.

GUS. Why not?

BEN. It isn't done.

BEN *goes to his bed.*

Well, that should be all right, anyway, for the time being.

GUS. You think so, eh?

BEN. Get dressed, will you? It'll be any minute now.

GUS *puts on his waistcoat.* BEN *lies down and looks up at the ceiling.*

GUS. This is some place. No tea and no biscuits.

BEN. Eating makes you lazy, mate. You're getting lazy, you know that? You don't want to get slack on your job.

GUS. Who me?

BEN. Slack, mate, slack.

GUS. Who me? Slack?

BEN. Have you checked your gun? You haven't even checked your gun. It looks disgraceful, anyway. Why don't you ever polish it?

GUS *rubs his revolver on the sheet.* BEN *takes out a pocket mirror and straightens his tie.*

GUS. I wonder where the cook is. They must have had a few, to cope with that. Maybe they had a few more gas stoves. Eh! Maybe there's another kitchen along the passage.

BEN. Of course there is! Do you know what it takes to make an Ormitha Macarounada?

GUS. No, what?

BEN. An Ormitha—! Buck your ideas up, will you?

GUS. Takes a few cooks, eh?

GUS *puts his revolver in its holster.*

The sooner we're out of this place the better.

He puts on his jacket.

Why doesn't he get in touch? I feel like I've been here years. (*He takes his revolver out of its holster to check the ammunition.*) We've never let him down though, have we? We've never let him down. I was thinking only the other day, Ben. We're reliable, aren't we?

He puts his revolver back in its holster.

Still, I'll be glad when it's over tonight.

He brushes his jacket.

I hope the bloke's not going to get excited tonight, or anything. I'm feeling a bit off. I've got a splitting headache.

Silence.
The box descends. BEN *jumps up.*
GUS *collects the note.*

(*Reading.*) One Bamboo Shoots, Water Chestnuts and Chicken. One Char Siu and Beansprouts.
BEN. Beansprouts?
GUS. Yes.
BEN. Blimey.
GUS. I wouldn't know where to begin.

He looks back at the box. The packet of tea is inside it. He picks it up.

They've sent back the tea.
BEN (*anxious*). What'd they do that for?
GUS. Maybe it isn't tea-time.

The box goes up. Silence.

BEN (*throwing the tea on the bed, and speaking urgently*). Look here. We'd better tell them.
GUS. Tell them what?
BEN. That we can't do it, we haven't got it.
GUS. All right then.
BEN. Lend us your pencil. We'll write a note.

GUS, *turning for a pencil, suddenly discovers*

the speaking-tube, which hangs on the right wall of the hatch facing his bed.

GUS. What's this?
BEN. What?
GUS. This.
BEN (*examining it*). This? It's a speaking-tube.
GUS. How long has that been there?
BEN. Just the job. We should have used it before, instead of shouting up there.
GUS. Funny I never noticed it before.
BEN. Well, come on.
GUS. What do you do?
BEN. See that? That's a whistle.
GUS. What, this?
BEN. Yes, take it out. Pull it out.

GUS *does so.*

That's it.
GUS. What do we do now?
BEN. Blow into it.
GUS. Blow?
BEN. It whistles up there if you blow. Then they know you want to speak. Blow.

GUS *blows. Silence.*

GUS (*tube at mouth*). I can't hear a thing.
BEN. Now you speak! Speak into it!

GUS *looks at* BEN, *then speaks into the tube.*

GUS. The larder's bare!
BEN. Give me that!

He grabs the tube and puts it to his mouth.

(*Speaking with great defence.*) Good evening. I'm sorry to—bother you, but we just thought we'd better let you know that we haven't got anything left. We sent up all we had. There's no more food down here.

He brings the tube slowly to his ear.

What?

To mouth.

What?

To ear. He listens. To mouth.

No, all we had we sent up.

To ear. He listens. To mouth.

Oh, I'm very sorry to hear that.

To ear. He listens. To GUS.

The Eccles cake was stale.

He listens. To GUS.

The chocolate was melted.

He listens. To GUS.

The milk was sour.
GUS. What about the crisps?
BEN (*listening*). The biscuits were mouldy.

He glares at GUS. *Tube to mouth.*

Well, we're very sorry about that.

Tube to ear.

What?

To mouth.

What?

To ear.

Yes. Yes.

To mouth.

Yes certainly. Certainly. Right away.

To ear. The voice has ceased. He hangs up the tube.

(*Excitedly*). Did you hear that?
GUS. What?

BEN. You know what he said? Light the kettle! Not put on the kettle! Not light the gas! But light the kettle!
GUS. How can we light the kettle?
BEN. What do you mean?
GUS. There's no gas.
BEN (*clapping hand to head*). Now what do we do?
GUS. What did he want us to light the kettle for?
BEN. For tea. He wanted a cup of tea.
GUS. *He* wanted a cup of tea! What about me? I've been wanting a cup of tea all night!
BEN (*despairingly*). What do we do now?
GUS. What are we supposed to drink?

BEN sits on his bed, staring.

What about us?

BEN sits.

I'm thirsty too. I'm starving. And he wants a cup of tea. That beats the band, that does.

BEN lets head sink on to his chest.

I could do with a bit of sustenance myself. What about you? You look as if you could do with something too.

GUS sits on his bed.

We send him up all we've got and he's not satisfied. No, honest, it's enough to make the cat laugh. Why did you send him up all that stuff? (*Thoughtfully.*) Why did I send it up?

Pause.

Who knows what he's got upstairs? He's probably got a salad bowl. They must have something up there. They won't get much from down here. You notice they didn't ask for any salads? They've probably got a salad bowl up there. Cold meat, radishes, cucumbers. Watercress. Roll mops.

Pause.

Hardboiled eggs.

Pause.

The lot. They've probably got a crate of beer too. Probably eating my crisps with a pint of beer now. Didn't have anything to say about those crisps, did he? They do all right, don't worry about that. You don't think they're just going to sit there and wait for stuff to come up from down here, do you? That'll get them nowhere.

Pause.

They do all right.

Pause.

And he wants a cup of tea.

Pause.

That's past a joke, in my opinion.

He looks over at BEN, *rises, and goes to him.*

What's the matter with you? You don't look too bright. I feel like an Alka-Seltzer myself.

BEN *sits up.*

BEN (*in a low voice*). Time's getting on.
GUS. I know. I don't like doing a job on an empty stomach.
BEN (*wearily*). Be quiet a minute. Let me give you your instructions.
GUS. What for? We always do it the same way, don't we?
BEN. Let me give you your instructions.

GUS *sighs and sits next to* BEN *on the bed. The instructions are stated and repeated automatically.*

When we get the call, you go over and stand behind the door.
GUS. Stand behind the door.
BEN. If there's knock on the door you don't answer it.
GUS. If there's a knock on the door I don't answer it.
BEN. But there won't be a knock on the door.
GUS. So I won't answer it.
BEN. When the bloke comes in—
GUS. When the bloke comes in—
BEN. Shut the door behind him.
GUS. Shut the door behind him.
BEN. Without divulging your presence.
GUS. Without divulging my presence.
BEN. He'll see me and come towards me.
GUS. Ye'll see you and come towards you.
BEN. He won't see you.
GUS (*absently*). Eh?
BEN. He won't see you.
GUS. He won't see me.
BEN. But he'll see me.
GUS. He'll see you.
BEN. He won't know you're there.
GUS. He won't know you're there.
BEN. He won't know *you're* there.
GUS. He won't know I'm there.
BEN. I take out my gun.
GUS. You take out your gun.
BEN. He stops in his tracks.
GUS. He stops in his tracks.
BEN. If he turns round—
GUS. If he turns round—
BEN. You're there.
GUS. I'm here.

BEN *frowns and presses his forehead.*

You've missed something out.
BEN. I know. What?
GUS. I haven't taken my gun out, according to you.
BEN. You take your gun out—
GUS. After I've closed the door.
BEN. After you've closed the door.
GUS. You've never missed that out before, you know that?
BEN. When he sees you behind him—
GUS. Me behind him—

BEN. And me in front of him—
GUS. And you in front of him—
BEN. He'll feel uncertain—
GUS. Uneasy.
BEN. He won't know what to do.
GUS. So what will he do?
BEN. He'll look at me and he'll look at you.
GUS. We won't say a word.
BEN. We'll look at him.
GUS. He won't say a word.
BEN. He'll look at us.
GUS. And we'll look at him.
BEN. Nobody says a word.

Pause.

GUS. What do we do if it's a girl?
BEN. We do the same.
GUS. Exactly the same?
BEN. Exactly.

Pause.

GUS. We don't do anything different?
BEN. We do exactly the same.
GUS. Oh.

GUS *rises, and shivers.*

Excuse me.

He exists through the door on the left. BEN *remains sitting on the bed, still.*
The lavatory chain is pulled once off left, but the lavatory does not flush.
Silence.
GUS *re-enters and stops inside the door, deep in thought. He looks at* BEN, *then walks slowly across to his own bed. He is troubled. He stands, thinking. He turns and looks at* BEN. *He moves a few paces towards him.*

(*Slowly in a low, tense voice.*) Why did he send us matches if he knew there was no gas?

Silence.

BEN *stares in front of him.* GUS *crosses to the left side of* BEN, *to the foot of his bed, to get to his other eat.*

Ben. Why did he send us matches if he knew there was no gas?

BEN *looks up.*

Why did he do that?
BEN. Who?
GUS. Who sent us those matches?
BEN. What are you talking about?

GUS *stares down at him.*

GUS (*thickly*). Who is it upstairs?
BEN (*nervously*). What's one thing to do with another?
GUS. Who is it, though?
BEN. What's one thing to do with another?

BEN *fumbles for his paper on the bed.*

GUS. I asked you a question.
BEN. Enough!
GUS (*with growing agitation*). I asked you before. Who moved in? I asked you. You said the people who had it before moved out. Well, who moved in?
BEN (*hunched*). Shut up.
GUS. I told you, didn't I?
BEN (*standing*). Shut up!
GUS (*feverishly*). I told you before who owned this place, didn't I? I told you.

BEN *hits him viciously on the shoulder.*

I told you who ran this place, didn't I?

BEN *hits him viciously on the shoulder.*

(*Violently.*) Well, what's he playing all these games for? That's what I want to know. What's he doing it for?
BEN. What games?
GUS (*passionately, advancing*). What's he doing it for? We've been through our tests,

haven't we? We got right through our tests, years ago, didn't we? We took them together, don't you remember, didn't we? We've proved ourselves before now, haven't we? We've always done our job. What's he doing all this for? What's the idea? What's he playing these games for?

The box in the shaft comes down behind them. The noise is this time accompanied by a shrill whistle, as it falls. GUS *rushes to the hatch and seizes the note.*

(*Reading.*) Scampi!

He crumples the note, picks up the tube, takes out the whistle, blows and speaks.

WE'VE GOT NOTHING LEFT! NOTHING! Do YOU UNDERSTAND?

BEN *seizes the tube and flings* GUS *away. He follows* GUS *and slaps him hard, back-handed, across the chest.*

BEN. Stop it! You maniac!
GUS. But you heard!
BEN (*savagely*). That's enough! I'm warning you!

Silence.
BEN *hangs the tube. He goes to his bed and lies down. He pickes up his paper and reads. Silence.*
The box goes up.
They turn quickly, their eyes meet. BEN *turns to his paper.*
Slowly GUS *goes back to his bed, and sits. Silence.*
The hatch falls back into place.
They turn quickly, their eyes meet. BEN *turns back to his paper.*
Silence.
BEN *throws his paper down.*

BEN. Kaw!

He picks up the paper and looks at it.

Listen to this!

Pause.

What about that, eh?

Pause.

Kaw!

Pause.

Have you ever heard such a thing?
GUS (*dully*). Go on!
BEN. It's true.
GUS. Get away.
BEN. It's down here in black and white.
GUS (*very low*). Is that a fact?
BEN. Can you imagine it.
GUS. It's unbelievable.
BEN. It's enough to make you want to puke, isn't it?
GUS (*almost inaudible*). Incredible.

BEN *shakes his head. He puts the paper down and rises. He fixes the revolver in his holster.*
GUS *stands up. He goes towards the door on the left.*

BEN. Where are you going?
GUS. I'm going to have a glass of water.

He exits. BEN *brushes dust off his clothes and shoes. The whistle in the speaking-tube blows. He goes to it, takes the whistle out and puts the tube to his ear. He listens. He puts it to his mouth.*

BEN. Yes.

To ear. He listens. To mouth.

Straight away. Right.

To ear. He listens. To mouth.

Sure we're ready.

To ear. He listens. To mouth.

Understood. Repeat. He has arrived and
will be coming in straight away. The
normal method to be employed. Understood.

To ear. He listens. To mouth.

Sure we're ready.

To ear. He listens. To mouth.

Right.

He hangs the tube up.

Gus!

*He takes out a comb and combs his hair,
adjusts his jacket to diminish the bulge of the
revolver. The lavatory flushes off left.* BEN
goes quickly to the door, left.

Gus!

The door right opens sharply. BEN *turns,
his revolver levelled at the door.*
GUS *stumbles in.*
*He is stripped of his jacket, waistcoat, tie,
hoslter and revolver.*
He stops, body stooping, his arms at his sides.
He raises his head and looks at BEN.
A long silence.
They stare at each other.

Curtain

THE IRONIC CON GAME IN
THE DUMB WAITER

Penelope Ann Prentice

In a room two men we later learn are
hired gunmen await orders, but instead of
orders an envelop of matches mysteriously

arrives. Discussion leads to argument—Ben,
the senior partner, strikes Gus. A dumb
waiter mysteriously descends with orders, but
food orders which the men nevertheless attempt to fill; the dumb waiter repeatedly
ascends empty until the men send up what
food they have. A voice at the other end
rejects the food—Ben again strikes Gus. The
men receive yet another order for food they
are unable to fill. While Gus is out of the
room Ben finally receives the awaited order
to proceed as usual (presumably as they just
rehearsed it). Ben calls Gus who enters
stripped of waistcoat and gun—Ben levels his
gun at Gus. One of the hired killers is now the
intended victim. Why?

In *The Dumb Waiter*, as in most of Harold
Pinter's work, much of the violence that at
first appears mysterious (Why does Ben
strike Gus?) is linked to the struggle for
dominance. The final threat of violence in
the play (Ben may shoot Gus.) is consistent
with the earlier violence—each time Ben's
position as the senior partner is seriously
threatened he strikes his subordinate, Gus.
When asked about violence in his work
Pinter himself traced it to the dominant-
subservient relationship:

> I think what you're talking about began in *The
> Dumb Waiter*, which from my point of view is a
> relatively simple piece of work. The violence is
> really only an expression of the question of
> dominance and subservience, which is possibly
> a repeated theme in my plays.[1]

Dominance and subservience operate
both technically and thematically in nearly
all of Pinter's work, but most simply in *The
Dumb Waiter*. Technically the struggle for
dominance generates much of the dramatic
tension—will Ben maintain authority over
Gus? He will try, even if he has to kill him.
In the dominant-subservient relationship the

[1] "Harold Pinter," [An interview with Lawrence M.
Bensky] *Writers at Work: The Paris Review*. Third series.
Ed. George Plimpton (New York: Viking Press, 1967),
p. 363.

characters are by definition symbiotically dependent upon each other; Gus submits to Ben's authority which largely derives from having someone to dominate. Mutual dependence is a precarious basis for a relationship that can thrive only so long as the dominant character, Ben, can maintain his superior position without threat by outside forces and without question by the subservient character, Gus. Since, however, outside forces are seldom absent, and since Gus is unwilling and unable to be wholly subservient, changes which must occur are bound to destroy the relationship, and may destroy Gus.

Dramatic tension is further enhanced because violence is the natural product of the struggle for dominance. Both characters fight with the reflexive action of trained athletes whenever their values are challenged. What makes for conflict is that their values are radically different. In over-simplified terms Ben subscribes to the authority manifested in the organization that sends them. Gus questions it.

Thematically the conflicting values of the two characters create two different roles which are ultimately equated with identity; being dominant or subservient apparently defines who one is. The dominant character gives orders, criticizes, and provides answers for all events, frequently mysterious, while the subservient character takes orders, receives criticism and asks questions. The dominant character, Ben, must always act self-confident and in control in order to keep command, while the subservient character, Gus, may admit to weakness and doubt, and may even offer sympathy for weakness which the dominant character cannot accept. Ben instead has contempt for weakness and doubt which he attempts to eradicate. When Gus admits that he has difficulty talking to their superior, Wilson, Ben says, "Scrub round it, will you."

Equipped at the outset with his position as senior partner, Ben is even in the opening scene in the superior position on the bed while Gus is in the lower position of the floor. Ben's first response to Gus is disapproving—"he glares after him" when Gus exits. Ben's position proceeds not, however, from superior strength, intelligence, experience or virtue, but largely as a given role Ben maintains as well as he can. Ironically he can remain dominant only so long as he is wholly subservient to the organization, and he willingly is.

Ben's newspaper reading about killing and death dramatizes his willing compliance with authority, any authority. When Gus questions one account, Ben says, "It's down here in black and white." Ben has no sympathy with anyone who gets himself into a position to be killed. "It's enough to make you want to puke," he says about the story of the old man who got run over. Ben never questions the order of a superior, and the questions he aims at Gus are used almost exclusively to confirm his own authority: "What are you doing, criticising me?" and "Who's the senior partner here, me or you?"

As senior partner Ben must supply an answer or a reason for all events, such as why the envelope of matches mysteriously appears under their door. Gus conjectures, "Well they'll come in handy," and Ben adopts that as fact. "Well they'll come in handy," Ben says in perfect echo that dramatizes his momentary interchangeability with Gus. Conjecture again functions as fact as real fears are deflected into minor concerns—focus on the strange appearance of the matches shifts to a quarrel over usage. Gus maintains that the matches were sent to "light the gas." Ben disagrees arguing that the correct expression is "light the kettle." Truth, in so relative a matter as usage where both are correct, is less important to Ben than maintaining position. Although Gus is the first to say "light the kettle," as soon as he says "put on the kettle," Ben defends "light the kettle," as his own. Since defense of position is roughly self-defense, Ben will use whatever methods he can to defend his position. First Ben resorts to authority: "It's common knowledge," and "It's common usage!" Failing here he resorts to verbal abuse and bullying:

BEN. (*Menacing*). What do you mean?
GUS. They say put on the kettle.
BEN. (*Taut*). Who says?
They stare at each other, breathing hard.

Being right becomes a deadly comic battle for life as Ben "vehemently" proceeds: "Nobody says light the gas!" To score the point he asks Gus what the gas lights, grabs Gus by the throat and shouts, "THE KETTLE, YOU FOOL!" Relieved and relaxed at having won, Ben lapses into saying, "Put on the bloody kettle," the usage he had just denounced.

In contrast to Ben's vicarious pleasure of reading about sports events and the news, Gus would like to go to see a football game, and prefers "a bit of a view," a window. Gus does see many things Ben is blind to until Gus points them out: Gus observes that this place is "worse than the last one"; he notices the number of burners on the stove, and he is the one who discovers the matches, the orders for food, and the speaking tube next to the dumb waiter. His observations lead to subsequent insights: the fact that the stove has only three burners leads him to conclude that they are not in the basement of a restaurant. Unfortunately his insights, if applied to their situation, make their attempts to fill food orders absurd. Yet what other choices do they have?

Ben has no better answers than Gus. When the dumb waiter clatters down for the first time both men draw their guns; neither seems to know who sent the order for steak and sago pudding. When the dumb waiter ascends empty Gus shouts, "Give us a chance." Both men equally desire to comply with the food order, both are equally mystified. As senior partner, however, Ben must supply an answer for the mysterious appearance of the dumb waiter. He conjectures, "It probably used to be a café here, that's all." But when Gus asks the crucial question, "WELL WHO'S GOT IT NOW?" Ben can

only hedge, "Well that all depends—." Pinter has nicely prepared for the divergent responses of the two men. While Gus continues to question the events, Ben adopts and acts on the implicit conjecture that the organization is operating the dumb waiter.

Mystery, however, operates throughout the play to undermine Ben's authority by revealing that his position has no ultimate value. Technically mystery enhances suspense. Who are Ben and Gus? They are hired killers. Each answer poses new questions. Who sent them? Wilson. Who sent him? The organization. Who runs the organization and why? The ultimate Who and Why remain mysterious, unknown, and possibly unknowable. Thematically, mystery suggests a world without a Prime Mover where a hierarchy of values and therefore one's position may be artificial, man made, without ultimate value.

What follows in the play is fairly easy to understand. Both the audience and the characters are at first perplexed by the discovery of the dumb waiter as they earlier were by the matches. Ben, not only used to giving orders but also used to taking them, responds to these orders for food as he would to any other order from above. But as the demands from the dumb waiter become increasingly difficult to meet (though they were always impossible) Ben becomes more aggressive in asserting his dominance over Gus.

Ben's violence against Gus proceeds in direct proportion to his being thwarted in maintaining his position which is being threatened from above. Ben can relieve pressure only momentarily by each new resolve to act. Although "they are both relieved at the decision," when Ben resolves, "We'd better send something up," they cannot really fill the order. Yet both eagerly try to comply even though they do not know who is sending the orders. Why? Several reasons are plausible. If the orders are not sent by the organization then the men do not wish to attract unnecessary attention to their clandestine activities. If they are sent by the organization this may be a test which they do not wish to fail. Gus asks, "We're reliable, aren't we?" and says, "We've been through our tests, haven't we?"

When a new order arrives Ben deflects his renewed frustration by reprimanding Gus for bringing only one Eccles cake, and only enough crisps for himself, which suggests an imbalance in the relationship, an erosion of Ben's power, and explains why he strikes Gus saying, "You're playing a dirty game my lad!"

To fill the order for Greek food the men send up all the food Gus brought: "One Lyons Red Label! One Smith's Crisps! One Eccles cake!" Because the threat seems alleviated by this action, Ben only mildly rebukes Gus for shouting up the hatch by noting Gus's impropriety; Ben says, "It isn't done." But when a moment later a new order for Chinese food appears and Gus blurts out, "The larder's bare!" Ben seizes the tube and "with great deference," reveals his absolute respect for the authority of the unknown superior:

> Good evening. I'm sorry to—bother you, but we just thought we'd better let you know that we haven't got anything left.

Although he receives complaints that the cake was stale, the chocolate melted, and the milk sour, he is elated by information that seems to confirm his position:

> You know what he said? Light the kettle! Not put on the kettle! Not light the gas! But light the kettle!

The victory is both comic and irrelevant. As Gus points out, "There is no gas." For the first and only time Ben is despondent: "Now what do we do?" Gus offers sympathy by delivering a tirade against those upstairs who he suspects have plenty of food. But Ben refuses sympathy and pulls himself out of despair by the resolve to act, to rehearse their plans. The situation is not of course

under control. Gus points out that Ben left out the part where Gus withdraws his gun, and he asks, "Why did he send us matches if he knew there is no gas?" The first mysterious event is still unsolved, and Ben "nervously" responds, "What's one thing to do with another?" Ben regains empty authority by hitting Gus "viciously on the shoulder."

Ben fails, however, to stop Gus's questions: "What's he playing these games for?" The unspoken threat implied by Gus's question is that the game is being played for survival; if they fail to comply with the orders they may be killed.

When the dumb waiter arrives with yet another order Gus impulsively shouts: "WE'VE GOT NOTHING LEFT! NOTHING! DO YOU UNDERSTAND!" This time Ben flings him away and "slaps him hard, back-handed across the chest." But his only alternative now is to ignore the box which ominously ascends empty. Ben returns to the familiar activity of newspaper reading —now devoid of all meaning: "Listen to this! (Pause). What about that, eh? (*Pause*). Kaw!"

Very little evidence suggests that Ben knows in advance who the victim will be. He receives the awaited order while Gus is out of the room, and his response, "Sure we're ready," would seem to indicate that both he and Gus are going to do the job. Yet when Gus returns Ben levels his gun at him and the two men merely stare at each other without surprise or recognition until the curtain falls.

Although the ultimate reasons for the final action remain mysterious, the more immediate reasons are carefully prepared for. It is no surprise that Gus not Ben, is on the receiving end of the gun. Ben, eager to comply with orders from above, finally receives an order he can fill. The effectively abrupt ending focuses on the precariousness of the relationship and the unresolved dilemma. Ben must choose whether or not to shoot Gus, but either way he may lose. Although Ben's violence culminates in his holding a gun on Gus, if he pulls the trigger he will destroy his own position which depends upon having someone to dominate.

Despite the numerous apparent differences between Ben and Gus the deeper reality is that neither the dominant nor the subservient character has much on which to base an identity when it grows solely or even primarily out of the dominant-subservient relationship. The violent means used to maintain dominance may destroy not only the subservient character but also the dominant character whose position is relative to the person he dominates. The obvious irony in this con game is that there can be no real winner, and possibly nothing to win. If Gus is destroyed, the best Ben can hope is that he will maintain what he has—his life and some continued subservient position with the organization. The organization may not, however, be sending the orders. Given the capriciousness of the events there are no guarantees that even by complying with the orders Ben can insure himself against being next on the receiving end of the gun. Yet if Ben fails to follow the order to shoot, the implicit threat is that he may be killed. Audience sympathy at the end is for both men, for any man in a situation where the awful irony is that all available choices seem wrong.

OUTSIDERS

HUGHIE

Eugene O'Neill

CHARACTERS

"ERIE" SMITH, a teller of tales
A NIGHT CLERK

Scene

The desk and a section of lobby of a small hotel on a West Side street in midtown New York. It is between 3 and 4 A.M. of a day in the summer of 1928.

It is one of those hotels, built in the decade 1900–10 on the side streets of the Great White Way sector, which began as respectable second class but soon were forced to deteriorate in order to survive. Following the First World War and Prohibition, it had given up all pretense of respectability, and now is anything a paying guest wants it to be, a third class dump, catering to the catch-as-catch-can trade. But still it does not prosper. It has not shared in the Great Hollow Boom of the twenties. The Everlasting Opulence of the New Economic Law has overlooked it. It manages to keep running by cutting the overhead for service, repairs, and cleanliness to a minimum.

The desk faces left along a section of seedy lobby with shabby chairs. The street entrance is off-stage, left. Behind the desk are a telephone switchboard and the operator's stool. At right, the usual numbered tiers of mailboxes, and above them a clock.

The NIGHT CLERK sits on the stool, facing front, his back to the switchboard. There is nothing to do. He is not thinking. He is not sleepy. He simply droops and stares acquiescently at nothing. It would be discouraging to glance at the clock. He knows there are several hours to go before his shift is over. Anyway, he does not need to look at clocks. He has been a night clerk in New York hotels so long he can tell time by sounds in the street.

He is in his early forties. Tall, thin, with a scrawny neck and jutting Adam's apple. His face is long and narrow, greasy with perspiration, sallow, studded with pimples from ingrowing hairs. His nose is large and without character. So is his mouth. So are his ears. So is his thinning brown hair, powdered with dandruff. Behind horn-rimmed spectacles, his blank brown eyes contain no discernible expression. One would say they had even forgotten how it feels to be bored. He wears an ill-fitting blue serge suit, white shirt and collar, a blue tie. The suit is old and shines at the elbows as if it had been waxed and polished.

Footsteps echo in the deserted lobby as someone comes in from the street. The NIGHT CLERK rises wearily. His eyes remain empty but his gummy lips part automatically in a welcoming The-Patron-Is-Always-Right grimace, intended as a smile. His big uneven teeth are in bad condition.

ERIE SMITH enters and approaches the desk. He is about the same age as the Clerk and has the same pasty, perspiry, night-life complexion. There the resemblance ends. Erie is around medium height but appears shorter because he is stout and his fat legs are too short for his body. So are his fat arms. His big head squats on a neck which seems part of his beefy shoulders. His face is round, his snub nose flattened at the tip. His blue eyes have drooping lids and puffy pouches under them. His sandy hair is falling out and the top of his head is bald. He walks to the desk with a breezy, familiar air, his gait a bit waddling because of his short legs. He carries a Panama hat and mops his face with a red and blue silk handkerchief. He wears a light grey suit cut in the extreme, tightwaisted, Broadway mode, the coat open to reveal an old and faded but expensive silk shirt in a shade of blue that sets teeth on edge, and a gay red and blue foulard tie, its knot stained by perspiration. His trousers are held up by a braided brown leather belt with a brass buckle. His shoes are tan and white, his socks white silk.

In manner, he is consciously a Broadway sport and a Wise Guy—the type of small fry gambler and horse player, living hand to mouth on the fringe of the rackets. Infesting corners, doorways, cheap restaurants, the bars of minor speakeasies, he and his kind imagine they are in the Real Know, cynical oracles of One True Grapevine.

Erie usually speaks in a low, guarded tone, his drooplidded eyes suspiciously wary of nonexistent eavesdroppers. His face is set in the prescribed pattern of gambler's dead pan. His small, pursy mouth is always crooked in the cynical leer of one who possesses superior, inside information, and his shifty once-over glances never miss the price tags he detects on everything and everybody. Yet there is something phoney about his characterization of himself, some sentimental softness behind it which doesn't belong in the hard-boiled picture.

Erie avoids looking at the Night Clerk, as if he resented him.

ERIE
Peremptorily.

Key.

Then as the Night Clerk gropes with his memory—grudgingly.

Forgot you ain't seen me before. Erie Smith's the name. I'm an old timer in this fleabag. 492.

NIGHT CLERK
In a tone of one who is wearily relieved when he does not have to remember anything—he plucks out the key.

492. Yes, sir.

ERIE
Taking the key, gives the Clerk the once-over. He appears not unfavorably impressed but his tone still holds resentment.

How long you been on the job? Four, five days, huh? I been off on a drunk. Come to now, though. Tapering off. Well, I'm glad they fired that young squirt they took on when Hughie got sick. One of them fresh wise punks. Couldn't tell him nothing. Pleased to meet you, Pal. Hope you stick around.

He shoves out his hand. The Night Clerk takes it obediently.

NIGHT CLERK
With a compliant, uninterested smile.

Glad to know you, Mr. Smith.

ERIE

What's your name?

NIGHT CLERK
As if he had half forgotten because what did it matter, anyway?

Hughes. Charlie Hughes.

ERIE
Starts.

Huh? Hughes? Say, is that on the level?

NIGHT CLERK

Charlie Hughes.

ERIE

Well, I be damned! What the hell d'you know about that!

Warming toward the Clerk.

Say, now I notice, you don't look like Hughie, but you remind me of him somehow. You ain't by any chance related?

NIGHT CLERK

You mean to the Hughes who had this job so long and died recently? No, sir. No relation.

ERIE
Gloomily.

No, that's right. Hughie told me he didn't have no relations left—except his wife and kids, of course.

He pauses—more gloomily.

Yeah. The poor guy croaked last week. His funeral was what started me off on a bat.

Then boastfully, as if defending himself against gloom.

Some drunk! I don't go on one often. It's bum dope in my book. A guy gets careless and gabs about things he knows and when he comes to he's liable to find there's guys who'd feel easier if he wasn't around no more. That's the trouble with knowing things. Take my tip, Pal. Don't never know nothin'. Be a sap and stay healthy.

His manner has become secretive, with sinister undertones. But the Night Clerk doesn't notice this. Long experience with guests who stop at his desk in the small hours to talk about themselves has given him a foolproof technique of self-defense. He appears to listen with agreeable submissiveness and be impressed, but his mind is blank and he doesn't hear unless a direct question is put to him, and sometimes not even then. Erie thinks he is impressed.

But hell, I always keep my noggin working, booze or no booze. I'm no sucker. What was I sayin'? Oh, some drunk. I sure hit the high spots. You shoulda seen the doll I made night before last. And did she take me to the cleaners! I'm a sucker for blondes.

He pauses—giving the Night Clerk a cynical, contemptuous glance.

You're married, ain't you?

NIGHT CLERK

Long ago he gave up caring whether questions were personal or not.

Yes, sir.

ERIE

Yeah, I'd'a laid ten to one on it. You got that old look. Like Hughie had. Maybe that's the resemblance.

He chuckles contemptuously.

Kids, too, I bet?

NIGHT CLERK

Yes, sir. Three.

ERIE

You're worse off than Hughie was. He only had two. Three, huh? Well, that's what comes of being careless!

He laughs. The Night Clerk smiles at a guest. He had been a little offended when a guest first made that crack—must have been ten years ago—yes, Eddie, the oldest, is eleven now—or is it twelve? Erie goes on with goodnatured tolerance.

Well, I suppose marriage ain't such a bum racket, if you're made for it. Hughie didn't seem to mind it much, although if you want my low-down, his wife is a bum—in spades! Oh, I don't mean cheatin'. With her puss and figure, she'd never make no one except she raided a blind asylum.

The Night Clerk feels that he has been standing a long time and his feet are beginning to ache and he wishes 492 would stop talking and go to bed so he can sit down again and listen to the noises in the street and think about nothing. Erie gives him an amused, condescending glance.

How old are you? Wait! Let me guess. You look fifty or over but I'll lay ten to one you're forty-three or maybe forty-four.

NIGHT CLERK

I'm forty-three.

He adds vaguely.

Or maybe it is forty-four.

ERIE
Elated.

I win, huh? I sure can call the turn on ages, Buddy. You ought to see the dolls get sored up when I work it on them! You're like Hughie. He looked like he'd never see fifty again and he was only forty-three. Me, I'm forty-five. Never think it, would you? Most of the dames don't think I've hit forty yet.

The Night Clerk shifts his position so he can lean more on the desk. Maybe those shoes he sees advertised for fallen arches—But they cost eight dollars, so that's out—Get a pair when he goes to heaven. Erie is sizing him up with another cynical, friendly glance.

I make another bet about you. Born and raised in the sticks, wasn't you?

NIGHT CLERK
Faintly aroused and defensive.

I come originally from Saginaw, Michigan, but I've lived here in the Big Town so long I consider myself a New Yorker now.

This is a long speech for him and he wonders sadly why he took the trouble to make it.

ERIE

I don't deserve no medal for picking that one. Nearly every guy I know on the Big Stem—and I know most of 'em—hails from the sticks. Take me. You'd never guess it but I was dragged up in Erie, P-a. Ain't that a knockout! Erie, P-a! That's how I got my moniker. No one calls me nothing but Erie. You better call me Erie, too, Pal, or I won't know when you're talkin' to me.

NIGHT CLERK

All right, Erie.

ERIE

Atta Boy.

He chuckles.

Here's another knockout. Smith is my real name. A Broadway guy like me named Smith and it's my real name! Ain't that a knockout!

He explains carefully so there will be no misunderstanding.

I don't remember nothing much about Erie, P-a, you understand—or want to. Some punk burg! After grammar school, my Old Man put me to work in his store, dealing out groceries. Some punk job! I stuck it till I was eighteen before I took a run-out powder.

The Night Clerk seems turned into a drooping waxwork, draped along the desk. This is what he used to dread before he perfected his technique of not listening: The Guest's Story of His Life. He fixes his mind on his aching feet. Erie chuckles.

Speaking of marriage, that was the big reason I ducked. A doll nearly had me hooked for the old shotgun ceremony. Closest I ever come to being played for a sucker. This doll in Erie—Daisy's her name—was one of them dumb wide-open dolls. All the guys give her a play. Then one day she wakes up and finds she's going to have a kid. I never figured she meant to frame me in particular. Way I always figured, she didn't have no idea who,

so she holds a lottery all by herself. Put about a thousand guys' names in a hat—all she could remember—and drew one out and I was it. Then she told her Ma, and her Ma told her Pa, and her Pa come round looking for me. But I was no fall guy even in them days. I took it on the lam. For Saratoga, to look the bangtails over. I'd started to be a horse player in Erie, though I'd never seen a track. I been one ever since.

With a touch of bravado.

And I ain't done so bad, Pal. I've made some killings in my time the gang still gab about. I've been in the big bucks. More'n once, and I will be again. I've had tough breaks too, but what the hell, I always get by. When the horses won't run for me, there's draw or stud. When they're bad, there's a crap game. And when they're all bad, there's always bucks to pick up for little errands I ain't talkin' about, which they give a guy who can keep his clam shut. Oh, I get along, Buddy. I get along fine.

He waits for approving assent from the Night Clerk, but the latter is not hearing so intently he misses his cue until the expectant silence crashes his ears.

NIGHT CLERK
Hastily, gambling on "yes."

Yes, Sir.

ERIE
Bitingly.

Sorry if I'm keeping you up, Sport.

With an aggrieved air.

Hughie was a wide-awake guy. He was always waiting for me to roll in. He'd say, "Hello, Erie, how'd the bangtails treat you?" Or, "How's luck?" Or, "Did you make the old bones behave?" Then I'd tell him how I'd done. He'd ask, "What's new along the

Big Stem?" and I'd tell him the latest off the grapevine.

He grins with affectionate condescension.

It used to hand me a laugh to hear old Hughie crackin' like a sport. In all the years I knew him, he never bet a buck on nothin'.

Excusingly.

But it ain't his fault. He'd have took a chance, but how could he with his wife keepin' cases on every nickel of his salary? I showed him lots of ways he could cross her up, but he was too scared.

He chuckles.

The biggest knockout was when he'd kid me about dames. He'd crack, "What? No blonde to-night, Erie? You must be slippin'." Jeez, you never see a guy more bashful with a doll around than Hughie was. I used to introduce him to the tramps I'd drag home with me. I'd wise them up to kid him along and pretend they'd fell for him. In two minutes, they'd have him hanging on the ropes. His face'd be red and he'd look like he wanted to crawl under the desk and hide. Some of them dolls was raw babies. They'd make him pretty raw propositions. He'd stutter like he was paralyzed. But he ate it up, just the same. He was tickled pink. I used to hope maybe I could nerve him up to do a little cheatin'. I'd offer to fix it for him with one of my dolls. Hell, I got plenty, I wouldn't have minded. I'd tell him, "Just let that wife of yours know you're cheatin', and she'll have some respect for you." But he was too scared.

He pauses—boastfully.

Some queens I've brought here in my time, Brother—frails from the Follies, or the Scandals, or the Frolics, that'd knock your eye out! And I still can make 'em. You watch. I ain't slippin'.

He looks at the Night Clerk expecting reassurance, but the Clerk's mind has slipped away to the clanging bounce of garbage cans in the outer night. He is thinking: "A job I'd like. I'd bang those cans louder than they do! I'd wake up the whole damned city!" Erie mutters disgustedly to himself.

Jesus, what a dummy!

He makes a move in the direction of the elevator, off right front—gloomily.

Might as well hit the hay, I guess.

NIGHT CLERK
Comes to—with the nearest approach to feeling he has shown in many a long night—approvingly.

Good night, Mr. Smith. I hope you have a good rest.

But Erie stops, glancing around the deserted lobby with forlorn distaste, jiggling the room key in his hand.

ERIE

What a crummy dump! What did I come back for? I shoulda stayed on a drunk. You'd never guess it, Buddy, but when I first come here this was a classy hotel—and clean, can you believe it?

He scowls.

I've been campin' here, off and on, fifteen years, but I've got a good notion to move out. It ain't the same place since Hughie was took to the hospital.

Gloomily.

Hell with going to bed! I'll just lie there worrying—

He turns back to the desk. The Clerk's face would express despair, but the last time he was able to feel despair was back around

World War days when the cost of living got so high and he was out of a job for three months. Erie leans on the desk—in a dejected, confidential tone.

Believe me, Brother, I never been a guy to worry, but this time I'm on a spot where I got to, if I ain't a sap.

NIGHT CLERK
In the vague tone of a corpse which admits it once overheard a favorable rumor about life.

That's too bad, Mr. Smith. But they say most of the things we worry about never happen.

His mind escapes to the street again to play bouncing cans with the garbage men.

ERIE
Grimly.

This thing happens, Pal. I ain't won a bet at nothin' since Hughie was took to the hospital. I'm jinxed. And that ain't all—But to hell with it! You're right, at that. Something always turns up for me. I was born lucky. I ain't worried. Just moaning low. Hell, who don't when they're getting over a drunk? You know how it is. The Brooklyn Boys march over the bridge with bloodhounds to hunt you down. And I'm still carrying the torch for Hughie. His checking out was a real K.O. for me. Damn if I know why. Lots of guys I've been pals with, in a way, croaked from booze or something, or got rubbed out, but I always took it as part of the game. Hell, we all gotta croak. Here today, gone tomorrow, so what's the good of beefin'? When a guy's dead, he's dead. He don't give a damn, so why should anybody else?

But this fatalistic philosophy is no comfort and Erie sighs.

I miss Hughie, I guess. I guess I'd got to like him a lot.

Again he explains carefully so there will be no misunderstanding.

Not that I was ever real pals with him, you understand. He didn't run in my class. He didn't know none of the answers. He was just a sucker.

He sighs again.

But I sure am sorry he's gone. You missed a lot not knowing Hughie, Pal. He sure was one grand little guy.

He stares at the lobby floor. The Night Clerk regards him with vacant, bulging eyes full of a vague envy for the blind. The garbage men have gone their predestined way. Time is that much older. The Clerk's mind remains in the street to greet the noise of a far-off El train. Its approach is pleasantly like a memory of hope; then it roars and rocks and rattles past the nearby corner, and the noise pleasantly deafens memory; then it recedes and dies, and there is something melancholy about that. But there is hope. Only so many El trains pass in one night, and each one passing leaves one less to pass, so the night recedes, too, until at last it must die and join all the other long nights in Nirvana, the Big Night of Nights. And that's life. "What I always tell Jess when she nags me to worry about something: 'That's life, isn't it? What can you do about it?'" Erie sighs again—then turns to the Clerk, his foolishly wary, wise-guy eyes defenseless, his poker face as self-betraying as a hurt dog's—appealingly.

Say, you do remind me of Hughie somehow, Pal. You got the same look on your map.

But the Clerk's mind is far away attending the obsequies of night, and it takes it some time to get back. Erie is hurt—contemptuously.

But I guess it's only that old night clerk look! There's one of 'em born every minute!

NIGHT CLERK
His mind arrives just in time to catch this last—with a bright grimace.

Yes, Mr. Smith. That's what Barnum said, and it's certainly true, isn't it?

ERIE
Grateful even for this sign of companionship, growls.

Nix on the Mr. Smith stuff, Charlie. There's ten of *them* born every minute. Call me Erie, like I told you.

NIGHT CLERK
Automatically, as his mind tiptoes into the night again.

All right, Erie.

ERIE
Encouraged, leans on the desk, clacking his room key like a castanet.

Yeah. Hughie was one grand little guy. All the same, like I said, he wasn't the kind of guy you'd ever figger a guy like me would take to. Because he was a sucker, see—the kind of sap you'd take to the cleaners a million times and he'd never wise up he was took. Why, night after night, just for a gag, I'd get him to shoot crap with me here on the desk. With *my* dice. And he'd never ask to give 'em the once-over. Can you beat that!

He chuckles—then earnestly.

Not that I'd ever ring in no phoneys on a pal. I'm no heel.

He chuckles again.

And anyway, I didn't need none to take Hughie because he never even made me knock 'em against nothing. Just a roll on the desk here. Boy, if they'd ever let me throw

'em that way in a real game, I'd be worth ten million dollars.

He laughs.

You'da thought Hughie woulda got wise something was out of order when, no matter how much he'd win on a run of luck like suckers have sometimes, I'd always take him to the cleaners in the end. But he never suspicioned nothing. All he'd say was "Gosh, Erie, no wonder you took up gambling. You sure were born lucky."

He chuckles.

Can you beat that?

He hastens to explain earnestly.

Of course, like I said, it was only a gag. We'd play with real jack, just to make it look real, but it was all my jack. He never had no jack. His wife dealt him four bits a day for spending money. So I'd stake him at the start to half of what I got—in chicken feed, I mean. We'd pretend a cent was a buck, and a nickel was a fin and so on. Some big game! He got a big kick out of it. He'd get all het up. It give me a kick, too—especially when he'd say, "Gosh, Erie, I don't wonder you never worry about money, with your luck."

He laughs.

That guy would believe anything! Of course, I'd stall him off when he'd want to shoot nights when I didn't have a goddamned nickel.

He chuckles.

What laughs he used to hand me! He'd always call horses "the bangtails," like he'd known 'em all his life—and he'd never seen a race horse, not till I kidnapped him one day and took him down to Belmont. What a kick he got out of that! I got scared he'd pass out with excitement. And he wasn't doing no betting either. All he had was four bits. It was just the track, and the crowd, and the horses got him. Mostly the horses.

With a surprised, reflective air.

Y'know, it's funny how a dumb, simple guy like Hughie will all of a sudden get something right. He says, "They're the most beautiful things in the world, I think." And he wins! I tell you, Pal, I'd rather sleep in the same stall with old Man o' War than make the whole damn Follies. What do you think?

NIGHT CLERK
His mind darts back from a cruising taxi and blinks bewilderedly in the light: "Say yes."

Yes, I agree with you, Mr.—I mean, Erie.

ERIE
With good-natured contempt.

Yeah? I bet you never seen one, except back at the old Fair Grounds in the sticks. I don't mean them kind of turtles. I mean a real horse.

The Clerk wonders what horses have to do with anything—or for that matter, what anything has to do with anything—then gives it up. Erie takes up his tale.

And what d'you think happened the next night? Damned if Hughie didn't dig two bucks out of his pants and try to slip 'em to me. "Let this ride on the nose of whatever horse you're betting on tomorrow," he told me. I got sore. "Nix," I told him, "if you're going to start playin' sucker and bettin' on horse races, you don't get no assist from me."

He grins wryly.

Was that a laugh! Me advising a sucker not to bet when I've spent a lot of my life tellin' saps a story to make 'em bet! I said, "Where'd you grab this dough? Outa the Little Woman's purse, huh? What tale you going to give her when you lose it? She'll start breaking up the furniture with you!" "No," he says, "she'll just cry." "That's worse," I said, "no guy can beat that racket. I had a doll cry on me once in a restaurant full of people till I had to promise her a diamond engagement ring to sober her up." Well, anyway, Hughie sneaked the two bucks back in the Little Woman's purse when he went home that morning, and that was the end of that.

Cynically.

Boy Scouts got nothin' on me, Pal, when it comes to good deeds. That was one I done. It's too bad I can't remember no others.

He is well wound up now and goes on without noticing that the Night Clerk's mind has left the premises in his sole custody.

Y'know I had Hughie sized up for a sap the first time I see him. I'd just rolled in from Tia Juana. I'd made a big killing down there and I was lousy with jack. Came all the way in a drawing room, and I wasn't lonely in it neither. There was a blonde movie doll on the train—and I was lucky in them days. Used to follow the horses South every winter. I don't no more. Sick of traveling. And I ain't as lucky as I was—

Hastily.

Anyway, this time I'm talkin' about, soon as I hit this lobby I see there's a new night clerk, and while I'm signing up for the bridal suite I make a bet with myself he's never been nothin' but a night clerk. And I win. At first, he wouldn't open up. Not that he was cagey about gabbin' too much. But like he couldn't think of nothin' about himself worth saying. But after he'd seen me roll in here the last one every night, and I'd stop to kid him along and tell him the tale of what I'd win that day, he got friendly and talked. He'd come from a hick burg upstate. Graduated from high school, and had a shot at different jobs in the old home town but couldn't make the grade until he was took on as night clerk in the hotel there. Then he made good. But he wasn't satisfied. Didn't like being only a night clerk where everybody knew him. He'd read somewhere—in the Suckers' Almanac, I guess—that all a guy had to do was come to the Big Town and Old Man Success would be waitin' at the Grand Central to give him the key to the city. What a gag that is! Even I believed that once, and no one could ever call me a sap. Well, anyway, he made the break and come here and the only job he could get was night clerk. Then he fell in love—or kidded himself he was—and got married. Met her on a subway train. It stopped sudden and she was jerked into him, and he put his arms around her, and they started talking, and the poor boob never stood a chance. She was a sales girl in some punk department store, and she was sick of standing on her dogs all day, and all the way home to Brooklyn, too. So, the way I figger it, knowing Hughie and dames, she proposed and said "yes" for him, and married him, and after that, of course, he never dared stop being a night clerk, even if he could.

He pauses.

Maybe you think I ain't giving her a square shake. Well, maybe I ain't. She never give me one. She put me down as a bad influence, and let her chips ride. And maybe Hughie couldn't have done no better. Dolls didn't call him no riot. Hughie and her seemed happy enough the time he had me out to dinner in their flat. Well, not happy. Maybe contented. No, that's boosting it, too. Resigned comes nearer, as if each was given' the other a break by thinking, "Well, what more could I expect?"

Abruptly he addresses the Night Clerk with contemptuous good nature.

How d'you and your Little Woman hit it off, Brother?

NIGHT CLERK
His mind has been counting the footfalls of the cop on the beat as they recede, sauntering longingly toward the dawn's release. "If he'd only shoot it out with a gunman some night! Nothing exciting has happened in any night I've ever lived through!" He stammers gropingly among the echoes of Erie's last words.

Oh—you mean *my* wife? Why, we get along all right, I guess.

ERIE
Disgustedly.

Better lay off them headache pills, Pal. First thing you know, some guy is going to call you a dope.

But the Night Clerk cannot take this seriously. It is years since he cared what anyone called him. So many guests have called him so many things. The Little Woman has, too. And, of course, he has, himself. But that's all past. Is daybreak coming now? No, too early yet. He can tell by the sound of that surface car. It is still lost in the night. Flat wheeled and tired. Distant the carbarn, and far away the sleep. Erie, having soothed resentment with his wisecrack, goes on with a friendly grin.

Well, keep hoping, Pal. Hughie was as big a dope as you until I give him some interest in life.

Slipping back into narrative.

That time he took me home to dinner. Was that a knockout! It took him a hell of a while to get up nerve to ask me. "Sure, Hughie," I told him, "I'll be tickled to death." I was thinking, I'd rather be shot. For one thing, he lived in Brooklyn, and I'd sooner take a trip to China. Another thing, I'm a guy that likes to eat what I order and not what somebody deals me. And he had kids and a wife, and the family racket is out of my line. But Hughie looked so tickled I

couldn't welsh on him. And it didn't work
out so bad. Of course, what he called home
was only a dump of a cheap flat. Still, it
wasn't so bad for a change. His wife had
done a lot of stuff to doll it up. Nothin' with
no class, you understand. Just cheap stuff to
make it comfortable. And his kids wasn't the
gorillas I'd expected, neither. No throwin'
spitballs in my soup or them kind of gags.
They was quiet like Hughie. I kinda liked
'em. After dinner I started tellin' 'em a story
about a race horse a guy I know owned once.
I thought it was up to me to put out something, and kids like animal stories, and this
one was true, at that. This old turtle never
wins a race, but he was as foxy as ten guys, a
natural born crook, the goddamnedest thief,
he'd steal anything in reach that wasn't
nailed down— Well, I didn't get far. Hughie's
wife butt in and stopped me cold. Told the
kids it was bedtime and hustled 'em off like
I was giving 'em measles. It got my goat,
kinda. I coulda liked her—a little—if she'd
give me a chance. Not that she was nothin'
Ziegfeld would want to glorify. When you
call her plain, you give her all the breaks.

Resentfully.

Well, to hell with it. She had me tagged for a
bum, and seein' me made her sure she was
right. You can bet she told Hughie never invite me again, and he never did. He tried to
apologize, but I shut him up quick. He says,
"Irma was brought up strict. She can't help
being narrow-minded about gamblers." I
said, "What's it to me? I don't want to hear
your dame troubles. I got plenty of my own.
Remember that doll I brung home night
before last? She gives me an argument I
promised her ten bucks. I told her, 'Listen,
Baby, I got an impediment in my speech.
Maybe it sounded like ten, but it was two,
and that's all you get. Hell, I don't want to
buy your soul! What would I do with it?'
Now she's peddling the news along Broadway I'm a rat and a chiseler, and of course
all the rats and chiselers believe her. Before
she's through, I won't have a friend left."

He pauses—confidentially.

I switched the subject on Hughie, see, on
purpose. He never did beef to me about his
wife again.

He gives a forced chuckle.

Believe me, Pal, I can stop guys that start
telling me their family troubles!

NIGHT CLERK
*His mind has hopped an ambulance clanging
down Sixth, and is asking without curiosity:
"Will he die, Doctor, or isn't he lucky?"
"I'm afraid not, but he'll have to be absolutely
quiet for months and months." "With a
pretty nurse taking care of him?" "Probably
not pretty." "Well, anyway, I claim he's
lucky. And now I must get back to the hotel.
492 won't go to bed and insists on telling me
jokes. It must have been a joke because he's
chuckling." He laughs with a heartiness
which has forgotten that heart is more than a
word used in "Have a heart," an old slang
expression.*

Ha—Ha! That's a good one, Erie. That's the
best I've heard in a long time!

ERIE
*For a moment is so hurt and depressed he
hasn't the spirit to make a sarcastic crack.
He stares at the floor, twirling his room key—
to himself.*

Jesus, this sure is a dead dump. About as
homey as the Morgue.

He glances up at the clock.

Gettin' late. Better beat it up to my cell and
grab some shut eye.

*He makes a move to detach himself from the
desk but fails and remains wearily glued to it.
His eyes prowl the lobby and finally come to
rest on the Clerk's glistening, sallow face.
He summons up strength for a withering
crack.*

Why didn't you tell me you was deef, Buddy? I know guys is sensitive about them little afflictions, but I'll keep it confidential.

But the Clerk's mind has rushed out to follow the siren wail of a fire engine. "A fireman's life must be exciting." His mind rides the engine, and asks a fireman with disinterested eagerness: "Where's the fire? Is it a real good one this time? Has it a good start? Will it be big enough, do you think?" Erie examines his face—bitingly.

Take my tip, Pal, and don't never try to buy from a dope peddler. He'll tell you you had enough already.

The Clerk's mind continues its dialogue with the fireman: "I mean, big enough to burn down the whole damn city?" "Sorry, Brother, but there's no chance. There's too much stone and steel. There'd always be something left." "Yes, I guess you're right. There's too much stone and steel. I wasn't really hoping, anyway. It really doesn't matter to me." Erie gives him up and again attempts to pry himself from the desk, twirling his key frantically as if it were a fetish which might set him free.

Well, me for the hay.

But he can't dislodge himself—dully.

Christ, it's lonely. I wish Hughie was here. By God, if he was, I'd tell him a tale that'd make his eyes pop! The bigger the story the harder he'd fall. He was that kind of sap. He thought gambling was romantic. I guess he saw me like a sort of dream guy, the sort of guy he'd like to be if he could take a chance. I guess he lived a sort of double life listening to me gabbin' about hittin' the high spots. Come to figger it, I'll bet he even cheated on his wife that way, using me and my dolls.

He chuckles.

No wonder he liked me, huh? And the bigger I made myself the more he lapped it up. I

went easy on him at first. I didn't lie—not any more'n a guy naturally does when he gabs about the bets he wins and the dolls he's made. But I soon see he was cryin' for more, and when a sucker cries for more, you're a dope if you don't let him have it. Every tramp I made got to be a Follies' doll. Hughie liked 'em to be Follies' dolls. Or in the Scandals or Frolics. He wanted me to be the Sheik of Araby, or something that any blonde'd go round-heeled about. Well, I give him plenty of that. And I give him plenty of gambling tales. I explained my campin' in this dump was because I don't want to waste jack on nothin' but gambling. It was like dope to me, I told him. I couldn't quit. He lapped that up. He liked to kid himself I'm mixed up in the racket. He thought gangsters was romantic. So I fed him some baloney about highjacking I'd done once. I told him I knew all the Big Shots. Well, so I do, most of 'em, to say hello, and sometimes they hello back. Who wouldn't know 'em that hangs around Broadway and the joints? I run errands for 'em sometimes, because there's dough in it, but I'm cagey about gettin' in where it ain't healthy. Hughie wanted to think me and Legs Diamond was old pals. So I give him that too. I give him anything he cried for.

Earnestly.

Don't get the wrong idea, Pal. What I fed Hughie wasn't all lies. The tales about gambling wasn't. They was stories of big games and killings that really happened since I've been hangin' round. Only I wasn't in on 'em like I made out—except one or two from way back when I had a run of big luck and was in the bucks for a while until I was took to the cleaners.

He stops to pay tribute of a sigh to the memory of brave days that were and that never were—then meditatively.

Yeah, Hughie lapped up my stories like they was duck soup, or a beakful of heroin. I sure took him around with me in tales and showed him one hell of a time.

He chuckles—then seriously.

And, d'you know, it done me good, too, in a way. Sure. I'd get to seein' myself like he seen me. Some nights I'd come back here without a buck, feeling lower than a snake's belly, and first thing you know I'd be lousy with jack, bettin' a grand a race. Oh, I was wise I was kiddin' myself. I ain't a sap. But what the hell, Hughie loved it, and it didn't cost nobody nothin', and if every guy along Broadway who kids himself was to drop dead there wouldn't be nobody left. Ain't it the truth, Charlie?

He again stares at the Night Clerk appealingly, forgetting past rebuffs. The Clerk's face is taut with vacancy. His mind has been trying to fasten itself to some noise in the night, but a rare and threatening pause of silence has fallen on the city, and here he is, chained behind a hotel desk forever, awake when everyone else in the world is asleep, except Room 492, and he won't go to bed, he's still talking, and there is no escape.

NIGHT CLERK
His glassy eyes stare through Erie's face. He stammers deferentially.

Truth? I'm afraid I didn't get—What's the truth?

ERIE
Hopelessly.

Nothing, Pal. Not a thing.

His eyes fall to the floor. Far a while he is too defeated even to twirl his room key. The Clerk's mind still cannot make a getaway because the city remains silent, and the night vaguely reminds him of death, and he is vaguely frightened, and now that he remembers, his feet are giving him hell, but that's no excuse not to act as if the Guest is always right: "I should have paid 492 more atten-

tion. After all, he is company. He is awake and alive. I should use him to help me live through the night. What's he been talking about? I must have caught some of it without meaning to." The Night Clerk's forehead puckers perspiringly as he tries to remember. Erie begins talking again but this time it is obviously aloud to himself, without hope of a listener.

I could tell by Hughie's face before he went to the hospital, he was through. I've seen the same look on guys' faces when they knew they was on the spot, just before guys caught up with them. I went to see him twice in the hospital. The first time, his wife was there and give me a dirty look, but he cooked up a smile and said, "Hello, Erie, how're the bangtails treating you?" I see he wants a big story to cheer him, but his wife butts in and says he's weak and he mustn't get excited. I felt like crackin', "Well, the Docs in this dump got the right dope. Just leave you with him and he'll never get excited." The second time I went, they wouldn't let me see him. That was near the end. I went to his funeral, too. There wasn't nobody but a coupla his wife's relations. I had to feel sorry for her. She looked like she ought to be parked in a coffin, too. The kids was bawlin'. There wasn't no flowers but a coupla lousy wreaths. It woulda been a punk showing for poor old Hughie, if it hadn't been for my flower piece.

He swells with pride.

That was some display, Pal. It'd knock your eye out! Set me back a hundred bucks, and no kiddin'! A big horseshoe of red roses! I knew Hughie'd want a horseshoe because that made it look like he'd been a horse player. And around the top printed in forget-me-nots was "Good-by, Old Pal." Hughie liked to kid himself he was my pal.

He adds sadly.

And so he was, at that—even if he was a sucker.

He pauses, his false poker face as nakedly forlorn as an organ grinder's monkey's. Outside, the spell of abnormal quiet presses suffocatingly upon the street, enters the deserted, dirty lobby. The Night Clerk's mind cowers away from it. He cringes behind the desk, his feet aching like hell. There is only one possible escape. If his mind could only fasten onto something 492 has said. "What's he been talking about? A clerk should always be attentive. You even are duty bound to laugh at a guest's smutty jokes, no matter how often you've heard them. That's the policy of the hotel. 492 has been gassing for hours. What's he been telling me? I must be slipping. Always before this I've been able to hear without bothering to listen, but now when I need company—Ah! I've got it! Gambling! He said a lot about gambling. That's something I've always wanted to know more about, too. Maybe he's a professional gambler. Like Arnold Rothstein."

NIGHT CLERK
Blurts out with an uncanny, almost lifelike eagerness.

I beg your pardon, Mr.—Erie—but did I understand you to say you are a gambler by profession? Do you, by any chance, know the Big Shot, Arnold Rothstein?

But this time it is Erie who doesn't hear him. And the Clerk's mind is now suddenly impervious to the threat of Night and Silence as it pursues an ideal of fame and glory within itself called Arnold Rothstein.

ERIE
With mournful longing.

Christ, I wish Hughie was alive and kickin'. I'd tell him I win ten grand from the bookies, and ten grand at stud, and ten grand in a crap game! I'd tell him I bought one of those Mercedes sport roadsters with nickel pipes sticking out of the hood! I'd tell him I lay three babes from the Follies—two blondes and one brunette!

The Night Clerk dreams, a rapt hero worship transfiguring his pimply face: "Arnold Rothstein! He must be some guy! I read a story about him. He'll gamble for any limit on anything, and always wins. The story said he wouldn't bother playing in a poker game unless the smallest bet you could make— one white chip!—was a hundred dollars. Christ, that's going some! I'd like to have the dough to get in a game with him once! The last pot everyone would drop out but him and me. I'd say, 'Okay, Arnold, the sky's the limit,' and I'd raise him five grand, and he'd call, and I'd have a royal flush to his four aces. Then I'd say, 'Okay, Arnold, I'm a good sport, I'll give you a break. I'll cut you double or nothing. Just one cut. I want quick action for my dough.' And I'd cut the ace of spades and win again." Beatific vision swoons on the empty pools of the Night Clerk's eyes. He resembles a holy saint, recently elected to Paradise. Erie breaks the silence—bitterly resigned.

But Hughie's better off, at that, being dead. He's got all the luck. He needn't do no worryin' now. He's out of the racket. I mean, the whole goddamned racket. I mean life.

NIGHT CLERK
Kicked out of his dream—with detached, pleasant acquiescence.

Yes, it is a goddamned racket when you stop to think, isn't it, 492? But we might as well make the best of it, because—Well, you can't burn it all down, can you? There's too much steel and stone. There'd always be something left to start it going again.

ERIE
Scowls bewilderedly.

Say, what is this? What the hell you talkin' about?

NIGHT CLERK
At a loss—in much confusion.

Why, to be frank, I really don't—Just something that came into my head.

ERIE
Bitingly, but showing he is comforted at having made some sort of contact.

Get it out of your head quick, Charlie, or some guys in uniform will walk in here with a butterfly net and catch you.

He changes the subject—earnestly.

Listen, Pal, maybe you guess I was kiddin' about that flower piece for Hughie costing a hundred bucks? Well, I ain't! I didn't give a damn what it cost. It was up to me to give Hughie a big-time send-off, because I knew nobody else would.

NIGHT CLERK

Oh, I'm not doubting your word, Erie. You won the money gambling, I suppose—I mean, I beg your pardon if I'm mistaken, but you are a gambler, aren't you?

ERIE
Preoccupied.

Yeah, sure, when I got scratch to put up. What of it? But I don't win that hundred bucks. I don't win a bet since Hughie was took to the hospital. I had to get down on my knees and beg every guy I know for a sawbuck here and a sawbuck there until I raised it.

NIGHT CLERK
His mind concentrated on the Big Ideal—insistently.

Do you by any chance know—Arnold Rothstein?

ERIE
His train of thought interrupted—irritably.

Arnold? What's he got to do with it? He

wouldn't loan a guy like me a nickel to save my grandmother from streetwalking.

NIGHT CLERK
With humble awe.

Then you do know him!

ERIE

Sure I know the bastard. Who don't on Broadway? And he knows me—when he wants to. He uses me to run errands when there ain't no one else handy. But he ain't my trouble, Pal. My trouble is, some of these guys I put the bite on is dead wrong G's, and they expect to be paid back next Tuesday, or else I'm outa luck and have to take it on the lam, or I'll get beat up and maybe sent to a hospital.

He suddenly rouses himself and there is something pathetically but genuinely gallant about him.

But what the hell. I was wise I was takin' a chance. I've always took a chance, and if I lose I pay, and no welshing! It sure was worth it to give Hughie the big send-off.

He pauses. The Night Clerk hasn't paid any attention except to his own dream. A question is trembling on his parted lips, but before he can get it out Erie goes on gloomily.

But even that ain't my big worry, Charlie. My big worry is the run of bad luck I've had since Hughie got took to the hospital. Not a win. That ain't natural. I've always been a lucky guy—lucky enough to get by and pay up, I mean. I wouldn't never worry about owing guys, like I owe them guys. I'd always know I'd make a win that'd fix it. But now I got a lousy hunch when I lost Hughie I lost my luck—I mean, I've lost the old confidence. He used to give me confidence.

He turns away from the desk.

No use gabbin' here all night. You can't do me no good.

He starts toward the elevator.

NIGHT CLERK
Pleadingly.

Just a minute, Erie, if you don't mind.

With awe.

So you're an old friend of Arnold Rothstein! Would you mind telling me if it's really true when Arnold Rothstein plays poker, one white chip is—a hundred dollars?

ERIE
Dully exasperated.

Say, for Christ's sake, what's it to you—?

He stops abruptly, staring probingly at the Clerk. There is a pause. Suddenly his face lights up with a saving revelation. He grins warmly and saunters confidently back to the desk.

Say, Charlie, why didn't you put me wise before, you was interested in gambling? Hell, I got you all wrong, Pal. I been tellin' myself, this guy ain't like old Hughie. He ain't got no sportin' blood. He's just a dope.

Generously.

Now I see you're a right guy. Shake.

He shoves out his hand which the Clerk clasps with a limp pleasure. Erie goes on with gathering warmth and self-assurance.

That's the stuff. You and me'll get along. I'll give you all the breaks, like I give Hughie.

NIGHT CLERK
Gratefully.

Thank you, Erie.

Then insistently.

Is it true when Arnold Rothstein plays poker, one white chip—

ERIE
With magnificent carelessness.

Sets you back a hundred bucks? Sure. Why not? Arnold's in the bucks, ain't he? And when you're in the bucks, a C note is chicken feed. I ought to know, Pal. I was in the bucks when Arnold was a piker. Why, one time down in New Orleans I lit a cigar with a C note, just for a gag, y'understand. I was with a bunch of high class dolls and I wanted to see their eyes pop out—and believe me, they sure popped! After that, I coulda made 'em one at a time or all together! Hell, I once win twenty grand on a single race. That's action! A good crap game is action, too. Hell, I've been in games where there was a hundred grand in real folding money lying around the floor. That's travelin'!

He darts a quick glance at the Clerk's face and begins to hedge warily. But he needn't. The Clerk sees him now as the Gambler in 492, the Friend of Arnold Rothstein—and nothing is incredible. Erie goes on.

Of course, I wouldn't kid you. I'm not in the bucks now—not right this moment. You know how it is, Charlie. Down today and up tomorrow. I got some dough ridin' on the nose of a turtle in the 4th at Saratoga. I hear a story he'll be so full of hop, if the joc can keep him from jumpin' over the grandstand, he'll win by a mile. So if I roll in here with a blonde that'll knock your eyes out, don't be surprised.

He winks and chuckles.

NIGHT CLERK
Ingratiatingly pally, smiling.

Oh, you can't surprise me that way. I've been a night clerk in New York all my life, almost.

He tries out a wink himself.

I'll forget the house rules, Erie.

ERIE
Dryly.

Yeah. The manager wouldn't like you to remember something he ain't heard of yet.

Then slyly feeling his way.

How about shootin' a little crap, Charlie? I mean just in fun, like I used to with Hughie. I know you can't afford takin' no chances. I'll stake you, see? I got a coupla bucks. We gotta use real jack or it don't look real. It's all my jack, get it? You can't lose. I just want to show you how I'll take you to the cleaners. It'll give me confidence.

He has taken two one-dollar bills and some change from his pocket. He pushes most of it across to the Clerk.

Here y'are.

He produces a pair of dice—carelessly.

Want to give these dice the once-over before we start?

NIGHT CLERK
Earnestly.

What do you think I am? I know I can trust you.

ERIE
Smiles.

You remind me a lot of Hughie, Pal. He always trusted me. Well, don't blame me if I'm lucky.

He clicks the dice in his hand—thoughtfully.

Y'know, it's time I quit carryin' the torch for Hughie. Hell, what's the use? It don't do him no good. He's gone. Like we all gotta go. Him yesterday, me or you tomorrow, and who cares, and what's the difference? It's all in the racket, huh?

His soul is purged of grief, his confidence restored.

I shoot two bits.

NIGHT CLERK
Manfully, with an excited dead-pan expression he hopes resembles Arnold Rothstein's.

I fade you.

ERIE
Throws the dice.

Four's my point.

Gathers them up swiftly and throws them again.

Four it is.

He takes the money.

Easy when you got my luck—and know how. Huh, Charlie?

He chuckles, giving the Night Clerk the slyly amused, contemptuous, affectionate wink with which a Wise Guy regales a Sucker.

CURTAIN

THE MISSING HALF OF *HUGHIE*

Doris Alexander

O'Neill was alive when *The Emperor Jones* was staged. And a good thing too. What if the director had been on his own? Perhaps he would have read the descriptions of Jones' visions and decided that these "thoughts" couldn't be staged. This did not happen to *The Emperor Jones*, but it is exactly what happened to *Hughie*, which was published and produced posthumously. O'Neill was not there to oversee the staging and the result was

First published in *The Drama Review*, Vol. 11 © 1967 by *The Drama Review*. Reprinted by permission. All Rights Reserved.

two weird productions, one in Stockholm and the other on Broadway.

Hughie is very much like *Jones* in structure, a monologue counterpointed by the visions of the title character. With *Jones*, O'Neill made sure that the visions were presented in pantomime, like the flowing images of silent film. He explained the technique to George Tyler; demanding "a new ingenuity and creative collaboration on the part of the producer," O'Neill said, it combines "the scope of the movies with all that is best of the spoken drama."

Shortly after the *Jones* production, O'Neill saw *The Cabinet of Dr. Caligari*. "It sure opened my eyes to wonderful possibilities," he said —and from then on he wanted to express himself directly in film. He made plans to film *Jones* with the help of Robert Edmond Jones and Francesco Bianco, the Italian film director. The film was never made, but O'Neill continued to write scenarios. In the fall of 1929 he saw his first talky. He wrote to George Jean Nathan that the new technique could help him get "a real Elizabethan treatment" of a theme. He thought of plays that could be done "either on the regular stage or as a 'talky.'" Above all, he had an idea of "a stage play combined with a screen talky background to make alive visually and vocally the memories, etc., in the minds of the characters."

At the beginning of 1940, despairing that he would ever finish this cycle of eleven plays, O'Neill turned to other matters. John Ford and Dudley Nichols began a film version of *The Long Voyage Home*. O'Neill started immediately to sketch the miniature cycle of one-act plays, *By Way of Obit*, of which *Hughie* is the only completed part. All plays in the cycle, it seems, were to combine film and live performance, but O'Neill was not explicit about this in the *Hughie* manuscript. This is not surprising. He had sworn Nathan to secrecy when he first told him the idea in 1929, afraid that news of his technique would leak and someone would steal his thunder.

Although there is nothing in the manu-

script, O'Neill's intentions are clear enough upon reading *Hughie*. Only two characters appear on stage. One speaks, the other daydreams. The drama is in the tension between the two. Erie's tormented monologue, punctuated sparsely by the monosyllabic replies of the Night Clerk, is only half the play. The other half—and the heart—is the Night Clerk's visions, and the overwhelming despair they convey. O'Neill did not use much dialogue in his screen scenario for the Night Clerk's visions: the Clerk is a simple, inarticulate man. But his visions are another matter; in them there is grandeur. For example, Erie has tried to wither the Clerk with the suggestion that he is "deaf."

> But the Clerk's mind has rushed out to follow the siren wail of a fire engine. "A fireman's life must be exciting." His mind rides the engine, and asks a fireman with disinterested eagerness: "Where's the fire? Is it a real good one this time? Has it a good start? Will it be big enough, do you think?" [*Erie interrupts, then:*] The Clerk's mind continues its dialogue with the fireman: "I mean, big enough to burn down the whole damn city?" "Sorry, Brother, but there's no chance. There's too much stone and steel. There'd always be something left." "Yes, I guess you're right. There's too much stone and steel. I wasn't really hoping, anyway. It really doesn't matter to me."

Clearly this is a scenario. Superimposed on the fiery images is the Clerk's naïve thought, "A fireman's life must be fun." Then the Clerk rides the engine, and so on. The directors in Stockholm and New York discarded this scene.

Even more baffling to them must have been passages like the Night Clerk's response to Erie's taunt that he'd better lay off headache pills or someone would call him an addict.

> But the Night Clerk cannot take this seriously. It is years since he cared what anyone called him. So many guests have called him so many things. The Little Woman has, too. And, of course, he has himself. But that's all past. Is daybreak coming now? No, too early yet. He

can tell by the sound of that surface car. It is still lost in the night. Flat wheeled and tired. Distant the carbarn, and far away the sleep.

Impossible to stage, these thoughts would make interesting film montage. In fact the whole of the Night Clerk's inner life can be conveyed on film—from his aching feet to his visions of a *danse macabre* of garbage cans (which follows ironically on Erie's brag about all the "frails from the Follies" he's made).

The job for the film-maker is not easy, but neither is it impossible. It would be stock-in-trade to an expressionist like Buñuel. Above all, the film-maker must project the terrible moment when a "spell of abnormal quiet presses suffocatingly upon the street," and the Night Clerk is left cowering before "the threat of Night and Silence"—a confrontation with death. This is the climax and turning point of *Hughie*. It drives the Night Clerk to grab at Erie's myth of gambler's glory and so give life to a lie that will allow both men to go on living.

A SON, COME HOME
Ed Bullins

CHARACTERS

MOTHER, Early 50's
SON, 30 Years Old
THE GIRL
THE BOY

The BOY *and the* GIRL *wear black tights and shirts. They move the action of the play and express the* MOTHER's *and the* SON's *moods and tensions. They become various embodiments recalled from memory and history: they enact a number of personalities and move from mood to mood.*

The players are Black.

At rise: Scene: Bare stage but for two chairs positioned so as not to interfere with the actions of the BOY *and the* GIRL.

The MOTHER *enters, sits in chair and begins to use imaginary iron and board. She hums a spiritual as she works.*

MOTHER: You came three times . . . Michael? It took you three times to find me at home?

[*The* GIRL *enters, turns and peers through the cracked, imaginary door.*]

SON'S VOICE: [*Offstage.*] Is Mrs. Brown home?
GIRL: [*An old woman.*] What?
MOTHER: It shouldn't have taken you three times. I told you that I would be here by two and you should wait, Michael.

[*The* SON *enters, passes the* GIRL *and takes his seat upon the other chair. The* BOY *enters, stops on other side of the imaginary door and looks through at the* GIRL.]

BOY: Is Mrs. Brown in?
GIRL: Miss Brown ain't come in yet. Come back later . . . She'll be in before dark.
MOTHER: It shouldn't have taken you three times . . . You should listen to me, Michael. Standin' all that time in the cold.
SON: It wasn't cold, Mother.
MOTHER: I told you that I would be here by two and you should wait Michael.
BOY: Please tell Mrs. Brown that her son's in town to visit her.
GIRL: You little Miss Brown's son? Well, bless the Lord.

[*Calls over her shoulder.*]

Hey, Mandy, do you hear that? Little Miss Brown upstairs got a son . . . a great big boy . . . He's come to visit her.
BOY: You'll tell her, won't you?
GIRL: Sure, I'll tell her.

[*Grins and shows gums.*]

I'll tell her soon as she gets in.

MOTHER: Did you get cold, Michael?

SON: No, Mother. I walked around some . . . sightseeing.

BOY: I walked up Twenty-third Street toward South. I had phoned that I was coming.

MOTHER: Sightseeing? But this is your home, Michael . . . always has been.

BOY: Just before I left New York I phoned that I was taking the bus. Two hours by bus, that's all. That's all it takes. Two hours.

SON: This town seems so strange. Different than how I remember it.

MOTHER: Yes, you have been away for a good while . . . How long has it been, Michael?

BOY: Two hours down the Jersey Turnpike, the trip beginning at the New York Port Authority Terminal . . .

SON: . . . and then straight down through New Jersey to Philadelphia . . .

GIRL: . . . and home . . . Just imagine . . . little Miss Brown's got a son who's come home.

SON: Yes, home . . . an anachronism.

MOTHER: What did you say, Michael?

BOY: He said . . .

GIRL: [*Late teens.*] What's an anachronism, Mike?

SON: Anachronism: 1: an error in chronology; *esp:* a chronological misplacing of persons, events, objects or customs in regard to each other 2: a person or a thing that is chronologically out of place—anachronistic/ *also* anachronic/ *or* anachronous—anachronistically/ *also* anachronously.

MOTHER: I was so glad to hear you were going to school in California.

BOY: College.

GIRL: Yes, I understand.

MOTHER: How long have you been gone, Michael?

SON: Nine years.

BOY: Nine years it's been. I wonder if she'll know me . . .

MOTHER: You've put on so much weight, son. You know that's not healthy.

GIRL: [*20 years old.*] And that silly beard . . . how . . .

SON: Oh . . . I'll take it off. I'm going on a diet tomorrow.

BOY: I wonder if I'll know her.

SON: You've put on some yourself, Mother.

MOTHER: Yes, the years pass. Thank the Lord.

BOY: I wonder if we've changed much.

GIRL: Yes, thank the Lord.

SON: The streets here seem so small.

MOTHER: Yes, it seems like that when you spend a little time in Los Angeles.

GIRL: I spent eighteen months there with your aunt when she was sick. She had nobody else to help her . . . she was so lonely. And you were in the service . . . away. You've always been away.

BOY: In Los Angeles the boulevards, the avenues, the streets . . .

SON: . . . are wide. Yes, they have some wide ones out West. Here, they're so small and narrow. I wonder how cars get through on both sides.

MOTHER: Why, you know how . . . we lived on Darby Street for over ten years, didn't we?

SON: Yeah, that was almost an alley.

MOTHER: Did you see much of your aunt before you left Los Angeles?

SON: What?

GIRL: [*Middle-aged woman.*] [*To* BOY.] Have you found a job yet, Michael?

MOTHER: Your aunt. My sister.

BOY: Nawh, not yet . . . Today I just walked downtown . . . quite a ways . . . this place is plenty big, ain't it?

SON: I don't see too much of Aunt Sophie.

MOTHER: But you're so much alike.

GIRL: Well, your bags are packed and are sitting outside the door.

BOY: My bags?

MOTHER: You shouldn't be that way, Michael. You shouldn't get too far away from your family.

SON: Yes, Mother.

BOY: But I don't have any money. I had to walk downtown today. That's how much money I have. I've only been here a week.

GIRL: I packed your bags, Michael.

MOTHER: You never can tell when you'll need or want your family, Michael.

SON: That's right, Mother.

MOTHER: You and she are so much alike.

BOY: Well, goodbye, Aunt Sophie.

GIRL: [*Silence.*]

MOTHER: All that time in California and you hardly saw your aunt. My baby sister.

BOY: Tsk tsk tsk.

SON: I'm sorry, Mother.

MOTHER: In the letters I'd get from both of you there'd be no mention of the other. All these years. Did you see her again?

SON: Yes.

GIRL: [*On telephone.*] Michael? Michael who? . . . Ohhh . . . Bernice's boy.

MOTHER: You didn't tell me about this, did you?

SON: No, I didn't.

BOY: Hello, Aunt Sophie. How are you?

GIRL: I'm fine, Michael. How are you? You're looking well.

BOY: I'm getting on okay.

MOTHER: I prayed for you.

SON: Thank you.

MOTHER: Thank the Lord, Michael.

BOY: Got me a job working for the city.

GIRL: You did now.

BOY: Yes, I've brought you something.

GIRL: What's this, Michael . . . ohhh . . . it's money.

BOY: It's for the week I stayed with you.

GIRL: Fifty dollars. But, Michael, you didn't have to.

MOTHER: Are you still writing that radical stuff, Michael?

SON: Radical?

MOTHER: Yes . . . that stuff you write and send me all the time in those little books.

SON: My poetry, Mother?

MOTHER: Yes, that's what I'm talking about.

SON: No.

MOTHER: Praise the Lord, son. Praise the Lord. Didn't seem like anything I had read in school.

BOY: [*On telephone.*] Aunt Sophie? . . . Aunt Sophie? . . . It's me, Michael . . .

GIRL: Michael?

BOY: Yes . . . Michael . . .

GIRL: Oh . . . Michael . . . yes . . .

BOY: I'm in jail, Aunt Sophie . . . I got picked up for drunk driving.

GIRL: You did . . . how awful . . .

MOTHER: When you going to get your hair cut, Michael?

BOY: Aunt Sophie . . . will you please come down and sign my bail. I've got the money . . . I just got paid yesterday . . . They're holding more than enough for me . . . but the law says that someone has to sign for it.

MOTHER: You look almost like a hoodlum, Michael.

BOY: All you need to do is come down and sign . . . and I can get out.

MOTHER: What you tryin' to be . . . a savage or something? Are you keeping out of trouble, Michael?

GIRL: Ohhh . . . Michael . . . I'm sorry but I can't do nothin' like that . . .

BOY: But all you have to do is sign . . . I've got the money and everything.

GIRL: I'm sorry . . . I can't stick my neck out.

BOY: But, Aunt Sophie . . . if I don't get back to work I'll lose my job and everything . . . please . . .

GIRL: I'm sorry, Michael . . . I can't stick my neck out . . . I have to go now . . . Is there anyone I can call?

BOY: No.

GIRL: I could call your mother. She wouldn't mind if I reversed the charges on her, would she? I don't like to run my bills up.

BOY: No, thanks.

MOTHER: You and your aunt are so much alike.

SON: Yes, Mother. Our birthdays are in the same month.

MOTHER: Yes, that year was so hot . . . so hot and I was carrying you . . .

[*As the* MOTHER *speaks the* BOY *comes over and takes her by the hand and leads her from the chair, and they stroll around the stage, arm in arm.*

The GIRL *accompanies them and she and the* BOY *enact scenes from the* MOTHER's *mind.*]

. . . . carrying you, Michael . . . and you were such a big baby . . . kicked all the time. But I was happy. Happy that I was having a baby of my own . . . I worked as long as I could and bought you everything you might need . . . diapers . . . and bottles . . . and your own spoon . . . and even toys . . . . and even books . . . And it was so hot in Philadelphia that year . . . Your Aunt Sophie used to come over and we'd go for walks . . . sometimes up on the avenue . . . I was living in West Philly then . . . in that old terrible section they called "The Bottom." That's where I met your father.

GIRL: You're such a fool, Bernice. No nigger . . . man or boy's . . . ever going to do a thing to me like that.

MOTHER: Everything's going to be all right, Sophia.

GIRL: But what is he going to do? How are you going to take care of a baby by yourself?

MOTHER: Everything's going to be all right, Sophia. I'll manage.

GIRL: You'll manage? How? Have you talked about marriage?

MOTHER: Oh, please, Sophia!

GIRL: What do you mean "please?" Have you?

MOTHER: I just can't. He might think . . .

GIRL: Think! That dirty nigger better think. He better think before he really messes up. And you better too. You got this baby comin' on. What are you going to do?

MOTHER: I don't know . . . I don't know what I can do.

GIRL: Is he still tellin' you those lies about . . .

MOTHER: They're not lies.

GIRL: Haaaa . . .

MOTHER: They're not.

GIRL: Some smooth-talkin' nigger comes up from Georgia and tell you he escaped from the chain gang and had to change his name so he can't get married 'cause they might find out . . . What kinda shit is that, Bernice?

MOTHER: Please, Sophia. Try and understand. He loves me. I can't hurt him.

GIRL: Loves you . . . and puts you through this?

MOTHER: Please . . . I'll talk to him . . . Give me a chance.

GIRL: It's just a good thing you got a family, Bernice. It's just a good thing. You know that, don't cha?

MOTHER: Yes . . . yes, I do . . . but please don't say anything to him.

SON: I've only seen my father about a half dozen times that I remember, Mother. What was he like?

MOTHER: Down in The Bottom . . . that's where I met your father. I was young and hinkty then. Had big pretty brown legs and a small waist. Everybody used to call me Bernie . . . and me and my sister would go to Atlantic City on the weekends and work as waitresses in the evenings and sit all afternoon on the black part of the beach at Boardwalk and Atlantic . . . getting blacker . . . and having the times of our lives. Your father probably still lives down in The Bottom . . . perched over some bar down there . . . drunk to the world . . . I can see him now . . . He had good white teeth then . . . not how they turned later when he started in drinkin' that wine and wouldn't stop . . . he was so nice then.

BOY: Awwww, listen, kid. I got my problems too.

GIRL: But Andy . . . I'm six months gone . . . and you ain't done nothin'.

BOY: Well, what can I do?

GIRL: Don't talk like that . . . What can you do? . . . You know what you can do.

BOY: You mean marry you? Now lissen, sweetheart . . .

GIRL: But what about our baby?

BOY: Your baby.

GIRL: Don't talk like that! It took more than me to get him.

BOY: Well . . . look . . . I'll talk to you later, kid. I got to go to work now.

GIRL: That's what I got to talk to you about too, Andy. I need some money.

BOY: Money! Is somethin' wrong with your head, woman? I ain't got no money.

GIRL: But I can't work much longer, Andy. You got to give me some money. Andy . . . you just gotta.

BOY: Woman . . . all I got to *ever* do is die and go to hell.

GIRL: Well, you gonna do that, Andy. You

sho are . . . you know that, don't you? . . .
You know that.

MOTHER: . . . Yes, you are, man. Praise the
Lord. We all are . . . All of us . . . even
though he ain't come for you yet to make
you pay. Maybe he's waitin' for us to go
together so I can be a witness to the retribution that's handed down. A witness to all
that He'll bestow upon your sinner's head
. . . A witness! . . . That's what I am,
Andy! Do you hear me? . . . A witness!

SON: Mother . . . what's wrong? What's the
matter?

MOTHER: Thank the Lord that I am not
blinded and will see the fulfillment of
divine . . .

SON: Mother!

MOTHER: Oh . . . is   something   wrong,
Michael?

SON: You're shouting and walking around . . .

MOTHER: Oh . . . it's nothing, son. I'm just
feeling the power of the Lord.

SON: Oh . . . is there anything I can get you,
Mother?

MOTHER: No, nothing at all.

[*She sits again and irons.*]

SON: Where's your kitchen? . . . I'll get you
some coffee . . . the way you like it. I bet I
still remember how to fix it.

MOTHER: Michael . . . I don't drink anything
like that no more.

SON: No?

MOTHER: Not since I joined the service of the
Lord.

SON: Yeah? . . . Well, do you mind if I get
myself a cup?

MOTHER: Why, I don't have a kitchen. All
my meals are prepared for me.

SON: Oh . . . I thought I was having dinner
with you.

MOTHER: No. There's nothing like that here.

SON: Well, could I take you out to a restaurant? . . . Remember how we used to go
out all the time and eat? I've never lost
my habit of liking to eat out. Remember
. . . we used to come down to this part of
town and go to restaurants. They used to

call it home cooking then . . . now, at least
where I been out West and up in Harlem
. . . we call it soul food. I bet we could find
a nice little restaurant not four blocks from
here, Mother. Remember that old man's
place we used to go to on Nineteenth and
South? I bet he's dead now . . . but . . .

MOTHER: I don't even eat out no more,
Michael.

SON: No?

MOTHER: Sometimes I take a piece of holy
bread to work . . . or some fruit . . . if it's
been blessed by my Spiritual Mother.

SON: I see.

MOTHER: Besides . . . we have a prayer meeting tonight.

SON: On Friday?

MOTHER: Every night. You'll have to be
going soon.

SON: Oh.

MOTHER: You're looking well.

SON: Thank you.

MOTHER: But you look tired.

SON: Do I?

MOTHER: Yes, those rings around your eyes
might never leave. Your father had them.

SON: Did he?

MOTHER: Yes . . . and cowlicks . . . deep cowlicks on each side of his head.

SON: Yes . . . I remember.

MOTHER: You do?

[*The* BOY *and the* GIRL *take crouching
positions behind and in front of them. They
are in a streetcar. The* BOY *behind the*
MOTHER *and* SON, *the* GIRL *across the aisle,
a passenger.*]

MOTHER: [*Young woman.*] [*To the* BOY.]
Keep your damn hands off him, Andy!

BOY: [*Chuckles.*] Awww, c'mon . . . Bernie.
I ain't seen him since he was in the crib.

MOTHER: And you wouldn't have seen neither
of us . . . if I had anything to do with it
. . . Ohhh . . . why did I get on this trolley?

BOY: C'mon . . . Bernie . . . don't be so stuck-
up.

MOTHER: Don't even talk to us . . . and stop
reaching after him.

BOY: Awww . . . c'mon . . . Bernie. Let me look at him.

MOTHER: Leave us alone. Look . . . people are looking at us.

[*The* GIRL *across the aisle has been peeking at the trio but looks toward front at the mention of herself.*]

BOY: Hey, big boy . . . do you know who I am?

MOTHER: Stop it, Andy! Stop it, I say . . . Mikie . . . don't pay any attention to him . . . you hear?

BOY: Hey, big boy . . . know who I am? . . . I'm your daddy. Hey, there . . .

MOTHER: Shut up . . . shut up, Andy . . . you nothin' to us.

BOY: Where you livin' at . . . Bernie? Let me come on by and see the little guy, huh?

MOTHER: No! You're not comin' near us. . . ever . . . you hear?

BOY: But I'm his father . . . look . . . Bernie . . . I've been an ass the way I've acted but . . .

MOTHER: He ain't got no father.

BOY: Oh, come off that nonsense, woman.

MOTHER: Mikie ain't got no father . . . his father's dead . . . you hear?

BOY: Dead?

MOTHER: Yes, dead. My son's father's dead.

BOY: What you talkin' about? . . . He's the spittin' image of me.

MOTHER: Go away . . . leave us alone, Andrew.

BOY: See there . . . he's got the same name as me. His first name is Michael after your father . . . and Andrew after me.

MOTHER: No, stop that, you hear?

BOY: Michael Andrew . . .

MOTHER: You never gave him no name . . . his name is Brown . . . Brown. The same as mine . . . and my sister's . . . and my daddy . . . . You never gave him nothin' . . . and you're dead . . . go away and get buried.

BOY: You know that trouble I'm in . . . I got a wife down there, Bernie. I don't care about her . . . what could I do?

MOTHER: [*Rises, pulling up the* SON.] We're leavin' . . . don't you try and follow us . . .

you hear, Andy? C'mon . . . Mikie . . . watch your step now.

BOY: Well . . . bring him around my job . . . you know where I work. That's all . . . bring him around on payday.

MOTHER: [*Leaving.*] We don't need anything from you . . . I'm working . . . just leave us alone.

[*The* BOY *turns to the* GIRL.]

BOY: [*Shrugs.*] That's the way it goes . . . I guess. Ships passing on the trolley car . . . Hey . . . don't I know you from up around 40th and Market?

[*The* GIRL *turns away.*]

SON: Yeah . . . I remember him. He always had liquor on his breath.

MOTHER: Yes . . . he did. I'm glad that stuff ain't got me no more . . . Thank the Lord.

GIRL: [*35 years old.*] You want to pour me another drink, Michael?

BOY: [*15 years old.*] You drink too much, Mother.

GIRL: Not as much as some people I know.

BOY: Well, me and the guys just get short snorts, Mother. But you really hide some port.

GIRL: Don't forget you talkin' to your mother. You gettin' more like your father every day.

BOY: Is that why you like me so much?

GIRL: [*Grins drunkenly.*] Oh, hush up now, boy . . . and pour me a drink.

BOY: There's enough here for me too.

GIRL: That's okay . . . when Will comes in he'll bring something.

SON: How is Will, Mother?

MOTHER: I don't know . . . haven't seen Will in years.

SON: Mother.

MOTHER: Yes, Michael.

SON: Why you and Will never got married? . . . You stayed together for over ten years.

MOTHER: Oh, don't ask me questions like that, Michael.

SON: But why not?

MOTHER: It's just none of your business.

SON: But you could be married now . . . not alone in this room . . .

MOTHER: Will had a wife and child in Chester . . . you know that.

SON: He could have gotten a divorce, Mother . . . Why . . .

MOTHER: Because he just didn't . . . that's why.

SON: You never hear from him?

MOTHER: Last I heard . . . Will had cancer.

SON: Oh, he did.

MOTHER: Yes.

SON: Why didn't you tell me? . . . You could have written.

MOTHER: Why?

SON: So I could have known.

MOTHER: So you could have known? Why?

SON: Because Will was like a father to me . . . the only one I've really known.

MOTHER: A father? And you chased him away as soon as you got big enough.

SON: Don't say that, Mother.

MOTHER: You made me choose between you and Will.

SON: Mother.

MOTHER: The quarrels you had with him . . . the mean tricks you used to play . . . the lies you told to your friends about Will . . . He wasn't much . . . when I thought I had a sense of humor I us'ta call him just plain Will. But we was his family.

SON: Mother, listen.

MOTHER: And you drove him away . . . and he didn't lift a hand to stop you.

SON: Listen, Mother.

MOTHER: As soon as you were big enough you did all that you could to get me and Will separated.

SON: Listen.

MOTHER: All right, Michael . . . I'm listening.

[*Pause.*]

SON: Nothing.

[*Pause. Lifts an imaginary object.*]

Is this your tambourine?

MOTHER: Yes.

SON: Do you play it?

MOTHER: Yes.

SON: Well?

MOTHER: Everything I do in the service of the Lord I do as well as He allows.

SON: You play it at your meetings.

MOTHER: Yes, I do. We celebrate the life He has bestowed upon us.

SON: I guess that's where I get it from.

MOTHER: Did you say something, Michael?

SON: Yes. My musical ability.

MOTHER: Oh . . . you've begun taking your piano lessons again?

SON: No . . . I was never any good at that.

MOTHER: Yes, three different teachers and you never got past the tenth lesson.

SON: You have a good memory, Mother.

MOTHER: Sometimes, son. Sometimes.

SON: I play an electric guitar in a combo.

MOTHER: You do? That's nice.

SON: That's why I'm in New York. We got a good break and came East.

MOTHER: That's nice, Michael.

SON: I was thinking that Sunday I could rent a car and come down to get you and drive you up to see our show. You'll get back in plenty of time to rest for work Monday.

MOTHER: No, I'm sorry. I can't do that.

SON: But you would like it, Mother. We could have dinner up in Harlem, then go down and . . .

MOTHER: I don't do anything like that any more, Michael.

SON: You mean you wouldn't come to see me play even if I were appearing here in Philly?

MOTHER: That's right, Michael. I wouldn't come. I'm past all that.

SON: Oh, I see.

MOTHER: Yes, thank the Lord.

SON: But it's my life, Mother.

MOTHER: Good . . . then you have something to live for.

SON: Yes.

MOTHER: Well, you're a man now, Michael . . . I can no longer live it for you. Do the best with what you have.

SON: Yes . . . Yes, I will, Mother.

GIRL'S VOICE: [*Offstage.*] Sister Brown . . . Sister Brown . . . hello.

MOTHER: [*Uneasy; peers at watch.*] Oh . . . it's Mother Ellen . . . I didn't know it was so late.

GIRL: [*Enters.*] Sister Brown . . . how are you this evening?

MOTHER: Oh, just fine, Mother.

GIRL: Good. It's nearly time for dinner.

MOTHER: Oh, yes, I know.

GIRL: We don't want to keep the others waiting at meeting . . . do we?

MOTHER: No, we don't.

GIRL: [*Self-assured.*] Hello, son.

SON: Hello.

MOTHER: Oh, Mother . . . Mother . . .

GIRL: Yes, Sister Brown, what is it?

MOTHER: Mother . . . Mother . . . this is . . . this is . . .

[*Pause.*]

. . . this is . . .

SON: Hello, I'm Michael. How are you?

MOTHER: [*Relieved.*] Yes, Mother . . . This is Michael . . . my son.

GIRL: Why, hello, Michael. I've heard so much about you from your mother. She prays for you daily.

SON: [*Embarrassed.*] Oh . . . good.

GIRL: [*Briskly.*] Well . . . I have to be off to see about the others.

MOTHER: Yes, Mother Ellen.

GIRL: [*As she exits; chuckles.*] Have to tell everyone that you won't be keeping us waiting, Bernice.

[*Silence.*]

SON: Well, I guess I better be going, Mother.

MOTHER: Yes.

SON: I'll write.

MOTHER: Please do.

SON: I will.

MOTHER: You're looking well . . . Thank the Lord.

SON: Thank you, so are you, Mother.

[*He moves toward her and hesitates.*]

MOTHER: You're so much like your aunt. Give her my best . . . won't you?

SON: Yes, I will, Mother.

MOTHER: Take care of yourself, son.

SON: Yes, Mother. I will.

[*The* SON *exits. The* MOTHER *stands looking after him as the lights go slowly down to . . .*]

BLACKNESS

BLACK IRONIES: PAST AND PRESENT

Sandra Marie Lee

An ironist can resolutely confront with assertions the "shifting ambiguities" of "unidealized" experience that Northrop Frye[1] identifies as the basis of the ironic vision, or, he may merely examine and question—both the experience and the questioning itself. Of the "two major branches in the mainstream of the new Black creativity" that dramatist Ed Bullins[2] identifies, one, "the dialectic of change," confronts the grotesque nature of the black/white reality of America as it is juxtaposed to a steady view of morality and truth; the other, the "dialectic of experience (or being)," simply presents the experience of black life in all of its contradictions and illusiveness. One dramatic vision protests, the other presents.

As the ironist presents any "unidealized experience"—either as satire or as phenomenon—he implicitly parodies the affirmations of comedy, tragedy, and romance. He parodies romantic quest and the idealization of

[1]Northrop Frye, *Anatomy of Criticism. Four Essays.* (Princeton: Princeton University Press, 1957), p. 223.

[2]Ed Bullins, ed., *The New Lafayette Theatre Presents. Plays with Aesthetic Comments by Six Black Playwrights* (Garden City, New York: Anchor Press/Doubleday, 1974), p. 4.

Reprinted by permission of the author, Indiana University Northwest.

the hero above time and nature, tragic sacrifice and isolated nobility, and the comic sense of new life and hope within a rejuvenated society. He denies the certainty of seeing existence in such positive designs. The modern unidealized black experience contradicts such certainties, too. Since the black ironist no longer focuses upon "the social and political aspects of Black existence in America" for the education and titillation of chiefly white audiences,[3] he can specifically parody those values that black people have ardently affirmed within the romantic, tragic and comic patterns: the romantic quest of coming "up from slavery" or going "back to the roots," the tragic sacrifice and isolated nobility of the black hero who willfully and individually separates himself from the strictures of both black community and white American society, and the comic sense of life and hope within the black ghetto with the black church and black family or matriarchy. For black ironists, the romantic quest is never really successful; the separated tragic hero too often ignoble and merely outcast; the warmth of the church and the comic family smothering or absent entirely.

The questioning ironist further parodies satire. The satirist would superimpose his own design upon the unidealized experience; the questioning ironist is not certain enough of the nature of the reality to either affirm or deny the existence or the value of the affirmations of romance, comedy, tragedy, or satire. Quite different from the questioning irony of Ed Bullins is the satirical irony of a dramatist like Brecht, with his epic theatre and alienation effect that indict a materialistic society and suggest, if not specific solutions, the necessity of questioning and change, or the satirical irony of Imamu Baraka (Le Roi Jones), with his black/white value system that castigates a moribund white American society (and that part of the black society that reflects its values) and praises a vital, natural, expressive black existence. Bullins identifies him-

self with those writers who merely present "the dreadful white reality of being a modern Black captive and victim."

This concept of the black experience unites two contradictory ironic states: the bondage of the black captive in the American society and the floating isolation of the accidental victim. Bullins, of course, recognizes the apparent patterns of captivity within the American system that crush black people into "gross distortions of what they can and should be because they were denied knowledge of themselves and a place to grow."[4] Like all of the contemporary black ironists, he recognizes the unidealized experience behind the affirmed and certain values. The black man, as the captive, is immersed in the collective identity of the group of black people in the American society and is, therefore, heir to a history that has defined the patterns of bondage—from the chains of slavery to the chains of coming up from slavery. For example, to affirm the quest of coming up from mental or physical slavery, the black man essentially must become a white-washed denial of himself. The black ironists present the design as so infused within the black man's existence that often the white society is not physically present in the plays.

Yet, Bullins suggests that even as black "being" seems to be almost deterministically the effect of a pre-ordained pattern within the American society, it is also accidental and without meaning, without a continuous past that provides a basis for motivated action—however ineffectual. The modern black victim is capriciously chosen and separated from the group of black people, loosed and freed, and without the certainty of even affirming those patterns of action that the ironists parody. Bullins recognizes the pattern of captivity and questions the possibility of recognizing a pattern; he questions whether the victimization is accidental as he recognizes that any design may be a falsifica-

---

[3] Ibid.

[4] Ed Bullins, "The Electric Nigger," *Ebony*, September, 1968, pp. 97–98.

tion of the reality. Consequently, Bullins cannot moralize about the black experience and present a more acceptable action pattern as the satirists do. ("If a writer moralized in an amoral world, he would be a contradiction of the times. Morality changes. To say what morality is, is letting yourself in for lies.")[5]

The stage presentation of Bullins' ironic vision requires a technique closer to Brecht's than Baraka's. Like most of the new black dramatists, he does not desire an emotional response that is so empathetic in nature that the black audience is lulled into a sense of the inevitability of the bondage within the black experience. Inevitability suggests design and Bullins is uncertain of design. Of course, the satirists want the audience to cast their eyes toward change. However, the satirists' chief, although not total, means to this end is emotional engagement of the black audience through censure of whites and praise of blacks. Bullins is uncertain of this moral system. Like Brecht, Bullins seeks a fluid emotional and intellectual examination during his plays. (Unlike Brecht, his examination can only suggest societal culpability, and cannot suggest solutions or even the possibility or the need for them.)

> I don't write to please the audience and reassure everyone that we agree. I don't care how they feel or what they think—whether they agree or disagree—just so it makes them examine themselves.[6]

In a play like *A Son, Come Home* the techniques used to effect the emotional and intellectual examination of the modern black captive/victim's "being" are complex. Bullins must present simultaneously both the bondage and the looseness of the black experience without suggesting the validity of one view over the other. Many of the devices used in this brief play are similar to the *presentational* devices of the epic theatre. There are no real

[5]Ed Bullins, "Is Rape a Symbol of Race Relations?," *New York Times*, 18 May 1975.
[6]Ibid.

props; two of the four actors perform multiple roles; fragmentation and distortion of the humanity of both Mother and Son is presented through the separation of the public roles of a mother and a son from what Bullins calls their private *"moods and tensions," "memory and history"*. These two roles are represented by two different actors and enacted simultaneously and in juxtaposition. The stage directions state that these scenes remembered by the Mother and Son, played by the Boy and the Girl, are the real action of the play. These presentational devices allow Bullins to move the audience from the patterns of affirmations and expectations that the ambiguous title sets up toward an examination, both emotional and intellectual, of the unidealized black experience presented during the course of the play.

The title, *A Son, Come Home*, focuses attention chiefly upon the affirmations of comedy —the nurturing black family, supported by the church, is to be reunited; a son will come home. The title is not without suggestions of the other patterns. The separation, with a comma, of the son and the action may imply a command to the son to return from the tragic and willful isolation of the black individual to immersion within the black community. The title may even promise a successful and romantic homecoming.

The first scene in the play parodies these affirmations as it presents the unidealized experience. The homecoming as a return to a supportive community is parodied by the physical and geographical details of the *place* of "home" in Philadelphia. The black society's reaction to the homecoming is represented by the Girl as a grinning, gum-showing old woman who insists upon imagining the mother not only as the matriarch but as a child. In the loudness of her "Well, bless the Lord" and haste to tell Mandy, another neighbor, about the "great big boy" that has come to visit "little Miss Brown" she is a ludicrous sample of black solidarity and community. With the grotesque societal response the audience also perceives the Mother's less than enthusiastic welcome. She has all of the usual trappings of the matriarch —humming her spiritual as she works with an imaginary iron and board, chastizing her son about his failure to listen to her about the time of her arrival home, and his standing in the cold, and his silly beard, and his weight. But she shows none of the expected radiating warmth. Her initial conversation with him is more monologue than real dialogue. The Mother's emotions are bound to the black church, the traditional insulator of the black captive or victim from the restraints of society; its promise of freedom is life-negating, not rejuvenating: "Yes, the years pass. Thank the Lord."

During the first scene, the tragically isolated Son is ironically inverted to a mere outsider. His self-image of being an anachronism ("a chronological misplacing of persons, events, objects, or customs in regard to each other; . . . a person or a thing that is chronologically out of place") states his belief in his individual separation from the black community. Such a "big" college word itself is incomprehensible to the Girl, now the society's teenager, and the Mother. Michael insists upon a causal design uniting his intentions and his actions and the action of his mother. Nevertheless, Michael is not willfully out of step with the black community. He wants to come home.

The rest of this visit is dramatized with seven scenes from the past recalled from the memory of either Mother or Son. The Son is first to remember three separate encounters with his aunt Sophia in Los Angeles; the Mother then recalls three scenes from her past—a talk with her sister Sophia about her pregnancy, a private discussion with Michael's father, Andrew, and a public quarrel with Andrew. Michael finally envisions a drunken moment with his mother fifteen years before. These scenes are performed by the Boy, in the roles of Michael or Andrew, and the Girl, as Sophia, as the Mother, or as a representative of the black community. Like most remembrances from the past, those in *A Son, Come Home* are evoked by the action of the present visit.

The audience at first sees the past embodied by the Boy and Girl beside the frozen action of the present visit, then the encircling action of Mother and Son as they *"stroll around the stage, arm and arm"*—with the Girl following as she and the Boy enact the Mother's past scenes, and finally the participating action of the Mother and Son with the Boy as Andrew and the Girl as the black community on the streetcar. The audience sees the present gradually flow into the past. They see the fragmented Mother and Son, those distortions of their expectations, unite with their inner selves and each other through the flashbacks. The audience also sees the communication finally deteriorate in the last scene as the Mother is summoned by her spiritual Mother Ellen and the Son must leave. In this last scene, the physical action of the play slows down—the Boy and Girl are no longer reenactors of the past (the Girl again represents the black religious community—now as Mother Ellen); pauses, silences, hesitations, and an exit punctuate the end of the visit of a mother and a son.

In *A Son, Come Home* the experience that the audience has witnessed is that of the black captive and victim. Contrary to the usual method of the satirists, Bullins does not employ the flashback as an Ibsen-like exposition that explains the causes of the unidealized experience presented during the visit. Such a use of the past would assert a causal world. Bullins cannot answer so positively the audience's question about the source of the unidealized situation in the first scene (the unsuccessful quest to go back to the roots, the non-nurturing mother, the outcast son). Even though the audience sees the present fuse with the past through the physical action of the play, Bullins leaves ambiguous the question of whether the quality of the fusion is a causal design, or a loose and accidental phenomenon. The accidental is always present with the design. It is even part of what the audience hears and sees as the action moves from present visit to past memory. The dialogue often moves the action directly into the past, as when the Mother asks—

"Did you see much of your aunt before you left Los Angeles?" But some present-past verbal connections are more tenuous; Michael's statement that he and his aunt were born in the same month is answered in a non-sequitor by his mother—"Yes, that year was so hot . . . so hot and I was carrying you. . . ." At this line, Michael and his mother begin the stroll around the stage "followed" by three embodiments of the past. During the play the audience must constantly question whether the dialogue that they hear and the action that they view are really causally designed or merely sequential, or, in some ambiguous manner, both.

This ambiguity of the gestic elements of the drama—that is quite similar to Brecht's alienation effect—heightens the audience's examination of their thoughts and feelings about the black experience that the play presents. After the first scene the Mother and the Son's experience is seen as a distortion of the affirmations of idealized black experience. The black woman representative of society seems grotesque; the Mother, a farcical shell of the black matriarch; the Son, a pitiful outcast. The essence of the initial scene is unchanged at the end of the play. The religious society is a ludicrous distortion of a truly rejuvenated black community; Mother Ellen who comes to summon Sister Brown is smothering. The Mother and the Son promise to correspond but are still not really communicating. The son is still not within this black community, back to his roots, however non-nurturing and non-supportive.

The experience of moving through the past with Mother and Son decreases the audience's emotional distance from them. Through the fusion of present and past, the audience sees beyond the present fragments of people to a vision of potential human beings, who were either victimized or captured in the course of their lives, a vision that makes detachment from the present Mother and Son impossible.

The flashbacks show the potential humanity of the Son and then the Mother and the past experiences that may or may not have distorted that humanity and that may or may not have caused the present mother-son relationship. The play's technique is to present experience without moralizing. Scenes echo one another without comment. The play does not label the precise relationship between Michael's present reality as the outcast, alienated son whose position in a combo has brought him to New York. The audience does not know whether the aunt's rejection has caused Michael to seek employment as a musician, a more acceptable pattern of striving and creativity in the black experience than poetry. They do not know whether no poetry and no family lead to alcohol. Nor do they know whether the Son and the aunt, who initially seem so patently opposite —one so spontaneous and expressive and open, the other so closed to life and bound to the American system's monetary, Puritan values—are really "so much alike" as the mother insists.

The Mother's three scenes are contrapuntal to the Son's; her testimony of life-negating religious fervor echoes the Son's statement that he is no longer a poet. The Mother's memory of rejection by Andrew is placed chronologically before her "spell" of religious fervor when talking to her son. This spell precedes her public rejection of Andrew. Therefore, her testimony of religion—"Thank the Lord that I am not blinded and will see the fulfillment of divine . . . . I'm just feeling the power of the Lord."—is placed between her private and public confrontations with Andrew. Its causal relationship is only a possibility.

This similarity of the flashback patterns of Mother and Son climaxes in the Son's remembrance of their common drinking, which both united and separated them as people and as mother and son.

GIRL: Don't forget you talkin' to your mother. You gettin' more like your father every day.

BOY: Is that why you like me so much?

GIRL: (*grins drunkenly.*) Oh, hush up now, boy . . . and pour me a drink.

The causes of the drinking are no more lucid than the other "causal" designs presented in the play—but the effects, or perhaps, the experience, is clearer. However, even though the scene seems to show the non-parental, nonsupportive, non-nurturing relationship of Mother and Son in the past, there may be more true warmth behind that banter than within the conversation of the present visit. This memory is presented before the most truly communicating exchange between the Mother and Son as they discuss Will, Michael's surrogate father. But the discussion of Will and his relationship to their family unit quickly builds to the silences of the last scene. The silence is the Son's answer to the Mother's charge that Michael drove good and plain Will away. Michael cannot explain why.

The silence is the essential silence of this play's moralizing about the black experience. Michael's "Nothing" voices the echoes of the entire play. One cannot ascertain the reason for the Mother's life-negating religious fervor and the Son's insistent, reaffirmation of his relationship to her. One can only examine the experience and feel the loss of humanity as one realizes that there is no pattern nor moral action that will recapture what was lost. Flashing back to the past will only present the experiences that are fused with the present; flashing back to the past will never elucidate the real relationship between memory and reality. It is all simply "being."

PART FOUR

ESSAYS

FROM THE POETICS

Aristotle

translated and edited by
G. M. A. Grube

... Tragedy, then, is the imitation of a good[1] action, which is complete and of a certain length, by means of language made pleasing for each part separately; it relies in its various elements not on narrative but on acting; through pity and fear it achieves the purgation (catharsis) of such emotions.

[1]The same question of Aristotle's moral view of drama arises in connection with the first clause of his definition of tragedy: "an imitation of an action which is *good*." Here the word is *spoudaios*, and those who want to empty it of moral implication translate "a serious action" or "an action of high importance." The action here is, of course, that of the whole play, not a particular incident. It is the commentators who create the problem by here again introducing the distinction between a moral and an aesthetic judgment which is foreign to Aristotle. He tells us himself a few lines later that an "action" derives its quality from the character and mind of the doer.

When the same word *spoudaios* is applied to a character, it is always in a context which we would call moral. However, Aristotle must use a fairly mild word, for characters who are completely virtuous or vicious are not, to him, fit subjects of tragedy (or of comedy either). It does not help us to speak of men "of a higher type," or "of a lower type" (*phauloteros*), for it would

By "language made pleasing" I mean language which has rhythm, melody, and music. By "separately for the parts" I mean that some parts use only meter while others also have music. And as it is through acting that the poets present their imitation, one first and necessary element of a tragedy is the arranging of the spectacle. Then come music and diction, for these are the means used in the imitation. By diction I mean the actual composition of the verses, while the effect of music is clear to all.

THE SIX ELEMENTS OR ASPECTS OF TRAGEDY

Since it is an action which is imitated, it is performed by persons who must have qualities of character and mind, and from them we transfer these predicates to the actions also. Character and thought are the two natural causes of action; through actions men suc-

have sorely puzzled Aristotle, I believe, how a man could be of a higher type without being a better man, or of a lower type without being a worse one, and the nature of the action is tied to the nature of the man who performs it. To Aristotle, the *éthos* of a man included his mind as well as his morals, in fact his whole personality. Our word "character" has a much more restricted sense.

Aristotle fully realized that an art must be judged on its own premises ("correctness for a poet is not the same as for a politician"), but that these premises were, in the case of tragedy, purely aesthetic, and therefore amoral, is a thought that simply could not have occurred to him, and there are other passages of the *Poetics* to prove it.

ceed or fail. The imitation of the action is the plot, for this is what I mean by plot, namely, the arrangement of the incidents. Character, on the other hand, is that which leads us to attribute certain qualities to the persons who act. Thought is present in all they say to prove a point or to express an opinion. Every tragedy, therefore, has these six necessary elements which make it what it is: plot, character, diction, thought, spectacle, and music. Two of these elements are the means of imitation, one is the manner, three belong to the objects imitated, and besides these there are no others. We may say that most poets use these elements; every tragedy, in much the same manner, has spectacle, character, plot, diction, music, and thought.

PLOT AND CHARACTER

The most important of these is the arrangement of incidents, for tragedy is an imitation, not of men but of action and life, of happiness and misfortune. These are to be found in action, and the goal of life is a certain kind of activity, not a quality. Men are what they are because of their characters, but it is in action that they find happiness or the reverse. The purpose of action on the stage is not to imitate character, but character is a by-product of the action. It follows that the incidents and the plot are the end which tragedy has in view, and the end is in all things the most important. Without action there could be no tragedy, whereas a tragedy without characterization is possible.

The tragedies of most of our recent poets have no characterization and, generally speaking, there are many such poets. This is the difference, among painters, between Zeuxis and Polygnotus, for Polygnotus expresses character very well, while Zeuxis does not express it at all. Moreover, a series of speeches expressing character, well written and well thought-out though they might be, would not fulfill the essential function of a tragedy; this would be better achieved by a play which had a plot and structure of incidents, even though deficient in respect to

character. Besides, the most important means by which a tragedy stirs the emotions reside in the plot, namely, Reversals and Recognitions. Another argument is that those who begin to write poetry attain mastery in diction and characterization before they attain it in plot structure. Nearly all our early poets are examples of this.

The plot is the first essential and the soul of a tragedy; character comes second. Pretty much the same is true of painting: the most beautiful colors, laid on at random, give less pleasure than a black-and-white drawing. It is the action which is the object of the imitation; the individual characters are subsidiary to it.

THOUGHT AND CHARACTER

Thought is the third element in tragedy. It is the capacity to express what is involved in, or suitable to, a situation. In prose this is the function of statesmanship and rhetoric. Earlier writers made their characters speak like statesmen; our contemporaries make them speak like rhetoricians. A person's character makes clear what course of action he will choose or reject where this is not clear. Speeches, therefore, which do not make this choice clear, or in which the speaker does not choose or reject any course of action at all, do not express character. Thought comes in where something is proved or disproved, or where some general opinion is expressed.

DICTION, MUSIC, SPECTACLE

Diction is the fourth of the elements we mentioned. By diction I mean, as I said before, the use of words to express one's meaning. Its function is the same in verse and prose. Of the remaining elements, music is most important among the features of tragedy which give pleasure. As for the spectacle, it stirs the emotions, but it is less a matter of art than the others, and has least to do with poetry, for a tragedy can achieve its effect even apart from the performance and the actors. Indeed, spectacular effects belong to the craft of the property man rather than to that of the poet.

VII

PLOT: BEGINNING, MIDDLE, AND END

Having now defined these elements, our next point is what the plot structure should be, as this is the first and most important part of a tragedy. We have established that a tragedy is the imitation of an action which is whole and complete, and also of a certain length, for a thing can be whole without being of any particular size. "Whole" means having a beginning, a middle, and an end. The beginning, while not necessarily following something else, is, by definition, followed by something else. The end, on the contrary, follows something else by definition, either always or in most cases, but nothing else comes after it. The middle both itself follows something else and is followed by something else. To construct a good plot, one must neither begin nor end haphazardly but make a proper use of these three parts.

SIZE OR LENGTH

However, an animal, or indeed anything which has parts, must, to be beautiful, not only have these parts in the right order but must also be of a definite size. Beauty is a matter of size and order. An extraordinarily small animal would not be beautiful, nor an extraordinarily large one. Our view of the first is confused because it occupies only an all but imperceptible time, while we cannot view the second all at once, so that the unity of the whole would escape us if, for example, it were a thousand miles long. It follows that, as bodies and animals must have a size that can easily be perceived as a whole, so plots must have a length which can easily be re-membered. However, the limit set to length by the circumstances of the dramatic presen-

tation or by the perceptive capacity of the audience is not a matter of dramatic art. If a hundred tragedies were competing at once, the poets would compete with their eye on the water clock, and this they say happened at one time. What is a matter of art is the limit set by the very nature of the action, namely, that the longer is always the more beautiful, provided that the unity of the whole is clearly perceived. A simple and sufficient definition is: such length as will allow a sequence of events to result in a change from bad to good fortune or from good fortune to bad in accordance with what is probable or inevitable.[2]

VIII

UNITY OF PLOT

A story does not achieve unity, as some people think, merely by being about one person. Many things, indeed an infinite num-ber of things, happen to the same individual, some of which have no unity at all. In the same way one individual performs many ac-tions which do not combine into one action. It seems, then, that all those poets who wrote a *Heracleid*, a *Theseid*, and the like, were in error, for they believed that, because Heracles is one person, a story about him cannot avoid having unity. Now Homer, outstanding as he is in other respects also, seems to have perceived this clearly, whether as a conscious artist or by instinct. He did not include in the *Odyssey* all that happened to Odysseus— for example, his being wounded on Parnassus or his feigning madness when the troops were being levied—because no thread of probability or necessity linked those events. He built his plot around the one action which we call the *Odyssey;* and the same is true of the *Iliad.* As in other kinds of imitative

[2]Aristotle's word *avaukaiov* refers to something that needs must happen and cannot be avoided. "Probable or necessary" is the usual translation, but the adjective "inevitable" is more natural, though "necessity" may be the better noun.

art each imitation must have one object, so with the plot: since it is the imitation of an action, this must be one action and the whole of it; the various incidents must be so constructed that, if any part is displaced or deleted, the whole plot is disturbed and dislocated. For if any part can be inserted or omitted without manifest alteration, it is no true part of the whole.

IX

TRAGEDY AND HISTORY

It also follows from what has been said that it is not the poet's business to relate actual events, but such things as might or could happen in accordance with probability or necessity. A poet differs from a historian, not because one writes verse and the other prose (the work of Herodotus could be put into verse, but it would still remain a history, whether in verse or prose), but because the historian relates what happened, the poet what might happen. That is why poetry is more akin to philosophy and is a better thing than history; poetry deals with general truths, history with specific events. The latter are, for example, what Alcibiades did or suffered, while general truths are the kind of thing which a certain type of person would probably or inevitably do or say. Poetry aims to do this by its choice of names; this is clearly seen in comedy, for when the writers of comedy have constructed their plots in accordance with probability, they give their characters typical names, nor are they, like the writers of iambic lampoons, concerned with a particular individual.

NAMES OF CHARACTERS: TRADITIONAL LEGENDS

The tragedians cling to the names of historical persons. The reason is that what is possible is convincing, and we are apt to distrust what has not yet happened as not possible, whereas what has happened is obviously possible, else it could not have happened. However, there are tragedies which use only one or two of the well-known names, the others being fictitious; indeed a few tragedies have no well-known names at all, the *Antheus* of Agathon for example. Both the names and the events of that play are fictitious, yet it is enjoyable nonetheless. It is not, therefore, absolutely necessary to cling to the traditional stories which are the usual subjects of tragedy. In fact, it is absurd to strive to do so, for even the familiar stories are familiar only to a few, yet are enjoyed by all. All this shows that it is the plot, rather than the verse, which makes a (tragic) poet, for he is a poet in virtue of his imitation, and he imitates actions. He is no less a poet if he happens to tell a true story, for nothing prevents some actual events from being probable or possible, and it is this probability or possibility that makes the (tragic) poet.

TYPES OF PLOTS

The episodic are the worst of all plots and actions; and by an episodic plot I mean one in which the episodes have no probable or inevitable connection. Poor poets compose such plots through lack of talent, good poets do it to please the actors. As they write in competition and stretch the plot too far, they are thereby compelled to distort the sequence of events.

The object of the imitation is not only a complete action but such things as stir up pity and fear, and this is best achieved when the events are unexpectedly interconnected. This, more than what happens accidentally and by chance, will arouse wonder. Even chance events arouse most wonder when they have the appearance of purpose, as in the story of the man who was responsible for the death of Mitys and was watching a festival at Argos when the statue of his victim fell upon him and killed him. Things like that do not seem to happen without purpose, and plots of this kind are necessarily better.

X

SIMPLE AND COMPLEX PLOTS

Some plots are simple, others are complex, just as the actions which they imitate are clearly one or the other. I call simple an action which is one and continuous, as defined above, and in the course of which the change of fortune occurs without recognition or reversal. A complex action is one wherein the change of fortune is accompanied either by recognition or reversal, or by both. These must emerge from the plot structure itself so that they are connected with what has gone before as the inevitable or probable outcome. It makes all the difference whether one incident is caused by another or merely follows it.

XI

REVERSALS AND RECOGNITIONS

Reversal (*peripeteia*) is a change of the situation into its opposite, and this too must accord with the probable or the inevitable.[3] So in the *Oedipus* the man comes to cheer Oedipus and to rid him of his fear concerning his mother; then, by showing him who he is, he does the opposite; also in the

[3]Peripety or reversal should not be confused with the change of fortune which Aristotle calls μετάβασις. The metabasis refers to this change only, from bad fortune to good or, and this Aristotle considered better, from good fortune to bad (see ch. 14), and it involves no more than this change. Reversal, on the other hand, means that a situation that seems to or is intended to develop in one direction suddenly develops in the reverse direction. In *Oedipus King,* a messenger brings news that the king of Corinth is dead. Hearing that Oedipus had left Corinth because of an oracle which foretold he would kill his father and marry his mother, the messenger seeks to rid him of this fear by showing that he is not the son of the Corinthian king. But instead of relief, this disclosure leads to the revelation that Laius (whom he killed) was his father and, ultimately, that Iocasta is his mother and that the oracle is fulfilled. The *Lynceus* is attributed to Theodectes, but is unknown to us.

Lynceus the hero is brought in to die and Danaus follows, intending to kill him, but in the event it is Danaus who dies and the other who is saved.

Recognition (*anagnorisis*), as the name implies, is a change from ignorance to knowledge of a bond of love or hate between persons who are destined for good fortune or the reverse. The finest kind of recognition is accompanied by simultaneous reversals, as in the *Oedipus*. There are, to be sure, other forms of recognition: the knowledge acquired may be of inanimate objects, indeed of anything; one may recognize that someone has, or has not, done something. But the recognition which is most fully part of the plot and of the action is the kind we noted first. This kind of recognition and reversal will evoke pity or fear. Tragedy is the imitation of such actions, and good or ill fortune results from them.

This recognition is between persons. Sometimes the identity of one person is known, and then only one person is recognized by the other; at other times both have to be recognized, as when Iphigenia is recognized by Orestes as soon as she sends the letter, but another recognition scene is necessary for her to recognize Orestes.

These things, reversal and recognition, are two parts of the plot. A third is suffering. We have discussed two of the three, namely reversal and recognition. Suffering (*pathos*) is a fatal or painful action like death on the stage, violent physical pain, wounds, and everything of that kind.

XII

THE SECTIONS OF A TRAGEDY

We have previously mentioned the parts of tragedy in the sense of its qualitative parts. The quantitative sections, on the other hand, into which a tragedy is divided are the following: *prologos, epeisodion, exodos,* and the choral part, itself subdivided into *parodos* and *stasima.* These occur in all tragedies; there may also be actors' songs and *kommoi.*

The *prologos* is that whole section which precedes the entrance of the chorus; the *epeisodion* is a whole section between complete choral odes; the *exodos* is that whole section of a tragedy which is not followed by a choral ode. In the choral part, the entrance song (*parodos*) is the first complete statement of the chorus, a *stasimon* is a song of the chorus without anapaests or trochees; a *kommos* is a dirge in which actors and chorus join.

We spoke previously of the parts which must be considered as qualitative elements of tragedy; these are the quantitative parts.

XIII

POSSIBLE CHANGES OF FORTUNE

We must discuss next what a writer should aim at and what he should avoid in constructing his plot, how tragedy will come to fulfill its proper function. As already stated, the plot of the finest tragedies must not be simple but complex, it must also represent what is fearful or pitiful, as this is characteristic of tragic imitation. It clearly follows that, in the first place, good men must not be seen suffering a change from prosperity to misfortune; this is not fearful or pitiful but shocking. Nor must the wicked pass from misfortune to prosperity; this, of all things, is the least tragic; nothing happens as it should, it is neither humane nor fearful nor pitiful. A thoroughly wicked man must not pass from prosperity to misfortune either; such a plot may satisfy our feeling of humanity, but it does not arouse pity or fear. We feel pity for a man who does not deserve his misfortune; we fear for someone like ourselves; neither feeling is here involved.

THE TRAGIC CHARACTER

We are left with a character in between the other two; a man who is neither out-standing in virtue and righteousness, nor is it through wickedness and vice that he falls into misfortune, but through some flaw.[4] He should also be famous or prosperous, like Oedipus, Thyestes, and the noted men of such noble families.

THE BEST PLOTS

A good plot must consist of a single and not, as some people say, of a double story; the change of fortune should not be from misfortune to prosperity but, on the contrary, from prosperity to misfortune. This change should not be caused by outright wickedness but by a serious flaw in a character such as we have just described, or one better rather than worse. This is proved by what has happened: at first tragic poets related any kind of story, but now the best tragedies are constructed around the fortunes of a few families, and are concerned with Alcmaeon, Oedipus, Orestes, Meleager, Thyestes, Telephus, and any other such men who have endured or done terrible things. The best products of the tragic art have this kind of plot structure.

People are therefore mistaken when they criticize Euripides on this very point, because

[4]Granted then that the *hamartia* is in the character, is it a moral weakness or an error of judgment? Those who hold the first view believe that the hero is morally responsible for his tragedy; those who hold the second view seem to think that he is not. But are we not, here again, forcing upon Aristotle a choice between clear alternatives that are ours, not his? He does not say the hero is responsible for his tragedy or that it is his fault. All he says is that there is some flaw or weakness in the personality of the hero which brings about his tragedy. Indeed, this follows logically from his previous statement, for if the hero were flawless he would be quite perfect and no tragic hero. I do not believe that Aristotle here makes any distinction between a moral flaw and a flaw in mental judgment. Each is a flaw or weakness in the personality of the hero, either may bring about the tragedy or bring it about at that particular time; neither makes him deserve it, but either again may make it seem natural that it should come about and is therefore dramatically satisfying. Besides, if pity is to be aroused, the misfortune must be undeserved in any case. Aristotle is not concerned to fix any responsibility or blame but to see that the tragedy should seem "probable or inevitable."

his tragedies are of this kind and many of them end unhappily, for this, as I said, is right. There is convincing proof of this: in the theater and in dramatic contests such dramas are seen to be the most tragic if they are well performed, and even though Euripides manages his plays badly in other respects, he obviously is the most tragic of the poets.

THE DOUBLE PLOT OF COMEDY

The double plot, such as we find in the *Odyssey*, where, at the end, the good are rewarded and the bad punished, is thought by some to be the best, but in fact it holds only second place. It is the weakness of our audiences that places it first, and the poets seek to please the spectators. The pleasure provided in this way, however, belongs to comedy rather than to tragedy; it is in comedy that those who, in the story, are the greatest enemies, like Orestes and Aegisthus, are reconciled in the end, walk off the stage as friends, and no one kills anybody.

XIV

Pity and Fear should be due to Plot, not to Spectacle

Fear and pity can be caused by the spectacle or by the plot structure itself. The latter way is better and argues a better poet. The story should be so constructed that the events make anyone who hears the story shudder and feel pity even without seeing the play. The story of Oedipus has this effect. To arouse pity and fear by means of the spectacle requires less art and a costly performance. And those plays which, by means of the spectacle, arouse not fear but only amazement have nothing in common with tragedy. We should not require from tragedy every kind of pleasure, but only its own peculiar kind.

The Tragic Situation

As the tragic poet must aim to produce by his imitation the kind of pleasure which results from fear and pity, he must do so through the plot. We must therefore investigate what sort of incidents are terrible or pitiful. Such actions must necessarily occur between people who are friends, enemies, or neither. Between enemies neither the action itself nor the intention excites pity, except in so far as suffering is pitiful in itself. The same is true between people who are neither friends nor enemies. When, however, suffering is inflicted upon each other by people whose relationship implies affection, as when a brother kills, or intends to kill, his brother, a son his father, a mother her son, a son his mother, or some other such action takes place—those are the situations to look for.

Acting in Ignorance

It is not possible to undo the traditional stories, the murder of Clytemnestra by Orestes or that of Eriphyle by Alcmaeon, but the poet must find ways to make good use of the given situation. Let us clarify what we mean by "good use." The deed can be done, as in the old poets, with full knowledge of the facts, as the Medea of Euripides kills her children. Or it can be done in ignorance of its terrible nature and this recognized later, as the Oedipus of Sophocles killed his father; this action, it is true, lies outside the drama, but it can happen in the course of a play, as with the Alcmaeon of Astydamas or with Telegonus in the *Wounded Odysseus*. There is still a third way: when someone who intends to do the deed is ignorant of the relationship but recognizes it before the deed is done. There is no further alternative, for one must act or not, either with knowledge or without it.

The worst of all these is to have full knowledge and intend to do the deed, and then not do it; this is not tragic but shocking, and there is no suffering; it is a type never or very rarely used, as when Haemon threatens his father Creon in the *Antigone*. It is better to commit the crime. Better still is to do it in ignorance and to recognize the truth afterwards. Then there is nothing to shock, and the recognition is frightening. Best of all is the last alternative, the way of Merope in the *Cresphontes* where she intends to kill her son but does not do it when she recognizes him, or, as in the *Iphigenia*, where the sister is about to kill the brother, or in the *Helle*, where the son, about to give up his mother, recognizes her.

That is the reason why the subjects of tragedy are, as we said some time ago, provided by a few families. By chance rather than intent, poets found the way to provide these situations in their plots, and this forces them to go to those families which were thus afflicted.

We have now said enough about the arrangement of the incidents and the right kinds of plot.

XV

FOUR AIMS IN CHARACTERIZATION

In expressing character there are four things to aim at. Of these the first and foremost is that the characters should be good. Words and action express character, as we stated, if they bring out a moral choice, and the character is good if the choice is right. This applies to every type: even a woman or a slave can be good, though the former of these is a weaker being and the slave is altogether inferior. In the second place, characters must be appropriate or true to type: there is a manly character, but it is not appropriate for a woman to be manly or a clever speaker. The third aim is to be true to life, and this is different from being good or true to type. The fourth is consistency. Even if the character represented displays inconsistency as a character trait, he must be consistent in his inconsistency.

Menelaus in the *Orestes* provides an example of a character which is unnecessarily evil; the lament of Odysseus in the *Scylla* and the speech of Melanippe are unsuitable and inappropriate; Iphigenia in *Iphigenia at Aulis* shows inconsistency: her supplication is quite unlike the character she displays later.

In characterization as in plot structure,

one must always aim at either what is probable or what is inevitable, so that a certain character will say or do certain things in a way that is probable or inevitable, and one incident will follow the other in the same way.

THE SUPERNATURAL

The solution of the plot should also emerge from the story itself; it should not require the use of the supernatural, as it does in the *Medea* and in the threatened departure of the Greeks in the *Iliad*. The supernatural should be used only in connection with events that lie outside the play itself, things that have happened long ago beyond the knowledge of men, or future events which need to be foretold and revealed, for we attribute to the gods the power of seeing all things. In the incidents of the play there should be nothing inexplicable or, if there is, it should be outside the actual play, as in the *Oedipus* of Sophocles.

CHARACTERIZATION

Since tragedy is the imitation of characters better than those we know in life, we should imitate good portrait painters. They too render the characteristic appearance of their subject in a good likeness which is yet more beautiful than the original. So when the poet is imitating men who are given to anger, indolence, and other faults of character, he should represent them as they are, and yet make them worthy. As such an example of violent temper we have the Achilles of Agathon and Homer.

CARE FOR DETAILS OF PRESENTATION

These things the poet must keep in mind. Besides these, he must also pay attention to the visual and other impressions which, apart from its essential effects, a poetic presentation inevitably makes upon the audience, for frequent errors are possible here also. These are adequately dealt with in my published works.

XVI

KINDS OF RECOGNITION

What recognition is has already been stated. As to its different kinds, the first, least artistic but most frequently used through lack of talent, is recognition by tokens or signs. Some of these signs are congenital, like the spearshaped birthmark of the Sons of Earth, or the stars which Carcinus used in his *Thyestes;* others are acquired, whether marks on the body like wounds, external possessions like necklaces, or the skiff which was the means of recognition in the *Tyro.* There is a better and a worse way of using these signs; both his old nurse and the swineherds recognize Odysseus by his scar, but the manner of their recognition is quite different. Recognitions deliberately brought about to prove one's identity are less artistic, as are all recognitions of this kind; but those that emerge from the circumstances of the reversal are better, as in the bath scene with Odysseus' old nurse.

The second kind of recognition is that contrived by the poet; it is inartistic for this very reason, as Orestes in the *Iphigenia* brings about the recognition that he is Orestes. The recognition of Iphigenia follows from the letter, but Orestes says himself what the poet, not the plot, requires him to say. This is why it comes very close to the fault mentioned above in the case of Odysseus and the swineherds, for Orestes too could have had some tokens with him. The cry of the shuttle in the *Tyreus* of Sophocles also belongs here.

The third kind of recognition is through memory: we see one thing and recall another, as a character in the *Cyprians* of Dicaeogenes saw the picture and wept, or the recognition scene in the play of Antinous, where Odysseus listens to the bard and weeps at his memories, and this leads to the recognition.

Recognition of the fourth kind is by inference, as in the *Choephori:* someone like me has come, there is no one like me except Orestes, therefore Orestes has come. The same applies to Iphigenia in the work of the sophist Polyidus, for it was likely for Orestes to reflect that his sister was sacrificed and that the same thing was now happening to him, or for Tydeus in the play of Theodectes to say that he had come to find his son and was being killed himself. Similarly, in the *Phineidae,* the women, on seeing the place, reflected on their fate: that they were fated to die in this place from which they had been cast out.

There is a further kind of composite recognition based upon a wrong inference by one of the two parties involved, as in *Odysseus the False Messenger,* where one said he would know the bow he had never seen, and the other understood him to say he would recognize it, and thus made a false inference.

Of all these, the best recognition is that which emerges from the events themselves, where the amazement and the surprise are caused by probable means, as in the *Oedipus* of Sophocles and the *Iphigenia,* for it was probable that Iphigenia should wish to send a letter. This is the only kind of recognition which dispenses with contrived tokens and necklaces. The second best is recognition based on a correct inference.

TRAGIC AND COMIC RHYTHMS
Susanne Langer

THE TRAGIC RHYTHM

As comedy presents the vital rhythm of self-preservation, tragedy exhibits that of self-consummation.

The lifting advance of the eternal life process, indefinitely maintained or temporarily lost and restored, is the great general vital pattern that we exemplify from day to day. But creatures that are destined, sooner or later, to die—that is, all individuals that do not pass alive into new generations, like jellyfish and algae—hold the balance of life only precariously, in the frame of a total movement that is quite different; the movement from birth to death. Unlike the simple metabolic process, the deathward advance of their individual lives has a series of stations that are not repeated; growth, maturity, decline. That is the tragic rhythm. . . .

Tragedy dramatizes human life as potentiality and fulfillment. Its virtual future, or Destiny, is therefore quite different from that created in comedy. Comic Destiny is Fortune —what the world will bring, and the man will take or miss, encounter or escape; tragic Destiny is what the man brings, and the world will demand of him. That is his Fate.

What he brings is his potentiality: his mental, moral and even physical powers, his powers to act and suffer. Tragic action is the realization of all his possibilities, which he unfolds and exhausts in the course of the drama. His human nature is his Fate. Destiny conceived as Fate is, therefore, not capricious, like Fortune, but is predetermined. Outward events are merely the occasions for its realization.

The idea of personal Fate was mythically conceived long before the relation of life history to character was discursively understood. The mythical tradition of Greece treated the fate of its "heroes"—the personalities springing from certain great, highly individualized families—as a mysterious power inherent in the world rather than in the man and his ancestry; it was conceived as a private incubus bestowed on him at birth by a vengeful deity, or even through a curse pronounced by a human being. Sometimes no such specific cause of his peculiar destiny is given at all; but an oracle foretells what he is bound to do. It is interesting to note that this conception of Fate usually centers in the mysterious predictability of *acts* someone is to perform. The occasions of the acts are not foretold; the world will provide them. . . .

For the development of tragedy, such determination of the overt acts without circumstances and motives furnished an ideal starting point, for it constrained the poets to invent characters whose actions would issue naturally in the required fateful deeds. The oracular prophecy, then, became an intensifying symbol of the necessity that was really given with the agent's personality; the "fable" being just one possible way the world might elicit his complete self-realizaton in endeavor and error and discovery, passion and punishment, to the limit of his powers. The prime example of this passage from the mythical idea of Fate to the dramatic creation of Fate as the protagonist's natural, personal destiny is, of course, the *Oedipus Tyrannus* of Sophocles. With that tremendous piece of self-assertion, self-divination and self-exhaustion, the "Great Tradition" of tragedy was born in Europe.

There is another mythical conception of Fate that is not a forerunner of tragedy, but possibly of some kinds of comedy: that is the idea of Fate as the will of supernatural powers, perhaps long decreed, perhaps spontaneous and arbitrary. It is the "Fate" of the true fatalist, who takes no great care of his life because he deems it entirely in the hand of Allah (or some other God), who will slay or spare at his pleasure no matter what one does. That is quite a different notion from the "oracular" Fate of Greek mythology; the will of a god who gives and takes away, casts down or raises up, for inscrutable reasons of his own, is Kismet, and that is really a myth of Fortune. Kismet is what a person encounters, not what he is. Both conceptions often exist side by side. The Scotsman who has to "dree his weird" believes nonetheless that his fortunes from moment to moment are in the hands of Providence. Macbeth's Weird Sisters were perfectly acceptable to a Christian audience. Even in the ancient lore of our fairy tales, the Sleeping Beauty is destined to prick herself—that is, she has a personal destiny. In Greek tradition, on the other hand, where the notion of "oracular Fate" was so generally entertained that the Oracle was a public institution, Fate as the momentary decree of a ruling Power is represented in the myth of the Norns, who spin the threads of human lives and cut them where they list; the Three Fates are as despotic and capricious as Allah, and what they spin is, really, Kismet. . . .

A dramatic act is a commitment. It creates a situation in which the agent or agents must necessarily make a further move; that is, it motivates a subsequent act (or acts). The situation, which is the completion of a given act, is already the impetus to another—as, in running, the footfall that catches our weight at the end of one bound already sends us forward to land on the other foot. The bounds need not be alike, but proportional, which means that the impetus of any specially great leap must have been prepared and gathered somewhere, and any sudden diminution be balanced by some motion that carries off the driving force. Dramatic acts are analogously connected with each other so that each one directly or indirectly motivates what follows it. In this way a genuine rhythm of action is set up, which is not simple like that of a physical repetitive process (e.g. running, breathing), but more often intricate, even deceptive, and, of course, not given primarily to one particular sense, but to the imagination through whatever sense we employ to perceive and evaluate action; the same general rhythm of action appears in a play whether we read it or hear it read, enact it ourselves or see it performed. That rhythm is the "commanding form" of the play; it springs from the poet's original conception of the "fable," and dictates the major divisions of the work, the light or heavy style of its presentation, the intensity of the highest feeling and most violent act, the great or small number of characters, and the degrees of their development. The total action is a cumulative form; and because it is constructed by a rhythmic treatment of its elements, it appears to *grow* from its beginnings.

That is the play-wright's creation of "organic form."

The tragic rhythm, which is the pattern of a life that grows, flourishes, and declines, is abstracted by being transferred from that natural activity to the sphere of a characteristically human action, where it is exemplified in mental and emotional growth, maturation, and the final relinquishment of power. In that relinquishment lies the hero's true "heroism"—the vision of life as accomplished, that is, life in its entirety, the sense of fulfillment that lifts him above his defeat. . . .

Tragic drama is so designed that the protagonist grows mentally, emotionally, or morally, by the demand of the action, which he himself initiated, to the complete exhaustion of his powers, the limit of his possible development. He spends himself in the course of the one dramatic action. This is, of course, a tremendous foreshortening of life; instead of undergoing the physical and psychical, many-sided, long process of an actual biography, the tragic hero lives and matures in some particular respect; his entire being is concentrated in one aim, one passion, one conflict and ultimate defeat. For this reason the prime agent of tragedy is heroic; his character, the unfolding situation, the scene, even though ostensibly familiar and humble, are all exaggerated, charged with more feeling than comparable actualities would possess. This intensification is necessary to achieve and sustain the "form in suspense" that is even more important in tragic drama than in comic, because the comic denouement, not marking an absolute close, needs only to restore a balance, but the tragic ending must recapitulate the whole action to be a visible fulfillment of a destiny that was implicit in the beginning. This device, which may be called "dramatic exaggeration," is reminiscent of "epic exaggeration," and may have been adopted quite unconsciously with the epic themes of ancient tragedy. But that does not mean that it is an accidental factor, a purely historical legacy from an older poetic tradition; inherited conventions do not maintain themselves long in any art unless they serve its own purposes. They may have their old *raison d'être* in new art forms, or take on entirely new functions, but as sheer trappings—traditional requirements—they would be discarded by the first genius who found no use for them.

Drama is not psychology, nor (though the critical literature tends to make it seem so) is it moral philosophy. It offers no discourse on the hero's or heroine's native endowments, to let us estimate at any stage in the action how near they must be to exhaustion. The action itself must reveal the limit of the protagonist's powers and mark the end of his self-realization. And so, indeed, it does: the turning point of the play is the situation he cannot resolve, where he makes his "tragic error" or exhibits his "tragic weakness." He is led by his own action and its repercussions in the world to respond with more and more competence, more and more daring to a constantly gathering challenge; so his character "grows," i.e. he unfolds his will and knowledge and passion, as the situation grows. His career is not change of personality, but maturation. When he reaches his limit of mental and emotional development, the crisis occurs; then comes the defeat, either by death or, as in many modern tragedies, by hopelessness that is the equivalent of death, a "death of the soul," that ends the career. . . .

In truth, I believe, the hero of tragedy must *interest* us all the time, but not as a person of our own acquaintance. His tragic error, crime, or other flaw is not introduced for moral reasons, but for structural purposes: it marks his limit of power. His potentialities appear on stage only as successful acts; as soon as his avowed or otherwise obvious intentions fail, or his acts recoil on him and bring him pain, his power has reached its height, he is at the end of his career. In this, of course, drama is utterly different from life. The moral failure in drama is not a normal incident, something to be lived down, presumably neither the doer's first trans-

gression nor his last; the act that constitutes the protagonist's tragic error or guilt is the high-water mark of his life, and now the tide recedes. His "imperfection" is an artistic element: that is why a single flaw will do.

THE COMIC RHYTHM

It is commonly assumed that comedy and tragedy have the same fundamental form, but differ in point of view—in the attitude the poet and his interpreters take, and the spectators are invited to take, toward the action. But the difference really goes deeper than surface treatment (i.e. relative levity or pathos). It is structural and radical. Drama abstracts from reality the fundamental forms of consciousness: the first reflection of natural activity in sensation, awareness, and expectation, which belongs to all higher creatures and might be called, therefore, the pure sense of life; and beyond that, the reflection of an activity which is at once more elaborate, and more integrated, having a beginning, efflorescence, and end—the personal sense of life, or self-realization. The latter probably belongs only to human beings, and to them in varying measure.

The pure sense of life is the underlying feeling of comedy, developed in countless different ways. To give a general phenomenon one name is not to make all its manifestations one thing, but only to bring them conceptually under one head. Art does not generalize and classify; art sets forth the individuality of forms which discourse, being essentially general, has to suppress. The sense of life is always new, infinitely complex, therefore infinitely variable in its possible expressions. This sense, or "enjoyment," is the realization in direct feeling of what sets organic nature apart from inorganic: self-preservation, self-restoration, functional tendency, purpose. Life is teleological, the rest of nature is, apparently, mechanical; to maintain the pattern of vitality in a non-living universe is the most elementary instinctual purpose. An organism tends to keep its equilibrium amid the bombardment of aimless forces that beset it, to regain equilibrium when it has been disturbed, and to pursue a sequence of actions dictated by the need of keeping all its interdependent parts constantly renewed, their structure intact. Only organisms have needs; lifeless objects whirl or slide or tumble about, are shattered and scattered, stuck together, piled up, without showing any impulse to return to some preeminent condition and function. But living things strive to persist in a particular chemical balance, to maintain a particular temperature, to repeat particular functions, and to develop along particular lines, achieving a growth that seems to be performed in their earliest, rudimentary, protoplasmic structure. . . .

But the impulse to survive is not spent only in defense and accommodation; it appears also in the varying power of organisms to seize on opportunities. Consider how chimney swifts, which used to nest in crevasses among rocks, have exploited the products of human architecture, and how unfailingly mice find the warmth and other delights of our kitchens. All creatures live by opportunities, in a world fraught with disasters. That is the biological pattern in most general terms. . . .

The sex impulse, which presumably belongs only to bisexual creatures (whatever equivalents it may have in other procreative processes), is closely intertwined with the life impulse; in a mature organism it is part and parcel of the whole vital impetus. But it is a specialized part, because the activities that maintain the individual's life are varied and adaptable to many circumstances, but procreation requires specific actions. This specialization is reflected in the emotional life of all the higher animals; sexual excitement is the most intense and at the same time the most elaborately patterned experience, having its own rhythm that engages the whole creature, its rise and crisis and cadence, in a much higher degree than any other emotive response. Consequently the whole development of feeling, sensibility, and temperament is wont to radiate from that source of vital consciousness, sexual action and passion.

Mankind has its rhythm of animal existence, too—the strain of maintaining a vital balance amid the alien and impartial chances of the world, complicated and heightened by passional desires. The pure sense of life springs from that basic rhythm, and varies from the composed well-being of sleep to the intensity of spasm, rage, or ecstasy. But the process of living is incomparably more complex for human beings than for even the highest animals; man's world is, above all, intricate and puzzling. The powers of language and imagination have set it utterly apart from that of other creatures. In human society an individual is not, like a member of a herd or a hive, exposed only to others that visibly or tangibly surround him, but is consciously bound to people who are absent, perhaps far away, at the moment. Even the dead may still play into his life. His awareness of events is far greater than the scope of his physical perceptions. Symbolic construction has made this vastly involved and extended world: and mental adroitness is his chief asset for exploiting it. The pattern of his vital feeling, therefore, reflects his deep emotional relation to those symbolic structures that are his realities, and his instinctual life modified in almost every way by thought —a brainy opportunism in the face of an essentially dreadful universe.

This human life-feeling is the essence of comedy. It is at once religious and ribald, knowing and defiant, social and freakishly individual. The illusion of life which the comic poet creates is the oncoming future fraught with dangers and opportunities, that is, with physical or social events occurring by chance and building up the coincidences with which individuals cope according to their lights. This ineluctable future—ineluctable because its countless factors are beyond human knowledge and control—is Fortune.

Destiny in the guise of Fortune is the fabric of comedy; it is developed by comic action, which is the upset and recovery of the protagonist's equilibrium, his contest with the world and his triumph by wit, luck, personal power, or even humorous, or ironical, or philosophical acceptance of mischance. Whatever the theme—serious and lyrical as in *The Tempest*, coarse slapstick as in the *Schwänke* of Hans Sachs, or clever and polite social satire —the immediate sense of life is the underlying feeling of comedy, and dictates its rhythmically structured unity, that is to say its organic form.

Comedy is an art form that arises naturally wherever people are gathered to celebrate life, in spring festivals, triumphs, birthdays, weddings, or initiations. For it expresses the elementary strains and resolutions of animate nature, the animal drives that persist even in human nature, the delight man takes in his special mental gifts that make him the lord of creation; it is an image of human vitality holding its own in the world amid the surprises of unplanned coincidence. The most obvious occasions for the performance of comedies are thanks or challenges to fortune. What justifies the term "Comedy" is not that the ancient ritual procession, the Comus, honoring the god of that name, was the source of this great art form—for comedy has arisen in many parts of the world, where the Greek god with his particular worship was unknown—but that the Comus was a fertility rite, and the god it celebrated a fertility god, a symbol of perpetual rebirth, eternal life.

Tragedy has a different basic feeling, and therefore a different form; that is why it has also quite different thematic material, and why character development, great moral conflicts, and sacrifice are its usual actions. *It is also what makes tragedy sad*, as the rhythm of sheer vitality makes comedy happy.

There are many ways of accepting death; the commonest one is to deny its finality, to imagine a continued existence "beyond" it— by resurrection, reincarnation, or departure of the soul from the body, and usually from the familiar world, to a deathless existence in hades, nirvana, heaven or hell. But no matter how people contrive to become reconciled to their mortality, it puts its stamp on their conception of life: since the instinctive struggle to go on living is bound to meet defeat in the end, they look for *as much life as possible* between birth and death—for adventure, variety and intensity of experience, and the sense of growth that increase of personality and social status can give long after physical growth has stopped. The known limitation of life gives form to it and makes it appear not merely as a process, but as a career. This career of the individual is variously conceived as a "calling," the attainment of an ideal, the soul's pilgrimage, "life's ordeal," or self-realization. The last of these designations is, perhaps, the most illuminating in the present context, because it contains the notion of a limited potential personality given at birth and "realized," or systematically developed, in the course of the subject's total activity. His career, then, appears to be preformed in him; his successive adventures in the world are so many challenges to fulfill his individual destiny.

Destiny viewed in this way, as a future shaped essentially in advance and only incidentally by chance happenings, is Fate; and Fate is the "virtual future" created in tragedy. The "tragic rhythm of action," as Professor Fergusson calls it, is the rhythm of man's life at its highest powers in the limits of his unique, death-bound career. Tragedy is the image of Fate, as comedy is of Fortune. Their basic structures are different; comedy is essentially contingent, episodic, and ethnic; it expresses the continuous balance of sheer vitality that belongs to society and is exemplified briefly in each individual; tragedy is a fulfillment, and its form therefore is closed, final and passional. Tragedy is a mature art form, that has not arisen in all parts of the world, not even in all great civilizations. Its conception requires a sense of individuality which some religions and some cultures— even high cultures—do not generate.

THE TRAGIC FORM

Richard B. Sewall

A discussion of tragedy is confronted at the outset with the strenuous objections of Croce, who would have no truck with genres. "Art is one," he wrote in his famous *Britannica* acticle,[1] "and cannot be divided." For convenience, he would allow the division of Shakespeare's plays into tragedies, comedies, and histories, but he warned of the dogmatism that lay in any further refining of distinctions. He made a special point of tragedy, which as usual was the fighting issue. No artist, he said, will submit to the servitude of the traditional definition: that a tragedy must have a subject of a certain kind, characters of a certain kind, and a plot of a certain kind and length. Each work of art is a world in itself, "a creation, not a reflection, a monument, not a document." The concepts of aesthetics do not exist "in a transcendent region" but only in innumerable specific works. To ask of a given work "is it a tragedy?" or "does it obey the laws of tragedy?" is irrelevant and impertinent.

Although this may be substituting one dogmatism for another, there is sense in it. Nothing is more dreary than the textbook categories; and their tendency, if carried too far, would rationalize art out of existence. The dilemma is one of critical means, not ends: Croce would preserve tragedy by insuring the autonomy of the artist; the schoolmen would preserve it by insuring the autonomy of the form.

But the dilemma is not insurmountable, as Eliot and a number of others have pointed out. There is a life-giving relationship between tradition and the individual talent, a "wooing both ways" (in R. P. Blackmur's phrase) between the form which the artist inherits and the new content he brings to it. This wooing both ways has been especially true of the development of tragedy, where values have been incremental, where (for instance) each new tragic protagonist is in some degree a lesser Job and each new tragic work owes an indispensable element to the Greek idea of the chorus. So I should say that, provided we can get beyond the stereotypes Croce seems to have had in mind, we should continue to talk about tragedy, to make it grow in meaning, impel more artists, and attract a greater and more discerning audience.

But we must first get a suitable idea of form. Blackmur's article[2] from which I have just quoted provides, I think, a useful suggestion. It is the concept of "theoretic form," which he distinguishes from technical or "executive" form. "Technical form," he writes, "is our means of getting at . . . and then making something of, what we feel the form of life itself is: the tensions, the stresses, the deep relations and the terrible disrelations that inhabit them. . . . This is the form that underlies the forms we merely practice. . . ." This (and here Croce's full concept of form is more adequately represented) is "what Croce means by theoretic form for feeling, intuition, insight, what I mean by the theoretic form of life itself." Discussion of the "form" of tragedy in this sense need be neither prescriptive nor inhibiting, but it may define a little more precisely a vital area of thought and feeling.

Here is the kind of situation in which such a discussion might be helpful: Two years ago, in *Essays in Criticism* (October 1952), Miss K. M. Burton defended what she called the "political tragedies" of Ben Jonson and George Chapman as legitimate tragedies, although non-Aristotelian. *Sejanus* was perhaps the clearest case in point. Herford and Simpson, in their commentary, had set the

[1] Eleventh edition, article "Aesthetics."

Richard B. Sewall, "The Tragic Form," *Essays in Criticism*, IV (October, 1954), pp. 345–358. Reprinted by Permission.

[2] "The Loose and Baggy Monsters of Henry James: Notes on the Underlying Classic Form in the Novel," *Accent*, Summer, 1951; see also Eliseo Vivas, "Literature and Knowledge," *Sewanee Review*, Autumn, 1952.

play down as at best "the tragedy of a satirist," a "proximate" tragedy, with no tragic hero and with no cathartic effect. "Whatever effect (Jonson) aimed at," they wrote, "it was not the purifying pity excited by the fatal errors of a noble nature." Miss Burton's reply lay in her concept of political tragedy. She saw Jonson's tragic theme as "the manner in which evil penetrates the political structure." The "flaw" that concerned him lay "within the social order," and whatever purifying pity we feel would come from contemplating the ordeal of society, not the fatal errors of a noble nature. The play for her had "tragic intensity"; it was both "dramatic, and a tragedy."

Whether one agrees with her or not, the question, despite Croce, is out: "Is the play a tragedy?" And many others follow. Can there be a tragedy without a tragic hero? Can "the social order" play his traditional role? Is catharsis the first, or only, or even a reliable test? In a recent article, Professor Pottle wrote, "I shall be told Aristotle settled all that." And added, "I wish he had." The disagreement on *Sejanus* is symptomatic. F. L. Lucas once pointed out that (on much the same issues) Hegel thought only the Greeks wrote true tragedy; and I. A. Richards, only Shakespeare. Joseph Wood Krutch ruled out the moderns, like Hardy, Ibsen and O'Neill; and Mark Harris ruled them in.[3] The question arises about every new "serious" play or novel; we seem to care a great deal about whether it is, or is not, a tragedy.

I have little hope of settling all this, but I am persuaded that progress lies in the direction of theoretic form, as Blackmur uses the term. Is it not possible to bring the dominant feelings, intuitions, insights that we meet in so-called tragic writings into some coherent relationship to which the word "form" could be applied without too great violence? This

is not to tell artists what to do, nor to set up strict *a priori* formulae, nor to legislate among the major genres. The problem of evaluating the total excellence of a given work involves much more than determining its status as a tragedy, or as a "proximate" tragedy, or as a non-tragedy. It involves, among other things, the verbal management within the work and the ordering of the parts. Furthermore, our discussion need not imply the superiority of tragedy over comedy (certainly not as Dante conceived of comedy) or over epic, although, if we look upon these major forms as presenting total interpretations of life, the less inclusive forms (lyric, satire) would seem to occupy inferior categories. But as we enter the world of any play or novel to which the term tragedy is at all applicable, we may well judge it by what we know about the possibilities of the form, without insisting that our judgment is absolute. If, set against the full dimensions of the tragic form, Jonson's *Sejanus* or Hemingway's *A Farewell to Arms* (for instance) reveal undeveloped possibilities or contrary elements, we can still respect their particular modes of expression.

In indicating these dimensions of tragedy, I shall be mindful of Unamuno's warning[4] that tragedy is not a matter, ultimately, to be systematized. He speaks truly, I think, about "the tragic sense of life." He describes it as a sub-philosophy, "more or less formulated, more or less conscious," reaching deep down into temperament, not so much "flowing from ideas as determining them." It is the sense of ancient evil, of the mystery of human suffering, of the gulf between aspiration and achievement. It colors the tragic artist's vision of life (his theoretic form) and gives his works their peculiar shade and tone. It speaks, not the language of systematic thought, but through symbolic action, symbol and figure, diction and image, sound and rhythm. Such a recognition should precede any attempt

[3]F. A. Pottle, "Catharsis," *Yale Review*, Summer, 1951; F. L. Lucas, *Tragedy in Relation to Aristotle's Poetics*, N. Y., 1928; Joseph Wood Krutch, *The Modern Temper*, N. Y., 1929; Mark Harris, *The Case for Tragedy*, N. Y., 1932.

[4]*The Tragic Sense of Life*, tr. J. E. C. Flitch, London, 1921, pp. 17–18.

to talk "systematically" about tragedy, while not denying the value of the attempt itself.

Two more comments remain to be made about method. The first is the problem of circular evidence,[5] the use of tragedies to define tragedy. I am assuming that we can talk meaningfully about a body of literature which reveals certain generic qualities and which can be distinguished from the body of literature called comedy, epic, satire, or the literature of pathos. My purpose is to isolate these qualities and to refer to the works themselves as illustrations rather than proof.

The second comment involves the problem of affectivism, which is the problem of catharsis: "This play is a tragedy because it makes me feel thus and so." As Max Scheler puts it, this method would bring us ultimately to the contemplation of our own ego. Thus, I would reverse the order of F. L. Lucas' discussion, which assumes that we must know what tragedy does before we can tell what it is: "We cannot fully discuss the means," Lucas wrote, "until we are clear about the ends." It is true that the usual or "scientific" way is to define natures by effects, which are observable. But rather than found a definition of tragedy on the infinite variables of an audience's reactions, I would consider first the works themselves as the "effects" and look in them for evidences of an efficient cause: a world-view, a form that "underlies the forms we merely practice." What are the generic qualities of these effects? Do they comprise a "form"? I think they do; and for convenience I shall use the term from the start as if I had already proved its legitimacy.

Basic to the tragic form is its recognition of the inevitability of paradox, of unresolved tensions and ambiguities, of opposites in precarious balance. Like the arch, tragedy never rests—or never comes to rest, with all losses restored and sorrows ended. Problems are put and pressed, but not solved. An occasional "happy ending," as in *The Oresteia* or *Crime and Punishment*, does not mean a full resolution. Though there may be intermittences, there is no ultimate discharge in the war. Although this suggests formlessness, as it must in contrast with certain types of religious orthodoxy or philosophical system, it would seem the essence of the tragic form. Surely it is more form than chaos. For out of all these tensions and paradoxes, these feelings, intuitions, insights, there emerges a fairly coherent attitude towards the universe and man. Tragedy makes certain distinguishable and characteristic affirmations, as well as denials, about (I) the cosmos and man's relation to it; (II) the nature of the individual and his relation to himself; (III) the individual in society.

(I) *The tragic cosmos.* In using the term cosmos to signify a theory of the universe and man's relation to it, I have, of course, made a statement about tragedy: that tragedy affirms a cosmos of which man is a meaningful part. To be sure, the characteristic locale of tragedy is not the empyrean. Tragedy is primarily humanistic. Its focus is an event in this world; it is uncommitted as to questions of ultimate destiny, and it is non-religious in its attitude toward revelation. But it speaks, however vaguely or variously, of an order that transcends time, space and matter.[6] It assumes man's connection with some supersensory or supernatural, or metaphysical being or principle, whether it be the Olympians, Job's Jehovah or the Christian God; Fate, Fortune's Wheel, the "elements" that Lear invoked, or Koestler's "oceanic sense," which comes in so tentatively (and pathetically) at the end of *Darkness at Noon*. The first thing that tragedy says about the cosmos is that, for good or ill, it is; and in this respect tragedy's theoretic opposite is naturalism or mechanism. Tragedy is witness (secondly) to the cosmic mystery, to the "wonderful" surrounding our lives; and in literature the opposite of tragedy is not only writing based

---

[5]Cf. Max Scheler, "On the Tragic," *Cross Currents*, Winter, 1954.

[6]Cf. Susan Taubes, "The Nature of Tragedy," *Review of Metaphysics*, December 1953.

upon naturalistic theory but also upon the four-square, "probable"[7] world of satire and rationalistic comedy. Finally, what distinguishes tragedy from other forms which bespeak this cosmic sense—for tragedy of course is not unique in this—is its peculiar and intense preoccupation with the evil in the universe, whatever it is in the stars that compels, harasses, and bears man down. Tragedy wrestles with the evil of the mystery—and the mystery of the evil. And the contest never ends.

But, paradoxically, its view of the cosmos is what sustains tragedy. Tragedy discerns a principle of goodness that coexists with the evil. This principle need be nothing so pat as The Moral Order, the "armies of unalterable law," and it is nothing so sure as the orthodox Christian God. It is nearer the folk sense that justice exists somewhere in the universe, or what Nietzsche describes as the orgiastic, mystical sense of oneness, of life as "indestructibly powerful and pleasurable." It may be a vision of some transcendent beauty and dignity against which the present evil may be seen as evil and the welter as welter. This is what keeps tragedy from giving up the whole human experiment, and in this respect its opposite is not comedy or satire but cynicism and nihilism, as in Schopenhauer's theory of resignation. The "problem of the good" plays as vital a part in tragedy as the "problem of evil." It provides the living tension without which tragedy ceases to exist.

Thus tragedy contemplates a universe in which man is not the measure of all things. It confronts a mystery. W. Macneile Dixon[8]

pointed out that tragedy started as "an affair with the gods"; and the extent to which literature has become "secularized and humanized," he wrote, is a sign of its departure from (to use our present term) the tragic form. While agreeing with him as to the tendency, one may question the wholesale verdict which he implies. The affair with the gods had not, in the minds of all our artists, been reduced to an affair with the social order, or the environment, or the glands. But certainly where it becomes so, the muse of tragedy walks out; the universe loses its mystery and (to invoke catharsis for a moment) its terror.

The terms "pessimism" and "optimism," in view of the universe as conceived in the tragic form, do not suggest adequate categories, as Nietzsche first pointed out.[9] Tragedy contains them both, goes beyond both, illuminates both, but comes to no conclusion. Tragedy could, it is true, be called pessimistic in its view of the evil in the universe as unremitting and irremediable, the blight man was born for, the necessary condition of existence. It is pessimistic, also, in its view of the overwhelming proportion of evil to good and in its awareness of the mystery of why this should be—the "unfathomable element" in which Ahab foundered. But it is optimistic in what might be called its vitalism, which is in some sense mystical, not earthbound; in its faith in a cosmic good; in its vision, however fleeting, of a world in which all questions could be answered.

[7]The "wonderful" and the "probable" are the basic categories in Albert Cook's distinction between tragedy and comedy. (*The Dark Voyage and the Golden Mean*, Cambridge, Mass., 1949, chap. I.)

[8]*Tragedy*, London, 1924. The extent of my indebtedness to this book, and to the other discussions of tragedy mentioned in this paper, is poorly indicated by such passing references as this. Since observations on tragedy and the theory of tragedy appear in innumerable discussions of particular authors, eras, and related critical problems, a complete list would be far too cumbersome. Among them would be, surely, the standard work of A. C. Bradley and Willard Farnham on Shakespearean tragedy; C. M. Bowra and Cedric Whitman on Sophocles; W. L. Courtney (*The Idea of Tragedy*, London, 1900); Maxwell Anderson, *The Essence of Tragedy*, Washington, 1939; Northrop Frye, "The Archetypes of Literature," *Kenyon Review*, Winter, 1951; Moody Prior, *The Language of Tragedy*, N.Y., 1947; and Herbert Weisinger, *Tragedy and the Paradox of the Fortunate Fall*, Michigan State College Press, 1953, which makes rich use of the archaeological and mythographic studies of the origin of tragedy (Cornford, Harrison, Murray). I am indebted, also, to my colleague Laurence Michel, for frequent conversations and helpful criticism.

[9]See also Reinhold Niebuhr, *Beyond Tragedy*, London, 1938.

(II) *Tragic man.* If the tragic form asserts a cosmos, some order behind the immediate disorder, what does it assert about the nature of man, other than that he is a being capable of cosmic affinities? What is tragic man as he lives and moves on this earth? Can he be distinguished meaningfully from the man of comedy, satire, epic, or lyric? How does he differ from "pathetic man" or "religious man"? or from man as conceived by the materialistic psychologies? Tragic man shares some qualities, of course, with each of these. I shall stress differences in the appropriate contexts.

Like the cosmos which he views, tragic man is a paradox and a mystery. He is no child of God; yet he feels himself more than a child of earth. He is not the plaything of Fate, but he is not entirely free. He is "both creature and creator" (in Niebuhr's phrase) —"fatefully free and freely fated" (in George Schrader's). He recognizes "the fact of guilt" while cherishing the "dream of innocence" (Fiedler), and he never fully abandons either position. He is plagued by the ambiguity of his own nature and of the world he lives in. He is torn between the sense in common-sense (which is the norm of satire and rationalistic, or corrective, comedy) and his own uncommon sense. Aware of the just but irreconcilable claims within and without, he is conscious of the immorality of his own morality and suffers in the knowledge of his own recalcitrance.

The dynamic of this recalcitrance is pride. It sustains his belief, however humbled he may become by later experience, in his own freedom, in his innocence, and in his uncommon sense. Tragic man is man at his most prideful and independent, man glorying in his humanity. Tragic pride, like everything else about tragedy, is ambiguous; it can be tainted with arrogance and have its petty side; but it is not to be equated with sin or weakness. The Greeks feared it when it threatened the gods or slipped into arrogance, but they honored it and even worshiped it in their heroes. It was the common folk, the chorus, who had no pride, or were "flaw-less."[10] The chorus invariably argues against pride, urging caution and moderation, because they know it leads to suffering; but tragedy as such does not prejudge it.

While many of these things, again, might be said of other than tragic man, it is in the peculiar nature of his suffering, and in his capacity for suffering, that his distinguishing quality lies. For instance (to ring changes on the Cartesian formula), tragic man would not define himself, like the man of corrective comedy or satire, "I think, therefore I am"; nor like the man of achievement (epic): "I act, or conquer, therefore I am": nor like the man of sensibility (lyric): "I feel, therefore I am": nor like the religious man: "I believe, therefore I am." Although he has all these qualities (of thought, achievement, sensibility, and belief) in various forms and degrees, the essence of his nature is brought out by suffering: "I suffer, I will to suffer, I learn by suffering; therefore I am." The classic statement, of course, is Aeschylus': "Wisdom comes alone through suffering" (Lattimore's translation); perhaps the most radical is Dostoevski's: "Suffering is the sole origin of consciousness."[11]

This is not to say that only tragic man suffers or that he who suffers is tragic. Saints and martyrs suffer and learn by suffering; Odysseus suffered and learned; Dante suffered and learned on his journey with Virgil. But tragic man, I think, is distinguishable from these others in the nature of his suffering as conditioned by its source and locus, in its characteristic course and consequences (that is, the ultimate disaster and the "knowledge" it leads to), and in his intense preoccupation with his own suffering.

But to consider these matters in turn and to illustrate them briefly:

I have already suggested the main sources and locus of tragic man's suffering. He suffers because he is more than usually sensitive to the "terrible disrelations" he sees about him

[10]Cf. Arthur Miller, "Tragedy and the Common Man," *New York Times*, February 27th, 1949.

[11]*Notes from Underground*, tr. B. G. Guerney.

and experiences in himself. He is more than usually aware of the mighty opposites in the universe and in man, of the gulf between desire and fulfilment, between what is and what should be. This kind of suffering is suffering on a high level, beyond the reach of the immature or brutish, and for ever closed to the extreme optimist, the extreme pessimist,[12] or the merely indifferent. It was Job on the ash-heap, the proto-type of tragic man, who was first struck by the incongruity between Jehovah's nature and His actions, between desert and reward in this life; and it was he who first asked, not so much for a release from physical suffering as a reasonable explanation of it. But above all, the source of tragic suffering is the sense, in the consciousness of tragic man, of simultaneous guilt and guiltlessness. Tillich called tragedy "a mixture of guilt and necessity." If tragic man could say, "I sinned, therefore I suffer" or "He (or They or God) sinned, therefore I suffer," his problem would be resolved, and the peculiar poignancy of his suffering would be removed. If he felt himself entirely free or entirely determined, he would cease to be tragic. But he is neither—he is, in short, a paradox and mystery, the "riddle of the world."

To draw further distinctions: The element of guilt in tragic suffering distinguishes it from the pathetic suffering of the guiltless and from the suffering of the sentimentalist's bleeding heart. On the other hand, tragic man's sense of fate, and of the mystery of fate, distinguishes his suffering from the suffering (which is little more than embarrassment) of the man of corrective comedy and satire. The suffering of the epic hero has little of the element of bafflement or enigma; it is not, characteristically, spiritual suffering. The Christian in his suffering can confess total guilt and look to the promise of redemption through grace.[13] The martyr seeks suffering, accepts it gladly, "glories in tribulation." Tragic

man knows nothing of grace and never glories in his suffering. Although he may come to acquiesce in it partly and "learn" from it (a stage I shall discuss below), his characteristic mood is resentment and dogged endurance. He has not the stoic's patience, although this may be part of what he learns. Characteristically, he is restless, intense, probing and questioning the universe and his own soul (Job, Lear, Ahab). It is true that, from Greek tragedy to tragedy written in the Christian era (Shakespeare and beyond) emphasis shifts from the universe to the soul, from the cosmic to the psychological. But Prometheus had an inner life; Antigone, for all her composure, suffered an ultimate doubt; Oedipus suffered spiritually as he grew to understand the dark ambiguities in his own nature. And we should be mistaken if we tried to interpret the divine powers in the plays of Shakespeare simply as "allegorical symbols for psychological realities."[14]

Tragic man, then, placed in a universe of irreconcilables, acting in a situation in which he is both innocent and guilty, and peculiarly sensitive to the "cursed spite" of his condition, suffers. What in the tragic view is the characteristic course of this suffering and what further aspects of tragic man are revealed by it? The tragic form develops, not only the partial outlines of a cosmology and psychology, but of an ethic.

(III) *Tragic man and society.* The tragic sufferer may now be viewed in his social and moral relationships. In the tragic world there are several alternatives. A man can default from the human condition—"Curse God and die"—and bring his suffering to an end: he can endure and be silent; he can turn cynic. Tragic man understands these alternatives, feels their attractions, but chooses a different way. Rising in his pride, he protests: he pits himself in some way against whatever, in the heavens above and in the earth beneath, seems to him to be wrong, oppressive, or personally thwarting. This is the hero's commitment, made early or late, but involving

---

[12]Cf. William Van O'Connor, *Climates of Tragedy*, Baton Rouge, La., 1943.

[13]Cf. Karl Jaspers, *Tragedy Is Not Enough*, tr. Reiche, Moore, Deutsch; Boston, 1952.

[14]Susan Taubes, *op. cit.*, p. 196.

him necessarily in society and in action—with Prometheus and Antigone early, with Hamlet late. What to the orthodox mind would appear to be the wisdom or folly, the goodness or badness, of the commitment is not, in the beginning, the essence of the matter. In the first phase of his course of suffering, the hero's position may be anarchic, individual, romantic. Herein tragedy tests all norms—as, by contrast, satire,[15] comedy, or epic tend to confirm them. The commitment may even be expressed in what society knows as a crime, but, as with tragic pride (of which the commitment is in part the expression) tragedy does not prejudge it. Thus it is said that tragedy studies "the great offenders," and Dostoevski sought among criminals and outcasts for his greatest spiritual discoveries. But the commitment must grow in meaning to include the more-than-personal. Ultimately, and ideally, the tragic hero stands as universal man, speaking for all men. The tragic sufferer, emerging from his early stage of lament or rebellion (Job's opening speech; the first scenes of Prometheus; Lear's early bursts of temper), moves beyond the "intermittences" of his own heart and makes a "pact with the world that is unremitting and sealed."[16]

Since the commitment cannot lead in the direction of escape or compromise, it must involve head-on collision with the forces that would oppress or frustrate. Conscious of the ambiguities without and within, which are the source of his peculiar suffering, tragic man accepts the conflict. It is horrible to do it, he says, but it is more horrible to leave it undone. He is now in the main phase of his suffering—the "passion."[17]

15Cf. Maynard Mack, "The Muse of Satire," *Yale Review*, Spring, 1952.

16Wallace Fowlie, "Swann and Hamlet: A Note on the Contemporary Hero," *Partisan Review*, 1942.

17Cf. Francis Fergusson, *The Idea of a Theater*, Princeton, N.J., 1949, chap. I, "The Tragic Rhythm of Action." Fergusson translates Kenneth Burke's formulation "Poiema, Pathema, Mathema" into "Purpose, Passion, Perception." (See *A Grammar of Motives*, pp. 38ff.) Cf. also Susan Taubes, *op. cit.*, p. 199.

In his passion he differs from the rebel, who would merely smash; or the romantic hero, who is not conscious of guilt; or the epic hero, who deals with emergencies rather than dilemmas. Odysseus and Aeneas, to be sure, face moral problems, but they proceed in a clear ethical light. Their social norms are secure. But the tragic hero sees a sudden, unexpected evil at the heart of things that infects all things. His secure and settled world has gone wrong, and he must oppose his own ambiguous nature against what he loves. Doing so involves total risk, as the chorus and his friends remind him. He may brood and pause, like Hamlet, or he may proceed with Ahab's fury; but proceed he must.

He proceeds, suffers, and in his suffering "learns." This is the phase of "perception." Although it often culminates in a single apocalyptic scene, a moment of "recognition," as in *Oedipus* and *Othello*, it need not be separate in time from the passion phase. Rather, perception is all that can be summed up in the spiritual and moral change that the hero undergoes from first to last and in the similar change wrought by his actions or by his example in those about him.

For the hero, perception may involve an all-but-complete transformation in character, as with Lear and Oedipus; or a gradual development in poise and self-mastery (Prometheus, Hamlet); or the softening and humanizing of the hard outlines of a character like Antigone's. It may appear in the hero's change from moody isolation and self-pity to a sense of his sharing in the general human condition, of his responsibility for it and to it. This was one stage in Lear's pilgrimage ("I have ta'en too little care of this") and as far as Dostoevski's Dmitri Karamazov ever got. In all the manifestations of this perception there is an element of Hamlet's "readiness," of an acceptance of destiny that is not merely resignation. At its most luminous it is Lear's and Oedipus' hard-won humility and new understanding of love. It may transform or merely inform, but a change there must be.

And it is more, of course, than merely a

moral change, just as the hero's problem is always more than a moral one. His affair is still with the gods. In taking up arms against the ancient cosmic evil, he transcends the human situation, mediating between the human and the divine. It was Orestes' suffering that, in the end, made the heavens more just. In the defeat or death which is the usual lot of the tragic hero, he becomes a citizen of a larger city, still defiant but in a new mood, a "calm of mind," a partial acquiescence. Having at first resented his destiny, he has lived it out, found unexpected meanings in it, carried his case to a more-than-human tribunal. He sees his own destiny, and man's destiny, in its ultimate perspective.

But the perception which completes the tragic form is not dramatized solely through the hero's change, although his pilgrimage provides the traditional tragic structure.[18] The full nature and extent of the new vision is measured also by what happens to the other figures in the total symbolic situation—to the hero's antagonists (King Creon, Claudius, Iago); to his opposites (the trimmers and hangers-on, the Osrics); to his approximates (Ismene, Horatio, Kent, the Chorus). Some he moves, some do not change at all. But his suffering must make a difference somewhere outside himself. After Antigone's death the community (even Creon) re-forms around her; the "new acquist" at the end of *Samson Agonistes* is the common note, also at the end of the Shakespearean tragedies. For the look-

[18]Indeed, it has been pointed out that, in an age when the symbol of the hero as the dominating center of the play seems to have lost its validity with artist and audience, the role is taken over by the artist himself, who is his own tragic hero. That is, "perception" is conveyed more generally, in the total movement of the piece and through all the parts. The "pact with the world" and the suffering are not objectified in a hero's ordeal but seem peculiarly the author's. This quality has been noted in Joyce's *Ulysses;* Berdiaev saw it in Dostoevski; Hardy, Conrad, Faulkner are examples that come to mind. At any rate, the distinction may be useful in determining matters of tone, although it is not clear cut, as distinctions in tone seldom are. But it is one way of pointing to the difference between the tragic tone and the Olympian distance of Meredithian comedy, or the ironic detachment of satire. . . .

ers-on there is no sudden rending of the veil of clay, no triumphant assertion of The Moral Order. There has been suffering and disaster, ultimate and irredeemable loss, and there is promise of more to come. But all who are involved have been witness to new revelations about human existence, the evil of evil and the goodness of good. They are more "ready." The same old paradoxes and ambiguities remain, but for the moment they are transcended in the higher vision.

THEATRE FOR PLEASURE OR THEATRE FOR INSTRUCTION

Bertolt Brecht

A few years back, anybody talking about the modern theatre meant the theatre in Moscow, New York and Berlin. He might have thrown in a mention of one of Jouvet's productions in Paris or Cochran's in London, or *The Dybbuk* as given by the Habima (which is to all intents and purposes part of the Russian theatre, since Vakhtangov was its director). But broadly speaking there were only three capitals so far as modern theatre was concerned.

Russian, American and German theatres differed widely from one another, but were alike in being modern, that is to say in introducing technical and artistic innovations. In a sense they even achieved a certain stylistic resemblance, probably because technology is international (not just that part which is directly applied to the stage but also that which influences it, the film for instance), and because large progressive cities in large industrial countries are involved. Among the older capitalist countries it is the Berlin theatre that seemed of late to be in the lead. For a period all that is common to the modern theatre received its strongest and (so far) maturest expression there.

The Berlin theatre's last phase was the so-called epic theatre, and it showed the modern theatre's trend of development in its purest form. Whatever was labelled '*Zeitstück*' or '*Piscatorbühne*' or '*Lehrstück*' belongs to the epic theatre.

THE EPIC THEATRE

Many people imagine that the term 'epic theatre' is self-contradictory, as the epic and dramatic ways of narrating a story are held, following Aristotle, to be basically distinct. The difference between the two forms was never thought simply to lie in the fact that the one is performed by living beings while the other operates via the written word; epic works such as those of Homer and the medieval singers were at the same time theatrical performances, while dramas like Goethe's *Faust* and Byron's *Manfred* are agreed to have been more effective as books. Thus even by Aristotle's definition the difference between the dramatic and epic forms was attributed to their different methods of construction, whose laws were dealt with by two different branches of aesthetics. The method of construction depended on the different way of presenting the work to the public, sometimes via the stage, sometimes through a book; and independently of that there was the 'dramatic element' in epic works and the 'epic element' in dramatic. The bourgeois novel in the last century developed much that was 'dramatic,' by which was meant the strong centralization of the story, a momentum that drew the separate parts into a common relationship. A particular passion of utterance, a certain emphasis on the clash of forces are hallmarks of the 'dramatic.' The epic writer Döblin provided an excellent criterion when he said that with an epic work, as opposed to a dramatic, one can as it were take a pair of scissors and cut it into individual pieces, which remain fully capable of life.

This is no place to explain how the opposition of epic and dramatic lost its rigidity after having long been held to be irreconcilable. Let us just point out that the technical advances alone were enough to permit the stage to incorporate an element of narrative in its dramatic productions. The possibility of projections, the greater adaptability of the stage due to mechanization, the film, all completed the theatre's equipment, and did so at a point where the most important transactions between people could no longer be shown simply by personifying the motive forces or subjecting the characters to invisible metaphysical powers.

To make these transactions intelligible the environment in which the people lived had to be brought to bear in a big and 'significant' way.

This environment had of course been shown in the existing drama, but only as seen from the central figure's point of view and not as an independent element. It was defined by the hero's reactions to it. It was seen as a storm can be seen when one sees the ships on a sheet of water unfolding their sails, and the sails filling out. In the epic theatre it was to appear standing on its own.

The stage began to tell a story. The narrator was no longer missing, along with the fourth wall. Not only did the background adopt an attitude to the events on the stage—by big screens recalling other simultaneous events elsewhere, by projecting documents which confirmed or contradicted what the characters said, by concrete and intelligible figures to accompany abstract conversations, by figures and sentences to support mimed transactions whose sense was unclear—but the actors too refrained from going over wholly into their role, remaining detached from the character they were playing and clearly inviting criticism of him.

The spectator was no longer in any way allowed to submit to an experience uncritically (and without practical consequences) by means of simple empathy with the characters in a play. The production took the subject-matter and the incidents shown and put them through a process of alienation: the alienation that is necessary to all understanding. When something seems 'the most obvious thing in the world' it means that any attempt to understand the world has been given up.

What is 'natural' must have the force of what is startling. This is the only way to expose the laws of cause and effect. People's activity must simultaneously be so and be capable of being different.

It was all a great change.

The dramatic theatre's spectator says: Yes, I have felt like that too—Just like me—It's only natural—It'll never change—The sufferings of this man appal me, because they are inescapable—That's great art; it all seems the most obvious thing in the world—I weep when they weep, I laugh when they laugh.

The epic theatre's spectator says: I'd never have thought it—That's not the way—That's extraordinary, hardly believable—It's got to stop—The sufferings of this man appal me, because they are unnecessary—That's great art: nothing obvious in it—I laugh when they weep, I weep when they laugh.

The Instructive Theatre

The stage began to be instructive.

Oil, inflation, war, social struggles, the family, religion, wheat, the meat market, all became subjects for theatrical representation. Choruses enlightened the spectator about facts unknown to him. Films showed a montage of events from all over the world. Projections added statistical material. And as the 'background' came to the front of the stage so people's activity was subjected to criticism. Right and wrong courses of action were shown. People were shown who knew what they were doing, and others who did not. The theatre became an affair for philosophers, but only for such philosophers as wished not just to explain the world but also to change it. So we had philosophy, and we had instruction. And where was the amusement in all that? Were they sending us back to school, teaching us to read and write?

Were we supposed to pass exams, work for diplomas?

Generally there is felt to be a very sharp distinction between learning and amusing oneself. The first may be useful, but only the second is pleasant. So we have to defend the epic theatre against the suspicion that it is a highly disagreeable, humourless, indeed strenuous affair.

Well: all that can be said is that the contrast between learning and amusing oneself is not laid down by divine rule; it is not one that has always been and must continue to be.

Undoubtedly there is much that is tedious about the kind of learning familiar to us from school, from our professional training, etc. But it must be remembered under what conditions and to what end that takes place.

It is really a commercial transaction. Knowledge is just a commodity. It is acquired in order to be resold. All those who have grown out of going to school have to do their learning virtually in secret, for anyone who admits that he still has something to learn devalues himself as a man whose knowledge is inadequate. Moreover the usefulness of learning is very much limited by factors outside the learner's control. There is unemployment, for instance, against which no knowledge can protect one. There is the division of labour, which makes generalized knowledge unnecessary and impossible. Learning is often among the concerns of those whom no amount of concern will get any forwarder. There is not much knowledge that leads to power, but plenty of knowledge to which only power can lead.

Learning has a very different function for different social strata. There are strata who cannot imagine any improvement in conditions: they find the conditions good enough for them. Whatever happens to oil they will benefit from it. And: they feel the years beginning to tell. There can't be all that many years more. What is the point of learning a lot now? They have said their final word: a grunt. But there are also strata 'waiting their turn' who are discontented with conditions, have a vast interest in the practical side of learning, want at all costs to find out where they stand, and know that they are lost without learning; these are the best and keenest learners. Similar differences apply to countries and peoples. Thus the pleasure of learning depends on all sorts of things; but none the less there is such a thing as pleasurable learning, cheerful and militant learning.

If there were not such amusement to be had from learning the theatre's whole structure would unfit it for teaching.

Theatre remains theatre even when it is instructive theatre, and in so far as it is good theatre it will amuse.

Theatre and Knowledge

But what has knowledge got to do with art? We know that knowledge can be amusing, but not everything that is amusing belongs in the theatre.

I have often been told, when pointing out the invaluable services that modern knowledge and science, if properly applied, can perform for art and specially for the theatre, that art and knowledge are two estimable but wholly distinct fields of human activity. This is a fearful truism, of course, and it is as well to agree quickly that, like most truisms, it is perfectly true. Art and science work in quite different ways: agreed. But, bad as it may sound, I have to admit that I cannot get along as an artist without the use of one or two sciences. This may well arouse serious doubts as to my artistic capacities. People are used to seeing poets as unique and slightly unnatural beings who reveal with a truly godlike assurance things that other people can only recognize after much sweat and toil. It is naturally distasteful to have to admit that one does not belong to this select band. All the same, it must be admitted. It must at the same time be made clear that the scientific occupations just confessed to are not pardonable side interests, pursued on days off after

a good week's work. We all know how Goethe was interested in natural history, Schiller in history: as a kind of hobby, it is charitable to assume. I have no wish promptly to accuse these two of having needed these sciences for their poetic activity; I am not trying to shelter behind them; but I must say that I do need the sciences. I have to admit, however, that I look askance at all sorts of people who I know do not operate on the level of scientific understanding: that is to say, who sing as the birds sing, or as people imagine the birds to sing. I don't mean by that that I would reject a charming poem about the taste of fried fish or the delights of a boating party just because the writer had not studied gastronomy or navigation. But in my view the great and complicated things that go on in the world cannot be adequately recognized by people who do not use every possible aid to understanding.

Let us suppose that great passions or great events have to be shown which influence the fate of nations. The lust for power is nowadays held to be such a passion. Given that a poet 'feels' this lust and wants to have someone strive for power, how is he to show the exceedingly complicated machinery within which the struggle for power nowadays takes place? If his hero is a politician, how do politics work? If he is a business man, how does business work? And yet there are writers who find business and politics nothing like so passionately interesting as the individual's lust for power. How are they to acquire the necessary knowledge? They are scarcely likely to learn enough by going round and keeping their eyes open, though even then it is more than they would get by just rolling their eyes in an exalted frenzy. The foundation of a paper like the *Völkischer Beobachter* or a business like Standard Oil is a pretty complicated affair, and such things cannot be conveyed just like that. One important field for the playwright is psychology. It is taken for granted that a poet, if not an ordinary man, must be able without further instruction to discover the motives that lead a man to commit murder; he must be able to give a picture of a murderer's mental state 'from within himself.' It is taken for granted that one only has to look inside oneself in such a case; and then there's always one's imagination. . . . There are various reasons why I can no longer surrender to this agreeable hope of getting a result quite so simply. I can no longer find in myself all those motives which the press or scientific reports show to have been observed in people. Like the average judge when pronouncing sentence, I cannot without further ado conjure up an adequate picture of a murderer's mental state. Modern psychology, from psychoanalysis to behaviourism, acquaints me with facts that lead me to judge the case quite differently, especially if I bear in mind the findings of sociology and do not overlook economics and history. You will say: but that's getting complicated. I have to answer that it *is* complicated. Even if you let yourself be convinced, and agree with me that a large slice of literature is exceedingly primitive, you may still ask with profound concern: won't an evening in such a theatre be a most alarming affair? The answer to that is: no.

Whatever knowledge is embodied in a piece of poetic writing has to be wholly transmuted into poetry. Its utilization fulfils the very pleasure that the poetic element provokes. If it does not at the same time fulfil that which is fulfilled by the scientific element, none the less in an age of great discoveries and inventions one must have a certain inclination to penetrate deeper into things—a desire to make the world controllable—if one is to be sure of enjoying its poetry.

Is the Epic Theatre Some Kind of 'Moral Institution'?

According to Friedrich Schiller the theatre is supposed to be a moral institution. In making this demand it hardly occurred to Schiller that by moralizing from the stage he might drive the audience out of the theatre. Audiences had no objection to moralizing in his day. It was only later that Friedrich Nietzsche attacked him for blowing a moral trumpet. To Nietzsche any concern with morality was a depressing affair; to Schiller it seemed thoroughly enjoyable. He knew of nothing that could give greater amusement and satisfaction than the propagation of ideas. The bourgeoisie was setting about forming the ideas of the nation.

Putting one's house in order, patting oneself on the back, submitting one's account, is something highly agreeable. But describing the collapse of one's house, having pains in the back, paying one's account, is indeed a depressing affair, and that was how Friedrich Nietzsche saw things a century later. He was poorly disposed towards morality, and thus towards the previous Friedrich too.

The epic theatre was likewise often objected to as moralizing too much. Yet in the epic theatre moral arguments only took second place. Its aim was less to moralize than to observe. That is to say it observed, and then the thick end of the wedge followed: the story's moral. Of course we cannot pretend that we started our observations out of a pure passion for observing and without any more practical motive, only to be completely staggered by their results. Undoubtedly there were some painful discrepancies in our environment, circumstances that were barely tolerable, and this not merely on account of moral considerations. It is not only moral considerations that make hunger, cold and oppression hard to bear. Similarly the object of our inquiries was not just to arouse moral objections to such circumstances (even though they could easily be felt—though not by all the audience alike; such objections were seldom for instance felt by those who profited by the circumstances in question) but to discover means for their elimination. We were not in fact speaking in the name of morality but in that of the victims. These truly are two distinct matters, for the victims are often told that they ought to be contented with their lot, for moral reasons. Moralists of this sort see man as existing for morality, not morality for man. At least it should be possible to gather from the above to what degree and in what sense the epic theatre is a moral institution.

CAN EPIC THEATRE BE PLAYED ANYWHERE?

Stylistically speaking, there is nothing all that new about the epic theatre. Its expository character and its emphasis on virtuosity bring it close to the old Asiatic theatre. Didactic tendencies are to be found in the medieval mystery plays and the classical Spanish theatre, and also in the theatre of the Jesuits.

These theatrical forms corresponded to particular trends of their time, and vanished with them. Similarly the modern epic theatre is linked with certain trends. It cannot by any means be practised universally. Most of the great nations today are not disposed to use the theatre for ventilating their problems. London, Paris, Tokyo and Rome maintain their theatres for quite different purposes. Up to now favourable circumstances for an epic and didactic theatre have only been found in a few places and for a short period of time. In Berlin Fascism put a very definite stop to the development of such a theatre.

It demands not only a certain technological level but a powerful movement in society which is interested to see vital questions freely aired with a view to their solution, and can defend this interest against every contrary trend.

The epic theatre is the broadest and most far-reaching attempt at large-scale modern theatre, and it has all those immense difficulties to overcome that always confront the vital forces in the sphere of politics, philosophy, science and art.

['Vergnügungstheater oder Lehrtheater?,' from *Schriften zum Theater,* 1957]

TRAGEDY, COMEDY, AND IRONY FROM *THE ANATOMY OF CRITICISM*
Northrop Frye

TRAGEDY

It is a commonplace of criticism that comedy tends to deal with characters in a social group, whereas tragedy is more concentrated on a single individual. We have given reasons in the first essay for thinking that the typical tragic hero is somewhere between the divine and the "all too human." This must be true even of dying gods: Prometheus, being a god, cannot die, but he suffers for his sympathy with the "dying ones" (*brotoi*) or "mortal" men, and even suffering has something subdivine about it. The tragic hero is very great as compared with us, but there is something else, something on the side of him opposite the audience, compared to which he is small. This something else may be called God, gods, fate, accident, fortune, necessity, circumstance, or any combination of these, but whatever it is the tragic hero is our mediator with it.

The tragic hero is typically on top of the wheel of fortune, half-way between human society on the ground and the something greater in the sky. Prometheus, Adam, and Christ hang between heaven and earth, between a world of paradisal freedom and a world of bondage. Tragic heroes are so much the highest points in their human landscape that they seem the inevitable conductors of the power about them, great trees more likely to be struck by lightning than a clump of grass. Conductors may of course be instruments as well as victims of the divine lightning: Milton's Samson destroys the Philistine

Selections from Northrop Frye, *Anatomy of Criticism: Four Essays* (copyright © 1957 by Princeton University Press; Princeton Paperback, 1971) pp. 207–211, 166–171, and 285–286. Reprinted by permission of Princeton University Press.

temple with himself, and Hamlet nearly exterminates the Danish court in his own fall. Something of Nietzsche's mountain-top air of transvaluation clings to the tragic hero: his thoughts are not ours any more than his deeds, even if, like Faustus, he is dragged off to hell for having them. Whatever eloquence or affability he may have, an inscrutable reserve lies behind it. Even sinister heroes—Tamburlaine, Macbeth, Creon— retain this reserve, and we are reminded that men will die loyally for a wicked or cruel man, but not for an amiable backslapper. Those who attract most devotion from others are those who are best able to suggest in their manner that they have no need of it, and from the urbanity of Hamlet to the sullen ferocity of Ajax, tragic heroes are wrapped in the mystery of their communion with that something beyond which we can see only through them, and which is the source of their strength and their fate alike. In the phrase which so fascinated Yeats, the tragic hero leaves his servants to do his "living" for him, and the center of tragedy is in the hero's isolation, not in a villain's betrayal, even when the villain is, as he often is, a part of the hero himself.

As for the something beyond, its names are variable but the form in which it manifests itself is fairly constant. Whether the context is Greek, Christian, or undefined, tragedy seems to lead up to an epiphany of law, of that which is and must be. It can hardly be an accident that the two great developments of tragic drama, in fifth-century Athens and in seventeenth-century Europe, were contemporary with the rise of Ionian and of Renaissance science. In such a world-view nature is seen as an impersonal process which human law imitates as best it can, and this direct relation of man and natural law is in the foreground. The sense in Greek tragedy that fate is stronger than the gods really implies that the gods exist primarily to ratify the order of nature, and that if any personality, even a divine one, possesses a genuine power of veto over law, it is most unlikely that he will want to exercise it. In Christianity much

the same is true of the personality of Christ in relation to the inscrutable decrees of the Father. Similarly the tragic process in Shakespeare is natural in the sense that it simply happens, whatever its cause, explanation, or relationships. Characters may grope about for conceptions of gods that kill us for their sport, or for a divinity that shapes our ends, but the action of tragedy will not abide our questions, a fact often transferred to the personality of Shakespeare.

In its most elementary form, the vision of law (*dike*) operates as *lex talionis* or revenge. The hero provokes enmity, or inherits a situation of enmity, and the return of the avenger constitutes the catastrophe. The revenge-tragedy is a simple tragic structure, and like most simple structures can be a very powerful one, often retained as a central theme even in the most complex tragedies. Here the original act provoking the revenge sets up an antithetical or counterbalancing movement, and the completion of the movement resolves the tragedy. This happens so often that we may almost characterize the total *mythos* of tragedy as binary, in contrast to the three-part saturnalia movement of comedy.

We notice however the frequency of the device of making the revenge come from another world, through gods or ghosts or oracles. This device expands the conceptions of both nature and law beyond the limits of the obvious and tangible. It does not thereby transcend those conceptions, as it is still natural law that is manifested by the tragic action. Here we see the tragic hero as disturbing a balance in nature, nature being conceived as an order stretching over the two kingdoms of the visible and the invisible, a balance which sooner or later *must* right itself. The righting of the balance is what the Greeks called *nemesis*; again, the agent or instrument of *nemesis* may be human vengeance, ghostly vengeance, divine vengeance, divine justice, accident, fate or the logic of events, but the essential thing is that *nemesis* happens, and happens impersonally, unaffected, as *Oedipus Tyrannus* illustrates, by the moral quality of human motivation involved.

In the *Oresteia* we are led from a series of revenge-movements into a final vision of natural law, a universal compact in which moral law is included and which the gods, in the person of the goddess of wisdom, endorse. Here *nemesis*, like its counterpart the Mosaic law in Christianity, is not abolished but fulfilled: it is developed from a mechanical or arbitrary sense of restored order, represented by the Furies, to the rational sense of it expounded by Athene. The appearance of Athene does not turn the *Oresteia* into a comedy, but clarifies its tragic vision.

There are two reductive formulas which have often been used to explain tragedy. Neither is quite good enough, but each is almost good enough, and as they are contradictory, they must represent extreme or limiting views of tragedy. One of these is the theory that all tragedy exhibits the omnipotence of an external fate. And, of course, the overwhelming majority of tragedies do leave us with a sense of the supremacy of impersonal power and of the limitation of human effort. But the fatalistic reduction of tragedy confuses the tragic condition with the tragic process: fate, in a tragedy, normally becomes external to the hero only *after* the tragic process has been set going. The Greek *ananke* or *moira* is in its normal, or pre-tragic, form the internal balancing condition of life. It appears as external or antithetical necessity only after it has been violated as a condition of life, just as justice is the internal condition of an honest man, but the external antagonist of the criminal. Homer uses a profoundly significant phrase for the theory of tragedy when he has Zeus speak of Aegisthus as going *hyper moron, beyond* fate.

The fatalistic reduction of tragedy does not distinguish tragedy from irony, and it is again significant that we speak of the irony of fate rather than of its tragedy. Irony does not need an exceptional central figure: as a rule, the dingier the hero the sharper the irony, when irony alone is aimed at. It is the admixture of heroism that gives tragedy its characteristic splendor and exhilaration.

The tragic hero has normally had an extraordinary, often a nearly divine, destiny almost within his grasp, and the glory of that original vision never quite fades out of tragedy. The rhetoric of tragedy requires the noblest diction that the greatest poets can produce, and while catastrophe is the normal end of tragedy, this is balanced by an equally significant original greatness, a paradise lost.

The other reductive theory of tragedy is that the act which sets the tragic process going must be primarily a violation of *moral* law, whether human or divine; in short, that Aristotle's hamartia or "flaw" must have an essential connection with sin or wrongdoing. Again it is true that the great majority of tragic heroes do possess hybris, a proud, passionate, obsessed or soaring mind which brings about a morally intelligible downfall. Such hybris is the normal precipitating agent of catastrophe, just as in comedy the cause of the happy ending is usually some act of humility, represented by a slave or by a heroine meanly disguised. In Aristotle the hamartia of the tragic hero is associated with Aristotle's ethical conception of *proairesis*, or free choice of an end, and Aristotle certainly does tend to think of tragedy as morally, almost physically, intelligible. It has already been suggested, however, that the conception of catharsis, which is central to Aristotle's view of tragedy, is inconsistent with moral reductions of it. Pity and terror are moral feelings, and they are relevant but not attached to the tragic situation. Shakespeare is particularly fond of planting moral lightning-rods on both sides of his heroes to deflect the pity and terror: we have mentioned Othello flanked by Iago and Desdemona, but Hamlet is flanked by Claudius and Ophelia, Lear by his daughters, and even Macbeth by Lady Macbeth and Duncan. In all these tragedies there is a sense of some far-reaching mystery of which this morally intelligible process is only a part. The hero's act has thrown a switch in a larger machine than his own life, or even his own society.

COMEDY

There are two ways of developing the form
of comedy: one is to throw the main emphasis on the blocking characters; the other is to
throw it forward on the scenes of discovery
and reconciliation. One is the general tendency of comic irony, satire, realism, and
studies of manners; the other is the tendency
of Shakespearean and other types of romantic comedy. In the comedy of manners the
main ethical interest falls as a rule on the
blocking characters. The technical hero and
heroine are not often very interesting people:
the *adulescentes* of Plautus and Terence are
all alike, as hard to tell apart in the dark as
Demetrius and Lysander, who may be parodies of them. Generally the hero's character
has the neutrality that enables him to represent a wish-fulfilment. It is very different
with the miserly or ferocious parent, the
boastful or foppish rival, or the other characters who stand in the way of the action.
In Molière we have a simple but fully tested
formula in which the ethical interest is
focussed on a single blocking character, a
heavy father, a miser, a misanthrope, a
hypocrite, or a hypochondriac. These are
the figures that we remember, and the plays
are usually named after them, but we can
seldom remember all the Valentins and An-
geliques who wriggle out of their clutches. . . .

Comedy usually moves toward a happy
ending, and the normal response of the audience to a happy ending is "this should be,"
which sounds like a moral judgement. So it is,
except that it is not moral in the restricted
sense, but social. Its opposite is not the villainous but the absurd, and comedy finds
the virtues of Malvolio as absurd as the vices
of Angelo. Moliere's misanthrope, being
committed to sincerity, which is a virtue, is
morally in a strong position, but the audience
soon realizes that his friend Philinte, who is
ready to lie quite cheerfully in order to
enable other people to preserve their self-
respect, is the more genuinely sincere of the
two. It is of course quite possible to have a
moral comedy, but the result is often the kind
of melodrama that we have described as

comedy without humor, and which achieves
its happy ending with a self-righteous tone
that most comedy avoids. It is hardly possible
to imagine a drama without conflict, and
it is hardly possible to imagine a conflict
without some kind of enmity. But just as love,
including sexual love, is a very different thing
from lust, so enmity is a very different thing
from hatred. In tragedy, of course, enmity
almost always includes hatred; comedy is
different, and one feels that the social judgement against the absurd is closer to the comic
norm than the moral judgement against the
wicked.

The question then arises of what makes
the blocking character absurd. Ben Jonson
explained this by his theory of the "humor,"
the character dominated by what Pope calls
a ruling passion. The humor's dramatic
function is to express a state of what might
be called ritual bondage. He is obsessed by
his humor, and his function in the play is
primarily to repeat his obsession. A sick man
is not a humor, but a hypochondriac is,
because, *qua* hypochondriac, he can never
admit to good health, and can never do anything inconsistent with the role that he has
prescribed for himself. A miser can do and
say nothing that is not connected with the
hiding of gold or saving of money. In *The
Silent Woman,* Jonson's nearest approach to
Molière's type of construction, the whole
action recedes from the humor of Morose,
whose determination to eliminate noise from
his life produces so loquacious a comic action.

The principle of the humor is the principle
that unincremental repetition, the literary
imitation of ritual bondage, is funny. In a
tragedy—*Oedipus Tyrannus* is the stock example—repetition leads logically to catastrophe.
Repetition overdone or not going anywhere
belongs to comedy, for laughter is partly a
reflex, and like other reflexes it can be conditioned by a simple repeated pattern. In
Synge's *Riders to the Sea* a mother, after losing
her husband and five sons at sea, finally
loses her last son, and the result is a very
beautiful and moving play. But if it had
been a full-length tragedy plodding glumly
through the seven drownings one after an-

other, the audience would have been helpless with unsympathetic laughter long before it was over. The principle of repetition as the basis of humor both in Jonson's sense and in ours is well known to the creators of comic strips, in which a character is established as a parasite, a glutton (often confined to one dish), or a shrew, and who begins to be funny after the point has been made every day for several months. Continuous comic radio programs, too, are much more amusing to habitués than to neophytes. The girth of Falstaff and the hallucinations of Quixote are based on much the same comic laws. Mr. E. M. Forster speaks with disdain of Dickens's Mrs. Micawber, who never says anything except that she will never desert Mr. Micawber: a strong contrast is marked here between the refined writer too finicky for popular formulas, and the major one who exploits them ruthlessly. . . .

The comic ending is generally manipulated by a twist in the plot. In Roman comedy the heroine, who is usually a slave or courtesan, turns out to be the daughter of somebody respectable, so that the hero can marry her without loss of face. The *cognitio* in comedy, in which the characters find out who their relatives are, and who is left of the opposite sex not a relative, and hence available for marriage, is one of the features of comedy that have never changed much: *The Confidential Clerk* indicates that it still holds the attention of dramatists. There is a brilliant parody of a *cognitio* at the end of *Major Barbara* (the fact that the hero of this play is a professor of Greek perhaps indicates an unusual affinity to the conventions of Euripides and Menander), where Undershaft is enabled to break the rule that he cannot appoint his son-in-law as successor by the fact that the son-in-law's own father married his deceased wife's sister in Australia, so that the son-in-law is his own first cousin as well as himself. It sounds complicated, but the plots of comedy often are complicated because there is something inherently absurd about complications. As the main character interest in comedy is so often focussed on the defeated characters, comedy regularly illustrates a victory of

arbitrary plot over consistency of character. Thus, in striking contrast to tragedy, there can hardly be such a thing as inevitable comedy, as far as the action of the individual play is concerned. That is, we may know that the convention of comedy will make some kind of happy ending inevitable, but still for each play the dramatist must produce a distinctive "gimmick" or "weenie," to use two disrespectful Hollywood synonyms for *anagnorisis*. Happy endings do not impress us as true, but as desirable, and they are brought about by manipulation. The watcher of death tragedy has nothing to do but sit and wait for the inevitable end; but something gets born at the end of comedy, and the watcher of birth is a member of a busy society.

The manipulation of plot does not always involve metamorphosis of character, but there is no violation of comic decorum when it does. Unlikely conversions, miraculous transformations, and providential assistance are inseparable from comedy. Further, whatever emerges is supposed to be there for good: if the curmudgeon becomes lovable, we understand that he will not immediately relapse again into his ritual habit. Civilizations which stress the desirable rather than the real, and the religious as opposed to the scientific perspective, think of drama almost entirely in terms of comedy. In the classical drama of India, we are told, the tragic ending was regarded as bad taste, much as the manipulated endings of comedy are regarded as bad taste by novelists interested in ironic realism.

Irony

As tragedy moves over towards irony, the sense of inevitable event begins to fade out, and the sources of catastrophe come into view. In irony catastrophe is either arbitrary and meaningless, the impact of an unconscious (or, in the pathetic fallacy, malignant) world on conscious man, or the result of more or less definable social and psychological forces. Tragedy's "this must be" becomes irony's "this at least is," a concentration on foreground facts and a rejection of mythical superstructures. Thus the ironic drama is a vision of what in theology is called the fallen world, of simple humanity, man as natural man and in conflict with both human and non-human nature. In nineteenth-century drama the tragic vision is often identical with the ironic one, hence nineteenth-century tragedies tend to be either *Schicksal* dramas dealing with the arbitrary ironies of fate, or (clearly the more rewarding form) studies of the frustrating and smothering of human activity by the combined pressure of a reactionary society without and a disorganized soul within. Such irony is difficult to sustain in the theatre because it tends toward a stasis of action. In those parts of Chekhov, notably the last act of *The Three Sisters*, where the characters one by one withdraw from each other into their subjective prison-cells, we are coming about as close to pure irony as the stage can get.

The ironic play passes through a dead center of complete realism, a pure mime representing human life without comment and without imposing any sort of dramatic form beyond what is required for simple exhibition. . . . In the theatre we usually find that the spectacle of "all too human" life is either oppressive or ridiculous, and that it tends to pass directly from one to the other. Irony, then, as it moves away from tragedy, begins to merge into comedy.

Ironic comedy presents us of course with "the way of the world," but as soon as we find sympathetic or even neutral characters in a comedy, we move into the more familiar comic area where we have a group of humors outwitted by the opposing group. Just as tragedy is a vision of the supremacy of *mythos* or thing done, and just as irony is a vision of *ethos*, or character individualized against environment, so comedy is a vision of *dianoia*, a significance which is ultimately social significance, the establishing of a desirable society. . . . The further comedy moves from irony, the more it becomes what we here call ideal comedy, the vision not of the way of the world, but of what you will, life as you

like it. Shakespeare's main interest is in getting away from the son-father conflict of ironic comedy towards a vision of a serene community, a vision most prominent in *The Tempest*. Here the action is polarized around a younger and an older man working in harmony together, a lover and a benevolent teacher.

CHEKHOV AND THE THEATRE OF THE ABSURD
Joyce Carol Oates

The faithful rendering of life as it is truly lived, its tragedy always conditioned by the relentless banality of life and so transformed into something akin to comedy; the insistence upon the unheroic, the unmelodramatic, the self-deceiving, the futile; the paralysis of will that is at once a mark of the cultured and a sign of their decadence: these are the obvious characteristics of Chekhov's drama. The point at which Chekhov's meticulous symbolic naturalism touches the inexplicable, the ludicrous, and the paradoxical is the point at which his relationship to our contemporary theater of the absurd is most clear. Much of what seems stunning and *avant garde* in the last two decades of theater has been anticipated in both theory and practice by Chekhov. For instance, one has only to examine the central issues of *The Cherry Orchard* and *The Three Sisters*—the hopeless, comic-pathetic loss of a tradition and the futile longing for Moscow—to see how closely Chekhov is echoed in Beckett's *Waiting for Godot* and other works.

The concept of the "absurd" must be defined. It is a confusing term, for we are accustomed to equating the works of many modern writers with the existential concept of "absurdity." Sartre and Camus systematically examine the bases and the consequences of an absurd world, a world without meaning, but their works of literature, particularly their plays, are traditional in structure and language. However, when the playwright attempts to give expression to the absurd through both the structure and language of his work, he is then considered a playwright in the theater of the absurd (a term that could be set off by quotation marks, since its meaning is by no means simple). Chekhov's philosophical basis is clearly nineteenth-century naturalism, but his technique is only apparently naturalistic: it is fundamentally symbolic. What is absurd in Chekhov is the content of his works—what actually happens—and several of the devices he uses, particularly those dealing with language. Again and again we are confronted with intelligent people who have somehow lost their capacity for self-expression, whether wealthy landowners and their offspring, or working-class people, or the "emancipated." And with this capacity for self-expression they have also lost their ability to live.

All literature deals with contests of will, but drama makes most clear the spiritual struggles that life demands through its ritualistic enactment of the agon. Lifelong conflicts —conflicts of an abstract and spiritual nature —are given body, compressed, and played out before us on the stage. On the stage someone is either being born or dying; if his struggle is not with the resisting forces of other people (as in much of Shakespeare), it is with the forces of his unknown self, or, as in the Ionesco play *Exit the King*, with the force of death. Chekhov's works are tragedies of the impotence of will about to transform themselves into comedies, because their protagonists are diminished human beings; as Chekhov says, *The Cherry Orchard* is almost farcical in places,[1] though it deals with the end of an entire social order and the splitting-up of a family. This kind of bitter comedy is, perhaps, tragedy that can no longer sustain faith in itself.

[1] Quoted in David Magarshack, *Chekhov the Dramatist* (London, 1952), p. 264.

In his philosophical grasp of his material, as well as in a number of particular dramatic devices, Chekhov anticipates the contemporary theater of the absurd. This essay will analyze the relationship between the techniques of Chekhov and the absurdist playwrights, mainly the distortions of dramatic and linguistic convention, the use of inexplicable incident and "arbitrary issue" or private poetic image, and the relentless rhythm of disintegration that pierces exteriors but deliberately fails to achieve a recognition of a solid underlying reality.

In some ways the absurdist playwrights are more conventional than Chekhov. With the exception of Beckett, they provide situations of tension that build up to climaxes—a rhythm of movement any audience can feel though perhaps it cannot understand. Beckett's works, like Chekhov's, are dramas of the loss of will, in which the unattainable salvation is deliberately vague, as in a dream, and in which language is man's sole occupation. Since salvation is transcendent and exterior to man, action is certainly needless; one sits and talks. In Chekhov the actions that occur are irrelevant to the willed desires of the characters. What is scrupulously denied is a catharsis of any recognizable sort, even a true dramatic climax. When climaxes are provided they are always out of focus, for Chekhov's people cannot see clearly enough to do what might be expected of them by ordinary standards. Treplev in *The Sea Gull* has already tried to kill himself, and so his successful suicide is somehow anticlimactic; moreover, the audience is denied, like Treplev, the meaning this action will have to the others. So the action is simply an action, and as long as it is not interpreted within the context of the play, it never achieves meaning. The climax of *The Three Sisters*—Tuzenbach's death in a duel—affirms the sisters' loss rather than tying it together in a single, compact image, the death being denied sentimental value and even meaning, for Irina does not love Tuzenbach. The climax of *The Cherry Orchard*—the merchant Lopakhin's revelation that it is he who has bought the estate on which his father was once a serf ("I bought it," he announces with pride and awe)—initiates wrong reactions from everyone, for Lopakhin is the central character and had wanted in some confused way recognition for what he had done; this leads into the strange fourth act, an act of abandonment and leave-taking conducted with the most banal of conversations. Technically, a climax occurs in each play, but thematically, it is somehow not the right climax. The true issues are always avoided. Only in *Uncle Vanya* does the "hero" accurately sight his enemy, but of course he is unable to kill him and unable to commit suicide. If there is a catharsis in any acceptable sense in Chekhov, it must be through the accumulation of detail and the revelation of character, through the history of a given moment in terms of numbers of people and not simply, as in most drama, in terms of one or two people. The cathartic recognition of the relationship between the reality on stage and the reality it is meant to mirror in the real world makes the works art, but this art is difficult because it guides the emotional expectations of the audience up to a certain point and then baffles these expectations, allows a tragic situation to turn comic, denies its heroes or heroines the knowledge that would make them noble, and, strangest of all, deliberately scatters the audience's emotions among a group of people. If the audience could focus its sympathies upon one person, this person might achieve a kind of elevation; but in Chekhov it is rather the relationships between people and not the "realistics" of the people themselves that are of interest. Such art is difficult because no audience is prepared for it.

By contrast, such well-known absurdist plays as Ionesco's *The Bald Soprano, The Lesson*, and *The Chairs* are structured along lines that are almost anecdotal, in each case ending with a catharsis of violence in which the accumulated tensions are exorcized by complete irrationality. *The Killer*, Ionesco's most interesting long play, ends with a final scene that is really an act in itself, in which a fairly

ordinary, intelligent, pseudo-heroic man confronts the mysterious killer, a deformed, giggling creature, and is finally overcome by his "infinitely stubborn will." Despite the metaphysical poetry of Ionesco's images—his "arbitrary issues" that remind us of the private, privately created world of Kafka—the accumulation and release of tension in these plays is actually classic. The audience's emotions are guided by an expert hand. Ionesco is concerned with *change*, and despite the difficulties one might have intellectually with this change, its emotional, visual reality is clear enough. He speaks of the two fundamental states of consciousness at the root of all his plays: feelings of evanescence and heaviness. Most often, "lightness changes to heaviness, transparence to thickness; the world weighs heavily; the universe crushes. . . . Matter fills everything, takes up all space, annihilates all liberty under its weight. . . . Speech crumbles."[2] If it is not matter precisely that annihilates, it is the savagery that weighs down upon the spiritual—the metamorphoses of men into beasts, never subtle, or the actual killing of characters onstage. In Chekhov this demonstration of the play's structure is never clear; the audience's emotions are dissipated, go off in several directions, cannot focus upon any single conflict. The meaning of Ionesco may be baffling, but the dramatic focus of his art is not. In Chekhov the meaning is perhaps inexplicable apart from the actual terms of the plays themselves, but the concentration of dramatic action is in itself baffling. Hence the notorious problems of staging Chekhov. When the dying old servant, Firs, limps in at the end of *The Cherry Orchard*, having been left alone in the big house by the departing characters, one does not know whether to laugh or cry; the conclusion is brilliantly appropriate, and yet impossible to define. Surely this is the real end of the "old order"— a faithful servant who sentimentally recalls serfdom, abandoned by his former owners

---

[2]Quoted in Martin Esslin, *The Theater of the Absurd* (New York, 1961), p. 105.

without a second thought. But in another sense, a more theatrical sense, it is simply absurd, gratuitous and unexpected, and distracts attention from what has been supposed the main action: the effects of selling the estate upon the main characters.

In Ionesco the play ends abruptly because the characters, who are soulless, have been accepted simply as theatrical approximations of life in its ludicrous or mysterious sense, and the meaning of the work is ultimately abstract and universal; in Chekhov the play ends technically, but the characters, given life so scrupulously, carry its meaning along with them and do not surrender it when the curtain falls. The absurdist theater has limited powers because its works are essentially parables whose success or failure depends entirely upon the ingenuity of the transformation of idea (for example, the idea that man waits endlessly for his true life, his real self, his salvation) into arresting images, and, as parables, they can evoke only an intellectual response in the audience. One can laugh at Beckett's people, since they deliberately invite laughter, but one cannot share their sorrow because it is not a human sorrow; it is a representation, at its most sterile an allegorical representation, of real sorrow that exists somewhere in the human world—a curious parallel to the assumptions of the medieval morality play. In Chekhov, even the most mysterious characters are made real for us by some abrupt switching of point of view, so that the character— Solyony or Charlotta—does not slip safely into caricature. Chekhov's stage "looks" real enough, and his characters speak a language that has the surface formlessness of that of real life, but in essence his conception of drama is more complex and more iconoclastic than that of the absurdists, whose revolt is chiefly in terms of a simplification of life and an attendant exaggeration of limited experiences.

One of the spectacular devices of the absurd stage is its use of language. Ionesco was driven to write *The Bald Soprano* out of his desire to express the "tragedy of language"—the breakdown in communication that is a result of the failure of man to know himself, to relate himself meaningfully to other men and to his world. At bottom, one feels, this is another manifestation of the mourning for the old, dead gods, whose presence or assumed presence is necessary for man to remain man. Humanism is a failure, the absurdists say, because man is not "human," cannot know himself, therefore cannot control himself, and, above all, cannot control his world. In Beckett, the world cannot be controlled, and nothing happens; in Ionesco, the hallucinatory movement of the world cannot be controlled, for the hero who attempts to do so (Bérenger in *The Killer* and *Rhinoceros*) discovers in himself an unconscious collaboration with the forces of destruction. The stasis of ordinary humanity in the drama of the absurd is an extreme working-out of the dilemma of the humanist or liberal writer: how to create tragedy, which is predicated upon the uniqueness of human beings, in a leveled world in which all are equal and all are perhaps without value. The stupid anguish of Ionesco's characters is eloquence for our time; as Raymond Williams says in a study of liberal tragedy (the tragedy of the "heroic liberator opposed and destroyed by a false society"), when one identifies with the false society, the society cannot then be opposed or challenged by death, but must simply be confessed, forgiven, and lived with. Suffering is "separate and finally isolated"; the deadlock is absolute and we are all victims."

The distortion and madness of language in the absurd theater relate, then, to the interior distortion and madness of a society that still can make itself understood on a conventional, cliché-ridden level. It is a theater of and for victims—creatures who have misplaced their souls or deliberately betrayed them—relating to an audience in the same condition that has not yet, as Nietzsche would say, heard the news. Their language reflects their deracination, for without absolute values the romantic imagination cannot endure sanity: it demands grotesque images, a frenzied dance of madness to express its anguish. If Chekhov does not seem romantic, it is because of his impersonality, his refusal to exaggerate or make particularly poetic the suffering his hollow people endure. Always their limitations are carefully exposed as self-induced limitations, not gross misfortunes that symbolize the evil of the universe. But the vision of man in absurdist drama and in Chekhov is similar, if not identical. The mournful poetry of *Waiting for Godot*—

"Have you not done tormenting me with your accursed time? . . . One day, is that not enough for you, one day like any other day, he went dumb, one day I went blind, one day we'll go deaf, one day we were born, one day we'll die, the same day, the same second. . . . They give birth astride of a grave, the light gleams an instant, then it's night once more."—is matched by the laments of a typical Chekhovian character (Andrei of *The Three Sisters* talking to a man who cannot hear well):

"Oh, where is it, where has it all gone, my past when I was young, gay, clever, when I dreamed and thought with grace, when my present and my future were lighted up with hope? Why is it that when we have barely begun to live, we grow dull, gray, uninteresting, lazy, indifferent, useless, unhappy. . . . Our town has been in existence now for two hundred years, there are a hundred thousand people in it, and not one who isn't exactly like all the others, not one saint . . . not one scholar, not one artist, no one in the least remarkable. . . . They just eat, drink, sleep, and then die . . . others are born and they, too, eat, drink, sleep, and to keep from being stupefied by boredom, they relieve the monotony of life with their odious gossip, with vodka, cards . . . and an overwhelmingly vulgar influence weighs on the children, the divine spark is extinguished in them, and they become the same pitiful, identical corpses as their fathers and mothers."

Beckett's outcasts seem to arrive at once at their insights, making no progress toward any kind of enlightenment; Chekhov's people, involved as they are in a three-dimensional drama, move in a way that is less a progression than a devastation of illusion. Ionesco's people are victims of their incapacity for expression and are therefore less than human. At the end of *The Bald Soprano*, the Smiths and Martins yell furiously at each other, having achieved a kind of passionate rapport beneath the level of rationality, but the achievement of passion marks the end of their humanity. *The Chairs* is a play about nothing but words—the first part being concerned with half-expressed, private anecdotes, and the second part with the desperate, pathetic attempt to turn private experience into universal knowledge, mocked cruelly by Ionesco's mute Orator, who either betrays the Old Man or delivers his message precisely; in either case the "message" is lost. The traditional farewell of tragedy—Othello's final words, Antony's final words—is parodied here, for when life has lost its meaning and there is only "metaphysical emptiness," words have no value.

Chekhov's naturalism when it is most "natural" arouses in the audience the same sense of mystery that Ionesco's deliberate absurdity does. When Masha, who takes snuff and is hopelessly in love with the young writer Treplev, walks off stage in act 2 of *The Seagull* and has to drag her leg along because it has gone to sleep, the detail is both naturalistic and gratuitously absurd; so also is the snoring of Sorin in the same scene. The governess Charlotta of *The Cherry Orchard*, who eats cucumbers that she carries in her pocket and performs bizarre sleight-of-hand tricks, remains inexplicable. . . .

In Ionesco's *The Bald Soprano*, all conversation is nonsense. It does not point toward any thematic sense, but is content to be a hilarious expression of the nonsense people do speak:

MR. SMITH.

One walks on his feet, but one heats with electricity or coal.

MR. MARTIN.

He who sells an ox today, will have an egg tomorrow.

MRS. SMITH.

In real life, one must look out the window.

MRS. MARTIN.

One can sit down on a chair, when the chair doesn't have any.

MRS. SMITH.

One must always think of everything.

MR. MARTIN.

The ceiling is above, the floor is below.

These aphorisms, which make as much sense as most clichés, then degenerate into pure sound, noise, bestiality, as the Smiths and the Martins yell furiously at each other. One regrets the unnecessary conclusion of "It's not that way, it's over here"—the "it" obviously meaning sanity—but the decision to end the play with the Martins taking the Smiths' places is an excellent one, emphasizing as it does the endlessness of this purgatorial condition. For Ionesco and Chekhov the condition of man is rather like Beckett's notion of the spherical purgatory, in which one can never make any progress and the "shadow in the end is no better than the substance."[3] That the "reality" is no better than its appearance would suggest, and that the appearance, which seems preferable to the reality precisely because of its being illusory, is ultimately "no better," is an ironic inversion of what one might expect; man is willfully deceived by his language and his conception of the world, but this deception does him no good because he himself lacks the imagination to give it beauty.

As in Ionesco and Beckett, one finds in Chekhov the substitution of language for action. All his plays are demonstrations of the impotence of will. The doctor in *Uncle Vanya* works very hard, hasn't had a single day free in ten years, but he regards his present work as meaningless drudgery and

looks to the misty future for a righting of present horrors. For most of the others, talk is unrelated to action. When Irina speaks ecstatically of "work," she is unable to anticipate her very natural and inevitable disgust with the work she can actually find to do. Vershinin, entrapped in an ugly marriage, echoes Astrov's prophecy that salvation lies somewhere in the future: "In two or three hundred years life on this earth will be unimaginably beautiful, wonderful. Man needs such a life, and so long as it is not here, he must foresee it, expect it, dream about it, prepare for it." The sisters and their brother, Andrei, learned French, German, and English from their father—the means of expressing themselves in three languages besides their own—and yet of course they have nothing to express; Masha says: "In this town, to know three languages is a needless luxury—not even a luxury, but a sort of superfluous appendage, like a sixth finger." In *The Cherry Orchard*, language is hardly shared by the characters. The merchant Lopakhin explains what the family must do in order to save their estate, but they cannot understand him. As the catastrophe nears, they expend themselves in useless dialogue calculated to distract them from reality. Even the student Trofimov, who expresses once again Chekhov's own hopes for an ideal future, is an "eternal student" who knows nothing of life and whose high-sounding words are perhaps ludicrous. He says of his relationship with Anya:

"We are above love. To avoid the petty and the illusory, which prevent our being free and happy—that is the aim and meaning of life. Forward! We are moving irresistibly toward the bright star that burns in the distance! Forward! Do not fall behind, friends!"

Anya, delighted, exclaims: "How well you talk!" And the emphasis surely is on the word "talk," an ironic emphasis since it implies the young man's own illusory condition. The same sort of substitution of talk for action is found everywhere in the absurdist

[3]Samuel Beckett, *Molloy* (New York, 1955), p. 33.

theater, most notably in Beckett's plays (and in his novels as well). In Ionesco's short play, *The Lesson*, a curious transformation of the eclipsing of life by language is effected when the tyrannical professor kills his student with the word "knife"—having complete control of the meanings of words, he controls the girl's reactions to them and hence her life. The totalitarian misuse of language suggested by the professor's omnipotence is sounded also in *The Killer*, where a fascistic woman named Mother Peep demonstrates the facility of believing that stupidity is intelligence, cowardice is bravery, clear-sightedness is blindness, liquidation is "only physical."

The Three Sisters demonstrates most clearly the progress of disintegration that is the basis of most absurdist plays. After the substitution of language for action there is the substitution of false rhetoric for the truth. When Olga says happily at the beginning of the play that she longs passionately to go "home" again (to Moscow) and that this dream "keeps growing stronger and stronger," one accepts this as perfectly truthful and admirable. When the same refrain is repeated throughout the play, however, it takes on a sinister and ironic note the sisters themselves do not understand. Thus, at the conclusion of act 2, while Natasha runs out to a very real man, Irina is left alone to yearn for her illusory paradise. "To Moscow!" she cries, and the cry is by now discomforting. The end of act 3 has Irina, the youngest, again yearning for Moscow, but by now she has had to agree to a marriage she does not really want: "I'll marry him, I'm willing, only let us go to Moscow! I implore you, let us go! There's nothing in the world better than Moscow!" Now the longing is hysterical and is intended to cover up the knowledge she has expressed earlier—that everything has somehow gone wrong, that she has forgotten her Italian, that they will never, never see Moscow. The end of the play has the sisters grouped together and consoling themselves with rhetoric, much like Sonya at the end of *Uncle Vanya*. We have here a brutal counter-pointing of idealism and nihilism, as the sisters hear the military music and say that they want to live, that "it seems as if just a little more and we shall know why we live, why we suffer . . . ," and the old doctor sits by "amiably," undisturbed by the death of Tuzenbach and singing "Ta-rara boom-de-ay, sit on the curb I may"; the last impression of this extraordinary play is one of frozen dialectic, intelligence deceiving itself with words and balanced by a mindlessness that uses words quite aptly to express its curb-sitting or moral paralysis, an image for the sisters as well as the doctor. Indeed, it is their idealism, their failure to make concrete and therefore active the words they use so charmingly, that has ruined their "real" lives. Natasha, who cannot talk well at all and whose French is embarrassingly poor, is significantly victorious over the sisters. Other symptoms of disintegration reflected in language are the change from the love duets of the second act (Masha and Vershinin; Irina and Tuzenbach) to the monologues of the last acts (the doctor's soliloquy on his ruined life; Andrei's in the presence of a deaf man); the interruptions, aimless talk, and the jokes of Solyony's that always miss their mark; the *non sequiturs* that are at once amusing and unsettling, suggesting as they do a serious failure of sane communication. Chekhov's plays are tragedies of language, like Ionesco's, assaults against the conventional language, which disguises by its very conventionality the hollowness of those who use it.

Most interesting of all the similarities between the Chekhovian and the *avant-garde* theater is the use of the "arbitrary issue" as poetic image. In absurdist theater the arbitrary issue is that which, despite its apparent inadequacy, is to carry the burden of the character's obsession. In Adamov's *Le Ping-Pong*, it is a pinball machine that captivates the imaginations of two men who grow old playing it, wasting their lives, transforming their natural human impulses toward transcendence into nonsensical trivialities about the machine itself. As Esslin notes in his excellent study of the play, the work is a powerful image of the "alienation of man through the worship of a false objective"[4]— the machine itself an obvious metaphor for anything that captivates men's lives without being worth the sacrifice. In Ionesco as well the arbitrary issue is that which is "given" without explanation: one must find out whether Mallot spelled his name with a "t" or a "d," one must get the growing corpse out of the apartment, one must resist to the end the metamorphosis into a rhinoceros. The images are not significant in themselves (except as theater), but only in what they suggest. This conception of writing differs from, for instance, the very real and not at all arbitrary issues of Ibsen, attacking the hypocrisy of society in *Ghosts*, or of Strindberg, passionately attacking the vampirish female. As if the world no longer offered real issues, these several playwrights create grotesque and parodying issues that will dominate their characters' imaginations and, when the play is successful, the audience's imagination as well. Such theater is really poetry, as Kafka's works are poetry: the creation of a sustained image that is the vehicle for symbolic meaning, yet never glibly contained by this meaning. But because the image is necessarily private and not social, historical, or mythical, the meaning must be expanded by the audience, which as a kind of unified consciousness can no longer be content to know—as Picasso says of most people—only what they already know. The difficulty with absurdist theater is its deliberate refusal to tell us what we already know, its unheroic heroes and unvillainous villains, its mock plots, its insistence upon baffling expectation, its taking over the prat-falls and rapid dialogue of vaudeville entertainment while leaving behind the "honest" foolishness. But as poetry, its images are closer to Pound's definition of the image than are, perhaps, such readily acceptable images as the paper lantern in Williams' *A Streetcar Named Desire*

[4]Esslin, p. 66.

and the doomed bird in *Miss Julie*. In 1913 Pound defined the "image" as "that which presents an intellectual and emotional complex in an instant of time. . . . It is the presentation of such a 'complex' instantaneously which gives that sense of sudden liberation; that sense of freedom from time limits and space limits; that sense of sudden growth, which we experience in the presence of the greatest works of art." The Imagists themselves created no images that broke so completely from the conventionally "poetic" as did the dramatists of the absurd.

In traditional theater the central issue is always acted upon; this is the only means of plot. One finally kills the king, though at great expense; one manages to marry the inevitable person; one breaks free from husband, children, and hypocritical society. Generally, in Chekhov and the absurd dramatists, the central issue is either not understood or not acted upon or both. The cherry orchard has all the makings of a symbol except—unlike the stuffed seagull in the earlier play—its symbolism points in several directions. It is various things to various people, and yet in itself it does not exist; it has no meaning. Never does anyone see the cherry orchard for what it is; they see wasted opportunities for making money, or they see ghostly faces in it, whether the student Trofimov's vision of the faces of serfs or Madame Ranevskaya's vision of her dead mother walking in it. They are capable of seeing only what they bring to it, of seeing only themselves. And when the orchard is finally sold, when the catastrophe happens, there is a queerly inappropriate relief; Gayev, though totally displaced by the change, says cheerfully:

"Yes, indeed, everything is all right now. Before the cherry orchard was sold we were all worried and miserable, but afterward, when the question was finally settled once and for all, everybody calmed down and felt quite cheerful."

One is reminded of Mann's famous definition of irony in his essay, "Goethe and Tolstoy": a technique that glances at both sides, playing "slyly and irresponsibly among opposites." With such irony there is no possibility of sentimental excess, since the writer does not choose sides.

If this is so, the theatergoer wants to ask, then what is the play about? Why has it been written? That the apparent central issue of a work should be declared quite trivial and insignificant after all the words and tears exerted for it is an extraordinary event in literature. It is as if the conventional form of art were calling itself into question, calling its very reason for existence into question, or calling, at least, the conventional audience's expectations into question. If it is ever appropriate to talk of genres in close relationship to actual works of art, one might say that for the tragic vision, deadly seriousness must always surround this central issue, and what the play undertakes is of real concern not only within the context of the play, but symbolically for its audience. Tragedy is a sacred art form. When self-consciousness or doubt or an impulse toward self-parody enter, tragedy disintegrates. In Chekhov this is precisely the case.

As in Beckett, the less tangible the means of salvation, the greater the urgency for salvation becomes. The intelligent human beings of such drama, caught in the purgatorial present, can only *talk*; it is the stupid—Natasha, Solyony, Arkadina, the professor of *Uncle Vanya*—who live on some level of existence, forcing others to submit to their wills, the simple fact of their being able to live involving a death for others. As one element

gains strength, so another element loses strength. The ghostliness of the central issue or image in Chekhov gives way abruptly to the flagrant mystery of the central issue of a play like *Godot*. Godot as image approaches the unfathomable just as Melville's white whale does—the former by its very absence, the latter by its tremendously detailed presence. Chekhov's imagery is more conventional than that of the absurdists, of course, since he is committed to a naturalistic stage, but his use of the image is similar: the truly poetic image whose meaning, as Pound says, gives one a sense of liberation and sudden growth by refusing to confine itself—in other words, to the easily explicable.

If there is intellectual deba⸱e in the theater of the absurd it is, like the "intellectual" discussions in Chekhov, ironic, exaggerated, and foolish, coming as it does at the point in history at which philosophy is divorced from the transcendental values it once tried to discover or support. Hence debate, talk, and duets of dialogue become meaningless, and characters are their own chorus, speaking and commenting endlessly upon their own speech. Are there images behind this speech? Are there realities behind these images? The prevailing tone in existential literature is that of mystery. In this art a strange, dissipated action, or the memory or vague desire for action, has replaced the older, more vital, ritualistic concerns of the stage. Chekhov and the absurdists remain true to their subject—life—by refusing to reduce their art to a single emotion and idea.